The American People

BRIEF SECOND EDITION

The American People

Creating a Nation and a Society

GARY B. NASH
University of California, Los Angeles

JULIE ROY JEFFREY
Goucher College

JOHN R. HOWE
University of Minnesota

PETER J. FREDERICK
Wabash College

ALLEN F. DAVIS
Temple University

ALLAN M. WINKLER
Miami University

HarperCollinsCollegePublishers

Executive Editor: Bruce Borland
Developmental Editor: John Matthews
Project Editor: Robert Ginsberg
Text and Cover Designer: Nancy Sabato
Cover Illustration: Christine Francis
Art Studio: Vantage Art, Inc.
Photo Researcher: Leslie Coopersmith
Electronic Production Manager: Valerie A. Sawyer
Desktop Administrator: LaToya Wigfall
Manufacturing Manager: Helene G. Landers
Electronic Page Makeup: Americomp
Printer and Binder: RR Donnelley & Sons Company
Cover Printer: The Lehigh Press, Inc.

For permission to use copyrighted material, grateful acknowledgment is made to the copyright holders on p. 711, which is hereby made part of this copyright page.

The American People: Creating a Nation and a Society, Brief Second Edition

Copyright © 1996 by HarperCollins College Publishers

Library of Congress Cataloging-in-Publication Data
The American People : creating a nation and a society / Gary B. Nash
   . . . [et al.]. — Brief 2nd ed.
         p.   cm.
   Includes index.
   ISBN 0-673-99526-7 (set). — ISBN 0-673-99527-5 (v. 1). —
ISBN 0-673-99528-3 (v. 2)
      1. United States — History.   I. Nash, Gary B.
E178 1. A49355   1995   95-887
973 — dc20   CIP

96 97 98 9 8 7 6 5 4 3 2

Contents in Brief

Detailed Contents

Maps and Charts

Preface

The Yoruba people of West Africa have an old saying: "However far the stream flows, it never forgets its source." Why, we wonder, do such ancient societies as the Yoruba find history so important, while modern American students question its relevance? This book aims to end such skepticism about the usefulness of history.

As we near the end of the twentieth century, in an ethnically and racially diverse country caught up in an interdependent global society, history is of central importance in preparing us to exercise our rights and responsibilities as free people. History cannot make good citizens, but without history we cannot understand the choices before us and think wisely about them. Lacking a collective memory of the past, we lapse into a kind of amnesia, unaware of the human condition and the long struggles of men and women everywhere to deal with the problems of their day and to create a better society. Unfurnished with historical knowledge, we deprive ourselves of knowing about the huge range of approaches people have taken to political, economic, and social life; to solving problems; and to conquering the obstacles in their way.

History has a deeper, even more fundamental importance: the cultivation of the private person, whose self-knowledge and self-respect provide the foundation for a life of dignity and fulfillment. Historical memory is the key to self-identity; to seeing one's place in the long stream of time, in the story of humankind.

When we study our own history, that of the American people, we see a rich and extraordinarily complex human story. This country, whose written history began with a convergence of Native Americans, Europeans, and Africans, has always been a nation of diverse peoples—a magnificent mosaic of cultures, religions, and skin shades. This book explores how American society assumed its present shape and developed its present forms of government; how as a nation we have conducted our foreign affairs and managed our economy; how as individuals and in groups we have lived, worked, loved, married, raised families, voted, argued, protested, and struggled to fulfill our dreams and the noble ideals of the American experiment.

Several ways of making the past understandable distinguish this book from most textbooks written in the past twenty years. The coverage of public events like presidential elections, diplomatic treaties, and economic legislation is integrated with the private human stories that underlie them. Within a chronological framework we have woven together our history as a nation, as a people, and as a society. When, for example, national political events are discussed, we analyze their impact on social and economic life at the state and local levels. Wars are described not only as they unfolded on the battlefield and in the salons of diplomats but also on the home front, where they are history's greatest motor of social change. The interaction of ordinary Americans with extraordinary events runs as a theme throughout this book.

Above all, we have tried to show the "humanness" of our history as it is revealed in people's everyday lives. The authors have often used the words of ordinary Americans to capture the authentic human voices of those who participated in and responded to epic events such as war, slavery, industrialization, and reform movements.

GOALS AND THEMES OF THE BOOK

Our primary goal is to provide students with a rich, balanced, and thought-provoking treatment of the American past. By this we mean a history that treats the lives and experiences of

Americans of all national origins and cultural backgrounds, at all levels of society, and in all regions of the country. It also means a history that seeks connections among the many factors—political, economic, technological, social, religious, intellectual, and biological—that have molded and remolded American society over four centuries. And finally it means a history that encourages students to think about how we have all inherited a complex past filled with both notable achievements and thorny problems. The only history befitting a democratic nation is one that inspires students to initiate a frank and searching dialogue with their past.

To speak of a dialogue about the past presumes that history is interpretive. Students should understand that historians are continually reinterpreting the past. New interpretations are often based on the discovery of new evidence, but more often new interpretations emerge because historians reevaluate old evidence in the light of new ideas that spring from the times in which they write and from their personal views of the world.

Through this book, we also hope to promote class discussions, which can be organized around six questions that we see as basic to the American historical experience:

1. How have Americans developed a stable, democratic political system flexible enough to address the wholesale changes that have occurred in the past two centuries, and to what degree has this political system been consistent with the principles of our nation's founding?
2. How has this nation been peopled, from the first inhabitants to many groups that arrived in slavery or servitude during the colonial period down to the voluntary immigrants of today? How have these waves of newcomers contributed to the American cultural mosaic, and how have they preserved elements of their ethnic, racial, and religious heritages?
3. How have economic and technological changes affected daily life, work, family or-

ganization, leisure, the division of wealth, and community relations in the United States?
4. What has been the role of our nation in the world?
5. How have the recurring reform movements in our history dealt with economic, political, and social problems in attempting to square the ideals of American life with the reality?
6. How have American beliefs and values changed over more than four hundred years of history, and how have they varied among different groups—women and men; people of different regions, racial and ethnic backgrounds, religions, and classes?

In writing a history that revolves around these themes, we have tried to describe two dynamics that operate in all societies. First, we observe people continually adjusting to new developments, such as industrialization and urbanization, over which they seemingly have little control; yet we realize that people are not paralyzed by history but rather are the fundamental creators of it. They retain the ability, individually and collectively, to shape the world in which they live and thus in considerable degree to control their own lives. Second, we emphasize the connections that always exist among social, political, economic, technological, and cultural events.

STRUCTURE OF THE BOOK

Part Organization

The chapters of this book are grouped into six parts relating to major periods in American history. Each part begins with a brief *introductory essay* that outlines how the six organizing questions described above are developed in the subsequent chapters.

Chapter Structure

Every chapter begins with a *personal story* recalling the experience of an ordinary or lesser-known American. Chapter 1, for example, starts with the tragic account of Opechancanough, a Powhatan tribesman whose entire life of nearly ninety years was consumed by a struggle against the land, hunger, and alien values brought by Spanish and English newcomers. This brief anecdote serves several purposes. First, it introduces the overarching themes and major concepts of the chapter, in this case the meeting in the North American wilderness of three societies—Native American, European, and African—each with different cultural values, life styles, and aspirations. Second, the personal story launches the chapter in a way that facilitates learning—by engaging the student with a human account. Last, the personal story suggests that history was shaped by ordinary as well as extraordinary people. At the end of the personal story a *brief overview* links the biographical sketch to the text by elaborating the major themes of the chapter.

We aim to facilitate the learning process for students in other ways as well. Every chapter ends with pedagogical features to reinforce and expand the presentation. A *conclusion* briefly summarizes the main concepts and developments elaborated in the chapter and serves as a bridge to the following chapter. A list of *recommended reading* provides supplementary sources for further study or research; novels contemporary to the period are often included. Finally, a *time line* reviews the major events and developments covered in the chapter. Each graph, map, and illustration has been chosen to relate clearly to the narrative.

THE BRIEF EDITION

This text is a Brief Edition of the very successful third edition of *The American People*. This shorter volume—approximately half the length of the complete version—will be particularly useful in one-semester courses and those courses that assign wide readings in primary sources, monographs, or articles in addition to the main text.

The foremost goal of the abridgement was to preserve the distinctive character of the complete text. The balance of political, social, economic, and cultural history remains the same, revolving around the same central, organizing themes previously described. The structure and organization of the text—parts, chapters, sections, and subsections—are largely unchanged. Deletions have been made on a careful line-by-line basis. All important topics are in place, as are the interpretive connections among the many factors molding our society. We have eliminated only detail, extra examples, and illustrative material within sections. While it might have been easier to delete more of the "humanness" of history, leaving room for facts and more facts, we have been careful to retain our focus on history as it is revealed through the lives of ordinary Americans, and the interplay of social and political factors.

We have also tried to provide the support materials necessary to make teaching and learning enjoyable and rewarding. The reader will be the judge of our success. The authors and HarperCollins welcome your comments.

ACKNOWLEDGMENTS

Over the years, as successive editions of this text were being developed, many of our colleagues read and criticized the various drafts of the manuscript. For their thoughtful evaluations and constructive suggestions, the authors wish to express their gratitude to the following reviewers:

Richard H. Abbott, Eastern Michigan University
Kenneth G. Alfers, Mountain View College
Gregg Andrews, Southwest Texas State University
Robert Asher, University of Connecticut, Storrs
Harry Baker, University of Arkansas at Little Rock
Michael Batinski, Southern Illinois University
Gary Bell, Sam Houston State University
Virginia Bellows, Tulsa Junior College

Spencer Bennett, Siena Heights College

James Bradford, Texas A&M University

Neal A. Brooks, Essex Community College

Jeffrey P. Brown, New Mexico State University

Sheri Bartlett Browne, Portland State University

David Brundage, University of California at Santa Cruz

Colin Calloway, University of Wyoming

D'Ann Campbell, Indiana University

James S. Chase, University of Arkansas

Vincent A. Clark, Johnson County Community College

Neil Clough, North Seattle Community College

Matthew Ware Coulter, Collin County Community College

David Culbert, Louisiana State University

John H. De Berry, Somerset Community College

Bruce Dierenfield, Canisius College

John Dittmer, DePauw University

Gordon Dodds, Portland State University

Richard Donley, Eastern Washington University

Robert Downtain, Tarrant County Community College

Mark Dyreson, Weber State University

Lori Clune Emerzian, California State University, Fresno

Rex L. Field, Palo Alto College

John L. Finnegan, Spokane Community College

Bernard Friedman, Indiana University–Purdue University at Indianapolis

Bruce Glasrud, California State University, Hayward

Richard Griswold del Castillo, San Diego State University

Colonel Williams L. Harris, The Citadel Military College

Robert Haws, University of Mississippi

Jerrold Hirsch, Northeast Missouri State University

Frederick Hoxie, McNickle Center for Study of American Indians

John S. Hughes, University of Texas

Donald M. Jacobs, Northeastern University

Delores Janiewski, University of Idaho, Mt. Holyoke

David Johnson, Portland State University

Richard Kern, University of Findlay

Monte Lewis, Cisco Junior College

William Link, University of North Carolina, Greensboro

Ronald Lora, University of Toledo

George M. Lubick, Northern Arizona University

John C. Massman, St. Cloud State University

Vern Mattson, University of Nevada at Las Vegas

Michael McCarthy, Community College of Denver

John McCormick, Delaware County Community College

Sylvia McGrath, Stephen F. Austin University

James E. McMillan, Denison University

Walter Miszczenko, Boise State University

Norma Mitchell, Troy State University

Gerald F. Moran, University of Michigan, Dearborn

William Morris, Midland College

Marian Morton, John Carroll University

Roger Nichols, University of Arizona

Paul Palmer, Texas A&I University

Al Parker, Riverside City College

Judith Parsons, Sul Ross State University

Neva Peters, Tarrant County Junior College

James Prickett, Santa Monica College

Noel Pugash, University of New Mexico

Juan Gomez-Quinones, University of California, Los Angeles

George Rable, Anderson College

Joseph P. Reidy, Howard University

Leonard Riforgiato, Pennsylvania State University

Randy Roberts, Purdue University

Mary Robertson, Armstrong State University

David Robson, John Carroll University

Sylvia Sebesta, San Antonio College

Herbert Shapiro, University of Cincinnati

David R. Shibley, Santa Monica College

Ellen Shockro, Pasadena City College

Sheila Skemp, University of Mississippi

Kathryn Sklar, Stanford University

Howard Smead, University of Maryland
Gary Scott Smith, Grove City College
James Smith, Virginia State University
John Snetsinger, California Polytechnic State
University
Tommy Stringer, Navarro College
Joan E. Supplee, Baylor University
Tom Tefft, Citrus College
John A. Trickel, Richland College
Donna Van Raaphorst, Cuyahoga Community
College
Morris Vogel, Temple University
Michael Wade, Appalachian State University
Jackie Walker, James Madison University

SUPPLEMENTS

For Instructors

- *Teaching the American People.* Authors Julie
  Roy Jeffrey and Peter J. Frederick have written this guide on the basis of ideas generated
  in the frequent "active learning" workshops
  held by the authors and have tied it closely to
  the text. In addition to suggestions on how to
  generate lively class discussion and involve
  students in active learning, this supplement
  also offers a file of exam questions and lists of
  resources, including films, slides, photo collections, records, and audiocassettes.

- *America Through the Eyes of Its People: A
  Collection of Primary Sources.* Prepared by
  Carol Brown of Houston Community
  College, this one-volume collection of primary documents portraying the rich and varied tapestry of American life contains documents concerning women, Native Americans,
  African-Americans, Hispanics, and others
  who helped to shape the course of U.S. history. Designed to be duplicated by instructors
  for student use, the documents have accompanying student exercises.

- *Discovering American History Through
  Maps and Views.* Created by Gerald Danzer
  of the University of Illinois at Chicago—the
  recipient of the AHA's 1990 James Harvey
  Robinson Prize for his work in the development of map transparencies—this set of 140
  four-color acetates is a unique instructional
  tool. It contains an introduction on teaching
  history through maps and a detailed commentary on each transparency. The collection includes cartographic and pictorial maps, views
  and photos, urban plans, building diagrams,
  and works of art.

- *Primary Sources in Gender in American
  History.* Prepared by Ellen Skinner of Pace
  University, this collection includes both classic and unique documents from diverse perspectives covering the history of women and
  gender in American history. The book includes critical thinking questions, bibliography, and contextual headnotes and is available shrinkwrapped with *The American
  People* at a low cost.

- *Primary Sources in African American History.*
  Prepared by Roy Finkenbine of Hampton
  University, this compelling collection includes
  both social and political documents and covers the history of African-Americans in
  America. The book includes critical thinking
  questions, bibliography, and contextual headnotes and is available shrinkwrapped with *The
  American People* at a low cost.

- *American Impressions: A CD-ROM for U.S.
  History, Volumes I and II.* This unique and
  ground-breaking CD-ROM for the U.S.
  History course is organized in a topical and the-
  matic framework which allows in-depth coverage with a media-centered focus. Hundreds of
  photos, maps, works of art, graphics, and historical film clips are organized into narrated
  vignettes and interactive activities to create a
  tool for both professors and students. The
  first volume includes: "The Encounter Period,"
  "Revolution to Republic," "A Century of
  Labor and Reform," and "The Struggle for
  Equality." A Guide for Instructors provides

teaching tips and suggestions for using advanced media in the classroom. The CD-ROM is available in both Macintosh and Windows formats.

- *Visual Archives of American History, 2nd ed.* This two-sided video laserdisc explores history from the meeting of three cultures to the present. It is an encyclopedic chronology of U.S. history offering hundreds of photographs and illustrations, a variety of source and reference maps—several of which are animated— plus 50 minutes of video. For ease in planning lectures, a manual listing barcodes for scanning and frame numbers for all the material is available.

- *A Guide to Teaching American History Through Film.* Written by Randy Roberts of Purdue University, this guide provides instructors with a creative and practical tool for stimulating classroom discussion. The sections include "American Films: A Historian's Perspective," a list of films, practical suggestions, and bibliography. The film listing is presented in narrative form, developing connections between each film and the topics being studied.

- *Video Lecture Launchers.* Prepared by Mark Newman, University of Illinois at Chicago, these video lecture launchers (each 2 to 5 minutes in duration) cover key issues in American history from 1877 to the present. The launchers are accompanied by an instructor's manual.

- *"This Is America" Immigration Videos.* Produced by the American Museum of Immigration, these two 20-minute videos tell the story of American immigrants, relating their personal stories and accomplishments. By showing how the richness of our culture is due to the contributions of millions of immigrant Americans, the videos make the point that America's strength lies in the ethnically and culturally diverse backgrounds of its citizens.

- *Visual Archives of American History.* This video laserdisc provides over 500 photos and 29 minutes of film clips of major events in American history. Each photo or film clip may be instantly accessed, making this collection ideal for classroom use.

- *Transparencies.* A set of more than 40 map transparencies drawn from the text.

- *Test Bank.* This test bank, prepared by Charles Cook, Houston Community College, and J. B. Smallwood, North Texas State University, contains more than 3,500 objective, conceptual, and essay questions. All questions are keyed to specific pages in the text.

- *TestMaster Computerized Testing System.* This flexible, easy-to-master computer test bank includes all the test items in the printed test bank. The TestMaster software allows you to edit existing questions and add your own items. Tests can be printed in several different formats and can include figures such as graphs and tables. Available for IBM and Macintosh computers.

- *QuizMaster.* This new program enables you to design TestMaster-generated tests that your students can take on a computer rather than in printed form. QuizMaster is available separately from TestMaster and can be obtained free through your sales representative.

- *Grades.* A grade-keeping and classroom management software program that maintains data for up to 200 students.

For Students

- *Study Guide and Practice Tests.* This two-volume study guide, created by Julie Roy Jeffrey and Peter J. Frederick, includes chapter outlines, significant themes and highlights, a glossary, learning enrichment ideas, sample test questions, exercises for identification and interpretation, and geography exercises based on maps in the text.

- *Learning to Think Critically: Films and Myths About American History.* Randy Roberts and Robert May of Purdue University use well-known films such as *Gone with the Wind* and *Casablanca* to explore some common myths about America and its past. Many widely held assumptions about our country's past come from or are perpetuated by popular films. Which are true? Which are patently not true? And how does a student of history approach documents, sources, and textbooks with a critical and discerning eye? This short handbook subjects some popular beliefs to historical scrutiny in order to help students develop a method of inquiry for approaching the subject of history in general.

- *Mapping America: A Guide to Historical Geography.* This workbook by Ken L. Weatherbie, Del Mar College, contains 35 sequenced exercises corresponding to the map program in the text, each culminating in a series of interpretive questions about the role of geographical factors in American history.

- *Mapping American History: Student Activities.* Written by Gerald Danzer of the University of Illinois at Chicago, this free map workbook for students features exercises designed to teach students to interpret and analyze cartographic materials as historical documents. The instructor is entitled to a free copy of the workbook for each copy of the text purchased from HarperCollins.

- *Concepts in American History.* This slim volume, written by Robert Asher of the University of Connecticut, contains brief essays on 13 key concepts in American history, including such topics as Republicanism, nativism, feminism, and capitalism.

- *SuperShell II Computerized Tutorial.* Prepared by Ken L. Weatherbie, Del Mar College, this interactive program for IBM computers helps students learn major facts and concepts through drill and practice exercises and diagnostic feedback. SuperShell II provides immediate correct answers, the text page number on which the material is discussed, and a running score of the student's performance maintained on the screen throughout the session. This free supplement is available to instructors through their sales representative.

- *TimeLink Computer Atlas of American History.* This atlas, compiled by William Hamblin of Brigham Young University, is an introductory software tutorial and textbook companion. This Macintosh program presents the historical geography of the continental United States from colonial times to the settling of the West and the admission of the last continental state in 1912. The program covers territories in different time periods, provides quizzes, and includes a special Civil War module.

GARY B. NASH
JULIE ROY JEFFREY
JOHN R. HOWE
PETER J. FREDERICK
ALLEN F. DAVIS
ALLAN M. WINKLER

About the Authors

Gary B. Nash received his Ph.D. from Princeton University in 1964. He is currently Director of the National Center for History in the Schools at the University of California, Los Angeles, where he teaches colonial and revolutionary American history. Among the books Nash has written are *Quakers and Politics: Pennsylvania, 1681–1726* (1968); *Red, White, and Black: The Peoples of Early America* (1974, 1982); *The Urban Crucible: Social Change, Political Consciousness, and the Origins of the American Revolution* (1979); and *Forging Freedom: The Black Urban Experience in Philadelphia, 1720–1840* (1988). His scholarship is especially concerned with the role of common people in the making of history. He wrote Part I and served as a general editor of this book.

Julie Roy Jeffrey earned her Ph.D. in history from Rice University in 1972. Since then she has taught at Goucher College. Honored as an outstanding teacher, Jeffrey has been involved in faculty development activities and curriculum evaluation. Jeffrey's major publications include *Education for Children of the Poor* (1978); *Frontier Women: The Trans-Mississippi West, 1840–1880* (1979); and *Converting the West: A Biography of Narcissa Whitman* (1991). She is the author of many articles on the lives and perceptions of nineteenth-century women. She wrote Parts III and IV in collaboration with Peter Frederick and acted as a general editor of this book.

John R. Howe received his Ph.D. from Yale University in 1962. At the University of Minnesota his teaching interests include early American politics and relations between Native Americans and whites. His major publications include *The Changing Political Thought of John Adams* (1966) and *From the Revolution Through the Age of Jackson* (1973). His major research currently involves a manuscript entitled "The Transformation of Public Life in Revolutionary America." Howe wrote Part II of this book.

Peter J. Frederick received his Ph.D. in history from the University of California, Berkeley, in 1966. Innovative student-centered teaching of American history has been the focus of his career at California State University, Hayward, and since 1970 at Wabash College (1992–1994 at Carleton College). Recognized nationally as a distinguished teacher and for his many articles and workshops for faculty on teaching and learning, Frederick has also written several articles on life-writing and a book, *Knights of the Golden Rule: The Intellectual as Christian Social Reformer in the 1890s*. He coordinated and edited all the "Recovering the Past" sections and co-wrote Parts III and IV of this book.

Allen F. Davis earned his Ph.D. from the University of Wisconsin in 1959. A former president of the American Studies Association, he is a professor of history at Temple University and Director of the Center for Public History. He is the author of *Spearheads for Reform: The Social Settlements and the Progressive Movement* (1967) and *American Heroine: The Life and Legend of Jane Addams* (1973). He is coauthor of *Still Philadelphia* (1983), *Philadelphia Stories* (1987), and *One Hundred Years at Hull-House* (1990). He is currently working on a book on masculine culture in America. Davis wrote Part V of this book.

Allan M. Winkler received his Ph.D. from Yale University in 1974. He is presently teaching at Miami University, where he chairs the History Department. His books include *The Politics of Propaganda: The Office of War Information, 1942–1945* (1978); *Modern America: The United States from the Second World War to the Present* (1985); *Home Front U.S.A.: America During World War II* (1986); and *Life Under a Cloud: American Anxiety About the Atom* (1993). His research centers on the connections between public policy and popular mood in modern American history. Winkler wrote Part VI of this book.

The American People

part 1

A Colonizing People

America has always been a nation of immigrants, an elaborate cultural mosaic created out of the unending streams of people who for four centuries have flocked to its shores from every corner of the world. This intermingling began with the convergence of people from the three continents of North America, Europe, and Africa. We examine the mingling of their values, institutions, and lifeways during the fifteenth and sixteenth centuries in Chapter 1, "Three Worlds Meet." Chapter 2, "Colonizing a Continent," explores five regions of settlement along the Atlantic seaboard.

Chapter 3, "Mastering the New World," explores how colonists struggled against Native Americans to expand their land base and turned to slave labor in the southern colonies. The colonists also had to deal with social and political tensions among themselves at the end of the seventeenth century. At the same time, French territorial ambitions in North America threatened another kind of conflict.

Chapter 4, "The Maturing of Colonial Society," traces the development of the colonies of England, Spain, and France in the first half of the eighteenth century. It shows how economic growth, religious revival, and political maturation prepared the English colonists by 1750 for the epic events that would follow. Chapter 5, "Bursting the Colonial Bonds," describes the coming of the American Revolution.

chapter 1

....

Three Worlds Meet

In the late 1550s, a few years after Catholic King Philip II and Protestant Queen Elizabeth assumed the throne in Spain and England, respectively, Opechancanough was born in Tsenacommacah. In the Algonquian language, the word Tsenacommacah meant "densely inhabited land." Later English colonizers would rename this place Virginia after their monarch, the virgin Queen Elizabeth. Before he died in the 1640s in the ninth decade of his life, Opechancanough had seen light-skinned, swarthy, and black-skinned newcomers from a half dozen European nations and African kingdoms swarm into his land.

Opechancanough was only an infant when Europeans first reached the Chesapeake Bay region. A small party of Spanish had explored the area in 1561, but they found neither gold nor silver nor anything else of value. Upon departing, they left behind something of unparalleled importance in the history of contact between the peoples of Europe and the Americas: a bacterial infection that spread like wildfire through a population that had no immunity against it. Many members of Opechancanough's tribe died.

In 1570, when Opechancanough was young, the Spanish returned and established a Jesuit mission near the York River. Violence occurred, and before the Spanish abandoned the Chesapeake in 1572, they put to death a number of captured Indians, including a chief who was Opechancanough's relative.

Opechancanough was in his forties when three ships of fair-skinned settlers disembarked in 1607 to begin the first permanent English settlement in the New World. As relations with the whites worsened, his half brother Powhatan, high chief of several dozen loosely confederated tribes in the region, sent him to capture the English leader John Smith and escort him to the Indians' main village. Smith was put through a mock execution but then released. He later got the best of Opechancanough, threatening him with a pistol, humiliating him in front of his warriors, and assaulting one of his sons.

Opechancanough saw English settlements slowly spread in the Chesapeake region. Then, in 1617, he assumed leadership of the Powhatan Confederacy. Five years later, Opechancanough led a determined assault on the English plantations that lay along the rivers and streams emptying into the bay. The Indians killed nearly one-third of the intruders. But they paid dearly in the retaliatory raids that the colonists mounted in succeeding years.

As he watched the land-hungry settlers swarm in during the next two decades, Opechancanough's patience failed him. Finally, in 1644, now in his eighties, he galvanized a new generation of warriors and led a final desperate assault on the English. It was a suicidal attempt, but the "great general" of the Powhatan Confederacy, faithful to the tradition of his people, counseled death over enslavement and humiliation. Though the warriors inflicted heavy casualties, they could not overwhelm the colonizers, who vastly outnumbered them. For two years, Opechancanough was kept prisoner by the Virginians. Nearly blind and "so decrepit that he was not able to walk alone," he was fatally shot in the back by an English guard in 1646.

Over a long lifetime, Opechancanough painfully experienced the meeting of people from three continents. The nature of this violent intermingling of Europeans, Africans, and Native Americans on Chesapeake Bay is an essential part of early American history. But to understand how the destinies of red, white, and black people became intertwined in Opechancanough's land, we must look at the precontact history and cultural foundations of life in the homelands of each of them.

THE PEOPLE OF AMERICA BEFORE COLUMBUS

The history of humankind in North America began thousands of years ago, as nomadic hunters from Siberia migrated across a land bridge connecting northeastern Asia with Alaska. Paleoanthropologists remain divided on the exact timing, but the main migration apparently occurred either about 12,000 to 14,000 or 25,000 to 28,000 years ago.

Hunters and Farmers

For thousands of years, these early hunters trekked southward and eastward, following vegetation and game. In time, they reached the tip of South America and the eastern edge of North America.

Archaeological evidence suggests that as centuries passed and population increased, the earliest inhabitants evolved into separate cultures, adjusting to a variety of environments in distinct ways. By the 1500s, as Europeans began to explore the New World, the "Indians" of the Americas were enormously diverse in the size and complexity of their societies, the languages they spoke, and their forms of social organization.

The first phase of "Native American" history, the long Beringian epoch, ended about 12,000 B.C. A rich archaeological record from that time indicates that the hunters had developed a new technology. Big-game hunters now flaked hard stones into spear points and chose "kill sites" where they slew whole herds of Pleistocene mammals. This more reliable food source allowed population growth, and nomadism began to give way to settled habitations or local migration within limited territories.

In the Archaic era, from about 8000 B.C. to 500 B.C., human populations adapted to a warmer climate as the glaciers retreated. The Pleistocene mammals could not survive, but the people learned to exploit new sources of food, especially plant life. In time a second technological breakthrough, the "agricultural revolution," occurred.

When Native Americans learned to "domesticate" plant life, they began the long process of transforming their relationship to the physical world. To learn how to harvest, plant, and nurture a seed was to gain partial control over natural forces that before had been ungovernable. Over the millennia, humans progressed from doorside planting of a few wild seeds to systematic clearing and planting of bean and maize fields. Sedentary village life began to replace a nomadic hunting and gathering existence. The increase in food supply brought about by agriculture triggered the growth of larger populations and greater social and political complexity. Many societies empowered religious figures, who organized the common followers, directed their work, exacted tribute, and undertook to protect the community from hostile forces.

Regional trading networks carried commodities such as salt, obsidian rock for projectile points, and copper for jewelry. Technology, religious ideas, and agricultural practices were also transmitted. By the end of the Archaic period (about 500 B.C.), hundreds of independent, kin-based groups, like people in other parts of the world, had learned to exploit the resources of their particular area and to trade with other groups in their region.

Native Americans in 1600

The last epoch of pre-Columbian development, the post-Archaic phase, occurred during the 2,000 years before contact with Europeans. It involved a complex process of growth and environmental adaptation among many distinct societies—and crisis in some of them. In the American Southwest, the ancestors of the present-day Hopi and Zuni developed carefully planned villages composed of large terraced buildings, each with many rooms. By the time the Spanish reached the American Southwest in the 1540s, the indigenous Pueblo people were using irrigation canals, check dams, and hillside terracing to bring water to their arid maize fields.

Far to the east were the mound-building societies of the Mississippi and Ohio valleys. These societies declined about 1,000 years before Europeans reached the continent, perhaps because of attacks from other tribes or severe climatic changes that undermined agriculture. Several centuries later, another culture, based on intensive cultivation of beans, maize, and squash, began to flourish in the Mississippi valley. Its center, a city of perhaps 40,000, called Cahokia, stood near present-day St. Louis and included a temple that rose in four terraces to a height of 100 feet. This was the urban center of a far-flung "Mississippi" culture that encompassed thousands of villages from Wisconsin to Louisiana and from Oklahoma to Tennessee.

The influence of the Mound Builders passed eastward to transform the woodlands societies along the Atlantic coastal plain. The numerous small tribes that settled from Nova Scotia to Florida had added limited agriculture to their skill in exploiting natural plants for food, medicine, dyes, and flavoring and had developed food-procurement strategies that used all the resources around them—cleared land, forests, streams, shore, and ocean.

Most of the eastern woodlands tribes lived in waterside villages. Locating their fields of maize near fishing grounds, they often migrated seasonally between inland and coastal village sites or situated themselves astride two ecological zones.

As European exploration of the Americas drew near, the continent north of the Rio Grande contained perhaps four million people, of whom perhaps 500,000 lived along the eastern coastal plain and in the piedmont region accessible to the early European settlers. The colonizers were not coming to a "virgin wilderness,"

An engraving showing the French discovery of the River of May in Florida on May 1, 1654. As the illustration shows, many initial encounters between Native Americans and Europeans were friendly. Here, a party of the locally indigenous people swims out to meet the French with gifts, and another Native American leads a small group of French inland to a village.

as they often described it, but to a land inhabited for thousands of years by people whose village existence in many ways resembled that of the arriving Europeans.

In some important ways, however, Indian culture also differed from that of Europeans. Horses, for example, were not available to the native peoples of the New World as they developed their methods of farming, transportation, and warfare. Without draft animals such as the horse or ox, they had not developed wheeled vehicles or, for that matter, the potter's wheel, which also uses the wheel-and-axle principle. Many inventions—such as the technology for the smelting of iron, which had diffused widely in the Old World—had not crossed the ocean barrier to reach the New World. The opposite was also true: Valuable New World crops, such as corn and potatoes, which had been developed by Indian agriculturalists, were unknown in the Old World before Columbus.

Contrasting World Views

Colonizing Europeans called themselves "civilized" and typically described the people they met in the Americas as "savage," "heathen," or "barbarian." The gulf separating people in Europe and North America was defined not only by their material cultures but also by how they viewed their relationship to the environment and how they defined social relations in their communities. Having evolved in complete isolation from each other, European and Indian cultures exhibited a wide difference in values.

In the view of Europeans, the natural world was a resource designed for use by humans. Native Americans, in contrast, were "contented with Nature as they find her," as one colonist phrased it. In their ethos, every part of the natural environment was sacred. Rocks, trees, and animals all possessed spiritual power, and all were linked to form a sacred whole. To injure the environment, by overfishing or abusing it in any way, was to offend the spiritual power present throughout nature and hence to risk spiritual retaliation.

Regarding the soil as a resource to be exploited for humans' benefit, Europeans believed that land should be privately possessed. Their social structure directly mirrored patterns of land ownership, with a land-wealthy elite at the apex of the social pyramid and a mass of propertyless individuals forming the broad base.

Native Americans also had concepts of property, and tribes recognized territorial boundaries. But they believed that land was invested with sacred qualities and should be held in common. Observing the Iroquois of the eastern woodlands in 1657, a French Jesuit noted with surprise that they had no almshouses because "their kindness, humanity and courtesy not only makes them liberal with what they have, but causes them to possess hardly anything except in common. A whole village must be without corn, before any individual can be obliged to endure privation." Not all Europeans were acquisitive, competitive individuals. The majority were peasants scratching a subsistence living from the soil, living in kin-centered villages with little contact with the outside world, and exchanging goods and labor through barter. But in Europe's urban centers a wealth-conscious, striving individual who celebrated wider choices and greater opportunities to enhance personal status was coming to the fore. In contrast, Native American traditions stressed the group rather than the individual. Holding land and other resources in common, Indian societies were usually more egalitarian and their members more concerned with personal valor than personal wealth.

The European newcomers to North America encountered a people whose cultural values differed strikingly from theirs. They also found disturbing the matrilineal organization of many tribal societies. Family membership among the Iroquois, for example, was determined through the female line. A typical family consisted of an old woman, her daughters with their husbands and children, and her unmarried granddaughters and grandsons. When a son or grandson married, he moved from this female-headed household to one headed by the matriarch of his wife's family. Divorce was also the woman's prerogative. If she desired it, she merely set her husband's possessions outside their dwelling door. Clans were composed of several matrilineal kin groups related by a blood connection on the mother's side.

European women, with rare exceptions, were entirely excluded from political affairs. By contrast, in Native American villages, again to take the Iroquois example, designated men sat in a circle to deliberate and make decisions, but the senior women of the village stood behind them, lobbying and instructing. The village chiefs were male, but they were named to their positions by the elder women of their clans. If they moved too far from the will of the women who appointed them, these chiefs were removed—or "dehorned."

In the tribal economy, men were responsible for hunting, fishing, and clearing land, but women controlled the cultivation, harvest, and distribution of food. When the men were away on hunting expeditions, women directed village life. Europeans perceived such a degree of sexual equality as another mark of the uncivilized nature of tribal society.

In the religious beliefs of Native Americans, the English saw a final cultural defect. Europeans built their religious life around the belief in a single god, written scriptures, an organized

Indian Societies During the Period of Early European Settlement

clergy, and churches. Most Native American societies believed in a spirit power dwelling throughout nature (polytheism).

AFRICA ON THE EVE OF CONTACT

Half a century before Columbus reached the Americas, a Portuguese sea captain, Antam Gonçalves, made the first European landing on the west coast of sub-Saharan Africa. If he had been able to travel the length and breadth of the immense continent, he would have encountered a rich variety of African peoples and cultures. The notion of African "backwardness" and cultural impoverishment was a myth perpetuated after the slave trade had begun transporting millions of Africans to the New World. During the period of early contact with Europeans, Africa, like pre-Columbian America, was recognized as a diverse continent with a long history of cultural evolution.

The Kingdoms of Africa

The peoples of Africa, estimated at about 50 million in the fifteenth century, when Europeans began making extensive contact with them, lived in vast deserts, grasslands, and tropical forests. As in Europe and the Americas at that time, most people tilled the soil. Part of their skill in farming derived from the development of iron production, which may have begun in West Africa while Europe was still in the Stone Age. More efficient iron implements increased agricultural productivity, which in turn spurred population growth.

By the time Europeans reached the west coast of Africa, a number of large empires had risen there. The first was the kingdom of Ghana, embracing an immense territory between the Sahara and the Gulf of Guinea and from the Atlantic Ocean to the Niger River. The development of large towns, skillfully designed buildings, elaborate sculpture and metalwork depicting humans and animals, long-distance commerce, and a complex political structure marked the Ghanaian kingdom from the sixth to eleventh centuries.

An invasion of North African Muslim people beginning in the eleventh century introduced a period of religious strife that eventually destroyed the kingdom of Ghana. But in the same region arose the Islamic kingdom of Mali, which flourished until the fifteenth century. Its city of Timbuktu contained a distinguished faculty of scholars with whom North Africans and even southern Europeans came to study. Lesser kingdoms such as Kongo, Songhay, and Benin had also been growing for centuries before Europeans reached Africa by water.

The African Ethos

The peoples of Africa had a rich diversity of cultures, but most of them shared certain ways of life that differentiated them from Europeans. As in Europe, the family was the basic unit of social organization. In many African societies, as in many Native American ones, the family was matrilineal. Property rights and political inheritance descended through the mother rather than the father. It was not the son of a chief who inherited his father's position but the son of the chief's sister. When a man married, he left his family to join that of his bride.

West Africans believed in a supreme creator of the cosmos, an assortment of lesser deities associated with natural forces such as rain, fertility, and animal life, and spirits that dwelt in trees, rocks, and rivers. Ancestors were also worshiped, for they mediated between the Creator and the living of the earth.

Social organization in much of West Africa by the time Europeans arrived was as elaborate as in fifteenth-century Europe. At the top of society stood the nobility and the priests, usually men of advanced age. Beneath them were the great masses of people. Most of them were farmers, but some worked as craftsmen, traders, teachers, and artists. At the bottom of society

The art of sixteenth-century West Africa, much of it ceremonial, shows a high degree of aesthetic development. On the left is Gou, god of war, a metal sculpture from the Fon culture in Dahomey; on the right is a pair of antelope headdresses (worn by running a cord through holes in the base and tying them atop the head) carved of wood by the Bambara tribe of Senegambia.

West African Cultures and Slaving Forts

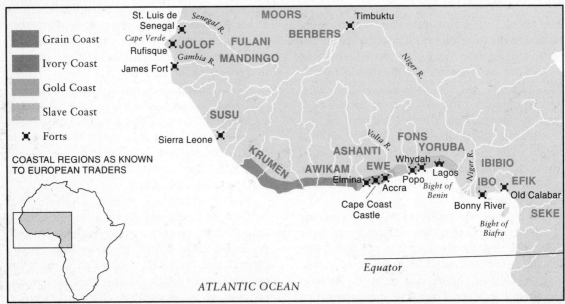

resided slaves. As in ancient Greece and Rome, they were "outsiders"—war captives, criminals, or sometimes persons who sold themselves into servitude to satisfy a debt. Slaves were entitled to protection under the law and allowed the privileges of education, marriage, and parenthood. Their servile condition was not permanent, nor was it automatically fastened onto their children, as would be the fate of Africans enslaved in the Americas.

EUROPE IN THE AGE OF EXPLORATION

In the ninth century, about the time that the Mound Builders of the Mississippi valley were constructing their urban center at Cahokia and the kingdom of Ghana was rising in West Africa, western Europe was an economic and cultural backwater. It was overshadowed by Christian Byzantium, which controlled Asia Minor, the Balkans, and parts of Italy, and by the Muslim culture of the Middle East, which had spilled across North Africa and penetrated Spain and West Africa south of the Sahara. Over the next six centuries, an epic revitalization of western Europe occurred, creating the conditions that enabled its leading maritime nations vastly to extend their oceanic frontiers. Thence began a 400-year epoch of the militant expansion of European peoples and European culture into other continents.

The Rise of Europe

The rebirth of western Europe, which began around A.D. 1000, owed much to a revival of long-distance trading from Italian ports on the Mediterranean. Venice, Genoa, Pisa, and other Italian ports grew wealthy and gradually evolved into merchant-dominated city-states that freed themselves from the rule of feudal lords in control of the surrounding countryside.

While merchants led the emerging city-states, western Europe's feudal system was grad-

ually weakening. In the thirteenth and fourteenth centuries, kings began to reassert their political authority and to undertake efforts to unify their realms.

Early developments in England led to a distinctive political system. In 1215, the English aristocracy curbed the powers of the king when they forced him to accept the Magna Charta. On the basis of this charter, a parliament composed of elective and hereditary members eventually gained the right to meet regularly to pass money bills. Parliament was thus in a position to act as a check on the Crown, an arrangement unknown on the Continent. During the sixteenth century, the Crown and Parliament worked together toward a more unified state, with the English kings wielding less political power than their European counterparts.

Economic changes of great significance also occurred in England during the sixteenth century. Members of the landed class began to combine their estates in order to practice more intensive and profitable agriculture. In this process, they threw peasant farmers off their plots, turning many of them into wage laborers. The formation of this working class was the crucial first step toward industrial development.

Continental Europe lagged behind England in two respects. First, it was far less affected by the move to consolidate, or "enclose," land. Part of the explanation lies in the values of continental aristocrats, who regarded the maximization of profit as unworthy of gentlemen. French nobles could lose their titles for commercial activities. Second, continental rulers were less successful in engaging the interests of their nobilities, and these nobles never shared governance with their king, as did English aristocrats through their participation in Parliament. In Spain, for example, the bloody expulsion of the Muslims and the Jews in 1492 strengthened the monarchy's hold, but regional cultures and leaders remained strong. The continental monarchs would thus warmly embrace doctrines of royal absolutism developed in the sixteenth century.

The New Monarchies and the Expansionist Impulse

In the second half of the fifteenth century, ambitious monarchs coming to power in France, England, and Spain sought social order and political stability in their kingdoms. Louis XI in France, Henry VII in England, Isabella of Castile, and Ferdinand of Aragon all created strong armies and bureaucratic state machinery. In these countries, and in Portugal as well, economic revival and Renaissance culture, with its secular emphasis on human abilities, nourished the impulse to expand beyond known frontiers. The exploratory urge had two initial objectives: to circumvent Muslim traders by finding an eastward oceanic route to Asia and to tap at its source the African gold trade.

Portugal launched Europe's age of exploration at the end of the fifteenth century. Led by Prince Henry the Navigator, for whom trade was secondary to the conquest of the Muslim world, Portugal breached the geographical unknown. In the 1420s, Henry began dispatching Portuguese mariners to probe the unknown Atlantic "sea of darkness." His intrepid sailors were aided by important improvements in navigation, mapmaking, and ship design, all promoted by the prince.

By the 1430s, Prince Henry's captains had reached Madeira, the Canaries, and the Azores, lying off the coasts of Portugal and northwestern Africa. These were soon developed as the first European agricultural plantations located on the Continent's periphery. From there, the Portuguese sea captains pushed farther south.

By the time of Prince Henry's death in 1460, Portuguese mariners had reached the west coast of Africa, where they began a profitable trade in ivory, slaves, and especially gold. By 1500, they had captured control of the African gold trade monopolized for centuries by North African Muslims. In 1497, Vasco da Gama became the first European to sail around the Cape of Africa, allowing the Portuguese to colonize the Indian Ocean and to establish trade concessions as far east as the Spice Islands and Canton by 1513.

Reaching the Americas

The marriage of Ferdinand and Isabella in 1469 united the independent states of Aragon and Castile and launched the Spanish nation into its golden age. Leading the way for Spain was an Italian sailor, Christopher Columbus. The son of a poor Genoese weaver, Columbus had married into a prominent family of Lisbon merchants and thus made important contacts at court.

Like many sailors, Columbus had listened to sea tales about lands to the west. He may have heard stories about the voyages of the Viking explorer Leif Eriksson, who around A.D. 1000 set sail from Greenland and landed at "Vinland," which may have been located somewhere between New England and Virginia. Columbus may also have heard accounts of the Viking settlement in Newfoundland. At any rate, he believed that ships could reach the Indies by sailing west across the Atlantic, but for nearly ten years he failed to secure financial backing and royal sanction in Portugal for exploratory voyages. Finally, in 1492, Queen Isabella of Spain commissioned him, and he sailed west with three tiny ships manned by about 90 men.

Strong winds, lasting ten days, blew the ships far into the Atlantic. There they were becalmed. In the fifth week at sea—longer than any European sailors had been out of the sight of land—mutinous rumblings swept through the crews. But Columbus pressed on. On the seventieth day, long after Columbus had calculated he would reach Japan, a lookout sighted land. On October 12, 1492, the sailors clambered ashore on a tiny island in the Bahamas, which Columbus named San Salvador (Holy Savior). Grateful sailors "rendered thanks to Our Lord, kneeling on the ground, embracing it with tears of joy."

Oceanic Exploration in the Fifteenth and Sixteenth Centuries

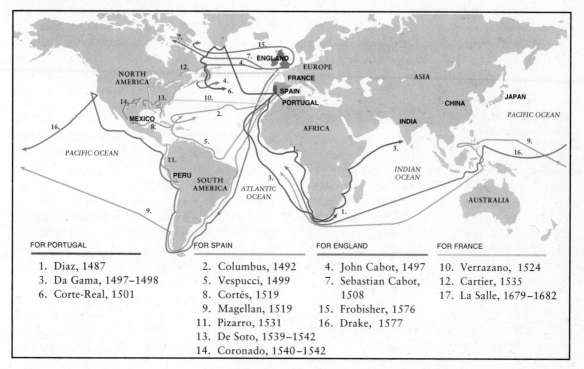

FOR PORTUGAL	FOR SPAIN	FOR ENGLAND	FOR FRANCE
1. Diaz, 1487	2. Columbus, 1492	4. John Cabot, 1497	10. Verrazano, 1524
3. Da Gama, 1497–1498	5. Vespucci, 1499	7. Sebastian Cabot,	12. Cartier, 1535
6. Corte-Real, 1501	8. Cortés, 1519	1508	17. La Salle, 1679–1682
	9. Magellan, 1519	15. Frobisher, 1576	
	11. Pizarro, 1531	16. Drake, 1577	
	13. De Soto, 1539–1542		
	14. Coronado, 1540–1542		

Believing he had reached Asia, Columbus explored the island-speckled Caribbean for ten weeks, landing on heavily populated islands that he named Hispaniola (shared today by Haiti and the Dominican Republic) and Cuba (which he thought was the Asian mainland). While homeward bound, he penned a report of his discoveries, still convinced that he had reached Asia.

Quickly printed and distributed throughout Europe, Columbus's report of his discoveries brought him financing for three much larger expeditions to explore the newfound lands. Though he led Spain to the threshold of a mighty empire, he reaped few rewards, dying unnoticed and penniless in 1506. To the end he believed that he had found the water route to Asia.

In time the real import of Columbus's discovery became clear, and he has long been celebrated as the bold explorer who initiated permanent contact between Europe and the Americas. He is attacked by some today as the ruthless exploiter of Indian peoples and lands, but Columbus is best understood in the context of his own times—an age of great brutality and violence, in which no race or nation had a monopoly on cruelty.

The expansion of Spain and Portugal into new areas of the world profoundly affected patterns of economic activity in Europe. Its commercial center now shifted away from the ports of the Mediterranean to the Atlantic ports facing the New World.

The New World also beckoned as a field of religious conquest. The heavily populated Americas offered millions of potential Christian converts. But the Catholic-Protestant division within Christianity complicated Christian dreams of converting a "heathen" continent. The people of western Europe, at precisely the time they were unlocking the secrets of the new worlds to the east and west in the sixteenth century, were being torn by religious schisms that magnified the era's national rivalries.

Religious Conflict During the Reformation

At the heart of Europe's religious strife was a continental movement to cleanse the Christian church of corrupt practices and return it to the purer ways of "primitive" Christianity, as practiced by the early Christians. While criticism of the worldliness of the Catholic church mounted during the Renaissance, a German monk, Martin Luther, became the first to break successfully with Rome and initiate a Protestant reformation of theology and practice. As Protestant sects multiplied, a Catholic Reformation grew up within the church, and the two groups began a long battle for the souls of Europeans.

Luther, an Augustinian monk, lost faith in the power of the age-old rituals of the church—prayer, the Mass, confession, pilgrimages to holy places, even crusades against Muslim infidels. He reasoned that salvation came through an inward faith, or "grace," that God conferred on those he chose. Good works, Luther believed, did not earn grace but were only the external evidence of grace won through faith. Luther had taken the revolutionary step of rejecting the church's elaborate hierarchy of officials, who presided over the rituals intended to guide individuals along the path toward salvation. The spread of printing, invented less than 70 years before, allowed the rapid circulation of his ideas.

Luther urged people to seek faith individually by reading the Bible, which he translated into German and made widely available for the first time in printed form. He also called on the German princes to assume control over religion

in their states, directly challenging the authority of Rome.

The basic issue dividing Catholics and Protestants thus centered on the source of religious authority. To Catholics, religious authority resided in the organized Church, headed by the pope. To Protestants, the Bible was the sole authority, and access to God's word or God's grace did not require the mediation of the Church.

Building on Luther's redefinition of Christianity, John Calvin, a Frenchman, brought new intensity and meaning to the Protestant Reformation. In 1536, at age 26, he published a ringing appeal to every Christian to form a direct, personal relationship with God. By Calvin's doctrine, God had saved a few souls at random before Creation and damned the rest. Human beings were too depraved to know or alter this predestination, but good Christians must struggle to believe in their hearts that they were saved. Without mediation of ritual or priest but by "straight-walking," one was to behave as one of God's elect, the "saints." This radical theology spread among elements in all classes throughout Europe.

Calvin proposed reformed Christian communities structured around the elect few. Communities of "saints" must control the state, rather than the other way around. Elected bodies of ministers and dedicated laymen, called presbyteries, were to govern the church, directing the affairs of society down to the last detail so that all, whether saved or damned, would work for God's ends.

Calvin's radical program converted large numbers of people to Protestantism throughout Europe. Sixteenth-century monarchs regarded attacks on the Catholic church with horror. But many local princes adopted some version of the reformed faith. The most important monarch to break with Roman Catholicism was Henry VIII of England. Although Henry did not consider himself a Protestant, when Pope Clement VII refused him permission to divorce and remarry, he broke relations with Rome and established the Church of England, with himself as head.

The countries most affected by the Reformation—England, Holland, and France—were slow in trying to colonize the New World, so Protestantism did not gain an early foothold in the Americas. Catholicism in Spain and Portugal remained almost immune from the Protestant Reformation. So even while under attack, it swept across the Atlantic almost unchallenged during the century after Columbus's voyages.

THE IBERIAN CONQUEST OF AMERICA

From 1492 to 1518, Spanish and Portuguese explorers opened up vast parts of Asia and the Americas to European knowledge. At first, only modest attempts at settlement were made, mostly by the Spanish on Caribbean islands. The three decades after 1518, however, became an age of conquest. In some of the bloodiest chapters in recorded history, the Spanish nearly exterminated the native peoples of the Caribbean islands, toppled and plundered the great inland empires of the Aztecs and Incas in Mexico and Peru, discovered fabulous silver mines, and built a westward oceanic trade of enormous importance to all of Europe. The consequences of this short era of conquest proved to be immense for the entire world.

Portugal, meanwhile, restricted by one of the most significant lines ever drawn on a map, concentrated mostly on building an eastward oceanic trade to southeastern Asia. In 1493, to settle a dispute, the pope had demarcated Spanish and Portuguese spheres of exploration in the Atlantic. Drawing a north-south line 100 leagues (about 300 miles) west of the Azores, the pope confined Portugal to the European side of the line. One year later, in the Treaty of Tordesillas, Portugal obtained Spanish agreement to move the line 270 leagues farther west. Nobody knew at the time that a large part of South America, as yet undiscovered by Europeans, bulged east of the new demarcation line and therefore fell within the Portuguese sphere. In time, Portugal would develop this region, called Brazil, into one of the most profitable areas of the New World.

The Spanish Onslaught

Within a single generation of Columbus's death in 1506, Spanish conquistadores explored, claimed, and conquered most of South America (except Brazil), Central America, and the southern parts of North America from Florida to California. They were motivated by religion, growing pride of nation, and dreams of personal enrichment. "We came here," explained one Spanish footsoldier in Cortés's legion, "to serve God and the king, and also to get rich."

In two bold and bloody strokes, the Spanish overwhelmed the ancient civilizations of the Aztecs and Incas. In 1519, Hernando Cortés set out with 600 soldiers from coastal Veracruz and marched over rugged mountains to attack Tenochtitlán (modern-day Mexico City), the capital of Montezuma's Aztec empire. In 1521, following two years of tense relations between the Spanish and Aztecs, it fell before Cortés's assault. From the Valley of Mexico, the Spanish extended their dominion over the Mayan people of the Yucatán and Guatemala in the next few decades.

In the second conquest, the intrepid Francisco Pizarro, marching from Panama through the jungles of Ecuador and into the towering mountains of Peru with a mere 168 men, most of them not even soldiers, toppled the Inca empire. Like the Aztecs, the populous Incas lived in a highly organized social system. But also like the Aztecs, violent internal divisions had weakened them. Pizarro captured their capital at Cuzco in 1533. From there, Spanish soldiers marched farther afield, plundering other gold- and silver-rich Inca cities. Further expeditions into Chile, New Granada (Colombia), Argentina, and Bolivia in

Before the arrival of Cortés in 1519, Tenochtitlán was the capital and showplace of Montezuma's Aztec empire. The Spanish were astounded to see such a magnificent city, larger than any in Spain at the time. This modern rendering is based on archaeological evidence.

the 1530s and 1540s brought under Spanish control an empire larger than any in the Western world since the fall of Rome.

By 1550, Spain had overwhelmed the major centers of native population throughout the Caribbean, Mexico, Central America, and the west coast of South America. Spanish ships carried gold, silver, dyewoods, and sugar east across the Atlantic and transported African slaves, colonizers, and finished goods west. In a brief half century, Spain had brought into harsh but profitable contact with one another the people of three continents and established the triracial character of the Americas.

For nearly a century after Columbus's voyages, Spain enjoyed almost unchallenged dominion over the fabulous hemisphere newly revealed to Europeans. Only Portugal, which staked out important claims in Brazil in the 1520s, challenged Spanish domination of the New World.

The Great Dying

Spanish contacts with the natives of the Caribbean basin, central Mexico, and Peru in the early sixteenth century triggered the most dramatic and disastrous population decline ever recorded. The population of the Americas on the eve of European arrival had grown to an estimated 50 million or more. Europeans were members of a population that for centuries had been exposed to nearly every lethal microbe that infects humans on an epidemic scale in the temperate zone. Over the centuries, Europeans had built up immunities to these diseases. Such biological defenses did not eliminate smallpox, measles, diphtheria, and other afflictions, but they limited their deadly power. In contrast, the people of the Americas had been geographically isolated from these diseases and had no immunity whatsoever.

The results were catastrophic. On Hispaniola, a population of about one million that had existed when Columbus arrived had only a few thousand survivors by 1530. Of some 25 million inhabitants of the Aztec empire prior to Cortés's arrival, about 90 percent were felled by disease within a half century. Demographic disaster also struck the populous Inca peoples of the Peruvian Andes. Smallpox "spread over the people as great destruction," an old Indian told a Spanish priest in the 1520s. "There was great havoc. Very many died of it. They could not stir, they could not change position, nor lie on one side, nor face down, nor on their backs. And if they stirred, much did they cry out.... And very many starved; there was death from hunger, [for] none could take care of [the sick]." In most areas where Europeans intruded in the hemisphere for the next three centuries, the catastrophe repeated itself. In Spanish territories, the enslavement and brutal treatment of the native people intensified the lethal effects of European diseases. After their spectacular conquests of the Incas and Aztecs, the Spanish enslaved thousands of native people and assigned them work regimens that severely weakened their resistance to disease.

Silver, Sugar, and Their Consequences

Though Europeans looked for gold in the New World, more than three centuries would pass before they found it in windfall quantities on the North American Pacific slope and in the Yukon. Silver, however, proved abundant. Bonanza strikes were made in Bolivia in 1545 and in northern Mexico in the next decade, and much of Spain's New World enterprise focused on its extraction. The Spanish empire in America, for most of the sixteenth century, was a vast mining community.

Native people, along with some African slaves, provided the labor supply for the mines. At

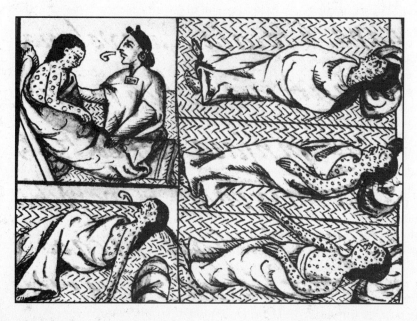

The devastating effects of smallpox on the Native American population were illustrated in this woodcut for a sixteenth-century book about Nueva España.

Potosí, in Bolivia, 58,000 workers labored at elevations of up to 13,000 feet to extract the precious metal from a fabulous sugarloaf "mountain of silver." The town's population reached 120,000 by 1570, making it larger than any in Spain at the time. Thousands of other workers toiled in the mines of Zacatecas, Taxco, and Guanajuato.

The massive flow of bullion from the Americas to Europe triggered profound changes. It financed further conquests and settlement in Spain's American empire, spurred long-distance trading in luxury items such as silks and spices from the Far East, and capitalized agricultural development in the New World of sugar, coffee, cacao, and indigo.

The enormous increase of silver in circulation in Europe after the mid–sixteenth century also caused a "price revolution." Between 1550 and 1600, prices doubled in many parts of Europe and then rose another 50 percent in the next half century. Landowning farmers got more for their produce, and merchants thrived on the increased circulation of goods. But artisans, laborers, and landless agricultural workers (the vast majority of the population) suffered because their wages did not keep pace with rising prices. The price revolution increased the number of people in western Europe living at the margins of society and thus built up the pressure to emigrate to the Americas.

While the Spaniards concentrated on the extraction of silver from the highlands of Mexico and Peru, the Portuguese staked their future on sugar production in the lowlands of Brazil. Adapting techniques of cultivation worked out earlier on their Atlantic islands, the Portuguese produced sugar for the export market. Whereas the Spanish mining operations used primarily Indian labor, the lowland Portuguese sugar planters scattered the indigenous people and replaced them with platoons of African slaves. By the 1630s this regimented work force was producing 32 million pounds of sugar annually. High in calories but low in protein, the sweet "drug food" revolutionized the tastes of millions of Europeans and caused the oceanic transport of millions of African slaves to the coast of Brazil and later to Colombia, Ecuador, and Peru.

From Brazil, sugar production jumped to the island-specked Caribbean. Here, in the early seventeenth century, England, Holland, and France challenged Spain for the riches of the New World. Once they secured a foothold in the West Indies, Spain's enemies stood at the gates of the Hispanic New World empire. In the seventeenth century they gradually sapped the strength of the first European empire outside of Europe.

Spain's Northern Frontier

The crown jewels of Spain's New World empire were silver-rich Mexico and Peru, with the islands and coastal fringes of the Caribbean representing lesser, yet valuable, gemstones. Distinctly third in importance were the northern borderlands of New Spain—the present-day Sun Belt of the United States. The early Spanish influence in Florida, the Gulf region, Texas, New Mexico, Arizona, and California indelibly marked the history of the United States.

Spanish explorers began charting the southeastern region of North America in the early sixteenth century, beginning with Juan Ponce de León's expeditions to Florida in 1515 and 1521. For the next half century, Spaniards planted small settlements there, and Franciscan priests attempted to gather the local tribes into mission villages and convert them to Catholicism.

The Spanish made several attempts to bring the entire Gulf of Mexico region under their control. From 1539 to 1542, Hernando de Soto, a veteran of Pizarro's conquest of the Incas, led an expedition deep into the homelands of the Creeks and explored westward across the Mississippi to Arkansas. In 1559, Spaniards marched northward from Mexico in an attempt to establish their authority in the lower Gulf region. Everywhere they went, they enslaved Indians and used them as provision carriers. In 1565, they built a fort at St. Augustine in Florida. They held Florida for more than two centuries.

The Southwest became the second region of Spanish activity in North America. Francisco Vásquez de Coronado explored the region from 1540 to 1542, never finding the legendary Seven Cities of Cíbola but opening much of Arizona, New Mexico, and Colorado to eventual Spanish control.

The Southwest, like Florida, proved empty of the fabled golden cities. Hence, in the seventeenth century, the region chiefly interested Jesuit and Franciscan missionaries. The Catholic mission became the primary institution of the Spanish borderlands. The Spanish missions operated differently, depending on the Indian cultures encountered. In Florida and California, where the native people lived in small, often seminomadic tribes, the Spanish used persuasion mixed with force to gather them within the sound of the mission bell. Setting the Indians to agricultural labor, the Spanish attempted slowly to convert them to European ways of life.

In New Mexico, however, the natives had lived in settled villages and practiced agriculture for centuries, so here the Spanish aimed to graft Catholicism onto Pueblo culture by building churches on the edges of ancient native villages. When they attempted to do more than overlay Indian culture with a veneer of Catholicism, they encountered fierce resistance. Such was the case in Popé's revolt in 1680. For five years, the Spanish padres had tried to root out traditional Pueblo religious practices. In response, a Pueblo leader named Popé led an Indian uprising that destroyed most of the churches in New Mexico and for more than a decade drove the Spanish from the region. Spaniards and Indians declared a kind of cultural truce: The Spaniards agreed to allow certain Pueblo rituals in return for nominal acceptance of Christianity.

ENGLAND LOOKS WEST

By the time England awoke to the promise of the New World, the two Iberian powers were firmly entrenched there. England was the most backward of the European nations facing the Atlantic in exploring and colonizing the New World. Only the voyages of John Cabot (the Genoa-born Giovanni Caboto) gave England any claim in the New World sweepstakes. But Cabot's voyages to Newfoundland and Nova Scotia a few years after Columbus's first voyage—the first northern crossing of the Atlantic since the Vikings—were never followed up.

At first, England's interest centered primarily on the rich fishing grounds of the Newfoundland Banks. Exploratory voyages along the eastern coast of North America hardly interested them. It was for the French that explorers Cartier and Verrazano sailed between 1524 and 1535. Looking for straits westward to India, through the northern landmass, which was still thought to be a large island, they made contact with many Indian tribes and charted the coastline from the St. Lawrence River to the Carolinas.

Changes occurred in the late sixteenth century that propelled the English overseas. The rising production of woolen cloth, a mainstay of the English economy, had sent merchants scurrying for new markets after 1550. Their success in establishing trading companies in Russia, Scandinavia, the Middle East, and India vastly widened England's commercial orbit and raised hopes that still other spheres could be developed. At the same time, population growth and rising prices depressed the existence of ordinary people and made them look to the transoceanic frontier for new opportunities.

England Challenges Spain

Queen Elizabeth, who ruled from 1558 to 1603, followed a cautious policy that did not include the promotion of overseas colonies. Ambitious and talented, she had to contend with Philip II, king of Spain and her fervently Catholic brother-in-law, whose long reign nearly coincided with hers. Regarding Elizabeth as a

Protestant heretic, Philip plotted incessantly against her.

The smoldering conflict between Catholic Spain and Protestant England broke into open flames. Elizabeth had been providing covert aid to the Protestant Dutch revolt against Catholic rule. Philip vowed to crush the rebellion and decided as well to launch an attack on England in order to wipe out this growing center of Protestant power. In 1585 Elizabeth sent 6,000 English troops to aid the Dutch Protestants. Three years later, Philip dispatched a Spanish armada of 130 ships, sails blazing with crusader's crosses, to conquer Elizabeth's England. For two weeks in the summer of 1588, a sea battle raged off the English coast. A motley collection of smaller English ships, with the colorful sea dog Francis Drake in the lead, defeated the Armada, sinking many of the lumbering Spanish galleons and then retiring as the legendary "Protestant wind" blew the crippled Armada into the North Sea. With Spanish naval power checked, both the English and the Dutch found the seas more open to their rising maritime and commercial interests.

The Westward Fever

In the last decades of the sixteenth century, the idea of overseas expansion captured the imagination of important elements of English society. Urging them on were two Richard Hakluyts, uncle and nephew. In the 1580s and 1590s, they devoted themselves to advertising the advantages of colonizing on the far side of the Atlantic. The New World offered land, opportunities for commerce, and heathen people in need of salvation. The Hakluyts publicized the idea that the time was ripe for England to break the Iberian monopoly on the riches of the New World.

England mounted its first attempts at colonizing, however, in Ireland. In the 1560s and 1570s, the English gradually extended their control over the country through brutal military conquest. Many of the leaders first involved in

New World colonizing had served in Ireland, and many of their ideas of how to deal with a "savage" and "barbaric" people stemmed from their Irish experience.

The first English attempts at overseas settlement in the 1580s and early 1600s were small, feeble, and ill fated. Beginning in 1583, they mounted several unsuccessful attempts to settle Newfoundland, but perhaps their most dramatic failure was the "Lost Colony" of Roanoke.

Sir Walter Raleigh, a veteran of the campaign in Ireland and a favorite courtier of Queen Elizabeth, organized two attempts to establish a colony at Roanoke Island, off the North Carolina coast. The first group of settlers landed in August 1585 but, failing to receive needed supplies from England, left the island the following spring, taking passage on ships of Sir Francis Drake, who paid them an unexpected but welcome visit. A second expedition of 117 colonists was sent to Roanoke in 1587 under the command of John White, whose pregnant daughter was among the settlers. White's granddaughter, Virginia Dare, was born in Roanoke soon after the colonists landed and became the first child of English parentage to be born in America. White soon sailed back to England to obtain more supplies and settlers for Roanoke, but England's war with Spain prevented his immediate return to the colony. When he finally revisited Roanoke in 1590, he found that the colonists had vanished. Their fate to this day remains unknown, but they probably perished in attacks by a local tribe after killing a tribal leader and displaying his head on a pike.

Small groups of men sent out to establish a tiny colony in Guiana, off the South American coast, failed in 1604 and 1609, and another group that set down in Maine in 1607 lasted only a year. Even the colonies founded in Virginia in 1607 and Bermuda in 1612, although they would flourish in time, floundered badly for several decades.

English merchants, sometimes supported by gentry investors, undertook these first tentative efforts. They risked their capital and had little backing from the government, in subsidies, ships, or naval protection, though they had the blessing of their queen. The Spanish and Portuguese colonizing efforts, by contrast, were national enterprises, sanctioned, capitalized, and coordinated by the Crown.

Not until these first merchant adventures solicited the wealth and support of the prospering middle class of English society could colonization succeed. This support grew steadily in the first half of the seventeenth century, but even then, investors were drawn far more to the quick profits promised in West Indian tobacco production than to the uncertainties of mixed farming, lumbering, and fishing on the North American mainland. In the 1620s and 1630s, most of the English capital invested overseas went into establishing tobacco colonies in the flyspeck Caribbean islands of St. Christopher (1624), Barbados (1627), Nevis (1628), Montserrat (1632), and Antigua (1632).

Apart from the considerable financing required, the vital element in launching a colony was a suitable body of colonists. About 80,000 streamed out of England between 1600 and 1640, as economic, political, and religious developments pushed them from their homeland at the same time that dreams of opportunity and adventure pulled them westward. In the next 20 years, another 80,000 departed.

Economic difficulties in England prompted many to try their luck in the New World. Probably half the households in England lived on the edge of poverty in the early seventeenth century. "This land grows weary of her inhabitants," wrote John Winthrop of East Anglia, "so as a man, which is the most precious of all creatures, is near more vile among us than a horse or a sheep."

Religious persecution and political considerations intensified the pressure to emigrate from England in the early seventeenth century. The largest number of emigrants went to the West Indies. The North American mainland colonies attracted perhaps half as many, and the Irish plantations in Ulster and Munster still fewer.

Anticipating North America

The early English settlers in North America were far from uninformed about the indigenous people of the New World. Beginning with Columbus's first description of the New World, published in several European cities in 1493 and 1494, reports and promotional accounts circulated among the participants in early voyages of discovery, trade, and settlement.

Colonists who read or listened to these accounts probably held a split image of the native people. On the one hand, the Indians were depicted by Columbus and Verrazano as a gentle people who eagerly received Europeans. The natives, "graceful of limb and tawny-colored," Verrazano related in 1524, "came toward us joyfully uttering loud cries of wonderment, and showing us the safest place to beach the boat."

This positive image of the Native Americans reflected both the friendly reception that Europeans often actually enjoyed and the European vision of the New World as an earthly paradise where war-torn, impoverished, or persecuted people could build a new life. The strong desire to trade with the native people also encouraged a favorable view because only a friendly Indian could become a suitable partner in commercial exchange.

A counterimage, of a savage, hostile Indian, however, also entered the minds of settlers coming to North America. As early as 1502, Sebastian Cabot had paraded in England three Eskimos he had kidnapped on an Arctic voyage. They were described as flesh-eating savages and "brute beasts" who "spake such speech that no man could understand them." Many other accounts portrayed the New World natives as crafty, brutal, loathsome half-men, who lived, as the Italian navigator and explorer Amerigo Vespucci put it, without "law, religion, rulers, immortality of the soul, and private property."

The English were also aware of the Spanish experience in the Caribbean, Mexico, and Peru—and the story was not pretty. Many books described in gory detail the wholesale violence that occurred when Spaniard met Mayan, Aztec, or Inca. Immigrants embarking for North America wondered if similar violent confrontations did not await them.

Another factor nourishing negative images of the Indian stemmed from the Indians' possession of the land necessary for settlement. For Englishmen, rooted in a tradition of the private ownership of property, this presented moral and legal, as well as practical, problems. As early as the 1580s, George Peckham, an early promoter

of colonization, had admitted that the English doubted their right to take the land of others. But many argued that in return for land, the settlers would offer the natives the advantages of a more advanced culture and, most important, the Christian religion.

A more ominous argument arose to justify English rights to native soil. By denying the humanity of the Indians, the English, like other Europeans, claimed that the native possessors of the land were disqualified from rightful ownership of it. Defining the Native Americans as "savage" and "brutish" gave the settlers moral justification for taking their land. For their part, people like Opechancanough probably perceived the arriving Europeans as impractical, irreligious, aggressive, and strangely intent on accumulating material wealth.

CONCLUSION

CONVERGING WORLDS

The English migrants who began arriving on the eastern edge of North America in the late sixteenth century came late to a New World that other Europeans had been colonizing for more than a century. The English immigrants to Virginia were but a small advance wave of the large, varied, and determined fragment of English society that would flock to the western Atlantic frontier during the next few generations. We turn now to the diversity of founding experiences of the English colonizers of the seventeenth century.

Recommended Reading

The rich pre-Columbian history of the Americas is surveyed in Dean Snow, *The Archaeology of North America: American Indians and Their Origins* (1980). Another fascinating analysis is Marshall Sahlins, *Stone Age Economics* (1972).

Excellent introductions to early African history include Basil Davidson, *The African Genius* (1969), and J. D. Fage, *A History of West Africa*, 4th ed. (1969).

Europe in the Age of Exploration can be studied in Ralph Davis, *The Rise of the Atlantic Economies* (1973); and Eric Wolf, *The People Without History* (1983).

A fine corrective to the much romanticized and often distorted story of the Spanish and Portuguese conquest of the Americas is James Lockhart and Stuart B. Schwartz, *Early Latin America* (1983). Also valuable is C. R. Boxer, *The Portuguese Seaborne Empire, 1415–1825* (1972).

The shape of English society as overseas colonization began is detailed in Carl Bridenbaugh, *Vexed and Troubled Englishmen, 1500–1642* (1968), and Peter Laslett, *The World We Have Lost* (1971). England's belated intervention in the Americas is followed in Nicholas P. Canny, *The Elizabethan Conquest of Ireland* (1976); David B. Quinn, *England and the Discovery of America, 1481–1620* (1974); and David B. Quinn, *North America from Earliest Discovery to First Settlements* (1977).

Time Line

	Pre-Columbian epochs	1513	Portuguese explorers reach China
12,000 B.C.	Beringian epoch ends	1515–1565	Spanish explore Florida and southern part of North America
6,000 B.C.	Paleo-Indian phase ends	1520s	Luther attacks Catholicism
500 B.C.	Archaic era ends	1521	Cortés conquers the Aztecs
		1530s	Calvin calls for religious reform
500 B.C.–A.D.	Post-Archaic era in North America	1533	Pizarro conquers the Incas
		1540–1542	Coronado explores the Southwest
1420s	Portuguese sailors explore west coast of Africa		
		1558	Elizabeth I crowned queen of England
1492	Christopher Columbus lands on Caribbean islands Spanish expel Moors (Muslims)	1585	Roanoke Island settlement
		1588	English defeat the Spanish armada
1494	Treaty of Tordesillas	1603	James I succeeds Elizabeth I
1497–1585	French and English explore northern part of the Americas	1607	English begin settlement at Jamestown, Virginia
1498	Vasco da Gama reaches India after sailing around Africa	1680	Popé's revolt in New Mexico
1500	Kingdoms of Ghana, Mali, Songhay in Africa		

chapter 2

Colonizing a Continent

John Mason had emigrated from southeastern England as part of the flock of John Warham, a Puritan minister from the village of Dorchester. In Massachusetts, the group commemorated their origins by giving the name Dorchester to the area assigned to them.

Four years later, in the fall of 1636, Mason followed many of his Dorchester friends out of Massachusetts to the Connecticut River, 100 miles to the west. At their journey's end, they founded the town of Windsor, on the west bank of the Connecticut.

Six months later, when his new village was no more than a collection of crude lean-tos, militia captain John Mason marched south against the Pequots. He commanded several hundred men whom the fledgling Connecticut River towns had dispatched to drive the Pequots from the area. In the years before the English arrival, the powerful Pequots had formed a network of tributary tribes. Finding it impossible to placate the English as they swarmed into the Connecticut River valley, the Pequots chose resistance.

At dawn on May 26, 1637, Captain Mason and his troops approached a Pequot village on the Mystic River. Supported by Narragansett allies, the English slipped into the town and torched the Pequot wigwams. Then they rushed from the fortified village. As flames engulfed the huts, the Pequots fled the inferno, only to be cut down with musket and sword by the English soldiers, who had ringed the community. Most of the terrified victims were noncombatants—old men, women, and children—for the Pequot warriors were preparing for war at another village about five miles away. Before the sun rose, a major portion of the Pequot tribe had been exterminated. Mason wrote that God had "laughed at his enemies and the enemies of his people, . . . making them as a fiery oven."

Captain John Mason's actions at the Mystic River testify that the European colonization of America involved a violent confrontation of two cultures. We often speak of the "discovery" and "settlement" of North America by English and other European colonists. But the penetration of the eastern edge of what today is the United States might more accurately be called "the invasion of America."

Yet mixed with violence was utopian idealism. The New World was a place to rescue humankind from the ruins of the Old World. This chapter reconstructs the manner of settlement and the character of immigrant life in five areas of early colonization: the Chesapeake Bay, southern New England, the St. Lawrence to the Hudson rivers, the Carolinas, and Pennsylvania.

THE CHESAPEAKE TOBACCO COAST

As we saw in the previous chapter, England gained a foothold in North America when Walter Raleigh tried to establish a colony on Roanoke Island off the Carolina coast in the 1580s. The colony was too small and poorly financed to succeed. It served only as a token of England's rising challenge to Spain in the western hemisphere and as a source of valuable information for colonists later settling the area.

The Roanoke colony also failed resoundingly as the first sustained contact between English and Native American peoples. Although one member of the first expedition reported that "we found the people most gentle, loving, and faithful, void of all guile and treason," relations with the local tribes quickly soured and then turned violent. In 1591, when a relief expedition reached Roanoke, none of the settlers could be found. It is likely that in spite of their Iron Age weaponry, these "lost colonists" of Roanoke succumbed to Indian attacks. It was an ominous beginning for England's overseas ambitions.

Jamestown

In 1607, a generation after the first Roanoke expedition, a group of merchants established the first permanent colony in North America at Jamestown, Virginia. Under a charter from James I, they operated as a joint-stock company, an early form of a modern corporation that allowed them to sell shares of stock in their company and use the pooled investment capital to outfit and supply overseas expeditions. Although the king's charter to the Virginia Company of London began with a concern for bringing Christian religion to native people, most of the settlers probably agreed with Captain John Smith, who described the company as "making religion their colour, when all their aim was profit."

Profits in the early years proved elusive, however. Most of the early Virginia colonists died miserably of dysentery, malaria, and malnutrition. More than 900 settlers, mostly men, arrived in the colony between 1607 and 1609; only 60 survived. Moreover, one-third of the first three groups of immigrants were gold-seeking adventurers with unroughened hands. Others were unskilled servants, some with criminal backgrounds, who "never did knowe what a days work was," observed John Smith. Both types adapted poorly to wilderness conditions, leaving Smith begging for "but thirty carpenters, husbandmen, gardeners, fishermen, and blacksmiths" rather than "a thousand such gallants as were sent to me, . . ."

The Jamestown colony was also hampered by the common assumption that Englishmen could exploit the Indians of the region as the Spanish had done in Mexico and Peru. But in the Chesapeake the English found that the indige-

As seen in this sixteenth-century watercolor by John White, a member of the expedition to Roanoke Island, the natives who inhabited the village of Secotan lived much like English or Irish peasants.

nous peoples were not densely settled and could not easily be subjugated. Relations with some 40 small tribes, grouped into a confederacy led by the able Powhatan, turned bitter almost from the beginning. Powhatan brought supplies of corn to the sick and starving Jamestown colony during the first autumn. However, John Smith, whose military experience in eastern Europe had schooled him in dealing with people he regarded as "barbarians," raided Indian corn supplies and tried to cow the local tribes by shows of force. In

response, Powhatan withdrew from trade with the English and sniped at their flanks. Many settlers died in the "starving times" of the first years.

Despite these early failures, merchants of the Virginia Company of London poured more money and settlers into the venture. Understanding the need for ordinary farmers who could raise the food necessary to sustain the colony, they reorganized the company in 1609, promising free land to settlers at the end of seven years' labor for the company. In 1618, they sweetened the terms by offering 50 acres of land outright to anyone journeying to Virginia. More than 9,000 voyaged to Virginia between 1610 and 1622, but only 2,000 remained alive at the end of that period. "Instead of a plantation," wrote one English critic, "Virginia will shortly get the name of a slaughter house."

Sot Weed and Indentured Servants

The promise of free land lured a steady stream of settlers to Virginia, even though the colony proved a burial ground for most immigrants within a few years of arrival. Also crucial to the continued growth of the colony was the discovery that tobacco grew splendidly in Chesapeake soil. Tobacco proved to be Virginia's salvation. The planters shipped the first crop in 1617. By 1624, Virginia was exporting 200,000 pounds of the "stinking weed"; by 1638, though the price had plummeted, the crop exceeded three million pounds. Tobacco became to Virginia in the 1620s what sugar was to the West Indies and silver to Mexico and Peru. In London, men gibed that Virginia was built on smoke.

The cultivation of tobacco obliged Virginia's planters to find a reliable supply of cheap labor. The "sot weed" required intensive care through the various stages of planting, weeding, thinning, suckering, worming, cutting, curing, and packing. To fill their need, planters recruited immigrants in England and Ireland and a scattering from Sweden, Portugal, Spain, Germany, and even Turkey and Poland. Such people, called indentured servants, willingly sold a portion of their working lives in exchange for free passage across the Atlantic. About four of every five seventeenth-century immigrants to Virginia—and later Maryland—came in this status. Nearly three-quarters of them were male, and most of them were between 15 and 24 years old.

Few servants survived long enough to achieve their freedom. If malarial fevers or dysentery did not quickly kill them, they often succumbed to the brutal work routine harsh masters imposed. Masters bought and sold their servants as property, gambled for them at cards, and worked them to death since there was little motive for keeping them alive beyond their term of labor. When servants neared the end of their contract, masters found ways to add time and were backed by courts controlled by the planter class.

Contrary to English custom, masters often put women servants to work at the hoe. Sexual abuse by masters was common. Servant women paid dearly for illegitimate pregnancies. The courts fined them heavily and ordered them to serve an extra year or two to repay the time lost during pregnancy and childbirth. They also deprived mothers of their illegitimate children, indenturing them out at an early age. For many servant women, marriage was the best release from this hard life. Many willingly accepted the purchase of their indenture by any man who suggested marriage.

Expansion and Indian War

As Virginia's population increased, violence mounted between white colonizers and the Powhatan tribes. In 1614, the sporadic hostility ended temporarily with the arranged marriage of Powhatan's daughter, the fabled Pocahontas, to planter John Rolfe. However, the profitable cultivation of tobacco created an intense demand for land, and more and more settlers pushed up the rivers that flowed into Chesapeake Bay.

In 1617, when Powhatan retired, the leadership of the Chesapeake tribes fell to Opechancanough, who began building military strength for an all-out attack on his English enemies. The English murder of Nemattanew, a Powhatan war captain and religious prophet, triggered a fierce Indian assault on Good Friday in 1622 that dealt Virginia a staggering blow. More than one-quarter of the white population fell before the marauding tribesmen; the casualties in cattle, crops, and buildings were equally severe.

The devastating attack led to the bankruptcy of the Virginia Company. As a result, the king annulled its charter in 1624 and established a royal government, which allowed the elected legislative body established in 1619, the House of Burgesses, to continue lawmaking in concert with the royal governor and his council. The Virginia House of Burgesses is significant as the first elected legislative body in colonial America.

The Indian assault of 1622 fortified the determination of the surviving planters to pursue a ruthless new Indian policy of "perpetual enmity." The Virginians sent annual military expeditions against the native villages west and north of the settled areas. Population growth after 1630 and the recurrent need for fresh acreage by settlers who planted soil-exhausting tobacco intensified the pressure on Indian land. The tough, ambitious planters soon encroached on Indian territories, provoking war in 1644 and again in 1675, reducing the native population of Virginia to less than 1,000 by 1680. The Chesapeake tribes, Virginians came to believe, had little to contribute to the goals of English colonization; they were merely obstacles to be removed from the path of English settlement.

Proprietary Maryland

By the time Virginia had achieved commercial success in the 1630s, another colony on the Chesapeake took root. Rather than hoping for profit, George Calvert sought to establish in

Early Chesapeake Settlement

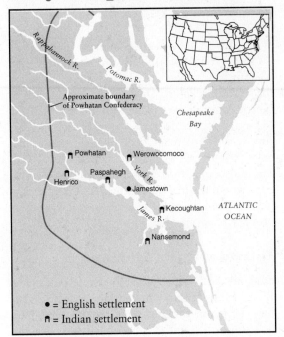

Rappahannock R.

Potomac R.

Approximate boundary
of Powhatan Confederacy

*Chesapeake
Bay*

⌂ Powhatan   ⌂ Werowocomoco

⌂ Paspahegh
⌂ Henrico   ⌂

York R.

● Jamestown

James R.

⌂ Kecoughtan   *ATLANTIC
OCEAN*

⌂ Nansemond

● = English settlement
⌂ = Indian settlement

Maryland a religious refuge for Catholics and a New World version of the English manorial countryside.

Catholics were an oppressed minority in England, and Calvert, Lord Baltimore, planned his colony as a place where they could start anew without fear of harassment. But knowing that he needed more than a small band of Catholic settlers, the proprietor planned to invite others as well. Catholics would never form a majority in his colony. They were quickly numerically overwhelmed by Protestants who jumped at the offer of free land with only a modest yearly fee to the proprietary family (a "quitrent") of two shillings per 100 acres.

Calvert died in 1632, leaving his 26-year-old son, Cecilius, to carry out his plans. The charter guaranteed the proprietor control over all branches of government and designated large estates for Calvert's relatives. Neither of these arrangements proved workable. Arriving in 1634, immigrants blithely ignored his plans, took up free land, imported as many indentured servants as they could afford, maintained generally peaceful relations with local Indian tribes, began to grow tobacco on scattered riverfront plantations like their Virginia neighbors, and governed themselves locally as much as possible. Although Maryland grew slowly at first, by 1700 its population of 33,000 was half that of Virginia's.

Daily Life on the Chesapeake

Though immigrants to the Chesapeake Bay region dreamed of bettering the life they had known in England, existence for most of them was dismally difficult. Only a minority could expect to marry and raise a family because marriage had to be deferred until after the indenture was completed, and there were three times more men than women. Once made, marriages were fragile. Either husband or wife was likely to succumb to disease within about seven years. The vulnerability of pregnant women to malaria frequently terminated marriages in the first few years, and death claimed half the children born before they reached adulthood. Few children could expect to have both parents alive while growing up. Grandparents were almost unknown. In a society so numerically dominated by men, widowed women were prized and remarried quickly. Such conditions produced complex families, full of stepchildren and stepparents, half sisters and half brothers.

The household of Robert Beverley of Middlesex County illustrates the tangled family relationships in this death-filled society. Between 1666 and 1687, Beverley had married in succession two widows who bore him nine children and had been stepfather to the eight children his two wives had produced with previous husbands. Not one of these 17 children, from an interlocking set of four marriages, reached adulthood with both a living mother and father.

Plagued by such mortality, the Chesapeake remained, for most of the seventeenth century, a land of immigrants rather than a land of settled families. Social institutions such as churches and schools took root very slowly amid such fluidity. The large number of indentured servants further increased the instability of community life.

The fragility of life showed clearly in the region's architecture. As in most New World colonies, the settlers at first erected only primitive huts and shanties, hardly more than windbreaks. After establishing crops, planters improved their habitats but still built ramshackle, one-room dwellings. "Their houses," it was observed in 1623, "stand scattered one from another, and are only made of wood . . . so as a firebrand is sufficient to consume them all." Even as Virginia and Maryland matured, cheaply built and cramped houses, usually no larger than 16 by 24 feet, remained the norm. Life was too uncertain, the tobacco economy too volatile, and the desire to invest every available shilling in field labor too great for men to build grandly.

The crudity of life also showed in the household possessions of the Chesapeake colonists. Struggling farmers and tenants were likely to own only a straw mattress, a simple storage chest, and the tools necessary for food preparation and eating—a mortar and pestle to grind corn, knives for butchering, a pot or two for cooking stews and porridges, wooden trenchers and spoons for eating. Most ordinary settlers owned no chairs, no dressers, no plates or silverware. Among middling planters the standard of living was raised only by possession of a flock mattress, coarse earthenware for milk and butter, a few pewter plates and porringers, a frying pan or two, and a few rough tables and chairs. Even one of Virginia's wealthiest planters, the prominent Robert Beverley, had "nothing in and about his house but what was necessary . . . good beds . . . but no curtains, and instead of cane chairs, he hath stools made of wood."

MASSACHUSETTS AND ITS OFFSPRING

While some English settlers in the reign of James I (1603–1625) scrambled for wealth on the Chesapeake, others in England were seized by the spirit of religion. They looked to the wilds of North America as a place to build a tabernacle to God, a society dedicated to reforming the corrupt world. American Puritanism nurtured a belief in America's special mission in the world. But it also sought to banish diversity on a continent where the arrival of streams of immigrants from around the globe was destined to become a primary phenomenon.

Puritanism in England

England had been officially Protestant since 1558. Many English in the late sixteenth century, however, thought the Church of England was still ridden with Catholic elements. Because they wished to purify the Church of England, they were dubbed Puritans.

The Puritan movement attracted men and women who hoped to find in religion an antidote to the changes sweeping over English society. Many feared for the future as they witnessed the growth of turbulent cities, the increase of wandering poor, rising prices, and accelerating commercial activity. In general, they disapproved of the growing freedom from the restraints of gentry-dominated medieval institutions such as the church, guilds, and local government. The concept of the individual operating as freely as possible, maximizing both opportunities and personal potential, is at the core of our modern system of beliefs and behavior. But many in England cringed at the crumbling of traditional restraints of individual action. They worried that individualistic behavior would undermine the notion of community—the belief that people were bound together by reciprocal rights, obligations, and responsibilities. Especially they decried the "degeneracy of the times," which they saw in the defiling of the Sabbath by maypole dancing, card playing, fiddling, and bowling. Puritans vowed not only to purify the Church of England but to reform society as well.

One part of their plan was a social ethic stressing work as a primary way of serving God. The "work ethic" would banish idleness and impart discipline throughout the community. Second, Puritans organized themselves into religious congregations where each member hoped for personal salvation but also supported all others in their quest. Third, Puritans assumed responsibility for the "unconverted" people around them, who might have to be controlled. Religious reform and social vision were in this way interlocked.

When King James VI of Scotland succeeded the childless Elizabeth as James I of England in 1603, he spoke stridently for the divine right of the monarch and his own role as head of the church. He deplored the rising power of the Puritans, who had occupied the pulpits in hundreds of churches, gained control of several colleges at Oxford and Cambridge, and obtained many seats in Parliament. James promised to "harry them out of the land, or else do worse."

Among those he succeeded in harrying out of the land were a congregation of Puritan Separatists, who from 1608 on escaped in small numbers and over a period of years to Leyden in Holland. Unlike other Puritans, the Separatists did not seek to reform the Church of England; they wanted only to be left alone to realize their vision of a pure life. They were allowed to practice their faith freely in Holland, but eventually a number of them turned to America for a permanent home.

When King Charles I ascended the English throne in 1625, the situation worsened for Puritans. Determined to strengthen the monarchy and stifle dissent, the king adjourned Parliament in 1629. He then appointed William Laud, the bishop of London, to high office and turned him loose on the Puritans, whom Laud called "wasps" and "the most dangerous enemies of the state."

By 1629, many Puritans were turning their eyes outward to Northern Ireland, Holland, the Caribbean islands, and especially North America. The depression in the cloth trades, most severe in Puritan strongholds, was an added motivation to emigrate. To some distant shore, many Puritans decided, they would transport a fragment of English society and carry out the completion of the Protestant Reformation. As they understood history, God had assigned them a special task in his plan for the redemption of humankind.

Puritan Predecessors in New England

Puritans were not the first Europeans to reach the shores of New England, but no permanent settlement took root until the Pilgrims arrived in Plymouth in 1620. The *Mayflower* left England in September 1620 carrying 35 Puritan Separatists and 67 other colonists. The "Pilgrims," as they called themselves, suffered greatly during their first winter in the new land, half of them dying of sickness, cold, and malnutrition. With the help of friendly Indians, however, the survivors learned to grow corn and exploit the waters for seafood.

For two generations, the Pilgrims tilled the soil and fished while trying to keep intact their religious vision. But with the much larger Puritan migration that began in 1630, the Pilgrim villages nestled on the shores of Cape Cod Bay became a backwater of the thriving, populous Massachusetts Bay colony, which absorbed them in 1691.

Errand into the Wilderness

In 11 ships, 1,000 Puritans set out from England in 1630 for the Promised Land. They were the

John Winthrop was one of the lesser gentry who joined the Puritan movement and in the 1620s looked westward for a new life. Always searching himself as well as others for signs of weakness, Winthrop was one of the Massachusetts Bay Colony's main leaders for many years.

vanguard of a movement that by 1642 had brought about 18,000 colonizers to New England's shores. Led by John Winthrop, they operated under a charter from the king to the Puritan-controlled Massachusetts Bay Company. The Puritans set about building their utopia with the characteristic fervor of people convinced they are carrying out a divine task.

Their intention was to establish communities of pure Christians who collectively swore a covenant with God to work for his ends. To accomplish this, the Puritan leaders agreed to employ severe means. Their historic mission was too important, they believed, to allow the luxury of diversity of opinion in religious matters. Likewise, participation in government would be

limited to church members. Civil and religious transgressors would be rooted out and severely punished.

To realize their utopian goals, the Puritans willingly gave up freedoms that their compatriots sought. An ideology of rebellion in England, Puritanism in America became an ideology of control. Much was at stake, for as Winthrop reminded the first settlers, "We shall be as a city upon a hill [and] the eyes of all people are upon us." That visionary sense of mission would help to shape a distinctive American self-image in future generations.

As in Plymouth and Virginia, the first winter tested the strongest souls. More than 200 of the first 700 settlers perished, but Puritans kept coming. They "hived out" along the Back Bay of Boston, along the rivers that emptied into the bay, south into what became Connecticut and Rhode Island a few years later, and north along the rocky Massachusetts coast.

Motivated by their militant work ethic and sense of mission, led by men experienced in local government, law, and the uses of exhortation, the Puritans thrived almost from the beginning. Most of the ordinary settlers came as freemen in families. Trained artisans and farmers, they established tightknit communities in which, from the outset, the brutal exploitation of labor rampant in the Chesapeake had no place.

An Elusive Utopia

The Puritans built a sound economy based on agriculture, fishing, timbering, and trading for beaver furs with local Indians. Even before leaving England, the directors of the Massachusetts Bay Company transformed their commercial charter into a rudimentary government and transferred the charter to New England. Once there, they laid the foundations of self-government. Free male church members annually elected a governor and deputies from each town who formed one house of a colonial legislature. The

Early New England

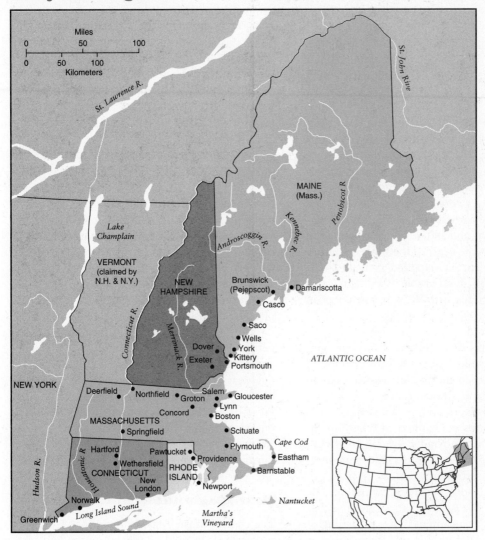

Miles
0   50   100

0   50   100
Kilometers

St. Lawrence R.

St. John Rive

MAINE
(Mass.)

Penobscot R.

Kennebec R.

Androscoggin R.

Lake Champlain

VERMONT
(claimed by
N.H. & N.Y.)

NEW
HAMPSHIRE

Brunswick
(Pejepscot) •   • Damariscotta

• Casco

• Saco

• Wells
• York
• Kittery
• Portsmouth

Connecticut R.

Merrimack R.

Dover •
Exeter •

ATLANTIC OCEAN

NEW YORK

Deerfield •   • Northfield   Salem
                • Groton •   • Gloucester
    Concord •   • Lynn
MASSACHUSETTS   • Boston
• Springfield
                • Scituate

Hartford •   Pawtucket •   • Plymouth   *Cape Cod*
    • Wethersfield   • Providence   • Eastham
CONNECTICUT   RHODE
    New   ISLAND   • Barnstable
    London •   • Newport

Housatonic R.

Hudson R.

Norwalk •
Greenwich •   *Long Island Sound*

Nantucket

*Martha's
Vineyard*

other house was composed of the governor's assistants, later to be called councillors. Consent of both houses was required to pass laws.

The Puritans established the first printing press in the English colonies and planted the seed of a university, Harvard College, which opened its doors in 1636 for the training of prospective clergymen. They also organized elementary and secondary schools, open to all.

In spite of these accomplishments, the Puritan colony experienced internal tensions and proved unable to reach a peaceful accommodation with the Native Americans, whose lands some colonists coveted. Others agitated for broader political rights and even briefly ousted Winthrop as governor in 1635.

Winthrop's troubles multiplied in 1633 when Salem's Puritan minister, Roger Williams, began to voice disturbing opinions on church and government policies. The visionary young man argued that the Massachusetts Puritans were not truly pure because they would not completely separate themselves from the polluted Church of England (which most Puritans still hoped to reform). He denounced mandatory worship and argued that government officials should not interfere with religious matters but confine themselves to civil affairs. Later to be celebrated as the earliest spokesman for the separation of church and state, Williams seemed in 1633 to strike at the heart of the Bible commonwealth, whose leaders regarded civil and religious affairs as inseparable. Williams also charged the Puritans with illegally intruding on Indian land.

In 1635, under threat of deportation to England, Williams fled southward through winter snow with a small band of followers to found Providence, a settlement on Narragansett Bay in what would become Rhode Island.

Even as they were driving Williams out, the Puritan authorities confronted another threat. Anne Hutchinson, who had arrived in 1634 with her husband and seven children, gained great respect among Boston's women as a practiced midwife, healer, and spiritual counselor. She soon began to discuss religion, suggesting that the "holy spirit" was absent in the preaching of some ministers. Before long Hutchinson was leading a movement labeled antinomianism, an interpretation of Puritan doctrine that stressed the mystical nature of God's free gift of grace while discounting the efforts the individual could make to gain salvation. She declared that God had communicated directly with her and that other true believers could also receive his message of grace and salvation directly. The importance of the clergy was thus diminished.

By 1636, Boston was dividing into two camps, those who followed the male clergy and those who cleaved to the theological views of a gifted though untrained woman with no official standing. Hutchinson doubly offended the male leaders of the colony because she boldly stepped outside the subordinate position expected of women. "The weaker sex" set her up as "a priest" and "thronged" after her, wrote one male leader.

In 1636 Hutchinson was tried and convicted of sedition and contempt and banished from the colony. Six months later, the Boston church excommunicated her for preaching 82 erroneous theological opinions. In the last month of her eighth pregnancy, Hutchinson, with a band of supporters, followed the route of Roger Williams to Rhode Island, the catch basin for Massachusetts Bay's dissidents.

But ideas proved harder to banish than people. The magistrates could never enforce uniformity of belief. Neither could they curb the appetite for land. Growth, geographic expansion, and commerce with the outside world all eroded the ideal of integrated, self-contained communities filled with religious piety. By 1636, groups of Puritans had swarmed not only to Rhode Island but also to Hartford and New Haven, where Thomas Hooker and John Davenport led new Puritan settlements in what became Connecticut.

New Englanders and Indians

The charter of the Massachusetts Bay Company proclaimed the goal of converting the natives to the Christian faith. But the instructions that Governor John Winthrop carried from England reveal other Puritan thoughts about the native inhabitants. According to Winthrop's orders, all men were to receive training in the use of firearms, Indians were prohibited from entering Puritan towns, and any colonist selling arms to an Indian or instructing one in their use was to be deported.

Only sporadic conflict with local tribes occurred at first because disease had catastrophically struck the Native American population of southern New England, which may have numbered as many as 125,000 in 1600, and left much of their land vacant. The settler pressure for new land, however, soon reached into areas untouched by disease. When land hunger mingled with the Puritan sense of mission, it proved an explosive mix. To a people charged with messianic zeal, the heathen Indians represented a mocking challenge to the building of a religious commonwealth that would "shine as a beacon" back to decadent England.

Making the "savages" of New England strictly accountable to the ordinances that governed white behavior was part of this quest for fulfilling their mission. In this the Puritans succeeded with the smaller, disease-ravaged tribes of eastern Massachusetts. But their attempts to control the stronger Pequots led to the bloody war in 1637 in which John Mason was a leader. The Puritan victory in that war removed the last obstacle to expansion into the Connecticut River valley. Missionary work, led by John Eliot, began among the remnant tribes in the 1640s. After a decade of effort, about 1,000 Indians had been settled in four "praying villages," learning to live according to the white man's ways.

The Web of Village Life

The village was the vital center of Puritan life. Unlike the Chesapeake tobacco planters, who dispersed along the streams and rivers of their area, the Puritans established small, tightly settled villages, and most pursued "open field" agriculture. Under this system, fields were divided into narrow strips of land that radiated out from the town, and a family might be allotted several disconnected strips. Each year a third or more of the village land was set aside to lie fallow so that it could regain its fertility. Farmers trudged out from the village each day to work on their fields. They grazed their cattle on common meadow and cut firewood on common woodland. Such a system re-created agricultural life in many parts of England.

In other towns, Puritans employed the "closed field" system of self-contained farms that they had known at home. But in either system, families lived close together in compact towns built around a common, where the meetinghouse and tavern were located. These small, communal villages kept families in close touch and perfectly served the need for moral surveillance, or "holy watching" among neighbors. Puritans also prohibited single men and women from living by themselves, for this would put individuals beyond patriarchal authority and group observation.

At the center of every Puritan village stood the meetinghouse. These plain wooden structures, sometimes called "Lord's barns," gathered within them every soul in the village twice a week—on the Lord's day and during mid-week as well. The minister was the spiritual leader in these small, family-based, community-oriented settlements, which viewed life as a Christian pilgrimage.

The unique Puritan mixture of strict authority and incipient democracy, of hierarchy and equality, can be seen in the way the Massachusetts town distributed land and devised local government. Each town was founded by a grant of the colony's General Court, sitting in Boston. Only groups of Puritans who had signed a compact signifying their unity of purpose received settlement grants.

After receiving a grant, townsmen met to parcel out land. They awarded individual grants according to the size of a man's household, his wealth, and his usefulness to the church and town. Such a system perpetuated existing differences in wealth and status. But Puritans also believed that every family should have enough land to sustain it, and prospering men were expected to use their wealth for the community's benefit, not for conspicuous consumption. Repairing the meetinghouse, building a school, aiding a widowed neighbor—such were the proper uses of wealth.

Having felt the sting of centralized power in church and state, Puritans emphasized local exercise of authority. Until 1684, only male church members could vote, and as the proportion of males who were church members declined, so did the proportion of men who could vote. These voters elected selectmen, who allocated land, passed local taxes, and settled disputes. Once a year, all townsmen gathered for the town meeting, at which they selected town officers for the next year and decided matters large and small: Should the playing of football in the streets be prohibited? Might Widow Thomas be allowed £10 for a kidney stone operation for her son? What salary should the schoolteacher be paid?

The predominance of families also lent cohesiveness to Puritan village life. Strengthening this family orientation was the remarkably healthy environment of the Puritans' "New Israel." While the germs carried by English colonizers devastated neighboring Indian societies, the effect on the newcomers of entering the new environment was the opposite because the low density of settlement prevented infectious diseases from spreading.

The result was a spectacular natural increase in the population and a life span unknown in Europe. The difference was not a higher birthrate. The crucial factor was that chances for survival after birth were far greater than in England because of the healthier climate and better diet. In New England, nearly 90 percent of the infants born in the seventeenth century survived to marriageable age, and life expectancy exceeded 60 years—longer than for the American population as a whole at any time until the early twentieth century. About 25,000 people immigrated to New England in the seventeenth century, but by 1700 they had produced a population of 100,000. By contrast, some 75,000 immigrants to the Chesapeake colonies had yielded a population of about 70,000 by the end of the century.

Women played a vital role in this family-centered society. In the household economies of the Puritan villages, the woman was not only wife, mother, and housekeeper but also custodian of the vegetable garden; processor of salted and smoked meats, diary products, and preserved vegetables; and spinner, weaver, and clothesmaker.

The presence of women and a stable family life strongly affected New England's regional architecture. Well-constructed one-room houses with sleeping lofts quickly replaced the early "wigwams, huts, and hovels." Families then added parlors and lean-to kitchens as soon as they could. Within a half century, New England immigrants accomplished a general rebuilding of their living structures, while the Chesapeake lagged far behind.

A final binding element in Puritan communities was the stress on literacy and education, eventually to become a hallmark of American society. Placing religion at the center of their lives, Puritans emphasized the ability to read catechisms, psalmbooks, and especially the Bible.

An event in England in 1642 affected the future development of the New England colonies. King Charles I pushed his people into revolution by violating the country's customary constitution and trying to continue the reformation in the Anglican church. The ensuing civil war climaxed with the trial and beheading of the king in 1649. Thereafter, during the so-called Commonwealth period (1649–1660), Puritans had the opportunity to complete the reform of English religion and society. Migration to New England abruptly ceased.

The 20,000 English immigrants who had come to New England by 1649 were scattered from Maine to Long Island. To combat disper-

Reconstructed Chesapeake planter's house, typical of such simply built and unpainted structures in the seventeenth century.

sion, Puritan leaders established a broad inter-colony political structure in 1643 called the Confederation of New England. This first American attempt at federalism functioned fitfully for a generation, though Massachusetts, the strongest and largest member, often refused to abide by group decisions when they ran counter to its objectives.

Although the Puritans fashioned stable communities and effective government, their leaders, as early as the 1640s, complained that the founding vision of Massachusetts Bay was faltering. Material concerns seemed to transcend religious commitment; the individual prevailed over the community. A generation later Puritans rarely mentioned the work of salvaging western Protestantism by example. Instead, they concentrated on keeping their children on the straight and narrow road.

Frequent complaints about moral laxness notwithstanding, New England had achieved economic success and political stability by the end of the seventeenth century. If social diversity increased and the religious zeal of the founding generation waned, that was only to be expected. One second-generation Bay colonist put the matter bluntly. His minister had noticed his absence

in church and found him late that day at the docks, unloading a boatload of cod. "Why were you not in church this morning?" asked the clergyman. Back came the reply: "My father came here for religion, but I came for fish."

FROM THE ST. LAWRENCE TO THE HUDSON

The New Englanders were not the only European settlers in the northern region, for both France and Holland created colonies there. At the same time that Jamestown was founded, the French repeated their attempt to settle Canada, more successfully than in the 1540s. French explorer Samuel de Champlain established a small settlement in Port Royal, Acadia (later Nova Scotia), in 1604, and another at what would become the capital of New France, Quebec, in 1608. The primary interest of the French was the fur trade. The holders of the fur monopoly in France did not encourage emigration to the colony because settlement would reduce the forests from which the furs were harvested. New France therefore remained so lightly populated that English marauders easily seized and held Quebec from 1629 to 1632.

In 1609, Champlain allied with the Algonquian Indians of the St. Lawrence region in attacking their enemies the Iroquois to the south, earning their eternal enmity. The Iroquois traded furs to the Dutch on the Hudson River for European goods, and when they exhausted the furs of their own territory, they turned north, determined to destroy the French-allied Hurons of the Great Lakes region and seize their rich forests. In the 1640s and 1650s, the Iroquois smashed the Hurons and the French Jesuit missions among them. That ended all commerce in New France for a time and menaced Quebec and Montreal. The bitterness bred in these years colored future colonial warfare, driving the Iroquois to ally with the English against the French. But for the time being, in the mid–seventeenth century, the English remained free of pressure from the beleaguered French colonists, who numbered only about 400.

By the mid–seventeenth century, the Chesapeake and New England regions each contained about 50,000 settlers. Between them lay the mid-Atlantic area controlled by the Dutch, who had planted a small colony named New Netherland at the mouth of the Hudson River in 1624 and in the next four decades had extended their control to the Connecticut and Delaware river valleys. To the south of the Chesapeake lay a vast territory where only the Spanish, on their mission frontier in Florida, challenged the power of Native American tribes.

These two areas, north and south of the Chesapeake, became strategic zones of English colonizing activity after the end of England's civil war in 1660 brought the reinstallation of the English monarchy.

England Challenges the Mighty Dutch

Although for generations they had been the Protestant bulwarks in a mostly Catholic Europe, England and Holland became bitter commercial rivals in the mid–seventeenth century. By the time the Puritans arrived in New England, the Dutch had become the mightiest carriers of seaborne commerce in western Europe. By one contemporary estimate, Holland owned 16,000 of Europe's 20,000 merchant ships. By 1650, the Dutch had temporarily overwhelmed the Portuguese in Brazil, and soon their vast trading empire reached the East Indies, Ceylon, India, and Formosa.

In North America, the Dutch West India Company's New Netherland colony was small but profitable. Agents fanned out from Fort Orange (Albany) and New Amsterdam (New York City) into the Hudson, Connecticut, and Delaware river valleys. There they established a lucrative fur trade with local tribes by hooking into the sophisticated trading network of the Iroquois Confederacy, which stretched to the Great Lakes. At Albany, the center of the Dutch-Iroquois trade, relations remained peaceful and profitable for several generations because both peoples admirably served each other's needs.

By 1650, England was ready to challenge Dutch maritime supremacy. Three times between 1652 and 1675, war broke out between the two Protestant competitors for control of the emerging worldwide capitalist economy. In the second and third wars, the Dutch colony on the Hudson River became an easy target for the English. They captured it in 1664, lost it to the Dutch in 1673, and recaptured it almost immediately. By 1675, the Dutch had been permanently dislodged from the North American mainland. But they remained mighty commercial competitors of the English in Europe, Africa, the Far East, and the Caribbean.

New Netherland, where from the beginning Dutch, French Huguenots, Walloons from present-day Belgium, Swedes, Portuguese, Finns, English, refugee Portuguese Jews from Brazil, and Africans had commingled in a babel of languages and religions, now became New York, named for James, duke of York, brother of the king and heir to the English throne.

Under English rule, gradual intermarriage between the Dutch, the Huguenots, and the English—the three main groups—diluted ethnic loyalties. But New York retained its polyglot, religiously tolerant character.

PROPRIETARY CAROLINA: A RESTORATION REWARD

In 1663, three years after he was restored to the throne taken from his father, Charles II granted a vast territory named Carolina to a group of men who had supported him when he was in exile. Its boundaries extended from ocean to ocean and from Virginia to central Florida. Within this miniature empire, eight proprietors, including several involved in Barbados sugar plantations, gained large powers of government and semifeudal rights to the land. To lure settlers, they promised religious freedom and offered land free for the asking. Onto this generous land offer they grafted plans for a semimedieval government that provided themselves, their deputies, and a small number of noblemen with a monopoly of political power. A hereditary aristocracy of wealthy manor lords, they thought, would bring social and political stability to the southern wilds of North America and would check boisterous small landholders.

However, the reality of settlement in Carolina bore faint resemblance to what the planners envisaged. The rugged sugar and tobacco planters who streamed in from Barbados and Virginia ignored proprietary regulations about settling in compact rectangular patterns and reserving two-fifths of every county for an appointed nobility. Meeting in assembly for the first time in 1670, they refused to accept the proprietors' Fundamental Constitutions of 1667 and ignored the orders of the governor appointed in London. In shaping local government, the planters were guided mostly by their experience in the slave society of Barbados, whence most of them had come.

The Indian Debacle

Carolina was the most elaborately planned colony in English history but the least successful in achieving amicable relations with the natives. The proprietors in London had anticipated a well-regulated Indian trade limited to their appointed Carolina agents. But the aggressive settlers from the West Indies and the Chesapeake openly flouted proprietary policy. Those from Barbados, accustomed to exploiting African slave labor, saw that if the major tribes of the Southeast—the Cherokees, Creeks, and Choctaws—could be drawn into trade, the planters might reap vast wealth.

It was not the beaver that beckoned in the Indian trade, as in the North, but the deerskin, much desired in Europe for making warm and durable clothing. But what began as a trade for the skins of deer soon became a trade for the skins of Indians. To the consternation of the London proprietors, capturing Indians for sale in New England and the West Indies became the cornerstone of commerce in Carolina in the early years.

The Indian slave trade plunged Carolina into a series of wars. Local planters and merchants selected a tribe, armed it, and rewarded it handsomely for bringing in captives from another tribe. Even strong tribes that allied for trade with the Carolinians found that after they had used English guns to enslave their weaker neighbors, they themselves were sometimes scheduled for elimination. By the early eighteenth century, the two main tribes of the coastal plain, the Westos and the Savannahs, were nearly extinct.

Early Carolina Society

Carolina's fertile land and warm climate convinced many that it was "a second Paradize." Into the country came Barbadians, Swiss, Scots, Irish, French Huguenots, English, and even

Restoration Colonies: New York, the Jerseys, Pennsylvania, and the Carolinas

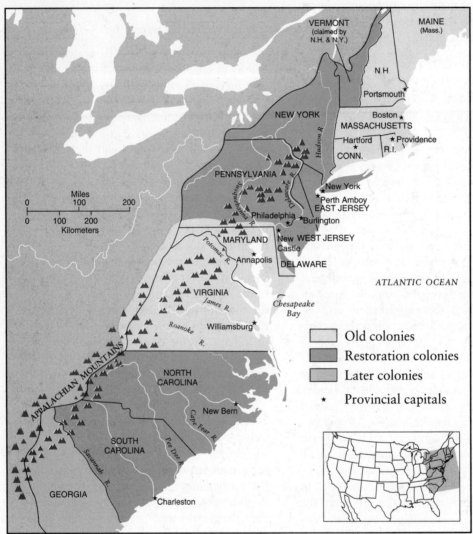

migrants from New England and New York. But far from creating paradise, this ethnically and religiously diverse people clashed abrasively in an atmosphere of fierce competition, brutal race relations, and stunted social institutions.

Settlements spread as the Indian population of the coastal region fell sharply. Planters experi-

mented with a variety of exotic crops, including sugar, indigo, tropical fruits, tobacco, and rice. It was this last that proved to be the staple crop upon which a flourishing economy could be built.

The cultivation of rice required backbreaking labor to drain the swampy lowlands, build

This painting of Mulberry Plantation in South Carolina shows the mansion house, built in 1708, and rows of slave huts constructed in an African style.

dams and levees, and hoe, weed, cut, thresh, and husk the crop. Since many of the early settlers had experience with African slaves in Barbados, their early reliance on slave labor came naturally to them. By 1720, when the colony's population had grown to 18,000, blacks outnumbered whites two to one.

As in Virginia and Maryland, the low-lying areas of coastal Carolina were so disease-ridden with malaria and yellow fever that population grew only slowly in the early years. "In the spring a paradise, in the summer a hell, and in the autumn a hospital," remarked one traveler. Malaria and yellow fever, especially dangerous to pregnant women, were the twin killers that retarded population growth, while the scarcity of women further limited natural increase."

In the healthier northern part of Carolina, mostly pine barrens along a sandy coast, a family-oriented society emerged. Populated largely by small tobacco farmers from Virginia seeking free land, the Albemarle region developed a mixed economy of livestock grazing, tobacco and food production, and the mining of the pine forests for naval stores—turpentine, resin, pitch, tar, and lumber. In 1701, North and South Carolina became separate colonies, but their distinctiveness had emerged before that. Slavery took root only slowly in North Carolina, which was still 85 percent white in 1720.

But in both North and South Carolina, several factors inhibited the growth of a strong corporate identity: the pattern of settlement, the ethnic and religious diversity, and the lack of shared assumptions about social and religious goals.

THE QUAKERS' PEACEABLE KINGDOM

Of all the utopian dreams imposed on the North American landscape in the seventeenth century, the most remarkable was that of the Quakers. During the English civil war, the Society of Friends, as the Quaker called themselves, had sprung forth as one of the many radical sects searching for a more just society and a purer religion. Their visionary ideas and their defiance of civil authority cost them dearly in fines, brutal punishment, and imprisonment. After Charles II and Parliament stifled radical dissent in the 1660s, they too sent many converts across the Atlantic. The society they founded in Pennsylvania foreshadowed more than any other colony the future religious and ethnic pluralism of the United States.

The Early Friends

Like their Puritan cousins, the Quakers regarded the English Protestant church (called the Church of England) as corrupt and renounced its formalities and rituals, which smacked of Catholicism. They also foreswore all church officials and institutions, persuaded that every believer could find grace through his or her own "inward light." By discarding the ideas of original sin and eternal predestination, the Quakers offered a radically liberating alternative to the reigning Calvinist doctrine. And their egalitarian doctrine of the light within elevated all lay persons to the position of the clergy and denied the primary place accorded the Scriptures.

Garbing themselves in plain black cloth and practicing civil disobedience, the Quakers presented a threat to social hierarchy and order. They refused to observe the customary marks of deference, such as doffing one's hat to a superior, believing that in God's sight no social distinctions existed. They used the familiar *thee* and *thou* instead of the formal and deferential *you,* they resisted taxes supporting the Church of England, and they refused to sign witnesses'

oaths on the Bible, regarding this as profane. They also renounced the use of force in human affairs and refused to perform militia service.

Quakers also affronted traditional views when they insisted on the spiritual equality of the sexes and the right of women to participate in church matters on an equal, if usually separate, footing with men. Quaker leaders urged women to preach and to establish separate women's meetings. Among Quakers who fanned out from England to preach the doctrine of the "inward light," 26 of the first 59 to cross the Atlantic were women. All but four of them were unmarried or without their husbands and therefore living, traveling, and ministering outside the bounds of male authority.

Intensely committed to converting the rest of the world to their beliefs, the Quakers ranged westward to North America and the Caribbean in the 1650s and 1660s. Nearly everywhere they were reviled, mutilated, imprisoned, and deported. Puritan Massachusetts warned them that their liberty in that colony consisted of "free liberty to keep away from us and such as will come to be gone as fast as they can, the sooner the better." The Bay Colony magistrates hanged several Quakers to show they meant business.

Early Quaker Designs

By the 1670s, the English Quakers were looking for a place in the New World to carry out their millennial dreams. Emerging as their leader in this dark period was William Penn, the son of Admiral Sir William Penn, who had captured Jamaica from the Spanish in 1654. Young William had been groomed for life in the English aristocracy, but he rebelled against his parents' designs for him. At age 23, he was converted by a spellbinding speech about the power of the Quaker inward light. After joining the Society of Friends in 1666, Penn devoted himself to their cause.

In 1674, Penn joined other Friends in establishing their own colony on former Dutch territory between the Hudson and Delaware rivers. They purchased the rights to the land, known as West Jersey, from Lord John Berkeley. Penn now helped fashion an extraordinarily liberal constitution for the budding Quaker colony. Legislative power and the authority to constitute courts were vested in an assembly chosen annually by virtually all free males in the colony. Election of justices of the peace and local officeholders was also mandated. Settlers were guaranteed freedom of religion and trial by jury. As Penn and the other trustees of the colony explained, "We lay a foundation for [later] ages to understand their liberty as men and Christians, that they may not be brought in bondage, but by their own consent; for we put the power in the people." Nowhere in the English world did ordinary citizens, especially those who owned no land, enjoy such extensive privileges.

Despite these idealistic plans, West Jersey sputtered at first. Only 1,500 immigrants arrived in the first five years. The focus of Quaker hopes lay across the Delaware River, where in 1681 Charles II granted William Penn a vast territory, almost as large as England itself, in payment of a large royal debt to Penn's father. To the Quakers' great fortune, the territory granted to Penn, the last unassigned segment of the eastern coast of North America, was also one of the most fertile.

Pacifism in a Militant World: Quakers and Indians

On the day Penn received his royal charter for Pennsylvania, he wrote a friend, "My God that has given it to me will, I believe, bless and make it the seed of a nation." The nation that Penn envisioned was unique among colonizing schemes. Penn intended to make his colony an asylum for the persecuted, a refuge from arbitrary state power. Puritans strove to nurture social homogeneity and religious uniformity, excluding all not of like mind. In the Chesapeake and Carolina colonies, aggressive, unidealistic men sought to exploit the region's resources. But

Penn dreamed of inviting to his sylvan colony people of all religions and national backgrounds and blending them together in peaceful coexistence. His state would claim no authority over the consciences of its citizens nor demand military service of them.

The Quakers who began streaming into Pennsylvania in 1682 quickly absorbed earlier Dutch, Finnish, and Swedish settlers. Primarily farmers, they fanned out from the capital city of Philadelphia, purchasing land from Penn at reasonable rates.

Even before arriving, Penn laid the foundation for peaceful relations with the Delaware tribe inhabiting his colony. He wrote to the Delaware chiefs: "The king of the Country where I live, hath given me a great Province; but I desire to enjoy it with your Love and Consent, that we may always live together as Neighbors and friends." Recognizing the Indians as the rightful owners of the land included in his grant, Penn pledged not to sell one acre until he had first purchased it from local chiefs. He also promised strict regulation of the Indian trade and a ban on the sale of alcohol.

A comparison between Pennsylvania and South Carolina shows the power of pacifism. A quarter century after initial settlement, Pennsylvania had a population of about 20,000 whites. Penn's peaceful policy had so impressed Native American tribes that Indian refugees began migrating into Pennsylvania from all sides. During the same 25 years, South Carolina had grown to only about 4,000 whites, but the area had become a cauldron of violence. Carolinians spread arms through the region to facilitate slave dealing, shipped some 10,000 members of local tribes off to New England and the West Indies as slaves, and laid waste to the Spanish mission frontier in Florida.

As long as the Quaker philosophy of pacifism and friendly relations with the Delawares and Susquehannocks held sway, interracial relations in the Delaware River valley contrasted sharply with those in other parts of North

Edward's Hick's Penn's Treaty with the Indians *was painted in the nineteenth century and in a romanticized version of the* Treaty of Shackamaxon *by which the Lenape Indians ceded the site of Philadelphia to Penn. The treaty was actually made in 1682, but Hicks was correct in implying that the Lenape held Penn in high regard for his fair treatment of them.*

America. But the Quaker policy of toleration, liberal government, and exemption from military service attracted to the colony, especially in the eighteenth century, thousands of immigrants whose land hunger and disdain for Indians undermined Quaker trust and friendship. Germans and Scots-Irish flooded in, swelling the population to 31,000 by 1720. Seeking farm land, neither of these groups shared Quaker idealism about racial harmony. They encroached on the lands of the local tribes, sometimes encouraged by the land agents of Penn's heirs. By the mid–eighteenth century, a confrontation of red and white inhabitants was occurring in Pennsylvania.

Building the Peaceable Kingdom

Although Penn's dream of a society that banished violence, religious intolerance, and arbitrary authority never completely materialized, the plain Quaker farmers prospered and retained a sense of common endeavor. They maintained their distinctive identity, allowing marriage only within their society, carefully providing land for their offspring, and guarding against too great a population increase (which would cause too rapid a division of farms) by limiting the size of their families.

Pennsylvania's countryside blossomed, and its port capital of Philadelphia also grew rapidly. By 1700, it had overtaken New York City in population, and a half century later it was the largest city in the colonies, bustling with a wide range of artisans, merchants, and professionals.

The Limits of Perfectionism

In spite of commercial success and peace with Native Americans, not all was harmonious in early Pennsylvania. Political affairs were often turbulent, in part because of Pennsylvania's weak leadership. Penn was a much-loved proprietor, but he did not tarry long in his colony to guide its course.

In England, Quakers had been bound to one another by decades of persecution. In Pennsylvania, the absence of persecution eliminated a crucial binding element, and factionalism developed. Meanwhile, Quaker industriousness and frugality led to such material success that after a generation, social radicalism and religious evangelicalism began to fade. As in other colonies, settlers discovered the door to prosperity wide open and surged across the threshold.

Where Pennsylvania differed from New England and the South was in its relations with Native Americans, at least for the first few generations. It also departed from the Puritan colonies in its immigration policy. Pennsylvania, it is said, was the first community since the Roman Empire to allow people of different national origins and religious persuasions to live together under the same government on terms of near equality. English, Highland Scots, French, Germans, Irish, Welsh, Swedes, Finns, and Swiss all settled in Pennsylvania. This ethnic mosaic was further complicated by a medley of religious groups, including Mennonites, Lutherans, Dutch Reformed, Quakers, Baptists, Anglicans, Presbyterians, Catholics, Jews, and a sprinkling of mystics. Their relations may not always have been friendly, but few attempts were made to discriminate against dissenting groups. Pennsylvanians thereby laid the foundations for the pluralism that was to become the hallmark of American society.

CONCLUSION

THE ACHIEVEMENT OF NEW SOCIETIES

Nearly 200,000 immigrants reached the coast of North America in the seventeenth century. Coming from a variety of social backgrounds, they represented the rootstock of distinctive societies that would mature in the North American colonies of England, France, Holland, and Spain. For three generations, North America served as a social laboratory for religious and social visionaries, political theorists, fortune seekers, social outcasts, and, most of all, ordinary men and women seeking a better life than they had known in their European homelands.

Nearly three-quarters of them came to the

Chesapeake and Carolina colonies. Most of them found this a region of disease and death rather than an arena of opportunity. In the northern colonies, to which the fewest immigrants came, life was more secure. Organized around family and community, favored by a healthier climate, and motivated by religion and social vision, the Puritan and Quaker societies thrived, even though utopian expectations were never completely fulfilled.

Recommended Reading

The early settlement of the Chesapeake is the subject of much exciting recent research. Newer works include Edmund S. Morgan, *American Slavery, American Freedom: The Ordeal of Colonial Virginia* (1975); Gloria L. Main, *Tobacco Colony: Life in Early Maryland* (1982); and Darrett B. Rutman and Anita H. Rutman, *A Place in Time: Middlesex County, Virginia, 1650–1750* (1984).

A good introduction to English Puritanism is Christopher Hill, *Society and Puritanism in Pre-Revolutionary England,* 2d ed. (1967). For information on the Puritans in their early New England communities, consult David G. Allen, *In English Ways* (1981); Philip Greven, Jr., *Four Generations* (1970); and Stephen Innes, *Labor in a New Land* (1983). Illuminating biographies of early Puritan leaders are Edmund S. Morgan, *The Puritan Dilemma: The Story of John Winthrop* (1958); and Robert Middlekauff,

The Mathers (1971). For rich analyses of Puritan-Indian relations, see Neal Salisbury, *Manitou and Providence* (1982); William Cronon, *Changes in the Land: Indians, Colonists, and the Ecology of New England* (1983); and James Axtell, *The Invasion Within* (1985).

Proprietary New York and Carolina are treated in Robert C. Ritchie, *The Duke's Province* (1977); Michael Kammen, *Colonial New York* (1975); M. Eugene Sirmans, *Colonial South Carolina* (1966); and Robert M. Weir, *Colonial South Carolina* (1983).

Quaker Pennsylvania is the subject of Gary B. Nash, *Quakers and Politics* (1968).

On indentured servitude, see David Galenson, *White Servitude in Colonial America* (1981), and Sharon V. Salinger, *"To Serve Well and Faithfully": Labor and Indentured Servitude in Pennsylvania* (1987).

Time Line

1590	Roanoke Island colony fails
1607	Jamestown settled
1616–1621	Native American population in New England decimated by European diseases
1617	First tobacco crop shipped from Virginia
1619	First Africans arrive in Jamestown
1620	Pilgrims land at Plymouth
1622	Powhatan tribes attack Virginia settlements
1624	Dutch colonize mouth of Hudson River
1630	Puritan migration to Massachusetts Bay
1632	Maryland grant to Lord Baltimore (George Calvert)
1633–1634	Native Americans in New England again struck by European diseases
1635	Roger Williams banished to Rhode Island
1636	Anne Hutchinson exiled to Rhode Island
1637	New England wages war against the Pequot tribe
1642–1649	English Civil War ends great migration to New England
1643	Confederation of New England
1659	Two Quaker men hanged on Boston Common
1660	Restoration of King Charles II in England
1663	Carolina charter granted to eight proprietors
1664	English capture New Netherland and rename it New York
	Royal grant of the Jersey lands to proprietors
1681	William Penn receives Pennsylvania grant

chapter 3

....

Mastering the
New World

Anthony Johnson, an African, arrived in
Virginia in 1621 with only the name "Antonio." Caught as a young man in the Portuguese slave-trading net, he was purchased by Richard Bennett and sent to work at
Bennett's tobacco plantation situated on the James River. On March 22, 1622, the
Powhatan tribes of tidewater Virginia fell upon the white colonizers in a determined
attempt to drive them from the land. Of the 57 persons on the Bennett plantation,
only black Antonio and four others survived.

Antonio—anglicized to Anthony—labored on the Bennett plantation for some 20
years, slave in fact if not in law, for legally defined bondage was still in the formative
stage. During this time he married Mary, another African, and fathered four children.
In the 1640s, Anthony and Mary Johnson gained their freedom and at some point
adopted their surname. Already past middle age, the Johnsons settled on Virginia's
eastern shore. By 1650, they owned 250 acres, a small herd of cattle, and two black
servants. By the late 1650s, however, as the lines of racial slavery tightened, the customs of the country began closing in on Virginia's free blacks.

In 1664, convinced that ill winds were blowing away the chances for their children
and grandchildren in Virginia, the Johnsons began selling their land to white neighbors.
The following spring, most of the clan moved north to Maryland, where they rented land
and again took up farming and cattle raising. Five years later, Anthony Johnson died,
leaving four children and his wife. A jury of white men in Virginia declared that because
Johnson "was a Negroe and by consequence an alien," the 50 acres he had deeded to his
son Richard before moving to Maryland should be awarded to a local white planter.

Johnson's children and grandchildren, born in America, could not duplicate the
modest success of the African-born patriarch. By the late seventeenth century, people
of color faced much greater difficulties. Anthony's sons never rose higher than tenant
farmer or small freeholder. John Johnson moved farther north into Delaware in the
1680s. Members of his family married local Indians and became part of a triracial
community that has survived to the present day. Richard Johnson stayed behind in
Virginia. His four sons became tenant farmers and hired servants. By now, in the early
eighteenth century, slave ships were pouring Africans into Virginia and Maryland to

replace white indentured servants, the backbone of the labor force for four generations. To be black had at first been a handicap. Now it became a fatal disability, an indelible mark of degradation and bondage.

Anthony and Mary Johnson and their children lived in a time of unrest and growing inequality. This chapter surveys the fluid, conflict-filled era from 1675 to 1715, a time when five overlapping struggles for mastery occurred. First, in determining to build a slave labor force, the colonists struggled to establish their mastery over resistant African captives. Second, the settlers sought mastery over Native American tribes. Third, the colonists resisted the attempts of English imperial administrators to bring them into a more dependent relationship. Fourth, within colonial societies, emerging elites struggled to establish their claims to political and social authority. Finally, the colonizers, aided by England, strove for mastery over French, Dutch, and Spanish contenders in North America.

BLACK BONDAGE

For almost four centuries after Columbus's voyages to the New World, European colonizers forcibly transported Africans out of their homelands and used their labor to produce wealth in their colonies. Estimates vary widely, but the number of Africans brought to the New World was probably not less than 12 million. Of all the people who populated the New World between the fifteenth and eighteenth centuries, the Africans were by far the most numerous, probably outnumbering Europeans two to one.

Slave traders took most Africans to the West Indies, Brazil, and Spanish America. Yet those who came to the American colonies, about 10,000 in the seventeenth century and 350,000 in the eighteenth, profoundly affected the destiny of American society. In a prolonged period of labor scarcity, their labor and skills were indispensable to colonial economic development. Their African culture mixed continuously with that of their European masters. And the race relations that grew out of slavery so deeply marked society that the problem of race has continued ever since to be the "American dilemma."

The Slave Trade

The African slave trade began as an attempt to fill a labor shortage in the Mediterranean world in the eighth century. Seven centuries later, Portuguese merchants reached the west coast of Africa by water and began buying slaves captured by other Africans and transporting them home by ship. These slaves were mostly criminals consigned to bondage in their own society or unfortunate individuals captured in tribal wars.

More than anything else, sugar transformed the African slave trade. By the seventeenth century, with Europeans developing a taste for sugar almost as insatiable as their craving for tobacco, they vied fiercely for possession of the tiny islands dotting the Caribbean and for control of the trading forts on the West African coast. African kingdoms, eager for European trade goods, warred against one another in order to supply the "black gold" demanded by white ship captains.

The economy of the former West African kingdom of Dahomey, for example, relied heavily for several centuries on commerce in slaves. Some black slave traders also joined in the carrying trade. One former slave, Francisco Felix de Sousa, came to own a fleet of slave ships. But the carrying trade was mainly in the hands of Europeans.

Many European nations competed for trading rights on the West African coast. In the seventeenth century, when about one million Africans were brought to the New World, the Dutch replaced the Portuguese as the major supplier. But by the 1790s, the English were the foremost slave-trading nation in Europe. All in all, in the eighteenth century, European traders carried at least six million Africans to the Americas, probably the greatest forced migration in history.

Even the most vivid accounts of the slave trade cannot convey the pain and demoralization that accompanied the capture and subsequent treatment of slaves. Olaudah Equiano, an eighteenth-century Ibo from what is now Nigeria, described how raiders from another tribe kidnapped him and his younger sister when he was only 11 years old. He passed from one trader to another while being marched to the coast. Many slaves attempted suicide or died from exhaustion or hunger on these forced marches. But Equiano survived. Reaching the coast, he and others were confined in barracoons, fortified enclosures on the beach, where a surgeon from an English slave ship inspected him. Equiano was terrified by the light skins, language, and long hair of the English and was convinced that he "had got into a world of bad spirits and that they were going to kill me."

More cruelties followed. Some slaves were branded with a hot iron. Then the slaves were ferried in large canoes to the ships anchored in the harbor. An English captain recounted the desperation of the captives: "The Negroes are so loath to leave their own country, that they have often leaped out of the canoes, boat and ship, into the sea, and kept under the water till they were drowned."

Conditions aboard the slave ships were miserable. Equiano recounted the scene below decks, where manacled slaves crowded together like corpses in coffins. "With the loathsomeness of the stench, and crying together, I became so sick and low that I was not able to eat, nor had I the least desire to taste anything." The refusal to take food was so common that ship captains devised special techniques to force feed resistant Africans.

The Atlantic passage usually took four to eight weeks. It was so physically depleting and psychologically wrenching that one of every seven captives died en route. Many others arrived in the Americas deranged or near death. In all, the relocation of any African may have averaged about six months from the time of capture to the time of arrival at the plantation of a colonial buyer. During this protracted personal crisis, the slave was completely cut off from the moorings of a previous life—language, family and friends, tribal religion, familiar geography, and status in a local community.

The Southern Transition to Black Labor

English colonists on the mainland of North America turned only slowly to Africa to solve their labor problem. Indentured white labor proved the best way to meet the demand for labor during most of the seventeenth century. Beginning in 1619, a small number of Africans were brought to Virginia and Maryland to labor in the tobacco fields alongside white servants. But as late as 1671, when some 30,000 slaves toiled in English Barbados, fewer than 3,000 served in Virginia. They were still outnumbered there at least three to one by white indentured servants.

The transformation of the southern labor force from mostly white to mostly black began in the last quarter of the seventeenth century.

Origins and Destinations of African Slaves, 1526-1810

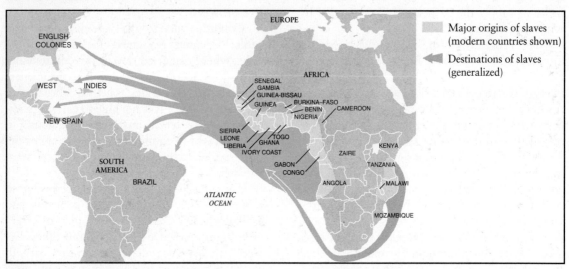

Three reasons explain this shift. First, the rising commercial power of England, at the expense of the Spanish and Dutch, swelled English participation in the African slave trade. Beginning in the 1680s, southern planters could purchase slaves more readily and cheaply than before. Second, the supply of white servants from England began drying up. Those who did arrive fanned out among a growing number of colonies. Finally, white servant unrest and a growing population of ex-servants who were landless, discontented, and potential challengers to established white planters led the southern elite to welcome a more pliable labor force. Consequently, by the 1730s, the number of white indentured servants had dwindled to insignificance.

Slavery in the Northern Colonies

Slavery never became the foundation of the northern colonial work force, for labor-intensive crops such as sugar and rice would not grow in colder climates. On the smaller family farms, household labor and occasional hired hands sufficed. Only in the cities, where slaves worked as artisans and domestic servants, and in a few scattered rural areas did slavery take substantial root.

Although the northern colonists employed few slaves, their economies were becoming enmeshed in the commercial network of the Atlantic basin, which depended on slavery and the slave trade. New England's merchant ships pursued profits in the slave trade as early as the 1640s. In New York and Philadelphia, building and outfitting slave vessels proved profitable. New England's seaports became centers for the distilling of rum, which was made from West Indian sugar and traded for slaves on the African coast. As the number of slaves in the Caribbean multiplied, the West Indies became a favorite market for codfish from New England, wheat from the middle colonies, and barrel staves and hoops from North Carolina. Thus, every North American colony participated in the racial exploitation in some way.

The System of Bondage

The first Africans brought to the American colonies came as bound servants. They served for a number of years; then, like Anthony and Mary Johnson, many of them eventually gained their freedom. Gradually during the seventeenth century, Chesapeake planters began to draw tighter lines around the activities of black servants. By the 1640s, Virginia forbade blacks, free or bound, to carry firearms. In the 1660s, marriages between white women and black servants were called "shameful matches" and "the disgrace of our Nation." Bit by bit, white settlers strengthened the association between black skin and slave status.

By the mid–seventeenth century, most white colonists were determined to fasten perpetual bondage on their black servants. In this dehumanization of Africans, which the English largely copied from their colonial rivals, the key step was instituting hereditary lifetime service. Once servitude became perpetual, relieved only by death, the elimination of all other privileges followed quickly. When the slave condition of the mother legally fell upon the black infant (not the case in other forms of slavery, such as in Africa), slavery became self-perpetuating, passing automatically from one generation to the next.

Slavery existed not only as a system of forced labor but also as a pattern of human relationships eventually legitimated by law. By the early eighteenth century, most provincial legislatures were enacting laws for controlling black rights and activities, known as "black codes." Slaves were forbidden to testify in court, engage in commercial activity, hold property, participate in the political process, congregate in public, travel without permission, or engage in legal marriage or parenthood. Nearly stripped of human status, they became defined as a form of property.

Eliminating all slave rights had both pragmatic and psychological dimensions. Every black man and woman in chains was a potential rebel. So the rapid increase in the slave population brought anxious demands to bring slaves under strict control. The desire to stifle black rebelliousness mingled with a need to justify brutal behavior toward slaves by defining

them as less than human. "The planters," wrote one Englishman in Jamaica, "do not want to be told that their Negroes are human creatures. If they believe them to be of human kind, they cannot regard them as no better than dogs or horses."

SLAVE CULTURE

Slave owners could set the external boundaries of existence for their slaves, controlling physical location, work roles, diet, and shelter. But the authority of the master class impinged far less on how slaves established friendships, fell in love, formed kin groups, raised children, worshiped their gods, buried their dead, and organized their leisure time.

In these aspects of daily life, slaves in America drew on their African heritage to shape their existence to some degree. In doing so, they laid the foundations for an African-American culture. At first, this culture had many variations because slaves came from many areas in Africa and lived under different conditions in the colonies. But common elements emerged, led by developments in the South, where about 90 percent of American slaves labored in the colonial period.

The Growth of Slavery

In contrast to other areas of the New World, in North America Africans reached a relatively healthy environment. In the southern colonies, where the ghastly mortality of the early decades had subsided by the time Africans were arriving in large numbers, their chances for survival were much better than in the West Indies or South America. This environmental advantage, combined with a more even sex ratio, led to a natural increase in the North American slave population that was unparalleled elsewhere.

In 1675, about 4,000 slaves were scattered across Virginia and Maryland. Most were men. A half century later, with the decline of white

The physical appearance of Africans captured the imaginations of some American artists. John Singleton Copley's Head of a Negro depicts a slave in the eighteenth century.

coastal low country they outnumbered whites three to one by 1760 and hence were able to maintain more of their African culture than slaves in the Chesapeake. Many slaves spoke Gullah, a "pidgin," or mixture, of several African languages. They often gave African names to their children, names like Cudjoe, Cuffe, Quashey, and Phibbi. And they kept alive their African religious customs.

In the northern colonies, slaves made up less than 10 percent of the population. Living in the same house as the master, slaves adapted to European ways much faster than in the South. Slavery was also less repressive in the North than in the South.

Slavery spread more extensively in the northern ports than across the countryside. Artisans, ship captains, and an emerging urban elite of merchants, lawyers, and landlords displayed their wealth and status by employing slaves. By the beginning of the eighteenth century, more than 40 percent of New York City's households owned slaves.

Resistance and Rebellion

While struggling to adapt to bondage in various regions of British America, slaves also rebelled in ways that constantly reminded their masters that slavery's price was eternal vigilance. "Saltwater" Africans fresh from their homelands often resisted slavery fiercely. "You would really be surprized at their perseverance," wrote one observer. "They often die before they can be conquered." Commonly this initial resistance took the form of escaping to the frontier to begin renegade settlements, to Indian tribes in the interior that sometimes offered refuge, or to Spanish Florida. Open rebellions, such as those in New York City in 1712 and at Stono, South Carolina, in 1739, mostly involved newly arrived slaves. There was no North American parallel, however, for the massive slave uprisings that erupted periodically in the West Indies and Brazil, where the slaves vastly outnumbered their masters.

servitude, 45,000 slaves labored on Chesapeake plantations. By 1760, when their number exceeded 185,000, the Chesapeake plantations relied almost entirely on black labor.

Although slave codes severely restricted the lives of slaves, the possibility for family life increased as the southern colonies matured. Larger plantations employed dozens and even hundreds of slaves, and the growth of roads and market towns permitted them greater opportunities to forge relationships beyond their own plantation. By the 1740s, a growing proportion of Chesapeake slaves were American-born, had established families, and lived in plantation outbuildings where from sundown to sunup they could fashion lives of their own.

In South Carolina, African slaves worked mostly on large plantations in swampy lowlands, and their knowledge of rice cultivation gave the colony a solid economic base. In the

In North America, slaves rarely outnumbered whites except in South Carolina, and the master class tried to cultivate tension between local Indians and slaves so that they would be "a check upon each other," as one worried planter explained. When rebellion did occur, white colonizers stopped at nothing to quell it. They tried to intimidate all slaves by torturing, hanging, dismembering, and even burning captured rebels at the stake.

Open rebelliousness often gave way to more subtle forms of resistance, such as dragging out the job, shamming illness, pretending ignorance, and breaking tools. Slaves also resisted through truancy, arson, crop destruction, pilfering to supplement their food supply, and direct assaults on masters, overseers, and drivers. In 1732, one South Carolina planter drove his slaves late into the night cleaning and barreling a rice crop. When he awoke in the morning, he found his barn, with the entire harvest in it, reduced to ashes.

Black Religion and Family

African-Americans struggled to find meaning and worth in their harsh existence. In this quest, religion and family played a central role—one destined to continue far into the post-slavery period.

Africans brought a complex religious heritage to the New World. No amount of desolation or physical abuse could wipe out these deeply rooted beliefs. Coming from cultures where the division between sacred and secular activities was less clear than in Europe, slaves made religion central to their existence. The black Christianity that emerged in the eighteenth century blended African religious practices with the religion of the master class. It laid the foundations for the black church that later became the central institution in African-American life.

The religious revival that began in the 1720s in the northern colonies and thereafter spread southward made important contributions to African-American religion. Evangelicalism stressed personal rebirth, used music and body motion, and caught individuals up in an intense emotional experience. The dancing, shouting, rhythmic clapping, and singing that came to characterize slaves' religious expression represented a creative mingling of West African and Christian religions.

Besides religion, the slaves' greatest refuge from their dreadful fate lay in their families. In West Africa, all social relations were centered in kinship lines, which stretched backward to include dead ancestors. Torn from their native societies, slaves placed great importance on rebuilding extended kin groups.

Most English colonies prohibited slave marriages. But in practice, domestic life was an area in which slaves and masters struck a bargain. Masters found that slaves would work harder if they were allowed to form families. Moreover, family ties stood in the way of escape or rebellion.

Slaves fashioned a family life only with difficulty, however. At first males outnumbered females, but as natural increase swelled the slave population in the eighteenth century, the sex ratio became more even.

The sale of either husband or wife could abruptly sever their fragile union. Young children usually stayed with their mothers until about age 8; then they were frequently torn from their families through sale, often to small planters needing only a hand or two. Few slaves escaped separation from family members at some time during their lives.

White male exploitation of black women represented another assault on family life. How many black women were coerced or lured with favors into sexual relations with white masters and overseers cannot be known. But the sizable mulatto (racially mixed) population at the end of the eighteenth century indicates that the number was large.

Not all interracial relationships were cruel. In some cases, black women sought the liaison to gain advantages for themselves or their children. These unions nonetheless threatened both the slave community and the white plantation ideal of separate racial categories.

While slave men struggled to preserve their family role, many black women assumed a position in the family that differed from that of white women. Plantation mistresses usually worked hard in helping to manage estates, but nonetheless the ideal grew that they should remain in the house to guard white virtue and set the standards for white culture. In contrast, the black woman remained indispensable to both the work of the plantation and the functioning of the slave quarters. She toiled in the fields and worked in the slave cabins. Paradoxically, black women's roles, which required constant labor, made them more equal to men than was the case of women in white society.

Above all, slavery was a set of power relationships designed to extract the maximum labor from its victims. Hence it regularly involved cruelties that filled family life with tribulation and uncertainty.

THE STRUGGLE FOR LAND

In the same period that slavery gained a permanent foothold in North America, both New England and Virginia fought major wars against Native Americans. The desire for land, a cause of both wars, produced a similar conflict somewhat later in South Carolina. The conflicts brought widespread destruction to the towns of both colonizers and Indians, inflicted heavy human casualties, and left a legacy of bitterness on both sides. For the coastal tribes, it was a disastrous time of defeat and decline.

King Philip's War in New England

Following the Pequot War of 1637 in New England, the Wampanoags and Narragansetts, whose fertile land lay within the boundaries of Plymouth and Rhode Island, attempted to maintain their distance from the New England colonists. But the New Englanders coveted Indian territories and gradually reduced the Indians' land base.

By the 1670s, when New England's population had grown to about 50,000, younger Indians began brooding over their situation. Their leader, Metacomet (named King Philip by the English), was the son of Massasoit, the Wampanoag who had allied himself with the first Plymouth settlers in 1620. As the Wampanoag leader, Metacomet faced one humiliating challenge after another. In 1671, for example, Plymouth forced Metacomet to surrender a large stock of guns and accept a treaty of submission acknowledging Wampanoag subjection to English law. Convinced that more setbacks would follow and humiliated by the discriminatory treatment of Indians brought before English courts, Metacomet began recruiting for a resistance movement.

The execution of three tribesmen in June 1675 was the catalyst for King Philip's War, but the root cause was the rising anger of the young Wampanoag males. As would happen repeatedly in the next two centuries as Americans pushed westward, these younger Native Americans refused to imitate their fathers, who had watched the colonizers erode their land base and compromise their sovereignty. Instead, they attempted a pan-Indian offensive against an intruder with far greater numbers and a much larger arsenal of weapons.

In the summer of 1675, the Wampanoags unleashed daring hit-and-run attacks on villages in the Plymouth colony. By autumn, many New England tribes, including the powerful Narragansetts, had joined King Philip's warriors. Towns all along the frontier reeled under Indian attacks. By the time the first snow fell in November, mobile Indian warriors had laid waste to the entire upper Connecticut River valley.

King Philip's offensive faltered in the spring

of 1676. Food shortages and disease sapped Indian strength, and the powerful Mohawks refused to support the New England tribes. By summer, groups of Indians were surrendering, while some moved westward seeking shelter among other tribes. King Philip fell in battle. His head was carried triumphantly back to Plymouth, where it remained on display for 25 years.

At war's end, several thousand colonists and perhaps twice as many Indians lay dead. Of some 90 Puritan towns, 52 had been attacked and 13 completely destroyed. Not for 40 years would the frontier advance beyond the line it had reached in 1675. Indian towns were devastated even more completely. Many of the survivors, including Metacomet's wife and son, were sold into slavery in the West Indies.

Bacon's Rebellion Engulfs Virginia

While New Englanders fought local tribes in 1675 and 1676, the Chesapeake colonies became locked in a struggle involving both a war between the red and white populations and civil war within the colonizers' society. This deeply tangled conflict was called Bacon's Rebellion after the headstrong Cambridge-educated planter Nathaniel Bacon, who arrived in Virginia at age 28.

Bacon and many other ambitious young planters detested the Indian policy of Virginia's royal governor, Sir William Berkeley. In 1646, at the end of the second Indian uprising against the Virginians, the Powhatan tribes had accepted a treaty granting them exclusive rights to territory north of the York River, beyond the limits of white settlement. Stable Indian relations suited the established planters, some of whom traded profitably with the Indians, but became obnoxious to new settlers arriving in the 1650s and 1660s. Nor did it please the white indentured servants who had served their time and were hoping to find cheap frontier land.

In the summer of 1675, a group of frontiersmen used an incident with a local tribe as an excuse to attack the Susquehannocks, whose rich land they coveted. Governor Berkeley denounced the attack, but few supported his position. He faced, he said, "a people where six parts of seven at least are poor, indebted, discontented, and armed."

Although badly outnumbered, the Susquehannocks prepared for war. They attacked during the winter of 1675–1676 and killed 36 Virginians. That spring, the hot-blooded Nathaniel Bacon became the frontiersmen's leader. Joined by hundreds of runaway servants and some slaves, he launched a campaign of indiscriminate warfare on friendly and hostile Indians alike. When Governor Berkeley declared Bacon a rebel and sent out 300 militiamen to drag him to Jamestown for trial, Bacon headed into the wilderness and recruited more followers, including many substantial planters. Frontier skirmishes with Indians had turned into civil war.

In the summer of 1676, Bacon and his followers captured the capital at Jamestown and put Governor Berkeley to flight across Chesapeake Bay.

Virginians at all levels had chafed under Berkeley's rule. High taxes, an increase in the governor's powers at the expense of local officials, and the monopoly that Berkeley and his friends held on the Indian trade were especially unpopular. Berkeley tried to rally public support by holding new assembly elections and extending the vote to all freemen, whether they owned property or not. The new assembly promptly turned on the governor, passing a set of reform laws intended to make government more responsive to the common people and to end rapacious officeholding. The assembly also made legal the enslavement of Native Americans.

Time was on the governor's side, however. Having crushed the Indians, Bacon's followers began drifting home to tend their crops. Meanwhile, Berkeley's reports of the rebellion brought the dispatch of 1,100 royal troops from England. By the time they arrived, in January 1677, Nathaniel Bacon lay dead of swamp fever and most of his followers had melted back into the frontier. After Bacon's death in October 1676, Berkeley rounded up 23 rebel leaders and hanged them without benefit of civil trial. Royal investigators who arrived in 1677 denounced Governor Berkeley as well as the rebels, whom they described as the "inconsiderate sort of men who so rashly and causelessly cry up a war and seem to wish and aim at an utter extirpation of the Indians."

The hatred of Indians did not die with the end of the rebellion. A generation later, in 1711, the Virginia legislature voted military appropriations of £20,000 "for extirpating all Indians without distinction of Friends or Enemys." The remnants of the once populous Powhatan Confederacy lost their last struggle for the world they had known. Now they moved farther west or submitted to a life on the margins of white society as tenant farmers, day laborers, or domestic servants.

After Bacon's Rebellion, an emerging planter aristocracy annulled most of the reform laws of 1676. But the war relieved much of the social tension among white Virginians. Newly available Indian land created fresh opportunities for small planters and former servants. Equally important, Virginians with capital to invest were turning to West Africa to supply their labor needs. A racial consensus, uniting whites of different ranks in the common pursuit of a prosperous, slave-based economy, began to take shape.

North and south of Virginia, Bacon's Rebellion caused insurrectionary rumblings. A dissident group in North Carolina's Albemarle County drove the governor from office and briefly seized the reins of power.

In Maryland, Protestant settlers chafed under high taxes, quitrents, and officeholders regarded as venal, Catholic, or both. Declining tobacco prices and a fear of Indian attacks increased their touchiness. A month after Bacon razed Jamestown, insurgent small planters tried to seize the Maryland government. Two of their leaders were hanged for the attempt. In 1681, another abortive uprising took place.

In all three southern colonies, the volatility of late-seventeenth-century life owed much to the region's peculiar social development. Where family formation was retarded by imbalanced sex ratios and fearsome mortality, and where geographic mobility was high, little social cohesion or attachment to community could grow. Missing in the southern colonies were mature local institutions, a vision of a larger purpose, and experienced and responsive political leaders.

AN ERA OF INSTABILITY

A dozen years after the major Indian wars in New England and Virginia, a series of insurrections and a major witchcraft incident rumbled through colonial society. The rebellions were triggered by the Revolution of 1688, known to Protestants in England thereafter as the Glorious Revolution because it ended forever the notion that kings ruled by a God-given "divine right" and marked the last serious Catholic challenge to Protestant supremacy. But these colonial disruptions also signified a struggle for social and political dominance in the expanding colonies, as did the Salem witchcraft trials in Massachusetts.

Organizing the Empire

From the earliest attempts at colonization, the English assumed that overseas settlements existed to promote the national interest at home. According to this mercantilist theory, colonies served as outlets for English manufactured goods, provided foodstuffs and raw materials, stimulated trade (and hence promoted a larger merchant navy), and contributed to the royal coffers by paying duties on exported commodities such as sugar and tobacco. Colonies benefited by the military protection and guaranteed markets provided from England.

England proceeded slowly in the seventeenth century to regulate its colonies accordingly. In 1621, the king's council forbade tobacco growers to export their crop to anywhere but England. Three years later, when the Virginia Company of London plunged into bankruptcy, the Crown made Virginia a royal colony, the first of many. In 1651, Parliament passed a navigation act requiring that English or colonial ships, manned by English or colonial sailors, carry all goods entering England, Ireland, and the colonies, no matter where those goods originated.

In 1660, after the monarchy was restored, Parliament passed a more comprehensive navigation act that listed colonial products (tobacco, sugar, indigo, dyewoods, cotton) that could be shipped only to England or to other English colonies. Like its predecessor, the act took dead aim at Holland's domination of Atlantic commerce while increasing England's revenues by imposing duties on the enumerated articles. In the following decades, other navigation acts closed loopholes in the 1660 law and added other enumerated articles. Nevertheless, this regulation bore lightly on the colonists because the laws lacked enforcement mechanisms.

After 1675, England tightened imperial control. That year marked the establishment of the Lords of Trade, a committee of the king's privy council vested with power to make and enforce decisions regarding the management of the colonies. Chief among their goals was the creation of more uniform governments in North America and the West Indies that would answer to the Crown's will. England was becoming the shipper of the world, and its state-regulated policy of economic nationalism, duplicating that of the Dutch, was essential to this rise to commercial greatness.

The Glorious Revolution in New England

When Charles II died in 1685, his brother, the duke of York, assumed the throne as James II. This set in motion a chain of events that nearly led to civil war. Like his brother, James II professed the Catholic faith. But unlike Charles II, who had disclosed this only on his deathbed, the new king announced his faith immediately upon assuming the throne. Consternation ensued. James proceeded to favor Catholics in various ways. When his wife gave birth to a son in 1688, a Catholic succession loomed.

Convinced that James was trying to seize absolute power and fearing a Catholic conspiracy, a group of Protestant leaders secretly plotted the king's downfall. In 1688, led by the earl of Shaftesbury, they invited William of Orange, a prince of the Netherlands, to invade England and take the throne with his wife, Mary, James's Protestant daughter. James abdicated rather than fight. It was a bloodless victory for Protestantism, for parliamentary power and the limitation of kingly prerogatives, and for the propertied merchants and gentry of England who stood behind the revolt.

The response of New Englanders to these events stemmed from their previous experience with royal authority and their fear of "papists." New England became a prime target for reform when the administrative reorganization of the empire began in 1675. In 1684, Charles II had annulled the Massachusetts charter. Two years later, James II appointed Sir Edmund Andros, former governor of New York, to rule over the newly created Dominion of New England that soon gathered under one government the colonies of New Hampshire, Massachusetts, Connecticut, Plymouth, Rhode Island, New York, New Jersey, and part of Maine. Puritans were now forced to swallow the bitter fact that they were subjects of London bureaucrats who cared more about shaping a disciplined empire than about the special religious vision of one group of overseas subjects.

At first, most New Englanders accepted Andros, but he soon earned their hatred. He imposed taxes without legislative consent, ended trial by jury, abolished the General Court of Massachusetts (which had met annually since 1630), muzzled Boston's town meeting, and challenged the validity of all land titles. He converted a Boston Puritan church into an Anglican chapel and rejected the Puritan practice of suppressing religious dissent.

When news reached Boston in April 1689 that William of Orange had landed in England, ending James II's hated Catholic regime, Bostonians streamed into the streets to the beat of drums. They imprisoned Andros, a suspected papist, and an interim government ruled Massachusetts for three years while the Bay colonists awaited a new charter and a royal governor.

Leisler's Rebellion in New York

In New York, the Glorious Revolution was similarly bloodless at first but far more disruptive. When news arrived of James II's abdication, the royal government simply melted away. A local militia captain, the German-born Jacob Leisler, appeared with his followers at Fort James at the lower tip of Manhattan. Governor Francis Nicholson made only a token show of resistance before quietly stepping down.

Leisler had come to New Amsterdam in 1660 as a common footsoldier of the Dutch West India Company, married into an established Dutch family, and become a successful merchant. After ousting Governor Nicholson, Leisler established an interim government and ruled with an elected Committee of Safety for 13 months, until a governor appointed by King William arrived.

Leisler's government enjoyed popularity among small landowners and urban laboring people. Most of the upper echelon, however, regarded him as an upstart commoner who had leapfrogged into the merchant class by marrying a wealthy widow. Leislerians were often labeled as people of "mean birth, and sordid education and desperate fortunes."

Much of this antipathy originated in the smoldering resentment lower- and middle-class Dutch inhabitants felt toward the town's English elite. Many Dutch merchants had readily adjusted to the English conquest of New Netherland in 1664, and many incoming English merchants had married into Dutch families. But beneath the upper class, incidents of Anglo-Dutch hostility were common. The feeling rose in the 1670s and 1680s among ordinary Dutch families that the English were crowding them out of the society they had built.

Leisler shared Dutch hostility toward New York's English elite, and his sympathy for the common people, mostly Dutch, earned him the hatred of the city's oligarchy. Leisler freed imprisoned debtors, planned a town-meeting system of government for New York City, and replaced merchants with artisans in important official posts. By the autumn of 1689, Leislerian mobs were attacking the property of some of New York's wealthiest merchants.

When a new English governor arrived in 1691, the anti-Leislerians embraced him and charged Leisler and seven of his assistants with treason for assuming the government without royal instructions. In the ensuing trial, Leisler and Jacob Milbourne, his son-in-law and chief lieutenant, were convicted of treason by an all-English jury and hanged. Leisler's popularity among the artisans of the city was evident when his wealthy opponents could find no carpenter in the city who would furnish a ladder to use at the scaffold. After his execution, peace gradually returned to New York, but for years provincial and city politics reflected the deep rift between Leislerians and anti-Leislerians.

Southern Rumblings

The Glorious Revolution also focused dissatisfactions in several southern colonies. Since Maryland was ruled by a Catholic proprietary family, the Protestant majority predictably seized on word of the Glorious Revolution and used it for their own purposes. Leading officials and planters formed a Protestant Association. Seizing control of the government in July 1689, they vowed to cleanse Maryland of its popish hue and to reform a corrupt customs service, cut taxes and fees, and extend the rights of the representative assembly. John Coode, formerly a fiery Anglican minister who had been involved in a brief rebellion in 1681, assumed the reins of government and held them until the arrival of Maryland's first royal governor in 1692.

In neighboring Virginia, the Catholic governor, Lord Howard of Effingham, had installed a number of Catholic officials. News of the revolution in England led a group of planters to attempt an overthrow of the governor. The uprising quickly faded when the governor's council asserted itself and took its own measures to remove Catholics from positions of authority.

The Glorious Revolution brought political changes to several colonies. The Dominion of New England was shattered. While Connecticut and Rhode Island were allowed to elect their own governors, Massachusetts and New Hampshire became royal colonies with governors appointed by the king. In Massachusetts, a new royal charter in 1691 eliminated church membership as a voting requirement. The Maryland proprietorship was abolished (to be restored in 1715 when the Baltimore family became Protestant), and Catholics were barred from office. Everywhere the liberties of Protestant Englishmen were celebrated.

The Social Basis of Politics

The colonial insurrections associated with the Glorious Revolution revealed social and political tensions in the immature societies. The colonial elite tried, of course, to foster social and political stability. The best insurance of this, they believed, was the maintenance of a stratified society where children were subordinate to parents, women to men, servants to masters, and the poor to the rich. In every settlement, leaders tried to maintain a system of social gradations and subordination. Churchgoers, for example, did not file into church on Sundays and occupy the pews in random fashion. Rather, the seats were "doomed," or assigned according to customary yardsticks of respectability—age, parentage, social position, wealth, and occupation.

This social ideal proved difficult to maintain on North American soil, however. Regardless of previous rank, settlers rubbed elbows so frequently and faced such raw conditions together that those without pedigrees often saw little reason to defer to men of superior rank. "In Virginia," explained John Smith, "a plain soldier that can use a pickaxe and spade is better than five knights." Colonists everywhere learned that basic lesson. They gave respect not to those who claimed it by birth but to those who earned it by deed.

Ambitious men on the rise, such as Nathaniel Bacon and Jacob Leisler, rose up against the constituted authorities. When they gained power during the Glorious Revolution, in every case only briefly, the leaders of these uprisings linked themselves with a tradition of English struggle against tyranny and oligarchical power. They vowed to make government more responsive to the ordinary people, who composed most of their societies.

Witchcraft in Salem

The ordinary people in the colonies, for whom Bacon and Leisler tried to speak, could sometimes be misled, as the tragic events of the Salem witch hunts demonstrated. The deposing of Governor Andros in 1689 left the Massachusetts colony in political limbo for three years, and this allowed what might have been a brief outbreak of witchcraft in the little community of Salem to escalate into a bitter and bloody battle to which the provincial government, caught in transition, reacted only belatedly.

On a winter's day in 1692, 9-year-old Betty Parris and her 11-year-old cousin Abigail Williams began to play at magic in the kitchen of a small house in Salem, Massachusetts. They enlisted the aid of Tituba, the slave of Betty's father, Samuel Parris, the minister of the small community. Tituba told voodoo tales handed down from her African past and baked "witch cakes." The girls soon became seized with fits and began making wild gestures and speeches. Soon other young girls in the village were behaving strangely. Village elders extracted confessions that they were being tormented by Tituba and two other women, one a decrepit pauper, the other a disagreeable hag.

What began as the innocent play of young girls turned into a ghastly rending of a farm community capped by the execution of 20 villagers accused of witchcraft. In the seventeenth century, people still took literally the biblical injunction "Thou shalt not suffer a witch to live." In Massachusetts, more than 100 people, mostly older women, had been accused of witchcraft before 1692, and more than a dozen had been hanged.

In Salem, the initial accusations against three older women quickly multiplied. Within a matter of weeks, dozens had been charged with witchcraft, including several prominent members of the community. But formal prosecution of the accused witches could not proceed because neither the new royal charter of 1691 nor the royal governor to rule the colony had yet arrived. When Governor William Phips arrived from England in May 1692, he ordered a special court to try the accused, but by now events had careened out of control. All through the summer the court listened to testimony. By September it had condemned about two dozen villagers. The authorities hanged 19 of them on barren "Witches Hill" outside the town, and 80-year-old Giles Corey was crushed to death under heavy stones. The trials rolled on into 1693, but by then colonial leaders, including many of the clergy, recognized that a feverish fear of one's neighbors, rather than witchcraft itself, had possessed the little village of Salem.

Many factors contributed to the hysteria. Among them were generational differences between older Puritan colonists and the sometimes less religiously motivated younger generation, old family animosities, population growth and pressures on the available farmland, and tensions between agricultural Salem Village and the nearby commercial center called Salem Town. An outbreak of food poisoning may also have caused hallucinogenic behavior. The fact that most of the individuals charged with witchcraft were women underscores the relatively weak position of women in Puritan society. The witch-hunting fever produced the greatest internal conflict in late-seventeenth-century America. Probably nobody will ever fully understand the underlying causes, but the fact that the accusations of witchcraft kept spreading suggests the anxiety of this tumultuous era, marked by war, economic disruption, the political takeover of the colony by Andros and then his overthrow, and the erosion of the early generation's utopian vision.

CONTENDING FOR A CONTINENT

At the end of the seventeenth century, following an era of Indian wars and internal upheaval, the colonists for the first time confronted an extended period of international war. The struggle for mastery of the New World among four contending European powers—Holland, Spain, France, and England—now became more overt, marking the beginning of nearly 100 years of conflict.

Anglo-French Rivalry

In 1661, the French king, Louis XIV, determined to make his country the most powerful in Europe, regarded North America and the Caribbean with renewed interest. New France's timber resources would build the royal navy, its fish would feed the growing mass of slaves in the French West Indies, and its fur trade, if greatly expanded, would fill the royal coffers.

Under the leadership of able governors such as Count Frontenac, New France grew in population, economic strength, and ambition in the late seventeenth century. In the 1670s, Louis Jolliet and Father Jacques Marquette, a Jesuit priest, explored an immense territory watered by the Mississippi and Missouri rivers, previously unknown to Europeans. A decade later, military engineers and priests began building forts and missions, one complementing the other, throughout the Great Lakes region and the Mississippi valley. In 1682, René Robert de La Salle canoed down the Mississippi all the way to the Gulf of Mexico.

The growth of French strength and ambitions brought New England and New France into deadly conflict for a generation, beginning in the late seventeenth century. Religious hostility overlaid commercial rivalry. Protestant New Englanders regarded Catholic New France as a satanic challenge to their divinely sanctioned mission. When the European wars began in 1689, armed conflict between England and France quickly extended into every overseas theater where the two powers had colonies. In North America, the battle zone was New York, New England, and eastern Canada.

In two wars, from 1689 to 1697 and 1702 to 1713, the English and French, while fighting in Europe, also sought to oust each other from the New World. The zone of greatest importance was the Caribbean, where slaves produced huge sugar fortunes. In the North American zone, problems of weather, disease, transport, and supply were so great that only irregular warfare was possible.

The English struck three times at the centers of French power. In 1690, during King William's War (1689–1697), their small flotilla captured Port Royal, the hub of Acadia (which was returned to France at the end of the war). The English assault on Quebec, however, failed disastrously. In Queen Anne's War (1702–1713), New England attacked Port Royal three times before finally capturing it in 1710. A year later, when England sent a flotilla of 60 ships and 5,000 men to conquer Canada, the land and sea operations foundered before reaching their destinations.

When European-style warfare failed miserably in America, both England and France attempted to subcontract military tasks to their Indian allies. This policy occasionally succeeded, especially with the French, who gladly sent their own troops into the fray alongside Indian partners. The French and Indians wiped out the frontier outpost of Schenectady, New York, in 1690; razed Wells, Maine, and Deerfield, Massachusetts, in 1703; and battered other towns along the New England frontier during both wars. In retaliation, the Iroquois, supplied by the English, stung several French settlements. Too powerful to be dictated to by either France or England, the Iroquois sat out the second war in the early eighteenth century.

The Results of War

The Peace of Utrecht in 1713, which ended the war, capped the century-long rise of England and the decline of Spain in the rivalry for the sources of wealth outside Europe. England, the big winner, received Newfoundland and Acadia (renamed Nova Scotia), and France recognized English sovereignty over the fur-rich Hudson Bay territory. France retained Cape Breton Island, controlling the entrance to the St. Lawrence River. In the Caribbean, France yielded St. Kitts and Nevis to England. In Europe, Spain lost its provinces in Italy and the last of its holdings in the Netherlands to the Austrian Hapsburgs. Spain also surrendered Gibraltar and Minorca to the English and awarded England the lucrative privilege of supplying the Spanish empire in America with African slaves, a favor formerly enjoyed by the French Senegal Company.

The French were the big losers in these wars, but they did not abandon their ambitions in the New World. Soon after Louis XIV died in 1715, the Regency government of the duke of Orleans tried to regain lost time in America by mounting

Visiting French Louisiana in 1735, Alexander de Batz painted members of the Illinois tribe who traded at New Orleans. Note the hatted African who apparently has been adopted by the Illinois.

a huge expedition to settle Louisiana. Because of mismanagement, however, this plan produced little result. French colonies expanded only in the Caribbean, where by 1750 the islands of Hispaniola, Martinique, and Guadeloupe counted 46,000 whites and 250,000 slaves.

At the Peace of Utrecht, Spain retained a vast empire in America. When France decided in 1762 that Louisiana was not worth the expense, Spain gladly accepted it and tried to make it a buffer against the British Americans migrating westward toward New Spain.

Though England had rebuffed France after a generation of war, New England suffered grievously. Massachusetts bore the brunt of the burden. Probably one-fifth of all able-bodied males in the colony participated in the Canadian campaigns, and of these about one-quarter never lived to tell of the terrors of New England's first major experience with international warfare. At the end of the first war in 1697, one leader bemoaned that Massachusetts was left "quite exhausted and ready to sink under the calamities and fatigue of a tedious consuming war." The war debt was £50,000 sterling in Massachusetts alone, a greater per capita burden than the na-

tional debt today. At the end of the second conflict in 1713, war widows were so numerous that the Bay Colony faced its first serious poverty problem.

The colonies south of New England were also affected by the wars. In Queen Anne's War, New York lost one of its best grain markets when Spain, allied with France, outlawed American foodstuffs in its West Indian colonies. The French navy plucked off nearly 30 New York merchant vessels, about one-quarter of the port's fleet, and disrupted the vital sea lanes between the mainland and the Caribbean, also to the detriment of Philadelphia's grain merchants.

One lesson of war, to be repeated many times in succeeding generations, was that the burdens and rewards fell unevenly on the participants. Some lowborn men could rise spectacularly. William Phips, the twenty-sixth child in his family, rose from sheep farmer and ship's carpenter in Maine to governor of Massachusetts in 1691. Other men, already rich, multiplied their wealth. Andrew Belcher of Boston, who had grown wealthy on provisioning contracts during King Philip's War in 1675 and 1676, combined patriotism with profit in King William's and Queen Anne's wars by supplying warships and outfitting the New England expeditions to Canada. However, most men, especially those who did the fighting, gained little, and many lost all.

CONCLUSION

CONTROLLING THE NEW ENVIRONMENT

By the second decade of the eighteenth century, the 12 English colonies on the eastern edge of North America had erected the basic scaffolding of colonial life. With the aid of England, they had ousted the Dutch, fought the French to a draw, and held their own against the Spanish. The coastal Indian tribes were reeling from disease and war. The settlers had overcome a scarcity of labor by copying the other European colonists in the hemisphere and importing slaves. Finally, the colonists had rebelled against what they viewed as arbitrary and tainted governments imposed by England.

Physically isolated from Europe, the colonists developed a large measure of self-reliance. Slowly, they began to identify themselves as the permanent inhabitants of a new land rather than transplanted English, Dutch, or Scots-Irish. The new land was a puzzling mixture of unpredictable opportunity and sudden turbulence, unprecedented freedom and debilitating wars, racial intermingling and racial separation. It was a New World in much more than a geographic sense, for the people of three cultures who now inhabited it had remade it; and, while doing so, they were remaking themselves.

Recommended Reading

The Atlantic slave trade is explored in Philip Curtin, *The Atlantic Slave Trade* (1969); and Martin Kilson and Robert I. Rotberg, eds., *The African Diaspora* (1976).

The origins and early history of slavery in the Americas are studied in H. Hoetink, *Slavery and Race Relations in the Americas* (1973); and Richard S. Dunn, *Sugar and Slaves* (1972).

For slavery in the American colonies, see Ira Berlin, "Time, Space, and the Evolution of Afro-American Society in British Mainland America," *American Historical Review* 85 (1980); Peter H. Wood, *Black Majority* (1974); and Daniel C. Littlefield, *Rice and Slaves* (1981).

Relations between colonizers and Native Americans after the founding period are examined in James Axtell, *The European and the Indian* (1981); Francis Jennings, *The Invasion of America* (1975); *The Ambiguous Iroquois Empire* (1984); J. Leitch Wright, *The Only Land They Knew: The Tragic Story of the American Indians in the Old South* (1981); and Gary B. Nash, *Red, White, and Black* (1974, 1982).

For the Glorious Revolution in America and the era of instability at the end of the seventeenth century, consult David Lovejoy, *The Glorious Revolution in America* (1972); Carol F. Karlsen, *The Devil in the Shape of a Woman* (1987); and Paul Boyer and Stephen Nissenbaum, *Salem Possessed* (1974).

Time Line

1600–1700	Dutch monopolize slave trade	1682	La Salle sails down Mississippi River and claims Louisiana for France
1619	First Africans imported to Virginia	1684	Massachusetts charter recalled
1637	Pequot War in New England	1686	Dominion of New England
1640s	New England merchants enter slave trade Virginia forbids blacks to carry firearms	1688	Glorious Revolution in England, followed by accession of William and Mary
1650–1670	Judicial and legislative decisions in Chesapeake colonies solidify racial lines	1689	Overthrow of Governor Andros in New England Leisler's Rebellion in New York
1660	Parliament passes first Navigation Act	1689–1697	King William's War
1664	English conquer New Netherland	1690s	Transition from white indentured to black slave labor begins in Chesapeake
1673–1685	French expand into Mississippi valley	1692	Witchcraft hysteria in Salem
1675–1676	King Philip's War in New England	1702–1713	Queen Anne's War
1676	Bacon's Rebellion in Virginia	1713	Peace of Utrecht

chapter 4

The Maturing of Colonial Society

Devereaux Jarratt was born in 1733 on the Virginia frontier, the third son of an immigrant yeoman farmer. In New Kent County, where Jarratt grew up, a farmer's "whole dress and apparel," he recalled later, "consisted in a pair of coarse breeches, one or two shirts, a pair of shoes and stockings, an old felt hat, and a bear skin coat." In a maturing colonial society that was six generations old by the mid–eighteenth century, such simple folk stepped aside and tipped their hats when prosperous neighbors went by.

As the colonies grew rapidly after 1700, economic development brought handsome gains for some, opened modest opportunities for many, but produced disappointment and privation for others. Jarratt was among those who advanced. His huge appetite for learning earned him some schooling. But at age 8, when his parents died, he had to take his place behind the plow alongside his brothers. Then, at 19, Jarratt was "called from the ax to the quill" by a neighboring planter's timely offer of a job tutoring his children.

Tutoring put Jarratt in touch with the world of wealth and status. Gradually he advanced to positions in the households of wealthy Virginia planters. His modest success also introduced him to the world of evangelical religion. In the eighteenth century, an explosion of religious fervor dramatically reversed the growing secularism of the settlers. Jarratt first encountered evangelicalism in the published sermons of George Whitefield, an English clergyman.

Later, at the plantation of John Cannon, he personally experienced conversion under the influence of Cannon's wife. Jarratt later became a clergyman in the Anglican church, but he never lost his religious zeal and desire to carry religion to the common people. In this, he was part of the first mass religious movement to occur in colonial society.

Colonial North America in the first half of the eighteenth century was a thriving, changing set of regional societies that had developed from turbulent seventeenth-century beginnings. New England, the mid-Atlantic colonies, the Upper and Lower

67

South, New France, and the northern frontier of New Spain were all distinct regions. Even within regions, diversity increased in the eighteenth century as newcomers, mostly from Africa, Germany, Ireland, and France, added new pieces to the emerging American mosaic.

Despite their bewildering diversity and lack of cohesion, the colonies along the Atlantic seaboard were affected similarly by population growth and economic development. Everywhere except on the frontier, class differences grew. A commercial orientation spread from north to south, especially in the towns, as local economies matured and forged links with the network of trade in the Atlantic basin. The exercise of political power of elected legislative assemblies and local bodies produced seasoned leaders, a tradition of local autonomy, and a widespread belief in a political ideology stressing the liberties that freeborn Englishmen should enjoy. All regions experienced a deep-running religious awakening that was itself connected to secular changes. All of these themes will be explored as we follow the way that scattered frontier settlements developed into mature provincial societies.

AMERICA'S FIRST POPULATION EXPLOSION

In 1680, some 150,000 colonizers clung to the eastern edge of North America. By 1750, they had swelled sevenfold to top one million. This growth rate, never experienced in Europe, staggered English policymakers. The population boom was fed from both internal and external sources. Natural increase accounted for much of the growth in all the colonies and nearly all of it in New England, where immigrants arrived only in a trickle in the eighteenth century. The black population also began to increase naturally by the 1720s. American-born slaves soon began to outnumber slaves born in Africa.

The Newcomers

While expanding through natural increase, the colonial population also received waves of newcomers. The eighteenth-century arrivals, who far outnumbered those who came before 1700, came overwhelmingly from Germany, Switzerland, Ireland, and Africa, and they were mostly indentured servants and slaves. Of all the groups arriving in the eighteenth century, the Africans were the largest. Numbering about 15,000 in 1690, they grew to 80,000 in 1730 and 325,000 in 1760.

German-speaking settlers, about 90,000 strong, flocked to the colonies in the eighteenth century. Most settled between New York and South Carolina, with Pennsylvania claiming the largest number of them.

Outnumbering the Germans were the Protestant Scots-Irish. Several thousand from Northern Ireland arrived each year after the Peace of Utrecht in 1713 reopened the Atlantic sea lanes. Mostly poor farmers, they streamed into the same backcountry areas where Germans were settling, though more of them followed the mountain valleys south into the Carolinas and Georgia. They washed over the ridges of Appalachia until their appetite for land brought

German Settlements, 1775

Scots-Irish Settlements, 1775

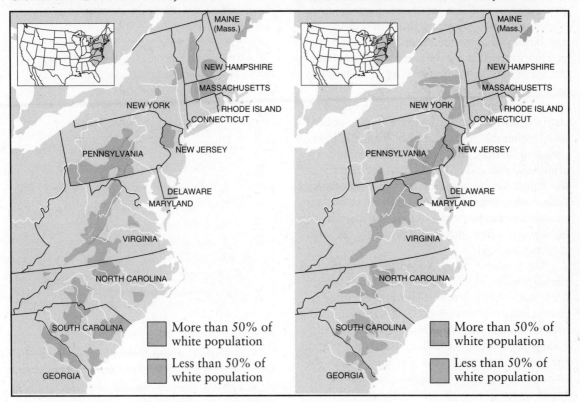

them face to face with the ancient occupiers of the land. No major Indian wars occurred between 1715 and 1754, but the frontier bristled with tension as the new settlers pushed westward.

In the enormous population growth occurring after 1715, New England nearly tripled in population, but the middle and southern colonies quadrupled, though in the South the fast-growing slave population accounted for much more of the growth than in the mid-Atlantic.

The social background of the new European immigrants differed substantially from that of their seventeenth-century predecessors. The early settlers included a number of men from the upper levels of the English social pyramid: university-trained Puritan ministers, sons of wealthy gentry, and merchants. The earlier immigrants had also included many from the middle rungs of the English social ladder—yeomen farmers, skilled craftsmen, and shopkeepers. But slaves and indentured servants made up most of the incoming human tide after 1713. The traffic in servants became a regular part of the commerce linking Europe and America.

Shipboard conditions for servants worsened in the eighteenth century and were hardly better than aboard the slave ships. Crammed between decks in stifling air, servants suffered from smallpox and fevers, rotten food, impure water, cold, and lice. "Children between the ages of one and seven seldom survive the sea voyage," bemoaned one German immigrant, "and parents must often watch their offspring suffer miserably, die, and be thrown into the ocean." The shipboard mortality rate of about 15 percent in the colonial era made this the most unhealthy of all times to seek American shores.

Like indentured servants in the seventeenth century, the servant immigrants who poured ashore after 1715 came mostly from the lower ranks of society. As earlier, some were petty criminals, political prisoners, and the castoffs of the cities. Yet, as one Englishman commented, "Men who emigrate are from the nature of their circumstances, the most active, hardy, daring, bold and resolute spirits, and probably the most mischievous also."

Once ashore, most indentured servants, especially males, found the labor system harsh. Merchants sold them, one shocked Britisher reported in 1773, "as they do their horses, and advertise them as they do their beef and oatmeal." Facing cruel treatment, thousands of servants ran away. Advertisements for them filled the colonial newspapers alongside notices for escaped slaves.

The goal of every servant was to secure a foothold on the ladder of opportunity. "The hope of buying land in America," a New Yorker noted, "is what chiefly induces people into America." However, many servants died before serving out their time. Others won freedom only to toil for years as poor day laborers and tenant farmers. Only a small proportion achieved the dream of becoming independent landholders. The chief beneficiaries of the system of bound white labor were not the laborers but their masters.

Africans in Chains

Among the thousands of ships crossing the Atlantic in the eighteenth century, the ones fitted out as seagoing dungeons for slaves were the

Population of European Colonies in North America, 1680–1770

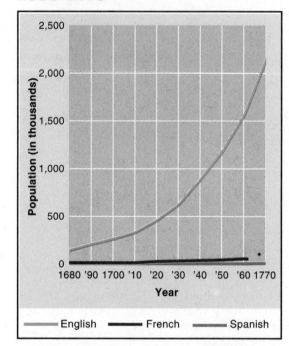

*France's North American colonies in Canada and Louisiana ceded to England and Spain, respectively, in 1763

most numerous. After the Peace of Utrecht, the slave trade to the southern colonies expanded sharply. The generation after 1730 witnessed the largest influx of African slaves in the colonial period, averaging about 5,000 a year. In the entire period from 1700 to 1775, more than 350,000 African slaves entered the American colonies.

Even as the traffic in slaves peaked, religious and humanitarian opposition to slavery arose. A few individuals, mostly Quaker, had objected to slavery on moral grounds since the late seventeenth century. But the idea grew in the 1750s that slavery contradicted the Christian concept of brotherhood and the Enlightenment notion of the natural equality of all humans. John Woolman, a Quaker tailor from New Jersey, dedicated his life in the 1750s to a crusade against slavery and planted the seeds of abolitionism.

BEYOND THE APPALACHIANS

By the mid–eighteenth century, the American colonists, though increasing rapidly in number, still occupied only a narrow strip of coastal plain in eastern North America. Of about 1.2 million settlers and slaves in 1750, only a tiny fraction lived farther than 100 miles from the shores of the Atlantic. Beginning in the 1750s, westward-moving colonists in pursuit of more land would encounter four other groups already established to their west: the populous interior Native American tribes, and smaller groups of French-Americans, Spanish-Americans, and African-Americans. Changes already occurring among these groups would affect settlers breaching the

Appalachian barrier and, in the third quarter of the eighteenth century, would even reach eastward to the original British settlements.

Cultural Changes Among Interior Tribes

During the first half of the eighteenth century, the inland tribes began to be affected by extensive contact with the French, Spanish, and English. The introduction of European trade goods, especially iron implements, textiles, firearms and ammunition, and alcohol, inescapably changed Indian lifeways. Subsistence hunting, limited to satisfying tribal food requirements, turned into commercial hunting, restricted only by the quantity of trade goods desired. Indian males spent far more time away from the villages trapping and hunting, and the increased importance of

The communalistic Moravian immigrants who came to Pennsylvania in the 1740s dedicated themselves, like the Quakers, to peaceful relations with the Indians. The Prussian John Jacob Schmick and his Norwegian wife Johanna were missionaries to the Delaware tribe

this activity to tribal life undermined the matrilineal basis of society. Women were also drawn into the new economic activities, helping to skin the beaver, marten, and fox, scrape and trim the pelts, and sew them into robes. Among some tribes, the trapping, preparation, and transporting of skins became so time-consuming that they had to procure food resources from other tribes.

Involvement in the fur trade altered the traditional Native American belief that the destinies of humans and animals were closely linked. In addition, the fur trade heightened intertribal tensions, often to the point of war. When a tribe depleted the furs in their hunting grounds, they could maintain their trade only by conquering more remote tribes with fertile hunting grounds or by forcibly intercepting the furs of other tribes as they were carried to European trading posts. The introduction of European weaponry, which Indians quickly mastered, further intensified intertribal conflict.

Tribal political organization among the interior tribes also changed in the eighteenth century. Most tribes had earlier been loose confederations of villages and clans, each exercising local autonomy. The Creek, Cherokee, and Iroquois gave primary loyalty to the village, not to the tribe or confederacy. But trade, diplomatic contact, and war with Europeans required more coordinated policies. To deal effectively with traders and officials, the villages gradually adjusted to more centralized leadership.

By 1750, the Cherokee, for example, had formed a more centralized tribal "priest state." When this proved inadequate, warriors began to assume the dominant role in tribal councils, replacing the civil chiefs. By this process the Cherokee reorganized their political structure so that dozens of scattered villages could amalgamate their strength.

While incorporating trade goods into their material culture and adapting their economies and political structures to new situations, the interior tribes held fast to tradition in many ways. They saw little reason to adopt the colonists' systems of law and justice, religion, education, family organization, or child rearing. Their refusal to accept the superiority of white culture frustrated English missionaries, eager to win Native Americans from "savage" ways. But a Carolinian admitted that "they are really better to us than we are to them. We look upon them with scorn and disdain, and think them little better than beasts in human shape, though if well examined, we shall find that, for all our religion and education, we possess more moral deformities and evils than these savages do."

Despite maintaining many cultural practices, the interior Indian tribes suffered from the contact with the British colonizers. Decade by decade, the fur trade spread epidemic diseases, raised the level of warfare, depleted their lands of game animals, and drew the Native Americans into a market economy where their trading partners gradually became trading masters.

France's Inland Empire

While the powerful Iroquois, Cherokee, Creek, and Choctaw tribes interacted with British colonists to their east, they also dealt with a growing French presence to their west. Between 1699 and 1754, the French developed a system of small forts, trading posts, and agricultural villages throughout the central area of the continent from French Canada to the Gulf of Mexico. The Indians retained sovereignty over the land but gradually succumbed to French diseases, French arms, and French-promoted intertribal wars. At the same time, however, because France's interior empire was organized primarily as a military and trading operation, soldiers, fur traders, and other men arriving without wives often exploited or married Indian women. French Louisiana had more mixed-race children and more white and black men who lived with Native Americans than any Anglo-American colony.

In 1718, France settled New Orleans at

France's Inland Empire, 1600-1720

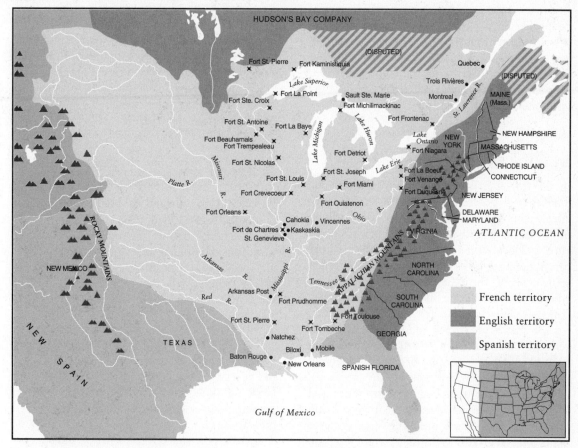

great cost by transporting almost 7,000 whites and 5,000 African slaves to the mouth of the Mississippi River. Disease rapidly whittled down these numbers, and an uprising of the powerful Natchez tribe in 1729 discouraged further French immigration. Most of the survivors settled around the little town of New Orleans and raised indigo, rice, and other crops.

In its economy and society, New Orleans much resembled early Charleston, South Carolina. What distinguished the people of New Orleans from those of Charleston, however, was that the French knew nothing of representative political institutions. Ruled by a governor, a

commissary and chief judge, and a small appointed council, the people had no elections or assembly, no newspapers or taxes.

From its first introduction in Louisiana in 1719, French plantation slavery grew so that by 1765, blacks outnumbered whites. Most slaves and a majority of whites lived in the New Orleans area. The conditions of life for slaves differed little from those in the southern English colonies. But the French had a paternalistic black legal code that gave slaves some protection in courts. When the Spanish took over the colony in 1769, they instituted their law guaranteeing slaves the right to buy freedom with money earned in their free time. Soon a large free black class emerged, headed by substantial people like Simon Colfat, who ran various enterprises, helped other slaves pay for their freedom, and headed the company of free black militia. When Americans acquired the colony in 1803, they suppressed freedom purchase and discouraged manumission.

Spain's North America

In the first half of the eighteenth century, the Spanish still possessed by far the largest American empire. Even as Spanish power declined in Europe, it spread in America. Spain strengthened its Florida military posts to challenge English settlement of the Carolinas and French settlement of the Mississippi valley. Also to counter the French, the Spanish established permanent military posts in Texas and New Mexico for the first time. At the end of the eighteenth century, however, fewer than 50,000 Spanish and Hispanicized people of color inhabited Texas, New Mexico, and California.

As in New France, racial intermixture and social fluidity were more extensive in New Spain than in the English colonies. The Spanish never defined racial groups as distinctly as the English. The word *Spaniard* on a census might mean a white immigrant from Mexico or a part-Indian person who "lived like a Spaniard." Social mobility was considerable because the Crown was willing to raise even a common person to the status of *hidalgo* (minor nobleman) as an inducement to settle in New Spain's remote northern frontier. Most of the immigrants became small ranchers, producing livestock, corn, and wheat for export to other Spanish provinces to the south.

The Native Americans of New Mexico were more successful in resisting Spanish domination than the tribes of California. In the 1770s, the Spanish rapidly completed their western land and sea routes from San Diego to the new port of Yerba Buena (San Francisco) to block Russian settlement south of their base in northern California. The Spanish pioneers were Franciscan missionaries, accompanied by soldiers provided by the Crown. The priests established missions and induced local Indians to settle nearby. These "mission" Indians lived under an increasingly harsh regimen until they were reduced to a condition of virtual slavery.

A LAND OF FAMILY FARMS

Population growth and economic development gradually transformed the landscape of eighteenth-century British America. Three distinct variations of colonial society emerged: the farming society of the North, the plantation society of the South, and the urban society of the seaboard commercial towns.

Northern Agricultural Society

In the northern colonies, especially New England, tightknit farming families, organized in communities of several thousand people, dotted the landscape by the mid–eighteenth century. They based their mixed economy on timber, fish, cultivation, and livestock.

The farmers of the middle colonies—Pennsylvania, Delaware, New Jersey, and New York—set their wooden plows to much richer soils than New Englanders did. They enjoyed the additional advantage of settling an area cleared by Native Americans who had relied more on agriculture than New England tribes. Thus favored, mid-Atlantic farm families produced modest surpluses of corn, wheat, beef, and pork, which were sold not only to the West Indies but also to areas that could no longer feed themselves—England, Spain, Portugal, and even New England.

In the North, the broad ownership of land distinguished farming society from every other agricultural region of the Western world. In most communities before 1750, the truly rich and abjectly poor were few and the gap between them small compared with European society. Most men other than indentured servants lived to purchase or inherit a farm of at least 50 acres. Settlers valued land highly, for freehold tenure ordinarily guaranteed both economic independence and political rights.

Amid widespread property ownership, a rising population pressed against a limited land supply by the eighteenth century, especially in New England. Family farms could not be divided and subdivided indefinitely, for it took at least 50 acres (of which only a quarter could usually be cultivated) to support a single family. The decreasing fertility of the soil compounded the problem of dwindling farm size. When land had been plentiful, farmers planted crops in the same field for three years and then let it lie fallow in pasturage seven years or more until it regained its fertility. But on the smaller farms of the eighteenth century, farmers had reduced fallow time to only a year or two. Inevitably, such intense use of the soil reduced crop yields.

The diminishing size and productivity of family farms forced many New Englanders in the eighteenth century to move to the frontier or out of the area altogether. Some drifted south to New York and Pennsylvania. Others sought opportunities as artisans in the coastal towns or took to the sea. More headed for the colony's western frontier or north into New Hampshire and the eastern frontier of Maine. Several thousand New England families migrated even farther north, to the Annapolis valley of Nova Scotia.

Wherever they took up farming, northern cultivators engaged in agricultural work routines that were far less intense than in the South. The growing season was much shorter, and the cultivation of cereal crops required incessant labor only during spring planting and autumn harvesting. This less burdensome work rhythm led many northern cultivators to fill out their calendars with intermittent work as clockmakers, shoemakers, carpenters, and weavers.

Changing Values

On April 29, 1695, an unusually severe hailstorm struck Boston. Merchant Samuel Sewall dined that evening with Cotton Mather, New England's most prominent Puritan clergyman. As Mather wondered why "more ministers houses than others proportionately had been smitten with lightning," hailstones began to shatter the windows of Sewall's house. Sewall and Mather fell to their knees and broke into prayer together "after this awful Providence."

As these two third-generation Massachusetts Puritans understood it, God was angry with them as leaders of a people whose piety and moral rectitude were being overtaken by worldliness. The people of Massachusetts had become "sermon-proof," as one dejected minister put it.

In other parts of the North, the expansive environment and the Protestant emphasis on self-discipline and hard work were also breeding qualities that would become hallmarks of American culture: an ambitious outlook, individualistic behavior, and a love of material things. In Europe, most tillers of the soil expected little from life. In America, one colonist remarked, "Every man expects one day or another to be upon a footing with his wealthiest neighbor."

Commitment to religion, family, and community did not disappear in the eighteenth century. But fewer men and women saw daily existence as a preparation for the afterlife. A slender almanac, written by the twelfth child of a poor Boston candlemaker, captured the new outlook with wit and charm. Born in 1706, Benjamin Franklin had abandoned a declining Boston for a rising Philadelphia. By age 23, he had learned the printer's trade and was publishing the *Pennsylvania Gazette*. Three years later, he began *Poor Richard's Almanack,* next to the Bible the most widely read book in the colonies.

Franklin spiced his annual almanac—the ordinary person's guide to weather and useful information—with quips, adages, and home-spun philosophy. Eventually this homely material added up to a primer for success published in 1747 as *The Way to Wealth*. "The sleeping fox gathers no poultry" and "Lost time is never found again," advised Poor Richard, emphasizing that time is money. "It costs more to maintain one vice than to raise two children," he counseled, advocating not morality but practicality. Ever cocky, Franklin caught the spirit of the rising secularism of the eighteenth century. He embodied the growing utilitarian doctrine that the good is whatever is useful and the notion that the community is best served through individual self-improvement and accomplishment.

Women and the Family in Northern Colonial Society

In 1662, Elnathan Chauncy, a Massachusetts schoolboy, copied into his writing book that "the soul consists of two portions, inferior and superior; the superior is masculine and eternal; the feminine inferior and mortal." This lesson had been taught for generations on both sides of the Atlantic. It was part of a larger conception of a world, of God's design, that assigned degrees of status and stations in life to all persons. In such a world, the place of women was, by definition, subordinate to that of men. As daughters they were subject to their fathers, as wives, to their husbands.

European women usually accepted these narrowly circumscribed roles. Few complained, at least openly, that their work was generally limited to housewifery and midwifery. They remained silent about exclusion from the early public schools and laws that transferred to their husbands any property or income they brought into a marriage. Nor could women speak in their churches or participate in governing them, and

they had no legal voice in political affairs. Most women did not expect to choose a husband for love; parental guidance prevailed in a society in which producing legal heirs was the means of transmitting property. Once wed, women expected to remain so until death, for they could rarely obtain a divorce.

On the colonial frontier, women's lives changed in modest ways. In Europe, about one of ten women did not marry. But in the colonies, where men outnumbered women for the first century, a spinster was almost unheard of, and widows remarried with astounding speed. *Woman* and *wife* thus became nearly synonymous.

A second difference concerned property rights. Single women and widows in the colonies, as in England, could make contracts, hold and convey property, represent themselves in court, and conduct business. Under English common law, a woman forfeited these rights, as well as all property, when she married. In the colonies, however, legislatures and courts gave wives more control over property brought into marriage or left at their husband's death. They also enjoyed broader rights to act for and with their husbands in business transactions. In addition, young colonial women slowly gained the right of consenting to a marriage partner—a right that came by default to the thousands of female indentured servants who completed their labor contracts and had no parents within 3,000 miles to dictate to them.

Women had limited career choices in colonial society, but the work spaces and daily routines of husband and wife overlapped and intersected far more than today. Farm women as well as men worked at planting, harvesting, and milking cows. Women also made candles and soap, butter and cheese, and smoked meat; they made cloth and sometimes marketed farm products. A merchant's wife kept shop, handled accounts when her husband voyaged abroad, and helped supervise the servants and apprentices. "Deputy husbands" and "yoke mates" were re-

Childbirth was an oft-repeated event in the lives of most colonial wives. In this portrait of the Cheney family, the older woman is a nanny or mother-in-law; the younger woman holding a baby is Mr. Cheney's second wife.

vealing terms used by New Englanders to describe eighteenth-century wives.

Women held vital responsibilities as midwives. Until the late eighteenth century, the "obstetrick art" was almost entirely in women's hands. Midwives counseled pregnant women, delivered babies, supervised postpartum recovery, and participated in ceremonies of infant baptism and burial. Mrs. Phillips, an immigrant to Boston in 1719, delivered more than 3,000 infants in her 42-year career. Because childbirth was a recurring and dangerous crisis, the circle of female friends and relatives who attended childbirth created strong networks of mutual assistance.

In her role as wife and mother, the eighteenth-century northern colonial woman differed somewhat from her English counterpart. American women married earlier and produced more children (on average seven, two of whom died in infancy). But gradually, as the coastal plain filled up in the eighteenth century, marriage age crept up and the number of children per family inched down.

Northern child-rearing patterns differed considerably. In the seventeenth century, stern fathers dominated Puritan family life, and few were reluctant to punish unruly children. "Better whip'd than damn'd," advised Cotton Mather. In Quaker families, however, mothers played a more active role in child rearing. More permissive, they relied on tenderness and love rather than guilt to mold their children. Attitudes toward choosing a marriage partner also separated early Puritan and Quaker approaches to family life. Puritan parents usually arranged their children's marriages but allowed them the right to veto. Young Quaker men and women made their own matches, subject to parental veto.

Despite this initial diversity in child rearing, the father-dominated family of New England gradually declined in the eighteenth century. In its place rose the mother-centered family, in which affectionate parents encouraged self-expression and independence in their children. This "modern" approach was closer to the parenting methods of the coastal Native Americans, who initially had been widely disparaged for their lax methods of rearing their young.

ECOLOGICAL TRANSFORMATION

Wherever Europeans settled in the Americas, they brought with them not only social and family traditions but also animals, plant life, diseases, and ways of viewing the natural resources they found—all of which had enormous consequences for the ecosystems they were entering. In New Spain, the Spanish introduction of grazing animals—cattle, horses, pigs, sheep, and goats—profoundly altered the landscape. Breeding prolifically, pigs and cattle devoured the tall grasses and most palatable plant species and within half a century left huge areas with little or no ground cover.

In England's North American colonies, the rapid increase of settlers after 1715 led to a swift depletion of the forests near the coast. Just for heating and cooking, the typical northern farmhouse required an acre of trees each year, and with the population explosion of the eighteenth century, the price of a cord of firewood quickly rose as woodcutters ventured farther inland.

Rapid harvesting of the forests had many effects. As the colonists chopped down the forest canopy that had previously moderated the weather, the summers became hotter and the winters colder. In deforested areas the snow melted sooner, and, as the winter's melting snow ran off more quickly, watersheds emptied faster. This, in turn, caused soil erosion and periods of drought.

The second ecological transformation came about as the result of the replacement of the animals already in North America by those brought by Europeans. European colonists were a livestock people, skilled in mixed farming and herding of domesticated cattle, horses, pigs, sheep, and goats. Such animals provided food, leather, fibers for clothmaking, and the sheer pulling and carrying power relied upon by a people who had no other source of energy than their own muscles. Multiplying rapidly in a favorable environment, pigs and cattle "swarm like vermin upon the earth," reported one Virginia account as early as 1700. In some areas, the animals multiplied so rapidly and denuded the native grasses and shrubs so quickly that they actually ate themselves out of subsistence and began to die for lack of grazing land. While European livestock filled the land, the native fur-bearing animals—beaver, deer, bear, wolf, raccoon, and marten—rapidly became extinct in the areas of settlement.

All these environmental changes were linked not only to the numbers of Europeans arriving in North America but also to their ways of thinking about nature. Looking out over wooded hills and fertile valleys, transplanted Europeans could only imagine the possibility of raising valuable crops as if the ecosystem were composed of unconnected elements, each ripe for exploitation. Land, lumber, fish, and fur-bearing animals could be converted into sources of cash that would buy imported commodities that improved one's material condition. The New England writer Edward Johnson described the process perceptively as early as 1653: Who would have imagined, he mused, "that this wilderness should turn a mart for merchants in so short a space, Holland, France, Spain, and Portugal coming hither for trade." Supplying these Europeans were the farmers, woodcutters, and fishermen who consigned to the marketplace huge portions of the ecosystem.

The "rage for commerce" and for an improved life produced wasteful practices on farms and in forests and fisheries. "The grain fields, the meadows, the forests, the cattle, etc.," wrote a Swedish visitor in the 1750s, "are treated with equal carelessness." Accustomed to the natural abundance once the native peoples had been driven from the land, the colonists embarked on ecologically destructive practices that over a period of many generations profoundly altered the natural world around them.

THE PLANTATION SOUTH

Between 1680 and 1750, the white tidewater settlements of the southern colonies made the transition from a frontier society marked by a high immigration rate, a surplus of males, and an unstable social organization to a settled society composed mostly of native-born families. Between the piedmont region and the ocean, a mature southern culture took form.

The Tobacco Coast

Tobacco production in Virginia and Maryland expanded rapidly in the seventeenth century, but war in Europe and the Americas for the two decades bridging the turn of the century drove up transportation costs and dampened the demand for tobacco. Stagnation in the tobacco market lasted from the mid-1680s until about 1715.

Yet it was in this period that the Upper South underwent a profound social transformation. First, slaves replaced indentured servants so rapidly that by 1730 the unfree labor force was overwhelmingly black. Second, the planters responded to the dull tobacco market by diversifying their crops. They shifted some of their tobacco fields to grain, hemp, and flax; increased their herds of cattle and swine; and became more self-sufficient by developing local industries to produce iron, leather, and textiles. By the 1720s, when a profitable tobacco trade with France created a new period of prosperity, their economy was much more diverse and resilient than it had been a generation before.

Third, the structure of the population changed rapidly. Black slaves grew from about 7 percent to 35 percent of the region's population between 1690 and 1750, and the drastic imbalance between white men and women disappeared.

Notwithstanding the influx of Africans, slave owning was far from universal. As late as 1750, a majority of families owned no slaves at all. Among slave owners, fewer than one-tenth held more than 20 slaves. Nonetheless, the common goal was the large plantation where black slaves made the earth yield up profits to support an aristocratic life for their masters.

The Chesapeake planters who acquired the best land and accumulated enough capital to invest heavily in slaves created a gentry life style that set them apart from ordinary farmers such as Devereaux Jarratt's father. Men such as Charles Carroll of Maryland and Robert "King" Carter and William Byrd of Virginia counted their slaves by the hundreds, their acres by the thousands, and their fortunes by the tens of thousands of pounds.

Ritual display of wealth marked southern gentry life. Racing thoroughbred horses and gambling on them recklessly became common sport for young gentlemen, who had often been educated in England. Planters began to construct stately brick Georgian mansions and fill them with imported furniture.

The emerging Chesapeake planter elite controlled the county courts, officered the local militia, ruled the parish vestries of the Anglican church, and made law in their legislative assemblies. To their sons they passed the mantle of political and social leadership.

For all their social display, southern planter squires were essentially agrarian businessmen. They spent their days obtaining credit, dealing in land and slaves, scheduling planting and harvesting routines, conferring with overseers, disciplining slaves, and arranging leases with tenants. A planter's reputation rose and fell with the quality of his crop. His wife also shouldered many responsibilities. She superintended cloth production and the processing and preparation of food while ruling over a household crowded with children, slaves, and occasional visitors. The farms were often so isolated from one another, however, that planter families lived a "solitary and unsociable existence," as one phrased it.

The Rice Coast

The plantation economy of the Lower South in the eighteenth century rested on the production of rice and indigo. Rice exports surpassed 1.5 million pounds per year by 1710 and reached 80 million pounds by the eve of the Revolution. Indigo, a blue dye obtained from plants for use in textiles, became a staple crop in the 1740s after Eliza Lucas Pinckney, a wealthy South Carolina planter's wife, experimented successfully with its cultivation. Within a generation, indigo production had spread into Georgia. It soon ranked among the leading colonial exports.

The expansion of rice production transformed the swampy coastal lowlands. In the rice-producing region radiating out from Charleston, planters imported thousands of slaves after 1720; by 1740, they composed nearly 90 percent of the region's inhabitants. White population declined as wealthy planters left their estates in the hands of resident overseers. At midcentury, a shocked New England visitor described local society as one "divided into opulent and lordly planters, poor and spiritless peasants, and vile slaves."

Throughout the plantation South, the courthouse became a central gathering place for men. Court day brought together men of all classes. They came to settle debts, dispute land boundaries, sue and be sued. When court was over, a multitude lingered on, drinking, gossiping, and staging horse races, cockfights, wrestling matches, footraces, and fiddling contests. Competition and assertiveness lay at the heart of all these demonstrations of male personal prowess.

The Backcountry

While the southern gentry matured along the tobacco and rice coasts, settlers poured into the upland backcountry. Thousands of land-hungry German and Scots-Irish settlers spilled into the interior valleys running along the eastern side of the Appalachians. Their enclaves of small farms remained isolated from the coastal region for several generations, which helped these pioneers cling fiercely to the folkways they had known on the other side of the Atlantic.

The crudity of backcountry life appalled many visitors from the more refined seaboard. In 1733, William Byrd described a large Virginia frontier plantation as "a poor, dirty hovel, with hardly anything in it but children that wallowed about like so many pigs." Charles Woodmason, a stiff-necked Anglican minister who spent three years tramping between settlements in the Carolina upcountry, wrote: "Many hundreds live in concubinage—swopping their wives as cattle and living in a state of nature more irregularly and unchastely than the Indians."

What Byrd and Woodmason were really observing was the poverty of frontier life and the lack of schools, churches, and towns. Most families lived in rough-hewn log cabins and planted their corn, beans, and wheat between the stumps of trees they had felled. Women toiled alongside men, in the fields, forest, and homestead. For a generation, these settlers endured a poor diet, endless work, and meager rewards.

By the 1760s, the southern backcountry began to emerge from the frontier stage. Small marketing towns became centers of craft activity, church life, and local government. Farms began producing surpluses for shipment east. Density of settlement increased. Class distinctions remained narrow compared with the older seaboard settlements, but many backcountry settlements acquired the look of permanence.

Family Life in the South

As the South emerged from the early era of withering mortality and stunted families, male and female roles gradually became more physically and functionally separated. In most areas, the white gender ratio reached parity by the 1720s. Women lost the leverage in the marriage market that scarcity had provided earlier. With the growth of slavery, the work role of white women also changed. The wealthy planter's wife became the domestic manager in the "great house."

The balanced sex ratio and the growth of slavery also brought changes for southern white males. The planter's son had always been trained in horsemanship, the use of a gun, and the rhythms of agricultural life. Ordering and disciplining slaves also became a part of his education. Bred to command, southern planters' sons also developed a self-confidence and authority that propelled many of them into leadership roles during the American Revolution.

On the small farms of the tidewater region and throughout the backcountry settlements, women's roles closely resembled those of northern women. Women labored in the fields alongside their menfolk. "She is a very civil woman," noted an observer of a southern frontierswoman, "and shows nothing of ruggedness or immodesty in her carriage; yet she will carry a gun in the woods and kill deer and turkeys, shoot down wild cattle, catch and tie hogs, knock down beeves with an ax, and perform the most manful exercises as well as most men in those parts."

Marriage and family life were also more informal in the backcountry. With vast areas unattended by ministers of any religion and courthouses out of reach, most couples married or "took up" with each other in matches unsanctioned by state or church until an itinerant clergyman passed through the area.

THE URBAN WORLD OF COMMERCE AND IDEAS

Only about 5 percent of the colonists lived in towns as large as 2,500, and none of the commercial centers boasted a population greater than 16,000 in 1750 or 30,000 in 1775. Yet the urban societies were at the leading edge of social change. Almost all the alterations associated with the advent of "modern" life occurred first in the seaport towns and radiated outward to the hinterland. In the seaboard centers, the transition first occurred from a barter to a commercial economy, from a social order based on assigned status to one based on achievement, from rank-conscious and deferential politics to participatory and contentious politics, and from small-scale craftsmanship to factory production. In addition, the cities were the centers of intellectual life and the conduits through which European ideas flowed into the colonies.

Sinews of Trade

In the half century after 1690, Boston, New York, and Philadelphia blossomed from urban villages into thriving commercial centers. This urban growth accompanied the development of the agricultural interior, to which the seaports were closely linked. Through the trade centers flowed colonial export staples such as tobacco, rice, wheat, timber products, and fish as well as the imported goods that colonists needed. The imports included manufactured and luxury goods from England such as glass, paper, iron implements, and cloth; wine, spices, coffee, tea, and sugar from other parts of the world; and the human cargo to fill the labor gap. In these seaports, the pivotal figure was the merchant. Frequently engaged in both retail and wholesale trade, the merchant was also moneylender (for no banks yet existed), shipbuilder, insurance agent, land developer, and often coordinator of artisan production.

By the eighteenth century, the American

economy was integrated into an Atlantic basin trading system that connected Great Britain, western Europe, Africa, the West Indies, and Newfoundland. The rulers of Great Britain, like those of other major trading nations of western Europe, pursued mercantilist trade policies. According to the principles of mercantilism, a country should strive to gain wealth by increasing its exports, levying duties on imports, regulating production and trade, and exploiting its colonies to its own advantage. The British followed these principles by controlling their colonies' trade, requiring the colonies to supply them with foodstuffs, lumber, and other non-manufactured products, and by selling the colonists British manufactured goods.

The colonists could never produce enough exportable raw materials to pay for the imported goods they craved, so they had to earn credits in England by supplying the West Indies and other areas with foodstuffs and timber products. They also accumulated credit by providing shipping and distributional services. New Englanders became the most ambitious participants in the carrying trade, sailing along the Atlantic seaboard, the Caribbean, and across the Atlantic.

The Artisan's World

Though merchants stood first in wealth and prestige in the colonial towns, artisans were far more numerous. About two-thirds of urban adult males, slaves excluded, labored at handicrafts. These "leather apron men" included not only the proverbial butcher, baker, and candlestick maker but also carpenters and coopers (who made barrels); shoemakers and tailors; silver-, gold-, pewter-, and blacksmiths; mast and sail makers; masons, plasterers, weavers, potters; and many more. They worked with hand tools, usually in small shops.

Work patterns for artisans were irregular, dictated by weather, hours of daylight, erratic delivery of raw materials, and shifting consumer demand. When ice blocked northern harbors,

mariners and dockworkers endured slack time. If prolonged rain delayed the slaughter of cows in the country or made impassable the rutted roads into the city, the tanner and the shoemaker laid their tools aside.

Urban artisans took fierce pride in their crafts. "Our professions rendered us useful and necessary members of our community," the Philadelphia shoemakers asserted. "Proud of that rank, we aspired to no higher." Yet the upperclass tended to view artisans as mere mechanics, part of the "vulgar herd."

In striving for respectability, artisans placed a premium on achieving economic independence. Every craftsman began as an apprentice, spending five or more teenage years learning the "mysteries of the craft" in the shop of a master "mechanick." After fulfilling his contract, the young artisan became a "journeyman." He sold his labor to a master craftsman and frequently lived in his house, ate at his table, and sometimes married his daughter. The journeyman hoped to complete within a few years the three-step climb from servitude to self-employment. After setting up his own shop, he could control his work hours and acquire the respect that came from economic independence. In trades requiring greater organization and capital, such as distilling and shipbuilding, the rise from journeyman to master proved impossible for many artisans. Nonetheless, the ideal of the independent craftsman prevailed.

In good times, urban artisans fared well. They expected to earn "a decent competency" and eventually to purchase a small house. But success was far from automatic, even for those following all of Poor Richard's advice about hard work and frugal living. An advantageous marriage, luck in avoiding illness, and the size of an inheritance were often the critical factors in whether an artisan moved up or down the ladder of success.

Urban Social Structure

Population growth, economic development, and a series of wars that punctuated the period from

1690 to 1765 altered the urban social structure. Stately townhouses rose as testimony to the fortunes acquired in trade, shipbuilding, war contracting, and urban land development. This last may have been the most profitable of all. "It is almost a proverb," a Philadelphian observed in the 1760s, "that every great fortune made here within these 50 years has been by land." By the late colonial era, some commercial titans had become America's first millionaires by accumulating estates of £10,000 to £20,000 sterling.

Alongside urban wealth grew urban poverty. From the beginning, every city had its disabled, orphaned, and widowed who required aid. But after 1720, poverty marred the lives of many more city dwellers. Boston was hit especially hard in the 1740s. The overseers of the poor groaned that their relief expenditures were double the outlays of any town of equal size "upon the face of the whole earth."

Burdened with mounting poor taxes, cities devised new ways of helping the needy. Rather than support the impoverished in their homes with "outrelief" payments, officials built large almshouses where the poor could be housed and fed more economically. Many of the indigent preferred "to starve in their homes."

The increasing gap between the wealthy and the poor in the colonial cities was recorded in the eighteenth-century tax lists. The top five percent of taxpayers increased their share of the cities' taxable assets between 1690 and 1770, while the bottom half of the taxable inhabitants saw their share of the wealth shrink. The urban middle classes, except in Boston, continued to make gains. But the growth of princely fortunes amid increasing poverty made some urban dwellers reflect that the conditions of the Old World seemed to be reappearing in the New.

The Entrepreneurial Ethos

As the cities grew, new values took hold. In the older, medieval, "corporate" view of society, economic life ideally operated according to what was equitable, not what was profitable. Citizens usually agreed that government should provide for the general welfare by regulating prices and wages, setting quality controls, licensing providers of service such as tavernkeepers and ferrymen, and supervising public markets where all food was sold. Such regulation seemed natural because a community was defined not as a collection of individuals, each entitled to pursue separate interests, but as a single body of interrelated parts where individual rights and responsibilities formed a seamless web.

In America, as in Europe, new ideas about economic life gathered support. The subordination of private interests to the commonweal became viewed as a lofty but unrealistic ideal. According to the new view, people should be allowed to pursue their own material desires competitively. The resulting impersonal market of producers and consumers would operate to everyone's advantage.

As the colonial port towns took their places in the Atlantic world of commerce, merchants became accustomed to making decisions according to the emerging commercial ethic that rejected traditional restraints on entrepreneurial activity. The underlying tension between the new economic freedom and the older concern for the public good erupted only with food shortages or galloping inflation.

Such a moment struck in Boston during Queen Anne's War. Merchant Andrew Belcher contracted to ship large quantities of wheat to the Caribbean, where higher prices would yield greater profit than in Boston. Ordinary neighbors, threatened with a bread shortage and angered that a townsman would put profit ahead of community needs, attacked one of Belcher's grain-laden ships in 1710. They sawed through the rudder and tried to run the vessel aground in order to seize the grain. Invoking the older ethic that the public welfare outweighed private interests, they took the law into their own hands. Even the grand jury, composed of substantial members of the community, hinted its approval of the violent action against Belcher by refusing to indict the rioters.

The two conceptions of community and economic life rubbed against each other for many decades. But by the mid–eighteenth century, the pursuit of a profitable livelihood, not the social compact of the community, animated most city dwellers.

The American Enlightenment

Ideas about not only economic life but also the nature of the universe and improving the human condition reached across the Atlantic to the colonies. In the eighteenth century, an American version of the European intellectual movement called the Enlightenment occurred, and the cities became centers for disseminating these new ideas.

European thinkers, in what is called the Age of Reason, rejected the pessimistic Calvinist concept of innate human depravity, replacing it with the optimistic notion that a benevolent God had blessed humankind with the supreme gift of reason. Thinkers like John Locke, in his influential *Essay Concerning Human Understanding* (1689), argued that God had not predetermined the content of the human mind but furnished it with the capacity to acquire knowledge. All Enlightenment thinkers prized this acquisition of knowledge, for it allowed humankind to improve its condition. As the great scientific thinker Isaac Newton demonstrated, systematic investigation could unlock the secrets of the physical universe. Moreover, scientific knowledge could be applied to human institutions in order to improve society.

Though only a small number of educated colonists read the Enlightenment authors, they began in the eighteenth century to make significant contributions to the advancement of science. Naturalists such as John Bartram of Philadelphia ranged the eastern part of the continent gathering and describing American plants as part of the transatlantic attempt to classify all plant life into one universal system of classification. Professor John Winthrop III of Harvard made an unusually accurate measurement of the earth's distance from the sun. Standing above them all was Benjamin Franklin, whose spectacular (and dangerous) experiments with electricity, the properties of which were just becoming known, earned him an international reputation.

Franklin's true genius as a figure of the Enlightenment came, however, in his practical application of scientific knowledge. Among his inventions were the lightning rod, which nearly ended the age-old danger of fires when lightning struck wooden buildings; bifocal spectacles; and an iron stove that heated rooms—in an age when firewood was a major item in the household budget—far more efficiently than the open fireplace commonly used. Franklin also made his adopted home of Philadelphia a center of the American Enlightenment. He played a leading role in founding America's first circulating library in 1731, an artisans' debating club for "mutual improvement" through discussion of the latest ideas from Europe, and an intercolonial scientific association that would emerge in 1769 as the American Philosophical Society.

The scientific and intellectual advances of the seventeenth- and eighteenth-century Enlightenment encouraged a belief in "natural law" and debate about the "natural" rights of human beings. In Europe issues of equality were explored by French philosophers François Voltaire and Denis Diderot. From 1750 to 1772, Diderot published his *Encyclopedia,* which treated such topics as equality, liberty, reason, and rights. The ideas of the Enlightenment spread in Europe and America and eventually found expression in movements for reform, democracy, and liberation. Though most American colonists were not educated enough to participate actively in the American Enlightenment, the efforts of men such as Franklin exposed thousands, especially in the cities, to new currents of thought. This led to the growing sense that the colonists, blessed by their abundant environment, might truly inhabit the part of the world where the Enlightenment ideal of achieving a perfect society might be fulfilled.

THE GREAT AWAKENING

Many of the social, economic, and political changes occurring in the eighteenth-century colonies converged in the Great Awakening, the first of many religious revivals that would sweep American society during the next two centuries. This quest for spiritual renewal challenged old sources of authority and produced patterns of thought and behavior that helped fuel a revolutionary movement in the next generation.

Fading Faith

Colonial America in the early eighteenth century remained an overwhelmingly Protestant culture. The Puritan, or Congregational, church dominated all of New England except Rhode Island. Anglicanism held sway in much of New York and throughout the South except the backcountry. In the mid-Atlantic and in the back settlements, a polyglot of German Mennonites, Dunkers, Moravians, and Lutherans; Scots-Irish Presbyterians; and English Baptists and Quakers mingled.

Yet these diverse groups commanded the allegiance of only about one-third of the colonists. Those who went to no church at all remained the majority. In many areas, ministers and churches were simply unavailable. In Virginia, the most populous colony, only 60 clergymen in 1761 served a population of 350,000—one parson for every 5,800 people.

In the eighteenth century, most colonial churches were voluntary or gathered ("congregated") groups, formed for reasons of conscience, not because of government compulsion. Catholics, Jews, and nonbelievers could not vote or hold office. But the persecution of Quakers and Catholics had largely passed, and some dissenting groups had gained the right by 1720 to use long-obligatory church taxes to support their own congregations.

The clergy often administered their congregations with difficulty. For example, Anglican ministers had to be ordained in England and make regular reports to the bishop of London. But once installed in Chesapeake parishes, Anglican priests faced wealthy planters who controlled the vestry (the local church's governing body), set the minister's salary, and drove out ministers who challenged them too forcefully.

Though governing their churches frustrated many clergymen, religious apathy was a far more pressing problem in the early eighteenth century. As early as 1662, the Congregational clergy of New England had attempted to return wandering sheep to the fold by adopting the Half-Way Covenant. It specified that children of church members, if they adhered to the "forms of godliness," might join the church even if they could not demonstrate that they had undergone a conversion experience. But despite compromises and innovations, most church leaders saw creeping religious apathy when they surveyed their towns.

The Awakeners' Message

The Great Awakening was not a unified movement but rather a series of revivals that swept different regions between 1720 and 1760 with varying degrees of intensity. The first stirrings came in the 1720s in New Jersey and Pennsylvania. Theodore Frelinghuysen, a Dutch Reformed minister, excited his congregation through emotional preaching. Avoiding theological abstractions, he concentrated on arousing among his parishioners a need to be "saved." A neighboring Presbyterian, Gilbert Tennent, soon took up the Dutchman's techniques, with similar success.

From New Jersey the Awakening spread to Pennsylvania in the 1730s, especially among Presbyterians, and then broke out in the Connecticut River valley. There it was led by Jonathan Edwards, pastor in Northampton. Edwards later became a philosophical giant in the colonies. But as a young man, he gained renown by lambasting his parishioners: "God and your

Jonathan Edwards (1703–1758) was the first major philosopher in the American colonies. A leader of the Great Awakening in Massachusetts, he was ousted by his congregation for reprimanding the children of church members for reading The Midwife Rightly Instructed, an obstetric guide that was as close as curious children could come to learning about sex.

own consciences know what abominable lasciviousness you have practised in things not fit to be named, when you have been alone; when you ought to have been reading, or meditating, or on your knees before God in secret prayer." After cataloging his parishioners' sins, Edwards drew such graphic pictures of the hell awaiting the unrepentant that his Northampton neighbors were soon preparing frantically for the conversion experience by which they would be "born again."

In 1739, these regional brushfires of evangelicalism began to spread. Instrumental in drawing together the separate local revivals and in inspiring a more scorching religious enthusiasm was George Whitefield, a 24-year-old Anglican priest from England. Whitefield made seven barnstorming tours along the American seaboard, the first in 1739 and 1740. Thousands turned out to see him, and with each success his fame and influence grew. In Boston, Whitefield preached to 19,000 in three days. Then, at a farewell sermon, he left 25,000 writhing in fear of damnation. In his wake came American preachers, mostly young men like Devereaux Jarratt, whom he had inspired.

The Awakeners preached that the established, college-trained clergy was too intellectual and tradition-bound to bring faith and piety to a new generation. Congregations were dead, Whitefield declared, "because dead men preach to them." "The sapless discourses of such dead drones," cried another Awakener, were worthless. The fires of Protestant belief could be reignited only if individuals assumed responsibility for their own conversion.

An important form of individual participation was "lay exhorting." In this personal religious testimony, any person—young or old, female or male, black or white—might spontaneously recount a conversion experience and preach "the Lord's truth." This horrified most established clergymen. Lay exhorting shattered the trained clergy's monopoly on religious discourse and permitted ordinary men and women, and even children, servants, and slaves, to defy traditionally assigned roles.

How religion, social change, and politics became interwoven in the Great Awakening can be seen by examining two regions swept by revivalism. Both Boston, the heartland of Puritanism, and interior Virginia, a land of struggling small planters and slave-rich aristocrats, experienced the Great Awakening, but in different ways and at different times.

The Urban North

In Boston, revivalism ignited in the midst of political controversy about remedies for the severe depreciation of the province's paper currency. Paper bills had been issued for years to finance military expeditions against French Canada. The

English government insisted that Massachusetts retire all paper money by 1741. Searching for a substitute circulating medium, one group proposed a land bank to issue private bills of credit backed by land. Another group proposed a silver bank to distribute bills of credit backed by silver. Large merchants preferred the fiscally conservative silver bank, while local traders, artisans, and the laboring poor preferred the land bank.

Whitefield's arrival in Boston coincided with the currency furor. At first, Boston's elite applauded Whitefield's ability to call the masses to worship. The master evangelist, it seemed, might restore social harmony by redirecting people from earthly matters such as the currency dispute to concerns of the soul.

When Whitefield left Boston in 1740, he was succeeded by others who were more critical of the "unconverted" clergy and the self-indulgent accumulation of wealth. Among them was James Davenport, who arrived in 1742. Finding every church closed to him, Davenport preached daily on Boston Common, aroused religious ecstasy among thousands, and stirred up feeling against Boston's leading figures. Respectable people grew convinced that revivalism had gotten out of hand, for by this time ordinary people were verbally attacking opponents of the land bank in the streets as "carnal wretches, hypocrites, fighters against God, children of the devil, cursed Pharisees." A revival that had begun as a return to religion now threatened polite culture, which stressed order and discipline from ordinary people.

The Rural South

The Great Awakening was ebbing in New England and the middle colonies by 1744, although aftershocks continued for years. But in Virginia, the movement rippled through society from the mid-1740s onward. As in Boston, the Awakeners challenged and disturbed the gentry-led social order.

Whitefield stirred some religious fervor during his early trips through Virginia. Traveling "New Light" preachers, led by the brilliant orator Samuel Davies, were soon gathering large crowds both in the backcountry and in the traditionally Anglican parishes of the older settled areas. By 1747, worried Anglican clergymen persuaded the governor to issue a proclamation restraining "strolling preachers." As one critic put it in 1745, the wandering preachers "have turned the world upside down."

New Light Presbyterianism, which challenged the religious monopoly of the gentry-dominated Anglican church, continued to spread in the 1750s. The evangelical cause advanced further with the rise of the Baptists in the 1760s. Renouncing finery and addressing one another as "brother" and "sister," the Baptists reached out to thousands of unchurched people. Like northern revivalists, they focused on the conversion experience. Many of their preachers were uneducated farmers and artisans who called themselves "Christ's poor." They stressed equality in human affairs, and their message penetrated deeply among Virginia's 140,000 slaves and other poor. As in New England, social changes had weakened the cultural authority of the upper class and, in the context of religious revival, produced a vision of a society drawn along more equal lines.

Legacy of the Awakening

By the time George Whitefield returned to America for his third tour in 1745, the revival had burned out in the North. Its effects, however, were long-lasting. The Awakening promoted religious pluralism and nourished the idea that all denominations were equally legitimate; none had a monopoly on the truth. The Great Awakening gave competing Protestant churches a theory for living together in relative harmony. From this framework of denominationalism came a second change—the separation of church and state. Once a variety of churches gained legitimacy, it was impossible for any one church to claim special privileges. This undermining of the church-state tie would be completed during the Revolutionary era.

A third effect of the revival was to bolster the view that diversity within communities, for better or worse, could not be prevented. Almost from the beginning. Rhode Island, the Carolinas, and the middle colonies had recognized this. But in Massachusetts and Connecticut, people learned through church schism caused by the Awakening that the fabric of community could be woven from threads of many hues.

New eighteenth-century colonial colleges reflected the religious pluralism symbolized by the Great Awakening. Before 1740 there existed only three. Puritans had founded Harvard in 1636 and Yale in 1701 to provide New England with educated ministers, and Anglicans had chartered William and Mary in 1693. To these small seats of higher education were added six new colleges between 1746 and 1769. But none of the new colleges were controlled by an established church, all had governing bodies composed of men of different faiths, and all admitted students regardless of religion.

Last, the Awakening nurtured a subtle change in values that crossed over into politics and daily life. Especially for ordinary people, the revival experience created a new feeling of self-worth. People assumed new responsibilities in religious affairs and became skeptical of dogma and authority. By learning to oppose authority and to take part in the creation of new churches, thousands of colonists unknowingly rehearsed for revolution.

POLITICAL LIFE

"Were it not for government, the world would soon run into all manner of disorders and confusions," wrote a Massachusetts clergyman early in the eighteenth century. Few colonists, wherever they lived, would have disagreed. A much less easily resolved matter was how political power should be divided within each colony. American colonists naturally drew heavily on in-

herited political ideas and institutions. These were almost entirely English because English charters sanctioned settlement, English governors ruled the colonies, and English common law governed the courts. But in a new environment, where they met unexpected circumstances, the colonists modified familiar political forms to suit their needs.

Structuring Colonial Governments

In England, the notion of the God-given supreme authority of the monarch was crumbling even before the planting of the colonies. In its place arose the belief that stable and enlightened government depended on balancing the interests of monarchy, aristocracy, and democracy. The Revolution of 1688 in England, by thwarting the king's pretensions to greater power, seemed to most colonists a vindication and strengthening of a carefully balanced political system.

In colonial governments, political balance was achieved somewhat differently. The governor was the king's agent or, in proprietary colonies, the agent of the king's delegated authority. The council, composed of wealthy appointees of the governor in most colonies, was a pale equivalent of the English House of Lords. The assembly, elected by white male freeholders, functioned as a replica of the House of Commons.

Bicameral legislatures developed in most of the colonies in the seventeenth century. The lower houses, or assemblies, represented the local interests of the people at large. The upper houses, or councils (which usually also sat as the highest courts), represented the nascent aristocracy. Except in Rhode Island and Connecticut, every statute required the governor's assent, and all colonial laws required final approval from the king's privy council. But during the months it took to receive such approval, the laws set down in the colonies took force.

Behind the formal structure of politics stood the rules governing who could participate in the

Table 4.1
Colonial Foundations of the American Political System

1606	Virginia companies of London and Plymouth granted patents to settle lands in North America.
1619	First elected colonial legislature meets in Virginia.
1634	Under a charter granted in 1632, Maryland's proprietor is given all the authority "as any bishop of Durham" ever held—more than the king possessed in England.
1635	The council in Virginia deports Governor John Harvey for exceeding his power, thus asserting the rights of local magistrates to contest authority of royally appointed governors.
1643	The colonies of Massachusetts, Plymouth, Connecticut, and New Haven draw up articles of confederation and form the first intercolonial union, the United Colonies of New England.
1647	Under a charter granted in 1644, elected freemen from the Providence Plantations draft a constitution establishing freedom of conscience, separating church and state, and authorizing referenda by the towns on laws passed by the assembly.
1677	The Laws, Concessions and Agreements for West New Jersey provide for a legislature elected annually by virtually all free males, secret voting, liberty of conscience, election of justices of the peace and local officeholders, and trial by jury in public so that "justice may not be done in a corner."
1689	James II deposed in England in the Glorious Revolution, and royal governors, accused of abusing their authority, ousted in Massachusetts, New York, and Maryland.
1701	First colonial unicameral legislature meets in Pennsylvania under the Frame of Government of 1701.
1735	John Peter Zenger, a New York printer, acquitted of seditious libel for printing attacks on the royal governor and his faction, thus widening the freedom of the press.
1754	First congress of all the colonies meets at Albany (with seven colonies sending delegates) and agrees on a Plan of Union (which is rejected by the colonies and the English government).
1765	The Stamp Act Congress, the first intercolonial convention called outside England's authority, meets in New York.

political process. In England since the fifteenth century, the ownership of land had largely defined electoral participation (women and non-Christians were uniformly excluded). Only those with property sufficient to produce an annual rental income of 40 shillings could vote or hold office. The colonists usually followed this principle closely, except in Massachusetts, where it took until 1691 to break the requirement of church membership for suffrage.

Whereas in England the 40-shilling freehold requirement was intended to restrict the size of the electorate, in the colonies, because of the cheapness of land, it conferred the vote on a large proportion of adult males. Between 50 and 75 percent of the adult free males could vote in most colonies. As the proportion of landless colonists increased in the eighteenth century, however, the franchise slowly became more limited.

Though voting rights were broadly based, the upper class assumed that only the wealthy and socially prominent were entitled to hold positions of political power. Lesser men, it was held, ought to defer to their betters. Balancing the elitist conception of politics, however, was the notion that the entire electorate should periodically judge the performance of those they entrusted with political power and reject those who represented them inadequately. Unlike the members of the English House of Commons, who by the seventeenth century thought of themselves as representing the entire nation, the colonial representatives were expected to reflect the views of those who elected them locally. Believing this, their constituents judged them accordingly. The people also felt justified in badgering their leaders, protesting openly, and, in extreme cases of abuse of power, assuming control.

The Crowd in Action

What gave special power to the common people when they assembled to protest oppressive authority was the general absence of effective police power. In the countryside, where most colonists lived, only the county sheriff, with an occasional deputy, insulated civil leaders from angry farmers. In the towns, police forces were still unknown. Only the sheriff, backed up by the night watch, safeguarded public order. Under these conditions, crowd action, frequently effective, gradually achieved a kind of legitimacy. The assembled people came to be perceived as the watchdog of government, ready to chastise or drive from office those who violated the collective sense of what was right and proper.

Boston's impressment riot of 1747 vividly illustrates the people's readiness to fight oppression. It began when Commodore Charles Knowles brought his Royal Navy ships to Boston for provisioning—and to replenish the ranks of mariners thinned by desertion. When Knowles sent press gangs out on a chill November evening with orders to fill the crew vacancies from Boston's waterfront population, they scooped up artisans, laborers, servants, and slaves, as well as merchant seamen from ships riding at anchor in the harbor.

But before the press gangs could hustle their victims back to the British men-of-war, a crowd of angry Bostonians seized several British officers, surrounded the governor's house, and demanded the release of their townsmen. When the sheriff and his deputies attempted to intervene, the crowd mauled them. The militia, called to arms by the governor, refused to respond. By dusk, a crowd of several thousand defied the governor's orders to disperse, stoned the windows of the governor's house, and dragged a royal barge from one of the British ships into the courtyard of his house, where they burned it amid cheers. After several days of negotiations amid further tumult, Knowles released the impressed Bostonians.

The Growing Power of the Assemblies

Incidents such as the impressment riot of 1747 demonstrated the touchiness of England's colonial subjects. But a more gradual and restrained change—the growing ambition and power of the legislative assemblies—was far more important. For most of the seventeenth century, royal and proprietary governors had exercised greater power in relation to the elected legislatures than did the king in relation to Parliament. The governors could dissolve the lower houses and delay their sitting, control the election of their speakers, and in most colonies initiate legislation with their appointed councils. Colonial governors also had authority to appoint and dismiss judges at all levels of the judiciary and to create chancery courts, which sat without juries. Governors also controlled the expenditure of public monies and had authority to grant land to individuals and groups, which they sometimes used to confer vast estates on their favorites.

In the seventeenth century, Virginia, Massachusetts, and New York had become royal colonies, with governors appointed by the Crown. By the 1730s, royal governments had replaced many of the proprietary governments, including New Jersey (1702), South Carolina (1719), and North Carolina (1729). Some of the royal governors were competent military officers or bureaucrats, but most were mediocre.

In the eighteenth century, elected colonial legislatures challenged the swollen executive powers of these colonial governors. Bit by bit, the representative assemblies won new rights—to initiate legislation, to elect their own speakers, to settle contested elections, to discipline their membership, and to nominate provincial treasurers who controlled the disbursement of public funds. The most important gain of all was acquiring the "power of the purse"—the authority to initiate money bills, which specified how much money should be raised by taxes and how it should be spent. Originally thought of as advisory bodies, the elected assemblies gradually transformed themselves into governing bodies reflecting the interests of the electorate.

Local Politics

Binding elected officeholders to their constituents became an important feature of the colonial political system. In England, the House of Commons was filled with representatives from "rotten boroughs," ancient places left virtually uninhabited by population shifts, and with men whose vote was in the pocket of the ministry because they had accepted Crown appointments, contracts, or gifts. The American assemblies, by contrast, contained mostly representatives sent by voters who often instructed them on particular issues and held them accountable for serving local interests. The voters mostly sent merchants, lawyers, and substantial planters and farmers to represent them in the lower houses, and by the mid–eighteenth century in most colonies, these men had formed political elites.

Local government was usually more important to the colonists than provincial government. In the North, local political authority generally rested in the towns. The New England town meeting decided a wide range of matters, striving for consensus, searching and arguing until it could express itself as a single unit. "By general agreement" and "by the free and united consent of the whole" were phrases denoting a decision-making process that sought participatory assent rather than a democratic competition among differing interests and points of view.

In the South, the county constituted the primary unit of government. No equivalent of the town meeting existed for placing local decisions before the populace. The planter gentry ruled the county courts and the legislature, while substantial farmers served in minor offices such as road surveyor and deputy sheriff. At court sessions, usually convened four times a year, deeds were read aloud and then recorded, juries impaneled and justice dispensed, elections held, licenses issued, and proclamations read aloud. On election days, gentlemen treated their neighbors (on whom they depended for votes) to "bumbo," "kill devil," and other alcoholic treats. By the mid–eighteenth century, a landed squirearchy of third- and fourth-generation families had achieved political dominance.

The Spread of Whig Ideology

Whether in local or provincial affairs, a political ideology called Whig or "republican" had spread widely by the mid–eighteenth century. The canons of this body of thought, inherited from England, flowed from the belief that concentrated power was historically the enemy of liberty and that too much power lodged in any person or group inevitably produced corruption and tyranny. The best defenses against concentrated power were balanced government, elected legislatures adept at checking executive authority, prohibition of standing armies (almost always controlled by tyrannical monarchs to oppress the people), and vigilance by the people for telltale signs of corruption in their leaders.

Much of this Whig ideology reached the people through the newspapers that began appearing in the seaboard towns in the early eighteenth century. The first was the *Boston News-Letter,* founded in 1704. By the 1730s, newspapers had become an important conduit of Whig political thought.

The new importance of the press was vividly illustrated in the Zenger case in New York. Young John Peter Zenger, a printer's apprentice,

had been hired in 1733 by the antigovernment faction of Lewis Morris to start a newspaper that would publicize the tyrannical actions of Governor William Cosby. In Zenger's *New-York Weekly Journal,* the Morris faction fired salvos at Cosby's interference with the courts and his alleged corruption in giving important offices to his henchmen.

These charges led to Zenger's arrest for seditious libel. He was brilliantly defended by Andrew Hamilton, a Philadelphia lawyer. Although the jury acquitted Zenger, the libel laws remained very restrictive. But the acquittal did reinforce the notion that the government was the people's servant, and it brought home the point that public criticism could keep people with political authority responsible to the people they ruled. Such ideas about liberty and corruption, raised in the context of local politics, would shortly achieve a much broader significance.

CONCLUSION

AMERICA IN 1750

The American colonies, robust and expanding, matured rapidly between 1700 and 1750. Churches, schools, and towns—the visible marks of the receding frontier—appeared everywhere. A balanced sex ratio and stable family life had been achieved throughout the colonies. Seasoned political leaders and familiar political institutions functioned from Maine to Georgia.

Yet the sinew, bone, and muscle of American society had not yet fully knit together. One-fifth of the population was bound in chattel slavery, and the Native American component was still unassimilated and uneasily situated on the frontier. Full of strength yet marked by awkward incongruities, colonial Americans in 1750 approached an era of strife and momentous decisions.

Recommended Reading

James A. Henretta and Gregory Nobles provide a good introduction to the growth and development of eighteenth-century colonial society in *Evolution and Revolution: American Society: 1620–1820* (1986). On immigration and immigration groups, see Jon But-

ler, *The Huguenots in Colonial America* (1983); Ned Landsman, *Scotland and Its First American Colony* (1985); and Bernard Bailyn, *Voyagers to the West* (1986).

On the development of the northern colonies,

rich material can be found in Laurel T. Ulrich, *Good Wives* (1982); and Sung Bok Kim, *Landlord and Tenant in the Colony of New York* (1976).

The transformation of eighteenth-century southern society is the subject of Allan Kulikoff, *Tobacco and Slaves* (1986); T. H. Breen, *Tobacco Culture: The Mentality of the Great Tidewater Planters on the Eve of the Revolution* (1985); and Mechal Sobel, *The World They Made Together: Black and White Values in Eighteenth-Century Virginia* (1987).

Much can be learned about commercial and intellectual life in the cities from Gary M. Walton and James F. Shepherd, *The Economic Rise of Early America* (1979); and Gary B. Nash, *The Urban Crucible* (1979).

Henry May addresses the American Enlightenment in *The American Enlightenment* (1976).

Excellent treatments of religious life and the Great Awakening include Harry S. Stout, *The New England Soul: Preaching and Religious Life in Colonial New England* (1986); and Patricia Bonomi, *Under the Cope of Heaven: Religion, Society, and Politics in Colonial America* (1986).

On the maturing colonial political systems, see Bernard Bailyn, *The Origins of American Politics* (1968); Edward M. Cook, Jr., *The Fathers of the Towns* (1976); and Patricia Bonomi, *A Factious People: Politics and Society in Colonial New York* (1977).

Time Line

1662	Half-Way Covenant in New England		1739–1740	Whitefield's first American tour spreads Great Awakening
1685–1715	Stagnation in tobacco market			Slaves compose 90 percent of population on Carolina rice coast
1704	*Boston News-Letter,* first regular colonial newspaper, published		1740s	Indigo becomes staple crop in Lower South
1713	Beginning of Scots-Irish and German immigration		1747	Benjamin Franklin publishes first *Poor Richard's Almanack*
1715–1730	Volume of slave trade doubles			Impressment riot in Boston
1718	French settle New Orleans		1760	Africans compose 20 percent of American population
1720s	Black population begins to increase naturally		1760s–1770s	Spanish establish California mission system
1734–1736	Great Awakening begins in Northampton, Massachusetts		1769	American Philosophical Society founded at Philadelphia
1735	Zenger acquitted of seditious libel in New York			

chapter 5

Bursting the Colonial Bonds

In 1758, when he was 21 years old, Ebenezer MacIntosh of Boston laid down his shoemaker's awl and enlisted in the Massachusetts expedition against the French on Lake Champlain. He contributed his mite to the climactic Anglo-American struggle that drove the French from North America.

But a greater role lay ahead for the poor Boston shoemaker. Two years after the Peace of Paris ended the Seven Years' War in 1763, England imposed a stamp tax on the American colonists. In the massive protests that followed, MacIntosh emerged as the street leader of the Boston crowd. In two nights of violent attacks on private property, a Boston crowd nearly destroyed the houses of two of the colony's most important officials. On August 14, they tore through the house of Andrew Oliver, a wealthy merchant and the appointed distributor of stamps for Massachusetts. Twelve days later, MacIntosh led the crowd in attacking the mansion of Thomas Hutchinson, a wealthy merchant who served as lieutenant governor and chief justice of Massachusetts. "The mob was so general," wrote the governor, "and so supported that all civil power ceased in an instant."

On November 5, 2,000 townsmen followed MacIntosh in an orderly march through the crooked streets of Boston to demonstrate their solidarity in resisting the hated stamps. Five weeks later, a crowd forced stamp distributor Oliver to announce his resignation publicly at the "Liberty Tree," which had become a symbol of resistance to England's new colonial policies. Few colonists in 1750 wanted to break the connection with England. Yet in a whirlwind of events, two million colonists moved haltingly toward a showdown with mighty England. Little-known men like Ebenezer MacIntosh as well as historically celebrated Samuel Adams, John Hancock, and John Adams were part of the struggle. Collectively, ordinary persons such as MacIntosh influenced—and in fact sometimes even dictated—the revolutionary movement in the colonies. Though we read and speak mostly of a small group of "founding fathers," the wellsprings of the American Revolution can be fully discovered only among a variety of people from different social groups, occupations, regions, and religions.

This chapter addresses the tensions in late colonial society, the imperial crisis that followed the Seven Years' War (in the colonies often called the French and Indian War), and the tumultuous decade that led to the "shots heard around the world" fired at Concord Bridge in April 1775. It portrays the origins of a dual American Revolution. Ebenezer MacIntosh, in leading the Boston mob against Crown officers and their colonial collaborators, helped set in motion a revolutionary movement to restore ancient liberties thought by the Americans to be under deliberate attack in England. This movement eventually escalated into the War of American Independence.

But MacIntosh's Boston followers were also venting years of resentment at the accumulation of wealth and power by Boston's aristocratic elite. Calls for the reform of a colonial society that had become corrupt, self-indulgent, and elite-dominated thus accompanied the movement to sever the colonial bond. As distinguished from the War for Independence, this was the American Revolution.

THE CLIMACTIC SEVEN YEARS' WAR

After a brief period of peace following King George's War (1744–1748), France and England fought the fourth, largest, and by far most significant of the wars for empire that had begun in the late seventeenth century. Known variously as the Seven Years' War, the French and Indian War, and the Great War for Empire, this global conflict in part represented a showdown for control of North America between the Atlantic Ocean and the Mississippi River. In North America, the Anglo-American forces ultimately prevailed, and their victory dramatically affected the lives of the great variety of people living in the huge region east of the Mississippi.

War and the Management of Empire

After the Glorious Revolution of 1688, England began constructing a more coherent imperial administration. In 1696, a professional Board of Trade replaced the old Lords of Trade; the Treasury strengthened the customs service; and Parliament created overseas vice-admiralty courts, which functioned without juries to prosecute smugglers who evaded the trade regulations set forth in the Navigation Acts. Royal governors received greater powers and more detailed instructions and came under more insistent demands from the Board of Trade to enforce British policies. England was quietly installing the machinery of imperial management and a corps of colonial bureaucrats.

The best test of an effectively organized state was its ability to wage war. Four times between 1689 and 1763, England matched its strength against France, its archrival in North America and the Caribbean. During this period, the English king and Parliament also increased their control over colonial affairs.

Parliament added new articles such as furs, copper, hemp, tar, and turpentine to the list of items produced in North America that had to be shipped to England before being exported to another country. Parliament also curtailed colonial production of articles important to England's economy: woolen cloth in 1699, beaver hats in 1732, finished iron products in 1750. Most important, Parliament passed the Molasses Act in

1733. Attempting to stop the trade between New England and the French West Indies, where Yankee traders exchanged fish, beef, and pork for molasses to convert into rum, Parliament imposed a prohibitive duty of six pence per gallon on molasses imported from the French islands. This turned many of New England's largest merchants, distillers, and ship captains and crews into smugglers.

The generation of peace ended abruptly in 1739 when England declared war on Spain. The cause of the war was England's determination to continue its drive toward commercial domination of the Atlantic basin. Five years after the war with Spain began in 1739, it merged into a much larger conflict between England and France, in Europe called the War of Austrian Succession, that lasted until 1748. The scale of King George's War (1744–1748) far exceeded previous conflicts. As military priorities became paramount, England pressed for increased discipline within the empire and larger colonial revenues. England asked its West Indian and American colonies to share in the costs of defending—and extending—the empire and to tailor their behavior to the needs of the home country.

Outbreak of Hostilities

The tension between English and French colonists in North America was intensified by the spectacular growth of the English colonies: from 0.25 million in 1700 to 1.25 million in 1750 and to 1.75 million in the next decade. Three-quarters of the increase came in the colonies south of New York. Such growth propelled thousands of land-hungry settlers toward the mountain gaps in the Appalachians in search of farmland.

Promoting this westward rush were eastern fur traders and speculators. But the farther west the settlement line moved, the closer it came to the western trading empire of the French and their Indian allies. Colonial pene-

tration of the Ohio valley in the 1740s established the first English outposts in the continental heartland. This challenged the French where their interest was vital. While the English controlled most of the eastern coastal plain of North America, the French had nearly encircled them to the west by building a chain of trading posts and forts along the St. Lawrence River, through the Great Lakes, and southward into the Ohio and Mississippi valleys all the way to New Orleans. The French attempted to block further English expansion by constructing new forts in the Ohio valley and by prying some tribes loose from their new English connections.

By 1755, the French had driven the English traders out of the Ohio valley and established forts as far east as the forks of the Ohio River, near present-day Pittsburgh. It was there, at Fort Duquesne, that the French smartly rebuffed an ambitious young Virginia militia colonel named George Washington, dispatched by his colony's government to expel them from the region.

Men in the capitals of Europe, not in the colonies, made the decision to force a showdown in the interior of North America. Urged on by England's powerful merchants, who were eager to destroy French overseas trade, the English ministry ordered several thousand troops to America in 1754; in France, 3,000 regulars embarked to meet the English challenge.

With war looming, the colonial governments attempted to coordinate their efforts. Representatives of seven colonies met with 150 Iroquois chiefs at Albany, New York, in June 1754. The twin goals were to woo the powerful Iroquois out of their neutrality and to perfect a plan of colonial union. Both failed. "Everyone cries a union is necessary," sighed Benjamin Franklin, "but when they come to the manner and form of the union, their weak noodles are perfectly distracted."

With his British army and hundreds of American recruits, General Edward Braddock slogged his way across Virginia in the summer of

1755, cutting a road through forests and across mountains at a few miles a day. A headstrong professional soldier, Braddock had contempt for the woods-wise French regiments and their stealthy Indian allies.

As Braddock neared Fort Duquesne, the entire French force and the British suddenly surprised each other in the forest. The French had 218 soldiers and militiamen and 637 Indian allies, while Braddock commanded twice that many men but few Indians. After an initial standoff, the French redeployed their Indian allies along both sides of the road in the trees. Unseen, the Indians poured murderous fire into Braddock's tidy lines of men. Braddock was mortally wounded, and two-thirds of his forces were killed or wounded. The Anglo-American force beat a hasty, ignominious retreat.

Throughout the summer, French-supplied Indian raiders put the torch to the Virginia and Pennsylvania backcountry. "The roads are full of starved, naked, indigent multitudes," observed one officer. One French triumph followed another during the next two years, and almost every tribe north of the Ohio River joined the French side.

The turning point in the war came after the energetic William Pitt became England's prime minister in 1757. Proclaiming "I believe that I can save this nation and that no one else can," he abandoned Europe as the main theater of action against the French and threw his nation's military might into the American campaign. About 23,000 British troops landed in America in 1757 and 1758, and the huge naval fleet that arrived in the latter year included 14,000 mariners. But even forces of this magnitude, when asked to engage the enemy in the forests of North America, were not necessarily sufficient to the task without Indian support, or at least neutrality.

Tribal Strategies

Anglo-American leaders knew that in a war fought mainly in the northern colonies, the support of the Iroquois Confederacy and their tributary tribes was crucial. Iroquois allegiance could be secured in only two ways, through purchase or by a demonstration of power that would convince the tribes that the English would prevail with or without their assistance. The Iroquois understood that their interest lay in playing off one European power against the other.

In 1758, the huge English military buildup began to produce victories. After a failed British and American assault on Fort Ticonderoga on Lake Champlain in June 1758, the tide turned. Troops under Sir Jeffrey Amherst captured Louisbourg, on Cape Breton Island, and Fort Duquesne fell to an army of 6,000 led by General John Forbes. The resolute Pitt had mobilized the fighting power of the English nation and put more men in the field than existed in all of New France. The colonists, in turn, had put aside intramural squabbling long enough to overwhelm the badly outnumbered French.

The victories of 1758 finally moved the Iroquois to join the Anglo-American side. In the South, however, back country skirmishes with the Cherokee from Virginia to South Carolina turned into a costly war from 1759 to 1761.

Other Anglo-American victories in 1759, the "year of miracles," decided the outcome of the bloodiest war yet known in the New World. The culminating stroke came with a dramatic victory at Quebec. Led by 32-year-old General James Wolfe, 5,000 troops scaled a rocky cliff and overcame the French on the Plains of Abraham. The capture of Montreal late in 1760 completed the shattering of French power in North America. The theater of operations shifted to the Caribbean, where fighting continued, as in Europe, for three years longer. But in the American colonies, the "Gallic menace" was gone.

Consequences of War

For the interior Indian tribes, the Treaty of Paris ending the Seven Years' War in 1763 dealt a harsh blow. Unlike the coastal Native Americans, whose population and independence had ebbed rapidly through contact with the colonizers, the inland tribes had maintained their strength and sometimes even grown more unified through relations with settlers. Although they came to depend on European trade goods, Native Americans had turned this commercial connection to their advantage so long as more than one source of trade goods existed.

The Indian play-off system ended with the French defeat. By the terms of the Treaty of Paris, France ceded Canada and all territory east of the Mississippi, except for New Orleans, to England. To Spain went New Orleans and France's trans-Mississippi empire. Spain yielded Florida to England. For the interior tribes, only one source of trade goods remained. Two centuries of European rivalry for control of eastern North America ended abruptly. Iroquois, Cherokee, Creek, and other interior peoples were now forced to adjust to this reality.

After concluding peace with the French, the English government launched a new policy in North America designed to separate Native Americans and colonizers by creating a racial boundary roughly following the crestline of the Appalachian Mountains from Maine to Georgia. The Proclamation of 1763 ordered the colonial governors to reserve all land west of the line for Indian nations. White settlers already living beyond the Appalachians were charged to withdraw to the east.

Though well intended, this attempt to legislate interracial accord failed completely. Even before the proclamation was issued, the Ottawa chief Pontiac was organizing a pan-Indian movement to drive the British out of the Ohio valley. Although his plan collapsed in 1764, it served notice that the interior tribes would fight for their lands.

The English government could not enforce its racial separation policy. Staggering under an immense wartime debt, England decided to maintain only small army garrisons in America to regulate the interior. Nor could royal governors stop land speculators and settlers from pri-

vately purchasing land from trans-Appalachian tribes or from simply encroaching on their land. Under such circumstances, the western frontier seethed with tension after 1763.

While the Seven Years' War marked an epic victory of Anglo-American arms over the French and redrew the map of North America, it also had important social and economic effects on colonial society. The war convinced the colonists of their growing strength yet left them debt-ridden and weakened in manpower. The wartime economy spurred economic development and poured British capital into the colonies yet rendered them more vulnerable to cyclic fluctuations in the British economy.

Military contracts, for example, brought prosperity to most colonies during the war years. Huge orders for ships, arms, uniforms, and provisions enriched northern merchants and provided good prices for farmers as well.

The war, however, required heavy taxes and took a huge human toll. The magnitude of the human losses in Boston indicates the war's impact. The wartime muster lists show that nearly every working-class Bostonian tasted military service at some point during the long war. When peace came, Boston had a deficit of almost 700 men in a town of about 2,000 families. The high rate of war widowhood produced a feminization of poverty and required expanded poor relief for the maintenance of husbandless women and fatherless children.

Peace ended the casualties but also brought depression. After the British forces left the American theater in 1760, the economy slumped badly, especially in the coastal towns. The greatest hardships fell on laboring people, although even some wealthy merchants went bankrupt. In Philadelphia, many poor people, unable to pay their property taxes, were "disposing of their huts and lots to others more wealthy than themselves." A New York artisan expressed a common lament in 1762. Although he still had employment, he had fallen into poverty and found it "beyond my ability to support my family . . . [which] can scarcely appear with decency or have necessaries to subsist." His situation, he added, "is really the case with many of the inhabitants of this city."

In spite of its heavy casualties and economic repercussions, the Seven Years' War paved the way for a far larger conflict in the next generation. The legislative assemblies, for example, which had been flexing their muscles at the expense of the governors in earlier decades, accelerated their bid for political power. During wartime, knowing that their governors must obtain military appropriations, they extracted concessions as the price for raising revenues. The war also trained a new group of military and political leaders. In carrying out military operations on a scale unknown in the colonies and in shouldering heavier political responsibilities, men such as George Washington, Samuel Adams, Benjamin Franklin, Patrick Henry, and Christopher Gadsden acquired the experience that would serve them well in the future.

The Seven Years' War, in spite of the severe costs, left many of the colonists with a sense of buoyancy. New Englanders rejoiced at the final victory over the "Papist enemy of the North." Frontiersmen, fur traders, and land speculators also celebrated the French withdrawal, for the West now appeared open for exploitation. The colonists also felt a new sense of their identity after the war. Surveying a world free of French and Spanish threats, they could not help but reassess the advantages and disadvantages of subordination to England.

THE CRISIS WITH ENGLAND

George Grenville became the chief minister of England's 25-year-old king, George III, at the end of the Seven Years' War. Struggling to reduce the large national debt, Grenville proposed new taxes in England and others in North America, where the colonists were asked to bear their share of running the empire. Grenville's particu-

lar concern was financing the 10,000 British regulars left in North America after 1763 to police French-speaking Canada and the frontier. His revenue program initiated a rift between England and its colonies that a dozen years later would culminate in revolution.

Sugar, Currency, and Stamps

In 1764, Grenville pushed through Parliament several bills that in combination pressed hard against the economic system of the colonies. First came the Revenue Act (or Sugar Act) of 1764, which imposed new taxes on the colonies and tightened up enforcement of old taxes. The new law reduced the tax on imported French molasses from six to three pence per gallon and added a number of colonial products to the list of commodities that could be sent only to England. It required American shippers to post bonds guaranteeing observance of the trade regulations before loading their cargoes. Finally, it strengthened the vice-admiralty courts, where violators of the trade acts were prosecuted.

Many of the colonial legislatures grumbled about the Sugar Act because a strictly enforced duty of three pence per gallon on molasses pinched more than the loosely enforced sixpence duty. But only New York objected that *any* tax by Parliament to raise revenue (rather than to control trade) violated the rights of overseas English subjects who were unrepresented in Parliament. On the heels of the Sugar Act came the Currency Act, which forbade the colonies to issue paper money as legal tender. In a colonial economy chronically short of hard cash, this constricted trade.

The move to tighten up the machinery of empire confused the colonists because many of the new regulations came from Parliament, which had heretofore been content to allow the king, his ministers, and the Board of Trade to run overseas affairs. In a world where history taught that power and liberty were perpetually at war, generations of colonists had viewed Parliament as a bastion of English liberty, the bulwark against despotic political rule. The Parliament on which colonial legislatures had modeled themselves now began to seem like a violator of colonial rights.

After Parliament passed the Sugar Act in 1764, Grenville announced his intention to extend to America the stamp duties that had already been imposed in England. However, he gave the colonies a year to suggest alternative ways of raising revenue. The colonies objected strenuously to the proposed stamp tax, but none provided another plan. The Stamp Act, effective November 1765, required revenue stamps on every newspaper, pamphlet, almanac, legal document, liquor license, college diploma, pack of playing cards, and pair of dice.

Colonial reaction to the Stamp Act ranged from disgruntled submission to mass defiance. In many cases, resistance involved not only discontent over England's tightening of the screws on the American colonies but also internal resentments born out of the play of local events. Especially in the cities, the defiance of authority and destruction of property by people from the middle and lower ranks redefined the dynamics of politics, setting the stage for a ten-year internal struggle for control among the various social elements alarmed by the new English policies.

Stamp Act Riots

The Virginia House of Burgesses was the first legislature to react to the news of the Stamp Act, which arrived in April 1765. In May, led by 29-year-old Patrick Henry, a fiery lawyer newly elected from a frontier county, the House of Burgesses debated seven strongly worded resolutions. Old-guard burgesses regarded some of them as treasonable. The legislature finally adopted the four more moderate resolves, including one proclaiming Virginia's right to impose taxes. They rejected the other resolves, which declared it "illegal, unconstitutional, and unjust" for anybody outside Virginia to lay taxes, asserted that Virginians did not have to obey any externally imposed tax law, and labeled as "an enemy to this, his Majesty's colony," anyone denying Virginia's exclusive right to tax its inhabitants. But within a month, all seven resolutions were broadcast in the newspapers of other colonies.

Governor Francis Bernard of Massachusetts called the Virginia resolves "an alarm bell for the disaffected." The events in Boston in August 1765 amply confirmed his view. On August 14, Bostonians reduced the luxurious mansion of stamp distributor Andrew Oliver to a shambles. Twelve days later, the shoemaker Ebenezer MacIntosh led the crowd again in attacks on the handsomely appointed homes of two British officials and Lieutenant-Governor Thomas Hutchinson. Military men "who have seen towns sacked by the enemy," one observer reported, "declare they never before saw an instance of such fury."

In attacking the property of men associated with the stamp tax, the Boston crowd demonstrated its opposition to parliamentary policy. But the crowd was also expressing hostility toward a local elite that for years had disdained lower-class political participation and had publicly denounced the working poor for their supposed lack of industry and frugality. For decades, ordinary Bostonians had aligned politically with the Boston "caucus," which led the colony's "popular party" against conservative aristocrats such as Hutchinson and Oliver. But the "rage-intoxicated rabble" had suddenly broken away from the leaders of the popular party and gone further than they had intended. The more cautious political leaders knew that they would have to struggle to regain control of the protest movement.

Violent protest against the Stamp Act also wracked New York and Newport, Rhode Island. Leading the resistance were groups calling themselves the Sons of Liberty, composed mostly of

From the time of his election to the Virginia House of Burgesses at the age of 29, Patrick Henry was an outspoken proponent of American rights. In this portrait, he pleads a case at a county courthouse crowded with local planters.

artisans, shopkeepers, and ordinary citizens. Protest took a more dignified form at the Stamp Act Congress, called by Massachusetts and attended by representatives of nine colonies, who met in New York in October 1765. The delegates formulated 12 restrained resolutions that accepted Parliament's right to legislate for the colonies but denied its right to tax them directly unless they had representation in the law-making body.

All over America by late 1765, effigy-burning crowds had convinced stamp distributors to resign their commissions. Some colonists defied

English authority even more directly by forcing most customs officers and court officials to open the ports and courts for business after November 1 without using the hated stamps required after that date. In March 1766, Parliament bowed to expediency and repealed the hated Stamp Act. The crisis had passed, yet nothing was really solved.

In the course of challenging parliamentary authority, the Stamp Act resisters politicized their communities as never before. The established leaders, generally cautious in their protests, were often displaced by those beneath them on the social ladder. Scribbled John Adams in his diary: "The people have become more attentive to their liberties, . . . and more determined to defend them."

An Uncertain Interlude

Ministerial instability in England hampered the quest for a coherent, workable American policy. Attempting to be a strong king, George III chose ministers who commanded little respect in Parliament. This led to strife between Parliament and the king's chief ministers; that in turn led to a shuffling of chief ministers and to a chaotic political situation at the very time that the king was attempting to overhaul the administration of the empire.

To manage the colonies more effectively, the Pitt-Grafton ministry that the king appointed in 1767 obtained new laws to reorganize the customs service, establish a secretary of state for American affairs, and install three new vice-admiralty courts in the port cities. Still hard pressed for revenue, the ministry also pushed through Parliament the Townshend duties on paper, lead, painters' colors, and tea. A final law suspended New York's assembly until that body ceased its noncompliance with the Quartering Act of 1765. This law not only required public funds for support of British troops garrisoned in the colonies but also spelled out how the colonial assemblies should allocate public funds for that purpose. Many colonists resented these new regulations, which they saw as more taxation without representation, but only the Massachusetts and New York assemblies refused to vote the mandated supplies to the troops.

Colonial reaction to the Townshend Acts, centered in Massachusetts, was more restrained than in 1765. New York buckled under to the Quartering Act rather than see its assembly suspended. But the Massachusetts House of Representatives sent a circular letter to each colony objecting to the new Townshend duties, small though they were. Written by Samuel Adams, the letter attacked as unconstitutional the plan to underwrite salaries for royal officials in America from customs duties.

"The Americans have made a discovery," declared Edmund Burke before Parliament, "that we mean to oppress them; we have made a discovery that they intend to raise a rebellion. We do not know how to advance; they do not know how to retreat."

While most of the colonists only grumbled and petitioned, Bostonians protested angrily. In the summer of 1768, after customs officials seized a sloop owned by John Hancock for a violation of the trade regulations, an angry crowd mobbed them. They fled to a British warship in Boston harbor and remained there for months. The newspapers warned of new measures designed "to suck the life blood" from the people and predicted that troops would be sent "to dragoon us into passive obedience."

Troops indeed came. The attack on the customs officials brought a resolute response from England. The ministry dispatched two regiments from England and two more from Nova Scotia. On October 1, 1768, red-coated troops marched into Boston without resistance.

After the troops occupied Boston, the colonists' main tactic of protest against the Townshend Acts became economic boycott. First in Boston and then in New York and Philadelphia, merchants and consumers adopted nonimportation and nonconsumption agreements. They pledged neither to import nor to use British articles. These measures promised to bring the politically influential English merchants to their aid, for half of British shipping was engaged in commerce with the colonies, and one-quarter of all English exports were consumed there.

Many colonial merchants, however, did not wish to support the boycott and had to be persuaded to comply by street brigades. Crowd action welled up again in the seaports, as determined patriot bands attacked the homes and warehouses of offending merchants and "rescued" incoming contraband goods seized by zealous customs officials. When the southern colonies also adopted nonimportation agreements in 1768, a new step toward intercolonial union had been taken.

England's attempts to discipline its American colonies and oblige them to share the costs of governing an empire lay in shambles by the end of the 1760s. The Townshend duties had failed miserably, yielding less than £21,000 by 1770 while costing British business £700,000 through the colonial nonimportation movement.

In London, on March 5, 1770, Parliament repealed all the Townshend duties except the one on tea. On that same evening in Boston, British troops fired on an unruly crowd of heckling citizens. When the smoke cleared, five bloody bodies lay dead in the snow-covered street. Among them were Ebenezer MacIntosh's brother-in-law and Crispus Attucks, a runaway slave who may have been the first black to lose his life in the American struggle against British authority. Bowing to furious popular reaction, Thomas Hutchinson, recently appointed governor, ordered the British troops out of town and arrested the commanding officer and the soldiers involved. They were later acquitted, with two young local lawyers, John Adams and Josiah Quincy, Jr., providing a brilliant defense.

The Growing Rift

After the "Boston massacre," opposition to English policies subsided for a time. From 1770 to 1772, relative quiet descended over the colonies. Not until June 1772 did England provide another inflammatory issue. Then, by announcing that it would pay the salaries of the royal governor and superior court judges in Massachusetts rather than allow the provincial legislature to continue supporting these positions, the Crown created a new furor. Even though the measure saved the colony money, it was seen as a dangerous innovation because it undermined a right set forth in the colony's charter. Judges paid from London, it was assumed, would respond to London.

Boston's town meeting protested loudly and created a Committee of Correspondence "to state the rights of the colonists . . . and to communicate and publish the same to the several towns and to the world." Crown supporters called the committee "the foulest, sublest, and most venomous serpent ever issued from the egg of sedition." By the end of 1772, another 80 towns in Massachusetts had created committees. In the next year, all but three colonies established Committees of Correspondence in their legislatures.

Samuel Adams was by now the leader of the Boston radicals. A man with deep roots among the laboring people despite his Harvard degree, he organized the working ranks through the taverns, clubs, and volunteer fire companies and also secured the support of wealthy merchants such as John Hancock. In England, Adams became known as one of the most dangerous firebrands in America.

In 1772, a band of Rhode Island colonists gave Adams new material to work with when they attacked a royal warship. The British commander of the *Gaspee* was roundly hated for hounding the fishermen and small traders of Narragansett Bay. When his ship ran aground, Rhode Islanders boarded the stranded vessel and burned it to the water's edge. A Rhode Island court then convicted the *Gaspee*'s captain of illegally seizing what he was convinced was smuggled sugar and rum. The government in London reacted with cries of high treason. Finding the lips of Rhode Islanders sealed regarding the identity of the arsonists, an investigating committee could do little. The event was tailor-made for Samuel Adams, who used it to "awaken the American colonies, which have been too long dozing upon the brink of ruin."

In early 1773, Parliament's passage of the Tea Act precipitated the final plunge into revolution. The act allowed the East India Company, which was on the verge of bankruptcy, to ship its tea directly to America. By eliminating English middlemen and English import taxes, this pro-

British Exports to North America, 1756–1775

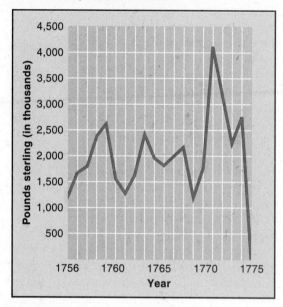

Source: U.S. Bureau of the Census.

vided Americans with the opportunity to buy their tea cheaply from the company's agents in the colonies. Even with the small tax to be paid in the colonies, Indian tea would now undersell smuggled Dutch tea.

Parliament monumentally miscalculated the American response. For several years, merchants in Philadelphia and New York had been flagrantly smuggling Dutch tea. As a consequence, imports of English tea plummeted. The merchants bitterly denounced the new act for giving the East India Company a monopoly on the North American tea market. Many colonists also objected that the government was shrewdly trying to gain implicit acceptance of Parliament's taxing power by offering tea at a new reduced rate. When Americans drank the taxed tea, they would also be swallowing the English right to impose taxes. Mass meetings in the port towns soon forced the resignation of the East India

Company's agents, and citizens vowed to stop the obnoxious tea at the water's edge.

Governor Hutchinson of Massachusetts brought the tea crisis to a climax. The popular party led by Samuel Adams wanted to send the tea back to England, but Hutchinson refused to grant the tea ships clearance papers to return to England with their cargoes. Finally, a band of Bostonians, dressed as Indians, boarded the tea ships at nightfall, broke open the chests of tea, and flung £10,000 worth of the East India Company's property into Boston harbor. Lord North, the king's chief minister, now argued that the dispute was no longer about taxes but about whether England had any authority at all over the colonies.

Thoroughly aroused by the Boston Tea Party, Parliament passed the Coercive Acts, which Bostonians promptly labeled the "Intolerable Acts." The acts closed the port of Boston to all shipping until the colony paid for the destroyed tea. They declared British soldiers and officials immune from local court trials for acts committed while suppressing civil disturbances. Parliament amended the Massachusetts charter to transform the council from an upper legislative chamber, elected by the lower house, to a body appointed by the governor. The acts also authorized the governor to prohibit all town meetings except for one annual meeting in each town to elect local officers of government. Finally, General Thomas Gage, commander in chief of British forces in America, replaced Thomas Hutchinson as governor. The Americans now found their maneuvering room severely narrowed.

When the Intolerable Acts arrived in May 1774, Boston's town meeting reacted belligerently. It dispatched a circular letter to all the colonies urging an end to trade with England. This met with faint support. But a second call, for a meeting in Philadelphia of delegates from all colonies, received a better response. The Continental Congress, as it was called, now began to transform a ten-year debate on constitutional rights conducted by separate colonies into a unified American cause.

Fifty-five delegates from all the colonies except Georgia converged on Carpenter's Hall in Philadelphia in September 1774. None were advocating American independence at this time. The discussions centered not on how to prepare for a war that many sensed was inevitable but on how to resolve differences that most delegates feared were irreconcilable.

Some delegates, led by cousins Samuel and John Adams from Massachusetts and Richard Henry Lee and Patrick Henry of Virginia, argued for outright resistance to Parliament's Coercive Acts. Moderate delegates from the middle colonies, led by Joseph Galloway of Pennsylvania and James Duane of New York, urged restraint and further attempts at reconciliation. After weeks of debate, the delegates agreed to issue a restrained Declaration of Rights and Resolves, which attempted to define American grievances and to justify the colonists' defiance of English policies and laws by appealing to the "immutable laws of nature, the principles of the English constitution, and the several [colonial] charters and compacts" under which they lived. More concrete was the Congress's agreement on a plan of resistance. If England did not rescind the Intolerable Acts by December 1, 1774, a ban on all imports and exports between the colonies and Great Britain, Ireland, and the British West Indies would take effect. Some exceptions were made for the export of southern staple commodities in order to keep reluctant southern colonies in the fold.

By the time the Congress adjourned in late October, Boston's cause had been transformed into a national movement. Patrick Henry declared, "The distinctions between Virginians, Pennsylvanians, New Yorkers, and New Englanders are no more. I am not a Virginian, but an American." Many of Henry's fellow delegates were more bound to their provincial identities, but in adjourning, the Congress agreed to reconvene in May 1775.

Even before the Second Continental Con-

Liberty always had to struggle against power, as American colonists saw it; in this cartoon, England (power) forces Liberty (America in the form of a woman) to drink the "Bitter Draught" of tea. Uncompliant, America spits the tea into England's face while another corrupt Englishman peeks under her petticoat.

gress met, the fabric of government had been badly torn in most colonies. Revolutionary committees, conventions, and congresses, entirely unauthorized by law, were replacing legal governing bodies. Assuming authority in defiance of royal governors, these extralegal bodies created and armed militia units, promoted observance of boycotts, levied taxes, operated the courts, and obstructed the work of English customs officials. By the end of 1774, all but three colonies defied their own charters by appointing provincial assemblies without royal authority. In the next year, this independently created power became evident in the nearly complete cessation of trade with England.

The Final Rupture

The final spark to the revolutionary powder keg was struck in early 1775. General Thomas Gage had assumed the governorship of Massachusetts 11 months earlier and occupied Boston with 4,000 troops—one for every adult male in the town. Ordered to arrest the leaders of the Boston insurrection, Gage sent 700 redcoats under cover of night to seize colonial arms and ammunition in nearby Concord. But Americans learned of the plan. When the troops reached Lexington at dawn, 70 "Minutemen"—townsmen available on a minute's notice—occupied the village green. In the skirmish that ensued, 18 Massachusetts farmers fell, 8 of them mortally wounded.

Marching six miles west, the British entered Concord, where another firefight broke out. Withdrawing, the redcoats made their way back to Boston, harassed by militiamen firing from farmhouses and barns and from behind stone walls. Before the bloody day ended, 273 British and 95 Americans lay dead or wounded. News of the bloodshed swept through the colonies. Within weeks, thousands of men besieged the British troops in Boston. One colonist reported that wherever one traveled, "you see the inhabitants training, making firelocks, casting mortars, shells, and shot."

The outbreak of fighting vastly altered the debates of the Second Continental Congress, which assembled in Philadelphia in May 1775. New delegates included Boston's wealthy merchant, John Hancock; a tall, young planter-lawyer from Virginia, Thomas Jefferson; and the much-applauded Benjamin Franklin, who had arrived from London only four days before the Congress convened.

The Congress had no power to legislate or command; it could only request and recommend. But setting to work, it authorized a continental army of 20,000 and chose George Washington as commander in chief. It issued a "Declaration of Causes of Taking-up Arms," sent the king an "Olive Branch Petition" humbly begging him to remove the obstacles to reconciliation, made moves to secure the neutrality of the interior Indian tribes, issued paper money, erected a postal system, and approved plans for a military hospital.

While debate continued over whether the colonies ought to declare themselves independent, military action grew hotter. The hotheaded Ethan Allen and his Green Mountain boys from eastern New York captured Fort Ticonderoga, controlling the Champlain valley, in May 1775. On New Year's Day in 1776, the British shelled Norfolk, Virginia. In March 1776, Washington's army forced the British to evacuate Boston. Hope for reconciliation with England crumbled at the end of 1775 when news arrived that the king, rejecting the Olive Branch Petition, had dispatched 20,000 additional British troops to quell the American insurrection and had proclaimed the colonies in "open and avowed rebellion." Those fatal words made all the Congress's actions treasonable and turned all who obeyed them into traitors.

By the time Thomas Paine's hard-hitting pamphlet *Common Sense* appeared in Philadelphia on January 9, 1776, members of the Congress were talking less gingerly about independence. Paine's blunt words and compelling rhetoric smashed through the remaining reserve. "O ye that love mankind! Ye that dare oppose not only the tyranny, but also the tyrant, stand forth!" wrote Paine. Within weeks the pamphlet was in bookstalls all over the colonies. "The public sentiment which a few weeks before had shuddered at the tremendous obstacles, with which independence was envisioned," declared Edmund Randolph of Virginia, now "overleaped every barrier."

The Continental Congress continued to debate independence during the spring of 1776, even as the war became bloodier. When an American assault on Quebec failed in May 1776, England embargoed all trade to the colonies and ordered the seizure of American ships. That convinced the Congress to declare its ports open to all countries. "Nothing is left now," Joseph Hewes of North Carolina admitted, "but to fight it out." On June 9 the Congress ordered a committee chaired by Jefferson to begin drafting a declaration of independence.

The declaration was not a highly original statement. It drew heavily on the addresses that the Congress had been issuing to justify American resistance, and it presented a theory of government that was embedded in the scores of pamphlets that had issued from the colonial presses over the previous decade. Jefferson's committee brought its handiwork before the Congress on June 28. On July 2, twelve delegations voted for the declaration, with New York's abstaining, thus allowing the Congress to say that the vote for independence was unanimous. Two days more were spent cutting and polishing the document.

In eloquent terms, the document declared that "all men are created equal" and "are endowed by their Creator with certain inalienable rights," including "life, liberty, and the pursuit of happiness." Governments rule by consent of the governed, and if a government becomes unjust and oppressive, the citizens have a right to "alter or abolish" it. After enumerating the many injuries inflicted on the colonies by the unjust British king, who was termed "unfit to be the ruler of a free people," the document finally declared the united colonies, or "United States of America," totally independent of Great Britain. On July 4, Congress sent the Declaration of Independence to the printer.

THE IDEOLOGY OF REVOLUTIONARY REPUBLICANISM

In the years after 1763, the colonists pieced together a political ideology, borrowed partly from English political thought, partly from the theories of the Enlightenment, and partly from their own experiences. Historians call this new ideology "revolutionary republicanism." But it is important to understand that because the colonists varied widely in interests and experiences, there was never a single coherent ideology to which they all subscribed.

A Plot Against Liberty

Many American colonists subscribed to the notion advanced by earlier English Whig writers that corrupt and power-hungry men were slowly extinguishing the lamp of liberty in England. The so-called "country" party represented by these Whig pamphleteers proclaimed itself the guardian of the true principles of the English constitution and opposed the "court" party representing the king and his appointees.

Every ministerial policy and parliamentary act in the decade after the Stamp Act appeared as a subversion of English liberties. The belief that England was carrying out "a deep-laid and desperate plan of imperial despotism . . . for the extinction of all civil liberty," as the Boston town meeting expressed it in 1770, spread rapidly in the next few years. By 1774, John Adams was writing of "the conspiracy against the public liberty [that] was first regularly formed and begun to be executed in 1763 and 1764." From London, America's favorite writer, Benjamin Franklin, described the "extreme corruption prevalent among all orders of men in this old rotten state."

Among many Americans, especially merchants, the attack on constitutional rights blended closely with the threats to their economic interests contained in the tough new trade policies. Merchants perceived a coordinated attack on their "lives, liberties, and property," as they frequently phrased it. Others saw in revolution an opportunity to restore and strengthen virtue in American life.

Revitalizing American Society

Many colonists believed that the growing commercial connection with the decadent and corrupt mother country was injecting deadly fluids into the American bloodstream. They worried about the luxury and vice they saw around them and came to believe that the resistance to England would return American society to a state of civic virtue, spartan living, and godly purpose.

The fervent support of the patriot movement by much of the colonial clergy, especially in New England, helped give a high-toned moral character to colonial protest. The notion of moral regeneration through battle against a corrupt enemy ennobled the cause.

The growth of a revolutionary spirit among common people also owed much to the plain style of polemical writers such as Thomas Paine and Patrick Henry. Paine's *Common Sense* attacked the idea of monarchy itself. Its astounding popularity—it sold more copies than any printed piece in colonial history—stemmed not only from its argument but also from its style. Paine wrote for the common people, using plain language and assuming their knowledge of nothing more than the Bible. He appealed to millennial yearnings: "We have it in our power to begin the world over again," if only the Americans would stand up for liberty, the goddess whom "Europe regards ... like a stranger, and England hath given ... warning to depart." Many Whig leaders denounced Paine as "crack-brained," but thousands who read or listened to *Common Sense* were radicalized by it and came to believe not only that independence could be wrested from England but also that a new social and political order could be created in North America.

THE TURMOIL OF REVOLUTIONARY SOCIETY

The long struggle with England over colonial rights between 1764 and 1776 did not occur in a unified society. Social and economic change, which accelerated in the late colonial period, brought deep unrest and calls for reform from many quarters.

As agitation against English policy intensified, previously acquiescent people took a more active interest in politics. Groups emerged—slaves, urban laboring people, backcountry farmers, evangelicals, women—who enunciated goals of their own that were sometimes only loosely connected to the struggle with England. The stridency and potential power of these groups raised for many upper-class leaders the frightening specter of a radically changed society. Losing control of the protests they had initially led, many of them would abandon the resistance movement against England.

Urban People

Although the cities contained only about 5 percent of the colonial population, they formed the vital cores of revolutionary agitation. They led the way in protesting English policy, and they soon contained the most politicized citizens in America. Local politics could be rapidly transformed as the struggle against England became enmeshed with calls for internal reform.

In Philadelphia, for example, economic difficulties in the 1760s and 1770s led craftsmen to band together within their craft and their community. Artisans played a central role in forging

In Common Sense, *Thomas Paine dared to articulate, in plain but muscular language, the thoughts of rebellion and independence that others had only alluded to.*

a nonimportation agreement in 1768, calling public meetings, publishing newspaper appeals, organizing secondary boycotts against foot-dragging merchants, and ferreting out and tarring and feathering opponents to their policies. By 1772, artisans were filling elected municipal positions and insisting on their right to participate equally with their social superiors in nominating assemblymen and other important office-holders.

By 1774, working-class intermeddling in state affairs had taken a bold new step—the de facto assumption of governmental powers by committees called into being by the people at large. Craftsmen had first clothed themselves in such extralegal authority in policing the nonimportation agreement in 1769. Five years later, in response to the Intolerable Acts, they put forward a radical slate of candidates for a committee to enforce a new economic boycott. Their ticket drubbed one nominated by the city's conservative merchants.

The political mobilization of laboring Philadelphians continued as the impasse with England reached a climax in 1775. Many pacifist Quaker leaders of the city had abandoned

politics by this time, and other conservative merchants had also concluded that mob rule had triumphed. Into the leadership vacuum stepped a group of radicals from the middling ranks: the fiery Scots-Irish doctor Thomas Young, who had agitated in Boston and Albany before migrating to Philadelphia; Timothy Matlack, a hardware retailer who was popular with the lower class for matching his prize bantam cocks against those of New York's aristocratic James Delancy; James Cannon, a young schoolteacher; Benjamin Rush, whose new medical practice took him into the garrets and cramped rooms of the city's poor; and Thomas Paine, a recent immigrant seeking something better in America than he had found as an ill-paid excise officer in England.

The political support of the new radical leaders was centered in the 31 companies of the Philadelphia militia, composed mostly of laboring men, and in the extralegal committees now controlling the city's economic life. Their leadership helped to overcome the conservatism of the regularly elected Pennsylvania legislature, which was resisting the movement of the Continental Congress toward independence. In addition, the new radical leaders demanded internal reforms: opening up opportunity; curbing the accumulation of wealth by "our great merchants" who were "making immense fortunes at the expense of the people"; abolishing the property requirement for voting; allowing militiamen to elect their officers; and imposing stiff fines, to be used for the support of the families of poor militiamen, on men who refused militia service.

Mobilization among artisans, laborers, and mariners, in other cities as well as Philadelphia, became part of the chain of events that led toward independence. Whereas most of the patriot elite fought only to change English colonial policy, the populace of the cities also struggled for internal reforms and raised notions of how an independent American society might be reorganized.

Women

Women also played a vital role in the relentless movement toward revolution, and they drew upon revolutionary arguments to define their own goals. Women signed nonimportation agreements, harassed noncomplying merchants, and helped organize "fast days," during which communities prayed for deliverance from English oppression. But the women's most important role was in facilitating the economic boycott of English goods. The success of the nonconsumption pacts depended on substituting homespun cloth for English textiles on which colonists of all classes had always relied. From Georgia to Maine, women and children began spinning yarn and weaving cloth. In 1769, the women of tiny Middletown, Massachusetts, set the standard by weaving 20,522 yards of cloth, about 160 yards each. After the Tea Act in 1773, patriotic women boycotted their favorite drink as well.

Women's perception of their role was also changed by colonial protests and petitions against England's arbitrary uses of power. The more male leaders talked about England's inten-

tions to "enslave" the Americans and England's callous treatment of its colonial "subjects," the more American women began to rethink their own domestic situations. Many American women felt that they too were badly treated "subjects" of their husbands. If there was to be independence, new laws must be passed, Abigail Adams reminded her husband, John, in March 1776. Choosing words and phrases that had been used over and over in the protests against England, she wrote: "Do not put such unlimited power into the hand of the husbands. . . . Put it out of the power of the vicious and the lawless to use us with cruelty and indignity," she insisted. "Remember, all men would be tyrants if they could." Abigail Adams warned that American women "will not hold ourselves bound by any laws in which we have no voice, or representation" and even promised that women would "foment a rebellion" if men did not heed their rightful claims.

Nothing came of Abigail Adams's plea on behalf of women, for there was no women's movement to take up her cause. The issues she raised about women's lack of power in society and in the family were largely ignored until the middle of the next century.

Protesting Farmers

In most of the agricultural areas of the colonies, where many settlers made their livelihoods, passions concerning English policies were aroused only slowly. After about 1740, farmers had benefited from a sharp rise in the demand for foodstuffs in England, southern Europe, and the West Indies. Living far from harping English customs officers, impressment gangs, and occupying armies, the colonists of the interior had to be drawn gradually into the resistance movement by their urban cousins. Even in Concord, Massachusetts, only a dozen miles from the center of colonial agitation, townspeople found little to protest in English policies until England closed the port of Boston in 1774.

Yet some parts of rural America seethed with social tension in the prewar era. The dynamics of conflict, shaped by the social development of particular regions, eventually became part of the momentum for revolution. In three western counties of North Carolina and in the Hudson River valley of New York, for example, widespread civil disorder marked the pre-Revolutionary decades. The militant rhetoric and tactics small farmers used to combat exploitation formed rivulets that fed the main stream of revolutionary consciousness.

For years, the small farmers of western North Carolina had suffered exploitation by corrupt county court officials appointed by the governor and a legislature dominated by eastern planter interests. Sheriffs and justices, allied with land speculators and lawyers, seized property when farmers could not pay their taxes and sold it, often at a fraction of its worth, to their cronies. In the mid-1760s, frustrated at getting no satisfaction from legal forms of protest, the farmers formed associations of so-called Regulators that forcibly closed the courts, attacked the property of their enemies, and whipped and publicly humiliated judges and lawyers. When their leaders were arrested, the Regulators stormed the jails and released them.

In 1768 and again in 1771, Governor William Tryon led troops against the Regulators, who were finally defeated. Seven leaders were executed in the ensuing trials. Though the Regulators lost on the field of battle, their protest against the self-interested behavior of a wealthy elite became part of the larger revolutionary struggle.

Rural insurgency in New York flared up in the 1750s and again in 1766 over land rights. The Hudson River valley had long been controlled by a few wealthy families with enormous landholdings, which they leased to small tenant farmers. The Van Rensselaer manor totaled a million acres, the Phillipses' manor nearly half as much. When tenants resisted rent increases or purchased land from Indians who swore that manor lords had extended the boundaries of their manors by fraud, the landlords began evicting their leaseholders.

The landlords had the power of government, including control of the courts, on their side, so the tenants, like the Carolina Regulators, went outside the law. By 1766, while New York City was absorbed in the Stamp Act furor, tenants led by William Prendergast began resisting sheriffs who tried to evict tenants from lands they claimed. The militant tenants threatened landlords with death and broke open jails to rescue their friends. British troops from New York were used to break the tenant rebellion. Prendergast was tried and sentenced to be hanged, beheaded, and quartered. Although he was pardoned, the bitterness of the Hudson River tenants endured through the Revolution, when most of them, unlike the Carolina Regulators, fought with the British because their landlords had joined the patriot cause.

CONCLUSION

FORGING A REVOLUTION

The Seven Years' War nurtured the colonists' sense of separate identity. Yet it left them with difficult economic adjustments, heavy debts, and growing social divisions. The Treaty of Paris in 1763 led to a reorganization of England's triumphant yet debt-torn empire that had profound repercussions in North America.

In the pre-Revolutionary decade, a dual disillusionment penetrated ever deeper into the colonial consciousness. Pervasive doubt arose concerning both the colonies' role, as assigned by England, in the economic life of the empire and the sensitivity of the government in London to the colonists' needs. At the same time, the colonists began to perceive British policies—instituted by Parliament, the king, and his advisers—as a systematic attack on the fundamental liberties and natural rights of British subjects in America.

The fluidity and diversity of colonial society and the differing experiences of Americans during and after the Seven Years' War evoked varying responses to the disruption that accompanied the English reorganization of the empire. In the course of resisting English policy, many previously inactive groups entered public life to challenge gentry control of political affairs. Often occupying the most radical ground in the opposition to England, they simultaneously challenged the growing concentration of economic and political power in their own communities.

When the Congress turned the 15-month undeclared war into a formally declared struggle for national liberation in July 1776, it steered its compatriots onto turbulent and unknown seas.

Recommended Reading

Further knowledge of the long, exhausting wars of empire that embroiled the colonies for four generations before 1763 can be derived from Douglas E. Leach, *Arms for Empire* (1973); and William Eccles, *The Canadian Frontier*, rev. ed. (1983).

The administration of the British Empire and the advent of the Seven Years' War are addressed in Michael Kammen, *Empire and Interest* (1970); and Francis Jennings, *Empire of Fortune: Crown, Colonies, and Tribes in the Seven Years' War in America* (1988).

For different points of view on the origins of the American Revolution, see Bernard Bailyn, *The Ideological Origins of the American Revolution* (1967);

Gary B. Nash, *The Urban Crucible* (1979); Joseph A. Ernst, *Money and Politics in America, 1755–1775* (1973); David Ammerman, *In the Common Cause* (1974); and Pauline Maier, *From Resistance to Rebellion* (1972).

Rich local studies of the Revolutionary crisis include Dirk Hoerder, *Crowd Action in Revolutionary Massachusetts* (1977); and Edward Countryman, *A People in Revolution* (1981). Excellent essays on various aspects of the coming of the Revolution can be found in Alfred F. Young, ed., *The American Revolution* (1976); and Jeffrey J. Crow and Larry E. Tise, eds., *The Southern Experience in the American Revolution* (1978).

Time Line

1696	Parliament establishes Board of Trade	1764	Pontiac's Rebellion in Ohio valley
1701	Iroquois set policy of neutrality	1765	Colonists resist Stamp Act Virginia House of Burgesses issues Stamp Act resolutions
1702–1713	Queen Anne's War	1766	Declaratory Act Tenant rent war in New York Slave insurrections in South Carolina
1713	Peace of Utrecht	1767	Townshend duties imposed
1733	Molasses Act	1768	British troops occupy Boston
1744–1748	King George's War	1770	"Boston Massacre" Townshend duties repealed (except on tea)
1754	Albany conference	1771	North Carolina Regulators defeated
1755	Braddock defeated by French and Indian allies	1772	*Gaspee* incident in Rhode Island
1756–1763	Seven Years' War	1773	Tea Act provokes Boston Tea Party
1759	Wolfe defeats the French at Quebec	1774	"Intolerable Acts" First Continental Congress meets
1759–1761	Cherokee War against the English	1775	Second Continental Congress meets Battles of Lexington and Concord
1760s	Economic slump	1776	Thomas Paine publishes *Common Sense* Declaration of Independence
1763	Treaty of Paris ends Seven Years' War Proclamation line limits westward expansion		
1764	Sugar and Currency acts		

part 2

A Revolutionary People

1775-1828

The American Revolution not only marked an epic military victory over the powerful mother country but also set the course of national development in ways that still affect American society. Members of the Revolutionary generation were inspired by the idea of building a model society based on principles of freedom and equality. Their attempt to construct a *novus ordo seclorum*, a new order of the ages, continued beyond the Revolutionary era and continues yet today.

Chapter 6, "A People in Revolution," traces the impact of the Revolutionary call to arms on the various groups—male and female, white, black, and Native American—that made up American society and traces the exhilarating yet divisive efforts to fashion a new, republican political

order. Chapter 7, "Consolidating the Revolution," examines the critical years of the 1780s, when the new nation struggled to forge national unity following the Revolutionary War and to find security in a hostile Atlantic world. Out of that struggle and the continuing competition for political power in the states emerged a great debate over the new nation's government. That debate led to the replacement of the Articles of Confederation with a new constitution. Learning to live under the new constitution during the 1790s is the focus for Chapter 8, "Creating a Nation."

Chapter 9, "Society and Politics in the Early Republic," delves into the political developments, foreign relations, and Indian-white relations of the first three decades of the nineteenth century.

chapter 6

....

A People in Revolution

Among the Americans wounded and captured at the Battle of Bunker Hill in the spring of 1775 was Lieutenant William Scott of Peterborough, New Hampshire. Asked by his captors how he had come to be a rebel, "Long Bill" Scott replied:

> The case was this Sir! I lived in a Country Town; I was a Shoemaker, & got [my] living by my labor. When this rebellion came on, I saw some of my neighbors get into commission, who were no better than myself. . . . I was asked to enlist, as a private soldier. My ambition was too great for so low a rank. I offered to enlist upon having a lieutenant's commission, which was granted. I imagined my self now in a way of promotion. If I was killed in battle, there would be an end of me, but if my Captain was killed, I should rise in rank, & should still have a chance to rise higher. These Sir! were the only motives of my entering into the service. For as to the dispute between Great Britain & the colonies, I know nothing of it; neither am I capable of judging whether it is right or wrong.

People fought in America's Revolutionary War for many reasons: fear, ambition, principle. We have no way of knowing whether Long Bill Scott's motives were typical. Certainly many Americans knew more than he about the colonies' struggle with England. But many did not.

In the spring of 1775, the Revolutionary War had just begun. So, as it turned out, had Long Bill's adventures. When the British evacuated Boston a year later, they transported Scott as a prisoner to Halifax, Nova Scotia. After more than a year's captivity, he managed to escape and make his way home to fight once more. He was recaptured near New York City when its garrison fell to a surprise British assault. Again Scott escaped, this time by swimming the Hudson River at night with his sword tied around his neck and his watch pinned to his hat.

During the winter of 1777, he returned to New Hampshire to recruit his own militia company. It included two of his sons. In the fall, he joined in the defeat of Burgoyne's army near Saratoga, New York, and later took part in the fighting around Newport, Rhode Island. In early 1778, Scott's health broke, and he was permitted to resign from the army. After only a few months, however, he was at it again. During the last year of the war, he served as a volunteer on a navy frigate.

For seven years, the war held Scott in its harsh grasp. Scott's oldest son died of camp fever after six years of service. In 1777, Long Bill sold his New Hampshire farm to meet family expenses. The note he took in exchange turned into a scrap of paper when the dollar of 1777 became worth less than two cents by 1780. He lost a second farm, in Massachusetts, when his military pay depreciated similarly. After his wife died, he helplessly turned their younger children over to his oldest son and set off to beg a pension or job from the government. He was employed by the government as a surveyor when he died of a fever in 1796, near Sandusky in the Ohio country.

American independence and the Revolutionary War that accompanied it were not as hard on everyone as they were on Long Bill Scott, yet together they transformed the lives of countless Americans. The war lasted for seven years, longer than any other of America's wars until Vietnam nearly two centuries later. And unlike the nation's twentieth-century contests, it was fought on American soil, among the American people. It called men by the thousands from shops and fields, disrupted families, killed civilians, spread diseases, and made a shambles of the economy.

While carrying on this struggle for independence, the American people also mounted a political revolution of profound importance. Politics, government, and elections were transformed in keeping with republican principles and the rapidly changing circumstances of political life. What did republican liberty mean? How should governmental power be organized? How democratic should American politics be? These were among the questions with which the American people wrestled at the nation's beginning.

Faced with the twin pressures of war and revolution, people turned increasingly to politics to solve their problems and achieve their goals. As the tempo of political activity increased, they clashed repeatedly over such explosive issues as slavery, the separation of church and state, paper money and debt relief, the regulation of prices, and the toleration of political dissent. They argued as well over the design of new state constitutions and the shape of a new national government. Seldom has America's political agenda been fuller or more troubled.

The American Revolution dominated the lives of all who lived through it. But it had different consequences for men than for women, for black slaves than for their white masters, for Native Americans than for frontier settlers, for overseas merchants than for urban workers, for northern businessmen than for southern planters. Our understanding of the experience out of which our nation emerged must begin with the Revolutionary War, for liberty came at a high cost.

The War for American Independence

As we know, the war began in Massachusetts in 1775. Within a year, the center of fighting shifted to the middle states. After 1779, the South was the primary theater. Why did this geographic pattern develop, what was its significance, and why did the Americans win?

The War in the North

For a brief time following Lexington and Concord, British officials thought of launching forays out from Boston into the surrounding countryside. They soon reconsidered, however, for the growing size of the continental army and the absence of significant Loyalist strength in the New England region urged caution. Even more important, American artillery on the strategic Dorchester Heights overlooking the city made its continued occupation untenable. On March 7, 1776, the British commander, General William Howe, decided to evacuate.

For a half dozen years after Boston's evacuation, British ships prowled the New England coast, attacking American commerce, confiscating supplies, and destroying towns. Yet away from the coast there was little fighting at all. Most New Englanders had reason to be thankful for their good fortune.

After evacuating Boston, British officials established their military headquarters in New York City, which offered important advantages over Boston. New York was more centrally located, and its spacious harbor lay at the mouth of the Hudson River, the major water route northward into the interior. Control of New York would, in addition, ensure access to the abundant grain and livestock of the Middle Atlantic states. Finally, Loyalist sentiment ran wide and deep among the inhabitants of the city and its environs.

In the summer of 1776, Washington tried to challenge the British for control of Manhattan, but he was outmaneuvered and badly outnumbered. By late October, the city was firmly in British hands. It would remain so until the war's end.

In the fall of 1776, King George III instructed his military commanders in North America to make one last effort at reconciliation with the colonists. When the British demanded that Congress revoke the Declaration of Independence, however, the negotiations collapsed.

For the next two years, the war swept back and forth across New Jersey and Pennsylvania. Reinforced by German mercenaries hired in Europe, the British moved virtually at will. Neither the state militias nor the continental army offered serious opposition. At Trenton in December 1776 and again at Princeton the following month, Washington surprised the British and scored victories that prevented the Americans' collapse. For the rebels, however, survival remained the primary goal.

American efforts during the first year of the war to invade Canada and bring that British colony into the rebellion also fared badly. In November 1775, American forces under General Richard Montgomery had taken Montreal. But the subsequent assault against Quebec ended with almost 100 Americans killed or wounded and more than 300 taken prisoner. The American cause could not survive many such losses.

At New York, Washington had learned the painful lesson that his troops were no match for the British in frontal combat. Thus he adopted a strategy of caution and delay. He would harass the British but avoid major battles. For the remainder of the war, Washington's posture was primarily defensive and reactive.

As a consequence, the war's middle years turned into a deadly chase that neither side proved able to win. In September 1777, the British took Philadelphia, sending the Congress fleeing into the countryside, but then failed to press their advantage. In October, the Americans won a victory at Saratoga, New York, where

Europeans were fascinated by news of the colonies' rebellion against England. Here a French artist offers a dramatic portrayal of the fateful encounter at Lexington in April 1775.

General Burgoyne surrendered with 5,700 British soldiers.

Congress and the Articles of Confederation

As the war erupted around them, members of the Continental Congress turned anxiously to the task of creating a more permanent and effective national government. It was a daunting assignment, for the American people had little experience working together across state lines.

Prior to independence, the colonies had repeatedly quarreled over territory, settlers, control of the fur trade, and commercial advantage within the British Empire. The crisis with England, however, forced them together, and the Continental Congress was the first embodiment of that union. The First Continental Congress sent resolutions of protest to England and functioned as a temporary assembly.

The Second Continental Congress, however, meeting in May 1775, in the midst of a war crisis, began to exercise some of the most basic responsibilities of a sovereign government: raising an army and conducting diplomatic relations. Its powers, though, were unclear, its legitimacy uncertain. As independence and the prospects of an extended war loomed, pressure grew to establish the Congress on a more sound footing. On June 20, 1776, shortly before independence was declared, Congress appointed a committee, chaired by John Dickinson of Pennsylvania, to draw up a plan of perpetual union. It was called the Articles of Confederation. While the war erupted around them, the delegates struggled with the new and difficult problem of creating a permanent government. They clashed over whether to form a strong, consolidated regime or a loosely joined confederation of sovereign states.

The final "Articles of Confederation" represented a compromise. Article 9 gave the Congress sole authority to regulate foreign affairs, declare war, mediate boundary disputes between the states, manage the post office, and administer relations with Indians living outside state boundaries. The Articles also stipulated that the citizens of each state were to enjoy "the privileges and immunities" of the citizens of every other state. Embedded in that clause was the basis for national, as distinguished from state, citizenship.

At the same time, the Articles sharply limited what Congress could do and reserved broad governing powers to the states. For example, the Congress could not raise troops or levy taxes on its own authority. Perhaps most important, Article 2 stipulated that each of the states was to "retain its sovereignty, freedom and independence, and every power, jurisdiction, and right which is not by this confederation expressly delegated to the United States in Congress assembled."

Though the Congress sent the Articles to the states for approval in November 1777, they were not ratified until March 1781. This was primarily because of disputes over the control of lands west of the Appalachian Mountains between states such as Virginia, South Carolina, and New York, which had western claims tracing back to their colonial charters, and states such as Maryland and New Jersey, which had none.

For several years, ratification hung in the balance while politicians and speculators jockeyed for advantage. A breakthrough finally came in 1780, when New York and Virginia agreed to transfer their western lands to the Congress. In early 1781, Maryland became the final state to approve the Articles, and their ratification was assured.

The war did not wait during the struggle over ratification. The Congress did the best it could, using the unratified Articles as a guide. Events, however, quickly proved the inadequacy of the powers allotted to the Congress, since it could do little more than pass resolutions and ask the states for support. If they refused, as they frequently did, the Congress could only protest and urge cooperation. Its ability to function was further limited by the stipulation that each state's delegation cast but one vote. On a number of occasions, disagreements within state delegations prevented them from voting at all. That could paralyze the Congress, since most important decisions required a nine-state majority.

During the war, Washington repeatedly criticized the Congress for its failure to support the army adequately. In 1778, acknowledging its own ineffectiveness, the body temporarily granted Washington extraordinary powers and asked him to manage the war on his own.

The War Moves South

As the war in the North bogged down in a costly stalemate, British officials adopted another strategy: invasion and pacification of the South. Royal officials in the South encouraged the idea with the promise that thousands of Loyalists would rally to the British standard. The southern coastline with its numerous rivers, moreover, offered maximum advantage to British naval strength. Then there were the slaves, that vast but imponderable force in southern society. If they could be lured to the British side, the balance might tip in Britain's favor. Persuaded by these arguments, British policymakers made the southern states the primary theater of military operations during the final years of the war.

Georgia—small, isolated, and largely defenseless—was the initial target. In December 1778, the British took Savannah, Georgia's major port, and on May 12, 1780, they occupied Charleston, South Carolina, after a month's siege. At a cost of only 225 casualties, the British captured the entire 5,400-man American garrison. It was the costliest American defeat of the war. The British then quickly extended their control north and south along the Carolina coast.

Their successes, however, proved deceptive, for British officers quickly learned the difficulty of extending their control into the interior. The distances were too large, the problems of supply too great, the reliability of Loyalist troops too problematic, and support for the Revolutionary cause among the people too strong.

Military Operations in the North, 1776-1780

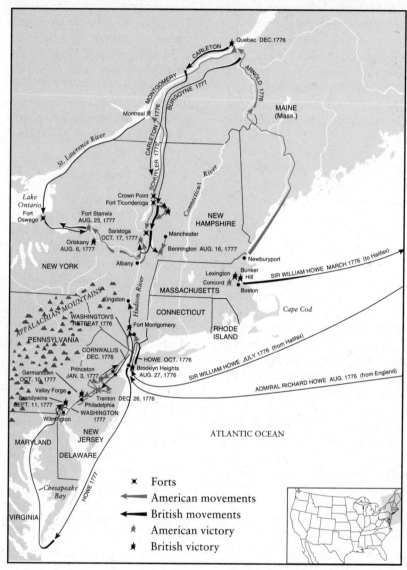

In October 1780, Washington sent Nathanael Greene south to lead the continental forces, for Greene knew the region and the kind of war that had to be fought. Dividing his army into small, mobile bands, he employed what today would be called guerrilla tactics, harassing the British and their Loyalist allies at every op-portunity, striking by surprise and then disap-pearing into the interior. Bands of private ma-rauders, roving the land and seizing advantage from the war's confusion, compounded the chaos.

In time, the tide began to turn. At Cowpens, South Carolina, in early 1781, American troops

Western Land Claims Ceded by the States, 1782–1802

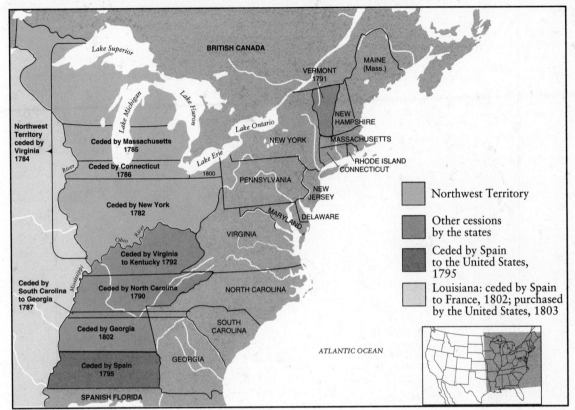

under General Daniel Morgan won a decisive victory. In April 1781, convinced that British authority could not be restored in the Carolinas while Virginia remained a supply and staging area for the rebels, British Commander Cornwallis moved north out of the Carolinas. With a force of 7,500, he raided deep into Virginia. In June, his forces sent Governor Jefferson and the Virginia legislature fleeing from Charlottesville into the mountains. But again Cornwallis had to turn toward the coast for protection and resupply. His goal was Yorktown, where he arrived on August 1.

So long as the British fleet controlled the waters of Chesapeake Bay, his position was secure. That advantage, however, did not last. In 1778, the French government, still smarting from its

defeat by England in the Seven Years' War and buoyed by the American victory at Saratoga in 1777, had signed a treaty of alliance with the American Congress, promising to send its naval forces into the war. On August 30, 1781, the French admiral Comte de Grasse arrived off Yorktown. Reinforced by a second French squadron from the North, de Grasse established naval superiority in the region. Cut off from the sea and caught on a peninsula between the York and James rivers by 17,000 French and American troops, Cornwallis found that his fate was sealed. On October 17, 1781, he opened negotiations for surrender.

In Philadelphia, upon hearing of the British surrender, citizens poured into the streets to celebrate while the Congress assembled for a solemn

Military Operations in the South, 1778–1781

ceremony of thanksgiving. Sporadic fighting continued for another several months; not until November 1782 were the preliminary articles of peace signed. But everyone knew after Yorktown that the war was over. Americans had won their independence.

Native Americans in the Revolution

The Revolutionary War involved more than Englishmen and colonists, for it drew in countless Native Americans as well. It could hardly have been otherwise, for the lives of all three peoples had been intimately connected since the first white settlements more than a century and a half before.

By the time of the Revolution, the coastal tribes were mostly gone, victims of white settlement and the ravages of European diseases. Between the Appalachian Mountains and the Mississippi River, however, powerful tribes remained. The Iroquois Six Nations, formed into a confederation numbering 15,000 people, controlled the area from Albany, New York, to the

Ohio country and dominated the "western" tribes of the Ohio valley—the Shawnee, Delaware, Wyandotte, and Miami. In the Southeast, five tribes—the Choctaw, Chickasaw, Seminole, Creek, and Cherokee, together numbering 60,000 people—occupied the interior.

When the Revolutionary War began, British and American officials urged neutrality on the Indians. But by the spring of 1776, both sides were actively seeking Indian alliances. Recognizing their immense stake in the Anglo-colonial conflict, Native Americans up and down the interior debated their options. Alarmed by the westward advance of white settlement and eager to take advantage of the colonists' troubles, a band of Cherokee, led by the warrior Dragging Canoe, launched a series of raids in July 1776

against white settlements in what is today eastern Tennessee. In a quick and devastating response, the Virginia and Carolina militias laid waste a group of Cherokee towns.

During the winter of 1780–1781, American militias again attacked the Cherokees. Though the Cherokees raided sporadically throughout the war, they never again mounted a sustained military effort against the patriots. Seeing what had become of their neighbors, the Creek stayed aloof. Their time for resistance would come decades later, when white settlers began to push aggressively onto their lands.

In the Ohio country—the home of the Shawnee, Delaware, Wyandotte, and Miami—white encroachment had begun several decades before the Revolution, with explorers such as

Indian Battles and the War in the West, 1775-1783

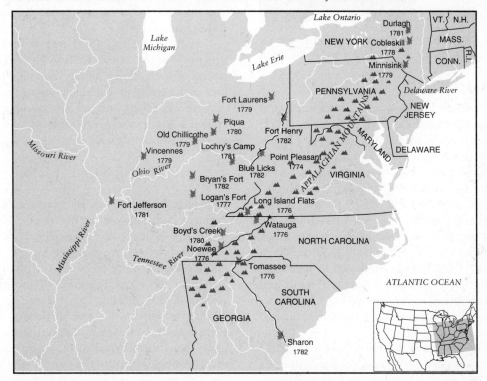

Though most battles were fought along the coastal plain, the British and their Indian allies opened a second front far to the west.

Mohawk chief Joseph Brant (Tayadaneega) played a major role in the Iroquois's decision to enter the war on the side of Britain.

Daniel Boone. The Revolution intensified conflict over control of the land. In February 1778, George Rogers Clark led a ragtag body of Kentuckians through icy rivers and across 180 miles of forbidding terrain to attack an English fort at Vincennes, in present-day Indiana. Though outnumbered nearly four to one by the 500 British regulars and their Indian allies, Clark fooled the British into believing that his force was much larger, and the fort's commander surrendered without a shot. Indians continued to fight sporadically for several years against English and American forces in the region, but Clark's victory tipped the balance in the western theater of the war.

To the northeast, a similar but more deadly scenario unfolded. A council of representatives of the Iroquois Six Nations, meeting at Albany, New York, at first opted for neutrality, but as the war spread and American troops raided deep into Mohawk territory west of Albany in the summer of 1777, most of the Iroquois abandoned neutrality and joined the struggle against the Americans. They did so at the urging of Joseph Brant, a Mohawk warrior who had visited England several years before and argued England's value as an ally against American expansion.

It was a fateful decision for Indians and whites alike. Over the next several years, the Iroquois and their English allies devastated large areas in central New York and Pennsylvania. The Americans' revenge came swiftly. During the summer of 1779, General John Sullivan led a series of raids into Iroquois country, burning the Iroquois villages, killing men, women, and children, and destroying fields of corn. The Iroquois recovered sufficiently to conduct punishing counter-raids during the final years of the war, but their losses in human lives and property were great.

At the peace talks that ended the Revolutionary War, the British entirely ignored the interests of their Indian allies. They received neither compensation for their losses nor any guarantees of their land, for the boundary of the United States was set far to the west, at the Mississippi River.

Negotiating Peace

In September 1781, formal peace negotiations began in Paris between the British commissioner and the American emissaries, Benjamin Franklin, John Adams, and John Jay. The negotiations were complicated by the fact that several European countries, seeking opportunity to weaken Great Britain, had become involved. France had entered the war in February 1778. Eight months later, Spain declared war on England, though it declined to recognize American independence. Between 1780 and 1782, Russia, the Netherlands, and six other European countries joined in a League of Armed Neutrality aimed at protecting their maritime trade against British efforts to control it. America's Revolutionary War had quickly become internationalized.

Dependent on French economic and military support, the Congress instructed the American commissioners to follow the advice of Vergennes, the French foreign minister. As the treaty talks began, the Americans learned to their distress that Vergennes was prepared to let the exhausting war continue in order to weaken England further and tighten America's dependence on France.

In the end, the American commissioners ignored their instructions and, without a word to Vergennes, arranged a provisional peace agreement with the British emissaries. In the Treaty of Paris, signed in September 1783, England agreed to recognize American independence. Moreover, Britain promised that U.S. fishermen would have the "right" to fish the waters off Newfoundland and that British forces would evacuate American territory "with all convenient speed" once hostilities had ceased. In return, the Congress agreed to recommend that the states restore the rights and property of the Loyalists. Both sides agreed that prewar debts owed the citizens of one country by the citizens of the other would remain valid. Each of these issues would trouble Anglo-American relations in the decades ahead, but for the moment it seemed a splendid outcome to a long and difficult struggle.

The Ingredients of Victory

How were the weak and disunited American states able to defeat Great Britain, the most powerful nation in the Atlantic world? Certainly the Dutch and French loans, war supplies, and military forces were crucially important. More decisive, though, was the American people's determination not to submit. Often the Americans were disorganized and uncooperative. As the war progressed, however, the people's estrangement from England and their commitment to the "glo-

rious cause" increased. To subdue the colonies, England would have had to occupy the entire eastern third of the continent, and that it could not do.

The American victory also owed much to the administrative and organizational talents of Washington. Against massive odds, he held the continental army together, often by the sheer force of his will. Had he failed, the Americans could not possibly have defeated the British.

In the end, however, it is as accurate to say that Britain lost the war as that the United States won it. With vast economic and military resources, Britain enjoyed clear military superiority over the American states and, until the closing months of the contest, naval superiority as well.

Britain had difficulty, however, extending its command structures and supply routes across several thousand miles of ocean. Because information flowed erratically back and forth across the water, strategic decisions made in London were often based on faulty or outdated intelligence. Given the difficulties of supply over such distances, British troops often had to live off the land. This reduced their mobility and antagonized the Americans whose crops and animals they commandeered. Faced with these circumstances, British leaders were often overly cautious.

British commanders also generally failed to adapt their battlefield tactics to the realities of the American war. They continued to fight in the European style, during specified times of the year and using set formations of troops deployed in formal battlefield maneuvers. Much of the American terrain, however, was rough and wooded and thus better suited to the use of smaller units and irregular troops. Washington and Greene were more flexible, often employing a patient strategy of raiding, harassment, and strategic retreat. Over time the costs of continuing the war became greater than the British government could bear. As a much later American war in Vietnam would also reveal, a guerrilla force can win if it does not lose; a regular army loses if it does not consistently win.

The Experience of War

In terms of loss of life and destruction of property, the Revolutionary War pales by comparison with America's more recent wars. Yet modern comparisons are misleading, for the War for American Independence was terrifying to the people caught up in it and destructive of lives and property.

Recruiting an Army

Estimates vary, but on the American side as many as 250,000 men may at one time or another have borne arms. That would amount to about one out of every two or three adult males.

Tens of thousands served in the state militias. At the time of independence, however, the militia in most of the states was not an effective fighting force. This was especially true in the South, where Nathanael Greene complained that the men came "from home with all the tender feelings of domestic life" and were not "sufficiently fortified . . . to stand the shocking scenes of war, to march over dead men, [or] to hear without concern the groans of the wounded."

The militia did serve as a convenient recruiting system. Given its grounding in local community life, it also served to secure people's commitment to the Revolutionary cause. What better way to separate the Patriots (those who supported the cause of independence) from the Loyalists (those who supported England) than by mustering the local militia company and seeing who turned out?

During the first year of the war, when enthusiasm ran high, men of all ranks volunteered to fight the British. But as the war progressed, it gradually became a battle by conscripts. Eventually it was transformed, as wars so often are, into a poor man's fight. Middle- and upper-class men increasingly hired substitutes to replace them, and communities filled their militia quotas with strangers lured by the promise of enlistment bonuses. This social transformation was even more evident in the continental army, where terms were longer, discipline was stiffer, and battlefields were more distant from the soldiers' homes.

For the poor and the jobless, whose ranks the war rapidly expanded, bonus payments and the promise of board and keep proved attractive. But often the bonuses failed to materialize, and pay was long overdue. Moreover, life in the camps was harsh, and soldiers frequently heard from their wives about their families' distress at home. Faced with such trials, soldiers often became disgruntled and insubordinate. As the war dragged on, Washington imposed harsher discipline on the continental troops in an effort to hold them in line.

Throughout the war, soldiers suffered from severe shortages of supplies. At Valley Forge during the terrible winter of 1777–1778, men hobbled about without shoes or coats. "I am sick, discontented, and out of humour," declared one despairing soul. "Poor food, hard lodging, cold weather, fatigue, nasty cloathes, nasty cookery, vomit half my time, smoked out of my senses. The Devil's in't, I can't Endure it. Why are we sent here to starve and freeze?"

The states possessed food and clothing enough but were often reluctant to strip their own people of wagons and livestock, blankets and shoes for use elsewhere. Moreover, mismanagement and difficulties in transportation stood in the way. Wagon transport was slow and costly, and the presence of the British fleet made water transportation along the coast perilous. Though many individuals served honorably as supply officers, others took advantage of the army's distress. Washington commented bitterly on the "speculators, various tribes of money makers, and stock-jobbers of all denominations"

The American rifleman, even as idealized in this engraving, lacked the pomp and formality—and often the discipline—of the British soldier.

whose "avarice and thirst for gain" threatened the country's ruin.

The Casualties of Combat

The death that soldiers dispensed to one another on the battlefield was intensely personal. Because the effective range of muskets was little more than 100 yards, combat was typically at close quarters. According to eighteenth-century military conventions, armies formed on the battlefield in ranks and fired in unison. After massed volleys, the lines often closed for hand-to-hand combat with knives and bayonets. The partisan warfare in the South, with its emphasis on ambush and small group actions, shocked British officers used to more distanced and dispassionate styles of warfare. One attributed to the American troops "a sort of implacable ardor and revenge."

The Americans' fervor in battle may be explained by the fact that this was in part a civil war. As many as 50,000 colonists fought for the king and engaged in some of the war's most bitter encounters. They figured importantly in Burgoyne's invasion from Canada and in the attacks on Savannah and Charleston. Benedict Arnold led a force of Loyalists on raids through the Connecticut and James river valleys, and Loyalist militia joined Indian allies in destructive sweeps through the Carolina backcountry. Throughout America, communities and families were divided against one another. The war's violent temper reflected this civil conflict.

Moreover, the war was fought in the midst of American society. Soldiers often found themselves fighting for the survival of their family and community. Finally, Americans believed fervently in the Revolutionary cause. The struggle, as they understood it, was for their own liberty. In such a crusade, against such a foe, nothing was to be spared that might bring victory.

Medical treatment, whether for wounds or diseases such as smallpox, dysentery, and typhus that raged through the camps, did little to help. Casualties poured into hospitals, overcrowding them beyond capacity. Dr. Jonathan Potts, the attending physician at Fort George in New York, reported that "we have at present upwards of one thousand sick crowded into sheds & labouring under the various and cruel disorders of dysentaries, bilious putrid fevers and the effects of a confluent smallpox: to attend to this large number we have four seniors and four mates, exclusive of myself."

Surgeons, operating without anesthetics and

with the crudest of instruments, as readily threatened life as preserved it. Doctoring consisted mostly of bleeding, blistering, inducing vomiting, and administering laxatives. Mercury, a highly toxic chemical, was a commonly administered drug.

How many soldiers actually died we do not know, but the most conservative estimate runs to more than 25,000, a higher percentage of the total population than for any other American conflict except the Civil War. About 12 percent of American soldiers died of wounds or disease, a rate virtually the equivalent of the Civil War and higher than any of America's other conflicts.

Civilians and the War

Noncombatants also suffered, most of all in the densely settled areas along the coast, where England focused its military efforts. At one time or another, British troops occupied every major port—Boston, New York, Philadelphia, Charleston, and Savannah. The resulting disruptions of urban life were profound.

The chaos in New York was typical. In September 1776, a fire consumed 500 houses, nearly a quarter of the city's dwellings. About half the town's inhabitants fled when the British occupation began and were replaced by an almost equal number of Loyalists who streamed in from the surrounding countryside. Ten thousand British and German troops added to the crowding. The growing numbers of poor erected makeshift shelters of sailcloth and timbers.

In Philadelphia, the occupation was shorter and the disruptions were less severe, but the shock of invasion was no less real. Elizabeth Drinker, living alone after local Patriots had exiled her Quaker husband, found herself the unwilling landlady of a British officer, Major Crammond, and his friends. Constantly anxious, she confided to her journal that "I often feel afraid to go to Bed." During the occupation, British soldiers frequently took what they wanted, tore down fences for their campfires,

and confiscated food to supplement their own tedious fare. Even the Loyalists commented on the "dreadful consequences" of occupation.

Along the entire coastal plain, British landing parties descended without warning to capture supplies or terrorize inhabitants. In 1780 and 1781, the British mounted a sustained attack along the Connecticut coast. Over 200 buildings in Fairfield were burned, and much of nearby Norwalk was destroyed.

The southern coast, with its broad rivers, was even more vulnerable. In December 1780, Benedict Arnold ravaged the James River valley, uprooting tobacco, confiscating slaves, and creating panic among the white population. Similar devastation befell the coasts of Georgia and the Carolinas. Such punishing attacks sent civilians fleeing into the interior. During the first years of the war, the port cities lost nearly half their population, while inland communities strained to cope with the thousands of migrants who streamed into them.

Not all the traffic was inland, away from the coast. In New York, Pennsylvania, Virginia, and the Carolinas, numerous frontier settlements collapsed in the face of British and Indian assaults. By 1783, the white population along the Mohawk River west of Albany, New York, had declined from 10,000 to 3,500. According to one observer, after nearly five years of warfare in Tryon County, 12,000 farms had been abandoned, 700 buildings burned, hundreds of thousands of bushels of grain destroyed, nearly 400 women widowed, and perhaps 2,000 children orphaned.

Wherever the armies went, they generated a swirl of refugees, who spread vivid tales of the war. This refugee traffic, added to the constant movement of soldiers back and forth between army and civilian life, brought the war home even to people who did not experience it at first hand. As they moved across the countryside, the armies lived off the land, commandeering the supplies they needed. During the desperate winter of 1777–1778, in an effort to protect the sur-

In September 1776, as American troops fought unsuccessfully for control of New York, nearly a quarter of the city was destroyed by fire. Not until the war ended did reconstruction and cleanup of the ruins begin.

rounding population, Washington issued an order prohibiting his troops from roaming more than a half mile from camp. In New Jersey, Britain's German mercenaries generated special fears among the citizenry. The Patriot press was filled with lurid stories of attacks on American civilians, especially women.

The Loyalists

No Americans suffered greater losses than those who remained loyal to the Crown. On September 8, 1783, Thomas Danforth, formerly a lawyer from Cambridge, Massachusetts, appeared in London before the King's Commission of Enquiry into the Losses and Services of the American Loyalists. Danforth was there to seek compensation for losses he had suffered at the

hands of the American Revolutionaries. He explained that

> ... now he finds himself near his fortieth year, banished under pain of death, to a distant country, where he has not the most remote family connection ... cut off from his profession—from every hope of importance in life, and in a great degree from social enjoyments.

The commission's response is unknown, but few of the several thousand Loyalists who appeared before it were reimbursed for more than one-third of their losses.

Though no count of the colonists who remained loyal to England can be exact, as many as 80,000 men, women, and children may have departed from the new nation, while several hundred thousand more remained in the United

States. These are substantial numbers when set against the total American population, black and white, of about 2.5 million. The incidence of loyalism differed dramatically from region to region. There were fewest Loyalists in New England and most in and around New York City, where British authority was most stable.

Why did so many Americans remain loyal, often at the cost of personal danger and loss? Customs officers, members of the governors' councils, and Anglican clergymen—all appointed to office in the King's name—often remained with the Crown. Loyalism was common as well among groups dependent on British authority— for example, settlers on the Carolina frontier who believed themselves mistreated by the planter elite along the coast; ethnic minorities, such as the Germans in the middle states, who feared domination by the Anglo-American majority; or tenants on some of the large estates along the Hudson River, who had struggled for years with their landlords over the terms of their leaseholds.

For many Loyalists, the prospect of confronting English military power proved sufficiently daunting. Others doubted the ability of a new, weak nation to survive in an Atlantic world dominated by competing empires, even if independence could be won.

William Eddis wondered what kind of society independence would bring when Revolutionary crowds showed no respect for the rights of Loyalist dissenters such as he. "If I differ in opinion from the multitude," he asked, "must I therefore be deprived of my character, and the confidence of my fellow-citizens; when in every station of life I discharge my duty with fidelity and honour?"

Whatever their motives, the Loyalists believed themselves advocates of reason and the rule of law in the midst of revolutionary passion. Tens of thousands of Americans believed strongly enough in their position to sacrifice home, community, and personal safety on its behalf.

Many who faced exile successfully established new lives in other parts of the empire. The majority settled in the Maritime Provinces of Canada. But even under the best of circumstances, forced resettlement was traumatic.

Loyalists came from all social classes but were most numerous among the upper and middle ranks of society, where individuals were most likely to have direct political and social connections with English officials and to fear the social consequences of revolution. Given their adherence to monarchical government and its values of hierarchy and subordination, their loss weakened the forces of social conservatism in America and facilitated the progress of revolutionary reform.

African-Americans and the Revolutionary War

American blacks were deeply involved in the Revolution. In fact, the conflict provoked the largest slave rebellion in American history prior to the Civil War. Once the war was under way, blacks found a variety of ways to turn events to their own advantage. For some, this meant applying Revolutionary principles to their own lives and calling for their personal freedom. For others, it meant seeking liberty behind English lines or in the continent's interior.

During the pre-Revolutionary decade, as their white masters talked excitedly about liberty, increasing numbers of black Americans questioned their own oppression. In the North, some slaves petitioned legislatures to set them free. In the South, pockets of insurrection appeared. In 1765, more than 100 South Carolina slaves fled to the interior, where they tried to establish a colony of their own. The next year, slaves paraded through the streets of Charleston, chanting, "Liberty, liberty!"

In November 1775, Lord Dunmore issued a proclamation offering freedom to all Virginia slaves and servants, "able and willing to bear arms," who would leave their masters and join the British forces in Norfolk. Within weeks, 500 to 600 slaves had responded. Among them was

Thomas Peters, from Wilmington, North Carolina.

Kidnapped from the Yoruba tribe in what is now Nigeria and brought to America by a French slave trader, Peters had been first purchased in Louisiana about 1760. He resisted enslavement so fiercely that his master sold him into the English colonies. By 1770, Peters belonged to William Campbell, an immigrant Scots planter on North Carolina's Cape Fear River, where he toiled while the storm brewed between England and the colonies. Four months after Dunmore issued his dramatic proclamation, Thomas Peters escaped and joined the British-officered Black Pioneers.

Many blacks saw in England the promise of freedom, not tyranny. From the Virginia slaves who responded to Dunmore's proclamation, a regiment of black soldiers was formed and marched into battle, their chests covered with sashes on which was emblazoned "Liberty to Slaves." At the war's end, several thousand former slaves were evacuated with the British to Nova Scotia, where they established their own settlements. Their reception by the white inhabitants there, however, was generally hostile. By the end of the century, most had left Canada to found the free black colony of Sierra Leone on the west coast of Africa. Thomas Peters was a leader among them.

Many of the slaves who fled behind English lines never won their freedom. In keeping with the terms of the peace treaty, hundreds were returned to their American owners. Several thousand others were transported to the West Indies and the harsher slavery of the sugar plantations.

Other blacks took advantage of the war's confusion to drift away in pursuit of a new life. Some sought refuge among the Indians. Some made their way north, following rumors that slavery had been abolished there.

Fewer blacks fought on the American side than on England's, because the Americans were not eager to see blacks armed. Of the blacks who served the Patriot cause, many received the freedom they were promised. The patriotism of untold others, however, went unrewarded.

THE FERMENT OF REVOLUTIONARY POLITICS

The Revolution altered people's lives in countless ways that reached beyond the sights and sounds of battle. No areas of American life were more powerfully changed than politics and government. What were the basic principles of the new republican ideology? How would the constitutions being written in each of the states balance the need for order against competing needs for democratic openness and accountability? Who among the American people would have political voice in revolutionary politics, and who would be excluded? These were some of the questions with which the revolutionaries wrestled.

Other explosive issues threatened to overwhelm Congress and the states—controlling the Loyalist "menace," deciding whether to abolish or retain slavery, arguing over religious freedom and the separation of church and state, apportioning taxes, regulating prices, issuing paper money and providing debt relief. Seldom has American politics been more heated, seldom has it struggled with a more daunting agenda, and seldom has it proved more creative than during the years of the nation's founding.

Mobilizing the People

Under the pressure of Revolutionary events, politics absorbed people's energies as never before. Newspapers multiplied in number, and between 1750 and 1783, more than 1,500 pamphlets joined the debate. Declared one contemporary in amazement, "Never ... were [political pamphlets] ... so cheap, so universally diffused, so easy of access." Pulpits rocked with political exhortations as well. Religion and politics had never been sharply separated in colonial America, but the Revolution drew them more tightly together. Some believed that God intended America as the place of Christ's Second Coming and that independence foretold that glorious day. Others thought of America as a New Israel, a covenanted people specially chosen by God to preserve liberty in a threatening world.

The belief that God sanctioned their Revolution strengthened American resolve. It also encouraged Americans to equate national interest with divine intent and thus offered convenient justification for whatever they believed necessary to do. This was not the last time Americans would make that dangerous equation.

Belief in the momentous importance of what they were doing intensified politics as well. In a letter from Philadelphia to his wife, Abigail, John Adams exalted independence as "the greatest question . . . which ever was debated in America."

As independence was declared, people in towns and hamlets throughout the land raised toasts to the great event: "Liberty to those who have the spirit to preserve it." "May the Crowns of Tyrants be crowns of thorns." They called themselves the Patriots of '76, a generation of Americans fused together by the searing experience of rebellion, war, and nation building and persuaded that they held in their hands the future of human liberty. Small wonder that they took politics so seriously.

The most dramatic evidence of America's expanding Revolutionary politics appeared in the array of extralegal committees and spontaneous gatherings that erupted across the states during the 1770s and 1780s. Electoral politics simply could not contain the political energies or resolve the political conflicts generated by the Revolution, and so people devised more direct forms of political action. Artisans, workingmen, and farmers, people formerly on the margins of political life, took seriously the talk about liberty, natural rights, and government by consent and applied those principles to their own lives.

The result was a growing demand for access to the political process. In addition, Patriot leaders, recognizing the need for popular support in the desperate struggle against England, organized committees of safety and correspondence to stimulate popular participation.

A Republican Ideology

Throughout history, as people have moved from colonial subordination to independence, they have struggled to define themselves as a free and separate nation. It was no different with the Revolutionary generation. No longer English, they were now Americans; but what exactly did that mean? "Our style and manner of thinking," observed Thomas Paine in amazement, "have undergone a revolution. . . . We see with other eyes, we hear with other ears, and think with other thoughts than those we formerly used." The ideology of revolutionary republicanism, pieced together from English political thought, theories of the Enlightenment, and people's own experience, constituted a revolution in thought.

The rejection of monarchy was one basic component of America's new republican faith. "The word *republic*," explained Paine, "means the public good of the whole, in contradistinction to the despotic form which makes the good of the sovereign, or of one man, the only object of government." It was Paine's unsparing rejection of monarchy that made his pamphlet *Common Sense* so radical. "Of more worth is one honest man to society, and in the sight of God," he scoffed, "than all the crowned ruffians that ever lived."

Limiting governmental power on behalf of preserving individual liberty was another basic postulate of republican belief. Those who wielded power, went the common refrain, inevitably used it for their own advantage rather than for the general good. It followed then that ways had to be found of controlling governmental power and maximizing liberty.

Given the dangers of governmental power,

how could political order be maintained? The Revolutionary generation offered an extraordinary answer to that question. Order was not to be imposed from above but would flow upward from the self-regulated behavior of the people, especially from their willingness to put the public good ahead of their own interests. The term for this extraordinary self-denial was "public virtue." It formed the core of republican ideology.

If public virtue provided the essential strength of republican politics, "faction," that is, organized self-interest, constituted its most dangerous enemy. Faction, or "party" as it was sometimes called, was the "mortal disease under which popular governments have everywhere perished." Given a republic's openness, factional conflict could easily spin out of control. It thus followed that republics could survive only in small territories, where society was homogeneous and where serious economic or religious conflicts were absent. This fear of party faction did not preclude political conflict in Revolutionary America, but it raised the ideological stakes and inclined people to question the basic motives of their political opponents.

Few Patriots were so naive as to believe that the American people were altogether virtuous. During the first years of independence, when Revolutionary enthusiasm ran high, however, many believed that public virtue was sufficiently widespread to support republican government. More than that, the American people would learn virtue by its practice. It was an extraordinarily hopeful but risk-filled undertaking.

The principle of political equality was another controversial touchstone of republicanism. Virtually everyone agreed that republican governments must be grounded in popular consent, that elections should be frequent, and that citizens must be vigilant in defense of their liberties. There, however, agreement often ended.

Some Americans took the principle of political equality literally, arguing that all citizens should have equal voice and that public office should be open to all. This position was argued most forcefully by individuals often excluded from the political process—farmers and tenants in the interior, workers and artisans in the coastal cities. More cautious citizens talked about the need for order as well as liberty and argued that stable republics depended on leadership by an "aristocracy of talent"—men of ability, wisdom, and experience. Merchants, planters, and large commercial farmers saw no need to alter radically the existing distribution of political power. These differences of principle and self-interest generated much of the conflict that lay at the heart of revolutionary politics.

Creating Republican Governments

With their English ties dissolved, the Revolutionaries set about the difficult task of creating new state governments. Connecticut and Rhode Island continued under their colonial charters, simply deleting all references to the British Crown. The other 11 states, however, set their charters aside and started anew. Within two years, all but Massachusetts had completed the task. By 1780, it had done so as well.

It was hard going, for the American people had no experience with government making on such a scale; they were embroiled in war, and they were sharply divided over the kind of government they wished to create.

In most states, the provincial congresses, extralegal successors to the defunct colonial assemblies, wrote the first constitutions. As the process went along, however, people became increasingly uneasy. Constitutions were intended to define and control government, but if governmental bodies wrote the documents, they could change them as well. If they could do that, what would guarantee against the abuse of governmental power? Some way had to be found of grounding the constitutions directly in the people's sovereign will.

Massachusetts was the first state to perfect

Occupational Composition of Several State Assemblies in the 1780s

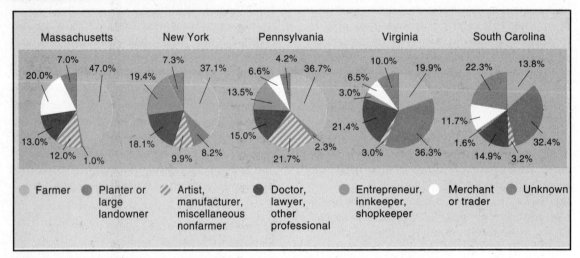

Membership in the Revolutionary assemblies reflected differences in the economies and societies of the various states. Those differences often generated political conflict throughout the Revolutionary era.
Source: Main, Political Parties Before the Constitution, *1973.*

the new procedures. In 1779, its citizens formed a special convention for the sole purpose of preparing a new constitution. The convention did its work, and the resulting constitution was returned to the people for ratification.

Through trial and argumentation, the Revolutionary generation worked out a practical understanding of what a constitution was and how it should be developed. In the process, it established some of the most basic doctrines of American constitutionalism: that sovereignty resides in the people; that written constitutions, produced by specially elected conventions and then ratified by the people, embody their sovereign will; and that government functions within constitutional limits. No doctrines have been more important to the preservation of American liberty.

The new state constitutions redefined American government in fundamental and lasting ways. For one thing, the new governments were considerably more democratic than the colonial

regimes had been. Most officials were now elected, many of them annually rather than every two or three years as before.

Most of the new constitutions also sharply reduced the governors' powers and increased the powers of the assemblies. Above all, the documents sharply reduced the governors' powers of appointment. "He who has the giving of . . . places in the government," went the common refrain, "will always be master."

The assemblies absorbed most of the powers stripped from the governors. Not only were the assemblies more powerful, but they were larger and more representative as well. Reflecting the spirit of republican reform as well as the demands of farmers and artisans for a larger voice in public affairs, the assemblies grew in size by half or more.

At the same time, constitution making generated heated conflicts over political principles and the competition for political power. Two examples, Pennsylvania and Massachusetts, illustrate how controversial the process was and how different the outcomes could be.

In Pennsylvania, a coalition of western farmers, Philadelphia artisans and shopkeepers, and radical leaders such as Thomas Paine, Timothy Matlack, and Thomas Young pushed through the most democratic state constitution of all. Drafted in 1776, during the most intense period of republican reform, it rejected the familiar English model of two legislative houses and an independent executive. Instead, the constitution provided for a single, all-powerful legislative house, its members annually elected, its debates open to the public. There was to be no governor. Legislative committees would assume executive duties. A truly radical assumption underlay this design: that only the "common interest of society" and not "separate and jarring private interests" should be represented in public affairs. Property-holding requirements for public office were abolished, and the franchise was opened to every male over 21 who paid taxes. The bill of rights introducing the document guaranteed every citizen religious freedom, trial by jury, and freedom of speech.

The most radical proposal of all called for the redistribution of property within the state, a step described as essential to preserving republican liberty. This was narrowly defeated.

Debate over the constitution divided the state deeply. Men of wealth led the opposition, but in 1776, the radicals had their way. The Pennsylvania constitution—together with its counterparts in Vermont and Georgia—represented the most radical thrust of Revolutionary republicanism. Its guiding principle, declared Thomas Young, was that "the people at large [are] the true proprietors of governmental power." The struggle for control of the Revolution in Pennsylvania was not over, for in 1790 a new and more moderate constitution would be approved. For the moment, however, the lines of political power had been decisively redrawn.

In Massachusetts, constitution making followed a more cautious course. There, the disruptions of the war were less severe and the continuity of political leadership was much greater. The main architect of the constitution, John Adams, readily admitted that the new government must be firmly grounded in the people. No principle was more fundamental to America's new republican faith. Yet Adams saw danger in reckless experimentation. A balance between two legislative houses and an independent executive was essential to preserving liberty, he believed, for "power must be opposed to power, force to force, ... interest to interest, ... and passion to passion."

Believing that society was inescapably divided between "democratic" and "aristocratic" forces, he sought to isolate them in separate legislative houses where they could guard against each other. The lower house, he explained, should be "an exact portrait, in miniature," of the people; it should "think, feel, act, and reason" like them. The senate, by contrast, should constitute a "natural aristocracy" of wealth, talent, and good sense intended to balance the popular excesses of the assembly and look after the interests of property. Following Adams's advice, the Massachusetts convention provided for a popular, annually elected assembly and a senate based on wealth, its members apportioned according to the amount of taxes paid in special senatorial districts. The constitution also provided for an independent governor with the power to veto legislation, make appointments, serve as commander in chief of the militia, and oversee state expenditures.

When the convention sent the document to the town meetings for approval in March 1779, farmers as well as artisans and working people attacked it as "aristocratic," too much like the old colonial regime. But when the convention reconvened in July 1779, it declared the constitution ratified. It went into effect the following year.

Two states, two very different outcomes to the politics of constitution making.

Women and the Limits of Republican Citizenship

Revolutionary leaders defined the boundaries of republican politics too narrowly to include all white Americans. Only people with property could vote in state elections. Most states reduced property requirements for the franchise, but nowhere were they abolished altogether.

Even more significant, republican citizenship did not encompass women. Except on scattered occasions, women had neither voted nor held public office during the colonial period. Nor, with rare exceptions, did they do so in Revolutionary America. The New Jersey constitution of 1776 opened the franchise to property-owning women, but the experiment did not last long. Declared one political leader: "It is evident that women, generally, are neither by nature, nor habit, nor education . . . fitted to perform this duty with credit to themselves, or advantage to the public." In 1807, the New Jersey assembly passed a bill specifically disenfranchising women. Its author, John Condict, had several years earlier narrowly escaped defeat when a number of women voted for his opponent. In no other state did women even temporarily secure the vote.

Most women did not press for political equality, for the idea flew in the face of long-standing social convention, and its advocacy often exposed a person to public ridicule. Some women did make the case, most often with one another or their husbands. "I cannot say, that I think you are very generous to the ladies," Abigail Adams chided her husband, John. "For whilst you are proclaiming peace and good will to men, emancipating all nations, you insist upon retaining an absolute power over all wives."

Prior to independence, most women had accepted the principle that political debate fell outside the feminine sphere, but the Revolution changed that. Women felt the urgency of the Revolutionary crisis as much as men. "How shall I impose a silence upon myself," wondered Anne Emlen in 1777, "when the subject is so very interesting, so much engrossing conversation—& what every member of the community is more or less concerned in?" With increasing frequency, women wrote and spoke to one another about public events, especially as they affected their own lives.

As the war progressed, increasing numbers of women ventured their opinions publicly. A few, such as Esther DeBerdt Reed of Philadelphia, published essays explaining women's urgent need to contribute to the Patriot cause. In her 1780 broadside, "The Sentiments of an American Woman," she called on women to renounce "vain ornament" as they had earlier renounced tea and English finery. The money no longer spent on clothing and hairstyles would be "the offering of the Ladies" to Washington's army. In Philadelphia, women responded by collecting $300,000 in continental currency from more than 1,600 individuals. Refusing Washington's proposal that the money be mixed with general funds in the national treasury, they insisted on using it to purchase materials for shirts so that each soldier might know he had received a contribution specifically from the women.

In the Revolutionary context, traditional female roles took on new political resonance. With English imports cut off and the army badly in need of clothing, spinning and weaving assumed increased importance. Often coming together as Daughters of Liberty, women made shirts, stockings, and other items of clothing. Charity Clarke, a New York teenager who knitted "stockens" for the soldiers, acknowledged that she "felt Nationaly."

Finally, the most traditional of female roles, the care and nurture of children, also took on political overtones during the Revolutionary era. Once independence was won, the republic would have to be sustained by the upcoming generation of republican citizens schooled in the principles of public virtue. They would have to be taught their responsibilities as citizens during their earliest years by their republican mothers, the women of the Revolution.

In a variety of ways, women developed new connections with the public realm during the Revolutionary years. Those connections re-

Abigail Adams, like many women of the Revolutionary generation, protested the contradiction in men's subordination of women while they extolled the principles of liberty and equality.

mained limited, for the assumption that politics and government belonged to men did not die easily. But challenges to that assumption would come, and when they did, women found guidance in the principles that the women of the Revolution had helped to define.

THE AGENDA OF REVOLUTIONARY POLITICS

Revolutionary politics followed different paths in different states. In Pennsylvania political change ran deep, while in other states, such as Connecticut and Virginia, change was more

muted. In each of the states, though, citizens struggled with a bewildering and often intractable array of issues that revealed the clash of conflicting ideologies, interests, and ambitions.

Separating Church and State

Among the most explosive questions was the proper relationship between church and state in a republican order. In most of the colonies prior to the Revolution, one religious group had enjoyed the benefits of endorsement by the government and public tax support for its clergy. At the time of independence, however, "dissenting" groups such as the Methodists and the Baptists were growing in numbers, especially among the lower classes of city and countryside, and were grudgingly tolerated by colonial authorities.

With independence, pressure built for severing church and state completely. Even before independence, Rhode Island, New Jersey, Pennsylvania, and Delaware had established full religious liberty. In five additional states, the Anglican church collapsed when English support was withdrawn.

In Massachusetts, Connecticut, and New Hampshire, the Congregationalists fought to retain their long-established privileges. Isaac Backus, the most outspoken of the New England Baptists, protested that "many, who are filling the nation with the cry of *liberty* and against oppressors are at the same time themselves violating that dearest of all rights, *liberty of conscience.*"

Massachusetts's new constitution guaranteed everyone the right to worship God "in the manner and season most agreeable to the dictates of his own conscience." But as Backus pointed out, it also empowered the legislature to require towns to lay taxes for "the public worship of *God,* and for the support and maintenance of public protestant teachers of piety, religion, and morality." During the decades following independence, New England's Congregational establishment continued to weaken. But not until the early nineteenth century—in Massachusetts not until 1833—were the laws linking church and state finally repealed.

In Virginia, the Baptists pressed their cause against the Protestant Episcopal church, successor to the Church of England. In 1786, the adoption of Thomas Jefferson's Bill for Establishing Religious Freedom, rejecting all connections between church and state and removing all religious tests for public office, finally settled the issue. Three years later, that statute served as a model for the First Amendment to the new federal Constitution.

Legal disestablishment did not end religious discrimination. But it did implant firmly the principle of religious liberty in American constitutional law.

Loyalists and the Public Safety

Emotions ran high between Patriots and Loyalists in Revolutionary America. "The rage of civil discord," lamented one individual, "hath advanced among us with an astonishing rapidity. The son is armed against the father, the brother against the brother, family against family." The security, perhaps the very survival, of the republic required stern measures against counterrevolutionaries. More than security was involved, however, for the Patriots were also determined to exact revenge against those who had rejected the Revolutionary cause.

During the war, each of the states passed a series of laws designed to deprive Loyalists of the vote, confiscate their property and banish them from their homes. In 1776, the Connecticut assembly passed a remarkably punitive law threatening anyone who criticized either the assembly or the Continental Congress with immediate fine and imprisonment. Probably not more than a few dozen Tories died at the hands of the Revolutionary regimes, but many others died in combat, and thousands found their livelihoods destroyed, their families ostracized, and themselves subject to physical attack.

Punishing Loyalists—or persons accused of loyalism—was a popular activity, especially since Loyalists were most numerous among the upper classes. Yet many of the more conservative Patriots wondered how safe their property was if others' property could be confiscated and sold.

Caught up in the Revolution's turmoil, many argued that the Loyalists had put themselves outside the protection of American law. Others worried about the implications of setting aside the protections of the law, even for Loyalists. Republics, after all, were supposed to be "governments of law, and not of men." Once that distinction disappeared, no one would be safe.

After the war ended and passions cooled, most states repealed their anti-Tory legislation. In the midst of the Revolution, however, no issue raised more clearly the troubling question of how to balance individual liberty against the needs of public security.

Slavery Under Attack

The place of human slavery in a republican society also vexed the Revolutionary generation. During the several decades preceding the imperial crisis, the trade in human chattels had flourished. Though several northern colonies abolished the slave trade, the 1760s witnessed the largest importations of slaves in colonial history.

The Revolution halted that trade almost completely. Once the war ended, southern planters sought to replace their lost slaves. But Revolutionary principles, a reduced need for fieldhands in the depressed tobacco economy, continuing natural increase in the slave population, and post-Revolutionary anxiety over black rebelliousness argued for the slave trade's extinction. By 1790, every state except South Carolina and Georgia had outlawed slave importations. Termination of the slave trade reduced the infusion of new Africans into the black population. This meant that over time an ever higher proportion of blacks were American-born, thus speeding the process of cultural transformation by which Africans became African-Americans.

Slavery itself came under attack during the Revolutionary era. As the crisis with England heated up, catchwords such as *liberty* and *tyranny,* employed by colonists protesting British policies, reminded citizens that one-fifth of the colonial population was in chains. Samuel Hopkins, a New England clergyman, chided his compatriots for "making a vain parade of being advocates for the liberties of mankind, while ... you at the same time are continuing this lawless, cruel, inhuman, and abominable practice of enslaving your fellow creatures." Following independence, the attacks intensified.

In Georgia and South Carolina, where blacks outnumbered whites more than two to one, slavery escaped significant challenge. In Virginia and Maryland, by contrast, whites argued openly over slavery's incompatibility with republicanism, and change did occur. The depression in the tobacco economy made the debate easier. Though neither state abolished slavery, both passed laws making it easier for owners to free their slaves. Moreover, increasing numbers of blacks petitioned for their own freedom, purchased it from their masters, or simply fled. By 1800, more than one of every ten blacks in the Chesapeake region were free, a dramatic increase over 30 years before. For many blacks in the Chesapeake region, the conditions of life slowly changed for the better.

The most dramatic breakthroughs occurred in the North, where slavery was either abolished or put on the road to extinction. Abolition was easier in the North because there were fewer slaves. In most areas, they constituted no more than 4 percent of the population.

Northern blacks joined in the attack on slavery. Following independence, they frequently petitioned state assemblies for their freedom. "Every Principle from which America has acted in the course of their unhappy difficulties with Great Britain," declared one group of Philadelphia blacks, "pleads stronger than a thousand arguments in favor of our petition." In 1780, the Pennsylvania assembly passed a law stipulating that all newborn blacks were to be free when they reached age 28. It was a cautious but decisive step. In the following decades, other northern states adopted similar policies of gradual emancipation.

Freed blacks continued to encounter pervasive discrimination. Still, remarkable progress had been made. Prior to the Revolution, slavery had been an accepted fact of northern life; after the Revolution, it no longer was. In addition, there now existed a coherent and publicly proclaimed antislavery argument, one closely linked in Americans' minds with the nation's founding. The first antislavery organizations had been created as well. Although another half century would pass before antislavery became a force in national political life, the groundwork for slavery's final abolition had been laid.

Politics and the Economy

The economic disruptions of independence and war also generated political conflict. The cutoff of long-established patterns of overseas trade sent American commerce into a tailspin from which it didn't recover for nearly 20 years. While English men-of-war prowled the coast, American ships rocked idly at empty wharves, as communities whose livelihood depended on the sea sank into depression. Virginia tobacco planters, their English markets gone and their plantations open to seaborne attack, struggled to survive. Farmers in the middle and New England states often prospered while hungry armies were nearby but saw their profits plummet when the armies moved on.

The war's impact on American manufacturing was uneven. With British goods excluded and wearing homespun deemed patriotic, American artisans and other producers took up the slack. (The familiar slogan "Buy American" has a long tradition.) Handsome profits were to be

Exports and Imports, 1768-1783

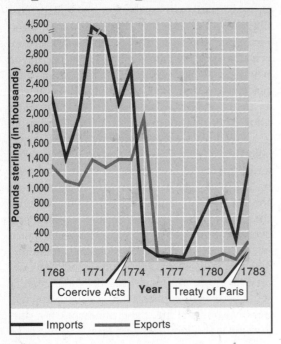

Source: U.S. Bureau of the Census.

made from government contracts by people with the right connections.

But even as some prospered, the war devastated major sectors of the economy. New England's booming shipbuilding industry virtually ceased production. The consequences for sailmakers, shipwrights, and blacksmiths were disastrous.

As major sectors of the economy fell into disarray and the costs of the war escalated, state governments struggled to cope. Price and wage inflation, skyrocketing taxation, mushrooming private and public debt—all demanded attention and often set people against one another. Debates raged, for example, over whether the public debt should be funded at face value or at some reduced rate. In support of full value were merchants and other people of wealth who had loaned the states money and had bought up large amounts of securities at deep discounts.

Others spoke out against full funding, arguing that speculators should reap no advantage from public distress.

The issue of taxation, seared into Americans' consciousness by their troubles with England, generated even greater controversy. As the costs of the war mounted, so did the tax burden. Between 1774 and 1778, Massachusetts levied a total of £408,976 in taxes, a dramatic increase over colonial days. Taxes, complained one anguished soul, equaled nearly one-third of the inhabitants' incomes. And Massachusetts was not unique.

As taxes rose, so did clashes over tax policy. Farmers, artisans, and others of modest means argued that taxes should be payable in depreciated paper money or government securities rather than only in specie, as some state laws required. In the New York assembly, men of property urged continuing dependence on the poll tax, a uniform assessment levied on all males 16 years of age and older. Working people, however, insisted that taxes should bear some relationship to people's ability to pay. As the demand for public revenue increased, pressure for taxing property rather than people grew.

Controversy swirled around the states' efforts to control soaring prices as well. Each of the states experimented with price controls at one time or another. Seldom were such efforts effective; always they generated political storms. In general, the poor and those not yet integrated into the market economy supported price controls. For merchants, shopkeepers, and others caught up in the commercial economy, however, the exchange of goods was an economic transaction that should be controlled by the laws of supply and demand.

Paper money was a final issue that energized state politics. Faced with the uncontrollable escalation of wartime expenses, Congress and the states did what colonial governments had done before and American governments have done ever since: They printed money. In the first year of the war alone, they issued more than $400 million in various kinds of paper, and that was only the beginning. Nothing supported the paper's value but the citizens' willingness to accept it in their dealings with the government and one another.

That willingness rapidly disappeared as the flood of paper grew and efforts lagged to draw it out of circulation through taxation. The result was a headlong collapse of the currency's value. Congressional bills of credit that in 1776 were pegged against gold at the ratio of 1.5 to 1 had slipped five years later to 147 to 1. State currencies depreciated even more alarmingly.

The flood of depreciated paper brought wild inflation of prices. In Massachusetts, a bushel of corn that sold for less than a dollar in 1777 went for nearly $80 two years later, while in Maryland the price of wheat increased several thousand-fold. In Boston, a crowd of women, angered by the escalating costs of food, tossed a merchant suspected of monopolizing commodities into a cart and dragged him through the city's streets while "a large concourse of men stood amazed."

In general, the poor and those not yet integrated into the market economy supported price controls. Faced with escalating prices, they had difficulty simply making ends meet. They also believed that goods should be sold for a "just price," one deemed fair to buyer and seller alike. In keeping with these principles, a crowd in New Windsor, New York, in 1777 seized a shipment of tea bound for Albany and sold it for what they deemed a fair price.

Merchants, shopkeepers, and others caught up in the commercial economy, however, believed that economic transactions should be controlled by the laws of supply and demand. "It is contrary to the nature of commerce," declared Benjamin Franklin, "for government to interfere in the prices of commodities." Attempts to regulate prices only created a disincentive to labor, which was "the principal part of the wealth of every country."

There were no ready solutions to the problems of debt, taxation, and price control. Thus they continued on the public agenda through the 1780s, heightening political tensions.

CONCLUSION

THE CRUCIBLE OF REVOLUTION

Independence and war redrew the contours of American life and changed the destinies of the American people. Though the Revolutionary War ended in victory, independence had its costs. Lives were lost, property was destroyed, local economies were deranged. The war changed relationships between Indians and whites, for it left the Iroquois and Cherokee severely weakened and opened the floodgates of western expansion. For black Americans, the Revolution had paradoxical results. It produced an ideology that decried slavery of all sorts and marked the first general debate over abolishing the oppressive institution. Yet the Revolutionary generation took steps to eradicate slavery only where it was least important, in the North, while preserving it in the South, where it was most important.

By 1783, a new nation had come into being, a nation based on the doctrines of republican liberty. That was the greatest change of all. The years immediately ahead would determine whether the republican experiment, launched with such hopefulness in 1776, would succeed.

Recommended Reading

Standard accounts of the Revolutionary War can be found in Don Higginbotham, *The War of American Independence* (1971); and Robert Middlekauff, *The Glorious Cause* (1982). Charles Royster, *A Revolutionary People at War* (1979), explains how the continental army embodied the Revolution's social and ideological goals. Jonathan Dull, *A Diplomatic History of the American Revolution* (1985), offers skillful discussion of Revolutionary War diplomacy.

The most vivid description of Native American involvement in the Revolution can be found in Anthony Wallace, *The Death and Rebirth of the Seneca* (1969). James O'Donnell discusses the situation in the Southeast in *Southern Indians in the American Revolution* (1973). Books that deal with the tangled history of slavery, race, and the Revolution include Duncan MacLeod, *Slavery, Race, and the American Revolution* (1974); and Ira Berlin and Ronald Hoffman, eds., *Slavery and Freedom in the Age of the American Revolution* (1983).

Linda Kerber, *Women of the Republic* (1980), examines the Revolutionary experience of women. Robert Calhoon, *The Loyalists in Revolutionary America, 1760–1781* (1973), deals with the experiences of Loyalist Americans. On daily life in the period, see Robert Gross, *The Minutemen and Their World* (1976); Jeffrey Crow and Larry Tise, eds., *The Southern Experience in the American Revolution* (1987); and Barbara Smith, *After the Revolution: The History of Everyday Life in the Eighteenth Century* (1985). Thomas Doerflinger, *A Vigorous Spirit of Enterprise* (1986), describes the Revolution's economic impact on Philadelphia.

For further information about the ideology of Revolutionary republicanism, see Bernard Bailyn, *The Ideological Origins of American Revolution* (1967).

State constitution making is discussed in Gordon Wood, *The Creation of the American Republic, 1776–1787* (1969). On Revolutionary state politics see Ronald Hoffman, *A Spirit of Dissension: Economics, Politics and the Revolution in Maryland* (1987); and Eric Foner, *Tom Paine and Revolutionary America* (1976).

Among many readable biographical accounts are Pauline Maier, *The Old Revolutionaries: Political Lives in the Age of Samuel Adams* (1980); Fawn Brodie, *Thomas Jefferson: An Intimate History* (1974); Claude Lopez and Eugenia Herbert, *The Private Franklin: The Man and His Family* (1975); and Marcus Cunliffe, *George Washington: Man and Monument* (1958).

Time Line

1775	Lord Dunmore's proclamation to slaves and servants in Virginia Iroquois Six Nations pledge neutrality Continental Congress urges "states" to establish new governments
1776	British evacuate Boston and seize New York City Declaration of Independence Eight states draft constitutions Cherokee raids and American retaliation
1777	British occupy Philadelphia Most Iroquois join the British Americans win victory at Saratoga Washington's army winters at Valley Forge
1778	War shifts to the South Savannah falls to British French treaty of alliance and commerce

1779	Massachusetts state constitutional convention Sullivan destroys Iroquois villages in New York
1780	Massachusetts constitution ratified Charleston surrenders to British Pennsylvania begins gradual abolition of slavery
1780s	Virginia and Maryland debate abolition of slavery Destruction of Iroquois Confederacy
1781	Cornwallis surrenders at Yorktown Articles of Confederation ratified by states
1783	Peace Treaty with England signed in Paris Massachusetts Supreme Court abolishes slavery King's Commission on American Loyalists begins work

chapter 7

Consolidating the Revolution

$\mathbf{T}$imothy Bloodworth of New Hanover County, North Carolina, knew what the American Revolution was about, for he had experienced it firsthand. A man of humble origins, Bloodworth had worked hard as an innkeeper and ferry pilot, self-styled preacher and farmer. By the mid-1770s, he owned nine slaves and 4,200 acres of land, considerably more than most of his neighbors.

His unpretentious manner and commitment to political equality earned Bloodworth the confidence of his community. In 1758, at the age of 22, he was elected to the North Carolina colonial assembly. Over the next three decades, he remained deeply involved in North Carolina's political life.

When the colonies' troubles with England drew toward a crisis, Bloodworth spoke ardently of American rights and mobilized support for independence. In 1784, shortly after the war ended, the North Carolina assembly named Bloodworth one of the state's delegates to the Confederation Congress. There he learned for the first time about the problems of governing a new nation. As the Congress struggled through the middle years of the 1780s, Bloodworth shared the growing conviction that the Articles of Confederation were too weak. He supported the Congress's call for a special convention to meet in Philadelphia in May 1787 to address this problem.

Like thousands of Americans, Bloodworth eagerly awaited the convention's work, but he was stunned by the result, for the proposed constitution seemed to him designed not to preserve republican liberty but to endanger it. Once again sniffing political tyranny on the breeze, he resigned his congressional seat in August 1787 and hurried back to North Carolina, where, over the next several years, he worked tirelessly to prevent its ratification.

A national government as strong as the one described in the proposed constitution, Bloodworth feared, would gobble up the states and destroy individual liberties. Alarmed by the provisions giving Congress the power of taxation as well as by the absence of explicit guarantees of trial by jury, Bloodworth demanded the addition of a federal bill of rights to protect individual liberties.

Bloodworth also feared the sweeping authority Congress would have "to make all laws which shall be necessary and proper for carrying into execution . . . all other powers vested . . . in the government of the United States." That language, he insisted, threatened the integrity of the states.

In North Carolina, the arguments of Bloodworth and his Anti-Federalist colleagues carried the day. By a vote of 184 to 84, the state ratifying convention declared that a bill of rights "asserting and securing from encroachment the great Principles of civil and religious Liberty, and the unalienable rights of the People" must be approved before North Carolina would concur. Not until November 1789—well after the new government had gotten under way and Congress had forwarded a national bill of rights to the states for approval—did North Carolina enter the new union.

As a member of the Confederation Congress, Timothy Bloodworth confronted the continuing vestiges of colonialism—the patronizing attitudes of England and France, their continuing imperial ambitions in North America, and the republic's ongoing economic dependence on Europe. He also observed the Congress's inability to reduce the war debt, open foreign ports to American commerce, and persuade the states to cooperate in solving the new nation's problems.

By 1786, Bloodworth, like countless other Americans, was caught up in the escalating debate between the Federalists, who believed that the Articles of Confederation were fatally deficient, and the Anti-Federalists, committed to retaining America's traditional localism and still deeply impressed by the dangers posed to individual liberties by consolidated power.

That debate came to a focus in the momentous Philadelphia convention of 1787, which produced not reform but revolutionary change in the national government and opened a portentous new chapter in the history of the American people.

STRUGGLING WITH THE PEACETIME AGENDA

As the war ended, difficult problems of demobilization and adjustment to the conditions of independence troubled the new nation. Whether the Confederation Congress could effectively deal with the problems of the postwar era remained unclear.

Demobilizing the Army

Demobilizing the army presented the Confederation government with some difficult moments, for when the fighting stopped, many of the troops refused to disband and go home until the Congress redressed their grievances. Trouble first arose in January 1783, when officers at the continental army camp in Newburgh, New York, sent a delegation to the Congress to complain about arrears in pay and other promised benefits. The Congress responded by calling for the army to be decommissioned. Almost immediately, an anonymous document circulated among the officers, attacking the "coldness and severity" of the Congress and hinting darkly at direct action if their grievances were not addressed. Washington urged the officers not to tarnish the victory they had so recently won. His efforts succeeded, for the officers reaffirmed their confidence in the Congress and agreed to disband.

In June, several hundred disgruntled continental soldiers and Pennsylvania militiamen gathered to express their frustrations in front of Independence Hall, causing Congress to flee to Princeton, New Jersey. Again, the crisis was eventually smoothed over, but the Congress's authority had been seriously challenged. During the mid-1780s, the Congress shuffled between Princeton and Annapolis, Trenton and New York, its transiency visible evidence of its steadily eroding position.

Opening the West

The Congress was not without important accomplishments during the postwar years. Most notable were the two great land ordinances of 1785 and 1787. The first provided for the systematic survey and sale of the region west of New York and Pennsylvania and north of the Ohio River. The area was to be laid out in townships six miles square, which were in turn to be subdivided into lots of 640 acres each. Thus began the rectangular grid pattern of land survey and settlement that to this day characterizes the nation's Midwest and distinguishes it so markedly from the irregular settlement patterns of the older colonial areas to the east.

Two years later, the Congress passed the Northwest Ordinance. It provided for the political organization of the same interior region, first with congressionally appointed officials, then with popularly elected assemblies, and ultimately as new states to be incorporated into the Union "on an equal footing with the original states in all respects whatsoever." Together these two pieces of legislation provided the legal mechanism for the nation's dramatic territorial expansion during the nineteenth century.

Despite its success in providing the legal framework for settlement of the trans-Appalachian frontier, however, Congress could nei-

ther secure removal of the British troops from the western posts after 1783 nor guarantee free navigation of the Mississippi. Nor could it clear the tribes of the Ohio region out of the white settlers' way.

During the immediate postwar years, the Congress operated as if the Native Americans of the interior were "conquered" peoples. The Treaty of Paris, American officials insisted, gave the United States political sovereignty over the tribes east of the Mississippi as well as ownership of their land.

For a few years the conquest strategy seemed to work. During the mid-1780s, the Congress negotiated several important land treaties with the interior tribes. At the Treaty of Fort Stanwix in 1784, the first congressional treaty with an Indian tribe, the Iroquois Six Nations made peace, ceded much of their land to the United States, and retreated to small reservations where they struggled for survival against disease and poverty, their traditional lifeways gone, their self-confidence broken.

The Iroquois were not the only tribes to lose their land. In January 1785, representatives of the Wyandotte, Chippewa, Delaware, and Ottawa tribes relinquished claim to most of present-day Ohio. The treaties with the Indians, however, were often exacted under the threat of force and generated widespread resentment. At Fort Stanwix, for example, negotiations were held at gunpoint, and hostages were taken to coerce the Indian delegates. Two years later, the Iroquois openly repudiated the treaty, asserting that they were still sovereigns of their own soil and "equally free as . . . any nation under the sun."

The Revolution, moreover, left behind a legacy of bitterness for both Indians and whites: for Indians because they had suffered betrayal and defeat, for white Americans because the Indians had sided with England and thus threatened the success of the Revolutionary cause. This bitterness would trouble Indian-white relations for years to come.

By the mid-1780s, tribal groups both above and below the Ohio River were actively resisting

Areas of White Settlement and Frontier in 1787

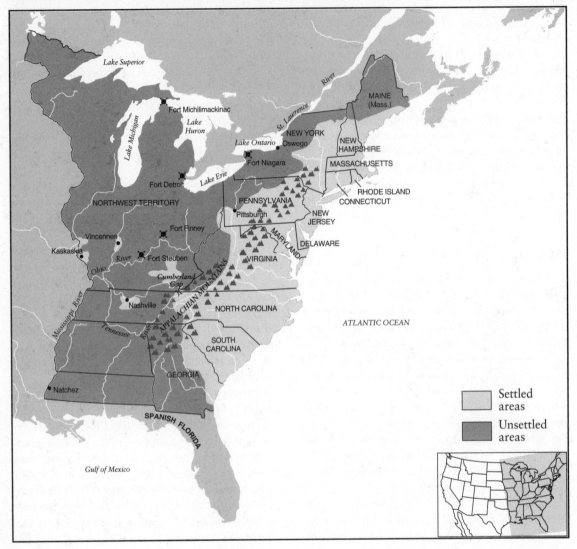

Settled areas

Unsettled areas

white expansion onto their land. In the summer of 1786, the Creek resumed hostilities in the backcountry of Georgia, while north of the Ohio, the Shawnee, Delaware, Wyandotte, and Miami moved to strengthen their Western Confederacy, reject the conquest theory, and prepare for the defense of their common homeland. When white settlers continued to press into the region, Native Americans launched a series of devastating raids, virtually halting white settlement. By 1786, the entire region from the Great Lakes to the Gulf of Mexico was embroiled in warfare. With the continental army disbanded and the nation in no position to raise a new one, there was little that Congress could do.

Settling the interior also involved relations

with other nations, and here, too, the Congress proved ineffective. In June 1784, Spain—still in possession of Florida, the Gulf Coast, and the trans-Mississippi West—closed the outlet of the Mississippi River at New Orleans to American shipping. Spain's action raised a storm of protest, especially among settlers in the West, who counted on the interior river system to float their produce downstream to outside markets. Land speculators from Virginia to South Carolina were aroused as well, for closure of the Mississippi would discourage development of the southern backcountry. Rumors spread that Spanish agents were urging backcountry American settlers to break away and seek affiliation with Spain. When Foreign Secretary John Jay offered to relinquish American claims to free transit of the Mississippi in return for a new commercial treaty opening Spanish ports to American shipping, the northern states supported the bargain. The southern states, however, angry at Jay's betrayal of their interests, refused. Thus stalemated, the Congress could take no action at all.

Wrestling with the National Debt

The Congress's inability to deal effectively with the massive war debt offered further evidence of the Confederation government's weakness. The public debt stood at about $35 million, much of it held abroad by French and Dutch bankers. Not only was the Congress unable to make regular payment against the loan's principal, but it had to borrow additional money abroad simply to pay the accumulating interest.

At home, things were no better. In response to the incessant demands of its creditors, the government could only delay and try to borrow more. Lacking the power to tax, the Congress continued to depend on the states' willingness to honor their obligations. This arrangement proved unworkable. By 1786, total federal revenue amounted to no more than $370,000 a

year—not a sufficient amount, as one official lamented, to provide for "the bare maintenance of the federal government [even] on the most economical establishment, and in a time of profound peace."

Not all Americans were alarmed. Some pointed out approvingly that several state governments were beginning to assume responsibility for portions of the national debt. Others saw that as additional evidence of the Congress's weakening condition and wondered how a government unable to maintain its credit could long endure.

Surviving in a Hostile World

The Congress's difficulties in countering Spain's decision to close the Mississippi River to American commerce and in dealing with its creditors overseas pointed to a broader problem in American foreign relations. Even after the United States had formally won independence, England, France, and Spain continued to harbor imperial ambitions in North America. France had lost its North American possessions following the Seven Years' War, but before the century was over, it would gain title to most of the continent west of the Mississippi River. England's Union Jack continued to fly over eastern Canada, while English troops retained possession of strategic outposts on American soil—at Detroit, Michilimackinac, and Niagara. Spain, in control of New Orleans and Florida, still conjured up grim memories of past New World conquests. The reason for America's diplomatic troubles was clear: The country was new, weak, and republican in a world dominated by monarchical governments and divided into warring empires.

Nothing revealed more starkly the difficulties of national survival than the Congress's largely futile efforts to rebuild America's overseas commerce. A flourishing overseas trade, across the Atlantic to markets in England and down the coast to the Caribbean, had been the foundation of colonial economic prosperity.

British and Spanish Possessions in Eastern North America, 1783

Lake Superior

BRITISH CANADA

St. Lawrence River

Fort Michillimackinac

Lake Huron   Lake Michigan   Lake Ontario

MAINE (Mass.)

Fort Niagara

NEW HAMPSHIRE

Lake Erie

NEW YORK

MASSACHUSETTS

Fort Detroit

RHODE ISLAND

PENNSYLVANIA   CONNECTICUT

NEW JERSEY

St. Louis

DELAWARE

SPANISH LOUISIANA

VIRGINIA   MARYLAND

Mississippi River   APPALACHIAN MOUNTAINS

NORTH CAROLINA

ATLANTIC OCEAN

SOUTH CAROLINA

Natchez   GEORGIA

New Orleans

SPANISH FLORIDA

Gulf of Mexico

✳ Military and administrative centers

British Canada
United States
Spanish possessions

Once the war was over, American traders sought eagerly to rebuild this trade. It proved a difficult task because the Congress could give them little support.

When the war ended, familiar English goods flooded American markets. Few American goods, however, flowed the other way, for English officials could command American markets without needing to grant trade concessions in return. Meanwhile, France and Spain gradually withdrew the special wartime trading privileges they had extended and returned to their policy of mercantile restrictions.

In an effort to rebuild American commerce, the Congress tried to secure the states' cooperation in a program of economic recovery. In 1784, however, it failed to obtain authorization from the states to regulate foreign commerce; each state wanted to channel its own trade for its own advantage. As a result, the Congress was unable to negotiate satisfactory commercial agreements abroad, and overseas trade continued to languish.

By the late 1780s, the per capita value of American exports had fallen a startling 30 percent from two decades earlier. In an Atlantic world divided into exclusive, imperial trading spheres, the United States stood outside and alone, lacking both the political unity and the economic power to protect its interests.

POLITICAL TUMULT IN THE STATES

As the Confederation Congress struggled to chart the nation's postwar course, controversy again embroiled state politics. Two issues carried over from the Revolutionary agenda came together with particularly explosive force: problems of debt relief and paper money on the one hand, and continuing arguments over political equality and the sharing of political power on the other.

The Limits of Republican Experimentation

In a pattern that would frequently recur in American history, the postwar era witnessed growing social and political conservatism. Popular voting declined, while leadership in the state governments fell increasingly to people convinced that republican experimentation had gone too far, that order had to balance liberty, and that the "better sort" of men, not democratic newcomers, should be in charge. The repeal of anti-Loyalist legislation and the occasional reappearance of Loyalists in public life provided evidence of the changing political climate.

In 1790, Pennsylvania replaced its radical constitution of 1776 with a more conservative document that provided for a strong governor with power to veto legislation and control the militia and a senate intended to balance the more democratic assembly. Gaining a majority in the assembly as early as 1786, the conservatives dismantled much of the radicals' program, repealing the revolutionary test oaths and thus reenfranchising thousands of conservatives, stopping the issuance of paper money, and rechartering the Bank of North America.

Shays's Rebellion

In other states, popular opposition to hard money and high-tax policies, problems still festering from the Revolution, provoked vigorous protest. The controversy that erupted in Massachusetts in 1786 echoed strongly of equal rights and popular consent, staples of the rhetoric of 1776.

The war vastly expanded the burden of debt among Massachusetts' citizens. By the mid-1780s, increasing numbers of people had to borrow money just to pay their taxes or support their families, while others borrowed to speculate in western land or government securities. Because there were no commercial banks in the state, people borrowed from one another in a complicated and vulnerable pyramid of credit and debt.

A crisis began to build shortly after the war's end. As English goods once again flooded the American market, American importers borrowed heavily in England to expand their purchases, which they sold to local retailers at a handsome profit. Some of those profits they loaned back to the retailers so that they could sell even more goods. The retailers in turn extended credit to their customers.

In time the flood of English goods glutted the American market and forced prices down. By 1785, a number of English banking houses, heavily overcommitted in the American trade, were in trouble. When they called in their American loans, American merchants in turn tried to collect the debts due them, sending a credit crisis surging through the economy.

The crisis was most acute among the small farmers and laboring people of country and town. Caught in a tightening bind, they turned to their state governments for "stay laws" suspending the collection of private debts. If not granted relief, they faced foreclosure and the loss of shops and farms. They also pressed for new issues of paper money so that they would have something with which to pay both private debts and public taxes.

The largest creditors, however, most of whom lived in commercial areas along the coast, fought these relief proposals, because they wanted to collect sums owed them in hard currency.

By 1786, Massachusetts farmers, made desperate by private debt and a lingering agricultural depression, petitioned the Massachusetts assembly for relief. Peter Wood, tax collector for the town of Marlborough, reported that "there was not . . . the money in possession or at command among the people . . . to discharge taxes." Between 1784 and 1786, fully 29 towns declared themselves unable to meet their tax payments. The farmers' appeals, however, fell on deaf ears, for commercial and creditor interests now controlled the government.

As frustrated citizens had done before and would do again when the law proved unresponsive to their needs, Massachusetts farmers stepped outside the law and took matters into their own hands. A Hampshire County convention of 50 towns condemned the state senate, lawyers, court fees, and the tax system. It advised against violence, but crowds soon began to form.

The county courts drew much of the farmers' wrath because they issued the writs of property foreclosure that state and private creditors demanded. On August 31, 1786, armed men prevented the county court from sitting at Northampton, and on September 5, angry citizens closed down the court at Worcester. When farmers threatened similar actions elsewhere, an alarmed Governor James Bowdoin dispatched 600 militiamen to protect the Supreme Court, then on circuit at Springfield.

About 500 insurgents had gathered near there under the leadership of Daniel Shays, a popular Revolutionary War captain recently fallen on hard times. Most of the men who gathered around Shays were also debtors and veterans. Worried about a possible raid on the federal arsenal at Springfield, the Continental Congress authorized 1,300 troops to be readied for use against Shays and his rebels. For a few weeks, Massachusetts seemed poised on the brink of civil war.

In late November, the insurrection collapsed in eastern Massachusetts, but things were far from over in the west. When several insurgent groups refused to disband at Governor Bowdoin's command, he called out a force of 4,400 men, financed and led by worried eastern merchants. On January 26, 1787, Shays led 1,200 men toward the federal arsenal. Frightened by the siege, its defenders opened fire, killing four of the attackers and sending the Shaysites into retreat.

Over the next several weeks, the militia chased the remnants of Shays's followers across the state and sent Shays himself fleeing into Vermont for safety. By the end of February, the rebellion was over. In March, the legislature pardoned all but Shays and three other leaders; in another year, they too had been forgiven.

Similar challenges to public authority, fired by personal troubles and frustration over unresponsive government, erupted in South Carolina in May 1785, in Maryland in June 1786, and in several other states. Across the nation, state politics was in turmoil.

TOWARD A NEW NATIONAL GOVERNMENT

By 1786, as a result of Shays's Rebellion and other rumbles of discontent, belief was spreading among members of the Congress and other political leaders that the nation was in crisis. Attention focused increasingly on the inadequacies of the Articles of Confederation. Within two years, following a raucous political struggle, a new and far more powerful constitution replaced the Articles. That outcome would change forever the course of American history.

The Rise of Federalism

The supporters of a stronger national government called themselves Federalists (leading their opponents to adopt the name Anti-Federalists). Led by men such as Washington, Hamilton, Madison, and Jay, they believed that the nation was in the midst of a social and political crisis that threatened its very survival. Such men had never been comfortable with the more radical impulses of the Revolution. While supporting the principles of moderate republicanism, they continued to believe in an aristocracy of talent and to place high value on social order and the rights of property.

They were now persuaded that social and political change had carried too far. The Revolution, Jay lamented, "laid open a wide field for the operation of ambition," especially for "men raised from low degrees to high stations and rendered giddy by elevation." It was time, he insisted, to find better ways of protecting "the worthy against the licentious." In 1776, American liberty had needed protection against English power. Danger now, however, came from too much liberty threatening to degenerate into license. "We have probably had too good an opinion of human nature," wrote Washington. "Experience has taught us, that men will not adopt and carry into execution measures the best calculated for their own good, without the intervention of a coercive power." In the Federalists' minds, America needed "a strong government, ably administered" by the "better sort."

Congressional inability to handle the national debt, establish public credit, and restore

James Madison of Virginia worked tirelessly between 1786 and 1788 to replace the Articles of Confederation with a new and more effective national constitution.

overseas trade also troubled the Federalists. They stressed the need for a new national government capable of extending American trade, spurring economic recovery, and protecting national interests against Anglo-European designs.

Beyond that, the Federalists shared a vision of an expanding commercial republic, its people spreading across the rich lands of the interior, its merchant ships connecting America with the markets of Europe and beyond. That vision, so rich in national promise, seemed also at risk.

The Grand Convention

The first step toward governmental reform came in September 1786, when delegates of five states, who had gathered in Annapolis, Maryland, to discuss interstate commerce, prepared an address to all 13 states. Written by the ardent nationalist Alexander Hamilton, it called for a new

convention to gather in Philadelphia in May 1787. In February, the Confederation Congress cautiously endorsed the idea of a convention to revise the Articles of Confederation. Before long, however, it became clear that more dramatic changes were in store.

During May, delegates representing every state except Rhode Island began assembling in Philadelphia. Eventually 55 delegates would participate in the convention's work, though daily attendance was usually between 30 and 40. The city bustled with excitement as they gathered, for the Grand Convention's roster read like an honor roll of the Revolution. From Virginia came the distinguished lawyer George Mason, chief author of Virginia's trailblazing bill of rights, and the already legendary George Washington. James Madison was there as well. No one, with perhaps the single exception of Alexander Hamilton, was more committed to nationalist reform. Madison brought to Philadelphia his own design for a new national government. That design, presented in the convention as the Virginia Plan, would serve as the basis for the new constitution. Nor did anyone rival the diminutive Madison's contributions to the convention's work. Tirelessly he took the convention floor to argue the nationalist cause or buttonhole wavering delegates to strengthen their resolve. In addition, he somehow found the energy to keep extensive notes in his personal shorthand. Those notes constitute our essential record of the convention's proceedings.

Two distinguished Virginians were conspicuously absent. Thomas Jefferson was abroad serving as minister to France, while the old patriot Patrick Henry, an ardent champion of state supremacy, wanted no part of the convention.

Other distinguished delegates included the venerable Benjamin Franklin, the erudite lawyer James Wilson, and the wealthy Robert Morris from Pennsylvania; Elbridge Gerry and Rufus King from Massachusetts; John Rutledge and Charles Pinckney from South Carolina; and Roger Sherman from Connecticut.

The New York assembly sent a deeply divided delegation that included Alexander Hamilton. Determined to protect New York's autonomy and his own political power, Governor George Clinton saw to it that several Anti-Federalist skeptics also made the trip to Philadelphia. They were no match for Hamilton, whose immense intelligence and ingratiating charm had enabled him to rise rapidly in the world. In 1777, while still in his early twenties, he became Washington's wartime aide-de-camp. That relationship served Hamilton well for the next 20 years. Returning from the war, Hamilton wooed and won the wealthy Elizabeth Schuyler, thereby securing his personal fortune and strengthening his political support. At Philadelphia, he was determined to drive his own nationalist vision ahead.

Meeting in Independence Hall, where the Declaration of Independence had been proclaimed little more than a decade before, the convention elected Washington its presiding officer, adopted rules of procedure, and, after spirited debate, voted to close the doors and conduct the convention's business in secret.

Debate focused first on Madison's Virginia Plan, which outlined a powerful national government and effectively set the convention's agenda. According to its provisions, there would be a bicameral congress, with the lower house elected by the people and the upper house, or senate, elected by the lower house from nominees proposed by the state legislatures. The plan also called for a president to be chosen by the congress, a national judiciary, and a council of revision, whose task was to review the constitutionality of legislation.

The smaller states quickly objected to the Virginia Plan's provision for proportional rather than equal representation. On June 15, William Paterson introduced a counterproposal, the New Jersey Plan, which would retain the Articles of Confederation while granting Congress the powers to tax and regulate both foreign and interstate commerce. After three days of heated debate, the delegates by a vote of seven states to three adopted the Virginia Plan as the basis for further discussions. It was now clear that the convention would set aside the Articles for a much stronger national government. Over the next four months, the convention struggled to shape that new government.

At times it seemed that the Grand Convention would collapse under the weight of its own disagreements and the oppressive summer heat as delegates wrestled over the sharply conflicting interests of large and small states, the balance of power between national and state governments, and the volatile issue of slavery. The delegates wrangled as well over the knotty problem of how to fashion an executive branch strong enough to govern but not so strong as to endanger republican liberty.

At one extreme was Hamilton's audaciously conservative proposal, made early in the convention's deliberations, for a congress and president elected for life and a national government so powerful that the states would survive as little more than administrative agencies. Finding his plan under attack and his influence among the delegates rapidly eroding, a disillusioned Hamilton withdrew from the convention in late June. He would return a month later but make few additional contributions.

At the other extreme stood the ardent Anti-Federalist Luther Martin of Maryland. Rude and unkempt, Martin voiced his uncompromising opposition to anything that threatened state sovereignty or smacked of aristocracy. Increasingly isolated by the convention's nationalist inclinations, Martin also returned home, in his case to warn of the convention's doings.

By early July, with tempers frayed and frustrated over the apparent deadlock, the delegates agreed to recess, ostensibly in recognition of Independence Day but actually to enable Franklin, Roger Sherman, and others to mount a final effort at compromise. All agreed that only a bold stroke could save the convention from collapse.

That stroke came on July 12, as part of what has become known as the Great Compromise.

The reassembled delegates agreed that representation in the lower house should be based on the total of each state's white population plus three-fifths of its black population. Though blacks were not accorded citizenship and could not vote, the southern delegates argued that they should be fully counted for this purpose. Delegates from the northern states, where relatively few blacks lived, did not want them counted at all, but the bargain was struck. As part of this compromise, the convention agreed that direct taxes would also be apportioned on the basis of population and that blacks would be counted similarly in that calculation as well. On July 16, the convention accepted the principle that each state should have an equal vote in the senate. The compromise thus accommodated the interests of both large and small states.

The convention then submitted its work to a committee of detail for drafting in proper constitutional form. That group reported on August 6, and for the next month the delegates hammered out the exact language of the document's seven articles.

Determined to give the new government the stability the state governments lacked, the delegates created an electoral process designed to bring only persons of standing and experience into national office. An electoral college of wise and experienced leaders would meet to choose the president. The process functioned exactly that way during the first several presidential elections.

Selection of the new Senate would be similarly indirect, for its members were to be named by the state legislatures. (Not until 1913, when the Seventeenth Amendment to the Constitution was ratified, would the people elect their senators.) Even the House of Representatives, the only popularly elected branch of the new government, was to be filled with persons of standing and wealth, for the Federalists were confident that only experienced and well-known leaders would be able to attract the necessary votes.

The delegates' final set of compromises touched the fate of black Americans. At the insistence of southerners, the convention agreed that the slave trade would not formally end for another 20 years. The delegates never used the words *slavery* or *slave trade* but spoke more vaguely about not prohibiting "the migration or importation of such persons as any of the states now existing shall think proper to admit." Their meaning, however, was clear.

More than that, they guaranteed slavery's protection, writing in Section 2 of Article 4 of the Constitution: "No person held to service or labour in one state, . . . [and] escaping into another, shall, in consequence of any law . . . therein, be discharged from such service, but shall be delivered up on claim of the party to whom such service or labour may be due." The delegates thus provided federal sanction for the capture and return of runaway slaves. This fugitive slave clause would return to haunt northern consciences in the years ahead, but at the time it seemed a small price to pay for sectional harmony and a new government. Northern accommodation to the demands of the southern delegates was eased, however, by knowledge that southerners in the Confederation Congress had recently agreed to prohibit the entry of new slaves into the Northwest Territory.

The document that emerged from the Philadelphia Convention, then, represented compromises between large states and small, as well as between North and South. Some of those compromises came at the expense of black Americans, who had no voice in the Constitution's drafting or ratification.

The Constitution decisively strengthened the national government, for Congress would now have authority to levy and collect taxes, regulate commerce, devise uniform rules for naturalization, and control the federal district in which it would eventually be located. Conspicuously missing was any statement reserving to the states all powers not explicitly conferred on the central government, which had been a crippling limitation of the Articles. On the contrary, the Constitution contained a number of clauses bestowing general grants of power on the new government. A final measure of the Federalists' determination to make the new government supreme over the states was the assertion in Article 6 that the Constitution and all laws passed under it were to be regarded as "the supreme Law of the Land."

When the convention had finished its business, 3 of the 42 remaining delegates refused to sign the document. The other 39, however, affixed their names and forwarded it to the Confederation Congress along with their request that it be sent on to the states for approval. On September 17, the Grand Convention adjourned.

Federalists Versus Anti-Federalists

Ratification presented the Federalists with more difficult problems than they had faced at Philadelphia. Now the debate shifted to the states, where sentiment was sharply divided and the situation was more difficult to control. Recognizing the unlikelihood of gaining quick agreement from all 13 states, the Federalists provided that the Constitution should go into effect when any nine agreed to it. Other states could then enter the Union as they were ready. They arranged for ratification by specially elected conventions rather than the state assemblies, since under the Constitution the assemblies would lose substantial amounts of power. Ratification by convention was also more constitutionally sound, since it would give the new government its own grounding in the people and free it from dependence on the state governments.

Word of the dramatic changes being proposed spread rapidly. In each state, Federalists and Anti-Federalists prepared to debate the new articles of government. Some critics feared that a stronger central government would threaten state interests or their own political power. Others, like Timothy Bloodworth, charged the Federalists with betraying Revolutionary republicanism. Like all "vigorous" and "energetic" governments, they warned, the new one would be corrupted by its own power.

The Anti-Federalists were aghast at the Federalists' vision of an expanding "republican empire." "The idea of . . . [a] republic, on an average of 1000 miles in length, and 800 in breadth, and containing 6 millions of white inhabitants all reduced to the same standards of morals, . . . habits . . . [and] laws," exclaimed one critic incredulously, "is itself an absurdity, and contrary to the whole experience of mankind." Such an attempt, the argument went, would guarantee factional conflict and disorder. Nor did the Anti-Federalists believe that the proposed separation of executive, legislative, and judicial powers or the balancing of state and national governments would prevent power's abuse. Government, they insisted, must be kept simple. Republican liberty could be preserved only in simple, homogeneous societies, where faction was absent and public virtue guided citizens' behavior.

Federalist spokesmen moved quickly to counter the criticism. The Federalists' most important effort was a series of essays penned by James Madison, Alexander Hamilton, and John Jay and published in New York under the pseudonym "Publius." Madison, Hamilton, and Jay moved systematically through the proposed constitution, explaining its virtues and responding to the Anti-Federalists' attacks. In the process, they described a political vision fundamentally different from that of their Anti-Federalist opponents.

Power, the Federalists now argued, was not the enemy of liberty but its guarantor. Nothing was more dangerous than the "mischievous effects of unstable government." Where government was not "energetic" and "efficient" (these were favorite Federalist words), demagogues and disorganizers did their work.

The *Federalist Papers* also countered the Anti-Federalists' warning that a single, extended republic encompassing the country's economic and social diversity would lead inevitably to factional warfare and the end of republican liberty. Factional divisions, they explained, could never be avoided, even in the smallest societies, because they were the inevitable by-products of economic and social development. Faction, moreover, was the necessary accompaniment of human liberty. Wrote Madison in *Federalist* No. 10: "Liberty is to faction what air is to fire, an ailment without which it instantly expires." To suppress faction would be to destroy liberty itself. Out of the clash and accommodation of social and economic interests would emerge public order and the best possible approximation of the public good.

The Federalist's arguments left the Anti-Federalists sputtering in amazement. What would become of public virtue in a system built on the notion of competing factional interests? They also accused their opponents of elitism, of wishing to join the government to wealth and privilege. Not all the Antis were democrats, but they were more consistently sympathetic to democratic principles than were their Federalist opponents. Certainly they believed more firmly that for government to be safe, it must be tied intimately to the people.

As the ratification debate revealed, the Federalists and Anti-Federalists held sharply contrasting visions of the new republic. The Antis remained much closer to the original republicanism of 1776, with its suspicion of power and wealth, its emphasis on the primacy of local government, and its fears of centralization. The Federalists, arguing that America's situation had changed dramatically since 1776, embraced the idea of nationhood and looked forward with anticipation to the development of a rising "republican empire" based on commercial development and led by men of wealth and talent. Both Federalists and Anti-Federalists claimed to be heirs of the Revolution, yet they differed dramatically on what the Revolution had meant.

The Struggle over Ratification

No one knows with certainty what most Americans thought of the proposed constitution. No national plebiscite on the Constitution was ever taken. A majority of the people probably opposed the document, either out of indifference or alarm. Fortunately for the Federalists, they did not have to persuade most Americans; they

needed only secure majorities in nine of the state ratifying conventions, a much less formidable task.

It took less than a year from the time the document left Congress to secure approval of the necessary nine states. Delaware, Pennsylvania, and New Jersey ratified first, in December 1787. Approval came a month later in Georgia and Connecticut. Massachusetts was next to ratify, but only after Federalist leaders forwarded a set of amendments outlining a federal "bill of rights" along with notice of ratification. Maryland and South Carolina were the seventh and eighth states to approve. The honor of being ninth and putting the Constitution over the top went to New Hampshire, which ratified on June 21.

Two massive gaps in the new Union remained—Virginia and New York. Clearly, the nation could not endure without them. In Virginia, careful politicking by Madison and other Federalist leaders made the difference. On June 25, the Virginia convention voted to ratify by the narrow margin of ten votes.

The New York convention met on June 17 at Poughkeepsie, with the Anti-Federalist followers of Governor Clinton firmly in command. Hamilton worked for delay, hoping that news of the results in New Hampshire and Virginia would turn the tide. For several weeks, approval hung in the balance while the two sides maneuvered for support. On July 27, approval squeaked through, 30 to 27. That left two states still uncommitted. North Carolina (with Timothy Bloodworth's cautious approval) finally ratified in November 1789. The final state, Rhode Island, did not enter the Union until May 1790, more than a year after the new government had gotten under way.

The Social Geography of Ratification

A glance at the geographic pattern of Federalist and Anti-Federalist strength indicates their different sources of political support. Federalist strength was concentrated along the coast and

Federalist and Anti-Federalist Areas, 1787–1788

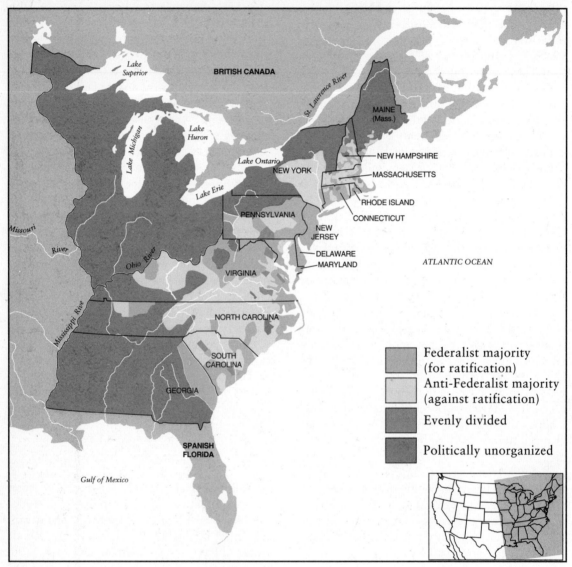

navigable rivers and was strongest in cities and towns. The centers of Anti-Federalist support lay away from the coast, in the interior of New England, upstate New York, the Virginia piedmont and southside, and the western regions of the Carolinas.

Merchants and businessmen supported the Constitution most ardently. Enthusiasm also ran high among urban laborers, artisans, and shopkeepers, who believed that a stronger government could better promote the overseas trade on which their prosperity depended and protect

American artisans from foreign competition. The Constitution also found support in the countryside, especially among commercial farmers and southern planters eager for profit and anxious about overseas markets. But Federalist enthusiasm waned and Anti-Federalist sentiment increased in the interior. Among most ordinary farmers living outside the market economy and immersed in their own localities, the republicanism of 1776 outweighed their interests in national affairs. They found the Federalist vision of an "American empire" both strange and alarming.

Why were the Federalists finally successful? Their task was simplified by the widespread perception that the Articles needed strengthening. In light of the obvious troubles of the Confeder-ation, the Federalists could argue that the Revolution was doomed to failure unless dramatic action was taken.

Most of all, however, the Federalists succeeded because of their determination and political skill. Most of the Revolution's major leaders were Federalists. Time and again these heroes spoke out for the Constitution in the state ratifying debates, and time and again their support proved decisive. Their experience as army officers and as members of the Continental and Confederation congresses caused them to identify with the nation and what it might become. They brought their vision to the ratification process and asked others to share it. With their success, the Federalists turned the American republic in a new and fateful direction.

CONCLUSION

COMPLETING THE REVOLUTION

Only five years had passed between England's acknowledgment of American independence in 1783 and ratification of the new national Constitution, yet to many Americans it seemed far longer. By war's end, the difficulties of sustaining American liberty were evident. The experience of the next half decade added to them. Americans continued to argue about their experiment in republicanism and to wonder whether it would actually work.

At the same time, the American people retained an immense reservoir of optimism about the future. Much would depend, of course, on their new constitution and the government soon to be created under it. As the ratification debate subsided and Congress prepared for the transition, the American people looked eagerly and anxiously ahead.

Recommended Reading

Among the major works dealing with the Articles of Confederation and the 1780s are Jack Rakove, *The Beginnings of National Politics: An Interpretive History of the Continental Congress* (1979); and Peter Onuf, *The Origins of the Federal Republic* (1983).

On the Philadelphia convention see Richard Morris, *Witnesses at the Creation: Hamilton, Madison, Jay and the Constitution* (1985); Christopher Collier and James Collier, *Decision in Philadelphia* (1986); and J. Jackson Barlow et al., *The American Founding: Essays on the Formation of the Constitution* (1988). Robert Rutland's *James Madison, the*

Founding Father (1987) is a readable biography of the most important constitution maker.

For postwar political and economic problems, see Ronald Hoffman and Peter Albert, eds., *Sovereign States in an Age of Uncertainty* (1918); and David Szatmary, *Shays's Rebellion: The Making of an Agrarian Rebellion* (1980).

Though several decades old, Jackson Main, *The*

Anti-Federalists: Critics of the Constitution, 1781–1788 (1961), is still important for an understanding of the Anti-Federalist opposition. See also Steven Boyd, *The Politics of Opposition: Antifederalists and the Acceptance of the Constitution* (1979). Dumas Malone et al., *Rhetoric and the Founding* (1987), examines the relationship between language and meaning in the constitutional debates.

Time Line

1784	Treaty of Fort Stanwix with the Iroquois Spain closes Mississippi River to American navigation	1786	Annapolis convention calls for revision of the Articles of Confederation
1785	Land Ordinance for the Northwest Territory Jay-Gardoqui negotiations	1786–1787	Shays's Rebellion
1786	Virginia adopts "Bill for Establishing Religious Freedom"	1787	Northwest Ordinance Constitutional Convention *Federalist Papers* published by Hamilton, Jay, and Madison
		1788	Constitution ratified

chapter 8

Creating a Nation

In October 1789, David Brown arrived in Dedham, Massachusetts. Born about 50 years before in Bethlehem, Connecticut, Brown served in the Revolutionary army and after the war shipped out on an American merchantman to see the world. His travels, as he later reported, took him to "nineteen different . . . Kingdoms in Europe, and nearly all the United States."

Though Brown had little formal schooling, he was a man with powerful opinions and considerable natural ability. His reading and personal experience had persuaded him that government was a conspiracy of the rich to exploit farmers, artisans, and other common folk, and he was quick to make his opinions known. "The occupation of government," Brown declared bluntly in one of his numerous pamphlets, "is to plunder and steal." The object of his wrath was the central government recently established under the new national constitution. The leaders of government, he charged, were engrossing the nation's western lands for themselves. "Five hundred [people] out of the union of five millions receive all the benefit of public property and live upon the ruins of the rest of the community."

In the highly charged political climate of the 1790s, Brown's attacks on the new government's leaders brought a sharp response. In 1798, John Davis, the federal district attorney in Boston, issued a warrant for Brown's arrest on charges of sedition. Brown fled to Salem on the Massachusetts coast but was caught and charged with intent to defame the government and aid the country's enemies. For want of $400 bail, he was clapped in prison.

In June 1799, Brown came before the U.S. Circuit Court, Justice Samuel Chase presiding. Determined to make Brown an example of what criticism of the government would bring, Chase sentenced him to a fine of $480 and 18 months in jail. For nearly two years, Brown languished in prison. Not until the Federalist party was defeated in the election of 1800 and the Jeffersonian Republicans had taken office was he freed.

David Brown discovered how easy it was for critics of the government to get into trouble during the 1790s, a decade of extraordinary political controversy. Even though the Revolutionary War was long past, the debate over Revolutionary principles and the struggle to create a republican political order continued. As Benjamin Rush, Philadelphia physician and Revolutionary patriot, explained: "The American War is over, but this is far from being the case with the American revolution. On the contrary, nothing but the first act of the great drama is closed. It remains . . . to establish and perfect our new forms of government."

As we have seen, the contest for ratification of the new Constitution had generated fierce debate over the familiar concerns about power, political equality, and the proper role of the central government in a republican society. As the new government got under way during the 1790s, that debate heated up once again, drawing countless people like David Brown into the struggle.

As the decade proceeded and the political debate escalated, Americans divided into two opposing political camps. The Federalists supported the presidential administrations of George Washington and John Adams; the Jeffersonian Republicans were the Federalists' increasingly vocal critics. Seldom has American political discourse been so virulent, and rarely has the survival of the republic seemed to hang more clearly in the balance.

In this chapter, we examine the new government's beginnings, and the domestic and foreign issues that polarized political divisions between Federalists and Jeffersonian Republicans during the administration of John Adams. The chapter ends with the election of 1800, which brought Federalist defeat and Thomas Jefferson's election to the presidency.

LAUNCHING THE NATIONAL REPUBLIC

Once ratification of the Constitution was achieved, many Anti-Federalists seemed ready to give the new experiment a chance. They determined, however, to watch it closely and raise the alarm at the first sign of danger. It was not many months before those alarms were sounded.

Beginning the New Government

On April 16, 1789, George Washington started north from Virginia toward New York City to be inaugurated as the first president of the United States. The first electoral college had convened under the Constitution and unanimously elected him to the nation's highest office. His feelings were mixed as he set forth. "I bade adieu to Mount Vernon, to private life, and to domestic felicity," he confided to his diary, "and with a mind oppressed with more anxious and painful sensations than I have words to express, set out for New York . . . with the best disposition to render service to my country in obedience to its call, but with less hope of answering its expectations."

Washington's journey through the countryside resembled a royal procession, for he was the object of constant adulation along the way. When he reached New York City, throngs of citizens and newly elected members of Congress greeted the weary traveler. Over the streets of the city stretched gaily decorated arches. During the parade uptown to the governor's mansion, young women in white flowing robes preceded him, strewing flowers in his path. That night, bonfires illuminated the city.

Already the transition from the old Confed-

This imaginative scene of President-elect Washington's reception in Trenton, New Jersey, during his trip from Virginia to New York City for his first inauguration depicts the popular adulation that surrounded him as well as the sharply different political roles of men and women.

eration Congress to the new government was under way. On October 10, the old Congress adjourned *sine die* after setting March 4, 1789, as the day for the new Congress to assemble.

Inaugural day was April 30. Shortly after noon, on a small balcony overlooking a Wall Street thronged with people, Washington took the oath of office. With the crowd roaring approval and 13 guns booming in the harbor, the president bowed his way off the balcony and into Federal Hall. The rest of the day and late into the night, celebrations filled the air.

The Bill of Rights

Among the new government's first items of business were the amendments that several states had made conditions of their ratification. After considerable debate Congress reached agreement on 12 amendments and sent them on to the states, which ratified ten of them. These ten became the Bill of Rights. Among other things, they guaranteed freedom of speech, press, and religion; pledged the right of trial by jury, the right to bear arms, and the right to due process of law; forbade "unreasonable searches and seizures"; and protected individuals against self-

incrimination in criminal cases. These constitutional amendments have protected individuals' basic rights throughout the nation's history.

During its first months in office, Washington's administration enjoyed almost universal support, both in Congress and among the people. The honeymoon, however, did not last long. Within a year criticism began, and by the middle of the decade, opposition groups came together in a political coalition known as the Jeffersonian Republicans. By 1800, the Jeffersonians had gained control of the government. The political conflict of this first decade revealed the fragility but also the resilience of this new government.

The People Divide

Disagreement began in January 1790, when Secretary of the Treasury Alexander Hamilton submitted the first of several major policy statements, the "Report on the Public Credit," to Congress. Seldom in the nation's history has a single official so dominated public affairs as Hamilton did during these years. A man of extraordinary intelligence and ambition, Hamilton was both a nationalist and a proponent of America's economic development. Perhaps more clearly than anyone else among the nation's founders, he foresaw the country's future strength and was determined to promote its growth. The United States, he was fond of saying, was "a Hercules in the cradle."

He believed that the proper role of the new government was to promote economic enterprise. The people he most admired were men of wealth, ambitious entrepreneurs eager to tie their own fortunes to America's rising empire. Hamilton regarded a close alliance between these people and government officials as essential to achieving American greatness.

If Hamilton's economic policies were liberal in looking forward to enhanced economic opportunity, his politics were profoundly conservative. He distrusted the people and doubted their

Alexander Hamilton used both the office of secretary of the treasury and his personal relationship with President Washington to shape national policy during the early 1790s.

wisdom. "The people," he asserted, "are turbulent and changing; they seldom judge or determine right." That stark belief guided much of what he did.

With the Constitution now in place, Hamilton set about to give it proper direction. His opportunity came when Washington named him secretary of the treasury. Hamilton had five objectives: stabilize the government's finances and establish its credit, build and demonstrate its power, tie the interests of the rich and well-born to the national government, promote the country's commercial expansion overseas and its economic development at home, and anchor the nation's foreign relations in a commercial and diplomatic alliance with England. All were essential to the nation's survival; each, he believed, was closely tied to the others.

In his first "Report on the Public Credit,"

Hamilton recommended funding the remaining Revolutionary War debt by encouraging the government's creditors to exchange their badly depreciated securities at full face value for new interest-bearing government bonds. The foreign debt, held chiefly in France and the Netherlands, Hamilton set at $11.7 million. The domestic debt, including back interest, he fixed at $40.4 million. Second, he proposed that the federal government assume responsibility for the $21.5 million in remaining state war debts. By these actions, he hoped to revive confidence in the government at home and abroad and tie business and commercial interests, which held most of the outstanding securities, firmly to the new government.

The proposal to fund the foreign debt aroused little controversy, but Hamilton's plans for handling the government's domestic obligations generated immediate opposition. In the House of Representatives, James Madison protested the unfairness of funding depreciated securities at their face value, especially since speculators, anticipating Hamilton's proposals, had acquired most of them at a fraction of their initial worth. In addition, Madison and many of his southern colleagues knew that northern businessmen held most of the securities and that funding would little benefit the South. After a bit of grumbling, Congress endorsed the funding plan.

Federal assumption of the remaining state debts aroused even greater criticism. States with the largest remaining unpaid obligations, such as Massachusetts, thought assumption a splendid idea. But others, such as Virginia and Pennsylvania, which had already retired much of their debt, were opposed. Critics also pointed out that assumption would strengthen the central government at the expense of the states, for wealthy individuals would now look to it rather than the states for a return on their investments. Moreover, with its increased need for revenue, the federal government would now have reason to exercise its newly acquired power of taxation. That was exactly what Hamilton intended.

Once again, Congress supported Hamilton's bill. Both Madison and Jefferson approved it as part of an agreement to move the seat of government from New York, first to Philadelphia and then, after 1800, to a special federal district on the Potomac River.

While the southern states continued to complain about the funding and assumption schemes, Hamilton introduced the second phase of his financial program in December 1790. He proposed a national bank capable of handling the government's financial affairs and pooling private investment capital for economic development. Though he was careful not to mention it publicly, he had the example of the Bank of England and its ties with the royal government clearly in mind.

Congressional opposition to the bank came almost entirely from the South. It seemed obvious that the bank would serve the needs of northern merchants and manufacturers far better than those of southern agrarians. Still, in February 1791, Congress approved the bank bill.

Before signing it, Washington asked his cabinet for advice. Following the constitutional doctrine of "implied powers"—the principle that the government possessed the authority to make any laws "necessary and proper" for exercising the powers specifically granted to it—Hamilton argued that Congress could charter such a bank under its power to collect taxes and regulate trade. Secretary of State Jefferson disagreed, maintaining that since the Constitution said nothing at all about chartering banks, the bill was unconstitutional and should be rejected.

Jefferson also opposed the bank because he feared it would promote a commercial republic filled with merchants and a dependent laboring class. He sought instead an agrarian republic populated by yeoman farmers committed to economic and political equality. To Jefferson's distress, Washington followed Hamilton's advice and signed the bank bill into law.

In December 1790, in his second "Report on the Public Credit," Hamilton broached the issue of federal taxation. He proposed a series of excise taxes, including one on the manufacture of distilled liquor. The power to tax and spend, Hamilton knew, was the power to govern. The Whiskey Tax became law in March 1791.

Finally, in his "Report on Manufactures," issued in December 1791, Hamilton called for a system of protective tariffs for American industry, bounties to encourage the expansion of commercial agriculture, and a network of federally sponsored internal improvements such as roadways and lighthouses. Neither the agrarian South nor northern seaport districts, however, wanted tariffs that might reduce trade and raise the cost of living. As a result, Congress never endorsed this report.

All the while, criticism of Hamilton's policies continued to grow, reaching a climax in January 1793 when Representative William Branch Giles of Virginia introduced a series of resolutions calling for an inquiry into the condition of the Treasury and urging censure of the secretary's conduct. None of Giles's accusations passed the House, but the debate was now spreading beyond the circle of governing officials in Philadelphia.

Among ordinary Americans, Hamilton's financial program drew a mixed response. In northern towns and cities, artisans and other working people generally approved. Closely dependent on the expansion of commerce and manufacturing, they supported efforts to improve credit and stimulate economic development. With their own economic circumstances improving, they seemed undisturbed by the special benefits that funding, assumption, and the bank brought to a few. Within several years, many of them would move into political opposition, but for the moment their support of the government was secure.

The Whiskey Rebellion

The farmers of western Pennsylvania provided the most dramatic expression of popular discontent with government policies. Their anger focused on the Whiskey Tax, for their livelihood depended on their ability to transport surplus grain eastward across the mountains to market. To ship it in bulk was prohibitively expensive, so they distilled the grain and moved it in the more cost-efficient form of whiskey. Hamilton's tax threatened to make this practice unprofitable. He knew that but cared little what the farmers thought.

Trouble was brewing by the summer of 1792 as angry farmers and their supporters gathered in mass meetings across western Pennsylvania. In August, a convention at Pittsburgh drew up a series of resolutions denouncing the tax and declaring that the people would prevent its collection. The convention's pronouncements echoed the Anti-Federalists' warnings against the centralizing and taxing tendencies of a national government. Like opponents of the Stamp Act in 1765, they decided that repression would follow if resistance did not soon begin.

Alarmed by the convention's resolutions, Washington quickly issued a proclamation warning against such "unlawful" gatherings and insisting on the enforcement of the excise. In July 1794, federal marshal David Lennox, in company with John Neville, a local excise inspector, attempted to serve papers on several western farmers, commanding their appearance in court at Philadelphia. An angry crowd gathered and stood in the way. Soon 500 armed men surrounded Neville's home just outside Pittsburgh and demanded his resignation. Learning that Neville had left, they ordered the dozen soldiers trapped in the house to lay down their arms and come out. The soldiers refused, and for several hours the two sides exchanged rifle fire. After several men had been wounded, the soldiers finally surrendered, whereupon Neville's house was put to the torch. Similar episodes involving angry crowds and the erection of Liberty Poles reminiscent of the Revolution erupted across the state. At Parkinson's Ferry, a convention of over 200 delegates debated both armed resistance and secession from the United States.

Alarmed that the protests might spread through the entire whiskey-producing backcountry from New York to Georgia, Washington ordered the insurgents home and called out troops from eastern Pennsylvania and surrounding states to restore order. Hamilton viewed the insurrection not as evidence of an unjust policy needing change but as a test of the administration's ability to govern. Suppressing the rebellion, Hamilton explained, "will . . . add to the solidity of everything in this country." He eagerly volunteered to accompany a federal army west.

In late August, a force of nearly 13,000 men, larger than the average strength of the continental army during the Revolutionary War, moved toward western Pennsylvania. At its center was Colonel William McPherson's "Pennsylvania Blues," an upper-class and strongly Federalist cavalry regiment. At its head rode the president of the United States and the secretary of the treasury. Washington soon returned to Philadelphia, persuaded by his aides of the danger to his safety, but Hamilton pressed ahead. The battle that Hamilton had anticipated never materialized, for as the federal army approached, the "Whiskey Rebels" dispersed. The army managed to take 20 prisoners, two of whom were convicted of high treason and sentenced to death. Later, in a calmer mood, Washington pardoned them both.

As people quickly realized, the "Whiskey Rebellion" had never threatened the government's safety. Even as ardent a Federalist as Fisher Ames was uneasy at the sight of federal troops marching against American citizens. Though a government "by overcoming an unsuccessful insurrection becomes stronger," he noted, "elective rulers can scarcely ever employ the physical force of a democracy without turning the moral force, or the power of public opinion, against the government." Americans would soon have additional reason to ponder Ames's warning.

THE REPUBLIC IN A THREATENING WORLD

Because the nation was so new and the outside world so threatening, issues of foreign policy during the 1790s generated extraordinary excitement. In the arguments over the French Revolution and its implications for the new American republic, the American people revealed once again how sharply they differed in values and beliefs.

The Promise and Peril of the French Revolution

France's revolution began in 1789 as an effort to reform an arbitrary monarchy weakened by debt and administrative decay. Pent-up demands for social justice, however, quickly outran the initial attempts at moderate, constitutional reform. By the early 1790s, France was embroiled in a radical social revolution. In January 1793, the monarch, Louis XVI, was beheaded. While the rest of Europe watched in horror and fascination, the forces of revolution and reaction struggled for the nation's soul.

As the revolution grew, the forces of conservatism across the Continent gathered in opposition. In response, France's revolutionary government launched a series of military thrusts into Belgium and Prussia. By the end of 1793, Europe was locked in a deadly war between revolutionary France and a counterrevolutionary coalition led by Prussia and Great Britain.

For more than a decade, the French Revolution dominated European affairs. It also cut like a plowshare through the surface of American politics, dividing Americans more deeply against one another.

The outbreak of European war posed a number of thorny problems for Washington's administration. Both England and France wanted America's raw materials, and each was determined to prevent them from reaching the other. Both nations attempted to control American trade for their own advantage by stopping American ships headed for the other's ports and confiscating American cargoes.

America's relations with England were further complicated by its practice of impressing American sailors into service aboard ships of the Royal Navy to meet its growing demand for seamen. Washington faced the problem of upholding the country's neutral rights and protecting its citizens without getting drawn into the European war.

The old French alliance of 1778 compounded the government's dilemma. If still in effect, it seemed to require the United States to aid France, much as France had assisted the American states a decade and a half before. But some insisted that the old treaty had been dissolved when the French monarchy collapsed.

The American people's intense reaction to the European drama further complicated the situation. At first, virtually everyone supported the French Revolution, viewing it as an extension of their own struggle for liberty. Even the swing toward social revolution did not immediately dampen American enthusiasm.

By the mid-1790s, however, especially after France's revolutionary regime launched its attacks on organized Christianity, many Americans pulled back in alarm. This certainly did not resemble their own revolution. What connection could there possibly be between the principles of 1776 and the chaos of revolutionary France? "There is a difference between the French and the American Revolution," insisted the *Gazette of the United States,* a Federalist newspaper. "In America no barbarities were perpetrated—no men's heads were stuck upon poles—no mangled ladies bodies were carried thro' the streets in triumph. . . . Whatever blood was shed, flowed gallantly in the field." The writer ignored the violence meted out by the supporters of monarchy in France and betrayed a selective memory of America's own revolution. But the differences were indeed profound.

For the Federalists, revolutionary France now symbolized social anarchy. With increasing vigor, they castigated the revolution and championed England as the defender of European stability and civilization.

Many Americans, however, continued to support France. While decrying the revolution's excesses, they believed that republican liberty would ultimately emerge from the turmoil. Jefferson wrote that although he regretted the shedding of innocent blood, he believed it necessary if true liberty were to be achieved.

Citizen Genêt and the Democratic-Republican Societies

Popular associations known as the Democratic-Republican societies provided the most vocal support for revolutionary France. As early as 1792, ordinary citizens began to establish "constitutional societies" dedicated to "watching over the rights of the people, and giving an early alarm in case of governmental encroachments." During the government's first years, several dozen such societies, modeled after the Sons of Liberty of 30 years before, formed to oppose Hamilton's financial program.

It was the French Revolution, however, that kindled democratic enthusiasm and stimulated the societies' growth. The arrival in April 1793 of Citizen Edmund Genêt, minister from the French republic to the United States, provided the spark. Genêt landed first at Charleston, South Carolina, to a tumultuous reception. His instructions were to woo public support and negotiate a commercial treaty with Washington's administration. However, he soon began commissioning American privateers to prey on British shipping in the Caribbean and enlisting American seamen for expeditions against Spanish Florida, both clear violations of American neutrality.

Later, despite a warning by Secretary of State Jefferson, Genêt, in open defiance of diplomatic protocol, urged Congress to reject Washington's recently issued neutrality proclamation and side with revolutionary France. That was the final straw. On August 2, the president demanded Genêt's recall, charging that his conduct threatened "war abroad and anarchy at home."

Although Genêt had little success as a diplomat, instead of returning to France, where the political situation was changing rapidly, he remained in the United States, fanning popular enthusiasm for the French revolution. In June 1793, with his open encouragement, the largest and most influential of the new societies, the Democratic Society of Pennsylvania, had been founded in Philadelphia. About 40 similar organizations scattered from Maine to Georgia sprang up during the next several years. Working people—mechanics, artisans, and laborers in the cities, small farmers and tenants in the countryside—provided the bulk of membership. The leaders, however, were doctors, lawyers, tradesmen, and landowners. All were united by a common dedication to what they called the "principles of '76" and a determination to preserve those principles against the "royalizing" tendencies of Washington's administration. They labeled Washington's proclamation of neutrality a "pusillanimous truckling to Britain." Declared the New York society: "We firmly believe that he who is an enemy to the French revolution cannot be a firm republican; and therefore . . . ought not to be entrusted with the guidance of any part of the machine of government." Several of the societies openly urged the United States to enter the war on France's behalf.

In western areas, local societies agitated against the continuing British occupation of the frontier posts around the Great Lakes and berated Spain for closing the Mississippi. In the East, they castigated England for its "piracy" against American shipping. In the Carolinas, they demanded fuller representation for the growing backcountry in the state's assembly. And almost to a person they protested the Excise Tax, opposed the administration's overtures to

England, and demanded that public officials, state and federal alike, attend to the people's wishes. Finally, they campaigned for a press free from the political control of Federalist "aristocrats." "The greater part of the American newspapers," they protested, "seem to be lock, stock, and barrel in the hands of the anti-democrats."

President Washington and his supporters were incensed by the societies' support of Genêt and their criticism of the government's domestic program. The "real design" of the societies, thundered the staunch Federalist Fisher Ames, was "to involve the country in war, to assume the reins of government and tyrannize over the people." Writing in the *Virginia Chronicle* of January 17, 1794, "Xantippe" berated Kentucky's Democratic Society as "that horrible sink of treason, that hateful synagogue of anarchy, that odious conclave of tumult, that frightful cathedral of discord, that poisonous garden of conspiracy, that hellish school of rebellion and opposition to all regular and well-balanced authority!" Such polemics illustrated how inflamed public discourse had become.

Jay's Controversial Treaty

Controversy over Jay's Treaty with England further heightened tensions at mid-decade. Alarmed by the worsening relations with England, Washington sent Chief Justice John Jay to London in the spring of 1794 with instructions to negotiate on a wide range of troublesome issues, including continued British occupation of the western posts, British interference with American neutral shipping, and impressment of American seamen.

Early in 1795, Jay returned home with a treaty that resolved almost none of America's grievances. England finally agreed to vacate the western posts, but not for another year and then only if it had uninterrupted access to the fur trade on American soil south of the Great Lakes. Jay failed to secure compensation for American slaves carried off by the British at the end of the Revolution. Nor would the British foreign minister offer guarantees against the future impress-

ment of American seamen, compromise on the issue of neutral rights, or open the British West Indies to American shipping.

When the terms of the treaty were made public, they triggered an explosion of protest. Southern planters were angry because the agreement brought no compensation for their slaves. Westerners complained that the British were not evacuating the posts, while merchants and sailors railed against Jay's capitulation on the West Indies trade and impressment. After a long and acrimonious debate, however, the Senate ratified the treaty by the narrowest of margins.

The administration made better progress on the still-volatile issue of free transit out the mouth of the Mississippi River. In the Treaty of San Lorenzo, negotiated by Thomas Pinckney in 1795, Spain for the first time recognized the United States' boundaries under the peace treaty of 1783 and thus gave up all claim to U.S. territory. Spain also granted free navigation of the Mississippi and the right of American merchants to unload their goods on shore for transshipment for the next three years.

By mid-decade, political harmony had disappeared, and the American people stood sharply divided on almost every significant issue of foreign and domestic policy. Increasingly estranged from administration policy, Jefferson resigned as secretary of state in July 1793 and soon joined politicians such as Madison and Albert Gallatin of Pennsylvania in open opposition to the Federalist administration.

In September 1796, Washington announced that he would not accept a third term. He had long been contemplating retirement, for he was now 64 and was exhausted by the political controversy swirling about him.

FEDERALISTS VERSUS JEFFERSONIANS

By 1796, bitter controversy surrounded the national government. That controversy intensified

As one of the first true elder statesmen of the early republic, Thomas Jefferson almost became the second president in the 1796 election after Washington declined to run for a third term. John Adams won that election by only three votes, and Jefferson—as the nominal leader of many of those in opposition to the Federalists—represented a powerful voice against many of Adams's policies

during the last half of the 1790s until it seemed to threaten the very stability of the country.

The Election of 1796

The presidential election of 1796 reflected the political storms buffeting the nation. In 1792, Washington and Adams had been reelected president and vice president, respectively, without significant opposition. Four years later, the situation was vastly different.

With Washington out of the picture, the presidential contest quickly narrowed to John Adams and Thomas Jefferson. Both were now elder statesmen. Both had played distinguished roles during the Revolution, when they had become friends and earned each other's respect. Though they had worked closely together, Adams and Jefferson differed in many ways. Short, round, and self-consciously neat, Adams contrasted sharply in physical appearance with the tall and frequently disheveled Jefferson. Intensely ambitious, Adams struggled self-consciously with his public career. Jefferson, by contrast, charted his course more quietly and repeatedly sought the solace of private life.

They differed in intellect and vision as well. Jefferson's mind was more expansive and his interests far more encompassing. Politician and political theorist, he was also an avid naturalist, architect, and philosopher. Adams's interests were more tightly focused on legal and constitutional affairs. By the mid-1790s, they differed as well in their visions of the new republic.

Adams, a committed Federalist, was appalled by the French Revolution and longed for political and social order. Jefferson, while firmly supporting the Constitution, was alarmed by Hamilton's financial program, viewed France's revolution as a logical if chaotic extension of America's struggle for freedom, and sought to expand political democracy. By 1796, he had become the vocal leader of an increasingly articulate political opposition, the Jeffersonian Republicans.

The election of that year bound Jefferson and Adams in a strained alliance. With Washington gone, Adams became the Federalists' candidate. He received 71 electoral votes and was declared president. Jefferson came in second with 68 and therefore, as specified in the Constitution, became vice president. The narrowness of Adams's majority gave indication of the Federalists' weakness and the growing strength of the Jeffersonians.

The War Crisis with France

Adams had no sooner taken office than he confronted a deepening crisis with France. Hoping to ease diplomatic relations between the two countries, he sent off a three-person commission to try to negotiate an accord.

When the commissioners arrived in Paris, agents of the French foreign minister, Charles Maurice de Talleyrand-Périgord, visited them and made it clear that the success of the negotiations depended on a prior loan to the French government and a $240,000 gratuity for them. The two staunchly Federalist commissioners, John Marshall and Charles Pinckney, indignantly rejected the demands and sailed home. The third commissioner, Elbridge Gerry, stayed behind, still hoping for an accommodation and alarmed by Talleyrand's intimation that if all three Americans left, France would declare war.

When Adams submitted a report to Congress on this incident, he substituted the letters X, Y, and Z for the names of the French agents involved, so the matter became known as the "XYZ affair." Americans were outraged at the French demands. Federalist congressmen thundered against the insult to American honor and demanded action. "Millions for defense, but not one cent for tribute" became their rallying cry. Adams now found himself an unexpected hero. Caught up in the anti-French furor, the president lashed out at "enemies" at home and abroad. "In the last extremity," he declared, "we shall find traitors who will unite with the invading enemy and fly within their lines."

For the moment, the Republicans were in disarray. Publicly they deplored the French government's behavior and pledged to uphold the nation's honor. But among themselves they talked with alarm about the Federalists' intentions. They had good reason for concern, because the Federalists quickly mounted a crash program to repel foreign invaders and roust out traitors in the country's midst.

The Alien and Sedition Acts

In May 1798, Congress created the Navy Department and called for the rapid development of a naval force to defend the American coast against French attack. In July, Congress unilaterally repeated the treaty of 1778, thus moving closer to an open breach with France, and then approved a 10,000-man army. The army's stated mission was to defend the country against an expected French invasion. The Jeffersonians, however, feared otherwise, for they remembered the speed with which the Federalists had used force against the Whiskey Rebels.

As criticism of the army bill mounted, Adams had second thoughts. He was still enough of a revolutionary to worry about the domestic dangers of standing armies. "This damned army," he burst out, "will be the ruin of the country." To the dismay of hard-line Federalists, he issued only a few of the officers' commissions that Congress had authorized. Without officers, the troops could not be mobilized.

Fearful of foreign subversion and aware that French immigrants were active in the Jeffersonian opposition, the Federalist-dominated Congress moved in the summer of 1798 to curb the flow of aliens into the country. The Naturalization Act extended from 5 to 14 years the residence requirement for citizenship, and the Alien Act authorized the president to expel "all such aliens as he shall judge dangerous to the peace and safety of the United States." Another bill, the Alien Enemies Act, empowered the president in time of war to arrest, imprison, or banish the subjects of any hostile nation without specifying charges against them or providing opportunity for appeal.

The implications of these acts for basic political liberties were ominous enough, but the Federalists had not yet finished. In July 1798, Congress passed the Sedition Act, aimed directly at the Jeffersonian opposition. The bill made it a high misdemeanor, punishable by fine and imprisonment, for anyone, citizen or alien, to conspire in opposition to "any measure or measures of the government" or to aid "any insurrection, riot, unlawful assembly, or combination." Fines and imprisonment were provided as well for persons who "write, print, utter, or publish . . . any false, scandalous and malicious writing" bringing the government, Congress, or the president into disrepute. The Federalists now equated preservation of their own political power with national survival. The Federalist moves stunned the Jeffersonians, for they threatened to smother political opposition.

Under the terms of the Alien Act, Secretary of State Timothy Pickering launched investigations intended to force the registration of all foreigners. The act's chilling effects were widespread. In July, Pickering noted approvingly that large numbers of aliens, especially persons of French ancestry, were leaving the country. Prosecutions under the Sedition Act were numerous. Twenty-five people, including David Brown of Dedham, were arrested and charged with violating the act. Fifteen were indicted, and ten were ultimately convicted, the majority of them Jeffersonian printers and editors.

Passage of the Alien and Sedition acts generated a firestorm of protest. The Virginia and Kentucky assemblies directly challenged the Federalist laws. The Kentucky Resolutions, drafted by Jefferson and passed on November 16, 1798, declared that the national government had violated the Bill of Rights. Faced with the arbitrary exercise of federal power, the resolutions continued, each state "has an equal right to judge by itself . . . infractions . . . [and] the mode and measure of redress." Nullification (declaring a law invalid within a state's borders) was the "rightful remedy" for unconstitutional laws. The Virginia Resolutions, written by Madison and passed the following month, asserted that when the central government threatened the people's liberties, the states "have the right and are in duty bound to interpose for arresting the progress of the evil." It would not be the last time that state leaders would claim authority to set aside a federal law.

The Kentucky and Virginia resolutions received little support elsewhere, but they indicated the depth of popular opposition to the Federalists' program. In Philadelphia, armed Federalist patrols walked the streets to protect government officials from angry crowds. As 1799 began, the country seemed on the brink of upheaval.

Within a year, however, the cycle turned again, this time decisively against the Federalists. The break came with Adams's dramatic decision to send a new emissary to France. From Europe, Adams's son, John Quincy Adams, sent assurances that Talleyrand was ready to negotiate an honorable accord. The president seized the opening, fearing that war with France "would convulse the attachments of the country." "The end of war is peace," Adams explained, "and peace was offered me." Moreover, he had concluded that his only chance of reelection lay in fashioning a peace coalition out of both parties.

Adams's cabinet strongly disapproved, for the entire Federalist war program depended on the credibility of the French crisis. But by year's end, the president's emissaries had secured an agreement providing for the restoration of peaceful relations between the two nations.

The "Revolution of 1800"

As the election of 1800 approached, the Federalists were bitterly divided. The Hamiltonians were furious at Adams's "betrayal" and demanded that he not seek reelection. When Adams did not withdraw, the Hamiltonians plotted his defeat.

Both sides believed that the republic's survival hung in the balance. Jefferson declared that this election would "fix our national character" and "determine whether republicanism or aristocracy" would prevail. The Federalists saw the choice as between republicanism and "anarchy." In Virginia, rumors of a slave insurrection briefly interrupted the feuding. But the scare passed quickly, and Federalists and Jeffersonians were soon at each others' throats once again.

Though election day was tense throughout the nation, it passed without serious interruption. As the results were tallied, it became clear that the Jeffersonians had handed the Federalists a decisive defeat. Jefferson, the Republicans' preferred candidate for president, and Aaron Burr, their other nominee, each had 73 votes. Adams followed with 65.

Presidential Election of 1800

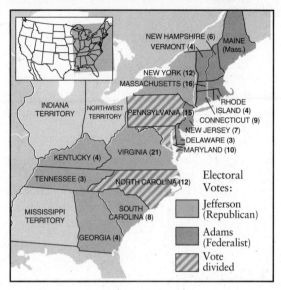

NEW HAMPSHIRE (6)
VERMONT (4)
MAINE (Mass.)
NEW YORK (12)
MASSACHUSETTS (16)
RHODE ISLAND (4)
PENNSYLVANIA (15)
CONNECTICUT (9)
NEW JERSEY (7)
DELAWARE (3)
MARYLAND (10)
INDIANA TERRITORY
NORTHWEST TERRITORY
KENTUCKY (4)
VIRGINIA (21)
TENNESSEE (3)
NORTH CAROLINA (12)
MISSISSIPPI TERRITORY
SOUTH CAROLINA (8)
GEORGIA (4)

Electoral Votes:
Jefferson (Republican)
Adams (Federalist)
Vote divided

Because of the tie vote, the election was thrown into the House of Representatives, where a deadlock quickly developed. After a bitter struggle, the House finally elected Jefferson, ten states to four, on the thirty-sixth ballot. (Seeking to prevent a recurrence of such a crisis, the new Congress soon passed, and the states ratified, the Twelfth Amendment, providing for separate electoral college ballots for president and vice president.) The magnitude of the Federalists' defeat was even more evident in the congressional elections, where they lost their majorities in both House and Senate.

The election's outcome revealed the strong sectional divisions now evident in the country's politics. The Federalists remained dominant in New England because of regional loyalty to Adams, the importance of the area's commercial ties with England, and fears that the Jeffersonians intended to import social revolution. From Maryland south, Jeffersonian control was almost as complete. In South Carolina, whites' fears of the black majority smothered every tendency toward political division, and the Federalists remained solidly in control. But

elsewhere, loyalty to Jefferson, strong anti-British and pro-French sentiment, and suspicion of the commercially oriented Federalists kept power in the hands of the Jeffersonians.

In the middle states, Federalists and Jeffersonians were more evenly balanced and the election was more fiercely contested because economic and social differences were greater and issues of foreign and domestic policy cut across society in more complicated ways. This sectional pattern would continue to shape American politics.

The distinctions between the Federalists and Jeffersonians were grounded in socioeconomic divisions as well. The Federalists were strongest among merchants, manufacturers, and commercial farmers located within easy reach of the coast—groups that had supported the Constitution in 1787 and 1788. In both New York City and Philadelphia, the Federalists' main strength was in the wards where assessments were highest and addresses most fashionable.

By contrast, the Jeffersonians included most of the old Anti-Federalists, agriculturalists in both North and South, and countless urban workers and artisans who resented Federalist arrogance. They also attracted people such as Irish and French immigrants and religious minorities—Baptists, Jews, and Catholics—restive under the lingering religious establishments.

The political alignment of 1800 resembled but did not exactly duplicate the Federalist–Anti-Federalist division of 1786–1788. The Jeffersonian coalition was much broader than the Anti-Federalists' had been, for it included countless individuals, from urban workers to leaders such as Madison and Jefferson, who had supported the Constitution and helped set the new government on its feet. Unlike the Anti-Federalists, the Jeffersonians were ardent supporters of the Constitution who called for the new government to be grounded in the principles of liberty, political equality, and a strong dependence on state authority. Nationally, the Jeffersonians now enjoyed a clear political majority. Their coalition would dominate American politics well into the nineteenth century.

CONCLUSION

TOWARD THE NINETEENTH CENTURY

The election of 1800 provided a remarkable outcome to more than a decade of political crisis. The series of events had begun in the late 1780s with the intensifying debate over the Articles of Confederation and the movement toward a stronger central government. Under the new Constitution, divisions began to form, first in Congress, then, increasingly, among the people. Hamilton's domestic policies first generated opposition, but it was foreign affairs—the French Revolution, the European war, Jay's Treaty, and the prospect of a war with France—that galvanized political energies and set the Federalists and Jeffersonians against each other.

After the election of 1800, control of the federal government passed for the first time from one political party to another, not easily but peacefully and legally. The Jeffersonians called it "The Revolution of 1800." The future would show whether the Jeffersonians were correct.

Recommended Reading

On politics in the states during the 1790s see Richard Beeman, *The Old Dominion and the New Nation, 1788–1801* (1972); Norman Risjord, *Chesapeake Politics, 1781–1800* (1978); and Charles Steffen, *The Mechanics of Baltimore: Workers and Politics in the Age of Revolution, 1763–1812* (1984).

For cogent discussions of the ideological debates between Federalists and Jeffersonians, see Joyce Appleby, *Capitalism and a New Social Order: The Republican Vision of the 1790s* (1984); and Lance Banning, *The Jeffersonian Persuasion: The Evolution of a Party Ideology* (1978).

Party development during the 1790s can be followed in John Hoadley, *Origins of American Political Parties, 1789–1803* (1986); and Merrill Peterson, *Thomas Jefferson and the New Nation* (1970).

The Bill of Rights and the problem of civil liberties are treated by Bernard Schwartz, *The Great Rights of Mankind* (1977); and Leonard Levy, *Legacy of Suppression: Freedom of Speech and Press in Early American History* (1960).

For a fuller understanding of foreign policy issues, turn to Harry Ammon, *The Genêt Mission* (1973); Jerald Combs, *The Jay Treaty* (1970); and Daniel Lang, *Foreign Policy in the Early Republic* (1985).

Thomas Slaughter explains the character of backwoods revolt in *The Whiskey Rebellion: Frontier Epilogue to the American Revolution* (1986). Aleine Austin, *Matthew Lyon: "New Man" of the Democratic Revolution, 1749–1822* (1981), traces the meaning of political equality in the life of an ardent Jeffersonian.

Time Line

Year	Event	Year	Event
1789	George Washington inaugurated as first president Outbreak of French Revolution	1793	Controversy over Citizen Genêt's visit
1790	Slave trade outlawed in all states except Georgia and South Carolina Hamilton's "Reports on the Public Credit"	1794	Whiskey Rebellion in Pennsylvania
		1795	Controversy over Jay's Treaty with England
1791	Bill of Rights ratified Whiskey tax and national bank established Hamilton's "Report on Manufactures"	1796	Washington's Farewell Address John Adams elected president
		1797	XYZ affair in France
		1798	Naturalization Act; Alien and Sedition Acts Virginia and Kentucky resolutions
1792	Washington reelected		
1793	Outbreak of war in Europe Washington's Neutrality Proclamation Jefferson resigns from cabinet	1798–1800	Undeclared naval war with France
		1801	Jefferson elected president by House of Representatives

chapter 9

....

Society and Politics in the Early Republic

In May 1809, Mary and James Harrod gathered their five children, loaded a few belongings (tools, seeds for the summer planting, and several prized pieces of furniture) on a wagon, closed the door on their four-room cabin, fell in line with a dozen other families, and headed west from Spotsylvania County, Virginia, toward a new life in Kentucky. They left behind 10 acres of marginal upland, 15 years of wearying effort at trying to wring a modest living from it, and a family cemetery holding two of their other children and Mary's parents.

The first years in central Kentucky would be especially hard for James and Mary as they "opened up" the land, planted the first crops, and erected a cabin. They would be lonesome as well, for the Harrods would be unlikely to see even the chimney smoke from their nearest neighbors. James and Mary were hopeful, though, and that sustained them as they trudged west.

In April 1795, Ben Thompson started north from Queen Anne's County, Maryland, for New York City. Ben knew little beyond farming, but he was ambitious and listened carefully to the ship's captains who talked about life at sea while they recruited men for their crews. Sailors were in demand, and pay was good. For five years, Ben sailed the seas. Having enough of travel, he returned to New York and hired out as an apprentice to a ship's carpenter.

About the same time, Phyllis Sherman left her home in Norwalk, Connecticut. She also headed for New York, where she took a job as a maid. As fate would have it, Phyllis and Ben met, fell in love, and in the spring of 1802 they were married.

There is little of note in this, except that Ben and Phyllis were former slaves and were married in the African Methodist Episcopal Zion church. Ben had purchased his freedom just as cotton production began to grow through the Chesapeake region. In another decade, he would have faced greater difficulty securing his freedom. Phyllis had been freed as a child when slavery ended in Connecticut. As she grew up, she tired of living as a servant with her former owner's family and longed for the companionship of other blacks. She had heard that there were people of color in New York City, and she was correct. In 1800, it contained 6,300 African-Americans, more than half of them free.

Though life in New York was better than either Ben or Phyllis had known before, it was hardly easy. They shared only marginally in the city's commercial prosperity. In 1804, they watched helplessly as yellow fever carried off their daughter and many of their friends. And while they found support in the expanding black community, they had to be on guard because slave ships still moved in and out of the port, and slave catchers pursued runaways from the South in the city's streets.

During the early years of the nineteenth century, thousands of people like Mary and James and Ben and Phyllis seized whatever opportunities they could find to improve their lives. Like countless others, they knew little about political theories or congressional debates between Federalists and Jeffersonians. Still they valued America's revolutionary origins and sought ways to make republican notions of opportunity and equality fit their lives. In the process, they helped shape the new republic.

The Jeffersonian Republicans, after their victory over the Federalists in 1800, implemented their vision of an expanding agrarian republic. At the local level, this meant increasing democratization of political life. Nationally, these years brought the collapse of the Federalist-Jeffersonian party system of the 1790s and set the stage for the dramatically new political era that Andrew Jackson's election to the presidency in 1828 would usher in. The Jeffersonians also reconstructed America's relationship with Europe, finally breaking free of a centuries-long pattern of dependence.

In 1800 one could speak of two Americas—one evolving via the decisions made by ordinary people in communities across the land, the other centered in the halls of Congress. In the early nineteenth century, political change would bring those two Americas closer together. In that gradual convergence is to be found much of the nation's history during those years.

RESTORING REPUBLICAN LIBERTY

The Jeffersonians entered office in March 1801 with several objectives in mind: calming the political storms that had threatened to rend the country, consolidating their recent victory, purging the government of Federalist holdovers, and setting it on a proper republican course.

The Jeffersonian Republicans Take Control

The government had moved from Philadelphia to the new capital in the District of Columbia in November 1800, while John Adams was still president. When the politicians arrived in Washington, they were stunned by its primitiveness and isolation, for the new capital was little more than a swampy clearing, holding about 5,000 residents, on the banks of the Potomac River.

In keeping with his desire to rid the government of Federalist embellishments, Jefferson planned a simple inauguration. Shortly before noon on March 4, 1801, the president-elect walked to the Capitol from his temporary lodgings at a nearby boardinghouse. "His dress," noted one observer, "was, as usual, that of a plain citizen, without any distinctive badge of office." Chief Justice John Marshall, a Virginian but a staunch Federalist as well, administered the oath of office, and a company of militia fired a 16-gun salute.

Though simple, the inauguration was filled with significance. This was the first time in the nation's brief history that control of the government had shifted from one political party to another. Mrs. Samuel Harrison Smith, Washington resident and political observer, described the occasion's drama: "I have this morning witnessed one of the most interesting scenes a free people can ever witness," she wrote a friend. "The changes of administration, which in every ... age have most generally been epochs of confusion, villainy, and bloodshed, in this our happy country take place without any species of distraction or disorder." Many Americans shared her sense of relief and pride.

In his inaugural speech, Jefferson enumerated "the essential principles of republican government" that would guide his administration: "equal and exact justice to all," support of the states as "the surest bulwarks against anti-republican tendencies," "absolute acquiescence" in the decisions of the majority, supremacy of civil over military authority, reduction of government spending, "honest payment" of the public debt, freedom of the press, and "freedom of the person under the protection of the *habeas corpus*." Though Jefferson never mentioned the Federalists by name, his litany of principles reverberated with the dark experience of the 1790s.

The president spoke also of political reconciliation. "Every difference of opinion," he explained, "is not a difference of principle. We

have called by different names brethren of the same principles. We are all republicans—we are all federalists."

Not all his followers welcomed that final flourish, for many were eager to root out the Federalists and scatter them to the political winds. Jefferson's goal, however, was to absorb the moderate Federalists, isolate the extremists, and destroy the Federalist Party as a political force. His strategy worked, for never again did the Federalists regain control of the national government.

Having swept both houses of Congress as well as the presidency in 1800, the Jeffersonians claimed a mandate to rid the government of Federalist officeholders. They were especially outraged by a flurry of last-minute appointments President Adams had pushed through the lame-duck Federalist Congress during the closing days of his administration in an effort to reward party loyalists and deny the Jeffersonians full control of the government.

Under pressure from party supporters, Jefferson reluctantly agreed that "a general sweep" of Federalist officeholders was necessary. By the time Jefferson left office in 1809, virtually all government personnel were solid Republicans.

Politics and the Federal Courts

Late in Adams's administration, the Federalists had introduced a new Judiciary Act calling for more circuit courts and judges with their attendant array of federal marshals, attorneys, and clerks. Congress passed the bill in February 1801, just before adjourning. This blatant effort to pack the judiciary aroused the Jeffersonians' wrath. "The Federalists," observed Jefferson bitterly, "defeated at the polls, have retired into the Judiciary, and from that barricade ... hope to batter down all the bulwarks of Republicanism." Something had to be done.

In January 1802, Senator John Breckinridge of Kentucky introduced a bill calling for repeal of the Judiciary Act of 1801. "The time will never arrive," Breckinridge naively asserted, "when America will stand in need of 38 federal judges."

The resulting controversy centered on the independence of the judiciary from political attack and the doctrine of judicial review, the notion that it was the federal courts' responsibility to judge the constitutionality of congressional laws and executive behavior. Gouverneur Morris, Federalist senator from New York, declared that an independent judiciary was necessary "to save the people from their most dangerous enemy, themselves." The Jeffersonians argued that each branch of the government—executive and legislative as well as judicial—must have the right to decide on the validity of an act. Congressional debate over repeal of the Judiciary Act drew wide public attention, for it offered a vivid contrast between Federalist and Jeffersonian notions of republican government. In February 1802, by a strict party vote, Congress repealed the Judiciary Act.

The Jeffersonians also sought to purge several highly partisan Federalist judges from the bench. In March 1803, the House of Representatives voted to impeach Federal District Judge John Pickering of New Hampshire. The grounds were not "high crimes and misdemeanors" as the Constitution required, but the Federalist diatribes with which Pickering regularly assaulted defendants and juries. The Senate convicted Pickering, by a strict party vote.

Spurred on by success, the Jeffersonians brought impeachment charges against Supreme Court Justice Samuel Chase, one of the most notorious Republican baiters. The trial, however, revealed that Chase had committed no impeachable offense. He was acquitted on every count and returned triumphantly to the bench.

After that defeat, the Jeffersonians pulled back, content to allow time and the regular turnover of personnel to cleanse the courts of Federalist control.

In several trailblazing decisions, the Supreme Court, led by Chief Justice John Marshall, soon established some of the most basic principles of American constitutional law. In *Marbury* v. *Madison* (1803), Marshall laid down in unmistakable terms the principle of judicial review. "It is emphatically the province and duty of the judicial department," he declared, "to say what the law is." This decision nullified the Judiciary Act of 1789, by which Congress had granted the Supreme Court certain powers. The Court decided that its powers, which were based on the Constitution, could not be extended by Congress. In so doing, the Court laid down a precedent for judicial review of laws as cases challenging specific laws came before it.

In another landmark decision, *McCulloch* v. *Maryland* (1819), the Court struck down a Maryland law taxing the Baltimore branch of the Second Bank of the United States. No state, explained Marshall, possessed the right to tax a nationally chartered bank, for "the power to tax involves the power to destroy." By affirming the constitutionality of the bank's congressional charter, Marshall laid down the constitutional argument for broad congressional authority. Let congressional intent "be within the scope of the Constitution," he wrote, "and all means which are appropriate ... which are not prohibited, but consist with the letter and spirit of the Constitution, are constitutional."

Dismantling the Federalist War Program

The Jeffersonians had regarded the Federalists' war program as a threat to republican liberty, so they moved quickly to dismantle it. Jefferson stopped prosecutions under the hated Sedition Act and freed its victims. In 1802, the act silently lapsed. The Jeffersonians, though not thoroughgoing civil libertarians, never duplicated the Federalists' campaign to stifle dissent.

Jefferson handled the Alien acts similarly, not bothering to seek their repeal but dismantling the Federalists' inspection system and allowing enforcement to lapse. In 1802, Congress passed a new and more liberal naturalization law, restoring the requirement of 5 rather than 14 years of residence for citizenship. The Federalists' provisional army was also reduced by 1802, to only 3,400. No longer would federal troops intimidate American citizens.

Finally, the Jeffersonians sought ways to reduce the size and operations of the federal government. The central government, Jefferson declared in his first message to Congress in 1801, was "charged with the external and mutual relations only of these states. The principal care of our persons, our property, and our reputation, constituting the great field of human concerns," should be left to the states.

The government inherited by the Jeffersonians was tiny by modern standards. In 1802, it had fewer than 3,000 civilian employees. In terms of domestic policy, it did little more than deliver the mail, deal with Native Americans, and administer the public lands. As the nation grew, however, so did pressures for a federal program of internal improvements. That reflected in part the growing political influence of the West, for the new states forming beyond the Appalachians sought closer ties of trade and communication with the East. The government responded by launching construction of several western routes, including the National Road (in 1811) connecting Cumberland, Maryland, with Wheeling on the Ohio River. The states, however, carried the major responsibility for internal improvements.

The Jeffersonians also reduced the national debt. In spite of the extraordinary costs of the Louisiana Purchase (1803), the debt dropped from $83 million in 1801 to $57 million a decade later. Though the Jeffersonians may not have "revolutionized" the government as they claimed, they clearly changed its character and direction.

BUILDING AN AGRARIAN REPUBLIC

The Jeffersonians worked vigorously to implement their vision of an expanding, agrarian republic. That vision was mixed and inconsistent, for the Jeffersonian party was an amalgam of different and often conflicting groups: southern patricians determined to maintain a privileged, slavery-based agrarian order; lower- and middle-class southern whites generally committed to black slavery though resentful of the patricians' social pretensions, and ardent proponents of political equality; northern artisans dedicated to honest toil and their own economic interests; and western farmers devoted to working the land and living free. In time, this diversity would splinter the Jeffersonian party. For the moment, however, these groups found unity not only against their common Federalist enemies but also in a set of broadly shared principles. Those principles guided Jeffersonian policies for over two decades, through the presidential administrations of Jefferson (1801–1809), James Madison (1809–1817), and James Monroe (1817–1825).

The Jeffersonian Vision

Political liberty, the Jeffersonians believed, could survive only under conditions of broad economic and social equality. The central task of Jeffersonian statecraft was thus to maintain an open and roughly equal society. The task was believed difficult because as societies grew in wealth and power, equality eroded and liberty was snuffed out. England's efforts to destroy colonial liberties had offered ample evidence of that.

The Jeffersonians, however, continued to believe that America, if properly guided, could escape England's fate. Their strategy centered on the independent yeoman farmer—self-reliant, secure in person and possessions, industrious and yet filled with concern for the public good. Such people exemplified the qualities essential to republican citizenship.

The Jeffersonian vision threatened to become clouded, however, because industriousness generated wealth, and wealth bred inequality. In short, economic and social development threatened to destroy the social bases of republicanism.

The solution to the problem of economic and social development, the Jeffersonians believed, lay in rapid territorial expansion. Land, constantly expanding and readily available to the nation's yeoman citizens, would offer opportunity to a restless people, draw them out of the cities and off the crowded lands of the East, and preserve the social equality that republican liberty required. The republic's growth across the North American continent would delay, perhaps even prevent, the cyclic process of growth, maturity, and decay through which all past societies had traveled.

Calls for expanding America's land base were strengthened by the arguments of an English clergyman and political economist named Thomas Malthus. In 1798, Malthus published an essay that jolted Europeans and Americans alike. Given the remarkable fecundity of human beings, Malthus argued, population increased more rapidly than agricultural production. Enlightenment notions of the steadily improving quality of human life, he warned, were a delusion, for the future would be filled with increasing misery and exploitation as population outran food. The future was most clear in Europe, where land was limited and poverty widespread, but the same fate awaited America.

Jefferson believed that America's vast reservoir of land would enable its people to escape Europe's fate. Rapid and continuing national expansion was thus indispensable to the Jeffersonian vision of the agrarian republic. Occupation of the West was also essential to secure America's borders against continuing threats from England, France, and Spain. The rapid sale of new public lands would in addition provide revenue for reducing the national debt. Finally, the Jeffersonians calculated that the creation of new western states would strengthen their political control and assure the Federalists' demise.

A Nation of Regions: The Northeast and the South

The growing young country continued to exhibit striking regional differences. While the long-established differences between Northeast and South that had originated during the colonial period persisted and even increased, an entirely new region of white settlement began to take shape beyond the Appalachians, in the nation's interior.

In the Northeast, a broad region stretching from eastern Pennsylvania through New England, family farms dominated the landscape. Because much of New England's land was poor, farmers there often turned their fields from tillage into pasture to take advantage of more profitable dairying and livestock raising. On the richer agricultural lands of New York and Pennsylvania, by contrast, farmers cultivated their land intensively, planting it in grain year after year rather than following the time-honored custom of allowing worn-out fields to lie fallow and recover their fertility.

Many northeastern farmers, especially in southern New England, along the Hudson River in New York, and in southeastern Pennsylvania, produced an agricultural surplus, which they exchanged in nearby towns for commodities such as tea, sugar, window glass, and tools. Many farm families, however, consumed nearly all they produced. As late as 1820, no more than 25 percent of agricultural output was available for export.

Across much of the rural Northeast, cash played only a small part in economic exchanges. "Instead of money going incessantly backwards and forwards into the same hands," declared an observant Frenchman, people "supply their

Although the cotton gin, invented in 1793, simplified one step of cotton processing, much of the work on a plantation continued to be done with rudimentary tools by slave labor. Here Benjamin Latrobe sketches An Overseer Doing His Duty.

needs in the countryside by direct reciprocal exchanges. The tailor and the bootmaker go and do the work of their calling at the home of the farmer ... who most frequently provides the raw material for it and pays for the work in goods. . . . They write down what they give and receive on both sides, and at the end of the year they settle a large variety of exchanges with a very small quantity of coin."

Most farms were not large. By 1800, the average farm in the longer-settled areas of New England and the mid-Atlantic states was no more than 100 to 150 acres, down substantially from half a century before, as a result of the continued division of farm property across generations of fathers and sons. Economic opportunity was also declining. Long and continuous cropping had robbed the soil of its fertility, forcing farmers to bring more marginal land under cultivation.

Though the vast majority of northeasterners made their living from the land, growing numbers worked as artisans or day laborers in the cities or labored in the small-scale manufactories—grain and saw mills, potash works, and iron forges—that dotted the rural landscape.

By 1800, the standard of living of many northeastern families was higher than it had been 30 years earlier, but for the countless families still outside the market system, life went on much as it had generations before.

Life was very different in the South. As the nineteenth century began, southern agriculture was in disarray. Falling prices, worn-out land, and the destruction wrought by the Revolutionary War had left the Chesapeake's tobacco economy in shambles. The extensive loss of slaves added to the region's economic woes.

Southern planters had experimented with wheat and other grains in an effort to bolster their sagging fortunes, but regional recovery began when they turned to a new staple crop—cotton. The fibers of the long-staple variety were highly valued and could easily be separated from the cotton's seeds. The delicate long-staple plant, however, grew only where soil and climate were right—on the sea islands off the coast of Georgia and South Carolina. The hardier short-staple variety could be cultivated across large areas of the South, but its fibers clung tenaciously to its sticky, green seeds. A slave could clean no more than a pound of short-staple cotton a day.

Demand for cotton of all sorts was growing, especially in England, where new textile factories created an insatiable appetite for the crop. In 1793 Eli Whitney, a Yankee schoolteacher seeking employment in the South, set his mind to the problem of short-staple cotton and its seeds. Within a few days, he had designed a "cotton gin," a box containing a roller, equipped with wire teeth, designed to pull the fibers through a comblike barrier, thus stripping them from the seeds. A hand crank activated the mechanism. The implications of Whitney's invention were immediately apparent, for with this crude device a laborer could clean up to 50 pounds of short-staple cotton per day.

During the next several decades, southern cotton production soared. In 1805, cotton accounted for 30 percent of the nation's agricultural exports; by 1820, it exceeded half. Across both the old coastal South and the newly developing states of Alabama, Mississippi, and Tennessee, cotton was becoming king.

As we shall see in later chapters, the swing to cotton marked a momentous turning point for the South and the nation, for it increased the demand for fieldhands and breathed new life into the institution of slavery. Some of the escalating demand was met from overseas, but much would be met by the internal slave trade that moved African-Americans from the worn-out lands of the Chesapeake to the booming cotton lands of the Deep South.

Trans-Appalachia

A third region, west of the Appalachian Mountains, was forming as the nineteenth century began. New, raw, repeatedly embroiled in warfare between Indian inhabitants and white intruders, Trans-Appalachia constituted a broad and shifting zone of cultural, political, economic, and military interaction between Native American and European-American peoples. It extended, east to west, from the Appalachian Mountains to the Mississippi River and from the Great Lakes on the north to the Gulf of Mexico. In 1790, scarcely 100,000 white settlers lived beyond the Appalachians. By 1800, their number had swollen to nearly a million; by 1820, fed by people like Mary and James Harrod, there were over a million more.

"The woods are full of new settlers," wrote an observer near Batavia, New York, in 1805. "Axes are resounding, and the trees literally falling around us as we passed." By 1812, some 200,000 souls lived in the western part of the state, where scarcely 30,000 whites had lived 20 years before. "America is breaking up and going west!" exclaimed the British traveler Morris Birkbeck.

Settlers were drawn by the promotions of land speculators. Between 1790 and 1820, land companies hawked vast areas of New York, Ohio, and Kentucky to prospective settlers such

as James and Mary Harrod. Individual settlers shared in the speculative fever, going into debt to buy extra land so they might sell it at a premium when population increased and land prices rose.

North of the Ohio River, settlement followed the grid pattern prescribed in the Land Ordinance of 1785, while south of the Ohio people distributed themselves more randomly across the land, much as their ancestors had done back east. Above the Ohio, mixed, free-labor agriculture took hold. Towns such as Columbus and Cincinnati emerged to provide services and cultural amenities for the surrounding population. In Kentucky and Tennessee, free-labor agriculture also developed but was soon challenged by the spread of slave-based cotton.

As people continued to spill into the region, they established churches, schools, and even colleges (Transylvania University, founded in Lexington, Kentucky, in 1780, was the first college west of the Appalachians). Even so, Trans-Appalachia retained a reputation for its rough and colorful ways. No characters were more famous in popular folklore than westerners like Daniel Boone. None were more colorful than the mythical riverman Mike Fink, "half man, half alligator," who could "whip his weight in grizzly bears."

As the settlers came, they began the long process of transforming the region's heavily forested land. In the mountainous areas of western Pennsylvania, entire hillsides were denuded of trees by anxious travelers who cut them down to drag behind their wagons as makeshift brakes during the jolting rides downhill. Regarding the unforested "oak openings" scattered through the woods of Ohio and southern Michigan as "barren" and infertile, many farmers staked their claims where the trees grew thickest and set about clearing the land.

Farmers followed the long-established practice of cutting a girdle of bark off the trees and leaving them to die in place, while planting crops around the decaying hulks. By this method, a family could clear from 3 to 5 acres a year for cultivation. The relentless demands for wood—for log cabins and barns, fences and fuel, potash and turpentine—added to the assault on the region's forests.

The Windfall Louisiana Purchase

The strategy of securing the agrarian republic by territorial expansion explains Jefferson's most dramatic accomplishment, his purchase of the Louisiana Territory in 1803. In 1800, Spain ceded the vast trans-Mississippi region known as Louisiana to France. When Jefferson learned of the secret agreement in 1801, he was profoundly disturbed. Especially upsetting were rumors that Spain would soon transfer New Orleans, the major outlet for western agricultural produce, to France. His fears were well grounded, for in October 1802 the Spanish commander at New Orleans, which Spain had retained, once again closed the Mississippi River to American commerce.

In January 1803, the president sent his young associate James Monroe to Paris with instructions to purchase New Orleans and West Florida, which contained Mobile, the only good harbor on the Gulf Coast, and the mouths of several rivers that drained the southern interior. When Monroe arrived, he found French Foreign Minister Talleyrand unwilling to sell West Florida but ready to sell all of Louisiana, a huge territory of nearly 830,000 square miles.

In April, the deal was struck. For $15 million, the United States obtained all of Louisiana, in one stroke doubling the nation's size. The public's response was overwhelmingly favorable, and Congress readily approved the purchase.

The Federalists reacted with alarm, fearing with good reason that the new states to be carved from Louisiana would be staunchly Jeffersonian and worrying that rapid expansion of the frontier would "decivilize" the nation. In New England, Federalist extremists talked of forming a northern confederacy and seceding from the Union.

National expansion did not stop with Louisiana. In 1810, American adventurers fomented a revolt in Spanish West Florida, proclaimed an independent republic, and sought annexation by the United States. In May 1812, over vigorous Spanish objections, Congress formally annexed the area. In 1819, in the Adams-Onis treaty, Spain ceded East Florida as well. As part of that agreement, the United States for the first time extended its territorial claims beyond Louisiana to include the Pacific Northwest. These impressive accomplishments set the stage for the final surge of continental expansion during the 1840s.

Opening the Trans-Mississippi West

If America's vast new domain was to serve the needs of the agrarian republic, it would have to be explored and made ready for settlement. In the summer of 1803, Jefferson dispatched an expedition led by his personal secretary, Meriwether Lewis, and William Clark, a young army officer, to explore the Far Northwest. For nearly 2½ years, the intrepid band of explorers, assisted by the Shoshoni woman Sacajawea, made its way across thousands of miles of unmapped terrain—up the Missouri River, through the Rockies via the Bitterroot Valley and Lolo Pass, down the Columbia to the Pacific coast, and back again, finally reemerging at St. Louis in September 1806. Lewis and Clark's reports of their journey fanned American interest in the trans-Mississippi West, established an American presence in the region, and demonstrated the feasibility of an overland route to the Pacific.

In 1805 and 1806, Lieutenant Zebulon Pike explored the sources of the Mississippi as far as Leech Lake in northern Minnesota. He followed that trek with an equally bold venture into New Mexico and Colorado, where he explored and named the peak that bears his name. In the

Important Routes Westward

decade after 1815, the government established a string of military posts from Fort Snelling, at the confluence of the Minnesota and Mississippi rivers, to Fort Atkinson on the Missouri and Fort Smith on the Arkansas. They were intended to secure the American frontier, promote the fur trade, and support white settlement.

The Jeffersonians' agrarian vision also guided changes in land policy. The primary objective of Federalist land policy had been to produce government revenue. The Jeffersonians were more interested in encouraging people to settle on the land.

The Land Act of 1801 reduced the minimum purchase of federal land to 320 acres, established a four-year credit system, and provided 8 percent discounts for cash sales. Over the next year and a half, settlers, speculators, and land

companies purchased nearly 400,000 acres of federal land, more than four times as much as during the entire 1790s. The amounts increased geometrically in the following decade.

In succeeding years, Congress established the principles of preemption, which enabled squatters to secure title to land, and pricing graduation, whereby lands that did not readily sell were offered at less than the established price or were even given away. All were efforts to speed the transfer of public land into private hands.

PERFECTING REPUBLICAN SOCIETY

During the Revolutionary era, politics and government had preoccupied the American people.

Exploring the Trans-Mississippi West, 1804–1807

Louisiana Purchase, 1803

In the early republic, there was increasing concern about fashioning a social order capable of supporting republican government. Spurred by that concern, Americans launched various projects of social reform intended to implement republican ideals.

The Principles of Reform

The first of these ideals was social equality. In part this meant equality of opportunity, the notion that people should have a chance to rise as far as ability and ambition would carry them. Privilege should be set aside, and everyone should have an equal chance.

Promises of equal opportunity had limited relevance for many Americans. Slaves, women, and working-class men understood all too well the limits of opportunity in preindustrial America. But the principle was bold and inspiring for countless others.

Social equality also had a powerful moral dimension, because it implied an equality of social worth among individuals, no matter what their wealth or social standing might be. That attitude showed up vividly in an episode that took place in New York City in 1795. Thomas Burke and Timothy Crady, two recent Irish immigrants, operated a ferry across the East River between lower Manhattan and Brooklyn. One day in early November, Gabriel Furman, a merchant and Federalist alderman, arrived on the Brooklyn shore a bit before the scheduled departure time and instructed the ferrymen to leave early. When they refused, he upbraided the "rascals" for their disrespect and threatened to have them arrested. Crady was especially angered by the alderman's arrogance. He and Burke, Crady exploded, "were as good as any buggers." When the ferry landed on the Manhattan shore, Furman had the two arrested.

Both Crady and Burke were eventually hauled before Mayor Richard Varick and three other Federalist aldermen, sitting as the Court of General Sessions. There was no jury. The judges quickly decided to make examples of the two insolent Irishmen. "You rascals, we'll trim you," Varick allegedly said; "we'll learn you to insult men in office." The magistrates quickly found the two guilty on charges of insulting an alderman and threatening the constable, sentenced them to two months at hard labor, and ordered 25 lashes for Crady as well.

Within a month, the two ferrymen had bolted from jail and disappeared into Pennsylvania, never to be heard from again. The episode, however, was not yet over, for a young Jeffersonian lawyer named William Keteltas took up the case and in time carried it all the way to the New York assembly. In a two-column newspaper account signed "One of the People," he castigated "the tyranny and partiality of the court" and concluded that Burke and Crady had been punished to "gratify the pride, the ambition and insolence of men in office." That, he argued, was intolerable in a republican society. The assembly, he charged, was protecting the mayor to save his reputation. But what of the ruined reputations of the ferrymen? Were they not just as important?

Before it was over, the incident generated wide public anger, and Keteltas earned a jail sentence for his efforts. When released, however, he was paraded through the streets by a throng carrying American and French flags and a banner inscribed "What, you rascal, insult your superi-

ors?" In the early republic, notions of equal social worth spread rapidly.

The doctrine of individualism was a second basic element of the new social faith. It asserted the primacy of individuals' needs and interests. During the colonial years, that idea had been carefully balanced by the opposing view that individuals must subordinate themselves to the general good. The Revolutionary experience, however, shifted the balance in favor of an emphasis on the primacy of the free and unfettered individual.

Patterns of Wealth and Poverty

In the early republic, as at other times in the nation's history, ideals jarred awkwardly against social reality. In that tension is to be found the primary impulse for social reform.

As the nineteenth century began, property was unequally distributed across gender and racial lines. Women continued to hold far less property than men. The large majority of blacks, moreover, were slaves; for them, ownership of anything more than the smallest items of personal property was beyond reach. Though the condition of free blacks such as Ben Thompson and his wife, Phyllis, was better, they too held little of the country's wealth.

Among white males, property was most broadly shared in rural areas of the North, where free labor and family-farm agriculture predominated, and least so in the South, where control of slave labor and the best land permitted tobacco, rice, and cotton planters to monopolize the region's wealth.

The class structure was also sharply drawn in the port cities where merchant capitalists controlled the sources of commercial and manufacturing wealth, while small artisans, sailors, and unskilled workers lived at the margins of the economy, their lives dominated by a relentless struggle for survival. The most even distribution of wealth existed on the edges of white settlement in the trans-Appalachian frontier, but that was an equality of want.

Taking the country as a whole, the pattern of wealth distribution had not changed much from pre-Revolutionary times. In 1800, the top 10 percent of property holders controlled about 42 percent of the nation's wealth, very close to what the situation had been 50 years before.

Though America contained no large destitute underclass such as could be found in the cities and countryside of Europe, poverty was real and was increasing. In the South, it was most evident among slaves and poor whites living on the sandy pine barrens of the backcountry. In the North, the port cities held growing numbers of the poor. In Boston, artisans and shopkeepers, who together had owned 20 percent of the city's wealth in 1700, held scarcely half as much a century later. During the winter of 1805, New York's mayor DeWitt Clinton worried publicly about the fate of 10,000 impoverished New Yorkers and asked the state legislature for help. During the winter of 1814–1815, relief agencies assisted nearly one-fifth of the city's population.

Even in rural New England and southeastern Pennsylvania, a lower class of transient and propertyless people was growing. The "strolling poor," they were called—landless men, and sometimes women, forced to roam the countryside searching for work.

Three other groups were conspicuous among the nation's poor. One consisted of old Revolutionary War veterans like Long Bill Scott, who had found poverty as well as adventure in the war. The others were women and children. Annual censuses of almshouse residents in New York City from 1816 to 1821 consistently listed more women and children than men.

Poverty was a continuing reality in the early republic. And for every American who actually suffered its effects, there were several others living just beyond its reach, their margin of safety alarmingly thin.

Just how thin became clear during the depression of 1819–1822. Triggered by a financial panic created by the unsound practices of hundreds of newly chartered state banks, a deep depression settled over the land, generating bankruptcies and sending unemployment soaring. In upstate New York, the pay of turnpike workers sank from 75 cents to 12 cents a day. In the South, farms and plantations stood abandoned as cotton and tobacco exports fell. By the early 1820s, the depression was lifting, but it left behind broken fortunes and shattered dreams.

Alleviating Poverty and Distress

Alleviating poverty was one goal of the early social reformers. In New York City during the early decades of the century, private and public authorities established more than 100 charitable and relief agencies to aid orphans and widows, aged females and young prostitutes, immigrants and imprisoned debtors, juvenile delinquents and poverty-stricken seamen. Across the nation as a whole, a "charitable revolution" increased benevolent institutions from 50 to nearly 2,000 by 1820.

Most of these ventures attempted to distinguish between the "worthy poor," respectable folk who were victims of circumstance and merited assistance, and the "idle" or "vicious poor," who were deemed to lack character and therefore deserved their fate.

Poverty was not the only object of public and private reform. Municipal authorities and private charities established orphanages for children, asylums for the insane, and hospitals for the sick. Most of these institutions were small and short-lived, but they provided a base for the more ambitious reform efforts to come several decades later.

Women's Lives

Though women's lives were not markedly altered during these years, changes that helped set the stage for later, more dramatic breakthroughs did occur. Divorce was one area where women achieved more equal treatment. When a neighbor asked John Backus, a silversmith in Great Barrington, Massachusetts, why he kicked and struck his wife, John replied that it was partly owing to the fact that his father had often treated his mother in the same way. We don't know whether John's mother tolerated such abuse, but his wife did not. She complained of cruelty and obtained a divorce. Her reaction was not unique, for more and more women were following her example.

Thomas and Sarah Mifflin, a well-to-do Quaker couple, sat for this portrait by John Singleton Copley. Note that Mrs. Mifflin's hands are busy weaving thread into a strip of fringe, while her husband marks his place in the book he is reading. Their activities suggest the different social roles men and women were expected to play.

The process of divorce was not easy. Most states allowed it only on the ground of adultery, while South Carolina did not permit it at all. Moreover, women typically had to present detailed evidence of their husbands' infidelities and face the discomfort of an all-male court, while accusations of a wife's transgressions could be more easily proven in court. Short of divorce, many women demonstrated their unwillingness to stay with a bad marriage by walking out. We know this from the increasing number of newspaper notices filed by deserted husbands announcing that their wives had left bed and board.

Changes also occurred in women's education. This was part of the general enthusiasm for educational reform, but it reflected a special concern for women's place in the new republic. Given women's role as keepers of public morality and nurturers of future citizens, their education was a subject of general concern. If the republic was to fulfill its destiny, young women would have to prepare for the responsibilities that motherhood would bring. During the 1790s, Judith Sargeant Murray published a series of essays, gathered under the title *The Gleaner,* in which she criticized parents who "pointed their daughters" toward marriage and dependence. "I would give my daughters every accomplishment which I thought proper," Murray wrote. "They should be enabled to procure for themselves the necessaries of life; independence should be placed within their grasp."

Between 1790 and 1820, a number of female academies were established, most of them in northeastern cities. Timothy Dwight, the future president of Yale, opened his academy at Greenfield Hill in Connecticut to girls and taught them the same subjects he taught boys, at the same time and in the same room; but he was the exception. Benjamin Rush, in his essay "Thoughts upon Female Education" (1787), prescribed bookkeeping, reading, grammar, penmanship, geography, natural philosophy, vocal music ("because it soothes cares and is good for the lungs"), and history. Traditionalists such as the Boston minister John Gardiner were decidedly less sympathetic. "Women of masculine minds," he warned, "have generally masculine manners, and a robustness of person ill calculated to inspire the tender passions."

The prediction that intellect would unsex women was accompanied by the warning that educated women would abandon their proper sphere as mothers and wives. Even the most ardent supporters of female learning insisted that they seek education so that they might function more effectively within their traditional sphere.

Race, Slavery, and the Limits of Reform

As we have seen (Chapter 7), the Revolution initiated the end of slavery in the northern states and raised challenges to its continued existence in the Upper South. As the new century began, however, antislavery sentiment was declining, while private manumission slowed as well. The reasons were several. The gradual abolition of slavery in the North soothed many consciences, while in the South, the spread of cotton increased the value of slave labor. Equally important were two slave rebellions that generated intense alarm.

Panic-stricken whites fleeing Hispaniola for their lives in 1791 carried word to the North American mainland of the black Haitians' successful rebellion against a French colonial army of 25,000. The news spread terror, especially through the South, where southern whites immediately tightened their black codes, cut the importation of new slaves from the Caribbean, and quizzed their slaves in an effort to root out suspected Haitian revolutionaries. The bloody rebellion and the prospect of a nearby island nation governed by blacks frightened northern whites as well.

A second shock followed in the summer of 1800, when a rebellion just outside Richmond, Virginia, was nipped in the bud. Gabriel Prosser,

a 24-year-old slave, had devised a plan to arm 1,000 slaves for an assault on the city. Betrayed by several black house servants, Prosser's plan failed. No white lives were lost, but scores of slaves and free blacks were arrested, and 25 suspects, including Prosser, were hanged at the personal order of Governor James Monroe.

In the early nineteenth century, antislavery appeals all but disappeared from the South, while proslavery arguments increased.

In the North, antislavery attitudes were increasingly conciliatory toward slave owners and unsympathetic toward blacks. Most of slavery's critics assumed that private manumission was the only safe approach, that it should be gradual so as to avoid social turmoil, and that freed blacks should be relocated to colonies in Africa. The American Colonization Society, founded in 1816, typified these attitudes. The Society never sent many blacks abroad, but it did help allay white anxieties.

Nor did free blacks living in the North find their lives much improved by the first stirrings of republican reform. During the half century following independence, strong and growing black communities appeared in the northern ports, notably in Boston, New York, Philadelphia, and Baltimore. Their growth was fed by people like Phyllis Sherman coming in from the northern countryside and Ben Thompson making his way up from the South. On the eve of independence, 4,000 slaves and a few hundred free blacks had called the four port cities home; 50 years later, more than 30,000 free blacks did so.

The men who came sought employment as laborers or sailors, the women as domestics. They sought as well the companionship of other people of color. The development of black neighborhoods was a result both of white discrimination and the black desire for community. In rural areas, free blacks lived in relative isolation and were largely defenseless against white hostility. In the cities, however, numbers provided some protection and greatly improved the chances of finding a marriage partner, establishing a family,

Blacks and Slavery, 1790–1820

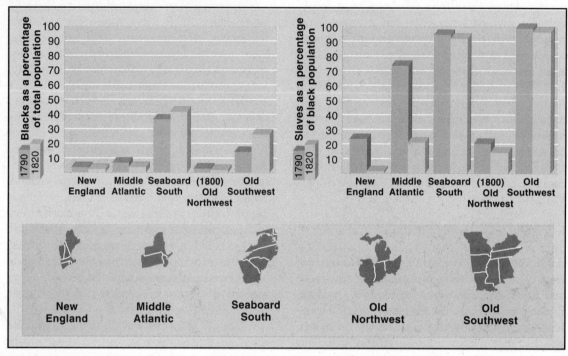

Though regions had differed in the importance of slavery and the number of blacks in their population as the Revolutionary era ended, those differences increased significantly over the next 30 years.
Source: *U.S. Bureau of the Census.*

and participating in community activities. Family formation was eased by the fact that many of the migrants were women, thus correcting a long-standing gender imbalance.

As their numbers increased, blacks organized community institutions. In 1794, Richard Allen and Absalom Jones founded the first two black churches in Philadelphia. By 1813, the two congregations had over 1,800 members. "African" schools, mutual-aid societies, and fraternal associations followed, first in Philadelphia and Boston, more slowly in New York and Baltimore, where slavery lingered longer.

By 1820, a rich institutional and cultural life had taken root in the black neighborhoods of the port cities. White hostility, however, re-

mained. Slavery's abolition actually increased rather than diminished white enmity in the North, in part because it pitted free blacks more directly against white laborers for employment and cheap housing. Race, as well as gender and class, continued to separate Americans from one another and reveal the limits of America's new social faith.

A FOREIGN POLICY FOR THE AGRARIAN REPUBLIC

During the early decades of the nineteenth century, the Jeffersonians struggled to fashion a foreign policy appropriate for the expanding agrarian republic. They had several major goals: protecting American interests on the high seas, clearing America's western territories of foreign troops and influence, and breaking free from the country's historic dependence on Europe. Those goals were not easily accomplished; yet by the 1820s, aided by changes taking place across the Atlantic, the Jeffersonians had fashioned a new relationship with Europe. In the Monroe Doctrine of 1823, they also projected a momentous new role for the United States within the Americas.

Jeffersonian Principles

Jeffersonian foreign policy was based on the doctrine of "no entangling alliances" with Europe that Washington had articulated in his Farewell Address of 1796. In the Jeffersonians' minds, England was still the prime enemy, but France was now suspect as well. By the time the Jeffersonians took office, the French Revolution had run its course and ended in the consulate of Napoleon. Second, the Jeffersonians emphasized the importance of overseas commerce to the security and prosperity of the agrarian republic, for trade provided markets for America's agricultural produce and fetched back manufactured goods in return. Third, they sought to maintain peace, because they feared war's effects on republican liberty. Not only did war kill people and destroy property, but it also inflamed politics, stifled freedom of speech, disrupted the economy, increased the public debt, and expanded governmental power.

The Jeffersonians' handling of the crisis leading into the War of 1812 against Great Britain illustrates how eagerly, and in this case how futilely, they sought to avoid conflict.

Struggling for Neutral Rights

After a brief interlude of peace, European war resumed in 1803. Once again England and France seized American shipping. England's overwhelming naval superiority made its attacks especially serious. British impressment of American seamen and continued occupation of the Great Lakes posts also increased tension between the two nations.

In response to increasing British seizures of American shipping, in April 1806 Congress passed the Non-Importation Act, prohibiting the importation of English goods that could be produced domestically or acquired elsewhere. On May 16, Britain replied by declaring a full blockade of the European coast. Threatened by Britain's action, Napoleon answered with the Berlin Decree, forbidding all commerce and communication with the British Isles. Americans were further angered by Britain's refusal to deal in good faith on issues of impressment and the reopening of the West Indian trade.

Tension between England and the United States reached the breaking point in June 1807, when the British warship *Leopard* stopped the American frigate *Chesapeake* off the Virginia coast. The British captain claimed that four *Chesapeake* crew members were British deserters and demanded their surrender. When the American commander refused, the *Leopard* opened fire, killing 3 men and wounding 18, and removed the alleged deserters. After the *Chesapeake* limped back into port with the story, cries of outrage rang across the land.

Fearing war and recognizing that the United States was not prepared to confront England, Jefferson decided to withdraw American ships from the Atlantic. In December 1807, Congress passed the Embargo Act, forbidding all American vessels from sailing for foreign ports. It was one of Jefferson's most ill-fated decisions.

The embargo had relatively little effect on England. British shipping actually profited from the withdrawal of American competition. The embargo's domestic impact, however, was far-reaching. American exports fell 80 percent in a year, and imports dropped by more than half.

New England ports were hardest hit, but up and down the coast, communities dependent on overseas commerce openly challenged the embargo. At Plattsburgh, New York, on Lake Champlain, federal officials declared martial law and sent in federal troops in an effort to stop smuggling into Canada. The result was guerrilla skirmishing as local citizens fired on U.S. revenue boats and recaptured confiscated goods. Throughout the largely Federalist Northeast, bitterness threatened to escalate into open rebellion. Connecticut's governor, in words reminiscent of the Virginia and Kentucky resolutions, warned that whenever Congress exceeded its authority, the states were duty-bound "to interpose their protecting shield between the rights and liberties of the people and the assumed power of the general government."

In the election of 1808, the Federalists rebounded after nearly a decade of decline. James Madison handily succeeded Jefferson in the presidency, but the Federalist candidates, C. C. Pinckney and Rufus King, garnered 47 electoral votes. Their party also made gains in Congress and recaptured several state legislatures.

Faced with the embargo's ineffectiveness abroad and its disastrous political consequences at home, Congress repealed the measure in 1809. In that year and the next, Congress tried more limited trade restrictions aimed at reducing English and French attacks on American shipping, but these strategies also failed, and American war fever continued to grow.

The War of 1812

The most vocal calls for war came from the West and the South. The election of 1810 had brought to Congress a new group of western and southern leaders, firmly Republican in their party loyalty but impatient with the Madison administration's bumbling policy and convinced of the need for tougher measures. The War Hawks, they were called, and an impressive group they proved to be: Henry Clay and Richard Johnson of Kentucky, John Calhoun and Langdon Cheves from South Carolina, Felix Grundy of Tennessee, and Peter Porter from western New York.

For too long, the War Hawks cried, the United States had tolerated Britain's presence on American soil, encouragement of Tecumseh's confederation, and attacks on American commerce. Their language echoed as well with talk of territorial expansion north into Canada and south into Florida. Their overriding goals were to secure the republic from European threats and demonstrate the Republican party's ability to govern.

Responding to the growing pressure, President Madison finally asked Congress for a declaration of war on June 1, 1812. Opposition came entirely from the New England and Middle Atlantic states—ironically, the regions British policies affected most adversely—while the South and West voted solidly for war. Seldom had sectional alignments been sharper.

The war itself was a curious affair, for its causes were uncertain and its goals unclear. England successfully fended off several American forays into Canada. The British navy once again blockaded American coastal waters, while British landing parties launched punishing attacks up and down the East Coast. On August 14, a British force occupied Washington, torched the Capitol and the president's house (which became known as the White House after being repaired and whitewashed), and sent the president, Congress, and a panic-stricken American army fleeing into Virginia. England, however, did not press its advantage, for it was preoccupied with Napoleon's armies in Europe and wanted to end the American quarrel.

On the American side, emotions ran high among both the war's Federalist critics and Republican supporters. In Baltimore, on the night of June 22, 1812, a Republican crowd demolished the printing office of the *Federal-Republican,* a local Federalist newspaper.

In late July, after copies of the *Federal-Republican* again appeared on Baltimore's

The War of 1812

The War of 1812 scarcely touched the lives of most Americans, but areas around the Great Lakes, Lake Champlain, Chesapeake Bay, and the Gulf Coast witnessed significant fighting.

streets, a thousand men and women once more surrounded the paper's office. This time, 50 armed Federalists were there to defend it. When the Federalist defenders opened fire, the crowd rolled up a cannon and sent a round of grapeshot into the building. Several people lay dead on both sides before the militia finally arrived to cart the Federalists off to the safety of jail.

On the following night, a crowd reassembled in front of the city jail and seized ten prisoners, including James Lingan, an old Revolutionary War general. The enraged mob beat Lingan and several others to death and left the bodies, stripped of their fine clothing, sprawling in the street.

Though the Baltimore riots were not duplicated elsewhere, emotions ran high throughout the country. In Federalist-dominated New England, opposition to "Mr. Madison's War" veered toward outright disloyalty. In December 1814, delegates from the five New England states met at Hartford, Connecticut, to debate proposals for secession. With the outcome of the war in doubt, some New England Federalists wanted to separate from the seemingly doomed republic, whose policies and administration they opposed. Cooler heads prevailed, but before adjourning, the Hartford Convention asserted the right of a state "to interpose its authority" against "unconstitutional" acts of the government. As the war dragged on, Federalist fortunes soared in the Northeast, while elsewhere bitterness grew over New England's disloyalty.

Before the war ended, American forces won several impressive victories, among them Commander Oliver Hazard Perry's defeat of the British fleet on Lake Erie in 1813. The most dramatic American triumph was Andrew Jackson's smashing victory in 1815 over an attacking British force at New Orleans. It occurred, however, after preliminary terms of peace had already been signed.

The treaty signed on Christmas Eve in 1814, at Ghent, Belgium, resolved almost nothing, for it ignored impressment, blockades, neutral rights, and American access to Canadian fisheries. England did agree to evacuate the western posts, but other than that, the treaty simply ended the conflict, provided for an exchange of prisoners and the restoration of conquered territory, and called for several joint commissions to deal with the remaining disputes.

The war did leave its mark on the American nation. It made Andrew Jackson a military hero and established him as a national political leader of major importance. The American people, moreover, regarded the contest as a "Second War of American Independence," in which they had whipped the British once again. The republic seemed finally secure. No longer would Americans have to worry about the vulnerability of their republican "experiment" to outside attack.

The years following 1815 brought an end to America's colonial-like dependence on Europe and a reorientation toward the tasks of internal development—occupying the continent, industrializing the economy, and reforming American society. At the same time, Europe entered nearly a century free from general conflict. In the past, European wars had involved the American people; in the twentieth century, they would do so again. For the remainder of the nineteenth century, however, that fateful link was missing. Also, the focus of European colonialism was shifting away from the Americas to Africa and Asia. From the 1820s on, Europe left the Americas relatively alone.

The United States and the Americas

While disengaging from Europe, the Jeffersonians fashioned new policies for Latin America that would guide the United States hemispheric relations for years to come. Although the American people gave little thought to Europe's Latin American colonies prior to 1800, when those colonies began their struggles for independence from Spain and Portugal in 1808, Americans voiced support. In the early 1820s, the United States recognized the new Latin American republics of Colombia, Mexico, Chile, and Argentina.

In November 1822, the Quadruple Alliance (France, Austria, Russia, and Prussia) talked of a plan to help Spain regain its American colonies, alarming both the United States and Great Britain. The British foreign secretary, George Canning, broached the idea of Anglo-American cooperation to thwart Spain's intentions.

Secretary of State John Quincy Adams opposed the idea. Son of the former Federalist president, Adams had joined the Jeffersonian camp some years before as part of the continuing exodus from the Federalist party. In the new spirit of nationalism so evident following the War of 1812, Adams declared that the United States should not "come in as a cockboat in the wake of the British man-of-war." He urged independent action based on two principles: a sharp separation between the Old World and the New, and the United States' dominance in the Western Hemisphere.

President Monroe, elected to a second term in 1820, soon agreed that the United States should issue its own policy statement. In his annual message of December 1823, he outlined a new Latin American policy. Though known as the Monroe Doctrine, its content was of Adams's devising.

Monroe asserted four basic principles: (1) the American continents were closed to new European colonization, (2) the political systems of the Americas were separate from those of Europe, (3) the United States would consider as dangerous to its peace and safety any attempts to extend Europe's political influence into the Western Hemisphere, and (4) the United States would neither interfere with existing colonies in the New World nor meddle in the internal affairs of Europe.

When Monroe issued his doctrine, the United States had neither the economic nor military power to enforce it. By the end of the nineteenth century, however, when the country's power had increased, it would become clear

what a fateful turning point in the history of the Americas Monroe's declaration had been.

INDIAN-WHITE RELATIONS IN THE EARLY REPUBLIC

The young country's power grew as it expanded westward. As white settlers surged across the interior, however, they found a land already occupied by Native American peoples. By 1800, white settlement, disease, and warfare had decimated Native Americans along the Atlantic coast. Powerful tribes, however, still controlled much of the trans-Appalachian interior. North of the Ohio River, the Shawnee, Delaware, Miami, and Potawatomi were allied in a Western confederacy capable of mustering several thousand warriors. South of the Ohio lived five major tribal groups: the Cherokee, Creek, Choctaw, Chickasaw, and Seminole. Together these southern tribes totaled nearly 60,000 people.

The years from 1790 to the 1820s brought a decisive shift in Indian-white relations throughout the trans-Appalachian interior. In 1790, the region was aflame with raids and warfare. As the pressures of white expansion increased, tribal groups devised various strategies of resistance and survival. The Cherokee followed a path of peaceful accommodation. Others, like the Shawnee and the Creek, rose in armed resistance. Neither strategy was altogether successful, for by the 1820s the balance of power in the interior had shifted, and the Indians faced a future of continued acculturation, military defeat, or forced migration to lands west of the Mississippi.

The Goals of Indian Policy

Between 1790 and 1820, the government established policies that would guide Indian-white relations for much of the nineteenth century.

Indian Land Cessions, 1750-1830

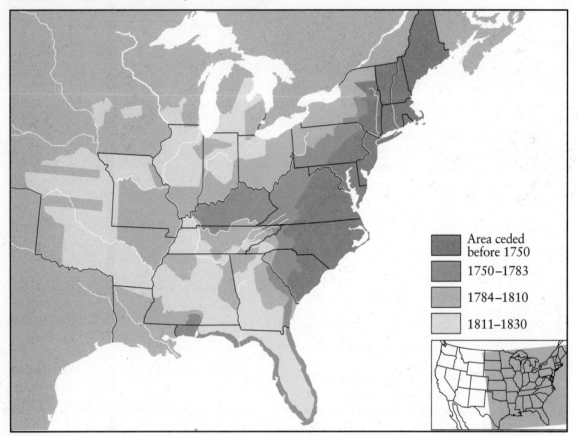

Area ceded before 1750

1750–1783

1784–1810

1811–1830

Though federal policymakers attempted to protect Native Americans from unscrupulous traders and aggressive settlers and to Christianize and civilize them in preparation for their admission into white society, the pace of territorial expansion created irresistible pressure to move the Indians out of the white settlers' way.

The acquisition of Native American land became the main objective of federal Indian policy. By 1790, the government had given up its earlier "conquest" theory, recognized Indian rights to the soil, and declared that land transfers would henceforth be accomplished through treaty agreements.

Responsibility for the management of Indian affairs rested with the War Department.

Henry Knox, Washington's first secretary of war, laid out the government's basic positions in 1789. The Indians, he said, "being the prior occupants of the soil, possess the right of the soil." It should not be taken from them "unless by their free consent, or by the right of conquest in case of just war." Few of the land treaties negotiated after 1789 represented the "free consent" of Native American people. Still, Knox had established a new, more humane principle, the acquisition of Native American land by formal treaty agreement.

The new treaty-based strategy was effective. Native American leaders were frequently willing to cede land in return for trade goods, yearly annuity payments, and assurances that no further

Sequoyah, who sat for this portrait in 1838, devised the Cherokee alphabet, which formed the basis for the first written Indian language in North America.

demands would be made on them. When tribal leaders proved reluctant, they could often be persuaded to cooperate by warnings about the inevitable spread of white settlement, or more tractable chieftains could be found. In these ways, state and national governments gained title to vast areas of tribal land throughout the trans-Appalachian interior. The continuing loss of land disastrously affected Native Americans, altering the balance of tribal power and forcing many to migrate west.

The fur trade was also a major concern of federal Indian policy. By 1790, most trans-Appalachian tribes served as intermediaries for hunters farther to the west. Both Native Americans and whites entered willingly into the trade. In return for furs, which they had in abundance, the Indians secured highly valued goods such as blankets, guns, rum, and ironware. White traders acquired valuable furs in exchange for relatively inexpensive trade items. Both sides also used the trade to cement diplomatic relations with each other.

The fur trade served white society very well. It had severe costs, however, for Native Americans, who fell victim to deadly diseases such as smallpox and measles and became dependent on renewed supplies of rum, firearms, and other goods. As the demand for furs and pelts increased, moreover, Native Americans over-trapped their hunting grounds, forcing them to reach farther west for fresh sources of supply. That process disturbed long-standing tribal patterns of trade and diplomatic relations.

A third objective of federal Indian policy was to civilize and Christianize the Native Americans and ultimately assimilate them into white society. In the trans-Appalachian West, where whites and Native Americans struggled openly for survival, most people believed that Indians would always remain "savage" and regarded them as impediments to be moved out of white settlement's way. Different attitudes, however, were evident in the East, where clergymen and government officials, newspaper editors and ordinary citizens displayed greater sympathy for the Native Americans' well-being.

A policy of assimilation seemed to offer hope for the Indians' survival in the face of continuing warfare, disease, and white expansion. Although the assimilationists cared deeply about the physical and spiritual fate of Native American people, they had little sympathy for Indian culture, for they demanded that Native Americans cease being Indian and adopt the ways of white society instead. Assimilation or continuing destruction were the alternatives posed by even the most benevolent whites.

Education and Christianization were the major instruments of assimilationist policy. Together Moravian, Quaker, Baptist, Congregationalist, and Dutch Reformed churches sent scores of missionaries to live among the Indians, preach the gospel, and teach the benefits of white civilization. Baptist missionary Isaac

McCoy ministered to the Shawnee tribe in Indiana from 1817 to 1829. John Stewart, a freeborn mulatto who was part Indian, preached to the Wyandotte near Sandusky, Ohio, from 1815 to his death in 1821. Among the most selfless were the Quaker missionaries who labored with the Iroquois in New York.

The missionaries' greatest success occurred where Indians had succumbed to white control or when missionaries blended Indian beliefs with the basic tenets of Christianity. Even so, most Native Americans remained aloof, for the chasm between Christianity and their own religions was wide (see Chapter 1), and the missionaries' denigration of Indian culture was obvious.

Education was the other weapon of the assimilationists. In 1793, Congress appropriated $20,000 to promote literacy, agriculture, and vocational instruction. Church groups established schools as well, and in 1819, the government handed over to the churches full responsibility for Indian education. Because federal officials thought that Christianity and civilization went hand in hand, they encouraged missionaries to teach their Indian students religious doctrine as well as reading, writing, and vocational skills.

Strategies of Survival: The Iroquois and the Cherokee

Faced with the steady loss of land and tribal autonomy, Native Americans devised various strategies of resistance and survival. Among the Iroquois, a prophet named Handsome Lake, who had fought with England during the Revolutionary War but who had succumbed to the despair of military defeat and reservation life, led his people through a process of cultural revitalization. In 1799, in a series of religious and social gospels, he preached a combination of Indian and white ways that included temperance, peace, land retention, and the rituals of Gaiwiio, a new religion joining elements of Christianity and traditional Iroquois belief. His vision, a new definition of "Indianness," offered hope and renewed pride for the Iroquois in their dramatically changed world.

Far to the south, the Cherokee followed a different path of accommodation. As the nineteenth century began, the Cherokee still controlled millions of acres in Tennessee, Georgia, and the western Carolinas. Their land base, however, was shrinking. By 1800, more than 40 Cherokee towns had disappeared, and over two-thirds of all Cherokee families had been forced to move into the increasingly crowded settlements that remained.

In 1801, the Tennessee legislature unilaterally expanded the boundaries of several counties to include Cherokee land and then claimed that the Indians fell under the authority of state law The Cherokee, declaring that they had their own system of justice and distrusting the state courts with their all-white juries and exclusion of Indian testimony, rejected white demands.

In Cherokee councils, a group of full-blood leaders argued for armed resistance. Others, however, including mixed-bloods such as John Ross, pointed out the futility of fighting and argued that accommodation offered the only hope for survival. In the early 1800s, following a bitter struggle for tribal control, the accomodationists won out.

Their first goal was to bring the tribe's scattered villages under a common government. In 1808, the Cherokee National Council adopted a written legal code combining elements of white and Indian law, and in July 1827, the Cherokee devised a written constitution patterned after those of nearby states, complete with executive, legislative, and judicial branches of government. They accompanied it with a bold declaration of their standing as an independent nation. In 1829, the Cherokee government formalized the "blood law," making it an offense punishable by death for any tribe member to transfer land to white ownership without the consent of tribal authorities.

Meanwhile, the process of social and cultural accommodation went forward. Missionaries opened a school for Cherokee youth on the Hiwanee River in 1804 and established a boarding school near present-day Chattanooga 12 years later. They stepped up their religious activities as well, baptizing Cherokee into the Christian faith.

As the Cherokee changed from a mixed hunting, gathering, and farming economy to one based predominantly on settled agriculture, many of them moved from traditional town settlements onto individual farmsteads. The majority continued to inhabit crude log cabins and live a hand-to-mouth existence. However, some prospered, especially mixed-bloods who learned English and understood how to deal with white society. A few of the most successful lived as well as upper-class whites. Joseph Vann, known as "Rich Joe," accumulated hundreds of acres of fertile land, scores of black slaves, and an assortment of mills, stores, and river ferries.

Changes in the Cherokee economy altered relations with blacks as well. Since the mid–eighteenth century, the Cherokee had held a few blacks in slavelike conditions. During the early nineteenth century, however, Cherokee slavery expanded and became more harsh. By 1820, there were nearly 1,300 black slaves in the Cherokee nation. Such changes came about primarily because the spread of cotton cultivation increased the demand for slave labor among Cherokee as well as whites.

By 1820, the strategy of peaceful accommodation had brought obvious rewards. Tribal government was stronger, the standard of living higher, and the sense of Cherokee identity reasonably secure. In the end, however, the Cherokee's success proved their undoing, for as their self-confidence grew, so did the hostility of southern whites, who were increasingly impatient to get them out of the way. That hostility would soon erupt in a final campaign to remove the Cherokee from their land forever (see Chapter 12).

Patterns of Armed Resistance: The Shawnee and the Creek

Not all tribes of the interior proved so accommodating to white expansion. Faced with growing threats to their political and cultural survival, the Shawnee and Creek nations rose in armed resistance during the War of 1812.

In the late 1780s, the tribes of the Old Northwest had launched a series of devastating raids across Indiana, Ohio, and western Pennsylvania, creating panic among white settlers. In September 1790, a force of 1,500, dispatched by President Washington to quell the uprising, fell into an ambush in northwestern Ohio, losing nearly 200 men. The following year, another army of 6,000 troops met a similar fate. Buoyed by their victories, the Shawnee and their allies followed up with a furious assault, virtually clearing northern and central Ohio of white settlement.

Faced with two humiliating defeats, Washington determined to smash the Indians' resistance. In the autumn of 1793, General Anthony Wayne led a third army of conquest into the Ohio wilderness. The following year, his army won a complete victory in the decisive Battle of Fallen Timbers. After the smoke of battle had cleared, the assembled chiefs ceded the southern two-thirds of Ohio in return for $20,000 in trade goods and a $10,000 annual annuity. It was the largest single transfer of Indian land yet, and it opened the heart of the Old Northwest to white control.

In subsequent years, additional treaties further reduced the Indians' land base, driving the Shawnee and Delaware, the Miami and Wyandotte more tightly in upon each other. In the early years of the nineteenth century, two Shawnee leaders, the brothers Tecumseh and Elskwatawa, the latter known to whites as "the Prophet," began to forge an alliance of the region's tribes against the invading whites. In 1809, they established headquarters at an ancient Indian town named Kithtippecanoe in northern Indiana.

Between 1809 and 1811, Tecumseh carried his message of Indian nationalism and military resistance south to the Creek and the Cherokee, calling for "a war of extermination against the paleface." The southern tribes refused to join, but by 1811, over 1,000 fighting men had gathered at Kithtippecanoe.

Alarmed by the Indians' growing militancy, the governor of the Indiana Territory, William Henry Harrison, mustering a force of 1,000 soldiers, attacked and burned Kithtippecanoe.

Over the next several months, Tecumseh's followers, taking advantage of the recent outbreak of the War of 1812 between the United States and England and aided by British troops from Canada, carried out devastating raids across Indiana and southern Michigan. Together they crushed American armies at Detroit and Fort Nelson. At the Battle of the Thames near Detroit, the tide finally turned, for there Harrison inflicted a grievous defeat on a combined British and Indian force. Among those slain was Tecumseh.

The American victory at the Thames signaled the end of Indian resistance in the Old Northwest. Beginning in 1815, American settlers surged once more across Ohio and Indiana and pressed on unimpeded into Illinois and Michigan.

To the south, the Creek challenged white intruders with similar militancy. As the nineteenth century began, white settlers were pushing onto Creek lands in northwestern Georgia and central Alabama. While some Creek leaders urged accommodation, others, called Red Sticks, prepared to fight. The embers of this smoldering conflict were fanned into flame by an aggressive Tennessee militia commander named Andrew Jackson. Citing Creek atrocities, Jackson urged President Jefferson in 1808 to endorse a campaign against the Creek.

Bristling at their treatment by Georgia and Alabama, the Red Sticks carried out a series of violent frontier raids in the spring and summer of 1813. They capped their campaign with an assault on Fort Mims on the Alabama River, where they killed as many as 500 people, women and children among them. News of that tragedy raised bitter cries for revenge. At the head of 5,000 Tennessee and Kentucky militia, augmented by Cherokee, Choctaw, and Chickasaw warriors eager to punish their traditional Creek enemies, Jackson launched his long-

awaited attack. As he moved south, the ferocity of the fighting grew.

The climactic battle of the Creek War came in March 1814 at Horseshoe Bend, on the Tallapoosa River in central Alabama. There, in the fortified town of Tohopeka, 1,000 Creek warriors made a futile stand against 1,400 state troops and 600 Indian allies. Over 800 Native Americans died, more than in any other single battle in the history of Indian-white warfare. With no hope left, Red Eagle, one of the few remaining Red Stick leaders, walked alone into Jackson's camp and addressed the American commander:

> General Jackson, I am not afraid of you.... for I am a Creek warrior.... You can kill me if you desire. But I come to beg you to send for the women and children of the war party, who are now starving in the woods.... If I could fight you any longer I would most heartily do so. Send for the women and children. They never did you any harm. But kill me, if the white people want it done.

The war against the Creek was finished, and Jackson allowed Red Eagle to return home.

But the general was not quite done. He built Fort Jackson on the Hickory Ground, the most sacred spot of the Creek nation, and seized 22 million acres of land, nearly two-thirds of their domain. Before his Indian-fighting days were over, Jackson would acquire through treaty and military conquest nearly three-fourths of Alabama and Florida, a third of Tennessee, and a fifth of both Georgia and Mississippi.

The Creek's defeat at Horseshoe Bend broke the back of Indian defenses in the South. With all possibility of armed resistance gone, the Native Americans of the Old Southwest gave way before the swelling tide of white settlement.

POLITICS IN TRANSITION

For two decades following Jefferson's election in 1800, the Jeffersonian Republicans monopolized the presidency and dominated Congress, while the Federalist Party, its reputation damaged by charges of disloyalty during the War of 1812 and by its continuing "aristocratic" image, gradually collapsed. By the 1820s, however, the Jeffersonian ascendancy was coming to an end as political changes ushered in a new era of American politics.

A New Style of Politics

By the 1820s, basic patterns of political behavior were changing. Most evident was the surge of voter participation in state and local elections. Women, blacks, and Native Americans continued to be excluded, but white men flocked to the polls in unprecedented numbers. The flood of voters resulted in part from removal of property-holding and taxpaying restrictions on the franchise in some states.

Equally important were the growing strength of democratic beliefs among the people and the appearance of a new generation of political leaders skilled in the techniques of mass, electoral politics.

Division Among the Jeffersonians

With the Federalists in disarray following the War of 1812, the Jeffersonian Republicans stood triumphant, their ranks swollen by fresh recruits in the East and the admission of new states in the West. The Jeffersonians' success, however, proved their undoing, for no single party could contain the nation's growing diversity of economic and social interests, sectional differences, and individual ambitions.

Following the War of 1812, largely in response to growing pressures from the West and Northeast, the government launched a Federalist-like program of national economic development. Wartime disorganization of the currency demonstrated the need for a new national bank to replace the First Bank of the United States,

whose charter had expired in 1811. In March 1816, President Madison signed a bill creating a second bank, intended to stimulate economic expansion and regulate the loose currency-issuing practices of the country's countless state-chartered banks. In his final message to Congress in December 1816, Madison called for a tariff to protect the country's infant industries. Congress responded with the first truly protective tariff in American history, a set of duties on imported woolen and cotton goods, iron, leather, hats, paper, and sugar.

The administration's program of national economic development drew sharp criticism from so-called Old Republicans, a group of southern politicians who regarded themselves as keepers of the Jeffersonian conscience. Thirty-three Old Republicans voted against the bank bill. Over the next decade, their strength dwindled, even as their cries of alarm became increasingly shrill. By the early 1820s, Henry Clay and others, taking up the name National Republicans, were proposing an ambitious "American system" of tariffs and internal improvements.

The Specter of Sectionalism

In spite of the postwar surge of national spirit, Federalist talk of disunion had illustrated just how uncertain national unity continued to be. Congressional debates over the tariff, internal improvements, and the national bank reverberated with the clash of state and sectional interests. The Missouri crisis of 1819–1820 revealed how deep-seated sectional rivalries had become.

Ever since 1789, politicians had labored to keep the explosive issue of slavery tucked safely beneath the surface of political life, for they recognized how quickly it could jeopardize national unity. Their fears were borne out in 1819 when Missouri applied for admission to the Union and raised anew the question of slavery's expansion. In the Northwest Ordinance of 1787, Congress had limited slavery north of the Ohio River while allowing its expansion to the south. But

Missouri Compromise of 1820

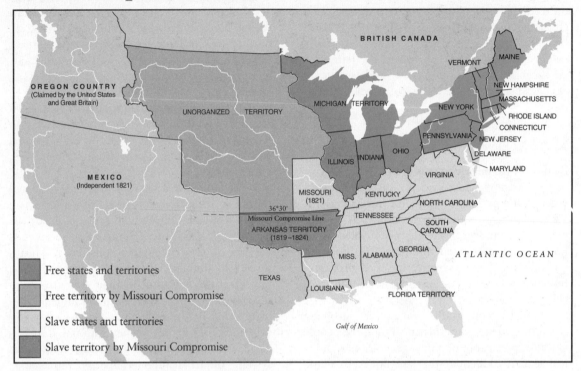

Free states and territories

Free territory by Missouri Compromise

Slave states and territories

Slave territory by Missouri Compromise

what about the vast new territory west of the Mississippi River?

Seizing the opportunity to deal with that question, Senator Rufus King of New York demanded that Missouri prohibit slavery before entering the Union. His proposal triggered a fierce debate over Congress's authority to prevent slavery's spread. Southerners were adamant that Congress could not close the trans-Mississippi West to their slave property and were determined to maintain the Senate's balance between slave and free states. Already by 1819, the North's more rapidly growing population had given it a 105-to-81 advantage in the House of Representatives. Equality in the Senate offered the only sure protection of southern interests. Northerners vowed to keep the trans-Mississippi West open to free labor. That meant closing it to slavery.

For nearly three months, Congress debated the issue. During much of the time, free blacks listening intently to northern antislavery speeches filled the House gallery. "This momentous question," worried the aged Jefferson, "like a fire-bell in the night, [has] awakened and filled me with terror." Northerners were similarly alarmed. The Missouri question, declared the editor of the New York *Daily Advertiser,* "involves not only the future character of our nation, but the future weight and influence of the free states. If now lost—it is lost forever."

In the end, compromise prevailed. Missouri gained admission as a slave state, while Maine came in as a counterbalancing free state, and a line was drawn west from Missouri at latitude 36°30' to the Rocky Mountains dividing the lands that would be open to slavery from those that would not. For the moment, the explosive issue of slavery's expansion had again been put to rest.

Collapse of the Federalist-Jeffersonian Party System

The final collapse of the Federalist-Jeffersonian party system came with the presidential election of John Quincy Adams in 1824. For the first time since 1800, when the "Virginia dynasty" of Jefferson, Madison, and Monroe began, there was competition for the presidency from every major wing of the Jeffersonian Party. Of the five candidates, Adams of Massachusetts and Henry Clay of Kentucky advocated strong federal programs of economic development. William Crawford of Georgia and Andrew Jackson of Tennessee clung to traditional Jeffersonian principles of limited government, agrarianism, and states' rights. In between stood John Calhoun of South Carolina, just beginning his fateful passage from nationalism to southern nullification.

A medical problem eliminated Crawford from the campaign, while Calhoun, attracting limited support, withdrew to become the vice-presidential partner of both Adams and Jackson. When none of the remaining candidates received an electoral majority, the election, as in 1800, moved into the House of Representatives. There, an alliance of Adams and Clay supporters gave the New Englander the election, even though he had trailed Jackson in electoral votes, 84 to 99. The Jacksonians' charges of a "corrupt bargain" gained credence when Adams appointed Clay secretary of state.

Adams's ill-fated administration revealed the disarray in American politics. His stirring calls for federal road and canal building, standardization of weights and measures, establishment of a national university, promotion of commerce and manufacturing, and government support for science and the arts quickly fell victim to sectional conflicts, political factionalism, and his own open scorn for the increasingly democratic politics of the day. Within a year of Adams's inauguration, his administration had foundered. For the rest of his term, politicians jockeyed for position in the political realignment that was under way.

CONCLUSION

THE PASSING OF AN ERA

During the first quarter of the nineteenth century, Americans saw their nation's territory more than double in size while the Jeffersonians labored to set the government on a proper republican course. They promoted agrarian expansion and transformed the country's relations with Europe and the Americas. They also sought, less successfully, to reconcile Native American rights with national expansion.

The 1820s brought an end to the era of founding, a turning point that was dramatized on July 4, 1826, the fiftieth anniversary of American independence, when two of the remaining Revolutionary patriarchs, John Adams and Thomas Jefferson, died within a few hours of each other. "The sterling virtues of the Revolution are silently passing away," wrote George McDuffie of South Carolina, "and the period is not distant when there will be no living monument to remind us of those glorious days of trial." A new and different era was at hand.

Recommended Reading

Drew McCoy, *The Elusive Republic* (1980), describes the importance of agrarian expansion for the Jeffersonians. For Jeffersonian politics and government, see also Noble Cunningham, *The Process of Government Under Jefferson* (1978); Daniel Jordan, *Political Leadership in Jefferson's Virginia* (1983); and Andrew Cayton, *The Frontier Republic: Ideology and Politics in the Ohio Country, 1780–1825* (1986). Discussions of the Federalists can be found in James Broussard, *The Southern Federalists, 1800–1816* (1978); and Linda Kerber, *Federalists in Dissent* (1970). Steven Watts, *The Republic Reborn: War and the Making of Liberal America, 1790–1820* (1987), traces the change from Revolutionary republicanism to liberal capitalism.

Robert Berkhofer discusses white attitudes toward Indians in *The White Man's Indian* (1978). See also William McLoughlin, *Cherokees and Missionaries, 1789–1839* (1984).

Foreign policy issues and the politics surrounding them are portrayed by Reginald Horsman, *The Diplomacy of the New Republic, 1776–1815* (1986); and Ernest May, *The Making of the Monroe Doctrine* (1975).

On politics and the Supreme Court, see Richard Ellis, *The Jeffersonian Crisis: Courts and Politics in the Young Republic* (1971).

Donald Jackson, *Thomas Jefferson and the Stony Mountains: Exploring the West from Monticello* (1981), discusses Jefferson's fascination with the West. For problems of cultural nationalism, see Joseph Ellis, *After the Revolution: Profiles of Early American Culture* (1979); Emory Elliott, *Revolutionary Writers: Literature and Authority in the New Republic, 1725–1810* (1985); and David Simpson, *The Politics of American English* (1986).

Time Line

1789	Treaty of Fort Harmar Knox's reports on Indian affairs	1810	Macon's Bill No. 2
1794	Battle of Fallen Timbers	1811	Battle of Kithtippecanoe
1795	Treaty of Greenville	1812	Madison reelected West Florida annexed War declared against Great Britain
1796	Congress establishes Indian Factory System	1813	Battle of the Thames
1800	Capital moves to Washington Thomas Jefferson elected president	1813– 1814	Creek War
1801	Judiciary Act New Land Act	1814	Treaty of Ghent Battle of Horseshoe Bend
1802	Judiciary Act repealed	1814– 1815	Hartford Convention
1803	*Marbury* v. *Madison* Louisiana Purchase	1815	Battle of New Orleans U.S. establishes military posts in trans-Mississippi West
1803– 1806	Lewis and Clark expedition		
1803– 1812	Napoleonic Wars resume British impress American sailors	1816	James Monroe elected president Second United States Bank chartered
1804	Jefferson reelected	1819	Adams-Onis Treaty with Spain Spain cedes East Florida to U.S. *McCulloch* v. *Maryland*
1805– 1807	Pike explores the West		
1806	Non-Importation Act	1820	Land Act Missouri Compromise Monroe reelected
1807	Embargo Act *Chesapeake-Leopard* affair Congress prohibits slave trade	1822	Diplomatic recognition of Latin American republics
1808	James Madison elected Cherokee legal code established	1823	Monroe Doctrine proclaimed
1809	Tecumseh's confederacy formed Non-Intercourse Act	1824	John Quincy Adams elected president
		1827	Cherokee adopt written constitution

part 3

An Expanding People

During the first half of the nineteenth century, the young nation expanded rapidly. As Americans surged west, and, in the 1840s, pushed on to the Pacific coast, the population soared and became more diverse. Expansion also sharpened regional differences, particularly between the North and the South, and the period ended with the most devastating conflict the nation has ever experienced.

Chapters 10, 11, and 12 cover roughly the same time period. Chapter 10, "Currents of Change in the Northeast and the Old Northwest," investigates the economic and social transformations that affected everyday life in these two regions. Chapter 11, "Slavery and the Old South," considers the South's distinctive economic and social system, which, based as it was on slavery, raised questions about the special virtue of the nation and the meaning of justice and equality.

In Chapter 12, "Shaping America in the Antebellum Age," we focus on economic and social changes that sharpened the familiar tension between narrowly defined self-interest and social concerns. The election of Andrew Jackson as president marked the advent of the second American party system and of a lively political culture firmly rooted in new economic and social conditions.

Chapter 13, "Moving West," shows the power of American expansionism and the limited meaning many Americans gave to terms like *liberty* and *equality*. During the 1840s, as settlers to new frontiers sought to re-create familiar institutions and patterns, the earlier inhabitants, mostly Mexicans and Native Americans, found themselves excluded from most of the promises of American life.

The expansion of slavery into the West threatened the political balance of power between the North and the South and raised the question of where power and authority lay to decide the future of the West.

Chapter 14, "The Union In Peril," traces the disintegration of the second party system and the eruption of civil war in Kansas. Secession and civil war soon followed. Chapter 15, "The Union Severed," examines the Civil War and the unanticipated results of the conflict. Chapter 16, "The Union Reconstructed," explores how Americans tried to resolve the many dilemmas of the postwar period.

chapter 10

Currents of Change in the Northeast and the Old Northwest

For her first eighteen years, Susan Warner was little touched by the far-reaching economic and social changes that were transforming the character of the country and her own city of New York. While some New Yorkers toiled to make a living by taking in piecework and others responded to unsettling new means of producing goods by joining trade unions to agitate for wages that would enable them to "live as comfortable as others," Susan was surrounded by luxuries and privilege. Much of the year was spent in the family's townhouse on St. Mark's Place, not far from the home of the enormously rich real estate investor and fur trader John Jacob Astor. There Susan acquired the social graces and skills appropriate for a girl of her position and background. She had dancing and singing lessons, studied Italian and French, and learned the etiquette involved in receiving visitors and making calls. When the hot weather made life in New York unpleasant, the Warners escaped to the cooler airs of Canaan, where they had a summer house.

All this changed after Susan's father, heretofore so successful a provider and parent, lost most of his fortune during the financial Panic of 1837. Like others experiencing a sharp economic reversal, the Warners had to make radical adjustments. The fashionable home on St. Mark's Place was exchanged for a more modest one on an island in the Hudson River. Susan turned "housekeeper" and learned how to do tasks once relegated to others: sewing and making butter, pudding sauces, and johnny cake. Prized possessions eventually went up for auction. "When at last the men and the confusion were gone," Susan's younger sister, Anna, recalled, "then we woke up to life."

Waking up to life meant facing the necessity of making money. But what could Susan do to reverse sliding family fortunes? True, some women labored as factory operatives, domestics, seamstresses, or schoolteachers, but it was doubtful Susan could even imagine herself in any of these occupations.

On the advice of her Aunt Fanny, Susan decided to try her hand at writing fiction. She constructed a story around the trials of a young orphan girl, Ellen Montgomery. As Ellen suffered one reverse after another, she learned the lessons that allowed her to survive and eventually triumph over adversity: piety, self-denial, discipline, and the power of a mother's love. Entitled *The Wide, Wide World,* the novel was accepted for publication only after the mother of the publisher, George Putnam, read it and told her son, "If you never publish another book, you must make *The Wide, Wide World* available for your fellow men." Much to Putnam's surprise, *The Wide, Wide World* became the first American novel to sell more than a million copies. It was one of the best-sellers of the century.

Susan Warner's second novel described the spiritual and intellectual life of a young girl thrust into poverty after an early life of luxury in New York. Entitled *Queechy,* this novel was also a great success.

The popularity of Susan's books suggested how well they spoke to the concerns and interests of a broad readership. The background of social and financial uncertainty, with its sudden changes of fortune, captured the reality and fears of a fluid society in the process of transformation. Pious heroines like Ellen Montgomery, who struggled to master their passions and urges toward independence, were shining exemplars of the new norms for middle-class women. Their successful efforts to mold themselves heartened readers who believed that the future of the nation depended on virtuous mothers and who struggled to live up to new ideals. Susan's novels validated their efforts and affirmed the importance of the domestic sphere.

This chapter explores the economic changes in the Northeast and Old Northwest that not only transformed the economy between 1820 and 1860, as Susan Warner discovered, but also shaped social, cultural, and political life. Though most Americans still lived in rural settings rather than in factory towns or cities, economic growth and the new industrial mode of production affected them through the creation of new goods, opportunities, and markets. In urban communities and factory towns, the new economic order ushered in new forms of work, new class arrangements, and new forms of social strife.

After discussing the factors that fueled antebellum growth, the chapter turns to the industrial world, where so many of the new patterns of work and life appeared. An investigation of urbanization reveals shifting class arrangements and values as well as rising social and racial tensions. Finally, an examination of rural communities in the East and on the frontier in the Old Northwest highlights the transformation of these two sections of the country. Between 1840 and 1860, industrialization and economic growth increasingly knit them together.

ECONOMIC GROWTH

Between 1820 and 1860, the American economy moved away from its reliance on agriculture as the major source of growth toward an industrial and technological future. Real per capita output of goods and services grew an average of 2 percent annually between 1820 and 1840 and slightly less between 1840 and 1860. But the economy, though expanding, was also unstable, lurching from periods of boom (1822–1834, mid-1840s–1850s) to periods of bust (1816–1821, 1837–1843). As never before, Americans faced dramatic shifts in the availability of jobs and goods and in prices and wages. Moreover, because regional economies were increasingly linked, problems in one area tended to affect conditions in others.

Factors Fueling Economic Development

What accounted for this new phase of growth and economic development? The United States, of course, had abundant natural resources, enormously increased by the Louisiana Purchase in 1803. An expanding population, soaring from 9 million in 1820 to over 30 million in 1860, represented the new workers, new households, and new consumers so essential to economic development. Until the 1840s, most of the growth in population came from natural increase. But as the size of American families gradually shrank—in 1800, the average white woman bore seven children; by 1860, the number had declined to five—foreign immigration took up the slack.

Improved transportation played a key role in bringing about economic and geographic expansion. Early in the century, high freight rates discouraged production for distant markets, and primitive transportation hindered western settlement. During the 1820s and 1830s, however, canal-building projects revolutionized travel and commerce and made migration much easier. The Erie Canal, completed in 1825, stretched 363 miles between Albany and Buffalo, New York. The canal was the last link in the chain of waterways binding New York City to the Great Lakes and the Northwest.

The Erie Canal and hundreds of other newly constructed canals fostered strong economic and social ties between the Northwest and the East.

Even at the height of the canal boom, politicians, promoters, and others, impressed with Britain's success with railways, also supported the construction of railroads. Only 73 miles of track were laid between 1828 and 1830, but by 1840, there were 3,000 miles of track, most in the Northeast. By the end of the 1850s, total mileage soared to 30,000. Like the canals, the new railroads strengthened the links between the Old Northwest and the East.

Improved transportation had such a profound influence on American life that some historians use the term *transportation revolution* to refer to its impact. Canals and railroads provided cheap and reliable access to distant markets and goods and encouraged Americans to settle the frontier and cultivate virgin lands. Eventually, the strong economic and social ties the waterways and then the railways fostered between the Northwest and the East led people living in the two regions to share political outlooks.

Especially in terms of the pattern of western settlement, railroads exerted enormous influence. Their routes could determine whether a city, town, or even homestead survived. The railroad transformed Chicago from a small settlement into a bustling commercial and transportation center. In 1850, the city contained not 1 mile of track, but within five years, 2,200 miles of track serving 150,000 square miles terminated in Chicago.

Improved transportation stimulated agricultural expansion and regional specialization. Farmers began to plant larger crops for the market, concentrating on those most suited to their soil and climate. By the late 1830s, the Old Northwest had become the country's granary, while New England farmers turned to dairy or produce farming. By 1860, American farmers

Growth of the Railroads, 1850–1860

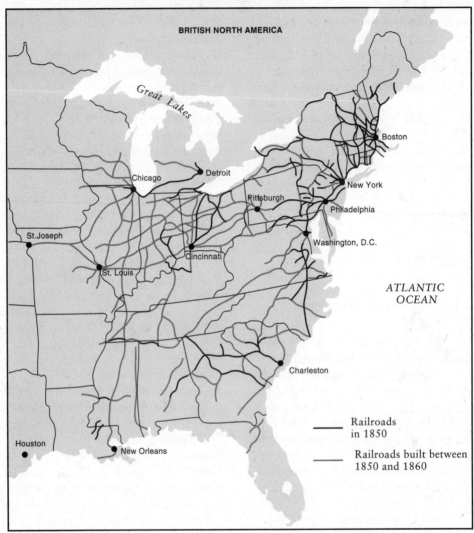

were producing four to five times as much wheat, corn, cattle, and hogs as they had in 1810.

Capital and Government Support

Internal improvements, the exploitation of natural resources, and the cultivation of new lands all demanded capital. Much of it came from European investors. Between 1790 and 1861, over $500 million flowed into the United States from Europe. Foreign investors from Europe, adding to funds brought by immigrant families, financed as much as a third of all canal construction and bought about a quarter of all railroad bonds.

American mercantile capital fueled growth

as well. The merchant class prospered in the half century after the Revolution, and merchants invested in schemes ranging from canals to textile factories. Many ventured into the production of goods and became manufacturers themselves.

Prosperous Americans eagerly sought opportunities to put their capital to work. Two New Yorkers, Arthur Bronson and Charles Butler, made a careful tour of the Northwest in 1833. Despite primitive conditions, both men saw wonderful opportunities. Detroit, Butler concluded, "is destined to be a very great city," while Chicago "presents one of the finest fields in America for industry & enterprise." Each man channeled funds into western projects. Bronson's investments ranged from Ohio banks to farmland in Wisconsin Territory, Illinois, Michigan, Ohio, and Indiana to real estate in Chicago and Detroit, all in addition to his holdings in New York ironworks and banks.

Local and state government played their part by enthusiastically supporting economic growth. States often helped new ventures raise capital by passing laws of incorporation, by awarding entrepreneurs special privileges such as tax breaks or monopolistic control, by underwriting bonds for improvement projects (which increased their investment appeal), and by providing loans for internal improvements. New York, Pennsylvania, Ohio, Indiana, Illinois, and Virginia publicly financed almost 75 percent of the canal systems in their states between 1815 and 1860.

The national government assisted some internal improvements such as the National Road linking Maryland and Illinois. Federal tariff policy shielded American products, and the second U.S. Bank provided the financial stability investors required. The line separating the public sector from the private often became unclear.

The law also helped to promote aggressive economic growth. The case of *Palmer* v. *Mulligan*, decided by the New York State Supreme Court in 1805, laid down the principle that property ownership included the right to develop property for business purposes. A series of important Supreme Court decisions between 1819 and 1824 clarified contract law, establishing the basic principle that contracts were binding.

A New Mentality

As the discussion of the links between law and economic growth suggests, economic expansion depends on intangible factors as well as more obvious ones such as improved transportation. The entrepreneurial mentality that encouraged investment, new business ventures, and land speculation was an important component of antebellum economic development. Another factor was American energy and openness to change. As one Frenchman explained in 1834, "All here is circulation, motion, and boiling agitation. Experiment follows experiment; enterprise succeeds to enterprise."

Others described an American mechanical "genius." The American was "a mechanic by nature," one Frenchman insisted. "In Massachusetts and Connecticut, there is not a labourer who had not invented a machine or tool." This observer exaggerated, but Americans did develop a number of efficient and productive tools and machines. The McCormick harvester, the Colt revolver, Goodyear vulcanized rubber products, and the sewing machine were developed, refined, and developed further. Such improvements cut labor costs and increased efficiency.

While the shortage of labor in the United States stimulated technological innovations that replaced humans with machines, the rapid spread of education after 1800 also contributed to innovation and increased productivity. By 1840, most whites were literate. In that year, public schools nationwide were educating 38.4 percent of white children between the ages of 5 and 19.

The belief that education spurred economic growth helped to foster enthusiasm for public education, particularly in the Northeast. Massachusetts moved first toward mass education by mandating in 1827 that taxes pay the whole cost of the state's public schools. At first, the Massachusetts school system did not function well. School buildings were often run-down and even unheated. Because school curricula were virtually nonexistent, students often lounged idly at their desks.

Under the leadership of Horace Mann, the reform of state education for white children began in 1837. Mann advocated graded schools, uniform curricula, teacher training, and reduced the power of local districts over schools. His campaigns made the Massachusetts system a model for reformers everywhere.

Mann believed that education promoted inventiveness. It "had a market value." Businessmen often agreed. Prominent industrialists in the 1840s believed that education produced workers who could handle complex machinery without undue supervision and were superior employees—reliable, punctual, industrious, and sober.

Ambivalence Toward Change

While supporting education as a means to economic growth, many Americans also firmly believed in its social value. Public schools could mold student character and promote "virtuous habits" and "rational self-governing" behavior. Students learned facts by rote because memory work and recitation taught them discipline and concentration. Nineteenth-century schoolbooks reinforced the classroom message. "It is a great sin to be idle," children read in one 1830 text, while another warned, "Poverty is the fruit of idleness."

The concern with education and character indicate that as much as Americans welcomed economic progress, they also feared social and economic change. Schools, which taught students to be deferential, obedient, and punctual, could counter the worst by-products of change. Schools served as much as a defense against change as its agents.

The touted virtues of diligence, punctuality, temperance, and thrift probably did assist economic growth, but the success of early nineteenth-century economic ventures frequently depended on the ability to take risks, to think daringly. The emphasis given to the safe but stolid virtues suggests that the fear of social disintegration ran through antebellum society.

The Advance of Industrialization

Significant economic growth between 1820 and 1860 resulted from the reorganization of production. Factory production reorganized work by breaking down the manufacture of an article into discrete steps. At first, manufacturers often relied on the putting-out system. Eventually, they centralized all the steps of production under one roof, where hand labor gradually gave way to power-driven machinery such as wooden "spinning jennies." Often they sought the help of British immigrants who had the practical experience and technical know-how no American possessed.

As factory workers replaced artisans and home manufacturers, the volume of goods rose, and prices dropped dramatically. The price of a yard of cotton cloth fell from 18 cents to 2 cents over the 45 years preceding the Civil War.

Between 1820 and 1860, textile manufacturing became the country's leading industry. Textile mills sprang up across the New England and the Middle Atlantic states, regions that contained swift-flowing streams to power the mills, capitalists eager to finance the ventures, children and women to tend the machines, and numerous cities and towns with ready markets for cheap textiles. Early mills were small affairs, containing only the machines for carding and spinning. The thread was then put out to home workers to be woven into cloth. The early mechanization of cloth production did not replace home manufacture but supplemented it.

Already underway in 1813, however, were experiments that would lead to the development

This calico factory, located in Manchester, New Hampshire, produced colorful fabrics for American consumers. In 1854, fully 1,250 of the 2,000 workers were female.

of the power loom. Eventually, the loom devised by Francis Cabot Lowell and Paul Moody was installed in a mill at Waltham, Massachusetts.

The most important innovation of the Waltham operation was Lowell's decision to bring all the steps of cotton cloth production together under one roof. By centralizing the entire manufacturing process and work force in one factory, cloth for the mass market could be produced more cheaply and more profitably. In 1823, the Boston Associates expanded their operations to East Chelmsford on the Merrimack River, a town they renamed Lowell.

Most New England mills followed the Lowell system. The cumulative impact of the rise of the textile industry was to supplant the home production of cloth, even though some women would continue to spin and weave for their families for some years to come, and hand-loom weavers would survive for another generation. In the process, Americans were transformed from a people clad in earth-colored homespun into a nation decked out in gayer, more colorful clothing.

Textile mills helped to account for the increasingly industrial character of the Northeast. By 1860, fully 71 percent of all manufacturing workers lived in this region of the country.

Other important manufacturing operations reached west and south from New England. The processing of wheat, timber, and hides using power-driven machinery was common in most communities of 200 families or more. Paper mills were widespread, although a third of them were clustered in Philadelphia. The iron and metalworking industry stretched from Albany, New York, south to Maryland and west to Cincinnati.

Environmental Consequences

The impact of this economic growth on the environment was far-reaching and often harmful. Steamboats and early railroads, for example, depended on wood for fuel. So too did the heating stoves that were keeping American families warm. Armed with new steel axes, lumbermen and farmers kept up with the increased demand for wood, and the eastern forest and the wildlife that lived there rapidly disappeared. Better transportation, which encouraged western settlement, also promoted forest clearance as individual settlers cleared land for crops and cut wood for housing. Sawmills and milldams interfered with spawning habits of fish, clogged their gills with sawdust, and even changed the flow of rivers. The process of ecological change, spurred by the desire for wood, recurred as lumber companies and entrepreneurs moved from the East to exploit the forests of the Great Lakes and of the Gulf states.

As late as 1840, wood was the main source for the country's energy needs. But the high price of wood and the discovery of anthracite coal in Pennsylvania signaled the beginning of a shift to coal as the major source of power. While the East gradually regained some of its forest cover, the heavy use of coal resulted in air pollution. Steam engines and heating stoves poured out dirty fumes into the air. In New York City, one could see the evidence of pollution everywhere— in the gray cloud hanging over the city, in the smoke rising from its machine shops, refineries, and private houses, in the acrid smells and black soot that were a part of daily life.

Some Americans were aware of the environmental consequences of rapid growth and change. Author James Fenimore Cooper had one of his characters in his novel *The Pioneers* condemn those who destroyed nature "without remorse and without shame." Yet most Americans accepted the changing environment as an inevitable part of progress.

EARLY MANUFACTURING

Industrialization created a more efficient means of producing more goods at much lower cost than had been possible in the homes and small shops of an earlier day. Philadelphian Samuel Breck's diary reveals some of the new profusion and range of goods. "Went to town principally to see the Exhibition of American Manufactures

at the Masonic Hall," he noted in 1833. "More than 700 articles have been sent. Among this great variety, I distinguished the Philadelphia porcelains, beautiful Canton cotton, made at York in this state, soft and capacious blankets, silver plate, . . . chymical drugs, hardware, saddlery, and the most beautiful black broadcloth I ever saw."

The Impact of Industrialization

Two examples illustrate how industrialization transformed American life. Before the nineteenth century, local printing shops depended on manual labor to produce books, newspapers, and journals. The cost of reading material was high enough to make a library a sign of wealth.

Between 1830 and 1850, however, adoption and improvement of British inventions, together with managerial and marketing innovations, revolutionized the printing and publishing industries.

As books and magazines dropped in cost and grew in number, far more people could afford them. No longer dependent solely on the words of the "better sort" for information, people could now form their views on the basis of what they read. The proliferation of printed matter had an enormous impact on people's stock of information, values, tastes, and use of leisure time. It also contributed to the rising literacy rate among white Americans.

Just as printed materials wrought great changes in American life, the making of inexpensive timepieces affected its pace and rhythms. Before the 1830s, when few Americans could afford a clock, it was difficult to make exact plans. But the production of timepieces soared in the 1830s, and by midcentury, inexpensive, mass-produced ones could be found everywhere. Clocks encouraged a more disciplined use of time and undergirded the economic changes taking place. Timepieces, for example, were essential for the successful operation of railroads, which ran on schedules. Clocks also imposed a new rhythm in many workplaces.

A New England Textile Town

To understand the process of industrialization and its impact on work and the work force, let us examine Lowell, the "model" Massachusetts textile town, and Cincinnati, a bustling midwestern industrial center.

Lowell was a new town, planned and built expressly for industrial purposes in the 1820s. Regarded as a model factory community, in 1836 Lowell, with 17,000 inhabitants, aspired to become the "Manchester of America," Manchester being the center of England's textile industry. Lowell was America's most important textile center.

By 1830, women composed nearly 70 percent of the Lowell textile work force. The women who came to Lowell for jobs were the first American women to labor outside their homes in large numbers. They were also among the first Americans to experience the full impact of the factory system.

Working and Living in a Mill Town

Mary Paul was typical of the young women drawn to work in Lowell and other New England textile towns. As the planners had anticipated, most were unmarried and young. In 1830, more than 63 percent of Lowell's population was female, and most were between the ages of 15 and 29.

These women, from New England's middling rural families, came to the mills for a variety of reasons ranging from the desire for economic independence to the decline of home manufacturing. As Sally Rice from Vermont explained, "I am almost nineteen years old. I must of course have something of my own before many more years have passed over my head. And where is that something coming from if I go home and earn nothing." Mill work paid women relatively well in the 1820s and 1830s. Domestic servants' weekly wages hovered around 75 cents and seamstresses' 90 cents, while in the mid-1830s women could make between $2.40 and $3.20 a week in the mill.

Few of the women considered their decision to come to Lowell a permanent commitment. They came to work for a few years, felt free to go home or to school for a few months, and then returned to mill work. Once married, they left the mill work force forever.

New manufacturing work was regimented and exhausting. The standard schedule was 12 hours a day, six days a week, with only a half hour for breakfast and lunch.

Within the factory, the organization of space facilitated production. In the basement was the waterwheel, the source of power. Above, successive floors were completely open, each containing the machines necessary for the different steps of cloth making: carding, spinning, weaving, and dressing. Elevators moved materials from one floor to another. On a typical floor, rows of machines stretched the length of the low room, tended by operatives who might watch over several machines at the same time. From his elevated desk at the end of the room, the overseer watched the workers.

Involving an adaptation to a completely new work situation, mill work also entailed an entirely new living situation for women operatives. The companies provided substantial quarters for their overseers and housing for male workers and their families. Hoping to attract respectable females to Lowell, the mill owners also constructed company boardinghouses where women workers had to live, usually four to six to a room. Headed by female housekeepers, the boardinghouse maintained strict rules, including a 10 o'clock curfew. Amid such intimate working and living conditions, young women formed close ties with one another and developed a strong sense of community.

Female Responses to Work

Although mill work offered better wages than other occupations open to women, all female workers had limited job mobility, because only men could hold supervisory positions. Most female operatives accepted such sexual discrimination as part of life. But the sense of sisterhood supported open protest when trouble arose.

Trouble broke out when hard times hit Lowell in February 1834. Falling prices, poor sales, and rising inventories prompted managers to announce a 15 percent wage cut. This was their way of protecting profits—at the expense of their employees. The mill workers sprang into action. Petitions circulated, threatening a strike. Meetings followed. At one lunchtime gathering, the company agent, hoping to end the protests, fired an apparent ringleader. But, as the agent re-

Work in textile mills was often tedious and repetitive. Although women were paid less than men, they often welcomed the opportunity to live independently and to earn their own money.

ported, "she declared that every girl in the room should leave with her," then "made a signal, and . . . they all marched out & few returned the ensuing morning." The strikers roamed the streets appealing to other workers and visited other mills. In all, about a sixth of the town's work force turned out.

Though this work stoppage was brief and failed to prevent the wage reduction, it demonstrated women workers' concern about the impact of industrialization on the labor force. Strikers, taunted as unfeminine for their "amazonian display," refused to agree that workers were inferior to bosses. Pointing out that they were daughters of free men, strikers called the bosses "Tories in disguise" and sought to link their protest to their fathers' and grandfathers' efforts to throw off the bonds of British oppression during the Revolution. Revolutionary rhetoric that once held only political meaning took on economic overtones as Lowell women confronted industrial work.

During the 1830s, wage cuts, long hours, increased work loads, and production speed-ups, mandated by owners' desires to protect profits, constantly reminded Lowell women and other textile workers of the possibility of "wage slavery." In Dover, New Hampshire, 800 women turned out and formed a union in 1834 to protest wage cuts. In the 1840s, women in several New England states agitated for the ten-hour day, while petitions from Lowell prompted the Massachusetts legislature to hold the first government hearing on industrial working conditions.

The Changing Character of the Work Force

Most protest efforts met with limited success. The short tenure of most women mill workers prevented permanent labor organizations. In addition, the waves of immigration that deposited so many penniless foreigners in northeastern cities in the 1840s and 1850s created a new pool of labor. The newcomers were desperate for jobs and would accept lower wages than New England farm girls. Gradually, the Irish began to replace Yankee women in the mills. Representing only 8 percent of the Lowell work force in 1845, the Irish composed nearly half the workers by 1860. As the ethnic makeup of the work force changed, so did its gender composition. More men came to work in the mills. By 1860, some 30 percent of the Lowell workers were male. All these changes made the women expendable and increased the costs of going "against the mill."

Lowell itself changed as the Irish crowded into the city and New England women gradually left the mills. With owners no longer feeling the need to continue paternalistic practices, boardinghouses disappeared. A permanent work force, once a nightmare to owners, had become a reality by 1860, and Lowell's reputation as a model factory town faded away.

Factories on the Frontier

Cincinnati, a small Ohio River settlement of 2,540 in 1810, grew to be the country's third largest industrial center by 1840. With a population of 40,382, it contained a variety of industries at different stages of development. Cincinnati manufacturers who turned out machines, machine parts, hardware, and furniture were quick to mechanize for increased volume and profits. Other trades like carriage making and cigar making moved far more slowly toward mechanization before 1860. Alongside these concerns, artisans like coopers, blacksmiths, and riverboat builders still labored in small shops using traditional hand tools. The new and the old ways coexisted in Cincinnati, as they did in most manufacturing communities.

In 1850, most Cincinnati workers worked in small or medium-size shops, but almost 20 percent labored in factories with over 100 employees. Some craftsmen continued to use a wide array of skills as they produced goods in time-honored ways. Others worked in new factories, performing more specialized and limited tasks. In furniture factories, for example, some artisans worked exclusively as varnishers, others as car-

penters, and still others as finishers. No single worker made a chair from start to finish. But all used some of their skills and earned steady wages. Though in the long run machines threatened to replace them, these skilled factory workers often had reason in the short run to praise the factory's opportunities. Less fortunate was the new class of unskilled factory laborers, who received low wages and had little job security.

Many of Cincinnati's female residents were "outworkers" who worked in small shops or at home as seamstresses for the city's growing ready-to-wear clothing industry. Manufacturers purchased the cloth, cut it into basic patterns, and then contracted the work out to be finished.

Paid by the piece, female outworkers were among the most exploited of Cincinnati's workers. The successful marketing of sewing machines in the 1850s contributed to worsening working conditions and lower pay. Since the sewing machine made stitching easier, the pool of potential workers increased and the volume of work that bosses expected grew.

Cincinnati employers claimed that the new industrial order offered great opportunities to most of the city's male citizens. Manufacturing work encouraged the "manly virtues" so necessary to the "republican citizen." Not all Cincinnati workers agreed. Like workers in Lowell and other manufacturing communities, Cincinnati's laborers rose up against their bosses in the decades before the Civil War.

The workingman's plight, as Cincinnati labor leaders analyzed it, stemmed from his loss of independence. The new industrial order was changing the nature of the laboring class itself. A new kind of worker had emerged. Rather than selling the products of his skills, he had only his raw labor to sell. His "wage slavery," or dependence on wages, promised to be lifelong. The reorganization of work signaled the end of the progression from apprentice to journeyman to master and undermined traditional skills. Few workers could expect to rise to the position of independent craftsman. Most would labor only for others, just as slaves labored for their mas-

In 1848, an unknown photographer took this picture of Cincinnati. The prominence of steamboats in the picture suggests the role location and improvements in transportation played in the city's growth. Although the countryside is visible in the background, the rows of substantial commercial and industrial buildings make Cincinnati's status as a bustling urban center clear.

ters. Nor would wages bring to most that other form of independence, the ownership of shop and home. The expression "wage slavery" contained a deep truth about the changed conditions of many American workingmen.

Workers also resented the masters' attempts to control their lives. In the new factories, owners insisted on a steady pace of work and uninterrupted production. Artisans who were used to working in spurts, stopping for a few moments of conversation or a drink, disliked the new routines.

The fact that workers' wages in Cincinnati, as in other cities, rose more slowly than food and housing costs compounded discontent over changing working conditions. The working class sensed it was losing ground at the very time the city's rich were visibly growing richer. In 1817, the top tenth of the city's taxpayers owned over half the wealth, while the bottom half possessed

only 10 percent. In 1860, the share of the top tenth had increased to two-thirds, while the bottom half's share had shrunk to 2.4 percent.

In the decades before the Civil War, Cincinnati workers formed unions, turned out for fair wages, and rallied in favor of the ten-hour day. Like the Lowell mill women, they cloaked their protest with the mantle of the Revolution. Striking workers staged parades with fifes and drums and appropriated patriotic symbols to bolster their demands for justice and independence. They insisted that masters were denying them a fair share of profits, thereby dooming them to economic dependency. Since the republic depended on a free and independent citizenry, the male workers warned that their bosses' policies threatened to undermine the republic itself.

Only in the early 1850s did Cincinnati workers begin to suspect that their employers formed a distinct class of parasitic "nonproducers." Although most strikes still revolved around familiar issues of better hours and wages, signs appeared of the more hostile labor relations that would emerge after the Civil War.

As elsewhere, skilled workers were in the forefront of Cincinnati's labor protest and union activities. But Cincinnati workers did not readily unite with them. The uneven pace of industrialization meant that these workers, unlike the Lowell mill women, had no common working experience. Moreover, growing cultural and ethnic diversity compounded differences in the workplace. By 1850, almost half the people in the city were foreign-born, most of them German, compared with 22 percent in 1825. Protestant workers frequently felt that they had more in common with their Protestant bosses than with Catholic Irish or German fellow workers.

These tensions exploded in Cincinnati in the spring of 1855. Americans attacked barricades erected in German neighborhoods, crying out death threats. Their wrath visited the Irish as well. In many cases, labor disunity served economic progress by undermining workers' efforts for higher pay, shorter hours, and better working conditions, thus favoring businesses.

URBAN LIFE

Americans experienced the impact of economic growth most dramatically in the cities. In the four decades before the Civil War, the rate of urbanization in the United States was faster than ever before or since. In 1820, about 9 percent of the American people lived in cities (defined as areas containing a population of 2,500 or more). Forty years later, almost 20 percent of them did.

The Process of Urbanization

Three distinct types of cities—commercial centers, mill towns, and transportation hubs—emerged during these years of rapid economic growth. Commercial seaports like Boston,

Philadelphia, and Baltimore expanded steadily and developed diversified manufacturing to supplement the older functions of importing, exporting, and providing services and credit. New York replaced Philadelphia as the country's largest and most important city. With the completion of the Erie Canal, New York merchants gained control of much of the trade with the West. By 1840, they had also secured the largest share of the country's import and export trade.

Access to waterpower fueled the development of a second kind of city like Lowell, Massachusetts; Trenton, New Jersey; and Wilmington, Delaware. Situated inland along the waterfalls and rapids that provided the power to run their mills, these cities burgeoned in the decades before the Civil War.

West of the Appalachian Mountains, a third type of city arose. Louisville, Cleveland, and St. Louis were typical of cities that had served as transportation service and distribution centers from the earliest days of frontier settlement. Chicago acted as "grand depot, exchange, counting-house, and metropolis" for its hinterlands.

As the number of urban dwellers grew, their needs helped to generate economic growth. Cities provided a growing market for farm products and manufactured goods such as shoes, clothing, furniture, carriages, cast-iron stoves, and building materials.

Until 1840, the people eagerly crowding into cities came mostly from the American countryside. Then a growing number of immigrants arrived in the seaport cities. Many moved on to the interior, but the penniless had little choice but to remain in eastern cities and search for work there. By 1860, fully 20 percent of the people living in the Northeast were immigrants. The Irish, fleeing famine and poverty at home, were the largest foreign group in the Northeast.

A look at Philadelphia reveals the character and tensions of urban life during the antebellum period. An inland port, Philadelphia stood second only to New York. Though William Penn's "green country town" boasted an attractive appearance and an orderly plan, the expanding nineteenth-century city merited little praise. Speculators interested only in profit relied on the grid pattern as the cheapest and most efficient way to divide land for development. They built monotonous miles of new streets, new houses, new alleys, with "not a single acre left for public use, either for pleasure or health," as merchant Samuel Breck observed.

Overwhelmed by rapid growth, city governments provided few of the services we consider essential today, and usually only to those who paid for them. Water is a case in point. Only by paying a special fee could Philadelphians have water brought into their homes, so most of the city's residents went without. An inspection carried out by Mathew Carey in 1837 had pointed to an even more basic problem: 253 persons crowded into 30 tenements without even one privy. The ability to pay for services determined not only comfort but health.

Class Structure in the Cities

The drastic differences in the quality of urban life reflected the growing economic inequality that characterized Philadelphia and other American cities. In sharp contrast to the colonial period, the first half of the nineteenth century witnessed a dramatic rise in the concentration of wealth in the United States. The pattern was most extreme in cities. By the late 1840s, the wealthiest 4 percent of Philadelphia's population (merchants, brokers, lawyers, bankers, and manufacturers) held about two-thirds of the wealth. The economic pattern was similar in other American cities.

This widening gap between the upper class and the working class did not translate into mass suffering because more wealth was being generated. But the growing inequality hardened class lines, nourished social tensions, and contributed to the labor protests of the antebellum period.

Between 1820 and 1860, Philadelphia's working class, like Cincinnati's, was transformed. As preindustrial ways yielded to factory production, some former artisans and skilled workers climbed into the middle class, becoming businessmen, factory owners, mill supervisors, and shopkeepers. But downward occupational mobility also increased. Fed by waves of immigrants, the lower class was growing at an accelerating rate. Moreover, within the working class itself, the percentage of unskilled wage earners living in poverty or on its brink increased.

The Urban Working Class

As with so much else in urban life, housing reflected social and economic divisions. The poorest rented quarters in crowded, flimsily constructed shacks, shanties, and two-room houses. The urban working class faced not just poverty but the transformation of family life. Men could no longer be sure of supporting their wives and children, even when they were employed, and they felt that they had lost much of their authority and power in the family. Some found their wives no longer subservient or seemingly careless with their hard-earned money. Family violence that spilled out onto the streets was not uncommon in working-class quarters.

Middle-Class Life and Ideals

Members of the comfortable middle class profited from the dramatic increase in wealth in antebellum America. The houses of the city's elite were spacious and filled with new conveniences. Samuel Breck's house in 1839 was elegant and luxurious, with "parlours 14 feet high, . . . furnaces, water closet and shower and common bath up stairs, marble mantels and fireplaces in dressing rooms."

For the urban middle and upper class, the rewards of economic success included residential comfort, choice, and stability. But working-class renters moved often, from one cramped lodging to another. This common pattern of repeated mobility made it difficult to create close-knit neighborhoods in urban settings.

As the gap between classes widened, new

middle-class norms emerged, nourished by the changing economy. Better transportation, new products, and the rise of factory production and large businesses changed family life. Falling prices for processed and manufactured goods made it unnecessary for women to continue making these items at home. As men increasingly involved themselves in a money economy, women's and children's contributions to the family economy became relatively less significant. Even the rhythm of their lives, oriented to housework rather than the demands of the clock, separated them from the bustling commercial world where their husbands now labored. By 1820, the notion emerged that the sexes occupied separate spheres.

While men pursued success in the public world, what were women's responsibilities? Sarah Hale, editor of the popular magazine *Godey's Lady's Book,* and Catharine Beecher, well-known lecturer and writer, argued that woman's sphere was at home, keeping house and creating a clean, wholesome, and private setting for family life.

Women also served as their families' moral and cultural guardians. Arguing that women had different characters from men, that they were innately pious, virtuous, unselfish, and modest, publicists maintained that mothers would train future citizens and workers to be obedient, moral, patriotic, and hardworking. Just as important, they would preserve important values in a time of rapid change. As one preacher explained, a wife was the guardian angel who "watches over" her husband's interests, "warns him against dangers, comforts him under trial; and by . . . pious, assiduous, and attractive deportment, constantly endeavors to render him more virtuous, more useful, more honourable, and more happy."

This view, characterizing women as morally superior to and different from men, had important consequences for many women's lives. The physical separation of the male and female worlds and the shift in women's status often meant that women shared more with one another than with men, even their husbands. Simi-

lar social experiences and perspectives made female friendships central for many women, the source of comfort, security, and happiness.

They also experienced both pleasure and frustration in their role as housekeepers. Now that most domestic production had disappeared from the household, the task of creating a comfortable and attractive home became primary. But new standards of cleanliness, order, and beauty were often impossible to achieve. Moreover, efforts to create a perfect home often worked against harmonious family life.

Although the concept of domesticity seemed to confine women to the domestic sphere, it actually prompted women to take on activities in the outside world. If women were the guardians of morality, why should they not carry out their tasks in the public sphere? This reasoning lay behind the tremendous growth of voluntary female associations in the early decades of the nineteenth century. Initially, most involved religious and charitable activities. In the 1830s, as we shall see in Chapter 12, women added specific moral concerns like the abolition of slavery to their missionary and benevolent efforts, often clashing with men and with social conventions about "woman's place."

Domesticity described norms, not the actual conduct of middle-class women. Obviously not all women were pious, disinterested, selfless, virtuous, cheerful, and loving. But these ideas influenced how women thought of themselves. The new norms, effectively spread by the publishing industry, influenced rural women and urban working women. The insistence on marriage and service to family discouraged married women from entering the work force. Those who had to work often bore a burden of guilt. Though the new feminine ideal may have seemed noble to middle-class women in cities and towns, it created difficult tensions in the lives of working-class women.

As family roles were reformulated, a new view of childhood emerged. Working-class children still worked or scavenged for goods to sell or use at home, but middle-class children were no longer expected to contribute economically to the family. Middle-class parents now came to see childhood as a special stage of life, a period of preparation for adulthood.

Children were to spend their early years learning important values from their mothers and through schooling. Children's fiction also presented dutiful, religious, loving, and industrious youngsters as role models.

The growing publishing industry helped to spread new ideas about family roles and appropriate family behavior. Novels, magazines, etiquette and child-rearing manuals, and schoolbooks all carried the message from northern and midwestern centers of publishing to the South, to the West, and to the frontier. Probably few Americans lived up to the new standards established for the model parent or child, but the standards increasingly influenced them.

New notions of family life supported the widespread use of contraception for the first time in American history. Since children required so much loving attention and needed careful preparation for adulthood, many parents desired smaller families. The declining birthrate was evident first in the Northeast, particularly in cities and among the middle class. Contraceptive methods included abortion, which was legal in many states until 1860. This medical procedure terminated perhaps as many as a third of all pregnancies. Other birth control methods included coitus interruptus and abstinence. The success of these methods for family limitation suggests that many men and women adopted the new definitions of the female sex as naturally affectionate but passionless and sexually restrained.

Mounting Urban Tensions

The social and economic changes transforming American cities in the half century before the Civil War produced urban violence on a scale never before witnessed in America, not even during the Revolution. Festering ethnic and racial tensions often triggered mob actions that lasted for days.

Racial tensions contributed to Philadelphia's disorders. An unsavory riot in August 1834 revealed other important sources of social antagonism as well as the inability of its police force to control disorder.

One hot August evening, several hundred white Philadelphians wrecked a building on South Street that contained the "Flying Horses," a merry-go-round patronized by both blacks and whites. A general melee followed. As the *Philadelphia Gazette* reported, "At one time it is supposed that four or five hundred persons were engaged in the conflict, with clubs, brickbats, paving stones, and the materials of the shed in which the flying horses were kept." Spurred by the taste of blood, the white mob moved into the center of the crowded, racially mixed neighborhood, where they continued their orgy of destruction, looting, and intimidation of black residents.

An investigation following the riots revealed that the white mob had caused at least $4,000 of damage to two black churches and more than 36 private homes. At least one black had been killed, and numerous others had been injured.

Many rioters bragged that they were "hunting the nigs." Riots, however, are complicated events, and this racial explanation does not reveal the range of causes underlying the rampage of violence and destruction.

The mob's composition hints at some of the reasons for participation. Many of the rioters were young and at the bottom of the occupational and economic ladder, competing with blacks for jobs. This was particularly true of the newly arrived Irish immigrants, who were attempting to replace blacks in low-status jobs. Subsequent violence against blacks suggested that economic rivalry was an important component of the riot. "Colored persons, when engaged in their usual vocations," the *Niles Register* observed, "were repeatedly assailed and maltreated. . . . Parties of white men have insisted that no blacks shall be employed in certain departments of labor."

Some rioters were skilled workers who had experienced the negative impact of a changing economic system that was undermining the small-scale mode of production. To them, blacks were scapegoats, but the real but intangible villain was the economic system itself. Trade union organizing and a general strike a year later would highlight the grievances of this group.

Rapid urban expansion also figured as a factor in the racial violence. Most of the rioters lived either in the riot area or nearby. All had experienced the overcrowded and inadequate living conditions caused by the city's rapid growth. The racial tensions generated by squalid surroundings and social proximity go far to explain the outbreak of violence. The same area would later become the scene of race riots and election trouble and became infamous for harboring criminals and juvenile gangs.

The city's small, newly formed police force proved unable to control the mob, thus prolonging the violence. Philadelphia, like other eastern cities, was in the midst of creating its police force. Only continued rowdiness, violence, and riots would convince residents and city officials in Philadelphia (and in other large cities) to support an expanded, quasi-military, preventive police force in uniforms. By 1855, most sizable eastern cities had established such forces.

Finally, the character of the free black community itself was a factor in producing those gruesome August events. Not only was the community large and visible, but it had also created its own institutions and its own elite. Whites resented "dressy blacks." The mob targeted the solid brick houses of middle-class blacks, robbing them of silver and watches.

The Black Underclass

Events in Philadelphia showed how hazardous life for free blacks could be. Northern whites,

like southerners, believed in black inferiority and depravity and feared black competition for jobs and resources. Although northern states had passed gradual abolition acts between 1780 and 1803 and the national government had banned slaves from entering new states to be formed out of the Northwest Territory, nowhere did any government extend equal rights and citizenship or economic opportunities to free blacks in their midst.

For a time in the early nineteenth century, some blacks living in the North were permitted to vote, but they soon lost that right. Beginning in the 1830s, Pennsylvania, Connecticut, and New Jersey disenfranchised blacks. New York allowed only those with three years' residence and property valued at $250 or more to vote. Only the New England states (with the exception of Connecticut), which had tiny black populations, preserved the right to vote regardless of color. By 1840, fully 93 percent of the northern free black population lived in states where law or custom prevented them from voting.

Other black civil rights were also restricted. In five northern states, blacks could not testify against whites or serve on juries. In most states, the two races were thoroughly segregated. Blacks increasingly endured separate and inferior facilities in railway cars, steamboats, hospitals, prisons, and other facilities. They sat in "Negro pews" in churches and took communion only after whites had left the church. Although most Protestant religious denominations in the antebellum period split into northern and southern branches over the issue of slavery, most northern churches were not disposed to welcome blacks as full members.

As the Philadelphia riot revealed, whites were driving blacks from their jobs. In 1839, *The Colored American* blamed the Irish. "These impoverished and destitute beings . . . are crowding themselves into every place of business . . . and driving the poor colored American citizen out." Increasingly after 1837, these "white niggers" became coachmen, stevedores, barbers, cooks, house servants—all occupations blacks had once held.

Educational opportunities for blacks were also severely limited. Only a few school systems admitted blacks, in separate facilities. The case of Prudence Crandall illustrates the lengths to which northern whites would go to maintain racial segregation. In 1833, Crandall, a Quaker schoolmistress in Canterbury, Connecticut, announced that she would admit "young colored ladies and Misses" to her school. The outraged townspeople, unable to persuade her to abandon her project, harassed and insulted students and teachers and finally demolished the school. Crandall was arrested, and after two trials—in which free blacks were declared to have no citizenship rights—she finally gave up and moved to Illinois.

Crandall would not have found the Old Northwest much more hospitable. The fast-growing western states were intensely committed to white supremacy and black exclusion. As an Indiana newspaper editor observed in 1854, informal customs made life dangerous for blacks. They were "constantly subject to insults and annoyance in traveling and the daily avocations of life; [and] are practically excluded from all social privileges, and even from the Christian communion."

RURAL COMMUNITIES

Although the percentage of families involved in farming fell from 72 to 60 percent between 1820 and 1860, Americans remained a rural people. Agriculture persisted as the country's most significant economic activity, and farm products still made up most of the nation's exports. The small family farm still characterized eastern and western agriculture.

Farming remained the dominant way of life, but agriculture changed in the antebellum period. Vast new tracts of land came under cultivation in the West. Railroads, canals, and better roads pulled rural Americans into the orbit of the wider world. Some crops were shipped to regional markets; others, like grain, hides, and

pork, stimulated industrial processing. Manufactured goods, ranging from cloth and tools to books and periodicals, flowed in return to farm families. Commercial farming encouraged different ways of thinking and acting and lessened the isolation so typical before 1820.

Farming in the East

During the antebellum period, economic changes created new rural patterns in the Northeast. Marginal lands in New England, New York, and Pennsylvania, cultivated as more fertile lands ran out, yielded discouraging returns. Gradually after 1830, farmers abandoned these farms, often to move westward. By 1860, almost 40 percent of people who had been born in Vermont had left their native state.

Farmers who did not migrate west had to transform their production. Realizing that they could not compete with western grain, they sought new agricultural opportunities created by better transportation and growing urban markets. One of the demands was for fresh milk. By the 1830s, some eastern cities had grown so large that milk was turning sour before it reached central marketplaces. To meet the desire for milk, several cities, including New York City, started urban dairies. As railroad lines extended into rural areas, however, farmers living as far away as Vermont and upper New York state discovered that they could ship cooled milk to urban centers. City residents had fresher and cheaper milk and drank more of it as a result.

Urban appetites encouraged other farmers to cultivate fruit and vegetables for sale in city markets. With fresh produce in regular supply, cookbooks began to include recipes calling for fresh ingredients.

As northern farmers adopted new crops, they began to consider farming as a scientific endeavor. After 1800, northern farmers started using manure as fertilizer rather than disposing of it as a smelly nuisance. By the 1820s, some

This 1856 print titled Preparing for Market *shows the farm as a center of human and animal activity. The goods this farmer is loading in his wagon suggest the shifts in agriculture that took place in the East as competition from the Midwest encouraged farmers to raise new crops for the market.*

farmers were rotating their crops and planting new grasses and clover to restore fertility to the soil. By 1860, American farmers had developed thousands of special varieties of plants for local conditions. Many improvements resulted from experimentation, but farmers also enjoyed more and better information, which they found in new journals like the *New England Farmer,* the *Farmers' Register,* and the *Cultivator.* Following New York's lead in 1819, many states established agricultural agencies to propagate new ideas. A "scientific" farmer in 1850 could often produce two to four times as much per acre as in 1820.

Farmers in the fertile area around Northampton, Massachusetts, illustrate the American farmer's adjustment to new economic conditions. As roads and canals improved, markets became more accessible. Farmers started to cultivate crops "scientifically" in order to increase profits. Farming was becoming a business. At home, women found themselves freed from many of their traditional tasks. Peddlers brought goods to the door. The onerous duty of making cloth and clothing disappeared with the coming of inexpensive ready-made cloth and even ready-made clothes in the 1820s. Daughters liberated from the chores of home manufacturing went off to the mills or earned money by taking in piecework from local merchants. Cash transactions replaced the exchange of goods. Country stores became more reluctant to accept wood, rye, corn, oats, and butter as payment for goods instead of cash.

Some farmers prospered as they became involved in the market economy; others just got along. Wealth inequality increased near Northampton, as it did elsewhere in the rural Northeast.

Frontier Families

Many people who left the North during these years headed for the Old Northwest, where they raised corn and pork, sending their products down the Ohio and Mississippi rivers to southern buyers. In 1820, less than one-fifth of the American population lived west of the Appalachians; by 1860, almost half did, and Ohio and Illinois had become two of the nation's most populous states.

In 1830, Chicago had only 250 residents. Conditions were often primitive, as Charles Butler and Arthur Bronson discovered during their 1833 trip. Their hotel in Michigan City, Indiana, was "a small log house, a single room, which answered the purpose of drawing room, sitting room, eating room & sleeping room; in this room some eleven or twelve persons lodged in beds & on the floor."

During the 1830s, land sales and settlement boomed in the Old Northwest. Eastern capital contributed to the boom with loans, mortgages, and speculative buying. Internal improvement schemes after 1830 also influenced new settlement patterns and tied the Old Northwest firmly to the East. Erasmus Gest, who as a 17-year-old had worked on canal projects in Indiana, recalled the settlers' enthusiasm for improvements: "We Engineers were favorites with the People wherever we went."

Wheat for the eastern market rather than corn and hogs for the southern market became increasingly important with the transportation links eastward. Between 1840 and 1860, Illinois, southern Wisconsin, and eastern Iowa turned into the country's most rapidly growing grain regions. In the 1850s, these three states accounted for 70 percent of the increase in national wheat production.

Settling in the Old Northwest required hard work and at least some money. Catharine Skinner, who moved from New York to Indiana with her husband when she was 24, wrote to her sister in 1849: "We have got 80 acres of land in the woods of Indiana, a very level country; we have got two acres cleared and fenced and four more pirty well under way; we have got about five acres of wheat in the ground; we raised corn enough for our use and to fat our pork . . . we have a cow so that we have milk and butter and plenty of corn bread but wheat is hard to be got in account of our not having mony."

The Skinners probably spent $500 to $600 to start farming. They invested perhaps $100 for 80 acres of government land, $300 for basic farming equipment, and another $100 or $150 for livestock. To buy an already "improved" farm cost more. Once farmers moved onto the prairies of Indiana and Illinois, they needed an initial investment of about $1,000 since they had to buy materials for fencing, housing, and expensive steel plows. If farmers invested in the new horse-drawn reapers, they could cultivate more land, but all their costs also increased.

Opportunities in the Old Northwest

It was possible to begin farming with less, however. Some farmers borrowed from relatives, banks, or insurance companies like the Ohio Life Insurance and Trust Company. Others rented land from farmers who had bought more acres than they could manage. Tenants who furnished their own seeds and animals could expect to keep about a third of the yield. Within a few years, some saved enough to buy their own farms. Even those without any capital could work as hired hands. Since labor was scarce, they earned good wages. Probably about a quarter of the western farm population consisted of young men laboring as tenants or hired hands.

Rural communities, unlike the cities, had no growing class of propertyless wage earners, but inequalities nevertheless existed in the Old Northwest. In Butler County, Ohio, for example, 16 percent of people leaving wills in the 1830s held half of the wealth. By 1860, the wealthiest 8 percent held half of the wealth. While wealth was not as concentrated in rural areas as in the cities, a few residents benefited more from rapid economic development than others. Nevertheless, the Northwest offered many American families the chance to become independent producers and to enjoy "a pleasing competence."

Agriculture and the Environment

Shifting agricultural patterns in the East and expanding settlement into the Old Northwest contributed to the changing character of the American landscape. As naturalist John Audubon mused in 1826, "a century hence," the rivers, swamps, and mountains "will not be here as I see them. Nature will have been robbed of many brilliant charms, the rivers will be tormented and turned astray from their primitive course, the hills will be levelled with the swamps, and perhaps the swamps will have become a mount surmounted by a fortress of a thousand guns."

When eastern farmers changed their agricultural practices as they became involved in the market economy, their decisions left an imprint on the land. As forests disappeared, so too did their wildlife. Even using mineral manures like gypsum or lime or organic fertilizers like guano to revitalize worn-out soil and increase crop yields meant the depletion of land elsewhere.

When farmers moved into the old Northwest, they used new steel plows, like the one developed in 1837 by Illinois blacksmith John Deere. Unlike older eastern plows, the new ones could cut through the dense, tough prairie cover. Deep plowing and the intensive cultivation of large cash crops had immediate benefits. But these practices could result in robbing the soil of necessary minerals like phosphorous, carbon, and nitrogen. When farmers built new timber houses as frontier conditions receded, they helped fuel the destruction of the country's forests.

CONCLUSION

THE CHARACTER OF PROGRESS

Between 1820 and 1860, the United States experienced tremendous growth and economic development. Visitors constantly remarked on the amazing bustle and rapid pace of American life. The United States was, in the words of one Frenchman, "one gigantic workshop, over the entrance of which there is the blazing inscription 'NO ADMISSION HERE, EXCEPT ON BUSINESS.' "

Although the wonders of American development dazzled foreigners and Americans alike, economic growth had its costs. Expansion was cyclic, and financial panics and depression punctuated the era. Industrial profits were based partly on low wages to workers. Time-honored routes to economic independence disappeared, and a large class of unskilled, impoverished workers appeared in American cities. Growing inequality characterized urban and rural life, prompting some labor activists to criticize new economic and social arrangements. But workers, still largely unorganized, did not speak with one voice. Ethnic, racial, and religious diversity divided Americans in new and troubling ways.

During these decades, many also noted that the paths between the East, Northwest, and South seemed to diverge. The rise of King Cotton in the South, where slave rather than free labor formed the foundation of the economy, created a new kind of tension in American life, as the next chapter will show.

Recommended Reading

Two useful introductions to economic change during this period are Stuart Bruchey, *The Roots of American Economic Growth, 1607–1861* (1965), and Albert W. Niemi, *U.S. Economic History: A Survey of the Major Issues* (1975).

Thomas C. Cochran provides an overview of industrial development in *Frontiers of Change: Early Industrialism in America* (1981), while technological innovation is the subject of David J. Jeremy, *Transatlantic Industrial Revolution: The Diffusion of Textile Technology Between Britain and America, 1790–1830* (1981).

On economic change in individual communities, see Thomas Dublin, *Women at Work: The Transformation of Work and Community in Lowell, Massachusetts, 1826–1860* (1979), and (as editor) *Farm to Factory: Women's Letters, 1830–1860* (1981); Allen F. Davis and Mark H. Haller, eds., *The Peoples of Philadelphia: A History of Ethnic Groups and Lower-Class Life, 1790–1940* (1973); and Steven J. Ross, *Workers on the Edge: Work, Leisure, and Politics in Industrializing Cincinnati, 1788–1890* (1985). See also Gary B. Nash, *Forging Freedom: The Formation of Philadelphia's Black Community, 1720–1840* (1988).

Alexis de Tocqueville analyzes American society in the 1830s in *Democracy in America* (1957 ed.). Edward Pessen shows the growth of inequality in four cities in *Riches, Class, and Power Before the Civil War* (1973). Mary P. Ryan focuses on the middle-class family in *Cradle of the Middle Class: The Family in Oneida County, New York, 1790–1865* (1981), while Christine Stansell focuses on lower-class urban women in *City of Women: Sex and Class in New York, 1789–1860* (1986). On family life see also Robert V. Wells, *Revolutions in Americans' Lives: A Demographic Perspective of the History of Americans, Their Families, and Their Society* (1982). Immigrant life is described in Stephan Thernstrom, ed., *Harvard Encyclopedia of American Ethnic Groups* (1980).

On the midwestern frontier, see Clarence Danhof, *Changes in Agriculture: The Northern United States, 1820–1870* (1969); Don H. Doyle, *The Social Order of a Frontier Community: Jacksonville, Illinois, 1825–1870* (1978); and John Mack Faragher, *Sugar Creek: Life on the Illinois Prairies* (1986).

Time Line

1805	*Palmer* v. *Mulligan*	1830s	Boom in the Old Northwest
1816	Second U.S. Bank chartered		Increasing discrimination against free blacks
1819–1824	Supreme Court decisions establish the principle that contracts are binding.		Public education movement spreads
		1833	Philadelphia establishes small police force
1820	Lowell, Massachusetts, founded by Boston Associates	1834	Philadelphia race riots
	The expression "woman's sphere" becomes current		Lowell work stoppage
1824–1850	Construction of canals in the Northeast	1837	Horace Mann becomes secretary of Massachusetts Board of Education
1825–1856	Construction of canals linking the Ohio, the Mississippi, and the Great Lakes	1837–1844	Financial panic and depression
		1840	Agitation for ten-hour day
1828	Baltimore and Ohio Railroad begins operation	1840s–1850s	Rising tide of immigration

chapter 11

Slavery and the Old South

As a young slave boy, Frederick Douglass was sent by his master to live in Baltimore. When he first met his mistress, Sophia Auld, she appeared to be "a woman of the kindest heart and finest feelings." He was "astonished at her goodness" as she began to teach him to read. Her husband, however, ordered her to stop because Maryland law forbade teaching slaves to read. In the seven years he lived with the Aulds, young Frederick had to use "various strategems" to teach himself to read and write, the key to his later escape to freedom.

Slaves and masters were inextricably bound to each other. After her husband's interference, Sophia Auld, Douglass observed, was transformed from an angel into a demon by the "fatal poison of irresponsible power." Her formerly tender heart turned to "stone" when she ceased teaching him. "Slavery proved as injurious to her," Douglass wrote, "as it did to me."

Such was also the case in Douglass's relationship with Mr. Covey, a slavebreaker to whom he was sent in 1833 to have his will broken. Covey succeeded for a time, Douglass reported, in breaking his "body, soul, and spirit" by brutal hard work and discipline. But one hot August day in 1833, the two men fought a long, grueling battle, which Douglass won. His victory, he said, "rekindled the few expiring embers of freedom, and revived within me a sense of my own manhood." Although it would be four more years before his escape to the North, the young man never again felt like a slave. The key to Douglass's successful resistance to Covey's power was not just his strong will, but rather his knowledge of how to jeopardize Covey's reputation and livelihood as a slavebreaker. The oppressed survive by knowing their oppressors.

As Sophia Auld and Covey discovered, as long as some people were not free, no one was free. After quarreling with a house servant, one plantation mistress complained that she "exercises dominion over me—or tries to do it. One would have thought . . . that I was the Servant, she the mistress." Many whites lived in constant fear of a slave revolt, sometimes sleeping with "a brace of loaded pistols at their sides."

Slavery, then, was an intricate web of human relationships as well as a labor system. After showing the economic growth and development of the Old South, in which slavery and cotton played vital roles, this chapter will emphasize the daily lives and relationships of masters and slaves who, like Douglass and the Aulds, lived, loved, learned, worked, and struggled with one another in the years before the Civil War.

Perhaps no issue in American history has generated quite as many interpretations or as much emotional controversy as slavery. As American attitudes toward that institution have changed over the years, three interpretive schools have developed, each adding to our knowledge of the "peculiar institution." The first saw slavery as a relatively humane and reasonable institution in which plantation owners took care of helpless, childlike slaves. The second depicted slavery as a harsh and cruel system of oppressive exploitation. The third, and most recent, interpretation described the slavery experience from the perspective of the slaves, who did indeed suffer brutal treatment in slavery but who also survived with individual self-esteem and a sense of community and culture.

The first and second interpretive schools emphasized workaday interactions among masters and slaves, while the third focused on life in the slave quarters from sundown to sunup. In a unique structure, this chapter follows these masters and slaves through their day, from morning in the Big House through hot afternoon in the fields to the slave cabins at night. But although slavery was the crucial institution in defining the Old South, many other social groups and patterns contributed to the tremendous economic growth of the South from 1820 to 1860. We will look first at these diverse aspects of antebellum southern life.

BUILDING THE COTTON KINGDOM

The vast region of the antebellum South was not a monolithic society filled only with large cotton plantations worked by hundreds of slaves. The realities of the South and slavery were much more complex. Large-plantation agriculture was dominant, but most southern whites were not even slaveholders, much less large planters. Most southern farmers lived in dark, cramped, two-room cabins. Cotton was a key cash crop in the South, but it was not the only crop grown there. Some masters were kindly, but many were not; some slaves were contented, but most were not.

There were many Souths, encompassing several geographic regions, each with different economic bases and social structures. The older Upper South of Virginia, Maryland, North Carolina, and Kentucky grew different staple crops from those grown in the newer, Lower or "Black Belt" South that stretched from South Carolina to eastern Texas. Within each state, moreover, the economies differed between flat, coastal areas and inland, up-country forests and pine barrens. A still further diversity existed between these areas and the Appalachian highlands of northern Alabama and Georgia, eastern Tennessee and Kentucky, and western Virginia and North Carolina. Finally, the cultural and economic life of New Orleans, Savannah,

Charleston, and Richmond differed dramatically from that of rural areas of the South. But although the South was diverse, agriculture dominated its industry and commerce.

Economic Expansion

In the 20 years preceding the Civil War, the South's economy grew slightly faster than the North's. Personal income in 1860 was 15 percent higher in the South than in the prosperous states of the Old Northwest. The cotton gin was fundamental to this economic growth, wedding the southern economy to cotton production for a century and stimulating the expansion of slavery into vast new territories.

As we learned in Chapter 9, most cotton farmers planted "long staple" cotton prior to the invention of Eli Whitney's cotton gin in 1793. After the cotton gin, the "short staple" variety, which could grow anywhere in the South, predominated. But only large-plantation owners could afford to buy gins and purchase the fertile bottomlands of the Gulf states. Thus the plantation system and slavery spread with the rise of cotton.

Although corn was a larger crop than cotton in total acreage, cotton was the largest cash crop and for that reason was called "king." In 1820, the South became the world's largest producer of cotton, and from 1815 to 1860 cotton represented more than half of all American exports. Cotton was not only the mainstay of the southern economy but also a crucial link in the national economy.

The supply of cotton from the South grew at an astonishing rate, soaring from 461,000 bales in 1817 to 1.35 million bales in 1840, 2.85 million bales in 1849, and 4.8 million bales in 1860. In the period from 1817 to 1860, cotton production jumped over tenfold. This rapid growth was stimulated by world demand, especially from English textile mills. The availability of new lands, a self-reproducing supply of cheap slave labor, and low-cost steamboat transportation

down the Mississippi River to New Orleans helped to keep cotton king.

White and Black Migrations

Southerners migrated southwestward in huge numbers between 1830 and 1860 to grow more and more cotton. They pushed the southeastern Indians and the Mexicans in Texas out of the way and were still moving into Texas as the Civil War began. The migration process made many planters rich.

By the 1830s, the center of cotton production had shifted from South Carolina and Georgia to Alabama and Mississippi. This process continued in the 1850s as southerners forged into Arkansas, Louisiana, and eastern Texas. As they moved, they carried their values and institutions, including slavery, with them.

Not only were these migrating southern families attracted by the pull of fresh land and cheap labor, but they were also pushed westward by worsening economic conditions and other pressures in the older Atlantic states. Beginning in the 1820s, the states of the Upper South underwent a long depression affecting tobacco and cotton prices. Moreover, years of constant use had exhausted their lands. Those who stayed in the Upper South continued to shift to grains, mainly corn and wheat. Because these crops required less labor than tobacco, slave owners began to sell some of their slaves.

The internal slave trade from Virginia "down the river" to the Old Southwest thus became a multimillion-dollar "industry" in the 1830s. Between 1830 and 1860, an estimated 300,000 Virginia slaves were transported south for sale. Although most southern states attempted occasionally to outlaw or control the traffic in slaves, these efforts were poorly enforced and usually short-lived. Besides, the reason for outlawing the slave trade was generally not humanitarian but rather originated in a fear of a rapid increase in the slave population, especially of "wicked" slaves sent south because they

The Varied Economic Life in the South

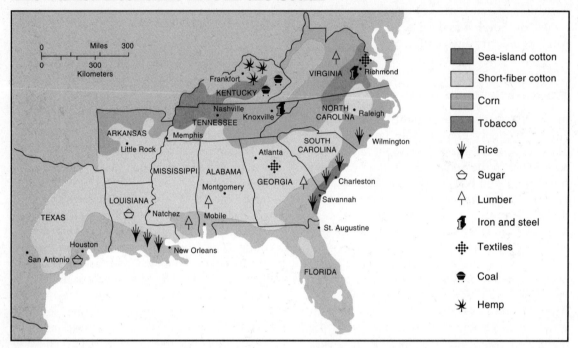

were considered unmanageable. Alabama, Mississippi, and Louisiana all banned the importation of slaves after the Nat Turner revolt in Virginia in 1831 (described later in this chapter). But all three states permitted the slave trade again during the profitable 1850s.

Congress formally ended the external slave trade on January 1, 1808, the earliest time permitted by the Constitution. Although many thousands of blacks continued to be smuggled to North America until the end of the Civil War, the tremendous increase in the slave population was the result not of this illegal trade but of natural reproduction, often encouraged by slaveowners eager for more laborers and salable human property.

The Dependence on Slavery

The rapid increase in the number of slaves, from 1.5 million in 1820 to 4 million in 1860, paral-leled the growth of the southern economy and its dependence on the slave labor system. Economic growth and migration southwestward changed the geographic distribution of slaves, thus hindering the cause of abolition.

Although most slaves worked on plantations and medium-size farms, they could be found in all segments of the southern economy. In 1850, some 75 percent of all slaves were engaged in agricultural labor. The 300,000 slaves in 1850 who were not domestics or agricultural laborers worked as lumberjacks and turpentine producers in Carolina and Georgia forests; gold, coal, and salt miners in Virginia and Kentucky; boiler stokers and deckhands on Mississippi River steamships; toilers on road and railroad construction gangs in Georgia and Louisiana; textile laborers in Alabama cotton mills; dockworkers in Savannah and Charleston; and tobacco and iron workers in Richmond factories.

Southern Cotton Production, 1821-1859

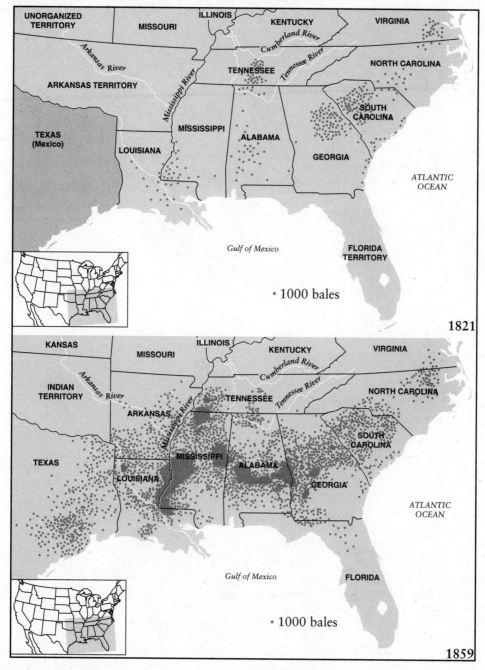

Concentration of Slavery, 1820-1860

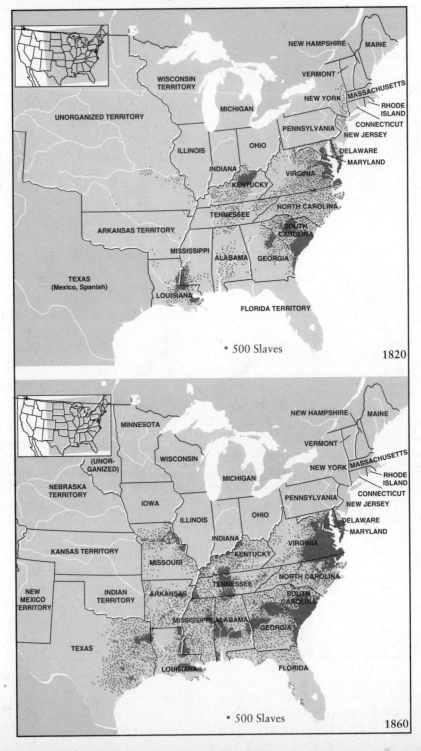

• 500 Slaves

1820

• 500 Slaves

1860

Slaves were also used in the industrial sector. The Tredegar Iron Company of Richmond decided in 1847 to shift from white labor "almost exclusively" to slave labor in order to destroy the potential power of organized white workers to strike. Tredegar's decision, though local, had enormous future implications. Although black and white workers have sometimes been able to agree on class issues, racial animosities based on white perceptions of threats to their job security by black workers continue to this day.

Whether in iron factories, coal mines, or cotton fields, slavery was profitable to owners. In 1859, the average plantation slave produced $78 in cotton earnings for his master annually while costing only about $32 to be fed, clothed, and housed. Slaves were also a good investment. In 1844, a "prime field hand" sold for $600. A cotton boom beginning in 1849 raised this price by 1860 to $1,800.

The economic growth of the slaveholding South was impressive, but it was limited because of the dependence on slavery. Generally, agricultural growth leads to the rise of cities and industry, facilitating sustained economic growth. In the planter-dominated antebellum South, however, agricultural improvements did not lead to industrialization and urbanization. On the eve of the Civil War, one southerner in 14 was a city dweller, compared with one of every three people in the North. The South would be economically backward as long as the whites with capital insisted on putting all their business energies toward cotton production.

Slavery and Class in the South

Slavery was more than an economic institution, for it also served social purposes. Although the proportion of southern white families that owned slaves slowly declined from 40 to 25 percent as some families sold off their slaves to cotton planters, the ideal of slave ownership still permeated all classes and determined the hierarchical character of the southern social structure. At the top stood the planter aristocracy, much of

it new wealth. Some 10,000 rich families owned 50 or more slaves in 1860; about 3,000 of these owned over 100. Below them was a slightly larger group of small planters who held from 10 to 50 slaves. But the largest group, 70 percent of all slaveholders in 1860, comprised 270,000 middle-level farm families with fewer than ten slaves. The typical slaveholder worked a small family farm of about 100 acres with eight or nine slaves, perhaps members of the same family. The typical slave, however, was more likely to be in a group of 20 or more other slaves on a large farm or small plantation.

In 1841, a young, white North Carolinian, John Flintoff, went to Mississippi to fulfil his dream of wealth and prestige. Beginning as an overseer managing an uncle's farm, he bought "a negro boy 7 years old" even before he owned any land. After several years of unrewarding struggle, Flintoff married and returned to North Carolina. There he finally bought 124 acres and a few more cheap, young blacks, and by 1860 he had a modest farm with several slaves growing corn, wheat, and tobacco. Although he never became as prosperous as he had dreamed, his son went to college, and his wife, he reported proudly, "has lived a *Lady*."

Like Flintoff, most southerners supported slavery for reasons of upward economic mobility, social prestige, and political influence. But they also defended the institution because it gave them a sense of superiority over at least one group and a sense of kinship, if not quite equality, with other whites. Although there was always a small element of southern society that believed in emancipation, most southerners did not. A small Alabama farmer told a northern visitor in the 1850s that if the slaves were given their freedom, "they'd all think themselves just as good as we.... How would you like to hev a nigger feelin' just as good as a white man?"

The Nonslaveholding South

Below Flintoff and other middling farmers lived the majority of white southerners, who owned no slaves but were equally, or even more, anti-black. Newton Knight, for example, worked a harsh piece of land cut out of the pines of southern Mississippi. He and his wife lived in a crude log cabin, scratching out their livelihood by growing corn and sweet potatoes and raising chickens and hogs. A staunch Baptist given to fits of violence, Knight had once killed a black.

The 75 percent of southern whites who owned no slaves were scattered throughout the South. Many were Scots-Irish. Most lived in the foothills of the mountains and worked generally poorer land than the large planters. Largely self-sufficient, they raised mostly corn and wheat, hogs, enough cotton for their own clothes and a little cash, and subsistence vegetable crops. They lived in two-room log houses separated by a "dog run." Families gathered at corn huskings and quilting parties, logrolling and wrestling matches, and political stump and revivalist camp meetings. In many ways the yeoman farmers were the solid backbone of the South. Fiercely proud of their independence, they had a share of political power, voting overwhelmingly for Andrew Jackson.

Another little-known group of southern whites were the herdsmen who raised hogs and other livestock. They supplied bacon and pork to local slaveholders (who often thought hog growing was beneath their dignity) and drove herds of hogs to stockyards in Nashville, Louisville, and Savannah. The South raised two-thirds of the nation's hogs. In 1860, the value of southern livestock was $500 million, twice that of cotton. However valuable the total size of the hog business, individual hog herdsmen did not stand very high on the southern social ladder.

Below them were the poor whites of the South, about 10 percent of the population. Often sneeringly called "hillbillies," "dirt eaters," "crackers," or "poor white trash," they eked out a living from the poor soil of pine barrens, sand hills, and marshes. Although they grew a little corn and vegetables, their livelihood came mostly from fishing, hunting small game,

and raising a few pigs. Some made corn whiskey, and many hired themselves out as farmhands for an average wage, with board, of about $14 per month. Because of poor diet and bad living conditions, these poor whites often suffered from diseases such as hookworm and malaria.

The poor whites were kept poor in part because the slave system allowed the planter class to accumulate a disproportionate amount of land and political power. High slave prices made entry into the planter class increasingly difficult, thus increasing class tensions within the South. Because the larger planters dominated southern life and owned the most slaves, an understanding of the character of slavery and the relationships between masters and slaves is best accomplished by looking at plantation life during a typical day from morning to night.

MORNING: MASTER IN THE BIG HOUSE

It is early morning on the southern plantation. Imagine three scenes. In the first, on the South Carolina plantation of James Hammond, the horn blows an hour before daylight to awaken the slaves for work in the fields. Hammond rises soon after, ever aware that "to continue" as a wealthy master, he must "draw the reign tighter and tighter" to hold his slaves "in complete check." He is as good as his word, recommending that "in general 15 to 20 lashes will be sufficient flogging" for most offenses but that "in extreme cases" the punishment "must not exceed 100 lashes in one day."

On an Alabama plantation, Hugh Lawson is up early, writing a sorrowful letter to Susanna Clay, telling her of the death of a "devotedly attached and faithful" slave, Jim. "I feel desolate," Hugh writes. "My most devoted friend is gone and *his place* can never be supplied by another." As Lawson pens his letter, a female slave has already awakened and "walked across a frosty field in the early morning and gone to the big house to build a fire" for her mistress. As the mistress wakes up to a warming house, she says to the slave, a grown woman responsible for the welfare of two families, "Well, how's my little nigger today?"

In a third household, this one a medium-size farm in up-country Georgia, not far from Hammond's huge plantation, Charles Brock wakes up at dawn and joins his two sons and four slaves to work his modest acreage of grains and sweet potatoes, while Brock's wife and a female slave tend the cows that provide milk and butter. On small and medium-size family farms with five or fewer slaves, blacks and whites commonly worked together, as one observer noted, with "the axe of master and man [slave] falling with alternate strokes . . . [and] ploughing side by side."

As these scenes suggest, slavery thoroughly permeated the lives of southern whites. For the slaves, morning was a time for getting up and going to work. But for southern whites, morning involved contact with slaves in many ways: as burdens of figuring profit and loss, as objects to be kept obedient and orderly, as intimates and fellow workers, and as ever-present reminders of fear, hate, and uncertainty.

The Burdens of Slaveholding

Robert Francis Withers Allston (1801–1864) was a major rice planter in a low, swampy, mosquito-infested tidal area of South Carolina. It was a perfect spot for growing rice, but so unhealthy that few whites wanted to live there. The death rate among slaves was appallingly high. In 1840, a total of 18,274 slaves toiled in the Georgetown district, but only 2,193 whites, many for only part of the year. By 1860, Allston owned seven plantations along the Peedee River, totaling some 4,000 acres. He held nearly 600 slaves, 236 of whom worked at the home plantation, Chicora Wood. Rich in land and labor, he nevertheless had large mortgages and outstanding debts.

Allston was an educated, talented, public-spirited man. He served in the South Carolina state senate for 24 years and as governor from 1856 to 1858. His political creed, he wrote in 1838, was one of "virtue and purity" based on "the principles of Thomas Jefferson." Allston was active in the Episcopal church and an ardent reformer, advocating liberalization of South Carolina's poor laws; an improved system of public education open to rich and poor alike; humanitarian care of the deaf, blind, insane, and other disabled persons; and the improvement of conditions on the reservations of the Catawba Indians.

In 1832, Allston married Adele Petigru, an equally enlightened and hardworking person. She participated fully in the management of the plantation and ran it while Robert was away on politics. After Robert's death during the Civil War, she assumed control of the Allston plantations, which had been abandoned when Union troops moved through the area.

State politics lured Robert from his land for part of each year, but he was by no means an absentee owner. Managing thousands of acres of rice required careful supervision of both the slaves and an elaborate irrigation system.

Allston's letters frequently expressed the serious burdens of owning slaves. Although he was careful to distribute enough cloth, blankets, and shoes to his slaves and to give them sufficient rest, the sickness and death of slaves, especially young field-workers, headed his list of concerns. "I lost in one year 28 negroes," Allston complained, "22 of whom were task hands." He tried to keep slave families together but sold slaves when necessary.

Other planters shared Allston's concerns, seeing slavery as both a duty and a burden. Many planters insisted that they worked harder than their slaves to feed and clothe them and to make their lives "as comfortable as possible." R. L. Dabney of Virginia exclaimed that "there could be no greater curse inflicted on us than to be compelled to manage a parcel of Negroes." Curse or not, Dabney and other planters profited from their burdens, a point they seldom admitted.

Adele and Robert F. W. Allston shared the work and burdens of managing their rice plantations.

Their wives experienced other kinds of burdens. "The mistress of a plantation," wrote Susan Dabney Smedes, "was the most complete slave on it." Plantation mistresses were expected to act as chaste ladies, while their husbands had virtually unrestricted sexual access to slave women. "God forgive us, but ours is a monstrous system," Mary Boykin Chestnut wrote in her diary. "Like the patriarchs of old, our men live all in one house with their wives and their concubines; and the mulattoes one sees in every family partly resemble the white children. Any lady is ready to tell you who is the father of all the mulatto children in everybody's household but her own. Those, she seems to think, drop from the clouds."

Chestnut called the sexual dynamics of slavery "the sorest spot." There were others. Southern white women had to tend to the food, clothing, health, and welfare not just of their husbands and children but of the plantation slave population as well. The plantation mistress, then, served many roles: as a potential hu-manizing influence on men; as a tough, resourceful, responsible manager of numerous plantation affairs; as a coercer of slaves and perpetuator of the system; and sometimes as a victim herself.

Justifying Slavery

As slavery was increasingly attacked as immoral, slaveholders felt compelled to justify their institution. Until the 1830s, their defense explained slavery as a "necessary evil." After the abolitionists stepped up their attack in that decade, however, the justification shifted to defending slavery, in John C. Calhoun's words, as "a positive good." Various arguments were used: biblical, historical, constitutional, scientific, and sociological.

The biblical justification was based in part (incorrectly) on the curse of Canaan, the son of Ham, who was condemned to eternal servitude because his father had looked on Noah's nakedness. Furthermore, in various places both the Old and New Testaments admonished servants to obey their masters and accept their earthly lot.

Southern apologists also cited historical arguments. Slavery had existed throughout history. In fact, the greatest civilizations—Egypt, Greece, and Rome—had all built their strength and grandeur in part on slave labor.

A third argument justified slavery on legal grounds. Southerners pointed out (correctly) that the United States Constitution clearly sanctioned slavery.

A fourth justification was "scientific." Southern ethnologists argued that blacks had been created separately (a theory called "polygenesis") and were an inherently inferior race with inferior brains. Therefore, the destiny of the inferior Africans was to serve the superior Caucasians (the "Adamic race") in work.

In a paternalistic defense of slavery based on racism and social control, George Fitzhugh argued that "the Negro is but a grown child and must be governed as a child." Social chaos would result if the slaves were freed. Emancipation, therefore, would be heartless and unthinkable, a burden to both blacks and whites.

Southern apologists for slavery faced the difficult intellectual task of justifying a system that ran counter to the main ideological directions of nineteenth-century American society: the expansion of individual liberty, mobility, economic opportunity, and democratic political participation. Moreover, the southern defense of slavery had to take into account the 75 percent of white families who owned no slaves and who envied those who did. Because of the potential for class anatagonisms among whites, wealthy planters developed a justification of slavery that deflected class differences by maintaining that all whites were superior to all blacks but equal to one another. The theory of democratic equality among whites, therefore, was made consistent with racism and the holding of slaves.

As the southern defense of slavery intensified in the 1840s and 1850s, it aroused greater opposition from northerners and from slaves themselves. Although slavery was cruel in many ways, perhaps its worst feature was not physical but psychological: to be enslaved at all and barred from economic advancement in a nation that put a high value on freedom and equality of opportunity.

NOON: SLAVES IN HOUSE AND FIELDS

It is two o'clock on a hot July afternoon on the plantation. The midday lunch break is over, and the slaves are returning to their work in the fields. Lunch was the usual nutritionally deficient fare of cornmeal and pork. Douglass remembered that "we worked all weathers. . . . It was never too hot, or too cold" for toiling in the fields.

Daily Toil

The daily work schedule for most slaves, whether in the fields or the Big House, was long and demanding. Aroused by a bell or horn before daybreak, they worked on an average day 14 hours in the summer and 10 hours in the winter. During harvest time, it was not uncommon to work for 18 hours. Depending on the size of the work force and the crop, the slaves were organized either in gangs or according to tasks. The gangs, usually of 20 to 25, worked their way along the cotton rows under the watchful eye and quick whip of a driver. Ben Simpson, a Georgia slave, remembered vividly how his master would use a "great, long whip platted out of rawhide" to hit a slave in the work gang who would "fall behind or give out."

Under the task system, each slave had a specific task to complete daily. This system gave slaves the incentive to work hard enough to finish early, but it meant that the quality of their work was scrutinized constantly. An overseer's weekly report to Robert Allston in 1860 noted that he had "flogged for hoeing corn bad Fanny 12 lashes, Sylvia 12, Monday 12, Phoebee 12, Susanna 12, Salina 12, Celia 12, Iris 12."

An average slave was expected to pick 130 to 150 pounds of cotton per day. The work on sugar and rice plantations was even harder. Sugar demanded constant cultivation and the digging of drainage ditches in snake-infested fields. At harvest time, cutting, stripping, and carrying the cane to the sugar house for boiling was exhausting. In addition, huge quantities of firewood had to be cut and carried. Working in the low-country rice fields was worse: Slaves spent long hours standing in water up to their knees.

House slaves, most of them women, had relatively easier assignments than the field slaves, though they were usually called on to help with the harvest. They also ate and dressed better than their fellow slaves in the fields. But house slaves were watched more closely, were on call at all hours of the day and night, and were more often involved in personality conflicts in the white household. The most feared punishment for a house slave, other than sale to the Deep South, was to be sent to the fields.

Slave Health

Although slave owners had an interest in keeping their slaves healthy by providing adequate care, slaves led sickly lives. Home was a crude, one-room log cabin with a dirt floor. Most cabins had a fireplace for heat and cooking, a table, some stools or boxes to sit on, an iron pot and wooden dishes, and perhaps a bed. The cabins were crowded, with usually more than one family living in each. Slave clothing was shabby and uncomfortable.

Studies on the adequacy of slave diet disagree, some showing that the food most slaves ate was deficient in calories and vitamins, others claiming that the energy value of the slave diet exceeded that of free whites in the general population. Compared with Latin American slaves, American slaves were well fed, receiving weekly rations of cornmeal, salt pork or bacon, molasses, and perhaps sweet potatoes. This bland fare was supplemented for some slaves, with the master's permission, by vegetables grown in a small garden and by fishing or hunting small game.

Most slaves, however, rarely enjoyed fresh meat, dairy products, fruits, or vegetables. To make up for these deficiencies, they sometimes stole from the master's kitchen, gardens, and barnyard. Inadequate diet led some slaves to become dirt eaters, which gave them worms and "swollen shiny skin, puffy eyelids, pale palms and soles." Others suffered regularly from skin disorders, cracked lips, and sore eyes. Many slaves, like poor whites, came down with vitamin deficiency diseases such as rickets, pellagra, beriberi, scurvy, and even mental illness.

Women slaves especially suffered weaknesses caused by vitamin deficiency, hard work, and disease, as well as those associated with the menstrual cycle and childbirth. Women were expected to do the same tasks in the fields as the men, in addition to cooking, sewing, child care, and traditional female jobs in the quarters when the fieldwork was finished. "Pregnant women," the usual rule stated, "should not plough or lift but must be kept at moderate work until the last hour" and were given a three-week recovery period after giving birth. But these guidelines were more often violated than honored. Infant mortality of slave children under 5 years of age was twice as high as for white children.

Life expectancy for American slaves was longer than for those in Latin America and the Caribbean, but not very high for either blacks or whites in the antebellum South (21.4 for blacks and 25.5 for whites in 1850). In part because of poor diet and climate, slaves were highly susceptible to disease. Many died from malaria, yellow fever, cholera, intestinal ailments, and respiratory diseases.

The relatively frequent incidence of whippings and other physical punishments aggravated the poor physical condition of the slaves. The slave William Wells Brown reported that on his plantation the whip was used "very frequently and freely" for inadequate or uncompleted work, stealing, running away, and even insolence and lying. Former slaves described a good owner as one who did not "whip too much" and a bad owner as one who "whipped till he'd bloodied you and blistered you." Other forms of punishment included isolation and confinement in stocks and jails during leisure hours, chains, muzzling, salting lash wounds, branding, burning, and castration.

Slave Law and the Family

Complicating master-slave relationships was the status of slaves as both persons and property, a legal and psychological ambiguity the South never resolved. On the one hand, the slaves had names, personalities, families, and wills of their own. This required dealing with them as fellow humans. On the other hand, they were items of property, purchased and maintained to perform specific profit-making tasks. As a Kentucky court put the problem, "Although the law of this state considers slaves as property, . . . it recognizes their personal existence, and, to a qualified extent, their natural right."

This ambiguity in the laws changed after the challenges to slavery in the early 1830s. As a result of Nat Turner's revolt and William Lloyd Garrison's publication of the abolitionist *Liberator* in 1831 (discussed later), the South tightened up the slave system. Laws prohibiting manumission were passed, but at the same time, laws protecting slaves from overly severe treatment were strengthened, and material conditions generally improved.

But whatever the law said, the practice was always more telling. Treatment varied with individual slaveholders. This was especially true with regard to the slave family. Most planters, like Robert Allston, generally encouraged their slaves to marry and did all they could to keep families intact. They believed that families made black males more docile and less inclined to revolt or run away. But some masters failed to respect slave marriages or broke them up because of financial problems. This tendency was supported by southern courts and legislatures, which did not legally recognize slave marriages or the right to family unity.

Adding to the pain of forced breakup of the slave family was the sexual abuse of black women. Although the frequency of such abuse is unknown, the presence of thousands of mulattoes in the antebellum era is testimony to this practice. White men in the South abused black slave women in several ways: by offering gifts for sexual "favors," by threatening those who refused with physical punishment or the sale of a child or loved one, by purchasing concubines, or by rape. As Frederick Douglass put it, the "slave woman is at the mercy of the fathers, sons or brothers of her master."

Because of the need to obtain cheap additional slaves for the work force, slaveholders encouraged young slave women to bear children, whether married or not. If verbal prodding and inducements such as less work and more rations did not work, masters would choose mates and foist them on slave women. More often, slaves chose their own mates on the basis of mutual attraction during an uneasy courtship complicated by the threat of white interferences. As among poor whites, premarital intercourse was frequent, but promiscuous behavior was rare. Most couples maintained affectionate, lasting relationships.

Although motherhood was the key event in a slave woman's life, bearing children and the double burden of work and family responsibilities challenged her resourcefulness. New mothers often had to choose between taking their babies into the fields to be fed or leaving them with others. Some masters would provide time off for nursing mothers, but the more common practice was for them to work in the fields with their newborn infants lying nearby, wrapped in cloth to protect them from the sun. Women developed networks of mutual support, looking after one another's children, meeting together to

Despite separation, sale, and sexual abuse by white masters, many slave families endured and provided love, support and self-esteem to their members. This 1862 photograph shows five generations of a slave family, all born on the plantation of J. J. Smith of Beaufort, South Carolina.

sew, quilt, cook, or do laundry, and attending births, caring for the sick and dying, and praying together.

The most traumatic problem for slaves was the separation of families, a haunting fear rarely absent from slave consciousness. The separation of husbands and wives (one-third according to one study of three Deep South states) challenged the couples to maintain contact. When Abream Scriven informed his wife, Dinah, of his sale to a trader in New Orleans, he had no idea where he would be sold but promised to "write and let you know where I am. . . . My Dear Wife for you and my Children my pen cannot Express the griffe I feel to be parted from you all."

There was much basis in fact for the abolitionists' contention that slavery was a harsh, brutal system. Yet, despite the travail of slavery, whether under relatively kind or cruel masters, the slaves endured with dignity, communal sensitivity, and even some joy. If daytime in the fields describes a view of slavery at its worst, nighttime in the quarters, as examined from the black perspective, reveals the slaves' survival powers and their capacity to mold an African-American culture under slavery.

NIGHT: SLAVES IN THEIR QUARTERS

It is near sundown, and the workday is almost over. Some of the slaves begin singing the gentle spiritual "Steal Away to Jesus," and others join in. Or perhaps they sing, "Dere's a meeting here tonight." To the unwary overseer or master, the humming, soothing sound of the song suggests happy slaves, content with their earthly lot and looking forward to deliverance in heaven, "in the sweet bosom of Jesus." To the slaves, however, the songs are a signal that, as an ex-slave, Wash Wilson, put it, they are to "steal away to Jesus" because "dere gwine be a 'ligious meetin' dat night." When evening arrived on the plantation, after a hard day of work in the hot sun or in the Big House, the slaves returned to their own quarters. There, as Wilson said, "sometimes us sing and pray all night."

In the slave quarters, away from white masters, overseers, and the burdens of daily work, an elaborate black community helped the slaves make sense out of their lives. In family life, religion, song, dance, the playing of musical instruments, and the telling of stories, the slaves both described their experiences and sought release from hardship and suffering. However burdensome their lives from sunup to sundown, after work the slaves experienced enjoyment and a sense of self-worth, hope, and group identity in their quarters.

Black Christianity

As suggested by the scene Wash Wilson described, Christian worship was an indispensable part of slave life in the quarters. The revivals of the early nineteenth century led to an enormous growth of Christianity among black Americans. Some independent black Baptist and Methodist churches, especially in border states and cities, served both slaves and free blacks and occasionally even whites. These separate churches had to steer a careful path to maintain their freedom and avoid white interference. But the vast majority of southern blacks were slaves, attending plantation missions set up by their masters.

For the slaveholders, religion often represented a form of social control. Black religious gatherings were usually forbidden unless white observers were present or white preachers led them. Whether in slave or white churches (where blacks sat in the back), preachers often delivered sermons from the biblical text "Servants, obey your masters."

Although some slaves accommodated themselves to the master's brand of Christianity and patiently waited for heavenly deliverance, others rebelled and sought earthly liberty. Douglass had an illegal Sabbath school on one plantation, where he and others risked being whipped while learning about Christianity and how to read. "The work of instructing my dear fellow-slaves," he wrote, "was the sweetest engagement with which I was ever blessed." Sarah Fitzpatrick, an Alabama slave, recalled that the slaves wanted so much to "go to church by de'-selves" that they were willing to sit through the "white fo'ks' . . . service in de mornin'." But when evening came, "a'ter dey clean up, wash de dishes, an' look a'ter ever'thing," the slaves would "steal away" to the nearby woods for their own service. Long into the night they would sing, dance, shout, and pray.

Although many of the expressive forms were African, the message reiterated over and over in the slave church was the Christian theme of suffering and deliverance from bondage. Slaves identified with the children of Israel and with the Exodus story, as well as with the suffering of Jesus and the inner turmoil of an unconverted "trebbled spirit." Nothing illustrated both the communal religious experience and these mixed Christian themes of suffering and redemption better than slave spirituals.

The Power of Song

A group of slaves gathers in the dark of night in the woods behind their quarters to sing and shout together.

O brothers, don't get weary
O brothers, don't get weary
O brothers, don't get weary
We're waiting for the Lord.
We'll land on Canaan's shore

We'll land on Canaan's shore
When we land on Canaan's shore
We'll meet forever more.

Music was a crucial form of expression in the slave quarters on both secular and religious occasions. The slaves were adept at creating a song, as one slave woman recalled, "on de spurn of de moment."

Although the spirituals were composed for many purposes, they reiterated one basic Christian theme: A chosen people, the children of God, were held captive in bondage but would be delivered. The titles and lyrics reveal the message: "We Are de People of de Lord," "To the Promised Land I'm Bound to Go," "Go Down, Moses," "Who Will Deliver Po' Me?" What they meant by "deliverance" was not always clear and often had a double meaning: freedom in heaven and freedom in the North.

"The songs of the slave," Douglass wrote, "represent the sorrows of his heart." Although they often expressed the sadness of broken families and the burdens of work, they also expressed joy, triumph, and deliverance. Slave songs did not always contain hidden meanings. Sometimes slaves gathered simply for music, to play fiddles, drums, and other instruments fashioned by local artists in imitation of West African models. Sacred and secular events such as weddings, funerals, holiday celebrations, family reunions, and a successful harvest were all occasions for a communal gathering, usually with music. So too was news of external events that affected their lives— a crisis in the master's situation, a change in the slave code, the outcome of a battle during the Civil War, or emancipation itself.

The Enduring Family

The role of music in births, weddings, funerals, and other milestones of family life suggests that the family was central to life in the slave quarters. Although the pain of sexual abuse and fam-

ily separation was a real or potential part of the experience of all slaves, so was the hope for family continuity.

The benefits of family cohesion were those of any group: love, protection, education, moral guidance, the transmission of culture, and the provision of status, role models, and basic support. All of these existed in the slave quarters. As the slaves gathered together at the end of the working day, parents passed on to their children the family story, language patterns and words, recipes, folktales, religious and musical traditions, and strong impressions of strength and beauty. In this way they preserved cultural tradition, which enhanced the identity and self-esteem of parents and children alike. Parents taught their children how to survive in the world and how to cope with life under slavery. As the young ones neared the age when they would work full time in the fields, their parents instructed them in the best ways to pick cotton or corn, how to avoid the overseer's whip, whom to trust and learn from, and ways of fooling the master.

The love and affection that slaves had for one another was sometimes a liability. Many slaves, women especially, were reluctant to run away because they did not want to leave their families. The slave family, though constantly endangered, played a crucial role in helping blacks adapt to slavery and achieve a sense of self-esteem.

RESISTANCE AND FREEDOM

Songs, folktales, and other forms of cultural expression enabled slaves to articulate their resistance to slavery. For example, Old Jim was going on a "journey" to the "kingdom" and, as he invited others to "go 'long" with him, he taunted his owner: "O blow, blow, Ole Massa, blow de cotton horn / Ole Jim'll neber wuck no mo' in de cotton an' de corn." From refusal to work it was a short step to outright revolt. In another song,

"Samson," the slaves clearly stated their determination to abolish the house of bondage: "An' if I had-'n my way / I'd tear the buildin' down! / . . . And now I got my way / And I'll tear this buildin' down." Every hostile song, story, or event, like Douglass's victory over Covey, was an act of resistance by which the slaves asserted their dignity and gained a measure of freedom. Some escaped slavery altogether to achieve such autonomy as was possible for free blacks in the antebellum South.

Forms of Black Protest

One way slaves protested the burdensome demands of continuous forced labor was in various "day to day" acts of resistance. These ranged from breaking or misplacing tools to burning crops, barns, and houses, from stealing or destroying animals and food to defending fellow slaves from punishment, from self-mutilation to deliberate work slowdowns, and from poisoning masters to feigning illness.

Overseers also suffered from these acts of disobedience, for their job depended on productivity, which in turn depended on the goodwill of the slave workers. No one knew this better than the slaves themselves, who adeptly played on the frequent struggle between overseer and master. Often the conflicts were ended by firing a bad overseer and hiring a more suitable replacement. Many slave-holders eventually resorted to using black drivers rather than overseers, but this created other problems.

The slave drivers were "men between," charged with the tricky job of getting the master's work done without alienating fellow slaves or compromising their own values. Although some drivers were as brutal as white overseers, many became leaders and role models for other slaves. A common practice of the drivers was to appear to punish without really doing so. Solomon Northrup reported that he "learned to handle the whip with marvellous dexterity and precision, throwing the lash within a hair's breadth of the back, the ear, the nose, without, however, touching either of them." As he did this, the "punished" slave would howl in pretended pain and complain loudly to his master about his harsh treatment.

Another form of resistance was to run away. The typical runaway was a young male, who ran off alone and hid out in a nearby wood or swamp. He left to avoid a whipping or because he had just been whipped, to protest excessive work demands, or, as one master put it, for "no cause" at all. But there was a cause—the need to experience a period of freedom away from the restraints and discipline of the plantation.

Some slaves left again and again. Remus and his wife, Patty, ran away from their master, James Battle, in Alabama. They were caught and jailed three times, but each time they escaped again. Battle urged the next jailer to "secure Remus well." Some runaways, called "Maroons," hid out for months and years at a time in communities of runaway slaves. Several Maroon colonies were located in the swamps and mountains of the South, especially in Florida, where Seminole and other Indian groups befriended them. In these areas, blacks and Indians, sharing a common hostility to local whites, frequently intermarried, though sometimes Indians were hired to track down runaway slaves.

The underground railroad, organized by abolitionists, was a series of safe houses and stations where runaway slaves could rest, eat, and spend the night before continuing. Harriet Tubman, who led some 300 slaves out of the South on 19 separate trips, was the railroad's most famous "conductor." It is difficult to know exactly how many slaves actually escaped to the North and Canada, but the numbers were not large. One estimate suggests that in 1850 about a thousand slaves (out of over three million) attempted to run away, and most of them were returned. Nightly patrols by white militiamen, an important aspect of southern life, reduced the chances for any slave to escape and probably deterred many slaves from even trying to run away.

Slave Revolts

The ultimate act of resistance, of course, was rebellion. Countless slaves committed individual acts of revolt. In addition, there were hundreds of conspiracies whereby slaves met to plan a group escape and often the massacre of whites. Most of these conspiracies never led to action, either because circumstances changed or the slaves lost the will to follow through or, more often, because some fellow slave—perhaps planted by the master—betrayed the plot. Such spies thwarted the elaborate conspiracies of Gabriel Prosser (Richmond, Virginia, 1800) and Denmark Vesey (Charleston, South Carolina, 1822). Both resulted in severe reprisals by whites, including mass executions of leaders and the random killing of innocent blacks.

Only a few organized revolts, in which slaves threatened white lives and property, ever actually took place. Latin American slaves challenged their masters more often than their North American counterparts. Weaker military control, easier escape to rugged interior areas, the greater imbalance of blacks to whites, and the continued dependence of Latin American slaveholders on the African slave trade for their supply of mostly male workers explain this pattern. The imbalance of males to females (156 to 100 in Cuba in 1860, for example, compared with a near one-to-one ratio in the United States) weakened family restraints on violent revolts.

The most famous slave revolt in North America, led by Nat Turner, occurred in Southampton County, Virginia, in 1831. Turner was an intelligent, skilled, unmarried, religious slave who had experienced many visions of "white spirits and black spirits engaged in bat-

tle." He believed that he was "ordained for some great purpose in the hands of the Almighty."

On a hot August night, Turner and a small band of fellow slaves launched their revolt. They intended, as Turner said, "to carry terror and devastation" throughout the country. They crept into the home of Turner's master, Joseph Travis, who Nat said was "a kind master" with "the greatest confidence in me," and killed the entire family. Before the revolt was finally put down, 55 white men, women, and children had been murdered and twice as many blacks killed in the aftermath. Turner hid in a hole in the woods for two weeks before he was apprehended and executed, but not before dictating a chilling confession to a white lawyer. Rarely thereafter would slaveholders go to sleep without the Southampton revolt in mind.

Free Blacks: Becoming One's Own Master

No matter how well they coped with their bondage, the slaves obviously preferred freedom. As Frederick Douglass said of the slave, "Give him a *bad* master, and he aspires to a *good* master; give him a good master, and he wishes to become his *own* master." Between 1820 and 1860, the number of free blacks in the United States doubled, from 233,500 to 488,000. This rise resulted from natural increase, successful escapes, "passing" as whites, purchasing freedom, and a continuation of some manumissions despite legal restriction in most states after the 1830s.

However freedom was achieved, what was life like for the 11 percent of the total black population who in 1860 were not slaves? More than half the free blacks lived in the South, most (85 percent in 1860) in the Upper South, where the total number of slaves had declined slightly. Free blacks generally lived away from the dense plantation centers, scattered on impoverished rural farmlands and in small towns and cities. One-

Frederick Douglass, photographed here in about 1855, spent his life working for freedom and improved opportunities for blacks after his own escape to freedom as a young man in 1838.

third of southern free blacks lived in cities such as Baltimore, Richmond, Charleston, and New Orleans. In part because it took a long time to buy their freedom, they tended to be older, more literate, and more skilled than other blacks. A great many were light-skinned women, reflecting the favored privileges these blacks received from slaveholders.

Most southern free blacks were poor, laboring as farmhands, day laborers, or woodcutters. In the cities, they lived in appalling poverty and worked in factories. A few skilled jobs, such as barbering, shoemaking, and plastering, were reserved for black men; they were barred from more than 50 other trades. Women worked as cooks, laundresses, and domestics. The 15 percent of free blacks who lived in the Lower South were divided into two distinct castes. Most were poor. But in New Orleans, Charleston, and other southern cities, a small, mixed-blood class of free blacks emerged as an elite group, closely connected to white society and removed from

the mass of poor blacks. A handful even owned land and slaves.

Most free blacks, however, had no such privileges. In most states, they could not vote, bear arms, buy liquor, assemble, speak in public, form societies, or testify against whites in court. In Richmond, efforts were also made to confine the free blacks to certain sections of the city or, increasingly by the 1850s, to compel them to leave the city, county, or state altogether. Those who stayed had trouble finding work, were required to carry licenses and freedom papers to be surrendered on demand, and often needed a white guardian to approve their actions. Nevertheless, free blacks and slaves often worked together in factories and fields, attended the same churches and places of entertainment, and sometimes even married.

The center of urban black community was the church. Martin Delaney wrote to Douglass in 1849 that "among our people ... the Church is the Alpha and Omega of all things." The church not only performed the usual religious functions but also provided and promoted education, social insurance, fraternal associations, and picnics, concerts, and other forms of recreation. Besides the church, black community identity and pride revolved around the African schools and various burial and benevolent societies for self-help and protection against poverty, illness, and other disasters. Like their counterparts among whites, these societies grew and took on a new and significant social importance in the two decades before the Civil War.

Free blacks faced a crisis of extinction in the 1850s, especially when pressures increased late in the decade either to deport the free blacks or to enslave them. In the wake of increasing threats to their already precarious free status, some black leaders not surprisingly began to look more favorably on migration to Africa. That quest was interrupted, however, by the outbreak of the Civil War, rekindling in Douglass and others the "expiring embers of freedom."

CONCLUSION

DOUGLASS'S DREAM OF FREEDOM

Frederick Douglass won his freedom by forging a free black sailor's pass and escaping through Chesapeake Bay to New York. In a real sense, he wrote himself into freedom. The *Narrative of the Life of Frederick Douglass,* "written by himself" in 1845, was a way both of exposing the many evils of slavery and of creating his own identity, even to the point of choosing his own name. Ironically, Douglass had learned to value reading and writing, we recall, from his Baltimore masters, the Aulds. This reminds us again of the intricate and subtle ways in which the lives of slaves and masters were tied together in the antebellum South.

In a poignant moment in his *Narrative,* Douglass described his dreams of freedom as he looked out at the boats on the waters of Chesapeake Bay as a boy. As we will see later, southern white planters also bemoaned their lack of freedom relative to the North and made their own plans to achieve independent status through secession. Meanwhile, as that struggle brewed beneath the surface of antebellum life, many other Americans were dismayed by various evil aspects in their society, slavery among them, and sought ways of shaping a better America. We turn to these other dreams in the next chapter.

Recommended Reading

Gavin Wright provides a difficult but thorough analysis of the economic development of the Old South in *The Political Economy of the Cotton South: Households, Markets, and Wealth in the Nineteenth Century* (1978). On the economics of slavery, see Paul David et al., *Reckoning with Slavery: A Critical Study of the Quantitative History of American Negro Slavery* (1976). Nonagricultural slaves are dealt with in Robert Starobin, *Industrial Slavery in the Old South* (1970). The most readable story of the lives of non-slaveholding whites in the South is an old one, Frank Owsley's *Plain Folk in the Old South* (1949).

A brilliant study of racism in America, including excellent chapters on the southern justification of slavery, is George Fredrickson, *The Black Image in the White Mind: The Debate on Afro-American Character and Destiny, 1817–1914* (1971). For a stunning portrayal of female slaves in the plantation South, see Deborah Gray White, *Arn't I a Woman?* (1985). A remarkable work that treats both white and slave women is Elizabeth Fox-Genovese, *Within the Plantation Household* (1988).

Of the many collections of primary source documents about slavery, the best is Willie Lee Rose, *A Documentary History of Slavery in North America* (1976). Among the best surveys of slavery are Nathan I. Huggins, *Black Odyssey: The Afro-American Ordeal in Slavery* (1977); and John Blassingame, *The Slave Community,* rev. ed. (1979). Slave culture and life in the quarters are treated brilliantly in Charles Joyner, *Down by the Riverside: A South Carolina Slave Community* (1984); and Lawrence Levine, *Black Culture and Black Consciousness: Afro-American Folk Thought from Slavery to Freedom* (1977). Frederick Douglass's experiences are told in three separate autobiographies, including *My Bondage and My Freedom* (1855), and *Life and Times of Frederick Douglass* (1881). A superb biography is *Frederick Douglass* (1990) by William S. McFeely.

The definitive work on free blacks in the South is Ira Berlin, *Slaves Without Masters: The Free Negro in the Antebellum South* (1976). Slave resistance and revolt are described in Vincent Harding, *There Is a River: The Black Struggle for Freedom in America* (1981), but a superb way to experience both slavery and the struggle for freedom is by reading an old classic, Harriet Beecher Stowe's *Uncle Tom's Cabin* (1852).

Time Line

1787	Constitution adopted with pro-slavery provisions		**1831**	Nat Turner's slave revolt in Virginia
1793	Eli Whitney invents cotton gin		**1845**	*Narrative of the Life of Frederick Douglass* published
1800	Gabriel Prosser conspiracy in Virginia		**1850s**	Cotton boom
1808	External slave trade prohibited by Congress		**1851**	Indiana state constitution excludes free blacks
1820	South becomes world's largest cotton producer		**1852**	Harriet Beecher Stowe publishes best-selling *Uncle Tom's Cabin*
1822	Denmark Vesey's conspiracy in Charleston		**1860**	Cotton production and prices peak
1830s	Southern justification of slavery changes from a necessary evil to a positive good			

chapter 12

Shaping America in the Antebellum Age

On November 19, 1836, 30-year-old Marius Robinson and Emily Rakestraw were married near Cincinnati, Ohio. Two months after their wedding, he went on the road to speak against slavery and to organize abolitionist societies throughout Ohio. Emily stayed in Cincinnati to teach in a school for free blacks. During their ten-month separation, they exchanged affectionate letters that reflected their love and work. Marius, who had experienced a series of conversions inspired by the revivalist Charles G. Finney and his abolitionist disciple Theodore Dwight Weld, described the reason for their separation: "God and humanity bleeding and suffering demand our services apart." Thus motivated by a strong religious commitment to serve others, these two young reformers dedicated themselves to several social causes: the abolition of slavery, equal rights and education for free blacks, temperance, and women's rights.

Their commitments cost more than separation. Emily's parents disapproved of Marius and of their reformist activities. Teaching at the school in Cincinnati was demanding, and the white citizens of the city resented the school and the young abolitionists in their midst. But Emily persisted in the work of "our school" while worrying about the health and safety of her husband on the road.

She had good reason for concern, for Marius's letters were full of reports of mob attacks, disrupted meetings, stonings, and narrow escapes. In June, he was dragged from the home of his Quaker host and beaten, tarred, and feathered. Never quite recovering his health, Marius spent half a year in bed, weak and dispirited. For nearly ten years after that, the Robinsons lived quietly on an Ohio farm, only slightly involved in the abolitionist movement. Despite the joyous birth of two daughters, they felt lonely, restless, and guilt-ridden, "tired of days blank of benevolent effort and almost of benevolent desires."

The work of Emily and Marius Robinson represents one response by the American people to the rapid social and economic changes of the antebellum era described in Chapters 10 and 11. In September 1835, a year before the Robinsons' marriage, the

Niles Register commented on some 500 recent incidents of mob violence and social upheaval. "*Society seems everywhere unhinged*, and the demon of 'blood and slaughter' has been let loose upon us. . . . [The] character of our countrymen seems suddenly changed." How did Americans adapt to these changes and maintain some sense of control over their lives?

One way was to embrace the changes fully. Thus some Americans became entrepreneurs in new industries; invested in banks, canals, and railroads; bought more land and slaves; and invented new machines. Others went west or to the new textile mills, enrolled in common schools, joined trade unions, specialized their labor both in the workplace and the home, and celebrated the practical benefits that resulted from modernization. Marius Robinson eventually went into life insurance, though he and Emily never fully abandoned their reformist efforts and idealism.

But many Americans were uncomfortable with the character of the new era. Some worried about the unrestrained power and selfish materialism symbolized by the slavemaster's control over his slaves. Others feared that institutions like the U.S. Bank represented a "monied aristocracy" capable of undermining the country's honest producers. Seeking positions of leadership and authority, these critics of the new order tried to shape a nation that retained the benefits of economic change without sacrificing humane principles of liberty, equality of opportunity, and community virtue. This chapter examines four ways in which the American people responded to change by attempting to influence their country's development: party politics, religious revivalism, utopian communitarianism, and social reform.

THE POLITICAL RESPONSE TO CHANGE

At the heart of American politics was the concern for the continued health of the republican experiment. As American society changed, so too did the understanding of political measures necessary to maintain that health. The economic dislocations after 1819 and in the late 1830s and the spirited presidential campaigns of Andrew Jackson helped to create widespread interest in politics in the era between 1820 and 1840.

Changing Political Culture

The presidency of Andrew Jackson was a crucial factor in bringing politics to the center of many Americans' lives. Styling himself as the people's candidate in 1828, Andrew Jackson derided the Adams administration as corrupt and aristocratic and promised a more democratic political system with the interests of the people at its center. Then as today, many Americans believed the campaign rhetoric. Four times more men turned out to vote in the election of 1828 than had gone to the polls four years earlier. They gave Jackson a resounding 56 percent of their ballots. No other president in the century would equal that percentage of popular support.

Despite campaign rhetoric, Jackson was not personally very democratic, nor did the era he symbolized involve any significant redistribution of wealth. Jackson himself owned slaves, defended slavery, and condoned mob attacks on abolitionists like Marius Robinson in the mid-1830s. And belying promises of widening opportunity, the rich got richer during the Jacksonian era, and most farming and urban laboring families did not prosper.

But the nation's political life had changed in important ways. The old system of politics based on elite coalitions and the deference of voters to their "betters" largely disappeared. In its place emerged a competitive party system, begun early in the republic but now oriented toward widespread voter participation in state and local politics. Political parties sponsored conventions, rallies, and parades. In the North, even women turned out for political rallies and speeches and rode on floats at party parades. Party-subsidized newspapers regularly indulged in scurrilous attacks on political candidates.

As depicted in this Robert Cruikshank lithograph, All Creation Going to the White House, *the first inauguration of Andrew Jackson in 1829 was the scene of wild festivities, a harbinger of the excesses in American life and politics in the ensuing years.*

Jackson's Path to the White House

Andrew Jackson's personality suited the new era. Orphaned at 14, young Jackson was rowdy, indecisive, and often in trouble. As a law student he was described as a "most roaring, rollicking, game-cocking, horse-racing, card-playing, mischievous fellow." He passed the bar and set out at the age of 21 to seek his fortune in the West. Settling in the frontier town of Nashville, the tall, red-headed young man built up a successful law practice in Tennessee and went on to become public prosecutor (called attorney general). Eventually, he became a substantial landowner and a prominent citizen of Nashville.

Jackson's national reputation stemmed mainly from his military exploits against American Indians and from his victory over the British at New Orleans in 1815. Careful political maneuvering in Tennessee in the early 1820s brought him election as U.S. senator and nomination for the presidency in 1824.

In the 1824 election, Jackson won both the popular and electoral votes but lost in the House of Representatives to John Quincy Adams.

When Henry Clay threw his support to Adams and was named secretary of state, Jackson condemned this deal as a "corrupt bargain." Jackson's loss convinced him of the importance of having an effective political organization. He organized his campaign by setting up loyal committees and newspapers in many states and by encouraging efforts to undermine Adams and Clay.

The loose coalition promoting Jackson's candidacy, which began to call itself the Democratic Party, was a mixed lot, drawing in politicians of diverse views from all sections of the country. Jackson played down his position on controversial issues, but he made clear his intentions of reforming government by throwing out of office anyone who was incompetent or who failed to represent the will of the people. Democratic newspapers picked up this theme and presented Jackson as a politician who would cleanse government of corruption and privileged interests.

The campaign between Jackson and Adams

in 1828 degenerated into a nasty but entertaining contest. Both sides engaged in slanderous personal attacks. Supporters of Adams and Clay, who called themselves National Republicans, claimed that Jackson was "an adulterer, a gambler, a cockfighter, a brawler, a drunkard, and a murderer." The Jacksonians in turn described Adams as a "stingy, undemocratic" aristocrat determined to destroy the people's liberties. Worse yet, Adams was an intellectual, "a man who can write." Jackson, by contrast, was the hero of the Battle of New Orleans, "a man who can fight." The efforts of Jackson and his party paid off as he won an astonishing 647,286 ballots, about 56 percent of the total.

Jackson's inauguration on a mild March 4 horrified many Americans. Washington was packed for the ceremonies. When Jackson appeared on the steps of the Capitol to take the oath of office, wild and unrestrained cheering broke out. After making a short address and taking the oath, Jackson was all but mobbed as he tried to make his way to his horse.

The White House reception soon got completely out of hand. A throng of people poured into the White House with muddy boots to overturn furniture in a rush for food and punch. The inauguration, according to Justice Joseph Story, illustrated "the reign of King Mob." Another observer called it "a proud day for the people." These contrasting views on the events of the inauguration captured the essence of the Jackson era. For some they symbolized the excesses of democracy; for others they represented democratic fulfillment.

Old Hickory's Vigorous Presidency

President Jackson's decisions, often controversial, helped to sharpen what it meant to be a Democrat and what it meant to be democracy's opponent. A few key convictions—the principle of majority rule, the limited power of the national government, the obligation of the national government to defend the interests of the nation's average people against the machinations of the "monied aristocracy"—guided Jackson's political behavior as president. Because he saw himself as the people's most authentic representative (only the president was elected by all the people), Jackson intended to be an effective, vigorous executive. More than any previous president, Jackson used presidential power in the name of the people and justified his actions by popular appeals to the electorate.

Jackson asserted his power most dramatically through use of the veto. The six preceding presidents had used the veto only nine times, most often against measures that they had believed unconstitutional. Jackson vetoed 12 bills during his eight years in office.

One of the abuses Jackson had promised to correct was what he described as an undemocratic and corrupt system of government officeholding. Too often "unfaithful or incompetent" men held onto their offices for years, making a mockery of the idea of representation. In the first year and a half of his presidency, Jackson removed 919 officeholders of a total of 10,093, fewer than one in ten. Most of these were for good reason—corruption or incompetence. The new Democratic appointees were not much better than their predecessors.

Jackson's similarly controversial Indian policy of forcible removal and relocation westward defined white American practice for the rest of the century. In the opening decades of the nineteenth century, the vast landholdings of the five "civilized nations" of the Southeast (the Cherokee, Choctaw, Chickasaw, Seminole, and Creek) had been seriously eroded by the pressures of land-hungry whites supported by successful military campaigns led by professional Indian fighters such as General Jackson. Land cessions to the government and private sales accounted for huge losses of Indian lands. In his first annual message to Congress in 1829, Jackson urged removal of the southeastern tribes. He argued that because the Indians were "surrounded by the whites with their arts of civilization," it was inevitable that the "resources of the savage" would be destroyed, dooming the Indians to "weakness and decay." Removal was justified, Jackson claimed, by both "humanity and national honor." He also endorsed the paramount right of state laws over the claims of either Indians or the federal government.

With the president's position clear, the crisis soon came to a head in Georgia. In 1829, the Georgia legislature declared the Cherokee tribal council illegal and its laws null and void in Cherokee territories and announced that the state had jurisdiction over both the tribe and its lands. Without legal recourse on the state level, the Cherokee carried their protests to the Supreme Court. In 1832, Chief Justice Marshall supported their position in *Worcester* v. *Georgia,* holding that the Georgia law was "repugnant to the Constitution" and did not apply to the Cherokee nation.

With Jackson's blessing, however, Georgians defied the Court ruling. By 1835, harassment, intimidation, and bribery had persuaded a minority of chiefs to sign a removal treaty. But most Cherokee refused to leave their lands. Therefore, in 1837 and 1838, the United States Army searched and seized the terrified Indians and gathered them in stockades prior to herding them west to the "Indian Territory" in Oklahoma. An eyewitness described how the Cherokee trek began:

> Families at dinner were startled by the sudden gleam of bayonets in the doorway and rose to be driven with blows and oaths along the weary miles of trail that led to the stockade. Men were seized in their fields, or going along the road, women were taken from their [spinning] wheels and children from their play. In many cases, on turning for one last look as they crossed the ridge they saw their homes in flames, fired by the lawless rabble that followed on the heels of the soldiers to loot and pillage.

The removal, the $6 million cost of which was deducted from the $9 million awarded the tribe for its eastern lands, brought death to perhaps a quarter of the 15,000 who set out. The Cherokee remember this event as the "Trail of Tears." Other southern and some northwestern tribes between 1821 and 1840 shared a similar fate. Although both Jackson and the Removal Act of 1830 had promised to protect and forever guarantee the Indian lands in the west, within a generation those promises, like others before and since, would be broken.

Indian removal left the eastern United States open for the enormous economic expansion described in Chapters 10 and 11. On the question of internal improvements to support that expansion, Jackson also imposed his enormous will.

When proposals for federal support for internal improvements seemed to rob local and state authorities of their proper function, Jackson, a firm believer in states' rights, opposed them. But projects of national significance, like the building of lighthouses or river improvements, were different matters. In fact, Jackson supported an annual average of $1.3 million in internal improvements while he was in office.

In a period of rapid economic change, tariffs were a matter of heated debate. New England and the Middle Atlantic states, the center of manufacturing operations, favored protective tariffs. But the South had long opposed such tariffs because they made it more expensive for southerners to buy manufactured goods from the North or abroad. Feelings against the high protective "Tariff of Abominations" were particularly strong in South Carolina, which was suffering from an economic depression.

Vice President John C. Calhoun, a brilliant political thinker from South Carolina, who aimed to defend southern agrarian interests against the more industrialized North, argued that minority rights could be protected by seeing the nation as "a confederacy of equal and sovereign states." In 1828, the same year as the hateful tariff, Calhoun published an anonymous essay, *Exposition and Protest,* which presented the doctrine of nullification as a means by which the southern states could protect themselves from harmful national action. According to this doctrine, when federal laws were deemed to overstep the limits of constitutional authority, a state had the right to declare that legislation null and void within its borders and refuse to enforce it.

In 1830, at a Jefferson birthday dinner, President Jackson declared himself on the issue. Despite his support of states' rights, Jackson did not believe that any state had the right to reject the will of the majority or to destroy the Union. He rose for a toast, held high his glass, and said, "Our Union—it must be preserved." Not to be outdone, Calhoun followed with his toast: "The Union—next to our liberty most dear." The split between them widened, and in 1833 Calhoun resigned as vice president. Final rupture came in a collision over the tariff and nullification.

In 1832, following Jackson's recommendation of a "middle course" for tariff revisions, Congress modified the tariff of 1828 by retaining high duties on goods such as wool, woolens, iron, and hemp and lowering other rates to an earlier level. Many southerners felt injured. In a special convention later that year in South Carolina, the delegates adopted an Ordinance of Nullification, declaring that the offending tariffs of 1828 and 1832 were null and void in that state. None of the duties would be collected. Furthermore, South Carolina threatened secession if the federal government should try to force the state to comply.

South Carolina's actions represented a direct attack on the concepts of federal union and majority rule. Jackson responded with a proclamation which stated emphatically that "the laws of the United States must be executed. . . . The Union will be preserved and treason and rebellion promptly put down."

Jackson's proclamation stimulated an outburst of patriotism and popular support all over the country. No other southern states supported nullification, and several state legislatures denounced it. South Carolina stood alone. When Jackson asked Congress for legislation to enforce tariff duties (the Force Bill of 1833), the crisis neared resolution. Tariff revisions, engineered by Henry Clay and supported by Calhoun, called for reductions over a ten-year period. South Carolina quickly repealed its nullification of the tariff laws but saved face by nullifying the Force Bill at the same time, an act that Jackson ignored. The crisis was over, but left unresolved were the constitutional issues it raised.

Jackson's Bank War and "Van Ruin's" Depression

As the people's advocate, Jackson could not ignore the Second Bank of the United States, which had been chartered for 20 years in 1816. Jackson believed that the bank threatened the people's liberties and called it a "monster." But the bank was not as irresponsible as Jacksonians imagined.

Guided since 1823 by the aristocratic Nicholas Biddle, the Philadelphia bank and its 29 branches performed many useful financial services and generally played a responsible economic role in an expansionary period. As the nation's largest commercial bank, the U.S. Bank was able to shift funds to different parts of the country as necessary and to influence state banking activity. It restrained state banks from making unwise loans by insisting that they back their notes with specie (gold or silver coin) and by calling in its own loans to these institutions. The bank accepted federal deposits, made commercial loans, and bought and sold government bonds. Businessmen, state bankers needing credit, and nationalist politicians such as Daniel Webster and Henry Clay, who were on the bank's payroll, all favored the bank.

Other Americans, however, led by the president, distrusted the bank. Jackson had long opposed the bank both for personal reasons (a near financial disaster in his own past) and because he and his advisers believed it was the chief example of a special privilege monopoly that hurt the common man—farmers, craftsmen, and debtors.

Aware of Jackson's persisting hostility, Clay and Webster persuaded Biddle to ask Congress to recharter the bank in 1832, four years ahead of schedule. They reasoned that in an election year, Jackson would not risk a veto. The bill to recharter the bank swept through Congress and landed on the president's desk one hot, muggy day in July. "The bank . . . is trying to kill me," he told his running mate, Martin Van Buren, *"but I will kill it."*

Jackson determined not only to veto the bill but also to carry his case to the public. His veto message condemned the bank as undemocratic, un-American, and unconstitutional. He denounced the bank as a dangerous monopoly that helped the rich and harmed "the humble members of society."

The furor over the bank helped to clarify party differences. In the election of 1832, the National Republicans, now becoming known as Whigs to show their opposition to "King Andrew," nominated Henry Clay. Democratic campaign rhetoric pitted Jackson, the people, and democracy against Clay, the bank, and aristocracy. A popular movement known as Anti-Masonry had formed in the 1820s and had become the first third party in American political life and the first to hold a nominating convention. The Anti-Masons' efforts revealed real issues more clearly than the two major parties. The anti-Masonic movement, which began in upstate New York, expressed popular resentments against the elitist Masonic order (Jackson was a member) and other secret societies. At a deeper level, anti-Masonry reflected tensions over commercialization as new groups vied with old families for political power.

When the ballots were counted, Jackson had once again won handsomely, garnering 124,000 more popular votes than the combined total for Clay and the Anti-Mason candidate, William Wirt, who said of Jackson, "He may be President for life if he chooses."

Although the election results suggest that the bank issue actually harmed Jackson, he interpreted the election as a victory for his bank policy and made plans to finish his war with Biddle. The bank still had four years before the charter expired, so Jackson and his advisers decided to weaken the bank by transferring $10 million in government funds to state banks. Although two secretaries of the treasury balked at the removal request as financially unsound, Jackson persisted until he found one, Roger Taney, willing to remove the funds. And when Chief Justice John Marshall, a Whig, died in 1835, Jackson replaced him with Taney.

Jackson's war with Biddle and the bank had serious economic consequences. A wave of speculation in western lands and ambitious new state internal improvement schemes in the mid-1830s led to rising land prices and a flood of paper money. Determined to curtail irresponsible economic activity, in July 1836 Jackson issued the Specie Circular, announcing that the government would accept only gold and silver in payment for public lands. Panicky investors rushed to change paper notes into specie, while banks started to call in loans. The result was the Panic of 1837. Although Jackson was blamed for this rapid monetary expansion followed by sudden deflation in the mid-1830s, international trade problems with Britain and China probably contributed more to the panic and to the ensuing seven years of depression than Jackson's erratic policies.

Whatever the primary cause, Jackson stuck his successor, Martin Van Buren, who was elected in 1836 over a trio of Whig opponents, with an economic crisis. Van Buren had barely taken the oath of office in 1837 when banks and businesses began to collapse. His term as president was marked by a depression so severe that it brought him the unfortunate nickname "Martin Van Ruin." As New York banks suspended credit and began calling in loans, an estimated $6 million was lost on defaulted debts.

By the fall of 1837, one-third of America's

workers were unemployed, and thousands of others found only sporadic, part-time work. Wages fell, while the price of necessities like flour, pork, and coal nearly doubled.

The pride of workers was damped as soup kitchens and bread lines grew faster than jobs. Moreover, the depression destroyed the trade union movement begun a decade earlier, leaving laboring families isolated and defenseless. In 1842, when Philadelphia textile employers lowered wages below subsistence levels, angry hand-loom weavers broke machinery, destroyed cloth, and wrecked the homes of Irish strike-breakers. Job competition, poverty, and ethnic animosities led to violent clashes in other eastern cities as well, as we saw in Chapter 10.

"How is it," a Philadelphia mechanic asked in 1837, that in a country as rich as the United States so many people were "pinched for the common necessaries of life?" President Van Buren's responses to the social misery behind this question were sympathetic but limited and inadequate. Political participation, as well as church membership, reached new heights during the depression, as Americans sought to alleviate their "gloom and despair."

The Second American Party System

By the mid-1830s, a new two-party system and a lively participatory national political culture had emerged in the United States. Although both parties included wealthy and influential, even despotic leaders, the Democrats had the better claim that they were the party of the common man with strength in all sections of the country.

Whigs represented greater wealth than Democrats and were strongest in New England and in areas settled by New Englanders across the Upper Midwest. Whigs generally favored a national bank, federally supported internal improvements, and tariff protection for industry. Artisans and laborers belonged equally to each party, making it difficult to draw clear regional or class distinctions between Whigs and Democrats. This blurring of party lines among social groups suggests that other factors, such as ethnic, religious, and cultural background, also influenced party choice.

In the Jeffersonian tradition, the Democrats espoused liberty and local rule. They wanted freedom from legislators of morality, from special privilege, and from too much government. Those who wanted to maintain religious or ethnic traditions found a home in the Democratic party. The Scots-Irish, German, French, and Irish Catholic immigrants, as well as free thinkers and labor organizers, tended to be Jacksonians. They were less moralistic than Whigs, especially on matters like temperance and slavery. Democrats sought to keep politics separate from moral issues.

By contrast, for many Whigs the line between reform and politics was hazy. Old-stock New England Yankee Congregationalists and Presbyterians were usually Whigs. So were Quakers and evangelical Protestants, who believed that positive government action could change moral behavior and eradicate sin. Whigs supported a wide variety of reforms, such as temperance, antislavery, public education, and strict observance of the Sabbath, as well as government action to promote economic development.

The election of 1840 illustrated the new style of political culture. Passing over Henry Clay, the Whigs nominated William Henry Harrison of Indiana, the aging hero of the Battle of Tippecanoe (Kithtippecanoe), fought nearly 30 years earlier. A Virginian, John Tyler, was nominated for vice president to underline the regional diversity of the party. The Democrats had no choice but to renominate Van Buren, who conducted a quiet campaign. The Whig campaign, however, featured every form of popularized appeals for votes—barbecues, torchlight parades, songs, and cartoons. Harrison (who lived in a mansion) was depicted in front of a rural log cabin with a barrel of hard cider, while the

Whigs labeled Van Buren an aristocratic dandy. Harrison reminded voters of General Jackson, and they swept him into office, 234 electoral votes to Van Buren's 60. In one of the largest turnouts in American history, over 80 percent of eligible voters marched to the polls. Commenting on the defeat, a Democratic party journal acknowledged that the Whigs had out-Jacksoned the Jacksonians: "We taught them how to conquer us."

Concern over the new politics outlasted Harrison, who died only a month after taking office. For many Americans, usually Whigs and often women, it was precisely the excesses of Jacksonian politics, most notably intemperance and the inherent violence of slavery, that led them to seek other ways than politics of imposing order and morality on American society. To gain a measure of control over their lives and reshape their changing world, the American people turned also to religion, social reform, and utopianism.

RELIGIOUS REVIVAL AND REFORM PHILOSOPHY

When the Frenchman Alexis de Tocqueville visited the United States in 1831 and 1832, he observed that he could find "no country in the whole world in which the Christian religion retains a greater influence over the souls of men than in America." What de Tocqueville was describing was a new and powerful religious enthusiasm among the American people.

Finney and the Second Great Awakening

From the late 1790s until the late 1830s, a wave of religious revivals that matched the intensity of the Great Awakening in the 1730s and 1740s swept through the United States. The camp meeting revivals of the frontier at the turn of the century and the New England revivals sparked by Lyman Beecher took on a new emphasis and location after 1830. Led by the spellbinding Charles G. Finney, revivalism shifted to upstate New York and the Old Northwest. Both areas had been experiencing profound economic and social changes, as the example of Rochester, New York, suggests.

By the 1830s, Rochester, like Lowell and Cincinnati, was a rapidly growing American city. Its location on the recently completed Erie Canal changed Rochester from a sleepy little village of 300 in 1815 to a bustling commercial and milling city of nearly 20,000 inhabitants by 1830. Saloons and unions sprang up in workingmen's neighborhoods, and workers became more transient, following the canal and other opportunities westward.

Prominent Rochester citizens, sensing a widening gulf between laborers and their masters, invited Charles Finney to come to town in 1830 to deliver some sermons. What followed was one of the most successful revivals of the Second Great Awakening. For six months Rochester went through a citywide prayer meeting in which one conversion led to another. The Rochester revival was part of the wave of religious enthusiasm in America that contributed to the tremendous growth of the Methodists, the Baptists, and other evangelical sects in the first half of the nineteenth century.

Most revivalists, especially in the South, sought individual salvation. The Finney revivals, however, were unique in that they nourished collective reform. Finney taught that humans were not passive objects of God's predestined plan but moral free agents who could choose good over evil, convince others to do the same, and thereby eradicate sin from the world. Conversion and salvation were not the end of religious experience but the beginning. Finney's idea of the "utility of benevolence" meant not only individual reformation but also the commitment to reform society. The Bible commanded humans, "Be ye therefore perfect even as your Father in heaven is perfect," and mid-nineteenth-century reformers took the challenge seriously.

Reform and Politics

The reform impulse ultimately involved antebellum activists in the broader politics of the Jacksonian era. Reformers and party politicians, especially Whigs, both faced timeless dilemmas about how best to effect change. Does one, for example, try to change attitudes first and then behavior, or the reverse? Which is more effective, to appeal to people's minds and hearts in order to change bad institutions or to change institutions first, assuming that altered behavior will change hearts and attitudes? Reformers, moreover, have to decide whether to attempt to improve on a partly defective system or tear down the entire system in order to build a utopian new one; whether to use or recommend force; and whether to enter into coalitions with less principled potential allies.

Advocates of change also experience enormous pressures, recriminations, and persecution, as Marius and Emily Robinson learned. Nevertheless, their duty to themselves, their society, and God sustains their commitment.

The Transcendentalists

No one knew this better than Ralph Waldo Emerson, a Concord, Massachusetts, essayist who was the era's foremost intellectual figure. The small but influential group of New England intellectuals who lived near Emerson were called Transcendentalists because of their belief that truth was found beyond experience in intuition. Casting off the European intellectual tradition, Emerson urged Americans to look inward and to nature for self-knowledge, self-reliance, and the spark of divinity burning within all persons. "To acquaint a man with himself," he wrote, would inspire a "reverence" for self and others, which would then lead outward to social reform.

"What is man born for," Emerson wrote, "but to be a Reformer?"

The Transcendentalists questioned not only slavery, an obvious evil, but also the obsessive competitive pace of economic life, the overriding concern for materialism, and the restrictive conformity of social life.

Although not considered Transcendentalists, Nathaniel Hawthorne and Herman Melville, two giants of midcentury American literature, also reflected these concerns in their fiction. In his greatest novel, *The Scarlet Letter* (1850), Hawthorne sympathetically told the story of a courageous Puritan woman's adultery and her eventual loving triumph over the narrowness of both cold intellect and intolerant social conformity.

Herman Melville's epic novel *Moby Dick* (1851), at one level a rousing story of pursuit of the great white whale, was actually an immense allegory of good and evil, bravery and weakness, innocence and experience. Like Emerson, Hawthorne and Melville mirrored the tensions of the age as they explored issues of freedom and control.

When Emerson wrote, "Whoso would be a man, must be a nonconformist," he described his friend Henry David Thoreau. On July 4, 1845, Thoreau went to live in a small hut by Walden Pond, near Concord, to confront "the essential facts of life." When Thoreau left Walden two years later, he protested against slavery and the Mexican War by refusing to pay his taxes. He went to jail briefly and wrote an essay, "On Civil Disobedience" (1849), and a book, *Walden* (1854), which are still considered classic statements of what one person can do to protest unjust laws and wars and live a life of principle.

UTOPIAN COMMUNITARIANISM

Thoreau tried to lead an ideal solitary life. Other reformers sought to create perfect communities. Emerson noted in 1840 that he hardly met a thinking, reading man who did not have "a draft of a new community in his waistcoat pocket."

Oneida and the Shakers

One such man was John Humphrey Noyes of Putney, Vermont, an instant, if unorthodox, convert of Charles Finney. Noyes believed that the act of final conversion led to absolute perfection and complete release from sin. Among those who were perfect, he argued, all men and women belonged equally to one another. For Noyes, complete sharing in family relationships was a step toward perfect cooperation and shared wealth in socioeconomic relationships. Others called his heretical doctrines "free love" and socialism. Noyes married a loyal follower, and when she delivered four stillborn children within six years, he revised even further his unconventional ideas about sex.

In 1848, Noyes and 51 devoted followers founded a "perfectionist" community at Oneida, New York. Sexual life at the commune was subject to many regulations, including sexual restraint and male continence except under carefully prescribed conditions. In a system of planned reproduction, only certain spiritually advanced males (usually Noyes) were allowed to father children. Other controversial practices included communal child rearing, sexual equality in work, the removal of the competitive spirit from both work and play, and an elaborate program of "mutual criticism" at community meetings presided over by "Father" Noyes.

The Oneida community grew and prospered through manufacturing. Oneida specialized at first in the fabrication of steel animal traps and later diversified into making silverware. Eventually abandoning religion to become a joint-stock company in which individual members held shares, Oneida thrived for many years and continues today as a silverware company.

Noyes greatly admired another group of communitarians, the Shakers, who also believed in perfectionism, the surrender of all worldly property to the community, and the devotion of one's labor and love to bringing about the millennial kingdom of heaven. But unlike the Oneidans, Shakers viewed sexuality as a sin and believed in absolute chastity, trusting in conversions to perpetuate their sect. They believed that God had a dual personality, male and female, and that their founder, Mother Ann Lee, was the female counterpart to the masculine Christ. The Shaker worship service featured frenetic dancing intended to release (or "shake") sin out through the fingertips. Shaker communities, some of which still survive, were characterized by communal ownership of property, the equality of women and men, simplicity, and beautifully crafted furniture.

Other Utopias

In an era of disruptive economic and social change, over 100 utopian communities like Oneida and the Shaker colonies were founded. Some were religiously motivated; others were secular. Most were small and lasted only a few months or years. All eventually failed.

Pietist German-speaking immigrants founded the earliest utopian communities in America to preserve their language, spirituality, and ascetic life style. The most notable of these were the Ephrata colonists in Pennsylvania, the Harmonists in Indiana, the Zoar community in Ohio, and the Amana Society in Iowa. In 1840, Adin Ballou founded Hopedale in Massachusetts as "a miniature Christian republic" based on the ethical teachings of Jesus. Hopedale's newspaper, *The Practical Christian*, advocated temperance, pacifism, women's rights, and other reforms.

The secular communities responded more directly to the social misery and wretched working conditions accompanying the industrial revolution. They believed that altered environments rather than new morals would eliminate or reduce poverty, ignorance, intemperance, and other ugly by-products of industrialism.

In 1824, Robert Owen, a Scottish industrialist, founded New Harmony in Indiana. But

In this sacred Shaker dance, sin is being shaken out of the body through the fingertips. Note the separation of women and men.

problems rather than harmony prevailed. Overcrowding, lazy and uncooperative members, Owen's frequent absences, splintered goals, and financial mismanagement ruined New Harmony within three years.

Brook Farm, founded by two Concord friends of Emerson, Bronson Alcott and George Ripley, was an experiment in integrating "intellectual and manual labor." Residents would hoe in the fields and shovel manure for a few hours each day and then study literature and recite poetry. The colony lasted less than three years.

Whether secular or religious, the utopian communities all failed for similar reasons. Americans seemed ill-suited to communal living and work responsibilities and were unwilling to share either their property or their spouses with others. Nor was celibacy greeted with much enthusiasm. Other recurring problems included unstable leadership, financial bickering, the hostility of local citizens, the indiscriminate admission of members, and a waning of enthusiasm after initial settlement. Emerson pinned the failure of the communities on their inability to confront the individualistic impulses of human nature. As he said of Brook Farm, "It met every test but life itself." That could serve as an epitaph for all the utopian communities.

Millerites and Mormons

If utopian communities failed to bring about the millennium, an alternative hope was to leap directly past the thousand years of peace and harmony to the Second Coming of Christ. William Miller, a shy farmer from upstate New York, became so absorbed with the idea of the imminent coming of Christ that he figured out mathematically the exact time of the event: 1843, probably in March. A religious sect, the Millerites, gathered around him to prepare for Christ's return and the Day of Judgment. When 1843 passed without the expected end, Miller and his followers recalculated and set a series of alternative dates. Each new disappointment diminished Miller's followers, and he died in 1848 a discredited man.

Other groups that emerged from the same religiously active area of upstate New York were more successful. As Palmyra, New York, was being swept by Finney revivalism, young Joseph Smith, a recent convert, claimed to be visited by the angel Moroni. According to Smith, Moroni led him to golden tablets buried in the ground near his home. On these plates were inscribed more than 500 pages of *The Book of Mormon,* which described the one true church and a "lost tribe of Israel" missing for centuries. The book also predicted the appearance of an American prophet who would establish a new and pure kingdom of Christ in America. Smith published his book in 1830 and soon founded the Church of Jesus Christ of Latter-day Saints.

Smith and a steadily growing band of converts migrated successively to Ohio and Missouri and then back to Illinois. Despite ridicule, persecution, and violence, the Mormons prospered and increased. By the mid-1840s, Nauvoo, Illinois, with a thriving population of nearly 15,000, was the showplace of Mormonism. Smith petitioned Congress for separate territorial status and ran for the presidency in 1844. This was too much for the citizens of nearby towns. Violence escalated and culminated in Smith's trial for treason and his murder by a mob. Under the brilliant leadership of Smith's successor, Brigham Young, the Mormons headed westward in 1846 in their continuing search for the "land of promise."

REFORMING SOCIETY

Most Americans sought to bring about "the promised land" by focusing in a practical way on a specific social evil rather than by embracing whole new religions or joining utopian colonies.

"We are all a little wild here," Emerson wrote in 1840, "with numberless projects of social reform." The reformers, including thousands of women, created and joined all kinds of societies for social betterment. They addressed such issues as alcohol consumption; diet and health; sexuality; institutional treatment of the mentally ill, the disabled, paupers, and criminals; education; the rights of labor; slavery; and women's rights.

Temperance

On New Year's Eve in 1831, a Finney disciple, Theodore Dwight Weld, delivered a four-hour temperance lecture in Rochester. In graphic detail he described the awful fate of those who refused to stop drinking and urged his audience not only to cease their tippling but to stop others as well. Several were converted to abstinence on the spot. The next day, Elijah and Albert Smith, the largest providers of whiskey in Rochester, rolled their barrels out onto the sidewalk and smashed them. Cheering Christians applauded as the whiskey ran out into Exchange Street.

Americans in the nineteenth century drank heavily. One man observed that "a house could not be raised, a field of wheat cut down, nor could there be a log rolling, a husking, a quilting, a wedding, or a funeral without the aid of alcohol." The corrosive effects of drinking were obvious: poverty, crime, illness, insanity, battered and broken families, and corrupt politics.

Religion, Reform, and Utopian Activity, 1830-1850

Early efforts at curbing alcohol consumption emphasized moderation. But the American Temperance Society, founded in 1826, was dedicated to total abstinence. Within a few years, thousands of local and state societies had formed, though some refused to prohibit drinking of hard cider and communion wine.

Temperance advocates copied successful revival techniques. Fiery lecturers expounded on the evil consequences of drink and distributed a deluge of graphic and sometimes gory temperance tracts.

By 1840, disagreements over goals and methods split the temperance movement into many separate organizations. The Washington Temperance Society, founded in a Baltimore tavern in 1840, was enormously popular with unemployed young workers and grew to an estimated 600,000 members in three years. The Washingtonians, arguing that alcoholism was a disease rather than moral failure, changed the shape of the temperance movement. They replaced revivalist techniques with those of the new party politics by organizing parades, picnics, melodramas, and festivals to encourage people to take the pledge.

Tactics in the 1840s also shifted away from moral suasion to political action. Temperance societies lobbied for local option laws, which allowed communities to prohibit the sale, manufacture, and consumption of alcohol. The Maine law in 1851 was the first in the nation. Fifteen other states followed with similar laws before the Civil War. Despite weak enforcement, the per capita consumption of alcohol declined dramatically in the 1850s. Interrupted by the Civil War, the movement did not reach its ultimate objective until passage of the Eighteenth Amendment to the Constitution in 1919.

The temperance crusade reveals the many practical motivations that attracted Americans to join reform societies. For some, as in Rochester, temperance provided an opportunity for the Protestant middle classes to exert some control over laborers, immigrants, and Catholics. For perfectionists, abstinence was a way of practicing self-control and reaching moral perfection. For many young men, especially after the onset of the depression of 1837, a temperance society provided entertainment, fellowship, and contacts to help their careers. In temperance societies as in political parties, Americans found jobs, purpose, support, spouses, and relief from the loneliness and uncertainty of a changing world.

For many women, the temperance effort was a respectable way to control the behavior of drunken men who beat wives and daughters. The movement also educated some women about their own political weakness. Women such as Susan B. Anthony, who worked as an organizer in the temperance movement, found a wall of prejudice against women's active participation. She also became aware that women could not provide effective financial support to a cause as long as their husbands controlled their earnings. (Several more decades elapsed before the founding in 1874 of the Women's Christian Temperance Union. See Chapter 19.)

Health and Sexuality

It was a short step from the physical and psychological ravages of drink to other potentially harmful effects on the body. Reformers were quick to attack excessive eating, use of stimulants of any kind, and, above all, the evils of too much sexual activity. Many endorsed a variety of special diets and exercise programs for maintaining good health. Some promoted panaceas for all ailments. One of these was hydropathy:

The temperance movement of the 1830s and 1840s used the tactics of religious revivalists to scare drinkers into taking the "teetotal" pledge. Who could resist this poignant 1846 portrayal of The Drunkard's Progress?

Clients sojourned at one of 70 special resorts for bathing and water purges of the body.

Another movement concerned sexual purity. In 1834, Sylvester Graham, a promoter of proper diet and hygiene, delivered a series of lectures on chastity, later published as a manual of advice. To those "troubled" by sexual desire, the inventor of the Graham cracker recommended taking "more active exercise in the open air" and using "the cold bath under proper circumstances." Women were advised to remain pure and to "have intercourse only for procreation."

The authors of antebellum "health" manuals advocated abstinence from sexual activity as vehemently as they recommended abstinence from alcohol. Semen was to be saved for reproductive purposes and should not be used for pleasure in either masturbation or intercourse. Such use, maintained the manuals on sexual purity, would lead to enervation, disease, insanity, and death. Some argued further that the "expenditure" of sperm meant a loss of needed energy from the economy. One doctor argued that women ought not to be educated because blood needed for the womb would be diverted to the head, thus breeding "puny men."

Humanizing the Asylum

In their effort to restore order to American society, some reformers preferred to work not for private influence over individuals but toward public changes in institutions. They wanted to transform such social institutions as asylums, almshouses, prisons, schools, and even factories. In many ways, Horace Mann, who led the struggle for common schools in Massachusetts (see Chapter 10), was a typical antebellum reformer. He blended dedicated idealism with a canny, practical sense of how to institutionalize educational improvements in one state: teacher training schools, higher teachers' salaries, and compulsory attendance laws.

Other reformers were less successful in achieving their goals. This was especially true of the treatment of society's outcasts. In 1843, Dorothea Dix, a frail New Englander, horrified the Massachusetts legislature with her famous report that imprisoned insane persons in the state were subject to "the extremest state of degradation and misery." They were confined in "cages, closets, stalls, pens! Chained, naked, beaten with rods, and lashed into obedience!" Dix recommended special hospitals or asylums where the insane could be "humanly and properly controlled" by trained attendants.

Many perfectionist reformers like Dix believed that special asylums could reform society's outcasts. But all too often, results were disappointing. Prison reformers believed that a properly built and administered penitentiary could bring a hardened criminal "back to virtue." Some assumed that by putting "penitents" into isolated cells to study the Bible and reflect on their wrongdoing, they would eventually decide to become good citizens. In practice, many criminals simply went mad or committed suicide. The institutions built by well-intentioned reformers became dumping places for society's outcasts. By midcentury, American prisons and mental asylums had become the impersonal, understaffed, overcrowded institutions we know today.

Working-Class Reform

For working-class Americans, the social institution most in need of transformation was the factory. Workers, many of whom were involved in other issues such as temperance, peace, and abolitionism, took it upon themselves to improve their own lives. As labor leader Seth Luther told a meeting of New England mechanics and laborers, "We must take our business into our own hands. Let us awake." And awake they did, forming both trade unions and workingmen's parties as Andrew Jackson neared the presidency.

Between 1828 and 1832, dozens of workingmen's parties were formed, advocating such programs as free, tax-supported schools, free public lands in the West, equal rights for the poor, and the elimination of all monopolistic privilege. Trade union activity began in Philadelphia in 1827 as skilled workers organized journeymen carpenters, plasterers, printers, weavers, tailors, and other tradesmen. That same year, 15 unions combined into a citywide federation, a process followed in other cities. The National Trades Union, founded in 1834, was the first attempt at a national labor organization.

The trade unions called for shorter hours, wages that would keep pace with rising prices, and ways (such as the closed shop) of warding off the competitive threat of cheap labor. In addition, both workers and their middle-class interlocutors called for the abolition of imprisonment for debt and of compulsory militia duty, both of which often cost workers their jobs; free public education; improved living conditions in workers' neighborhoods; and the right to organize.

With union membership of near 300,000, workers struck some 168 times between 1834 and 1836, usually for higher wages. The Panic of 1837 and the ensuing depression dashed the hopes and efforts of American workers. But the organizational work of the 1830s promised that the labor movement would reemerge with greater strength later in the century.

ABOLITIONISM AND WOMEN'S RIGHTS

As American workers struggled in Lowell and other eastern cities for better wages and hours in 1834, Emily and Marius Robinson arrived in Cincinnati to fight for their causes. They had been attracted there, along with scores of other young idealists, by the newly founded Lane Seminary, a school to train abolitionist leaders. Lane soon became a center of reformist activity. When nervous local residents persuaded President Lyman Beecher to crack down on the students,

40 "Lane rebels," led by Theodore Weld, fled to Oberlin in northern Ohio. As the Robinsons remained in southern Ohio, the group in the north turned Oberlin College into the first institution in the United States open equally to women and men, blacks and whites. Thus the movements to abolish slavery and to grant equal rights to women and free blacks were joined. Whether seeking to eliminate coercion in the cotton fields or in the kitchen, reformers faced the dual challenge of pursuing distant and elusive goals while at the same time achieving practical changes in everyday life.

Tensions Within the Antislavery Movement

Although the antislavery movement had a smaller membership than temperance reform, it revealed more clearly the difficulties of trying to achieve significant social change in America. On January 1, 1831, eight months before Nat Turner's revolt, William Lloyd Garrison published the first issue of *The Liberator*, soon to become the leading antislavery journal in the United States. "I am in earnest," he wrote. "I will not equivocate—AND I WILL BE HEARD." After first organizing the New England Anti-Slavery Society with a group of blacks and whites in a church basement in Boston, in 1833 Garrison and 62 others established the American Anti-Slavery Society.

Until Garrison's publication, most people opposed to slavery, other than blacks, had advocated gradual emancipation by individual slave owners and colonization of the freed blacks on the west coast of Africa. Garrison opposed the moderation and gradualism of the colonizationists, declaring that compromise was unthinkable. There would be "no Union with slaveholders," he cried, condemning the Constitution that perpetuated slavery as *"a covenant with death, an agreement with Hell."* The American Anti-Slavery Society called for the immediate and total abolition of slavery. But the abolitionists did not always agree, splitting into factions over ideological differences between colonizationists, gradualists, and immediatists.

Abolitionists also differed over the tactics of ending slavery. Their primary method was moral suasion, by which they sought to convince slaveholders and their supporters that slavery was a sin. In an outpouring of sermons, petitions, resolutions, pamphlets, and speeches, abolitionists tried to overwhelm slaveholders with moral guilt to get them to free their slaves as an act of repentance. In 1839, Weld published *American Slavery As It Is,* which described in gory detail every conceivable form of inhumane treatment of the slaves.

Other abolitionists preferred more direct methods. Some brought antislavery petitions before Congress or formed third parties. Another tactic was to boycott goods made by slave labor. A fourth approach, although rare, was to call for slave rebellion, as did two northern blacks, David Walker in a pamphlet in 1829 and Henry Highland Garnet in a speech at a convention of black Americans in 1843.

Disagreement over tactics helped to splinter the abolitionist movement. Class differences and race further divided abolitionists. Northern workers, though fearful of the job competition implications of emancipation, nevertheless saw their "wage slavery" as similar to chattel slavery. Strains between northern labor leaders and middle-class abolitionists, who minimized the seriousness of workingmen's concerns, were similar to those between white and black antislavery forces. Whites like Wendell Phillips decried slavery as a moral blot on American society, while blacks like Douglass were more concerned with the effects of slavery and discrimination on black people. Moreover, white abolitionists tended to see slavery and freedom as absolute moral opposites: A person was either slave or free. Blacks, however, knew that there were degrees of freedom and that discriminatory restrictions on freedom existed for blacks in the North just as did relative degrees of servitude in the South.

Furthermore, black abolitionists themselves experienced prejudice, not just from ordinary northern citizens but also from their white abolitionist colleagues, many of whom refused to hire black workers. One free black described a white abolitionist as one who hated slavery, "especially that slavery which is 1000 to 1500 miles away," but who hated even more "a man who wears a black skin."

The celebrated conflict between Garrison and Douglass reflected these tensions. The famous runaway slave was one of the most effective orators in the movement. But after a while, rather than simply describing his life as a slave, Douglass began skillfully to analyze abolitionist policies. Garrison warned him that audiences would not believe he had ever been a slave, and other whites told him to stick to the facts and let them take care of the philosophy. Douglass gradually moved away from Garrison's views, endorsing political action and sometimes even slave rebellion.

Moving beyond Garrison, a few black nationalists, like the fiery Martin Delany, totally rejected white American society and advocated emigration and a new destiny in Africa. Most blacks, however, agreed with Douglass to work to end slavery and discrimination in the United States, which, for better or worse, was their home. These black leaders organized a National Negro Convention Movement, which began annual meetings in 1830. They met not only to condemn slavery but also to discuss concrete issues of discrimination facing free blacks in the North.

Flood Tide of Abolitionism

Black and white abolitionists, however, agreed more than they disagreed and usually worked together well. They supported each other's publications, stayed in each other's homes when they traveled, and cooperated on the underground railroad.

The two races worked together fighting discrimination as well as slavery. When David Ruggles was dragged from the "white car" of a New Bedford, Massachusetts, railway in 1841, Garrison, Douglass, and 40 other protesters organized what may have been the first successful integrated "sit-in" act of civil disobedience in American history. Blacks and whites also worked harmoniously in protesting segregated schools. In 1855, Massachusetts became the first state to outlaw segregated public education.

White and black abolitionists united in defending themselves against the attacks of people who regarded them as dangerous fanatics. Mob attacks like the one on Marius Robinson in Ohio in 1836 occurred frequently in the mid-1830s. Abolitionists were stoned, dragged through streets, ousted from their jobs and homes, and reviled by northern mobs, often led or encouraged by leading citizens. Theodore Weld, known as "the most mobbed man in the United States," could hardly finish a speech without disruption. In 1837, an antislavery editor in Illinois, Elijah Lovejoy, was murdered and his printing press destroyed.

Antiabolitionists were as fervid as the abolitionists themselves and equally determined to publicize their cause. "I warn the abolitionists, ignorant and infatuated barbarians as they are," growled one South Carolinian, "that if chance shall throw any of them into our hands, they may expect a felon's death." President Jackson denounced the abolitionists in his annual message in 1835 as "incendiaries" who deserved to have their "unconstitutional and wicked" activities broken up by mobs. The president went on to urge Congress to ban antislavery literature from the U.S. mails. A year later, southern Democratic congressmen, with the crucial support of Van Buren, succeeded in passing a "gag rule," which stopped the flood of abolitionists petitions in Congress until the rule was repealed in 1844.

By the 1840s, many northerners, including many workers otherwise unsympathetic to the goal of ending slavery, decried the mob violence, supported the right of free speech, and denounced the South and its northern defenders as undemocratic. The gag rule, interference with the mails, and the killing of Lovejoy seemed proof of the growing pernicious influence of slave power.

Women's Rights

Another important source of tension within the antislavery movement was disagreement over the participation of women. In an age when women were not supposed to speak in public, those who dared to do so encountered rude and humiliating treatment. The reception women experienced in the antislavery movement directly inspired some of them to launch a campaign for women's rights.

Abby Kelley, a young teacher in Massachusetts in 1836, circulated petitions for the local antislavery society. She came to reform from revivalism and in 1837 wrote, " 'Tis a great joy to see the world grow better. . . . Indeed I think endeavors to improve mankind is the only object worth living for." A year later, she braved the threats of an angry crowd in Philadelphia by delivering an abolitionist speech to a convention of antislavery women. Her speech was so eloquent that Weld told her that if she did not join the movement full time, "God will smite you." Before the convention was over, a mob, incensed by both abolitionists and women speaking in public, attacked with stones and torches and burned the hall to the ground.

After a soul-searching year, Kelley left teaching to devote all her efforts to antislavery and women's rights. When she married Stephen Foster, she retained her own name and went on lecture tours of the West while her husband stayed home to care for their daughter.

Angelina and Sarah Grimké, two demure but outspoken Quaker sisters from Philadelphia who had grown up in slaveholding South Carolina, went to New England in 1837 to lecture to disapproving audiences on behalf of abolitionism and the rights of women. After the tour, Angelina married Theodore Weld and stopped her public speaking to show that she could also be a good wife and mother.

Young couples like Grimké and Weld, the Robinsons, and Kelley and Foster, while pursuing reform, experimented with equal private relationships in an age that assigned distinctly unequal roles to husbands and wives.

Catharine Beecher argued that it was by accepting marriage and the home as woman's sphere and by mastering domestic duties there that women could best achieve moral power and autonomy. In another form of "domestic feminism," American wives exerted considerable control over their own bodies by convincing their husbands to practice abstinence, coitus interruptus, and other forms of birth control. Some women found an outlet for their role as moral guardians by attacking the sexual double standard. They worked to convert prostitutes to evangelical Protestantism and to close houses of prostitution.

Women reformers sought more legally protected equal rights with men. Campaigns to secure married women control of their property and custody of their children involved many women, who discovered striking similarities between their own oppression and that of slaves. American women "have good cause to be grateful to the slave," Kelley wrote, for in "striving to strike his iron off, we found most surely, that we were manacled *ourselves.*"

Activist antislavery women encountered hostility, especially from clergymen, who quoted the Bible to justify female inferiority and servility. Sarah Grimké struck back in 1837 with a series called *Letters on the Condition of Women and the Equality of the Sexes,* claiming that "men and women were CREATED EQUAL" and that "whatever is *right* for man to do, is *right* for woman."

Male abolitionists were divided about women's rights. At the World Anti-Slavery Convention in 1840, attended by many American abolitionists, the delegates refused to let women participate. Two upstate New Yorkers, Elizabeth Cady Stanton and Lucretia Mott, were compelled to sit behind curtains and not even be seen, much less be permitted to speak. When they returned home, they resolved to "form a society to advocate the rights of women." In 1848, in Seneca Falls, New York, their intentions, though delayed, were fulfilled in one of the most significant protest gatherings of the antebellum era.

In preparing for the meeting, Mott and Stanton drew up a list of women's grievances. They discovered that even though some states had awarded married women control over their property, they still had none over their earnings. Modeling their Declaration of Sentiments on the Declaration of Independence, the women at Seneca Falls proclaimed it a self-evident truth that "all men and women are created equal," and that men had usurped women's freedom and dignity. A man, the Declaration of Sentiments charged, "endeavored in every way he could, to destroy [woman's] confidence in her own powers, to lessen her self-respect, and to make her willing to lead a dependent and abject life." The remedy was expressed in 11 resolutions calling for equal opportunities in education and work, equality before the law, and the right to appear on public platforms. The most controversial resolution called for women's "sacred right to the elective franchise." The convention approved Mott and Stanton's list of resolutions.

Throughout the 1850s, led by Stanton and Susan B. Anthony, women continued to meet in annual conventions, working by resolution, persuasion, and petition campaign to achieve equal political, legal, and property rights with men. The right to vote, however, was considered the cornerstone of the movement. It remained so for 72 years of struggle until 1920, when passage of the Nineteenth Amendment made woman suffrage part of the Constitution. The Seneca Falls convention was crucial in beginning the cam-

Elizabeth Cady Stanton (1815–1902) and Lucretia Mott (1793–1880) were the leaders of the 1848 gathering for women's rights at Seneca Falls, New York.

paign for equal public rights. The seeds of gaining psychological autonomy and self-respect, however, were sown in the struggles of countless women like Abby Kelley, Sarah Grimké, and Emily Robinson. The struggle for that kind of liberation continues today.

CONCLUSION

PERFECTING AMERICA

Advocates for women's rights and temperance, abolitionists, and other reformers carried on very different crusades from those waged by Andrew Jackson against Indians, nullificationists, and the U.S. Bank. In fact, Jacksonian politics and antebellum reform were often at odds. Most abolitionists and temperance reformers were anti-Jackson Whigs. Jackson and most Democrats repudiated the passionate moralism of reformers.

Yet both sides shared an abiding faith in change and the idea of progress. Whether inspired by religious revivalism or political party loyalty, both believed that by stamping out evil forces, they could shape a better America.

As the United States neared midcentury,

slavery emerged as the most divisive issue. Although both major political parties tried to evade the question, westward expansion and the addition of new territories to the nation would soon make avoidance impossible. Would new states be slave or free? The question increasingly aroused the deepest passions of the American people. For the pioneer family, the driving force behind the westward movement, however, questions involving their fears and dreams seemed more important. We turn to this family and that movement in the next chapter.

Recommended Reading

Richard McCormick, *The Second Party System: Party Formation in the Jacksonian Era* (1966); and Richard Latner, *The Presidency of Andrew Jackson: White House Politics, 1829–1837* (1979), are the definitive works on those topics. See also Richard Ellis, *The Union at Risk: Jacksonian Democracy, States' Rights, and The Nullification Crisis* (1987); Ronald Formisano, *The Transformation of Political Culture* (1983); and Jean Baker, *Affairs of Party* (1983). On Jackson's popular appeal, see two books by Robert Remini, *Andrew Jackson and the Course of American Freedom, 1822–1832* (1981), and *Andrew Jackson and the Course of American Democracy* (1984). Jackson's political opponents are best understood by reading biographies of his major rivals: Clement Eaton, *Henry Clay and the Art of American Politics* (1957); Irving H. Bartlett, *Daniel Webster* (1978); and Margaret Coit, *John P. Calhoun: American Portrait* (1950).

The best single volume on antebellum religion and reform is Ronald Walters, *American Reformers, 1815–1860* (1978). A fascinating account of revivalism is William McLoughlin, *Modern Revivalism:* *From Charles G. Finney to Billy Graham* (1959). Paul Johnson, *A Shopkeeper's Millennium: Society and Revivals in Rochester, New York, 1815–1837* (1978), details the social impact of both economic change and revivalism in one community. To understand the Transcendentalists, read Perry Miller, ed., *The Transcendentalists* (1957), or Thoreau's *Walden*.

The standard work on utopian communities is Arthur Bestor, *Backwoods Utopias* (1950); but John Humphrey Noyes's *History of American Socialisms* (1870) is indispensable.

On the temperance crusade, see Ian Tyrrell, *Sobering Up: From Temperance to Prohibition in Antebellum America, 1800–1860* (1979). The experience of most efforts at institutional reforms is superbly analyzed in David Rothman, *The Discovery of the Asylum: Social Order and Disorder in the New Republic* (1971). Working-class reformers are the focus in Edward Pessen, *Most Uncommon Jacksonians: The Radical Leaders of the Early Labor Movement* (1967). On women's suffrage, see Eleanor Flexner, *Century of Struggle: The Woman's Rights Movement in the United States*, rev. ed. (1975).

Time Line

1824	New Harmony established
1825	John Quincy Adams chosen president by the House of Representatives
1826	American Temperance Society founded
1828	Calhoun publishes *Exposition and Protest* Jackson defeats Adams for the presidency Tariff of Abominations
1828–1832	Rise of workingmen's parties
1830	Webster-Hayne debate and Jackson-Calhoun toast Joseph Smith publishes *The Book of Mormon* Indian Removal Act
1830–1831	Charles Finney's religious revivals
1831	Garrison begins publishing *The Liberator*
1832	Jackson vetoes U.S. Bank charter Jackson reelected *Worcester* v. *Georgia*
1832–1833	Nullification crisis
1832–1836	Removal of funds from U.S. Bank to state banks
1833	Force Bill Compromise tariff Calhoun resigns as vice president American Anti-Slavery Society founded
1834	National Trades Union founded Whig Party established
1835–1836	Countless incidents of mob violence
1836	"Gag rule" Specie circular Van Buren elected president
1837	Financial panic and depression Sarah Grimké publishes *Letters on the Equality of the Sexes* Emerson's "American Scholar" address
1837–1838	Cherokee "Trail of Tears"
1840	William Henry Harrison elected president American Anti-Slavery Society splits World Anti-Slavery Convention Ten-hour day for federal employees
1840–1841	Transcendentalists found Hopedale and Brook Farm
1843	Dorothea Dix's report on treatment of the insane
1844	Joseph Smith murdered in Nauvoo, Illinois
1846–1848	Mormon migration to the Great Basin
1847	First issue of Frederick Douglass's *North Star*
1848	Oneida community founded First women's rights convention at Seneca Falls, New York
1850	Nathaniel Hawthorne, *Scarlet Letter*
1851	Maine prohibition law Herman Melville, *Moby Dick*
1853	Children's Aid Society established in New York City
1854	Thoreau publishes *Walden*
1855	Massachusetts bans segregated public schools

chapter 13

Moving West

By the 1840s, the frontier was retreating across the Mississippi. As Americans contemplated the lands west of the great river, they debated the question of expansion. Some, like Michigan's senator Lewis Cass, saw the Pacific Ocean as the only limit to territorial expansion. Cass believed that the West represented not only economic opportunity for Americans but political stability for the nation as well. People crowded into cities and confined to limited territories endangered the republic, he told fellow senators in a speech. But if they headed west to convert "the woods and forests into towns and villages and cultivate[d] fields" and to extend "the dominion of civilization and improvement over the domain of nature," they would find rewarding personal opportunities that would ensure political and social harmony.

Thousands of men seconded Cass's sentiments by volunteering to join American forces in the war against Mexico in the summer of 1845. Largely untrained, the companies hurried south. But before long these supporters of expansion saw the ugly side of territorial adventures: insects, bad weather, poor food, unsanitary conditions, and illnesses such as the "black vomit" (yellow fever), dysentery, and diarrhea. As a member of the American occupying army, Henry Judah also experienced the hostility of conquered peoples. In his diary, he reported, "It is dangerous to go out after night. . . . Four of our men were stabbed today."

Thomas Gibson, a captain of Indiana volunteers, described a battlefield "still covered with [Mexican] dead" where "the stench is most horrible." Indiana friends had been killed, and Gibson himself had narrowly escaped. His wife, Mary, had not escaped the heady propaganda for national expansion. She had heard that Indiana soldiers had "shode themselves great cowards by retreating during battle," and she disapproved. "We all would rather you had stood like good soldiers," she told her husband.

Lewis Cass, Henry Judah, Thomas and Mary Gibson, and thousands of other Americans played a part in the nation's expansion into the trans-Mississippi West. The differences and similarities in their perspectives and in their responses to territorial growth unveil the complex nature of the western experience. Lewis Cass's speech illustrates the hold the West had on people's imagination and how some Americans linked expansion to individual opportunity and national progress. Yet his assumption that the West was vacant points to the costs of white expansion for Mexican-Americans and Native Americans.

This chapter concerns movement into the trans-Mississippi West between 1830 and 1865. First, we will consider how and when Americans moved west, by what means the United States acquired the vast territories that in 1840 belonged to other nations, and the meaning of "Manifest Destiny," the slogan used to defend the conquest of the continent west of the Mississippi River. Then, we explore the nature of life on the western farming, mining, and urban frontiers. Finally, the chapter examines responses of Native Americans and Mexican-Americans to expansion and illuminates the ways in which different cultural traditions intersected in the West.

PROBING THE TRANS-MISSISSIPPI WEST

Until the 1840s, most Americans lived east of the Mississippi. The admission of new states between 1815 and 1840 symbolized the steady settlement of the eastern half of the continent. By 1860, some 4.3 million Americans had moved west of the great river.

Foreign Claims and Possessions

With the exception of the Louisiana Territory, Spain held title to most of the trans-Mississippi region in 1815. Spanish holdings stretched south to Mexico and west to the Pacific and included present-day Texas, Arizona, New Mexico, Nevada, Utah, western Colorado, California, and small parts of Wyoming, Kansas, and Oklahoma. When Mexico won its independence from Spain in 1821, it inherited these lands and the 75,000 Spanish-speaking inhabitants and numerous Native Americans living there.

To the north of California was the Oregon country, a vaguely defined area extending from California to Alaska. Both Great Britain and the United States claimed the Oregon country on the basis of explorations in the late eighteenth century and fur trading in the early nineteenth. Joint occupation, agreed on in the Convention of 1818 and the Occupation Treaty of 1827, temporarily deferred settling the boundary question.

Traders, Trappers, and Cotton Farmers

Americans made commercial forays into the trans-Mississippi West long before the migrations of the 1840s and 1850s and became familiar with some of its people and terrains. As early as 1811, Americans engaged in the fur trade in Oregon, and within ten years, fur trappers and traders were exploiting the resources of the Rocky Mountain region. By the mid-1830s, trappers had almost exterminated the beaver, but trade in bison robes prepared by the Plains tribes flourished in the area around the upper Missouri River and its tributaries until after 1860.

With the collapse of the Spanish Empire in 1821, American traders were able to penetrate the Southwest. Each year, caravans from "the States" followed the Santa Fe Trail over the plains and mountains, loaded with weapons, tools, and brightly colored calicoes, which they traded for metals and furs.

To the south, in Texas, land for cotton

rather than trade attracted settlers and squatters in the 1820s. By 1835, almost 30,000 Americans were living in Texas, the largest group of Americans living outside the nation's boundaries at that time.

On the Pacific, New England traders acquired California cowhides and tallow in exchange for clothes, boots, hardware, and furniture manufactured in the East.

Among the earliest easterners to settle in the trans-Mississippi West were tribes from the South and the Old Northwest whom the American government forcibly relocated in present-day Oklahoma and Kansas. Ironically, some of these eastern tribes acted as agents of white civilization by introducing cotton, the plantation system, and schools. Other tribes triggered conflicts that weakened the western tribes with whom they came into contact. The Cherokee, Shawnee, and Delaware forced the Osages out of their Missouri and Arkansas hunting grounds, while tribes from the Old Northwest claimed hunting areas long used by Kansas plains tribes. These disruptions foreshadowed white incursions later in the century.

The facts that much of the trans-Mississippi West lay outside U.S. boundaries and that the government had guaranteed Indian tribes permanent possession of some western territories did not curtail American economic activities. By the 1840s, a growing volume of published information fostered dreams of possession. Lansford Hastings's *Emigrants' Guide to Oregon and California* (1845) provided not only the practical information that emigrants would need but also the encouragement that heading for the frontier was the right thing to do.

In his widely read guide, Hastings minimized the importance of Mexican and British sovereignty. His belief that Americans would obtain rights to foreign holdings in the West came true within a decade. In the course of the 1840s, the United States acquired the Southwest and Texas as well as the Oregon country up to the 49th parallel. Later, with the Gadsden Purchase

in 1853, the total area of all these new lands amounted to over 1,500,000 square miles.

Manifest Destiny

Bursts of rhetoric accompanied territorial growth and its slogan, "Manifest Destiny." The phrase, coined in 1845 by the editor of the *Democratic Review,* suggests that the country's superior institutions and culture gave Americans a God-given right to spread their civilization across the entire continent.

This sense of a unique mission was a legacy of early Puritan utopianism and revolutionary republicanism. By the 1840s, however, an argument for territorial expansion merged with the belief that the United States possessed a unique civilization. States could successfully absorb new territories. Publicists of Manifest Destiny proclaimed that the nation must.

WINNING THE TRANS-MISSISSIPPI WEST

Manifest Destiny justified expansion but did not cause it. Concrete events in Texas triggered the national government's determination to acquire territories west of the Mississippi River.

The Texas question originated in the years when Spain held most of the Southwest. Although some settlements such as Santa Fe, founded in 1609, were almost as old as Jamestown, the Spanish considered the sparsely populated and underdeveloped Southwest primarily a buffer zone for Mexico. In the Adams-Onís treaty with Spain in 1819, the United States accepted a southern border excluding Texas, to which the Americans had vague claims stemming from the Louisiana Purchase.

Annexing Texas, 1845

By the time the treaty was ratified in 1821, Mexico had won its independence from Spain. The

United States Territorial Expansion by 1860

Oregon Territory
(Treaty of 1846
with Great Britain)

Ceded by Great Britain,
1818

CANADA

NEW HAMPSHIRE

VERMONT

MAINE

MASSACHUSETTS

WISCONSIN

MICHIGAN

NEW YORK

RHODE
ISLAND

Louisiana Purchase
(from France, 1803)

PENNSYLVANIA

CONNECTICUT

NEW JERSEY

ILLINOIS

OHIO

Original
colonies

DELAWARE

INDIANA

Mexican Cession
(acquired from Mexico, 1848)

United States after
Peace of Paris,
1783

MARYLAND

VIRGINIA

KENTUCKY

TENNESSEE

NORTH CAROLINA

MISSISSIPPI

SOUTH
CAROLINA

ATLANTIC
OCEAN

ALABAMA

GEORGIA

PACIFIC
OCEAN

Gadsden Purchase
(from Mexico, 1853)

Texas
Annexation
(1845)

Louisiana
(1810–1813)

Florida
Territory
(purchased from
Spain, 1819)

MEXICO

Gulf of Mexico

new nation inherited the borderlands, their people, and their problems. Mexicans soon had reason to fear American expansionism, after several attempts by the United States to buy Texas and continuing aggressive American statements.

In 1823, the Mexican government determined to strengthen border areas by increasing population. To attract settlers, it offered land in return for token payments and pledges to become Roman Catholics and Mexican citizens. Stephen F. Austin, who gained rights to bring 300 families into Texas, was among the first of the American *empresarios*, or contractors, to take advantage of this opportunity. By the end of the decade, some 15,000 white Americans and 1,000 slaves lived in Texas, far outnumbering the 5,000 Mexican inhabitants.

Mexican officials soon questioned their invitation. Few American settlers became Catholics, and they remained more American than Mexi-

can. Some of the settlers disliked Mexican laws and customs, and in late 1826, a small group raised the flag of rebellion and declared the Republic of Fredonia. Although settlers like Austin assisted in putting down the brief uprising, American newspapers hailed the rebels as "apostles of democracy" and called Mexico "an alien civilization."

Mexican anxiety grew apace. In 1829, the Mexican government, determined to curb American influence, abolished slavery in Texas. The next year, it forbade further American immigration, and officials began to collect customs duties on goods crossing the Louisiana border. But little changed in Texas. American slave owners freed their slaves and forced them to sign life indenture contracts. Emigrants still crossed the border and continued to outnumber Mexicans.

Tensions escalated to the brink of war. In October 1835, a skirmish between the colonial militia and Mexican forces signaled the beginning of hostilities. Sam Houston, onetime governor of Tennessee and army officer, became commander in chief of the Texas forces.

Mexican dictator and general Antonio López de Santa Anna hurried north to crush the rebellion with an army of 6,000 conscripts. Santa Anna and his men won the initial engagements of the war: The Alamo at San Antonio fell to him, taking Davy Crockett and Jim Bowie with it. So too did the fortress of Goliad, to the southeast.

As he pursued Houston and the Texans toward the San Jacinto River, carelessness proved Santa Anna's undoing. When the Mexican general and his men settled down to their usual siesta on April 21, 1836, without posting an adequate guard, the Americans attacked. With cries of "Remember the Alamo! Remember Goliad!" the Texans overcame the army, captured its commander in his slippers, and won the war within 20 minutes. Their casualties numbered only two, while 630 Mexicans lay dead.

With the victory at San Jacinto, Texas gained its independence. But although Texans immediately sought admission to the Union, their request failed. Many northerners violently opposed annexation of another slave state. The Union was precariously balanced, with 13 free and 13 slave states. Texas would upset that equilibrium in favor of the South.

For the next few years, the Lone Star Republic led a precarious existence. Mexico refused to recognize its independence, and Texans skirmished with Mexican bands. Financial ties with the United States increased, however, as trade grew and many Americans invested in Texas bonds and lands.

Texas became headline news again in 1844, when President John Tyler (who had assumed office after William Henry Harrison's death one month into his term) reopened the question of annexation, hoping that Texas would ensure his reelection. The issue exploded, however, bringing to life powerful sectional, national, and political tensions. Southern Democrats insisted that the South's future hinged on the annexation of Texas.

Democrats Lewis Cass, Stephen Douglas of Illinois, and Robert Walker of Mississippi vigorously supported annexation, not because it would expand slavery, a topic they avoided, but because it would spread the benefits of American civilization. Their arguments, classic examples of the tenets of Manifest Destiny, put the question into a national context of expanding American freedom. So successfully did they link Texas to Manifest Destiny and avoid sectional issues that their candidate, James Polk of Tennessee, secured the Democratic nomination in 1844. Polk called for "the reannexation of Texas at the earliest practicable period" and the occupation of the Oregon Territory. Manifest Destiny had come of age.

Polk won a close election in 1844. But by the time Polk took the oath of office in March 1845, Tyler, in his last months in office, had pushed through Congress a joint resolution admitting Texas to the Union. Nine years after its revolution, Texas finally became part of the Union. The agreement gave Texas the unusual right to divide into five states if it chose to do so.

War with Mexico, 1846-1848

When Mexico learned of Texas's annexation, it promptly severed diplomatic ties with the United States. It was easy for Mexicans to interpret the events from the 1820s on as part of a gigantic American plot to steal Texas. Now that the Americans had gained Texas, would they want still more?

Polk, like many other Americans, failed to appreciate how the annexation of Texas humiliated Mexico and increased pressures on its government to respond belligerently. Aware of its weakness, the president anticipated that Mexico would grant his grandiose demands: a Texas bounded by the Rio Grande rather than the Nueces River 150 miles to its north, as well as California and New Mexico.

Even before the Texans could accept the

The Mexican-American War, 1846–1848

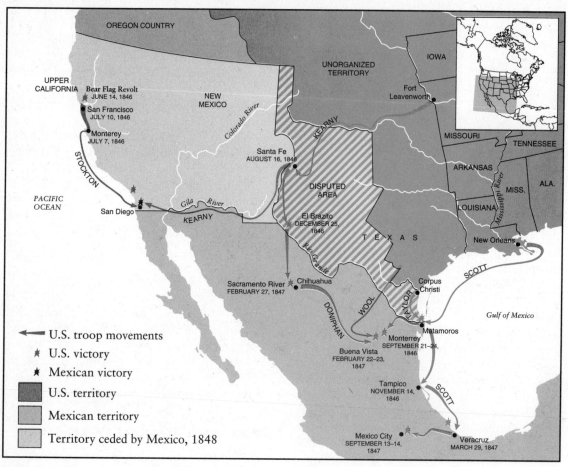

long-awaited invitation to join the Union, rumors of a Mexican invasion were afloat. As a precautionary move, Polk ordered General Zachary Taylor to move "on or near the Rio Grande." By October 1845, Taylor and 3,500 American troops had reached the Nueces River. In November, the president sent his secret agent, John L. Slidell, to Mexico City with instructions to secure the Rio Grande border and to buy Upper California and New Mexico. When the Mexican government refused to receive Slidell, an angry Polk decided to force Mexico into accepting American terms. He ordered Taylor

south of the Rio Grande. To the Mexicans, who insisted that the Nueces River was the legitimate boundary, their presence constituted an act of war.

In late April, the Mexican government declared a state of defensive war. Two days later, a skirmish broke out between Mexican and American troops, resulting in 16 American casualties. When Polk received Taylor's report, he quickly drafted a war message for Congress. The president claimed that Mexico had "passed the boundary of the United States . . . invaded our territory and shed American blood upon American soil." "War exists," he claimed and, he added untruthfully, "notwithstanding all our efforts to avoid it, exists by act of Mexico."

Although Congress declared war, the conflict bitterly divided Americans. Many Whigs, including Abraham Lincoln, questioned the accuracy of Polk's initial account of the events, and their opposition grew more vocal as time passed. In 1847, a month after General Winfield Scott took Mexico City, Philadelphian Joseph Sills wrote in his diary, "There is a widely spread conviction . . . that it is a wicked & disgraceful war."

Yet Polk enjoyed the enthusiastic support of expansionists. Thomas Gibson's men, like most other soldiers, were eager volunteers. Some expansionists even urged permanent occupation of Mexico.

In the end, chance helped draw hostilities to a close. Mexican moderates approached Polk's diplomatic representative, Nicholas Trist, who accompanied the American army in Mexico. In Trist's baggage were detailed, though out-of-date, instructions outlining Polk's requirements: the Rio Grande boundary, Upper California, and New Mexico. Although the president had lost confidence in Trist and had ordered him home in chains, Trist stayed in Mexico to negotiate an end to the war. Having obtained most of Polk's objectives, Trist returned to Washington to an ungrateful president. Apparently Polk had wanted more territory from Mexico for less money. Firing him from his job at the State Department, Polk denounced Trist as an "impudent and unqualified scoundrel."

California and New Mexico

Polk made it clear from the early days of his presidency that California and New Mexico were part of any resolution of the Mexico crisis. Serious American interest in California dated only from the late 1830s. A few Americans had settled in California during the 1820s and 1830s. But gradual recognition of California's fine harbors, its favorable position for the China trade, and the suspicion that other countries, especially Great Britain, had designs on the region nourished the conviction that it must become part of the United States. As more Americans poured into California in the early 1840s, one resident realized, "The American population will soon be sufficiently numerous to play the Texas game."

Polk tried to purchase California, but Santa Anna, who bore the burden of having lost Texas, was in no position to sell. Thus in 1846, a few armed American settlers rose up against Mexican "tyranny" and established the "Bear Flag Republic."

New Mexico was also on Polk's list. Ties with the United States began in the 1820s, when American traders began to bring their goods to Santa Fe. New Mexicans had little desire for annexation, however, and the unsuccessful attempt by the Texans to capture Santa Fe in 1841 and border clashes in the following two years did not enhance the attractiveness of their Anglo neighbors. But standing awkwardly in the path of American westward expansion, New Mexico faced an uncertain future.

In June 1846, shortly after the declaration of war with Mexico, the Army of the West, led by Colonel Stephen W. Kearny, left Fort Leavenworth, Kansas, for New Mexico. Two months later, the army took Santa Fe without a shot. New Mexico's upper class, who had already begun to intermarry with American merchants and send some sons to colleges in the United States, readily accepted the new rulers. However, ordinary Mexicans and Pueblo Indians did not take conquest so lightly. After Kearny departed, resistance erupted in New Mexico. Californians also fought the American occupation force. Kearny was wounded, and the first appointed American governor of New Mexico was killed. In the end, however, superior American military strength won the day. By January 1847, both California and New Mexico were firmly in American hands.

The Treaty of Guadalupe Hidalgo, 1848

Negotiated by Trist and signed on February 2, 1848, the Treaty of Guadalupe Hidalgo dictated the fate of most people living in the Southwest. The United States absorbed the region's 75,000 Spanish-speaking inhabitants and its 150,000 Native Americans and increased its territory by 529,017 square miles, almost a third of Mexico's extent. Mexico received $15 million and in 1853 would receive another $10 million for large tracts of land in southern Arizona and New Mexico (the Gadsden Purchase). In the treaty, the United States guaranteed the civil and political rights of former Mexican citizens and their rights to land and also agreed to satisfy all American claims against Mexico. The war had cost the United States 13,000 American lives, lost mostly to diseases such as measles and dysentery, and $97 million expended for military operations.

The Oregon Question, 1844-1846

Belligerence and war secured vast areas of the Southwest and California for the United States. In the Pacific Northwest, the presence of mighty Great Britain rather than the weak, crisis-ridden Mexican government suggested more cautious tactics. There diplomacy became the means for territorial gains.

Despite the disputed nature of claims to the Oregon Territory, Polk assured the inauguration day crowd huddled under umbrellas that "our title to the country of Oregon is 'clear and unquestionable,' . . . already our people are preparing to perfect that title by occupying it with their wives and children." Polk's words reflected American confidence that settlement carried the presumption of possession. But the British did not agree.

Between 1842 and 1845, the number of Americans in Oregon grew from 400 to over 5,000. Most located south of the Columbia River in the Willamette valley. By 1843, these settlers had written a constitution and soon after elected a legislature. At the same time, British interests in the area were declining as the fur trade dwindled.

The Democratic platform and the slogan that had helped elect Polk laid claim to a boundary of 54°40′. In fact, Polk was not willing to go to war with Great Britain for Oregon. Privately, he considered reasonable a boundary at the 49th parallel, which would extend the existing Canadian-American border to the Pacific and secure the harbors of Puget Sound for the United States. But Polk could hardly admit this to his Democratic supporters, who had so enthusiastically shouted "Fifty-four forty or fight" during the recent campaign.

Soon after his inaugural, Polk offered his compromise to Great Britain. But his tone offended the British minister, who rejected the offer at once. However, most Americans did not want to fight for Oregon and preferred to resolve the crisis diplomatically. As war with Mexico loomed, this task became more urgent.

The British, too, were eager to settle. In June 1846, the British agreed to accept the 49th parallel boundary if Vancouver Island remained British. With overwhelming Senate approval, Polk ended the crisis just a few weeks before the declaration of war with Mexico.

As these events show, Manifest Destiny was an idea that supported and justified expansionist policies. It corresponded, at the most basic level, to what Americans believed, that expansion was both necessary and right.

GOING WEST

After diplomacy and war clarified the status of the western territories, Americans lost little time in moving there. A trickle of emigrants became a flood. During the 1840s, 1850s, and 1860s, thousands of Americans left their homes for the frontier. By 1860, California alone had 380,000 settlers.

Some chose to migrate by sea, sailing around South America to the West Coast or taking a ship to Panama, crossing the isthmus by land, and then continuing by sea. Most emigrants, however, chose land routes. In 1843, the first large party succeeded in crossing the plains and mountains to Oregon. More followed. Between 1841 and 1867, some 350,000 traveled over the overland trails to California or to Oregon, while others trekked part of the way to intermediate points like Colorado and Utah.

The Emigrants

Most of the emigrants who headed for the Far West, where slavery was prohibited, were white and American-born. They came from the Midwest and the Upper South. A few free blacks made the trip as well. Pioneer Margaret Frink remembered seeing "a Negro woman . . . tramping along through the heat and dust, carrying a cast iron black stove on her head, with her provisions and a blanket piled on top . . . bravely pushing on for California." Emigrants from the Deep South usually selected Arkansas or Texas as their destination, and many brought their slaves with them. By 1840, over 11,000 slaves toiled in Texas and 20,000 in Arkansas.

The many pioneers who kept journals during the five- to six-month overland trip captured the human dimension of emigrating. One migrant, Lodisa Frizzell, described her feelings of parting in 1852:

> Who is there that does not recollect their first night when started on a long journey, the well known voices of our friends still ring in our ears, the parting kiss feels still warm upon our lips, and that last separating word FAREWELL! sinks deeply into the heart. It may be the last we ever hear from some or all of them, and to those who

start . . . there can be no more solemn scene of parting only at death.

Most emigrants traveled with family and relatives. Only during the gold rush years did large numbers, usually young men, travel independently. Migration was a family experience, mostly involving men and women from their late twenties to early forties. A sizable number of them had recently married, and many had moved before. The difference was the vast distance to this frontier and the seemingly final separation from home.

Migrants' Motives

What led so many Americans to sell most of their possessions and embark on an unknown future thousands of miles away? Many believed that frontier life would offer rich opportunities. Thousands sought riches in the form of gold. Others anticipated making their fortune as merchants, shopkeepers, peddlers, land speculators, or practitioners of law or medicine.

Most migrants dreamed of bettering their life by cultivating the land. Federal and state land policies made the acquisition of land increasingly alluring. Preemption acts during the 1830s and 1840s gave "squatters" the right to settle public lands before the government offered them for sale and then allowed them to purchase these lands at the minimum price once they came on the market. At the same time, the amount of land a family had to buy shrank to only 40 acres. In 1862, the Homestead Act went further by offering 160 acres of government land free to citizens or future citizens over 21 who lived on the property, improved it, and paid a small registration fee. Oregon's land policy, which predated the Homestead Act, was even more generous. It awarded a single man 320 acres of free land and a married man 640 acres provided he occupied his claim for four years and made improvements.

Some emigrants hoped the West would restore them to health. Others pursued religious or cultural missions in the West. Missionary couples like David and Catherine Blaine, who settled in Seattle when it was a frontier outpost, determined to bring Protestantism and education west. Stirred by the stories they had heard of the "deplorable morals" on the frontier, they left the comforts of home to evangelize and educate westerners. Still others, like the Mormons, made the long trek to Utah to establish a society in conformity with their religious beliefs.

Not everyone who dreamed of setting off for the frontier could do so. The trip to the Far West involved considerable expense. The sea route around Cape Horn came to perhaps $600 per person. For the same sum, four people could make the overland trip. And if the emigrants sold their wagons and oxen at the journey's end, the final expenses might amount to only $220. Clearly, however, the initial financial outlay was considerable enough to rule out the trip for the very poor. Despite increasingly liberal land policies, migration to the Far West (with the exception of group migration to Utah) was a movement of middle-class Americans.

The Overland Trails

The trip started for most emigrants in the late spring, when they left their homes and headed for starting points in Iowa and Missouri: Council Bluffs, Independence, Westport, St. Joseph. There companies of wagons gathered, and when grass was up for the stock, usually by the middle of May, they set out. Emigrant trains first followed the valley of the Platte River. Making only 15 miles a day, they slowly wound their way through the South Pass of the Rockies, heading for destinations in California or Oregon.

Emigrants found the first part of the trip novel and even enjoyable. The Indians, one woman noted, "proved better than represented." Men drove and repaired the wagons,

Overland Trails to the West

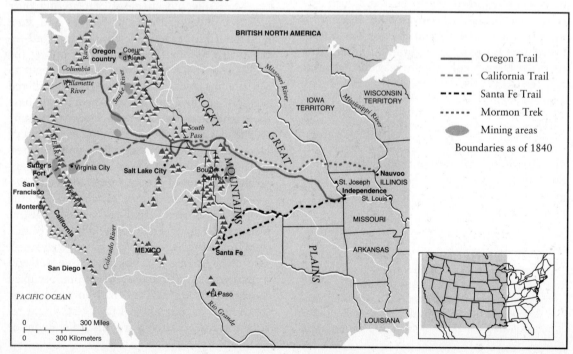

———	Oregon Trail
– – –	California Trail
– · – ·	Santa Fe Trail
· · · ·	Mormon Trek
⬭	Mining areas

Boundaries as of 1840

This undated photograph of two emigrant wagons and their occupants gives a good idea of the family character of emigration and the limited space that the wagons had for family possessions and items needed at the end of the trip. Note that the children are barefoot.

ferried cattle and wagons across rivers, hunted, and stood guard at night. Women labored at domestic chores, caring for children, cooking meals, and washing clothes. Many of the children later remembered the trip as an exciting adventure.

As the trip lengthened, difficulties multiplied. Cholera often took a heavy toll. Conflict with Indians became a problem only in the 1850s and made emigrants jumpy during the second half of the trip. (Between 1840 and 1860, Indians killed about 400 emigrants, most during the second half of the trip; the emigrants themselves killed at least that many Indians.) Traveling grew more arduous as deserts and mountains replaced rolling prairies.

Since emigrants had to cross the final mountain ranges of the Sierras and the Cascades before the first snowfall, there was a pressing need to push ever onward. Animals weakened by constant travel, poor feed, and bad water sickened, collapsed, and often died. As families faced the harsh realities of travel, they had to lighten their wagons by throwing out possessions lovingly brought from home. Food grew scarce.

Finally, five or six months after setting out, emigrants arrived, exhausted and often penniless, in Oregon or California. As one wrote on a

September day in 1854, her journey had ended "which for care, fatigue, tediousness, perplexities and dangers of various kinds, can not be excelled."

LIVING ON THE FRONTIER

When emigrants finally reached their destinations and began building a new life, they naturally drew on their experiences back east. "Pioneers though we are, and proud of it, we are not content with the wilds ... with the idleness of the land, the rudely construct[ed] log cabin," one Oregon settler explained. "Pioneers are not that kind of folks."

The Agricultural Frontier

Pioneer farmers faced the urgent task of establishing their homesteads and beginning farming. First, the family had to locate a suitable claim. Clearing the land and constructing a crude shelter followed. Only then could crops be planted. Since emigrants brought few of their possessions west, their work was more difficult. A young Oregon bride who set up housekeeping in the

1840s with only a stew kettle and three knives was not unusual.

After months of intense interaction with other travelers, families were now alone on their claims. The typical frontier household consisted of parents with one to four children. For several years, isolation was the rule. One pioneer remembered, "We were . . . 'all told,' eleven families within a radius of six or eight miles, widely separated by our holdings and three hundred and twenty acres to each family. In those days anyone residing within twenty miles was considered a neighbor." But the isolation usually ended within a few years as most areas attracted new emigrants and old settlers seeking better claims.

In Oregon, the pioneers set up a political system based on eastern models before the status of the territory was resolved. Before permanent schools or churches existed, men resumed the familiar political rituals of voting, electioneering, and talking politics. They were also going to court to resolve controversies and to ensure law and order. Although modern movies and novels suggest that violence was a part of everyday life on the frontier, this was not true on the farming frontier. Courts, rather than rough-and-ready vigilante groups, usually handled the occasional violence.

The chronic shortage of cash on the frontier retarded the growth of both schools and churches. Until farmers could send their goods to market, they had little cash to spare. Geographic mobility also contributed to institutional instability. Up to three-quarters of the population of a frontier county might vanish within a ten-year period as emigrants left to seek better land. Some farmed in as many as four locations until they found a satisfactory claim. Institutions relying on continuing personal and financial support suffered accordingly.

Yet even if their efforts to re-create familiar institutional life often faltered, settlers did not lose sight of their goals. Newspapers, journals, and books, which circulated early on the frontier, reinforced familiar values and norms and kept determination strong. As more and more settlers arrived, the numbers willing to support educational, religious, and cultural institutions grew. In the end, as one pioneer pointed out, "We have a telegraph line from the East, a daily rail road train, daily mail and I am beginning to feel quite civilized. And here ended my pioneer experience." Only 16 years had passed since she had crossed the Plains.

Although the belief in the frontier's special economic and social opportunities encouraged emigration, the dream was often illusory. The appearance of workers for hire and tenant farmers also pointed to real economic differences and hinted at the difficulties those on the bottom would face as they tried to improve their situation. Their widespread geographic mobility also indicates that many found it difficult to capitalize on the benefits of homesteading. Census data show that those who moved were generally less successful than the core of stable residents.

The Mining Frontier

On the mining frontier, tales of prospectors who had reportedly struck it rich fueled the fantasies of fortune hunters. News of the discovery of gold in 1848 in California swept the country like wildfire. Thousands raced to cash in on the bonanza. Within a year, California's population ballooned from 14,000 to almost 100,000. By 1852, that figure had more than doubled.

The forty-niners were mostly young, unmarried, predominantly male, and heterogeneous. Of those pouring into California in 1849, about 80 percent came from the United States, 8 percent from Mexico, and 5 percent from South America. The rest came from Europe and Asia. Few were as interested in settling the West as they were in extracting its precious metals and returning home rich.

California was the first and most dramatic of the western mining frontiers. Later gold strikes drew prospectors to the Pacific Northwest and British Columbia, Colorado, and Montana in the 1850s and 1860s. In the mid-1870s, yet another discovery of gold, this time in the

Black Hills of South Dakota, attracted hordes of fortune seekers.

The discovery of gold or silver spurred immediate, if usually short-lived, growth. Merchants, saloonkeepers, cooks, druggists, gamblers, and prostitutes hurried into boom areas as fast as prospectors. Usually about half of the residents of any mining camp were there to relieve the miners of their profits, not to prospect themselves.

Life in the mining boomtowns was often disorderly. Racial antagonism between American miners and foreigners, whom they labeled "greasers" (Mexicans), "chinks" (Chinese), "keskedees" (Frenchmen), and lesser "breeds," led to ugly riots and lynchings. Fistfights, drunkenness, and murder occurred often enough to become part of the lore of the gold rush. Wrote one woman, "In the short space of twenty four days, we have had murders, fearful accidents, bloody deaths, a mob, whippings, a hanging, an attempt at suicide, and a fatal duel."

Although the lucky few struck it rich or at least made enough money to return home with pride intact, miners' journals and letters reveal that many made only enough to keep going. The problem was that easily mined silver and gold deposits soon ran out. The remaining rich deposits lay deeply embedded in rock or gravel.

Extraction required cooperative efforts, capital, technological experience, and expensive machinery. Eventually, mining became a corporate industrial concern, with miners as wage earners. As early as 1852, the changing nature of mining in California had transformed most of the shaggy miners into wage workers.

Probably 5 percent of early gold rush emigrants to California were women and children. Many of the women also anticipated getting "rich in a hurry." Because there were so few of them, the cooking, nursing, laundry, and hotel services women provided had a high value. Yet it was wearying work, and some wondered if the money compensated for the exhaustion. As Mary Ballou thought it over, she decided, "I would not advise any Lady to come out here and suffer to toil and fatigue I have suffered for the sake of a little gold." As men's profits shrank, so too did those of the women who served them.

Some of the first women to arrive on the mining frontier were prostitutes, who may have made up as much as 20 percent of California's female population in 1850. During boom days, they made good money and sometimes won a recognized place in society. But they were more often the victims of murder and violence than the recipients of courtesy.

The Mexicans, South Americans, Chinese,

Although there were only a few women on the early mining frontier, they often found that the predominantly male environment offered them good opportunities to earn money.

and small numbers of blacks seeking their fortunes in California soon discovered that racial discrimination flourished vigorously in the land of golden promise. At first, American miners hoped to force foreigners out of the gold fields altogether. But an attempt to declare mining illegal for all foreigners failed. A high tax on foreign miners proved more successful. Thousands of Mexicans and Chinese left the mines. As business stagnated in mining towns, however, white miners had second thoughts about the levy and reduced it. In 1870, the tax was declared unconstitutional.

Black Americans found that color placed them in a situation akin to that of foreigners. Deprived of the vote, forbidden to testify in civil or criminal cases involving whites, excluded from the bounties of the state's homestead law, blacks led a precarious existence. When news arrived of the discovery of gold in British Columbia in the late 1850s, hundreds of blacks as well as thousands of Chinese left the state hoping that the Canadian frontier would be more hospitable than California.

Although men's and women's fantasies of dazzling riches rarely came true, gold had a huge impact on the West as a whole. Between 1848 and 1883, California mines supplied two-thirds of the country's gold. This gold transformed San Francisco from a sleepy town into a bustling metropolis. It fueled the development of California and Oregon, and it built harbors, railroads, and irrigation systems all over the West.

The Mormon Frontier

In the decades before 1860, many emigrants heading for the Far West stopped to rest and buy supplies in Salt Lake City, the heart of the Mormon state of Deseret. There they encountered a society that seemed familiar and orderly, yet foreign and shocking. Visitors admired the attractively laid out town with its irrigation ditches, gardens, and tidy houses, but they deplored

polygamy. They were amazed that so few Mormon women seemed interested in escaping from the bonds of plural marriage.

Violent events had driven the Mormons to the arid Great Basin area. Joseph Smith's murder in 1844 marked no end to the persecution of his followers. By the fall of 1846, angry mobs had chased the last of the "Saints" out of Nauvoo, Illinois. Smith's successor, Brigham Young, realized that flight from the United States represented the best hope for survival.

Young selected the Great Basin area, technically part of Mexico, as the best site for his future kingdom. It was arid and remote, 1,000 miles from its nearest "civilized" neighbors. But if irrigated, Mormon leaders concluded, it might prove as fertile as the fields and vineyards of ancient Israel.

In April 1847, Young led an exploratory expedition of 143 men, three women, and two children to this promised land. By September 1847, fully 566 wagons and 1,500 of the Saints had made the arduous trek to Salt Lake City. By 1850, the Mormon frontier had attracted over 11,000 settlers. Missionary efforts in the United States and abroad, especially in Great Britain and Scandinavia, drew thousands of converts to the Great Basin. By the end of the decade, over 30,000 Saints lived in Utah. Though hardship marked these early years, the Mormons thrived. As one early settler remarked, "We have everything around us we could ask."

Non-Mormon or "Gentile" emigrants passing through Utah found much that was recognizable but also perceived profound differences, for the heart of Mormon society was not the individual farmer living on his own homestead but the cooperative village. Years of persecution had nourished a strong sense of group identity and acceptance of church leadership. Organized by the church leaders, who made the essential decisions, farming became a collective enterprise. All farmers were allotted land. All had irrigation rights, for water did not belong to individuals but to the community. During Sunday services, the local bishop might give farming instructions to his congregation along with his sermon.

The church was omnipresent in Utah; in fact, nothing separated church and state. When it became clear that Utah would become a territory, Mormon leaders drew up a constitution that divided religious and political power. But once in place, powers overlapped. As one Gentile pointed out, "This intimate connection of church and state seems to pervade everything that is done. The supreme power in both being lodged in the hands of the same individuals, it is difficult to separate their two official characters, and to determine whether in any one instance they act as spiritual or merely temporal officers."

The Treaty of Guadalupe Hidalgo officially incorporated Utah into the United States but little affected political and religious arrangements. Brigham Young became territorial governor. Local bishops continued to act as spiritual leaders as well as civil magistrates in Mormon communities.

Other aspects of the Mormon frontier were distinctive. Mormon policy toward the Indian tribes was remarkably enlightened. As one prominent Mormon pointed out, "It has been our habit to shoot Indians with tobacco and bread biscuits rather than with powder and lead, and we are most successful with them." After two expeditions against the Timpanagos and Shoshone in 1850, Mormons concentrated on converting rather than killing Native Americans. Mormon missionaries learned Bannock, Ute, Navajo, and Hopi languages in order to bring the faith to these tribes. They also encouraged Native Americans to ranch and farm.

While most Gentiles could tolerate some of the differences they encountered on the Mormon frontier, few could accept polygamy and the seemingly immoral extended family structure that plural marriage entailed. Although Joseph Smith and other church leaders had secretly practiced polygamy in the early 1840s, Brigham Young publicly revealed the doctrine only in 1852, when the Saints were safely in Utah.

Actually, relatively few families were polygamous. During the 40-year period in which Mormons practiced plural marriage, only 10 to 20 percent of Mormon families were polygamous. Few men had more than two wives. Because of the expense of maintaining several families and the personal strains involved, usually only the most successful and visible Mormon leaders practiced polygamy. To the shock of outsiders, Mormon women defended polygamy to the outside world. Polygamy was preferable to monogamy, which left the single woman without the economic and social protection of family life and forced some of them into prostitution.

Although the Mormon frontier seemed alien to outsiders, it succeeded in terms of its numbers, its growing economic prosperity, and its group unity. Long-term threats loomed for this community, however, once the area became part of the United States. Attacks on Young's power as well as heated verbal denunciations of polygamy proliferated. Efforts began in Congress to outlaw polygamy. In the years before the Civil War, Mormons withstood these assaults on their way of life. But as Utah became more connected to the rest of the country, the tide would turn against them.

The Urban Frontier

Many emigrants went west to settle in cities like San Francisco, Denver, and Portland. There they hoped to find business and professional opportunities or, perhaps, the chance to make a fortune by speculating in town lots.

Cities were an integral part of frontier life and sometimes preceded agricultural settlement. Some communities turned into bustling cities as they catered to the emigrant trade. St. Joseph, Missouri, outfitted families setting out on the overland journey. Salt Lake City offered pioneers headed for California an opportunity to rest and restock. Portland was the destination of many emigrants and became a market and supply center for homesteaders.

Some cities, like San Francisco and Denver, sprang up almost overnight. In a mere 12 years, San Francisco's population zoomed from 812 to 56,802.

Young, single men seeking their fortunes made up a disproportionate share of the urban population. Frontier Portland had more than three men for every woman. Predictably, urban life was often noisy, rowdy, and occasionally violent. Eventually the sex ratio became balanced, but as late as 1880, fully 18 of the 24 largest western cities had more men than women.

Although western cities began with distinctive characters, they soon resembled eastern cities. As a western publication boasted, "Transport a resident of an Eastern city and put him down in the streets of Portland, and he would observe little difference between his new surroundings and those he beheld but a moment before in his native city."

The history of Portland suggests the common pattern of development. In 1845, Portland was only a clearing in the forest. By the early 1850s, it had grown into a small trading center. As farmers poured into Oregon, the city became a regional commercial center. More permanent structures were built, giving the city an "eastern" appearance.

The belief that urban life in the West abounded with special opportunities initially drew many young men to Portland and other western cities. Many of them did not find financial success there. Opportunities were greatest for newcomers who brought assets with them. These residents became the elite of the community.

CULTURES IN CONFLICT

Looking at westward expansion through the eyes of white emigrants provides only one view of the frontier experience. An entry from an Oregon Trail journal suggests other perspectives. On May 7, 1864, Mary Warner, a bride of only a few months, described a frightening event. That day, a "fine-looking" Indian had visited the wagon train and tried to buy her. Mary's husband, probably uncertain how to handle the situation, played along, agreeing to trade his wife for two ponies. The Indian generously offered three. "Then," wrote Mary, "he took hold of my shawl to make me understand to get out [of the wagon]. About this time I got frightened and really was so hysterical [that] I began to cry." Everyone laughed at her, she reported, though surely the Indian found the whole incident no more amusing than she had. This ordinary encounter on the overland trail only begins to hint at the social and cultural differences separating white Americans moving west and the peoples with whom they came into contact.

Confronting the Plains Tribes

During the 1840s, white Americans first came into extensive contact with the powerful Plains tribes. Probably a quarter million Native Americans occupied the area from the Rocky Mountains to the Missouri River and from the Platte River to New Mexico. Nearest the Missouri and Iowa frontier lived the "border" tribes—the Pawnee, Omaha, Oto, Ponca, and Kansa. These Indians, unlike other Plains tribes, lived in villages and raised crops, though they supplemented their diet with buffalo meat during the summer months. On the Central Plains lived the Brulé and Oglala Sioux, the Cheyenne, the Shoshone, and the Arapaho, aggressive tribes that followed the buffalo and often raided the border tribes. In the Southwest were the Comanche, Ute, Navajo, and some Apache bands, while the Kiowa, Wichita, Apache, and southern Comanche claimed northern and western Texas as their hunting grounds.

Although there were differences among these tribes, they shared certain characteristics. Most had adopted a nomadic way of life after the introduction of horses in the sixteenth century increased their seasonal mobility from 50

Artists were fascinated by Plains Indian life, which they captured in sketches and paintings. Most anticipated that native culture would disappear with the coming of whites to the West.

miles to 500 miles. Horses allowed Indian braves to hunt the buffalo with such success that tribes (with the exclusion of the border groups) came to depend on the beasts for food, clothing, fuel, tepee dwellings, and trading purposes. Because women were responsible for processing buffalo products, some men had more than one wife to tan skins for trading.

Mobility also increased tribal contact and conflict. War played a central part in the lives of the Plains tribes. But tribal warfare was not like the warfare of white men. Indians sought not to exterminate their enemies or to claim territory but rather to steal horses and to prove individual prowess. They considered it braver to touch an enemy than to kill or scalp him.

The Plains tribes, though disunified, posed a fearsome obstacle to white expansion. They had signed no treaties with the United States and had few friendly feelings toward whites. Their contact with white society had brought gains through trade in skins, but the trade had also brought alcohol and destructive epidemics.

When the first emigrants drove their wagons across the plains and prairies in the early 1840s, relations between Indians and whites were peaceable. But the intrusion of whites set in motion an environmental cycle that eventually drew the two groups into conflict. Indian tribes depended on the buffalo and slaughtered only what they needed. Whites, however, adopted the "most exciting sport," the buffalo hunt. As the great herds began to shrink, Native American tribes began to battle one another for hunting grounds and food. In an 1846 petition to President Polk, the Sioux requested compensation for damages caused by whites. When the president denied their request, they tried to extract taxes

Indian Tribes in 1840

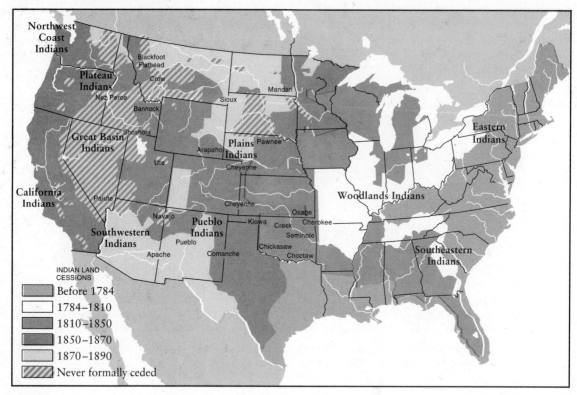

from the emigrants passing over their lands. Emigrants were outraged.

The discovery of gold in California, which lured over 20,000 across the Plains in 1849 alone, became the catalyst for federal action. The vast numbers of gold seekers and their animals wrought such devastation in the Platte valley that it rapidly became a wasteland for the Indians. The dreaded cholera that whites carried with them spread to the Indians, killing thousands.

To meet the crisis, government officials devised a two-pronged plan. The government would construct a chain of forts to protect emigrants and, simultaneously, call the tribes to a general conference. Officials expected that in return for generous presents, Indians would end

tribal warfare and limit their movements to prescribe areas. They instructed tribes to select chiefs to speak for them at the conference.

The Fort Laramie Council, 1851

In 1851, the council convened at Fort Laramie. As many as 10,000 Indians, hopeful of ending the destruction of their way of life and eager for the promised presents, gathered at the fort. Tribal animosities simmered, however. Skirmishes occurred on the way to the fort, and the border tribes, fearful of the Sioux, declined to participate. The Comanche, Kiowa, and Apache also refused to come since their enemies, the Sioux and the Crow, were to be there.

At the conference, whites told the gathered tribes that times had changed. In the past, "you had plenty of buffalo and game ... and your Great Father well knows that war has always been your favorite amusement and pursuit. He then left the question of peace and war to yourselves. Now, since the settling of the districts West of you by the white men, your condition has changed." There would be compensation for the destruction of their grass, timber, and buffalo and annual payments of goods and services. But in return, the tribes had to give up their rights of free movement. The government drew tribal boundaries, and chiefs made promises to stay within them. In most cases, some tribal lands were sold.

The Fort Laramie Treaty was the first agreement between the Plains tribes and the United States government. It expressed the conviction of whites that Indians must stay in clearly defined areas apart from white civilization.

But ominous signs appeared that more trouble would precede any "resolution" of Indian-white affairs. Sioux chief Black Hawk told whites, "You have split the country and I do not like it." His powerful tribe refused to be restricted to lands north of the Platte. In the following years, it would become evident that Americans and Sioux had conflicting interests south of the Platte. Elsewhere in the trans-Mississippi West, other tribes, like the fierce Navajo of New Mexico, also resisted white attempts to confine them.

Overwhelming the Mexicans

In the Southwest, in Texas, and in California, Americans contended with a Spanish-speaking population. Americans regarded Mexicans as lazy, ignorant, and cunning, the "dregs of society." Although Mexicans easily recognized such cultural arrogance, they lacked the numbers to fend off American aggression.

Although Anglo-Mexican interaction differed from place to place, few Anglos heeded the Treaty of Guadalupe Hidalgo's assurances that Mexicans would have citizens' rights and the "free enjoyment of their liberty and property." The greatest numbers of Spanish-speaking people lived in New Mexico, and, of all former Mexican citizens, they probably fared the best. Most were of mixed blood, living marginally as ranch hands for rich landowners or as farmers and herdsmen in small villages dominated by a *patron* or headman. As the century wore on, Americans produced legal titles and took over lands long occupied by peasant farmers and stock raisers. But despite economic reversals, New Mexicans survived, carrying their rural culture well into the twentieth century.

Light-skinned, upper-class landowners fared better. When the United States annexed New Mexico, this substantial and powerful class contracted strategic marriage and business alliances with the Anglo men who slowly trickled into the territory. During the 1850s, they maintained their influence and prestige and their American connections. Only rarely did they bother with the plight of their poor countrymen. Class outweighed ethnic or cultural considerations.

In Texas, the Spanish-speaking residents, only 10 percent of the population in 1840, shrank to a mere 6 percent by 1860. Although the upper class also intermarried with Americans, they lost most of their power as Germans, Irish, French, and Americans poured into the state. Poor, dark-skinned Hispanics clustered in low-paying and largely unskilled jobs.

In California, the discovery of gold radically changed the situation for Hispanic-Americans. In 1848, there were 7,000 Californios and about twice as many Anglos. By 1860, the Anglo population had ballooned to 360,000. Hispanic-Americans were hard pressed to cope with the rapid influx of outsiders.

In 1851, Congress passed the Gwin Land Law, which forced California landowners to defend what was already theirs and encouraged squatters to settle on land in the hopes that the Californios' titles would prove false. It took an average of 17 years to establish clear title to land. A victory at court often turned into a defeat when legal expenses forced owners to sell their lands to pay debts. In the south, where Anglos judged land less valuable than in the mining north, the process of dispossession was slower. But by the early 1860s, the ranching class there had also lost most of its extensive holdings.

Many working-class Hispanic-Americans lived marginal existences in California's growing towns and cities. Others became cowboys on American ranches or lived on their own small ranches in the backcountry. For them, the coming of the Anglos presented not opportunity but oppression. By 1870, the average Hispanic-American worker's property was worth only about a third of its value of 20 years earlier.

As the career of Tiburcio Vásquez, a notorious *bandido* in southern California, suggests, some Hispanics felt that they could protest events only through violence:

> My career grew out of the circumstances by which I was surrounded. . . . As I grew to manhood I was in the habit of attending balls and parties given by the native Californians, into which the Americans, then beginning to become numerous, would force themselves and shove the native born men aside, monopolizing the dance and the women. This was about 1852. A spirit of hatred and revenge took possession of me. I had numerous fights in defense of my countrywomen. The officers were continually in pursuit of me. I believed we were unjustly and wrongfully deprived of the social rights that belonged to us.

What Anglos called crime, Vásquez called self-defense.

CONCLUSION

FRUITS OF MANIFEST DESTINY

Like Lewis Cass, many nineteenth-century Americans were convinced that the country had merely gained western territories to which it was entitled. The expanding nation did gain vast natural wealth in the trans-Mississippi West. But only a small fraction of the hopeful emigrants heading for the frontier realized their dreams of success. And the move west had a dark side as Americans clashed with Mexicans and Native Americans in their drive to fulfill their "Manifest Destiny."

Recommended Reading

Ray Allen Billington gives an overview of the move west in *America's Frontier Heritage* (1966). Gilbert C. Fite treats agriculture in *The Farmer's Frontier, 1865–1900* (1966). The cities of the West are the subject of *The Urban West at the End of the Frontier* (1978) by Lawrence H. Larson.

Frederick Merk explores Manifest Destiny in *Manifest Destiny and Mission in American History* (1963). Robert W. Johanssen treats the Mexican War in *To the Halls of Montezuma: The Mexican War in the American Imagination* (1985). George Pierre Castile treats cultural conflict in

North American Indians: An Introduction to the Chichimeca (1979). Peter Nabakov has edited a collection of Indian responses, *Native American Testimony: An Anthology of Indian and White Relations* (1978).

Julie Roy Jeffrey compensates for the neglect of women in older frontier studies in *Frontier Women: The Trans-Mississippi West, 1840–1880* (1979). Sandra Myres edited women's diaries in *Ho for California! Women's Overland Diaries from the Huntington Library* (1980). See also John D. Unruh, Jr., *The Plains Across: The Overland Emigrants and the Trans-Mississippi West, 1840–1860* (1979). For details of

the mining frontier, consult Rodman W. Paul, *California Gold: The Beginning of Mining in the Far West* (1974). Although there were not many blacks on the frontier, William Loren Katz studies them in *The Black West* (1971). As for the Mormons, see Richard L. Bushman's *Joseph Smith and the Beginnings of Mormonism* (1984). Studies of Mexicans include Leonard Pitt, *The Decline of the Californios: A Social History of the Spanish-Speaking Californians, 1846–1890* (1970); M. S. Meir and Feliciano Rivera, *The Chicanos: A History of Mexican-Americans* (1972); and Alfredo Mirande and Evangeline Enriquez, *La Chicana: The Mexican-American Woman* (1979).

Time Line

Year	Event	Year	Event
1803–1806	Lewis and Clark expedition	1844	James Polk elected president
1818	Treaty on joint U.S.-British occupation of Oregon	1845	"Manifest Destiny" coined United States annexes Texas and sends troops to the Rio Grande Americans attempt to buy Upper California and New Mexico
1819	Spain cedes Spanish territory in United States and sets transcontinental boundary of Louisiana Purchase, excluding Texas	1846	Mexico declares defensive war United States declares war and takes Santa Fe Resolution of Oregon question
1821	Mexican independence Opening of Santa Fe Trail Stephen Austin leads American settlement of Texas	1847	Attacks on Veracruz and Mexico City Mormon migration to Utah begins
1821–1840	Indian removals	1848	Treaty of Guadalupe Hidalgo
1829	Mexico abolishes slavery in Texas	1849	California gold rush begins
1836	Texas declares independence Battles of the Alamo and San Jacinto	1850	California admitted to the Union
1840s	Emigrant crossings of Overland Trail	1851	Fort Laramie Treaty
		1853	Gadsden Purchase
		1862	Homestead Act

chapter 14

The Union in Peril

The election of 1860 confronted Abraham Lincoln and the American people with the most serious crisis since the founding of the Republic. Feeling deeply "the responsibility that was upon me," Lincoln won an unusual four-party election with only 39 percent of the popular vote. He had appealed almost exclusively to northern voters in a blatantly sectional campaign, defeating his three opponents by carrying every free state except New Jersey.

Other Americans sensed the mood of crisis that fall and faced their own fears and responsibilities. A month before the election, plantation owner Robert Allston wrote his oldest son, Benjamin, that "disastrous consequences" would follow from a Lincoln victory. After the election, Allston corresponded with a southern colleague about the need for "an effective military organization" to resist "Northern and Federal aggression." In this shift from sewing machines to military ones, Robert Allston prepared for what he called the "impending crisis."

Frederick Douglass, however, greeted the election with characteristic optimism. "Slaveholders," he said, "know that the day of their power is over when a Republican President is elected." But no sooner had Lincoln's victory been determined than Douglass's hopes turned sour. He noted that Republican leaders, in their desire to keep southern border states from seceding, sounded more antiabolitionist than antislavery. Slavery would, in fact, Douglass bitterly concluded, "be as safe, and safer" with Lincoln than with a Democrat.

Michael Luark, an Iowa farmer, was not so sure. Born in Virginia, Luark was a typically mobile nineteenth-century American. After growing up in Indiana, he followed the mining booms of the 1850s to Colorado and California before returning to the Midwest to farm. Writing in his diary on the last day of 1860, Luark looked ahead to 1861 with a deep sense of fear. "Startling" political changes would occur, he predicted, perhaps even the "Dissolution of the Union and Civil War with all its train of horrors." Within four months of this diary entry, the guns of the Confederate States of America fired on a federal fort in South Carolina, and the Civil War began.

Such a calamitous event had numerous causes, large and small. But as Douglass understood, by 1860 it was clear that "slavery is the real issue, the single bone of contention between all parties and sections."

This chapter analyzes how the momentous issue of slavery disrupted the political system and eventually the Union itself. We will look at how four major developments between 1848 and 1861 contributed to the Civil War: first, a sectional dispute over the extension of slavery into the western territories; second, the breakdown of the political party system; third, growing cultural differences in the views and life styles of southerners and northerners; and fourth, intensifying emotional and ideological polarization between the two regions over losing their way of life and sacred republican rights at the hands of the other. All four of these developments were tied to the central issue of slavery, and the election of Lincoln, the antislavery candidate, was the spark that touched off the conflagration.

SLAVERY IN THE TERRITORIES

The North and the South had managed to contain their differences over slavery, with only occasional difficulties, during the 60 years after the Constitutional Convention. Political compromise in 1787 had resolved the questions of the slave trade and how to count slaves for congressional representation. In 1820, the Missouri Compromise had established a workable way of balancing the admission of free and slave states to the Union and had also defined a geographic line (36°30′) to determine future decisions. In 1833, compromise had defused South Carolina's nullification of the tariff, and the gag rule in 1836 had kept divisive abolitionist petitions to end slavery off the floor of Congress.

One reason these compromises were temporarily successful was the existence of a two-party system with intersectional membership. Whigs and Democrats lived on both sides of the Mason-Dixon line. This changed in the late 1840s with territorial expansion, and the change would prove catastrophic to the Union.

Free Soil or Constitutional Protection?

When the Mexican War broke out in 1846, it seemed likely that the United States would acquire new territories in the Southwest. Would they be slave or free? To an appropriations bill to pay for the war, David Wilmot, a congressman from Pennsylvania, added a short amendment declaring that "neither slavery nor involuntary servitude shall ever exist" in any territories acquired from Mexico. The debates in Congress over the Wilmot Proviso were significant because legislators voted not as Whigs and Democrats but as northerners and southerners.

When the Mexican War ended, several solutions were presented to deal with this question of slavery in the territories. The first was the "free soil" idea of preventing any extensions of slavery. Supporters of "free soil" had mixed motives. For some, slavery was a moral evil. But for many northern white farmers looking to move westward, the threat of economic competition with an expanding system of large-scale slave labor was even more serious. Nor did they wish to compete for land with free blacks. As Wilmot put it, his proviso was intended to preserve the area for "the sons of toil, of my own race and own color." Other northerners resented the "insufferable arrogance" of the "spirit and demands of the Slave Power."

Opposed to the free-soil position were the arguments of Senator John C. Calhoun of South Carolina, expressed in several resolutions introduced in the Senate in 1847. Not only did Congress lack the constitutional right to exclude slavery from the territories, Calhoun argued, but it had a positive duty to protect it. The Wilmot Proviso, therefore, was unconstitutional, as was the Missouri Compromise and any other federal act that prevented slaveholders from taking their slave property into the territories of the United States.

Economic, political, and moral considerations stood behind the Calhoun position. Many southerners hungered for new cotton lands in the West and Southwest. Politically, southerners wanted to protect their institutions against destructive abolitionists. Southern leaders saw the Wilmot Proviso as a moral issue that raised questions about basic republican principles. Senator Robert Toombs of Georgia warned that if Congress passed the proviso, he would favor disunion rather than "degradation."

Popular Sovereignty and the Election of 1848

With such divisive potential, it was natural that many Americans sought a compromise solution to keep slavery out of politics. "Popular sovereignty," as promulgated by Senator Lewis Cass, left the decision of whether to permit slavery in a territory to the local territorial legislature. The Democratic Party, attracted to the idea that popular sovereignty could mean all things to all people, nominated Cass for president in 1848. He denounced abolitionists and the Wilmot Proviso but otherwise avoided the issue of slavery.

The Whigs found an even better way to evade the slavery issue. They nominated the Mexican War hero General Zachary Taylor, a

Louisiana slaveholder, who compared himself to Washington as a "no party" man above politics. This was nearly the only thing he stood for. Southern Whigs supported Taylor because they thought he might understand the burdens of slave-holding, while northern Whigs were pleased that he took no stand on the Wilmot Proviso.

The evasions of the two major parties disappointed Calhoun, who tried to create a new unified southern party. Threatening secession, Calhoun called for a united effort against further attempts to interfere with the southern right to extend slavery, but his effort failed.

Warnings also issued from the North. Disaffected Democrats in New York and "conscience" Whigs from Massachusetts met in Buffalo, New York, to form the Free-Soil party and nominate Martin Van Buren as president. The platform of the new party, composed of an uneasy mixture of ardent abolitionists and racist opponents of free black mobility into western lands, pledged to fight for "free soil, free speech, free labor and free men."

General Taylor won the election largely because defections from Cass in New York and Pennsylvania to the Free-Soilers cost the Democrats the electoral votes from those states. Although weakened, the two-party system survived, and purely sectional parties were prevented.

The Compromise of 1850

Taylor won the election by avoiding slavery issues, but as president he could no longer do so. As he was inaugurated in 1849, four compelling issues faced the nation. The rush of some 80,000 unruly gold miners to California qualified that territory for admission to the Union. But California's entry as a free state would upset the balance between slave and free states in the Senate that had prevailed since 1820.

The unresolved status of the Mexican cession in the Southwest posed a second problem. The boundary between Texas and the New Mexico Territory was also in dispute, with Texas claiming lands all the way to Santa Fe. This increased northern fears that Texas might be divided into five or six slave states.

The existence of slavery and one of the largest slave markets in North America in the nation's capital was a third problem, especially to abolitionists. Fourth, Southerners resented the lax federal enforcement of the Fugitive Slave Act of 1793. They called for a stronger act that would end the protection northerners gave runaway slaves as they fled along the underground railroad to Canada.

Early in 1850, therefore, the old compromiser Henry Clay introduced a series of resolutions in an omnibus package intended to settle these issues once and for all. Despite some 70 speeches on behalf of the compromise, however, the Senate defeated Clay's Omnibus Bill, and the tired and disheartened 73-year-old Clay left

Washington. Into the gap stepped a new compromiser, Senator Stephen Douglas of Illinois, who understood that Clay's resolutions had a better chance of passing if voted on individually rather than as a package. Under Douglas's leadership, and with the support of Millard Fillmore, who succeeded to the presidency upon Taylor's untimely death, a series of bills was finally passed.

The so-called Compromise of 1850 put Clay's resolutions, slightly altered, into law. First, California entered the Union as a free state, upsetting the balance of free and slave states, 16 to 15. Second, the territorial governments of New Mexico and Utah were organized by letting the people of those territories decide for themselves whether to permit slavery. The Texas–New Mexico border was settled in a compromise that denied Texas the disputed area. In turn, the federal government compensated Texas with $10 million to pay off debts owed to Mexico. Third, the slave trade, but not slavery itself,

The Compromise of 1850

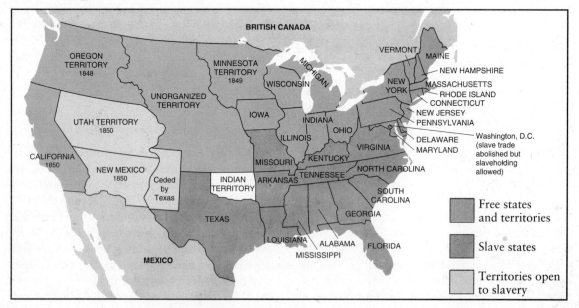

CAUTION!!

COLORED PEOPLE

OF BOSTON, ONE & ALL,

You are hereby respectfully CAUTIONED and advised, to avoid conversing with the

Watchmen and Police Officers of Boston,

For since the recent ORDER OF THE MAYOR & ALDERMEN, they are empowered to act as

KIDNAPPERS

AND

Slave Catchers,

And they have already been actually employed in KIDNAPPING, CATCHING, AND KEEPING SLAVES. Therefore, if you value your LIBERTY, and the *Welfare of the Fugitives* among you, *Shun* them in every possible manner, as so many *HOUNDS* on the track of the most unfortunate of your race.

Keep a Sharp Look Out for KIDNAPPERS, and have TOP EYE open.

APRIL 24, 1851.

THEODORE PARKER'S PLACARD.

Placard written by Theodore Parker and printed and posted by the Vigilance Committee of Boston after the rendition of Thomas Sims to slavery in April, 1851.

The dangers of the Fugitive Slave Act are evident in this 1851 broadside published by Boston abolitionist Theodore Parker, which alerted the city's black community to the dangers posed by the new law.

was abolished in the District of Columbia. Fourth, a strengthened Fugitive Slave Act went into effect; it contained many provisions that offended northerners.

Consequences of Compromise

The Compromise of 1850 was the last attempt to keep slavery out of politics. The intersectional party system was severely tested but for a while was preserved. Douglas celebrated the acts of 1850 as a "final settlement" of the slavery question.

The Compromise, however, only delayed more serious sectional conflict. It added two new ingredients to American politics. The first hinted at the realignment of parties along sectional lines. Second, although repudiated by most ordinary citizens, ideas like secessionism, disunion, and a "higher law" than the Constitution entered more and more into political discourse.

The new fugitive slave law angered many northerners because it brought the evils of slavery right into their midst, compelling northerners to turn in runaways. The owners of escaped slaves hired agents, labeled "kidnappers" in the North, to hunt down fugitives. Ralph Waldo Emerson said it was "a filthy law" that he would not obey.

Frederick Douglass would not obey it either. As a runaway slave himself, he was threatened with arrest and return to the South until friends overcame his objections and purchased his freedom. Arguing the "rightfulness of forcible resistance," he urged free blacks to arm themselves and even wondered whether it was justifiable to kill kidnappers. Douglass raised money for black fugitives, hid runaways in his home, and helped hundreds escape to Canada. Other northerners, white as well as black, increased their work for the underground railroad in response to the fugitive slave law.

Douglass and others also spoke out on the wrongs of slavery. In an Independence Day speech in 1852, Douglass wondered, "What, to the American slave, is your 4th of July?" It was, he said, the day that revealed to the slave "the gross injustice and cruelty to which he is the constant victim." To a slave, the American claims of national greatness were vain and empty; the "shouts of liberty and equality" were "hollow mockery." Douglass's speeches, like those of another ex-slave, Sojourner Truth, took on an increasingly strident tone in the early 1850s.

At a women's rights convention in Akron, Ohio, in 1851, Truth made one of the decade's boldest statements for minority rights. The convention was attended by clergymen, who kept interrupting the proceedings to heckle female speakers. Up stood Sojourner Truth. She pointed to her many years of childbearing and hard, backbreaking work as a slave, crying out in a repetitive refrain, "And ar'n't I a woman?" Referring to Jesus, she asked where he came from: "From God and a woman: Man had nothing to do with Him." Referring to Eve, she concluded, "If the first woman God ever made was strong enough to turn the world upside down all alone, these women together ought to be able to turn it back, and get it right side up again! And now they is asking to do it, the men better let them." Her brief speech silenced the hecklers.

As Truth spoke, another American woman, Harriet Beecher Stowe, was finishing a novel, *Uncle Tom's Cabin*. Stowe's novel gave readers an absorbing indictment of the horrors of slavery and its immoral impact on both northerners and southerners. The book was published initially in serial form, and each month's chapter ended at a nail-biting dramatic moment. Readers throughout the North cheered Eliza's daring escape across the ice floes on the Ohio River, cried over Uncle Tom's humanity and Little Eva's death, suffered under the lash of Simon Legree, and rejoiced in the reuniting of black family members. When published in full in 1852, *Uncle Tom's Cabin* became one of the all-time best-sellers in American history.

POLITICAL DISINTEGRATION

The response to *Uncle Tom's Cabin* and the Fugitive Slave Act indicated that politicians had congratulated themselves too soon for saving the Republic in 1850. Political developments, not all dealing with slavery, were already weakening the ability of political parties—and ultimately the nation—to withstand the passions slavery aroused.

The Apathetic Election of 1852

Political parties must convince voters that their party stands for moral values and economic policies crucially different from those of the opposition. In the period between 1850 and 1854, these differences were blurred, thereby undermining party loyalty. First, both parties scrambled to convince voters that they had favored the Compromise of 1850. In addition, several states rewrote their constitutions and remodeled their laws in the early 1850s, standardizing many political and economic procedures. One effect of these changes was to reduce the number of patronage jobs available for party victors to dispense. Another effect was to regularize the process, begun in the 1830s, for securing banking, railroad, and other corporate charters, removing the role formerly played by the legislature. Both of these weakened the importance of the party in citizens' lives.

The third development that weakened parties was economic. During the prosperity of the early 1850s, party distinctions over economic policies seemed less important. Economic issues persisted, but the battles were fought at the local rather than national level. Around such issues as temperance, free blacks, taxes for internal improvements, and a ten-hour working day, local politicians formed fleeting alliances. As a Baltimore businessman said, "The two old parties are fast melting away."

The election of 1852 illustrated the lessening significance of political parties. After 52 ballots, the Whigs nominated General Winfield Scott, another Mexican War hero. Democrats had their own problems deciding on a candidate. After 49 ballots, in which Cass, Douglas, and James Buchanan each held the lead for a time, the party turned to the lackluster Franklin Pierce of New Hampshire as a compromise candidate.

The two parties offered little choice. The

Baltimore *Sun* remarked that "there is no issue that much interests the people." Democratic prospects were aided by thousands of new Catholic immigrants from Ireland and Germany. Party officials often bought their votes with bribes and drinks. Internal conflicts and defections seriously weakened the Whigs, and Pierce won easily, 254 to 42 electoral votes.

The Kansas-Nebraska Act

The Whig party's final disintegration came on a February day in 1854 when southern Whigs stood to support Stephen Douglas's Nebraska bill, thus choosing to be more southern than Whig. The Illinois senator had many reasons for introducing a bill organizing the Nebraska Territory (which included Kansas). As an ardent nationalist and chairman of the Committee on Territories, he was concerned for the continuing development of the West. As an Illinoisan in a period of explosive railroad building, he wanted the eastern terminus for a transcontinental railroad in Chicago rather than in rival St. Louis. This meant organizing the lands west of Iowa and Missouri. Douglas also wanted to recapture the party leadership he had held when he led the fight to pass the Compromise of 1850, and he harbored presidential ambitions.

The entire Nebraska Territory lay north of the line where slavery had been prohibited by the Missouri Compromise. But Douglas's bill, introduced early in 1854, recommended using the principle of popular sovereignty in organizing the Kansas and Nebraska territories. This meant that inhabitants could vote slavery in, thereby violating the Missouri Compromise. Douglas reasoned, however, that the climate and soil of the prairies in Kansas and Nebraska would never support slavery-based agriculture, and the people would decide to be a free state. Therefore, he could win the votes he needed for the railroad without also getting slavery.

Douglas miscalculated. Northerners from his own party immediately attacked him and his bill as a "criminal betrayal of precious rights."

The outrage among Whigs and abolitionists was even greater.

But Stephen Douglas was a fighter. The more he was attacked, the harder he fought. Eventually his bill passed, but not without seriously damaging the political party system. What began as a railroad measure ended in reopening the question of slavery in the territories that Douglas and others had thought finally settled in 1850. What began as a way of avoiding conflict ended up in violence. What began as a way of strengthening party lines ended up destroying one party (the Whigs), planting deep, irreconcilable divisions in another (the Democrats), and creating two new ones (Know-Nothings and Republicans).

Expansionist "Young America"

The Democratic Party was weakened in the early 1850s not only by the Kansas-Nebraska Act but also by an ebullient, expansive energy that led Americans to adventures far beyond Kansas. As republican revolutions erupted in Europe in 1848, Americans greeted them as evidence that the American model of free republican institutions was the wave of the future. Those dedicated to the idea of this continuing national mission, which ironically included the spread of slavery, were called "Young America."

President Pierce's platform in 1852 recalled the successful expansionism of the Polk years, declaring that the Mexican War had been "just and necessary." Many Democrats took their overwhelming victory as a mandate to continue adding territory to the Republic. Pierce's ambassador to Mexico, for example, James Gadsden, tried without success to purchase large parts of Mexico. But he did manage to purchase a strip of desert along the southwest border in order to build a transcontinental railroad linking the Deep South with the Pacific Coast.

The failure to acquire more territory from Mexico legally did not discourage expansionist Americans from pursuing illegal means. During the 1850s, Texans and Californians staged dozens of raids (called "filibusters") into Mexico. The most daring adventurer of the era was William Walker, a 100-pound Tennesseean with a zest for danger and power. After migrating to southern California, Walker made plans to add slave lands to the country. In 1853, he invaded Lower California with fewer than 300 men and declared himself president of the independent Republic of Sonora. Although eventually arrested and tried in the United States, he was acquitted after eight minutes of deliberation. He later took it upon himself to invade Nicaragua. Walker came to a fitting end in 1860 when he was captured and shot by a Honduran firing squad after invading that country.

Undaunted by failures in the Southwest, the Pierce administration looked more seriously to the acquisition of Cuba, a Spanish colony many Americans thought destined to be a part of their country. Secretary of State William Marcy instructed the emissary to Spain, Pierre Soulé, to offer $130 million for Cuba. If that failed, Marcy suggested stronger measures. In 1854, the secretary arranged for Soulé and the American ministers to France and England to meet in Belgium to consider options. The result was the Ostend Manifesto, a document intended to pressure Spain to sell Cuba to the United States.

The manifesto argued that Cuba "belongs naturally" to the United States. Both geographically and economically, the fortunes and interests of Cubans and southerners were so "blended" that they were "one people with one destiny." Trade and commerce in the hemisphere would "never be secure" until Cuba was part of the United States.

If Spain refused to sell the island, the ministers threatened a revolution in Cuba with American support. If that should fail, the manifesto warned, "we should be justified in wresting it from Spain." Even Secretary Marcy was shocked when he received the document from Belgium, and he quickly rejected it. Like the Kansas-Nebraska Act, the Ostend Manifesto was urged most by Democrats who advocated the expansion of slavery. The outraged reaction of northerners in both cases divided and further weakened the Democratic Party.

Nativism, Know-Nothings, and Republicans

Foreign immigration damaged an already enfeebled Whig Party and created concern among many native-born Americans. To the average hard-working Protestant American, the foreigners pouring into the cities and following the railroads westward spoke unfamiliar languages, wore funny clothes, drank alcohol freely in grogshops, and increased crime and pauperism. Still worse, they attended Catholic churches, sent children to their own schools, and worked for lower wages in worse conditions than American workers. Perhaps worst of all, these nativists said, the new immigrants corrupted American politics.

Catholic immigrants preferred the Democratic Party out of traditional loyalties and because Democrats were less inclined than Whigs to interfere with religion, schooling, drinking, and other aspects of personal behavior. It was mostly former Whigs, therefore, who in 1854 founded the American Party to oppose the new immigrants. Members wanted a longer period of naturalization and pledged themselves never to vote for Irish Catholics for public office since it was assumed that their highest loyalty was to the pope in Rome. They also agreed to keep information about their order secret. If asked, they would say, "I know nothing." Hence, they were dubbed the Know-Nothing Party.

The Know-Nothings were overwhelmingly a party of the middle and lower classes, workers who worried about their jobs and wages, and farmers and small-town Americans who worried about disruptive new forces in their lives. In the 1854 and 1855 elections, the Know-Nothings gave anti-Catholicism a national political focus for the first time. They did so well that they

The American (Know-Nothing) Party campaign against the immigrants is dramatically shown in this cartoon of a whiskey-drinking Irishman and beer-barreled German stealing the ballot box while native-born Americans fight at the election poll in the background.

threatened to replace the Whigs as the second major party.

Meanwhile, a group of ex-Whigs and Free-Soilers met and formed the nucleus of another new party, called the Republican Party. Its first challenge was to respond to popular sentiments by mobilizing sectional fears and ethnic and religious concerns.

Composed almost entirely of northerners, former "conscience" Whigs, and disaffected Democrats, the Republican Party combined four main elements. The first group sought to prohibit slavery in the territories and to repeal the Fugitive Slave Act. A more moderate and larger group, typified by Abraham Lincoln of Illinois, opposed slavery in the western territories but indicated that they would not interfere with it where it already existed.

A third element of the party was anti-Catholic, reflecting the traditional Whig position. The fourth element wanted the federal government to promote commercial and industrial development and the dignity of labor. This fourth group, which Lincoln was in as well, believed that a system of free labor led to progress. As the Springfield *Republican* said in 1856, the Republican Party's strength came from "those who work with their hands, who live and act independently, who hold the stakes of home and family, of farm and workshop, of education and freedom—these as a mass are enrolled in the Republican ranks."

The strengths of the Republican and Know-Nothing (American) parties were tested in 1856. Which party could best oppose the Democrats? The American Party nominated Fillmore, who had strong support in the Upper South and border states. The Republicans chose John C. Frémont, a Free-Soiler from Missouri with virtually no political experience. The Democrats nominated James Buchanan of Pennsylvania, commonly known as "a northern man with southern principles." Frémont won several free states, while Fillmore won only Maryland. Buchanan, taking advantage of the divided opposition, won the election, but with only 45 percent of the popular vote. After 1856, the Know-Nothings died out, but nativism did not.

KANSAS AND THE TWO CULTURES

As slaveholders sought ways of expanding slavery westward across the Plains and south into Cuba in the mid-1850s, Republicans wanted to halt the advance of slavery. In 1854, Lincoln worried that it was slavery that "deprives our republican example of its just influence in the world."

Competing for Kansas

Lincoln was concerned about the passage of the Kansas-Nebraska Act in 1854, which opened the way for proslavery and antislavery forces to meet physically and to compete over whether Kansas would become a slave or free state. No sooner had the bill passed Congress than Eli Thayer founded the Massachusetts Emigrant Aid Society to recruit Free-Soil settlers to go to Kansas. From New York, Frederick Douglass called for "companies of emigrants from the free states . . . to possess the goodly land." By the summer of 1855, about 1,200 New England colonists had migrated to Kansas.

David Atchison, Democratic senator from Missouri, believed that Congress had an obligation to protect slavery in the territories, thereby permitting Missouri slaveholders to move into Kansas. He described New England migrants as "negro thieves" and "abolition tyrants." He recommended to fellow Missourians that they defend their property and interests "with the *bayonet* and with *blood*" and, if need be, "to kill every God-damned abolitionist in the district."

Under Atchison's inflammatory leadership, secret societies sprang up in the Missouri counties adjacent to Kansas. They vowed to combat the Free-Soilers. Rumors of 20,000 Massachusetts migrants spurred Missourians to action. Thousands poured across the border late in 1854 to vote in the first territorial election. Twice as many ballots were cast as the number of registered voters, and in one polling place only 20 of over 600 voters were legal residents.

In March 1855, a second election was held to select a territorial legislature. The pattern of border crossings, intimidation, and illegal voting was repeated. Atchison himself, drinking "considerable whiskey" along the way, led a band of armed men across the state line to vote and frighten would-be Free-Soil voters away. Not surprisingly, a small minority of eligible voters elected a proslavery territorial legislature. Free-Soilers, meanwhile, staged their own constitutional convention in Lawrence and created a Free-Soil government at Topeka. It banned blacks from the state. The proslavery legislature settled in Lecompton, giving Kansas two governments.

Neither President Pierce nor Congress could do anything except send an investigating committee, which further inflamed passions. Throughout 1855, the call to arms grew more strident. One proslavery newspaper invited southerners to bring their weapons and "send the scoundrels" from the North "back to whence they came, or . . . to hell, it matters not which." At Yale University, the noted minister Henry Ward Beecher presented Bibles and rifles to young men who would go fight for the Lord in Kansas. Missourians dubbed the rifles "Beecher's Bibles" and vowed, as one newspaper put it, "Blood for Blood! . . . for each drop spilled, we shall require one hundred fold!"

"Bleeding Kansas"

Inevitably, blood flowed in Kansas. In May 1856, supported by a prosouthern federal Marshall, a mob entered Lawrence, smashed the offices and presses of a Free-Soil newspaper, fired several cannonballs into the Free State Hotel,

"Bleeding Kansas"

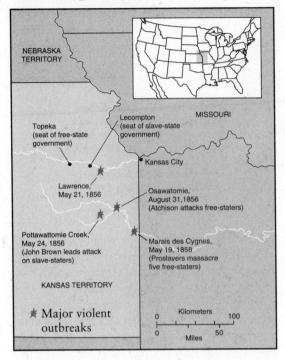

NEBRASKA TERRITORY

MISSOURI

Topeka (seat of free-state government)

Lecompton (seat of slave-state government)

Kansas City

Lawrence, May 21, 1856

Osawatomie, August 31, 1856 (Atchison attacks free-staters)

Pottawattomie Creek, May 24, 1856 (John Brown leads attack on slave-staters)

Marais des Cygnes, May 19, 1858 (Proslavers massacre five free-staters)

KANSAS TERRITORY

★ Major violent outbreaks

Kilometers
0   100

0   50
Miles

and destroyed homes and shops. Three nights later, motivated by vengeance and a feeling that he was doing God's will, John Brown led a small New England band, including four of his sons, to a proslavery settlement near Pottawatomie Creek. There they dragged five men out of their cabins and despite the terrified entreaties of their wives, hacked them to death with swords.

Violence also entered the halls of Congress. That same week, abolitionist senator Charles Sumner accused proslavery Senate leaders, especially Atchison and Andrew Butler of South Carolina, of cavorting with "the harlot, Slavery." Two days later, Butler's nephew, Congressman Preston Brooks, avenged the honor of his colleague by beating Sumner senseless with his cane as he sat at his Senate desk.

The sack of Lawrence, the massacre at Pottawatomie Creek, and the caning of Sumner set off a minor civil war, which historians have called "Bleeding Kansas." It lasted throughout the summer. Crops were burned, homes were destroyed, fights broke out in saloons and streets, and night raiders tortured and murdered their enemies. For residents like Charles Lines, who just wanted to farm his land in peace, it was impossible to remain neutral. Lines hoped his neighbors near Lawrence would avoid "involving themselves in trouble." But when proslavery forces seized a mild-mannered neighbor, bound him, tortured him, and left him to die, Lines joined the battle. He wrote to a friend that "blood must end in the triumph of the right."

Even before the bleeding of Kansas began, the New York *Tribune* warned, "We are two peoples. We are a people for Freedom and a people for Slavery. Between the two, conflict is inevitable." The competing visions of two separate cultures for the future destiny of the United States were at stake.

Northern Views and Visions

The North saw itself as a prosperous land of bustling commerce and expanding, independent agriculture. Northern farmers and workers were typically self-made men who believed that individualism, equality of opportunity, and government support for free labor and industrial growth would lead to economic progress. Although the North contained many growing cities, northerners revered the values of the small towns that spread from New England across the Upper Midwest. These values included a respect for the rights of the people, tempered by the rule of law; individual enterprise, balanced by a concern for one's neighbors; and a fierce morality rooted in Calvinist Protestantism. Many northerners would regulate morality—by persuasion if possible but by legislation if necessary—to remove the sins of irreligion, illiteracy, and intemperance from American society. It was no accident that the ideas of universal public education and laws against the sale and consumption of alcohol both began in New England.

BORDER RUFFIANS "GOING OVER TO WIPE OUT LAWRENCE."

Led by Senator David Atchison, thousands of gun-toting Missourians crossed into Kansas in 1854 and 1855 in order to vote illegally for a proslavery territorial government. The ensuing bloodshed made Kansas a preview of the Civil War.

Most northerners also believed that only free men could achieve economic progress and moral society. Therefore, the worst sin in the northerner's view was the loss of one's freedom. Slavery was the root of all evil, and for many, the South represented the antithesis of everything that northerners saw as good. Northern migrants to Kansas described southerners as subhuman, unclean, and uncivilized. They were, as one put it, "drunken ourang-outans," "wild beasts" who drank whiskey, ate dirt, uttered oaths, raped slave women, and fought or dueled at the slightest excuse. In the popular language of the day, they were known as "Pukes."

The Southern Perspective

Epithets aside, southerners were a diverse people who, like northerners, shared certain broad values, generally those of the planter class. If in the North the values of economic enterprise were most important, southerners revered social values most. Like the English gentry they sought to emulate, they saw themselves as courteous, refined, hospitable, and chivalrous. By contrast, they saw northerners as coarse, ill-mannered, aggressive, materialistic "Yankees." In a society

where one person in three was a black slave, racial distinctions and paternalistic relationships were crucial in maintaining order and white supremacy. Fear of slave revolt was ever present. The South had five times more military schools than the North. Northerners educated the many for economic utility, but southerners educated the few for grace and character. In short, the South saw itself as a genteel, ordered society guided by the aristocratic code of the gentleman planter.

Southerners believed that the democratic principle of self-government was best preserved in local political units such as the state. They cherished the Union but preferred the loose confederacy of the Jeffersonian past to the centralized nationalism New York senator William Seward kept invoking.

Two images dominated the South's view of northerners: either they were stingy, hypocritical, moralizing Puritans, or they were grubby, slum-dwelling, Catholic immigrants.

Each side, then, saw the other threatening its freedom and infringing on its view of a proper republican society. As hostilities increased, the views each section had of the other grew steadily more rigid and conspiratorial. Northerners saw the South as a "slave power," determined to foist the slave system on free labor throughout the land. Southerners saw the North as full of "black Republicanism," determined to destroy the southern way of life.

POLARIZATION AND THE ROAD TO WAR

Because of the national constituencies of the two major political parties, northern and southern cultural stereotypes and conspiratorial accusations had been largely held in check. But events in Kansas solidified the image of the Republicans as a northern party and seriously weakened the Democrats. Further events, still involving the question of slavery in the territories, soon split the Democratic Party irrevocably into sectional halves: the *Dred Scott* decision of the Supreme Court (1857), the constitutional crisis in Kansas (1857), the Lincoln-Douglas debates in Illinois (1858), John Brown's raid in Virginia (1859), and Lincoln's election (1860). These incidents also further polarized the two cultures and set the nation on the final road to civil war.

The *Dred Scott* Case

The events of 1857 reinforced the arguments of those who believed in a slave power conspiracy. Two days after James Buchanan's inauguration, the Supreme Court finally ruled in *Dred Scott* v. *Sandford*. The case had been pending before the Court for nearly three years, but the slave family of Dred Scott had been waiting longer for the decision. In 1846, Dred and Harriet Scott had filed suit in Missouri for their freedom. They argued that their master had taken them into Minnesota, Wisconsin, and other territories where the Missouri Compromise prohibited slavery, and therefore they should be freed.

When the Court, which had a majority of southern judges, issued its decision, by a vote of 7 to 2, it made three rulings. First, since blacks were, as Chief Justice Roger Taney put it, "be-ings of an inferior order [who] had no rights which white men were bound to respect," Dred Scott was not a citizen and had no right to sue in federal courts. The second ruling stated that the Missouri Compromise was unconstitutional because Congress did not have the power to ban slavery in a territory. And third, the fact that the Scotts had been taken in and out of free states did not affect their status. Despite two eloquent dissenting opinions, Dred and Harriet Scott remained slaves.

The implications of these decisions went far beyond the Scotts' personal freedom. The arguments about black citizenship insulted and infuriated many northerners. Even more troublesome was the possibility hinted at in the decision that slavery might be permitted in the free states of the North, where it had long been banned. One issue that remained unresolved by the Court was whether or not a territorial legislature could write a constitution that permitted the introduction of new slaves.

Douglas and the Democrats

The *Dred Scott* decision, endorsed by Buchanan, fed northern suspicions of a slave power conspiracy to impose slavery everywhere. Events in Kansas, which still had two governments, heightened these fears. In the summer of 1857, Kansas had still another election, called by the proslavery legislature at Lecompton. Free-Soldiers refused to vote, charging gross irregularities in drawing district boundaries, so that only 2,000 out of a possible 24,000 voters participated. They elected a proslavery slate of delegates to a constitutional convention meeting at Lecompton as a preparation for statehood. The convention decided to exclude free blacks from the state, to guarantee the property rights of the few slaveholders in Kansas, and to ask voters to decide in a referendum whether to permit more slaves.

The proslavery Lecompton constitution,

clearly unrepresentative of the wishes of the majority of the people of Kansas, was sent to Congress for approval. Eager to retain the support of southern Democrats, Buchanan endorsed it. Stephen Douglas, a northern Democrat, opposed it. Congress sent the Lecompton constitution back to the people of Kansas for another referendum. This time they defeated it, which meant that Kansas remained a territory rather than becoming a slave state. While Kansas was left in an uncertain status, the larger political effect of the struggle was to split the Democratic party almost beyond repair.

Lincoln and the Illinois Debates

No sooner had Douglas settled the Lecompton question than he faced reelection in Illinois in 1858. Opposing him was Abraham Lincoln, who had emerged to challenge William Seward for leadership of the Republican Party. Lincoln's character was shaped on the midwestern frontier, where he had educated himself, developed antislavery views, and dreamed of America's greatness.

Since Douglas was clearly the leading Democrat, the Senate election in Illinois appeared to be a preview of the presidential election of 1860. The Illinois campaign featured a series of seven debates between Lincoln and Douglas in different cities. With a national as well as a local audience, the debates provided a remarkable opportunity for the two men to state their views on the heated racial issues before the nation.

Lincoln set a solemn tone when he accepted the Republican senatorial nomination in Chicago in June. The American nation, he said, was in a "crisis" and building toward a worse one: "A House divided against itself cannot stand. I believe this government cannot endure, permanently half *slave* and half *free*." Lincoln said he did not expect the Union "to be dissolved" or "the house to fall" but rather that "it will become *all* one thing, or *all* the other." In the ensuing debates with Douglas, Lincoln skillfully staked out a moral position not only in advance of Douglas but well ahead of his time.

Lincoln was also very much a part of his time. He believed that whites were superior to blacks and opposed equal rights for free blacks. He believed, furthermore, that the physical and moral differences between whites and blacks would "forever forbid the two races from living together on terms of social and political equality." However, he not only believed that blacks were "entitled to all the natural rights ... in the Declaration of Independence" but also that they had many specific economic rights as well, like "the right to put into his mouth the bread that his own hands have earned." In these rights, blacks were, Lincoln said, "my equal and the equal of Judge Douglas, and the equal of every living man."

Unlike Douglas, Lincoln hated slavery. At Galesburg, he said, "I contemplate slavery as a moral, social, and political evil." In Quincy, he said that the difference between a Republican and a Democrat was quite simply whether one thought slavery wrong or right. Douglas advocated "popular sovereignty," the doctrine that the people of a territory should have the right to determine whether they wanted to permit slavery or not. Douglas's moral indifference to slavery was clear in his admission that he did not care if a territorial legislature voted it "up or down." Republicans did care, Lincoln affirmed, sounding a warning that by stopping the expansion of slavery, the course toward its "ultimate extinction" had begun.

Douglas won the election. When he and Lincoln met again two years later, the order of their finish would be reversed. Elsewhere in 1858, however, Democrats did poorly, losing 18 congressional seats to the Republicans.

John Brown's Raid

The slavery issue grew more heated on October 16, 1859, when John Brown and a band of 22

This 1860 photograph of Lincoln shows him without the look of strain and overwhelming stress commonly seen in photographs taken during the Civil War.

men attacked a federal arsenal at Harpers Ferry, Virginia (now West Virginia). He hoped that the action might provoke a general uprising of slaves throughout the Upper South or at least provide the arms by which slaves could make their way to freedom. Although he seized the arsenal, federal troops soon overcame him. Nearly half his men were killed, including two sons. Brown himself was captured, tried, and hanged for treason. So ended a lifetime of failures.

In death, however, he was not a failure. Brown's daring if foolhardy raid, and his impressively dignified behavior during his trial and speedy execution, unleashed powerful passions, further widening the gap between North and South. Northerners responded to his death with an outpouring of admiration and sympathy, for both the man and his cause. But many southerners concluded that northerners would stop at nothing, including armed force, to free the slaves. Brown's raid stimulated a wave of fear and suspicion. In response to the Brown raid, southerners also became more convinced, as the governor of South Carolina put it, that a "black Republican" plot in the North was "arrayed against the slaveholders."

The Election of 1860

The conflict between Buchanan and Douglas took its toll on the Democratic Party. When the nominating convention met in Charleston, South Carolina, a hotbed of secessionist sentiments, it met for a record ten days without being able to name a presidential candidate. The Democrats went through 59 ballots, adjourned, and then met again, acknowledging their irreparable division by naming two candidates. Douglas represented northern Democrats, and John C. Breckinridge, Buchanan's vice president, carried the banner of the proslavery South. The Constitutional Union Party, made up of former southern Whigs and border-state nativists, claimed the middle ground of compromise and nominated John Bell, a slaveholder from Tennessee with mild views.

With Democrats split in two and a new party in contention, the Republican strategy aimed at keeping the states carried by Frémont in 1856 and adding Pennsylvania, Illinois, and Indiana. Lincoln, a moderate midwesterner with widespread appeal, won his party's nomination.

The Republican platform also reflected moderation, reducing attacks on slavery to oppose only its extension. Most of the platform spoke to the concerns of the several elements of the party: tariff protection, subsidized internal improvements, free labor, and a homestead bill. Above all, the Republicans, like southern Democrats, defended their view of what republican values meant for America's future. It did not include the kind of society of equal rights envisioned by Frederick Douglass. An English traveler in 1860 observed that in America "we see, in effect, two nations—one white and another black—growing up together within the same political circle, but never mingling on a principle of equality."

The Republican strategy for electoral victory worked exactly as planned, as Lincoln swept the entire Northeast and Midwest. Although he received less than 40 percent of the popular vote nationwide, his triumph in the North was decisive. Even a united Democratic Party could not have defeated him. With victory assured, Lincoln prepared for the consequences and awesome responsibilities of his election. They came even before his inauguration.

THE DIVIDED HOUSE FALLS

The Republicans overestimated the extent of Unionist sentiment in the South. They could not believe that the secessionists would prevail after Lincoln's victory. A year earlier, some southern congressmen had walked out in protest of the selection of an antislavery speaker of the House. A Republican leader, Carl Schurz, recalling this act, said that the southerners had taken a drink and then come back. After Lincoln's election, Schurz predicted, they would walk out, take two drinks, and come back again. He was wrong.

Secession and Uncertainty

On December 20, 1860, South Carolina seceded from the Union, declaring the "experiment" of putting people with "different pursuits and institutions" under one government a failure. By February 1, the other six Deep South states (Mississippi, Florida, Alabama, Georgia, Louisiana, and Texas) had seceded. A week later, delegates met in Montgomery, Alabama, created the Confederate States of America, adopted a consti-

tution, and elected Jefferson Davis, a Mississippi senator and cotton planter, its provisional president. The divided house had fallen, as Lincoln had predicted it would.

The nation waited and watched, wondering what Virginia and the border states would do, what outgoing President Buchanan would do, and what Congress would do. Buchanan did nothing, and so the entire nation waited for Abraham Lincoln.

Frederick Douglass waited too, without much hope. Seeing northern politicians and businessmen "granting the most demoralizing concessions to the Slave Power," Douglass began to explore possibilities for emigration and colonization in Haiti, an idea he had long opposed. In February, Douglass said, "Let the conflict come." He opposed all compromises, hoping that with Lincoln's inauguration in March it would "be decided, and decided forever, which of the two, Freedom or Slavery, shall give law to this Republic."

Lincoln and Fort Sumter

As Douglass penned these thoughts, Lincoln began a long, slow train ride from Springfield, Illinois, to Washington, writing and rewriting his inaugural address. Lincoln was firmly opposed to secession and to any compromises with the principle of stopping the extension of slavery. He would neither conciliate secessionist southern states nor force their return.

But Lincoln believed in his constitutional responsibility to uphold the laws of the land, and on this significant point he would not yield. The focus of his attention was a federal fort in the harbor of Charleston, South Carolina. Major Robert Anderson, the commander of Fort Sumter, was running out of provisions and had requested new supplies from Washington. Lincoln would enforce the laws and protect federal property at Fort Sumter.

Table 14.1

Major Causes of and Events Leading to the Civil War

DATE	EVENT	IMPACT OR EFFECT AS CAUSE OF CIVIL WAR
1600s–1860s	Slavery in the South	Major underlying pervasive cause
1700s–1860s	Development of two distinct socioeconomic systems and cultures	Further reinforced slavery as fundamental socioeconomic, cultural, moral issue
1787–1860s	States' rights, nullification doctrine	Ongoing political issue, less fundamental as cause
1820	Missouri Compromise (36°30′)	Background for conflict over slavery in territories
1828–1833	South Carolina tariff nullification crisis	Background for secession leadership in South Carolina
1831–1860s	Antislavery movements, southern justification	30 years of emotional preparation for conflict
1846–1848	Mexican War (Wilmot Proviso, Calhoun, popular sovereignty)	Options for slavery in territories issue
1850	Compromise of 1850	Temporary and unsatisfactory "settlement" of divisive issue
1851–1854	Fugitive slaves returned and rescued in North; personal liberty laws passed in North; Harriet Beecher Stowe's *Uncle Tom's Cabin*	Heightened northern emotional reactions against the South and slavery
1852–1856	Breakdown of Whig Party and national Democratic Party; creation of a new party system with sectional basis	Made national politics an arena where sectional and cultural differences over slavery were fought
1854	Ostend Manifesto and other expansionist efforts in Central America	Reinforced image of Democratic Party as favoring slavery
	Formation of Republican party	Major party identified as opposing the expansion of slavery
	Kansas-Nebraska Act	Reopened "settled" issue of slavery in the territories
1856	"Bleeding Kansas"; Senator Sumner physically attacked in Senate	Foretaste of civil war (200 killed, $2 million in property lost) inflamed emotions and polarized North and South

(continued)

Table 14.1 (continued)

Major Causes of and Events Leading to the Civil War

DATE	EVENT	IMPACT OR EFFECT AS CAUSE OF CIVIL WAR
1857	*Dred Scott* decision; proslavery Lecompton constitution in Kansas	Made North fear a "slave power conspiracy," supported by President Buchanan and the Supreme Court
1858	Lincoln-Douglas debates in Illinois; Democrats lose 18 seats in Congress	Set stage for election of 1860
1859	John Brown's raid and reactions in North and South	Made South fear a "black Republican" plot against slavery; further polarization and irrationality
1860	Democratic party splits in half; Lincoln elected president; South Carolina secedes from Union	Final breakdown of national parties and election of "northern" president; no more compromises
1861	Six more southern states secede by February 1; Confederate constitution adopted February 4; Lincoln inaugurated March 4; Fort Sumter attacked April 12	Civil War begins

As the new president rose to deliver his inaugural address on March 4, he faced a tense and divided nation. Federal troops, fearing a Confederate attack on the nation's capital, were everywhere. Lincoln asserted his unequivocal intention to enforce the laws of the land, arguing that the Union was constitutionally "perpetual" and indissoluble. He reminded the nation that the "only substantial dispute" was that "one section of our country believes slavery is *right,* and ought to be extended, while the other believes it is *wrong,* and ought not to be extended." Still hoping to appeal to Unionist strength among southern moderates, Lincoln indicated that he would make no attempts to interfere with existing slavery or the law to return fugitive slaves. He urged against rash actions and put the burden of initiating a civil war on the "dissatisfied fellow-countrymen" who had seceded. His deepest hope was that

the mystic chords of memory, stretching from every battlefield, and patriot grave, to every living heart and hearthstone, all over this broad land, will yet swell the chorus of the Union, when again touched, as surely they will be, by the better angels of our nature.

On April 6, Lincoln notified the governor of South Carolina that he was sending "provisions only" to Fort Sumter. No effort would be made "to throw in men, arms, or ammunition" unless the fort were attacked. On April 10, Jefferson Davis directed General P. G. T. Beauregard to demand the surrender of Fort Sumter. Davis told Beauregard to reduce the fort if Major Anderson refused.

On April 12, as Lincoln's relief expedition neared Charleston, Beauregard's batteries began shelling Fort Sumter, and the Civil War began. Frederick Douglass was about to leave for Haiti when he heard the news. He immediately changed his plans: "This is no time . . . to leave the country." He announced his readiness to help end the war by aiding the Union to organize freed slaves "into a liberating army" to "make war upon . . . the savage barbarism of slavery." Benjamin Allston, who was in Charleston, described the events to his father. On April 14, he reported exuberantly "the glorious, and astonishing news that Sumter has fallen." With it fell America's divided house.

CONCLUSION

THE "IRREPRESSIBLE CONFLICT"

Lincoln had been right. The nation could no longer endure half slave and half free. The collision between North and South, William Seward said, was not an "accidental, unnecessary" event but "an irrepressible conflict between opposing and enduring forces." Those forces had been at work for many decades but developed with increasing intensity after 1848 in the conflict over the question of the extension of slavery into the territories. Although economic, cultural, political, constitutional, and emotional forces all contributed to the developing opposition between North and South, slavery was the fundamental, enduring force that underlay all others, causing what poet Walt Whitman called "the red blood of civil war."

Recommended Reading

Easily the finest overall account of the political history of the 1850s is David Potter's superb narrative, *The Impending Crisis, 1848–1861* (1976), completed by Donald Fehrenbacher after Potter's death. See also James McPherson, *Ordeal by Fire: The Civil War and Reconstruction* (1982). Essay collections on recent Civil War scholarship are Eric Foner, ed., *Politics and Ideology in the Age of the Civil War* (1980); and William E. Gienapp, Thomas B. Alexander, Michael F. Holt, Stephen E. Mazlish, and Joel H. Silbey, *Essays on American Antebellum Politics, 1840–1860* (1982). Kenneth Stampp has compiled the most useful combination of primary and secondary sources representing differences of opinion, *The Causes of the Civil War*, rev. ed. (1974), a good book in which to explore various historical interpretations.

Michael F. Holt, *The Political Crisis of the 1850s* (1978), is the best overall work of "new politics" showing the breakdown of political parties as a major cause of the Civil War. On ethnic and religious politics and the effects of nativism on political behavior, see Paul Kleppner, *The Third Electoral System, 1853–1892: Parties, Voters, and Political Cultures* (1979). For a monumental new synthesis and interpretation, see William E. Gienapp, *The Origins of the Republican Party, 1852–1856* (1987). Specialized works on the effects of the issue of slavery in the territories on sectional rivalry and political parties are William J. Cooper, *The South and the Politics of Slavery* (1978); and Richard Sewell, *Ballots for Freedom: Antislavery Politics in the United States, 1837–1865* (1976).

On racism in the West, see James Rawley, *Race and Politics: "Bleeding Kansas" and the Coming of the Civil War* (1969). The definitive work on the *Dred Scott* case is Donald Fehrenbacher, *Slavery, Law, and Politics: The Dred Scott Case in Historical Perspective* (1981). The final road to war after Lincoln's election in 1860 is detailed in William Barney, *The Road to Secession* (1972); and Steven Channing, *Crisis of Fear: Secession in South Carolina* (1970).

Among biographies of major figures see Robert Johannsen, *Stephen Douglas* (1973); Stephen Oates, *To Purge This Land with Blood: A Biography of John Brown* (1970) and *With Malice Toward None: The Life of Abraham Lincoln* (1982). The emotional flavor of the decade is captured in Harriet Beecher Stowe's novel *Uncle Tom's Cabin* (1852); and Walt Whitman's poetry in *Leaves of Grass* (any edition).

Time Line

1832	Nullification crisis	1855	Walt Whitman publishes *Leaves of Grass*
1835–1840	Intensification of abolitionist attacks on slavery Violent retaliatory attacks on abolitionists	1855–1856	Thousands pour into Kansas, creating months of turmoil and violence
1840	Liberty party formed	1856	John Brown's massacre in Kansas Sumner-Brooks incident in Senate James Buchanan elected president
1846	Wilmot Proviso		
1848	Free-Soil party founded Zachary Taylor elected president	1857	*Dred Scott* decision legalizes slavery in territories Lecompton constitution in Kansas
1850	Compromise of 1850, including Fugitive Slave Act	1858	Lincoln-Douglas debates
1850–1854	"Young America" movement	1859	John Brown's raid at Harpers Ferry
1851	Women's rights convention in Akron, Ohio	1860	Democratic Party splits Four-party campaign Abraham Lincoln elected president
1852	Harriet Beecher Stowe publishes *Uncle Tom's Cabin* Franklin Pierce elected president	1860–1861	Seven southern states secede
1854	Ostend Manifesto Kansas-Nebraska Act nullifies Missouri Compromise Republican and Know-Nothing parties formed	1861	Confederate States of America founded Attack on Fort Sumter begins Civil War

chapter 15

The Union Severed

"We cannot escape history," Abraham Lincoln reminded Congress in 1862. "We of this Congress and this administration will be remembered in spite of ourselves." Lincoln's conviction that Americans would long remember him and other major actors of the Civil War—Jefferson Davis, Robert E. Lee, Ulysses S. Grant—was correct. Whether seen as heroes or villains, these great men have dominated the story of the Civil War.

Yet from the earliest days, the war touched the lives of even the most uncelebrated Americans. From Indianapolis, 20-year-old Arthur Carpenter wrote to his parents in Massachusetts begging for permission to enlist in the volunteer army: "I have always longed for the time to come when I could enter the army and be a military man, and when this war broke out, I thought the time had come, but you would not permit me to enter the service . . . now I make one more appeal to you." The pleas worked, and Carpenter enlisted, spending most of the war fighting in Kentucky and Tennessee.

In that same year, in Tennessee, George and Ethie Eagleton faced anguishing decisions. Though not an abolitionist, George, a 30-year-old Presbyterian preacher, was unsympathetic to slavery and opposed to secession. But when his native state left the Union, George felt compelled to follow and enlisted in the 44th Tennessee Infantry. Ethie, his 26-year-old wife, despaired over the war, George's decision, and her own forlorn situation:

> *Pres. Lincoln has done what no other Pres. ever dared to do—he has divided these once peaceful and happy United States. And Oh! the dreadful dark cloud that is now hanging over our country—'tis enough to sicken the heart of any one. . . . Mr. E. is gone. . . . What will become of me, left here without a home and relatives, a babe just nine months old and no George?*

Both Carpenter and the Eagletons survived the war, but the conflict transformed all of their lives. Carpenter had difficulty settling down to civilian life. Filled with bitter memories of the war years in Tennessee, the Eagletons moved to Arkansas.

For thousands of Americans, from Lincoln and Davis to Carpenter and the Eagletons, war was both a profoundly personal and a major national event. Its impact reached far beyond the four years of hostilities. The war that was fought to conserve two political, social, and economic visions ended by changing familiar ways of political, social, and economic life in both North and South. War was a transforming force, both destructive and creative in its effect on the structure and social dynamics of society and on the lives of ordinary people. This theme underlies this chapter's analysis of the war's three stages: the initial months of preparation, the years of military stalemate between 1861 and 1865, and, finally, resolution.

ORGANIZING FOR WAR

The Confederate bombardment of Fort Sumter on April 12, 1861, and the surrender of Union troops the next day ended the uncertainty of the secession winter. The North's response to Fort Sumter was a virtual declaration of war as President Lincoln called for state militia volunteers to crush southern "insurrection." His action pushed several slave states (Virginia, North Carolina, Tennessee, Arkansas) off the fence and into the southern camp. Other states (Maryland, Kentucky, and Missouri) agonizingly debated which way to go. The "War Between the States" was now a reality.

Many Americans were unenthusiastic about the course of events. Southerners like George Eagleton only reluctantly followed Tennessee out of the Union. Robert E. Lee of Virginia was initially hesitant to resign his federal commission. Many southern whites and residents of border states were dismayed at secession and war. Many would eventually join the Union forces.

In the North, large numbers had supported neither the Republican Party nor Lincoln. Nevertheless, the days following Fort Sumter and Lincoln's call for troops saw an outpouring of support on both sides, fueled in part by relief at decisive action, in part by patriotism and love of adventure, in part by unemployment. Sisters, wives, and mothers set to work making uniforms. A New Yorker, Jane Woolsey, described the drama of those early days "of terrible excitement."

> Outside the parlor windows the city is gay and brilliant with excited crowds, the incessant movement and music of marching regiments and all the thousands of flags, big and little, which suddenly came fluttering out of every window and door.

The war fever produced so many volunteers that neither northern nor southern officials could handle the throng. Northern authorities turned aside offers from blacks to serve. Both sides sent thousands of white would-be soldiers home. The conviction that the conflict would rapidly come to a glorious conclusion fueled the eagerness to enlist. Lincoln's call for 75,000 state militiamen for only 90 days of service and a similar enlistment term for Confederate soldiers supported the notion that the war would be short.

The Balance of Resources

Despite the bands, parades, cheers, and confidence, the outcome of the approaching civil conflict was much in doubt. The military stalemate in 1861 and 1862 proved that in the short term, North and South were not unevenly matched. Almost 187,000 Union troops bore arms in July 1861, while just over 112,00 men marched under Confederate colors.

Secession of the Southern States

The Union, however, enjoyed impressive economic advantages. In the North, one million workers in 110,000 manufacturing concerns produced goods valued at $1.5 billion annually, while 110,000 southern workers in 18,000 manufacturing concerns produced goods valued at only $155 million a year. The North had one factory for every southern industrial worker, and 70 percent of the nation's railroad tracks were in the North. Producing 17 times as much cotton cloth and woolen goods, 32 times as many firearms, and 20 times as much pig iron as the South, the North could clothe and arm troops and move them and their supplies on a scale that the South could not match. But to be effective, northern industrial resources had to be mobilized for war. Furthermore, the depleted northern treasury made the government's first task the raising of funds to pay for military necessities.

The South traditionally depended on imported manufactured goods from the North and from Europe. If Lincoln cut off that trade, the South would face the enormous task of creating its industry almost from scratch. Moreover, its railroad system was organized to move cotton, not armies and supplies. Yet the agricultural South did have important resources of food, draft animals, and, of course, cotton, which southerners believed would secure British and French support. Finally, in choosing to wage a defensive war, the South could tap regional loyalty and would enjoy protected lines of supply and support, while Union forces, embarked on an expensive war of conquest, would have extended supply lines vulnerable to attack.

The Border States

When the seven states of the Deep South seceded during the winter of 1860–1861, the strategically important border states adopted a wait-and-see attitude. Delaware identified with the Union camp, but the others vacillated. Lincoln's call for troops precipitated decisions in several states, however. Between April 17 and May 20, 1861, Virginia, Arkansas, Tennessee, and North Carolina joined the Confederacy.

In Maryland, sympathies were divided, but

Confederate enthusiasts abounded in Baltimore. On April 19, the 6th Massachusetts Regiment arrived in Baltimore headed for Washington. Because the regiment had to change railroad lines, the soldiers set out across the city on foot and in horsecars. As they marched through the streets, a mob of some 10,000 southern sympathizers, flying Confederate flags, attacked them with paving stones, then bayonets and bullets. The soldiers fought back, but would-be secessionists burned the railroad bridges connecting Baltimore to the North and to the South. Washington found itself cut off from the rest of the Union, an island in the middle of hostile territory.

Lincoln took stern measures to secure Maryland. Hundreds of southern sympathizers, including 19 state legislators and Baltimore's mayor, were arrested and languished in prison without trial. Although the chief justice of the United States, Roger B. Taney, challenged the legality of the president's action, Lincoln ignored him. A month later, Taney ruled in *Ex parte Merryman* that if the public's safety was endangered, only Congress had the right to suspend a writ of habeas corpus. By then, Lincoln had secured Maryland for the Union.

Though Lincoln's quick and harsh response ensured Maryland's loyalty, he was more cautious elsewhere, for any hasty action would push border states into the waiting arms of the Confederacy. In the end, after some fighting and much maneuvering, Kentucky and Missouri, like Maryland, stayed in the union.

Challenges of War

During the tense weeks after Fort Sumter, both the North and the South faced enormous organizational problems as they readied for war. The South had to create everything from a constitution and governmental departments to a flag and postage stamps.

In February 1861, the original seceding states sent delegates to Montgomery, Alabama, to begin work on a provisional framework and to select a provisional president and vice president. The delegates swiftly wrote a constitution, much like the federal constitution of 1787 except in its emphasis on the "sovereign and independent character" of the states and its explicit recognition of slavery. The provisional president, Jefferson Davis of Mississippi, put together a geographically and politically balanced cabinet, but it had few men of political stature. As time passed, it turned out to be unstable as well. In a four-year period, 14 men held six positions.

Davis's cabinet appointees faced the formidable challenge of creating government departments from scratch. The president's office was in a hotel parlor. The Confederate Treasury Department was housed in a room in an Alabama bank "without furniture of any kind." Treasury Secretary Christopher G. Memminger bought furniture with his own money; operations lurched forward in fits and starts. Other departments faced similar difficulties.

Lincoln never had to set up a postal system or decide whether laws passed before 1861 were valid, but the new president also faced organizational problems. The treasury was empty. The Republicans had won their first presidential election, and floods of office seekers who had worked for Lincoln now thronged into the White House looking for rewards.

Not knowing many of the "prominent men of the day," Lincoln appointed important Republicans from different factions of the party to cabinet posts whether they agreed with him or not. Most were almost strangers to the president. Several scorned him as a bumbling backwoods politician.

Lincoln and Davis

A number of Lincoln's early actions illustrated that he was no malleable backcountry bumbler. After Sumter, he swiftly called up the state militias, expanded the navy, and suspended habeas corpus. He ordered a naval blockade of the South and approved the expenditure of funds for military purposes, all without congressional sanction, since Congress was not in session. As Lincoln told legislators later, "The dogmas of the quiet past are inadequate to the stormy present. . . . As our case is new, so must we think anew, and act anew . . . and then we shall save our country." This willingness to "think anew" was a valuable personal asset, even though some critics called his expansion of presidential power despotic.

By coincidence, Lincoln and his rival, Jefferson Davis, had been born only 100 miles apart in Kentucky. However, the course of their lives had diverged radically. Lincoln's father had migrated north and eked out a simple existence as a farmer in Indiana and Illinois. Abraham had only a rudimentary formal education and was largely self-taught. Davis's family, however, had moved south to Mississippi and become cotton planters. Davis grew up in comfortable circumstances, went to Transylvania University and West Point, fought in the Mexican War before his election to the U.S. Senate, and served as secretary of war under Franklin Pierce (1853–1857). Tall and distinguished-looking, he appeared every inch the aristocratic southerner.

Davis reassured southerners in his inaugural address that his aims were conservative, "to preserve the Government of our fathers in spirit." Yet under the pressure of events, he moved toward creating a new kind of South.

CLASHING ON THE BATTLEFIELD, 1861-1862

The Civil War was the most brutal and destructive conflict in American history. Much of the bloodshed resulted from the application of the theories of Henri Jomini, a French military historian, to the battlefield. Jomini argued that an army seized victory by concentrating its infantry attack at the weakest point in the enemy's defenses. At the time Jomini wrote, this offensive strategy made military sense. The artillery, sta-

tioned well outside the range of enemy fire, could prepare the way for the infantry attack by bombarding enemy lines. By 1861, however, the range of rifles had increased from 100 yards to 500 yards. It was no longer possible to position the artillery close enough to the enemy to allow it to soften up the opposing line in preparation for the infantry charge. During the Civil War, then, enemy fire mowed down attacking infantry soldiers as they ran the 500 fatal yards to the front lines. Battles based on Jomini's theories produced a ghastly crop of dead men.

War in the East

The war's brutal character only gradually revealed itself. The Union commanding general, 70-year-old Winfield Scott, at first pressed for a cautious, long-term strategy, known as the Anaconda Plan. Scott proposed weakening the South gradually through blockades on land and at sea. The excited public, however, hungered for action and quick victory. So did Lincoln, who knew that the longer the war lasted, the more embittered the South and the North would both become, making reunion ever more difficult. Under the cry of "Forward to Richmond!" 35,000 partially trained men led by General Irwin McDowell headed out from Washington in sweltering July weather.

On July 21, 1861, only 25 miles from the capital at Manassas Creek, or Bull Run, as it is also called, inexperienced northern troops confronted 25,000 raw Confederate soldiers commanded by Brigadier General P.G.T. Beauregard, a West Point classmate of McDowell's. Although sightseers, journalists, and politicians accompanied the Union troops, expecting only a Sunday outing, the encounter at Bull Run was no picnic. The course of battle swayed back and forth before the arrival of 2,300 fresh Confederate troops, brought by trains, decided the day. Union soldiers and sightseers fled toward Washington in terror and confusion.

Yet inexperienced Confederate troops failed

Eastern Theater of the Civil War, 1861-1862

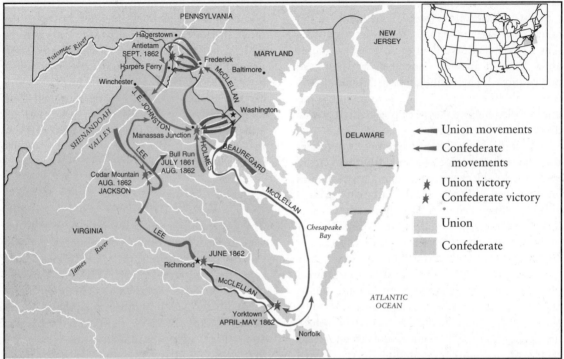

to turn the rout into the quick and decisive victory they sought. As General Joseph E. Johnston pointed out, his men were disorganized, confused by victory, and not well enough supplied with food to chase the Union army back toward Washington.

In many ways, the Battle of Bull Run was prophetic. Victory would be neither quick nor easy. As the disorganization and confusion of both sides suggested, the armies were unprofessional.

For the Union the loss at Bull Run was sobering. Replacing McDowell with 34-year-old General George McClellan, Lincoln began his search for a northern commander capable of winning the war. McClellan, formerly an army engineer, confronted the task of transforming the Army of the Potomac into a fighting force. Short-term militias went home. When Scott re-

tired in the fall of 1861, McClellan became general in chief of the Union armies.

McClellan had considerable organizational ability but no desire to be a daring leader on the battlefield. Convinced that the North must combine military victory with efforts to persuade the South to return to the Union, he sought to avoid unnecessary and embittering loss of life and property. He intended to win the war "by maneuvering rather than fighting."

Pushed by an impatient Lincoln, in June 1862 McClellan advanced with 130,000 troops toward Richmond, now the Confederate capital, but failed to take it. Other Union defeats followed in 1862 as commanders came and went. In September, the South boldly invaded Maryland but suffered a costly defeat at Antietam in which more than 5,000 soldiers were slaughtered and another 17,000 wounded on the grisli-

Trans-Mississippi Campaign of the Civil War

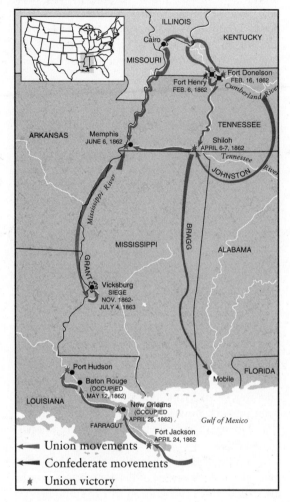

← Union movements

← Confederate movements

★ Union victory

vital river trade and its great port, New Orleans. Here both George Eagleton and Arthur Carpenter served. Beyond lay the trans-Mississippi West—Louisiana, Arkansas, Missouri, Texas, and the Great Plains—where Native American tribes joined the conflict on both sides.

In the western theater, the Union had two strategic objectives: the domination of Kentucky and eastern Tennessee, the avenues to the South and West, and control of the Mississippi River in order to split the South in two. Major campaigns sought strategic points along rivers and railroads.

It was in the western theater that Ulysses S. Grant rose to prominence. He had attended West Point and served creditably in the Mexican War. Soon after Fort Sumter, Grant enlisted as a colonel in an Illinois militia regiment. Within two months, he was a brigadier general.

Grant realized that the Tennessee and Cumberland rivers were the paths for the successful invasion of Tennessee. Assisted by gunboats, he was largely responsible for the capture of Fort Henry and Fort Donelson, key points on the rivers, in February 1862. His army was nearly destroyed, however, by a surprise Confederate attack at Shiloh Church in Tennessee. The North won this battle but suffered over 13,000 casualties, while 10,000 Confederates lay dead or wounded. More men fell in this single battle than in the American Revolution, the War of 1812, and the Mexican War combined. Because neither army offered sufficient care on the battlefield, many men died of untreated wounds and exposure.

The war in the trans-Mississippi West was a sporadic, far-flung struggle for the control of this vast area. California was one prize that lured both armies into the Southwest. Confederate troops from Texas held Albuquerque and Santa Fe briefly in 1862. Volunteer soldiers from the Colorado mining fields, joined by Mexican-Americans and other soldiers, drove the Texas Confederates from New Mexico. A Union force recruited in California arrived after the Confederates were gone. They spent the remainder of

est day of the war. Lee withdrew to Virginia, and the war in the East was stalemated.

War in the West

The East was only one of three theaters of actions. Between the Appalachian Mountains and the Mississippi lay the western theater, the states of Kentucky, Tennessee, Mississippi, and Alabama. At its edge lay the Mississippi, with its the Civil War years fighting the Apache and the Navajo and with brutal competence crushed both Native American nations.

Farther east was another prize, the Missouri River, which flowed into the Mississippi River, bordered Illinois, and affected military campaigns in Kentucky and Tennessee. Initially, Confederate troops were successful here, but in March 1862, at Pea Ridge in northern Arkansas, the Union forces defeated a Confederate army of 16,000 that included a brigade of Native Americans from the Five Civilized Nations. Missouri entered the Union camp for the first time in the war, and fierce guerrilla warfare continued in the region.

Naval Warfare

Lincoln's naval blockade of southern ports was not immediately effective. With no more than 33 ships, the Union navy tried to close up 189 ports along a 3,500-mile coastline. In 1861, the navy intercepted only about one blockade runner in ten and in 1862, one in eight. In the short run, the blockade did little damage to the South.

More successful were operations to gain footholds along the southern coast. In November 1861, a Union expedition took Port Royal Sound, where it freed the first slaves, and the nearby South Carolina Sea Islands. A few months later, the navy defeated a Confederate force on Roanoke Island. But the Union's greatest naval triumph in the early war years was the capture of New Orleans, the South's most important port, in 1862.

The Confederate leadership, recognizing that the South could not match the Union fleet, concentrated on developing new weapons like torpedoes and formidable ironclad vessels. They raised the *Merrimac,* a sunken U.S. warship, and covered it with heavy iron armor. Rechristened the *Virginia,* the ship steamed out of Norfolk in March 1862, heading directly for the Union ships blocking the harbor. Using its 1,500-pound ram and guns, the *Virginia* drove a third of the

ships aground and destroyed the squadron's largest ships. Victory was short-lived. The next day, the *Virginia* confronted the *Monitor,* a newly completed Union iron vessel. Their duel was inconclusive, and the *Virginia* withdrew. It was burned during the evacuation of Norfolk that May.

The Confederate navy's policy of harming northern commerce was moderately successful. Confederate raiders wreaked havoc on northern shipping. In its two-year career, the raider *Alabama* destroyed 69 Union merchant vessels valued at more than $6 million.

Throughout the first two years of conflict, both sides achieved victories, but the war remained deadlocked. The costs in manpower and supplies far exceeded what either side had anticipated. The need to replace lost men and supplies thus loomed ever more serious at the end of 1862.

Cotton Diplomacy

Both sides in the Civil War realized that attitudes in Europe could be critical. The Confederacy hoped to gain European diplomatic recognition and European loans and assistance. The European powers, however, consulted their own national interests and one by one declared a policy of neutrality.

Southerners were sure that the need of English and French textile mills for cotton would eventually force recognition of the Confederacy and an end to the North's blockade. But European industrialists found new sources for cotton in India and Egypt, and Southern hopes were dashed.

Union Secretary of State Seward sought above all else to prevent diplomatic recognition of the Confederacy. He daringly threatened Great Britain with war if it interfered in what he insisted was an internal matter. Some called his boldness reckless, even mad. Nevertheless, his policy succeeded. Even though England allowed the construction of Confederate raiders in its

Many deaths resulted from inadequate care for the wounded and sick soldiers of both armies. This wounded soldier receives water from a canteen rather than medical attention.

ports, it did not intervene in American affairs in 1861 or 1862. Nor did the other European powers.

Common Problems, Novel Solutions

As the conflict dragged on into 1863, unanticipated problems appeared in both the Union and the Confederacy, and leaders devised novel approaches to solve them.

Both treasuries had been empty initially, and the war was proving extraordinarily expensive. Eventually both sides initiated taxation on a small scale. Ultimately taxes financed 21 percent of the North's war expenses (but only one percent of southern expenses). Both treasuries also tried borrowing. Northerners bought over $2 billion worth of bonds, but southerners proved reluctant to buy their government's bonds.

Finally, both sides resorted to printing paper money. In August 1861, the Confederacy put into circulation $100 million in crudely engraved bills. Millions more followed the next year. Five months later, the Union issued $150 million in paper money, soon nicknamed "greenbacks" because of their color. The resulting inflation was particularly troublesome in the Confederacy, but it also caused an 80 percent increase in food prices for Union city families.

Both sides confronted manpower problems as initial enthusiasm for the war evaporated. Young men were shocked at the deadliness of diseases that accompanied the army wherever it went, and they were unprepared for the boredom of camp life. Those in the service longed to go home. The swarm of volunteers disappeared. Rather than fill their military quotas from within, rich northern communities began offering bounties of $800 to $1,000 to outsiders who would join up.

Arthur Carpenter's letters reveal growing disillusionment with the war as his regiment moved into Kentucky and Tennessee in the winter of 1862. "Soldiering in Kentucky and Tennessee," he complained, "is not so pretty as it was in Indianapolis. . . . We have been half starved, half frozen, and half drowned." Soldiering often meant marching over rutted roads carrying 50 or 60 pounds of equipment with insufficient food, water, or supplies. One blanket was not enough in the winter. In the summer, stifling woolen uniforms attracted lice and other vermin. Poor food, bugs, inadequate sanitation, and exposure invited disease. Carpenter marched through Tennessee suffering from diarrhea and then fever. His regiment left him behind in a convalescent barracks in Louisville, which he fled as soon as he could. He feared the hospital at least as much as the sickness. "[Ninety-nine] Surgeons out of a hundred," he wrote his parents, "would not know whether his patient had the horse distemper, lame toe, or any other disease."

Confederate soldiers, even less well supplied

than their northern counterparts, complained similarly. In 1862, a Virginia captain wrote:

> During our forced marches and hard fights, the soldiers have been compelled to throw away their knapsacks ... Hundreds of men are perfectly barefooted and there is no telling when they can be supplied with shoes.

Desertion was common, and as the manpower problems became critical, both governments resorted to the draft. Ultimately, over 30 percent of the Confederate army and six percent of the Union forces were draftees.

The Confederacy relied more heavily on the draft than the Union did because the North's initial manpower pool was larger and growing. During the war, 180,000 foreigners of military age poured into the northern states. Some came specifically to claim bounties and fight. Immigrants made up at least 20 percent of the Union army.

The draft laws were very unpopular. The first Confederate conscription declared all able-bodied men between 18 and 35 eligible for military service but allowed numerous exemptions and the purchase of substitutes. Critics complained that the provision entitling every planter with more than 20 slaves to one exemption from military service favored rich slave owners. The legislation fed class tension and encouraged disloyalty and desertion among the poorer classes, particularly among southern mountaineers. One woman shouted after her husband as he was dragged off to the army, "You desert again, quick as you kin. . . . Desert, Jake!"

The northern draft law of 1863 also allowed the hiring of substitutes, and $300 bought exemption from military service. Workers resented the ease with which moneyed citizens could avoid army duty. In July 1863, the resentment boiled over in New York City in the largest civil disturbance of the nineteenth century. Several Irish draftees destroyed draft records and the Enrollment Office. Events then spun out of control as a mob also burned the armory, plundered the houses of the rich, and looted jewelry stores. Blacks, whom the Irish hated as economic competitors and the cause of the war, became special targets. Mobs beat and lynched blacks and even burned the Colored Orphan Asylum. More than 100 people died in the three days of rioting. There was much truth in the accusation that the war on both sides was a rich man's war but a poor man's fight.

Political Dissension, 1862

As the war continued, rumbles of dissension grew louder. In the South, criticism of Confederate leaders mounted. Wrote one southerner to a friend, "Impeach Jeff Davis for incompetency & call a convention of the States. . . . West Point is death to us & sick Presidents & Generals are equally fatal." Because the South had no party system, dissatisfaction with Davis and his handling of the war tended to be factional, petty, and personal.

Although Lincoln has since become a folk hero, at the time many northerners derided his performance and hoped for a new president in 1864. Peace Democrats, called Copperheads, claimed that Lincoln betrayed the Constitution and that working-class Americans bore the brunt of his policy of conscription. Immigrant workers had little sympathy for abolitionism or blacks, and they supported the antiwar stance of the Copperheads. Even Democrats favoring the war effort found Lincoln arbitrary and tyrannical, while some Republicans judged him indecisive and inept.

Republicans split gradually into two factions. The moderates favored a cautious approach toward winning the war and feared the possible consequences of emancipating the slaves, confiscating Confederate property, or arming blacks. The radicals, however, urged Lincoln to make emancipation a wartime objective. The reduction of the congressional Republican majority in the fall elections of 1862 made it imperative that Lincoln listen not only to both factions but also to the Democratic opposition.

THE TIDE TURNS, 1863-1865

Hard political realities made Lincoln delay an emancipation proclamation until 1863. Like congressional Democrats, many northerners supported a war for the Union but not one for emancipation. Many, if not most, whites saw blacks as inferior. They also suspected that emancipation would trigger a massive influx of former slaves who would steal white men's jobs and political rights. Race riots in New York, Brooklyn, Philadelphia, Buffalo, and Cincinnati dramatized white attitudes.

The Emancipation Proclamation, 1863

If the president moved too fast on emancipation, he risked losing the allegiance of people like Carpenter, offending the border states, and increasing the Democrats' chances for political victory. But if he did not move at all, he would alienate abolitionists and lose the support of radical Republicans, which he could ill afford.

For these reasons, Lincoln proceeded cautiously. In the early spring of 1862, he urged Congress to pass a joint resolution offering federal compensation to states beginning a "gradual abolishment of slavery." Border-state opposition killed the idea. Abolitionists and northern blacks, however, greeted Lincoln's proposal with "a thrill of joy."

That summer, Lincoln told his cabinet he intended to emancipate the slaves. Secretary of State Seward urged the president to delay any general proclamation until the North won a decisive military victory. Otherwise, he warned, Lincoln would appear to be urging racial insurrection behind the Confederate lines to compensate for northern military bungling.

Lincoln followed Seward's advice, using that summer and fall to prepare the North for the shift in the war's purpose. In August, Horace Greeley, the influential abolitionist editor of the New York *Tribune*, printed an open letter to Lincoln attacking him for failing to act on slavery. In his reply, Lincoln linked the idea of emancipation to military necessity. His primary goal, he wrote, was to save the Union:

> If I could save the Union without freeing *any* slave, I would do it; and if I could save it by freeing *all* the slaves, I would do it; and if I could do it by freeing some and leaving others alone, I would also do that. What I do about Slavery and the colored race, I do because I believe it helps to save this Union.

In September 1862, the Union victory at Antietam gave Lincoln the opportunity to issue a preliminary emancipation proclamation. It stated that unless rebellious states (or parts of states in rebellion) returned to the Union by January 1, 1863, the president would declare their slaves "forever free." Although supposedly aimed at bringing the southern states back into the Union, Lincoln never expected the South to lay down arms after two years of bloodshed. Rather, he was preparing northerners to accept the eventuality of emancipation on the grounds of necessity. Frederick Douglass greeted the president's action with jubilation. "We shout for joy," he wrote, "that we live to record this righteous decree."

Cautious cabinet members begged Lincoln to forget about emancipation, but on New Year's Day, 1863, he issued the final Emancipation Proclamation. It was "an act of justice, warranted by the Constitution upon military necessity." Thus what had started as a war to save the Union now also became a struggle that, if victorious, would free the slaves. Yet the proclamation had no immediate impact on slavery. It affected only slaves living in the unconquered portions of the Confederacy. It was silent about slaves in the border states and in parts of the

Black soldiers, some from southern states, were accepted for combat duty in the Union army as the war progressed. Here the First Carolina Volunteers gather to celebrate emancipation on January 1, 1863.

South already in northern hands. These limitations led Elizabeth Cady Stanton and Susan B. Anthony to establish the women's Loyal National League to lobby Congress to emancipate all southern slaves.

Though the Emancipation Proclamation did not immediately liberate southern slaves from their masters, it had a tremendous symbolic importance. Blacks realized that the proclamation had changed the nature of the war. For the first time, the government had committed itself to freeing slaves. Jubilant blacks could believe only that the president's action heralded a new era for their race. More immediately, the proclamation sanctioned the policy of accepting blacks as soldiers into the military.

Diplomatic concerns also lay behind the Emancipation Proclamation. Lincoln and his advisers anticipated that the commitment to abolish slavery would favorably impress foreign powers. European statesmen, however, did not abandon their cautious stance toward the Union. The English prime minister called the proclamation "trash." But important segments of the English public who opposed slavery now came to regard any attempt to help the South as immoral.

Unanticipated Consequences of War

The Emancipation Proclamation was but one example of the war's surprising consequences. Innovation was necessary for victory, and one of the Union's experiments involved using black troops for combat duty. Blacks had offered themselves as soldiers in 1861 but had been turned away. They were serving as cooks, laborers, teamsters, and carpenters in the army, however, and composed as much as a quarter of the navy. But as white casualties mounted, so did the interest in black service on the battlefield. The Union government allowed states to escape draft quotas if they enlisted enough volunteers and allowed them to count southern black enlistees on their state rosters.

Black leaders like Frederick Douglass pressed for military service. "Once let the black man get upon his person the brass letter, U.S., let him get an eagle on his button, and a musket on his shoulder and bullets in his pocket," Douglass believed, "there is no power on earth that can deny that he has earned the right to citizenship." By the war's end, 186,000 blacks (10 percent of the army) had served the Union cause, 134,111 of them escapees from slave states.

Enrolling blacks in the Union army was an important step toward citizenship and acceptance of blacks by white society. But the black experience in the army highlighted some of the obstacles to racial acceptance. Black soldiers, usually led by white officers, were second-class soldiers for most of the war, receiving lower pay ($10 a month as compared to $13), poorer food, often more menial work, and fewer benefits than whites. "If we are good enough to fill up white men's places and fight, we should be treated then, in all respects, the same as the white man," one black soldier protested.

The faith in Jomini's military tactics was another wartime casualty. The infantry charge, so valued at the war's beginning, resulted in horrible carnage. Military leaders came to realize the importance of the strong defensive position. Although Confederate soldiers criticized General Lee as "King of Spades" when he first ordered them to construct earthworks, the epithet evolved into one of affection as it became obvious that earthworks saved lives. By the end of 1862, both sides were digging defensive earthworks and trenches.

Gone, too, was the courtly idea that war involved only armies. Early in the war, many officers tried to protect civilians and their property, but such restraint soon vanished, and along with it went chickens, corn, livestock, and, as George Eagleton noted with disgust, even the furnishings of churches. War touched all of society, not just the battlefield participants.

Changing Military Strategies, 1863–1865

In the early war years, the South's military strategy combined defense with selective maneuvers. This policy, however, did not change the course of the war, and Lee concluded that the South had to win victories in the North in order to gain the peace it so desperately needed and European recognition.

In the summer of 1863, Lee led the Confederate Army of Northern Virginia across the Potomac into Maryland and southern Pennsylvania. His goal was a victory that would threaten both Philadelphia and Washington.

At Gettysburg on a hot and humid July 1, Lee came abruptly face to face with a Union army led by General George Meade. During three days of fighting, the fatal obsession with the infantry charge returned as Lee ordered costly assaults that probably lost him the battle. On July 3, Lee sent three divisions, about 15,000 men in all, against the Union center. The assault, known as Pickett's Charge, was as futile as it was gallant. At 700 yards, the Union artillery opened

fire. One southern officer described the scene: "Pickett's division just seemed to melt away in the blue musketry smoke which now covered the hill. Nothing but stragglers came back."

Lee's dreams of victory died that hot week, with grave consequences for the southern cause. Gettysburg marked the turn of the military tide in the East.

Despite the Gettysburg victory, Lincoln was dissatisfied with General Meade, who had failed to finish off Lee's demoralized and exhausted army as it retreated. His disappointment soon faded with news of a great victory at Vicksburg in the western theater on July 4. The commander, Ulysses S. Grant, completed the Union campaign to gain control of the Mississippi River and to divide the South.

Grant's successful capture of Vicksburg illustrated the boldness and flexibility that Lincoln sought in a commander, and in March 1864, Lincoln appointed him general in chief of the Union armies. Grant planned for victory within a year. "The art of war is simple enough," he reasoned. "Find out where your enemy is. Get at him as soon as you can. Strike at him as hard as you can, and keep moving on."

Grant proposed a grim campaign of annihilation, using the North's superior resources of men and supplies to wear down and defeat the South. He aimed "to consume everything that could be used to support or supply armies." Following this new policy of "total war," he set out after Lee's army in Virginia. General William Tecumseh Sherman, who pursued Confederate General Joseph Johnston from Tennessee toward Atlanta, further refined this plan.

Sherman wanted to make southerners "fear and dread" their foes. Therefore, his campaign to seize Atlanta and his march to Savannah spread destruction and terror. A Georgia woman described in her diary the impact of Sherman's march:

> There was hardly a fence left standing all the way from Sparta to Gordon. The fields were trampled

The Tide Turns, 1863–1865

Gettysburg
JULY 1–3, 1863 ★

Washington

Chancellorsville
MAY 1–4, 1863 ★

× Appomattox
LEE SURRENDERS
APRIL 9, 1865

• Richmond

Ohio River

Potomac River

Mississippi River

Atlanta

★ Vicksburg
SIEGE
MAY 22–
JULY 4, 1863

Sherman's March
SEPT.–DEC. 1864

Savannah

ATLANTIC OCEAN

Gulf of Mexico

← Union movements
★ Union victories
★ Confederate victories
Union
Confederate

down and the road was lined with carcasses of horses, hogs and cattle that the invaders, unable either to consume or to carry away with them, had wantonly shot down, to starve out the people. . . . The dwellings that were standing all showed signs of pillage, and on every plantation we saw . . . charred remains.

This destruction, with its goal of total victory, showed once more how conflict produced the unexpected. The war that both North and South had hoped would be quick and relatively painless was ending after four long years with great cost to both sides.

CHANGES WROUGHT BY WAR

As bold new tactics emerged both on and off the battlefield, both governments took steps that changed their societies in surprising ways. Of the two, the South, which had left the Union to conserve a traditional way of life, experienced the more radical transformation.

A New South

The expansion of the central government's power in the South, starting with the passage of the 1862 Conscription Act, continued in the last years of the war. Secession grew out of the concept of states' rights, but, ironically, winning the war depended on central direction and control. Many southerners denounced Davis as a tyrant and a despot because he recognized the need for the central government to take the lead. Despite the accusations, the Confederate Congress cooperated with him and established important precedents. In 1863, it enacted a comprehensive tax law and an impressment act that allowed government agents to requisition food, horses, wagons, and other necessary war materials, often for only about half their market price. These were prime examples of the central government's power to interfere with private property. Government impressment of slaves for war work in 1863 affected the very form of private property that had originally driven the South from the Union.

The Conscription Act of 1862 was followed in 1864 by an expanded conscription measure that made all white males between the ages 17 and 50 subject to the draft. By 1865, the necessities of war had led to the unthinkable: arming slaves as soldiers. Black companies were recruited in Richmond and other southern towns. However, because the war soon ended, no blacks actually fought for the Confederacy.

Southern agriculture also changed under the pressure of war. Earlier, the South had imported food from the North, concentrating on the production of staples such as cotton and tobacco for market. Now, more and more land was turned over to food crops. Cotton production declined from 4.5 million bales in 1861 to 300,000 bales in 1864, but food remained in short supply.

The war also triggered the expansion of military-related industries in the South. The war and navy offices directed industrial development, awarding contracts to private manufacturing firms like Richmond's Tredegar Iron Works and operating other factories themselves. The number of southerners working in industry rose dramatically. In 1861, the Tredegar Iron Works employed 700 workers; two years later, it employed 2,500, more than half of them black. At the end of the war, the soldiers were better supplied with arms and munitions than with food.

Although the war did not transform the southern class structure, relations between the classes began to change. Draft resistance and desertion reflected growing alienation from a war perceived as serving only the interests of upper-class plantation owners. More and more yeoman families suffered grinding poverty as the men went off to war and government officials and armies requisitioned needed resources. This new poverty was an ominous hint of the decline of the yeoman farming class in postwar years.

The Victorious North

Although changes in the South were more noticeable, the Union's government and economy also responded to the demands of war. Like Davis, Lincoln was accused of being a dictator. Although he rarely tried to control Congress, veto its legislation, or direct government departments, Lincoln did use executive power freely. He violated the writ of habeas corpus by suspending the civil rights of over 13,000 northerners, who languished in prison without trials; curbed the freedom of the press because of supposedly disloyal and inflammatory articles; established conscription; issued the Emancipation Proclamation; and removed army generals. Lincoln argued that this vast extension of presidential power was temporarily justified because, as president, he was responsible for defending and preserving the Constitution.

Many of the wartime changes in government proved more permanent than Lincoln had imagined. The financial necessities of war helped to revolutionize the country's banking system. Ever since Andrew Jackson's destruction of the Bank of the United States, state banks had served American financial needs. Treasury Secretary Salmon P. Chase found this banking system inadequate and chaotic and proposed to replace it. In 1863 and 1864, Congress passed banking acts that established a national currency issued by federally chartered banks and backed by government bonds. The country had a federal banking system once again.

The northern economy also changed under wartime demands. Agriculture expanded, as did investment in farm machinery, notably McCormick reapers, which performed the work of four to six men. During the war, McCormick sold 165,000 of his machines. Northern farmers

Ruined buildings and mourning women were common sights in Richmond as the war came to an end. This photograph gives a vivid sense of the devastation of the South in 1865.

not only grew enough grain to feed civilians and soldiers but gathered a surplus to export as well.

The war also selectively stimulated manufacturing, although it retarded overall economic growth. Industries that produced for the war machine, especially those with advantages of scale, expanded and made large profits. Each year, the Union army required 1.5 million uniforms and 3 million pairs of shoes; the woolen and leather industries grew accordingly. Meatpackers and producers of iron, steel, and pocket watches all profited from wartime opportunities. Cincinnati was one city that flourished from supplying soldiers with everything from pork to soap and candles.

On the Home Front, 1861–1865

In numerous, less tangible ways, the war transformed northern and southern society. Civilians read newspapers and national weekly magazines with a new eagerness. The use of the mails increased dramatically as they corresponded with faraway relatives and friends. The war helped to make Americans less parochial, integrating them into the larger world.

For some Americans, like John D. Rockefeller and Andrew Carnegie, war brought army contracts and profits. In the South, blockade runners made fortunes slipping luxury goods past Union ships. For the majority of Americans, however, war meant deprivation. To be sure, the demand for workers ended unemployment. Large numbers of women and blacks entered the work force, a phenomenon that would be repeated in all future American wars. But while work was easy to get and wages appeared to increase, real income actually declined. Inflation, especially destructive in the South, was largely to blame. By 1864, eggs sold in Richmond for $6 a dozen; butter brought $25 a pound. Strikes and union organizing pointed to working-class discontent.

Low wages particularly harmed women workers. As more women entered the work force, employers cut costs by slashing wages. In 1861, the Union government paid Philadelphia seamstresses 17 cents per shirt. At the height of inflation, three years later, the government reduced the piecework rate to 15 cents per shirt. Private employers paid even less, about eight cents a shirt. Working women in the South fared no better. War may have brought prosperity to a few Americans, North and South, but for most it meant trying to survive on an inadequate income.

Shortages and hardships were severe in the South, especially in cities, where carts brought in vital supplies since trains were reserved for military use. Hunger was rampant. Food riots erupted in Richmond and other cities; crowds of hungry whites broke into stores to steal food. The very cleanliness of southern cities pointed to urban hunger. As one Richmond resident noted, everything was so "cleanly consumed that no garbage or filth can accumulate."

Thousands of southerners who fled as Union armies advanced suddenly found themselves homeless. "The country for miles around is filled with refugees," noted an army officer in 1862. "Every house is crowded and hundreds are living in churches, in barns and tents."

One slave described the upsetting arrival of the Yankees at his plantation in Arkansas: "Them folks stood round there all day. Killed hogs ... killed cows.... Took all kinds of sugar and preserves.... Tore all the feathers out of the mattresses looking for money. Then they put Old Miss and her daughter in the kitchen to cooking." So frightened was this slave's mother that she hid in her bed, only to be roused by the lieutenant, who told her, "We ain't a-going to do you no hurt.... We are free-ing you." But the next day, the Yanks were gone and the Confederates back. "Pa was 'fraid of both" and resolved the problem by hiding out in the cotton patch.

Wartime Race Relations

The journal kept by Emily Harris in South Carolina conveys some of the character of life behind the lines. Emily and her husband, David, lived on a 500-acre farm with their seven young children and ten slaves. When David went to war, Emily had to manage the farm, even though David worried that she would be "much at a loss with the ... farm and the negroes."

Indeed, Emily's relations with her slaves proved a major problem. As so many southerners discovered, war transformed the master-slave relationship. Because Emily was not the master David had been, her slaves gradually began to take unaccustomed liberties. At Christmas in 1864, several left the farm without her permission; others stayed away longer than she allowed. "Old Will" boldly requested his freedom. Worse yet, she discovered that her slaves had helped three Yankees who had escaped from prison camp.

The master-slave relationship was crumbling, and Emily reported in her journal, "It seems people are getting afraid of negroes." In March she wrote, "The Negroes are all expect-

ing to be set free very soon and it causes them to be very troublesom."

Such scenes, which occurred throughout the South, and the thousands of blacks (probably 20 percent of all slaves) who fled toward Union lines after the early months of the war were proof of the changing nature of race relations and the harm slaves could do to the southern cause.

Women and the War

Emily Harris's journal illustrates how the war affected women's lives. So many men on both sides had gone off to fight that women had to find jobs and had to carry on farming operations. During the war years, southern women who had no slaves to help with the farmwork and northern farm wives who labored without the assistance of husbands or sons carried new physical and emotional burdens.

Women also participated in numerous war-related activities. In the North, hundreds of women became military nurses. Under the supervision of Drs. Emily and Elizabeth Blackwell; Dorothea Dix, superintendent of army nurses; and Clara Barton, northern women nursed the wounded and dying for low pay or even for none at all. They also attempted to improve hospital conditions by attacking red tape and bureaucracy. The diary of a volunteer, Harriet Whetten, revealed the activist attitude of many others:

> I have never seen such a dirty disorganized place as the Hospital. The neglect of cleanliness is inexcusable. All sorts of filth, standing water, and the embalming house near the Hospital.... No time had to be lost. Miss Gill and I set the contrabands at work making beds & cleaning.

Although men largely staffed southern military hospitals, Confederate women also played an important part in caring for the sick and wounded in their homes and in makeshift hospitals behind the battle lines. Women also worked as volunteers in soldiers' aid societies and in the United States Sanitary Commission. Many others made bandages and clothes, put together packages for soldiers at the front, helped army wives and disabled soldiers find jobs, and joined in war-related fund-raising activities.

Many of the changes women experienced during war years ended when peace returned and the men came home. But for women whose men came home maimed or not at all, the work had not ended.

The Election of 1864

In the North, the election of 1864 brought some of the transformations of wartime into the political arena. The Democrats, capitalizing on war weariness, nominated General George McClellan for president and demanded an armistice with the South. They accused Lincoln of arbitrarily expanding executive power and insinuated that if the Republicans won, a fusion of blacks and whites would result.

Although Lincoln easily gained Republican renomination because of his tight control over party machinery and patronage, his party did not unite behind him. His veto of the radical reconstruction plan for the South, the Wade-Davis bill, led to cries of "usurpation." The Emancipation Proclamation did not sit well with conservatives. But Sherman's capture of Atlanta in September 1864 and the march through Georgia to Savannah helped swing voters to Lincoln. He won 55 percent of the popular vote and swept the electoral college.

Why the North Won

In the months after Lincoln's reelection, the war drew to an agonizing conclusion. Sherman moved north from Atlanta to North Carolina, while Grant pummeled Lee's forces in Virginia. The losses Grant would sustain were staggering: 18,000 in the Battle of the Wilderness, over

8,000 at Spotsylvania, and another 12,000 at Cold Harbor. On April 9, 1865, Grant accepted Lee's surrender at Appomattox, and the war was finally over.

Grant's military strategy succeeded because the Union could survive staggering losses of men and equipment while the Confederacy could not. As Union armies pushed back the borders of the Confederacy, the South lost control of territories essential for their war effort. Finally, naval strategy eventually paid off because the North could build enough ships to make its blockade work. In 1861, fully 90 percent of the blockade runners were slipping through the naval cordon. By the war's end, only half made it.

The South had taken tremendous steps toward meeting war needs. But, as one civilian realized, "The question of bread and meat . . . is beginning to be regarded as a more serious one even than that of War." Women farming alone or with disgruntled slaves and worn-out farm equipment could not produce enough food. The government's impressment of slaves and animals cut production. The half million blacks who fled to Union lines also played their part in pulling the South down in defeat.

Advancing Union forces destroyed many industries. A Confederate officer in northern Virginia observed, "Many of our soldiers are thinly clothed and without shoes and in addition to this, very few of the infantry have tents. With this freezing weather, their sufferings are indescribable." By 1864, the Union armies were so well supplied that soldiers often threw away heavy blankets and coats as they advanced.

The South's woefully inadequate transportation system also contributed to defeat. Primitive roads became all but impassable without repairs. The railroad system, geared to the needs of cotton, not war, was inefficient. When tracks wore out or were destroyed, they were not replaced. Thus food intended for the army rotted awaiting shipment. Food riots in southern cities pointed to the hunger, anger, and growing demoralization of civilians.

Ironically, measures the Confederacy took to win the war undermined its own war effort. Conscription, impressment, and taxes all contributed to resentment and sometimes open resistance. The many southern governors who refused to contribute men, money, and supplies on the scale Davis requested implicitly condoned disloyalty to the cause. The belief in states' rights and the sanctity of private property that gave birth to the Confederacy also helped kill it.

It is tempting to compare Lincoln and Davis as war leaders. There is no doubt that Lincoln's humanity, eloquence, and determination to save the Union set him apart as one of this country's most extraordinary presidents. Yet the men's personal characteristics were probably less important than the differences between the political and social systems of the two regions. Without the support of a party behind him, Davis failed to engender enthusiasm or loyalty. Lincoln, commanding considerable resources of patronage, was able to line up federal, state, and local officials behind his party and administration.

Just as the northern political system provided Lincoln with more flexibility and support, its social system also proved more able to meet the war's extraordinary demands. Northerners were more cooperative, disciplined, and aggressive in meeting the organizational and production challenges of wartime. In the southern states, old attitudes, habits, and values impeded the war effort. Southern governors, wedded to states' rights, refused to cooperate with the Confederate government. North Carolina, the center of the southern textile industry, actually kept back most uniforms for its own regiments. At the war's end, 92,000 uniforms and thousands of blankets, shoes, and tents still lay in its warehouses. Even slaveholders whose property had

been the cause for secession resisted the impressment of their slaves for war work.

One northerner described southerners as they surrendered at Appomattox:

> Before us in proud humiliation stood the embodiment of manhood: men whom neither toils and sufferings, nor the fact of death, nor disaster, nor hopelessness could bend from their resolve; standing before us now, thin, worn, and famished, but erect, and with eyes looking level into ours, waking memories that bound us together as no other bond.

The Costs of War

In the end, the Confederacy collapsed, exhausted and bleeding. The long war was over, but the memories of that event would fester for years to come. About three million American men, a third of all free males between the ages of 15 and 59, had served in the army. Each would remember his own personal history of the war. For George Eagleton, who had worked in army field hospitals, the history was one of "Death and destruction! Blood! Blood! Agony! Death! Gaping flesh wounds, broken bones, amputations, bullet and bomb fragment extractions." Of all wars Americans have fought, none has been more deadly. The death rate during this war was over five times as great as the death rate during World War II. About 360,000 Union soldiers and another 258,000 Confederate soldiers died, about a third of them because their wounds were either improperly treated or not treated at all. Disease claimed more lives than combat.

Many men would be reminded of the war by the missing limbs that marked them as Civil War veterans. About 275,000 on each side were maimed. Another 410,000 (195,000 northerners and 215,000 southerners) would recall their time in wretchedly overcrowded and unsanitary prison camps, such as Andersonville in Georgia, where 31,000 Union soldiers were confined. At the war's end, over 12,000 graves were counted there.

Some Americans found it hard to throw off wartime experiences and return to civilian routines. Even those who adjusted successfully discovered that they looked at life from a different perspective. The experience of fighting, of mixing with all sorts of people from many places, of traveling far from home had lifted former soldiers out of their familiar local world and widened their vision. Fighting the war made the concept of national union real.

Unanswered Questions

What, then, had the war accomplished? On the one hand, death and destruction. The South suffered an estimated 43 percent decline in wealth during the war years, exclusive of the value of slaves. Great cities like Atlanta, Columbia, and Richmond lay in ruins. Fields lay uncultivated, much livestock had disappeared, and two-thirds of the railroads had been destroyed. Thousands were hungry, homeless, and bitter, and over three million slaves, a vast financial investment, were free.

On the other hand, the war had resolved the question of union and ended the debate over the relationship of the states to the federal government. During the war, Republicans seized the opportunity to pass legislation that would foster national union and economic growth: the Pacific Railroad Act of 1862, which set aside huge tracts of public land to finance the transcontinental railroad; the Homestead Act of 1862, which was to provide yeoman farmers cheaper and easier access to the public domain; the Morrill Act of 1862, which established support for agricultural (land-grant) colleges; and the banking acts of 1863 and 1864.

The war had also resolved the issue of slavery, but new questions had to be faced. What would happen to the former slaves? Were blacks to have the same civil and political rights as

whites? Would they be given land, the means for economic independence? What would be their relations with their former owners?

What, indeed, would be the status of the conquered South in the nation? Should it be punished for the rebellion? Some people thought so. But Lincoln, as early as December 1863, had announced a generous plan of reconciliation. He was willing to recognize the government of former Confederate states established by a group of citizens equal to 10 percent of those voting in 1860, as long as the group swore to support the Constitution and to accept the abolition of slavery. He began to restore state governments in three former Confederate states on that basis. But not all northerners agreed with his leniency, and the debate continued.

In his 1865 inaugural address, Lincoln urged Americans to harbor "malice towards none . . . and charity for all." "Let us strive," he urged, "to finish the work we are in; to bind up the nation's wounds . . . to do all which may achieve a just and lasting peace." Generosity and goodwill would pave the way for reconciliation. On April 14, he pressed the point home to his cabinet. His wish was to avoid persecution and bloodshed.

That same evening, only five days after the surrender at Appomattox, the president attended a play at Ford's Theater. There, as one horrified eyewitness reported,

> a pistol was heard and a man . . . dressed in a black suit of clothes leaped onto the stage apparently from the President's box. He held in his right hand a dagger whose blade appeared about 10 inches long. . . . Every one leaped to his feet, and the cry of 'the President is assassinated' was heard—Getting where I could see into the President's box, I saw Mrs. Lincoln . . . in apparent anguish.

John Wilkes Booth, a southern sympathizer, had killed the president.

CONCLUSION

AN UNCERTAIN FUTURE

As the war ended, many Americans grieved for the man whose decisions had so marked their lives for five years. "Strong men have wept tonight & the nation will mourn tomorrow," wrote one eyewitness to the assassination. Many more wept for friends and relations who had not survived the war but whose actions had in one way or another contributed to its outcome. Perhaps not all Americans realized how drastically the war had altered their lives, their futures, their nation. It was only as time passed that the war's impact became clear to them. And it was only with time that they recognized how many problems the war had left unsolved. It is to these years of Reconstruction that we turn next.

Recommended Reading

Good general introductions are Peter J. Parrish, *The American Civil War* (1985); and James McPherson, *Battle Cry of Freedom: The Civil War Era* (1988). Careful studies of the Confederacy include Emory M. Thomas, *The Confederate Nation, 1861–1865* (1979); and Paul D. Escott, *After Secession: Jefferson Davis and the Failure of Confederate Nationalism* (1978). For economic matters, consult David Gilchrist and W. David Lewis, eds., *Economic Change in the Civil War Era* (1965). On social history, see Maris Vinovskis, ed., *Toward a Social History of the American Civil War* (1990).

The military aspects of the war can be followed in Richard E. Beringer, Herman Hattaway, Archer Jones, and William N. Still, Jr., *Why the South Lost the Civil War* (1986); and Henry S. Commager, ed., *The Blue and the Gray: The Story of the Civil War as Told by Participants,* 2 vols. (1950).

Eric Foner's essays, collected in *Politics and Ideology in the Age of Civil War* (1980), are valuable for understanding the political context of the Civil War. Also helpful is John L. Thomas, ed., *Abraham Lincoln and the American Political Tradition* (1986). For a biography, see Stephen B. Oates, *With Malice Towards None: The Life of Abraham Lincoln* (1977).

Benjamin Quarles studies southern blacks in *The Negro in the Civil War* (1968 ed.), while Leon F. Litwack illuminates changing race relations in *Been in the Storm So Long: The Aftermath of Slavery* (1979). A good primary source is James M. McPherson, ed., *The Negro's Civil War* (1965). The strength of white racism is portrayed in George M. Frederickson, *The Black Image in the White Mind* (1971); and in C. Vann Woodward, *American Counterpoint: Slavery and Racism in the North-South Dialogue* (1971).

The experience of women is treated in Catherine Clinton and Nina Silber, eds., *Divided Houses: Gender and the Civil War* (1993); John P. Bugardt, ed., *Civil War Nurse* (1980); and in more general works such as Sara M. Evans, *Born for Liberty: A History of Women in America* (1989); and Eleanor Flexner, *Century of Struggle: The Woman's Rights Movement in the United States* (1975). Although Mary Boykin Chesnut's diary was actually written after the war, her vivid account, *Mary Chesnut's Civil War* (1981), is well worth consulting. Southern Unionists are explored in Phillip Shaw Paludan's *Victims: A True Story of the Civil War* (1981).

Novels about the Civil War include Stephen Crane, *The Red Badge of Courage* (any ed.), and MacKinlay Kantor, *Andersonville* (1955).

Time Line

1861	Lincoln calls up state militia and suspends habeas corpus First Battle of Bull Run Union blockades the South
1862	Battles at Shiloh, Bull Run, and Antietam *Monitor* and *Virginia* battle First black regiment authorized by Union Union issues greenbacks South institutes military draft Pacific Railroad Act Homestead Act Morrill Land-Grant College Act
1863	Lincoln issues Emancipation Proclamation
1863	Congress adopts military draft Battles of Gettysburg and Vicksburg Union Banking Act Southern tax laws and impressment act New York draft riots Southern food riots
1864	Sherman's march through Georgia Lincoln reelected Union Banking Act
1865	Lee surrenders at Appomattox Lincoln assassinated Andrew Johnson becomes president Congress passes Thirteenth Amendment, abolishing slavery

chapter 16

....

The Union
Reconstructed

In April 1864, one year before Lincoln's assassination, Robert Allston died of pneumonia. His wife, Adele, and daughter, Elizabeth, took over the affairs of their many rice plantations. With Yankee troops moving through coastal South Carolina in the late winter of 1864–1865, Elizabeth's sorrow over the loss of her father turned to "terror" as Union soldiers arrived seeking liquor, firearms, and hidden valuables. The Allston women endured an insulting search and then fled. In a later raid, Yankee troops encouraged the Allston slaves to take furniture and other household goods from the Big Houses, some of which the blacks returned when the Yankees were gone. But before they left, the Union soldiers, in their role as liberators, gave the keys to the crop barns to the semifree slaves.

When the war was over, Adele Allston took an oath of allegiance to the United States and secured a written order commanding the blacks to relinquish these keys. She and Elizabeth made plans to return in the early summer of 1865 to resume control of the family plantations, thereby reestablishing white authority. Possession of the keys to the barns, Elizabeth wrote, would be the "test case" of whether former masters or their former slaves would control land and labor.

Not without some fear, Adele and Elizabeth Allston rode up in a carriage to their former home, Nightingale Hall, to confront their ex-slaves. To their surprise, a pleasant reunion took place. A trusted black foreman handed over the keys to the barns. This harmonious scene was repeated elsewhere.

But at Guendalos, a plantation owned by a son absent during most of the war fighting with the Confederate army, the Allston women met a very different situation. As their carriage arrived, a defiant group of armed ex-slaves lined both sides of the road, following the carriage as it passed by. Tension grew when the carriage stopped. A former black driver, Uncle Jacob, was unsure whether to yield the keys to the barns full of rice and corn, put there by black labor. An angry young man shouted out: "Ef yu gie up de key, blood'll flow." Uncle Jacob slowly slipped the keys back into his pocket.

The tension increased as the blacks sang freedom songs and brandished hoes, pitchforks, and guns in an effort to discourage anyone from going to town for help.

The Allstons spent the night safely, if restlessly, in their house. Early the next morning, they were awakened by a knock at the unlocked front door. Adele slowly opened the door, and there stood Uncle Jacob. Without a word, he gave her the keys.

⋅>═══◍═══<⋅

The story of the keys reveals most of the essential human ingredients of the Reconstruction era. Despite defeat and surrender, southern whites were determined to resume control of both land and labor. Rebellion aside, the law, property titles, and federal enforcement were generally on the side of the original owners of the land.

In this encounter between former slaves and the Allston women, the role of the northern federal officials is most revealing. The Union soldiers, literally and symbolically, gave the keys of freedom to the blacks but did not stay around long enough to guarantee that freedom. Understanding the limits of northern help, Uncle Jacob handed the keys to land and liberty back to his former owner. The blacks at Guendalos knew that if they wanted to ensure their freedom, they had to do it themselves.

The goals of the groups at the Allston plantations were in conflict. The theme of this chapter is the story of what happened to people's various dreams as they sought to form new social, economic, and political relationships during Reconstruction.

For much of the twentieth century, Reconstruction was seen as a disgraceful period in which vindictive northern Radical Republicans imposed a harsh rule of evil carpetbaggers, scalawags, and illiterate blacks on the helpless, defeated South. *Gone with the Wind* reflects this view. In 1935, the black scholar W. E. B. Du Bois challenged this interpretation, suggesting instead that an economic struggle over land and the exploitation of black workers was the crucial focus of Reconstruction. Other historians have shown the beginnings of biracial cooperation and political participation in some southern states and the eventual violent repression of the freedmen's dreams of land, schooling, and votes. This chapter reflects this later interpretation, enriched by an awareness of the ambiguity of human motives and the devastation and divisions of class and race in pursuit of conflicting goals.

THE BITTERSWEET AFTERMATH OF WAR

"There are sad changes in store for both races," the daughter of a Georgia planter wrote in her diary early in the summer of 1865, adding, "I wonder the Yankees do not shudder to behold their work." In order to understand the bittersweet nature of Reconstruction, we must look at the state of the nation in the spring of 1865, shortly after the assassination of President Lincoln.

The United States in 1865

The "Union" was in a state of constitutional crisis in April 1865. The status of the 11 states of the former Confederate States of America was unclear. Lincoln's official position had been that the southern states had never left the Union, which was "constitutionally indestructible." As a result of their rebellion, they were only "out of their proper relation" with the United States. The president, therefore, as commander in chief, had the authority to decide on the basis for setting relations right and proper again.

Lincoln's congressional opponents argued that by declaring war on the Union, the Confederate states had broken their constitutional ties and reverted to a kind of prestatehood status like territories or "conquered provinces." Congress, therefore, which decided on the admission of new states, should resolve the constitutional issues and assert its authority over the reconstruction process. This conflict between Congress and the president reflected the fact that the president had taken on broad powers necessary for rapid mobilization of resources and domestic security during the war. As soon as the war was over, Congress sought to reassert its authority, as it would do after every subsequent war.

In April 1865, the Republican Party ruled victorious and virtually alone. Although less than a dozen years old, the Republicans had won the war, preserved the Union, and enacted a program for economic growth. The Democratic Party, by contrast, was in shambles. Nevertheless, it had been politically important in 1864 for the Republicans to show that the war was a bipartisan effort. A Jacksonian Democrat and Unionist from Tennessee, the tactless Andrew Johnson, had therefore been nominated as Lincoln's vice president. In April 1865, he headed the government.

The United States in the spring of 1865 was a picture of stark economic contrasts. Northern cities hummed with productive activity while southern cities lay in ruins. Roadways and railroad tracks laced the North, while in the South railroads and roads had been devastated. Southern financial institutions were bankrupt, while northern banks flourished. Northern farms,

under increasing mechanization, were more productive than ever before. Southern farms and plantations, especially those that had lain in the path of Sherman's march, were like a "howling waste."

Despite pockets of relative wealth, the South was largely devastated as soldiers demobilized and returned home in April 1865. Yet, as a later southern writer, Wilbur Cash, explained, "If this war had smashed the Southern world, it had left the essential Southern mind and will . . . entirely unshaken." Many southerners wanted nothing less than to resist Reconstruction and restore their old world.

The dominant social reality in the spring of 1865, however, was that nearly four million former slaves were on their own, facing the challenges of freedom. After an initial reaction of joy and celebration, the freedmen quickly became aware of their continuing dependence on former owners.

Hopes Among Freedmen

Throughout the South in the summer of 1865, there were optimistic expectations in the old slave quarters. As Union soldiers marched through Richmond, prisoners in slave-trade jails chanted: "Slavery chain done broke at last! Gonna praise God till I die!" The slavery chain, however, was not broken all at once but link by link. After Union soldiers swept through an area, Confederate troops would follow, or master and overseer would return, and the slaves learned not to rejoice too quickly or openly. "Every time a bunch of No'thern sojers would come through," recalled one slave, "they would tell us we was free and we'd begin celebratin'. Before we would get through somebody else would tell us to go back to work, and we would go." So former slaves became cautious about what freedom meant.

Gradually, the freedmen began to test their new freedom. The first thing they did was to leave the plantation, if only for a few hours or days. Some former slaves cut their ties entirely, leaving cruel and kindly masters alike.

Many freedmen left the plantation in search of members of their families. For some, freedom meant getting married legally. Legal marriage was important morally, but it also served such practical purposes as establishing the legitimacy of children and gaining access to land titles and other economic opportunities. Marriage also meant special burdens for black women who took on the now familiar double role as housekeeper and breadwinner. For many newly married blacks, however, the initial goal was to create a traditional family life, resulting in the widespread withdrawal of women from plantation field labor.

Another way in which freedmen demonstrated their new status was by choosing surnames; names associated with the concept of independence, such as Washington, were common. Emancipation changed black manners around whites as well. Masks were dropped, and old expressions of humility—tipping a hat, stepping aside, feigning happiness, addressing whites with titles of deference—were discarded. For the blacks, these were necessary symbolic expressions of selfhood; they proved that things were now different. To whites, these behaviors were seen as acts of "insolence," "insubordination," and "puttin' on airs."

However important were choosing names, dropping masks, moving around, getting married, and testing new rights, the primary goal for most freedmen was the acquisition of their own land. During the war, some Union generals had placed liberated slaves in charge of confiscated and abandoned lands. In the Sea Islands off the coast of South Carolina and Georgia, blacks had been working 40-acre plots of land and harvesting their own crops for several years. Some blacks held title to these lands. Northern philanthropists had organized others to grow cotton for the Treasury Department to prove the superiority of free labor over slavery.

Many freedmen expected a new economic order as fair payment for their years of involuntary work on the land. As one freedman put it, "Gib us our own land and we take care ourselves; but widout land, de ole massas can hire us or starve us, as dey please." However cautiously expressed, the freedmen had every expectation, fed by the intensity of their dreams, that "forty acres and a mule" would be provided.

The White South's Fearful Response

White southerners had mixed goals at the war's end. Yeoman farmers and poor whites stood side by side with rich planters in bread lines as together they looked forward to the restoration of their land and livelihood. Suffering from "extreme want and destitution," as a Georgia resident put it, white southerners responded with feelings of outrage, loss, and injustice. "I tell you it is mighty hard," said one man, "for my pa paid his own money for our niggers; and that's not all they've robbed us of. They have taken our horses and cattle and sheep *and everything.*"

A more dominant emotion, however, was fear. The entire structure of southern society was shaken, and the semblance of racial peace and order that slavery had provided was shattered. Many white southerners could hardly imagine a society without blacks in bondage. Having lost control of all that was familiar and revered, whites feared everything from losing their cheap labor supply to having to sit next to blacks on trains.

The mildest of their fears was the inconvenience of doing various jobs and chores they had rarely done before, like housework. The worst fears of southern whites were rape and revenge. The presence of black soldiers touched off fears of violence. Although demobilization occurred rapidly after Appomattox, a few black militia units remained in uniform, parading with guns in southern cities. Acts of violence by black soldiers against whites, however, were rare.

Believing that their world was turned upside

Both white southerners and their former slaves suffered in the immediate aftermath of the Civil War, as illustrated by this engraving from Frank Leslie's Illustrated Newspaper.

down, the former planter aristocracy set out to restore the old plantation order and appropriate racial relationships. The key to reestablishing white dominance were the "black codes" that state legislatures passed in the first year after the end of the war. Many of the codes granted freedmen the right to marry, sue and be sued, testify in court, and hold property. But these rights were qualified. Complicated passages in the codes explained under exactly what circumstances blacks could testify against whites or own property (mostly they could not) or exercise other rights of free persons. Some rights were denied, including racial intermarriage and the right to bear arms, possess alcoholic beverages, sit on trains except in baggage compartments, be on city streets at night, or congregate in large groups.

Many of the alleged rights guaranteed by the black codes—testimony in court, for example—were passed to induce the federal government to withdraw its remaining troops from the South. This was a crucial issue, for in many

places marauding groups of whites were assaulting and terrorizing virtually defenseless freedmen, who clearly needed protection and the right to testify in court against whites.

Because white planters needed the freedmen's labor, the crucial provisions of the black codes were intended to regulate the freedmen's economic status. "Vagrancy" laws provided that any blacks not "lawfully employed," which usually meant by a white employer, could be arrested, jailed, fined, or hired out to a man who would assume responsibility for their debts and future behavior. The codes regulated the work contracts by which black laborers worked in the fields for white landowners, including severe penalties for leaving before the yearly contract was fulfilled and rules for proper behavior, attitude, and manners. In this way, southern leaders sought to reestablish their dominance.

NATIONAL RECONSTRUCTION

The question facing the national government in 1865 was whether it would use its power to support the black codes and the reimposition of racial intimidation in the South or to uphold the newly sought rights of the freedmen. Would the federal government side with the democratic reform impulse in American history, which stressed human rights and liberty, or with the forces emphasizing property, order, and self-interest? Although the primary drama of Reconstruction took place in the conflict between white landowners and black freedmen over land and labor in the South, the struggle over Reconstruction policy among politicians in Washington played a significant role in the local drama, as well as the next century of American history.

The Presidential Plan

After initially calling for punishment of the defeated Confederates for "treason," President

Johnson soon adopted a more lenient policy. On May 29, 1865, he issued two proclamations setting forth his reconstruction program. Like Lincoln, he maintained that the southern states had never left the Union. His first proclamation continued Lincoln's policies by offering "amnesty and pardon, with restoration of all rights of property" to all former Confederates who would take an oath of allegiance to the Constitution and the Union of the United States. However, he made exceptions: ex–Confederate government leaders and rich rebels whose taxable property was valued at over $20,000. Any southerners not covered by the amnesty proclamation could, however, apply for special individual pardons, which Johnson granted to nearly all applicants. By the fall of 1865, only a handful remained unpardoned.

Johnson's second proclamation laid out the steps by which southern states could reestablish state governments. First, the president would appoint a provisional governor, who would call a state convention representing "that portion of the people of said State who are loyal to the United States." This included those who took the oath of allegiance or were otherwise pardoned. The convention should ratify the Thirteenth Amendment, which abolished slavery, void secession, repudiate all Confederate debts, and then elect new state officials and members of Congress.

Under this lenient plan, each of the southern states successfully completed reconstruction and sent newly elected members to the Congress that convened in December 1865. Southern voters defiantly elected dozens of former officers and legislators of the Confederacy, including a few not yet pardoned. Some state conventions hedged on ratifying the Thirteenth Amendment, and some asserted their right to compensation for the loss of slave property. No state provided for black suffrage, and most did nothing to guarantee civil rights, schooling, or economic protection for the freedmen. Less than eight months after Appomattox, Reconstruction seemed to be over.

Congressional Reconstruction

As they looked at the situation late in 1865, northern leaders painfully saw that almost none of their postwar goals were being fulfilled. The South was taking advantage of the president's program to restore the power of the prewar planter aristocracy. The freedmen were receiving neither equal citizenship nor economic independence. And the Republicans were not likely to maintain their political power and stay in office. Would the Democratic Party and the South gain by postwar politics what they had been unable to achieve by civil war?

Congressional Republicans, led by Congressman Thaddeus Stevens of Pennsylvania and Senator Charles Sumner of Massachusetts, decided to assert their own policies for reconstructing the nation. Although branded as "radicals," only for a brief period in 1866 and 1867 did "radical" rule prevail. Rejecting Johnson's notion that the South had already been reconstructed, Congress asserted its constitutional authority to decide on its own membership and refused seats to the newly elected senators and representatives from the old Confederate states. Congress then established the Joint Committee on Reconstruction to investigate conditions in the South. Its report documented disorder and resistance and the appalling treatment and conditions of the freedmen. Even before the report was made final in 1866, Congress passed a civil rights bill to protect the fragile rights of the blacks and extended for two more years the Freedmen's Bureau, an agency providing emergency assistance at the end of the war. President Johnson vetoed both bills, arguing that they were unconstitutional and calling his congressional opponents "traitors."

Johnson's growing anger forced moderates into the radical camp, and Congress passed both bills over his veto. Both, however, were watered down by weakening the power of enforcement.

A white mob burned this freedmen's school during the Memphis riot of May 1866.

Southern civil courts, therefore, regularly disallowed black testimony against whites, acquitted whites charged with violence against blacks, sentenced blacks to compulsory labor, and generally made discriminatory sentences for the same crimes. In this judicial climate, racial violence erupted with discouraging frequency.

In Memphis, for example, a race riot occurred in May 1866 that typified race relations during the Reconstruction period. A street brawl erupted between the police and some recently discharged but armed black soldiers. After some fighting and an exchange of gunfire, the soldiers went back to their fort. That night, white mobs, led by prominent local officials, invaded the black section of the city. With the encouragement of the Memphis police, the mobs engaged in over 40 hours of terror, killing, beating, robbing, and raping virtually helpless residents and burning houses, schools, and churches. When it was over, 48 persons, all but two of them black,

had died in the riot. The local Union army commander took his time intervening to restore order, arguing that his troops had "a large amount of public property to guard [and] hated Negroes too." A congressional inquiry found that in Memphis, blacks had "no protection from the law whatever."

A month later, Congress proposed to the states the ratification of the Fourteenth Amendment, the single most significant act of the Reconstruction era. The first section of the amendment sought to provide permanent constitutional protection of the civil rights of freedmen by defining them as citizens. States were prohibited from depriving "any person of life, liberty, or property, without due process of law," and all persons were guaranteed "the equal protection of the laws." In section 2, Congress paved the way for black male suffrage in the South by declaring that states not enfranchising black males would have their "basis of representation reduced" proportionally. Other sections of the amendment denied leaders of the Confederacy the right to hold national or state political office (except by act of Congress), repudiated the Confederate debt, and denied claims of compensation by former slave owners for their lost property.

President Johnson urged the southern states not to ratify the Fourteenth Amendment, and ten states immediately rejected it. Johnson then went on the campaign trail in the midterm election of 1866 to ask voters to throw out the radical Republicans. Vicious name calling and other low forms of electioneering marked this first political campaign since the war's end. The result of the election was an overwhelming victory for the Republicans and a repudiation of Andrew Johnson and his policies.

Therefore, early in 1867, Reconstruction Acts were passed dividing the southern states into five military districts to maintain order and protect the rights of property and persons and defining a new process for readmitting a state.

Qualified voters, which included blacks and excluded unreconstructed rebels, would elect delegates to state constitutional conventions, which then would write new constitutions guaranteeing black suffrage. After the new voters of the states had ratified the constitutions, elections would be held to choose governors and state legislatures. When a state ratified the Fourteenth Amendment, its representatives to Congress would be accepted, thus completing readmission to the Union.

The President Impeached

At the same time as it passed the Reconstruction Acts, Congress also approved bills to restrict the powers of the president and to establish the dominance of the legislative branch over the executive. The Tenure of Office Act, designed to protect the outspoken secretary of war, Edwin Stanton, from removal by Johnson, limited the president's appointment powers. Other measures restricted his power as commander in chief. Johnson behaved exactly as congressional Republicans had anticipated, vetoing the Reconstruction Acts, issuing orders to limit military commanders in the South, and removing cabinet and other government officials sympathetic to Congress's program. The House Judiciary Committee investigated, charging the president with "usurpations of power," but moderate House Republicans defeated impeachment resolutions to remove Johnson from office.

In August 1867, Johnson finally dismissed Stanton and asked for Senate consent. When the Senate refused, the president ordered Stanton to surrender his office, which he refused, barricading himself inside. This time the House rushed impeachment resolutions to a vote, charging the president with "high crimes and misdemeanors" as detailed in 11 offenses while in office, mostly focusing on alleged violations of the Tenure of Office Act. The three-month trial in the Senate early in 1868 featured impassioned oratory, but in the end, seven moderate Republicans joined

Democrats against conviction, and the effort to find the president guilty as charged fell short of the two-thirds majority required by a single vote.

As the moderate or regular Republicans gained strength in 1868 through their support of the presidential election winner, Ulysses S. Grant, radicalism lost much of its power within Republican ranks. Not for another 100 years would a president again face removal from office through impeachment.

Congressional Moderation

The impeachment crisis revealed that most Republicans were more interested in protecting themselves than the freedmen and in punishing Johnson rather than the South. It is revealing to look not only at what Congress did during Reconstruction but also at what it did not do.

With the exception of Jefferson Davis, Congress did not imprison Confederate leaders, and only one person, the commander of the infamous Andersonville prison camp, was put to death. Congress did not insist on a long-term probationary period before southern states could be readmitted to the Union. It did not reorganize southern local governments. It did not mandate a national program of education for the four million ex-slaves. It did not confiscate and redistribute land to the freedmen, nor did it prevent President Johnson from taking land away from freedmen who had gained possessory titles during the war. It did not, except indirectly, provide economic help to black citizens.

What Congress did do, and that only reluctantly, was grant citizenship and suffrage to the freedmen. Black suffrage gained support after the election of 1868, when General Grant, a military hero regarded as invincible, barely won the popular vote in several states. Congressional Republicans, who had twice rejected a suffrage amendment, took another look at the idea as a way of adding grateful black votes to party rolls. After a bitterly contested fight, repeated in several state ratification contests, the Fifteenth

Amendment, forbidding all states to deny the vote to anyone "on account of race, color, or previous condition of servitude," became part of the Constitution in 1870. A black preacher from Pittsburgh observed that "the Republican party had done the Negro good, but they were doing themselves good at the same time."

For political reasons, therefore, Congress gave blacks the vote but not the land, the opposite priority of what the freedmen wanted. Almost alone, Thaddeus Stevens argued that "forty acres . . . and a hut would be more valuable . . . than the . . . right to vote." But Congress never seriously considered his plan to confiscate the land of the "chief rebels" and to give a small portion of it, divided into 40-acre plots, to the freedmen.

Although most Americans, in the North as well as the South, opposed confiscation and black independent landownership, Congress passed an alternative measure. Proposed by George Julian of Indiana, the Southern Homestead Act of 1866 made public lands available to blacks and loyal whites in five southern states. But the land was of poor quality and inaccessible, and claimants had only until January 1, 1867, to claim their land. But that was nearly impossible for most blacks because they were under contract with white employers until that date. Only about 4,000 black families even applied for the Homestead Act lands, and fewer than 20 percent of them saw their claims completed. The record of white claimants was not much better. Congressional moderation, therefore, left the freedmen economically weak as they faced the challenges of freedom.

Women and the Reconstruction Amendments

One casualty of the Fourteenth and Fifteenth amendments was the goodwill of the women who had been petitioning and campaigning for suffrage for two decades. They had hoped that grateful male legislators would recognize their support for the Union effort during the war and the suspension of their own demands in the interests of the more immediate concerns of preserving the Union, nursing the wounded, and emancipating the slaves. They were therefore shocked to see the wording of the Fourteenth Amendment, which for the first time inserted the word *male* in the Constitution in referring to a citizen's right to vote. Stanton and Anthony campaigned actively against the Fourteenth Amendment, and when the Fifteenth Amendment was proposed, they wondered why the word *sex* could not have been added to the "conditions" no longer a basis for denial of the vote.

Disappointment over the suffrage issue was one of several reasons that led to a split in the women's movement and the formation of two competing organizations in 1869. While some women's rights activists felt that the struggle for black rights should have its day and should not be hindered by linkage to women's demands for the vote, others pointed out that some blacks were also women. Anthony and Stanton, determined to continue their fight for a national amendment for woman suffrage and a long list of other rights, founded the National Woman Suffrage Association (NWSA). The rival American Woman Suffrage Association (AWSA) concentrated its hopes on securing the vote on a state-by-state basis. In the end, both blacks and women would have a long path of struggle ahead of them.

LIFE AFTER SLAVERY

Clinton Fisk, a well-meaning white who helped to found a black college in Tennessee, told freedmen in 1866 that they could be "as free and as happy" working again for their "old master . . . as any where else in the world." For many blacks such pronouncements sounded familiar, reminding them of white preachers' exhortations during slavery to work hard and obey their masters. Ironically, though, Fisk was an agent of the Freedmen's Bureau, the crucial agency intended to ease the transition from slavery to freedom for the four million ex-slaves.

The Freedmen's Bureau

Never in American history has one small agency—underfinanced, understaffed, and undersupported—been given a harder task than was the Bureau of Freedmen, Refugees and Abandoned Lands. Its purposes and mixed successes illustrate the tortuous course of Reconstruction.

The activities of the Freedmen's Bureau included issuing emergency rations of food and providing clothing and shelter to the homeless, hungry victims of the war; establishing medical care and hospital facilities; providing funds for transportation for the thousands of freedmen and white refugees dislocated by the war; helping blacks search for and put their families back together; and arranging for legal marriage ceremonies. The bureau also served as a friend in local civil courts to ensure that the freedmen got fair trials. Although not initially empowered to do so, the agency was responsible for the education of the ex-slaves. To bureau schools came many idealistic teachers from various northern Freedmen's Aid societies.

In addition, the largest task of the Freedmen's Bureau was to serve as an employment agency, tending to the economic well-being of the blacks. This included settling them on abandoned lands and getting them started with tools, seed, and draft animals, as well as arranging work contracts with white landowners. In the area of work contracts, the Freedmen's Bureau served more to "reenslave" the freedmen as impoverished fieldworkers than to set them on their way as independent farmers.

Although some agents were idealistic young New Englanders eager to help slaves adjust to freedom, others were Union army officers more concerned with social order than social trans-formation. On a typical day, these overworked and underpaid agents would visit courts and schools in their district, supervise the signing of work contracts, and handle numerous complaints, most involving contract violations between whites and blacks or property and domestic disputes among blacks. They were helpful in finding work for the freedmen, but more often than not the agents found themselves defending white landowners by telling the blacks to obey orders, to trust their employers, and to sign and live by disadvantageous contracts.

Despite mounting pressures to support white landowners, personal frustrations, and even threats on their lives, the agents accomplished a great deal. In little more than two years, the Freedmen's Bureau issued 20 million rations (nearly one-third to poor whites), reunited families and resettled some 30,000 displaced war refugees, treated some 450,000 cases of illness and injury, built 40 hospitals and hundreds of schools, provided books, tools, and furnishings—and even some land—to the freedmen, and occasionally protected their economic and civil rights. The historian W. E. B. Du Bois wrote an epitaph for the bureau that might stand for the whole of Reconstruction: "In a time of perfect calm, amid willing neighbors and streaming wealth," he wrote, it "would have been a herculean task" for the bureau to fulfill its many purposes. But in the midst of hunger, sorrow, spite, suspicion, hate, and cruelty, "the work of any instrument of social regeneration was . . . foredoomed to failure."

Economic Freedom by Degrees

The economic failures of the Freedmen's Bureau forced the freedmen into a new economic dependency on their former masters, and both were affected by the changing character of southern agriculture in the postwar years. First, land ownership was concentrated into fewer and even larger holdings than before the Civil War. From South Carolina to Louisiana, the wealthiest tenth of the population owned about 60 percent of the real estate in the 1870s. Second, these large planters increasingly concentrated on one crop, usually cotton, and were tied into the international market. This resulted in a steady drop in food production in the postwar period. Third, reliance on one-crop farming meant that a new credit system emerged whereby most farmers, black and white, depended on local merchants for renting seed, farm implements and animals, provisions, housing, and land. These changes affected race relations and class tensions among whites.

This new system, however, took a few years to develop after emancipation. At first, most freedmen signed contracts with white landowners and worked in gangs in the fields as farm laborers very much as during slavery. But what the freedmen wanted, a Georgia planter correctly observed, was "to get away from all overseers, to hire or purchase land, and work for themselves."

Many blacks therefore broke contracts, ran away, engaged in work slowdowns or strikes, burned barns, and otherwise expressed their displeasure with the contract labor system. Blacks' insistence on autonomy and land of their own was the major impetus for the change from the contract system to tenancy and sharecropping. As a South Carolina freedman put it, "If I can't own de land, I'll hire or lease land, but I won't contract." The sharecroppers were given seed, fertilizer, farm implements, and all necessary food and clothing to take care of their families. In return, the landlord (or a local merchant) told them what to grow and how much and took a share—usually half—of the harvest. The half retained by the cropper, however, was usually needed to pay for goods bought on credit (at huge interest rates) at the landlord's store. Thus the sharecroppers were semiautonomous but remained tied to the landlord's will for economic survival.

Sharecroppers and tenant farmers, though more autonomous than contract laborers, remained dependent on the landlord for their survival.

Under the tenant system, farmers had only slightly more independence. In advance of the harvest, a tenant farmer promised to sell his crop to a local merchant in return for renting land, tools, and other necessities. He was also obligated to purchase goods on credit (at higher prices than whites paid) against the harvest from the merchant's store. At "settling up" time, the income from the sale of the crop was matched with debts accumulated at the store. But tenants usually remained in debt at the end of each year and were then compelled to pledge the next year's crop. Thus a system of debt peonage replaced slavery. Only a very few blacks became independent landowners—about 2 to 5 percent by 1880, but closer to 20 percent in some states by 1900.

These changes in southern agriculture affected yeoman and poor white farmers as well as the freedmen, especially as cotton production doubled between the Civil War and 1880. Like the freedmen, whites, too, were forced to concentrate on growing staples, to pledge their crops against high-interest credit from local merchants, and to face perpetual indebtedness.

Larger planters' reliance on cotton meant fewer food crops, which led to greater dependence on local merchants for provisions and a poorer diet. Poor whites thus faced diminishing fortunes throughout the South. Some became farmhands, earning $6 a month (with board) from other farmers. Other fled to low-paying jobs in urban cotton mills.

In part because their lives were so hard, poor whites persisted in their belief in white superiority. As a federal officer reported in 1866, "The poorer classes of white people ... have a most intense hatred of the Negro, and swear he shall never be reckoned as part of the population." Many poor whites, therefore, joined the Ku Klux Klan and other southern white terror groups that emerged between 1866 and 1868. But however hard life was for poor whites, blacks were far more often sentenced to chain gangs for the slightest crimes and were bound to a life of debt, degradation, and dependency. The

high hopes with which the freedmen had greeted emancipation turned slowly to resignation and disillusionment. Felix Haywood, a former Texas slave, recalled:

> We thought we was goin' to be richer than white folks, 'cause we was stronger and knowed how to work, and the whites ... didn't have us to work for them anymore. But it didn't turn out that way. We soon found out that freedom could make folks proud but it didn't make 'em rich.

Black Self-Help Institutions

It was clear to many black leaders that since white institutions could not fulfill the promises of emancipation, black freedmen would have to do it themselves. Fortunately, the tradition of black community self-help survived in the organized churches and schools of the antebellum free Negro communities and in the "invisible" cultural institutions of the slave quarters. Religion, as usual, was vital. Emancipation brought an explosion in the growth of membership in black churches. The Negro Baptist church grew from 150,000 members in 1850 to 500,000 in 1870. The various branches of the African Methodist Episcopal church increased fourfold in the decade after the Civil War, from 100,000 to over 400,000 members.

Black ministers continued their tradition of community leadership and revivalist preaching. An English visitor to the South in 1867 and 1868, after observing a preacher in Savannah arouse nearly 1,000 people to "sway, and cry, and groan," noted the intensity of black "devoutness."

The freedmen's desire for education was as strong as for religion. A school official in Virginia echoed the observation of many when he said that the freedmen were "down right crazy to learn." This enthusiasm was dampened by the demands of fieldwork and scarce resources for black schools. The first teachers of the black children in the South were unmarried northern women, the legendary "Yankee schoolmarms," sent by groups such as the American Missionary

Along with equal civil rights and land of their own, what the freedmen most wanted was education. Despite white opposition and limited facilities for black schools, one of the most positive outcomes of the Reconstruction era was education in freedmen's schools.

Association. But blacks increasingly preferred their own teachers, who could better understand former slaves. To ensure the training of black preachers and teachers, northern philanthropists founded Howard, Atlanta, Fisk, Morehouse, and other black universities in the South between 1865 and 1867.

Black schools, like churches, became community centers. They published newspapers, provided training in trades and farming, and promoted political participation and land ownership. These efforts made black schools objects of local white hostility. In 1869, in Tennessee alone, 37 black schools were burned to the ground.

White opposition to black education and land ownership stimulated the rise of black nationalism and separatism. In the late 1860s, Benjamin "Pap" Singleton, a former Tennessee slave who had escaped to Canada, organized a land company in 1869 and promoted relocation of blacks to separatist communities in Kansas, where they would be able to manage their own affairs apart from white interference. When these schemes failed, Singleton and other nationalists urged emigration to Canada and Liberia. Other black leaders, notably Frederick Douglass, continued to assert that suffrage would eventually lead to full citizenship rights within the United States.

RECONSTRUCTION IN THE STATES

Douglass's confidence in the power of the ballot seemed warranted in the enthusiastic early months under the Reconstruction Acts of 1867. With President Johnson neutralized, national Republican leaders were finally in a position to accomplish their political goals. Local Republicans, taking advantage of the inability or refusal of many southern whites to vote, overwhelmingly elected their delegates to state constitutional conventions in the fall of 1867. With guarded optimism and a sense of the "sacred importance" of their work, black and white Republicans turned to the task of creating new state governments.

Republican Rule

Despite popular belief, the southern state governments under Republican rule were not dominated by illiterate black majorities intent on "Africanizing" the South by passing compulsory racial intermarriage laws, as many whites feared. Nor were these governments unusually corrupt or financially extravagant. Nor did they use massive numbers of federal troops to enforce their will. Rather, they tried to do their work in a climate of economic distress and increasingly violent harassment.

A diverse combination of political groups made up the new governments elected under congressional Reconstruction. Labeled the "black and tan" governments by their opponents to suggest domination by former slaves and mulattoes, they were actually predominantly white, with the one exception of the lower house of the South Carolina legislature. The new leadership included an old Whiggish elite class of bankers, industrialists, and others interested far more in economic growth than in radical social reforms; northern Republican capitalists seeking investment opportunities; retired Union veterans; and missionaries and teachers. Such people were unfairly labeled "carpetbaggers."

Moderate blacks also participated in the Republican state governments. A large percentage of black officeholders were mulattoes, many of them well-educated preachers, teachers, and soldiers from the North. Others, such as John Lynch of Mississippi, were self-educated tradesmen or representatives of the small landed class of southern blacks. This class composition meant that black leaders often supported land policies that largely ignored the economic needs of the black masses.

These black politicians were more interested in pursuing political influence and education than land redistribution or state aid to black peasants. They sought no revenge or reversal of power, only, as an 1865 petition said, "that the same laws which govern white men shall govern black men [and that] we be dealt with as others are—in equity and justice."

The primary accomplishment of Republican rule in the South was in eliminating the undemocratic features of earlier state constitutions. All states provided universal men's suffrage and loosened requirements for holding office. The basis of state representation was made fairer by apportioning more legislative seats to the interior regions of southern states. Social and penal laws were also modernized.

Republican governments undertook the task of financially and physically reconstructing the South, overhauling tax systems, and approving generous railroad and other capital investment bonds. Most important, the Republican governments provided for a state-supported system of public schools, absent before in most of the South. As in the North, these schools were largely segregated, but for the first time, rich and poor, black and white alike had access to education. As a result, black school attendance increased from 5 to over 40 percent and white from 20 to over 60 percent by the 1880s. All of this cost money, and the Republicans did indeed greatly increase tax rates and state debts. All in all, the Republican governments "dragged the South, screaming and crying, into the modern world."

Despite its effectiveness in modernizing southern state governments, the Republican coalition did not last very long. In fact, as the map indicates, Republican rule lasted for different periods of time in different states. In some

The Return to the Union During Reconstruction

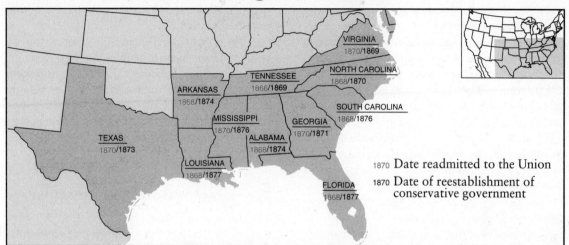

VIRGINIA
1870/**1869**

NORTH CAROLINA
1868/1870

TENNESSEE
1866/**1869**

ARKANSAS
1868/**1874**

SOUTH CAROLINA
1868/1876

MISSISSIPPI
1870/**1876**

GEORGIA
1870/**1871**

ALABAMA
1868/1874

TEXAS
1870/**1873**

LOUISIANA
1868/1877

FLORIDA
1868/1877

1870 Date readmitted to the Union
1870 Date of reestablishment of conservative government

states, Virginia, for example, the Republicans ruled hardly at all. In South Carolina, the unwillingness of black leaders to use their power to help black laborers contributed to their loss of political control to the Democrats. Class tensions and divisions among blacks in Louisiana helped to weaken that Republican regime as well. Republican rule lasted the longest in the black-belt states of the Deep South, where the black population was equal to or greater than the white.

Violence and "Redemption"

Democrats used racial violence, intimidation, and coercion to restore their power. The Ku Klux Klan was only one of several secret organizations that used force and violence against black and white Republicans. The cases of North Carolina and Mississippi are representative in showing how conservative Democrats were able to regain control.

After losing a close election in North Carolina in 1868, conservatives waged a concen-

trated campaign of terror in several counties in the piedmont area. If the Democrats could win these counties in 1870, they would most likely win statewide. In the year prior to the election, several prominent Republicans were killed, including a white state senator, whose throat was cut, and a leading black Union League organizer, who was hanged in the courthouse square with a sign pinned to his breast: "Bewar, ye guilty, both white and black." Scores of citizens were flogged, tortured, fired from their jobs, or forced to flee in the middle of the night from burning homes and barns. The courts consistently refused to prosecute anyone for these crimes. Local papers, in fact, charged that "disgusting negroes and white Radicals" had committed the crimes. The conservative campaign worked. In the election of 1870, some 12,000 fewer Republicans voted in the two crucial counties than had voted two years earlier, and the Democrats swept back into power.

In the state election in Mississippi in 1875, Democrats used similar tactics. In what was called the Mississippi Plan, local Democratic clubs organized themselves into armed militias, marching defiantly through black areas, breaking up Republican meetings, and provoking riots to justify the killing of hundreds of blacks. Armed men were posted during voter registration to intimidate Republicans. At the election itself, anyone still bold enough to attempt to vote was either helped by gun-toting whites to cast a Democratic ballot or driven away from the polls with cannon and clubs. Counties that had earlier given Republican candidates majorities in the thousands managed in 1875 a total of less than a dozen votes!

Democrats called their victory "redemption." As conservative Democratic administrations resumed control of each state government, Reconstruction came to an end. Redemption resulted from a combination of the persistence of white southern resistance, including violence and other coercive measures, and a loss of will to persist in the North.

Congress and President Grant did not totally ignore the violence in the South. Three Force Acts, passed in 1870 and 1871, gave the president strong powers to use federal supervisors to make sure that citizens were not prevented from voting by force or fraud. The third act, known as the Ku Klux Klan Act, declared illegal secret organizations that used disguise and coercion to deprive others of equal protection of the laws. Congress created a joint committee to investigate Klan violence, which reported in 1872 in 13 huge volumes of horrifying testimony. Grant issued proclamations condemning lawlessness and sent some additional troops to South Carolina. However, as reform Republicans realized that black voters supported Grant, they lost interest in defending those voters. Regular Republicans were also not very supportive, since many felt that they could do without black voters. In 1875, Grant's advisers told him that Republicans might lose important Ohio elections if he continued to protect blacks. Thus he decided that year to reject appeals by Mississippi blacks that troops be stationed in their state to guarantee free elections. Grant declared instead that he and the nation "had tired of these annual autumnal outbreaks."

The federal government did little to stop the reign of terror against black and white Republicans throughout the South. The Force Acts were wholly inadequate and were themselves weakly enforced. Although the Ku Klux Klan's power was officially ended, the attitudes (and tactics) of Klansmen would continue long into the next century.

Reconstruction, Northern Style

The American people, like their leaders, were tired of battles over the freedmen and were shifting their attention to other matters. Frustrated with the difficulties of trying to transform an unwilling South and seemingly ungrateful blacks, the easiest course was to give blacks their citizenship and the vote and move on to something else. After the interruptions of civil war and its aftermath, most Americans were primarily interested in starting families, finding work, and making money. This meant firing furnaces in the new steel plant in Wheeling, West Virginia, pounding in railroad ties for the Central Pacific in the Nevada desert, struggling to teach in a one-room schoolhouse in Vermont for $23 a month, or battling heat, locusts, and railroad rates on a family homestead in Kansas.

At both the individual and national levels, Reconstruction, northern style, meant the continuation of the enormous economic revolution of the nineteenth century. Although failing to effect a smooth transition from slavery to freedom for ex-slaves, Republican northerners were able to accelerate and solidify their program of economic growth and industrial and territorial expansion.

The years between 1865 and 1875 featured not only the rise (and fall) of Republican governments in the South but also the spectacular rise of working-class activity and organization. Stimulated by the Civil War to improve working conditions in northern factories, such groups as trade unions, labor reform associations, and labor parties flourished, culminating in the founding of the National Labor Union in 1866. Before the depression of 1873, an estimated 300,000 to 500,000 American workers had enrolled in some 1,500 trade unions, the largest such increase in the nineteenth century. This growth would inevitably affect class tensions. In 1876, hundreds of freedmen in the rice region along the Combahee River in South Carolina went on strike to protest a 40-cent-per-day wage cut, clashing with local sheriffs and white Democratic rifle clubs. A year later, also over wage cuts, thousands of railroad workers in Pittsburgh, St. Louis, Omaha, and other northern cities went out in a nationwide wave of strikes, clashing with local police and the National Guard.

As economic relations changed, so did the Republican Party. It changed from the party of moral reform to one of material interest. In the continuing struggle in American politics between "virtue and commerce," self-interest was again winning. No longer willing to support an agency like the Freedmen's Bureau, Republican politicians had no difficulty backing huge grants of money and land to the railroads. As blacks were told to go to work and help themselves, the Union Pacific was being given subsidies of between $16,000 and $48,000 for each mile of track laid across western plains and mountains.

By 1869, the year financier Jay Gould almost succeeded in cornering the gold market, the nation was increasingly defined by materialistic "go-getters" and by sordid grasping for wealth and power. Ulysses Grant himself was an honest man, but his judgment of others was flawed. His administration featured a series of scandals that touched several cabinet officers and relatives and even two vice presidents. Under Grant's appointments, outright graft flourished in a half dozen departments. Most scandals involved large sums of public money. The Whiskey Ring affair, for example, cost the public millions of dollars in lost tax revenues siphoned off to government of-

ficials. Gould's gold scam received the unwitting aid of Grant's Treasury Department and the knowing help of his brother-in-law.

Nor was Congress pure in these various schemes. Crédit Mobilier figured in the largest of several scandals in which construction companies for transcontinental railroads (in this case a dummy company) received generous bonds and work contracts in exchange for giving congressmen gifts of money, stocks, and railroad lands. Henry Adams spoke for many Americans when he said that Grant's administration "outraged every rule of decency."

The election of 1872 marked the decline of public interest in moral issues. A "liberal" faction of the Republican Party, unable to dislodge Grant and disgusted with his administration, formed a third party with a reform platform and nominated Horace Greeley, editor of the New York *Tribune,* for president. Democrats, lacking notable presidential candidates, also nominated Greeley, even though he had spent much of his earlier career assailing Democrats as "rascals." Despite his wretched record, Grant easily won a second term.

The End of Reconstruction

Soon after Grant's second inauguration, a financial panic, caused by overconstruction of railroads and the collapse of some crucial eastern banks, created a terrible depression that lasted throughout the mid-1870s. In times of hardship, economic issues dominated politics, further pulling attention away from the plight of the freedmen. As Democrats took control of the House of Representatives in 1874 and looked toward winning the White House in 1876, politicians talked about such issues as new scandals in the Grant administration, unemployment, various proposals for public works expenditures for relief, the availability of silver and greenback dollars, and high tariffs.

No one, it seemed, talked much about the rights and conditions of southern freedmen. In 1875, a guilt-ridden Congress passed Senator

Charles Sumner's civil rights bill, intended to put teeth into the Fourteenth Amendment. But the act was not enforced and was declared unconstitutional by the Supreme Court eight years later. Congressional Reconstruction, long dormant, had ended. The election of 1876 sealed the conclusion.

As their nominee for president in 1876, the Republicans turned to a former governor of Ohio, Rutherford B. Hayes, partly because of his reputation for honesty, partly because he had been an officer in the Union army (a necessity for post–Civil War candidates), and partly because, as Henry Adams put it, he was "obnoxious to no one." The Democrats chose Governor Samuel J. Tilden of New York, who achieved national recognition as a civil service reformer in breaking up the corrupt Tweed Ring.

Tilden won a majority of the popular vote and appeared to have enough electoral votes for victory. Of 20 disputed electoral votes, all but one came from states in the Deep South, where Democrats had applied various versions of the Mississippi Plan to intimidate voters. To resolve the disputed votes, Congress created a special electoral commission, which awarded Hayes all 20 votes, enough to win, 185 to 184.

Outraged Democrats threatened to stop the Senate from officially counting the electoral votes, thus preventing Hayes's inauguration. The country was in a state of crisis, and some Americans wondered if civil war might break out again.

As the inauguration date approached and newspapers echoed outgoing President Grant's call for "peace at any price," the forces of mutual self-interest concluded the "compromise of 1877." The Democrats agreed to suspend resistance to the counting of the electoral votes, and on March 2, Rutherford B. Hayes was declared president. In exchange for the presidency, Hayes ordered the last remaining troops out of the South (South Carolina, Louisiana, and Florida being the last states under military Reconstruction), appointed a former Confederate general to his cabinet, supported federal aid to bolster economic and railroad development in the South, and announced his intentions to let southerners handle race relations themselves. Hayes let it be known that he would not enforce the Fourteenth and Fifteenth amendments, thus initiating a pattern of executive inaction not broken until the middle of the twentieth century. The immediate crisis was averted, officially ending the era of Reconstruction, but the unfulfilled hopes of freedmen continued to smolder beneath the surface of everyday life.

CONCLUSION

A MIXED LEGACY

In the 12 years between Appomattox and Hayes's inauguration, the diverse dreams of victorious northern Republicans, defeated white southerners, and hopeful black freedmen conflicted. There was little chance that all could be realized, yet each group could point to a modest fulfillment of its goals. The compromise of 1877 cemented the reunion of South and North, thus providing new opportunities for economic development in both regions. The Republican Party achieved its economic goals and preserved its political hold on the White House, though not Congress, with two exceptions, until 1932. The ex–Confederate states were brought back into the Union, and southerners retained their firm control of southern lands and black labor, though not without struggle and some changes. To the extent that the peace of 1877 was preserved "at any price," that price was paid by the freedmen.

In 1880, Frederick Douglass summarized Reconstruction for the freedmen, saying that it was a wonder to him "not that freedmen have made so little progress, but, rather, that they have made so much; not that they have been standing still, but that they have been able to stand at all." Indeed, despite their liabilities, the freedmen had made admirable gains in education and in economic and family survival. Although sharecropping and tenancy were harsh systems, black laborers organized themselves to achieve a measure of autonomy and opportunity in their lives that could never be diminished. Moreover, the three great Reconstruction amendments to the Constitution, despite flagrant violation over the next 100 years, held out the promise that the rights of equal citizenship and political participation would yet be fulfilled.

Recommended Reading

The best overviews of the Reconstruction era are John Hope Franklin, *Reconstruction After the Civil War* (1961); Kenneth Stampp, *The Era of Reconstruction, 1865–1877* (1965); and the brilliant work by Eric Foner, *Reconstruction: America's Unfinished Revolution, 1863–1877* (1988).

The fullest, most moving account of the black experience in the transition from slavery to freedom is Leon Litwack's massive and sensitive work, *Been in the Storm So Long: The Aftermath of Slavery* (1980). The southern white response to emancipation is described in Dan T. Carter, *When the War Was Over: The Failure of Self-Reconstruction in the South, 1865–1867* (1985).

The economy of the South and the freedmen's experience with land and labor are described in Roger Ransom and Richard Sutch, *One Kind of Freedom: The Economic Consequences of Emancipation* (1977); and Eric Foner, *Nothing but Freedom: Emancipation and Its Legacy* (1983). An excellent work showing the white experience with tenancy in the changing economy of the South is Stephen Hahn, *The Roots of Southern Populism* (1983). The Freedmen's Bureau is the subject of Donald Nieman, *To Set the Law in Motion: The Freedmen's Bureau and the Legal Rights of Blacks, 1865–1868* (1979). Continuing racial prejudice in the South and North is the subject of C. Vann Woodward, *The Strange Career of Jim Crow,* 3d rev. ed. (1974). See also W. E. B. Du Bois's *Black Reconstruction* (1935) and *The Souls of Black Folk* (1903).

Northern politics during Reconstruction have been widely discussed. See David Donald, *The Politics of Reconstruction* (1965); and Michael Les Benedict, *A Compromise of Principle: Congressional Republicans and Reconstruction, 1863–1869* (1974). Southern politics is best seen in Michael Perman, *The Road to Redemption: Southern Politics, 1869–1879* (1984). Grant's presidency and the abandonment of the freedmen by northern Republicans can be traced in William McFeeley, *Grant: A Biography* (1981); and William Gillette, *Retreat from Reconstruction, 1869–1879* (1979). The campaign of violence that ended the Republican governments in the South is told with gripping horror in George C. Rable, *But There Was No Peace: The Role of Violence in the Politics of Reconstruction* (1984).

Five novels written at different times and representing different interpretations of the story of Reconstruction are Albion Tourgée, *A Fool's Errand* (1879); Thomas Dixon, *The Clansman* (1905); W. E. B. Du Bois, *The Quest of the Silver Fleece* (1911); Howard Fast, *Freedom Road* (1944); and Ernest Gaines, *The Autobiography of Miss Jane Pittman* (1971).

Time Line

1865	Civil War ends	**1870**	Fifteenth Amendment ratified
	Lincoln assassinated; Andrew Johnson becomes president	**1870s–1880s**	Black followers of Pap Singleton migrate to Kansas
	Johnson proposes general amnesty and reconstruction plan	**1870–1871**	Force Acts
	Racial confusion, widespread hunger, and demobilization		North Carolina and Georgia reestablish Democratic control
	Thirteenth Amendment ratified	**1872**	General Amnesty Act
	Freedmen's Bureau established		Grant reelected president
1865–1866	Black codes	**1873**	Crédit Mobilier scandal
	Repossession of land by whites and freedmen's contracts		Panic causes depression
1866	Freedmen's Bureau renewed and Civil Rights Act passed over Johnson's veto	**1874**	Alabama and Arkansas reestablish Democratic control
	Southern Homestead Act	**1875**	Civil Rights Act
	Ku Klux Klan formed		Mississippi reestablishes Democratic control
	Tennessee readmitted to Union		
1867	Reconstruction Acts passed over Johnson's veto	**1876**	Hayes-Tilden election
	Impeachment controversy	**1876–1877**	South Carolina, Louisiana, and Florida reestablish Democratic control
	Freedmen's Bureau ends		
1868	Fourteenth Amendment ratified	**1877**	Compromise of 1877; Rutherford B. Hayes assumes presidency and ends Reconstruction
	Johnson acquitted		
	Ulysses S. Grant elected president		
1868–1870	Ten states readmitted under congressional plan	**1880s**	Tenancy and sharecropping prevail in the South
1869	Georgia and Virginia reestablish Democratic Party control		Disfranchisement and segregation of southern blacks begins

part 4

An Industrializing People

1865-1900

In the last quarter of the nine-teenth century Americans turned their energies toward transforming their society from one based on agriculture to one based on heavy industry. This era of technological change, industrial growth, and national expansion deeply affected rural Americans and Native Americans as well as urban labor. By 1900, the United States had emerged as one of the world's great industrial powers and had entered the international arena as a new aspiring contender.

Chapters 17, 18, and 19 form a unit. Chapter 17, "Rural America in the Industrial Age," examines the ways in which American farmers modernized and vastly expanded production after the Civil War. Even though agriculture provided the basis for urban industrial development, many farmers did not win the rewards they had anticipated. While the postwar period was difficult for some farmers, it was disastrous for Native Americans. By 1900, the power of the Plains Indians had been broken and the reservation system firmly set in place.

Chapter 18, "The Rise of Smoke-stack America," focuses on the character of industrial progress and urban expansion. The labor conflicts of the period indicate the difficulty of these years for most working-class Americans.

In Chapter 19, "Politics and Reform," we see how the national politics of the Gilded Age largely ignored the needs of farmers, workers, and other ordinary Americans and how the 1890s became a turning point in American attitudes and political party alignments.

Chapter 20, "Becoming a World Power," demonstrates the international consequences of the country's successful industrialization, its emerging sense of national identity, and its

chapter 17

Rural America in the Industrial Age

In 1873, Milton Leeper, his wife, Hattie, and their baby, Anna, climbed into a wagon piled high with their possessions and set out to homestead in Boone County, Nebraska. From their claim, Hattie wrote to her sister in Iowa, "When we get a fine house and 100 acres under cultivation, I wouldn't trade with any one." But Milton had broken in only 13 acres when disaster struck. Hordes of grasshoppers appeared, and the Leepers fled their claim and took refuge in the nearby town of Fremont.

There they stayed for two years. Milton worked first at a store, then hired out to other farmers. Hattie sewed, kept a boarder, and cared for chickens and a milk cow. The family lived on the brink of poverty but never gave up hope. In 1876, the Leepers triumphantly returned to their claim with the modest sum of $27 to help them start over.

The grasshoppers were gone, there was enough rain, and preaching was only half a mile away. The Leepers, like others, began to prosper. Two more daughters were born and cared for in the comfortable sod house, "homely" on the outside but plastered and cozy within. As Hattie explained, the homesteaders lived "just as civilized as they would in Chicago."

Their luck did not last. Hattie, pregnant again, fell ill and died in childbirth along with her infant son. Heartbroken, Milton buried his wife and child and left the claim. The last frontier had momentarily defeated him, although he would try farming in at least four other locations before his death in 1905.

The story of the Leepers illustrates some of the problems confronting rural Americans in the last quarter of the nineteenth century. As a mature industrial economy transformed agriculture and shifted the balance of economic power permanently away from America's farmlands to the country's cities and factories, many farmers found it impossible to realize the traditional dream of rural independence and prosperity. Even bountiful harvests no longer guaranteed success. "We were told . . . to go to work and raise a big crop; that was all we needed," said one farmer. "We went to work and plowed and planted; the rains fell, the sun shone, nature smiled, and we raised the big crop they told us to; and what came of it? Eight cent corn, ten cent oats, two cent beef and no price at all for butter and eggs—that's what came of it." Native Americans also discovered that changes in rural life threatened their values and dreams. As the Sioux leader Red Cloud told railroad surveyors in Wyoming, "We do not want you here. You are scaring away the buffalo."

This chapter explores the agricultural transformation of the late nineteenth century and highlights the ways in which rural Americans—red, white, and black—joined the industrial world and responded to new conditions. The rise of large-scale agriculture in the West, the exploitation of its natural resources, and the development of the Great Plains form a backdrop for the discussion of the impact of white settlement on western tribes and their reactions to white incursions. In an analysis of the South, the efforts of whites to create a "New South" form a contrast to the underlying realities of race, cotton, and economic peonage. The chapter also highlights the protests of blacks and farmers against their places in American life.

MODERNIZING AGRICULTURE

Between 1865 and 1900, the nation's farms more than doubled in number as Americans pushed west of the Mississippi and broke virgin land. In both newly settled and older areas, farmers raised specialized crops with the aid of modern machinery and relied on the expanding railroad system to send them to market. The character of agriculture became increasingly capitalistic. Farmers, as one New Englander pointed out, "must understand farming as a business; if they do not it will go hard with them."

Rural Myth and Reality

The number of Americans still farming the land testified to the continuing vitality of the rural tradition. In the late eighteenth century, Benjamin Franklin praised the country's "industrious frugal farmers," while Thomas Jefferson viewed them as the "deposit for substantial and genuine virtue" and fundamental to the health of the republic.

The notion that the farmer and the farm life symbolized the essence of America persisted as the United States industrialized. The popularity of inexpensive Currier and Ives prints, depicting idyllic rural scenes with sturdy, happy people, suggests how the idealized view of country life captivated Americans.

The prints obscured the often harsh reality of American agriculture. Farmers were no longer the backbone of the work force. In 1860, they represented almost 60 percent of the labor force; by 1900, less than 37 percent of employed Americans were farmers. At the same time, farmers' contribution to the nation's wealth declined from a third to a quarter.

Farmers were increasingly affected by the industrial and urban world. Reliable, cheap transportation allowed them to specialize. Farmers on the Great Plains now grew most of the country's wheat, while those in the Midwest replaced that

This Currier and Ives print expresses an idealized view of rural life, which helps explain the great popularity of these illustrations.

crop with corn used to feed hogs and cattle. Eastern farmers turned to vegetable, fruit, and dairy farming. Cotton continued to dominate the economy of the South, although farmers also raised tobacco, wheat, and rice. In the Far West, grain, fruits, and vegetables predominated.

As farmers specialized in cash crops for national and international markets, their success depended increasingly on outside forces, such as banks, loan companies, middlemen, railroads, and exporters. After 1870, exports of wheat, flour, and animal products rose, with wheat becoming the country's chief cash crop. Thus the cultivation of wheat in Russia and Argentina meant fewer foreign buyers for American grain, and the opening of the Canadian high plains in the 1890s added another competitor.

Farming had become a modern business. "Watch and study the markets and the ways of marketmen . . . learn the art of 'selling well,'" one rural editor advised his readers in 1887. "The work of farming is only half done when the crop is out of the ground."

Like other businesses of the post–Civil War era, farming also increasingly depended on machinery. Harvesters, binders, and other new machines, pulled by work animals, made farm work easier and more efficient. Moreover, they allowed farmers to cultivate far more land than they had been able to do with hand tools, so that by 1900 more than twice as much land was in cultivation as in 1860. But machinery was expensive, and many American farmers had to borrow to buy it. In the decade of the 1880s, mortgage indebtedness grew 2½ times faster than agricultural wealth.

New Farmers, New Farms

As farmers became more like other nineteenth-century businessmen, some became large-scale entrepreneurs. Small family farms still typified American agriculture, but vast mechanized operations devoted to the cultivation of one crop appeared, especially west of the Mississippi River. These farms had huge barns for storage of machinery and a handful of other farm buildings but few gardens, trees, or outbuildings. No churches or villages interrupted the monotony of the landscape.

The bonanza farms, huge wheat farms established in the late 1870s on the northern plains, symbolized the trend to large-scale agriculture. The North Dakota farm that Oliver Dalrymple operated for two Northern Pacific Railroad directors used 200 pairs of harrows and 125 seeders for planting and required 155 binders and 26 steam threshers for harvesting. At peak times, the farm's work force numbered 600 men. The result was a harvest of 600,000 bushels of wheat in 1882.

Overproduction and Falling Prices

Farmers did not initially realize that the new technology might cause problems. As productivity rose, however, the yields for some crops like wheat became so large that the domestic market could not absorb them. The prices farm products commanded steadily declined. In 1867, corn sold for 78 cents a bushel. By 1873, it had fallen to 31 cents and by 1889 to 23 cents. Wheat and cotton prices also spiraled downward.

Because the federal government gradually withdrew paper money from circulation after the Civil War and did not coin much silver, the supply of money rose more slowly than productivity. As a result, prices fell by more than half between the end of the Civil War and 1900. In a deflationary period, farmers received less for their crops but also paid less for their purchases. But deflation increased the real value of debts. In 1888, it took 174 bushels of wheat to pay the interest on a $2,000 mortgage at 8 percent. By 1895, it took 320 bushels.

Farming on the Western Plains, 1880s–1890s

Between 1870 and 1900, the acreage devoted to farming tripled west of the Mississippi as settlers flocked to the Great Plains (North and South Dakota, Kansas, Nebraska, Oklahoma, and Texas). In the mid–nineteenth century, emigrants had deemed the Plains unsuitable for farming and had headed for the Far West. Views of the farming potential of the Plains changed after the Civil War, however. Railroads eager for business as they laid down new lines, town boosters eager for inhabitants, and land speculators eager to sell their holdings all undertook major promotional efforts to lure settlers to the Plains.

Late-nineteenth-century industrial innovations also helped settlers overcome the natural obstacles that made farming on the plains so problematic at midcentury. Because there was so little timber for fencing or housing on the plains, early emigrants had chosen to settle elsewhere. But in the 1870s, Joseph Glidden developed barbed wire as a cheap alternative to timber fencing. Barbed wire fencing could be used to enclose fields on the plains. Other helpful innovations included twine binders, which speeded up grain harvesting, reducing the threat of losing crops to the unpredictable weather, and mail-order steel windmills for pumping water from deep underground wells.

In the first boom period of settlement, lasting from 1879 to the early 1890s, tens of thousands of eager families like the Leepers moved onto the Great Plains and began farming. Some made claims under the Homestead Act, which granted 160 acres to any family head or adult who lived on the claim for five years or who paid $1.25 an acre after six months of residence. Because homestead land was frequently less desirable than land held by railroads and speculators, however, most settlers bought land outright rather than taking up claims. The costs of getting started were thus more substantial than the Homestead Act would suggest. In 1880, some 20 percent of the Plains farmers were tenants who lacked the capital to buy land, and this percentage rose over time.

Many of the new settlers were immigrants, most of whom arrived from Germany, the

Agriculture in the 1880s

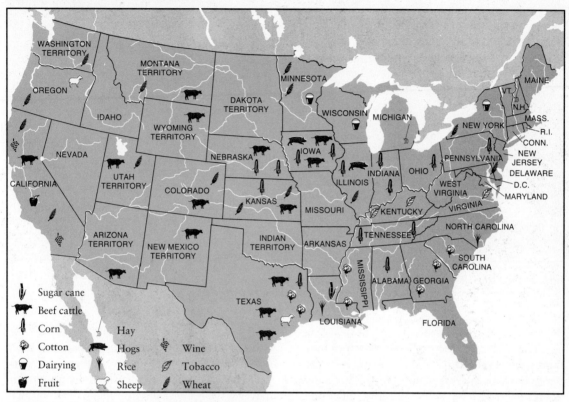

This map reveals the patterns of regional agricultural specialization in the 1880s.

British Isles, and Canada. Many Scandinavians, Czechs, and Poles also moved to the new frontier.

Life on the Plains frontier often proved difficult. The costs of machinery, the vagaries of crops and markets, the pests and natural disasters, the shortage of cash all contributed to the uncertainties of frontier life. Survival was often precarious, and the chances of failure were great. In addition, many settlers found the vast treeless plains depressing. One New England visitor explained, "It has been terrible on settlers, on the women especially, for there is no society and they get doleful and feel almost like committing suicide for want of society." O. E. Rölvaag's novel *Giants in the Earth* (1927) depicts the wife of a Norwegian immigrant farmer driven to madness and death.

But life on the Plains was not always so discouraging as Rölvaag suggested. Willa Cather, who spent her childhood in Nebraska, showed both the harshness and the lure of prairie life in her novels, while letters and diaries also provide a more positive view of farming life. In 1880, six years after Elam Bartholomew had settled in northern Kansas, his journal reveals that 1,081 people stopped at his home. His wife served 783 meals to visitors. Trips to church, parties, sings, and neighborhood get-togethers brightened family life.

Plains settlers had to devise new forms of shelter, using materials readily at hand. The Rawding family posed with their most prized possessions in front of their Nebraska sod house in 1886.

The Plains frontier required many adjustments, however. Scarce water and violent temperature changes demanded resourcefulness and new modes to behavior. Without firewood, farmers learned to burn corncobs and twisted wheat for warmth. The inventive settlers also discovered how to build houses of sod "bricks." Although from a distance such houses often looked like mounds of earth, they were comfortable, cozy, and practical.

The first wave of expansion into the Great Plains halted abruptly by the early 1890s. Falling agricultural prices cut profits. Then, the unusually plentiful rainfall of the 1880s, which had lured farmers to settle semiarid regions, disappeared. A devastating drought followed. The destitute survived on boiled weeds, a few potatoes, and a little bread and butter. Many farmers could not pay their debts and lost their farms to creditors. Some stayed on as tenants. By 1900, two-thirds of homesteaded farms had failed.

Whether individual farmers remained on the Great Plains or whether they retreated to more promising climates, collectively these new agricultural efforts had a significant long-term impact on the region's environment. When farmers removed sod to build their sod houses and broke the prairies with their ploughs in order to plant their crops, they were removing the earth's protective covering. The heavy winds so common on the prairies could lift exposed topsoil and carry it miles away. The deep plowing, which was essential for dry farming techniques introduced after the drought of the 1880s, worsened this situation. The dust bowl of the 1930s was the eventual outcome of these agricultural interventions.

The Early Cattle Frontier, 1860–1890

In the mid-1870s, a clash between two Plains settlers, John Duncan, a cattleman, and Peter Schmidt, a farmer, symbolized the meeting of the farming and cattle frontiers. Some of Duncan's cattle wandered onto Schmidt's property and destroyed his garden. Schmidt ran the cattle off but was outraged at the damage. For years, such incidents had been rare, but as settlement increased in the 1880s and 1890s, they became more common.

The commercial cattle frontier had its roots in Union military strategy. During the war, the North had cut Texas off from its Confederate markets. At the end of the war, five million longhorns were roaming the Texas range. The postwar burst of railroad construction provided a way of turning cattle into dollars. If ranchers drove the cattle north from Texas to railroad connections for shipment to slaughtering and packing houses in cities like Chicago and Kansas City, their value would soar. Thus started the first cattle drives, celebrated in stories, movies, and television. In the late 1860s, cowboys herded thousands of longhorns north to towns like Abilene, Wichita, and Dodge City.

Ranchers on the Great Plains bought some of the cattle. In the late 1870s and early 1880s, huge ranches appeared in eastern Colorado, Wyoming, and Montana and in western Kansas, Nebraska, and the Dakotas. Because the cattle could roam at will over the public domain, they cost owners little as they fattened up.

By the mid-1880s, the first phase of the cattle frontier was ending as farmers moved onto the Plains, bought up public lands once used for grazing, and fenced them in. But the struggle between cattle ranchers and farmers was only one factor in the cattle frontier's collapse. Eager for fat profits, ranchers overstocked their herds. Hungry cattle ate everything in sight, then grew weak as grass became scarce. As one Texan realized, "Grass is what counts. It's what saves us all—as far as we get saved. . . . Grass is what holds the earth together." When cattlemen overstocked the range, their herds devoured the perennial grasses. In their place tough, less nutritious annual grasses sprang up, and sometimes even these grasses disappeared. Lands once able to support large herds of cattle eventually were transformed into deserts of sagebrush, weeds, and dust.

A winter of memorable blizzards in 1886 killed 90 percent of the cattle. Frantic owners dumped their remaining cattle on the market, getting $8 or even less per animal, compared with the $60 to $70 they had gotten previously. In the aftermath, the ranchers who remained stock raisers adopted new techniques. Experimenting with new breeds, they began to replace their longhorns, to fence in their herds, and to feed them grain during the winter months. Ranching, like farming, was becoming more of a modern business.

Cornucopia on the Pacific

Ranching and farming had a somewhat different history in California. When gold was discovered there in 1849, Americans had rushed west to find it. But as one father told his eager son, "Plant your lands; these be your best gold fields." Little of California's land, however, was actually homesteaded or developed as small family farms. When California entered the Union, Mexican ranchers held vast tracts of land, which never became part of the public domain. Neither Mexican-Americans nor small farmers profited from the 20 years of confusion over the legitimacy of Mexican land titles. Speculators did, however, acquiring much of the Mexican-Americans' land. Consequently, small farmers needed substantial sums to buy land.

California farms were typically larger than farms in the rest of the country. In 1870, the average California farm was 482 acres, whereas the national average farm was only 153 acres. By 1900, two-thirds of the state's agricultural land was occupied by farms of 1,000 acres or more. Small farmers and ranchers did exist, of course, but they found it difficult to compete with large, mechanized operators using cheap migrant laborers, usually Mexican or Chinese.

The value of much of California's agricultural land, especially the southern half of the Central Valley, depended on water. Dams and canals were built to irrigate the parched earth. By 1890, over a quarter of California's farms benefited from irrigation.

Although grain was initially California's most valuable crop, it faced stiff competition from farmers on the Plains and in other parts of the world. Some argued that

> land capable of raising Adriatic figs, Zante currants, French prunes, Malaga raisins, Batavia oranges, Sicily lemons, citrons, limes, dates and olives, and our own incomparable peaches, apricots, nectarines, pears, quinces, plums, pomegranates, apples, English and native walnuts, chestnuts, pecans and almonds, in a climate surpassing that of Italy, is too valuable for the cultivation of simple cereals.

As railroad managers in the 1880s realized the potential profit California's produce represented, they lowered rates and introduced refrigerated railroad cars. Fruit and vegetable production rose. In June 1888, fresh apricots and cherries successfully survived the trip from California to New York. Two years later, 9,000 carloads of navel oranges headed east. Before long California fruit was available in London.

Exploiting Natural Resources

The perspective that led Americans to treat farming as a business was also evident in the ways in which they dealt with the country's abundant natural resources. Gold had been the precious metal originally drawing prospectors to California, but the discovery of other precious materials—silver, iron, copper, coal, lead, zinc, tin—lured thousands west to Colorado, Montana, Idaho, and Nevada as well as to states like Minnesota. The popular conception of the miner as a hardy forty-niner searching for loose placer deposits of gold captures the early days of mining. But by the late nineteenth century, mining

relied on machinery, railroads, engineers, and a large work force. It was a big business with high costs and an underlying philosophy that encouraged rapid and thorough exploitation of the earth's resources.

The decimation of the nation's forests went hand in hand with large-scale mining and the railroads that provided the links to markets. Both railroads and mining depended on wood—railroads for wooden ties, mines for shaft timber and ore reduction. The California State Board of Agriculture estimated in the late 1860s that one-third of the state's forests had already disappeared.

The idea that the public lands belonging to the federal government ought to be rapidly developed supported such exploitation of the nation's natural resources. In 1878, Congress passed the Timber and Stone Act, which initially applied to Nevada, Oregon, Washington, and California. This legislation allowed the sale of 160-acre parcels of the public domain that were "unfit for cultivation" and "valuable chiefly for timber." Timber companies were quick to see the possibilities in the new law. They hired men willing to register for claims and then to turn them over to timber interests. By the end of the century, more than 3.5 million acres of the public domain had been acquired under the legislation, and most of it was in corporate hands.

The rapacious exploitation of resources made some Americans uneasy. Many believed that forests played a part in causing rainfall and that their destruction would have an adverse impact on the climate. Others, like the early environmentalist John Muir, lamented the destruction of the country's great natural beauty. In 1868 Muir came upon the Great Valley of California, "all one sheet of plant gold, hazy and vanishing in the distance . . . one smooth, continuous bed of honey-bloom." He soon realized, however, that a "wild, restless agriculture" and "flocks of hoofed locusts, sweeping over the ground like a fire" would destroy this vision of loveliness. Muir became a conservation champion. He played a part in the creation of Yosemite National Park in 1890 and participated in a successful effort to allow President Benjamin Harrison to classify certain parts of the public domain as forest reserves (the Forest Reserve Act of 1891). In 1892, Muir established the Sierra Club. Conservation ideas were more popular in the East, however, than in the West, where the seeming abundance of natural resources and the profit motive diminished support.

THE SECOND GREAT REMOVAL

As farmers settled the western frontier and became entangled in a national economy, they clashed with the Indian tribes who lived on the land. Black Elk, an Ogalala Sioux, recalled an ominous dream:

> A long time ago my father told me what his father told him, that there was once a Lakota [Sioux] holy man, called Drinks Water, who dreamed what was to be; and this was long before the coming of the Wasichus [white men]. He dreamed . . . that a strange race had woven a spider's web all around the Lakotas. And he said: "When this happens, you shall live in square gray houses, in a barren land, and beside those square gray houses you shall starve."

During Black Elk's lifetime, the nightmarish prophecy came true.

Background to Hostilities

As Chapter 13 explained, the lives of most Plains Indians centered on hunting the buffalo. Increased emigration to California and Oregon in the 1840s and 1850s interrupted tribal pursuits and animal migration patterns. During the Civil War, tribes that President Andrew Jackson had earlier resettled in Oklahoma divided in their

Black Elk, pictured here on the left, was a perceptive observer of the deleterious changes experienced by Indians during the latter part of the nineteenth century.

support of the Union and the Confederacy. After the war, however, all "were treated as traitors." The federal government nullified earlier pledges and treaties, leaving Indians defenseless against further incursions on their lands. As settlers pushed into Kansas, the tribes living in Kansas were shunted into Oklahoma.

The White Perspective

At the end of the Civil War, a state of war existed between Indians and whites on the Plains. The shameful massacre of friendly Cheyenne at Sand Creek, Colorado, by the Colorado Volunteers in

1864 sparked widespread hostilities. A congressional commission authorized to make peace on the Plains concluded that "an industrious, thrifty, and enlightened population" of whites would occupy most of the West. All Native Americans should relocate in either the western half of present-day South Dakota, or Oklahoma. There they would learn the ways of white society and "civilized" life.

At two major conferences in 1867 and 1868, Native American chiefs listened to these proposals with mixed feelings. As a Kiowa chief explained, "I don't want to settle. I love to roam over the prairies." None of the agreements extracted were binding since the chiefs had no authority to speak for their tribes. The U.S. Senate dragged its feet in approving the treaties. Supplies promised to Indians who settled in the reserved areas failed to materialize, and wildlife proved too sparse to support them. These Indians soon drifted back to their former hunting grounds.

As General William T. Sherman, Commander of the Army in the West, warned, however, "All who cling to their old hunting ground are hostile and will remain so till killed off." In 1867, he entrusted General Philip Sheridan with the duty of dealing with the tribes. Sheridan introduced a new tactic of winter campaigning. He proposed to seek out the Indians who divided into small groups during the winter and to exterminate them.

The completion of the transcontinental railroad in 1869 added another pressure for "solving" the Indian question. Transcontinental railroads wanted rights-of-way through tribal lands and needed white settlers to make their operations profitable. They carried not only thousands of hopeful settlers to the West but miners and hunters as well.

In his 1872 annual report, the commissioner for Indian affairs, Francis Amasa Walker, proposed a solution for the Indian problem: reservations, where the Indians would be subjected to "a rigid reformatory discipline."

Though Walker considered himself a "friend of humanity" and wished to save the Indians from destruction, he also thought they must "yield or perish."

The Tribal View

Native Americans did not yield passively to such attacks on their ancient way of life and to the violation of treaties. As Black Elk related, his father and many others soon decided that fighting was the only way "to keep our country." But "wherever we went, the soldiers came to kill us, and it was all our country."

Broken promises fed Indian resistance. In 1875, the federal government allowed gold prospectors to stream into the Black Hills, part of the Sioux reservation and one of their sacred places. The Sioux, led by chiefs Sitting Bull, Crazy Horse, and Rain-in-the-Face, took to the warpath. Despite their victory over General George Custer at the Battle of Little Big Horn in 1876, the well-supplied and well-armed U.S. Army finally overwhelmed them. Crazy Horse was murdered. Elsewhere, General Sherman defeated Native American tribes in Texas, while in the Pacific Northwest, Nez Percé chief Joseph surrendered in 1877.

The wholesale destruction of the buffalo contributed to white victory. The animals were central to Indian life, culture, and religion. As one Pawnee chief explained, "Am afraid when we have no meat to offer, Great Spirit . . . will be angry & punish us." Although Plains Indians could be wasteful of buffalo in areas where the animals were abundant, white miners and hunters ultimately destroyed the herds.

The slaughter, which had claimed 13 million animals by 1883, was in retrospect disgraceful. The Indians considered white men demented. "They just killed and killed because they like to do that," said one, whereas when "we hunted the bison . . . [we] killed only what we needed."

The Dawes Act, 1887

Changing federal policy also undermined Native American culture and life. In 1871, Congress ended the practice, in effect since the 1790s, of treating the tribes as sovereign nations. The government urged tribes to establish court systems in place of tribal justice and extended federal jurisdiction to the reservations. Tribes were also warned not to gather for religious ceremonies.

The Dawes Severalty Act of 1887 set the course of federal Indian policy for the rest of the century. Believing that tribal bonds kept Indians in savagery, reformers intended to destroy them. Rather than allotting reservation lands to tribal groups, the act allowed the president to distribute these lands to individuals. Those who accepted allotments would become citizens and presumably forget their tribal identity. Although Indian agents explained that Native Americans opposed the Dawes Act, Congress did not hesitate to legislate on their behalf.

Another motive was also at work. Even if each Indian family head claimed a typical share of 160 acres, millions of "surplus" acres would remain for sale to white settlers. Within 20 years of the Dawes Act, Native Americans had lost 60 percent of their lands.

The Ghost Dance: An Indian Renewal Ritual

By the 1890s, the grim reality of their plight made many Native Americans responsive to the message of Paiute prophet Wovoka, who predicted that natural disasters would eliminate the white race. Dancing Indians would not only avoid this destruction but also gain new strength thanks to the return to life of their ancestors. Believers expressed their faith and hope through the new rituals of ghost dancing and meditation.

Although Wovoka's prophecies discouraged hostile actions against whites, American settlers were uneasy. Indian agents tried to prevent the ghost dances and filed hysterical reports. One

agent determined that the Sioux medicine man, Sitting Bull, was a leading troublemaker and attempted to arrest him. In the confusion, Indian police killed Sitting Bull.

Bands of Sioux fled the reservation with the army in swift pursuit. In late December 1890, the army caught up with the Sioux at Wounded Knee Creek and massacred over 200 men, women, and children. An eyewitness described the desolate scene a few days later. "Among the fragments of burned tents . . . we saw the frozen bodies lying close together or piled one upon another."

Thus arose the lament of Black Elk, who saw his people diminished, starving, despairing:

> Once we were happy in our own country and we were seldom hungry, for then the two-leggeds and the four-leggeds lived together like relatives, and there was plenty for them and for us. But then the Wasichus came, and they have made little islands for us and other islands for the four-leggeds, and always these islands are becoming smaller, for around them surges the gnawing flood of the Wasichus; and it is dirty with lies and greed.

THE NEW SOUTH

As the Indians faced an uncertain future, some inhabitants of the South hoped to lift their region out of poverty. Of all the nation's agricultural regions, the South was the poorest. In 1880, southerners' yearly earnings were only half the national average. Some southern publicists during the late nineteenth century, however, dreamed of making the agricultural South the rival of the industrial North.

Postwar Southerners Face the Future

The publicists of the movement for a "New South" argued that southern backwardness did not stem from the Civil War, as so many southerners believed, but from long-standing conditions in southern life, especially a rural economy

Indian Lands and Communities in the United States

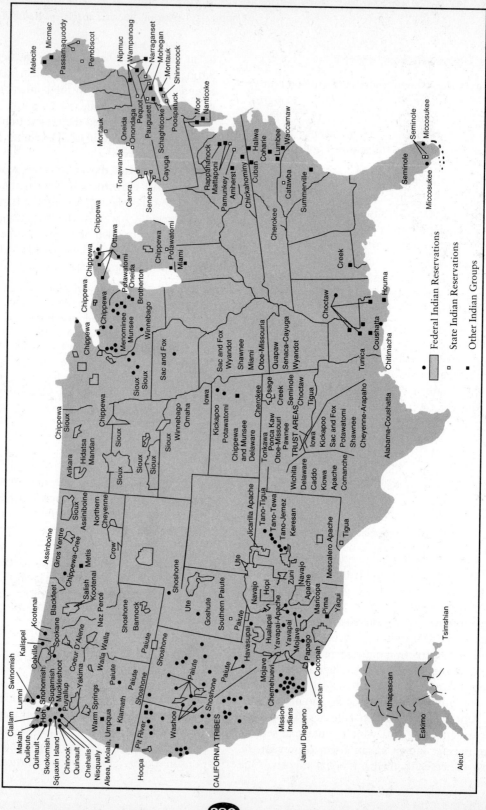

Federal Indian Reservations

State Indian Reservations

Other Indian Groups

Malecite
Micmac
Passamaquoddy
Penobscot
Nipmuc
Wampanoag
Narraganset
Mohegan
Montauk
Shinnecock
Montauk
Oneida
Onondaga
Pequot
Paugusett
Schaghticoke
Poospatuck
Moor
Nanticoke
Tonawanda
Cayuga
Carora
Seneca
Rappahanock
Mattaponi
Pamunkey
Amherst
Chickahominy
Haliwa
Coharie
Lumbee
Waccamaw
Cuban
Catawba
Summerville
Cherokee
Seminole
Seminole
Miccosukee
Miccosukee
Chippewa
Chippewa
Ottawa
Chippewa
Potawatomi
Chippewa
Chippewa
Oneida
Miami
Potawatomi
Munsee
Brotherton
Menominee
Winnebago
Creek
Houma
Chippewa
Sac and Fox
Choctaw
Coushatta
Sioux
Sioux
Sac and Fox
Wyandot
Shawnee
Miami
Otoe-Missouria
Quapaw
Seneca-Cayuga
Wyandot
Tunica
Chitimacha
Chippewa
Iowa
Winnebago
Omaha
Kickapoo
Potawatomi
Chippewa and Munsee
Delaware
Cherokee
Osage
Creek
Seminole
Choctaw
Tigua
Arikara
Hidatsa
Mandan
Sioux
Sioux
Sioux
Sioux
Sioux
Tonkawa
Ponca
Kaw
Otoe-Missouri
Pawnee
Wichita
Delaware
Caddo
Kiowa
Apache
Comanche
Iowa
Kickapoo
Sac and Fox
Potawatomi
Shawnee
Cheyenne-Arapaho
Alabama-Coushatta
Sioux
Assiniboine
Northern Cheyenne
Gros Ventre
Chippewa-Cree
Metis
Crow
Jicarilla Apache
Tano-Tigua
Tano-Tewa
Tano-Jemez
Keresan
Tigua
Blackfeet
Kootenai
Salish
Kootenai
Nez Percé
Coeur D'Alene
Walla Walla
Shoshone
Bannock
Ute
Goshute
Southern Paiute
Paiute
Navajo
Hopi
Zuni
Navajo
Apache
Mescalero Apache
Tigua
Spokane
Kalispel
Colville
Swinomish
Lumni
Makah
Quileute
Skokomish
Squaxin Island
Chinook
Quinault
Chehalis
Nisqually
Alsea, Molala, Umpqua
Hoopa
Suquamish
Muckleshoot
Puyallup
Yakima
Warm Springs
Klamath
Pit River
Washoe
Shoshone
Paiute
Paiute
Paiute
Paiute
Havasupai
Hualapai
Yavapai-Apache
Yavapai
Mojave
Mojave
Maricopa
Pima
Papago
Cocopah
Quechan
Jamul Diegueno
CALIFORNIA TRIBES
Chemehuevi
Mission Indians
Clallam
Coushatta
Tsimshian
Athapascan
Eskimo
Aleut
TRUST AREAS

based on cotton. Power and wealth came not from cotton, they asserted, but from factories, machines, and cities.

In hundreds of speeches, editorials, pamphlets, articles, and books, spokesmen for the New South tried to persuade fellow southerners to abandon prewar ideals that glorified leisure and gentility and adopt the ethic of hard work. To attract essential capital, New South advocates held out inviting opportunities. Several southern state governments offered tax exemptions and cheap convict labor. Texas and Florida awarded the railroads land grants, and cities like Atlanta and Louisville mounted huge industrial exhibitions as incentives to industrial progress. Middle-class southerners increasingly accepted new entrepreneurial values.

During the late nineteenth century, northern money flowed into the southern cotton industry and railroad system. Northern capital helped southern cities to embark on an extended period of expansion. By 1900, some 15 percent of all southerners lived in cities, compared with 7 percent in 1860. (The national averages for these years were 40 percent and 20 percent, respectively.)

The city of Birmingham, Alabama, symbolized the New South. In 1870, the site of the future city was a peaceful cornfield. The next year, two northern real estate speculators arrived on the scene, attracted by the area's rich iron deposits. Despite a siege of cholera and the depression of the 1870s, Birmingham rapidly became the center of the southern iron and steel industry. By 1890, a total of 38,414 people lived in the city. Other southern cities like Richmond and Augusta, Georgia, flourished as well by developing a variety of industries.

The Other Side of Progress

Despite the optimism of New South leaders about matching or even surpassing the North's economic performance, the South made slow progress. Older values persisted, impeding full

acceptance of a new economic order. And the southern school system lagged far behind that of the North.

Although new industries and signs of progress abounded, the South did not better its position relative to the North. Whereas in 1860 the South had 17 percent of the country's manufacturing concerns, by 1904 it had only 15 percent. During the same period, the value of its manufactures grew from 10.3 percent of the total value of manufactures in the United States to only 10.5 percent.

Moreover, the South failed to reap many benefits from industrialization. As in the antebellum period, the South remained an economic vassal of the North. Southern businessmen grew in number, but with the exception of the American Tobacco Company, no great southern corporations arose. Instead, southerners worked for northern companies and corporations, which absorbed southern businesses or dominated them financially. By 1900, for example, five corporations directed three-quarters of the railroad mileage in the South (excluding Texas), and northern bankers controlled all five. Northerners also took over the southern steel industry.

As this happened, profits and the power to make decisions flowed north. In many cases, northern directors determined that southern mills and factories could handle only the early stages of processing, while northern factories finished the goods. Thus southern cotton mills sent yarn and coarse cloth north for completion. Southern manufacturers who did finish their products, hoping to improve their chances in the marketplace, found that railroad rate discrimination robbed their goods of any competitive edge.

Individual workers in the new industries received meager rewards. The thousands of women and children in factories were silent testimony to the fact that their husbands and fathers could not earn sufficient wages to keep them at home. As usual, women and children earned lower wages than men. Justifying these policies, one Augusta factory president claimed that the employment of children was "a matter of charity with us; some of them would starve if they were not given employment." In general, all workers earned lower wages and worked longer hours in the South than elsewhere. Per capita income was the same in 1900 as it had been in 1860—and only half the national average. Black workers, who made up 6 percent of the southern manufacturing force in 1890, usually had the worst jobs and the lowest wages.

Cotton Still King

Although New South advocates envisioned an industrial society, they always recognized the need for agricultural change. The overdependence on "King Cotton" hobbled southern agriculture by making farmers the victims of far-away market forces and an oppressive credit system. Subdivide old cotton plantations into small diversified farms, Henry Grady, editor of the Atlanta *Constitution,* urged. Truck farming could produce "simply wonderful profits."

A new agricultural South with new class and economic arrangements did emerge, but it was not the one Grady and others envisioned. Despite the breakup of some plantations following the Civil War, large landowners proved resourceful in holding on to their property and in dealing with postwar conditions, as Chapter 16 showed. As landowners adopted new agricultural arrangements, former slaves sank into debt peonage.

White farmers on small and medium-size holdings fared only slightly better than black tenants and sharecroppers. Immediately after the war, high cotton prices tempted them to raise as much cotton as they could. Then prices began a disastrous decline, from 11 cents a pound in 1875 to less than 5 cents in 1894. Yeoman farmers became entangled in debt. Each year, farmers found themselves buying supplies on credit so that they could plant the next year's crop and support their families until harvest time. Each year, thousands of indebted farmers fell further behind. Many lost their land and became tenant

farmers. By 1900, over half the South's white farmers and three-quarters of its black farmers were tenants. Although tenancy was increasing all over rural America, nowhere did it rise more rapidly than in the Deep South.

These patterns had baneful results for individual southerners and for the South as a whole. Caught in a cycle of debt and poverty, few farmers could think of improving agricultural techniques or diversifying crops. In their desperate attempt to pay off debts, they concentrated on cotton, despite falling prices. "Cotton brings money, and money pays debt" was the small farmer's slogan. Landowners also pressured tenants to raise a market crop. Far from diversifying, as Grady had hoped, farmers increasingly limited the number of crops they raised. By 1880, the South was not growing enough food to feed its people adequately. Poor nutrition contributed to chronic bad health and sickness.

The Nadir of Black Life

Grady and other New South advocates painted a picture of a strong, prosperous, and industrialized South, a region that could deal with the troublesome race issue without the interference of any "outside power." Realizing that black labor would be crucial to the transformation he sought, Grady advocated racial cooperation. But since he assumed that blacks were racially inferior, he supported an informal system of segregation.

By the time of Grady's death in 1889, a much harsher perspective on southern race relations was emerging. In 1891, at a national assembly of women's clubs in Washington, D.C., a black woman, Frances Ellen Watkins Harper, anticipated efforts to strip the vote from blacks and appealed to the white women at the meeting not to abandon black suffrage. "Instead of taking the ballot from his hands, teach him how to use it, and add his quota to the progress, strength, and durability of the nation."

The positive approach urged by Harper had no chance of adoption in the late-nineteenth-century political climate. The decision by congressional leaders in 1890 to shelve a proposed civil rights act and the defeat of the Blair bill providing federal assistance for educational institutions made black Americans vulnerable. The traditional sponsor of the rights of freedmen, the Republican Party, left blacks to fend for themselves as a minority in the white South. The courts also abandoned blacks. In 1878, the Supreme Court declared unconstitutional a Louisiana statute banning discrimination in transportation. In 1882, the Court voided the Ku Klux Klan Act of 1871, deciding that the civil rights protections of the Fourteenth Amendment applied to states rather than to individuals. In 1883, the provisions of the Civil Rights Act of 1875, which assured blacks of equal rights in public places, were declared unconstitutional.

Northern leaders did not oppose these actions. In fact, northerners increasingly promulgated negative stereotypes, picturing blacks as either ignorant, lazy, childlike fools or as lying, stealing, raping degenerates. *Atlanta Monthly* in 1890 anticipated a strong current in magazine literature when it expressed doubts that this "lowly variety of man" could ever be brought up to the intellectual and moral standards of whites. Encouraged by northern public opinion, and with the blessing of Congress and the Supreme Court, southern citizens and legislatures sought to make blacks permanently second-class members of southern society.

In the political sphere, white southerners amended state constitutions to disfranchise black voters. By various legal devices—the poll tax, literacy tests, "good character" and "understanding" clauses administered by white voter registrars, and all-white primary elections— blacks lost the right to vote. The most ingenious method was the "grandfather clause," which specified that only citizens whose grandfathers were registered to vote on January 1, 1867, could cast their ballots. This virtually excluded blacks. Although the Supreme Court outlawed such blatantly discriminatory laws as grandfather clauses, a series of other constitutional changes, beginning in Mississippi in 1890 and

spreading to all 11 former Confederate states by 1910, effectively excluded the black vote.

In a second tactic in the 1890s, state and local laws legalized informal segregation in public facilities. Beginning with railroads and schools, "Jim Crow" laws, upheld by the Supreme Court in 1896 in *Plessy v. Ferguson*, were extended to libraries, hotels, restaurants, hospitals, asylums, prisons, theaters, parks and playgrounds, cemeteries, toilets, morgues, sidewalks, drinking fountains, and most places where blacks and whites might mingle.

Political and social discrimination made it ever more possible to keep blacks permanently confined to agricultural and unskilled labor and dependent on whites for their material welfare. In 1900, nearly 84 percent of black workers nationwide engaged in some form of agricultural labor as farmhands, overseers, sharecroppers, or tenant or independent farmers or in service jobs, primarily domestic service and laundry work. These had been the primary slave occupations. At the end of the Civil War, at least half of all skilled craftsmen in the South had been black. But by the 1890s, the percentage had decreased to less than 10 percent, as whites systematically excluded blacks from the trades. Such factory work as blacks had been doing was also reduced, largely in order to drive a wedge between poor blacks and whites to prevent unionization. The exclusion of blacks from industry prevented them from acquiring the skills and habits that would enable them to rise into the middle class.

Blacks did not accept their declining position passively. In the mid-1880s, they enthusiastically joined the mass worker organization, the Knights of Labor (discussed in Chapter 18), first in cities such as Richmond and Atlanta, then in rural areas. But as blacks joined, whites withdrew. The flight of whites weakened the organization in the South, and a backlash of white violence finally smashed it.

Against this backdrop, lynchings and other violence against blacks increased. On February 21, 1891, the New York *Times* reported that in Texarkana, Arkansas, a mob apprehended a 32-

year-old black man, Ed Coy, charged with the rape of a white woman, tied him to a stake, and burned him alive. As Coy proclaimed his innocence, his alleged victim herself somewhat hesitatingly put the torch to his oil-soaked body. The *Times* report concluded that only by the "terrible death such as fire ... can inflict" could other blacks "be deterred from the commission of like crimes." Ed Coy was one of more than 1,400 black men lynched or burned alive during the 1890s. About a third were charged with sex crimes. The rest were accused of a variety of "crimes" related to not knowing their place: marrying or insulting a white woman, testifying in court against whites, having "a bad reputation."

Diverging Black Responses

White discrimination and exploitation nourished new black protest tactics and ideologies. For years, Frederick Douglass had been proclaiming that blacks should remain loyal Americans and count on the promises of the Republican Party. But on his deathbed in 1895, his last words were allegedly, "Agitate! Agitate! Agitate!"

Among black expressions of protest, one was a woman's. In Memphis, Tennessee, editor Ida B. Wells launched a campaign against lynching in 1892. So hostile was the white community's response that Wells carried a gun to protect herself. When white citizens finally destroyed the press and threatened her partner, Wells left Memphis to pursue her activism elsewhere.

Other voices called for black separatism within white America. T. Thomas Fortune wrote in the black New York *Freeman* in 1887 that "there will one day be an African Empire." Three years later, he organized the Afro-American League (a precursor of the NAACP), insisting that blacks must join together to fight the rising tide of discrimination. The league encouraged independent voting, opposed segregation and lynching, and urged the establishment of black institutions like banks to support black businesses.

While some promoted black nationalism, most blacks worked patiently within white society for equality and social justice. In 1887, J. C. Price formed the Citizens Equal Rights Association, which opposed segregation and called for state laws to guarantee equal rights.

Efforts to escape oppression in the South, like "Pap" Singleton's movement to found black towns in Tennessee and Kansas, continued. Blacks founded 25 towns in Oklahoma Territory, as in other states and even Mexico. But these attempts, like earlier ones, were short-lived, crippled by limited funds and the hostility of white neighbors. Singleton eventually recommended migration to Canada or Liberia as a final solution, and later black nationalist leaders also looked increasingly to Africa. But as Douglass had long argued, no matter how important African roots might be, blacks had been in the Americas for generations and would have to win justice and equal rights here.

Most black Americans responded to the slow, moderate self-help program of Booker T. Washington, the best-known black leader in America. Born a slave, Washington had risen through hard work to become the founder (in 1881) and principal of Tuskegee Institute in Alabama, which became the nation's largest and best-known industrial training school. At Tuskegee, young blacks received a highly disciplined education in scientific agricultural techniques and vocational skilled trades. Washington believed that economic self-help and the familiar Puritan virtues of hard work, frugality, cleanliness, and moderation were the way to success. He spent much of his time traveling through the North to secure philanthropic gifts to support Tuskegee. In time, he became a favorite of the American entrepreneurial elite.

Although Washington worked actively behind the scenes for black civil rights, in 1895 in Atlanta he publicly urged that blacks postpone for the time being their pursuit of the vote, civil rights, and social equality with whites and concentrate on gaining an education, vocational training, and economic improvement, especially in agriculture and the trades. Whites throughout the country enthusiastically acclaimed Washington's address, but many blacks called his "Atlanta Compromise" a serious setback in the struggle for black rights. They also believed that if blacks were to improve their lives, they would have to organize.

FARM PROTEST

During the post–Civil War period, many farmers, both black and white, began to realize that only by organizing could they hope to ameliorate the conditions of rural life. Not all were dissatisfied with their lot, however. Farmers in the Midwest and near city markets successfully adjusted to new economic conditions and had little reason for discontent. Farmers in the South and West, by contrast, faced new problems and difficulties that led to the first mass organization of farmers in American history.

The Grange in the 1860s and 1870s

The earliest effort to organize white farmers came in 1867 when Oliver Kelley founded the Order of the Patrons of Husbandry. At first the organization emphasized the improvement of rural social and cultural life, but more aggressive goals soon evolved. Dudley Adams, speaking to an Iowa group in 1870, emphasized the powerlessness of "the immense helpless mob" of farmers, victims of "human vampires." Salvation, Adams maintained, lay in organization.

More and more farmers, especially those in the Midwest and the South, agreed with Adams. The depression of the 1870s (discussed in Chapter 18) sharpened discontent. By 1875, an estimated 800,000 had joined Kelley's organization, now known as the National Grange. The "Farmers' Declaration of Independence," read before local granges on July 4, 1873, called upon farmers to rouse themselves and cast off "the tyranny of monopoly."

Some Granger "reforms" attempted to bypass money-hungry middlemen by establishing buying and selling cooperatives. Although many cooperatives failed, they indicated that farmers realized they could not respond to new conditions on an individual basis but needed to act collectively. Operators of grain elevators drew fire for cheating midwestern farmers. But Grangers saw the railroads, America's first big business, as the greatest offenders. As Chapter 18 will show, cutthroat competition among railroad companies generally brought lower rates. But even though rates dropped nationwide, the railroads often set high rates in rural areas and awarded discriminatory rebates to large shippers.

Other groups also wished to see controls imposed on the railroads. Railroad policies that favored large Chicago grain terminals and long-distance shippers over local concerns victimized many western businessmen. Between 1869 and 1874, both businessmen and farmers in Illinois, Iowa, Wisconsin, and Minnesota lobbied for state railroad laws. The resulting Granger Laws established maximum rates railroads and grain elevators could charge. Other states also sought to control railroads by establishing state regulatory commissions.

Railroad companies and grain elevators quickly challenged the new laws. In 1877, the Supreme Court upheld the legislation in *Munn* v. *Illinois*. Even so, state commissions failed to control long-haul rates, and railroads often raised long-haul charges.

Although the Granger Laws failed to control the railroads, they established an important principle: State legislatures had the power to regulate businesses of a public nature like the railroads. But the failure of the Granger Laws and the Supreme Court's reversal of *Munn* v. *Illinois* in its 1886 *Wabash* v. *Illinois* decision led to greater pressure on Congress to continue the struggle against big business.

The Interstate Commerce Act, 1887

In 1887, Congress responded to farmers, railroad managers who wished to regulate the fierce competition that threatened to bankrupt their companies, and shippers who objected to transportation rates by passing the Interstate Commerce Act. That legislation required that railroad rates be "reasonable and just," that rate schedules be made public, and that practices such as rebates be discontinued. The act also set up the first federal regulatory agency, the Interstate Commerce Commission (ICC), but limited its authority to control over commerce conducted between states.

Like state railroad commissions, the ICC found it difficult to define a reasonable rate. Moreover, thousands of cases overwhelmed the tiny staff in the early months of operation. In the long run, the lack of enforcement power was most serious.

The Farmers' Alliances in the 1880s and 1890s

The Grange declined in the late 1870s as the depression receded. But neither farm organizations nor farm protest died. Depression struck again in the late 1880s and worsened in the 1890s. Official statistics told the familiar story of falling prices for cereal crops grown on the plains and prairies. A bushel of wheat that had sold for $1 in 1870 was worth 60 cents in the 1890s. And while prices declined, the load of debt climbed.

A Kansas farmer's letter reveals some of the human consequences of such trends:

> At the age of 52 years, after a long life of toil, economy and self-denial, I find myself and family virtually paupers. With hundreds of cattle, hundreds of hogs, scores of good horses, and a farm that rewarded the toil of our hands with 16,000 bushels of golden corn, we are poorer by many dollars than we were years ago. What once seemed a neat little fortune and a house of refuge for our declining years . . . has been rendered valueless.

Under these pressures, farmers turned again to organization, education, and cooperation. Farmers' alliances sprang up, grew, and coalesced, and by the late 1880s two organizations dominated: the Northwestern Farmers' Alliance, which was active in Kansas, Nebraska, Iowa, Minnesota, and the Dakotas; and the Southern Farmers' Alliance, which originated in Texas and proceeded to absorb farmers' groups in Arkansas and Louisiana. The Southern Farmers' Alliance, one of the most important reform organizations of the 1880s, sent lecturers throughout the South and onto the western plains. The Alliance's newspaper, the *National Economist,* maintained that "agriculture, as a class, can only be rendered prosperous by radical changes in the laws governing money, transportation, and land." Alliance lecturers proposed various programs that would help realize their slogan: "Equal rights to all, special privileges to none."

On the one hand, the Alliances experimented with buying and selling cooperatives in order to free farmers from the clutches of supply merchants, banks, and other credit agencies. Although these efforts often failed in the long run, they taught the value of cooperation to achieve common goals. On the other hand, the Alliances supported legislative efforts to regulate powerful monopolies and corporations, which they believed gouged the farmer. Many Alliance members also felt that increasing the money supply was critical to improving the position of farmers and supported a national banking system empowered to issue paper money. Finally, the Alliances called for better public schools, state agricultural colleges, and an improvement in the status of women.

By 1890, rural discontent was spreading. In Kansas, hundreds of farmers packed their families into wagons to set off for Alliance meetings or to parade in long lines through the streets of nearby towns and villages. Similar scenes occurred through the West and the South. Never had there been such a wave of organizational activity in rural America. In 1890, more than a million farmers counted themselves as Alliance members.

The Alliance network also included black farmers. In 1888, black and white organizers established the Colored Farmers' Alliance, headed by a white Baptist minister, R. M. Humphrey. The Colored Farmers' Alliance recognized that black and white farmers faced common economic problems, but few initially confronted the fact that many southern cotton farmers depended on black labor and had a different perspective from that of blacks.

The Ocala Platform, 1890

In December 1890, the National Alliance gathered in Ocala, Florida, to develop an official platform. Most delegates felt that the federal government had failed to address the farmers' problems. "Congress must come nearer the people or the people will come nearer the Congress," warned the Alliance's president. The platform called for the direct election of U.S. senators. Alliance members also supported lowering the tariff, emphasizing the need to reduce prices for "the poor of our land." Their money plank proposed a new banking system controlled by the federal government and an increased amount of money in circulation, which, they believed, would lead to inflation, higher prices, and a reduction in debt.

Other platform measures were aimed at freeing farmers from the twin evils of the credit merchant and depressed prices at harvest time. Other demands included a graduated income tax and support for the regulation of transportation and communication networks. If regulation failed, the government was called upon to take over both networks and run them for the public benefit.

These planks, with the demand for aggressive governmental action, departed radically from conventional political norms. Many Americans feared that the organization could upset political arrangements. The New York *Sun* newspaper reported that the Alliance had caused a "panic" in

the two major parties. Although the Alliance was not formally in politics, it supported sympathetic candidates in the state and local elections of 1890. A surprising number of these candidates won. Alliance victories in the West harmed the Republican Party enough to cause President Harrison to refer to "our election disaster."

Before long, many Alliance members were pressing for an independent political party, as legislators who had courted Alliance votes conveniently forgot their pledges. One Texas farmer reported that the chairman of the state Democratic executive committee "calls us all skunks" and observed that "anything that has the scent of the plowhandle smells like a polecat" to the Democrats. Among the first to realize the necessity of forming an independent third party was Georgia's Tom Watson. He also recognized that electoral success in the South would depend on unity between white and black farmers.

The People's Party, 1892

In February 1892, the People's, or Populist, Party was established, with almost 100 black delegates in attendance. The party nominated James B. Weaver, Union army veteran from Iowa, as its presidential candidate, and James G. Field, a former Confederate soldier, for vice president.

The platform preamble captured the urgent spirit of the agrarian protest movement in the 1890s:

> We meet in the midst of a nation brought to the verge of moral, political and material ruin. Corruption dominates the ballot box, the legislatures, the Congress.... The fruits of the toil of millions are boldly stolen to build up colossal fortunes ... we breed two great classes—paupers and millionaires.

The charge was clear: "The controlling influences dominating the old political parties have allowed the existing dreadful conditions to develop without serious effort to restrain or prevent them."

The Omaha platform demands, drawn from

the Ocala platform of 1890, were greatly expanded. They included more means of direct democracy, like the secret ballot, and several planks intended to enlist the support of urban labor. The People's Party also endorsed a graduated income tax; the free and unlimited coinage of silver, at a ratio of 16 to 1; and government ownership of railroads, telephone, and telegraph.

The Populist Party attempted to widen the nature of the American political debate by promoting a new vision of the government's role with respect to farmers' problems. But the tasks of weaning the South away from the Democratic Party, encouraging southern whites to work with blacks, and persuading voters of both parties to abandon familiar political ties were monumental.

Despite these obstacles, the new party pressed forward. Unlike the candidates of the major parties in 1892, Weaver campaigned actively. In the South, he faced hostile Democrats who disapproved of attempts to form a biracial political coalition. The results of the campaign were mixed. Although Weaver won over a million popular votes (the first third-party candidate to do so), he carried only four states (Kansas, Colorado, Idaho, and Nevada) and parts of two others for a total of 22 electoral votes. The attempt to break the stranglehold of the Democratic Party on the South had failed, as had its effort to attract urban workers and farmers in the Great Lakes region.

Although the People's Party did not succeed in recruiting a cross-section of American voters in 1892, it gained substantial support. Miners and mine owners in states like Montana and Colorado and in territories like New Mexico favored the demand for coinage of silver. Most Populists, however, were rural Americans in the South and West who stood outside the mainstream of American life. They often lived far from towns, villages, and railroads. Frustrated by the workings of their political, social, and economic world, they responded to a party offering to act as their advocate. They succeeded in electing governors in Kansas and North Dakota, and the party swept the state offices in Colorado. In the South, their losses stemmed from violent opposition and fraud on the part of the Democrats.

Farmers who were better integrated into their world tended to believe that they could work through existing political parties. In 1892, when thousands of farmers and others were politically and economically discontented, they voted for Grover Cleveland and the Democrats, not the Populists.

CONCLUSION

CHANGING RURAL AMERICA

The late nineteenth century brought turbulence to rural America. The "Indian problem," which had plagued Americans for 200 years, was tragically solved for a while, but not without resistance and bloodshed. Few whites found these events troubling. Most were caught up in the challenge of responding to a fast-changing world. White farmers, ranchers, and miners moved into western lands. Southerners struggled to catch up with the North. Blacks protested as they saw their hopes for equal rights thwarted. Some farmers met with success, but others, like Milton Leeper, whose experience was a far cry from the idyllic Currier and Ives depictions of life in the country, found only hardship. Many were caught in a cycle of poverty and debt. Some fled to the cities, where they joined the industrial work force described in the next chapter. Many farmers turned to collective action and politics.

Their actions demonstrate that they did not merely react to events but attempted to shape them.

Recommended Reading

Gilbert C. Fite provides a detailed study of the last agricultural frontier in *The Farmer's Frontier, 1865–1900* (1966). Annette Kolodny deals with women's perceptions of the West in *The Land Before Her: Fantasy and Experience of the American Frontiers, 1630–1860* (1984). Fred C. Luebke has edited a collection of essays dealing with immigrants on the Plains frontier, *Ethnicity on the Great Plains* (1980). Earl Pomeroy covers the Far West in *The Pacific Slope: A History of California, Oregon, Washington, Idaho, Utah, and Nevada* (1965). See also David Montejano, *Anglos and Mexicans in the Making of Texas, 1831–1986* (1987).

R. W. Paul writes of the mining frontier in *Mining Frontiers of the Far West, 1848–1880* (1963). Robert R. Dykstra explores urban development and social tensions on the cattle frontier in *The Cattle Towns: A Social History of the Kansas Cattle Trading Centers* (1970).

On relations between whites and Native Americans, see William T. Hagan, *American Indians* (1979 ed.); and Wilcomb E. Washburn, *The Indian in America* (1975). John G. Neihardt's *Black Elk Speaks* (1932) is the account of a holy man of the Ogalala Sioux.

For views of the New South, see C. Vann Woodward, *The Origins of the New South, 1877–1913* (1951); and Gavin Wright, *Old South, New South: Revolutions in the Southern Economy Since the Civil War* (1986). Also helpful are Robert C. McMath and Orville V. Burton, eds., *Toward a New South: Studies in Post–Civil War Southern Communities* (1982); and Lawrence H. Larsen, *The Rise of the Urban South* (1985). On race relations, see H. N. Rabinowitz, *Race Relations in the Urban South* (1978); and Jacqueline Jones, *Labor of Love, Labor of Sorrow: Black Women, Work, and the Family from Slavery to the Present* (1985).

Lawrence Goodwyn provides a provocative study of Populism in *The Populist Moment: A Short History of the Agrarian Revolt in America* (1978). Other studies include Bruce Palmer, *"Men over Money": The Southern Populist Critique of American Capitalism* (1980); and Peter H. Argersinger, *Populism and Politics: William Alfred Peffer and the People's Party* (1974).

Good novels include Willa Cather, *My Antonia* (1918); and O. E. Rölvaag, *Giants in the Earth* (1927).

Time Line

1860s	Cattle drives from Texas begin		1884	Southern Farmers' Alliance founded
1865–1867	Sioux wars on the Great Plains		1886	Severe winter ends cattle boom *Wabash* v. *Illinois*
1867	National Grange founded		1887	Dawes Severalty Act Interstate Commerce Act Farm prices plummet
1869	Transcontinental railroad completed			
1869–1874	Granger Laws		1888	Colored Farmers' Alliance founded
1873	Financial panic triggers economic depression		1890	Afro-American League founded Sioux Ghost Dance movement Massacre at Wounded Knee Ocala platform
1874	Barbed wire patented			
1875	Black Hills gold rush incites Sioux War		1890s	Black disfranchisement in the South Jim Crow laws passed in the South Declining farm prices
1876	Custer's last stand at Little Big Horn			
1877	*Munn* v. *Illinois* Bonanza farms in the Great Plains		1892	Populist Party formed
			1895	Booker T. Washington's "Atlanta Compromise" address
1880s	"New South"			
1881	Tuskegee Institute founded		1896	*Plessy* v. *Ferguson*
1883–1885	Depression			

chapter 18

The Rise of Smokestack America

By 1883, Thomas O'Donnell, an Irish immigrant, had lived in the United States for over a decade. He was 30 years old, married, with two young children. His third child had died in 1882, and O'Donnell was still in debt for the funeral. Money was scarce, for O'Donnell was a textile worker in Fall River, Massachusetts, and not well educated. "I went to work when I was young," he explained, "and have been working ever since." However, O'Donnell worked only sporadically at the mill. New machines needed "a good deal of small help," and the mill owners preferred to hire man-and-boy teams. Since O'Donnell's children were only 1 and 3, he often saw others preferred for day work. Once, when he was passed over, he recalled, "I said to the boss . . . what am I to do; I have got two little boys at home . . . how am I to get something for them to eat; I can't get a turn when I come here. . . . I says, 'Have I got to starve; ain't I to have any work?' "

O'Donnell was describing his family's marginal existence to a Senate committee that was gathering testimony in Boston in 1883 on the relations between labor and capital. As the senators heard the tale, they asked him why he did not go west. "It would not cost you over $1,500," said one senator. The gap between senator and worker could not have been more dramatic. O'Donnell replied, "Well, I never saw over a $20 bill . . . if some one would give me $1,500 I will go."

From the vantage point of the senator, who had no comprehension of the realities of O'Donnell's life, the fruits of industrial progress were clear. As the United States became a world industrial leader in the years after the Civil War, its factories poured forth an abundance of ever-cheaper goods ranging from steel rails and farm reapers to mass-produced parlor sets. Manufacturing replaced agriculture as the leading source of economic growth between 1860 and 1900. A rural nation of farmers was becoming a nation of industrial workers and city dwellers.

As O'Donnell's testimony illustrates, industrial growth did not benefit everyone. Estimates suggest that perhaps half of the American population was too poor to take advantage of the new goods of the age.

This chapter examines the new order that resulted from the maturing of the American industrial economy between 1865 and 1900. The chapter's central theme grows out of O'Donnell's story: As the United States built up its railroads, cities, and factories, its production and profit orientation resulted in the maldistribution of wealth and power. The social problems that accompanied the country's industrial development would capture the attention of reformers and politicians for decades to come.

THE TEXTURE OF INDUSTRIAL PROGRESS

When Americans went to war in 1861, agriculture was the country's leading source of economic growth. Forty years later, manufacturing had taken its place. As American manufacturing progressed, new regions grew in industrial importance. From New England to the Midwest lay the country's industrial heartland. New England was still a center of light industry, and the Midwest continued to process natural resources. Now, however, the production of iron, steel, and transportation equipment joined the older manufacturing operations there. In the Far West, manufacturers concentrated on processing the region's natural resources, but heavy industry made strides as well. In the South, the textile industry put down roots by the 1890s, although the South as a whole was far less industrialized than either the North or the Midwest.

The Rise of Heavy Industry from 1880 to 1900

Although many factors contributed to the dramatic rise in industrial productivity, the changing nature of the industrial sector itself explains many of the gains. Heavy industry, which produced goods like steel, iron, petroleum, and machinery, grew rapidly and fueled further economic growth. Farmers, who bought machinery for their farms; manufacturers, who installed new equipment; and railroads, which bought steel rails—all contributed to rising productivity figures.

Technological innovations that revolutionized production lay behind the rise of heavy industries such as steel. The introduction of the Bessemer converter and the open-hearth steelmaking method in the 1870s transformed the production process. Both techniques converted iron ore into steel while reducing the need for so many skilled workers.

Dramatic changes in the steel industry resulted. Steel companies developed new forms of vertical organization that provided them with access to raw materials and markets and brought all stages of steel manufacturing, from smelting to rolling, into one mill. Production soared and prices fell.

The production of a cheaper, stronger, more durable material than iron created new goods, new demands, and new markets. Millions of tons of steel went into the making of rails and locomotives, cable suspension bridges, ships, and humbler items such as wire and nails.

New sources of power facilitated the conversion of American industry to mass production. Early manufacturers depended on water power, but with the opening of new anthracite coal deposits, the cost of coal dropped, and American industry rapidly shifted to steam. By 1900, steam engines accounted for 80 percent of the nation's industrial energy supply.

The emergence of a national transportation and communications network was central to economic growth. In 1860, most railroads were located in the East and the Midwest. From 1862 on, the federal and state governments vigorously promoted railroad construction with land grants from the public domain. The first transcontinental railroad, completed in 1869, led to a burst of railroad construction. Four additional transcontinental lines and miles of feeder and branch roads were laid down in the 1870s and 1880s. As railroads crisscrossed the country, Western Union lines arose alongside them. Mass production and distribution depended on fast, efficient, and regular transportation. The completion of the national system both encouraged and supported the adoption of mass production and mass marketing.

Financing Postwar Growth

Such changes demanded huge amounts of capital and the willingness to accept financial risks. The creation of the railroad system alone cost over $1 billion by 1859. Completion of the network required another $10 billion, and foreigners contributed a third of the sum. Americans also eagerly supported new ventures and began to devote an increasing percentage of the national income to investment rather than consumption.

Although savings and commercial banks continued to invest their depositors' capital, investment banking houses like Morgan & Co. played a new and significant role in matching resources with economic enterprises. Investment bankers marketed investment opportunities in corporate bonds (which offered set interest rates and eventually the repayment of principal) and stocks (which paid dividends only if the company made a profit). The market for industrial

securities expanded rapidly in the 1880s and 1890s.

Railroads: Pioneers of Big Business

As the nature of the American economy changed, big businesses became the characteristic form of economic organization. The railroads were the pioneers of big business and a great modernizing force in America. After the Civil War, railroad companies expanded rapidly. In 1865, the typical railroad was only 100 miles long. Twenty years later, it was 1,000.

Railroads faced constant high costs of maintaining equipment and lines. In addition, they carried a heavy load of debt, incurred to pay for construction and expansion. Yet railroad freight charges dropped steadily during the last quarter of the century. When two or more lines competed for the same traffic, railroads often offered lower rates than their rivals or secret rebates (cheaper fares in exchange for all of a company's business). Rate wars helped customers, but they could plunge a railroad into bankruptcy. Instability plagued the railroad industry even as it expanded.

In the 1870s, railroad leaders sought stability by eliminating ruinous competition. They established "pools," informal agreements that set uniform rates or divided up the traffic. Yet pools never completely succeeded. Too often, individual companies disregarded their agreements, especially when the business cycle took a downturn. Railroad leaders often tried to offset falling prices by slashing their workers' wages. As a result, railroads faced powerful worker unrest (described later in this chapter).

The size of railroads, the huge costs of construction, maintenance, and repair, and the complexity of operations required unprecedented amounts of capital and new management techniques. In 1854, the directors of the Erie Railroad hired engineer and inventor Daniel McCallum to devise a system to make railroad managers and their employees more accountable. McCallum's system, emphasizing division of responsibilities and a regular flow of information, attracted widespread interest, and railroads became pioneers in rationalized administrative practices and management techniques and models for other businesses in decision making, scheduling, and engineering. Because other big businesses faced similar economic conditions, they also emulated the behavior of the railroads—their competitiveness, their attempts to underprice one another, their eventual interest in merger, and their tendency to cut workers' wages.

Growth in Other Industries

By the last quarter of the century, the textile, metal, and machinery industries equaled the railroads in size. Business expansion was accomplished in one of two ways (or a combination of both). Some owners, like steel magnate Andrew Carnegie, integrated their businesses vertically, by adding operations either before or after the production process. Even though he had introduced the most up-to-date innovations in his steel mills, Carnegie realized he needed his own sources of pig iron, coal, and coke in order to avoid dependence on suppliers. He also acquired steamships and railroads to transport his finished products. Companies that integrated vertically frequently achieved economies of scale through more efficient management techniques.

Other companies copied the railroads and integrated horizontally by combining similar businesses. They sought to gain a monopoly of the market in order to eliminate competition and to stabilize prices. John D. Rockefeller used this strategy to gain control of the oil market.

As giant businesses competed intensely, often cutting wages and prices, they absorbed or eliminated smaller and weaker producers. As a result, business ownership became increasingly concentrated. In 1870, some 808 American iron and steel firms competed in the marketplace. By 1900, the number had dwindled to fewer than 70.

Like the railroads, many big businesses chose to incorporate. Incorporation offered many benefits. Through the sale of stock, businesses could raise funds for large-scale operations. The principle of limited liability protected investors, while the corporation's legal identity ensured its survival after the death of original and subsequent shareholders. Longevity suggested a measure of stability that heightened the attractiveness of a corporation as an investment.

The Erratic Economic Cycle

The transformation of the economy was neither smooth nor steady. Two depressions, one from 1873 to 1879 and the other from 1893 to 1897, surpassed the severity of economic downturns before the Civil War. They were accompanied by widespread unemployment, a phenomenon new to American life.

During expansionary years, manufacturers flooded markets with goods. When the market was finally saturated, sales and profits declined, and the economy spiraled downward. Owners slowed production and laid off workers, who in turn bought less food. As farm prices plummeted, farmers had to cut back on purchases. Business and trade stagnated, and the railroads were finally affected. Eventually, the cycle bottomed out, but in the meantime, millions of workers lost their jobs, thousands of businesses went bankrupt, and many Americans suffered deprivation and hardship.

Pollution

Another negative by-product of the industrial age was widespread pollution. Industrial processes everywhere had an adverse impact on the environment. In the iron and steel city of Birmingham, Alabama, for example, the coke ovens poured smoke, soot, and ashes into the air. Coal tar, a by-product of the coking process, was dumped, and it made the soil so acid that nothing would grow in it.

There was little awareness, however, of the extent or seriousness of environmental damage caused by pollution. Few were concerned that when industrial, human, and animal wastes were disposed of in rivers, they killed off fish and other forms of marine life and the plants that were part of that ecosystem. By the late nineteenth century, pollution of eastern and midwestern rivers as well as lakes had become pronounced. Although Presidents Grover Cleveland and Benjamin Harrison both set aside forest reserves, and there was growing interest in creating national parks, these sorts of actions were limited in scope and did not begin to touch the problems created by the rise of heavy industry and the rapid urban expansion that it stimulated.

URBAN EXPANSION IN THE INDUSTRIAL AGE

The new industrial age engendered rapid urban expansion. Before the Civil War, manufacturers had relied on water power and chosen rural sites for their factories. Now as they shifted to steam power, most favored urban locations that offered them workers, specialized services, local markets, and railroad links to materials and to distant markets.

Cities of all sizes grew. The population of New York and Philadelphia doubled and tripled. Smaller cities in the industrial Midwest, the South, and the Far West also shared in the dramatic growth. In 1870, some 25 percent of Americans lived in cities; by 1900, fully 40 percent of them did.

A Growing Population

What accounted for the dramatic increase in urban population? Certainly not a high birthrate.

The general pattern of declining family size that had emerged before the Civil War continued. By 1900, the average woman bore only 3.6 children, in contrast to 5.2 in 1860. Urban families, moreover, tended to have fewer children than their rural counterparts, and urban infants and children had a higher death rate.

American Urban Dwellers

The swelling population of late-nineteenth-century cities came both from the nation's small towns and farms and from abroad. For rural Americans, the "push" came from the modernization of agricultural life. As farm machines replaced human hands, farm workers increasingly sought work in cities.

By 1890, manufacturing workers were earning hundreds of dollars more a year than farm laborers. Part of the difference between rural and urban wages was eaten up by the higher cost of living in the city, but not all of it. City life also offered excitement and variety to young men and women who had grown up on farms and in small towns.

Novelist Theodore Dreiser captured both the fascination and the dangers of city life. Writing in a style termed literary realism, he examined social problems and cast his characters in carefully depicted local settings. Dreiser's novel *Sister Carrie* (1900) follows a typical country girl as she comes to Chicago. Carrie fantasizes a life of luxury, beyond her means as a mere factory employee. Her desire for comfort and pleasure leads her to affairs with prosperous men. Many readers were shocked that Dreiser never punished Carrie for her "sins."

Southern blacks, often single and young, also migrated to the cities. In the West and the North, blacks made up a tiny part of the population. In southern cities they were more numerous. About 44 percent of Atlanta's residents in the late nineteenth century were black, 38 percent of Nashville's. No matter where they were,

These women and children, photographed as they landed at the Battery in New York City, were part of the new immigration from eastern Europe and Russia.

however, the city offered them few rewards, little glamor, and many dangers.

The New Immigration

In 1870, a "brokenhearted" Annie Sproul stole away from her parents' home in Londonderry, Ireland, to seek a new future in Philadelphia. Probably the disgrace of a love affair prompted Annie's desperate flight, but the young woman was one of many who left their homelands in the nineteenth century. In the 40 years before the Civil War, five million immigrants poured into the United States; from 1860 to 1900, that volume almost tripled. Three-quarters of the newcomers stayed in the Northeast, and many of the rest settled in cities across the nation, where they soon outnumbered native-born whites.

As the flow of immigration increased, the national origin of immigrants shifted. Until 1880, three-quarters of the immigrants, often called the "old immigrants," hailed from the British Isles, Germany, and Scandinavia. Irish and Germans were the largest groups. Then the pattern slowly changed, as the ethnic and religious heterogeneity of the American people was transformed. By 1890, old immigrants composed only 60 percent of the total number of newcomers, while the "new immigrants" from

southern and eastern Europe (Italy, Poland, Russia, Austria-Hungary, Greece, Turkey, and Syria) made up most of the rest. Italian Catholics and eastern European Jews were the most numerous, followed by Slavs.

Efforts to modernize European economies stimulated immigration. New agricultural techniques led European landlords to consolidate their land, evicting longtime tenants. Many younger European farmers emigrated to the United States. Similarly, artisans and craftsmen whose skills were obsolete headed for the United States and other destinations. Government policies pushed others to leave. In eastern Europe, especially in Russia, official persecution of minorities and expansion of the draft for the czar's army led millions of Jewish families and others to emigrate.

Opportunity in the "golden land" of America also attracted thousands. Friends and relatives in America encouraged others to follow. Their letters described favorable living and working conditions and contained promises to help newcomers find work. The phenomenon of immigrants' being recruited through the reports and efforts of their predecessors is known as "chain migration."

Like rural and small-town Americans, Europeans came primarily to work. When times were good and American industry needed large numbers of unskilled laborers, migration was heavy. When times were bad, numbers fell off. Perhaps as many as a third eventually returned to their native lands.

Adding to the stream of foreigners coming to the United States were Mexicans and Chinese laborers. In Mexico, modernization, overpopulation, and new land policies uprooted many inhabitants. Gonzalo Plancarte, a cattle raiser, lost his livelihood in the 1890s when the owner of the hacienda determined to turn his land over to producing goods for export and ended the family's grazing privileges. Eventually Gonzalo headed for the American border. Perhaps 280,000 Mexicans crossed into the United States between 1899 and

Immigration to the United States, 1870–1920

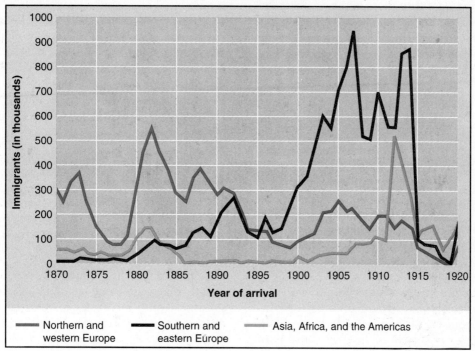

Northern and western Europe   *Southern and eastern Europe*   *Asia, Africa, and the Americas*

1914, many of them finding work on the railroads and in western mines.

Overpopulation, depressed conditions, unemployment, and crop failures brought Asians, most of them from southern China, to the "Land of the Golden Mountains." Although only 264,000 Chinese came to the United States between 1860 and 1900, they constituted a significant minority on the West Coast. Most were unskilled male contract laborers who promised to work for a number of years and then return to their homelands.

The Industrial City, 1880–1900

The late-nineteenth-century industrial city had new physical and social arrangements. By the last quarter of the century, the jumbled arrangements of the antebellum city, whose size and configuration had been limited by the necessity of walking to work, disappeared. Where once substantial houses, businesses, and small artisan dwellings had stood side by side, central business districts emerged. Few people lived downtown, although many worked or shopped there. Surrounding the business center were areas of light manufacturing and wholesale activity with housing for workers. Beyond these working-class neighborhoods stretched middle-class residential areas. Then came the suburbs, with "pure air, peacefulness, quietude, and natural scenery." Scattered throughout the city were pockets of industrial activity surrounded by crowded working-class housing.

This new pattern, with the poorest city residents clustered near the center, is familiar today. However, it reversed the early-nineteenth-century urban form, where much of the most desirable housing was in the heart of the city. New living arrangements were also more segregated by race and class than those in the preindustrial walking city. Homogeneous social and economic neighborhoods emerged, and it became more unusual than before for a poor, working-class family to live near a middle- or upper-class family. Better transportation increasingly allowed middle- and upper-class residents to live away from their work and from grimy industrial districts.

Neighborhoods and Neighborhood Life

Working-class neighborhoods clustered near the center of most industrial cities. Here lived newcomers from the American countryside and crowds of foreigners as well.

Ethnic groups frequently chose to gather in particular neighborhoods, often located near industries requiring their labor. In Detroit in 1880, for example, 37 percent of the city's native-born families lived in one area, while 40 percent of the Irish inhabited the "Irish West Side." Over half the Germans and almost three-quarters of the Poles settled on the city's east side. Although such neighborhoods often had an ethnic flavor, with small specialty shops and foreign-language signs, they were not ethnic ghettos. Immigrants and native-born Americans often lived in the same neighborhoods, on the same streets, and even in the same houses.

Working-class neighborhoods were often what would be called slums today. They were crowded and unsanitary and had inadequate public services. Outdoor privies, often shared by several families, were the rule. Water came from outdoor hydrants, and women had to carry it inside for cooking, washing, and cleaning. Piles of garbage and waste stank in the summer and froze in the winter. In such an environment, death rates were high. Only at the turn of the century did the public health movement, particularly the efforts to treat water supplies with germ-killing chemicals, begin to ameliorate these conditions.

Not every working-class family lived in abject circumstances. Skilled workers might rent comfortable quarters, and a few even owned their own homes. But the unskilled and semi-skilled workers were not so fortunate. A Massachusetts survey described the family of an unskilled ironworker crammed into a tenement of four rooms,

> in an overcrowded block, to which belong only two privies for about fifty people. When this place was visited the vault had overflowed in the yard and ... created a stench that was really frightful.... The house inside, was badly furnished and dirty, and a disgrace to Worcester.

A wide range of institutions and associations ameliorated the drabness of urban life. Frequently they were based on ethnic ties. Irish associational life, for example, centered on the Roman Catholic parish church, Irish nationalist organizations, and ward politics. Irish saloons were convivial places where men socialized, drank, and talked politics. Jews gathered in their synagogues, Hebrew schools, and Hebrew- and Yiddish-speaking literary groups. Germans had family saloons and educational and singing societies. While such activities may have slowed assimilation into American society and discouraged intergroup contact, they provided companionship, social life, and a bridge between life in the "old country" and life in America. Working-class men and women were far from mere victims of their environment. They found the energy, squeezed out the time, and even saved the money to support networks of social ties and associations.

Black Americans faced the most wretched living conditions of any group in the city. Northern blacks often lived in segregated neighborhoods. In southern cities, they gathered in back alleys and small streets. Many could afford only rented rooms. However, a rich associational life tempered the suffering. Black denominations like the African Methodist Episcopal Church enjoyed phenomenal growth.

Some urban blacks in the late nineteenth century rose into the middle class and, in spite of the heavy odds against them, created the nucleus of professional and artistic life. Henry Ossawa Tanner gained international recognition as a painter by 1900, black educators such as George Washington Williams wrote some of the first African-American histories, and novelists such as Charles W. Chesnutt and William Wells Brown produced noteworthy novels and short stories.

Beyond working-class neighborhoods and pockets of black housing lay streets of middle-class houses, many of which boasted up-to-date gas lighting and bathrooms. Outside, the neighborhoods were cleaner and more attractive than in the inner city. Residents could pay for garbage collection, gaslights, and other improvements.

Streetcar Suburbs

On the fringes of the city were houses for the upper middle class and the rich, who either made their money in business, commerce, and the professions or inherited family fortunes.

Public transportation sped them downtown to their offices and then home again. Robert Work, a modestly successful cap and hat merchant, moved his family to a $5,500 house in West Philadelphia in 1865 and commuted more than four miles to work. The 1880 census revealed his family's comfortable life style. The household included two servants to do the domestic work. The Works enjoyed running hot and cold water, indoor bathrooms, central heating, and other modern conveniences of the age.

The Social Geography of the Cities

In industrial cities of this era, people were sorted by class, occupation, and race. The physical distances between upper- and middle-class neighborhoods and working-class neighborhoods meant that city dwellers often had little first-hand knowledge of people who were different from themselves. Ignorance led to distorted views and social disapproval. Middle-class newspapers unsympathetically described laboring men as "loafing in the sunshine" and criticized the "crowds of idlers, who, day and night,

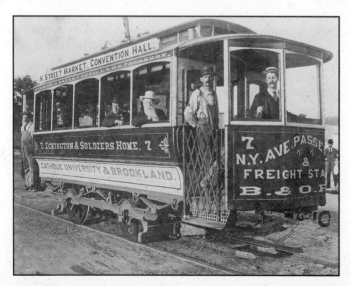

For the middle class, commuting to work from the suburbs became part of the daily routine.

infect Main Street." Yet those "crowds of idlers" were often men who could not find work.

THE LIFE OF THE MIDDLE CLASS

Newspaper comments suggest the economic polarization and social conflict that late-nineteenth-century industrialization spawned. Middle-class Americans found they had much to value in the new age: job and education opportunities, material comforts, and leisure time. By 1900, fully 36 percent of urban families owned their homes.

The expansion of American industry had raised the living standard for increasing numbers of Americans, who were better able to purchase consumer products manufactured, packaged, and promoted in an explosion of technological inventions and shrewd marketing techniques. Among the still familiar products and brands invented or mass-produced for the first time in the 1890s were Del Monte canned fruits and vegetables, Van Camp's pork and beans, Wesson oil, Lipton tea, and Wrigley's Juicy Fruit chewing gum.

More time for recreation like bicycling or watching professional baseball and greater access to consumer goods signaled the power of industrialism to transform the lives of middle-class Americans. Shopping for home furnishings, clothes, and other items became an integral part of many middle-class women's lives. A plentiful supply of immigrant servant girls relieved urban middle-class wives of many housekeeping chores, and smaller families lessened the burdens of motherhood. The new department stores that began to appear in the 1870s profited from women's leisure time and encouraged their desire for material possessions.

New Freedoms for Middle-Class Women

Middle-class women were also gaining new freedoms. Several states granted women more property rights in marriage. Women, moreover, finally cast off confining crinolines and bustles in favor of a shirtwaist blouse and ankle-length skirt. This "new woman" was celebrated as *Life* magazine's attractively active, slightly rebellious "Gibson girl."

Using their new freedom, women joined literary societies, charity groups, and reform clubs like the Women's Christian Temperance Union. The General Federation of Women's Clubs, founded in 1890, boasted one million members by 1920. The depression of 1893 stimulated many women to become socially active, investigating slum and factory conditions.

Job opportunities for these educated middle-class women were generally limited to the social services and teaching. Women teachers, frequently hired because they accepted lower pay than men, often faced classes of 40 to 50 children in poorly equipped rooms. By the 1890s, the willingness of middle-class women to work for low pay opened up new forms of employment in office work, nursing, and clerking in department stores.

After the Civil War, educational opportunities for women expanded. New women's colleges such as Smith, Mount Holyoke, Vassar, Bryn Mawr, and Goucher offered programs similar to those at competitive men's colleges, while state schools in the Midwest and the West dropped prohibitions against women. The number of women attending college rose. In 1890, some 13 percent of all college graduates were women; by 1900, this had increased to nearly 20 percent.

Many medical schools refused to accept women students. As a Harvard doctor explained in 1875, a woman's monthly period "unfits her from taking those responsibilities which are to control questions often of life and death." Despite the obstacles, 2,500 women managed to become physicians and surgeons by 1880 (making up 2.8 percent of the total). Women were less successful at breaking into the legal world.

One reason for the greater independence of

American women was that they were having fewer babies. Decreasing family size and an increase in the divorce rate (one out of 12 marriages in 1905) fueled men's fears that the new woman threatened the family, traditional sex roles, and social order. Theodore Roosevelt called this "race suicide" and argued that the falling white birthrate endangered national self-interest.

Arguments against the new woman intensified as many men reaffirmed Victorian stereotypes of "woman's sphere." One male orator in 1896 attacked the new woman's public role because "a woman's brain involves emotions rather than intellect."

Male Mobility and the Success Ethic

As the postwar economy expanded and the structure of American business changed, middle-class men's lives were affected. New job opportunities appeared. Where once the census taker had noted only the occupation of "clerk," now he listed "accountant," "salesman," and "shipping clerk." As the lower ranks of the white-collar world became more specialized, the number of middle-class jobs increased.

To prepare for these new careers, Americans required more education. The number of public high schools in the United States increased from 160 in 1870 to 6,000 in 1900. By 1900, a majority of states and territories had compulsory school attendance laws.

Higher education also expanded in this period. The number of students in colleges and universities nearly doubled, from 53,000 in 1870 to 101,000 in 1900.

Greater specialization and professionalism in education, medicine, law, and business affected male careers. By the 1890s, with government licensing and the rise of professional schools, no longer were tradesmen likely to read up on medicine and become doctors. In this period, organizations like the American Medical Association and the American Bar Association were regulating and professionalizing membership. The number of law schools doubled in the last quarter of the century, and 86 new medical schools were founded in the same period. Dental schools increased from 9 to 56 between 1875 and 1900.

This age of increasing professionalism also gave rise to some new professions. The disciplines of history, economics, sociology, psychology, and political science all date from the last 20 years of the nineteenth century.

The social ethic of the age stressed the availability of economic rewards. Many argued that unlike Europe, where family background and social class determined social rank, in America few barriers held back those of good character and diligent work habits. Anyone doubting this opportunity needed only to be reminded of the rise of two giants of industry, John D. Rockefeller and Andrew Carnegie, who had risen spectacularly through their own efforts.

The best-known popularizer of the rags-to-riches myth was Horatio Alger, Jr. Millions of boys read his 119 novels, with titles like *Luck and Pluck, Strive and Succeed,* and *Bound to Rise.* In a typical Alger novel, the story opens with the hero leading the low life of a shoeshine boy in the streets and wasting what little money he has on tobacco, liquor, gambling, and the theater. A chance opportunity occurs, like diving into the icy waters of the harbor to save the life of the daughter of a local banker, and changes the Alger hero's life. He gives up his slovenly ways to work hard, save his money, and study. Eventually he rises to a prominent position at the bank.

Unlimited and equal opportunity for upward advancement in America has never been as easy as the "bootstraps" ethic maintains. In fact, the typical big businessman was a white, Anglo-Saxon Protestant from a middle- or upper-class family whose father was most likely in business, banking, or commerce.

INDUSTRIAL WORK AND THE LABORING CLASS

David Lawlor, an Irish immigrant who came to the United States as a child in 1872, read Horatio Alger in his free time. Like Alger's heroes, he went to night school and rose in the business world, eventually becoming an advertising executive. But Lawlor's success was exceptional. As industrialization transformed the nature of work and the composition of the work force, traditional opportunities for mobility and even for a secure livelihood seemed to slip away from the grasp of many working-class Americans.

The Impact of Ethnic Diversity

Immigrants made up a sizable portion of the urban working class in the late nineteenth century. They made up 20 percent of the labor force and over 40 percent of laborers in the manufacturing and extractive industries. In cities, where they tended to settle, they accounted for more than half the working-class population.

The fact that more than half of the urban industrial class was foreign and unskilled and often had only a limited command of English influenced industrial work, urban life, labor protest, and local politics. Eager for the unskilled positions rapidly being created as mechanization and mass production took hold, immigrants often had little in common with native-born workers or even with one another. American working-class society became a mosaic of nationalities, cultures, religions, and interests.

The ethnic diversity of the industrial work force helps explain its occupational patterns. At the top of the working-class hierarchy, native-born Protestant whites held a disproportionate share of well-paying skilled jobs. Beneath them, skilled northern European immigrants filled most of the positions in the middle ranks of the occupational structure. Germans, who had training as tailors, bakers, brewers, and shoe-makers, moved into similar jobs in this country, while Jews became the backbone of the garment industry.

But most of the "new immigrants" from southern and central Europe had no urban industrial experience. They labored in the unskilled, dirty jobs such as relining blast furnaces in steel mills, carrying raw materials or finished products from place to place, or digging ditches. Hiring was often on a daily basis, often arranged through middlemen like the Italian *Padrone*.

At the bottom, blacks occupied the most marginal positions as janitors, servants, porters, and laborers. Racial discrimination generally excluded them from industrial jobs, even though their occupational background differed little from that of rural white immigrants.

The Changing Nature of Work

The rise of big business changed the size and shape of the work force and the nature of work itself. More and more Americans were wage earners rather than independent artisans. The number of manufacturing workers doubled between 1880 and 1900, with the fastest expansion in the unskilled and semiskilled ranks.

But the need for skilled workers remained. New positions, as in steam fitting and structural iron-work, appeared as industries expanded and changed. Increasingly, older skills became obsolete. And all skilled workers faced the possibility that technical advances would eliminate their favored status or that employers would eat away at their jobs by having unskilled helpers take over parts of them.

Work Settings and Experiences

While increasing numbers of American manufacturing workers now labored in factories, some Americans still toiled in small shops and sweatshops tucked away in basements, lofts, or immigrant apartments. Even in these smaller settings, the pressure to produce was almost as relentless as in the factory, for volume, not hours, determined pay. When contractors cut wages, workers had to speed up to earn the same pay.

The organization of work divided workers from one another. In large factories, workers were separated into small work groups and mingled only rarely with the rest of the work force. The clustering of ethnic groups in certain types of work also undermined working-class solidarity. But all workers had one thing in common: a very long working day—usually ten hours a day, six days a week.

Work was usually unhealthy, dangerous, and comfortless. Few owners paid attention to regulations on toilets, drinking facilities, or washing areas. Nor did they concern themselves with the health or safety of their employees. Women bent over sewing machines developed digestive illnesses and curved spines. New drilling machinery introduced in western mines filled the shafts with tiny stone particles that caused lung disease. Accident rates in the United States far exceeded those of Europe's industrial nations. Each year, 35,000 American workers died from industrial mishaps. Iron and steel mills were the main killers, although the railroads alone accounted for 6,000 fatalities a year during the 1890s. The law placed the burden of avoiding accidents on workers.

Industrial jobs were also increasingly specialized and monotonous. Even skilled workers did not produce a complete product, and the range of their skills was narrowing. Cabinetmakers found themselves not crafting cabinets but putting together and finishing pieces made by others. In such circumstances, many skilled workers complained that they were being reduced to drudges and wage slaves.

The Worker's Share in Industrial Progress

The huge fortunes accumulated by industrialists like Andrew Carnegie and John D. Rockefeller during the late nineteenth century dramatized the pattern of wealth concentration that had begun in the early period of industrialization. In 1890, the top one percent of American families possessed over a quarter of the wealth, while the share held by the top 10 percent was about 73 percent. Economic growth still benefited people who influenced its path, and they claimed the lion's share of the rewards.

But what of the workers who tended the machines that lay at the base of industrial wealth? Industry still needed skilled workers and paid them well. Average real wages rose over 50 percent between 1860 and 1900. Skilled manufacturing workers, about a tenth of the nonagricultural working class in the late nineteenth century, saw their wages rise by about 74 percent. But wages for the unskilled increased by only 31 percent. The differential was substantial and widened as the century drew to a close.

A U.S. Bureau of Labor study of working-class families in 1889 revealed great disparities of income: A young girl in a silk mill made $130 a year; a laborer earned $384 a year; a carpenter took home $686. The carpenter's family lived comfortably and breakfasted on meat or eggs, hotcakes, butter, cake, and coffee. The silk worker and the laborer, by contrast, ate bread and butter as the main portion of two of their three daily meals.

For workers without steady employment, rising real wages were meaningless. When times were slow or conditions depressed, as they were between 1873 and 1879 and 1893 and 1897, employers, especially in small firms, laid off both skilled and unskilled workers and reduced wages. Even in a good year like 1890, one out of every five men outside of agriculture had been unemployed at least a month. Since unemployment insurance did not exist, workers had no cushion against losing their jobs.

Although nineteenth-century ideology pictured men as breadwinners, many working-class married men could not earn enough to support their families alone. A working-class family's

Women in the Labor Force, 1870-1900

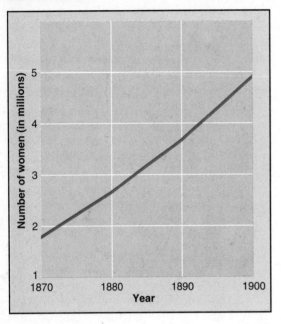

standard of living thus often depended on its number of workers. Married women did not usually take outside employment, although they contributed to family income by taking in sewing, laundry, and boarders. In 1890, only 3.3 percent of married women were to be found in the paid labor force.

The Family Economy

If married women did not work for pay outside their homes, their children did. In 1880, one-fifth of the nation's children between the ages of 10 and 14 held jobs.

Child labor was closely linked to a father's income, which in turn depended on skill, ethnic background, and occupation. Immigrant families more frequently sent their young children out to work (and also had more children) than native-born families. Sending children to work was a means of coping with the immediate

threat of poverty, of financing the education of one of the children, or even of ensuring that children stay near their family.

Women at Work

Many more young people over 14 were working for wages than children. Half of all Philadelphia's students had quit school by that age. Daughters as well as sons were expected to take positions, although young women from immigrant families were more likely to work than young American women. As *Arthur's Home Magazine* for women pointed out, a girl's earnings would help "to relieve her hard-working father of the burden of her support, to supply home with comforts and refinements, to educate a younger brother." By 1900, nearly 20 percent of American women were in the labor force.

Employed women earned far less than men. An experienced female factory worker might be paid between $5 and $6 a week, while an unskilled male laborer could make about $8. About a quarter of working women secured factory jobs. Italian and Jewish women (whose cultural backgrounds virtually forbade domestic work) clustered in the garment industry, while Poles and Slavs went into textiles, food processing, and meatpacking. In some industries, like textiles, women composed an important segment of the work force. But about 40 percent of them, especially those from Irish, Scandinavian, or black families, took jobs as maids, cooks, laundresses, and nurses.

Domestic service meant low wages, unpleasant working conditions, and little free time, usually one evening a week and part of Sunday. A servant received room and board plus $2 to $5 a week. The fact that so many women took domestic work despite the job's disadvantages speaks clearly of their limited opportunities.

The dismal situation facing working women drove some, like Rose Haggerty, into prostitution. Burdened with a widowed and sickly mother and four young brothers and sisters,

Rose was only 14 when she started work at a New York paper bag factory. She earned $10 a month, but $6 went for rent. Her fortunes improved when a friend helped her buy a sewing machine. Rose then sewed shirts at home, often working as long as 14 hours a day, to support her family. Suddenly, the piecework rate for shirts was slashed in half. In desperation, Rose contemplated suicide. But when a sailor offered her money for spending the night with him, she realized she had an alternative. Prostitution meant food, rent, and heat for her family. "Let God Almighty judge who's to blame the most," the 20-year-old Rose reflected, "I that was driven, or them that drove me to the pass I'm in." Prostitution appears to have increased in the late nineteenth century, although there is no way of knowing the actual numbers of women involved.

The unpaid domestic labor of married working-class women was critical to family survival. With husbands away for 10 to 11 hours a day, women bore the burden and loneliness of caring for children and doing the domestic chores, which were time-consuming and arduous without a refrigerator, washing machine, or other labor-saving appliances.

As managers of family resources, married women had important responsibilities. Domestic economies were vital to survival. "In summer and winter alike," one woman explained, "I must try to buy the food that will sustain us the greatest number of meals at the lowest price." Women also supplemented family income by taking in work. Jewish and Italian women frequently did piecework and sewing at home. In the Northeast and the Midwest, between 10 and 40 percent of all working-class families kept boarders.

Black women's working lives reflected the obstacles blacks faced in late-nineteenth-century cities. Although few married white women worked outside the home, black women did so both before and after marriage. In southern cities in 1880, about three-quarters of single

black women and one-third of married women worked outside the home. This contrasted to rates for white women of 24 and 7 percent, respectively. Since industrial employers would not hire black women, most of them had to work as domestics or laundresses. The high percentage of married black women in the labor force reflected the marginal wages their husbands earned.

CAPITAL VERSUS LABOR

Class conflict characterized late-nineteenth-century industrial life. While owners reaped most of the profits, bad pay, poor working conditions, and long hours were turning workers into wage slaves. Fashioning their arguments from their republican legacy, workers claimed that the degradation of the country's citizen laborers threatened to undermine the republic itself.

On-the-Job Protests

Workers and employers engaged in a struggle over who would control the workplace. Skilled workers, like iron puddlers and glassblowers, had indispensable knowledge about the production process and practical experience and were in a key position to direct on-the-job actions. Sometimes their goal was to retain control over critical work decisions or to humanize work. Cigar makers clung to their custom of having one worker read to others as they performed their tedious chores. Often workers sought to control the pace of production. Workers also resisted owners' attempts to grasp large profits through unlimited production. Too many goods meant an inhuman pace of work and might result in overproduction, massive layoffs, and a reduction in the prices paid for piecework.

A newspaper account of a glassblowers' strike in 1884 illustrates the clash between capital and labor. With an eye toward bigger profits, the boss tried to increase production. "He knew if the limit was taken off, the men could work ten or twelve hours every day in the week; that in their thirst for the mighty dollar they would kill themselves with labor." But his employees resisted his proposal. Their goal was not riches but a decent pace of work and a respectable wage. Thus "they thundered out no. . . . Threats and curses would not move them."

To protect themselves and preserve the dignity of their labor, workers devised ways of combating employer attempts to speed up the production process. In three industrial firms in the late nineteenth century, one-quarter of the workers stayed home at least one day a week. Some of these lost days were due to layoffs, but not all. The efforts of employers to impose stiff fines on absent workers suggested their frustration at uncooperative workers.

To a surprising extent, workers made the final protest by quitting their jobs altogether. A Massachusetts labor study in 1878 found that although two-thirds of them had been in the same occupation for more than ten years, only 15 percent of the workers surveyed were in the same job. A similar rate of turnover occurred in the industrial work force in the early twentieth century. Workers unmistakably and clearly voted with their feet.

Strike Activity After 1876

The most direct and strenuous attempts to change conditions in the workplace came in the form of thousands of strikes punctuating the late nineteenth century. In 1877, railroad workers staged the first and most violent nationwide industrial strike of the nineteenth century. The immediate cause of the disturbance was the railroad owners' decision to reduce wages. But the rapid spread of the strike from Baltimore to Pittsburgh and then to cities as distant as San Francisco, Chicago, and Omaha, as well as the violence of the strikers, who destroyed railroad property and kept trains idle, indicated more fundamental discontent. An erratic economy, high unemployment rates, and the lack of job se-

curity all contributed to the conflagration. Over 100 people died before federal troops ended the strike. The frenzied response of the propertied class, which saw the strike as the beginning of revolution and favored the intervention of the military, forecast the pattern of later conflicts. Time and time again, middle- and upper-class Americans would turn to the power of the state to crush labor activism.

A wave of confrontations followed the strike of 1877. Between 1881 and 1905, a total of 36,757 strikes erupted, involving over six million workers—three times the strike activity in France. These numbers indicate that far more than the "poorest part" of the workers were involved. Strikes, sabotage, and violence were most often linked to demands for higher wages and shorter hours.

In the period of early industrialization, discontented laborers rioted in their neighborhoods rather than at their workplaces. Between 1845 and the Civil War, however, strikes at the workplace began to replace neighborhood riots. Although workers often called for higher wages, they had only a murky sense that the strike could be a weapon to force employers to improve working conditions.

As an increasing percentage of the work force entered factories, collective actions at the workplace spread. Local and national unions played a more important role in organizing protest, conducting 60 percent of the strikes between 1881 and 1905. By 1891, more than one-tenth of the strikes called by unionized workers were sympathy strikes. Finally, wages became less of an issue among the most highly unionized workers. Workers sought more humane conditions. By the early 1890s, over one-fifth of strikes involved the rules governing the workplace.

Labor Organizing, 1865–1900

The Civil War experience colored labor organizing in the postwar years. As one working-class song pointed out, workers had borne the brunt of that struggle. "You gave your son to the war /

The rich man loaned his gold / And the rich man's son is happy to-day, / And yours is under the mold." Now workers who had fought to save the Union argued that wartime sacrifices justified efforts to gain justice and equality in the workplace.

Labor leaders quickly realized the need for national as well as local organizations to protect the laboring class against "despotic employers." In 1866, several craft unions and reform groups formed the National Labor Union (NLU). Claiming 300,000 members by the early 1870s, the organization supported a range of causes including temperance, women's rights, and the establishment of cooperatives to bring the "wealth of the land" into "the hands of those who produce it," thus ending "wage slavery." They called for an eight-hour day to allow workers the time to cultivate the qualities necessary for republican citizenship. Many of the NLU's specific goals survived, although the organization did not.

The Knights of Labor and the AFL

As the depression of 1873 wound down, a new mass organization, the Noble Order of the Knights of Labor, rose to national importance. Founded as a secret society in 1869, the order became public and national when Terence V. Powderly, an Irish-American, was elected Grand Master Workman in 1879. The Knights of Labor sought "to secure to the workers the full enjoyment of the wealth they create." Since the industrial system denied workers their fair share as producers, the Knights of Labor proposed a cooperative system of production alongside the existing system. Cooperative efforts would give workers the economic independence necessary for citizenship, while an eight-hour day would provide them with the leisure for moral, intellectual, and political pursuits.

The Knights of Labor opened its ranks to all American "producers," defined as all contributing members of society—skilled and unskilled,

black and white, men and women. Only the idle and the corrupt (bankers, speculators, lawyers, saloon keepers, and gamblers) were to be excluded.

The organization grew in spurts, attracting miners between 1874 and 1879 and skilled urban tradesmen between 1879 and 1885. Although Powderly frowned on using the strike as a labor weapon, the organization gained members following grass-roots strike activity. In 1886, the Haymarket Riot in Chicago contributed to such a growth in labor militancy that in that single year the membership of the Knights of Labor ballooned from 100,000 to 700,000.

The "riot" at Haymarket was, in fact, a peaceful protest meeting connected with a lockout at the McCormick Reaper Works. When the Chicago police arrived to disperse the crowd, a bomb exploded, killing seven policemen. Although no one knows who planted the bomb, eight anarchists were tried and convicted. Three were executed, one commited suicide, and the others served prison terms.

Labor agitation and turbulence spilled over into politics. In 1884 and 1885, the Knights of Labor lobbied to secure a national contract labor law and state anticonvict labor laws. The organization also pressed successfully for the creation of a federal Department of Labor. Between 1885 and 1888, the Knights of Labor sponsored candidates in 200 towns and cities in 34 states and 4 territories and achieved many electoral victories. Despite local successes, no national labor party emerged.

The Knights of Labor could not sustain their momentum as the voice for the American laboring people. Consumer and producer cooperatives fizzled; the policy of accepting both black and white workers led to strife and discord in the South. The two major parties proved adept at coopting labor politicians. Powderly also bore responsibility for the organization's decline. He was never able to unify or direct his diverse following or control the militant elements that opposed him. Local, unauthorized strike actions were often ill-considered and violent and hurt his cause. By 1890, the membership had dropped to 100,000, although the Knights continued to play a role well into the 1890s.

In the 1890s, the American Federation of Labor (AFL), founded in 1886, replaced the Knights of Labor as the nation's dominant union. The history of the Knights pointed up the problems of a national union that admitted all who worked for wages but officially rejected strike action in favor of the ballot box and arbitration. The leader of the AFL, Samuel Gompers, had a different notion of effective worker organization. Gompers's experience as head of the Cigarmakers' Union in the 1870s and as a founder of the Federation of Organized Trades and Labor Unions in 1881 convinced him that skilled workers should put their specific occupational interests before the interests of workers as a whole. By so doing, they could control the supply of skilled labor and keep wages up.

Gompers organized the AFL as a federation of skilled trades—cigar makers, iron molders, iron workers, carpenters, and others—each one autonomous yet linked through an executive council to work together for prolabor national legislation and mutual support during boycott and strike actions. Gompers was a practical man. He believed in the value of the strike, and he knew from bitter experience the importance of dues high enough to sustain a strike fund through a long, tough fight.

Under Gompers's leadership, the AFL grew from 140,000 in 1886 to nearly one million by 1900. Although his notion of a labor organization was elitist, he succeeded in steering his union through a series of crises, fending off challenges from socialists on his left and corporate opposition to strikes from his right. But there was no room in his organization for the unskilled or for blacks. Nor did the AFL welcome women.

Hostile male attitudes constituted a major barrier against organizing women. Change was slow in coming. When the International Ladies Garment Workers Union (ILGWU) was estab-lished in 1900, women were the backbone of the organization, but men dominated the leadership.

Working-Class Setbacks

Despite the growth of working-class organizations, workers lost many of their battles with management. Some of the more spectacular clashes reveal why working-class activism often ended in defeat and why so many workers lived precariously on the edge of poverty.

In 1892, silver miners in Coeur d'Alene, Idaho, went on strike when their employers installed machine drills in the mines, reduced skilled workers to shovelmen, and announced a wage cut. The owners, supported by state militiamen and the federal government, successfully broke the strike by using scabs, but not without armed fighting. Several hundred union men were arrested, herded into huge bull pens, and eventually tried and found guilty of a wide variety of charges. Out of the defeat emerged the Western Federation of Miners (WFM), whose chief political goal was an eight-hour law for miners. The pattern of struggle in Coeur d'Alene was followed in many subsequent strikes. In spite of the intimidation tactics of mine owners, the WFM won as many strikes as it lost.

The Homestead and Pullman Strikes of 1892 and 1894

The most serious setback to labor occurred in 1892 at the Homestead steel mills near Pittsburgh, Pennsylvania. Andrew Carnegie had recently purchased the Homestead plant and put Henry Clay Frick in charge. Together they wanted to eliminate the Amalgamated Association of Iron, Steel, and Tin Workers. When the union refused to accept wage decreases, Frick resorted to a lockout. He fenced in the entire plant and hired 300 armed Pinkerton agents to guard it. As they arrived on July 6, they engaged armed steelworkers in a daylong gun battle. Several men on both sides were killed, and the Pinkertons retreated.

Pinkerton detectives are pictured in a Harper's Weekly *engraving of 1892 as they leave the scene of the Homestead steel strike.*

Frick telegraphed Pennsylvania's governor, who sent 8,000 troops to crush both the strike and the union. Two and a half weeks later, Alexander Berkman, a New York anarchist sympathetic to the plight of the oppressed Homestead workers, attempted to assassinate Frick.

Observing these events, Eugene Victor Debs of Terre Haute, Indiana, for many years an ardent organizer of railroad workers, wrote, "If the year 1892 taught the workingmen any lesson worthy of heed, it was that the capitalist class, like a devilfish, had grasped them with its tentacles and was dragging them down to fathomless depths of degradation."

Despite a new depression in 1893, Debs succeeded in combining several of the separate railroad brotherhoods into a united American Railway Union (ARU). Within a year, over 150,000 railroadmen joined the ARU, and Debs won a strike against the Great Northern Railroad.

Debs faced his toughest crisis at the Pullman Palace Car Company in Chicago. Pullman was a model company town where management controlled all aspects of workers' lives. "We are born in a Pullman house, fed from the Pullman shop, taught in the Pullman school, catechized in the Pullman church, and when we die we shall be buried in the Pullman cemetery and go to the Pullman hell," said one worker wryly.

Late in 1893, as the depression worsened, Pullman cut wages by one-third and laid off many workers but made no reductions in rents or prices in the town stores. Those still at work suffered speedups, intimidations, and further wage cuts. Desperate and "without hope," the Pullman workers joined the ARU in the spring of 1894 and went out on strike.

In late June, Debs led the ARU into a sympathy strike in support of the striking Pullman workers. His instructions were to boycott trains handling Pullman cars throughout the West. As the boycott spread, the General Managers Association, which ran the 24 railroads centered in Chicago, came to the Pullman's support, hiring some 2,500 strikebreakers and obtaining state, federal, and judicial support in stopping the strike.

On July 4, President Grover Cleveland ordered federal troops in to crush the strikers. Violence escalated rapidly, and scores of workers were killed.

Debs appealed for wider labor support. When Samuel Gompers refused his support, the strike collapsed. Debs and several other leaders were arrested and found guilty of contempt of a court injunction to end the strike. While in prison, the disillusioned Debs, a lifelong Democrat, became a confirmed socialist. His arrest and the defeat of the Pullman strike provided a deathblow to the American Railway Union. In 1895, the Supreme Court upheld the legality of using an injunction to stop a strike and provided management with a powerful weapon to use against unions in subsequent years.

Many people claimed to accept the idea of worker organizations, but they would not concede that unions should participate in making economic or work decisions. Most employers violently resisted union demands as infringements of their rights to make production decisions, to hire and fire, to lock workers out, to hire scabs, or to reduce wages in times of depression. The sharp competition of the late nineteenth century, combined with a pattern of falling prices, stiffened employers' resistance to workers' demands. State and local governments and the courts frequently supported them in their battles to curb worker activism.

The severe depressions of the 1870s and 1890s also undermined working-class activism. Many unions collapsed during hard times. Of the 30 national unions in 1873, fewer than one-third managed to survive the depression. A far more serious problem was the reluctance of most workers to organize even in favorable times. In 1870, less than one-tenth of the industrial work force belonged to unions. Thirty years later, despite the expansion of the work force, only 8.4 percent (mostly skilled workers) were union members.

Why were workers so slow to join unions? Certainly, diverse work settings and ethnic differences made it difficult for workers to recognize common bonds. Moreover, many native-born Americans still clung to the tradition of individualism. Others continued to nourish dreams of escaping from the working class and entering the ranks of the middle class.

The comments of an Irish woman highlight another important point. "There should be a law . . . to give a job to every decent man that's out of work," she declared, "and another law to keep all them I-talians from comin' in and takin' the bread out of the mouths of honest people." The ethnic and religious diversity of the work force made it difficult to forge a common front.

The perspective of immigrant workers contributed to their indifference to unions and to tension with native-born Americans. Many foreigners planned to return to their homeland and had limited interest in changing conditions in the United States. Moreover, since their goal was to work, they took jobs as scabs. Much of the violence that accompanied working-class actions erupted when owners brought in strikebreakers. Some Americans blamed immigrants for both low wages and failed worker actions. Divisions among workers were often as bitter as those between strikers and employers. When workers divided, employers benefited.

In the 1870s and 1880s, white workers in the West began to blame the Chinese for economic hardships. A meeting of San Francisco workers in 1877 in favor of the eight-hour day exploded into a rampage against the Chinese. In the following years, angry mobs killed Chinese workers in Tacoma, Seattle, Denver, and Rock Springs, Wyoming. "The Chinese must go! They are stealing our jobs!" became a rallying cry for American workers.

Hostility was also expressed at the national level with the Chinese Exclusion Act of 1882. The law, which had the support of the Knights of Labor in the West, prohibited the immigration of both skilled and unskilled Chinese workers for a ten-year period. It was extended in 1892 and made permanent in 1902.

At the same time, many immigrants, especially those who were skilled, did support unions and cooperate with native-born Americans. Irish-Americans played important roles in the Knights of Labor and the AFL. British and Germans also helped build up the unions. Often ethnic bonds served labor causes by tying members to one another and to the community.

The importance of workers' organizations lay not so much in their successful struggles and protests as in the implicit criticism they offered of American society. Using the language of republicanism, many workers lashed out at an economic order that robbed them of their dignity and humanity. As producers of wealth, they protested that so little of it was theirs. As members of the working class, they rejected the middle-class belief in individualism and social mobility.

The Balance Sheet

Except for skilled workers, most laboring people found it impossible to earn much of a share in the material bounty industrialization created. Yet our perception of the harshness of working-class life partly grows out of our own standards of what is acceptable today. Immigrant workers had their own perspectives. The family tenement, one Polish immigrant remarked, "seemed quite advanced when compared with our home" in Poland. American poverty was preferable to Russian pogroms. A ten-hour job in the steel mill might be an improvement over dawn-to-dusk farmwork that brought no wages.

Studies of several cities show that nineteenth-century workers achieved some occupational mobility. One worker in five in Los Angeles and Atlanta during the 1890s, for example, managed to climb into the middle class. Most immigrant workers were stuck in ill-paid, insecure jobs, but their children ended up doing better. Native-born whites, Jews, and Germans rose more swiftly and fell less often than Irish, Italians, or Poles. Cultural attitudes, family size, education, and group leadership all contributed to different ethnic mobility patterns. Jews, for example, valued education and sacrificed to keep children in school. With an education, they moved upward. The Slavs, however, who valued a steady income over mobility and education, sent their children to work at an early age, believing that these jobs not only helped the family but also provided a head start in securing reliable, stable employment. The southern Italian proverb "Do not make your child better than you are" suggests the value Italians placed on family rather than individual success. Differing attitudes and values led to different aspirations and career patterns.

Two groups enjoyed little mobility. African-Americans were largely excluded from the industrial occupational structure and restricted to unskilled jobs. A study in Los Angeles suggests that Hispanic residents made minimal gains. Their experiences elsewhere may have been much the same.

Although occupational mobility was limited for immigrants, other rewards often compensated for the lack of success at the workplace. Home ownership loomed important for groups like the Irish, while political success or mobility in institutions like the Catholic church provided satisfactions. Likewise, participation in social clubs and fraternal orders compensated in part for lack of advancement at work. Ethnic associations, parades, and holidays provided a sense of identity and security that offset the limitations of the job world.

CONCLUSION

THE COMPLEXITY OF INDUSTRIAL CAPITALISM

The rapid growth of the late nineteenth century made the United States one of the world's industrial giants. Many factors contributed to the "wonderful accomplishments" of the age. They ranged from sympathetic government policies to the rise of big business and the emergence of a cheap industrial work force. But it was also a turbulent period. Many Americans benefited only marginally from the new wealth. Some of them protested by joining unions, by walking out on strike, or by initiating on-the-job actions. Most lived their lives more quietly and never had the opportunity that Thomas O'Donnell did of telling their story to others. But middle-class Americans began to wonder about the O'Donnells of the country. It is to their concerns, worries, and aspirations that we now turn.

Recommended Reading

The late-nineteenth-century industrial world has been the subject of lively historical investigation. A helpful overview of economic change is provided by Stuart Bruchey, *Growth of the Modern American Economy* (1975); and Robert L. Heilbroner, *The Economic Transformation of America* (1977). Samuel P. Hays gives a useful analysis in *The Response to Industrialism, 1885–1914* (1957).

On big business, see Glenn Porter, *The Rise of Big Business, 1860–1910* (1973); and Olivier Zunz, *Making America Corporate, 1870–1929* (1990). Advertising and its effects are discussed in James D. Norris, *Advertising and the Transformation of American Society, 1865–1920* (1990). Edward C. Kirkland illuminates the business mind in *Dream and Thought in the Business Community, 1860–1900* (1964).

Zane Miller's *Urbanization of America* (1973) provides a good introduction to city growth in the late nineteenth century. Gunther Barth examines urban culture in *The Rise of Modern City Culture in Nineteenth-Century America* (1980). James Borchert explores the black experience in *Alley Life in Washington: Family, Community, Religion, and Folklife in the City, 1850–1970* (1980).

For the immigrant experience, consult Thomas J. Archdeacon, *Becoming American: An Ethnic History* (1983). Alan M. Kraut brings together varied material on immigrants in *The Huddled Masses: The Immigrant in American Society, 1880–1921* (1982).

Studies of the working class include Herbert G. Gutman, *Work, Culture, and Society in Industrializing America* (1976); David M. Gordon, Richard Edwards, and Michael Reich, *Segmented Work, Divided Workers: The Historical Transformation of Labor in the United States* (1982); David T. Rodgers, *The Work Ethic in Industrial America* (1978); David Montgomery, *The Fall of the House of Labor: The Workplace, The State, and American Labor Activism, 1865–1925* (1987); and Theodore Hershberg, ed., *Philadelphia: Work, Space, Family, and Group Experience in the Nineteenth Century* (1981).

Labor conflicts are the focus of Nell Irvin Painter's *Standing at Armageddon in The United States, 1877–1919* (1987). Leon Fink explores the Knights of Labor in several communities in *Workingmen's Democracy: The Knights of Labor and American Politics* (1983). The issue of safety for miners is treated by James Whiteside in *Regulating Danger: The Struggle for Mine Safety in the Rocky Mountain Coal Industry* (1990).

Women and work are the subject of Alice Kessler-Harris, *Out to Work: A History of Wage-Earning Women in the United States* (1982); and Julie Matthaei, *An Economic History of Women in America: Women's Work, the Sexual Division of Labor, and the Development of Capitalism* (1982).

Stephen Thernstrom explores the realities of mobility and assimilation in *Poverty and Progress: Social Mobility in a Nineteenth Century City* (1964) and *The Other Bostonians: Poverty and Progress in the American Metropolis, 1880–1970* (1973). Similar works include Clyde and Sally Griffen, *Natives and Newcomers: The Ordering of Opportunity in Mid-Nineteenth-Century Poughkeepsie* (1978).

Novels depicting the period include Theodore Dreiser, *Sister Carrie* (1900); Stephen Crane, *Maggie: A Girl of the Streets* (1893); Abraham Cahan, *The Rise of David Levinsky* (1917); and Thomas Bell, *Out of This Furnace* (1976 ed.).

Time Line

1843–1884	"Old immigration"	1879	Thomas Edison invents incandescent light
1844	Telegraph invented	1882	Chinese Exclusion Act
1850s	Steam power widely used in manufacturing	1885–1914	"New immigration"
1859	Value of U.S. industrial production exceeds value of agricultural production	1886	American Federation of Labor founded Haymarket Riot in Chicago
1866	National Labor Union founded	1887	Interstate Commerce Act
1869	Transcontinental railroad completed Knights of Labor organized	1890	Sherman Anti-Trust Act
1870	Standard Oil of Ohio formed	1892	Standard Oil of New Jersey formed Coeur d'Alene strike Homestead steelworkers strike
1870s–1880s	Consolidation of continental railroad network	1893	Chicago World's Fair
1873	Bethlehem Steel begins using Bessemer process	1893–1897	Depression
1873–1879	Depression	1894	Pullman railroad workers strike
1876	Alexander G. Bell invents telephone	1900	International Ladies Garment Workers Union founded Corporations responsible for two-thirds of U.S. manufacturing
1877	Railroad workers hold first nationwide industrial strike		

chapter 19

Politics and Reform

At the start of his best-seller *Looking Backward* (1888), Edward Bellamy likened the American society of his day to a huge stagecoach. Dragging the coach along sandy roads and over steep hills were "the masses of humanity," straining "under the pitiless lashing of hunger." At the top sat the favored few, riding well in breezy comfort. The fortunate few, however, were constantly fearful that they might lose their seats from a sudden jolt, fall to the ground, and have to pull the coach themselves.

Bellamy's famous coach allegory introduced a utopian novel in which the class divisions and pitiless competition of the nineteenth century were replaced by a classless, caring, cooperative new world. Economic anxieties and hardships were supplanted by satisfying labor and leisure.

The novel opens in 1887. The hero, Julian West, a wealthy Bostonian, falls asleep worrying about the effect local labor struggles might have on his upcoming wedding. When he wakes up, it is the year 2000. Utopia had been achieved peacefully through the development of one gigantic trust, owned and operated by the national government. All citizens between 21 and 45 work in an industrial army with equalized pay and work difficulty. In a special division of the industrial army, women worked shorter hours in "lighter occupations." The purpose of equality of the sexes and more leisure, the novel made clear, was to enable women to cultivate their "beauty and grace" and, by extension, to feminize culture and politics.

Bellamy's book was immensely popular. Educated middle-class Americans were attracted by his vision of a society in which humans were both morally good and materially well off. Although the collectivist features of Bellamy's utopia were socialistic, he and his admirers called his system "nationalism." This appealed to a new generation of Americans who had put aside Civil War antagonisms to embrace the greatness of a growing, if now economically divided, nation. In the early 1890s, with Americans buying nearly 10,000 copies of *Looking Backward* every week, over 160 Nationalist clubs were formed to crusade for the adoption of Bellamy's ideas.

The inequalities of wealth described in Bellamy's coach scene reflected a political life in which many participated but only a few benefited. The wealthiest 10 percent, who rode high on the social coach, dominated national politics, while untutored bosses (mostly Irish) held sway in governing cities. Except for token expressions of support, national political leaders ignored the cries of factory workers, immigrants, farmers, blacks, Native Americans, and other victims of the vast transformation of American industrial, urban, and agrarian life in the late nineteenth century. But as the century drew to a close, middle-class Americans like Bellamy, as well as labor and agrarian leaders, proposed various reforms.

In this chapter, we will examine American politics at the national and local level from the end of Reconstruction to the 1890s and look at the growing social and political involvement of educated middle-class reformers. We will conclude with an account of the pivotal importance of the 1890s, which shook many comfortable citizens out of their apathy.

POLITICS IN THE GILDED AGE

In a satirical book in 1873, Mark Twain, with Charles Dudley Warner, used the expression "Gilded Age" to describe the political corruption of Ulysses S. Grant's presidency. The phrase, with its suggestion of shallow glitter, has come to characterize social and political life in the last quarter of the nineteenth century. Ironically, although Gilded Age politics was tainted by corruption and tinted by more color than substance, the period was one of high party vitality: Voter participation in national elections between 1876 and 1896 hovered at an all-time high of 73 to 82 percent of all registered voters.

Behind the pomp, parades, free beer, and lengthy speeches of Gilded Age politics occurred two gradual changes that would greatly affect twentieth-century politics. The first was the development of a professional bureaucracy, which served as a counterfoil to the perceived dangers of majority rule represented by high voter participation. Second, after a period of close elections and party stalemate based on Civil War divisions between Democrats and Republicans, new issues and concerns fostered a party realignment in the 1890s.

Politics, Parties, Patronage, and Presidents

American government in the 1870s and 1880s clearly supported the interests of riders at the top of the coach. Nineteenth-century Americans believed in laissez-faire, a doctrine that argued that all would benefit from an economic life free of government interference. As Republican leader Roscoe Conkling explained, the primary role of government was "to clear the way of impediments and dangers, and leave every class and every individual free and safe in the exertions and pursuits of life." Government regulation of business was in disfavor, but government cooperation with business through policies such as protective tariffs and currency legislation beneficial to financial and commercial interests was another matter.

The Gilded Age, Henry Adams observed, was the most "thoroughly ordinary" period in American politics since Columbus. "One might search the whole list of Congress, Judiciary, and

Politicians in the evenly contested electoral campaigns of the Gilded Age avoided real issues in favor of parades, pomp, patronage, and patriotism. Republican campaigns, invoking Lincoln, reminded voters to "vote as you shot" in the Civil War.

Executive during the twenty-five years 1870–95 and find little but damaged reputation." Adams was especially sensitive to this decline in the quality of democratic politics. His autobiography, *The Education of Henry Adams* (1907), contrasted the low political tone of his own age with the exalted political morality of the days of his grandfather John Quincy Adams and great-grandfather John Adams.

As a result of the weak Johnson and Grant presidencies, Congress emerged in the 1870s as the dominant branch of government. With power in the committee system, the moral quality of congressional leadership was typified by men such as the popular James G. Blaine, who

was involved in a bribery scandal in which he was paid for supporting favors to railroads, and Roscoe Conkling, who spent most of his career in patronage conflicts with fellow Republican Party leaders. Though he served in Congress for over two decades, Conkling never drafted a bill. His career was unharmed, for legislation was not Congress's primary purpose.

In 1879, a student of legislative politics, Woodrow Wilson, expressed his disgust with the degradation of Gilded Age politics in eight words: "No leaders, no principles; no principles, no parties." Little differentiated the two major parties. They diverged not over principles but patronage, not over issues but over awarding thousands of government jobs to the winning candidate and his party. An English observer concluded that the most cohesive force in American politics was "the desire for office and for office as a means of gain." The two parties, like two bottles of liquor, bore different labels, yet "each was empty."

Republican votes still came from northeastern Yankee industrial interests and from New England migrants across the Upper Midwest. The main support for Democrats still came primarily from southern whites, northern workers, and Irish Catholic and other urban immigrants. For a few years, Civil War and Reconstruction issues generated clear, ideological party differences. But after 1876, on national issues at least, party labels did indeed mark "empty" bottles.

One reason for avoiding issues in favor of bland platforms and careful campaigning was that the two parties were evenly matched. In three of the five presidential elections between 1876 and 1892, one percent of the vote separated the two major candidates. Although all the presidents in the era except Grover Cleveland were Republicans, the Democrats controlled the House of Representatives in eight of the ten sessions of Congress between 1875 and 1895. As a result, political interest shifted away from Washington to states and cities.

Gilded Age presidents were an undistinguished group. None of them—Rutherford B. Hayes (1877–1881), James Garfield (1881), Chester A. Arthur (1881–1885), Grover Cleveland (1885–1889 and 1893–1897), and Benjamin Harrison (1889–1893)—served two consecutive terms. None was strongly identified with any particular issue. Although Cleveland was the only Democrat in the group, he differed little from the Republicans.

Most Americans expected their presidents to take care of party business by rewarding the faithful with government positions. The scale of patronage was enormous. Garfield complained of having to dispense thousands of jobs as he took office in 1881. He is remembered primarily

for being shot early in his administration by a disappointed office seeker. His successor, Chester Arthur, was so closely identified with Conkling's patronage operation that when the shooting of the president was announced, a friend said with shocked disbelief, "My God! Chet Arthur in the White House!"

National Issues

Arthur surprised his doubters by proving himself a capable and dignified president, responsive to the growing demands for civil service reform. Four issues were important at the national level in the Gilded Age: the tariff, currency, civil service, and government regulation of railroads (see Chapter 17). In confronting these issues, legislators tried to serve both their own self-interest and the national interest of an efficient, productive economy. Two additional issues, Indian "reform" and black rights, were submerged in these interests (see Chapter 17).

The tariff was one issue where party, as well as regional attitudes toward the use of government power, made some difference. Republicans believed in using the national government to support business interests and stood for a high protective tariff. Democrats stressed that a low tariff exemplified the "economic axiom . . . that the government is best which governs least." In practice, politicians accommodated local interests in tariff adjustments. Democratic senator Daniel Vorhees of Indiana explained, "I am a protectionist for every interest which I am sent here by my constituents to protect."

Tariff revisions were bewilderingly complex in their acceding to these many special interests. As one senator knowingly said, "The contest over a revision of the tariff brings to light a selfish strife which is not far from disgusting." Most tariffs included a mixture of higher and lower rates that defied understanding.

The question of money was even more complicated. During the Civil War, the federal government had circulated paper money (greenbacks) that could not be exchanged for gold or silver. In the late 1860s and 1870s, proponents of a hard-money policy supported either withdrawing all paper money from circulation or making it convertible to specie. They opposed increasing the volume of money because they thought it would lead to higher prices. Greenbackers, who advocated soft money (currency not exchangeable for gold or silver) urged increasing the supply of paper money. An inadequate money supply, they believed, led to falling prices and an increase in interest rates, which harmed farmers, industrial workers, and all people in debt.

Hard-money interests had more power and influence, and in 1875 Congress put the nation firmly on the gold standard. But as large supplies of silver were discovered and mined in the West, pressure was resumed for increasing the money supply by coining silver. In 1878, the Bland-Allison Act required the Treasury to buy between $2 million and $4 million of silver each month and to coin it as silver dollars. Despite the increase in money supply, the period was not inflationary, but prices fell, disappointing the supporters of soft money. Their response was to push for more silver, which continued the controversy into the 1890s.

The issue of civil service reform was, Henry Adams observed, "a subject almost as dangerous in political conversation in Washington as slavery itself in the old days before the war." The worst feature of the spoils system was that parties financed themselves by assessing holders of patronage jobs, often as much as one percent of their annual salaries. The assassination of Garfield, however, created enough public support to force Congress to take action. The Pendleton Act of 1883 established a system of merit examinations covering about one-tenth of federal offices. Gradually, more bureaucrats fell under its coverage, but parties became no more honest. As campaign contributions from government employees dried up, parties turned to other financial sources, such as corporate contributions.

The Lure of Local Politics

The fact that the major parties did not disagree substantially on issues like money and civil service does not mean that nineteenth-century Americans found politics dull or uninteresting. In fact, far more eligible voters turned out in the late nineteenth century than at any time since. The 78.5 percent average turnout to vote for president in the 1880s contrasts sharply with the less than 55 percent of eligible Americans who voted for president in the 1980s.

Americans were drawn to the polls in part by the fun and games of party parades, buttons, and banners but also by the lure of local issues. For example, Iowa corn farmers turned out to vote for state representatives who favored curbing the power of the railroads to set high grain-shipping rates. But emotional issues of race, religion, nationality, and life style often overrode economic self-interest. While Irish Catholics in New York sought political support for their parochial schools, third-generation middle-class American Protestants from Illinois or Connecticut voted for laws that would compel attendance at public schools.

The influx of the new immigrants, especially in the mushrooming cities, facilitated the rise of urban bosses, whose power to control city government rested on an ability to deliver the votes of poor, uneducated immigrants. In return for votes, bosses like "Big Tim" Sullivan of New York and "Hinky Dink" Kenna of Chicago operated informal welfare systems. They handed out jobs and money for rent, fuel, and bail.

Party leaders also won votes by making political participation exciting. Nineteenth-century campaigns were punctuated by parades, rallies, and oratory. Campaign buttons, handkerchiefs, songs, and other paraphernalia generated color and excitement in political races where substantive issues were not at stake. In the election of 1884, for example, Democrats campaigned against Blaine's record of dishonesty, while Republicans focused on Cleveland's illegitimate child. Cleveland won, in part because a Republican clergyman unwisely called the Democrats the party of "rum, Romanism, and rebellion" on election eve in New York, which delivered the state, and the election, to Cleveland.

Voters may have been cool toward the tariff and civil service, but they expressed strong interest in temperance, anti-Catholicism, compulsory school attendance and Sunday laws, aid to parochial schools, racial issues, restriction of immigration, and "bloody shirt" reminders of the Civil War.

Party membership reflected voter interest in cultural, religious, and ethnic questions. Since the Republican Party had proved its willingness in the past to mobilize the power of the state to reshape society, people who wished to regulate moral and economic life were attracted to it. Catholics and various immigrant groups found the Democratic Party more to their liking because it opposed government efforts to regulate morals. Said one Chicago Democrat, "A Republican is a man who wants you t' go t' church every Sunday. A Democrat says if a man wants t' have a glass of beer on Sunday he can have it."

These differences caused spirited local contests, particularly over prohibition. Many Americans considered drinking a serious social problem. Annual consumption of brewery beer had risen from 2.7 gallons per capita in 1850 to 17.9 in 1880. Rather than trying to persuade individuals to give up drink, as the temperance movement had done earlier in the century, many now sought to make drinking a crime.

In the 1870s in San Jose, California, temperance reformers put on the ballot a local option referendum to ban the sale of liquor in San Jose. Women erected a temperance tent where they held conspicuous daily meetings. On election eve, a large crowd appeared at the temperance tent, but a larger one turned up at a proliquor rally. In the morning, women roamed the streets, urging men to adopt the referendum. Children were marched around to the polls and saloons, singing, "Father, dear father, come home with me now." By afternoon the mood grew ugly, and the women were harassed and threatened by drunken men. The prohibition proposal lost by a vote of 1,430 to 918.

Similarly emotional conflicts occurred in the 1880s at the state level over other issues, especially education. In Iowa, Illinois, and Wisconsin, Republicans sponsored laws mandating that children attend schools that provided instruction in English. The intent of these laws was to undermine parochial schools, which taught in the language of immigrants. In Wisconsin, a law for compulsory school attendance was so strongly anti-Catholic that it backfired. Many voters, disillusioned with Republican moralism, shifted to the Democratic Party.

MIDDLE-CLASS REFORM

Middle-class Americans moved by moral issues such as education and temperance were also concerned by the corruption of urban life and saw the value of the sophisticated and moral thinking they could bring to national life.

Frances Willard and the Women's Christian Temperance Union (WCTU) is an example. As president of the WCTU from 1879 until her death in 1898, Willard headed the largest women's organization in the country. Most members, like Willard, believed drunkenness caused poverty and family violence. But after 1886, the WCTU reversed its position, seeing drunkenness as a result of poverty, unemployment, and bad labor conditions. Willard joined the Knights of Labor in 1887 and by the 1890s had influenced the WCTU to extend its programs in a "do-everything" policy to alleviate the problems of workers, particularly women and children.

The Gospel of Wealth

Frances Willard called herself a Christian socialist because she believed in applying the ethical principles of Jesus to economic life with the aim of reducing inequalities of wealth. But for most Americans in the Gilded Age, Christianity supported the competitive individualistic ethic that justified the lofty place of those at the top. This ethic was endorsed by prominent ministers and others. Episcopal bishop William Lawrence wrote that it was "God's will that some men should attain great wealth."

Industrialist Andrew Carnegie in an article, "The Gospel of Wealth" (1889), celebrated the benefits of better goods and lower prices that resulted from competition. The concentration of wealth in the hands of a few leading industrialists, he concluded, was "not only beneficial but essential to the future of the race." Those most fit would bring order and efficiency out of the chaos of rapid industrialization. Carnegie also insisted that the rich were obligated to spend some of their wealth to benefit their "poorer brethren." He practiced what he preached, establishing over 2,500 libraries and providing substantial funding for education.

Carnegie's ideas about wealth were drawn from an ideology known as social Darwinism, based on the work of Charles Darwin, whose famous *Origin of Species* was published in 1859. Herbert Spencer, an English social philosopher, adopted Darwin's notions of natural selection and the "survival of the fittest" and applied them to human society. Progress, he said, resulted from relentless competition in which the weak failed and were eliminated while the strong climbed to the top. He believed that "the whole effort of nature is to get rid of such as are unfit, to clear the world of them, and make room for better."

Spencer's American followers, like Carnegie and William Graham Sumner, a professor of political economy at Yale, familiarized the American public with the basic ideas of social Darwinism. They emphasized that poverty was the inevitable consequence of the struggle for existence and that attempts to end it were pointless, if not immoral. Sumner, who opposed the monopolistic aims of industrial giants such as John D. Rockefeller, nevertheless scoffed at those who would take power or money away from millionaires. That, he said, would be "like killing off our generals in war."

Social Darwinists also believed in the superiority of the Anglo-Saxon race, which they maintained had reached the highest stage of evolution. Their theories were used to justify race supremacy and imperialism as well as the monopolistic efforts of American businessmen. Railroad magnate James J. Hill said that the absorption of smaller railroads by larger ones was the industrial analogy of the victory in nature of the fit over the unfit. John D. Rockefeller, Jr., told a YMCA class in Cleveland that "the growth of a large business is merely a survival of the fittest." Like the growth of a beautiful rose, "the early buds which grow up around it" must be sacrificed. This was, he said, "merely the working out of a law of nature and a law of God."

Others questioned this rosy outlook. Brooks Adams, brother of Henry, wrote that social philosophers like Spencer and Sumner were "hired by the comfortable classes to prove that everything was all right."

Reform Darwinism and Pragmatism

A number of intellectual reformers directly challenged the gloomy social Darwinian notion that nothing could be done to alleviate poverty and injustice.

Henry George observed that wherever the

highest degree of "material progress" had been realized, "we find the deepest poverty." George's book *Progress and Poverty* (1879) was an early statement of the contradictions of American life. With Bellamy's *Looking Backward,* it was the most influential book of the age, selling two million copies by 1905. George admitted that economic growth had produced wonders but pointed out the social costs and the loss of Christian values. His remedy was to break up landholding monopolists who profited from the increasing value of their land and rents they collected from those who actually did the work. He proposed a "single tax" on the unearned increases in land value received by landlords.

Henry George's optimistic faith in the capacity of humans to effect change appealed to many middle-class intellectuals. Some went beyond George to develop social scientific models that justified reform energy rather than inaction. A sociologist, Lester Frank Ward, and an economist, Richard T. Ely, both found examples of cooperation in nature and demonstrated that competition and laissez-faire had proved both wasteful and inhumane. These reform Darwinists urged instead an economic order marked by caring cooperation and social regulation.

Two pragmatists, John Dewey and William James, established a philosophical foundation for reform. James, a professor at Harvard, argued that while environment was important, so also was human will. People could influence the course of human events. He made it clear that the expression of human sympathies and the aversion to both economic and international war was moral conduct with the most ethical consequences.

James and young social scientists like Ward and Ely rejected the social determinism of Spencer and provided intellectual justification for the struggle against the inequalities of wealth found in many sectors of their society.

Settlements, Revivalism, and the Social Gospel

Jane Addams understood the gap between progress and poverty. She saw it in the misery of the working-class people in Chicago. Addams founded Hull House in Chicago in 1889 "to aid in the solution of the social and industrial problems which are engendered by the modern conditions of life in a great city." Vida Scudder, too, "felt the agitating and painful vibrations" of the depression. This young professor of literature at Wellesley College resolved to do something to alleviate the suffering of the poor. She and six other Smith College graduates formed an organization of college women in 1889 to work in settlement houses.

Other middle-class activists who worried about social conditions were mostly profession-

The young Jane Addams was one of the college-educated women who chose to remain unmarried and pursue a career as an "urban housekeeper" and social reformer, serving immigrant families in the Chicago neighborhood near her Hull House.

als—lawyers, ministers, teachers, journalists, and academic social scientists. The message they began to preach in the 1890s was highly idealistic, ethical, and Christian. They preferred a society marked by cooperation rather than competition, where, as they liked to say, people were guided by the "golden rule rather than the rule of gold." As middle-class intellectuals, they tended to stress an educational approach to problems, but they also ran for public office, crusaded for legislation, mediated labor disputes, and lived in poor neighborhoods.

The settlement house movement typified the blend of idealism and practicality characteristic of middle-class reformers in the 1890s. Addams opened Hull House, and Scudder started Denison House in Boston. A short time later, on New York's Lower East Side, Lillian Wald opened her "house on Henry Street." The primary purpose of the settlement houses was to help immigrant families, especially women, adapt to the realities of urban living in America. This meant launching day nurseries, kindergartens, boarding rooms for working women, and classes in sewing, cooking, nutrition, health care, and English. The settlements also frequently organized sports clubs and coffeehouses for young people as a way of keeping them out of the saloons.

A second purpose of the settlement house movement was to provide college-educated women with meaningful work at a time when they faced professional barriers and to allow them to preserve the strong feelings of sisterhood they had experienced in college. A third goal was to gather data exposing social misery in order to spur legislative action, such as developing city building codes for tenements, abolishing child labor, and improving safety in factories. Hull House, Addams said, was intended in part "to investigate and improve the conditions in the industrial districts of Chicago."

By contrast, another Chicagoan, Dwight Moody, led a wave of urban revivals in the 1870s, which appealed to lower-class rural folk who were either drawn to the city by expectant

opportunities or pushed there by economic ruin. Supported by businessmen, who felt that religion would make workers and immigrants more docile, revivalists battled sin through individual conversion rather than by the settlement workers' focus on reform. The revivals helped nearly to double Protestant church membership in the last two decades of the century.

In the 1890s, many Protestant ministers immersed themselves in the Social Gospel movement, which tied salvation to social betterment. Like the settlement house workers, these religious leaders sought to make Christianity relevant to industrial and urban problems. A young Baptist minister in the notorious Hell's Kitchen area of New York City, Walter Rauschenbusch, unleashed scathing attacks on the selfishness of capitalism and church ignorance of socioeconomic issues. His progressive ideas for social justice and a welfare state were later published in two landmark Social Gospel books, *Christianity and the Social Crisis* (1907) and *Christianizing the Social Order* (1912).

Perhaps the most influential book promoting social Christianity was a best-selling novel, *In His Steps,* published in 1897 by Charles Sheldon. *In His Steps* portrayed the dramatic transformations in business relations, tenement life, and urban politics made possible by the work of a few community leaders who resolved to base all their actions on a single question: "What would Jesus do?" Although streaked with naive sentimentality characteristic of much of the Social Gospel, Sheldon's novel prepared thousands of influential middle-class Americans for progressive civic leadership after the turn of the century.

Reforming the City

No late-nineteenth-century institution needed reforming as much as urban government. The president of Cornell University described American city governments as "the worst in Christendom—the most expensive, the most inefficient, and the most corrupt."

Rapid urban growth overburdened city leaders. Population increase and industrial expansion created new demands for service. As city governments struggled to respond to new needs, they raised taxes and incurred vast debts. This combination of rapid growth, indebtedness, and poor services, coupled with the influx of new immigrants, prepared fertile ground for graft and "bossism."

The rise of the boss was directly connected to the growth of the city. As immigrant voters appeared, traditional native-born ruling groups left city government for business, where more money and status beckoned. Into the resulting power vacuum stepped the boss. In an age of urban expansion, bosses dispensed patronage jobs in return for votes and contributions to the party machine. They awarded street railway, gas line, and other utility franchises and construction contracts to local businesses in return for kickbacks and other favors. They also passed on tips to friendly real estate men about the location of projected city improvements. Worse yet, the bosses received favors from the owners of saloons, brothels, and gambling clubs in return for their help with police protection, bail, and influence with the courts. These institutions, however unsavory we might think them today, were vital to the urban economy and played an important role in easing the immigrants' way into American life. For many young women, the brothel was a means of economic survival. For men, the saloon was the center of social life, as well as a place for cheap meals and information about work and aid to their families.

"Bossism" deeply offended middle-class urban reformers, who opposed not only graft and vice but also the perversion of democracy by the exploitation of ignorant immigrants. Urban reformers, whose programs were similar in most cities, not only worked for the "Americanization" of immigrants in public schools (and opposed parochial schooling) but also formed clubs or voters' leagues to discuss the failings of municipal government. Political considerations pervaded every reform issue. Many Anglo-Saxon men favored prohibition partly to remove ethnic saloon owners from politics and supported woman suffrage in part to gain a middle-class political advantage against the predominantly male immigrant community. They proposed to replace the bosses with expert city managers. They hoped to make government less costly and thereby lower taxes. One effect of their emphasis on cost efficiency was to cut services to the poor. Another was to disfranchise working-class and ethnic groups, whose political participation depended on the old ward boss system.

Not all urban reformers were elitist, managerial types. Samuel Jones, for example, both opposed the boss system and had a passionate commitment to democratic political participation by the urban immigrant masses. An immigrant himself, Jones was a self-made man in the rags-to-riches mold, working his way up to the ownership of several oil fields and a factory in Toledo, Ohio. In 1894, Jones resolved "to apply the Golden Rule as a rule of conduct" in his factory. He instituted an eight-hour day for his employees, a $2 minimum wage per day (50 to 75 cents higher than the Toledo average for ten hours), a cooperative insurance program, and an annual 5 percent Christmas dividend. He hired ex-criminals and outcasts that no one else would employ and plastered the Golden Rule all over his factory walls.

Beginning in 1897, Jones was elected to an unprecedented four terms as mayor of Toledo. As a pacifist, he did not believe in violence or coercion of any kind. Therefore, he took away policemen's side arms and heavy clubs. When he sat as judge in police court, he regularly dismissed most cases of petty theft and drunkenness brought before him, charging that the accused were victims of an unjust social order and that only the poor went to jail for such crimes. He refused to advocate closing the saloons or brothels, and when prostitutes were brought before him, he usually dismissed them after fining every man in the room 10 cents—and himself a dollar—for permitting prostitution to exist. The crime rate in Toledo, a notoriously sinful city, decreased during his tenure, and Jones was adored by the plain people. When he died in 1904, nearly 55,000 persons, "tears streaming down their faces," filed past his coffin.

The Struggle for Woman Suffrage

Women served, in Jane Addams's phrase, as "urban housekeepers" in the settlement house and good government movements, which reflected the tension many women felt between their public and private lives, between their obligations to self, family, and society.

Some middle-class women, Addams and Scudder, for example, avoided marriage altogether, preferring the supportive relationships found in the female settlement house community. In fact, the generation of women that came of age in the 1890s married less—and later—than any other in American history.

One way women reconciled the conflicting pressures between their private and public lives, as well as deflected male criticism, was to see their work as maternal. Addams called Hull House "the great mother breast of our common humanity." Frances Willard told Susan B. Anthony in 1898 that "government is only housekeeping on the broadest scale," a job men had botched, thus requiring women's saving participation. But how could they be municipal housekeepers if they could not yet even vote?

In the years after the Seneca Falls Convention in 1848, women's civil and political rights advanced very slowly. Although in several western states they received the right to vote in municipal and schoolboard elections, only the territory of Wyoming, in 1869, had granted full political equality before 1890. Colorado, Utah, and Idaho enfranchised women in the 1890s, but no other states granted suffrage until 1910.

In the 1890s, leading suffragists reappraised the situation. The two wings of the women's rights movement, split since 1869, combined in 1890 as the National American Woman Suffrage Association (NAWSA). Although Elizabeth Cady Stanton and Susan B. Anthony continued to head the association, they were both in their seventies, and effective leadership soon passed to younger leaders, who concentrated on the single issue of the vote rather than dividing their energies among the many causes Stanton and Anthony had espoused. Women of widely divergent political and philosophical views were able to come together on this one issue.

Changing leadership meant a shift from principled to expedient arguments for the suffrage. Since 1848, suffragists had made their argument primarily from principle, citing, as Stanton argued at a congressional hearing in 1892, "our republican idea, individual citizenship." Finding that appeals to principle did not work, the younger generation shifted to three expedient arguments. The first was that women needed to vote to pass self-protection laws that would guard them against rapists, state age-of-consent laws, and unsafe industrial work. The second argument, Addams's notion of urban housekeeping, pointed out that political enfranchisement would further women's role in cleaning up morals, tenements, saloons, factories, and corrupt politics. The third expedient argument was that educated, native-born American women should be given the vote to counteract the undesirable influence of ignorant, illiterate, and immoral male immigrants. In a speech in Iowa in 1894, Carrie Chapman Catt, who would succeed Anthony as president of NAWSA in 1900, argued that the "Government is menaced with great danger . . . in the votes possessed by the males in the slums of the cities," a danger that could be averted only by cutting off that vote and giving it instead to women. In the new century, under the leadership of capable organizers like Catt, suffrage would finally be secured.

THE PIVOTAL 1890s

For years, many Americans have mistakenly called the last decade of the nineteenth century the "gay nineties." The 1890s were, indeed, a decade of sports and leisure, the electrification of the city, and the enormous wealth of the few. But for many more Americans it was also a decade of dark tenement misery, grinding work or desperate unemployment, and poverty.

The 1890s, far from gay, were years of contrasts and crises. The obvious contrast, as Bellamy had anticipated, was between the rich and the poor. The pivotal nature of the decade hinged on this feeling of polarizing unrest and upheaval as the nation underwent the traumas of change. America was transforming itself from a rural to an urban society and experiencing the pressures of rapid industrialization and accompanying changes in the workplace and on farms. Moreover, the new immigration from Europe and the northward, westward, and cityward internal migrations of blacks and farmers added to the "great danger" against which Carrie Catt warned. The depression of 1893 worsened the gaps between rich and poor and accelerated the demands for reform. Government bureaucratic structures began to adapt to the needs of governing a complex specialized society, and Congress slowly shifted away from laissez-faire in order to confront national problems.

Republican Legislation in the Early 1890s

Benjamin Harrison's election to the presidency in 1888 was accompanied by Republican control of both houses of Congress. Though by no means reformers, the Republicans moved forward in the first six months of 1890 with legislation in five areas: pensions for Civil War veterans and their dependents, trusts, the tariff, the money question, and rights for blacks. The De-pendent Pensions Act, providing generous support of $160 million a year for Union veterans and their dependents, sailed through Congress.

The Sherman Anti-Trust Act declared illegal "every contract, combination ... or conspiracy in restraint of trade or commerce." Although the bill was vague and not really intended to break up large corporations, the Sherman Act was an initial attempt to restrain large business combinations. But in 1895 the Supreme Court ruled that the law applied only to commerce, not manufacturing.

A bill for higher tariffs, introduced in 1890 by Ohio Republican William McKinley, passed after nearly 500 amendments were added.

The Sherman Silver Purchase Act, a compromise measure that momentarily satisfied almost everyone, ordered the Treasury to buy 4.5 million ounces of silver monthly and to issue treasury notes for it. Silverites were pleased by the proposed increase in the money supply. Opponents felt they had averted the worst, free coinage of silver. The gold standard remained secure.

Republicans were also prepared to confront violations of the voting rights of southern blacks in 1890. President Harrison told the editor of the New York *Tribune*, "I feel very strong upon the question of a free ballot." An elections bill, proposed by Massachusetts senator Henry Cabot Lodge, would protect voter registration and ensure fair elections by setting up mechanisms for investigating charges of bribery and fraud. A storm of disapproval from Democrats greeted the measure. Senate Democrats delayed action with a filibuster.

Meanwhile, Republicans worried that they could not pass both the elections bill and the McKinley Tariff, which was languishing in the Senate. Pennsylvania senator Matt Quay, who had skillfully directed Harrison's election in 1888, proposed that if the Democrats ceased their delaying tactics so that the tariff could come to a vote, the Republicans would agree to put off consideration of the elections bill. The ploy worked, marking the end of major party efforts to protect black voting rights in the South until the 1960s.

The legislative efforts of the summer of 1890, impressive by nineteenth-century standards, fell far short of solving the nation's problems. Trusts grew more rapidly after the Sherman Act than before. Union veterans were pleased by their pensions, but southerners were incensed that Confederate veterans were not covered. Farm prices continued to decline, and gold and silver advocates were only momentarily silenced. Black rights were put off to another time. Polarizing inequalities of wealth remained. Voters abandoned the GOP in droves in the 1890 congressional elections, dropping the number of Republicans in the House from 168 to 88.

Two years later, Cleveland won a presidential rematch with Harrison. His inaugural address underlined the lesson he drew from Republican legislative activism in 1890. "The lessons of paternalism ought to be unlearned," he said, "and the better lesson taught that while the people should ... support their government, its functions do not include the support of the people."

The Depression of 1893

Cleveland's philosophy of government soon faced a difficult test. No sooner had he taken office than began one of the worst depressions ever to grip the American economy, lasting from 1893 to 1897. The depression started in Europe and spread to the United States as overseas buyers cut back on their purchases of American products. Shrinking markets abroad soon crippled American manufacturing. As gold left the country to pay for securities dumped by foreign investors, the nation's supply of money declined.

The collapse in 1893 was also caused by serious overextensions of the economy at home, especially in railroad construction. Farmers, troubled by falling prices, planted more and more crops, hoping somehow that the market would pick up. As the realization of overextension spread, confidence faltered, then gave way to financial panic. When the stock market crashed early in 1893, investors frantically sold their shares, companies plunged into bankruptcy, and disaster spread. People rushed to exchange paper notes for gold, reducing gold reserves and confidence in the economy even further. Banks called in their loans, which by the end of the year led to 16,000 business bankruptcies and 500 bank failures. Factories closed, and within a year, an estimated three million Americans, 20 percent of the work force, were unemployed. Suddenly people began to look fearfully at the tramps wandering from city to city looking for work. "There are thousands of homeless and starving men in the streets," one young man reported from Chicago, indicating that he had seen "more misery in this last week than I ever saw in my life before."

As in Bellamy's coach image, the misery of the many was not shared by the few, which only increased discontent. While unemployed men foraged in garbage dumps for food, the wealthy gave lavish parties sometimes costing $100,000. At one such affair, diners ate their meal while seated on horses; at another, many guests proudly proclaimed that they had spent over $10,000 on their dresses. While Lithuanian immigrants walked or rode streetcars to Buffalo steel factories to work, wealthy men skimmed across lakes and oceans in huge pleasure yachts. J. P. Morgan owned three, one with a crew of 85 sailors.

Nowhere were these inequalities more apparent than in Chicago during the World's Columbian Exposition, which opened on May 1, 1893, five days before plummeting prices on the stock market began the depression. Built at a cost of $31 million, the Chicago World's Fair celebrated the marvelous mechanical accomplishments of American enterprise. The elegant

The depression of 1893 accentuated contrasts between rich and poor. While well-to-do children enjoyed the giant Ferris wheel and other midway attractions at the Chicago World's Columbian Exposition, slum children played in filthy streets nearby.

design of its buildings and lagoons stimulated a "City Beautiful" movement that made many cities more attractive and enjoyable for their residents. But as well-to-do fairgoers sipped pink champagne, men, women, and children in the immigrant wards of Chicago less than a mile away drank contaminated water, crowded into packed tenements, and looked in vain for jobs.

Despite the magnitude of despair during the depression, national politicians and leaders were reluctant to respond. Only mass demonstrations forced city authorities to provide soup kitchens and places for the homeless to sleep. When an army of unemployed led by Jacob Coxey marched into Washington in the spring of 1894 to press for some form of public work relief, its leaders were arrested for stepping on the grass of the Capitol. Cleveland's reputation for callous disregard for citizens suffering from the depres-

sion worsened later that summer when he sent federal troops to Chicago to crush the Pullman strike.

The president focused his efforts on tariff reform and repeal of the Silver Purchase Act, which he blamed for the depression. Although repeal was ultimately a necessary measure to establish business confidence, in the short run it worsened the financial crisis.

The Crucial Election of 1896

The campaign of 1896, waged during the continuing depression, was one of the most critical in American history. Known as the "battle of the standards," the election was fought in part over the ratio of gold and silver as the standard national currency. Although Cleveland was in disgrace for ignoring depression woes, few leaders in either major party thought the federal government was responsible for alleviating the suffering of the people. But unskilled workers wondered where relief might be found.

As the election of 1896 approached, Populist leaders focused on the issues of silver and whether to fuse with one of the major parties by agreeing on a joint ticket. But fusion required abandoning much of the Populist platform, thus weakening the party's distinctive character. Under the influence of silver mine owners, many Populists became convinced that the hope of the party lay in a single-issue commitment to the free and unlimited coinage of silver at the ratio of 16 to 1. James Weaver expected both parties to nominate gold candidates, which would send disappointed silverites to the Populist standard.

The Republicans, holding their convention first, nominated Senator William McKinley of Ohio on the first ballot. They also cited the familiar argument that prosperity depended on the gold standard and protection and blamed the depression on Cleveland's attempt to lower the tariff.

William Jennings Bryan, surprise nominee at the 1896 Democratic convention, was a vigorous proponent of the "cause of humanity." His surprise nomination threw the country into a frenzy of fear and the Populist Party into a fatal decision over "fusion."

The excitement of the Democratic convention in July contrasted with the staid, smoothly organized Republican one, a pattern to be repeated throughout most of the twentieth century. The surprise nominee of the Democratic convention was an ardent young silverite, William Jennings Bryan, a 36-year-old congressman from Nebraska. Few saw him as presidential material, but as a member of the Resolutions Committee, Bryan arranged to give the closing argument for a silver plank himself. His dramatic speech swept the convention for silver and ensured his own nomination. At the conclusion of what was to become one of the most famous political speeches in American history, Bryan attacked the "goldbugs" and promised, "You shall not press down upon the brow of labor this crown of thorns, you shall not crucify mankind upon a cross of gold."

Populist strategy lay in shambles with the nomination of a Democratic silver candidate. The Democratic vice-presidential candidate, Arthur Sewall, was an East Coast banker and a hard-money man. The Populist convention ultimately nominated Bryan (who thus became the simultaneous nominee of two party conventions), but instead of Sewall chose Populist Tom Watson of Georgia as his running mate. The existence of two silverite slates damaged Bryan's electoral hopes.

During the campaign, McKinley stayed at his home in Canton, Ohio. Republican strategy featured an unprecedented effort to reach voters through a highly sophisticated mass-media campaign, heavily financed by such major corporations as Standard Oil and the railroads. Party leaders hired thousands of speakers to support McKinley and distributed over 200 million pamphlets to a voting population of 15 million. The literature, distributed in 14 languages, was designed to appeal to particular national, ethnic, regional, and occupational groups. To all these people, McKinley was advertised as "the advance agent of prosperity."

In sharp contrast to the Republican stay-at-home policy, Bryan took his case to the people. Three million people in 27 states heard him speak as he traveled over 18,000 miles, giving as many as 30 speeches a day. Bryan's message was simple. Prosperity would return with free coinage of silver. Government policies should attend to the needs of the producing classes rather than the vested interests that believed in the gold standard. "That policy is best for this country," Bryan proclaimed, "which brings prosperity first to those who toil." But his rhetoric favored rural toilers. Few urban workers were inspired by this rhetoric, nor were most immigrants impressed by Bryan's prairie moralizing.

To influential easterners, the brash young

Nebraskan represented a threat to social harmony. Theodore Roosevelt wrote that "this silver craze surpasses belief. Bryan's election would be a great calamity." One newspaper editor said of Bryan that he was just like Nebraska's Platte River: "six inches deep and six miles wide at the mouth." Others branded him a "madman" and an "anarchist."

With such intense interest in the election, it was predictable that voters would turn out in record numbers. When the voting was over, McKinley had won 271 electoral votes to Bryan's 176. Millionaire Mark Hanna jubilantly wired McKinley: "God's in his heaven, all's right with the world." Bryan had been defeated by the largest popular majority since Grant trounced Greeley in 1872.

Although Bryan won over six million votes, more than any previous Democratic winner, he failed to carry the Midwest and the industrial masses. McKinley's promise of a "full dinner pail" was more convincing than the untested formula for free silver. Chance also played a part in Bryan's defeat. Bad wheat harvests in India, Australia, and Argentina drove up grain prices in the world market. Many of the complaints of American farmers evaporated amid rising farm prices.

The New Shape of American Politics

The landslide Republican victory marked the end of the political stalemate that had characterized American politics since the end of the Civil War. Republicans lost their identification with the politics of piety and strengthened their image as the party of prosperity and national greatness, which gave them a party dominance that lasted until the 1930s. The Democrats, who would remain under Bryan's leadership until 1912, took on the mantle of populist moralism but were largely reduced to a sectional party, reflecting

narrow southern views on money, race, and national power. The 1896 election demonstrated that the Northeast and the Great Lakes states had acquired so many immigrants that they now controlled the entire nation's political destiny. Populists, demoralized by fusion with a losing campaign, fell apart and disappeared. Asked a despondent Populist, Ignatius Donnelly, "Will the sun of triumph never rise? I fear not." His pessimism was premature, for within the next 20 years most Populist issues were taken over and adopted by politicians of the major parties.

Another result of the election of 1896 was a change in the pattern of political participation. Because the Republicans were so dominant, voters had less and less motivation to cast a ballot. Many black voters in the South, moreover, were disfranchised, and middle-class good government reformers succeeded in reducing the high voter turnout achieved by urban party bosses. Thus the tremendous rate of political participation that had characterized the nineteenth century since the Jackson era gradually declined. In the twentieth century, the low political involvement among poorer Americans was unique among western industrial countries.

McKinley had promised that Republican rule meant prosperity, and as soon as he took office, the economy recovered. Discoveries of gold in the Yukon and the Alaskan Klondike increased the money supply, thus thwarting silver mania until the early 1930s. Industrial production returned to full capacity.

McKinley's election marked not only the return of an era of economic health but also the emergence of the executive as the preeminent focus of the American political system. Just as McKinley's campaign set the pattern for the extravagant efforts to win office that have dominated modern times, his conduct as president foreshadowed the nature of the twentieth-century presidency. McKinley rejected traditional views of the president as the passive executor of laws, instead playing an active role in dealing with Congress and the press. His frequent trips away from Washington testified to his respect for public opinion. Some historians regard McKin-ley as the first modern president in his emphasis on the role of the chief executive in contributing to industrial growth and national power.

CONCLUSION

LOOKING FORWARD

McKinley's triumph in 1896 indicated that in a decade marked by depression, Populist revolt, and cries for action to close the inequalities of wealth, the established order remained intact and politics remained as unresponsive as ever. But in the areas of personal action and the philosophical bases for social change, intellectual middle-class reformers like Edward Bellamy, Henry George, William James, Jane Addams, "Golden Rule" Jones, and many others were showing the way to progressive reforms in the new century.

As the year 1900 approached, Henry Adams, still the pessimist, saw an ominous future, predicting the explosive and ultimately destructive energy of unrestrained industrial development. But others, more optimistic, saw America as an exemplary nation, demonstrating to the world the moral superiority of its economic system, democratic institutions, and middle-class Protestant values. Surely the new century, most thought, would see not only the continued perfection of these values and institutions but also the spread of American influence throughout the world.

Recommended Reading

The politics of the Gilded Age is treated usefully in the context of other developments of late-nineteenth-century life in H. Wayne Morgan, *From Hayes to McKinley: National Party Politics, 1877–1896* (1969); and Morton Keller, *Affairs of State: Public Life in Late Nineteenth Century America* (1977). An analysis of politics in the 1890s (and a good example of the "new political history") is R. Hal Williams, *Years of Decision: American Politics in the 1890s* (1978). The new social and political history is well represented by Paul Kleppner, *The Third Electoral System, 1853–1892: Parties, Voters, and Political Cultures* (1979).

The lives of middle-class men and women are understood best by a variety of different approaches. See relevant chapters in Mary Ryan's excellent survey, *Womanhood in America* (1983 ed.). See also Ruth Bordin, *Frances Willard: A Biography* (1986). Social

Darwinism and the success ethic are covered in Richard Hofstadter, *Social Darwinism in American Thought* (1955 ed.); and John Cawelti, *Apostles of the Self-Made Man: Changing Concepts of Success in America* (1965).

Novels that capture the flavor of middle-class life in the late nineteenth century include Mark Twain and Charles Dudley Warner, *The Gilded Age* (1873); Edward Bellamy, *Looking Backward* (1888); William Dean Howells, *The Rise of Silas Lapham* (1885) and *A Hazard of New Fortunes* (1889). Theodore Dreiser, *Sister Carrie* (1900); and Frank Norris, *The Octopus* (1901), depict a middle-class view of both middle- and lower-class life.

On late-nineteenth-century reform see John Sproat, *"The Best Men": Liberal Reformers in the Gilded Age* (1968); and Ralph Luker, *The Social*

Gospel in Black and White: American Racial Reform, 1885–1912 (1991). A study of middle-class urban reformers and the bossism they opposed is John Allswang, *Bosses, Machines, and Urban Voters* (1977). See also William Riordon's delightful recovery of the words of a typical boss, *Plunkitt of Tammany Hall* (1963, originally published in 1905). Biographical or autobiographical accounts of urban reformers include Peter Frederick, *Knights of the Golden Rule: The Intellectual as Christian Social Reformer in the 1890s*

(1976); Jane Addams, *Twenty Years at Hull House* (1910); and Vida Scudder, *On Journey* (1937).

The profound impact of the depression of 1893 is seen in Charles Hoffman, *The Depression of the Nineties: An Economic History* (1970). Populism and the election of 1896 are covered in a straightforward account by Paul Glad, *McKinley, Bryan and the People* (1964). A more recent examination of Populism is Gene Clanton, *Populism: The Humane Preference in America, 1890–1900* (1991).

Time Line

1873	Congress demonetizes silver		Sherman Anti-Trust Act
1875	Specie Resumption Act		Sherman Silver Purchase Act
			McKinley Tariff
1877	Rutherford B. Hayes becomes president		Elections bill defeated
1878	Bland-Allison Act	1890s	Wyoming, Colorado, Utah, and Idaho grant woman suffrage
1879	Henry George, *Progress and Poverty*	1892	Cleveland elected president for the second time; Populist Party wins over a million votes
1880	James A. Garfield elected president		
1881	Garfield assassinated; Chester A. Arthur succeeds to presidency		Homestead steel strike
1883	Pendleton Civil Service Act	1893	World's Columbian Exposition, Chicago
1884	Grover Cleveland elected president W. D. Howells, *The Rise of Silas Lapham*	1893– 1897	Financial panic and depression
1887	College Settlement House Association founded	1894	Pullman strike Coxey's march on Washington
1888	Edward Bellamy, *Looking Backward* Benjamin Harrison elected president	1895	*United States v. E. C. Knight*
		1896	Charles Sheldon, *In His Steps* (serialized version) Populist Party fuses with Democrats William McKinley elected president
1889	Jane Addams establishes Hull House Andrew Carnegie promulgates "The Gospel of Wealth"	1897	"Golden Rule" Jones elected mayor of Toledo, Ohio Economic recovery begins
1890	General Federation of Women's Clubs founded		

chapter 20

....

Becoming a World Power

In January 1899, the United States Senate was locked in a dramatic debate over whether to ratify the Treaty of Paris concluding the recent war with Spain over Cuban independence. At the same time, American soldiers uneasily faced Filipino rebels across a neutral zone around the outskirts of Manila, capital of the Philippines. Until recent weeks, the Americans and Filipinos had been allies, together defeating the Spanish to liberate the Philippines. The American fleet under Admiral George Dewey had destroyed the Spanish naval squadron in Manila Bay on May 1, 1898. Three weeks later, an American ship brought from exile the native Filipino insurrectionary leader, Emilio Aguinaldo, to lead rebel forces on land while U.S. gunboats patrolled the seas.

At first, the Filipinos looked on the Americans as liberators, helping them win their independence, but when an armistice ended the war in August, American troops denied Filipino soldiers an opportunity to liberate their own capital city and shunted them off to the suburbs. The armistice agreement recognized American rights to "the harbor, city, and bay of Manila," while the proposed Treaty of Paris gave the United States the entire Philippine Island archipelago.

Consequently, tension mounted in Manila. Barroom skirmishes and knifings pervaded the city at night; American soldiers searched houses without warrants and looted stores. Their behavior was not unlike that of the English soldiers in Boston in the 1770s.

On the night of February 4, 1899, Privates William Grayson and David Miller of Company B, 1st Nebraska Volunteers, were on patrol in Santa Mesa, a Manila suburb surrounded on three sides by insurgent trenches. The Americans had orders to shoot any Filipino soldiers found in the neutral area. As the two Americans cautiously worked their way to a bridge over the San Juan River, they encountered four Filipinos and shot three of them. A full-scale battle followed.

The outbreak of hostilities ended the Senate debates. On February 6, the Senate ratified the Treaty of Paris, thus formally annexing the Philippines and sparking a war between the United States and Filipino nationalists.

In a guerrilla war similar to those fought later in the twentieth century in Asia and Central America, Filipino nationalists held out until July 1902, three years longer than the Spanish-American War that caused it and involving far more troops, casualties, and monetary and moral costs.

How did all this happen? What brought Private Grayson halfway around the world to the Philippines? For the first time in history, regular American soldiers found themselves fighting outside North America. The "champion of oppressed nations," as Aguinaldo said, had turned into an oppressor nation itself, imposing the American way of life and American institutions on faraway peoples against their will.

The war in the Philippines marked a critical transformation of America's role in the world. Within a few years at the turn of the century, the United States acquired an empire, however small by European standards, and established itself as a world power. In this chapter, we will review the historical dilemmas of America's role in the world; we will examine the motivations for the intensified expansionism of the 1890s; and we will look at how the fundamental patterns of modern American foreign policy were established for Latin America, Asia, and Europe in the early twentieth century. We will see that the tension between idealism and self-interest that has permeated America's domestic history has guided its foreign policy as well.

STEPS TOWARD EMPIRE

The circumstances that brought Privates Grayson and Miller from Nebraska to the Philippines originated deep in American history. Just as the Puritan John Winthrop sought to set up a "city on a hill" in the New World, a model community of righteous living for others in the world to behold, such idealism became a permanent goal of American policy toward the outside world.

America as a Model Society

Nineteenth-century Americans continued to believe in the nation's special mission. The Monroe Doctrine in 1823 pointed out moral differences between the monarchical, arbitrary governments of Europe and the free republican institutions of the New World. The American Revolutionary model seemed irresistible. In a world that was evil, Americans believed that they stood as a transforming force for good. Many others agreed. The problem was how a nation committed to isolationism was to do the transforming. One way was to encourage other nations to observe and imitate the good example set by the United States. But often other nations preferred their own society or were attracted to competing models of modernization, as has frequently happened in the twentieth century. This implied a more aggressive foreign policy.

Americans have rarely simply focused on perfecting the good example at home, waiting for others to copy it. This requires patience and passivity, two traits not prevalent in Americans. Rather, throughout history, the American people have actively and sometimes forcefully imposed their ideas and institutions on others. The international crusades of the United States, well intentioned if not always well received, have usually been motivated by a mixture of idealism and self-interest.

Early Expansionism

A consistent expression of continental expansionism marked the first century of American independence. Jefferson's purchase of the Louisiana Territory in 1803 and the grasping for Florida and Canada by War Hawks in 1812 signaled an intense American interest in territorial growth. The Cherokee, Seminole, Lakota, Apache, Cheyenne, and other Native American nations found the United States to be far from isolationist. Until midcentury, the United States pursued its "Manifest Destiny"—its conviction that Americans had a mission to spread their civilization across the continent from ocean to ocean (see Chapter 13). But in the 1850s, Americans began to look beyond their own continent. This trend was marked most significantly by Commodore Perry's visit to Japan, the expansion of the China trade, and various expeditions into the Caribbean in search of more cotton lands and a canal connecting the two oceans.

Lincoln's secretary of state, William Seward, believed that the United States was destined to exert commercial domination "on the Pacific ocean, and its islands and continents." His goal was that from markets, raw materials, and trade would come the "regeneration of . . . the East." Toward this end, Seward purchased Alaska from Russia in 1867 for $7.2 million. He also acquired a coaling station in the Midway Islands in the mid-Pacific and paved the way for American commercial expansion in Korea, Japan, and China. Seward dreamed of "possession" of the entire North and Central American continent and ultimately "control of the world."

Expansion After Seward

In 1870, foreshadowing the Philippine debates 30 years later, supporters of President Grant tried without success to force the Senate to annex Santo Domingo (Hispaniola). Senatorial opponents responded that expansionism violated the American principle of self-determination and government by the consent of the governed. They pointed out, moreover, that the native peoples of the Caribbean were brown-skinned, culturally inferior, non-English-speaking, and therefore unassimilable. Finally, they suggested that expansionism might involve foreign entanglements, necessitating a large and expensive navy, growth in the size of government, and higher taxes. The Senate rejected the treaty to annex Santo Domingo.

In 1881, Secretary of State James G. Blaine sought to convene a conference of American nations to promote hemispheric peace and trade. Although motivated mostly by his presidential ambitions, his effort nevertheless led to the first Pan-American Conference eight years later. The Latin Americans may have wondered what Blaine intended, for in 1881 he intervened in three separate border disputes in Central and South America, in each case at the cost of goodwill and trust.

Ten years later, relations with Chile were harmed when several American sailors on shore leave were involved in a barroom brawl in Valparaiso. Two Americans were killed and several others injured. American pride was also injured, and President Benjamin Harrison sent an ultimatum calling for a "prompt and full reparation." After threats of war, Chile complied.

Similar incidents occurred as American expansionists pursued Seward's goals in the Pacific. In the mid-1870s, American sugar-growing interests in the Hawaiian Islands were strong enough to place whites in positions of influence over the native monarchy. In 1875, they obtained a reciprocity treaty admitting Hawaiian sugar duty-free to the United States. When the treaty was renewed and approved in 1887, the United States also gained exclusive rights to build a naval base at Pearl Harbor on the island of Oahu.

In 1891, the strongly nationalist Queen Liliuokalani assumed the throne in Hawaii and promptly abolished the constitution, seeking to establish control over whites in the name of "Hawaii for the Hawaiians." In 1893, with the help of U.S. gunboats and marines, the whites staged a palace coup (a revolution later called

Princess Liliuokalani of Hawaii, in a portrait from the late 1870s or early 1880s. She assumed the Hawaiian throne in 1891 and was deposed in a palace coup two years later.

one "of sugar, by sugar, for sugar") and waited patiently for annexation by the United States, which came during the war in 1898.

U.S. naval forces in the Pacific had skirmishes with Canadian sealing and fishing vessels in the 1880s, and with German naval forces in 1889 in the Samoan Islands. More serious was a conflict with England. In 1895 a long-standing boundary dispute between Venezuela and British Guiana flared up anew after gold was discovered in both lands. The British threatened to intervene against the Venezuelans. President Cleveland, in need of a popular political issue to deflect attention from the depression, discovered the political value of a tough foreign policy by defending a weak sister American republic against the British bully. A strong note citing the Monroe Doctrine was sent to the British, and the possibility of war loomed until both Britain and

Venezuela agreed to allow an impartial American commission settle the boundary.

These increasing conflicts in the Caribbean and the Pacific signaled the rise of American presence beyond the borders of the United States. Yet as of 1895, the nation had neither the means nor a consistent policy for enlarging its role in the world. The diplomatic service was small, inexperienced, and unprofessional, and it exhibited insensitive behavior toward native cultures. The U.S. Army, numbering about 28,000 men in the mid-1890s, ranked thirteenth in the world, behind that of Bulgaria. The navy ranked no higher than tenth in size.

EXPANSIONISM IN THE 1890s

In 1893, historian Frederick Jackson Turner wrote that for three centuries, "the dominant fact in American life has been expansion." Turner believed that the frontier played an important role in the development of democracy and liberty in America. He observed that the "extension of American influence to outlying islands and adjoining countries" indicated that expansionism would continue. Turner's observations struck a responsive chord in a country that had always been restless, mobile, and optimistic. With the western American frontier closed, Americans would surely look for new frontiers, for mobility and markets as well as for morality and missionary activity. The motivations for the expansionist impulse of the late 1890s resembled those that had prompted people to settle the New World in the first place: greed, glory, and God. We will examine expansionism as a reflection of profits, patriotism, piety (or moral mission), and politics.

Profits: Searching for Overseas Markets

Senator Albert Beveridge of Indiana bragged in 1898 that "American factories are making more

United States Territorial Expansion to 1900

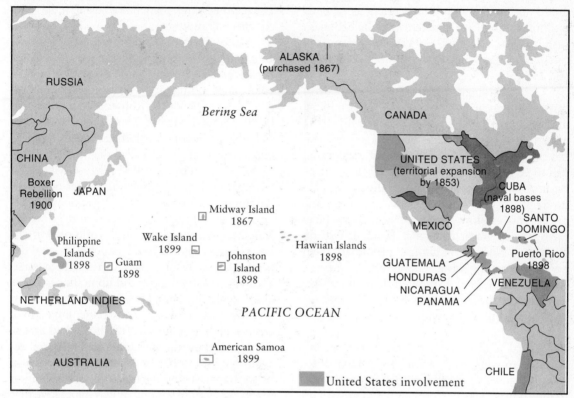

than the American people can use; American soil is producing more than they can consume. Fate has written our policy for us; the trade of the world must and shall be ours." Beveridge believed in the dream of a commercial empire in the islands and adjoining countries of the Caribbean Sea and the Pacific Ocean. American businessmen saw huge profits beckoning in the heavily populated areas of Latin America and Asia, and they began to shape diplomatic and military strategy. As Senator Orville Platt of Connecticut said in 1893, "A policy of isolation did well enough when we were an embryo nation, but today things are different."

Not all businessmen in the 1890s approved of risky new ventures in Asia and Latin America. Some thought it more important in 1897 to se-cure recovery from the depression than little islands in Asia.

But the decrease in domestic consumption during the depression also encouraged businessmen to expand into new markets to sell surplus goods. They were led by the newly formed National Association of Manufacturers, which emphasized in 1896 "that the trade centres of Central and South America are natural markets for American products."

Despite the depression of the 1890s, products spewed from American factories at a staggering rate. The United States moved from fourth in the world in manufacturing in 1870 to first in 1900. The United States led the world not only in railroad construction (206,631 miles of tracks in 1900, four times more than in 1870) but also in agricultural machinery and mass-produced technological products such as sewing machines, electrical implements, telephones, cash registers, elevators, and cameras. Manufactured goods grew nearly fivefold between 1895 and 1914.

Correspondingly, the total value of American exports tripled, jumping from $434 million in 1866 to nearly $1.5 billion in 1900. By 1914, exports had risen to $2.5 billion, a 67 percent increase over 1900. The increased trade continued to go mainly to Europe. Nevertheless, interest in Asian markets grew, especially as agricultural production continued to increase and prices remained low. Farmers dreamed of selling their surplus wheat to China. James J. Hill of the Great Northern Railroad promoted their hopes by printing wheat cookbooks in various Asian languages and distributed them in the Far East, hoping to fill his westward-bound boxcars and merchant ships with wheat and other grains.

American direct investments abroad also increased, growing from about $634 million to $2.6 billion between 1897 and 1914. At the turn of the century came the formation and growth of America's biggest multinational corporations—the United Fruit Company, Alcoa Aluminum, Amalgamated Copper, Du Pont, American Tobacco, and others, which supported an aggressive foreign policy and the expansion of America's role in the world.

Patriotism: Asserting National Power

American interest in investments, markets, and raw materials abroad reflected a determination not to be left out of the international competition among European powers and Japan for commercial spheres of influence and colonies in Asia, Africa, and Latin America. In 1898, a State Department memorandum stated that "we can no longer afford to disregard international rivalries now that we ourselves have become a com-

petitor in the world-wide struggle for trade." The national state, then, had a role in supporting commercial interests.

More Americans, however, saw national glory and greatness as legitimate motivations for expansionism. In the late 1890s, a group of young men centered on Assistant Secretary of the Navy Theodore Roosevelt and Senator Henry Cabot Lodge of Massachusetts emerged as highly influential in shifting from "continentalism" to what Lodge called the "large policy."

The writings of Alfred Thayer Mahan, a naval strategist and author of several books on the importance of sea power to national greatness, greatly influenced the new foreign policy elite. Mahan argued that in a world of Darwinian struggle for survival, national power depended on naval supremacy, control of sea lanes, and vigorous development of domestic resources and foreign markets. He advocated colonies in both the Caribbean and the Pacific, linked by a canal built and controlled by the United States. Strong nations, Mahan wrote, had a special responsibility to dominate weak ones. In a world of constant "strife," where "everywhere nation is arrayed against nation," it was imperative that Americans begin "to look outward." National pride and glory would surely follow.

Piety: The Missionary Impulse

As Mahan's statements suggest, a strong sense of duty and the missionary ideal of doing good for others also motivated expansionism. A statesman once boasted that "with God's help, we will lift Shanghai up and up, ever up, until it is just like Kansas City." Secretary of State Richard Olney agreed, saying in 1898 that "the mission of this country is . . . to forego no fitting opportunity to further the progress of civilization." Motivated by America's sense of itself as a model nation, such statements sometimes rationalized the exploitation and oppression of weaker peoples.

As a missionary put it in 1885, "The Christian nations are subduing the world in order to make mankind free." Josiah Strong, a Congregational minister, was one of the most ardent advocates of American missionary expansionism. Although his book *Our Country* (1885) focused on internal threats to American social order, in a long chapter titled "The Future of the Anglo-Saxon Race," Strong argued that in the struggle for survival among nations, the United States had emerged as the center of Anglo-Saxonism and was "divinely commissioned" to spread the blessings of political liberty, Protestant Christianity, and civilized values over the earth. "This powerful race," he wrote, "will move down upon Mexico, down upon Central and South America, out upon the islands of the sea, over upon Africa and beyond."

Missionaries carried similar Western values to non-Christian lands around the world. China was a favorite target. The number of American Protestant missionaries in China increased from 436 in 1874 to 5,462 in 1914. The estimated number of Christian converts in China jumped from 5,000 in 1870 to nearly 100,000 in 1900. Many Chinese reformist intellectuals who absorbed Western ideas in Christian mission colleges went on to lead the Revolution of 1912 that ended the Manchu dynasty. Economic relations between China and the United States increased at approximately the same rate as missionary activity. The number of American firms in China grew from 50 to 550 between 1870 and 1930, while trade increased 1,500 percent.

Politics: Manipulating Public Opinion

During the expansionist 1890s, public opinion over international issues loomed large in presidential politics for the first time in American history. This process was helped by the growth of a highly competitive popular press, the penny daily newspaper, which brought international issues before a mass readership. When several newspapers in New York City, notably William

Randolph Hearst's *Journal* and Joseph Pulitzer's *World,* competed to see which could stir up more public support for the Cuban rebels in their struggle for independence from Spain, politicians ignored the public outcry at their peril. Daily reports of Spanish atrocities in 1896 and 1897 kept public moral outrage constantly before President McKinley as he considered his course of action.

Politics, then, joined profits, patriotism, and piety in motivating the expansionism of the 1890s. These four impulses interacted to influence the Spanish-American War, the annexation of the Philippine Islands, and the foreign policy of President Theodore Roosevelt.

CUBA AND THE PHILIPPINES

Lying 90 miles off the southern tip of Florida, Cuba had been the object of intense American interest for a half century. Although successful in thwarting American adventurism in Cuba in the 1850s, Spain was unable to halt the continuing struggle of the Cuban people for relief from exploitive labor on the sugar plantations, even after slavery itself ended, and for a measure of autonomy. The most recent uprising, which lasted from 1868 to 1878, had raised tensions between Spain and the United States; it also whetted the Cuban appetite not just for reforms but for complete independence.

The Road to War

When the Cuban revolt flared up anew in 1895, the Madrid government sent General "Butcher" Weyler with 50,000 troops to quell the disturbance. When Weyler began herding rural Cuban citizens into "reconcentration" camps, Americans were outraged. An outpouring of sympathy swept the nation, especially as reports came back of the horrible suffering in the camps.

The Cuban struggle appealed to a country convinced of its role as protector of the weak and defender of the right of self-determination. One editorial deplored Spanish "injustice, oppression, extortion, and demoralization" while describing the Cubans as heroic freedom fighters "largely inspired by our glorious example of beneficent free institutions and successful self-government." But neither President Cleveland nor President McKinley wanted a war over Cuba.

Self-interested motives also played a role. American companies had invested extensively in Cuban sugar plantations. By 1897, trade with Cuba reached $27 million per year. Appeals for reform had much to do with ensuring a stable environment for further investments, as well as for the protection of sugar fields against the ravages of civil war.

A new government in Madrid recalled Weyler, but conditions in Cuba worsened. Although McKinley skillfully resisted the pressure for war, the fundamental causes of the war—Spanish intransigence in the face of persistent Cuban rebellion and American sugar interests and sympathies for the underdog—were seemingly unstoppable.

Events early in 1898 sparked the outbreak of hostilities. Rioting in Havana intensified both Spanish repression and American outrage. As pressures for war increased, a letter from the Spanish minister to the United States, Depuy de Lôme, calling McKinley a "weak" hypocritical politician, was intercepted by spies and made public. Hearst's New York *Journal* called de Lôme's letter "the worst insult to the United States in its history."

A second event was the sinking of the U.S. battleship *Maine*, sent to Havana harbor to protect American citizens. Early in the evening on February 15, a tremendous explosion blew up the *Maine*, killing 262 men. American advocates of war, who assumed Spanish responsibility, called immediately for intervention. Newspaper publishers broadcast slogans like "Remember the *Maine*! To hell with *Spain*!"

Assistant Secretary of the Navy Theodore

Roosevelt, who had been preparing for war for some time, said that he would "give anything if President McKinley would order the fleet to Havana tomorrow." Although an official board of inquiry concluded that an external submarine mine caused the disaster, probably a faulty boiler or some other internal problem set off the explosion, a possibility even Roosevelt later conceded.

After the sinking of the *Maine*, Roosevelt took advantage of Secretary of the Navy John D. Long's absence from the office one day to send a cable to Commodore George Dewey, commander of the United States' Pacific fleet at Hong Kong. Roosevelt ordered Dewey to fill his ships with coal and, "in the event" of a declaration of war with Spain, to sail to the Philippines and make sure "the Spanish squadron does not leave the Asiatic coast."

Roosevelt's act was not impetuous, as Long thought, but consistent with naval policies he had been urging upon his more cautious superior for more than a year. Influenced by Mahan, Roosevelt wanted to enlarge the navy, whose growth had been restricted for years. He also believed that the United States should construct an interoceanic canal, acquire the Danish West Indies (the Virgin Islands), annex Hawaii outright, and oust Spain from Cuba. As Roosevelt told McKinley late in 1897, he was putting the navy in "the best possible shape" for "when war began."

The public outcry over the *Maine* drowned out McKinley's efforts to calm the populace and avoid war. Nor was he successful in wringing concessions from Spain. On April 11, 1898, therefore, the president sent an ambiguous message to Congress that seemed to call for war. Two weeks later, Congress authorized the use of troops against Spain and passed a resolution recognizing Cuban independence, actions amounting to a declaration of war. In a significant additional resolution, the Teller Amendment, Congress stated that the United States had no intentions of annexing Cuba, guaranteeing the Cubans the right to determine their own destiny.

An imaginative reconstruction of the celebrated charge of "Teddy's Rough Riders" up Kettle Hill, which so greatly helped Roosevelt's political career.

"A Splendid Little War"

As soon as war was declared, Theodore Roosevelt resigned his post in the Navy Department and prepared to lead a cavalry unit in the war. Black regiments as well as white headed to Tampa, Florida, to be shipped to Cuba. Blacks were especially sympathetic to the Cuban people's struggle. As one soldier wrote in his journal, "Oh, God! at last we have taken up the sword to enforce the divine rights of a people who have been unjustly treated." As the four-month war neared its end in August, John Hay wrote Roosevelt that "it has been a splendid little war; begun with the highest motives, carried on with magnificent intelligence and spirit."

It was a "splendid" war. It was short and relatively easy. Naval battles were won almost without return fire. At both major naval engagements, Manila Bay and Santiago Bay, only two Americans died, one of them from heat prostration while stoking coal. The islands of Guam and Puerto Rico were taken virtually without a shot. Only 385 men died from Spanish bullets, but over 5,000 succumbed to tropical diseases.

The Spanish-American War was splendid in other ways, as letters from American soldiers suggest. One young man wrote that his comrades were all "in good spirits" because oranges and coconuts were so plentiful and "every trooper has his canteen full of lemonade all the time." Another, however, wrote that "words are inadequate to express the feeling of pain and sickness when one has the fever. For about a week every bone in my body ached and I did not care much whether I lived or not."

Roosevelt's brush with death at Las Guásimas and his celebrated charge up Kettle Hill near Santiago, his flank protected by black troops, made three-inch headlines and advanced not only his political career but also the cause of expansion and national glory.

The Philippines Debates and War

Roosevelt's ordering Dewey to Manila initiated a chain of events that led to the annexation of the Philippines. The most crucial battle of the Spanish-American War occurred on May 1, 1898, when Dewey destroyed the Spanish fleet in Manila Bay. McKinley then began the process of shaping American public opinion to accept the "political, commercial [and] humanitarian" reasons for annexing all 7,000 Philippine islands, Guam, and Puerto Rico. The Treaty of Paris gave the United States all of them in exchange for a $20 million payment to Spain.

The treaty was sent to the Senate for ratification during the winter of 1898–1899. As we have seen, the Senate debate was ended when fighting broke out between American soldiers and Aguinaldo's insurgents near Manila. The Filipino-American War triggered national debates over what to do with the Philippines. After several months of quietly seeking advice and listening to public opinion, McKinley finally recommended annexation. Fellow Republicans confirmed McKinley's arguments for annexation, adding even more racist ones. Filipinos were described as childlike, savage, stunted in size, dirty, and backward. Roosevelt called Aguinaldo "a renegade Pawnee" and said that the Filipinos had no right "to administer the country which they happen to be occupying." The attitudes favoring annexation, therefore, asserted Filipino inferiority and incapacity for self-rule while also reflecting America's proud sense of itself in 1900 as a nation of civilized order and progress.

Other Americans were not so positive about such "progress." A small but vocal group, the Anti-Imperialist League, vigorously opposed war and annexation. They included a cross-section of American dignitaries: ex-Presidents Harrison and Cleveland, Samuel Gompers and Andrew Carnegie, William James, Jane Addams, Mark Twain, and many others.

The major anti-imperialist arguments pointed out how imperialism in general and annexation in particular were unconstitutional and contradicted American ideals regarding the right of self-determination. Moreover, social reforms needed at home demanded American energies and money before foreign expansionism.

Not all anti-imperialist arguments were so noble. One position alleged that since the Filipinos were nonwhite, Catholic, and inferior in size and intelligence, they were unassimilable. Annexation would lead to miscegenation and contamination of Anglo-Saxon blood. Senator Ben Tillman of South Carolina opposed "incorporating any more colored men into the body politic." Some saw the Philippines as a burden that would require American troops to fight distant Asian wars.

The last argument became fact when Private Grayson's encounter started the Filipino-American War. Before it was over in 1902, some 126,500 American troops served in the Philippines, 4,234 died there, and 2,800 more were wounded. The cost was $400 million. Filipino casualties were much worse. In addition to the 18,000 killed in combat, an estimated 200,000 Filipinos died of famine and disease as American soldiers burned villages and destroyed crops and livestock in order to disrupt the economy and deny rebel fighters their food supply. General Jacob H. Smith ordered his troops to "kill and

burn and the more you kill and burn, the better you will please me."

As U.S. treatment of the Filipinos during the war became more and more like Spanish mistreatment of the Cubans, the hypocrisy of American behavior became even more evident, especially to black American soldiers who identified with the dark-skinned insurgents. "I feel sorry for these people," a sergeant in the 24th Infantry wrote. "You have no idea the way these people are treated by the Americans here."

The war starkly exposed the hypocrisies of shouldering the white man's burden. Upon reading a report that 8,000 Filipinos had been killed in the first year of the war, Carnegie wrote a letter, dripping with sarcasm, congratulating McKinley for "civilizing the Filipinos. . . . About 8,000 of them have been completely civilized and sent to Heaven. I hope you like it." Another writer penned a devastating one-liner: "Dewey took Manila with the loss of one man—and all our institutions."

The anti-imperialists failed either to prevent annexation or to interfere with the war effort. They were seen as an older, conservative, elite group of Americans, out of tune with the period of exuberant national pride, prosperity, and promise.

Expansionism Triumphant

By 1900, the United States had acquired several island territories, thereby joining the other great world powers. But questions arose over what to do with the new territories. What was their status? Were they colonies? Would they be granted statehood? Did the native peoples of Hawaii, Puerto Rico, Guam, and the Philippines have the same rights as American citizens on the mainland? The answers to these difficult questions emerged in a series of Supreme Court cases, congressional acts, and presidential decisions.

Although slightly different governing systems were worked out for each new territory, the solution in each was to define its status somewhere between subject colony and candidate for statehood. Territorial status came closest. The native people were usually allowed to elect their own legislature for internal lawmaking but had governors and other judicial and administrative officials appointed by the American president. The question of constitutional rights was resolved by deciding that Hawaiians and Puerto Ricans, for example, would be treated differently from Texans and Oregonians. In the "insular cases" of 1901, the Supreme Court ruled that these people would achieve citizenship and constitutional rights only when Congress said they were ready. To the question "Does the Constitution follow the flag?" the answer, as Secretary of State Elihu Root put it, was, "Ye-es, as near as I can make out the Constitution follows the flag— but doesn't quite catch up with it."

McKinley's resounding defeat of Bryan in 1900 clearly revealed the optimistic, nationalistic spirit of the American people, who strongly favored annexation of the Philippines. In the closing weeks of the campaign, Bryan and the Democrats shied away from criticizing the war as imperialist, but Bryan fared no better on other issues. The McKinley forces rightly claimed that under four years of Republican rule, more money, jobs, thriving factories, and manufactured goods had been created. Moreover, McKinley pointed to the tremendous growth in American prestige abroad. Spain had been kicked out of Cuba, and the American flag flew in many places around the globe.

Within one year, the active expansionist, Theodore Roosevelt, went from assistant secretary of the navy to colonel of the Rough Riders to governor of New York. Some Republican politicos sought to slow him down by nominating him for vice president at the Republican convention in 1900. But six months into McKinley's second term, the president was shot and killed by an anarchist, the third presidential assassination in less than 40 years. "Now look," exclaimed party boss Mark Hanna, who had opposed putting Roosevelt on the ticket, "that damned cowboy is President of the United States!"

ROOSEVELT'S ENERGETIC DIPLOMACY

As president from 1901 to 1909, and as the most dominating American personality for the 15 years between 1897 and 1912, Roosevelt made much fuss and noise about the activist role he thought the United States should play in the world. His energetic foreign policy in Latin America, Asia, and Europe paved the way for the vital role of the United States as a world power.

Foreign Policy as Darwinian Struggle

Roosevelt's personal principles and presidential policies went together. He was an advocate of both individual physical fitness and collective national strength. His ideal was "a nation of men, not weaklings." To be militarily prepared and to fight well were the tests of racial superiority and national greatness. Powerful nations, like individuals, Roosevelt believed, had a duty to cultivate qualities of vigor, strength, courage, and moral commitment to civilized values. In practical terms this meant developing natural resources, building large navies, and being ever prepared to fight. "I never take a step in foreign policy," he wrote, "unless I am assured that I shall be able eventually to carry out my will by force."

Although known for his advice to "speak softly and carry a big stick," Roosevelt often not only wielded a large stick but spoke loudly as well. Despite his bluster, Roosevelt was usually restrained in the exercise of force. He won the Nobel Peace Prize in 1906 for helping to end the Russo-Japanese War. The purpose of the big stick and the loud talk was to preserve order and peace in the world. "To be prepared for war," he

The "big stick" became a memorable image in American diplomacy as Teddy Roosevelt sought to make the United States a policeman not only of the Caribbean basin but also of the whole world.

said, "is the most effectual means to promote peace."

Roosevelt divided the world into civilized and uncivilized nations, the former usually defined as Anglo-Saxon and English-speaking. The civilized nations had a responsibility to "police" the uncivilized, not only maintaining order but also spreading superior values and institutions. Roosevelt regarded this "international police power" as the "white man's burden," a phrase originated by English imperialist author Rudyard Kipling.

Roosevelt also believed in the balance of power. Strong, advanced nations like the United States had a duty to use their power to preserve order and peace. The 1900 census had recently revealed that the United States, with 75 million people, was much more populous than Great Britain, France, or Germany. Since all of these

nations had many colonies in Asia and Africa it seemed time for Americans to exercise a greater role in world affairs, and to assert its primacy in the Western Hemisphere.

Roosevelt developed a highly personal style of diplomacy. Rather than relying on the Department of State, he preferred face-to-face contact and personal exchange of letters with foreign ambassadors, ministers, and heads of state. A British emissary observed that Roosevelt had a "powerful personality" and a commanding knowledge of the world. As a result, ministries from London to Tokyo respected both the president and the power of the United States.

"In a crisis the duty of a leader is to lead," Roosevelt said. When he wanted Panama, Roosevelt bragged later, "I took the Canal Zone," and while Congress debated his actions, the building of the canal across Panama began. Roosevelt's energetic executive activism in foreign policy set a pattern followed by nearly every twentieth-century American president.

Taking the Panama Canal

In justifying the intervention of 2,600 American troops in Honduras and Nicaragua in 1906, Philander Knox, secretary of state from 1909 to 1913, said, "We are in the eyes of the world, and because of the Monroe Doctrine, held responsible for the order of Central America, and its proximity to the Canal makes the preservation of peace in that neighborhood particularly necessary." The Panama Canal was not yet finished when Knox spoke, but it had already become a vital cornerstone of United States policy in the region.

Panama was a province of Colombia and could not negotiate with the United States. In 1903, the Colombian senate rejected a treaty negotiated by Secretary of State John Hay, but mostly on nationalistic, not financial, grounds. Roosevelt, angered by this rebuff, called the Colombians "Dagoes" and "foolish and homicidal corruptionists," who tried to "hold us up" like highway robbers.

Aware of Roosevelt's fury, encouraged by hints of American support, and eager for the economic benefits the building of a canal would bring, Panamanian nationalists in 1903 staged a revolution led by several rich families and a Frenchman, Philippe Bunau-Varilla of the New Panama Canal Company. The bloodless revolution occurred on November 3; the next day, Panama declared its independence. On November 6, the United States officially recognized the new government in Panama. Although Roosevelt did not formally encourage the revolution, it would not have occurred without American money and the presence of American troops, who prevented Colombian troops from landing to suppress the rebellion.

On November 18, Hay and Bunau-Varilla signed a treaty establishing the American right to build and operate a canal through Panama and to exercise "titular sovereignty" over the 10-mile-wide Canal Zone. The Panamanian government protested the treaty, to no avail, and a later government called it "the treaty that no Panamanian signed."

Policeman of the Caribbean

As late as 1901, the Monroe Doctrine was still regarded, according to Roosevelt, as the "equivalent to an open door in South America." To the United States, this meant that although no nation had a right "to get territorial possessions," all nations had equal commercial rights in the Western Hemisphere south of the Rio Grande. But as American investments poured into Central America and Caribbean islands, that policy changed to one of the primary right of the United States to dominant influence in the lands of the Caribbean basin. Order was indispensable for profitable economic activity.

After the Spanish were expelled from Cuba, the United States supervised the island under Military Governor General Leonard Wood until 1902, when the Cubans elected their own congress and president. The United States honored Cuban independence, as it had promised to do in the Teller Amendment. But through the Platt Amendment, which Cubans reluctantly attached to their constitution in 1901, the United States obtained many economic rights in Cuba, a naval base at Guantanamo Bay, and the right of intervention if Cuban sovereignty were ever threatened. Newspapers in Havana assailed this violation of their newfound independence.

American policy intended to make Cuba a model of how a newly independent nation could achieve orderly self-government with only minimal guidance. When in 1906 an internal political crisis threatened the infant nation, however, Roosevelt sent warships and troops, at Cuba's request "to restore order and peace and public confidence." As he left office in 1909, Roosevelt proudly proclaimed that "we have done our best to put Cuba on the road to stable and orderly government." The road was paved with sugar. United States trade with Cuba increased from $27 million in the decade before 1898 to an average of $43 million per year during the following decade. Along with economic development, American political and even military involvement in Cuban affairs continued throughout the century. The Platt Amendment provided the excuse for United States intervention at nearly every Cuban election, because the losing side would call on the United States to overturn the results—a pattern that hampered the independent development of the Cuban political system.

The pattern repeated itself throughout the Caribbean region. United States warships discouraged European intervention in the Dominican Republic in 1904. Two years later, the United States intervened in Guatemala and Nicaragua, where American bankers controlled nearly 50 percent of all trade.

Roosevelt's policy of intervention as "an international police power," he said in his annual message in 1904, was necessary to have "stable, orderly and prosperous neighbors." This doctrine, known as the Roosevelt Corollary to the Monroe Doctrine, justified American intervention in Caribbean countries to protect property, loans, and investments and to maintain order. This meant supporting the brutal regimes of wealthy elites who owned most of the land, suppressed the poor and efforts for reform, and acted as surrogates of American policy.

After 1904, the Roosevelt Corollary was invoked in several Caribbean countries. Intervention usually required the landing of U.S. Marines to counter the threat posed by political instability and bankruptcy to American economic interests: railroads, mines, and the production of sugar, bananas, and coffee. Roosevelt's successors, William Howard Taft and Woodrow Wilson, pursued the same interventionist policy. Later presidents, including Lyndon Johnson, Ronald Reagan, George Bush, and Bill Clinton, would do likewise.

Opening the Door to China

Another area that attracted American commercial interest was China. Throughout the nineteenth century, American relations with China were restricted to a small but profitable trade. While Britain, France, Germany, and Russia had advantageous trade treaties with China as well as spheres of influence, Americans tended to disdain European imperialism, though they, too, wanted to participate in the trade. American attitudes toward the Chinese people reflected this confusion of motives. Some Americans held an idealized view of China as the center of Eastern wisdom and saw a "special relationship" between the two nations. But the dominant American attitude viewed the Chinese as heathen, exotic, backward, and immoral.

The annexation of Hawaii, Samoa, and the Philippines in 1898–1899 convinced Secretary of State Hay that the United States should announce its own policy for China. The result was the Open Door notes of 1899–1900, which declared the principle of equal access to commercial rights in China by all nations and called on all countries to respect the "territorial and administrative integrity" of China. This second principle opened the way for a larger American role in Asia, offering China protection from foreign invasions and preserving a balance of power in the Far East.

An early test of this new role came during the Boxer Rebellion in 1900. The Boxers were a society of young traditionalist Chinese in revolt against both the Manchu dynasty and the growing Western presence and influence in China. During the summer of 1900, fanatical Boxers killed some 242 missionaries and other foreign-

United States Involvement in Central America and the Caribbean, 1898-1939

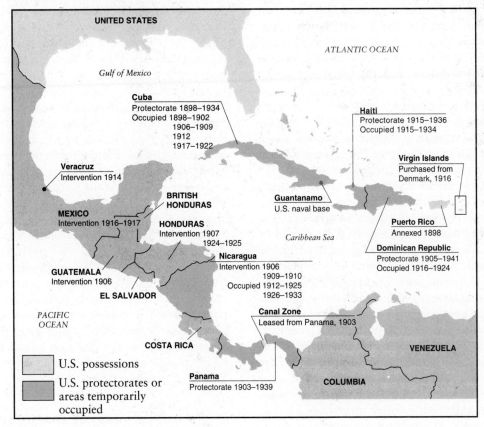

UNITED STATES

ATLANTIC OCEAN

Gulf of Mexico

Cuba
Protectorate 1898–1934
Occupied 1898–1902
1906–1909
1912
1917–1922

Haiti
Protectorate 1915–1936
Occupied 1915–1934

Virgin Islands
Purchased from
Denmark, 1916

Veracruz
Intervention 1914

BRITISH HONDURAS

Guantanamo
U.S. naval base

MEXICO
Intervention 1916–1917

HONDURAS
Intervention 1907
1924–1925

Caribbean Sea

Puerto Rico
Annexed 1898

Dominican Republic
Protectorate 1905–1941
Occupied 1916–1924

Nicaragua
Intervention 1906
1909–1910
Occupied 1912–1925
1926–1933

GUATEMALA
Intervention 1906

EL SALVADOR

PACIFIC OCEAN

Canal Zone
Leased from Panama, 1903

COSTA RICA

VENEZUELA

U.S. possessions

U.S. protectorates or
areas temporarily
occupied

Panama
Protectorate 1903–1939

COLUMBIA

ers and besieged the foreign legation quarter of Peking. Eventually, an international military force of 19,000 troops, including some 3,000 Americans sent from the Philippines, marched on Peking to end the siege.

Although the American relationship with China was plagued by the exclusionist immigration policy, the idea that the United States had a unique guardian relationship with China persisted into the twentieth century. Since Japan had ambitions in China, this created a rivalry between Japan and the United States, testing the American commitment to preserve the Open Door in China, the territorial integrity of China, and the balance of power in Asia.

Japan and the Balance of Power

Because of population pressures on the limited land mass of Japan, as well as war and the quest for economic opportunities, Japanese immigration to the United States dramatically increased around the turn of the century. Coming first as unmarried males working on western railroads and in Pacific Coast canneries, mines, and logging camps, immigrants from Japan increased from 25,000 in the 1890s to 125,000 between 1901 and 1908. Like the earlier Chinese immigrants, they were met with nativist hostility and discrimination. At Roosevelt's instigation, the Japanese agreed to limit the migration of unskilled workers to the United States in a gentleman's agreement signed in 1907.

Roosevelt also relied on the use of diplomacy and negotiation in his effort to balance Asian powers against one another. The Boxer Rebellion of 1900 left Russia, which had 50,000 troops in Manchuria, the strongest nation in eastern Asia. Roosevelt's admiration for the Japanese as a "fighting" people and a valuable factor in "the civilization of the future" contrasted with his low respect for the Russians, whom he described as "corrupt," "treacherous," and "incompetent." As Japan moved into Korea and Russia into Manchuria, Roosevelt hoped that each would check the growing power of the other.

Because of increasing Russian strength, Roosevelt welcomed news in 1904 that Japan had launched a successful surprise attack on Port Arthur in Manchuria, beginning the Russo-Japanese War. He was equally pleased when the Japanese expressed interest in ending the war. His goal was to achieve peace and leave a balanced situation. "It is best," he wrote, that Russia be left "face to face with Japan so that each may have a moderative action on the other." The negotiations and resulting treaty were carried out in the summer of 1905 near Portsmouth, New Hampshire. No single act better symbolizes the new posture of American power and presence in the world than the signing of a peace treaty ending a war in Manchuria between Russia and Japan halfway around the globe in New Hampshire!

The Treaty of Portsmouth left Japan dominant in Manchuria, but in return, in the Root-Takahira Agreement of 1908, Japan promised to honor U.S. control in the Philippines and to make no further encroachments into China.

These agreements over territorial divisions barely covered up the tensions in Japanese-American relations. Some Japanese were angry that they had not received in the Portsmouth Treaty the indemnities they had wanted from Russia, and they blamed Roosevelt. American insensitivity to the immigration issue also left bad feelings. In Manchuria, U.S. Consul General Willard Straight aggressively pushed an anti-Japanese program of financing capital investment projects in banking and railroads. The United States was in Japan's way, and rumors of war circulated in the world press.

It was clearly time for Roosevelt's version of the "big stick." In 1907, he told Secretary of State Root that he was "more concerned over the Japanese situation than almost any other. Thank Heaven we have the navy in good shape." From 1900 to 1905, outlays to the navy rose from $56 to $117 million. Such a naval spending binge was without precedent in peacetime. In 1907, Roosevelt sent his new, modernized "Great White Fleet" on a goodwill tour around the world. The first stop was the Japanese port of Yokohama. For the time being, the balance of power in Asia was preserved.

Preventing War in Europe

Although the United States was actively involved in Latin America and Asia, toward Europe the traditional policies of neutrality and nonentanglement continued. Still, there was an American role to be played even there, and Roosevelt was eager to play it.

Roosevelt believed that the most serious threats to world peace and civilized order lay in relationships among Germany, Great Britain, and France. He established two fundamental policies toward Europe that with only minor variations would define the U.S. role throughout the century. The first was to make friendship with Great Britain the cornerstone of U.S. policy. The second was to prevent the outbreak of a general war in Europe among strong nations.

Toward this end, Roosevelt depended on his personal negotiating skills and began the practice of summit diplomacy.

Throughout most of the nineteenth century, England was America's chief enemy and commercial rival. But the Venezuelan crisis and a number of other events at the turn of the century shocked the United States and England into an awareness of their mutual interests. Roosevelt supported British imperialism because he favored the dominance of "the English-speaking race" and believed that England was "fighting the battle of civilization." Furthermore, both nations worried about growing German power in Europe, Africa, and East Asia. As German naval power increased, England had to bring its fleet closer to home. Friendly allies were needed to police parts of the world formerly patrolled by the British navy. England therefore concluded a mutual-protection treaty with Japan in 1902 and willingly let the Americans police Central America and the Caribbean Sea. As Roosevelt left the presidency in 1909, one of his final acts was to proclaim the special American friendship with Great Britain.

German Kaiser Wilhelm II often underestimated the solidity of Anglo-American friendship and thought that Roosevelt was really pro-German, an error the American president skillfully used. The Moroccan crisis in 1905 and 1906 is illustrative. European powers competed for colonies and spheres of influence in Africa as well as in Asia. Germany resented French dominance along the North African coast in Morocco. The kaiser precipitated a crisis in the summer of 1905 by delivering a bellicose speech in Casablanca, Morocco, intended to split the British and French entente and to force an opening of commercial doors in Morocco. As war threatened, Roosevelt intervened, arranging a conference of European powers in Algeciras, Spain, to avert conflict. The treaty signed in 1906 prevented war and settled the issues of commerce and police administration in Morocco favorably for the French.

In 1911 retired president Roosevelt wrote that there would be nothing worse than that "Germany should ever overthrow England and establish the supremacy in Europe she aims at." German interest "to try her hand in America," he thought, would surely follow. To avert such horrors, Roosevelt's policy for Europe included cementing friendship with England and, while maintaining official neutrality, using diplomacy to prevent hostilities among European powers. The relationship between Great Britain and Germany continued to deteriorate, however, leading to the outbreak of World War I in 1914.

CONCLUSION

THE RESPONSIBILITIES OF POWER

Since the earliest settlements in Massachusetts Bay, Americans had struggled with the dilemma of how to do good in a world that did wrong. Roosevelt said in 1910 that because of "strength and geographical situation," the United States had itself become "more and more, the balance of power of the whole world." This ominous responsibility was also an opportunity to extend American economic, political, and moral influence around the globe.

As president in the first decade of the twentieth century, Roosevelt established aggressive American policies toward the rest of the world. Americans dominated and policed Central

America and the Caribbean Sea, annexed the Philippines, and worked to preserve the balance of power in Asia. In Europe, the United States sought to remain neutral, cement Anglo-American friendship, and prevent "civilized" nations from going to war.

Throughout the period, the fundamental ambivalence of America's sense of itself as a model "city on a hill," an example to others, remained. But Americans learned that it was difficult for the United States to be both responsible and good, both powerful and loved. The American people thus learned to experience both the satisfactions and the burdens, the profits and the costs, of the missionary role.

Recommended Reading

The best overviews of the emergence of America as a world power in the late nineteenth century, each emphasizing different motives for expansion, are Walter La Feber, *The New Empire: An Interpretation of American Expansion, 1860–1898* (1963); Robert Beisner, *From the Old Diplomacy to the New, 1865–1900* (1975); and Charles Campbell, *The Transformation of American Foreign Relations, 1865–1900* (1976).

On the immediate causes of expansionism in the 1890s and the war with Spain, see David Healy, *U.S. Expansion: Imperialist Urge in the 1890s* (1970). Particular aspects of American expansion are discussed in William Widenor, *Henry Cabot Lodge and the Search for an American Foreign Policy* (1980); and Emily Rosenberg, *Spreading the American Dream: American Economic and Cultural Expansion, 1890–1945* (1982). McKinley's leadership is covered in Lewis Gould, *The Presidency of William McKinley* (1980); and John Dobson, *Reticent Expansionism: The Foreign Policy of William McKinley* (1988).

On the Spanish-American War, see David Trask, *The War with Spain in 1898* (1981); and a fascinating account of the war experiences of black soldiers, Willard Gatewood, Jr., *"Smoked Yankees" and the Struggle for Empire: Letters from Negro Soldiers, 1898–1902* (1971). The brutal suppression of the Philippine rebels is described in Stanley Karnow, *In Our Image: America's Empire in the Philippines* (1989); and Richard Welch, *Response to Imperialism: The United States and the Philippine-American War, 1899–1902* (1979). Some anti-imperialists are treated in Robert Beisner, *Twelve Against Empire: The Anti-Imperialists, 1898–1900* (1975). Relations with Asian countries are discussed in Ronald Takaki, *Strangers from a Different Shore: A History of Asian Americans* (1989).

The standard work on Roosevelt's foreign policy is Howard Beale, *Theodore Roosevelt and the Rise of America to World Power* (1956). Newer interpretations can be found in Raymond Esthus, *Theodore Roosevelt and the International Rivalries* (1970); and Frederick Marks II, *Velvet on Iron: The Diplomacy of Theodore Roosevelt* (1979). Walter La Feber has documented how thoroughly American interests have dominated Central America in *The Panama Canal* (1978) and *Inevitable Revolutions: The United States in Central America* (1983).

Time Line

1823	Monroe Doctrine
1857	Trade opens with Japan
1867	Alaska purchased from Russia
1870	Failure to annex Santo Domingo (Hispaniola)
1875	Sugar reciprocity treaty with Hawaii
1877	United States acquires naval base at Pearl Harbor
1878	United States acquires naval station in Samoa
1882	Chinese Exclusion Act
1889	First Pan-American Conference
1890	Alfred Mahan publishes *Influence of Sea Power upon History*
1893	Hawaiian coup by American sugar growers
1895	Cuban revolt against Spanish Venezuelan boundary dispute
1896	Weyler's reconcentration policy in Cuba McKinley-Bryan presidential campaign
1897	Theodore Roosevelt's speech at Naval War College

1898		
	January	De Lôme letter
	February	Sinking of the battleship *Maine*
	April	Spanish-American War; Teller Amendment
	May	Dewey takes Manila Bay
	July	Annexation of Hawaiian Islands
	August	Americans liberate Manila; war ends
	December	Treaty of Paris; annexation of the Philippines

1899	Senate ratifies Treaty of Paris Filipino-American War begins American Samoa acquired
1899–1900	Open Door notes
1900	Boxer Rebellion in China William Mckinley reelected president
1901	Supreme Court insular cases McKinley assassinated; Theodore Roosevelt becomes president
1902	Filipino-American War ends U.S. military occupation of Cuba ends Platt Amendment Venezuela debt crisis
1903	Panamanian revolt and independence Hay–Bunau-Varilla Treaty
1904	Theodore Roosevelt elected president Roosevelt Corollary
1904–1905	Russo-Japanese War ended by treaty signed at Portsmouth, N.H.
1904–1906	United States intervenes in Nicaragua, Guatemala, Cuba
1905–1906	Moroccan crisis
1906	Roosevelt receives Nobel Peace Prize
1907	Gentleman's agreement with Japan
1908	Root-Takahira Agreement
1909	U.S. Navy ("Great White Fleet") sails around the world
1911	U.S. intervenes in Nicaragua
1914	Opening of the Panama Canal World War I begins
1916	Partial home rule granted to the Philippines

part 5

A
Modernizing People

1900-1945

The first half of the twentieth century was filled with tumultuous changes: two world wars, the worst economic depression the modern world has endured, and spectacular advances in technology. By 1945, the automobile, the airplane, plastics, radio, television, and the atomic bomb had transformed the country, and most Americans lived in urban areas.

Chapter 21, "The Progressives Confront Industrial Capitalism," discusses progressivism, the first modern American reform movement. It examines the nation's struggle to maintain democratic order in an urban and industrial age and to adapt its institutions to the arrival of millions of immigrants.

Chapter 22, "The Great War," describes U.S. involvement in World War I, a crusade to "make the world safe for democracy," in Woodrow Wilson's words. The wartime situation gave new opportunities to blacks and other minorities and began the process of government–business cooperation that would increase bureaucracy and change the very nature of the American system of free enterprise.

Chapter 23, "Affluence and Anxiety," covers the period between World War I and the stock market crash of 1929—a time of prosperity for some, and of fear and intolerance for others.

Chapter 24, "The Great Depression and the New Deal," focuses on the Depression decade, a time of unprecedented economic collapse, and the New Deal, a major American reform movement that promoted the power of the federal government to stimulate the economy and to pass a variety of social programs.

In Chapter 25, "World War II," we discover that war, rather than the New Deal, ended the Depression. World War II stimulated the economy and at the same time released American crusading zeal in an all-out effort to defeat Germany and Japan. During the war, Americans tended to see the world divided between good and evil; yet the United States emerged as the most prosperous and most powerful nation on earth. The euphoria would not last long as peace devolved into the Cold War and competition with the Soviet Union for world domination.

chapter 21

....

The Progressives Confront Industrial Capitalism

Frances Kellor received her law degree in 1897 from Cornell University but decided that she was more interested in solving the nation's social problems than in practicing law. She moved to Chicago, studied sociology, and trained herself as a social reformer. Kellor believed passionately that poverty and inequality could be eliminated in America.

Like many progressives, Kellor believed that environment was more important than heredity in determining ability, prosperity, and happiness. Better schools and better housing, she thought, would produce better citizens. Even criminals, she argued, were simply victims of environment. Kellor demonstrated that poor health and deprived childhoods explained the only differences between criminals and college students.

Kellor was an efficient professional. Like the majority of the professional women of her generation, she never married but devoted her life to social research and social reform. She lived for a time at Hull House in Chicago and at the College Settlement in New York, centers not only of social research and reform but also of lively community.

While staying at the College Settlement, Kellor researched and wrote a muckraking study of employment agencies, published in 1904 as *Out of Work*. She revealed how employment agencies exploited immigrants, blacks, and other recent arrivals in the city. Kellor's book, like the writing of most progressives, spilled over with moral outrage. But Kellor went beyond moralism to suggest corrective legislation at the state and national levels.

Convinced of the need for a national movement to push for reform legislation, Kellor helped to found the National Committee for Immigrants in America, which tried to promote a national policy "to make all these people Americans," and a federal bureau to organize the campaign. Eventually she helped establish the Division of Immigrant Education within the Department of Education. A political movement led by

455

Theodore Roosevelt excited her most. More than almost any other single person, Kellor had been responsible for alerting Roosevelt to the problems the immigrants faced in American cities. When Roosevelt formed the new Progressive Party in 1912, she was one of the many social workers and social researchers who joined him. She campaigned for Roosevelt and directed the Progressive Service Organization, to educate voters in all areas of social justice and welfare after the election. After Roosevelt's defeat and the collapse of the Progressive Party in 1914, Kellor continued to work for Americanization. She spent the rest of her life promoting justice, order, and efficiency and trying to find ways for resolving industrial and international disputes.

Frances Kellor's life illustrates two important aspects of progressivism, the first nationwide reform movement of the modern era: first, a commitment to promote social justice, to assure equal opportunity, and to preserve democracy; and second, a search for order and efficiency in a world complicated by rapid industrialization, immigration, and spectacular urban growth. Progressivism reached a climax in the years from 1900 to 1914. The reform impulse seems to run in cycles in American history, and the progressive movement was one of those times in American history (others were the 1830s, the 1930s, and the 1960s) when a majority of Americans agreed that changes were needed in American society. This chapter traces the important aspects of progressivism, a broad and diverse movement that influenced almost all areas of American life. It examines the social justice movement, life among workers, the reform movements in the cities and states, and finally, progressivism at the national level during the administrations of Theodore Roosevelt and Woodrow Wilson, the first thoroughly modern presidents.

THE SOCIAL JUSTICE MOVEMENT

The "progressive movement" was actually a number of movements focusing on the problems created by a rapidly expanding urban and industrial world. Progressivism had roots in the 1890s, when many reformers were shocked by the devastation caused by the depression of 1893, and they were influenced by reading Henry George's *Progress and Poverty* (1879) and Edward Bellamy's *Looking Backward* (1888), as well as literature of the Social Gospel movement.

The Progressive World View

Intellectually, the progressives were influenced by the Darwinian revolution. They believed that the world was in flux, and they rebelled against the fixed and the formal in every field. One of the philosophers of the movement, John Dewey, wrote that ideas could become instruments for change. William James, in his philosophy of pragmatism, denied that there were universal truths; ideas should be judged by their usefulness. Most of the progressives were environmentalists who were convinced that environment was much more important than heredity in forming character. Thus if one could build better schools and houses, one could make better people and a more perfect society. But they also believed that some groups could be molded and changed more easily than others. Thus progressivism did not usually mean progress for blacks.

Progressivism sought to bring order and efficiency to a world that had been transformed by rapid growth and new technology. The progressive leaders were almost always middle-class, and they quite consciously tried to teach their middle-class values to the immigrants and the working class. They were part of a statistics-minded, realistic generation. They conducted surveys, gathered facts, wrote reports about every conceivable problem, and usually had faith that their reports would lead to change. Their urge to document came out in haunting photographs of young workers taken by Lewis Hine, in the stark and beautiful city paintings by John Sloan. They pondered such questions as: What is the proper relation of government to society? To big business? How much responsibility does society have to care for the poor and needy?

The Muckrakers

One group of writers who exposed corruption and other evils in American society were labeled "muckrakers" by Theodore Roosevelt. Not all muckrakers were reformers—some merely wanted to profit from the scandals—but the reformers learned from their techniques of exposé. Editors of magazines such as *American, McClure's,* and *Cosmopolitan* eagerly published the articles of investigative reporters who wanted to tell the public what was wrong in American society.

Lincoln Steffens, a young California journalist, wrote articles for *McClure's* exposing the connections between respectable urban businessmen and corrupt politicians. When published in 1904 as *The Shame of the Cities,* Steffens's account became a battle cry for people determined to clean up the graft in city government. Ida Tarbell, a teacher turned journalist, revealed John D. Rockefeller's ruthless ways and his unfair business practices in her *History of the Standard Oil Company* (1904).

After Steffens and Tarbell achieved popular success, many others followed. Realistic fiction also portrayed social problems. For example, Frank Norris in *The Octopus* (1901) dramatized the railroads' stranglehold on the farmers.

Working Women and Children

Nothing disturbed the social justice progressives more than the sight of children, sometimes as young as 8 or 10, working long hours in dangerous and depressing factories. Young people had worked in factories since the beginning of the industrial revolution, but that did not make the practice any less repugnant to the reformers. "Children are put into industry very much as we put in raw material," Jane Addams objected, "and the product we look for is not better men and women, but better manufactured goods."

Florence Kelley was one of the most important leaders in the crusade against child labor. Raised in an upper-class Philadelphia family, she studied law when she could find no attorney in Chicago to argue a child labor case against some of the prominent corporations. She passed the bar exam and argued the cases herself.

Although Kelley and the other child labor reformers won a few cases, they quickly recognized the need for state laws if they were going to have any real influence. Reformers, marshaling their evidence about the tragic effects on growing children of long working hours in dark and damp factories, pressured the Illinois state legislature into passing an anti–child labor law.

Nothing tugged at the heartstrings of the reformers more than the sight of little children, sullen and stunted, working long hours in factory, farm, and mine. These children, coal miners in Pennsylvania, were carefully posed by Lewis Hine while he worked for the National Child Labor Committee in 1911.

A few years later, however, the state supreme court declared the law unconstitutional.

Judicial opposition was one factor leading reformers to the national level in the first decade of the twentieth century. Florence Kelley again led the charge. In 1899, she had become secretary of the National Consumers League, an organization that enlisted consumers in a campaign to lobby elected officials and corporations to ensure that products were produced under safe and sanitary conditions. It was not Kelley, however, but Edgar Gardner Murphy, an Alabama clergyman, who suggested the formation of the National Child Labor Committee. Like many other Social Gospel ministers, Murphy believed that the church should reform society as well as save souls. He was appalled by the number of young children working in southern textile mills, where they were exposed to great danger and condemned to "compulsory ignorance" (because they dropped out of school).

The National Child Labor Committee led a campaign for child labor legislation. While two-thirds of the states passed some form of child labor law between 1905 and 1907, many had loopholes that exempted a large number of children, including newsboys and youngsters who worked in the theater. Despite reformers' efforts, compulsory school attendance laws did more to reduce the number of children who worked than federal and state laws, which proved difficult to pass and even more difficult to enforce.

The crusade against child labor was a typical social justice reform effort. Its orgins lay in the moral indignation of middle-class reformers. But reform went beyond moral outrage as reformers gathered statistics, took photographs documenting the abuse of children, and used their evidence to push for legislation first on the local level, then in the states, and eventually in Washington.

Like other progressive reform efforts, the battle against child labor was only partly successful. Too many businessmen, both small and large, were profiting from employing children at low wages. And some parents, who often desperately needed the money their children earned in the factories, opposed the reformers and even broke the law to allow their children to work.

In Denver and Chicago, reformers organized juvenile courts where judges had the authority to put delinquent youths on probation, take them from their families and make them wards of the state, or assign them to an institution. The juvenile court often helped prevent young delinquents from adopting a life of crime. Yet the juvenile offender was frequently deprived of all rights of due process, a fact that the Supreme Court finally recognized in 1967, when it ruled that children were entitled to procedural rights when accused of a crime.

Closely connected with the anti–child labor movement was the effort to limit the hours of women's work. It seemed inconsistent to protect a girl until she was 16 and then give her the "right to work from 8 A.M. to 10 P.M., thirteen hours a day, seventy-eight hours a week for $6." Florence Kelley and the National Consumers League led the campaign. In 1908, the Supreme

Lewis Hine, Carolina Cotton Mill, *1908.*

Court, in *Muller* v. *Oregon,* upheld the Oregon ten-hour law largely because reformer Josephine Goldmark had detailed the danger and disease that factory women faced. Most states fell into line with the Supreme Court decision and passed protective legislation for women, though many companies found ways to circumvent the laws. Even ten hours work a day seemed too long to some women. One factory worker stated. "I have four children and have to work hard at home. Make me awful tired. I would like nine hours. I get up at 5:30. When I wash, I have to stay up till one or two o'clock."

By contending that "women are fundamentally weaker than men," the reformers won some protection for women workers. But their arguments that women were weaker than men would eventually be used to reinforce gender segregation of the work force for the next half century.

In addition to working for protective legislation for working women, the social justice pro-

gressives also campaigned for woman suffrage. Addams argued that urban women not only could vote intelligently but also needed the vote to protect, clothe, and feed their families. Women in an urban age, she suggested, needed to be municipal housekeepers. The progressive insistence that all women needed the vote helped to push woman suffrage toward the victory that would come during World War I.

Much more controversial than either votes for women or protective legislation was the movement for birth control. The Comstock Law of 1873 made it illegal to promote or even write about contraceptive devices, but Margaret Sanger, a nurse who had watched poor women suffer from too many births and even die from dangerous illegal abortions, spoke out. Sanger obtained the latest medical and scientific European studies of birth control methods and in 1914 explained in her magazine, *The Woman Rebel,* and in a pamphlet, *Family Limitation,* that women could separate sex from procreation. She was promptly indicted for violation of the postal code and fled to Europe to avoid arrest. Birth control remained controversial and in most states illegal for many years. Yet Sanger helped to bring the topic of sexuality and contraception out into the open. When she returned to the United States in 1921, she founded the American Birth Control League, which became the Planned Parenthood Federation in 1942.

Home and School

The reformers believed that better housing and education could transform the lives of the poor and create a better world. Books such as Jacob Riis's *How the Other Half Lives* (1890) horrified them. With vivid language and haunting photographs, Riis had documented the overcrowded tenements, the damp, dark alleys, and the sickness and despair that affected people who lived in New York's slums. He labored to replace New York's worst slums with parks and playgrounds. In the first decade of the twentieth century, the progressives called attention to the effect of urban overcrowding and tried to pass tenement house laws in several cities, but the laws were often evaded or modified. In 1910, they organized the National Housing Association, and some of them looked ahead to federal laws and even to government-subsidized housing.

The housing reformers combined moral zeal with practical tactics. One reformer's guide, *How to Furnish and Keep House in a Tenement Flat,* recommended "wood-stained and uncluttered furniture surfaces, iron beds with mattresses, and unupholstered chairs. . . . Walls must be painted not papered . . . screens provide privacy in the bedrooms; a few good pictures should grace the walls." But often immigrant family ideals and values differed from those of the middle-class reformers. Despite the reformers' efforts to separate life's functions into separate rooms, most immigrants still crowded into the kitchen and hung religious objects rather than "good pictures" on the walls.

While some middle-class women reformers were concerned about immigrants' housekeeping, others began to realize that the domestic tasks expected of women of all classes kept many of them from taking their full place in society. Charlotte Perkins Gilman, author of *Women and Economics* (1898), dismantled the traditional view of "woman's sphere" and sketched an alternative. Suggesting that entrepreneurs ought to build apartment houses designed to allow women to combine motherhood with careers, she advocated shared kitchen facilities and a common dining room, a laundry run by efficient workers, and a roof-garden day nursery with a professional teacher.

Next to better housing, the progressives stressed better schools as a way to produce better citizens. Public school systems were often rigid and corrupt. Far from producing citizens who would help to transform society, the schools seemed to reinforce the conservative habits that blocked change. A reporter who traveled around the country in 1892 discovered mindless teachers who drilled pupils through repetitious rote learning.

Progressive education, like many other aspects of progressivism, revolted against the rigid and the formal in favor of flexibility and change. John Dewey was the key philosopher of progressive education. Having grown up in Vermont, he tried throughout his life to create a sense of the small rural community in the city. In his laboratory school at the University of Chicago, he experimented with new educational methods. He replaced the school desks, which were bolted down and always faced the front, with seats that could be moved into circles and arranged in small groups. The movable seat, in fact, became one of the symbols of the progressive education movement.

Dewey insisted that the schools be child-centered, not subject-oriented. Teachers should teach children rather than teach history or mathematics. History and math should be related to the students' experience. Students should learn by doing. They should not just learn about democracy; the school itself should operate like a democracy.

Crusades Against Saloons, Brothels, and Movie Houses

Given their faith in the reforming potential of healthy and educated citizens, it was logical that most social justice progressives opposed the sale of alcohol. They saw eliminating drinking as part of the process of reforming the city and conserving human resources.

Americans did drink great quantities of beer, wine, and hard liquor, and the amount they consumed rose rapidly after 1900, peaking between 1911 and 1915. The modern antiliquor movement was spearheaded in the 1880s and 1890s by the Women's Christian Temperance Union and after 1900 by the Anti-Saloon League and a coalition of religious leaders and social reformers. During the progressive era, temperance forces had considerable success in influencing legislation. Seven states passed temperance laws between 1906 and 1912.

The reformers tended to focus on the saloon and its social life. Drug traffic, prostitution, and political corruption all seemed linked to the saloon. Although they never quite understood the role alcohol played in the social life of many ethnic groups, Jane Addams and other settlement workers appreciated the saloon's importance as a neighborhood social center. Addams started a coffeehouse at Hull House in an attempt to lure the neighbors away from the evils of the saloon.

The progressives joined forces with other prohibition groups, and their combined efforts led to victory on December 22, 1917, when Congress sent to the states for ratification a constitutional amendment prohibiting the sale, manufacturing, or importing of intoxicating liquor within the United States. The spirit of sacrifice for the war effort facilitated its rapid ratification.

In addition to the saloon, the progressives saw the urban dance hall and the movie theater as threats to the morals and well-being of young people, especially young women. The motion picture, invented in 1889, developed as an important form of entertainment during the first decade of the twentieth century. But not until World War I, when D. W. Griffith produced long feature films, did the movies begin to attract a middle-class audience. The most popular of these early films was Griffith's *The Birth of a Nation* (1915), a blatantly racist and distorted epic of black debauchery during Reconstruction. Many early films had plots that depicted premarital sex, adultery, and violence, and, unlike later films, many attacked authority and had tragic endings. *The Candidate* (1907) showed an upper-class reform candidate who gets dirt thrown at him for his efforts to clean up the town. The film *Down with Women* (1907) showed well-dressed men denouncing woman suffrage and the incompe-

tence of the weaker sex, but throughout the film only strong women are depicted. In the end, when the hero is arrested, a woman lawyer defends him.

Although reformers disapproved of the dark theaters, often located near saloons, for young immigrant women, who made up the bulk of the audience at most urban movie theaters, the films provided rare exciting moments in their lives. One daughter of strict Italian parents remarked, "The one place I was allowed to go by myself was the movies. I went to the movies for fun. My parents wouldn't let me go anywhere else, even when I was twenty-four."

Saloons, dance halls, and movie theaters all seemed dangerous to progressives interested in improving life in the city because all appeared to be somehow connected with the worst evil of all, prostitution. Campaigns against prostitution had been waged since the early nineteenth century, but they were nothing compared with the progressives' crusade to wipe out what they called "the social evil." All major cities and many smaller ones appointed vice commissions and made elaborate studies of prostitution.

The progressive antivice crusade attracted many kinds of people, for often contradictory reasons. Racists and immigration restrictionists maintained that inferior people—blacks and recent immigrants, especially those from southern and eastern Europe—became prostitutes and pimps. Others had a variety of motives. Most progressives, however, stressed the environmental and especially the economic causes of vice. "Do you suppose I am going back to earn five or six dollars a week in a factory," one prostitute asked an investigator, "when I can earn that amount any night and often much more?"

Despite all their reports and all the publicity, the progressives failed to end prostitution and did virtually nothing to address its roots in poverty. They wiped out a few red-light districts, closed a number of brothels, and managed to push a bill through Congress (the Mann Act of 1910) that prohibited the interstate transport of women for immoral purposes. Perhaps more important, in several states they got the age of consent for women raised, and in 20 states they made the Wassermann test for syphilis mandatory for both men and women before a marriage license could be issued.

THE WORKER IN THE PROGRESSIVE ERA

Progressive reformers sympathized with industrial workers who struggled to earn a living for themselves and their families. The progressives sought protective legislation—particularly for women and children—unemployment insurance, and workers' compensation. But often they had little understanding of what it was really like to sell one's strength by the hour. For example, they supported labor's right to organize at a time when labor had few friends, yet they often opposed the strike as a weapon against management.

Adjusting to Industrial Labor

John Mekras arrived in New York from Greece in 1912 and traveled immediately to Manchester, New Hampshire, where he found a job in the giant Amoskeag textile mill. He did not speak a word of English. He later remembered,

> the man who hands out the jobs sent me to the spinning room. There I don't know anything about the spinning. I'm a farmer . . . I don't know what the boss is talking about.

Mekras didn't last long at the mill. He was one of the many industrial workers who had difficulty adjusting to factory work in the early twentieth century.

Many workers, whether they were from Greece, from eastern Europe, from rural Vermont, or from Michigan, confronted a bewildering world based on order and routine. Unlike farm or craft work, factory life was dominated

by the clock, the bell tower, and the boss. The workers continued to resist the routine and pace of factory work, and they subtly sabotaged the employers' efforts to control the workplace as they had done in an earlier period (see Chapters 11 and 18). They stayed at home on holidays, took unauthorized breaks, and set their own informal productivity schedules. Often they were fired or quit. In the woolen industry, the annual turnover of workers between 1907 and 1910 was more than 100 percent. In New York needle-worker shops in 1912 and 1913, the turnover rate was over 250 percent. Overall in American industry, one-third of the workers stayed at their jobs less than a year.

This industrial work force, still composed largely of immigrants, had a fluid character. Many migrants, especially those from southern and eastern Europe, expected to stay only for a short time and then return to their homeland. Many men came alone—70 percent in some years. They saved money by living in a boardinghouse. In 1910, two-thirds of the workers in Pittsburgh made less than $12 a week, but by lodging in boardinghouses and paying $2.50 a month for a bed, they could save perhaps one-third of their pay. "Here in America one must work for three horses," one immigrant wrote home. "The work is very heavy, but I don't mind it," another wrote.

About 40 percent of those who immigrated to America in the first decade of the twentieth century returned home, according to one estimate. In years of economic downturn, such as 1908, more Italians and Austro-Hungarians left the United States than entered it. For many immigrants, the American dream never materialized.

The nature of work continued to change in the early twentieth century as industrialists extended late-nineteenth-century efforts to make their factories and their work forces more efficient, productive, and profitable. In some industries, the introduction of new machines revolutionized work and eliminated highly paid

Immigration to the United States, 1900–1920

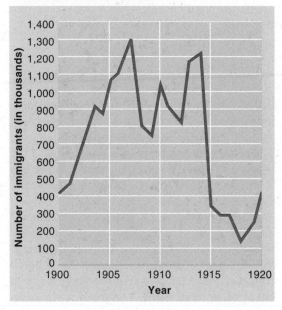

Source: U.S. Bureau of the Census

skilled jobs. Glassblowing machines invented about 1900, for example, replaced thousands of glassblowers or reduced them from craftsmen to workers. Power-driven machines, better-organized operations, and, finally, the moving assembly line, perfected by Henry Ford, transformed the nature of work and turned many laborers into unskilled tenders of machines.

While some skilled weavers and glassblowers were transformed into unskilled operators, the introduction of the machines themselves created the need for new skilled workers. In the auto industry, for example, the new elite workers were the mechanics and tool and die men who kept the assembly line running. Although these new skilled artisans survived, the trend toward mechanization was unstoppable, and even the most skilled workers were eventually removed from making decisions about the production process.

More than machines changed the nature of industrial work. The principles of scientific management, which set out new rules for organizing work, were just as important. The key figure was Frederick Taylor, an engineer at Midvale Steel Company in Philadelphia. Taylor was obsessed with efficiency. He emphasized centralized planning, systematic analysis, and detailed instructions. Most of all, he studied all kinds of workers and timed the various components of their jobs with a stopwatch.

As Taylor himself explained, scientific management meant "the deliberate gathering in on . . . management's side of all of the great mass of traditional knowledge, which in the past has been in the heads of the workmen, and in the physical skill and knack of the workman which he has acquired through years of experience." Taylor's approach was designed to reduce the need for skilled workers, to limit workers' scope for self-direction, and to control closely their productivity. Not surprisingly, many workers resented the drive for efficiency and control. "We don't want to work as fast as we are able to," one machinist remarked. "We want to work as fast as we think it comfortable for us to work."

Union Organizing

The progressive reformers had little understanding of the revolution going on in the factory. Samuel Gompers, head of the American Federation of Labor, however, was quick to recognize that Taylorism would reduce workers to "mere machines." Under his guidance the AFL prospered during the progressive era. Between 1897 and 1904, union membership grew from 447,000 to over two million, with three out of every four union members claimed by the AFL. By 1914, the AFL alone had over two million members. Gompers's "pure and simple unionism" was most successful among coal miners, railroad workers, and the building trades. As we saw in Chapter 18, Gompers ignored the growing army of unskilled and immigrant workers and concentrated on raising the wages and improving the working conditions of the skilled craftsmen who were members of unions affiliated with the AFL.

For a time, Gompers's strategy seemed to work. Several industries negotiated with the AFL as a way of avoiding disruptive strikes. But cooperation was short-lived. Labor unions were defeated in a number of disastrous strikes, and the National Association of Manufacturers launched an aggressive counterattack. The NAM and other employer associations provided strikebreakers, used industrial spies, and blacklisted union members to prevent them from obtaining other jobs.

The Supreme Court came down squarely on management's side, ruling in the *Danbury Hatters* case in 1908 that trade unions were subject to the Sherman Anti-Trust Act. Thus union members themselves could be held personally liable for money lost by a business during a strike. Courts at all levels sided overwhelmingly with employers. They often declared strikes illegal and were quick to issue restraining orders, making it impossible for workers to interfere with the operation of a business.

Working women and their problems aroused more sympathy among progressive reformers than the plight of working men. The number of women working outside the home increased steadily during the progressive era, from over 5 million in 1900 to nearly 8.5 million in 1920. But few belonged to unions, and the policy of Gompers and the other labor leaders was generally to oppose organizing women workers.

Many upper-class women reformers tried to help these working women in a variety of ways. Tension and misunderstanding often cropped up between the reformers and the working women, but one organization in which there was genuine cooperation was the Women's Trade Union League. Founded in 1903, the league was organized by Mary Kenney and William English Walling, a socialist and reformer. The league established branches in most large eastern and midwestern cities and served for more than a decade as an important force in helping to organize women into unions.

Garment Workers and the Triangle Fire

Thousands of young women, most of them Jewish and Italian, were employed in the garment industry in New York City. Most were between 16 and 25; some lived with their families, and others lived alone or with a roommate. They worked a 56-hour, six-day week and made about $6 for their efforts. Like other industries, garment manufacturing had changed in the first decade of the twentieth century. Once conducted in thousands of dark and dingy tenement rooms, now all the operations were centralized in large loft buildings in lower Manhattan. These buildings were an improvement over the sweating labor of the tenements, but many were overcrowded, and they had few fire escapes or safety features. In addition, the owners applied scientific management techniques in order to increase their profits, making life miserable for the workers. Most of the women had to rent their sewing machines and even had to pay for the electricity they used. They were penalized for mistakes or for talking too loudly. They were usually supervised by a male contractor, who badgered and sometimes even harassed them.

In 1909, some of the women went out on strike to protest the working conditions. The International Ladies' Garment Workers Union (ILGWU) and the Women's Trade Union League supported them. But strikers were beaten and sometimes arrested by unsympathetic policemen and by strikebreakers on the picket lines. At a mass meeting held at Cooper Union in New York on November 22, 1909, Clara Lemlich, a young shirtwaist worker who had been injured on the picket line and was angered by the long speeches and lack of action, rose and in an emotional speech in Yiddish demanded a general strike. The entire audience pledged its agreement. The next day, all over the city, the shirtwaist workers went out on strike. "The uprising of the twenty thousand," as the strike was called, startled the nation.

The shirtwaist workers won, and in part the success of the strike made the garment union one of the most powerful in the AFL. But the victory was limited. Over 300 companies accepted the union's terms, but others refused to go along. The young women went back to work amid still oppressive and unsafe conditions. That became dramatically obvious on Saturday, March 25, 1911, when a fire broke out on the eighth floor of the ten-story loft building housing the Triangle Shirtwaist Company near Washington Square in New York. Within minutes, the top three floors of the factory were a raging inferno. Many exit doors were locked. The elevators broke down. There were no fire escapes. Forty-six women jumped to their deaths, some of them in groups of three and four holding hands. Over 100 died in the flames.

Shocked by the Triangle fire, the state legislature appointed a commission to investigate working conditions in the state. The result was state legislation limiting the work of women to 54 hours a week, prohibiting labor by children under 14, and improving safety regulations in factories. One supporter of the bills in Albany was a young state senator named Franklin Delano Roosevelt.

Another investigative commission, the federal Industrial Relations Commission, which was created in 1912 to study the causes of industrial unrest and violence, conducted a detailed study of a violent labor-management conflict in Colorado, known as the Ludlow Massacre. A strike broke out in the fall of 1913 in the vast mineral-rich area of southern Colorado, much of it controlled by the Colorado Fuel and Iron Industry, a company largely owned by the Rockefeller family. It was a paternalistic empire where workers lived in company towns and sometimes in tent colonies. They were paid in company scrip and forced to shop at the company store.

When the workers, supported by the United Mine Workers, went on strike demanding an eight-hour day, better safety precautions, and the removal of armed guards, the company refused to negotiate. The strike turned violent, and in the spring of 1914, strikebreakers and national guardsmen fired on the workers. Eleven children and two women were killed in an attack on a tent city near Ludlow, Colorado.

The Industrial Relations Commission stated in its report that violent class conflict could be avoided only by limiting the use of armed guards and detectives, by restricting monopoly, by protecting the right of the workers to organize, and, most dramatically, by redistributing wealth through taxation. The commission's report, not surprisingly, fell on deaf ears. Most progressives, like most Americans, denied the commission's conclusion that class conflict was inevitable.

Radical Labor

In 1905, a group of about 200 radicals met in Chicago to form a new union as an alternative to the AFL. The Industrial Workers of the World, or IWW, would welcome all workers: the unskilled, and even the unemployed, as well as women, blacks, Asians, and all other ethnic groups. Attending the organizational meeting were Daniel De Leon of the Socialist Labor Party, Eugene Debs, one of the outstanding radical leaders in the country, and Mary Harris Jones, widely known as "Mother" Jones. Jones had been a dressmaker, a Populist, and a member of the Knights of Labor. During the 1890s, she had marched with miners' wives on the picket line in western Pennsylvania. She was imprisoned and denounced, but by 1905 she was already a legend.

Presiding at the Chicago meeting was "Big Bill" Haywood. He had been a cowboy, a miner, and a prospector. Somewhere along the way he had lost an eye and mangled a hand, but he had a booming voice and a passionate commitment to "the emancipation of the working class from the slave bondage of capitalism." Denouncing Gompers and the AFL, he talked of class conflict. "The purpose of the IWW," he proclaimed, "is to bring the workers of this country into the possession of the full value of the product of their toil."

The IWW remained a small organization, troubled by internal squabbles and disagreements. It succeeded in organizing textile workers in the Northeast as well as itinerant lumbermen and migratory workers in the Northwest. But in other places, especially in times of high unemployment, the Wobblies, as they were called, helped the unskilled workers vent their anger against their employers.

Many American workers still did not feel, as European workers did, that they were engaged in a perpetual class struggle with their capitalist employers. The AFL, not the IWW, became the dominant American labor movement. But for a few, the IWW represented a dream of what might have been. For others, its presence, though small and largely ineffective, meant that perhaps someday a European-style working-class movement might develop in America.

REFORM IN THE CITIES AND STATES

The reform movements of the progressive era usually started at the local level, then moved to the state and finally to the nation's capital. Progressivism in the cities and states had roots in the depression and discontent of the 1890s. The movement's leaders were often the professional and business classes. They intended to bring order out of chaos and to modernize the city and the state during a time of swift growth.

Municipal Reformers

American cities grew rapidly in the last part of the nineteenth and the first part of the twentieth centuries. New York, which had a population of

1.2 million in 1880, grew to 3.4 million by 1900 and 5.6 million in 1920. Chicago expanded even more dramatically, from 500,000 in 1880 to 1.7 million in 1900 and 2.7 million in 1920. Los Angeles was a town of 11,000 in 1880 but multiplied ten times by 1900, and then increased another five times, to more than a half million, by 1920.

The spectacular and continuing growth of the cities caused problems and created a need for housing, transportation, and municipal services. But it was the kind of people who were moving into the cities that worried many observers. Americans from the small towns and farms continued to throng to the urban centers, but immigration produced the greatest surge in population. Fully 40 percent of New York's population and 36 percent of Chicago's was foreign-born in 1910; if one included the children of the immigrants, the percentage approached 80 percent in some cities. The new immigrants from eastern and western Europe, according to Francis Walker, the president of MIT, were "beaten men from beaten races, representing the worst failures in the struggle for existence." They seemed to threaten the American way of life and the very tenets of democracy.

Fear of the city and its new inhabitants motivated progressive municipal reform efforts. Urban problems seemed to have reached a crisis stage.

The twentieth-century reformers, mostly middle-class citizens like those in the nineteenth, wanted to regulate and control the sprawling metropolis, restore democracy, reduce corruption, and limit the power of the political bosses and their immigrant allies. When these reformers talked of restoring power to the people, they usually meant ensuring control for people like themselves. The chief aim of municipal reform was to make the city more organized and efficient for the business and professional classes who were to control its workings.

Municipal reform movements varied from city to city. In Boston, the reformers tried to

Cities grew so rapidly that they often ceased to work. This 1909 photograph shows Dearborn Street looking south from Randolph in Chicago. Horse-drawn vehicles, streetcars, pedestrians, and even a few early autos clogged the intersection and created the urban inefficiency that angered municipal reformers.

strengthen the power of the mayor, break the hold of the city council, and eliminate council corruption. They succeeded in removing all party designations from city election ballots, and they extended the term of the mayor from two to four years. But to their chagrin, in the election of 1910, John Fitzgerald, grandfather of John F. Kennedy and foe of reform, defeated their candidate. In other cities, the reformers used different tactics, but they almost always conducted elaborate studies and campaigned to reduce corruption.

The most dramatic innovation was the replacement of both mayor and council with a nonpartisan commission of administrators. This innovation began quite accidentally when a hurricane devastated Galveston, Texas, in September 1900. The existing government was helpless to deal with the crisis, so the state legislature appointed five commissioners to run the city during the emergency. The idea spread and proved most popular in small to medium-size cities in the Midwest and the Pacific Northwest. By World War I, more than 400 cities had adopted the commission form. Dayton, Ohio, went one step further: After a disastrous flood in 1913, the city hired a city manager to run the city and to report to the elected council. Government by experts was the perfect symbol of what most municipal reformers had in mind.

The commission and the expert manager did not replace the mayor in most large cities. One of the most flamboyant and successful of the progressive mayors was Tom Johnson, elected mayor of Cleveland in 1901. During his two terms in city hall, he managed to reduce transit fares and to build parks and municipal bath houses throughout the city. Johnson also broke the connection between the police and prostitution in the city by promising the madams and the brothel owners that he would not bother them if they would be orderly and not steal from their customers or pay off the police. His most controversial move, however, was to advocate city ownership of the street railroads and utilities (sometimes called municipal socialism). Johnson was defeated in 1909 in part because he alienated many powerful business interests, but one of his lieutenants, Newton D. Baker, was elected mayor in 1911 and carried on many of his programs. Cleveland was one of many cities that began to regulate municipal utilities or to take them over from the private owners.

The City Beautiful

In Cleveland, both Tom Johnson and Newton Baker promoted the arts, music, and adult education. They also supervised the construction of a civic center, a library, and a museum. Most other American cities during the progressive era set out to bring culture and beauty to their centers. They were influenced at least in part by the great, classical White City constructed for the Chicago World's Fair of 1893 and by the grand European boulevards such as the Champs-Elysées in Paris. The architects of the "city beautiful movement" tried to make the city more attractive and meaningful for the middle and upper classes. The museums and the libraries were closed on Sundays, the only day the working class could possibly visit them.

The social justice progressives, especially those connected with the social settlements, were more concerned with neighborhood parks and playgrounds than with the ceremonial boulevards and grand buildings. Hull House established the first public playground in Chicago.

Most progressives had an ambivalent atti-

tude toward the city. They feared it, and they loved it. One of Tom Johnson's young assistants, Frederic C. Howe, wrote a book called *The City: The Hope of Democracy* (1905). Hope or threat, the progressives realized that the United States had become an urban nation and that the problems of the city had to be faced.

Reform in the States

The progressive movements in the states had many roots and took many forms. In some states, especially in the West, progressive attempts to regulate railroads and utilities were simply an extension of populism. In other states, the reform drive bubbled up from reform efforts in the cities. Most states passed initiative and referendum laws, allowing citizens to originate legislation and to overturn laws passed by the legislature, and recall laws, which gave the people a way to remove elected officials. Many states passed social justice measures as well. Maryland enacted the first workers' compensation law in 1902, paying employees for days missed because of job-related injuries. Illinois approved a law aiding mothers with dependent children. Several states passed anti–child labor bills, and Oregon's ten-hour law restricting women's labor became a model for other states.

The states with the most successful reform movements elected strong and aggressive governors: Charles Evans Hughes in New York, Hoke Smith in Georgia, Hiram Johnson in California, Woodrow Wilson in New Jersey, and Robert La Follette in Wisconsin. After Wilson, La Follette was the most famous and in many ways the model progressive governor.

The depression of 1893 hit Wisconsin hard. More than a third of the state's citizens were out of work; farmers lost their farms, and many small businesses went bankrupt. At the same time, the rich seemed to be getting richer. As grass-roots discontent spread, several newspapers joined the battle and denounced special privilege and corruption. Everyone could agree on the need for tax reform, railroad regulation, and more participation of the people in government.

La Follette, a lawyer who had had little interest in reform, took advantage of the general mood of discontent to win the governorship in 1901. A shrewd politician, he used professors from the University of Wisconsin, in the capital, to prepare reports and do statistical studies. Then he worked with the legislature to pass a state primary law and an act regulating the railroads. "Go back to the first principles of democracy; go back to the people" was his battle cry. He became a national figure and was elected to the Senate in 1906.

Although the progressive movement had mixed results, it did improve government and make it more responsible to the people in states like Wisconsin. The spirit of reform that swept the country was real, and progressive movements on the local level did eventually have an impact on Washington, especially during the administrations of Theodore Roosevelt and Woodrow Wilson.

THEODORE ROOSEVELT AND THE SQUARE DEAL

President William McKinley was shot in Buffalo, New York, on September 6, 1901, by Leon Czolgosz, an anarchist. He died eight days later, making Theodore Roosevelt, at 42, the youngest man ever to become president. The nation mourned its fallen leader, while in many cities anarchists and other radicals were rounded up for questioning.

No one knew what to expect from Roosevelt, but under his leadership, progressivism reshaped the national political agenda. While early progressive reformers had attacked problems at the state or local level, the emergence of a national industrial economy had spawned conditions that demanded national solutions.

Progressives at the national level turned their attention to the workings of the economic

system. They examined the railroads and other large corporations, threats to the natural environment, and the quality of the products of American industry. As they fashioned legislation to remedy the flaws in the economic system, they vastly expanded the power of the national government.

A Strong and Controversial President

Roosevelt came to the presidency with considerable experience. He had served a term in the New York state assembly, spent four years as a United States civil service commissioner, and served two years as the police commissioner of New York City. His exploits in the Spanish-American War brought him to the public's attention, but he had also been an effective assistant secretary of the navy and a reform governor of New York. While police commissioner and governor, he had been influenced by housing reformer Jacob Riis and other progressives. He came from an upper-class family, had written a number of books, and was one of the most intellectual presidents since Thomas Jefferson. But none of these things assured that he would be a progressive in office.

Roosevelt loved being president. He called the office a "bully pulpit," and he enjoyed talking to the people and the press. The American people quickly adopted him as their favorite. They called him "Teddy" and named a stuffed bear after him.

Roosevelt became the strongest president since Lincoln. He revitalized the executive branch, reorganized the army command structure, and modernized the consular service. He established the Bureau of Corporations, appointed independent commissions staffed with experts, and enlisted talented and well-trained men to work for the government. "TR," as he became known, also called a White House conference on the care of dependent children. He angered many social justice progressives by not going far enough. But he was the first president to listen to the pleas of the progressives and to learn from them.

Dealing with the Trusts

One of Roosevelt's first actions as president was to attempt to control the large industrial corporations. He took office in the middle of an unprecedented wave of business consolidation. Between 1897 and 1904, some 4,227 companies combined to form 257 large corporations. The Sherman Anti-Trust Act of 1890 had been virtually useless in controlling the trusts, but a new outcry from muckrakers and progressives called for regulation. Roosevelt opposed neither bigness nor the right of businessmen to make money. But he thought some businessmen arrogant, greedy, and irresponsible. "We draw the line against misconduct, not against wealth," he said.

To the shock of much of the business community, he directed his attorney general to file suit to dissolve the Northern Securities Company, a giant railroad monopoly put together by James J. Hill and financier J. P. Morgan. The government won its case and proceeded to prosecute some of the largest corporations, including Standard Oil of New Jersey and the American Tobacco Company. Although Roosevelt's antitrust policy did not end the power of the giant corporations or even alter their methods of doing business, it did breathe some life into the Sherman Anti-Trust Act, and it increased the role of the federal government as regulator. It also caused large firms such as U.S. Steel to diversify in order to avoid antitrust suits.

Roosevelt sought to strengthen the power of the Interstate Commerce Commission (ICC) to regulate rate and rebate abuses by the railroads through two proposed bills. Although opponents in Congress weakened the bills, the legislative effort resulted in the Elkins Act of 1903, which attempted to end the railroads' practice of granting rebates to shippers, and the Hepburn Act of 1906, which authorized the ICC to examine the account books of corporations and determine a maximum shipping rate. Despite their intent, however, these laws failed to end abuses or satisfy the farmers and small businessmen who had always been the railroads' chief critics.

Roosevelt firmly believed in corporate capitalism. He detested socialism and felt much more comfortable around business executives than labor leaders. Yet he saw his role as mediator and regulator. His view of the power of the presidency was illustrated in 1902 during the anthracite coal strike. Led by John Mitchell of the United Mine Workers, the coal miners went on strike to protest low wages, long hours, and unsafe working conditions. In 1901, a total of 513 coal miners had been killed. The mine owners refused to talk to the miners. They hired strikebreakers and used private security forces to threaten and intimidate the workers.

In the fall of 1902, schools began closing for lack of coal, and it looked like many citizens would suffer through the winter. Coal, which usually sold for $5 a ton, rose to $14. Roosevelt called the owners and representatives of the union to the White House. He appointed a commission that included representatives of the union as well as the community. Within weeks, the miners went back to work with a 10 percent raise.

Meat Inspection and Pure Food and Drugs

Roosevelt's first major legislative reform began almost accidentally in 1904 when Upton Sinclair, a 26-year-old muckraking journalist, started research on the Chicago stockyards. Sinclair boarded at the University of Chicago Settlement while he did research, conducted interviews, and wrote the story that would be published in 1906 as *The Jungle*.

Sinclair's novel told of the Rudkus family, who emigrated from Lithuania to Chicago filled with ambition and hope. But the American dream failed for them. Sinclair documented exploitation in his fictional account, but his description of contaminated meat drew more attention.

Selling 25,000 copies in its first six weeks, *The Jungle* disturbed many people, including Roosevelt, who ordered a study of the meat-packing industry. The resulting Meat Inspection Act of 1906 was a compromise. It enforced some federal inspection and mandated sanitary conditions in all companies selling meat in interstate commerce, but it did not require the dating of all meat. But the bill was a beginning. It illustrates how muckrakers, social justice progressives, and public outcry eventually led to reform legislation. It also shows how Roosevelt used the public mood and manipulated the political process to get a bill through Congress.

Taking advantage of the publicity that circulated around *The Jungle,* a group of reformers, writers, and government officials pushed for legislation to regulate the sale of food and drugs. Many packaged and canned foods contained dangerous chemicals and impurities. One popular remedy, Hosteter's Stomach Bitters, was revealed on analysis to contain 44 percent alcohol. Coca-Cola, a popular soft drink, contained a small amount of cocaine, and many medicines were laced with opium. Many people, including women and children, became alcoholics or drug addicts in their quest to feel better. The Pure Food and Drug Act, which passed Congress on the same day in 1906 as the Meat Inspection Act, was not a perfect bill, but it prevented some of the worst abuses, including eliminating the cocaine from Coca-Cola.

Conservation Versus Preservation

Although Roosevelt was pleased with the new legislation regulating the food and drug industries, he considered his conservation program his most important domestic achievement. For more than a century, American natural resources ap-peared to be inexhaustible, but by 1900 it had become obvious to many that forests had been destroyed, rivers polluted and filled with silt, land eroded, and other resources exploited for private gain. In 1902, with Roosevelt's enthusiastic support, Congress passed the Newlands Acts, named after Francis Newlands, an ardent conservationist from Nevada. Officially known as the National Reclamation Act, it set aside the proceeds from the sale of public land in sixteen western states to pay for the construction of irrigation projects in those states. Although it tended to help big farmers more than small producers, the Newlands Act federalized irrigation for the first time.

In 1908, Roosevelt convened a White House Conservation Conference, which resulted in the appointment of a National Conservation Commission charged with making an inventory of the natural resources of the entire country. To chair the commission Roosevelt appointed Gifford Pinchot, forestry expert and ardent conservationist, who advocated selective logging, fire control, and limited grazing on public lands.

Pinchot's policies pleased many in the timber and cattle industries but angered some as too restrictive. Preservationist John Muir, who believed passionately in preserving the land in a wilderness state, denounced the Pinchot approach. Muir helped to organize the Sierra Club in 1892 and also led the successful campaign to create Yosemite National Park in California.

An outdoorsman since his youth, Roosevelt used his executive authority to more than triple the land set aside for national forests, bringing the total to over 150 million acres. Use of such areas increased as many middle-class Americans took up hiking, camping, and other outdoor activities, while children joined the Boy Scouts (founded 1910) and the Camp Fire Girls (1912).

The conflicting philosophies of Pinchot and Muir were dramatically demonstrated by the controversy over Hetch-Hetchy, a remote valley deep within Yosemite National Park. Muir and his followers wanted to keep it an unspoiled wilderness, but the mayor of San Francisco wanted a dam and reservoir to supply his growing city with water. The Hetch-Hetchy affair was fought out in newspapers, magazines, and the halls of Congress, but in the end, the conservationists won out over the preservationists. Roosevelt and Congress sided with Pinchot, the dam was built, and the valley was turned into a lake. But the debate over how to use the nation's land and water would continue throughout the twentieth century.

Progressivism for Whites Only

Like most of his generation, Roosevelt thought in stereotyped racial terms. Although he appointed several qualified blacks to minor federal posts, notably Dr. William D. Crum to head the Charleston, South Carolina, customs house in 1905, at other times he seemed insensitive to the needs and feelings of black Americans. This was especially true in his handling of the Brownsville, Texas, riot of 1906. Members of a black army unit stationed there, angered by discrimination against them, rioted one hot August night. Exactly what happened no one was sure, but one white man was killed and several wounded. Waiting until after the midterm elections of 1906, Roosevelt ordered all 167 members of three companies dishonorably discharged. It was an unjust punishment for an unproved crime, and 66 years later the secretary of the army granted honorable discharges to the men, most of them by that time dead.

During the progressive era, even the most advanced progressives seldom included blacks in their reform schemes. Hull House, like most social settlements, was segregated, although Jane Addams spoke out repeatedly against lynching and supported the founding of the National Association for the Advancement of Colored People in 1909.

The most important black leader who argued for equality and opportunity for his people was W. E. B. Du Bois. As revealed in Chapter 18, Du Bois differed dramatically with Booker T. Washington on strategies to improve the position of blacks in American life. While Washington advocated vocational education, Du Bois argued for the best education possible for the most talented tenth of the black population. While Washington preached compromise and accommodation to the dominant white society, Du Bois increasingly urged militant action to assure equality. Du Bois called a meeting of young and militant blacks in 1905. They met in Canada, not far from Niagara Falls, and issued an angry statement. "We want to *pull down* nothing but we don't propose to be pulled down," the platform announced. "We believe in *taking what we can get* but we don't believe in being satisfied with it and in permitting anybody for a moment to imagine we're satisfied." The Niagara movement, as it came to be called, combined with the NAACP in 1910, and Du Bois became editor of its journal, *The Crisis*. The NAACP was a typical progressive organization, seeking to work within the American system to promote reform. But to Roosevelt and many others who called themselves progressives, the NAACP seemed dangerously radical.

William Howard Taft

After eight years as president, Roosevelt decided to step down. He handpicked as his successor William Howard Taft, who had been a distinguished lawyer, federal judge, and Roosevelt's secretary of war. After defeating William Jennings Bryan for the presidency in 1908, Taft quickly ran into difficulties. In some ways, he seemed more progressive than Roosevelt. His administration instituted more suits against monopolies in one term than Roosevelt had in his nearly two full terms. He supported the eight-hour workday and legislation to make mining safer and urged the passage of the Mann-Elkins Act in 1910, which strengthened the ICC

Tuskegee Institute followed Booker T. Washington's philosophy of black advancement through accommodation to the white status quo. Here students study American history, but most of their time was spent in vocational training.

by giving it more power to set railroad rates and extending its jurisdiction over telephone and telegraph companies. Taft and Congress also authorized the first tax on corporate profits. He also encouraged the process that eventually led to the passage of the federal income tax, which was authorized under the Sixteenth Amendment, ratified in 1913. That probably did more to transform the relationship of the government to the people than all other progressive measures combined.

Taft's biggest problem was his style. He was a huge man, weighing over 300 pounds. An uninspired speaker, he also lacked Roosevelt's political skills. Many progressives were annoyed when he signed the Payne-Aldrich Tariff, which midwesterners thought left rates on cotton and

wool cloth and other items too high and played into the hands of the eastern industrial interests. Even Roosevelt was infuriated when his successor reversed many of his conservation policies. Roosevelt broke with Taft, letting it be known that he was willing to run again for president. This set up one of the most exciting and significant elections in American history.

The Election of 1912

Woodrow Wilson won the Democratic nomination for president in 1912. Born two years before Roosevelt, Wilson was the son and grandson of Presbyterian ministers. Well educated, with a Ph.D. from the Johns Hopkins University in Baltimore, Wilson published a book, *Congressional Government* (1885), that established his reputation as a shrewd analyst of American politics. He taught history briefly at Bryn Mawr College near Philadelphia and at Wesleyan in Connecticut before moving to Princeton. Less flamboyant than Roosevelt, he was an excellent public speaker with the power to convince people with his words.

In 1902, Wilson was elected president of Princeton University. Later, as governor of New Jersey, he showed courage as he quickly alienated some of the conservatives who had helped to elect him. Building a coalition of reformers, he worked with them to pass a direct primary law and a workers' compensation law. He also created a commission to regulate transportation and public utility companies. By 1912, Wilson not only was an expert on government and politics but had also acquired the reputation of a progressive.

Roosevelt, who lost the Republican nomination to Taft, startled the nation by walking out of the convention and forming a new political party, the Progressive Party. The new party would not have been formed without Roosevelt, but the party was always more than Roosevelt. It appealed to progressives from all over the country who had become frustrated with the conservative leadership in both major parties.

Many social workers and social justice progressives supported the Progressive Party because of its platform, which contained provisions they had been advocating for years. The Progressives supported an eight-hour day, a six-day week, the abolition of child labor under age 16, and a federal system of accident, old age, and unemployment insurance. Unlike the Democrats, the Progressives also endorsed woman suffrage. Most supporters of the Progressives in 1912 did not realistically think they could win, but they were convinced that they could organize a new political movement that would replace the Republican Party, just as the Republicans had replaced the Whigs after 1856.

The enthusiasm for Roosevelt and the Progressive Party was misleading, for behind the unified facade lurked many disagreements. Roosevelt had become more progressive on many issues since leaving the presidency. He even attacked the financiers "to whom the acquisition of untold millions is the supreme goal of life, and who are too often utterly indifferent as to how these millions are obtained." But he was not as committed to social reform as some of the delegates. Perhaps the most divisive issue was the controversy over seating black delegates from several southern states. A number of social justice progressives fought hard to include a plank in the platform supporting equality for blacks and for seating the black delegation. Roosevelt, however, did not agree with them, and in the end, he prevailed.

The political campaign in 1912 became a contest primarily between Roosevelt and Wilson, with Taft, the Republican candidate and incumbent, ignored by most reporters who covered the campaign. Roosevelt spoke of the "New Nationalism." In a modern industrial society, he argued, large corporations were "inevitable and necessary." What was needed was not the breakup of the trusts but a strong president and increased power in the hands of the federal government to regulate business and industry and to ensure the rights of labor, women and children, and other groups.

Wilson talked of the "New Freedom." He emphasized the need for the Jeffersonian tradition of limited government with open competition. He spoke of the "curse of bigness" and argued against too much federal power: "If America is not to have free enterprise, then she can have freedom of no sort whatever." "What I fear is a government of experts," Wilson declared, implying that Roosevelt's New Nationalism would lead to regulated monopoly and even collectivism.

The level of debate during the campaign was impressive, making this one of the few elections in American history when important ideas were actually discussed. It also marked a watershed for political thought for liberals who rejected Jefferson's distrust of a strong central government. It is easy to exaggerate the differences between Roosevelt and Wilson. Both of them urged reform within the American system. Both defended corporate capitalism, and both opposed socialism and radical labor organizations such as the IWW. Both wanted to promote more democracy and to strengthen conservative labor unions. Both were very different in style and substance from the fourth candidate, Eugene Debs, who ran on the Socialist Party ticket in 1912.

Debs, in 1912, was the most important socialist leader in the country. Although socialism was always a minority movement in the United States, it had its greatest success in the first decade of the twentieth century. Thirty-three cities including Milwaukee, Wisconsin; Reading, Pennsylvania; Butte, Montana; Jackson, Michigan; and Berkeley, California, chose socialist mayors. Socialists Victor Berger from Wisconsin and Meyer London from New York were elected to Congress. The most important socialist periodical, *Appeal to Reason,* published in Girard, Kansas, increased its circulation from about 30,000 in 1900 to nearly 300,000 in 1906. Socialism appealed to some reformers, frustrated with the slow progress of reform, and to recent immigrants, who brought with them a European sense of class differences.

A tremendously appealing figure and a great orator, Debs had run for president in 1900, 1904, and 1908, but in 1912 he reached much wider audiences in more parts of the country. His message called for "wresting control of government and industry from the capitalists and making the working class the ruling class of the nation and the world." Debs polled almost 900,000 votes in 1912 (6 percent of the popular vote), the best showing ever for a socialist in the United States. Wilson received 6.3 million votes, Roosevelt a little more than 4 million, and Taft

3.5 million. Wilson garnered 435 electoral votes, Roosevelt 88, and Taft only 8.

WOODROW WILSON AND THE NEW FREEDOM

Wilson was elected largely because Roosevelt and the Progressive Party split the Republican vote. But once elected, Wilson became a vigorous and aggressive chief executive. Like Roosevelt, Wilson became more progressive during his presidency.

Tariff and Banking Reform

Wilson was not as charismatic as Roosevelt, but he was an outstanding orator who dominated through the force of his intellect. His ability to push his legislative program through Congress during his first two years in office was matched only by Franklin Roosevelt during the first months of the New Deal and by Lyndon Johnson in 1965.

Within a month of his inauguration, Wilson went before a joint session of Congress to outline his legislative program. By appearing in person before Congress, he broke a precedent established by Thomas Jefferson. First on his agenda was tariff reform. The Underwood Tariff, passed in 1913, was not a free-trade bill, but it did reduce the schedule for the first time in many years.

Attached to the Underwood bill was a provision for a small and slightly graduated income tax, which had been made possible by the passage of the Sixteenth Amendment. The income tax was enacted to replace the money lost from lowering the tariff. Wilson seemed to have no interest in using it to redistribute wealth in America.

The next item on Wilson's agenda was reform of the banking system. A financial panic in 1907 had revealed the need for a central bank, but few people could agree on the exact nature of the reforms. A congressional committee, led by Arsène Pujo of Louisiana, had revealed a massive consolidation of banks and trust companies and a system of interlocking directorates and informal arrangements that concentrated resources and power in the hands of a few firms such as the J. P. Morgan Company. But talk of banking reform alarmed conservative Democrats and the business community.

The bill that passed Congress established the Federal Reserve System, providing for 12 Federal Reserve Banks and a Federal Reserve Board appointed by the president. The bill also created a flexible currency, based on federal reserve notes, that could be expanded or contracted as the situation required. The Federal Reserve System, while not perfect, appealed to the progressives' desire for order and efficiency.

Despite these reform measures, Wilson was not very progressive in some of his actions during his first two years in office. He failed to support proposed long-term rural credit financed by the federal government, a woman suffrage amendment, and an anti–child labor bill. He also ordered the segregation of blacks in several federal departments. When southern Democrats, suddenly in control in many departments, began dismissing black federal officeholders, especially those "who boss white girls," Wilson did nothing.

Moving Closer to a New Nationalism

How to control the great corporations in America was a question Wilson and Roosevelt debated extensively during the campaign. Wilson's solution was the Clayton Act, submitted to Congress in 1914. The bill prohibited a number of unfair trading practices, outlawed the interlocking directorate, and made it illegal for corporations to purchase stock in other corporations if this tended to reduce competition. Labor leaders protested that the bill had no provision exempting labor organizations from prosecution under the Sherman Anti-Trust Act. When a section was added exempting both labor and agricultural organizations, Samuel Gompers hailed it as labor's Magna Carta. It was hardly that, because the courts interpreted the provision so that labor unions remained subject to court injunctions during strikes despite the Clayton Act.

More important than the Clayton Act, which both supporters and opponents realized was too vague to be enforced, was the creation of the Federal Trade Commission (FTC), modeled after the ICC, with enough power to move directly against corporations accused of restricting competition. The Federal Trade Commission, however, did not end monopoly, and the courts in the next two decades did not increase the government's power to regulate business.

Neither Roosevelt nor Wilson satisfied the demands of the advanced progressives. Most of the efforts of the two progressive presidents were spent trying to regulate economic power rather than to promote social justice. Their most important legacy, however, was that they reasserted presidential authority, modernized the executive branch, and began the creation of the federal bureaucracy, which has had a major impact on the lives of Americans in the twentieth century.

Both Roosevelt and Wilson used the presidency as a "bully pulpit" to make pronouncements, create news, and influence policy. For example, both presidents called White House conferences and appointed committees and commissions. Roosevelt strengthened the Interstate Commerce Commission and Wilson created the Federal Trade Commission, both of which were the forerunners of many other federal regulatory bodies. And by breaking precedent and actually delivering his annual message in person before a joint session of Congress, Wilson symbolized the new power of the presidency.

The new bureaus, committees, and commissions brought to Washington a new kind of expert, trained in the universities, at the state and local level, and in the voluntary organizations.

The expert, the commission, the statistical survey, and the increased power of the executive branch were all legacies of the progressive era.

CONCLUSION

THE LIMITS OF PROGRESSIVISM

The progressive era was a time when many Americans set out to promote reform because they saw poverty, despair, and disorder in a country transformed by immigration, urbanism, and industrialism. The progressives, largely middle-class whites, sought to help the poor, the immigrants, and the working class, but they rarely worried about blacks. They talked of the need for more democracy, but they often succeeded in promoting bureaucracy and a government run by experts. They believed there was a need to regulate business, promote efficiency, and spread social justice, but their regulatory laws tended to aid business and to strengthen corporate capitalism. By contrast, most of the industrialized nations of western Europe passed legislation during this period providing for old-age pensions and health and unemployment insurance.

Progressivism had its roots in the 1890s and reached a climax in the early twentieth century. Women played important roles in organizing reform and eventually began to fill positions in the new agencies in the state capitals and in Washington. Neither Theodore Roosevelt nor Woodrow Wilson was an advanced progressive, but during both their administrations, progressivism achieved some success. Progressivism would be altered by World War I, but it survived, with its strengths and weaknesses, to affect American society through most of the twentieth century.

Recommended Reading

A good starting point for exploring the progressive movement is Arthur S. Link and Richard L. McCormick, *Progressivism* (1983). Intellectual background is provided in David Noble, *The Progressive Mind, 1890–1917* (1970). Paul Boyer, *Urban Masses and Moral Order in America, 1820–1920* (1978), finds a continuity of the reform impulse across a century and rates fear of immigrants and a desire for social control as the most important ingredients of progressivism. Robert M. Crunden, *Ministers of Reform* (1982), stresses the religious motivation and includes art, architecture, literature, and music in his analysis. More recent studies include Robert B. Westbrook,

John Dewey and American Democracy (1991); and Susan Curtis, *Consuming Faith: The Social Gospel and Modern American Culture* (1991).

Allen F. Davis, *Spearheads for Reform* (1967), emphasizes the social justice movement. Ruth Rosen, *The Lost Sisterhood* (1982); and Mark T. Connelly, *The Response to Prostitution in the Progressive Era* (1980), tell the fascinating story of the crusade against prostitution. Louis Filler, *The Muckrakers* (1976), is the best place to begin a study of the journalists who helped to create a social movement. Dewey W. Grantham, *Southern Progressivism* (1983), details the impact of the movement in a region often thought to have missed much of the reform impulse. The struggle for women's rights can be followed in Aileen S. Kraditor, *The Ideas of the Woman Suffrage Movement, 1890–1920* (1965). August Meier, *Negro Thought in America, 1880–1915* (1963), is still the best introduction to black movements during the progressive period. David Montgomery, *The Fall of the House of Labor* (1988), tells the story of workers and the labor movement during the period.

John Morton Blum, *The Progressive Presidents* (1980), and John Milton Cooper, Jr., *The Warrior and the Priest* (1983), give interesting interpretations of Roosevelt and Wilson. Nick Salvatore, *Eugene V. Debs* (1982), is the best biography of America's most influential radical.

Relevant novels include Theodore Dreiser, *Sister Carrie* (1900), a classic of social realism; Upton Sinclair, *The Jungle* (1906), a muckraking novel about the meatpacking industry; and Charlotte Perkins Gilman, *Herland* (1915), the story of a female utopia.

Time Line

1901	McKinley assassinated; Theodore Roosevelt becomes president Robert La Follette elected governor of Wisconsin Tom Johnson elected mayor of Cleveland U.S. Steel formed	**1909**	Herbert Croly publishes *The Promise of American Life* NAACP founded
1902	Anthracite coal strike	**1910**	Ballinger-Pinchot controversy Mann-Elkins Act
1903	Women's Trade Union League founded	**1911**	Frederick Taylor publishes *The Principles of Scientific Management* Triangle Shirtwaist Company fire
1904	Roosevelt elected president Lincoln Steffens publishes *The Shame of the Cities*	**1912**	Progressive Party founded by Theodore Roosevelt Woodrow Wilson elected president Children's Bureau established Industrial Relations Commission founded
1905	Frederic C. Howe writes *The City: The Hope of Democracy* Industrial Workers of the World formed	**1913**	Sixteenth Amendment (income tax) ratified Underwood Tariff Federal Reserve System established Seventeenth Amendment (direct election of senators) passed
1906	Upton Sinclair publishes *The Jungle* Meat Inspection Act Pure Food and Drug Act	**1914**	Clayton Act AFL has over two million members Ludlow Massacre in Colorado
1907	Financial panic		
1908	*Muller* v. *Oregon* *Danbury Hatters* case William Howard Taft elected president		

chapter 22

The Great War

On April 7, 1917, the day after the United States officially declared war on Germany, Edmund P. Arpin, Jr., a young man of 22 from Grand Rapids, Wisconsin, decided to enlist in the army. It was not patriotism that led him to join the army but his craving for adventure and excitement. After training at Fort Sheridan, Illinois, Arpin finally arrived with his unit in Liverpool on December 23, 1917, aboard the *Leviathan*, a German luxury liner that the United States had interned when war was declared and pressed into service as a troop transport. In England, he discovered that American troops were not greeted as saviors. Hostility against the Americans simmered partly because of the previous unit's drunken brawls. Drinking also seems to have been a preoccupation of the soldiers in Arpin's outfit, but Arpin spent most of the endless waiting time learning to play contract bridge.

Arpin saw some of the horror of war when he went to the front with a French regiment as an observer, but his own unit did not engage in combat until October 1918, when the war was almost over. He took part in the bloody Meuse-Argonne offensive, which helped end the war. Wounded in the leg in an assault on an unnamed hill and awarded a Distinguished Service Cross for his bravery, Arpin later learned that the order to attack had been recalled but word had not reached him in time. When the armistice came, Arpin was recovering in a field hospital.

Edward Arpin was in the army for two years. He was one of 4,791,172 Americans who served in the army, navy, or marines. He was one of the two million who went overseas, and one of the 230,074 who were wounded. Some of his friends were among the 48,909 who were killed. When he was mustered out of the army in March 1919, he felt lost and confused, but in time, he settled down. He became a successful businessman, married, and raised a family. A member of the American Legion, he periodically went to conventions and reminisced with men from his division about their escapades in France.

Just as the Great War changed the life of Edmund P. Arpin, Jr., so too did it alter the lives of most Americans. Trends begun during the progressive era accelerated. The power and influence of the federal government increased. Not only did the war promote woman suffrage, prohibition, and public housing, but it also helped to create an administrative bureaucracy that blurred the lines between public and private, between government and business—a trend that would continue throughout the twentieth century.

Woodrow Wilson talked of a "war to end all wars" and a war "to make the world safe for democracy." His optimism, moralism, and missionary zeal helped to transform the war into a great crusade, which most Americans enthusiastically joined.

In this chapter, we travel the twisted path that led the United States into the war and share the wartime experiences of American men and women overseas and at home. The chapter concludes with a look at the idealistic efforts to promote peace at the end of the war.

THE EARLY WAR YEARS

Few Americans expected the Great War that erupted in Europe in the summer of 1914 to affect their lives. When a Serbian student terrorist assassinated Archduke Franz Ferdinand of Austria-Hungary in Sarajevo, the capital of the province of Bosnia, a place most Americans had never heard of, it precipitated a series of events leading to the most destructive war the world had ever known.

The Causes of War

Despite Theodore Roosevelt's successful peacekeeping attempts in the first decade of the century (see Chapter 20), relationships among the European powers had not improved. Intense rivalries for empire turned minor incidents in Africa, Asia, or the Balkans into events that threatened world peace. As European nations armed, they drew up a complex series of treaties. Austria-Hungary and Germany (the Central Powers) became military allies, while Britain, France, and Russia (the Allied Powers) agreed to assist one another in case of attack.

The incident in Sarajevo destroyed the precarious balance of power. The leaders of Austria-Hungary determined to punish Serbia for the assassination. Russia mobilized to aid Serbia. Germany, supporting Austria-Hungary, declared war on Russia and France. England hesitated, but when Germany invaded Belgium in order to attack France, England declared war, and the slaughter began. Europeans "have reverted to the condition of savage tribes roaming the forests and falling upon each other in a fury of blood and carnage," the New York *Times* announced.

The American sense that the nation would never succumb to the barbarism of war, combined with the fact that the Atlantic Ocean separated Europe from the United States, contributed to a great sense of relief after the first shock of the war began to wear off. Woodrow Wilson's official proclamation of neutrality on August 4, 1914, reinforced the belief that the United States had no major stake in the outcome of the war and would stay uninvolved. The president was preoccupied with his own personal tragedy. His wife, Ellen Axson Wilson, died of Bright's disease the day after his proclamation. Two weeks later, still engulfed by his own grief, he urged all Americans to "be neutral in fact as well as in name, . . . impartial in thought as well as in action."

American Reactions

Many social reformers despaired when they heard the news from Europe. Even during its first months, the war seemed to deflect energy

Europe During the Great War

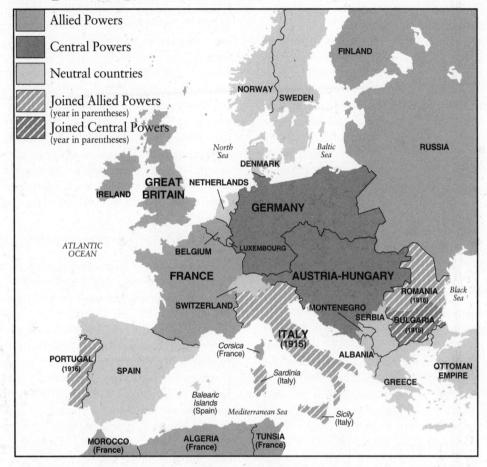

- Allied Powers
- Central Powers
- Neutral countries
- Joined Allied Powers (year in parentheses)
- Joined Central Powers (year in parentheses)

The Great War had an impact on all of Europe, even on the few countries that managed to remain neutral. Russia left the war in 1917, the same year that the United States joined the fight.

away from reform. Jane Addams of Hull House helped to organize the Woman's Peace Party.

While many people worked to promote an international plan to end the war through mediation, others could hardly wait to take part in the great adventure. Hundreds of young American men, most of them students or recent college graduates, volunteered to join ambulance units, to take part in the war effort without actually fighting. Among the most famous of them were Ernest Hemingway, John Dos Passos, and E. E. Cummings, who later turned their wartime adventures into literary masterpieces. Others volunteered for service with the French Foreign Legion or joined the Lafayette Escadrille, a unit of pilots made up of well-to-do American volunteers attached to the French army. Many of these young men were inspired by an older generation who pictured war as a romantic and manly adventure. One college president talked of the chastening and purifying effect of armed conflict, while Theodore Roosevelt projected an image of war that was something like a football game, where red-blooded American men could test their idealism and manhood.

Alan Seeger, a writer and poet who believed in the noble purpose of the war, joined the French Foreign Legion. "You have no idea how beautiful it is to see the troops undulating along the road . . . with the captains and lieutenants on horse back at the head of the companies," he wrote his mother. When Seeger was killed in 1916, he became an instant hero.

Many Americans visualized war as a romantic struggle for honor and glory because the only conflict they remembered was the "splendid little war" of 1898. But this would be a cruel modern war in which men died by the thousands, cut down by a more efficient technology of killing.

The New Military Technology

The German Schlieffen plan called for a rapid strike through Belgium to attack Paris and the French army from the rear. However, the French stopped the German advance at the Battle of the Marne in September 1914, and the fighting soon bogged down in a costly and bloody routine. Soldiers on both sides dug miles of trenches and strung out barbed wire to protect them. Thousands died in battles that gained only a few yards or nothing at all. Rapid-firing rifles, improved explosives, incendiary shells, smokeless bullets, and tracer bullets all added to the destruction. Most devastating of all, however, was the improved artillery, sometimes mounted on trucks and directed by spotters using wireless radios, that could fire over the horizon and hit targets many miles behind the lines.

The technology of defense, especially the machine gun, neutralized the frontal assault, the most popular military tactic since the American Civil War. As one writer explained: "Three men and a machine gun can stop a battalion of heroes." But the generals on both sides continued to order their men to charge to their almost certain deaths.

The war was both a traditional and a revolutionary struggle. It was the last war in which cavalry was used and the first that employed new military technologies. By 1918, airplanes, initially used only for observation, were creating terror below with their bombs. Tanks made their first tentative appearance in 1916, but it was not until the last days of the war that this new offensive weapon began to neutralize the machine gun. Poison gas, first used in 1914, added a new element of fear to a war of already unspeakable horror. But then military technicians on both sides developed the gas mask, allowing the defense to counter the new offensive weapons.

Difficulties of Neutrality

Despite Wilson's efforts to promote neutrality, ties of language and culture tipped the balance for most Americans in favor of the Allied cause. About eight million Austrian- and German-Americans lived in the United States, and some supported the cause of the Central Powers. They viewed Kaiser Wilhelm II's Germany as a progressive parliamentary democracy. The anti-British sentiment of some Irish-Americans led them to take sides not so much for Germany as against England. A few Swedish-Americans distrusted Russia so vehemently that they had difficulty supporting the Allies. A number of American scholars, physicians, and intellectuals fondly remembered studying in Germany. To them, Germany meant great universities and cathedrals, music and culture. It also represented social planning, health insurance, unemployment compensation, and many programs for which the progressives had been fighting.

Other reasons made real neutrality nearly impossible. American trade with the Allies was much more important than with the Central Powers. Wilson's advisers, especially Robert Lansing and Edward House, openly supported the French and the British, as did most newspaper owners and editors. Gradually for Wilson, and probably for most Americans, the perception that England and France were fighting to preserve civilization from the forces of Prussian evil replaced the idea that all Europeans were barbaric and decadent. But the American people were not yet willing to go to war to save civilization. Let France and England do that.

Woodrow Wilson also sympathized with the Allies for practical and idealistic reasons. He believed that by keeping the United States out of the war, he might control the peace. The war, he hoped, would show the futility of imperialism and would usher in a world of free trade in products and ideas.

Remaining neutral while maintaining trade with the belligerents became increasingly difficult. Remaining neutral while speaking out about the peace eventually became impossible. The need to trade and the desire to control the peace finally led the United States into the Great War.

World Trade and Neutrality Rights

The United States was part of an international economic community in 1914 in a way that it had not been a hundred years earlier during the Napoleonic Wars. The outbreak of war in the summer of 1914 caused an immediate economic panic in the United States. On July 31, 1914, the Wilson administration closed the stock exchange to prevent the unloading of European securities and panic selling. It also adopted a policy discouraging loans by American banks to belligerent nations. Most difficult was the matter of neutral trade. Wilson insisted on the rights of Americans to trade with both the Allies and the Central Powers, but Great Britain instituted an illegal naval blockade, mined the North Sea, and began seizing American ships, even those carrying food and raw materials to Italy, the Netherlands, and other neutral nations.

Wilson eventually accepted British control of the seas. His conviction that the destinies of the United States and Great Britain were inter-

twined outweighed his idealistic belief in free trade. Consequently, American trade with the Allies rose while with the Central Powers it declined. At the same time, the United States government eased restrictions on private loans to belligerents, and the British and French quickly obtained loans.

Germany retaliated against British control of the seas with submarine warfare. The new weapon, the U-boat (*Unterseeboot*), created unprecedented problems. Nineteenth-century international law obligated a belligerent warship to warn a passenger or merchant ship before attacking, but the chief advantage of the submarine was surprise. Rising to the surface to issue a warning would have meant being blown out of the water by an armed merchant ship.

On February 4, 1915, Germany announced a submarine blockade of the British Isles. Until Britain gave up its campaign to starve the German population, the Germans would sink even neutral ships. Wilson warned Germany that it would be held to "strict accountability" for illegal destruction of American ships or lives.

On May 7, 1915, a German U-boat torpedoed the British luxury liner *Lusitania* off the Irish coast. The liner, which was not armed but was carrying war supplies, sank in 18 minutes. Nearly 1,200 people, including many women and children, drowned. Among the dead were 128 Americans. Suddenly Americans confronted the horror of total war fought with modern weapons, a war that killed civilians, including women and children, just as easily as it killed soldiers.

Although some Americans called for a declaration of war, Wilson and most Americans had no idea of going to war in the spring of 1915, but the president refused to take William Jennings Bryan's advice and prevent further loss of American lives by simply prohibiting all Americans from traveling on belligerent ships. Instead, he sent a series of protest notes demanding reparation for the loss of American lives and a pledge from Germany that it would cease attacking ocean liners without warning. Bryan resigned as secretary of state over the tone of the notes and charged that the United States was not being truly neutral. The president replaced him with Robert Lansing, who was much more eager than Bryan to oppose Germany, even at the risk of war.

The tense situation eased late in 1915. After a German U-boat sank the British steamer *Arabic,* claiming two American lives, the German ambassador promised that Germany would not attack ocean liners without warning (the *Arabic* pledge). But the *Lusitania* crisis caused an outpouring of books and articles urging the nation to prepare for war. Preparedness groups called for a bigger army and navy and a system of universal military training.

Wilson sympathized with the preparedness groups, and despite great opposition, especially from southern and western congressmen, he signed the Army Reorganization Bill in June 1916. This law increased the regular army to just over 200,000 and integrated the National Guard into the defense structure. Few Americans, however, expected those young men to go to war. One of the most popular songs of 1916 was "I Didn't Raise My Boy to Be a Soldier." Even before American soldiers arrived in France, however, Wilson used the army and the marines in Mexico and Central America.

Intervening in Mexico and Central America

Woodrow Wilson came to office in 1913 planning to promote liberal and humanitarian ends, not only in domestic policies but also in foreign affairs. Wilson had a vision of a world purged of imperialism, a world of free trade, but a world where American ideas and American products would find their way. With his secretary of state, William Jennings Bryan, Wilson denounced the "big stick" and "dollar diplomacy" of the Roosevelt and Taft years. Yet in the end, his administration used force more systematically than those of his predecessors.

The diplomacy of idealism did not last long. After a disastrous civil war in the Dominican Republic, the United States offered in 1915 to take over the country's finances and police force. But when the Dominican leaders rejected a treaty making their country virtually a protectorate of the United States, Wilson ordered in the marines. They took control of the government in May 1916. Although Americans built roads, schools, and hospitals, people resented their presence. In neighboring Haiti, the situation was different, but the results were similar. The marines landed at Port-au-Prince in the summer of 1915 to prop up a pro-American regime. In Nicaragua, the Wilson administration kept in place the marines sent by Taft in 1912 to preserve the pro-American regime of Adolfo Díaz and acquired the right, through treaty, to intervene at any time to preserve order and protect American property. Except for a brief period in the mid-1920s, the marines remained until 1933.

Wilson's policy of intervention ran into greatest difficulty in Mexico, a country whose rulers had long welcomed American investors. By 1910, Americans controlled 75 percent of the mines, 70 percent of the rubber, and 60 percent of the oil. In 1911, however, Francisco Madero, a reformer, came to power. Two years later, he was deposed and murdered by order of Victoriano Huerta, the head of the army. This was the situation when Wilson became president.

To the shock of many diplomats and businessmen, Wilson refused to recognize the Huerta government. Instead, he set out to remove what he called a "government of butchers" and "to exert every influence [the U.S.] can to secure Mexico a better government under which all contracts and business concessions will be safer than they have ever been." When the United States landed troops at Veracruz, angry Mexican mobs destroyed American property wherever they could find it. Wilson's action outraged many Europeans and Latin Americans as well as Americans.

Wilson's military intervention succeeded in forcing Huerta out of power, but a civil war had erupted between forces led by Venustiano Carranza and those led by General Francisco "Pancho" Villa. With arms from the United States, Carranza, who was considered less radical than Villa, was victorious. When an angry Villa led what was left of his army in a raid on Columbus, New Mexico, in March 1916, Wilson sent an expedition under Brigadier General John Pershing to track down Villa and his men. Pershing's army charged 300 miles into Mexico but was unable to catch the retreating rebel. Tensions rose as Wilson refused to withdraw the American troops. In January 1917, just as war with Mexico seemed inevitable, Wilson agreed to recall the troops and to recognize the Carranza government. If it had not been for the growing crisis in Europe, it is likely that war would have resulted.

The tragedy was that Wilson, who idealistically wanted the best for the people of Mexico and Central America and who thought he knew exactly what they needed, managed to intervene too often and too blatantly to protect the strategic and economic interests of the United States. In the process, his policy alienated onetime friends of the United States.

THE UNITED STATES ENTERS THE WAR

A significant minority of Americans opposed going to war in 1917, but once involved, the government and the American people made the war into a patriotic crusade.

The Election of 1916

As 1915 turned to 1916, Wilson had to think of reelection as well as of preparedness, submarine warfare, and the Mexican campaign. At first glance, the president's chances of reelection seemed poor. He had won in 1912 only because Theodore Roosevelt and the Progressive Party had split the Republican vote.

Wilson was aware that he had to win over progressive voters who had favored Roosevelt in 1912. In January 1916, he appointed Louis D. Brandeis to the Supreme Court. The first Jew ever to sit on the High Court, Brandeis had always championed reform causes. In August, Wilson put heavy pressure on Congress and obtained passage of the Workmen's Compensation Bill, which gave some protection to federal employees, and the Keatings-Owen Child Labor Bill, which prohibited the shipment in interstate commerce of goods produced by children under 14 and in some cases under 16. The Keatings-Owen bill, later declared unconstitutional, was a far-reaching proposal that for the first time used federal control over interstate commerce to dictate the conditions under which businessmen could manufacture products.

To attract farm and labor support, Wilson supported the Federal Farm Loan Act, which created 12 Federal Farm Loan Banks to extend long-term credit to farmers, and the Adamson Act, which established an eight-hour day for all interstate railway workers. Within a few months, Wilson reversed the New Freedom doctrines he had earlier supported and brought the force of the federal government into play on the side of reform. The flurry of legislation early in 1916 provided one climax to the progressive movement. The strategy seemed to work, for progressives of all kinds enthusiastically endorsed the president.

The Republicans nominated Charles Evans Hughes, a former governor of New York and future Supreme Court justice. Their platform called for neutrality and preparedness. As the campaign progressed, the peace issue became more and more important, and the cry "He kept us out of war" echoed through every Democratic rally.

The election was extremely close. In fact, Wilson went to bed on election night thinking he had lost the presidency. He won by carrying the West as well as the South.

Deciding for War

In January 1917, Wilson went before the Senate and outlined a plan for a negotiated settlement before either side had achieved victory. It would be a peace among equals, "a peace without victory," a peace without indemnities and annexations.

The German government refused to accept a peace without victory and on January 31, 1917, announced that it would sink on sight any ship, belligerent or neutral, sailing toward England or France. In retaliation, the United States broke diplomatic relations with Germany. As goods began to pile up in warehouses and American ships stayed idly in port, however, pressure mounted to arm American merchant ships. An intercepted telegram from the German foreign secretary, Arthur Zimmermann, to the German minister in Mexico increased anti-German feeling. If war broke out, the German minister was to offer Mexico the territory it had lost in Texas, New Mexico, and Arizona in 1848. In return, Mexico would join Germany in a war against the United States. When this telegram was released to the press on March 1, 1917, many Americans demanded war against Germany. Wilson still hesitated.

As the country waited on the brink of war, news of revolution in Russia reached Washington. In the long run, that event would prove as important as the war itself. The March 1917 revolution in Russia was a spontaneous uprising of the workers, housewives, and soldiers against the oppressive government of Czar Nicholas II and its inept conduct of the war. At first, Wilson and other Americans were enthusiastic about the new republic led by Alexander Kerensky. The overthrow of the feudal aristocracy seemed in the spirit of the American Revolution. But within months, the revolution took a more extreme turn. Vladimir Ilyich Ulyanov, known as Lenin, returned from exile in Switzerland and led the radical Bolsheviks to victory over the Kerensky regime in November 1917.

Lenin, a brilliant lawyer and revolutionary tactician, was a follower of Karl Marx (1818–1883), a German intellectual and radical philosopher. Believing that capitalism and imperialism went hand in hand, Lenin argued that the only way to end imperialism was to end capitalism. The new Soviet Union, not the United States, was the model for the rest of the world to follow; communism, Lenin predicted, would eventually dominate the globe. The Russian Revolution posed a threat to Wilson's vision of the world and to his plan to bring the United States into the war "to make the world safe for democracy."

More disturbing than the first news of revolution in Russia, however, was the situation in the North Atlantic, where German U-boats sank five American ships between March 12 and March 21, 1917. Wilson no longer hesitated. On April 2, he urged Congress to declare war. The war resolution swept the Senate 82 to 6 and the House of Representatives 373 to 50.

A Patriotic Crusade

Not all Americans applauded the declaration of war. Some pacifists and socialists opposed the war. But whether they supported the war or not, for most Americans in the spring of 1917, the war seemed remote. A few days after the war was declared, one senator, hearing a report on supplies that would be needed by an American army in France, exclaimed, "Good Lord! You're not going to send soldiers over there, are you?"

To convince senators and citizens alike that the war was real and that American participation was just, Wilson appointed a Committee on Public Information, headed by George Creel, a muckraking journalist from Denver. The Creel Committee launched a gigantic propaganda campaign to win support for the war.

The patriotic crusade soon became stri-

The Great War, which seemed to some to be an idealistic crusade, was incredibly costly in lives and property.

dently anti-German and anti-immigrant. Most school districts banned the teaching of German, "a language that disseminates the ideals of autocracy, brutality and hatred." Anything German became suspect. Occasionally, the patriotic fever led to violence. The most notorious incident happened in East St. Louis, which had a large German population. A mob seized Robert Prager, a young German-American, in April 1918, stripped off his clothes, dressed him in an American flag, marched him through the streets, and lynched him. The eventual trial led to the acquittal of the ringleaders on the grounds that the lynching was a "patriotic murder."

The Wilson administration, of course, did not condone domestic violence and murder, but heated patriotism led to irrational hatreds and fears of subversion. Suspect were not only German-Americans but also radicals, pacifists, and others. In New York, the black editors of *The Messenger* were given 2½-year jail sentences for the paper's article "Pro-Germanism Among Negroes." The Los Angeles police ignored complaints that Mexicans were being harassed because after learning of the Zimmer-

mann telegram, they believed that all Mexicans were pro-German. In his home state of Wisconsin, Senator Robert La Follette, who had voted against the war resolution, was burned in effigy.

On June 15, 1917, Congress, at Wilson's behest, passed the Espionage Act, which provided imprisonment of up to 20 years or a fine of up to $10,000, or both, for persons who aided the enemy or who "willfully cause . . . insubordination, disloyalty, mutiny or refusal of duty in the military . . . forces of the United States. . . ." The act also authorized the postmaster general to prohibit from the mails any matter he thought advocated treason or forcible resistance to United States laws. Using the act, Postmaster General Albert S. Burleson banned the magazines *American Socialist* and *The Masses* from the mails.

Congress later added the Trading with the Enemy Act and a Sedition Act. The latter prohibited disloyal, profane, scurrilous, or abusive remarks about the form of government, flag, or uniforms of the United States. Eugene Debs was sentenced to ten years in prison for opposing the war. In 1919, the Supreme Court upheld the conviction, even though Debs had not explicitly urged the violation of the draft laws. Not all Americans agreed with the decision, for while still in prison, Debs polled close to one million votes in the presidential election of 1920. Ultimately, the government prosecuted 2,168 persons under the Espionage and Sedition acts and convicted about half of them. But these figures do not include the thousands informally persecuted and deprived of their liberties and their right of free speech. The attorney general of the United States, speaking of opponents of government policies, said, "May God have mercy on them for they need expect none from an outraged people and an avenging government."

The Civil Liberties Bureau, an outgrowth of the American Union Against Militarism, protested the blatant abridgment of freedom of speech during the war, but the protests fell on deaf ears at the Justice Department and in the White House. Rights and freedoms have been reduced or suspended during all wars, but the massive disregard for basic rights was greater during World War I than during the Civil War. Wilson was so convinced his cause was just that he ignored the rights of those who opposed him.

Raising an Army

How should a democracy recruit an army in time of war? The debate over a volunteer army versus the draft had been going on for several years before the United States entered the war. Wilson and his secretary of war, Newton Baker, both initially opposed the draft. In the end, however, both concluded that it was the most efficient way to organize military manpower. Ironically, it was Theodore Roosevelt who tipped Wilson in favor of the draft. Even though his health was failing and he was blind in one eye, the old Rough Rider was determined to recruit a volunteer division and lead it personally against the Germans. The thought of his old enemy Theodore Roosevelt blustering about Europe so frightened Wilson that he supported the Selective Service Act in part, at least, to prevent such volunteer outfits as Roosevelt planned. On June 5, 1917, some 9.5 million men between the ages of 21 and 31 registered, with little protest. In August 1918, Congress extended the act to men 18 to 45. In all, over 24 million men registered and over 2.8 million were inducted, making up over 75 percent of soldiers who served in the war.

The draft worked well, but not perfectly. Because local draft boards had so much control, favoritism and political influence allowed some to stay at home. Draft protests erupted in a few places, the largest in Oklahoma, where a group of tenant farmers planned a march on Washington to take over the government and end the "rich man's war." The Green Corn Rebellion, as it came to be called, died before it got started. A local posse arrested about 900 rebels and took them off to jail.

Some men escaped the draft. Some were deferred because of war-related jobs, while others resisted by claiming exemption for reasons of conscience. However, thousands of conscientious objectors were inducted. Some accepted noncombat positions; others went to prison for refusing to serve.

THE MILITARY EXPERIENCE

Family albums in millions of American homes contain photographs of young men in uniform, some of them stiff and formal, some of them candid shots of soldiers on leave in Paris or Washington or Chicago. These photographs testify to the importance of the war to a generation of Americans. For some, the war was a tragic event as they saw the horrors of the battlefield firsthand. For others, it was a liberating experience and the most exciting period in their lives.

The American Doughboy

The typical soldier, according to the Medical Department, stood 5 feet 7½ inches tall, weighed 141½ pounds, and was about 22 years old. He probably watched a movie called *Fit to Fight*, which warned him about the dangers of venereal disease. The majority of the American soldiers had not attended high school. The median amount of education for native whites was 6.9 years and for immigrants 4.7 years but was only 2.6 years for southern blacks. As many as 31 percent of the recruits were declared illiterate. Fully 29 percent of the recruits were rejected as physically unfit for service, which shocked the health experts.

Most World War I soldiers were ill-educated and unsophisticated young men. The military experience changed their lives and often their attitudes. Women also contributed to the war effort as telephone operators and clerk-typists in the navy and the marines. Some went overseas as army and navy nurses. Others volunteered for a tour of duty with the Red Cross, the Salvation Army, or the YMCA. Yet the military experience in World War I was predominantly male. Even going to training camp was a new and often frightening experience. A leave in Paris or London, or even in New York or New Orleans, was an adventure to remember for a lifetime. Even those who never got overseas or who never saw a battle experienced subtle changes. Many soldiers saw their first movie in the army or had their first contact with trucks and cars, safety razors, or cigarettes. The war experience also caused many men to abandon the pocket watch for the more convenient wristwatch, which had been considered effeminate before the war.

The Black Soldier

Blacks had served in all American wars, but black soldiers had most often performed menial work and belonged to segregated units. Black leaders hoped it would be different this time. Shortly after the United States entered the war, W. E. B. Du Bois, the black leader and editor of *The Crisis,* predicted that the war experience would cause the "walls of prejudice" to crumble. But the walls did not crumble, and the black soldier never received equal or fair treatment during the war.

White draft boards were more generous in exempting whites than blacks. Jim Crow laws also posed problems for black soldiers. In August 1917, violence erupted in Houston, Texas, involving soldiers from the regular army's all-black 24th Infantry Division. Harassed by the Jim Crow laws, which had been tightened for their benefit, a group of soldiers went on a rampage, killing 17 white civilians. Over 100 soldiers were court-martialed; 13 were condemned to death. Those convicted were hanged three days later before any appeals could be filed. Sec-

retary of War Baker made it clear that the army had no intention of upsetting the status quo. The basic government policy was of complete segregation and careful distribution of black units throughout the country.

Some blacks were trained as junior officers and were assigned to the all-black 92nd Division, where the high-ranking officers were white. But most of the black soldiers, including about 80 percent of those sent to France as stevedores and common laborers, worked under the supervision of white noncommissioned officers. Other black soldiers acted as servants, drivers, and porters for the white officers. It was a demeaning and ironic policy for a government that advertised itself as standing for justice, honor, and democracy.

Over There

The conflict that Wilson called the war "to make the world safe for democracy" had become a contest of stalemate and slaughter. Hundreds of thousands had died on both sides, but victory remained elusive. To this ghastly war Americans made important contributions. In fact, without their help, the Allies might have lost. But the American contribution was most significant only in the war's final months. When the United States entered the conflict in the spring of 1917, the fighting had dragged on for nearly three years. After a few rapid advances and retreats, the war in western Europe had settled down to a tactical and bloody stalemate. By the spring of 1917, the British and French armies were down to their last reserves. Italy's army had nearly collapsed. In the east, the Russians were engaged in a bitter internal struggle, and in November, the Bolshevik Revolution would cause them to sue for a separate peace.

A few token American regiments arrived in France in the summer of 1917 under the command of General John J. "Black Jack" Pershing, who had fought in the Spanish-American War

Assigned to segregated units, black soldiers were also excluded from white recreation facilities. Here black women in Newark, New Jersey, aided by white social workers, entertain black servicemen.

and led the Mexican expedition in 1916. The first Americans saw action near Verdun in October 1917. By March 1918, over 300,000 American soldiers had reached France, and by the time the war ended in November 1918, more than two million.

The United States forces were kept separate from the French and British divisions, with the exception of four regiments of black soldiers who were assigned to the French army. Despite the American warning to the French not to "spoil the Negroes" by allowing them to mix with the French civilian population, these soldiers fought so well that the French later awarded three of the regiments the Croix de Guerre, their highest unit citation.

In the spring of 1918, with Russia out of the war, the Germans launched an all-out, desperate offensive to win the war before full American military and industrial power became a factor in the contest. By late May, the Germans had pushed to within 50 miles of Paris. American troops were thrown into the line and helped stem the German advance. Americans also took part in the Allied offensive led by General Ferdinand Foch of France in the summer of 1918. In September, over one-half million American troops fought near St. Mihiel in the first battle where large numbers of Americans were pressed into action. The Americans suffered over 7,000 casualties, but they captured more than 16,000 German soldiers.

In the fall of 1918, the combined British, French, and American armies drove the Germans back. Faced with low morale among the German soldiers and finally the mutiny of the German fleet and the surrender of Austria, Kaiser Wilhem II abdicated on November 8, and the Armistice was signed on November 11. More than a million American soldiers took part in the final Allied offensive near the Meuse River and the Argonne forest. It was in this battle that

Edmund Arpin was wounded. Many of the men were inexperienced, and some, who had been rushed through training as "90-day wonders," had never handled a rifle before arriving in France. There were many disastrous mistakes and bungled situations.

The all-black 92nd Division, which had been deliberately dispersed around the United States and had never trained as a unit, was ordered at the last minute to a particularly difficult position on the Meuse-Argonne line. They had no maps and no wire-cutting equipment. Battalion commanders lost contact with their men, and on several occasions the men broke and ran in the face of enemy fire. The division was withdrawn in disgrace, and for years politicians and military leaders used this incident to point out that black soldiers would never make good fighting men, ignoring the difficulties under which the 92nd fought and the valor shown by black troops assigned to the French army.

The war produced a few American heroes. Joseph Oklahombie, a Choctaw, overran several German machine gun nests and captured more than 100 German soldiers. Sergeant Alvin York, a former conscientious objector from Tennessee, single-handedly killed or captured 160 Germans using only his rifle and pistol. The press made him a celebrity, but his heroics were not typical. Artillery, machine guns, and, near the end, tanks, trucks, and airplanes won the war.

With few exceptions, the Americans fought hard and well. While the French and British criticized American inexperience and disarray, they admired their exuberance, their "pep," and their ability to move large numbers of men and equipment efficiently. Sometimes it seemed that Americans simply overwhelmed the enemy with their numbers.

The United States entered the war late but still lost more than 48,000 service personnel and had many more wounded. Disease claimed 15 of every 1,000 American soldiers each year (compared with 65 per 1,000 in the Civil War). But the British lost 900,000 men, the French 1.4 million, and the Russians 1.7 million. The United States contributed huge amounts of men and supplies in the last months of the war, and that finally tipped the balance. But it had entered late and sacrificed little compared to France and England. That would influence the peace settlement.

The end of the Great War brought relief and joy to many, but the fall of 1918 also witnessed the outbreak of an unusually lethal flu epidemic. The conditions of life in the war zones and the movement of large numbers of troops and civilian refugees apparently contributed to the emergence of an extremely virulent form of influenza that spread around the world and claimed over 20 million lives. In a two-year period, the virus struck in three waves, becoming more lethal with each advance and killing young men, women, and children as well as the old and weak. In the United States, over half a million died in what may be considered an indirect legacy of the war.

DOMESTIC IMPACT OF THE WAR

For at least 30 years before the United States entered the Great War, a debate raged over the proper role of the federal government in regulating industry and protecting people who could not protect themselves. Even within the Wilson administration, advisers disagreed on the proper role of the federal government. The war and the problems it raised increased the power of the federal government in a variety of ways. The wartime experience did not end the debate, but the United States emerged from the war a more modern nation, with more power residing in Washington.

Financing the War

The war, by one calculation, cost the United States over $33 billion. Interest and veterans' benefits bring the total to nearly $112 billion. Early on, when an economist suggested that the war might cost the United States $10 billion, everyone laughed. Yet many in the Wilson administration knew the war was going to be expensive, and they set out to raise the money by borrowing and by increasing taxes.

Secretary of the Treasury William McAdoo shouldered the task of financing the war. A war must be "a kind of crusade," he remarked. His campaign to sell liberty bonds to ordinary American citizens at a very low interest rate called forth patriotic sentiment. "Lick a Stamp and Lick the Kaiser," one poster urged. Celebrities such as film stars Mary Pickford and Douglas Fairbanks promoted the bonds, and McAdoo employed the Boy Scouts to sell them. "Every Scout to Save a Soldier" was the slogan. The public responded enthusiastically, but they discovered after the war that their bonds had dropped to about 80 percent of face value.

McAdoo's other plan to finance the war involved raising taxes. The War Revenue Act of 1917 boosted the tax rate sharply, levied a tax on excess profits, and increased estate taxes. Another bill the next year raised the tax on the largest incomes to 77 percent. The wealthy protested, but a number of progressives were just as unhappy with the bill, for they wanted to confiscate all income over $100,000 a year. Despite taxes and liberty bonds, however, World War I, like the Civil War, was financed in large part by inflation. Food prices, for example, nearly doubled between 1917 and 1919.

Increasing Federal Power

At first, Wilson tried to work through a variety of state agencies to mobilize the nation's resources. The need for more central control and authority soon led Wilson to create a series of federal agencies to deal with the war emergency. The first crisis was food. Poor grain crops for two years and an increasing demand for American food in Europe caused shortages. To solve the problem, Wilson appointed Herbert Hoover, a young engineer who had won great prestige as head of the Commission for Relief of Belgium, to direct the Food Administration. Hoover set out to meet the crisis not so much through government regulation as through an appeal to the patriotism of farmers and consumers alike. He instituted a series of "wheatless" and "meatless" days and urged housewives to cooperate. In Philadelphia, a large sign announced, "FOOD WILL WIN THE WAR; DON'T WASTE IT."

The War Industries Board, led by Bernard Baruch, a shrewd Wall Street broker, used the power of the government to control scarce materials and, on occasion, to set prices and priorities. The government itself went into the shipbuilding business. The largest shipyard, at Hog Island, near Philadelphia, employed as many as 35,000 workers, but the yard did not launch its first ship until the late summer of 1918—too late to affect the outcome of the war.

The government also got into the business of running the railroads. When a severe winter and a lack of coordination brought the rail system near collapse in December 1917, Wilson put all the nation's railroads under the control of the United Railway Administration. The government spent more than $500 million to improve the rails and equipment, and in 1918 the railroads did run more efficiently than they had under private control. Some businessmen resented government rules and regulations, but most came to agree with Baruch that a close working relationship with government could improve the quality of their products, promote efficiency, and increase profits.

War Workers

The Wilson administration sought to protect and extend the rights of organized labor during the war, while at the same time mobilizing the workers necessary to keep the factories running. The National War Labor Board insisted on adequate wages and reduced hours, and it tried to prevent the exploitation of women and children working under government contracts. On one

Women proved during the war that they could do "men's work." These shipyard workers even dressed like men, but the war did not change the American ideal that a woman's place was in the home.

occasion, when a munitions plant refused to accept the War Labor Board's decision, the government simply took over the factory. When workers threatened to strike, the board often ruled that they either work or be drafted into the army.

The Wilson administration favored the conservative labor movement of Samuel Gompers and the AFL, while the Justice Department put the radical Industrial Workers of the World "out of business." Beginning in September 1917, federal agents conducted massive raids on IWW offices and arrested most of the leaders.

Samuel Gompers took advantage of the crisis to strengthen the AFL's position to speak for labor. He made it clear that he opposed the IWW as well as socialists and communists. Convincing Wilson that it was important to protect the rights of organized labor during wartime, he announced that "no other policy is compatible with the spirit and methods of democracy." As the AFL won a voice in homefront policy, its membership increased from 2.7 million in 1916 to over 4 million in 1917. Organized labor's wartime gains, however, would prove only temporary.

The war opened up industrial employment

opportunities for black men. With four million men in the armed forces and the flow of immigrants interrupted by the war, American manufacturers for the first time hired blacks in large numbers. Northern labor agents and the railroads actively recruited southern blacks, but the news of jobs in northern cities spread by word of mouth as well. By 1920, more than 300,000 blacks had joined the "great migration" north. As blacks moved north, thousands of Mexicans crossed into the United States as immigration officials relaxed the regulations because of the need for labor in the farms and factories of the Southwest.

The war also created new employment opportunities for women. One poster announced, "Stenographers, Washington Needs You." Women responded to these appeals out of patriotism, as well as out of a need to increase their earnings and to make up for inflation, which diminished real wages. Women went into every kind of industry. They labored in brickyards and in heavy industry, became conductors on the railroad, and turned out shells in munition plants. They even organized the Woman's Land Army to mobilize female labor for the farms. They demonstrated that women could do any kind of job, whatever the physical or intellectual demands. One black woman who gave up her position as a live-in servant to work in a paper-box factory declared:

> I'll never work in nobody's kitchen but my own any more. No indeed, that's the one thing that makes me stick to this job, but when you're working in anybody's kitchen, well you out of luck. You almost have to eat on the run; you never get any time off.

As black women moved out of domestic service, they took jobs in textile mills or even in the stockyards. Racial discrimination, however, even in the North, prevented them from moving very far up the occupational ladder.

The war accelerated trends already under way in women's employment. It increased the need for telephone operators, sales personnel, secretaries, and other white-collar workers, and in these occupations women soon became a majority. Telephone operator, for example, became an almost exclusively female job. There were 15,000 operators in 1900 but 80,000 in 1910, and by 1917 women represented 99 percent of all operators as the telephone network spanned the nation. In the end, the war provided limited opportunities for some women, but after the soldiers returned home, the gains made by women almost disappeared. There were 8 million women in the work force in 1910 and only 8.5 million in 1920.

The Climax of Progressivism

Many progressives, especially the social justice progressives, opposed the United States' entry into the war until a few months before the nation declared war. But after April 1917, many began to see the "social possibilities of war." They deplored the death and destruction, the abridgment of freedom of speech, and the patriotic spirit that accompanied the war. But they praised the social planning stimulated by the conflict. They approved the Wilson administration's support of collective bargaining, the eight-hour day, and protection for women and children in industry. They welcomed the experiments with government-owned housing projects, woman suffrage, and prohibition. Many endorsed the government takeover of the railroads and control of business during the war.

One of the best examples of the progressives' influence on wartime activities was the Commission on Training Camp Activities, set up early in the war to solve the problem of mobilizing, entertaining, and protecting American servicemen at home and abroad. Chairman of the commission was Raymond Fosdick, a former settlement worker. The commission organized community singing, baseball, post exchanges, theaters, and even university extension lectures for the servicemen.

The Commission on Training Camp Activi-

ties also incorporated the progressive crusades against alcohol and prostitution. The Military Draft Act prohibited the sale of liquor to men in uniform and gave the president power to establish zones around military bases where prostitution and alcohol would be prohibited. Some military commanders protested, and at least one city official argued that prostitutes were "God-provided means for the prevention of the violation of innocent girls, by men who are exercising their 'God-given passions.'" Yet the commission, with the full cooperation of the Wilson administration, set out to wipe out sin, or at least to put it out of the reach of servicemen. When the boys go to France, the secretary of war remarked, "I want them to have invisible armour to take with them. I want them to have armour made up of a set of social habits replacing those of their homes and communities."

France tested the "invisible armour." It proved impossible to keep the soldiers away from sex and liquor. Both the British and the French armies had tried to solve the problem of venereal disease by licensing and inspecting prostitutes. Georges Clemenceau, the French premier, found the American attitude toward prostitution difficult to comprehend. On one occasion, he offered to provide the Americans with licensed prostitutes. General Pershing considered the letter containing the offer "too hot to handle." So he gave it to Fosdick, who showed it to Baker, who remarked, "For God's sake, Raymond, don't show this to the President or he'll stop the war." The Americans never accepted Clemenceau's offer, and he continued to be baffled by the American progressive mentality.

Suffrage for Women

In the fall of 1918, while American soldiers were mobilizing for the final offensive in France and hundreds of thousands of women were working in factories and serving as Red Cross and Salvation Army volunteers near the army bases, Woodrow Wilson spoke before the Senate to ask its support of woman suffrage, which he maintained was "vital to the winning of the war." Wilson had earlier opposed the vote for women, and many people still argued that the vote would make women less feminine, more worldly, and less able to perform their primary tasks as wives and mothers.

Carrie Chapman Catt, an efficient administrator and tireless organizer from Iowa, devised the strategy that finally secured the vote for women. In 1915, Catt became president of the National American Woman Suffrage Association (NAWSA), the organization founded in 1890 and based in part on the society organized by Elizabeth Cady Stanton and Susan B. Anthony in 1869. Catt coordinated the state-campaigns with the work in Washington, directing a growing army of dedicated workers. The Washington headquarters sent precise information to the states on ways to pressure congressmen in local districts. In Washington, they maintained a file on each congressman and senator.

The careful planning began to produce results, but a group of more militant reformers, impatient with the slow progress, broke off from NAWSA to form the National Woman's Party (NWP) in 1916. This group was led by Alice Paul, a Quaker from New Jersey, who had participated in some of the suffrage battles in England. Paul and her group picketed the White House, chained themselves to the fence, and blocked the streets. They carried banners that asked, "MR. PRESIDENT, HOW LONG MUST WOMEN WAIT FOR LIBERTY?" In the summer of 1917, the government arrested more than 200 women and charged them with "obstructing the sidewalk." It was just the kind of publicity the militant group sought, and it made the most of it. Wilson, fearing even more embarrassment, began to cooperate with the more moderate reformers.

The careful organizing of the NAWSA and the more militant tactics of the NWP both contributed to the final success of the woman suffrage crusade. Early in 1919, the House of Representatives passed the suffrage amendment 304 to 90, and the Senate approved by a vote of 56 to 25. Fourteen months later, the required 36 states had ratified the amendment, and women at last had the vote.

PLANNING FOR PEACE

On January 8, 1918, in part to counteract the Bolshevik charge that the war was merely a struggle among imperialist powers, Woodrow Wilson announced his plan to organize the peace. Called the Fourteen Points, it argued for "open covenants of peace openly arrived at," freedom of the seas, equality of trade, the self-determination of all peoples. But his most important point, the fourteenth, called for an international organization, a "league of nations," to preserve peace.

The Paris Peace Conference

Late in 1918, Wilson announced that he would head the American delegation in Paris. Wilson's entourage included Secretary of State Lansing, Edward House, and a number of other advisers. Conspicuously missing, however, was Henry Cabot Lodge or any other Republican senator. This would prove a serious blunder, for the Republican-controlled Senate would have to approve any treaty negotiated in Paris. In Paris, Wilson faced the reality of European power politics and ambitions and the personalities of David Lloyd George of Great Britain, Vittorio Orlando of Italy, and Georges Clemenceau of France.

Though Wilson was more naive and more idealistic than his European counterparts, he was a clever negotiator who won many concessions at the peace table, sometimes by threatening to go home if his counterparts would not compromise. The European leaders were determined to punish Germany and enlarge their empires. Wilson, however, believed that he could create a new kind of international relations based on his Fourteen Points. He achieved limited acceptance of the idea of self-determination, his dream that each national group could have its own country and that the people should decide in what country they wanted to live.

The peacemakers carved the new countries of Austria, Hungary, and Yugoslavia out of what had been the Austro-Hungarian Empire. In addition, they created Poland, Czechoslovakia, Finland, Estonia, Latvia, and Lithuania, in part to help contain the threat of bolshevism in eastern Europe. France was to occupy the industrial Saar region of Germany for 15 years, with a plebiscite at the end of that time to determine whether the people wanted to become a part of Germany or France. Italy gained the port city of Trieste.

Wilson won some points at the peace negotiations, but he also had to make major concessions. He was forced to agree that Germany should pay reparations (later set at $56 billion), lose much of its oil- and coal-rich territory, and admit to its war guilt. He accepted a mandate system, to be supervised by the League of Nations, that allowed France and Britain to take over portions of the Middle East and allowed Japan to occupy Germany's colonies in the Pacific. He acquiesced when the Allies turned Germany's African colonies into "mandate possessions" because they did not want to allow the self-determination of blacks in areas they had colonized. Wilson also did not win approval for freedom of the seas or the abolition of trade barriers, but he did gain endorsement for the League of Nations, the organization he hoped would prevent all future wars.

Women for Peace

While the statesmen met at Versailles to sign the peace treaty hammered out in Paris and to divide up Europe, a group of prominent women from all over the world, including many from the Central Powers, met in Zurich, Switzerland. The American delegation was led by Jane Addams and included Florence Kelley of the National Consumers League; Alice Hamilton, a professor at Harvard Medical School; and Jeannette Rankin, a congresswoman from Montana (one

of the few states where women could vote). They met amid the devastation of war to promote a peace that would last. At their conference they formed the Women's International League for Peace and Freedom. Electing Addams president of the new organization, they denounced the harsh peace terms, which called for disarmament of only one side and exacted great economic penalties against the Central Powers. Prophetically, they predicted that the peace treaty would result in the spread of hatred and anarchy and "create all over Europe discords and animosities which can only lead to future wars."

Hate and intolerance were indeed legacies of the war. Also hanging over the peace conference was the Bolshevik success in Russia. The threat of revolution seemed so great that Wilson and the Allies sent American and Japanese troops into Russia in 1919 to attempt to defeat the Bolsheviks and create a moderate republic. But by 1920, the troops had failed in their mission and withdrew.

Wilson's Failed Dream

Probably most Americans supported the concept of the League of Nations in the summer of 1919. Yet in the end, the Senate refused to accept American membership in the League. The League of Nations treaty, one commentator has suggested, was killed by its friends and not by its enemies.

First there was Lodge, who had earlier endorsed the idea of some kind of international peacekeeping organization but who objected to Article 10, claiming that it would force Americans to participate in the wars of foreigners. Then there was Wilson, whose only hope of passage of the treaty in the Senate was a compromise to bring moderate senators to his side. But Wilson refused to compromise or to modify Article 10 to allow Congress the opportunity to decide whether or not the United States would support the League in time of crisis. While stumping the country to win popular support for the League treaty, Wilson collapsed in Pueblo, Colorado. He was rushed back to Washington, where a few days later he suffered a massive stroke. For the next year and a half, the president was incapable of running the government. Protected by his second wife and his closest advisers, Wilson became irritable and depressed and unable to lead a fight for the League. For a year and a half the country limped along without a president.

After many votes and much maneuvering, the Senate finally killed the League treaty in March 1920. Had the United States joined the League of Nations, it probably would have made little difference in the international events of the 1920s and 1930s. Nor would American participation have prevented World War II. The United States did not resign from the world of diplomacy or trade, nor did the United States with that single act become isolated from the rest of the world. But the rejection of the League treaty was symbolic of the refusal of many Americans to admit that the world and America's place in it had changed dramatically since 1914.

CONCLUSION

THE DIVIDED LEGACY OF THE GREAT WAR

For Edmund Arpin and many of his friends, the war was a great adventure. For others who served, the war's results were more tragic. Many died. Some came home injured, disabled by poison gas, or unable to cope with the complex world that had opened up to them.

The war created job opportunities for blacks and women, and farmers suddenly discovered a demand for their products. The passage of the woman's suffrage amendment and the use of federal power to promote justice and order pleased reformers. Once the war ended, however, much federal legislation was dismantled or reduced in effectiveness, and votes for women had little initial impact on social legislation.

The Great War marked the coming of age of the United States as a world power, but the country seemed reluctant to accept the new responsibility. The war stimulated patriotism and pride in the country, but it also increased intolerance. The shared experience of the Great War years, including contact among soldiers from various regions of the country, expanded employment opportunities for blacks and women, and with the growth of advertising, also contributed to the development of a more uniform mass culture. With this mixed legacy from the war, the country entered the new era of the 1920s.

RECOMMENDED READING

On Woodrow Wilson's foreign policy, see Arthur S. Link, *Woodrow Wilson: Revolution, War, and Peace* (1979). Ellis W. Hawley, *The Great War and the Search for Modern Order* (1979), emphasizes the long-term impact of the war.

The best general account of the American military involvement in the Great War is Edward M. Coffman, *The War to End All Wars* (1968). Arthur D. Barbeau and Florette Henri, *The Unknown Soldiers: Black American Troops in World War I* (1974), describes the experience of blacks in the military. David M. Kennedy, *Over Here* (1980), is the most comprehensive survey of the impact of the war on American society.

More specialized studies include Carol S. Gruber, *Mars and Minerva* (1975), on the impact of the war on higher education; and Nancy F. Cott, *The Grounding of Modern Feminism* (1987), on the relationship between suffrage and feminism. Frederick C. Luebke, *Bonds of Loyalty* (1974), details the experience of German-Americans. On the impact of the Russian Revolution on American policy and attitudes, see John L. Gaddis, *Russia, the Soviet Union, and the United States* (1978). For the Mexican intervention,

see P. Edward Haley, *Revolution and Intervention* (1970).

Paul Fussell, *The Great War and Modern Memory* (1975), focuses primarily on the British experience but is indispensable for understanding the importance of the war for the generation that lived through it.

Many novels focus on the war. Erich Maria Remarque highlights the horror of war from the European point of view in *All Quiet on the Western Front* (1929). John Dos Passos shows war as a bitter experience in *Three Soldiers* (1921), and Ernest Hemingway portrays its futility in *Farewell to Arms* (1929).

Time Line

1914	Archduke Ferdinand assassinated; World War I begins American troops invade Mexico and occupy Veracruz
1915	Germany announces submarine blockade of Great Britain *Lusitania* sunk *Arabic* pledge
1916	Expedition into Mexico Wilson reelected Workmen's Compensation Bill Keatings-Owen Child Labor Bill Federal Farm Loan Act National Woman's Party founded
1917	Germany resumes unrestricted submarine warfare United States breaks relations with Germany Zimmermann telegram Russian Revolution

1917	United States declares war on Germany Espionage Act Committee on Public Information established Trading with the Enemy Act Selective Service Act War Industries Board formed
1918	Sedition Act Flu epidemic sweeps nation Wilson's Fourteen Points American troops intervene in Russian Revolution
1919	Paris peace conference Eighteenth Amendment prohibits alcoholic beverages Senate rejects Treaty of Versailles
1920	Nineteenth Amendment grants woman suffrage

chapter 23

Affluence and Anxiety

John and Lizzie Parker were black share-croppers in central Alabama. They had two daughters, one age 6, the other already married. The whole family worked hard in the cotton fields, but they had little to show for their labor. One day in 1917, Lizzie straightened her shoulders and declared, "I'm through. I've picked my last sack of cotton. I've cleared my last field."

Like many southern blacks, the Parkers sought opportunity and a better life in the North. During World War I there was a shortage of workers, and some companies sent special trains into the South to recruit blacks. John Parker signed up with a mining company in West Virginia. The company offered free transportation for his family. "You will be allowed to get your food at the company store and there are houses awaiting for you," the agent promised.

They soon discovered that life in the company town in West Virginia was little better than the life they left in Alabama. John ran away and drifted to Detroit, where he got a job with the American Car and Foundry Company. It was 1918, and the pay was good. After a few weeks, he rented an apartment and sent for his family. For the first time, Lizzie had a gas stove and an indoor toilet, and Sally, who was now 7, started school. It seemed as if their dream had come true.

Detroit was not quite the dream, however. Many whites did not welcome blacks in their neighborhoods. Sally was beaten up by a gang of white youths at school. The Ku Klux Klan also made life uncomfortable for the blacks who had moved north to seek jobs and opportunity.

Suddenly the war ended, and almost immediately John lost his job. The Parkers were forced to leave their apartment for housing in a section just outside the city near Eight Mile Road. This black ghetto had dirt streets and the shack had no indoor plumbing and no electricity, only a pump in the yard and an outhouse.

The recession winter of 1921–1922 was particularly difficult. John could find only part-time employment, while Lizzie worked as a domestic servant for white families. The shack they called home was freezing cold, and it was cramped because their married daughter and her husband had joined them in Detroit.

Lizzie did not give up her dream, however. With strength, determination, and a sense of humor, she kept the family together. By the end of the decade, Sally had graduated from high school, and the Parkers finally had electricity and indoor plumbing in the house, though the streets were still unpaved. The Parkers had improved their lot, but they still lived outside Detroit—and, in many ways, outside America.

Like most Americans in the 1920s, the Parkers pursued the American dream of success. For them, a comfortable house and a steady job, a new bathroom, and an education for their younger daughter constituted that dream. The 1920s has often been referred to as the "jazz age," a time when the American people supposedly had one long party complete with flappers, speakeasies, illegal bathtub gin, and the Charleston. This frivolous interpretation has some basis in fact, but most Americans did not share in the party, for they were too busy struggling to make a living in a tumultuous time of social, economic, and technological change.

In this chapter, we will explore some of the conflicting trends of an exciting decade. First, we will examine the currents of intolerance that influenced almost all the events and social movements of the time. We will also look at some developments in technology, especially the automobile, which changed life for almost everyone during the 1920s and created the illusion of prosperity for all. We will then focus on groups—women, blacks, industrial workers, and farmers—who had their hopes raised but not always fulfilled during the decade. We will conclude by looking at the way business, politics, and foreign policy were intertwined during the age of Harding, Coolidge, and Hoover.

POSTWAR PROBLEMS

The years immediately following the end of World War I were marked by domestic dissension. The enthusiasm for social progress and the sense of common purpose that had energized Americans during the war evaporated. During 1919 Americans experienced strikes, violence, and a wave of fear that Bolsheviks, blacks, foreigners, and others were destroying the American way.

Red Scare

Americans have often feared radicals and other groups that seemed to be conspiring to overthrow the American way. In the 1840s, the 1890s, and at other times in the past, Catholics, Mormons, Populists, immigrants, and holders of many political views have all been attacked as dangerous and "un-American." But before 1917, anarchists seemed to pose the worst threat. After the Russian Revolution, *Bolshevik* became the most dangerous radical, while *communist* was transformed from a member of a utopian community to a dreaded, menacing subversive. In the spring of 1919, with the Russian announcement of a policy of worldwide revolution and with Communist uprisings in Hungary and Bavaria, many Americans feared that the Communists planned to take over the United States. There were a few American Communists, but they never really threatened the United States or the American way of life.

However, some idealists, like John Reed, found developments in Russia inspiring. Reed, the Harvard-educated son of a wealthy businessman, converted to socialism. In Europe shortly after the war began, he witnessed the bloody Bolshevik takeover in 1917. His eyewitness account, *Ten Days That Shook the World*, optimistically predicted a worldwide revolution. However, when he saw how little hope there was for that revolution in postwar America, he returned to the Soviet Union. By the time he died from typhus in 1920, the authoritarian nature of the new Russian regime had disillusioned him.

Working-Class Protest

Relatively few Americans, even among those who had been socialists, and fewer still among the workers, joined the Communist Party. Perhaps in all there were 25,000 to 40,000, and those were split into two groups, the American Communist Party and the Communist Labor Party. The threat to the American system of government was very slight. But in 1919, the Communists seemed to be a threat, particularly as a series of devastating strikes erupted across the country. Workers in the United States had suffered from wartime inflation, which had almost doubled prices between 1914 and 1919, while most wages remained the same. During 1919, more than four million workers took part in 4,000 strikes. Few wanted to overthrow the government; they demanded higher wages, shorter hours, and in some cases more control over the workplace.

On January 21, 1919, some 35,000 shipyard workers went on strike in Seattle, Washington. Within a few days, a general strike paralyzed the city; transportation and business stopped. The mayor of Seattle called for federal troops. Within five days, using strong-arm tactics, the mayor put down the strike and was hailed across the country as a "red-blooded patriot."

Yet the strikes continued, spreading in September to U.S. Steel and Bethlehem Steel. Blaming the strikes on the Bolsheviks, the owners imported strikebreakers, provoked riots, broke up union meetings, and finally used police and soldiers to end the strike. While the steel strike was still in progress, the police in Boston went on strike. The Boston newspapers blamed the strike on Communist influence. Calvin Coolidge, then governor of Massachusetts, quickly broke the strike and fired the policemen.

Several bomb incidents in 1919 also convinced some that revolution was around the corner, even though most American workers wanted only shorter hours, better working conditions, and a chance to realize the American dream.

The strikes and bombs, combined with the general postwar mood of distrust and suspicion, persuaded many people of a real and immediate threat to the nation. No one was more convinced than Attorney General A. Mitchell Palmer. From a Quaker family in a small Pennsylvania town, the attorney general had graduated from Swarthmore College and had been admitted to the Pennsylvania bar in 1893 at the age of 21. After serving three terms as a congressman, he helped swing the Pennsylvania delegation to Wilson at the 1912 convention. Wilson offered him the post of secretary of war, but Palmer's pacifism led him to refuse. He did support the United States' entry into the war, however, and served as alien property custodian, a job created by the Trading with the Enemy Act. This position apparently convinced him of the danger of radical subversive activities in America. The bombing of his home intensified his fears, and in the summer of 1919, he determined to find and destroy the Red network. He organized a special antiradical division within the Justice Department and put a young man named J. Edgar Hoover in charge of coordinating information on domestic radical activities.

Obsessed with the "Red menace," Palmer instituted a series of raids, beginning in November 1919. Simultaneously, in several cities, his men rounded up 250 members of the Union of

Russian Workers, many of whom were beaten and roughed up in the process. In December, 249 aliens, including the famous anarchist Emma Goldman, were deported, although very few were Communists and even fewer had any desire to overthrow the government of the United States. Palmer's men arrested 500 people in Detroit and 800 in Boston.

The Palmer raids, which probably constituted the most massive violation of civil liberties in America history to this date, found few dangerous radicals but did fan the flames of fear and intolerance in the country. In Indiana, a jury quickly acquitted a man who had killed an alien for yelling, "To hell with the United States."

Palmer became a national hero for ferreting out Communists, but Assistant Secretary of State Louis Post insisted that the arrested aliens be given legal rights, and in the end only about 600 were deported, out of the more than 5,000 arrested. The worst of the "Red Scare" was over by the end of 1920, but the fear of radicals and the emotional patriotism colored the rest of the decade.

The Red Scare promoted many patriotic organizations, such as the American Legion, the American Defense Society, the Sentinels of the Republic, the United States Flag Association, and the Daughters of the American Revolution. Such groups were often united by an obsessive fear of Communists and radicals.

Some organizations targeted women social reformers. One group attacked the "Hot-House, Hull House Variety of Parlor Bolshevists." Even the Needlework Guild and the Sunshine Society were accused of being influenced by Communists. The connections were made only through the use of half-truths, innuendo, and outright lies. To protest their charges did little good, for the accusers knew the truth and would not be deflected from their purpose of exterminating dangerous radicals.

The Sacco-Vanzetti Case

One result of the Red Scare was the conviction of two Italian anarchists, Nicola Sacco and Bar-

tolomeo Vanzetti. Arrested in 1920 for allegedly murdering a guard during a robbery of a shoe factory in South Braintree, Massachusetts, the two were convicted and sentenced to die in the summer of 1921 on what many liberals considered circumstantial and flimsy evidence. Indeed, it seemed to many that the two Italians, who spoke in broken English and were admitted anarchists, were punished because of their radicalism and their foreign appearance. Many intellectuals in Europe and America rallied to their defense, but all appeals failed, and the two were executed in the electric chair on August 23, 1927.

Ku Klux Klan

While the superpatriotic societies exploited the fear that radicals and Bolsheviks were subverting the American way of life from within, the Ku Klux Klan went further. The Klan was organized in Georgia by William J. Simmons, a lay preacher, salesman, and member of many fraternal organizations. He adopted the name and white-sheet uniform of the old antiblack Reconstruction organization that was glorified in 1915 in the immensely popular but racist feature film *Birth of a Nation*. Simmons appointed himself head ("Imperial Wizard") of the new Klan.

Unlike the original organization, which took almost anyone who was white, the new Klan was thoroughly Protestant and explicitly antiforeign, anti-Semitic, and anti-Catholic. It opposed the teaching of evolution; glorified old-time religion; supported immigration restriction; denounced short skirts, petting, and "demon rum"; and upheld patriotism and the purity of women. The Klan grew rapidly after the war because of aggressive recruiting but also because of the fear and confusion of the period.

The Klan flourished in small towns and rural areas in the South, where it set out to keep the returning black soldiers in their "proper place," but it soon spread throughout the country, and at least half the members came from urban areas. At the peak of its power, the Klan

The Klan, with its elaborate rituals and its white uniforms, exploited the fear of blacks, Jews, liberals, and Catholics while preaching "traditional" American values.

had several million members. The Klan's power declined after 1924, but widespread fear of Catholicism and everything perceived as un-American remained.

A PROSPERING ECONOMY

Although the decade after World War I was a time of considerable intolerance and anxiety, it was also a time of industrial expansion and widespread prosperity. Fueled by new technology, more efficient planning and management, and innovative advertising, industrial production almost doubled during the decade, and the gross national product rose by an astonishing 40 percent. A construction boom created new suburbs around American cities, while a new generation of skyscrapers transformed the cities themselves. However, the benefits of this prosperity fell unevenly on the many social groups comprising American society.

The Rising Standard of Living

Signs of the new prosperity appeared in many forms. Millions of sturdy homes and apartments were built and equipped with the latest conveniences. The number of telephones installed nearly doubled between 1915 and 1930. Plastics, rayon, and cellophane altered the habits of millions of Americans, while new products, such as cigarette lighters, reinforced concrete, dry ice, and Pyrex glass, created new demands unheard of a decade before.

In sharp contrast to the nineteenth century, Americans had more leisure time, a shorter work week, and often vacation with pay. The American diet also improved during the decade. Health improved and life expectancy increased.

Educational opportunities also expanded. In 1900, only one in ten young people of high school age remained in school. By 1930, that number had increased to six in ten, and much of the improvement came in the 1920s. In 1900, only one college-age person in 33 attended an institution of higher learning; by 1930, the ratio was one in seven, and over a million people were enrolled in the nation's colleges.

The Evolution of the Modern Corporation

The structure and practice of American business were transformed in the 1920s. After a crisis created by the economic downturn of 1920–1922, business boomed until the crash of 1929. Mergers increased during the decade, creating such giants as General Electric, General Motors, Sears Roebuck, Du Pont, and U.S. Rubber. By 1930, the 200 largest corporations controlled almost half the corporate wealth in the country. Large businesses also diversified during the decade. GE and Westinghouse began to produce household appliances and radios; Du Pont moved into plastics, paints, dyes, and film.

But perhaps the most important business trend of the decade was the emergence of a new kind of manager. No longer did family entrepreneurs make decisions relating to prices, wages, or output. Alfred P. Sloan, Jr., an engineer who reorganized General Motors, was a prototype of the new kind of manager. He divided the company into components, freeing the top managers to concentrate on planning new products, controlling inventory, and integrating the whole operation. Marketing and advertising became as important as production, and many businesses began to spend more money on research. The new manager often had a large staff but owned no part of the company. He was usually an expert at cost accounting and analyzing data. Increasingly, he was a graduate of one of the new business colleges.

The new managers introduced pensions, recreation facilities, cafeterias, and, in some cases, paid vacations and profit-sharing plans. The managers were not being altruistic, however; "welfare capitalism" was designed to reduce worker discontent and to discourage labor unions. Planning was the key to the new corporate structure, and planning often meant a continuation of the business-government cooperation that had developed during World War I. All the planning and the new managerial authority failed to prevent the economic collapse of 1929, but the modern corporation survived the Depression to exert a growing influence on American life in the 1930s and after.

Electrification

The 1920s also marked the climax of the "second industrial revolution." During the late nineteenth century, American industry had primarily manufactured goods intended for other producers. In the first quarter of the twentieth century, as industries like coal, textiles, and steel stabilized or declined, new manufacturing concerns that produced rubber, synthetic fabrics, chemicals, and petroleum arose. They focused on goods for consumers, such as silk stockings, washing machines, and cars.

Powering the second industrial revolution was electricity. Between 1900 and 1920, the replacement of steam power by electricity worked as profound a change as had the substitution of steam power for water power after the Civil War. In 1902, electricity supplied a mere 2 percent of all industrial power; by 1929, this figure rose to fully 80 percent. Less than one of every ten American homes was supplied with electricity in 1907, but more than two-thirds were by 1929. Powered by electricity, American industries reached new heights of productivity. By 1929, the work force was turning out twice as many goods as a similarly sized work force had ten years before.

Electricity brought dozens of gadgets and labor-saving devices into the home; washing machines, electric irons, vacuum cleaners, electric toasters, and sewing machines lightened housework. The "Great White Ways" of the cities symbolized progress, but they also made the darkness of slums and hamlets seem even more forbidding.

Automobile Culture

Automobile manufacturing, like electrification, underwent spectacular growth in the 1920s. The automobile was one major factor in the postwar economic boom. It stimulated and transformed the petroleum, steel, and rubber industries. The auto forced the construction and improvement of streets and highways and caused the spending of millions of dollars on labor and concrete.

The auto changed American life in myriad ways. It led to the decline of the small crossroads store as well as many small churches because the rural family could now drive to the larger city or town. The tractor changed methods of farming. Trucks replaced the horse and wagon and altered the marketing of farm products. Buses began to eliminate the one-room school, because it was now possible to transport students to larger schools. The automobile allowed young people for the first time to escape the chaperoning of parents. It was hardly the "house of prostitution on wheels" that one judge called it, but it did change courting habits in all parts of the country.

Gradually, as the decade progressed, the automobile became not just transportation but a sign of status. Advertising helped create the impression that it was the symbol of the good life, of sex, freedom, and speed. The auto in turn transformed advertising and design. It even altered the way products were purchased. By 1926, three-fourths of the cars sold were bought on some kind of deferred-payment plan. Installment credit, first tried by a group of businessmen in Toledo, Ohio, in 1915 to sell more autos, was soon used to promote sewing machines, refrigerators, and other consumer products. "Buy now, pay later" became the American way.

The United States had a love affair with the auto from the beginning. The number of registered motor vehicles rose from 8,000 in 1900 to nearly 27 million in 1929. Automobile culture was a mass movement.

The auto industry, like most American businesses, went through a period of consolidation in the 1920s. In 1908, more than 250 companies were manufacturing automobiles in the United States. By 1929, only 44 remained.

A pioneer of the auto industry, Henry Ford is often credited with inventing the assembly line. In actuality it was the work of a team of engineers. But the Ford Motor Company was the first organization to perfect the moving assembly line and mass-production technology. Introduced in 1913, the new method reduced the time it took to produce a car from 14 hours to an hour and a half.

In 1914, Ford startled the country by announcing that he was increasing the minimum pay of the Ford assembly-line worker to $5 a day (almost twice the national average pay for factory workers). Ford did not do so for humanitarian reasons. He wanted a dependable work force and understood that skilled workers were less likely to quit if they received good pay.

Henry Ford was not easy to work for. One newspaper account in 1928 called him "an industrial fascist—the Mussolini of Detroit." He ruthlessly pressured his dealers and used them to bail him out of difficult financial situations. Instead of borrowing money from a bank, he forced dealers to buy extra cars, trucks, and tractors. He used spies on the assembly lines and fired workers and executives at the least provocation. But he did produce a car that transformed America.

The Model T, which cost $600 in 1912, was reduced gradually in price until it sold for only $290 in 1924. The "Tin Lizzie," as it was affectionately called, was light and easily repaired. Replacement parts were standardized and widely available. The Model T did not change from year to year, and it did not deviate from its one color, black. The Model A, introduced in 1927, was never as popular or as successful as the Model T.

The Exploding Metropolis

The automobile enabled American cities to expand into the countryside. In the late nineteenth century, railroads and streetcars had created suburbs near the major cities, but the great expansion of suburban population occurred in the 1920s. Shaker Heights, a Cleveland suburb, was in some ways a typical development. Built on the site of a former Shaker community, the new suburb was planned and developed by two businessmen. They controlled the size and style of the homes and restricted buyers. No blacks were allowed. Curving roads led off the main auto boulevards, while landscaping and natural areas contributed to a parklike atmosphere. The suburb increased in population from 1,700 in 1919 to over 15,000 in 1929, and the price of lots multiplied by 10 during the decade. Other suburbs grew in an equally spectacular manner. The biggest land boom of all occurred in Florida, where the city of Miami mushroomed from 30,000 in 1920 to 75,000 in 1925.

The automobile transformed every city, but the most spectacular growth of all took place in two cities that the car virtually created. Detroit grew from 300,000 in 1900 to 1,837,000 in 1930, while Los Angeles expanded from 114,000 in 1900 to 778,000 in 1930. With sprawling subdivisions connected by a growing network of roads, Los Angeles was the city of the future.

While cities expanded horizontally during the 1920s, sprawling into the countryside, city centers grew vertically. A building boom that peaked near the end of the decade created new skylines for most urban centers. Even cities such as Tulsa, Dallas, Kansas City, Memphis, and Syracuse built skyscrapers.

A Communications Revolution

Changing communications altered the way many Americans lived as well as the way they conducted business. The telephone, first demonstrated in 1876, was found in 13 million homes by the end of the 1920. Commercial radio broadcasting, begun by WWJ in Detroit in the summer of 1920, was an immediate success. Five hundred stations took to the airwaves in 1922 alone. By the end of the decade, people in all sections of the country were humming the same popular songs. Actors and announcers became celebrities. The music, voice, and sound of the radio marked the end of silence and, to a certain extent, the end of privacy. Even more dramatic was the phenomenon of the movies. Forty million viewers a week went to the movies in 1922, and by 1929, that had increased to over 100 million. Charlie Chaplin, Rudolph Valentino, Lillian Gish, and Greta Garbo were more famous and more important to millions of Americans than most government officials were.

Not only movie stars became celebrities in the 1920s. Sports figures such as Babe Ruth, Bobby Jones, Jack Dempsey, and Red Grange were just as famous. The great spectator sports of the decade owed much to the increase of leisure time and to the automobile, the radio, and the mass-circulation newspaper. Thousands drove automobiles to college towns to watch football heroes perform. Millions listened for scores or read about the results the next day. One writer in 1924 called this era "the age of play." He might better have called it "the age of the spectator." The popularity of sports, like the movies and radio, was in part the product of technology.

The year 1927 seemed to mark the beginning of the new age of mechanization and progress. That was the year Henry Ford produced his 15-millionth car and introduced the Model A. During that year, radio-telephone service was established between San Francisco and Manila. The first radio network was organized (CBS), and the first talking movie was released (*The Jazz Singer*). In 1927, the Holland Tunnel, the first underwater vehicular roadway, connected New York and New Jersey. It was also the year that Charles Lindbergh flew from New York to Paris in his single-engine plane in 33½ hours. Lindbergh was not the first to fly the Atlantic, but he was the first to fly it alone, an accomplishment that won him $25,000 in prize money and captured the world's imagination. He was young and handsome, and his feat seemed to represent not only the triumph of an individual but also the triumph of the machine. When Americans cheered Lindbergh, they were reaffirming their belief in the American dream and their faith in individual initiative as well as in technology.

HOPES RAISED, PROMISES DEFERRED

The 1920s was a time when all kinds of hopes seemed realizable. "Don't envy successful salesmen—be one!" one advertisement screamed.

Buy a car. Build a house. Start a career. Invest in land. Invest in stocks. Make a fortune.

Not all Americans, of course, were intent on making a stock market killing or expected to win a huge fortune. Some merely wished to retain traditional values in a society that seemed to question them. Others wanted a steady job or perhaps a new appliance. Many discovered, however, that no matter how modest their hopes might be, they lay tantalizingly out of reach.

Clash of Values

During the 1920s, radio, movies, advertising, and mass-circulation magazines promoted a national, secular culture. But this new culture, which emphasized consumption, pleasure, upward mobility, even sex, clashed with traditional values of hard work, thrift, church, family, and home. Still, many Americans feared that new cultural values, scientific breakthroughs, and new ideas like bolshevism, relativism, Freudianism, and biblical criticism threatened their familiar way of life. A trial over the teaching of evolutionary ideas in high school in the little town of Dayton, Tennessee, symbolized the clash of the old versus the new.

The scientific community and most educated people had long accepted the basic concepts of evolution, if not all the details of Charles Darwin's theories. But many Christians, especially those from Protestant evangelical churches, accepted the Bible as the literal truth and opposed Darwin's ideas. Several states, including Tennessee, passed laws forbidding the teaching of evolution.

John Scopes, a young biology teacher, volunteered to test the law by teaching evolutionary theory to his class, and the state of Tennessee brought him to trial. The American Civil Liberties Union hired Clarence Darrow, perhaps the country's most famous defense lawyer, to defend Scopes; the World Christian Fundamentalist Association engaged William Jennings Bryan, former presidential candidate and secretary of state, to assist the prosecution. Bryan was old and

tired (he died only a few days after the trial), but he was still an eloquent and deeply religious man. In cross-examination, Darrow reduced Bryan's statements to intellectual rubble and revealed also that Bryan was at a loss to explain much of the Bible. He could not explain how Eve was created from Adam's rib or where Cain got his wife. Nevertheless, the jury declared Scopes guilty, for he had clearly broken the law. He was fined $100, though the case was later dismissed by a higher state court. But the press from all over the country covered the trial and upheld science and academic freedom.

Immigration and Migration

Just as the Scopes trial demonstrated a degree of resistance to change, a similar attitude was apparent in many Americans' views on immigration. Anyone perceived as "un-American" seemed to threaten the old ways. A movement to restrict immigration had existed for decades. An act passed in 1882 prohibited the entry of criminals, paupers, and the insane, and special agreements between 1880 and 1908 restricted both Chinese and Japanese immigration. But it was the fear and intolerance of the war years and the period right after the war that resulted in major restrictive legislation.

The first strongly restrictive immigration law passed in 1917 over President Wilson's veto. It required a literacy test for the first time (an immigrant had to read a passage in one of a number of languages). The bill also prohibited the immigration of certain political radicals. The literacy test did not stop the more than one million immigrants who poured into the country in 1920 and 1921, however.

In 1921 Congress limited European immigration in any one year to 3 percent of the number of each nationality present in the country in 1910. Congress changed the quota in 1924 to 2 percent of those in the country in 1890, in order to limit immigration from southern and eastern Europe and ban all immigration from Asia. The

John Steuart Curry was one of the 1920s regionalist painters who found inspiration in the American heartland. In Baptism in Kansas, he depicts a religious ritual that underscores the conflict between rural and urban values.

National Origins Act of 1927 set an overall limit of 150,000 European immigrants a year, with more than 60 percent coming from Great Britain and Germany but less than 4 percent from Italy. Restrictive immigration laws, sponsored by Republicans, helped to attract American Jews, Italians, and Poles to the Democratic Party.

The immigration acts of 1921, 1924, and 1927, in sharply limiting European immigration and virtually banning Asian immigrants, cut off the streams of cheap labor that had provided muscle for an industrializing country since the early nineteenth century. At the same time, by exempting immigrants from the Western Hemisphere, the new laws opened the country to Mexican laborers who were eager to escape poverty in their own land and to work in the fields and farms of California and the Southwest.

Mexican immigrants soon became the country's largest first-generation immigrant group. Nearly half a million arrived in the 1920s, in contrast to only 31,000 in the first decade of the century. Some worked on farms; others migrated to industrial cities such as Detroit, St. Louis, and Kansas City. Northern companies recruited them and paid their transportation. During the 1920s, El Paso, Texas, became more than half Mexican, San Antonio a little less than half. Like black Americans, the Mexicans found opportunity by migrating, but they did not escape prejudice or hardship.

Just as foreign immigrants were attracted to jobs in the United States, from 1915 to 1920 blacks migrated north in great numbers seeking a better life. One young black man wrote to the Chicago *Defender* from Texas that he would prefer to go to Chicago or Philadelphia, but, "I don't care where so long as I go where a man is a man." Most black migrants were young and unskilled. They found work in the huge meatpacking plants of Chicago, East St. Louis, Omaha, and Kansas City and in the shipyards and steel mills. The black population of Chicago increased from 44,000 in 1910 to 234,000 by 1930. Cleveland's black population grew eightfold between 1910 and 1930.

Blacks unquestionably improved their lives by moving north. But most were like the Parkers, their dreams only partly fulfilled. Most crowded into segregated housing and faced prejudice and hate. "Black men stay South," the Chicago *Tribune* advised and offered to pay the transportation for any who would return. The presence of more blacks in the industrial cities of the North led to the development of black ghettos and increased the racial tension that occasionally flared into violence.

One of the worst race riots took place in Chicago in 1919. The riot began at a beach on a hot July day. A black youth drowned in a white swimming area. Blacks claimed he had been hit by stones, but the police refused to arrest any of the white men. A group of blacks attacked the police, and the riot was on. It lasted four days. Several dozen people were killed and hundreds were wounded.

Race riots broke out in other places as well in the early 1920s. The wave of violence and racism angered and disillusioned W. E. B. Du Bois, who had urged blacks to close ranks and support the American cause during the war. In an angry editorial for *The Crisis,* he called upon blacks

to fight a sterner, longer more unbending battle against the forces of hell in our own land. *We return. We return from fighting. We return fighting.* Make way for Democracy; we saved it in France, and by the Great Jehovah, we will save it in the United States of America, or know the reason why.

Marcus Garvey: Black Messiah

Du Bois was not the only militant black leader in the postwar years. A flamboyant Jamaican fed a growing sense of black pride during that time. Marcus Garvey arrived in New York at the age of 29. Largely self-taught, he was an admirer of Booker T. Washington. Although he never abandoned Washington's philosophy of self-help, he thoroughly transformed it. Washington focused on economic betterment through self-help; Garvey saw self-help as a means of political empowerment by which African peoples would reclaim their homelands from European powers.

In Jamaica, Garvey had founded the Universal Negro Improvement Association. By 1919, he had established 30 branches in the United States and the Caribbean. He also set up the newspaper *The Negro World,* the Black Cross Nurses, and a chain of grocery stores, millinery shops, and restaurants. His biggest project was the Black Star Line, a steamship company, to be owned and operated by blacks. Advocating the return of blacks to Africa, he declared himself the "provisional president of Africa," a title he adopted from Eamon De Valera, the first "provisional president of Ireland." He glorified the African past and preached that God and Jesus were black.

Garvey won converts, mostly among lower-middle-class blacks, through the force of his oratory and the power of his personality, but especially through his message of black pride. Thousands of his followers invested their money in the Black Star Line. The line soon collapsed, however, in part because white entrepreneurs sold Garvey inferior ships and equipment. Garvey was arrested for using the mails to defraud shareholders and was sentenced to five years in prison. President Coolidge commuted the sentence. Ordered deported as an undesirable alien,

Marcus Garvey (second from right), shown dressed in his favorite uniform, became a hero for many black Americans.

Garvey left America in 1927. Despite Garvey's failures, he convinced thousands of American blacks that they could join together and accomplish something and that they should feel pride in their heritage and their future.

The Harlem Renaissance and the Lost Generation

A group of black writers, artists, and intellectuals who settled in Harlem after the war sought a way to be both black and American. Alain Locke, the first black Rhodes scholar and a dapper professor of philosophy at Howard University, was in one sense the father of the renaissance. His collection of essays and art, *The New*

Negro (1925), announced the movement to the outside world and outlined black contributions to American culture and civilization. Langston Hughes, a poet and novelist born in Missouri, went to high school in Cleveland, lived in Mexico, and traveled in Europe and Africa before settling in Harlem. He wrote bitter but laughing poems, using black vernacular to describe the pathos and the pride of American blacks. In *Weary Blues,* he adapted the rhythm and beat of black jazz and the blues to his poetry. Jazz was an important force in Harlem in the 1920s, and many prosperous whites came from downtown to listen to Louis Armstrong, Fletcher Henderson, Duke Ellington, and other black musicians.

The Harlem writers struggled with how to be both black and intellectual. They worried that they depended on white patrons, who introduced them to writers and artists in Greenwich Village and made contacts for them at New York publishing houses. Many of the white patrons pressured the black writers to conform to the white elite idea of black authenticity. Jean Toomer wrote haunting poems trying to explore the difficulty of black identity, and in a novel, *Cane* (1923), he sketched maladjusted, almost grotesque characters who expressed some of the alienation that many writers felt in the 1920s.

Many black writers felt alienated from American society. They tried living in Paris or in Greenwich Village, but most felt drawn to Harlem, which in the 1920s was rapidly becoming the center of black population in New York City. Much of the work of the Harlem writers was read by very small numbers, but another generation of young black intellectuals in the 1960s still struggling with the dilemma of how to be both black and American would rediscover it.

One did not need to be black to be disillusioned with society. Many white intellectuals, writers, and artists also felt alienated from what they perceived as the materialism, conformity, and provincial prejudice that dominated American life. Many writers of this postwar "Lost

Generation," including F. Scott Fitzgerald, Ernest Hemingway, E. E. Cummings, and T. S. Eliot, moved to Europe, where they wrote novels, plays, and poems about America.

For many writers, the disillusionment began with the war itself. Hemingway eagerly volunteered to go to Europe as an ambulance driver. But when he was wounded on the Italian front, he reevaluated the purpose of the war and the meaning of all the slaughter. His novel *The Sun Also Rises* (1926) is the story of the purposeless European wanderings of a group of Americans. But it is also the story of Jake Barnes, made impotent by a war injury. His "unreasonable wound" is a symbol of the futility of life in the postwar period.

F. Scott Fitzgerald epitomized some of the despair of his generation, which had "grown up to find all Gods dead, all wars fought, all faiths in man shaken." His best novel, *The Great Gatsby* (1925), was a critique of the American success myth. The book describes the elaborate parties given by a mysterious businessman, who, it turns out, has made his money illegally as a bootlegger. Gatsby hopes to win back a beautiful woman who has forsaken him for another man. But wealth won't buy happiness, and Gatsby's life ends tragically, as so many lives seemed to end in the novels written during the decade.

Sherwood Anderson's novel *Winesburg, Ohio* (1919) and Sinclair Lewis's *Main Street* (1920) and *Babbitt* (1922) criticized the narrowness of midwestern small-town middle-class culture. H. L. Mencken, who edited the *American Mercury* in Baltimore, denounced what he called "the booboisie."

Ironically, while intellectuals despaired over American society and complained that art could not survive in a business-dominated civilization, literature flourished. The novels of Hemingway, Fitzgerald, Lewis, William Faulkner, and Gertrude Stein, the plays of Eugene O'Neill and Maxwell Anderson, the poetry of T. S. Eliot, Hart Crane, E. E. Cummings, and Marianne Moore, and the work of many black writers marked the 1920s as one of the most creative decades in American literature.

Women Struggle for Equality

In the eventful postwar decade, women not only won the right to vote, as seen in Chapter 22; they also adopted changes in their ways of living and working. Any mention of the role of women in the 1920s brings to mind the image of the flapper—a young woman with a short skirt, bobbed hair, and a boyish figure doing the Charleston, smoking, drinking, and being very casual about sex. F. Scott Fitzgerald's heroines in novels like *This Side of Paradise* (1920) and *The Great Gatsby* (1925) provided the role models for young people to imitate, and movie stars such as Clara Bow and Gloria Swanson, aggressively seductive on the screen, supplied even more dramatic examples of flirtatious and provocative behavior.

Without question, women acquired more sexual freedom and more control over their reproductive lives in the 1920s. Contraceptives, especially the diaphragm, became more readily available during the decade, and Margaret Sanger, who had been indicted for sending birth control information through the mail in 1914, organized the first American birth control conference in 1921. Family size declined during the decade (from 3.6 children in 1900 to 2.5 in 1930), and young people were apparently more inclined to marry for love than for security.

Despite more freedom for women, however, the double standard persisted. "When lovely woman stoops to folly, she can always find someone to stoop with her," one male writer announced, "but not always someone to lift her up again to the level where she belongs."

Women's lives were shaped by other innovations of the 1920s. Electricity, running water, washing machines, vacuum cleaners, and other labor-saving devices made housework easier for the middle class but did not reduce time spent doing housework. Standards of cleanliness rose, and women were urged to make their houses more spotless than any nineteenth-century housekeeper would have felt necessary. At the same time, magazines and newspapers bombarded women with advertising urging them to buy products to make themselves better housekeepers.

More women worked outside the home. The greatest expansion of jobs for women was in white-collar occupations that were being feminized—secretary, bookkeeper, clerk, telephone operator. In 1930, fully 96 percent of stenographers were women. Although more married women had jobs (an increase of 25 percent during the decade), most of them held low-paying jobs, and most single women assumed that marriage would terminate their employment.

For some working women—secretaries and teachers, for example—marriage often led to dismissal. According to one businessman, married women are "very unstable in their work; their first claim is to home and children." Considering these attitudes, it is not surprising that the disparity between male and female wages widened during the decade. By 1930, women earned only 57 percent of what men were paid. Although the proportion of women lawyers and bankers increased slightly during the decade, the rate of growth declined, and the number of women doctors and scientists dropped. In the 1920s, women acquired some sexual freedom and a limited amount of opportunity outside the home, but the promise of the prewar feminist movement and the hopes that accompanied the suffrage amendment remained unfulfilled.

Winning the vote for women did not assure equality. In most states, a woman's service belonged to her husband. Women could vote, but often they could not serve on juries. In some states, women could not hold office, own a business, or sign a contract without their husbands' permission. Women were usually held responsible for an illegitimate birth, and divorce laws almost always favored men.

Alice Paul, who had led the militant Na-

tional Women's Party in 1916, chained herself to the White House fence once again to promote an equal rights amendment to the Constitution. The amendment received support in Wisconsin and several other states, but many women opposed it on the grounds that such an amendment would cancel the special legislation to protect women in industry that had taken so long to enact in the two decades before.

Rural America in the 1920s

Most farmers did not share in the prosperity of the 1920s. Responding to worldwide demands and rising prices for wheat, cotton, and other products, many farmers invested in more land, tractors, and farm equipment during the war. The prices tumbled. In the postwar depression, many farmers could not pay their debts. Because the value of land fell, they often lost both mortgage and land and still owed the bank money.

The changing nature of farming was part of the problem. The use of chemical fertilizers and new hybrid seeds increased the yield per acre. The use of tractors and trucks made farming more efficient and released for cash crops land formerly used to raise feed for horses and mules. Production increased at the very time that worldwide demand for American farm products declined.

Large commercial operations, using mechanized equipment, produced most of the cash crops. Many small farmers found themselves unable to compete with agribusiness. Some of them, along with many farm laborers, solved the problem of declining rural profitability by leaving the farms. In 1900, fully 40 percent of the labor force worked on farms; by 1930, only 21 percent earned their living from the land.

Few farmers could afford the products of the new technology. While many middle-class urban families were buying new cars, radios, and bathrooms, only one farm family in ten had electricity in the 1920s. The lot of the farm wife had not changed for centuries. She ran a domestic factory, did all the household chores, and helped on the farm as well.

As they had done in the nineteenth century, farmers tried to act collectively. They sought to influence legislation in the state capital and in Washington. Most of their effort went into the McNary-Haugen Farm Relief Bill, which would have provided for government support for key agricultural products. The bill was introduced a number of times between 1924 and 1928 without success, but farm organizations in all parts of the country learned how to work together to influence Congress. That would have important ramifications for the future.

The Workers' Share of Prosperity

Hundreds of thousands of workers improved their standard of living in the 1920s, yet inequality grew. Real wages increased 21 percent between 1923 and 1929, but corporate dividends went up by nearly two-thirds in the same period. The workers did not profit from the increased production they helped to create, and that boded ill for the future. The richest 5 percent of the population increased their share of the wealth from a quarter to a third, and the wealthiest one percent controlled a whopping 19 percent of all income. Even among workers there was great disparity. Those employed on the auto assembly lines or in the new factories producing radios saw their wages go up, and many saw their hours decline. Yet the majority of American working-class families did not earn enough to move them much beyond the subsistence level.

While some workers prospered in the 1920s, organized labor fell on hard times. Labor union membership fell from about 5 million in 1921 to less than 3.5 million in 1929. A number of large employers lured workers away from unions with promises that seemed to equal union benefits: profit-sharing plans, pensions, and their own company unions.

The more aggressive unions like the United Mine Workers, led by the flamboyant John L. Lewis, also encountered difficulties. The union's attempt to organize the mines in West Virginia had led to violent clashes between union members and imported guards. President Harding called out troops in 1921 to put down an "army organized by the strikers." The next year, Lewis called the greatest coal strike in history, and further violence erupted, especially in Williamson County, Illinois. Internal strife also weakened the union, and Lewis had to accept wage reductions in the negotiations of 1927.

Organized labor, like so many other groups, struggled desperately during the decade to take advantage of the prosperity. It won some victories, and it made some progress. But American affluence was beyond the reach of many groups during the decade. Eventually the inequality would lead to disaster.

THE BUSINESS OF POLITICS

Business, especially big business, prospered in the 1920s, and the image of businessmen, enhanced by their important role in World War I, rose further. The government reduced regulation, lowered taxes, and cooperated to aid business expansion at home and abroad. Business and politics, always intertwined, were especially allied during the decade. Republican presidents Harding, Coolidge, and Hoover favored an activist federal government whose main interest was big business. Wealthy financiers such as Andrew Mellon and Charles Dawes played important roles in formulating both domestic and foreign policy. Even more significant, a new kind of businessman was elected president in 1928. Herbert Hoover, international engineer and efficiency expert, was the very symbol of the modern techniques and practices that many people confidently expected to transform the United States and the world.

Harding and Coolidge

The Republicans, almost assured of victory in 1920 because of bitter reaction against Woodrow Wilson, nominated Warren G. Harding, a former newspaper editor from Ohio. To balance the ticket, the Republicans chose as their vice-presidential candidate Calvin Coolidge of Massachusetts, who had gained attention by his firm stand during the Boston police strike. The Democrats, after 44 roll calls, finally nominated Governor James Cox of Ohio and picked Franklin D. Roosevelt, a young politician from New York, as his running mate. Harding won in a record landslide, but less than 50 percent of the eligible voters went to the polls.

In contrast to the reform-minded Presidents Roosevelt and Wilson, Harding reflected the conservatism of the 1920s. He was a jovial man who brought many Ohio friends to Washington and placed them in positions of power. At a little house a few blocks from the White House on K Street, Harry Daugherty, Harding's attorney general and longtime associate, held forth with a group of friends. Amid bootleg liquor and the atmosphere of a brothel, they did a brisk business in selling favors, taking bribes, and organizing illegal schemes. Harding was not personally corrupt, and the nation's leading businessmen approved of his policies of higher tariffs and lower taxes. Nor did he spend all his time drinking with his cronies. He called a conference on disarmament and another to deal with the problems of unemployment, and he pardoned Eugene Debs, who had been in prison since the war. When he died suddenly in August 1923, the American people genuinely mourned him.

Only after Harding's vice president, Calvin Coolidge, succeeded to the presidency did the full extent of the corruption and scandals of the Harding administration come to light. A Senate committee discovered that the secretary of the interior, Albert Fall, had illegally leased government-owned oil reserves in the Teapot Dome section of Wyoming to private business interests in return for over $300,000 in bribes. Illegal activities were also discovered in the Veterans Administration and elsewhere in government. Harding's attorney general resigned in disgrace, the secretary of the navy barely avoided prison, two of Harding's advisers committed suicide, and the secretary of the interior was sentenced to jail.

Coolidge was dour and taciturn, but honest. No hint of scandal infected his administration or his personal life. He ran for election in 1924 with the financier Charles Dawes as his running mate. There was little question that he would win. The Democrats were so equally divided between northern urban Catholics and southern rural Protestants that it took 103 ballots before they nominated John Davis, an affable corporate lawyer with little national following. A group of dissidents, mostly representing the farmers and the laborers dissatisfied with both nominees, formed a new Progressive Party and nominated Robert La Follette of Wisconsin for president. They drafted a platform calling for government ownership of railroads and ratification of the child labor amendment. La Follette received nearly 5 million votes, only 3.5 million short of

Warren G. Harding (left) and Calvin Coolidge were immensely popular in the 1920s, but later historians criticized them and rated them among the worst of American presidents.

Davis's total. But Coolidge and prosperity won easily.

Symbolizing the pro-business attitude of the Harding and Coolidge administrations was the wealthy Andrew Mellon, appointed secretary of the treasury by Harding and retained in that post by the next two presidents. Mellon set out to lower individual and corporate taxes. In 1922, Congress, with Mellon's endorsement, repealed the wartime excess profits tax, and increased tax exemptions for families. In 1928, Congress reduced taxes further, removed most excise taxes, and lowered the corporate tax rate. The 200 largest corporations increased their assets during the decade from $43 billion to $81 billion. Coolidge observed, "The chief business of the American people is business."

Herbert Hoover

One bright light in the lackluster Harding and Coolidge administrations was Herbert Hoover, who served as secretary of commerce under both presidents. Hoover had made a fortune as an international mining engineer before 1914 and then earned the reputation of a great humanitarian for his work managing the Belgian Relief Committee and directing the Food Administration.

While secretary of commerce, Hoover used the force of the federal government to regulate, stimulate, and promote, but he believed first of all in American free enterprise and local volunteer action to solve problems. In 1921, he convinced Harding of the need to do something about unemployment during the postwar recession. The president's conference on unemployment, convened in September 1921, marked the first time the national government had admitted any responsibility to the unemployed. The result of the conference (the first of many on a variety of topics that Hoover was to organize) was a flood of publicity, pamphlets, and advice from experts. Most of all, the conference urged state and local governments and businesses to cooper-

ate on a volunteer basis to solve the problem. The primary responsibility of the federal government, Hoover believed, was to educate and promote. With all his activity and his organizing, Hoover got the reputation during the Harding and Coolidge years as an efficient and progressive administrator, and he became one of the most popular figures in government service.

Foreign Policy in the 1920s

The decade of the 1920s is often remembered as a time of isolation, when the United States rejected the League of Nations treaty and turned its back on the rest of the world. In fact, the United States remained involved—indeed, increased its involvement—in international affairs during the decade. Although the United States never joined the League of Nations or the World Court, it cooperated with many League agencies and conferences and took the lead in trying to reduce naval armaments and to solve the problems of international finance caused in part by the war.

Indeed, business, trade, and finance marked the decade as one of international expansion. With American corporate investments overseas growing sevenfold during the decade, the United States was transformed from a debtor to a creditor nation. The United States also continued its involvement in the affairs of South and Central American countries. Yet the United States took up its role of international power reluctantly and with a number of contradictory and disastrous results.

"We seek no part in directing the destiny of the world," Harding announced in his inaugural address, but even Harding discovered that international problems would not disappear. One that required immediate attention was the naval arms race.

At the Washington Conference on Naval Disarmament, which convened in November 1921, Secretary of State Charles Evans Hughes startled the delegates by proposing a ten-year "holiday" on the construction of warships and by offering to sink or scrap 845,000 tons of American ships, including 30 battleships. He urged Britain and Japan to do the same.

The conference participants ultimately agreed to fix the tonnage of capital ships at a ratio of the United States and Great Britain, 5; Japan, 3; and France and Italy, 1.67. Japan agreed only reluctantly, but when the United States promised not to fortify its Pacific island possessions, the Japanese yielded. The conference was hailed as the first time in history that the major nations of the world had agreed to disarm. And it was the United States that took the lead by offering to be the first to scrap its battleships.

American foreign policy in the 1920s tried to reduce the risk of international conflict, resist revolution, and make the world safe for trade and investment. American diplomats argued for an open door to trade in China, but in Latin America the United States had always assumed a special and distinct role. Throughout the decade, American investment in agriculture, minerals, petroleum, and manufacturing increased in the countries to the south.

The United States also continued the process of intervention begun earlier. By the end of the decade, the United States controlled the financial affairs of ten Latin American nations. The marines were withdrawn from the Dominican Republic in 1924, but that country remained a virtual protectorate of the United States until 1941. The government ordered the marines from Nicaragua in 1925 but sent them back the next year when a liberal insurrection, led by the charismatic Augusto Sandino, threatened the conservative government. One American coffee planter decided in 1931 that the American intervention had been a disaster. "Today we are hated and despised," he announced. "This feeling has been created by employing American marines to hunt down and kill Nicaraguans in their own country." In 1934, Sandino was murdered by General Anastasio Somoza, a ruthless leader

supported by the United States. For more than 40 years, Somoza and his two sons ruled Nicaragua as a private fiefdom, a legacy not yet resolved in that strife-torn country.

Mexico frightened American businessmen in the mid-1920s by beginning to nationalize foreign holdings in oil and mineral rights. Coolidge appointed Dwight W. Morrow of the J. P. Morgan Company as ambassador, and his conciliatory attitude led to agreements protecting American investments. Throughout the decade, the goal of U.S. policy toward Central and South America, whether in the form of negotiations or intervention, was to maintain a special sphere of influence.

The United States' policy toward Europe during this period was not always consistent or carefully thought out. At the end of the war, European countries owed the United States over $10 billion, with Great Britain and France responsible for about three-fourths of that amount. Nearly the only way European nations could repay the United States was by exporting products, but in a series of tariff acts, especially the Fordney-McCumber Tariff of 1922 and the Hawley-Smoot Tariff of 1930 Congress erected a protective barrier to trade. American policy of high tariffs (a counterproductive policy for a creditor nation) caused retaliation and restrictions on American trade, which American corporations were trying to increase.

The inability of the European countries to export products to the United States and to repay their loans was intertwined with the reparation agreement made with Germany. Germany's economy was in disarray after the war, with inflation raging and its industrial plant throttled by the peace treaty. By 1921, Germany was defaulting on its payments. The United States, which believed a healthy Germany important to the stability of Europe and of world trade, instituted a plan engineered by Charles Dawes whereby the German debt would be renegotiated and spread over a longer period. In the meantime, American bankers and the American government loaned Germany hundreds of millions of dollars. In the end, the United States loaned money to Germany so it could make payments to Britain and France so that those countries could continue their payments to the United States.

The United States had replaced Great Britain as the dominant force in international finance, but the nation in the 1920s was a reluctant and inconsistent world leader. Although the United States was hesitant to get involved in multinational agreements, in 1928 it signed the idealistic Kellogg-Briand pact, which outlawed war. Eventually 62 nations signed, but the only power behind the treaty was moral force rather than economic or military sanctions.

The Survival of Progressivism

The decade of the 1920s was a time of reaction against reform, but progressivism did not simply die. It survived in many forms through the period that Jane Addams called a time of "political and social sag." For example, child labor reformers worked through the Women's Trade Union League, the Consumers League, and other organizations to promote a child labor amendment to the Constitution after the 1919 law was declared unconstitutional in 1922.

The greatest success of the social justice movement was the 1921 Sheppard-Towner Maternity Act, one of the first pieces of federal social welfare legislation, the product of long progressive agitation. A study conducted by the Children's Bureau discovered that more than 3,000 mothers died in childbirth in 1918 and that more than 250,000 infants also died. The United States ranked eighteenth out of 20 countries in maternal mortality and eleventh in infant deaths. Josephine Baker, the pioneer physician and founder of the American Child Health Association, was not being ironic when she remarked, "It's six times safer to be a soldier in the trenches in France than to be born a baby in the United States."

The maternity bill called for a million dollars a year to assist the states in providing medical aid, consultation centers, and visiting nurses to teach expectant mothers how to care for themselves and their babies. The bill was controversial from the beginning. The American Medical Association and others attacked this bill as leading to socialism. Some opponents argued that it was put forward by extreme feminists or "inspired by foreign experiments in Communism."

Despite the opposition, the bill passed Congress and was signed by President Harding in 1921. The appropriation for the bill was only for six years, and the opposition, again raising the specter of a feminist-socialist-communist plot, succeeded in repealing the law in 1929.

Temperance Triumphant

Another survival of progressivism was the the temperance movement. Prohibition, like child labor reform and maternity benefits, was an important effort to conserve human resources. By 1918, over three-fourths of the people in the country lived in dry states or counties, but it was the war that allowed the anti-saloon advocates to associate prohibition with patriotism. "We have German enemies across the water," one prohibitionist announced. "We have German enemies in this country too. And the worst of all our German enemies, the most treacherous, the most menacing are Pabst, Schlitz, Blatz and Miller." In 1919, Congress passed the Volstead Act banning the brewing and selling of beverages containing more than one-half of one percent alcohol. The thirty-sixth state ratified the Eighteenth Amendment in June 1919, but the country had, for all practical purposes, been dry since 1917.

The prohibition experiment probably did reduce the total consumption of alcohol in the country, but most people who wanted to drink during the "noble experiment" found a way. Speakeasies replaced saloons, and people consumed bathtub gin, home brew, and many strange and dangerous concoctions. Bartenders invented the cocktail to disguise the poor quality of liquor, and women, at least middle- and upper-class women, began to drink in public for the first time. Prohibition also created great bootlegging rings, which were tied to organized crime in many cities. Al Capone of Chicago was the most famous underworld figure whose power and wealth were based on the sale of illegal alcohol. Many supporters of prohibition slowly came to favor its repeal, some because it reduced the power of the states, others because it stimulated too much illegal activity and because it did not seem to be worth the social and political costs.

The Election of 1928

The decade of the 1920s ended as it had begun, with a Republican administration. On August 2, 1927, President Coolidge announced simply, "I do not choose to run for President in 1928." Hoover immediately became the logical Republican candidate and easily won the nomination. In a year when the country was buoyant with optimism and when prosperity seemed as if it would go on forever, few doubted that Hoover would be elected.

The Democrats nominated Alfred Smith, a Catholic Irish-American from New York. With his New York accent, his opposition to prohibition, and his flamboyant style, he contrasted sharply with the more sedate Hoover. Racial and religious prejudice played a role in this campaign, as it had in others. But looked at more closely, the two candidates differed little. Both were self-made men, both were "progressives."

Hoover won in a landslide, 444 electoral votes to 76 for Smith, who carried only Massachusetts and Rhode Island outside the Deep South. But the 1928 campaign revitalized the Democratic Party. Smith polled nearly twice as many votes as the Democratic candidate in 1924, and for the first time the Democrats carried the nation's 12 largest cities.

Stock Market Crash

Hoover, as it turned out, had only six months to apply his progressive and efficient methods to running the country because in the fall of 1929, the prosperity that seemed endless suddenly came to a halt. In 1928 and 1929, rampant speculation made the stock market boom. Money could be made everywhere—in real estate and business ventures, but especially in the stock market.

Only a small percentage of the American people had previously invested in the stock market, but a large number got into the game in the late 1920s because it seemed a safe and sure way to make money. The economy was booming. The New York *Times* index of 25 industrial stocks, which had reached 100 in 1924, rose to 245 by the end of 1927.

Then the orgy started. During 1928, the market rose to 331. Many investors and speculators began to buy on margin (borrowing in order to invest). Businessmen and others began to invest money in the market that would ordinarily have gone into houses, cars, and other goods. Yet even at the peak of the boom, probably only about 1.5 million Americans owned stock.

In early September 1929, the New York *Times* index peaked at 452 and then began to drift downward. On October 23, the market lost 31 points. The next day ("Black Thursday"), it first seemed that everyone was trying to sell, but at the end of the day the panic appeared over. It was not. By mid-November, the market had plummeted to 224, about half what it had been two months before. This represented a loss on paper of over $26 billion. The market continued to go down. Tens of thousands of investors lost everything. There was panic and despair, but the legendary stories of executives jumping out of windows were grossly exaggerated.

CONCLUSION

A NEW ERA OF PROSPERITY AND PROBLEMS

The stock market crash ended the decade of prosperity and revealed the weakness of the economy. The fruits of economic expansion had been unevenly distributed. Not enough people could afford to buy the autos, refrigerators, and other products pouring from American factories. Prosperity had been built on a shaky foundation. When that foundation crumbled in 1929, the nation slid into a major depression.

More than most decades, the 1920s was a time of paradox and contradictions. It was a time of prosperity, yet a great many people, including farmers, blacks, and other ordinary Americans, did not prosper. It was a time of reaction against reform, yet progressivism survived. It was a time when intellectuals felt disillusioned with America, yet it was one of the most creative and innovative periods for American writers, who described its foibles and intolerance.

Recommended Reading

Lively reading about the 1920s is Frederick Lewis Allen, *Only Yesterday* (1931). Much better balanced, however, is William E. Leuchtenburg, *The Perils of Prosperity* (1958). Two very different views of foreign policy during the decade can be found in L. Ethan Ellis, *Republican Foreign Policy, 1921–33* (1968), and William Appleman Williams, *The Tragedy of American Diplomacy* (1959).

Robert K. Murray, *Red Scare* (1955), describes the hate and intolerance that erupted after the war. See also Kenneth Jackson, *The Ku Klux Klan and the City, 1915–1930* (1967). On Hispanic migration to the Southwest, see Sarah Deutsch, *No Separate Refuge* (1987). Nancy F. Cott, *The Grounding of Modern Feminism* (1987), tracks the role of women during the decade. The experiences of ordinary Americans are treated in Margaret Marsh, *Suburban Lives* (1990); and Lizabeth Cohen, *Making a New Deal: Industrial Workers in Chicago, 1919–1939* (1990).

Nathan Huggins, *Harlem Renaissance* (1971), and Frederick Hoffman, *The Twenties* (1955), are indispensable for the study of the literary trends during this innovative decade. Robert T. Sklar, *Movie-Made America* (1976), is excellent on Hollywood and the film industry. Roland Marchand, *Advertising the American Dream* (1985), is the best place to begin a study of the impact of advertising. On the Scopes trial and religious fundamentalism, see George M. Marsden, *Fundamentalism and American Culture* (1980).

Andrew Sinclair, *The Available Man* (1965); Donald R. McCoy, *Calvin Coolidge* (1967); Oscar Handlin, *Al Smith and His America* (1958); and Joan Hoff Wilson, *Herbert Hoover: The Forgotten Progressive* (1975), chart the lives and activities of some of the political leaders. John Kenneth Galbraith, *The Great Crash, 1929* (1954), explains how the 1920s came to a tragic end.

Time Line

1900–1930	Electricity powers the "second industrial revolution"		**1924**	Coolidge elected president Peak of Ku Klux Klan activity Immigration Quota Law
1917	Race riot in East St. Louis, Illinois		**1925**	Scopes trial in Dayton, Tennessee F. Scott Fitzgerald, *The Great Gatsby* Alain Locke, *The New Negro* Claude McKay, *Home to Harlem* 5 million enameled bathroom fixtures produced
1918	World War I ends			
1919	Treaty of Versailles Strikes in Seattle, Boston, and elsewhere Red Scare and Palmer raids Race riots in Chicago and other cities Marcus Garvey's Universal Negro Improvement Association spreads		**1926**	Ernest Hemingway, *The Sun Also Rises*
			1927	National Origins Act McNary-Haugen Farm Relief bill Sacco and Vanzetti executed Lindbergh flies solo, New York to Paris First talking movie, *The Jazz Singer* Henry Ford produces 15-millionth car
1920	Warren Harding elected president Women vote in national elections First commercial radio broadcast Sacco and Vanzetti arrested Sinclair Lewis, *Main Street*			
1921	Immigration Quota Law Disarmament Conference First birth control conference Sheppard-Towner Maternity Act		**1928**	Herbert Hoover elected president Kellogg-Briand Treaty Stock market soars
1921–1922	Postwar depression		**1929**	27 million registered cars in country 10 million households own radios 100 million people attend movies Stock market crash
1922	Fordney-McCumber Tariff Sinclair Lewis, *Babbitt*			
1923	Harding dies; Coolidge becomes president Teapot Dome scandal			

chapter 24

The Great Depression and the New Deal

Diana Morgan grew up in a small North Carolina town, the daughter of a prosperous cotton merchant. She lived the life of a "southern belle," oblivious to the country's social and political problems. But the Depression changed that. She came home from college for Christmas vacation during her junior year to discover that her world had fallen apart. Her father's business had failed, her family didn't have a cook or a cleaning woman anymore, and their house was being sold for back taxes. She was confused and embarrassed. Sometimes it was the little things that were the hardest to bear. Friends would come from out of town, and there would be no ice because her family did not own an electric refrigerator and they could not afford to buy ice. "There were those frantic arrangements of running out to the drug store to get Coca-Cola with crushed ice, and there'd be this embarrassing delay, and I can remember how hot my face was." Like many Americans, Diana Morgan and her family blamed themselves for what happened to them during the Depression.

Diana Morgan had never intended to work outside the home. But she found a position with the Civil Works Administration, a New Deal agency, where at first she had to ask humiliating questions of the people applying for assistance to make sure they were destitute. "Do you own a car?" "Does anyone in the family work?" One day, a woman who had formerly cooked for her family came in to apply for help. Each was embarrassed to see the other in changed circumstances.

She had to defend the New Deal programs to many of her friends, who accused her of being sentimental and told her that the poor, especially poor blacks, did not know any better than to live in squalor. "If you give them coal, they'd put it in the bathtub," was a charge she often heard. But she knew "they didn't have bathtubs to put coal in. So how did anybody know that's what they'd do with coal if they had it?"

Diana Morgan's experience working for a New Deal agency influenced her life and her attitudes; it made her more of a social activist. Her Depression experience gave her a greater appreciation for the struggles of the country's poor and unlucky.

The Great Depression changed the lives of all Americans and separated that generation from the one that followed. An exaggerated need for security, the fear of failure, a nagging sense of guilt, and a real sense that it might happen all over again divided the Depression generation from everyone born after 1940.

The Depression dominated the decade of the 1930s despite imaginative efforts and massive spending by Franklin Roosevelt's New Deal. The New Deal was not a radical movement; but it did establish a minimum welfare state, as the government accepted limited responsibility to manage the economy, subsidize farmers, and promote social insurance and minimum wage laws. Greater government involvement in the social welfare of the country had important consequences for the American people and nation.

This chapter explores the causes and consequences of the Great Depression. We will look at the efforts of Herbert Hoover and Franklin Roosevelt to combat the Depression. We will also examine the great strides in technology during the 1930s, when innovative developments in radio, movies, and the automobile affected the lives of most Americans.

THE GREAT DEPRESSION

There had been recessions and depressions in American history, notably in the 1830s, 1870s, and 1890s, but nothing compared to the devastating economic collapse of the 1930s. The Great Depression was all the more shocking because it came after a decade of unprecedented prosperity when most experts assumed that the United States was immune to a downturn in the business cycle. The Great Depression had an impact on all areas of American life; perhaps most important, it destroyed American confidence in the future.

The Depression Begins

Few people anticipated the stock market crash in the fall of 1929. But even after the collapse of the stock market, few expected the entire economy to go into a tailspin. By 1932, at least one of every four American breadwinners was out of work, and industrial production had almost ground to a halt.

Why did the nation sink deeper and deeper into depression? The answer is complex, but the prosperity of the 1920s, it appears in retrospect, was superficial. Farmers and coal and textile workers had suffered all through the 1920s from low prices, and the farmers were the first group in the 1930s to plunge into depression. But other aspects of the economy also lurched out of balance. Two percent of the population received about 28 percent of the national income, while the lower 60 percent only got 24 percent. Businesses increased profits while holding down wages and the prices of raw materials. The result was that American workers, like American farmers, did not have the money to buy the goods they helped to produce.

Well-to-do Americans were speculating a significant portion of their money in the stock market. Their illusion of permanent prosperity helped fire the boom of the 1920s, just as their pessimism and lack of confidence helped exaggerate the depression in 1931 and 1932.

Other factors were also involved. The stock

market crash revealed serious structural weaknesses in the financial and banking systems (7,000 banks had failed during the 1920s). The Federal Reserve Board, fearing inflation, tightened credit—exactly the opposite of the action it should have taken to fight a slowdown in purchasing. Economic relations with Europe contributed to deepening depression. High American tariffs during the 1920s had reduced trade. When American investment in Europe declined in 1928 and 1929, European economies declined. As the European financial situation worsened, the American economy spiraled downward.

Hoover and the Depression

Initial business and government reactions to the stock market crash were optimistic. "All the evidence indicates that the worst effects of the crash upon unemployment will have been passed during the next sixty days," Herbert Hoover reported. His upbeat first statements were calculated to prevent further panic.

The Agricultural Marketing Act of 1929 set up a $500-million revolving fund to help farmers organize cooperative marketing associations and to establish minimum prices. But as agricultural prices plummeted and banks foreclosed on farm mortgages, the available funds proved inadequate. The Farm Board was helpless to aid the farmer who could not meet mortgage payments because the price of grain had fallen so rapidly. Nor could it help the Arkansas woman who stood weeping in the window as her possessions, including the cows, which all had names, were sold one by one.

Hoover acted aggressively to stem the economic collapse. More than any president before him, he used the power of the federal government and the office of the president to deal with an economic crisis. Nobody called it a depression for the first year at least, for the economic problems seemed very much like earlier cyclic recessions. Hoover called conferences of business-

men and labor leaders. He met with mayors and governors and encouraged them to speed up public works projects. He created agencies and boards, such as the National Credit Corporation and the Emergency Committee for Employment, to obtain voluntary action to solve the problem. Hoover even supported a tax cut, which Congress enacted in December 1929, but it did little to stimulate spending. Hoover also went on the radio in his effort to convince the American people that the fundamental structure of the economy was sound.

The Collapsing Economy

Voluntary action and psychological campaigns could not stop the Depression. The stock market, after appearing to bottom out in the winter of 1930–1931, continued its decline, responding in part to the European economic collapse that threatened international finance and trade.

But more than a collapsing market afflicted the economy. Over 1,300 additional banks failed in 1930. Despite Hoover's pleas, many factories cut back on production, and some simply closed. U.S. Steel announced a 10 percent wage cut in 1931. As the auto industry laid off workers, the unemployment rate rose to over 40 percent in Detroit. More than 4 million Americans were out of work in 1930, and at least 12 million by 1932. Foreclosures and evictions created thousands of personal tragedies. While the middle class watched in horror as their life savings disappeared, the rich began to hoard gold and to fear revolution.

There was never any real danger of revolution. Some farmers organized to dump their milk to protest low prices, and when a neighbor's farm was sold, they gathered to hold a penny auction, bidding only a few cents for equipment and returning it to their dispossessed neighbor. But everywhere people despaired as the Depression deepened in 1931 and 1932. For unemployed blacks and for many tenant farmers, the Depression had little immediate effect because

Unemployment Rate, 1929–1940

Source: U.S. Bureau of the Census

their lives were already so depressed. Most Americans (the 98 percent who did not own stock) hardly noticed the stock market crash; for them, the Depression meant the loss of a job or a bank foreclosure. For Diana Morgan, it was learning that her father's business and the family home had been lost; for some farmers, it was burning corn rather than coal because the price of corn had fallen so low that it was not worth marketing.

For some in the cities, the Depression meant not having enough money to feed the children. "Have you ever heard a hungry child cry?" asked Lillian Wald of the Henry Street Settlement. "Have you seen the uncontrollable trembling of parents who have gone half starved for weeks so that the children may have food?" In Chicago, children fought with men and women over the garbage dumped by the city trucks.

Many Depression victims blamed themselves. A businessman who lost his job and had

to stand in a relief line remembered years later how he would bend his head low so nobody would recognize him.

The Depression probably disrupted women's lives less than men's. There were many exceptions, of course, but when men lost their jobs, their identity and sense of purpose as the family breadwinner were shattered. For women, however, even when money was short, there was still cooking, cleaning, and mending. Many women, in addition, took in laundry, found room for a boarder, and made the clothes they formerly would have bought. Many families were forced to move in with relatives. The marriage rate, the divorce rate, and the birthrate all dropped during the decade.

Hoover reacted to growing despair by urging more voluntary action. "We are going through a period," he announced in February 1931, "when character and courage are on trial, and where the very faith that is within us is under test." He insisted on maintaining the gold standard and a balanced budget, but so did almost everyone else. Hoover increasingly blamed the Depression on international economic problems, and he was not entirely mistaken. The whole world was gripped by depression, but as it deepened, Americans began to blame Hoover for some of the disaster. The president became isolated and bitter. The shanties that grew near all the large cities were called "Hoovervilles," and the privies, "Hoover villas."

Hoover did try innovative schemes. More public works projects were built during his administration than in the previous 30 years. He attempted to rescue banks and businesses that were near failure. When private effort failed, he turned reluctantly to Congress, which passed a bill early in 1932 authorizing the Reconstruction Finance Corporation. The RFC was capitalized at $500 million, but a short time later that was increased to $3 billion. It was authorized to make loans to banks, insurance companies, farm mortgage companies, and railroads. Its effectiveness was limited, however, because it funded

The worst result of the Depression was hopelessness and despair. Those emotions are captured in this painting of an unemployment office by Isaac Soyer.

only those financial institutions capable of putting up collateral, so that small, weak banks, for example, could not qualify for support. Similarly, public works projects had to include potential earnings for repayment. The RFC did help shore up a number of shaky financial institutions and remained the major government finance agency until World War II. But it became much more effective under Roosevelt because it provided loans directly to industry.

Hoover also asked Congress to make home mortgages more readily available. The Federal Home Loan Bank Act of 1932 became the basis for the Federal Housing Administration of the New Deal years. He also pushed the passage of the Glass-Steagall Banking Act of 1932, which expanded credit in order to make more loans available to businesses and individuals. Hoover

firmly believed in loans, but not direct subsidies, and he thought it was the responsibility of state and local governments, as well as of private charity, to provide direct relief to the unemployed and the needy.

The Bonus Army

Many World War I veterans lost their jobs during the Depression, and beginning in 1930, they lobbied for the payment of their veterans' bonuses, not due until 1945. In May 1932, about 17,000 veterans marched on Washington. Some took up residence in a shantytown, called Bonus City, in the Anacostia flats outside the city.

The House passed a bonus bill, but in mid-June, the Senate defeated it. Most of the veterans, disappointed but resigned, accepted a free railroad ticket home. Several thousand remained, however, along with some wives and children, in the unsanitary shacks during the steaming summer heat. Among them were a small group of committed Communists and other radicals. Hoover finally called out the U.S. Army to disperse them. General Douglas MacArthur, the army chief of staff, ordered the army to disperse the veterans. He described the Bonus marchers as a "mob . . . animated by the essence of revolution." With tanks, guns, and tear gas, the army routed the veterans. Two Bonus marchers were killed, and several others were injured. "What a pitiful spectacle is that of the great American Government, mightiest in the world, chasing unarmed men, women and children with Army tanks," commented a Washington newspaper. The army was not attacking revolutionaries in the streets of Washington but was routing bewildered, confused, unemployed men who had seen their American dream collapse.

The Bonus army fiasco, bread lines, and Hoovervilles became the symbols of Hoover's presidency. He deserved better because he tried to use the power of the federal government to solve growing and increasingly complex economic problems. But in the end, his personality and background limited him. Willing to use the federal government to support business, he could not accept federal aid for the unemployed. He feared an unbalanced budget and a large federal bureaucracy. Ironically, his policies led in the next years to a massive increase in federal power and in the federal bureaucracy.

ROOSEVELT AND THE FIRST NEW DEAL

The Republicans nominated Herbert Hoover for a second term, but in the summer of 1932, the Depression and Hoover's unpopularity opened the way for the Democrats. After a shrewd campaign, Franklin D. Roosevelt, governor of New York, emerged from the pack and won the nomination. Roosevelt, distantly related to Theodore

Roosevelt, had served as an assistant secretary of the navy during World War I and had been the Democratic vice-presidential candidate in 1920. Crippled by infantile paralysis not long after, he had recovered enough to serve as governor of New York for two terms, though he was not especially well known by the general public in 1932.

Governor Roosevelt had become the first governor to support state aid for the unemployed. But it was difficult to tell during the presidential campaign exactly what he stood for. The truth was that Roosevelt did not have a master plan to save the country. Yet he won overwhelmingly, carrying more than 57 percent of the popular vote.

In his inaugural address, Roosevelt announced confidently, "The only thing we have to fear is fear itself." This, of course, was not true, for the country faced the worst crisis since the Civil War, but Roosevelt's confidence and his ability to communicate with ordinary Americans were obvious early in his presidency. He instituted a series of radio "fireside chats" to explain to the American people what he was doing to solve the nation's problems. When he said "my friends," millions believed that he meant it, and they wrote letters to him in unprecedented numbers to explain their needs.

Roosevelt surrounded himself with intelligent and innovative advisers. His cabinet was made up of a mixture of people from different backgrounds who often did not agree with one another. Harold Ickes, the secretary of the interior, was a Republican lawyer from Chicago. Another Republican, Henry Wallace of Iowa, a plant geneticist and agricultural statistician, became the secretary of agriculture. Frances Perkins, the first woman ever appointed to a cabinet post, became the secretary of labor. A disciple of Jane Addams and Florence Kelley, she had been a settlement resident, secretary of the New York Consumers League, and an adviser to Al Smith.

In addition to the formal cabinet, Roosevelt created an informal "Brain Trust," which included Adolph Berle, Jr., Rexford Tugwell, and

Harry Hopkins. Eleanor Roosevelt, the president's wife, traveled widely, giving speeches and listening to the concerns of women, minorities, and ordinary Americans. Attacked by critics who thought she had too much power, she courageously took stands on issues of social justice and civil rights. She helped push the president toward social reform.

Roosevelt proved to be an adept politician. He took ideas, plans, and suggestions from conflicting sources and combined them. He had "a flypaper mind," one of his advisers decided. Roosevelt was an optimist and opportunist by nature. And he believed in action.

His first New Deal, lasting from 1933 to early 1935, focused mainly on recovery from the Depression and relief for the poor and unemployed. Congress passed legislation to aid business, the farmers, and labor and authorized public works projects and massive spending to put Americans back to work. No single ideological position united all the programs, for Roosevelt was a pragmatist who was willing to try a variety of programs. More than Hoover, he believed in economic planning and in government spending to help the poor.

Roosevelt's caution and conservatism shaped the first New Deal. He did not promote socialism or suggest nationalizing the banks. He was even careful in authorizing public works projects to stimulate the economy. The New Deal was based on the assumption that it was possible to create a just society by superimposing a welfare state on the capitalistic system, leaving the profit motive undisturbed. During the first New Deal, Roosevelt believed he would achieve his goals through cooperation with the business community. Later he would move more toward reform, but at first his primary concern was simply relief and recovery.

One Hundred Days

Because Roosevelt took office in the middle of a major crisis, a cooperative Congress was willing to pass almost any legislation that he put before

it. Not since Woodrow Wilson's first term did a president orchestrate Congress so effectively. In three months, a bewildering number of bills were rushed through. Many would have far-reaching implications for the relationship of government to society. Unlike Hoover, Roosevelt was willing to use direct government action to solve the problems of depression and unemployment. As it turned out, none of the bills passed during the first 100 days cured the Depression, but taken together, the legislation constituted one of the most innovative periods in American political history.

The most immediate problem Roosevelt faced was the condition of the banks. Many had closed. Using a forgotten provision of a World War I law, Roosevelt declared a four-day bank holiday. Three days later, an emergency session of Congress approved his action and within hours passed the Emergency Banking Relief Act. The bill gave the president broad powers over financial transactions, prohibited the hoarding of gold, and allowed for the reopening of sound banks, sometimes with loans from the Reconstruction Finance Corporation. Within the next few years, Congress passed additional legislation that gave the federal government more regulatory power over the stock market and over the process by which corporations issued stock. It also passed the Banking Act of 1933, which strengthened the Federal Reserve System, established the Federal Deposit Insurance Corporation, and insured individual deposits up to $5,000.

The Democratic platform in 1932 called for reduced government spending and an end to prohibition. Roosevelt moved quickly on both. The Economy Act, which passed Congress easily, reduced government salaries and cut veterans' pensions. However, other bills passed the same week called for increased spending. The Beer-Wine Revenue Act legalized 3.2 beer and light wines and levied a tax on both. The Twenty-first Amendment, ratified on December 5, 1933, repealed the Eighteenth Amendment and ended the prohibition experiment.

Congress granted Roosevelt great power to devalue the dollar and to manipulate inflation. Bankers and businessmen feared inflation, but farmers and debtors favored an inflationary policy as a way to raise prices and put more money in their pockets. "I have always favored sound money," Roosevelt announced, "and I do now, but it is 'too darned sound' when it takes so much of farm products to buy a dollar." He rejected the more extreme inflationary plans supported by many congressmen from the agricultural states, but he did take the country off the gold standard. No longer would paper currency be redeemable in gold. After experimenting with pushing the price of gold up by buying it in the open market, Roosevelt and his advisers fixed the price at $35 an ounce in January 1934 (against the old price of $20.63). This inflated the dollar by about 40 percent, but some still cried for more inflation.

Relief Measures

Roosevelt believed in economy in government and in a balanced budget, but he also wanted to help the unemployed and the homeless. One survey estimated in 1933 that 1.5 million Americans were homeless. One man with a wife and six children from Latrobe, Pennsylvania, who was being evicted wrote, "I have 10 days to get another house, no job, no means of paying rent, can you advise me as to which would be the most humane way to dispose of myself and family, as this is about the only thing that I see left to do."

Roosevelt's answer was the Federal Emergency Relief Administration (FERA), which Congress authorized with an appropriation of $500 million in direct grants to cities and states. A few months later, Roosevelt created a Civil Works Administration (CWA) to put more than four million people to work on various state, municipal, and federal projects. Hopkins, who ran both agencies, believed it was much better to pay people to work than to give them charity. An

accountant working on a road project said, "I'd rather stay out here in that ditch the rest of my life than take one cent of direct relief."

The CWA was not always effective, but in just over a year, the agency built or restored a half million miles of roads and constructed 40,000 schools and 1,000 airports. Roosevelt, however, feared that the program was costing too much and might create a permanent class of relief recipients. In the spring of 1934, he ordered the CWA closed down.

The Public Works Administration (PWA), directed by Harold Ickes, in some respects overlapped the work of the CWA, but it lasted longer. Between 1933 and 1939, the PWA built hospitals, courthouses, school buildings, low-cost housing, and other projects. One purpose of the PWA was economic pump priming—the stimulation of the economy and consumer spending through the investment of government funds. Afraid that there might be scandals in the agency, Ickes spent money slowly and carefully. PWA projects, however, did little to stimulate the economy.

Agricultural Adjustment Act

In 1933, most farmers were desperate as mounting surpluses and falling prices drastically cut their incomes. Congress passed a number of bills in 1933 and 1934 to deal with the agricultural crisis, but the New Deal's principal solution to the farm problem was the Agricultural Adjustment Act (AAA), which sought to control the overproduction of basic commodities so that farmers might regain the purchasing power they had enjoyed before World War I. To guarantee these "parity prices" (the average prices in the years 1909–1914), the production of major agricultural staples—wheat, cotton, corn, hogs, rice, tobacco, and milk—would be controlled by paying the farmers to reduce their acreage under cultivation. The AAA levied a tax at the processing stage to pay for the program.

The act aroused great disagreement among

farm leaders and economists, but the controversy was nothing compared with the outcry from the public over the initial action of the AAA in the summer of 1933. To prevent a glut on the cotton and pork markets, the agency ordered 10 million acres of cotton plowed up and 6 million little pigs slaughtered. It seemed unnatural, even immoral, to kill pigs and plow up cotton when millions of people were underfed and in need of clothes.

The Agricultural Adjustment Act did raise the prices of some agricultural products. But it helped the larger farmers more than the small operators, and it was often disastrous for the tenant farmers and sharecroppers, whom crop reduction made expendable. Many tenant farmers were simply cast out on the road with a few possessions and nowhere to go. The long-range significance of the AAA, which was later declared unconstitutional, was the establishment of the idea that the government should subsidize farmers for limiting production.

Industrial Recovery

The flurry of legislation during the first days of the Roosevelt administration contained something for almost every group. The National Industrial Recovery Act (NIRA) was designed to help business, raise prices, control production, and put people back to work. The act established the National Recovery Administration (NRA) with the power to set fair competition codes in all industries. To run the NRA, Roosevelt appointed Hugh Johnson, who had helped organize the World War I draft and served on the War Industries Board. Johnson used his wartime experiences and the enthusiasm of the bond drives to rally the country around the NRA. There were parades and rallies, even a postage stamp; and industries that cooperated could display a blue eagle, the symbol of the NRA. "We Do Our Part," the posters and banners proclaimed, but the results were somewhat less than the promise.

Section 7a of the NIRA established the National Labor Board to see that workers' rights were respected. But the board, usually dominated by businessmen, often interpreted the labor provisions of the contracts loosely. In addition, small businessmen complained that the NIRA was unfair to their interests. Any attempt to set prices led to controversy.

When the Supreme Court declared the NIRA unconstitutional in 1935, few people complained. The labor provisions of the act were picked up later by the National Labor Relations Act, sponsored by New York's Democratic senator Robert Wagner.

Civilian Conservation Corps

One of the most popular and successful of the New Deal programs, the Civilian Conservation Corps (CCC), combined work relief with the preservation of natural resources. It put young unemployed men between the ages of 18 and 25 to work on reforestation, road and park construction, flood control, and other projects. The men lived in the more than 1,500 work camps and earned $30 a month, $25 of which had to be sent home to their families. Some complained that the CCC camps, run by the U.S. Army, were too military. Others protested that the CCC did nothing for unemployed young women, so a few special camps were organized for them; however only 8,000 women took part in a program that by 1941 had included 2.5 million men. Overall, the CCC was one of the most successful and least controversial of all the New Deal programs.

Tennessee Valley Authority

Roosevelt, like his Republican namesake, believed in conservation. He promoted flood control projects and added millions of acres to the country's national forests, wildlife refuges, and fish and game sanctuaries. But the most important New Deal conservation project was the Tennessee Valley Authority (TVA).

For many people, the Depression meant homeless despair. Here an Oklahoma family who have lost their farm walk with all their possessions along the highway.

Congress authorized the TVA as an independent public corporation with the power to sell electricity and fertilizer and to promote flood control and land reclamation. The TVA built nine major dams and many minor ones between 1933 and 1944, affecting parts of Virginia, North Carolina, Georgia, Alabama, Mississippi, Tennessee, and Kentucky. It promoted everything from flood control to library bookmobiles. For residents of the valley, it meant cheaper electricity, radios, electric irons, washing machines, and other appliances for the first time. The largest federal construction project ever launched, it also created jobs for many thousands who helped build the dams. But government officials and businessmen who feared that the experiment would lead to socialism always curbed the regional planning possibilities of the TVA.

Critics of the New Deal

The furious legislative activity during the first 100 days of the New Deal helped alleviate the pessimism and despair hanging over the country. Stock market prices rose slightly, and industrial production was up 11 percent at the end of 1933. Still, the country remained locked in depression, and nearly 12 million Americans were without jobs. Yet Roosevelt captured the imagination of ordinary Americans everywhere. Hundreds of thousands of letters poured into the White House, so many that eventually 50 people had to be hired to answer them. "If ever there was a saint, he is one," declared a Wisconsin woman.

But conservatives were not so sure that Roosevelt was a savior; in fact, many businessmen began to fear that the president was leading the country toward socialism.

The conservative revolt against Roosevelt surfaced in the summer of 1934 as the congressional elections approached. A group of disgruntled politicians and businessmen formed the Liberty League, which supported conservative or at least anti–New Deal candidates for Congress, but it had little influence. In the election of 1934, the Democrats increased their majority from 310 to 319 in the House and from 60 to 69 in the Senate (only the second time in the twentieth century that the party in power had increased its control of Congress).

While some thought the New Deal too radical, others maintained that the government had not done enough to help the poor. One source of criticism was the Communist Party, which increased its membership from 7,500 in 1930 to 75,000 in 1938. While a majority who joined the party came from the working class, communism had a special appeal to writers, intellectuals, and some college students during a decade when the American dream had turned into a nightmare.

A larger number of Americans, however, were influenced by other movements promising easy solutions to poverty and unemployment. In Minnesota, Governor Floyd Olson, elected on a Farm-Labor ticket, accused capitalism of causing the Depression and startled some listeners when he thundered, "I hope the present system of government goes right to hell." In California, old-age pension schemes were promoted by Upton Sinclair and Dr. Francis E. Townsend.

More threatening to Roosevelt were the protest movements led by Father Charles E. Coughlin and Senator Huey P. Long. Father Coughlin, a Roman Catholic priest from a Detroit suburb, attracted an audience of 30 to 45 million to his national radio show. At first, he supported Roosevelt's policies, but later he savagely attacked the New Deal as excessively pro-business. Mixing religious commentary with visions of a society operating without bankers and big businessmen, he roused his audience with blatantly anti-Semitic appeals. Most often the "evil" bankers he described were Jewish—the Rothschilds, Warburgs, and Kuhn-Loebs. Anti-Semitism reached a peak in the 1930s, so Jews, rather than Catholics, bore the brunt of nativist fury. Groups like the Silver Shirts and the German-American Bund lashed out against Jews. To members of these groups and others like them, Father Coughlin's attacks made sense.

Huey Long, like Coughlin, had a charisma that won support from the millions still trying to survive in a country where the continuing depression made day-to-day existence a struggle. Elected governor of Louisiana in 1928, he promoted a "Share the Wealth" program. He taxed the oil refineries and built hospitals, schools, and thousands of miles of new highways. By 1934, he was the virtual dictator of his state, personally controlling the police and the courts. Long talked about a guaranteed income for all American families and promised pensions for the elderly and college educations for the young. He would pay for these programs by taxing the rich and liquidating the great fortunes. Had not an assassin's bullet cut Long down in September 1935, he might have mounted a third-party challenge to Roosevelt.

THE SECOND NEW DEAL

Responding in part to the discontent of the lower middle class but also to the threat of various utopian schemes, Roosevelt moved his programs in 1935 toward the goals of social reform and social justice. At the same time, he departed from attempts to cooperate with the business community.

Work Relief and Social Security

The Works Progress Administration (WPA), authorized by Congress in April 1935, was the first massive attempt to deal with unemployment. The WPA employed about three million people a year on a variety of socially useful projects, such as bridges, airports, libraries, roads, and golf courses. A minor but important part of the WPA funding supported writers, artists, actors, and musicians.

Only one member of a family could qualify for a WPA job, and first choice always went to the man. A woman could qualify only if she headed the household. But eventually more than 13 percent of the people who worked for the WPA were women, although their most common employment was in the sewing room, where old clothes were made over. "For unskilled men we have the shovel. For unskilled women we have only the needle," one official remarked.

The WPA inevitably aroused some criticism, but it did useful work; the program built nearly 6,000 schools, more than 2,500 hospitals, and 13,000 playgrounds. More important, it gave millions of unemployed Americans a chance to support their families. The National Youth Administration (NYA) supplemented the work of the WPA and assisted young men and women between the ages of 16 and 25, many of them students.

By far the most enduring reform came with the passage of the Social Security Act of 1935. By the 1930s, the United States remained the only major industrial country without such a program. The number of people over 65 in the country increased from 5.7 million in 1925 to 7.8 million in 1935, and that group demanded action.

The Social Security Act of 1935 was a compromise. It provided old-age and survivor insurance to be paid for by a tax of one percent on both employers and employees. The benefits initially ranged from $10 to $85 a month. The act also established a cooperative federal-state system of unemployment compensation. Other provisions authorized federal grants to the states to assist in caring for the crippled and the blind. Finally, the Social Security Act provided some aid to dependent children. This provision would eventually expand to become the largest federal welfare program.

Although the National Association of Manufacturers denounced social security, it was actually a conservative and incomplete system. In no other country was social insurance paid for in part by a regressive tax on the workers' wages. The law also excluded many people, including those who needed it most, such as farm laborers and domestic servants. It discriminated against married women wage earners, and it failed to protect against sickness. Yet for all its weaknesses, it was one of the most important New Deal measures. A landmark in American social legislation, it marked the beginning of the welfare state that would expand significantly after World War II.

Aiding the Farmers

The flurry of legislation in 1935 and early 1936, often called the "second New Deal," also included an effort to help American farmers. Over 1.7 million farm families had incomes of under $500 annually in 1935, and 42 percent of all those who lived on farms were tenants. The Resettlement Administration (RA) set out to relocate tenant farmers on land purchased by the government. Lack of funds and fears that the Roosevelt administration was trying to establish Soviet-style collective farms limited the effectiveness of the RA program.

Much more important in improving the lives of farm families was the Rural Electrification Administration (REA), which was authorized in 1935 to loan money to cooperatives to generate and distribute electricity in isolated rural areas not served by private utilities. When the REA's lines were finally attached, they dramatically changed the lives of millions of farm families.

In the hill country west of Austin, Texas, for example, no electricity existed until the end of the 1930s. There were no bathrooms because bathrooms required running water, and running water depended on an electric pump. Women

A farmer and his sons race to find shelter from a dust storm in Cimarron County, Oklahoma, in 1936. A combination of factors, including overplanting that destroyed the natural sod of the Great Plains, resulted in the devastating dust storms of the 1930s. Without sod to protect the soil from the wind, thousands of acres of the Great Plains just blew away.

and children hauled water constantly—for infrequent baths, for continuous canning (because without a refrigerator, fruits and vegetables had to be put up almost immediately or they spoiled), and for washday. Washday, always Monday, meant scrubbing clothes by hand with harsh soap on a washboard; it meant boiling clothes in a large copper vat over a wood stove and stirring them with a wooden fork.

It was memory of the difficult life in the hill country that inspired a young congressman from Texas, Lyndon Johnson, to work to bring rural electrification to the area. In November 1939, the lights finally came on in the hill country, plugging the area into the twentieth century.

The Dust Bowl: An Ecological Disaster

Some farmers profited from the agricultural legislation of the 1930s, but most of those who tried to farm on the Great Plains fell victim to years of drought and dust storms. Record heat waves and below-average rainfall in the 1930s turned an area from the Oklahoma panhandle to western Kansas into a giant dust bowl. A single storm on May 11, 1934, removed 300 million tons of topsoil and turned day into night. Between 1932 and 1939 there was an average of fifty dust storms a year. Cities kept their street lights on for twenty-four hours a day. Dust covered everything from food to bedspreads and piled up in dunes in city streets and barnyards. Thousands died of "dust pneumonia." One woman remembered what it was like at night: "A trip for water to rinse the grit from our lips, and then back to bed with washcloths over our noses, we try to lie still, because every turn stirs the dust on the blankets."

A 1936 survey of twenty counties in the heart of the dust bowl concluded that 97.6 percent of the land suffered from erosion and more than 50 percent was seriously damaged. By the end of the decade 10,000 farm homes were abandoned to the elements, 9 million acres of farmland was reduced to a wasteland, and three and a half million people had abandoned their farms and joined a massive migration to find a better life. More than 350,000 left Oklahoma during the decade and moved to California, a place that seemed to many like the promised land. But the name Okie came to mean any farm migrant. The plight of these wayfarers was immortalized by John Steinbeck in his novel about the Joad family, *The Grapes of Wrath* (1939).

The dust bowl was a natural disaster, but it was aided and exaggerated by human actions and inactions. The semiarid plains west of the 98th meridian were not suitable for intensive agriculture. Overgrazing, too much plowing, and indiscriminate planting over a period of sixty years exposed the thin soil to the elements. When the winds came in the 1930s, much of the land simply blew away.

The Roosevelt administration did try to deal with the problem. The Taylor Grazing Act of 1934 restricted the use of the public range in an attempt to prevent overgrazing, and it also closed 80 million acres of grassland to further settlement. The Civilian Conservation Corps and other New Deal agencies planted trees, and the Soil Conservation Service promoted drought-resistant crops and contour plowing, but it was too little and too late. Even worse, according to some authorities, government measures applied after the disaster of 1930 encouraged farmers to return to raising wheat and other inappropriate crops, leading to more dust bowl crises in the 1950s and 1970s.

Controlling Corporate Power and Taxing the Wealthy

In the summer of 1935, Roosevelt also moved to control the large corporations, and increase taxes paid by the well-to-do. The Public Utility Holding Company Act, passed in 1935, gave various government commissions the authority to regulate and control the power companies, 12 of which controlled over half of the country's power. The act gave each company five years to demonstrate that its services were efficient. This was one of the most radical attempts to control corporate power in American history.

In 1935, Roosevelt criticized the "unjust concentration of wealth and economic power" and persuaded Congress to increase estate and gift taxes and raise the income tax rates at the top.

The New Deal for Labor

Like many progressive reformers, Roosevelt was more interested in improving the lot of working people by passing social legislation than by strengthening the bargaining position of organized labor. Yet he saw labor as an important balance to the power of industry, and he listened to his advisers, especially to Frances Perkins and to Senator Robert Wagner of New York, who

Distribution of Income, 1935–1936

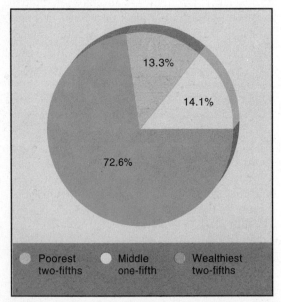

Source: U.S. Bureau of the Census

persistently brought up the needs of organized labor.

After strikes in San Francisco, Minneapolis, and Toledo, Roosevelt supported the Wagner Act, officially called the National Labor Relations Act, which outlawed blacklisting and a number of other practices and reasserted labor's right to organize and to bargain collectively. The act also established a Labor Relations Board with the power to certify a properly elected bargaining unit. The act did not require workers to join unions, but it made the federal government a regulator, or at least a neutral force, in management-labor relations. That alone made the National Labor Relations Act one of the most important New Deal reform measures.

The Roosevelt administration's friendly attitude toward organized labor helped to increase union membership from under 3 million in 1933 to 4.5 million by 1935. Many groups, however, were left out, including farm laborers, unskilled workers, and women. Only about 3 percent of working women belonged to unions, and women earned only about 60 percent of wages paid to men for equivalent work.

Still, many people resented the fact that women were employed at all. The Brotherhood of Railway and Steamship Clerks ruled that no married woman whose husband could support her was eligible for a job. One writer had a perfect solution for the unemployment problem: "Simply fire the women, who shouldn't be working anyway, and hire the men." The American Federation of Labor had little interest in organizing unskilled workers, but a new group of committed and militant labor leaders emerged in the 1930s to take up that task. John L. Lewis, the eloquent head of the United Mine Workers, was the most aggressive. He was joined by David Dubinsky of the International Ladies' Garment Workers and Sidney Hillman, president of the Amalgamated Clothing Workers. Both were socialists who believed in economic planning, but both had worked closely with social justice progressives. These new progressive

labor leaders formed the Committee of Industrial Organization (CIO) within the AFL and set out to organize workers in the steel, auto, and rubber industries. Rather than separating workers by skill or craft as the AFL preferred, they organized everyone into an industrywide union much as the Knights of Labor had done in the 1880s. They also used new and aggressive tactics. When a foreman tried to increase production or enforce discipline, the union leaders would simply pull the switch and declare a spontaneous strike. This "brass knuckle unionism" worked especially well in the auto and rubber industries.

In 1936, the workers at three rubber plants in Akron, Ohio, went on strike without permission from the leaders. Instead of picketing outside the factory, they occupied the buildings and took them over. The "sit-down strike" became a new protest technique. After sit-down strikes against General Motors plants in Atlanta, Georgia, and Flint, Michigan, General Motors finally accepted the United Auto Workers as their employees' bargaining unit.

The General Motors strike was the most important event in a critical period of labor upheaval. A group of workers using disorderly but largely nonviolent tactics (as would the civil rights advocates in the mid-1960s) demanded their rights under the law. They helped to make labor's voice heard in the decision-making process in major industries where labor had long been denied any role. They also helped to raise the status of organized labor in the eyes of many Americans.

"Labor does not seek industrial strife," Lewis announced. "It wants peace, but a peace with justice." As the sit-down tactic spread, violence often accompanied justice. Chrysler capitulated. But the Ford Motor Company used hired gunmen to discourage the strikers. A bloody struggle ensued before Ford agreed to accept the UAW as the bargaining agent. Even U.S. Steel came to terms with the Steel Workers Organizing Committee, but other steel companies refused to go along. In Chicago on Memorial Day in 1937, a confrontation between the police and peaceful pickets at the Republic Steel plant resulted in ten deaths. In the "Memorial Day Massacre," as it came to be called, the police fired without provocation into a crowd of workers and their families, who had gathered near the plant in a holiday mood. All ten of the dead were shot in the back.

Despite the violence and management's use of undercover agents within unions, the CIO gained many members. William Green and the leadership of the AFL were horrified at the aggressive tactics of the new labor leaders. They expelled the CIO leaders from the AFL only to see them form a separate Congress of Industrial Organization (the initials stayed the same). By the end of the decade, the CIO had infused the labor movement with a new spirit. Accepting unskilled workers, blacks, and others who had never belonged to a union before, they won increased pay, better working conditions, and the right to bargain collectively in most of the basic American industries. Jim Cole, a black butcher at one of the meatpacking plants in Chicago, tried to join the Amalgamated Butchers and Meat Cutters, an AFL union, but they turned him away because he was black. He later joined the CIO.

America's Minorities in the 1930s

A half million blacks joined unions through the CIO during the 1930s, and many blacks were aided by various New Deal agencies. Yet the familiar pattern of discrimination, low-paying jobs, and intimidation through violence persisted. Lynchings in the South actually increased in the New Deal years, rising from 8 in 1932 to 28 in 1933 and 20 in 1935.

The migration of blacks to northern cities, which had accelerated during World War I, continued during the 1930s. The collapse of cotton prices forced black farmers and farm laborers to flee north for survival. But since most were poorly educated, they were eligible for only the most menial jobs.

Black leaders attacked the Roosevelt administration for supporting or allowing segregation in government-sponsored facilities. The TVA model town of Norris, Tennessee, was off limits for blacks, and AAA policies actually drove blacks off the land in the South. The CCC segregated black and white workers, and the PWA financed segregated housing projects. Blacks ought to realize, a writer in the NAACP journal *The Crisis* warned in 1935, "that the powers-that-be in the Roosevelt administration have nothing for them."

Roosevelt, fearing that he might antagonize southern congressmen whose backing he needed, refused to support the two major civil rights bills of the era, an antilynching bill and a bill to abolish the poll tax. Yet Harold Ickes and Harry Hopkins worked to ensure that blacks were given opportunities in the CCC, the WPA, and other agencies. By 1941, black federal employees totaled 150,000, more than three times the number during the Hoover administration.

Partly responsible for the presence of more black employees was the "black cabinet," a group of more than 50 young blacks who had appointments in almost every government department and New Deal agency. The group met on Friday evenings at the home of Mary McLeod Bethune, promoter of black education and member of the advisory committee of the National Youth Administration. Bethune had a large impact on New Deal policy and on the black cabinet. She spoke out forcefully, she picketed and protested, and she intervened shrewdly to obtain civil rights and more jobs for black Americans.

W. E. B. Du Bois, in the meantime, had become disillusioned with the reform of race relations through integration with white society. He resigned from the NAACP in 1934 and eventually joined the Communist Party and moved to Ghana, where he died in 1963.

Eleanor Roosevelt, who was educated in

part by Mary McLeod Bethune, was committed to civil rights for blacks. In 1939, when the Daughters of the American Revolution refused to allow Marian Anderson, a black concert singer, to use their stage, Mrs. Roosevelt publicly protested and resigned her membership in the DAR. She also arranged for Anderson to sing from the steps of the Lincoln Memorial, where 75,000 people gathered to listen and to support civil rights for all black citizens.

Many Mexicans who had been actively recruited for American farms and businesses in the 1920s lost their jobs in the Depression decade. Hundreds of thousands drifted from the urban barrios to small towns and farms in the Southwest looking for work.

A few found work with the CCC or the WPA, but to be employed, an applicant had to qualify for state relief, and that eliminated most migrants. The primary solution was not to provide aid for Mexicans but to ship them back to Mexico. A trainload of repatriates left Los Angeles every month during 1933, and officials deported thousands from other cities. One estimate placed the number sent back in 1932 at 200,000, including some American citizens.

During the Depression, Native Americans also experienced hunger, disease, and despair, and their plight was compounded by years of exploitation. Since the Dawes Act of 1887 (described in Chapter 17), government policy had sought to make the Indian into a property-owning farmer and to limit tribal rights. Native Americans lost over 60 percent of the 138 million acres granted them in 1887. The government declared some of the land surplus and encouraged individuals to settle on 160 acres and adopt the "habits of civilized life." Few Native Americans profited from this system, but many whites did. Just as other progressives sought the quick assimilation of immigrants, the progressive era Indian commissioners sped up the allotment process to increase Indian detribalization. But many Native Americans who remained on the reservations were not even citizens. Finally,

in 1924, Congress granted citizenship to all Indians born in the United States. The original Americans became United States citizens, but that did not end their suffering.

Franklin Roosevelt brought a new spirit to Indian policy by appointing John Collier as commissioner of Indian affairs. Collier, who had organized the American Indian Defense Association in 1923 was primarily responsible for the passage of the Indian Reorganization Act of 1934, which sought to restore the political independence of the tribes and to end the allotment policy of the Dawes Act.

The bill also sought to promote "the study of Indian civilization" and to "preserve and develop the special cultural contributions and achievements of such civilization, including Indian arts, crafts, skills and traditions." Not all Indians agreed with the new policies. Some chose to become members of the dominant culture, and the Navajos voted to reject the Reorganization Act. Still, the Indian Reorganization Act and a more concerned attitude during the New Deal led to a reversal of land policy, a revival of interest in tribal identity, and a recognition of the importance of Indian culture, language, and ritual.

Women and the New Deal

Like some minorities, women made certain gains during the 1930s, but obstacles remained. While employment in general for women was not easy during a period of high unemployment for men, more women occupied high government positions in the Roosevelt administration than in any previous administration. The most visible was Frances Perkins, whose appointment as secretary of labor made her the first woman member of the cabinet. Katharine Lenroot, director of the Children's Bureau, and Mary Anderson, head of the Women's Bureau, selected many other women to serve in their agencies. With the support of Eleanor Roosevelt, Molly Dewson, a social worker who became head of the Women's

Division of the Democratic Committee and then an adviser to the president, worked to achieve a number of firsts: two women appointed ambassadors, a judge on the U.S. Court of Appeals, the director of the mint, and many women in government agencies.

Despite the number of women working for the government, feminism declined in the 1930s, and the image of woman's proper role continued to be housewife and mother.

THE LAST YEARS OF THE NEW DEAL

The New Deal was not a consistent or well-organized effort to end the Depression and restructure society. Roosevelt was a politician and a pragmatist, unconcerned about ideological or programmatic consistency. The first New Deal in 1933 and 1934 concentrated on relief and recovery, while the legislation passed in 1935 and 1936 was more involved with social reform. In many ways, the election of 1936 marked the high point of Roosevelt's power and influence. After 1937, in part because of the growing threat of war, but also because of increasing opposition in Congress, the pace of social legislation slowed. Yet several measures passed in 1937 and 1938 had such far-reaching significance that some historians refer to a third New Deal. Among the new measures were bills that provided for a minimum wage and for housing reform.

The Election of 1936

The Republicans in 1936 nominated a moderate, Governor Alfred Landon of Kansas. Roosevelt, helped by signs that the economy was recovering and supported by a coalition of the Democratic South, organized labor, farmers, and urban voters, won easily. A majority of black Americans for the first time deserted the party of Lincoln, not because of Roosevelt's interest in civil rights for blacks but because New Deal re-

lief programs assisted many poor blacks. Roosevelt won by over 10 million votes, carrying every state except Maine and Vermont. "To some generations much is given," Roosevelt announced in his acceptance speech; "of other generations much is expected. This generation has a rendezvous with destiny." Now he had a mandate to continue his New Deal social and economic reforms.

The Battle of the Supreme Court

The president's first action in 1937 was to announce a plan to reform the Supreme Court and the judicial system. The Court had invalidated a number of New Deal bills, including the NIRA and the first version of AAA. Increasingly angry at the "nine old men" who seemed to be destroying New Deal initatives and defying Congress's will, Roosevelt determined to create a more sympathetic Court. He hoped to gain power to appoint an extra justice for each justice over 70 years of age, of whom there were six. His plan also called for modernizing the court system at all levels, but that plan got lost in the public outcry over the Court-packing scheme.

Roosevelt's plan to nullify the influence of the older and more reactionary justices foundered. Many congressmen from his own party refused to support him. After months of controversy, Roosevelt withdrew the legislation and admitted defeat.

Ironically, though he lost the battle of the Supreme Court, Roosevelt won the war. By the spring of 1937, the Court began to reverse its position and in a 5–4 decision upheld the National Labor Relations Act. When Justice Willis Van Devanter retired, Roosevelt was able to make his first Supreme Court appointment, thus assuring at least a shaky liberal majority on the Court. But Roosevelt triumphed at great cost. His attempt to reorganize the Court was the most unpopular action he took as president, and even some of his supporters were dismayed by what they regarded as an attack on the principle of the separation of powers.

The economy improved in late 1936 and early 1937, but in August, the fragile prosperity collapsed. Unemployment shot back up, industrial production fell, and the stock market plummeted. Facing an embarrassing economic slump that evoked charges that the New Deal had failed, Roosevelt resorted to "deficit spending," as recommended by John Maynard Keynes, the British economist.

Keynes argued that to get out of a depression, the government must spend massive amounts of money on goods and services in order to increase demand and revive production. The economy responded slowly to increased government spending but never fully recovered until wartime expenditures, beginning in 1940, eliminated unemployment and ended the Depression.

The Third New Deal

Despite increasing hostility, Congress passed a number of important bills in 1937 and 1938 that completed the New Deal reform legislation. In 1937, the Farm Security Administration (FSA) was created to aid tenant farmers, sharecroppers, and farm owners who had lost their farms. More than a million men, women, and children were drifting aimlessly and hopelessly looking for work. The drought that had created a "dust bowl" in the Southwest worsened their plight. The FSA, which provided loans to grain collectives, also set up camps for migratory workers.

Congress passed a new Agricultural Adjustment Act in 1938 that tried to solve the continuing problem of farm surpluses. The new act replaced the processing tax, which the Supreme Court had declared unconstitutional, with direct payments from the federal treasury to farmers; added a soil conservation program; and provided for the marketing of surplus crops. Like its predecessor, the new act tried to stabilize farm prices by controlling production. But only the outbreak of World War II would end the problem of farm surplus, and then only temporarily.

In the cities, housing continued to be a problem. The Reconstruction Finance Corporation made low-interest loans to housing projects, and the Public Works Administration constructed some apartments. The National Housing Act of 1937 provided federal funds for slum clearance projects and for the construction of low-cost housing. By 1939, however, only 117,000 units had been built, and many of them soon became problems rather than solutions.

In the long run, New Deal housing legislation had a greater impact on middle-class housing policies and patterns. During the first 100 days of the New Deal, at Roosevelt's urging, Congress passed a bill creating the Home Owners Loan Corporation (HOLC), which over the next two years made more than $3 billion in low-interest loans and helped over a million people save their homes from foreclosure. The HOLC also introduced the first long-term fixed-rate mortgages and established a uniform system of real estate appraisal that tended to undervalue urban property, especially in neighborhoods that were old, crowded, and ethnically mixed. This was the beginning of the practice later called "redlining" that made it nearly impossible for certain prospective homeowners to obtain a mortgage in many urban areas.

The Federal Housing Administration (FHA), created in 1934 by the National Housing Act, expanded and extended many of these HOLC policies. New Deal housing policies helped to make the suburban home with the long FHA mortgage part of the American way of life, but the policies also contributed to the decline of many urban neighborhoods.

Just as important as housing legislation was the Fair Labor Standards Act, which Congress passed in June 1938. It applied to industries engaged in interstate commerce and called for a minimum wage of 25 cents an hour, to rise in two years to 40 cents an hour, and a maximum workweek of 44 hours, to be reduced to 40 hours. Congress exempted many groups, including farm laborers and domestic servants. Nevertheless, when it went into effect, 750,000 workers immediately received raises, and by 1940, some 12 million had had pay increases. The law also prohibited child labor in interstate commerce, making it the first permanent federal law to prohibit youngsters under 16 from working. And without emphasizing the matter, the law made no distinction between men and women.

The New Deal had many weaknesses, but it did dramatically increase government support for the needy. In 1913, local, state and federal governments spent $21 million on public assistance. By 1932, that had risen to $218 million; by 1939, it was $4.9 billion.

THE OTHER SIDE OF THE 1930s

The Great Depression and the New Deal so dominate the history of the 1930s that it is easy to conclude that nothing else happened, that there were only bread lines and relief agencies. But there is another side of the decade. A communications revolution changed the lives of middle-class Americans. The sale of radios and attendance at movies increased during the 1930s, and literature flourished. And automobiles facilitated travel.

Taking to the Road

"People give up everything in the world but their car," a banker in Muncie, Indiana, remarked during the Depression. Although automobile production dropped off after 1929 and did not recover until the end of the 1930s, the number of motor vehicles registered had swelled to over 32 million by 1940. People who could not afford new cars drove used ones. The fact that even many poor Americans owned cars shocked visitors from Europe, where automobiles were still only for the rich. Tourist courts sprang up across the country to accommodate travelers. In these predecessors of the motel there were no doormen, no bellhops, no register to sign. At the tourist court, all the owner wanted was the automobile license number.

The Electric Home

Just as travel became more convenient for families that owned automobiles, life at home also benefited from new technological developments. The sale of electrical appliances increased throughout the decade, with refrigerators leading the way. In 1930, the number of refrigerators produced exceeded the number of iceboxes for the first time.

Replacing an icebox with an electrical refrigerator, as many middle-class families did in the 1930s, altered more than the appearance of the kitchen. It also changed habits and life styles, especially for women. An icebox was part of a culture that included icemen, ice wagons (or ice trucks), picks, tongs, and a pan that had to be emptied continually. The refrigerator required no attention beyond occasional defrosting of the freezer compartment. Like the streamlined automobile, the sleek refrigerator became a symbol of progress and modern civilization in the 1930s. At the end of the decade, in 1939, the World's Fair in New York glorified the theme of a streamlined future, carefully planned and based on new technology.

The electric washing machine and electric iron revolutionized washday. Packaged and canned goods became more widely available during the decade, making food preparation easier.

Popular Pastimes

During the Depression, many people found themselves with time on their hands and sought out ways of spending it. The 1920s was a time of spectator sports, of football and baseball heroes, of huge crowds that turned out to see boxing matches. Those sports continued during the Depression decade, although attendance suffered. Softball and miniature golf also became popular.

Many popular games of the period had elaborate rules and directions. Contract bridge swept the country during the decade, and Monopoly was the most popular game of all. Produced by Parker Brothers, Monopoly was a fantasy of real estate speculation in which chance, luck, and the roll of the dice determined the winner.

The 1930s was also a time of fads and instant celebrities, created by radio, newsreels, and businessmen ready to turn almost anything to commercial advantage. The leading box office attraction between 1935 and 1938 was Shirley Temple, an adorable child star. She inspired dolls, dishes, books, and clothes. The media also focused on five identical girl babies born to a couple in northern Ontario in 1934. The Dionne quintuplets appeared on dozens of magazine covers and endorsed every imaginable product. Both Shirley Temple and the Dionne quintuplet craze were products of the new technology, especially radio and the movies.

Radio's Finest Hour

The number of radio sets purchased increased steadily during the 1930s. In 1929, slightly more than 10 million households owned radios; by 1939, fully 27.5 million households had radio sets. Families gathered around the radio at night to listen to and laugh at Jack Benny or Edgar Bergen and Charlie McCarthy or to try to solve a murder mystery with Mr. and Mrs. North. "The Lone Ranger," another popular program, had 20 million listeners by 1939. During the day there were soap operas.

The magic of radio allowed many people to feel connected to distant places and to believe they knew the radio performers personally. Radio was also responsible for one of the biggest hoaxes of all time. On October 31, 1938, Orson Welles broadcast "The War of the Worlds" so realistically that thousands of listeners really believed that Martians had landed in New Jersey. If anyone needed proof, that single program demonstrated the power of the radio.

The Silver Screen

The 1930s was the golden decade of the movies. Between 60 and 90 million Americans went to the movies every week. Talking films had replaced the silent variety in the late 1920s, and attendance soared. Though it fell off slightly in the early 1930s, by 1934 movie viewing was climbing again. For many families, even in the depth of the Depression, movie money was as important as food money.

The movies were a place to take a date, to go with friends, or to go as a family. Movies could be talked about for days. Young women tried to speak like Greta Garbo or to hold a cigarette like Joan Crawford. Jean Harlow and Mae West so popularized blonde hair that sales of peroxide shot up. Young men tried to emulate Clark Gable or Cary Grant, and one young man admitted that it was "directly through the movies that I learned to kiss a girl on her ears, neck, and cheeks, as well as on the mouth." The animated cartoons of Walt Disney, one of the true geniuses of the movie industry, were so popular that Mickey Mouse was more famous and familiar than most human celebrities.

Literary Reflections of the 1930s

Though much of the literature of the 1930s reflected the decade's troubled currents, reading continued to be a popular and cheap entertainment. John Steinbeck, whose later novel *The Grapes of Wrath* (1939) followed the fortunes of the Joad family, described the plight of Mexican migrant workers in *Tortilla Flat* (1935). John Dos Passos's trilogy *U.S.A.* (1930–1936) conveyed a deep pessimism about American capitalism. William Faulkner's fictional Yoknapatawpha County, brought to life in *The Sound and the Fury, As I Lay Dying, Sanctuary,* and *Light* in August (1929–1932), documented the South's racial problems, poverty, and stubborn pride. But the book about the South that became one of the decade's best-sellers was far more optimistic and far less complex than Faulkner's work—Margaret Mitchell's *Gone with the Wind* (1936). Its success suggested that many Americans read to escape, not to explore, their problems.

CONCLUSION

THE AMBIVALENCE OF THE GREAT DEPRESSION

The New Deal, despite its great variety of legislation, did not end the Depression, nor did it solve the problem of unemployment. For many Americans looking back on the decade of the 1930s, the most vivid memory was the shame and guilt of being unemployed, the despair and fear that came from losing a business or being evicted from a home or an apartment.

New Deal legislation did not solve the country's problems, but it did strengthen the federal government, especially the executive branch. Federal agencies like the Federal Deposit Insurance Corporation and programs like social security influenced the daily lives of most Americans, and rural electrification, the WPA, and the CCC changed the lives of millions. The New Deal also established the principle of federal responsibility for the health of the economy, initiated the concept of the welfare state, and dramatically increased government spending to help the poor.

The New Deal promoted social justice and social reform, but it provided little for people at the bottom of American society. The New Deal did not prevent business consolidation, and, in the end, it probably strengthened corporate capitalism. Roosevelt, with his colorful personality and his dramatic response to the nation's crisis, dominated his times in a way few presidents have done.

Recommended Reading

Robert S. McElvaine, *The Great Depression* (1984), is the best single volume on the subject. Donald Worster, *Dust Bowl* (1979), describes the impact of the Depression and the drought in the Southwest. Robert S. McElvaine, ed., *Down and Out in the Great Depression* (1983), uses letters written to Eleanor and Franklin Roosevelt to describe the reaction of ordinary Americans.

On the New Deal, see Paul K. Conkin, *The New Deal* (1967); Anthony J. Badger, *The New Deal: The Depression Years* (1989); and Steve Fraser and Gary Gertstle, eds., *The Rise and Fall of the New Deal Order* (1989). James MacGregor Burns, *Roosevelt: The Lion and the Fox* (1956), is still the best one-volume biography.

Specialized studies of the Depression and the New Deal abound. Harvard Sitkoff, *A New Deal for Blacks* (1978), discusses the limited attention given to blacks during the decade. On Collier and the Indian New Deal, see Kenneth R. Philip, *John Collier's Crusade for Indian Reform* (1977). Mark Reisler, *By the Sweat of Their Brow* (1976), descri'>es the plight of Mexican-Americans. Susan Ware, *3eyond Suffrage* (1981), depicts the lot of women durir.g the New Deal era. Irving Bernstein, *Turbulent Years* (1969), discusses the American worker and organized labor. Alan Brinkley, *Voices of Protest* (1982), tells the story of Father Coughlin and Huey Long. The other side of the 1930s can be followed in Warren Sussman, ed., *Culture and Commitment* (1973).

John Steinbeck shows Okies trying to escape the dust bowl in his novel *The Grapes of Wrath* (1939). James Farrell describes growing up in Depression Chicago in *Studs Lonigan* (1932–1935). Richard Wright details the trials of a young black man in *Native Son* (1940).

Time Line

1929	Stock market crashes Agricultural Marketing Act
1930	Depression worsens
1932	Reconstruction Finance Corporation established Glass-Steagall Banking Act Bonus march on Washington Franklin D. Roosevelt elected president
1933	Emergency Banking Relief Act Federal Emergency Relief Act Twenty-first Amendment repeals Eighteenth, ending prohibition Agricultural Adjustment Act National Industrial Recovery Act Civilian Conservation Corps Tennessee Valley Authority established Public Works Administration established
1934	Unemployment peaks Federal Housing Administration established Indian Reorganization Act
1935	Second New Deal begins Works Progress Administration established Social Security Act Rural Electrification Act National Labor Relations Act Public Utility Holding Company Act Committee for Industrial Organization (CIO) formed
1936	United Auto Workers hold sit-down strikes against General Motors Roosevelt reelected president Economy begins rebound
1937	Attempt to expand the Supreme Court Economic collapse Farm Security Administration established National Housing Act
1938	Fair Labor Standards Act Agricultural Adjustment Act

chapter 25

World War II

N. Scott Momaday, a Kiowa Indian born at Lawton, Oklahoma, in 1934, grew up on Navajo, Apache, and Pueblo reservations. He was only 11 when World War II ended, yet the war changed his life. Shortly after the United States entered the war, Momaday's parents moved to New Mexico, where his father got a job with an oil company and his mother worked in the civilian personnel office at an Army Air Force base. Like many couples, they had struggled through the hard times of the Depression. The war meant jobs.

Momaday's best friend was Billy Don Johnson, "a reddish, robust boy of great good humor and intense loyalty." Together they played war, digging trenches and dragging themselves through imaginary mine fields. Like most Americans, they believed that World War II was a good war fought against evil empires. The United States was always right, the enemy always wrong. It was an attitude that would influence Momaday and his generation for the rest of their lives.

Momaday's only difficulty was that his Native American face was often mistaken for that of an Asian. Almost every day on the school playground, someone would yell, "Hi ya, Jap," and a fight was on.

Near the end of the war, his family moved again, as so many families did, so that his father might get a better job. This time they lived right next door to an air force base, and Scott fell in love with the B-17 "Flying Fortress" bomber.

Looking back on his early years, Momaday reflected on the importance of the war in his growing up. "I see now that one experiences easily the ordinary things of life," he decided, "the things which cast familiar shadows upon the sheer, transparent panels of time, and he perceives his experience in the only way he can, according to his age." Though Momaday's youth was affected by the fact that he was male, was an Indian, and lived in the Southwest, the most important influence was that he was an American growing up during the war. Ironically, his parents, made U.S. citizens by an act of Congress in 1924 like all Native Americans living in Arizona and New Mexico, were denied the right to vote by state law.

Still, Momaday thought of himself not so much as an Indian as an American, and that too was a product of his generation. But as he grew to maturity, he became a successful writer and spokesman for his people. In 1969, he won the Pulitzer Prize for his novel *House Made of Dawn*. He also recorded his experiences and memories in a book called *The Names* (1976).

-◆-◇══◇-◆-

Despite the fact that no American cities were bombed and the country was never invaded, World War II influenced almost every aspect of American life. The war ended the Depression and unemployment. It also ended the last remnants of American isolationism. The United States emerged from the war in 1945 as the most powerful and most prosperous nation in the world.

This chapter traces the events during the 1930s that finally led to American participation in the most devastating war the world had seen. It recounts the diplomatic and military struggles of the war and the search for a secure peace. It also seeks to explain the impact of the war on ordinary Americans on their attitudes, and on their way of life. The war brought prosperity to some as it brought death to others.

THE TWISTING ROAD TO WAR

Looking back on the events between 1933 and 1941 that eventually led to American involvement in World War II, it is easy to be critical of decisions made or actions not taken. Leaders who must make decisions, however, never have the advantage of retrospective vision; they have to deal with situations as they find them, and they never have all the facts.

Foreign Policy in the 1930s

In March 1933, Roosevelt faced not only overwhelming domestic difficulties but also international crisis. The worldwide depression had caused near financial disaster in Europe. Germany had defaulted on its reparations installments, and most European countries were unable to keep up the payments on their debts to the United States.

Roosevelt had no master plan in foreign policy, just as he had none in the domestic sphere. At first, it seemed that the president would cooperate in some kind of international economic agreement on tariffs and currency. But during the June 1933 international economic conference in London, he undercut the American delegation by refusing to go along with any international agreement. Solving the American domestic economic crisis seemed more important to Roosevelt in 1933 than international economic cooperation. His actions signaled a decision to go it alone in foreign policy in the 1930s.

Roosevelt did, however, alter some of the foreign policy decisions of previous administrations. For example, he recognized the Soviet government, hoping to gain a market for surplus American grain. Although the expected trade bonanza never materialized, the Soviet Union agreed to pay the old debts and to extend rights to American citizens living in the Soviet Union. Diplomatic recognition opened communications between the two emerging world powers.

Led by Secretary of State Cordell Hull, Roosevelt's administration extended the Good Neighbor policy Hoover had initiated and completed the removal of American military forces from Haiti and Nicaragua in 1934. In a series of pan-American conferences, Roosevelt joined in pledging that no country in the hemisphere would intervene in the "internal or external affairs" of any other.

The first test of that pledge came in Cuba, where a revolution threatened American investments of more than a billion dollars. But the United States did not send troops. Instead Roosevelt dispatched special envoys to work out a conciliatory agreement with the revolutionary government. A short time later, when a coup led by Fulgencio Batista overthrew the revolutionary government, the United States not only recognized the Batista government but also offered a large loan and agreed to abrogate the Platt Amendment (which made Cuba a virtual protectorate of the United States) in return for the rights to a naval base.

Using presidential powers granted by the Trade Agreements Act of 1934, the Roosevelt administration negotiated a series of agreements that improved trade. By 1935, half of American cotton exports and a large proportion of other products were going to Latin America. So the Good Neighbor policy was also good business for the United States.

Another test for Latin American policy came in 1938 when Mexico nationalized the property of a number of American oil companies. Instead of intervening, as many businessmen urged, the State Department patiently worked out an agreement that included some compensation for the companies.

Neutrality in Europe

Around the time that Roosevelt was elected president, Adolf Hitler came to power in Germany. Born in Austria in 1889, Hitler had served as a corporal in the German army during World War I. Like many other Germans, he was angered by the Treaty of Versailles. But he blamed Germany's defeat on the Communists and the Jews.

Hitler, the leader of the National Socialist Party of the German Workers (*Nazi* is short for *National*), became chancellor of Germany on January 30, 1933, and within months the Reichstag (parliament) suspended the constitution, making Hitler *Führer* (leader) and dictator. His Fascist regime concentrated political and economic power in a centralized state. He intended to conquer Europe and to make the German Third Reich (empire) the center of a new civilization.

In 1934, Hitler announced a program of German rearmament, violating the Versailles Treaty of 1919. Meanwhile, in Italy, a Fascist dictator, Benito Mussolini, was building a powerful military force and threatening to invade the East African country of Ethiopia. These ominous rumblings in Europe frightened Americans, who never again wanted to get involved in a European conflict.

On many college campuses, students demonstrated against war. On April 13, 1934, a day of protest around the country, students at Smith College placed white crosses on the campus as a memorial to the people killed in the Great War and those who would die in the next one. The next year, even more students went on strike for a day. Students joined organizations like Veterans of Future Wars and Future Gold Star Mothers and protested the presence of the Reserve Office Training Corps on their campuses. They were determined never again to support a foreign war. But in Europe, Asia, and Africa, there were already rumblings of another great international conflict.

Ethiopia and Spain

In May 1935, Italy invaded Ethiopia and made quick work of the small and poorly equipped Ethiopian army. The Ethiopian war, remote as it seemed, frightened Congress, which passed a Neutrality Act authorizing the president to prohibit all arms shipments to nations at war and to advise all United States citizens not to travel on belligerents' ships except at their own risk. Remembering the process that led the United States into World War I, Congress was determined that it would not happen again. Roosevelt used the authority of the Neutrality Act of 1935 to impose an arms embargo. The embargo had little impact on Italy, but it was disastrous for the poor African nation. Italy quickly defeated Ethiopia, and by 1936, Mussolini had joined forces with Germany to form the Rome-Berlin Axis.

"We shun political commitments which might entangle us in foreign war," Roosevelt announced in 1936. "We are not isolationist except in so far as we seek to isolate ourselves completely from war." But isolation became more difficult when a civil war broke out in Spain in 1936. General Francisco Franco, supported by the Catholic church and large landowners, revolted against the republican government. Germany and Italy aided Franco, sending planes and other weapons, while the Soviet Union came to the support of the Spanish republican Loyalists. Most American Catholics and many anticommunists sided with Franco. But many American radicals, even those opposed to all war a few months before, found the Loyalist cause worth fighting and dying for. Over 3,000 Americans joined the Abraham Lincoln Brigade, and hundreds were killed fighting fascism in Spain.

The U.S. government tried to stay neutral and to ship arms and equipment to neither side. In 1937, Congress passed another Neutrality Act, this time making it illegal for American citizens to travel on belligerents' ships. The act extended the embargo on arms and made even nonmilitary items available to belligerents only on a cash-and-carry basis.

In a variety of ways, the United States tried to avoid repeating the mistakes that had led it into World War I. Unfortunately, World War II, which moved closer each day, would be a different kind of war, and the lessons of the first war would be of little use.

War in Europe

Roosevelt had no carefully planned strategy to deal with the rising tide of war in Europe in the late 1930s. He was by no means an isolationist, but he wanted to keep the United States out of the European conflagration.

Hitler, however, was on the move. In 1936 Hitler's troops marched into the Rhineland, an area demilitarized by the peace terms following World War I. In March 1938 he annexed Austria. Six months later he demanded the cession of Sudetenland, an adjacent part of Czechoslovakia. In a meeting at Munich on September 29, 1938, Britain and France agreed that Hitler could take Sudetenland, and Hitler, in turn, agreed to make no further territorial demands. The Munich Accords have since been held up as a lesson on the price of appeasing a dictator. Within six months, Hitler's armies had overrun the rest of Czechoslovakia.

Little protest came from the United States. Most Americans sympathized with the victims of Hitler's aggression, and eventually some were horrified at rumors of the murder of hundreds of thousands of Jews. August 23, 1939, brought news of a Nazi-Soviet pact. Fascism and communism were political philosophies supposedly in deadly opposition, but Nazi Germany and Soviet Russia had now signed a nonaggression pact. A week later, Hitler's army attacked Poland, marking the official beginning of World War II. Britain and France honored their treaties and came to Poland's defense. "This nation will remain a neutral nation," Roosevelt announced, "but I cannot ask that every American remain neutral in thought as well."

Roosevelt asked for a repeal of the embargo section of the Neutrality Act and for the approval of the sale of arms on a cash-and-carry basis to France and Britain. The United States would help the countries struggling against Hitler, but not at the risk of entering the war or even at the threat of disrupting the civilian economy. Yet Roosevelt did take some secret risks. In August 1939, Albert Einstein, a Jewish refugee from Nazi Germany, and other distinguished scientists warned the president that German researchers were at work on an atomic bomb. Fearing the consequences of a powerful new weapon in Hitler's hands, Roosevelt authorized funds for a top-secret project to build an American bomb first. Only a few advisers and key members of Congress knew of the project, which was officially organized in 1941 and would ultimately change the course of human history.

The war in Poland ended quickly. With Germany attacking from the west and the Soviet Union from the east, the Poles were overwhelmed in a month. The fall of Poland in September 1939 brought a lull in the fighting.

Great Britain sent several divisions to aid the French against the expected German attack, but for months nothing happened. Then on April 9, 1940, Germany attacked Norway and Denmark with a furious air and sea assault. A few weeks later, using armed vehicles supported by massive air strikes, the German *Blitzkrieg* swept through Belgium, Luxembourg, and the Netherlands. A week later, the Germans stormed into France. The famed Maginot line, a series of fortifications designed to repulse a German invasion, was useless as German mechanized forces swept around the end of the line and attacked from the rear. The French guns, solidly fixed in concrete and pointing toward Germany, were never fired. France surrendered in June as the British army fled back across the English Channel from Dunkirk.

Roosevelt reacted cautiously to events in Europe. He approved the shipment to Britain of 50 overage American destroyers. In return, the United States received the right to establish naval and air bases on British territory from Newfoundland to Bermuda and British Guiana.

In July 1940, Roosevelt also signed a measure authorizing $4 billion to increase the number of American naval warships. In September, Congress passed the Selective Service Act, which provided for the first peacetime draft in the history of the United States. As the war in Europe reached a crisis in the fall of 1940, the American people were still undecided about the proper response.

The Election of 1940

Part of Roosevelt's reluctance to aid Great Britain more energetically came from his genuine desire to keep the United States out of the war, but it was also related to the presidential campaign waged during the crisis months of the summer and fall of 1940. Roosevelt broke a long tradition by seeking a third term. He marked the increasing support he was drawing from the liberal wing of the Democratic party by selecting liberal farm economist Henry Wallace of Iowa as his running mate. The Republicans chose Wendell Willkie of Indiana, the most persuasive and exciting Republican candidate since Theodore Roosevelt. Yet in an atmosphere of international crisis, most voters chose to stay with Roosevelt. He won, 27 million to 22 million, and carried 38 of 48 states.

Lend-Lease

After the election, Roosevelt invented a scheme for sending aid to Britain without demanding payment, which Britain could not afford. He called the arrangement "lend-lease," and compared it to lending a garden hose to a neighbor whose house was on fire. The Lend-Lease Act, which Congress passed in March 1941, allowed the United States to lend or lease armaments to any country considered essential to American defense. The receiving country had only to agree to return the items after the war. The lend-lease program destroyed the fiction of neutrality.

By that time, German submarines were sinking a half million tons of shipping each month in the Atlantic. In June, Roosevelt proclaimed a national emergency and ordered the closing of German and Italian consulates in the United States. On June 22, Germany suddenly attacked the Soviet Union. It was one of Hitler's biggest blunders of the war, for now his armies had to fight on two fronts. In November 1941, Roosevelt extended lend-lease aid to Russia.

By the autumn of 1941, the United States was virtually at war with Germany in the Atlantic. It was not Germany, however, but Japan that catapulted the United States into World War II.

The Path to Pearl Harbor

Japan, controlled by ambitious military leaders, was the aggressor in the Far East as Hitler's Germany was in Europe. Intent on becoming a major world power yet desperately needing natural resources, especially oil, Japan was willing to risk war with China, the Soviet Union, and even the United States to get those resources. Japan invaded Manchuria in 1931 and launched an all-out assault on China in 1937. The Japanese leaders assumed that at some point the United States would go to war if Japan tried to take the Philippines, but the Japanese attempted to delay that moment as long as possible by diplomatic means. For its part, the United States feared the possibility of a two-front war and was willing to delay the confrontation with Japan until it had dealt with the German threat. Thus between 1938 and 1941, the United States and Japan engaged in a kind of diplomatic shadow boxing.

The United States did exert economic pressure on Japan, demanding that the Japanese withdraw from China. Beginning in July 1939, the United States gradually reduced trade shipments to Japan, but Japan continued on its course of expansion, occupying French Indochina in 1940 and 1941. In July 1941, Roosevelt froze all Japanese assets in the United States, effectively embargoing trade with Japan.

As the crisis developed, Roosevelt had an advantage in the negotiations with Japan, for the United States had broken the Japanese diplomatic code. But Japanese intentions were hard to decipher from the intercepted messages. The American leaders knew Japan was planning an attack, but they did not know when or where. In September 1941, the Japanese decided to strike at the United States sometime after November

unless the United States offered real concessions. The strike came at Pearl Harbor, the main American Pacific naval base, in Hawaii.

On the morning of December 7, 1941, Japanese airplanes launched from aircraft carriers attacked the United States fleet at Pearl Harbor. The surprise attack destroyed or disabled 19 ships (including 5 battleships) and 150 planes and killed 2,335 soldiers and sailors and 68 civilians. On the same day, the Japanese launched attacks on the Philippines, Guam, and the Midway Islands, as well as on the British colonies of Hong Kong and Malaya. The next day, with only one dissenting vote, Congress declared war on Japan. Jeannette Rankin, a member of Congress from Montana who had voted against the war resolution in 1917, voted no again on December 8, 1941. Three days later, Japan's allies, Germany and Italy, declared war on the United States. This time, Congress replied unanimously in declaring war on them.

December 7, 1941, was a day that would "live in infamy," in the words of Franklin Roosevelt. It was also a day that would have far-reaching implications for American foreign policy and for American attitudes toward the world. The surprise attack united the country as nothing else could have. Even isolationists quickly rallied behind the war effort.

After the shock and anger subsided, Americans searched for a villain. A myth persists to this day that the villain was Roosevelt, who, the story goes, knew of the Japanese attack but failed to warn the military commanders so that the American people might unite behind the war effort against Germany. But Roosevelt did not know. There was no specific warning that the attack was coming against Pearl Harbor, and the American ability to read the Japanese coded messages was no help because the fleet kept radio silence. The irony was that the Americans, partly because of racial prejudice against the Japanese, underestimated their ability.

Even more important in the long run than

An exploding American battleship at Pearl Harbor, December 7, 1941. The attack on Pearl Harbor united the country and came to symbolize Japanese treachery and American lack of preparedness. Photographs such as this were published throughout the war to inspire Americans to work harder.

the way the attack on Pearl Harbor united the American people was its effect on a generation of military and political leaders. Pearl Harbor became the symbol of unpreparedness. For a generation that experienced the anger and frustration of the attack on Pearl Harbor by an unscrupulous enemy, the lesson was to be prepared and ready to stop an aggressor before it had a chance to strike at the United States. The smoldering remains of the sinking battleships at Pearl Harbor on the morning of December 7, 1941, and the history lesson learned there would influence American policy not only during World War II but also in Korea, Vietnam, and the international confrontations of the 1980s.

THE HOME FRONT

World War II had an impact on all aspects of society—the economy, the movies and radio, even attitudes toward women and blacks. For many people, the war represented opportunity and the end of the Depression. For others, the excitement of faraway places meant that they could never return home again. For still others, the war left lasting scars.

Mobilizing for War

Converting American industry to war production was a complex task. Many corporate executives refused to admit that an emergency existed. Shortly after Pearl Harbor, Roosevelt created the War Production Board (WPB) and appointed Donald Nelson, executive vice president of Sears, Roebuck, to mobilize the nation's resources for an all-out war effort. The WPB offered businesses cost-plus contracts, guaranteeing a fixed and generous profit. Often the government also financed new plants and equipment.

The Roosevelt administration leaned over backward to gain the cooperation of businessmen. The president appointed many business executives to key positions, some of whom, like Nelson, served for a dollar a year. He also abandoned antitrust actions in all industries that were remotely war related.

The policy worked. Both industrial production and net corporate profits nearly doubled during the war. Large commercial farmers also profited. The war years accelerated the mechanization of the farm. At the same time, the farm population declined by 17 percent. The consolidation of small farms into large ones and the dramatic increase in the use of fertilizer made farms more productive and farming more profitable for the large operators.

Many government agencies in addition to the War Production Board helped to run the war effort efficiently. The Office of Price Administration (OPA) set prices on thousands of items to control inflation and also rationed scarce products. The National War Labor Board (NWLB) had the authority to set wages and hours and to monitor working conditions and could, under the president's wartime emergency powers, seize industrial plants whose owners refused to cooperate.

Membership in labor unions grew rapidly during the war, from a total of 10.5 million in 1941 to 14.7 million in 1945. This increase was aided by government policy. In return for a "no-strike pledge," the NWLB allowed agreements that required workers to retain their union membership through the life of a contract. Labor leaders, however, were often not content with the raises permitted by the NWLB. In the most famous incident, John L. Lewis broke the no-strike pledge of organized labor by calling a nationwide coal strike in 1943. When Roosevelt ordered the secretary of the interior to take over the mines, Lewis called off the strike. But this bold protest did help raise miners' wages.

In addition to wage and price controls and rationing, the government tried to reduce inflation by selling war bonds and by increasing taxes. The war made the income tax a reality for most Americans for the first time.

Despite some unfairness and much confusion, the American economy responded to the wartime crisis and turned out the equipment and supplies that eventually won the war. American industries built 300,000 airplanes, 88,140 tanks, and 3,000 merchant ships. Although the national debt grew from about $143 billion in 1943 to $260 billion in 1945, the government policy of taxation paid for about 40 percent of the war's cost. In a limited way, the tax policy also tended to redistribute wealth, which the New Deal had failed to do. The top 5 percent income bracket, which controlled 23 percent of the disposable income in 1939, accounted for only 17 percent in 1945.

Patriotic Fervor

In European and Asian cities, the horror and destruction of war were everywhere. But in the United States, the war was remote. The government tried to keep the country united behind the war effort. The Office of War Information, staffed by writers and advertising executives, controlled the news the American public received about the war. It promoted patriotism and presented the American war effort in the best possible light.

The government also sold war bonds, not only to help pay for the war and reduce inflation but also to sell the war to the American people. As had been true during World War I, movie stars and other celebrities appeared at war bond rallies. Schoolchildren purchased war stamps and faithfully pasted them in an album until they had accumulated stamps worth $18.75, enough to buy a $25 bond (redeemable ten years later). In the end, the government sold over $135 billion in war bonds.

Those too old or too young to join the armed forces served in other ways. Thousands became air raid wardens or civilian defense and Red Cross volunteers. They raised victory gardens and took part in scrap drives. Even small children could join the war effort by collecting old rubber, waste paper, and kitchen fats. Some items, including gasoline, sugar, butter, and meat, were rationed, but few people complained. Newspaper and magazine advertising characterized ordinary actions as speeding victory or impeding the war effort. "Hoarders are the same as spies," one ad announced. "Everytime you decide *not* to buy something you help win the war."

Internment of Japanese-Americans

Wartime campaigns not only stimulated patriotism but also promoted hate for the enemy. "You and I don't hate the Nazis because they are Germans. We hate the Germans because they are Nazis," announced a character in one of Helen MacInnes's novels. But before long, most Americans ceased to make distinctions. All Germans seemed evil, although the anti-German hysteria that had swept the country during World War I never developed.

The Japanese were easier to hate than the Germans. The attack on Pearl Harbor created a special animosity toward the Japanese, but the depiction of the Japanese as warlike and subhuman owed something to a long tradition of fear of the so-called yellow peril and a distrust of all Asians. The movies, magazine articles, cartoons, and posters added to the image of the Japanese soldier or pilot with a toothy grin murdering innocent women and children or shooting down helpless Americans.

The racial stereotype of the Japanese played a role in the treatment of Japanese-Americans during the war. Some prejudice was shown against German- and Italian-Americans, but Japanese-Americans were the only group confined in concentration camps in the greatest mass abridgment of civil liberties in American history.

At the time of Pearl Harbor, about 127,000 Japanese-Americans lived in the United States, most on the West Coast. About 80,000 were nisei (Japanese born in the United States and holding American citizenship) and sansei (the sons and daughters of nisei); the rest were issei (aliens born in Japan who were ineligible for U.S. citizenship). Although many retained cultural and linguistic ties to Japan, they posed no

more threat to the country than did the much larger groups of Italian-Americans and German-Americans. But their physical characteristics made them stand out as the others did not. After Pearl Harbor, an anti-Japanese panic seized the West Coast.

West Coast politicians and ordinary citizens urged the War Department and the president to evacuate the Japanese. The president capitulated and issued Executive Order 9066 authorizing the evacuation in February 1942.

Eventually, the government built the "relocation centers" in remote, often arid, sections of the West. The camps were primitive and unattractive. "When I first entered our room, I became sick to my stomach," a Japanese-American woman remembered. "There were seven beds in the room and no furniture nor any partitions to separate the males and the females of the family. I just sat on the bed, staring at the bare wall." The government evacuated about 110,000 Japanese. Those who were forced to leave their homes, farms, and businesses lost almost all their property and possessions.

The evacuation of the Japanese-Americans appears in retrospect to have been unjustified. Even in Hawaii, where a much larger Japanese population existed, the government attempted no evacuation, and no sabotage and little disloyalty occurred. The government allowed Japanese-American men to volunteer for military service, and many served bravely in the European theater. The 442nd Infantry Combat Team, made up entirely of nisei, became the most decorated unit in all the military service—another indication of the loyalty and patriotism of the Japanese-Americans. In 1988, Congress belatedly voted limited compensation for the Japanese-Americans relocated during World War II.

Black and Hispanic Americans at War

The United States in 1941, even in much of the North, remained a segregated society. Blacks

Japanese-American children on their way to a "relocation center." For many Japanese-Americans, but especially for the children, the nightmare of the relocation camp experience would stay with them all their lives.

could not live, eat, travel, work, or go to school with the same freedom whites enjoyed. Blacks profited little from the revival of prosperity and the expansion of jobs early in the war. Blacks who joined the military were usually assigned to menial jobs as cooks or laborers and were always assigned to segregated units with whites as the high-ranking officers. The myth that black soldiers had failed to perform well in World War I persisted.

Some black leaders found it especially ironic that as the country prepared to fight Hitler and his racist policies, the United States persisted in its own brand of racism. "A jim crow Army cannot fight for a free world," announced *The Crisis,* the journal of the NAACP. In 1941, A. Philip Randolph, who had organized and led the Brotherhood of Sleeping Car Porters, planned a march on Washington to demand equal rights.

The threat of as many as 100,000 blacks marching in protest in the nation's capital alarmed Roosevelt. At first he sent his assistants, including his wife, Eleanor, who was greatly admired in the black community, to dissuade Randolph from such drastic action. Finally, he talked to Randolph in person on June 18, 1941. Randolph and Roosevelt struck a bargain. Roosevelt refused to desegregate the armed forces, but in return for Randolph's calling off the march, the president issued Executive Order 8802, which stated that it was the policy of the United States that "there shall be no discrimination in the employment of workers in defense industries or government because of race, creed, color or national origin." He also established the Committee on Fair Employment Practices (FEPC) to carry out the order, but it was never effectively enforced.

Blacks continued to experience discrimination in other areas of life as well. Many black soldiers were angered and humiliated throughout the war by being made to sit in the back of buses and being barred from hotels and restaurants. Years later, one former black soldier recalled being refused service in a restaurant in Salina, Kansas, while the same restaurant served German prisoners from a camp nearby. "We continued to stare," he recalled. "This was really happening. . . . The people of Salina would serve these enemy soldiers and turn away black American G.I.'s."

Many black Americans improved their economic conditions during the war by taking jobs in war industries in northern and western cities. But they did not escape racial prejudice. In Detroit, a major race riot broke out in the summer of 1943. Polish-Americans had protested a public housing development that promised to bring blacks into their neighborhood. In one year, more than 50,000 blacks moved into that city, already overcrowded with many others seeking wartime jobs.

The riot broke out on a hot, steamy day at a municipal park where a series of incidents led to fights between black and white young people

Even before the United States entered the war, black families like this one moved north to look for work and a better life. This massive migration would change the racial mix in northern cities.

and then to looting in the black community. Before federal and state troops restored order, 34 had been killed (25 blacks and 9 whites), and rioters had destroyed more than $2-million worth of property. Other riots broke out in Mobile, Los Angeles, New York, and Beaumont, Texas. In all these cities, and in many others where the tension did not lead to open violence, the legacy of bitterness and hate lasted long after the war.

Mexican-Americans, like most minority groups, profited during the war from the increased job opportunities provided by wartime industry. But they, too, faced prejudice and discrimination.

In California and in many parts of the Southwest, Mexicans and Mexican-Americans could not use public swimming pools. Often lumped together with blacks, they were excluded from certain restaurants. Usually they were limited to menial jobs and were constantly harassed by the police, picked up for minor offenses, and jailed on the smallest excuse. In Los Angeles, the anti-Mexican prejudice flared into violence. The increased migration of Mexicans into the city and old hatreds created a volatile situation. Most of the hostility and anger focused on Mex-

ican gang members, or *pachucos,* especially those wearing zoot suits (long, loose coats with padded shoulders, ballooned pants pegged at the ankles, and a wide-brimmed hat).

The zoot-suiters especially angered soldiers and sailors who were stationed or on leave in Los Angeles. After a number of provocative incidents, the violence reached a peak on June 7, 1943, when gangs of servicemen, often in taxicabs, combed the city, attacking all the young zoot-suiters they could find or anyone who looked Mexican. The servicemen, joined by others, beat up the Mexicans, stripped them of their clothes, and then gave them haircuts. The police, both civilian and military, looked the other way, and when they did move in, they arrested the victims rather than their attackers. *Time* magazine called the riots "the ugliest brand of mob action since the coolie race riots of the 1870s."

THE SOCIAL IMPACT OF THE WAR

Modern wars have been incredibly destructive of human lives and property, and they have social results as well. The Civil War ended slavery and ensured the triumph of the industrial North for years to come; it left a legacy of bitterness and transformed the race question from a sectional to a national problem. World War I assured the success of woman suffrage and prohibition, caused a migration of blacks to northern cities, and ushered in a time of intolerance. World War II also had many social results. It altered patterns of work, leisure, education, and family life; caused a massive migration of people; created jobs; and changed life styles. It is difficult to overemphasize the impact of the war on the generation that lived through it.

Wartime Opportunities

The war caused many Americans to move to other parts of the country. More than 15 million civilians moved during the war, flocking to cities, where defense jobs were readily available. They moved west: California alone gained more than two million people during the war. But they also moved out of the South into the northern cities, while a smaller number moved from the North to the South. Late in the war, when a shortage of farm labor developed, some reversed the trend and moved back onto the farms.

The World War II migrants poured into industrial centers; 200,000 came to the Detroit area, nearly a half million to Los Angeles, and about 100,000 to Mobile, Alabama. They put pressure on the schools, housing, and other services. Often they had to live in new Hoovervilles, trailer parks, or temporary housing. Bill Mauldin, the war cartoonist, showed a young couple with a child buying tickets for a movie, with the caption: "Matinee, heck—we want to register for a week."

For the first time in years, many families had money to spend, but they had nothing to spend it on. The last new car rolled off the assembly line in February 1942. There were no washing machines, refrigerators, or radios in the stores, little gasoline and few tires to permit weekend trips.

The war required major adjustments in American family life. With several million men in the service and others far away working at defense jobs, the number of households headed by a woman increased dramatically. The number of marriages also rose sharply. Early in the war, a young man could be deferred if he had a dependent, and a wife qualified as a dependent. Later, many servicemen got married, often to women they barely knew, because they wanted a little excitement and perhaps someone to come home to. The birthrate also began to rise in 1940, reversing a long decline. The illegitimacy rate also went up, and from the outset of the war, the divorce rate began to climb sharply. Yet most of the wartime marriages survived, and many of the women left at home looked ahead to a time after the war when they could settle down to a normal life.

Women Workers for Victory

Another impact of the war was the opening of industrial jobs to women. Thousands of women took jobs in heavy industry that formerly would have been considered unladylike. They built tanks, airplanes, and ships, but they still earned less than men.

By 1943, with many men drafted and male unemployment virtually nonexistent, the government was quick to suggest that it was women's patriotic duty to take their place on the assembly line. A popular song was "Rosie the Riveter," who was "making history working for victory."

At the end of the war, the labor force included 19.5 million women. In 1944, women's weekly wages averaged $31.21, compared with $54.65 for men, reflecting women's more menial tasks and their low seniority as well as outright discrimination. Still, many women enjoyed factory work. "Boy have the men been getting away with murder all these years," exclaimed a Pittsburgh housewife. "Why I worked twice as hard selling in a department store and got half the pay." In addition to lower pay, women workers often had to endure catcalls, whistles, and more overt sexual harassment on the job.

Black women faced the most difficult situation during the war, and often when they applied for work, they were told, "We have not yet installed separate toilet facilities" or "We can't put a Negro in the front office." Not until 1944 did the telephone company in New York City hire a black telephone operator. Married women with young children also found it difficult to find work. They found few day-care facilities and were often informed that they should be home with their children.

Many women war workers quickly left their jobs after the war ended. Some left by choice, but many were laid off, because the law guaranteed to returning male veterans their former jobs. As war industries slowed down, dismissals ran twice as high for women as for men. The war had only temporarily shaken the notion that a woman's place was at home.

Entertaining the People

According to one survey, Americans listened to the radio an average of 4½ hours a day during the war. The major networks increased their news programs from less than 4 percent to nearly 30 percent of broadcasting time. Americans heard Edward R. Murrow broadcasting from London during the German air blitz with the sound of the air raid sirens in the background. They listened to Eric Sevareid cover the battle of Burma and describe the sensation of jumping out of an airplane. They also relied on commentators like H. V. Kaltenborn or Gabriel Heatter to explain what was happening around the world.

The serials, the standard fare of daytime radio, also adopted wartime themes. Dick Tracy tracked down spies, while Stella Dallas took a job in a defense plant.

Music, which took up a large proportion of radio programming, also conveyed a war theme. There was "Goodbye, Mama (I'm Off to Yokohama)" and "Praise the Lord and Pass the Am-

munition." But more numerous were songs of romance and love, songs about separation and hope for a better time after the war. The danceable tunes of Glenn Miller and Tommy Dorsey became just as much a part of wartime memories as ration books and far-off battlefields.

For many Americans, the motion picture became the most important leisure activity and a part of their fantasy life during the war. Attendance at the movies averaged about 100 million individuals a week. There might not be gasoline for weekend trips or Sunday drives, but the whole family could go to the movies.

Musical comedies, cowboy movies, and historical romances remained popular during the war, but the conflict intruded even on Hollywood. Newsreels that offered a visual synopsis of the war news, always with an upbeat message and a touch of human interest, preceded most movies. Their theme was that the Americans were winning the war, even if early in the conflict there was little evidence to that effect. Many feature films also had a wartime theme, picturing the war in the Pacific complete with grinning, vicious Japanese villains (usually played by Chinese or Korean character actors). In the beginning of these films, the Japanese were always victorious, but in the end, they always got "what they deserved."

The movies set in Europe differed somewhat from those depicting the Far Eastern war. British and Americans, sometimes spies, sometimes downed airmen, could dress up like Germans and get away with it. They outwitted the Germans at every turn, sabotaging important installations and finally escaping in a captured plane.

The GIs' War

GI, the abbreviation for *government issue,* became the affectionate designation for the ordinary soldier in World War II. The GIs came from every background and ethnic group. Ernie Pyle, one of the war correspondents who chronicled the authentic story of the ordinary GI, wrote of soldiers "just toiling from day to day in a world full of insecurity, discomfort, homesickness, and a dulled sense of danger."

Bill Mauldin, another correspondent, told the story of the ordinary soldier in a series of cartoons featuring two tired and resigned infantrymen, Willie and Joe. In one cartoon Willie says, "Joe, yestiddy ya saved my life an' I swore I'd pay you back. Here's my last pair of dry socks." For the soldier in the front line, the big strategies were irrelevant. The war seemed a constant mixup; much more important were the little comforts and staying alive.

In the midst of battle, the war was no fun, but only one soldier of eight who served ever saw combat, and even for many of those the war was a great adventure (just as World War I had been). World War II catapulted young men and women out of their small towns and urban neighborhoods into exotic places where they met new people and did new things.

The war was important for Mexican-Americans, who were drafted and volunteered in great numbers. A third of a million served in all branches of the military, a larger percentage than for many other ethnic groups.

Many Native Americans also served. In fact, many Indians were recruited for special service in the Marine Signal Corps. One group of Navajos completely befuddled the Japanese with a code based on their native language. "Were it not for the Navajos, the Marines would never have taken Iwo Jima," one Signal Corps officer declared. But the Navajo code talkers and all other Indians who chose to return to the reservations after the war were ineligible for veterans' loans, hospitalization, and other benefits. They lived on federal land, and that, according to the law, canceled all the advantages that other veterans enjoyed after the war.

For black Americans, who served throughout the war in segregated units and faced prejudice wherever they went, the military experience also had much to teach. Fewer blacks were sent overseas, and fewer were in combat outfits, so the percentage of black soldiers killed and wounded was low. Many illiterate blacks, especially from the South, learned to read and write in the service. Blacks who went overseas began to realize that not everyone viewed them as inferior. One black army officer said, "What the hell do we want to fight the Japs for anyhow? They couldn't possibly treat us any worse than these 'crackers' right here at home."

Because the war lasted longer than World War I, its impact was greater. In all, over 16 million men and women served in some branch of the military service. About 322,000 were killed in the war, and more than 800,000 were wounded. The 12,000 listed as missing just disappeared. The war claimed many more lives than World War I and was the nation's costliest after the Civil War. But because of penicillin, blood plasma, sulfa drugs, and rapid battle-field evacuation, the wounded in World War II were twice as likely to survive as in World War I.

Women in Uniform

Women had served in all wars as nurses and cooks and in other support capacities, and during World War II many continued in these traditional roles. A few nurses landed in France just days after the Normandy invasion. Nurses served with the army and the marines in the Pacific. They dug their own foxholes and treated men under enemy fire. Sixty-six nurses spent the entire war in the Philippines as prisoners of the Japanese. Most nurses, however, served far behind the lines tending the sick and wounded. Army nurses who were given officer rank were forbidden to date enlisted men.

Though nobody objected to women's serving as nurses, not until April 1943 did women physicians win the right to join the Army and Navy Medical Corps. Congress authorized full military participation for women (except for combat) because of the military emergency and the argument that women could free men for combat duty. World War II thus became the first war in which women were given regular military status. About 350,000 women joined up, most in the Women's Army Corps (WACS) and the women's branch of the navy (WAVES), but others served in the coast guard and the marines.

Men were informed about contraceptives and encouraged to use them, but information about birth control was explicitly prohibited for women. Rumors charged many servicewomen with sexual promiscuity. One cause for immediate discharge was pregnancy; yet the pregnancy rate for both married and unmarried women remained low.

Despite difficulties, women played important roles during the war, and when they left the service (unlike the women who had served in other wars), they had the same rights and privileges as the male veterans. And like male soldiers, many of the women who served had their lives changed and their horizons expanded.

A War of Diplomats and Generals

Pearl Harbor catapulted the country into war with Japan, and on December 11, 1941, Hitler declared war on the United States, forcing it to fight the Axis powers in both Europe and Asia.

War Aims

Why was the United States fighting the war? What did it hope to accomplish in a peace settlement once the war was over? Roosevelt and the other American leaders never really decided. In a speech before Congress in January 1941, Roosevelt had mentioned the four freedoms: freedom of speech and expression, freedom of worship, freedom from want, and freedom from fear. For many Americans, this was what they were fighting for. Roosevelt spoke vaguely of the need to extend democracy and to establish a peacekeeping organization, but in direct contrast to Woodrow Wilson's Fourteen Points, he never spelled out in any detail the political purposes for fighting.

Roosevelt and his advisers, realizing that it would be impossible to mount an all-out war against both Japan and Germany, decided to fight a holding action in the Pacific at first while concentrating efforts against Hitler in Europe, where the immediate danger seemed greater. The United States joined the Soviet Union and Great Britain in a difficult but ultimately effective alliance to defeat Nazi Germany. British prime minister Winston Churchill and Roosevelt got along well, although they often disagreed on strategy and tactics. Roosevelt's relationship with Soviet leader Joseph Stalin was much more strained, but often he agreed with the Russian leader about the way to fight the war. Stalin, a ruthless leader who had maintained his position of power only after eliminating hundreds of thousands of opponents, distrusted both the British and the Americans, but he needed them, just as they depended on him. Without the tremendous sacrifices of the Soviet army and people in 1941 and 1942, Germany would have won the war before the vast American military and industrial might could be mobilized.

1942: Year of Disaster

The first half of 1942 was disastrous for the Allied cause. In the Pacific, the Japanese captured the Dutch East Indies with their vast riches in rubber, oil, and other resources. They swept into Burma, took Wake Island and Guam, and invaded the Aleutian Islands of Alaska. They pushed the American garrison on the Philippines onto the Bataan peninsula and finally onto the tiny island of Corregidor, where U.S. General Jonathan Wainwright surrendered more than 11,000 men to the Japanese. American reporters tried to play down the disasters, concentrating their stories on the few American victories and on tales of American heroism against overwhelming odds.

In Europe, the Germans pushed deep into

World War II: Pacific Theater

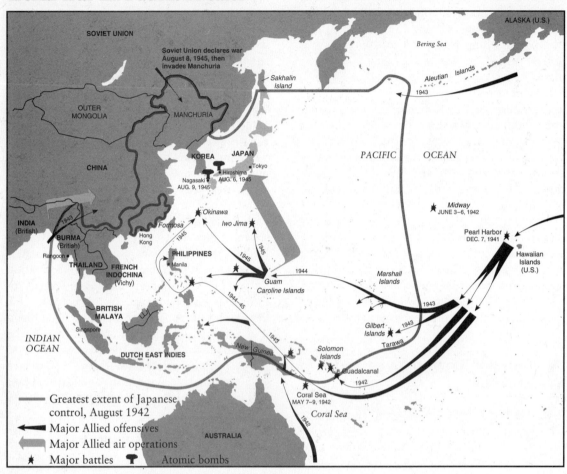

After the surprise attack on Pearl Harbor, the Japanese extended their control in the Pacific from Burma to the Aleutian Islands and almost to Australia. But after American naval and air victories at Coral Sea and Midway in 1942, the Japanese were increasingly on the defensive.

Russia, threatening Moscow. In North Africa, General Erwin Rommel and his mechanized divisions, the Afrika Korps, drove the British forces almost to Cairo in Egypt and threatened the Suez Canal. In contrast to World War I, which had been a war of stalemate, the opening phase of World War II was marked by air strikes and swift advances. In the Atlantic, German submarines sank British and American ships more

rapidly than they could be replaced. For a few dark months in 1942, it seemed that the Berlin-Tokyo Axis would win the war before the United States got itself ready to fight.

The Allies could not agree on the proper military strategy in Europe. Stalin demanded a second front, an invasion of Europe in 1942, to relieve the pressure on the Soviet army, which faced 200 German divisions along a 2,000-mile front. Roo-

World War II: European and North African Theaters

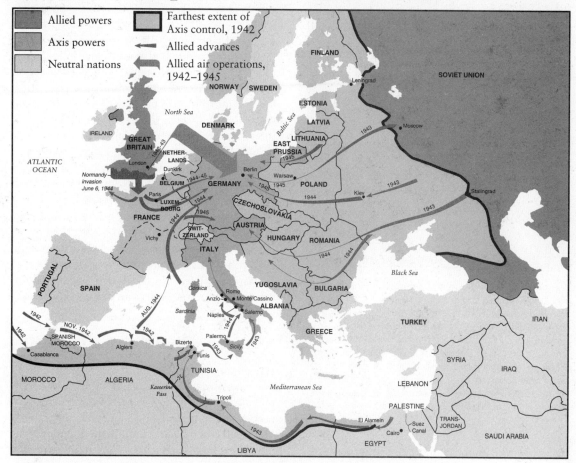

The German war machine swept across Europe and North Africa and almost captured Cairo and Moscow, but after major defeats at Stalingrad and El Alamein in 1943, the Axis powers were in retreat. Many lives were lost on both sides before the Allied victory in 1945.

sevelt agreed to an offensive in 1942. But in the end, the invasion in 1942 came not in France but in North Africa. The decision was probably right from a military point of view, but it taught the Soviets to distrust Britain and the United States. The delay in opening the second front probably contributed indirectly to the Cold War after 1945.

Attacking in North Africa in November 1942, American and British troops tried to link up with a beleaguered British army. The Ameri-

can army, enthusiastic but inexperienced, met little resistance in the beginning, but at Kasserine Pass in Tunisia, the Germans counter attacked and destroyed a large American force, inflicting 5,000 casualties.

To gain a cease-fire in conquered French territory in North Africa, the United States recognized Admiral Jean Darlan as head of its provisional government. Darlan persecuted the Jews, exploited the Arabs, imprisoned his opponents, and

The death camp Buchenwald, established by the Nazis in 1937, was liberated by American troops on April 13, 1945. One of the survivors was Elie Wiesel (shown here third from the right, middle level), whose mother and sister died in Auschwitz and whose father died in Buchenwald. Wiesel emigrated to the United States in 1956 and subsequently published an autobiographical novel, Night, *in which he described the horrors of existence in the concentration camp. For his efforts in exposing the evils of the Holocaust, he received the Nobel Prize for Peace in 1986.*

collaborated with the Nazis. The Darlan compromise reinforced Soviet distrust of the United States and angered many Americans as well.

Roosevelt also aided General Francisco Franco, the Fascist dictator in Spain, in return for safe passage of American shipping into the Mediterranean. But the United States also supplied arms to the left-wing resistance in France, to the Communist Tito in Yogoslavia, and Ho Chi Minh, the anti-French resistance leader in Indochina. Roosevelt also authorized large-scale lend-lease aid to the Soviet Union. Although liberals criticized his support of dictators, Roosevelt was willing to do almost anything to win the war. Military expediency often dictated his political decisions.

Even on one of the most sensitive issues of the war, the plight of the Jews in occupied Europe, Roosevelt's solution was to win the war as quickly as possible. By November 1942, confirmed information had reached the United States that the Nazis were systematically exterminating Jews. Yet the Roosevelt administration did nothing for more than a year, and even then it did scandalously little to rescue European Jews from the gas chambers. Widespread anti-Semitic feelings in the United States in the 1940s and the fear of massive Jewish immigration help to explain the failure of the Roosevelt administration to act. Roosevelt could not have prevented the Holocaust, but vigorous action on his part could have saved many thousands of lives during the war.

Roosevelt was not always right, nor was he even consistent, but people who assumed he had a master strategy or a fixed ideological position misunderstood the American president.

A Strategy for Ending the War

The commanding general of the Allied armies in the North African campaign emerged as a genuine leader. Born in Texas, Dwight D. Eisenhower spent his boyhood in Abilene, Kansas. His small-town background made it easy for biographers and newspaper reporters to make him into an American hero. Eisenhower was only a lieutenant colonel when World War II erupted. He was quickly promoted to general and achieved a reputation as an expert planner and organizer. Not a brilliant field commander, he had the ability to get diverse people working together, which was crucial where British and American units had to cooperate.

The American army moved slowly across North Africa, linked up with the British, invaded Sicily in July 1943, and finally stormed ashore in Italy in September. The Italian campaign proved long and bitter. The Allies did not reach Rome until June 1944, and they never controlled all of Italy.

President Roosevelt inspects General Eisenhower's troops in Sicily before returning home from the Cairo-Tehran Conference in 1943. These were two of the dominant personalities of the war years.

Despite the decision to make the war in Europe the first priority, American ships and planes halted the Japanese advance in the spring of 1942. In the Battle of Coral Sea in May 1942, American carrier-based planes inflicted heavy damage on the Japanese fleet and prevented the invasion of the southern tip of New Guinea and probably of Australia as well. It was the first naval battle in history in which no guns were fired from one surface ship against another; airplanes caused all the damage. In World War II, the aircraft carrier proved more important than the battleship. A month later, at the Battle of Midway, American planes sank four Japanese aircraft carriers and destroyed nearly 300 planes. This was the first major Japanese defeat; it restored some balance of power in the Pacific and ended the threat to Hawaii.

In 1943, the American sea and land forces leapfrogged from island to island, gradually retaking territory from the Japanese, often at terrible cost.

The Invasion of Europe

Operation Overlord, the code name for the largest amphibious invasion in history, the invasion Stalin had wanted in 1942, began only on June 6, 1944. It was, according to Churchill, "the most difficult and complicated operation that has ever taken place." The initial assault along a 60-mile stretch of the Normandy coast was conducted with 175,000 men supported by 600 warships and 11,000 planes. Within a month, over a million troops and more than

170,000 vehicles had landed. Eisenhower, now bearing the title Supreme Commander of the Allied Expeditionary Force in Western Europe, coordinated and planned the operation.

For months before the invasion, American and British planes had bombed German transportation lines, industrial plants, and even cities. However, in retrospect, the bombing of the cities may have strengthened the resolve of the German people to fight to the bitter end. The most destructive bombing raid of the war was carried out against Dresden on the night of February 13–14, 1945, to help demonstrate to Stalin that the British and Americans were aiding the Russian offensive. Three waves of planes dropped 650,000 incendiary bombs, causing a firestorm that swept over eight square miles, destroyed everything in its path and killed 135,000 civilians. One of the American pilots remarked, "For the first time I felt sorry for the population below."

With the dashing and eccentric General George Patton leading the charge and the more staid General Omar Bradley in command, the American army broke out of the Normandy beachhead in July 1944. Led by the tank battalions, it swept across France. American productive capacity and the ability to supply a mobile and motorized army eventually brought victory.

By late 1944, the American and British armies had swept across France, while the Russians had pushed the German forces out of much of eastern Europe. The war seemed nearly over. However, just before Christmas in 1944, the Germans launched a massive counterattack along an 80-mile front, much of it held by thinly dispersed and inexperienced American troops. During the Battle of the Bulge, as it was called, the Germans drove 50 miles inside the American lines before they were checked.

The Politics of Victory

As the American and British armies raced across France into Germany in the winter and spring of 1945, the political and diplomatic aspects of the war began to overshadow military concerns. It became a matter not only of defeating Germany but also of determining who was going to control Germany and the rest of Europe once Hitler fell. The relationship between the Soviet Union and the other Allies had been badly strained during the war; with victory in sight, the tension became even greater. High-level American diplomats and presidential advisers distrusted the Soviets and urged Roosevelt to make military decisions with the postwar political situation in mind.

The main issue in the spring of 1945 concerned who would capture Berlin. The British wanted to beat Stalin's forces to the capital city. Eisenhower, however, fearing that the Germans might barricade themselves in the Austrian Alps and hold out indefinitely, ordered the armies south rather than toward Berlin. Soviet and American troops met on April 25, 1945, at the Elbe River. On May 2, the Soviets took Berlin. Hitler committed suicide. The long war in Europe finally came to an end on May 8, 1945, but political problems remained.

In 1944, the United States continued to tighten the noose on Japan. American long-range B-29 bombers began sustained strikes on the Japanese mainland in June 1944, and by November they were dropping firebombs on Tokyo. American planes destroyed most of the remaining Japanese navy. By the end of 1944, an American victory in the Pacific was all but assured. American forces recaptured the Philippines early the next year, yet the American forces had barely touched Japan itself.

While the military campaigns reached a critical stage in both Europe and the Pacific, Roosevelt took time off to run for an unprecedented fourth term. To appease members of his own party, he replaced Vice President Henry Wallace, regarded by some as too radical, with a relatively unknown senator from Missouri, Harry S Truman. The Republicans nominated Thomas Dewey, the colorless and politically moderate governor of New York, who had a difficult time criticizing Roosevelt without appearing unpatriotic. Roosevelt seemed haggard and ill during much of the campaign, but he won the election easily. He would need all his strength to deal with the difficult political problems of ending the war and constructing a peace settlement.

The Big Three at Yalta

Roosevelt, Churchill, and Stalin, together with many of their advisers, met at Yalta in the Crimea in February 1945 to discuss the problems of the peace settlements. Most of the agreements reached at Yalta were secret, and in the atmosphere of the subsequent Cold War, many would become controversial. Roosevelt wanted the help of the Soviet Union in ending the war in the Pacific. In return for a promise to enter the war within three months after the war in Europe was over, the Soviet Union was granted the Kurile Islands, the southern half of Sakhalin, and railroads and port facilities in North Korea, Manchuria, and Outer Mongolia. Later that seemed like a heavy price to pay for the promise, but realistically the Soviet Union controlled most of this territory and could not have been dislodged short of going to war.

The European section of the Yalta agreement proved even more controversial than its Far Eastern provisions. It was decided to partition Germany and to divide the city of Berlin. The Polish agreements were even more difficult to swallow. Stalin demanded that the eastern half of Poland be given to the Soviet Union to protect its western border. Churchill and Roosevelt finally agreed to the Russian demands with the proviso that Poland be compensated with German territory on its western border. Stalin also agreed to include some members of the London-based Polish group in the new Polish government. He also promised to carry out "free and unfettered elections as soon as possible." The Polish settlement would prove divisive after the war. Yet at the time it seemed imperative that the Soviet Union enter the war in the

Pacific, and the reality was that in 1945 the Soviet army occupied most of eastern Europe.

The most potentially valuable accomplishment at Yalta was agreement on the need to construct a United Nations, an organization for preserving peace and fostering the postwar reconstruction of battered and underdeveloped countries.

Spirited debate occurred in San Francisco in April 1945 when the representatives of 50 nations gathered for this task. As finally accepted, amid optimism about a quick end to the war, the charter provided for a General Assembly in which every member nation had a seat. However, this General Assembly was designed mainly as a forum for discussing international problems. The responsibility for keeping global peace was lodged in the Security Council, composed of five permanent members (the United States, the Soviet Union, Great Britain, France, and China) and six other nations elected for two-year terms. The Security Council's responsibility was to suppress international violence by applying economic, diplomatic, or military sanctions against any nation that all permanent members agreed threatened the peace. In addition, the charter established an International Court of Justice and a number of agencies to promote "collaboration among the nations through education, science, and culture." Among these agencies were the International Monetary Fund, the World Health Organization, and the UN Educational, Scientific, and Cultural Organization (UNESCO).

The Atomic Age Begins

Two months after Yalta, on April 12, 1945, as the United Nations charter was being drafted, Roosevelt died suddenly of a massive cerebral hemorrhage. The nation was shocked. Roosevelt, both hated and loved to the end, was replaced by Harry Truman, who was both more difficult to hate and harder to love. In the beginning, Truman seemed tentative and unsure of himself. Yet it fell to the new president to make some of the most difficult decisions of all time. The most momentous of all was the decision to drop the atomic bomb.

The Manhattan Project, first organized in 1941, was one of the best kept secrets of the war. The task of the distinguished group of scientists whose work on the project was centered at Los Alamos, New Mexico, was to manufacture an atomic bomb before Germany did. By the time the bomb was successfully tested in the New Mexico desert on July 16, 1945, the war in Europe had ended. But a presidential committee made up of scientists, military leaders, and politicians recommended that it be used on a military target in Japan as soon as possible.

"The final decision of where and when to use the atomic bomb was up to me," Truman later remembered. "Let there be no doubt about it. I regarded the bomb as a military weapon and never had any doubt that it should be used." Even though Japan had lost most of its empire by the summer of 1945, it still had a military force of several million men and thousands of kamikaze planes that had already wreaked havoc on the American fleet. The kamikaze pilots gave up their own lives to make sure that their planes, heavily laden with bombs, crashed on an American ship. There was little defense against such fanaticism.

The monthlong battle for Iwo Jima, only 750 miles from Tokyo, had resulted in over 4,000 American dead and 15,000 wounded, and an invasion of Japan would be much more expensive.

The bomb, many thought, could end the war without an invasion of the home islands of Japan, thus saving many American lives. The timing of the first bomb, however, indicates that the decision was also intended to impress the Soviets.

On August 6, 1945, two days before the Soviet Union had promised to enter the war against Japan, a B-29 bomber dropped a single atomic bomb over Hiroshima. It killed or severely wounded 160,000 civilians and destroyed four square miles of the city. One of the men on the plane saw the thick cloud of smoke and thought that they had missed their target. "It looked like it had landed on a forest. I didn't see any sign of the city." The Soviet Union entered the war on August 8. When Japan refused to surrender, a second bomb was dropped on Nagasaki on August 9. The Japanese surrendered five days later. The war was finally over, but the problems of the atomic age were just beginning to come to light, as radioactive fallout from the bombs continued to cause radiation sickness, deaths, and birth defects among exposed Japanese.

Truman's decision to use atomic weapons against Japan generated decades of controversy. Some Americans maintain that Japan would have surrendered soon in any event, and that use of the terrible new weapon was not justified; others believe that many American lives were saved by Japan's quick surrender in response to the bombs. The issues of moral justification and military necessity are still being debated fifty years after the event.

CONCLUSION

PEACE, PROSPERITY, AND INTERNATIONAL RESPONSIBILITIES

The United States emerged from World War II as the world's most powerful industrial and military nation. The demands of the war had finally ended the Great Depression and increased the power of the federal government. The war had also ended American isolationism and made the

United States into the dominant international power.

Americans greeted the end of the war with joy and relief. They looked forward to the peace and prosperity for which they had fought. Yet within two years, the peace would be jeopardized by the Cold War, and the United States would be rearming its former enemies, Japan and Germany, to oppose its former friend, the Soviet Union. The irony of that situation reduced the joy of the hard-won peace and made the American people more suspicious of their government and its foreign policy.

Recommended Reading

On the process by which the United States got involved in World War II, see Robert Dallek, *Franklin D. Roosevelt and American Foreign Policy* (1979); Waldo Heinricks, *Threshold of War* (1988); and Robert A. Divine, *The Reluctant Belligerent* (1979). For United States policy toward Central America, see Walter La Feber, *Inevitable Revolutions: The United States in Central America* (1983).

On the war, see Robert Leckie, *Delivered from Evil* (1987); Martin J. Sherwin, *A World Destroyed* (1975); Warren Kimball, *The Juggler: Franklin Roosevelt as Wartime Statesman* (1991); Herbert Feis, *The Atomic Bomb and the End of World War II* (1966); and Stephen Ambrose, *Eisenhower* (1983). John W. Dower, *War Without Mercy* (1986), and Akira Iriye, *The Origins of the Second World War in Asia and the Pacific* (1988), deal with the war against Japan.

Ross Gregory, *America 1941* (1988), is a fascinating account of the United States on the eve of the war. John Morton Blum, *V Was for Victory* (1976), and Richard Polenberg, *War and Society* (1972), are excellent books about the home front. Ruth Milkman, *Gender at Work* (1987), describes women during the war. Richard M. Dalfuime, *Desegregation of the U.S. Armed Forces* (1975), describes race relations in the military during the war. Roger Daniels, *Concentration Camp U.S.A.* (1971), details the relocation of Japanese-Americans during the war. David S. Wyman, *The Abandonment of the Jews* (1984), tells the story of American policy toward the victims of the Holocaust. Other books about the domestic scene include Nicholas Lemann, *The Promised Land: The Great Black Migration and How It Changed America* (1991); Mauricio Mazon, *The Zoot-Suit Riots* (1984); and Bill Gilbert, *They Also Served: Baseball and the Homefront* (1992).

Irwin Shaw's novel *The Young Lions* (1948) tells what fighting the war was like.

Time Line

1931–1932	Japan seizes Manchuria	1941	Lend-Lease Act
			Proposed black march on Washington
1933	Hitler becomes German chancellor		Germany attacks Russia
	United States recognizes the Soviet Union		Japanese assets in United States frozen
	Roosevelt extends Good Neighbor policy		Japanese attack Pearl Harbor; United States declares war on Japan
1934	Germany begins rearmament		Germany declares war on the United States
1935	Italy invades Ethiopia	1942	Internment of Japanese-Americans
	First Neutrality Act		Second Allied front in Africa launched
1936	Spanish civil war begins	1943	Invasion of Sicily
	Second Neutrality Act		Italian campaign; Italy surrenders
	Roosevelt reelected		United Mine Workers strike
1937	Third Neutrality Act		Race riots in Detroit and other cities
1938	Hitler annexes Austria, occupies Sudetenland	1944	Normandy invasion (Operation Overlord)
	German persecution of Jews intensifies		Congress passes GI Bill
			Roosevelt elected for a fourth term
1939	Nazi-Soviet Pact	1945	Yalta conference
	German invasion of Poland; World War II begins		Roosevelt dies; Harry Truman becomes president
1940	Roosevelt elected for a third term		Germany surrenders
	Selective Service Act		Successful test of atomic bomb
1941	FDR's "Four Freedoms" speech		Hiroshima and Nagasaki bombed; Japan surrenders
	Executive order outlaws discrimination in defense industries		

part 6

A
Resilient
People

1945-1993

The final section of *The American People* traces the recent history of the United States and highlights themes developed earlier in the text. We will explore the sense of mission the Cold War with the Soviet Union inspired, the growing role of the federal government in promoting the well-being of its citizens, and the reaction against that role. Finally, we will examine the continuing struggle to realize national ideals of liberty and equality in racial, gender, and social relations as new waves of immigration from Latin America and Asia increased the diversity of the American people.

Chapters 26 and 27 are paired. Chapter 26, "Chills and Fever During the Cold War," shows how the United States moved from an uneasy friendship with the Soviet Union to disillusionment and hostility. Chapter 27, "Postwar Growth and Social Change," describes the expansion of self-interest in an age of extensive material growth and new patterns of regulation.

Chapters 28 and 29 are paired as well. Chapter 28, "The Rise and Fall of the Liberal State," describes the debate in the 1960s and 1970s over the appropriate role of government with regard to ensuring the welfare of all citizens. Chapter 29, "The Struggle for Social Reform," examines the continuing reform impulse that had its roots in the earliest days of American society.

In Chapter 30, "The Triumph of Conservatism," we explore the 1970s and 1980s in terms of economic and demographic developments, and we examine the 1992 presidential election.

chapter 26

....

Chills and Fever During the Cold War

Val Lorwin was in Paris in November 1950 when word of the charges against him arrived. A State Department employee, on leave of absence after 16 years of government service, he was in France working on a book. Now he had to return to the United States to defend himself against the accusation that he was a member of the Communist Party and thus a loyalty and security risk.

Lorwin had begun to work for the government in 1935, serving in a number of New Deal agencies, then in the Labor Department and on the War Production Board before he was drafted during World War II. While in the army, he was assigned to the Office of Strategic Services, an early intelligence agency, and he was frequently granted security clearances in the United States and abroad.

Lorwin, however, did have a left-wing past as an active Socialist in the 1930s. He had supported the unionization of southern tenant farmers and the provision of aid to the unemployed. He and his wife, Madge, drafted statements or stuffed envelopes to support their goals. But that activity was wholly open and legal, and Lorwin had from the start been aggressively anticommunist in political affairs.

Suddenly, Lorwin, like others in the period, faced the nightmare of secret charges against which the burden of proof was entirely on him and the chance of clearing his name slim. Despite his spotless record, Lorwin was told that an unnamed accuser had identified him as a Communist. He was entitled to a hearing if he chose, or he could resign.

Lorwin requested a hearing, held late in 1950. Still struck by the absurdity of the situation, he refuted all accusations but made little effort to cite his own positive achievements. At the conclusion, he was informed that the government no longer doubted his loyalty but considered him a security risk, grounds nonetheless for dismissal from his job.

When he appealed the judgment, Lorwin was again denied access to the identity of his accuser. This time, however, he thoroughly prepared his defense. At the hearing, a total of 97 witnesses either spoke under oath on Lorwin's behalf or left sworn written depositions testifying to his good character and meritorious service. In March 1952, Lorwin was finally cleared for both loyalty and security.

Though he thought he had weathered the storm, Lorwin's troubles were not yet over. His name appeared on one of the lists produced by Senator Joseph McCarthy of Wisconsin, the most aggressive anticommunist of the era, and Lorwin was again victimized. The next year, he was indicted for making false statements to the State Department Loyalty-Security Board. The charges this time proved as specious as before. Finally, in May 1954, admitting that its special prosecutor had deliberately lied to the grand jury and had no legitimate case, the Justice Department asked for dismissal of the indictment. Lorwin was cleared at last and went on to a distinguished career as a labor historian.

⟨⟩══◉══⟨⟩

Lorwin was more fortunate than some victims of the anticommunist crusade. People rallied around him and he survived the witch-hunt of the early 1950s. Not everyone was as lucky.

The Cold War, which unfolded soon after the end of World War II, powerfully affected all aspects of American life. The same sense of mission that had infused America in the Spanish-American War, World War I, and World War II now impelled most Americans to see themselves struggling against communism at home and abroad. This chapter explores that continuing sense of mission and its consequences.

CONFLICTING WORLD VIEWS

The Cold War was rooted in long-standing disagreements between the major powers regarding the shape of the postwar world. The United States, strong and secure, was intent on spreading its vision of freedom and economic opportunity around the world. The Soviet Union, concerned about its own security after a devastating war, demanded politically sympathetic neighbors on its borders. Each nation felt threatened by the interests of the other, and actions by both sides sparked reactions that culminated in the Cold War.

The American Stance

The United States emerged from World War II more powerful than any nation ever before. Now it sought to use that might to achieve the kind of order that could sustain American aims. American policymakers, following in Woodrow Wilson's footsteps, hoped to spread the values that provided the underpinning of the American dream—liberty, equality, and democracy. They also hoped for a world where economic enterprise could thrive. With the American economy operating at full speed as a result of the war, world markets were needed once the fighting stopped. Government officials wanted to eliminate trade barriers—imposed by the Soviet Union and other nations—to provide outlets for industrial products and for surplus farm commodities like wheat, cotton, and tobacco. As the largest source of goods for world markets, with exports totaling $14 billion in 1947, the United States required open channels for growth to continue.

Soviet Aims

The Soviet Union formulated its own goals after World War II. Historically, Russia had usually had a strongly centralized, sometimes even autocratic, government, and that tradition—as much as communist ideology, with its stress on class struggle and the inevitable triumph of a proletarian state—guided Soviet policy.

During the war, the Soviets had played down the notion of world revolution they knew the other allies found threatening and had mobilized support for more nationalistic goals. As the struggle drew to a close, they talked little of world conquest, emphasizing socialism within the nation itself.

Rebuilding was a necessary priority. Devastated by the war, the Soviet Union concentrated on reconstruction as its first priority. Soviet agriculture and industry were a shambles and had to be revived. But revival demanded internal security. The Soviets feared vulnerability along their western flank. Such anxieties had a historical basis, for in the early nineteenth century, Napoleon had reached the gates of Moscow. Twice in the twentieth century, invasions had come from the west, most recently when Hitler had attacked in 1941. Haunted by fears that the Germans would recover quickly, the Soviets demanded defensible borders and neighboring regimes sympathetic to their aims.

Cold War Leadership

Both the United States and the Soviet Union had strong leadership as the Cold War unfolded. On the American side, first Harry Truman, then Dwight Eisenhower accepted the centralization of authority Franklin Roosevelt had begun, as the executive branch became increasingly powerful in guiding foreign policy. In the Soviet Union, first Joseph Stalin, then Nikita Khrushchev provided equally forceful direction.

Harry S Truman served as president of the United States in the first postwar years. He was an unpretentious man who took a straightforward approach to public affairs. He was, however, ill prepared for the office he assumed in the final months of World War II. His three months as vice president had done little to school him in the complexity of postwar issues.

Yet Truman matured swiftly. Impulsive and aggressive, he made a virtue out of rapid response. At his first press conference, he answered questions so quickly that reporters could not record his answers. A sign on the president's White House desk read "The Buck Stops Here." His rapid-fire decisions had important consequences for the Cold War.

Truman served virtually all of the term to which Roosevelt had been elected, then won another for himself in 1948. In 1952, war hero Dwight D. Eisenhower, who won the presidency for the Republican Party for the first time in 20 years, succeeded him.

Eisenhower stood in stark contrast to his predecessor. His easy manner and warm smile made him widely popular. On occasion, in press conferences or other public gatherings, his comments came out convoluted and imprecise. Yet appearances were deceiving, for beneath his casual approach was real shrewdness.

Eisenhower had not taken the typical route to the presidency. After his World War II success, he served as army chief of staff, president of Columbia University, and then head of the North Atlantic Treaty Organization. Despite his lack of formal political background, he had a genuine ability to get people to compromise and to work together.

Ike's limited experience with everyday politics conditioned his sense of the presidential role. Whereas Truman was accustomed to political infighting and wanted to take charge, Eisenhower saw things differently. "You do not *lead* by hitting people over the head. Any damn fool can do that," he said, "but it's usually called 'assault'—not 'leadership.'" Even so, Ike knew exactly where he wanted to go and worked behind the scenes to get there.

Though the personal styles of Truman and Eisenhower differed, they both subscribed to traditional American attitudes about self-determination and the superiority of American political institutions and values. Both distrusted Soviet ventures during and after the war.

Truman accepted collaboration with the Soviet Union during the struggle as a marriage of necessity, but he became increasingly hostile to Soviet moves as the war drew to an end. Like Truman, Eisenhower believed that communism was a monolithic force struggling for world supremacy and that the Kremlin in Moscow was orchestrating subversive activity around the globe. Like Truman, he viewed the Soviet system as "a tyranny that has brought thousands, millions of people into slave camps and is attempting to make all mankind its chattel." Yet Eisenhower was still a military man with a measure of caution who could practice accommodation when it served his ends.

The leader of the Soviet Union at the war's end was Joseph Stalin. Possessing almost absolute power, he had presided over monstrous purges against his opponents in the 1930s. Now he was determined to rebuild Soviet society, if possible with Western assistance, and to keep eastern Europe within the Soviet sphere of influence.

Stalin's death in March 1953 left a vacuum in Soviet political affairs. His successor, Nikita S. Khrushchev, used his position as party secretary to consolidate his power. Purges of the party bureaucracy took place, and five years after Stalin's death, Khrushchev held the offices of both prime minister and party secretary. Known for rude behavior, Khrushchev once pounded a table at the United Nations with his shoe while the British prime minister was speaking. During Khrushchev's regime, the Cold War continued, but there were now brief periods when relations between the two powers became less hostile.

ORIGINS OF THE COLD WAR

The Cold War developed by degrees. With the Fascist threat defeated, disagreements about the shape of the postwar world brought the Soviet Union and the United States into conflict. Such conflicts caused suspicion and distrust. As confrontation followed confrontation, the two nations behaved, according to Senator J. William Fulbright, "like two big dogs chewing on a bone."

Disillusionment with the USSR

In September 1945, more than half (54 percent) of a U.S. national sample trusted the Soviets to cooperate with the Americans in the postwar years. Two months later, the figure had dropped to 44 percent, and by February 1946, to 35 percent.

As Americans soured on the Soviet Union, they began to equate the Nazi and Soviet systems and to transfer their hatred of Hitler's Germany to the Soviet Communists. Just as they had in the 1930s, authors, journalists, and public officials began to point to similarities between the regimes, some of them quite legitimate. Both states, they contended, maintained total control over communications and could eliminate political opposition whenever they chose. Both states used terror to silence dissidents. Soviet labor camps in Siberia were now compared to German concentration camps. After the American publication in 1949 of George Orwell's frightening novel *1984*, *Life* magazine noted in an editorial that the ominous figure Big Brother was but a "mating" of Hitler and Stalin. Truman spoke for many Americans when he said in 1950 that "there isn't any difference between the totalitarian Russian government and the Hitler government. . . . They are all alike. They are . . . police state governments."

The lingering sense that the nation had not acted quickly enough to resist totalitarian aggression in the 1930s heightened American fears. Had the United States stopped the Germans, Italians, or Japanese, it might have prevented the long, devastating war. The free world had not responded quickly enough before and was determined never to repeat the same mistake.

The Polish Question

The first clash between East and West came, even before the war ended, over Poland. Soviet demands for a government willing to accept Soviet influence clashed with American hopes for a more representative structure patterned after the Western model.

"We must stand up to the Russians," Truman said, "and not be easy with them." Truman's unbending stance in an April 1945 meeting with Soviet foreign minister Vyacheslav Molotov on the question of what kind of government should lead Poland contributed to the deterioration of Soviet-American relations.

Truman and Stalin met face to face for the first time at the Potsdam Conference in July 1945, the last of the meetings held by the Big Three during the war. There, as they considered the Soviet-Polish boundary, the fate of Germany, and the American desire to obtain an unconditional surrender from Japan, the two leaders sized each other up. It was Truman's first exposure to international diplomacy at the highest level, and it left him confident of his abilities. When he learned during the meeting of the first successful atomic bomb test in New Mexico, he became even more determined to insist on his positions.

Economic Pressure on the USSR

One major source of controversy in the last stage of World War II was the question of American aid to its allies. Responding to congressional pressure at home to limit foreign assistance as hostilities ended, Truman acted impulsively. Six days after V-E Day signaled the end of the European war in May 1945, he issued an executive order cutting off lend-lease supplies to the Allies. Although the policy affected all nations receiving aid, it hurt the Soviet Union most of all.

The United States intended to use economic pressure in other ways as well. The USSR desperately needed financial assistance to rebuild after the war and, in January 1945, had requested a $6 billion loan. Roosevelt hedged, hoping to win concessions in return. In August, the Soviets renewed their application, this time for only $1 billion. The new president dragged his heels, hoping to use the loan as a lever to gain access to new markets in areas traditionally dominated by the Soviet Union. Unwilling to help promote American trade in such areas, Stalin refused the offer of a loan with such conditions and launched his own five-year plan instead.

Declaring the Cold War

As Soviet-American disagreements increased, both sides stepped up their rhetorical attacks. Stalin spoke out first, in 1946, asserting his confidence in the triumph of the Soviet system. Capitalism and communism were on a collision course, he argued, and a series of cataclysmic disturbances would tear the capitalist world apart.

Supreme Court Justice William O. Douglas called Stalin's ominous speech "the declaration of World War III." In response, England's former prime minister, Winston Churchill, declared that "from Stettin in the Baltic to Trieste in the Adriatic, an iron curtain has descended across the Continent."

CONTAINING THE SOVIET UNION

Containment formed the basis of postwar American policy. Both political parties determined to check Soviet expansion. In an increasingly contentious world, the American government formulated rigid policies to maintain the upper hand. The Soviet Union responded in an equally rigid manner.

Containment Defined

George F. Kennan was primarily responsible for defining the new policy. Chargé d'affaires at the American embassy in the Soviet Union, he sent off an 8,000-word telegram to the State Department after Stalin's speech in February 1946. Kennan argued that Soviet-American hostility stemmed from "the Kremlin's neurotic view of world affairs," which in turn came from "the traditional and instinctive Russian sense of insecurity." Soviet fanaticism would not soften, regardless of how accommodating American policy became. Therefore, it had to be opposed at every turn.

Kennan's analysis struck a resonant chord in Washington. It made his diplomatic reputation, led to his assignment to an influential position in the State Department, and encouraged him to publish an extended analysis, under the pseudonym "Mr. X," in *Foreign Affairs*. "The whole Soviet governmental machine, including the mechanism of diplomacy," he wrote, "moves inexorably along the prescribed path, like a persistent toy automobile wound up and headed in a given direction, stopping only when it meets with some unanswerable force." Many Americans agreed with Kennan that Soviet pressure had to "be contained by the adroit and vigilant application of counter-force at a series of constantly shifting geographical and political points."

The concept of containment provided the philosophical justification for the hard-line stance that Americans, both in and out of government, adopted. Containment created the framework for military and economic assistance around the globe.

The Truman Doctrine

The Truman Doctrine represented the first major application of containment policy. The new pol-

icy was devised to respond to conditions in the eastern Mediterranean. The Soviet Union was pressuring Turkey for joint control of the Dardanelles, the passage between the Black Sea and the Mediterranean. Meanwhile, a civil war in Greece pitted Communist elements against the ruling English-aided right-wing monarchy. Revolutionary pressures threatened to topple the government.

In February 1947, the British ambassador to the United States informed the State Department that his exhausted country could no longer give Greece and Turkey economic and military aid. Would the United States now move into the void? The State Department was willing, but the conservative Congress had to be persuaded.

Administration leaders knew they needed bipartisan support to accomplish such a major policy shift. Senator Arthur Vandenberg of Michigan, a key Republican, warned that the administration had to begin "scaring hell out of the country" if it was serious about a bold new course of containment.

Truman took Vandenberg's advice to heart. On March 12, 1947, he told Congress, in a statement that came to be known as the Truman Doctrine, "I believe that it must be the policy of the United States to support free peoples who are resisting subjugation by armed minorities or by outside pressures." Unless the United States acted, the free world might not survive. To avert that calamity, he urged Congress to appropriate $400 million for military and economic aid to Turkey and Greece. Not everyone agreed with Truman's overblown description of the situation, but Congress passed his foreign aid bill.

In its assumption that Americans could police the globe, the Truman Doctrine was a major step in the advent of the Cold War. Truman's address, observed financier Bernard Baruch, "was tantamount to a declaration of . . . an ideological or religious war." Journalist Walter Lippmann was more critical. He termed the new containment policy a "strategic monstrosity" that could embroil the United States in disputes around the world. In the two succeeding decades, Lippmann proved correct.

The Marshall Plan, NATO, and NSC-68

The next step involved extensive economic aid for postwar recovery in western Europe. At the war's end, most of Europe was economically and politically unstable, thereby offering opportunities to the Communist movement. Decisive action was needed, for as the new secretary of state, George Marshall, declared, "The patient is sinking while the doctors deliberate." Another motive was eagerness to bolster the European economy to provide markets for American goods.

Marshall revealed the administration's willingness to assist European recovery in June 1947. He asked all troubled European nations to draw up an aid program that the United States could support, a program "directed not against any country or doctrine but against hunger, poverty, desperation, and chaos." The proposed program would assist the ravaged nations, provide the United States with needed markets, and advance the nation's ideological aims. American aid, Marshall pointed out, would permit the "emergence of political and social conditions in which free institutions can exist." The Marshall Plan and the Truman Doctrine, Truman noted, were "two halves of the same walnut."

In the end, American officials agreed to provide $17 billion over a period of four years to 16 cooperating nations. Though some members of Congress feared spreading American resources too thin, in early 1948 Congress committed the nation to funding European economic recovery, and the containment policy moved forward another step.

Closely related to the Marshall Plan was a concerted Western effort to rebuild Germany and to reintegrate it into a reviving Europe. At Yalta, Allied leaders had agreed on zonal occupation of Germany and on reparations Germany would pay the victors. Four zones, occupied by the Soviets, Americans, British, and French, had been established for postwar administration. A year after the end of the war, however, the balance of power in Europe had shifted. With the Soviet Union threatening to dominate eastern Europe, the West moved to fill the vacuum in central Europe. In late 1946, the Americans and British merged their zones for economic purposes and began to assign administrative duties to Germans. By the middle of 1947, the process of rebuilding West German industry was under way.

In mid-1948, the Soviet Union attempted to force the other nations out of Berlin, which, like Germany itself, was divided into zones after the war. Soviet refusal to allow the other Allies land access to West Berlin, located in the Soviet zone of Germany, led to a U.S. and Royal Air Force airlift that flew over two million tons of supplies to the beleaguered Berliners. The fliers named it Operation Vittles, and it broke the Soviet blockade.

The next major link in the containment strategy was the creation of a military alliance in Europe to complement the economic program. After the Soviets tightened their control of Hungary and Czechoslovakia, the United States in 1949 took the lead in establishing NATO, the North Atlantic Treaty Organization. Twelve nations formed the alliance, vowing that an attack against any one member would be considered an attack against all, to be met by appropriate armed force.

The Senate, formerly opposed to such military pacts, approved this time, and the United States established its first military treaty ties with Europe since the American Revolution. Congress also voted military aid for its NATO allies. The Cold War had softened long-standing American reluctance to become closely involved with European affairs.

In 1949, two significant events—the success of the Communists in the Chinese civil war and the Soviet detonation of an atomic device—led the United States to define its aims still more

An American and British airlift in 1948 brought badly needed supplies to West Berliners isolated behind a Soviet blockade of the city. By refusing to allow the Western powers to reach the city, located within the Soviet zone, the Russians hoped to drive them from Berlin, but the airlift broke the blockade.

specifically. The National Security Council, organized in 1947 to provide policy coordination, produced a paper, NSC-68, which shaped American policy for the next 20 years.

NSC-68 built on the Cold War rhetoric of the Truman Doctrine. It assumed that conflict between East and West was unavoidable, and that negotiation was useless, for the Soviets could never be trusted to bargain in good faith.

Having eliminated important options to resolving differences through traditional channels of diplomacy, NSC-68 then called for a massive increase in defense spending from the $13 billion set for 1950 to as much as $50 billion per year. The costs were huge, the document argued, but

necessary for the United States if the free world was to survive.

Containment in the 1950s

Containment, the keystone of American policy throughout the Truman years, was the rationale for the Truman Doctrine, the Marshall Plan, NATO, and NSC-68. In the 1950s, however, under Eisenhower's administration, containment came under attack as too cautious to counter the threat of communism.

For most of Eisenhower's two terms, John Foster Dulles was secretary of state. A devout Presbyterian who hated atheistic communism,

Cold War Europe in 1950

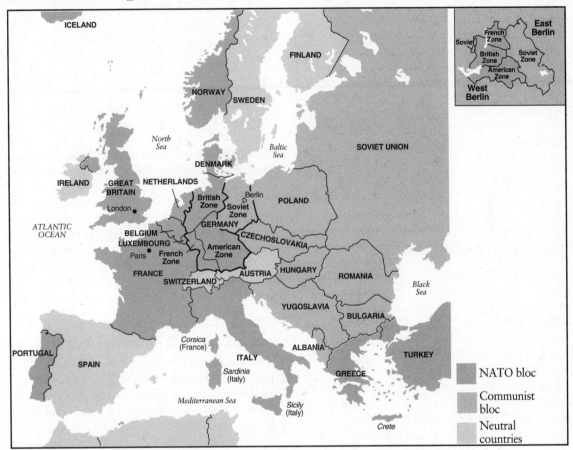

This map shows the rigid demarcation between East and West during the Cold War. Although there were a number of neutral countries in Europe, the other nations found themselves in a standoff, as each side tried to contain the possible advances of the other. The small inset map in the upper right-hand corner shows the division of Berlin that paralleled the division of Germany itself after World War II.

he sought to move beyond containment to a holy crusade to promote democracy and to free the countries under Soviet domination.

Eisenhower, more conciliatory and realistic than Dulles, recognized the impossibility of changing the governments of Russia's satellites. He also understood the need for caution. In mid-1953, as East Germans mounted anti-Soviet demonstrations, the United States kept its dis-

tance. In 1956, when Hungarian "freedom fighters" rose up against Soviet domination, the United States again stood back as Soviet forces smashed the rebels. Because Western action could have precipitated a more general conflict, Eisenhower refused to translate rhetoric into action. Throughout the 1950s, the policy of containment, largely as it had been defined earlier, remained in effect.

AMERICAN POLICY IN ASIA, THE MIDDLE EAST, AND LATIN AMERICA

Although containment resulted from the effort to promote European stability, the United States, in a dramatic departure from its history of non-involvement, extended the policy to meet challenges around the globe. In Asia, the Middle East and Latin America, the United States discovered the tremendous appeal of communism as a social and political system and found that ever greater efforts were required to advance American aims.

The Chinese Revolution

America's commitment to containment became stronger with the Communist victory in the Chinese civil war in 1949. China, an ally during World War II, had struggled against the Japanese, while at the same time it fought a domestic conflict rooted deep in the Chinese past—in widespread poverty, disease, oppression by the landlord class, and national humiliation at the hands of foreign powers. Mao Zedong (Mao Tse-tung),* founder of a branch of the Communist Party, wished to reshape China in a Communist mold. Opposing the Communists were the Nationalists, led by Jiang Jieshi (Chiang Kai-shek). By the early 1940s, Jiang Jieshi's regime was exhausted, hopelessly inefficient, and corrupt. Mao's movement, meanwhile, grew stronger during the Second World War as he opposed the Japanese invaders and won the loyalty of the peasant class.

After the war, Jiang fled in 1949 to the island of Taiwan. There he nursed the improbable belief that his was still the rightful government of all China and that he would one day return.

The United States failed to understand the long internal conflict in China or the immense popular support Mao had generated. As the Communist army moved toward victory, the New York *Times* termed the group a "nauseous force," a "compact little oligarchy dominated by Moscow's nominees."

Secretary of State Dean Acheson considered granting diplomatic recognition to the new regime but backed off after the Communists seized American property, harassed American citizens, and openly allied themselves with the Russians.

Tension with China increased during the Korean War and then again in 1954 when Mao's government began shelling Nationalist positions on the offshore islands of Quemoy and Matsu. Eisenhower, now president, was again unwilling to respond forcefully.

The War in Korea

The Korean War marked America's growing intervention in Asian affairs. Concern about China and determination to contain communism led the United States into the struggle, but American objectives were not always clear and were largely unrealized after three years of war.

The conflict in Korea stemmed from tensions lingering after World War II. Korea, long under Japanese control, hoped for independence after Japan's defeat. But the Allies temporarily divided Korea along the 38th parallel when the rapid end to the Pacific struggle allowed Soviet troops to accept Japanese surrender in the north while American forces did the same in the south. The Soviet-American line, initially intended as a matter of military convenience, hardened after 1945, just as a similar division rigidified in Germany, and in time the Soviets set up a government in the north and the Americans a government in the south. Each Korean government hoped to reunify the country on its own terms.

North Korea moved first. On June 25, 1950, North Korean forces invaded South Korea

---

*Chinese names are rendered in their modern *Pinyin* spelling. At first occurrence, the older (usually Wade-Giles) spelling is given in parentheses.

The Korean War

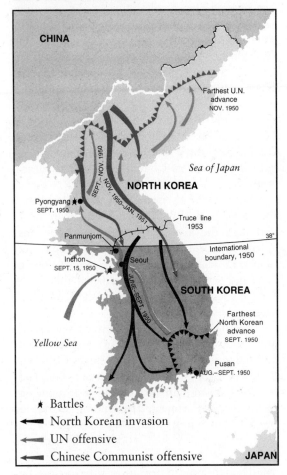

This map shows the ebb and flow of the Korean War. North Korea crossed the 38th parallel first, then the UN offensive drove the North Koreans close to the Chinese border, and finally the Chinese Communists entered the war and drove the UN forces back below the 38th parallel. The armistice signed at Panmunjom in 1953 provided a dividing line very close to the prewar line.

mean a third world war, just as similar incidents had brought on the second world war."

Truman readied American naval and air forces and directed General Douglas MacArthur in Japan to supply South Korea. The United States also went to the United Nations Security Council, which branded North Korea an aggressor and called on members of the organization to assist the south in repelling aggression and restoring peace.

The president first ordered American air and naval forces into battle south of the 38th parallel, then American ground forces as well. Following a daring amphibious invasion that pushed the North Koreans back to the former boundary line, United Nations troops crossed the 38th parallel, hoping to reunify Korea under an American-backed government. Despite Chinese signals that this movement toward their border threatened their security, the United States pressed on. In October, Chinese troops appeared briefly in battle, then disappeared. The next month, the Chinese mounted a full-fledged counterattack, which pushed the UN forces back below the dividing line again.

The resulting stalemate provoked a bitter struggle between Douglas MacArthur and his civilian commander in chief. A brilliant but arrogant general, MacArthur called for retaliatory air strikes against China, but Truman was trying to conduct a limited war.

MacArthur's public statements, issued from the field, finally went too far. In April 1951, he argued that the American approach in Korea was wrong, and that "there is no substitute for victory." Truman had no choice but to relieve him for insubordination.

The Korean War continued into Eisenhower's presidency. During the campaign of 1952, Eisenhower promised to go to Korea, and three weeks after his election, he did so. When truce talks bogged down again in May 1953, the new administration privately threatened the Chinese with the use of atomic weapons and a massive military campaign. This brought about a resumption of the peace talks. Finally, on July 27,

by crossing the 38th parallel. Following Soviet-built tanks, North Korean troops steadily advanced against South Korean soldiers.

The United States was taken by surprise, but Truman responded vigorously. He declared, "If this was allowed to go unchallenged it would

1953, an armistice was signed. The Republican administration had managed to do what the preceding Democratic administration could not. After three long years, the unpopular war had ended.

American involvement carried a heavy price: 54,000 Americans dead and many more wounded. But those figures paled beside the numbers of Korean casualties. As many as two million may have died in North and South Korea, and countless others were maimed.

The war also significantly changed American attitudes and institutions. This was the first war in which United States forces fought in integrated units. President Truman, as commander in chief, had ordered the integration of the armed forces in 1948, over the opposition of many generals, and blacks became part of all military units. Their successful performance led to acceptance of military integration.

The Korean War years also saw military expenditures soar from $13 billion in 1950 to about $47 billion three years later as defense spending followed the guidelines proposed in NSC-68. Whereas the military absorbed less than a third of the federal budget in 1950, a decade later it took one-half. More than a million military men were stationed around the world. At home, an increasingly powerful military establishment became closely tied to corporate and scientific communities and created a military-industrial complex that employed 3.5 million Americans by 1960.

The Korean War had important political effects as well. It led the United States to sign a peace treaty with Japan in September 1951 and to rely on that nation to maintain the balance of power in the Pacific. At the same time, the struggle poisoned relations with the People's Republic of China and ensured a diplomatic standoff that lasted more than 20 years.

Civil War in Vietnam

Indochina had been under French control since the middle of the nineteenth century. During World War II, the Japanese occupied the area but allowed French collaborators to direct internal affairs. An independence movement, led by the Communist organizer and revolutionary Ho Chi Minh, sought to expel the Japanese conquerors. In 1945, the Allied powers faced the decision of how to deal with Ho and his nationalist movement.

Franklin Roosevelt, like Woodrow Wilson, believed in self-determination and wanted to end colonialism. But France was determined to regain its colony, and by the time of his death, Roosevelt had backed down.

Ho Chi Minh meanwhile had established the Democratic Republic of Vietnam in 1945. Although the new government enjoyed widespread support, the United States refused to recognize it. The head of the American Office of Strategic Services mission predicted that if the French sought to regain control, the Vietnamese would fight to the death.

A long, bitter struggle between the French and the forces of Ho Chi Minh did break out and became entangled with the larger Cold War. President Truman was less concerned about ending colonialism than with checking growing Soviet power in Europe and around the world. He needed France to balance Soviet strength in Europe, and that meant cooperating with the French in Vietnam.

Though Ho did not, in fact, have close ties to the Soviet state and was committed to his independent nationalist crusade, Truman and his advisers, who saw communism as a monolithic force, assumed wrongly that Ho took orders from Moscow. Hence in 1950, the United States formally recognized the French puppet government in Vietnam. The United States also provided economic assistance to France. By 1954, the United States was paying over three-quarters of the cost of the war.

After Eisenhower took office, France's position deteriorated. Dulles was eager to assist the French; the chairman of the Joint Chiefs of Staff even contemplated using nuclear weapons. But

Eisenhower refused to intervene directly. The French fortress at Dien Bien Phu finally fell, and an international conference in Geneva divided Vietnam along the 17th parallel, with elections promised in 1956 (but never held) to unify the country and determine its political fate.

As a result of that division, two new states emerged. Ho Chi Minh held power in the north, while in the south Premier Ngo Dinh Diem, a fierce anticommunist, formed a separate government. Intent on taking France's place in Southeast Asia, the United States supported the Diem government and refused to sign the Geneva agreement. In the next few years, American aid increased and military advisers began to assist the South Vietnamese. The United States had taken the first steps toward involvement in a ruinous war halfway around the world that would later escalate out of control.

The Middle East

Cold War attitudes also influenced American responses to events in the Middle East. That part of the world had tremendous strategic importance as the supplier of oil for the industrialized nations. During World War II, the major Allied powers occupied Iran, with the provision that they would leave within six months of the war's end. As of early 1946, both Great Britain and the United States had withdrawn, but the Soviet Union, which bordered on Iran, remained. Stalin claimed that earlier security agreements had not been honored and, further, demanded oil concessions. A threat of vigorous American action, however, forced the Soviets to back down and withdraw.

The Eisenhower administration maintained its interest in Iran. In 1953, the CIA helped the local army overthrow the government of Mohammed Mossadegh, which had nationalized oil wells formerly under British control, and place the shah of Iran securely on the Peacock Throne.

After the coup, British and American companies regained command of the wells, and thereafter the United States government provided military assistance to the shah.

A far more serious situation emerged west of Iran. In 1948, the United Nations attempted to partition Palestine into an Arab state and a Jewish state. Truman officially recognized the new state of Israel 15 minutes after it was proclaimed. But recognition could not end bitter animosities between Arabs, who felt they had been robbed of their territory, and Jews, who felt they had finally regained a homeland after the horrors of the Holocaust. As Americans looked on, Arab forces from Egypt, Trans-Jordan, Syria, Lebanon, and Iraq invaded Israel, but the Israelis won the war and added territory to what they had been given by the UN.

The United States cultivated close ties with Israel but could not afford to lose the friendship of oil-rich Arab states or allow them to fall into the Soviet orbit. In Egypt, Arab nationalist General Gamal Abdel Nasser planned a great dam on the Nile River to produce electricity, while he proclaimed his country neutral in the Cold War. Dulles offered American financial support for the Aswan Dam project, but Nasser also began discussions with the Soviet Union. The secretary of state furiously withdrew the American offer. Left without funds for the dam, Nasser seized and nationalized the British-controlled Suez Canal in July 1956. At the same time, he closed the canal to Israeli ships. All of Europe feared that Nasser would disrupt the flow of oil from the Middle East.

In October and November, Israeli, British, and French military forces invaded Egypt. Eisenhower, who had not been consulted, was irate. Realizing that the attack might push Nasser into the arms of Moscow, the United States sponsored a UN resolution condemning the attacking nations and cut off oil from England and France. These actions persuaded them to withdraw.

In 1958, the United States again intervened

The Middle East in 1949

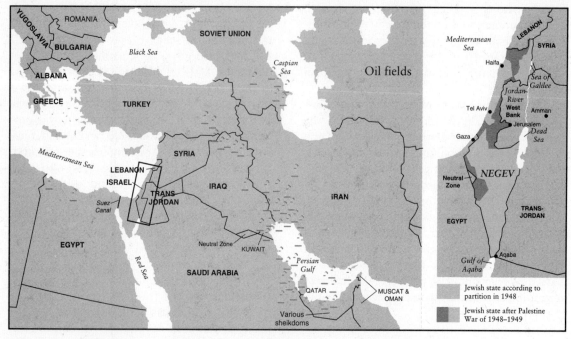

This map shows the extensive oil resources that made the Middle East such an important region, and the shifting boundaries of Israel as a result of the war following its independence in 1948. Notice how its size increased after its victory in the first of a series of Middle Eastern conflicts.

in the Middle East. Eisenhower authorized the landing of 14,000 soldiers in Lebanon to prop up a right-wing government challenged from within.

Restricting Revolt in Latin America

The Cold War also affected relations in Latin America, the United States' traditional sphere of influence. In 1954, Dulles sniffed Communist activity in Guatemala and ordered CIA support for a right-wing coup that overthrew the elected government of reform-minded Colonal Jacobo Arbenz Guzmán. The property of the United Fruit Company that Arbenz had seized was restored, but at the cost of aborting needed reform. The effort in Guatemala also fed strong anti-American feeling throughout Latin America.

In 1959, when Fidel Castro overthrew the dictatorial regime of Fulgencio Batista in Cuba, the shortsightedness of American policy became even clearer. Nationalism and the thrust for social reform were powerful forces in Latin America, as in the rest of the Third World. But when Castro confiscated American property in Cuba, the Eisenhower administration cut off exports and severed diplomatic ties. In response, Cuba turned to Russia for support.

ATOMIC WEAPONS AND THE COLD WAR

Throughout the Cold War period, the atomic bomb was a crucial factor in world affairs. Atomic weapons were destructive enough, but when the United States and the Soviet Union both developed hydrogen bombs, an age of overkill began.

Sharing the Secret of the Bomb

The United States, with British aid, had built the first atomic bomb in secrecy. Soviet spies, however, discovered that the Americans were at work on the bomb. By 1943, a program to create a Soviet atomic bomb was under way.

The question of sharing the atomic secret was pressing in the immediate postwar years. Secretary of War Henry L. Stimson favored co-operating with the Soviet Union. Recognizing the futility of trying to cajole the Soviets while "having this weapon ostentatiously on our hip," he suggested that "their suspicions and their distrust of our purposes and motives will increase." Only mutual accommodation could bring international cooperation.

But the United States never followed Stimson's advice. Truman, increasingly worried about the Soviet presence in eastern Europe, vowed to retain the technological advantage. He resisted a more flexible approach until the creation of a "foolproof method of control" over atomic weapons. Most Americans agreed.

For a time the administration sought a means of international arms control. The United States proposed an international agency to provide atomic energy control. This plan failed as negotiations collapsed.

The United States then moved toward its own internal mechanism of control. The Atomic Energy Act of 1946 established the Atomic Energy Commission to supervise all atomic energy development in the United States. It also opened the way to a nuclear arms race once the USSR developed its own bomb.

Nuclear Proliferation

As the atomic bomb found its way into popular culture, Americans at first showed more excite-

ment than fear. In Los Angeles, the "Atom Bomb Dancers" appeared at the Burbank Burlesque Theater. In 1946, the Buchanan Brothers recorded a song called "Atomic Power."

In September 1949, reporters were called to the White House and told: "We have evidence that within recent weeks an atomic explosion occurred in the U.S.S.R." Over the Labor Day weekend, a U.S. Air Force weather reconnaissance plane on a routine mission had picked up air samples showing higher than normal radioactivity counts. Other samples confirmed this, and scientists soon concluded that the Soviets had conducted a nuclear test.

The American public was shocked. Suddenly the security of being the world's only atomic power vanished. Harold C. Urey, a Nobel Prize–winning scientist, summed up the feelings of many Americans: "There is only one thing worse than one nation having the atomic bomb—that's two nations having it."

In early 1950, Truman authorized the development of a new hydrogen superbomb, potentially far more devastating than the atomic bomb. Edward Teller, a physicist on the Manhattan Project, had contemplated the possibility that fusion might release energy in even greater amounts. Now he had his chance to proceed.

By 1953, both the United States and the Soviet Union had unlocked the secret of the hydrogen bomb. Rumors circulated that the first test of a hydrogen device in the Pacific Ocean in 1952 had created a hole in the ocean floor 175 feet deep and a mile wide. Later, after the 1954 BRAVO test, Lewis Strauss, Atomic Energy Commission chairman, admitted that "an H-bomb can be made . . . large enough to take out a city." Then, in 1957, shortly after the news that the Soviets had successfully tested their first intercontinental ballistic missile (ICBM), Americans learned that the Soviets had fired the first satellite, *Sputnik,* into outer space. The apparent inferiority of American rocketry and the openness of the country to attack caused serious concern.

The discovery of radioactive fallout added another dimension to the nuclear dilemma. Fallout became publicly known after the BRAVO blast showered Japanese fishermen 85 miles away with radioactive dust. They became ill with radiation sickness, and several months later, one of them died. The Japanese, who had been the first to experience the effects of atomic weapons, were outraged and alarmed. Elsewhere people began to realize the terrible impact of the new weapons.

Authors in both the scientific and the popular press focused attention on radioactive fallout. Radiation, physicist Ralph Lapp observed, "cannot be felt and possesses all the terror of the unknown." Nevil Shute's best-selling 1957 novel *On the Beach,* and the film that followed, described a war that released so much radioactive waste that all life in the Northern Hemisphere disappeared, while the Southern Hemisphere waited for the residue to come closer and bring the same deadly end. In 1959, when *Consumer Reports* warned of the contamination of milk with strontium-90 as a result of nuclear fallout, public alarm grew.

The discovery of fallout provoked a bomb shelter craze. More and more companies advertised ready-made shelters to eager consumers. A firm in Miami reported many inquiries about shelters costing between $1,795 and $3,895, depending on capacity, and planned 900 franchises. By the end of 1960, an estimated one million family shelters had been built.

"Massive Retaliation"

As Americans grappled with the consequences of nuclear weapons, government policy came to depend increasingly on an atomic shield. Truman authorized the development of a nuclear arsenal but also stressed conventional forms of defense. After his election in 1952, Eisenhower decided to rely on atomic weapons rather than combat forces as the key to American defense. Dulles developed the policy of "massive retaliation." The United States was willing and ready to use nuclear weapons against communist aggression "at places of our own choosing." The policy allowed troop cutbacks and promised to be cost-effective by giving "more bang for the buck."

Massive retaliation provided for an all-or-nothing response, leaving no middle course, no alternatives between nuclear war and retreat. Critics called Dulles's foreign policy "brinkmanship" and wondered what would happen if the line were crossed in the new atomic age. Eisenhower himself was horrified when he saw reports indicating what nuclear weapons could do, and with characteristic caution he did his best to ensure that the rhetoric of massive retaliation did not lead to war.

THE COLD WAR AT HOME

The Cold War also affected domestic affairs and led to the creation of an internal loyalty program that produced serious violations of civil liberties. As Americans began to suspect Communist infiltration at home, some determined that they must root out any traces of communism inside the United States.

Truman's Loyalty Program

As the Truman administration mobilized support for its containment program in the immediate postwar years, its rhetoric became increasingly shrill and unrealistic. According to Attorney General J. Howard McGrath, there were "many Communists in America," each bearing "the germ of death for society."

When administration officials perceived an internal threat to security, Truman responded by appointing a Temporary Commission on Employee Loyalty. He also wanted to undercut the

Republican charge that the Democrats were "soft on communism."

On the basis of the report from his temporary commission, Truman established a new Federal Employee Loyalty Program by executive decree in 1947. In the same week he announced his containment policy, Truman ordered the FBI to check its files for evidence of subversive activity and then to bring suspects before a new Civil Service Commission Loyalty Review Board. Initially, the program included safeguards and assumed that a challenged employee was innocent until guilt had been proved. But as the Loyalty Review Board assumed more and more power, it came to overlook individual rights. Employees could now be attacked with little chance to fight back. Although the Truman loyalty program examined several million employees and found grounds for dismissing only several hundred, it still bred fear of subversion.

The Congressional Loyalty Program

While Truman's loyalty probe investigated government employees, Congress embarked on its own program. The Smith Act of 1940 had made it a crime to advocate or teach the forcible overthrow of the U.S. government. In 1949, Eugene Dennis and ten other Communist leaders were found guilty under its terms. In 1951, the Supreme Court upheld the Smith Act, clearing the way for the prosecution of nearly 100 other Communists.

The McCarran Internal Security Act of 1950 further circumscribed Communist activity by declaring that it was illegal to conspire to act in a way that would "substantially contribute" to establishing a totalitarian dictatorship in America. Members of Communist organizations had to register with the attorney general and could not obtain passports or work in areas of national defense. Congress passed the measure

over Truman's veto and provided further legal backing for the anticommunist crusade. The American Communist Party, which had never been large, even in the Depression, declined still further. Membership, numbering about 80,000 in 1947, fell to 55,000 in 1950 and 25,000 in 1954.

The investigations of the House Committee on Un-American Activities (HUAC) contributed to that decline. Intent on rooting out subversion, HUAC probed the motion picture industry in 1947. Protesting its scare tactics, some people the committee summoned refused to testify under oath. They were scapegoated for their stand. The so-called Hollywood Ten, a group of writers, were cited for contempt of court and sent to federal prison. At that, Hollywood knuckled under and blacklisted anyone with even a marginally questionable past. No one on these lists could find jobs at the studios anymore.

Congress made a greater splash with the Hiss-Chambers case. Whittaker Chambers, a former Communist who had broken with the party in 1938 and had become a successful editor of *Time*, charged that Alger Hiss had been a Communist in the 1930s. Hiss was a distinguished New Dealer who had served in the Agriculture Department before becoming assistant secretary of state. Now out of the government, he was president of the Carnegie Endowment for International Peace. He denied Chambers's charge, and the matter might have died there had not freshman congressman Richard Nixon taken up the case. Nixon finally extracted from Hiss an admission that he had once known Chambers. Outside the hearing room, Hiss sued Chambers for libel, whereupon Chambers changed his story and charged that Hiss was a Soviet spy.

Hiss was indicted for perjury, for lying under oath about his former relationship with Chambers. The case made front-page news around the nation. Chambers appeared unstable and changed his story several times. Yet Hiss, too, seemed contradictory in his testimony and never adequately explained how some copies of stolen State Department documents had been typed on a typewriter he had once owned. The first trial ended in a hung jury; the second trial, in January 1950, sent Hiss to prison for almost four years.

After Hiss's conviction but before his appeal, Dean Acheson supported his friend. Regardless of what happened, he said, "I do not intend to turn my back on Alger Hiss." Decent though his affirmation was, it caused the secretary of state political trouble. Truman too was broadly attacked for his comments about the case. The dramatic Hiss case helped to discredit the Democrats and to justify the even worse witch-hunt that followed.

The Second Red Scare

The key anticommunist warrior in the 1950s was Joseph R. McCarthy, senator from Wisconsin, who claimed he had in his hand a list of 205 known Communists in the State Department, then reduced the number of names to 57. He prompted mixed reactions. A subcommittee of the Senate Foreign Relations Committee, after investigating, called his charge a "fraud and a hoax." As his support grew, however, Republicans realized his partisan value and egged him on.

McCarthy selected assorted targets. In the elections of 1950, he attacked Millard Tydings, the Democrat from Maryland who had chaired the subcommittee that dismissed McCarthy's first accusations. A doctored photograph, showing Tyding with deposed American Communist party head Earl Browder, helped bring about Tydings's defeat. McCarthy called Dean Acheson the "Red Dean of the State Department" and slandered George C. Marshall as "a man steeped in falsehood."

A demagogue throughout his career, McCarthy liked to play tough for press and televi-

sion coverage. He did not mind appearing disheveled, unshaven, and half sober. He used obscenity and vulgarity freely.

McCarthy's tactics worked because the public was alarmed about the Communist threat. The arrest in 1950 of Julius and Ethel Rosenberg further aroused fears of subversion from within. The Rosenbergs, a seemingly ordinary American couple with two small children, were charged with stealing and transmitting atomic secrets to the Russians. To many Americans, it was inconceivable that the Soviets could have developed the bomb on their own. Only treachery could explain the Soviet explosion of an atomic device.

The next year, the Rosenbergs were found guilty of espionage and sentenced to death. Although some argued, then and today, that the Rosenbergs were victims of hysteria, efforts to prevent their execution failed. In 1953, they were put to death, but anticommunism continued unabated.

When the Republicans won control of the Senate in 1952, McCarthy's power grew. He became chairman of the Government Operations Committee and head of its Permanent Investigations Subcommittee. He now had a stronger base and two dedicated assistants, Roy Cohn and G. David Schine.

As McCarthy's anticommunist witch-hunt continued, Eisenhower became uneasy. He disliked the senator but, recognizing his popularity, was reluctant to challenge him.

With the help of Cohn and Schine, McCarthy pushed on, and finally he pushed too hard. In 1953, the army drafted Schine and then refused to allow the preferential treatment that Cohn insisted his colleague deserved. Angered, McCarthy began to investigate army security and even top-level army leaders themselves. When the army charged that McCarthy was going too far, the Senate investigated the complaint.

The Army-McCarthy hearings began in April 1954 and lasted 36 days. Televised to a fascinated nationwide audience, they demonstrated

COMMUNIST PARTY ORGANIZATION U.S.A-FEB. 9, 1950

Senator Joseph McCarthy's spurious charges inflamed anticommunist sentiment in the 1950s. Here he uses a chart of Communist Party organization in the United States to suggest that the nation was at risk unless subversives were rooted out.

the power of TV to shape people's opinions. Americans saw McCarthy's savage tactics on screen. He came across to viewers as irresponsible and destructive, particularly in contrast to Boston lawyer Joseph Welch, who argued the army's case with quiet eloquence.

The hearings shattered McCarthy's mystical appeal. In broad daylight, before a national television audience, his ruthless methods no longer made sense. The Senate finally summoned the courage to condemn him for his conduct. Conservatives there turned against McCarthy because by attacking Eisenhower and the army, he was no longer limiting his venom to Democrats and liberals. Although McCarthy remained in office, his influence disappeared. Three years later, at the age of 48, he died a broken man.

Yet for a time he had exerted a powerful hold in the United States. Some members of both parties spoke out against him, but most did not.

His crusade thus encouraged, McCarthy pressed on until he went too far.

The Casualties of Fear

The anticommunist crusade promoted a pervasive sense of suspicion in American society. In the late 1940s and early 1950s, dissent no longer seemed safe. Civil servants, government workers, academics, and actors all came under attack and found that the right of due process often evaporated as the Cold War Red Scare gained ground. Seasoned China experts lost their positions in the diplomatic service, and social justice legislation faltered.

This paranoia affected American life in countless ways. In New York, subway workers were fired when they refused to answer questions about their own political actions and beliefs. Navajos in Arizona and New Mexico, facing starvation in the bitter winter of 1947–1948, were denied government relief because of charges that their communal way of life was communistic and therefore un-American. Black actor Paul Robeson, who along with W. E. B. Du Bois criticized American foreign policy, was accused of Communist leanings, found few opportunities to perform, and eventually, like Du Bois, lost his passport. Hispanic laborers faced deportation for membership in unions with left-wing sympathies. In 1949, the Congress of Industrial

Organizations (CIO) expelled 11 unions with a total membership of more than one million for alleged domination by Communists. Val Lorwin, introduced at the beginning of the chapter, weathered the storm of malicious accusations and was finally vindicated, but others were less lucky. They were the unfortunate victims as the United States became consumed by the passions of the Cold War.

CONCLUSION

THE COLD WAR IN PERSPECTIVE

The Cold War was the greatest single force affecting American society in the decade and a half after World War II. In the early years after the war, policymakers and commentators justified the American stance as a bold and courageous effort to meet the Communist threat. Later, particularly in the 1960s, as the public started to have doubts about the course of American foreign policy, revisionist historians began to argue that American policy was misguided, insensitive

to Soviet needs, and a contributing factor to the worsening frictions.

The Cold War stemmed from a competition for international influence between the two great world powers. After World War II, the American vision of what the postwar world should be like clashed with the goals of Communist powers and with anticolonial movements in Third World countries. The Cold War, with its profound effects at home and abroad, was the unfortunate result.

Recommended Reading

Walter LaFeber, *America, Russia, and the Cold War, 1945–1990* (6th ed., 1991), is the best brief account of the Cold War from beginning to end. Other good sources include John Lewis Gaddis, *Strategies of Containment: A Critical Appraisal of Postwar American National Security Policy* (1982); and Thomas G. Patterson, *On Every Front: The Making of the Cold War* (1979).

For foreign policy in the Eisenhower period, see Robert A. Divine, *Eisenhower and the Cold War* (1981); and H. W. Brands, Jr., *Cold Warriors: Eisenhower's Generation and American Foreign Policy* (1988).

On the Korean War, see Burton I. Kaufman, *The*

Korean War: Challenges in Crisis, Credibility, and Command (1986), for an excellent survey of the foreign policy implications of the war. Joseph C. Goulden, *Korea: The Untold Story of the War* (1982), is a popular account of the struggle. James A. Michener's novel *The Bridges at Toko-Ri* (1953) provides a sense of the frustrations during the war.

On the anticommunist crusade, see Thomas C. Reeves, *The Life and Times of Joe McCarthy: A Biography* (1982), and David M. Oshinsky, *A Conspiracy So Immense: The World of Joe McCarthy* (1983). See also Allen Weinstein, *Perjury: The Hiss-Chambers Case* (1978); and Ronald Radash and Joyce Milton, *The Rosenberg File: A Search for Truth* (1984).

Time Line

1945	Yalta Conference Roosevelt dies; Harry Truman becomes president Potsdam Conference	1950– 1953	Korean War
1946	American plan for control of atomic energy fails Atomic Energy Act Iran crisis Churchill's "Iron Curtain" speech	1951	Japanese-American Treaty *Dennis* v. *United States*
		1952	Dwight D. Eisenhower elected president McCarthy heads Senate Permanent Investigations Subcommittee
1947	Truman Doctrine Federal Employee Loyalty Program House Un-American Activities Committee (HUAC) investigates the movie industry	1953	Stalin dies; Khrushchev consolidates power East Germans stage anti-Soviet demonstrations Shah of Iran returns to power in CIA-supported coup
1948	Marshall Plan launched Berlin airlift Israel created by UN Hiss-Chambers case Truman elected president	1954	Fall of Dien Bien Phu ends French control of Indochina Geneva Conference Guatemalan government overthrown with CIA help Mao's forces shell Quemoy and Matsu Army-McCarthy hearings
1949	Soviet Union tests atomic bomb North Atlantic Treaty Organization (NATO) established George Orwell publishes *1984* Mao Zedong's forces win Chinese civil war; Jiang Jieshi flees to Taiwan	1956	Suez incident Hungarian "freedom fighters" suppressed Eisenhower reelected
		1957	Soviets launch *Sputnik* satellite
1950	Truman authorizes development of the hydrogen bomb Alger Hiss convicted Joseph McCarthy's Wheeling (W. Va.) speech on subversion NSC-68 McCarran Internal Security Act	1958	U.S. troops sent to support Lebanese government
		1959	Castro deposes Batista in Cuba

chapter 27

Postwar Growth and Social Change

Ray Kroc, an ambitious salesman, headed toward San Bernardino, California, on a business trip in 1954. For more than a decade he had been selling "multimixers"—stainless steel machines that could make six milkshakes at once—to restaurants and soda shops around the United States. On this trip he was particularly interested in checking out a hamburger stand run by Richard and Maurice McDonald, who had bought eight of his "contraptions" and could therefore make 48 shakes at the same time.

Always eager to increase sales, Kroc wanted to see the McDonald's operation for himself. As he watched the lines of people at the San Bernardino McDonald's, he saw the reason for their success. The McDonald brothers sold only standard hamburgers and french fries, but they had developed a system that was fast, efficient, and clean. It drew on the automobile traffic that moved along Route 66. And it was profitable indeed. Sensing the possibilities, Kroc proposed that the two owners open other establishments as well. When they balked, he negotiated a 99-year contract that allowed him to sell the fast-food idea and the name—and their golden arches design—wherever he could.

On April 15, 1955, Kroc opened his first McDonald's in Des Plaines, a suburb of Chicago. Three months later, he sold his first franchise in Fresno, California. Others soon followed. Kroc persuaded people to put up the capital, and he provided them with specifications guaranteed to ensure future success. For his efforts, he received a percentage of the gross take.

From the start, Kroc insisted on standardization. Every McDonald's looked the same. All menus and prices were exactly the same, and Kroc demanded that the establishments be clean. No pinball games or cigarette machines were permitted.

McDonald's, of course, was an enormous success. When Kroc died in 1984, a total of 45 billion burgers had been sold at 7,500 outlets in 32 countries.

The success of McDonald's provides an example of the development of new trends in the 1950s in the United States. Kroc capitalized on the changes of the automobile age.

He understood that a restaurant, not in the city but along the highways, where it could draw on heavier traffic, had a better chance of success. He understood that the franchise notion provided the key to rapid growth. He sensed, too, the importance of standardization and uniformity.

This chapter describes the structural changes in American society in the decade and a half after World War II. We will examine how economic growth, spurred by technological advances, transformed the patterns of American life at home and at work. Self-interest triumphed over idealism as most Americans obtained material comfort previously unknown. But even as it promoted economic growth, the government was obliged to acknowledge the claims of minorities. In their protests against continuing social and economic injustice, blacks, Indians, and Hispanics highlighted the limits of the postwar American dream.

ECONOMIC BOOM

In spite of anxieties about the Cold War, most Americans were optimistic after 1945. As servicemen returned home and resumed their lives, a baby boom brought unprecedented population growth. The simultaneous economic boom that took the nation by surprise had an even greater impact as new technology and new products flooded the market.

The Peacetime Economy

The wartime prosperity continued in the postwar years. Americans enjoyed one of the most sustained periods of economic expansion the United States had ever known, as it solidified its position as the richest nation in the world.

The statistical evidence of economic success was impressive. The gross national product (GNP) jumped from just over $200 billion in 1940 to about $300 billion in 1950 and by 1960 had climbed above $500 billion. Per capita income rose from $2,100 in 1950 to $2,435 in 1960. Almost 60 percent of all families in the country were now part of the middle class, a dramatic change from the class structure in the nineteenth and early twentieth century.

Personal resources fueled economic growth. During World War II, American consumers had been unable to spend all they earned because production had been concentrated in the manufacture of weapons needed for the war. With accumulated savings of $140 billion at war's end, consumers were ready to purchase whatever they could. Equally important was the 22 percent rise in real purchasing power between 1946 and 1960.

The automobile industry was a key part of the economic boom. Limited to the production of military vehicles during World War II, the auto industry expanded dramatically in the postwar period. Two million cars were made in 1946, four times as many in 1955.

The development of a massive interstate highway system also stimulated auto production and so contributed to prosperity. The Interstate Highway Act of 1956 provided $26 billion, the largest public works expenditure in American history, to build over 40,000 miles of federal highways, linking all parts of the United States.

Though highways added to the problem of pollution and triggered urban flight, the interstate complex was hailed as a key to the country's material development. President Eisenhower wrote: "More than any single action by the government since the end of the war, this one would change the face of America."

House construction contributed to economic growth as well. Much of the stimulus came from the GI Bill of 1944. In addition to giving returning servicemen priority for many jobs and providing educational benefits, it offered low-interest home mortgages, and millions of former soldiers took advantage of the measure to buy into the American dream.

Federal policy also helped sustain the expansion by allowing businesses to buy almost 80 percent of the factories built by the government during the war for much less than they cost. Even more important was the dramatic rise in defense spending as the Cold War escalated. In 1947, when the Department of Defense was established, the defense budget stood at $13 billion. With the onset of the Korean War, it rose to $22 billion in 1951 and to about $47 billion in 1953. Between 1949 and 1960, spending for space research increased from $49 million to $401 million. As federal expenditures reached 20 percent of the GNP by the 1950s, it was clear that a major economic transformation had occurred.

Peaceful, prosperous, and productive, the country had become "the affluent society," in economist John Kenneth Galbraith's phrase. The concentration of income remained the same— the bottom half of the population still earned less than the top tenth—but the ranks of middle-class Americans grew.

The Corporate World

After 1945, the major corporations increased their hold on the American economy. Government policy in World War II had encouraged the growth of big business and produced tremendous industrial concentration. During the war, half of all military contracts were awarded to three dozen giants. In 1940, some 100 companies accounted for 30 percent of all manufacturing output in the United States. Three years later, that figure had risen to 70 percent.

Industrial concentration continued after the war, making oligopoly—domination of a given industry by a few firms—a feature of American capitalism. At the same time, the booming economy encouraged the development of conglomerates—firms that diversified with holdings in a variety of industries. International Telephone and Telegraph, for example, purchased Avis Rent-a-Car, Continental Baking, Sheraton Hotels, Levitt and Sons Home Builders, and Hartford Fire Insurance. That pattern, widely duplicated, protected companies against instability in one particular area. It also led to the further development of finance capitalism to help put the deals together, just as the demands of consolidation in the late nineteenth century had opened the way for bankers like J.P. Morgan (see Chapter 19).

While expanding at home, large corporations also moved increasingly into foreign markets, as they had in the 1890s. But at the same time they began to build plants overseas, where labor costs were cheaper. In the decade after 1957, General Electric built 61 plants abroad, and numerous other firms did the same.

In the post-1945 period, the close business-government ties that had developed during the war grew stronger. Federal dollars fueled research that in turn accounted for new industrial expansion.

Corporate planning, meanwhile, developed rapidly, as firms hired managers, trained in business schools, who could maximize profit.

The Workers' World

As corporations changed, so did the world of work. In the years after World War II, the United

States reversed a 150-year trend and became less a nation of goods producers and more a country of service providers. By 1956, a majority of the American people held white-collar jobs. Salaried rather than paid by the hour, these white-collar workers served as corporate managers, teachers, salespersons, and office workers.

Work in the huge corporations became even more impersonal than before. Money and material well-being were the prizes of corporate life. But white-collar employees paid a price for comfort. Corporations, preaching that teamwork was far more important than individuality, indoctrinated employees and conveyed the appropriate standards of conduct. RCA issued company neckties. IBM had training programs to teach employees the company line. Some large firms set up training programs to show wives how their own behavior could help their husbands' careers. Social critic C. Wright Mills observed, "When white-collar people get jobs, they sell not only their time and energy but their personalities as well."

Blue-collar workers also prospered in the postwar years. Labor union strength peaked as the war ended. The American Federation of Labor and the Congress of Industrial Organizations merged into the AFL-CIO in 1955. The new organization, led by building trade unionist George Meany, represented more than 90 percent of the country's 17.5 million union members. Union activity brought real improvements in income.

With higher, more predictable incomes, workers were more willing to limit strike activity. Labor peace prevailed, but at the expense of the last vestiges of autonomy in the workplace. Workers fell increasingly under the control of middle-level managers and watched anxiously as companies automated at home or expanded abroad, where labor was cheaper.

The union movement stalled in the mid-1950s. The heavy industries providing workers who gravitated to the union movement were no longer growing. As membership began to fall, unions tried to expand their base by reaching out to new groups—less skilled minority workers and white-collar service-oriented employees—but they proved difficult to organize.

The Agricultural World

The agricultural world changed even more than the industrial world in postwar America. New technology revolutionized farming. Improved planting and harvesting machines and better fertilizers and pesticides brought massive gains in productivity.

Increasing profitability led to agricultural consolidation. In the 25 years after 1945, average farm size almost doubled, and farmers left the land in increasing numbers. At the end of World War II, farmers made up one-fourth of the nation's work force (down from one-third in 1935). Over the next 25 years, 25 million people left the rural life behind, until only 5 percent of the population remained on farms in 1970.

Population Shifts and the New Suburbs

In post–World War II America, a growing population marked prosperity's return. During the Great Depression, the birthrate had dropped to an all-time low of 19 births per 1,000 population as hard times obliged people to delay marriage and parenthood. As World War II boosted the economy, the birthrate began to rise again, as millions of Americans began families. The "baby boom" peaked in 1957, with a rate of more than 25 births per 1,000. In that year, 4.3 million babies were born, one every seven seconds.

The rising birthrate was the dominant factor affecting population growth, but the death rate was also declining. Miracle drugs, such as streptomycin and aureomycin, played a large part in curing illnesses. Life expectancy rose: Midway through the 1950s, the average was 70 years for whites and 64 for blacks, compared with 55 for whites and 45 for blacks in 1920.

Birth and Population Rates, 1900-1960

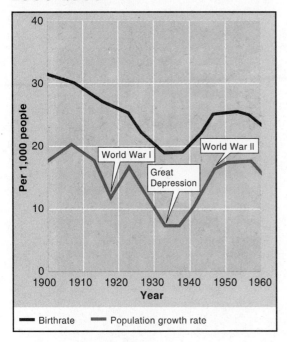

Source: *U.S. Bureau of the Census*

The baby boom had a powerful impact on family and social patterns and material needs. Many women who had taken jobs during the war now left the work force to raise their children and care for their homes. The demand grew for diaper services and baby foods. When they entered school, the members of the baby boom generation strained the educational system.

As Americans became more populous, they also became more mobile. For many generations, lower-class Americans had been the most likely to move; now geographic mobility spread to the middle class. Each year in the 1950s, over a million farmers left their farms in search of new employment. Other Americans moved to look for better jobs. Bob Moses of Baltimore simply wandered a while after returning home from the war. Traveling in a 1937 Chevrolet with some high school friends, Moses was going

"nowhere in particular, just roaming. We'd see a kink in a river on the map, and head there." After regimented military life, it was good to be free.

The war had produced increasing movement, most of it westward, as people gravitated toward the cities where shipyards, airplane factories, and other industrial plants were located. After the war, that migration pattern persisted, as the West and the Southwest continued to grow. Sun Belt cities like Houston, Albuquerque, Tucson, and Phoenix underwent phenomenal expansion. In the 1950s, Los Angeles pulled ahead of Phildelphia as the third largest city in the United States. By 1963, California had passed New York as the nation's most populous state.

After the war, another form of movement became even more important in the United States. Millions of white Americans fled the inner cities to suburban fringes. As central cities became places where poor nonwhites clustered, new urban and racial problems emerged.

For people of means, cities were places to work and then to leave at 5 o'clock. In Manhattan, south of City Hall, the noontime population of 1.5 million dropped to 2,000 during the night. The area, said writer John Brooks, was "left pretty much to thieves, policemen, and rats" after nightfall.

As the cities declined, the suburbs blossomed. If the decade after World War I had witnessed a rural-to-urban shift, the decades after World War II saw a reverse shift to the regions outside the central cities, usually accessible only by car. By the end of the 1950s, a third of all Americans resided in suburbs.

A key figure in the suburbanization movement was William J. Levitt, a builder eager to gamble and reap the rewards of a growing demand. Levitt recognized the advantages of mass production during World War II, when his firm put up dwellings for war workers. Aware that the GI Bill made mortgage money readily available, he felt that suburban development was a

Step-by-step mass production, with units completed in assembly-line fashion, was the key to William Levitt's approach to housing. But the suburban developments he and others created were marked by street after street of houses that all looked the same.

sure bet. But to cash in, Levitt knew he had to use new construction methods.

Mass production was the key. Working on a careful schedule, Levitt's team brought precut and preassembled materials to each site, put them together, and then moved on to the next location. As on an assembly line, tasks were broken down into individual steps. Groups of workers performed but a single job, moving from one tract to another. By this method, construction costs at Levittown, New York, a new community of 17,000 homes built in the late 1940s, were only $10 per square foot, compared with the $12 to $15 common elsewhere. Levitt provided a model for other developers.

Government-insured mortages, especially for veterans, fueled the housing boom. So did fairly low postwar interest rates. Mortgage interest rates were in the affordable 5 percent range.

Suburbanization changed the landscape of the United States. Huge tracts of land now contained acres of standardized squares, each bearing a house with a two-car garage and a manicured lawn. Woods disappeared, for it was cheaper to cut down all trees than to work around them. Folksinger Malvina Reynolds described the new developments she saw:

Little boxes on the hillside
Little boxes made of ticky tacky

Little boxes on the hillside
Little boxes all the same.
There's a green one and a pink one
And a blue one and a yellow one
And they're all made out of ticky tacky
And they all look just the same.

As suburbs flourished, businesses followed their customers out of the cities. Shopping centers catered to the suburban clientele, offering easy parking and convenient late hours. They also undermined the downtown department stores.

The Environmental Impact

Rapid development of the suburbs often took place without extensive planning and encroached on some of the nation's most attractive rural areas. Before long, virtually every American city was ringed by an ugly highway lined with eating places, shopping malls, and auto dealerships. Billboard advertisements dotted the landscape.

Responding to the increasingly cluttered terrain, architect Peter Blake ruthlessly attacked the practices of the 1950s in his muckraking book *God's Own Junkyard: The Planned Deterioration of America's Landscape,* published in 1964. The largely pictorial account indicted the careless attitudes toward the environment that led to the "uglification" of a once lovely land.

Despite occasional accounts like Blake's, there was little real consciousness of environmental issues in the post–World War II years. Yet the very prosperity that created the dismal highway strips in the late 1940s and 1950s was leading more and more Americans to appreciate natural environments as necessary parts of their rising standard of living. The shorter workweek provided more free time, and many Americans now had the means for longer vacations. They began to explore mountains and rivers and ocean shores, and to consider how to protect them. In 1958, Congress established the Na-

tional Outdoor Recreation Review Commission, a first step toward consideration of environmental issues that became far more common in the next decade.

Technology Supreme

Rapid technological change occurred in the postwar years. Computers led the way. Wartime advances led to large but workable calculators, followed in the postwar years by machines that contained their own internal instructions and memories. After the development of the transistor by three scientists at Bell Laboratories in 1948, the computer became faster and more reliable, and transformed American society as surely as industrialization had changed it a century before.

Television was even more important commercially. Developed in the 1930s, it became a major influence on American life after World War II. In 1946, there were fewer than 17,000 sets; by 1949, Americans bought some 250,000 a month; and by 1960, three-quarters of all American families owned at least one set. In 1955, the average American family tuned in four to five hours each day.

Young Americans grew up to the strains of "Winky Dink and You," "The Mickey Mouse Club," and "Howdy Doody Time" in the 1950s. Older viewers enjoyed situation comedies like "I Love Lucy" and "Father Knows Best" and live dramas such as "Playhouse 90."

Americans maintained an ardent love affair with new appliances and gadgets. Tiny transistors powered not only computers and radios but also miniature hearing aids that could fit into the frame of a pair of eyeglasses. Stereophonic hi-fi sets, using new transistor components, provided better sound. By the end of the 1950s, most families had at least one automobile, as well as a refrigerator, washing machine, television, and vacuum cleaner.

One ominous technological trend was the advent of automation. Mechanization was not new, but now it became far more widespread, threatening both skilled and unskilled workers. In 1952, the Ford Motor Company began using automatic drilling machines in an engine plant and found that 41 workers could do a job 117 had done before. The implications of falling purchasing power as machines replaced workers were serious for an economy dependent on consumer demand.

The Consumer Culture

The modern American economy depended on consumption. Purchasing new goods and gadgets became easier with the expansion of consumer credit. Installment plans facilitated buying a new car, while credit cards encouraged other expenditures. Consumer credit mushroomed from $8.4 billion in 1946 to nearly $45 billion in 1958.

Advertising, which had faltered when the economy collapsed in the 1930s, began to revive during the war as firms sought to keep the public aware of consumer goods, even those in short supply. With the postwar boom, advertisers again began to hawk their wares.

Motivational research became more sophisticated, uncovering new ways of persuading people to buy. Taking the place of radio, television played an important part in conveying the spirit of consumption to millions of Americans. Shows like "The Price Is Right" stressed consumption in direct ways: Contestants won goods for quoting their correct retail price. Drawing on a talent that was sharpened in the shopping centers and department stores, the show encouraged the acquisition of ever more material goods.

Americans welcomed the postwar affluence. They had weathered the poverty and unemployment of the 1930s, made sacrifices during a long war, and now intended to enjoy their newfound abundance and leisure time. By 1950, most wage laborers worked a 40-hour week, and 60 percent of nonagricultural workers enjoyed paid vacations, whereas few had in 1930. Most Ameri-

cans regarded all this as their due, sometimes neglecting to look beyond the immediate objects of their desire. The decade, journalist William Shannon wrote, was one of "self-satisfaction and gross materialism. . . . The loudest sound in the land has been the oink and grunt of private hoggishness. . . ."

CONSENSUS AND CONFORMITY

As the economy grew, an increasing sense of sameness pervaded American society. This was the great age of conformity, when members of all social groups learned to emulate those around them rather than strike out on their own. Television contributed to growing conformity by providing young and old with a common, visually seductive experience. Escaping the homogenizing tendencies was difficult.

Conformity in School and Religious Life

The willingness to conform to group norms affected colleges and universities, where cautious students sought security. They joined fraternities and sororities and engaged in panty raids and other pranks but took little interest in world affairs.

Americans also returned to their churches in record numbers. Church membership doubled between 1945 and 1970. In part, church attendance reflected a desire to challenge "godless communism" at the height of the Cold War and to find some solace from the threat of annihilation in a nuclear war; in part, it resulted from the power of suggestion that led Americans to do what others did. By the end of the 1950s, fully 95 percent of all Americans identified with some religious denomination.

Dwight Eisenhower reflected the national mood when he observed that "our government makes no sense unless it is founded in a deeply felt religious faith—and I don't care what it is."

In 1954, Congress added the words "under God" to the pledge to the flag and the next year voted to require the phrase "In God We Trust" on all American currency.

Back to the Kitchen

During World War II, as servicemen went overseas, women left their homes to work. After 1945, there was a period of adjustment as the men returned. In the 1950s, traditional gender roles were reaffirmed, even though, paradoxically, more women entered the work force than ever before.

Men viewed themselves as the primary breadwinners and wanted their jobs waiting for them after the war. For women, the situation was more difficult. Many had enjoyed working during the war and were reluctant to retreat to the home, although the government and employers persistently encouraged them to do so.

By the 1950s, the issue was settled. The baby boom increased average family size and made the decision to remain home easier. The flight to the suburbs gave women more to do, and they settled into the routines of redecorating their homes and gardens and transporting children to and from activities and schools.

In 1956, *Life* magazine produced a special issue on women. Profiling Marjorie Sutton, the magazine spoke of the "Busy Wife's Achievements" as "Home Manager, Mother, Hostess, and Useful Civic Worker." Married at 16, Marjorie was now busy with the PTA, Campfire Girls, and charity causes. She cooked and sewed for her family, which included four children, supported her husband by entertaining 1,500 guests a year, and worked out on the trampoline "to keep her size 12 figure." Marjorie Sutton reflected the widespread social emphasis on marriage and home.

Despite the reaffirmation of the old ideology that a woman's place was in the home, the decade of the 1950s was a period of unnoticed but important change. Because the supply of single women workers was diminished by the low birthrate of the Depression years and by increased schooling and early marriage, older married women began entering the labor force in large numbers for the first time. In 1940, only 15 percent of American wives had jobs. By 1950, 21 percent were employed, and ten years later, the figure had risen to 30 percent. Moreover, married women now accounted for more than half of all working women, a dramatic reversal of earlier patterns.

Women stepped into the new jobs created by economic expansion, clustering in office, sales, and service positions, occupations already defined as female. They and their employers considered their work subordinate to their primary role as wives and mothers.

Black women worked as always but often lost the jobs they had won during the war. As the total percentage of women in the Detroit automobile industry dropped from 25 to 7.5, for example, jobs for black women nearly disappeared. Their median income at the end of the 1940s was less than half of white women. But during the 1950s, they succeeded both in moving into white-collar positions and improving their income. By 1960, more than a third of all black women had clerical, sales, service, or professional jobs, and their paychecks were 70 percent of those of white women.

Despite women's mixed experiences, society continued to view women in traditional ways. The belief that women's main role was still at home justified paying them low wages and denying them promotions. This view was reinforced by the portrayal of women in movies, television programs, and popular literature.

Sexuality was a troublesome if compelling topic in the postwar years. In 1948, Alfred C. Kinsey published *Sexual Behavior in the Human Male*. Kinsey was an Indiana University zoologist who had previously studied the gall wasp. When asked to teach a course on marriage problems, he found little published material about human sexual activity and decided to collect his own. He compiled case histories of 5,300 white males, analyzed their personal backgrounds, and recorded patterns of sexual behavior.

Kinsey shocked the country with his statistics on premarital, extramarital, and otherwise illicit sexual activity. Among males who went to college, he concluded, 67 percent had engaged in sexual intercourse before marriage; 84 percent of those who went to high school but not beyond had done the same. Thirty-seven percent of the total male population had experienced some kind of overt homosexual activity. One out of every six farm boys in America had copulated with animals. Kinsey published a companion volume, *Sexual Behavior in the Human Female* (1953), that detailed many of the same sexual patterns. Although critics denounced the books, both sold widely, for they opened the door to a subject that had previously been considered taboo. Interest in sexuality was reflected in the fascination with sex goddesses like actress Marilyn Monroe and with male fantasies of women, visible in *Playboy,* which first appeared in 1953.

Cultural Rebels

Not all Americans fit the stereotypes of the 1950s. Some were alienated from the culture and rebelled against its values. Even as young people struggled to meet the standards and expectations of their peers, they were intrigued by Holden Caulfield, the main figure in J. D. Salinger's popular novel *The Catcher in the Rye* (1951). Holden, a sensitive student at boarding school, felt surrounded by "phonies" who threatened his individuality and independence. Holden's ill-fated effort to preserve his own integrity in the face of pressures to conform struck a resonant chord in many readers.

A group of writers, often called the "beat generation," espoused unconventional values in their stories, poems, and "happenings." Confronting apathy and conformity, they insisted there were alternatives. Stressing spontaneity and spirituality, they claimed that intuition was more important than reason, Eastern mysticism more valuable than Western faith. The "beats" went out of their way to challenge the norms of respectability. They rejected materialism, engaged in overt sexual activity designed to shock, and helped popularize the use of marijuana.

Their literary work reflected their approach to life. Jack Kerouac typed his best-selling novel *On the Road* (1957), describing free-wheeling trips across country, on a 250-foot roll of paper. Lacking conventional punctuation and paragraph structure, the book was a paean to the free life the beats espoused.

Poet Allen Ginsberg, like Kerouac a Columbia University dropout, became equally well known for his poem "Howl." Written during a wild weekend in 1955 while Ginsberg was under the influence of drugs, the poem was a scathing critique of the modern, mechanized culture and its effects.

The popularity of Salinger, Kerouac, and Ginsberg owed much to a revolution in book publishing and to the democratization of education that accompanied the program of GI educational benefits. More Americans than ever before acquired a taste for literature, and they found huge numbers of inexpensive books available because of the "paperback revolution." The paperback, introduced in 1939, dominated the book market after World War II. By 1965, readers could choose among some 25,000 titles.

The signs of cultural rebellion also appeared in popular music and art. A young Tennessee singer named Elvis Presley made "rock and roll" the new music of the young. American painters, led by Jackson Pollock and his "New York school," discarded the easel, laid gigantic canvases on the floor, and then used trowels, putty knives, and sticks to apply paint, glass shards, sand, and other materials in wild explosions of color. Known as abstract expressionists, these painters regarded the unconscious as the source of their artistic creations. Like much of the literature of rebellion, abstract expressionism reflected the artist's alienation from a world becoming filled with nuclear threats, computerization, and materialism.

DOMESTIC POLICY UNDER TRUMAN AND EISENHOWER

In the prosperous postwar era, pressures from the expanding middle class and from rapid growth influenced public policy. Two dissimilar men exercised presidential leadership in the decade and a half after World War II. Democrat Harry S Truman took the same aggressive stance at home as he adopted in foreign affairs. A conservative Congress, however, blocked him at every turn. His Republican successor, Dwight D. Eisenhower, created a very different imprint. Genial and calm, even when facing an opposition Congress himself, the war hero conveyed to Americans the feeling that everything was all right.

Reconversion

Truman's first priority when the war ended was reconversion—the transition to a peacetime economy. Servicemen returned rapidly. The number on active duty dropped from 12 million in 1945 to 1.6 million in mid-1947, causing competition in the housing and employment markets.

Truman also recognized the need to keep the cap on inflation. When wartime price controls ended, prices rose. A year and a half after the end of the war, the consumer price index was up almost 25 percent.

Finally, Truman had to deal with the problem of labor unrest. Massive layoffs left 2.7 million workers without jobs by March 1946. Wage issues were unresolved as well. After the wartime years of restraint, workers wanted pay increases they regarded as long overdue. Furthermore, many more of them belonged to unions. The percentage of nonagricultural workers who were union members rose from 13 percent in 1935 to 27 percent in 1940 and to 35 percent by

1945. When wage demands were refused, millions of workers walked out. In 1946, some 4.6 million workers marched on picket lines, more than had turned out ever before in the history of the United States. They struck in the automobile, steel, and electrical industries, the railroads, and the soft-coal mines. When Truman argued that the national interest was compromised by strikes in those industries, he alienated many working-class Americans, a major segment of the Democratic coalition that his predecessor, Franklin Roosevelt, had put together in the 1930s.

Postwar Public Policy

Even as he grappled with the immediate problems of postwar reconversion, Truman addressed broader questions. Less than a week after the end of World War II, Truman called on Congress to pass legislation guaranteeing all Americans jobs, decent housing, educational opportunities, and a variety of other rights outlined in a 21-point program. During the next ten weeks, Truman sent blueprints of further proposals to Congress, including health insurance and atomic energy legislation. This liberal program soon ran into fierce political opposition.

The debate surrounding the Employment Act of 1946 hinted at the fate of Truman's proposals. The Employment Act was a deliberate effort to apply the theory of English economist John Maynard Keynes to maintain economic equilibrium and prevent depression. The initial bill committed the government to maintaining full employment by monitoring the economy and taking remedial actions in case of decline. Those actions included tax cuts and spending programs to stimulate the economy and reduce unemployment.

Liberals hailed the measure, but business groups opposed it. Congress cut the proposal to bits. As finally passed, the act created a Council of Economic Advisers to make recommendations to the president, who was to report annually on the state of the economy. But it stopped short of committing the government to using fiscal tools to maintain full employment when economic indicators turned downward. The act was only a modest continuation of New Deal attempts at economic planning.

Truman Against a Conservative Congress

As the midterm elections of 1946 approached, Truman and his supporters knew they were vulnerable. Often seeming like a petty, bungling administrator, Truman became the butt of countless political jokes. Support for Truman dropped from 87 percent of those polled after he assumed the presidency to 32 percent in November 1946. Republicans won majorities in both houses of Congress for the first time since the 1928 elections, and a majority of the governorships as well.

After the 1946 election, Truman faced an unsympathetic 80th Congress. Republicans and conservative Democrats, dominating both houses, sought to reverse the liberal policies of the Roosevelt years. When the new Congress met, it moved to cut federal spending and reduce taxes.

Congress also struck at Democratic labor policies. Republicans wanted to check labor unions, and in 1947, they passed the Taft-Hartley Act, which intended to limit the power of unions by restricting the weapons they could employ. Revising the Wagner Act of 1935, the legislation spelled out unfair labor practices (such as preventing workers from working if they wished) and outlawed the closed shop whereby an employee had to join a union before getting a job. The law allowed states to prohibit the union shop, which forced workers to join the union after they had been hired. The act also gave the president the right to call for an 80-day cooling-off period in strikes affecting national security and required union officials to sign non-Communist oaths in order to use governmental machinery designed to protect their rights. Tru-

man vigorously opposed the bill, but Congress passed it over his veto.

The Fair Deal and Its Critics

In 1948, Truman won the Democratic nomination despite his waning popularity, but the Democratic Party was split by the civil rights issue.

When liberals defeated a moderate platform proposal and pressed for a stronger stand on black civil rights; angry delegates from Mississippi and Alabama stormed out of the convention. They later formed the States' Rights, or "Dixiecrat," party, nominated Governor J. Strom Thurmond of South Carolina as their presidential candidate, and affirmed their support for continued racial segregation.

Meanwhile, Henry A. Wallace, for seven years secretary of agriculture, then vice president during Roosevelt's third term and secretary of commerce after that, was mounting his own challenge. Truman had fired Wallace from his cabinet for supporting a more temperate stand on Soviet relations. Now Wallace became the presidential candidate of the Progressive Party.

In that fragmented state, against the first real third-party challenges since 1912, the Democrats faced the Republicans, who coveted the White House after 16 years out of power. Once again they nominated Thomas E. Dewey, the governor of New York. Egocentric and stiff, Dewey was hardly a charismatic figure. Still, the polls uniformly picked the Republicans to win.

Truman, as the underdog, conducted a vigorous campaign. He appealed to ordinary Americans as an unpretentious man engaged in an uphill fight. Speaking without a prepared text in his choppy, aggressive style, he warmed to crowds, and they warmed to him. "Give 'em hell, Harry," they yelled. "Pour it on." He did.

All the polls predicted a Republican win. But the pollsters were wrong. On election day, despite the bold headline "Dewey Defeats Truman" in the Chicago *Daily Tribune*, the incumbent president scored one of the most unex-

In one of the nation's most extraordinary political upsets, Harry Truman beat Thomas E. Dewey in 1948. Here an exuberant Truman holds a newspaper headline printed while he slept, before the vote turned his way.

pected political upsets in American history, winning 303–189 in the electoral college. Democrats also swept both houses of Congress.

Truman won primarily because he was able to revive the major elements of the Democratic coalition that Franklin Roosevelt had constructed more than a decade before. Despite the rocky days of 1946, Truman managed to hold on to labor, farm, and black votes.

With the election behind him, Truman pursued his liberal program, which became known as the "Fair Deal." Some parts of Truman's Fair Deal worked; others did not. The minimum wage was raised, and social security programs were expanded. A housing program brought modest gains but did not really meet housing needs. A farm program, aimed at providing income support to farmers if prices fell, never made it through Congress. Most of his civil rights program failed to win congressional support. The American Medical Association undermined the effort to provide national health insurance, and Congress rejected a measure to provide federal aid to education.

Committed to checking the perceived Soviet threat, Truman allowed his domestic program to suffer. As defense expenditures mounted, correspondingly less money was available for projects at home.

The Election of Eisenhower

In 1952, Truman had the support of only 23 percent of the American people, and all indicators pointed to a political shift. The Democrats nominated Adlai Stevenson, Illinois's able, articulate, and moderately liberal governor. The Republicans turned to Dwight D. Eisenhower, the World War II hero Americans knew as Ike.

The Republicans called the Democrats "soft

on communism." They criticized assorted scandals surrounding Truman's cronies and friends. The president himself was blameless, but some of the people near him were not. The Republicans also promised to end the unpopular Korean War.

Eisenhower won a massive victory at the polls. He received 55 percent of the vote and carried 41 states. The new president took office with a Republican Congress as well and had little difficulty gaining a second term four years later.

"Modern Republicanism"

Eisenhower believed firmly in limiting the presidential role. He wanted to reduce the growth of the federal government. Eisenhower sometimes termed his approach "dynamic conservatism" or "modern Republicanism," which, he explained, meant "conservative when it comes to money, liberal when it comes to human beings."

Above all, economic concerns dominated the Eisenhower years. The president and his chief aides wanted desperately to preserve the value of the dollar, pare down levels of funding, cut taxes, and balance the budget after years of deficit spending.

To achieve those aims, the president appointed George Humphrey, a fiscal conservative, as secretary of the treasury. Humphrey's approach to reducing spending did not exclude "using a meat axe." The business-oriented administration was willing to risk unemployment to keep inflation under control.

Eisenhower supported the passage of the Submerged Lands Act in 1953. That measure transferred control of about $40 billion worth of oil lands from the federal government to the states. The New York *Times* called it "one of the greatest and surely the most unjustified giveaway programs in all the history of the United States."

The administration also sought to reduce federal activity in the electric-power field. Eisenhower favored private rather than public development of power. He opposed a TVA proposal for expansion to provide power to the Atomic Energy Commission and instead authorized a private group, the Dixon-Yates syndicate, to build a plant in Arkansas to meet the need. Later, when charges of scandal arose, the administration canceled the agreement, but the basic preference for private development remained.

As a result of the administration's reluctance to stimulate the economy too much, the annual rate of economic growth declined from 4.3 percent between 1947 and 1952 to 2.5 percent between 1953 and 1960. The country suffered three recessions in Eisenhower's eight years. During the slumps, the deficits that Eisenhower so wanted to avoid increased.

Eisenhower's understated approach led to a legislative stalemate, particularly when the Democrats regained control of Congress in 1954. Opponents of the president gibed at Ike's restrained stance. Yet he was often active behind the scenes pursuing his favorite programs. By accepting the fundamental features of the welfare state the Democrats had created, he ensured that it would not be rolled back. For all the jokes at his expense, Eisenhower remained popular with the voters.

THE OTHER AMERICA

In the years after World War II, not all Americans enjoyed the prosperity and privileges of the growing middle class. Poverty existed in inner cities and rural areas. Minorities began to press for equal treatment and equal rights. Black Americans and Jews, in the forefront of the civil rights struggle, were joined by Hispanics and Native Americans, who built their protest movements on the model of black protest but moved more slowly than blacks.

Poverty amid Affluence

Many people in the "affluent society" lived in poverty. Economic growth favored the upper and middle classes. Although the popular "trickle-down" theory argued that economic expansion brought benefits to all classes, little, in fact, reached the citizens at the bottom of the ladder. In 1960, according to the Federal Bureau of Labor Statistics, a yearly subsistence-level income for a family of four was $3,000 and for a family of six, $4,000. The Bureau reported that 40 million people (almost a quarter of the population) lived below those levels and nearly the same number only marginally above the line.

Michael Harrington, Socialist author and critic, exposed those conditions in *The Other America*, a devastating account that shocked the country when it appeared in 1962. The poor were everywhere. Harrington described the "economic underworld" in New York City, where "Puerto Ricans and Negroes, alcoholics, drifters, and disturbed people" sought daily positions as "dishwashers and day workers, the fly-by-night jobs" at employment agencies. He also explained the plight of the rural poor—tenant farmers and migrant workers.

Black Americans and Civil Rights

Blacks became increasingly restive in the post–World War II years, particularly as economic changes affected traditional employment patterns. In the South, as cotton farmers turned to less labor-intensive crops like soybeans and peanuts, they ousted their tenants. Between 1930 and 1960, the southern agricultural population declined from 16 million to 6 million. Millions of blacks moved to southern cities, where they found better jobs, better schooling, and freedom from landlord control. Some achieved middle-class status. Still not entirely free, these southern blacks were now ready to attack Jim Crow.

Millions of blacks also headed for northern cities between 1940 and 1960. And since northern blacks could vote and usually voted for the Democrats, civil rights became an issue that northern Democratic leaders could not avoid.

Blacks had increased their demands for change during World War II. They had won some concessions (see Chapter 26) but not enough to satisfy rising black aspirations. Meanwhile, black servicemen returning from the war vowed to reject second-class citizenship and helped mobilize a grass-roots movement. Adam Clayton Powell, a Harlem preacher (and later congressman), warned that the black man "is ready to throw himself into the struggle to make the dream of America become flesh and blood, bread and butter, freedom and equality. He walks conscious of the fact that he is no longer alone—no longer a minority."

The racial question was dramatized in 1947 when Jackie Robinson broke the color line and began playing major league baseball with the Brooklyn Dodgers. After Robinson's trailblazing effort, other blacks, formerly confined to the old Negro leagues, started to move into the major leagues, then into professional football and basketball.

A somewhat reluctant Truman supported the civil rights movement. A moderate on questions of race who believed in political equality, not social equality, he yielded to the growing strength of the black vote. In 1946, Truman appointed a Committee on Civil Rights to investigate the problem of lynchings and other brutalities against blacks and to make recommendations. The committee's report, released in October 1947, showed that blacks remained second-class citizens in every area of American life. The report set a civil rights agenda for the next two decades.

Though Truman hedged at first, in February 1948 he sent a ten-point civil rights program to

Congress—the first presidential civil rights program since Reconstruction. When the southern wing of the Democratic Party bolted later that year, he moved forward even more aggressively. First he issued an executive order barring discrimination in the federal establishment. Then he ordered equality of treatment in the military services. Manpower needs in the Korean War led to the elimination of the last restrictions, particularly when the army found that integrated units performed well.

Elsewhere the administration pushed reforms. The Justice Department, not previously supportive of NAACP litigation on behalf of equal rights for blacks, entered the battle against segregation and filed briefs challenging the constitutionality of restrictions in housing, education, and interstate transportation. Those helped build the pressure for change that influenced the Supreme Court. Congress, however, did little.

Integrating the Schools

In the 1950s, as the civil rights struggle gained momentum, the judicial system played a crucial role. The NAACP was determined to overturn the doctrine established in *Plessy* v. *Ferguson* in 1896. In that decision, the Supreme Court had declared that segregation of the black and white races was constitutional if the facilities used by each were "separate but equal." The decree had been used for generations to sanction rigid segregation, primarily in the South, even though separate facilities were seldom, if ever, equal.

A direct challenge came in 1951 when Oliver Brown, the father of 8-year-old Linda Brown, sued the school board of Topeka, Kansas, to allow his daughter to attend a school for white children that she passed as she walked to the bus that carried her to a black school farther away. The case reached the Supreme Court, which on May 17, 1954, released its bombshell ruling in *Brown* v. *Board of Education*. For more than a decade, Supreme Court decisions had gradually expanded black civil rights, and

now the Court unanimously decreed that "separate facilities are inherently unequal" and concluded that the "separate but equal" doctrine had no place in public education. A year later, the Court turned to the question of implementation and declared that local school boards, acting with the guidance of lower courts, should move "with all deliberate speed" to desegregate their facilities.

Charged with the ultimate responsibility for executing the law was Dwight Eisenhower, who privately thought the decision was wrong but knew that according to the Constitution it was his duty to see that the law was carried out. Even while urging sympathy for the South in its period of transition, he acted immediately to desegregate the Washington, D.C., schools as a model for the rest of the country. He also ordered desegregation in navy yards and veterans' hospitals.

Even so, the South resisted. In district after district, vicious scenes occurred. The crucial confrontation came in Little Rock, Arkansas, in 1957. A desegregation plan, to begin with the token admission of a few black students to Central High School, was ready to go into effect. Just before the school year began, Governor Orval Faubus declared on television that it would not be possible to maintain order if integration took place. National Guardsmen, posted by the governor to keep the peace and armed with bayonets, turned away nine black students as they tried to enter the school. After three weeks, a federal court ordered the troops to leave. When the black children entered, the white students, spurred on by their elders, belligerently opposed them, chanting such slogans as "Two, four, six, eight, we ain't gonna integrate." In the face of hostile mobs, the black children left the school.

With the lines drawn, attention focused on the moderate man in the White House, who faced a situation in which Little Rock whites were clearly defying the law. As a former military officer, Ike knew that such resistance could not be tolerated. He called out federal troops to protect the rights of black citizens, ordered paratroopers to Little Rock, and placed National Guardsmen under federal command. The black children entered the school and attended classes with the military protecting their rights. Thus desegregation began.

Black Gains on Other Fronts

Meanwhile, blacks themselves began organizing in ways that advanced the civil rights movement. The crucial event occurred in Montgomery, Alabama, in December 1955. Rosa Parks, a 42-year-old black seamstress who was also secretary of the state NAACP, sat down in the front of a bus in a section reserved by custom for whites. Tired from a hard day's work, she refused when ordered to move back. The police were called at the next stop, and Parks was arrested for violating the segregation laws. Although she had not intended to challenge the law or cause a scene, her stance marked a new phase in the civil rights movement.

In Montgomery, black civil rights officials seized the issue. The next evening, resistance began. Fifty black leaders met to discuss the case and decided to organize a massive boycott of the bus system. Martin Luther King, Jr., the 27-year-old minister of the Baptist church where the meeting was held, soon emerged as the preeminent spokesman of the protest.

Fifty thousand blacks walked or formed car pools to avoid the transit system. Their actions cut gross revenue on city buses by 65 percent. Almost a year later, the Supreme Court ruled that bus segregation, like school segregation, violated the Constitution, and the boycott ended. But the mood it fostered continued, and peaceful protest became a way of life for many blacks.

Meanwhile, a concerted effort developed to guarantee black voting rights. The provisions of

Baptist minister Martin Luther King, Jr., emerged as the black spokesman in the Montgomery, Alabama, bus boycott and soon became the most eloquent African-American leader of the entire civil rights movement. Drawing on his religious background, he was able to mobilize blacks and whites alike in the struggle for equal rights.

the Fifteenth Amendment notwithstanding, many states had circumvented the law for decades (see Chapter 16). Some required a poll tax or a literacy test or an examination of constitutional understanding. Blacks often found themselves excluded from the polls.

Largely because of the legislative genius of Senate majority leader Lyndon B. Johnson of Texas, the civil rights bill, the first since Reconstruction, moved toward passage. With his eye on the presidency, Johnson wanted to establish his credentials as a man who could look beyond narrow southern interests. Paring the bill down to the provisions he felt would pass, Johnson pushed the measure through.

The Civil Rights Act of 1957 created a Civil Rights Commission and empowered the Justice Department to go to court in cases where blacks were denied the right to vote. The bill was a compromise measure, yet it was the first successful effort to protect civil rights in 82 years.

Again led by Johnson, Congress passed the Civil Rights Act of 1960, which set stiffer punishments for people who interfered with others' right to vote but again stopped short of authorizing federal registrars to register blacks to vote and so was generally ineffective.

The civil rights movement made important strides during the Eisenhower years, though little of the progress resulted from the president's leadership. Rather, the efforts of blacks themselves and the ruling of the Supreme Court brought significant change. The period of grassroots civil rights activities, now launched, would continue in the 1960s.

Mexican Migrant Laborers

In the years after World War II, Spanish-speaking groups in the United States suffered from many of the same problems as blacks. They came mainly from Puerto Rico, Mexico, and Central America. Often unskilled and illiterate, they gravitated to the cities like other less fortunate Americans.

Chicanos, or Mexican-Americans, the most numerous newcomers, faced peculiar difficulties and widespread discrimination. During World War II, as the country faced a labor shortage at home, American farmers sought Mexican *braceros* (helping hands) to harvest their crops. A program to encourage the seasonal immigration of farm workers continued after the war when the government signed a Migratory Labor Agreement with Mexico. Between 1948 and 1964, some 4.5 million Mexicans were brought to the United States for temporary work. *Braceros* were expected to return to Mexico at the end of their labor contract, but they often stayed, hoping to better their lives in America. Joining them were millions more who entered the country illegally.

Conditions were harsh for the *braceros* even in the best of times. In periods of economic difficulty, they worsened. During the 1953–1954 recession, the government mounted Operation Wetback to deport illegal entrants and *braceros* who had remained in the country illegally. Deportations numbered 1.1 million. But the *bracero* program continued, and in 1956 a record 445,000 *braceros* crossed the border to work on American farms.

The political attacks in the heated days of the Red Scare also brought persecution to Chicanos active in radical causes. Agapito Gómez had lived in the United States for 25 years. He had an American-born wife. Nonetheless, he found himself questioned for past union activities. In the 1930s, he had been part of a Depression relief organization and had joined the CIO. When he refused to divulge the names of people with whom he had worked, immigration officials took away his alien card.

In addition to economic oppression, Chicanos in all walks of life faced discrimination in the schools, uncertain access to public facilities, and occasional exclusion from the governing process, which they did not always understand. Like blacks, they protested such restrictions and sometimes met with success. The post–World War II years saw increasing political awareness on the part of Mexican-Americans and new aggressiveness in fighting for their rights.

Sometimes action resulted from a particular event. Chicanos, for example, established the American GI Forum when a Texas funeral home refused to bury a Mexican-American casualty of World War II. When the group's protest led to a burial in Arlington National Cemetery, it was clear that concerted action could succeed.

Meanwhile, in the waning months of the war, a court case challenging Mexican-American segregation in the schools began. Gonzalo Méndez, an asparagus grower and a U.S. citizen who had lived in Orange County, California, for 25 years, filed suit to permit his children to attend the school reserved for Anglo-Americans, which was far more attractive than the Mexican one to which they had been assigned. A federal district court upheld his claim in the spring of 1945, and two years later, the circuit court affirmed the original ruling. With the favorable decision, other communities filed similar suits and began to press for integration of their schools.

Chicanos also faced police brutality, particularly in the cities with the largest Chicano populations. Los Angeles, with its large number of Chicanos, was the scene of numerous unsavory racial episodes.

Protests continued, yet in the 1950s, Chicano activism was fragmented. Some Mexican-Americans considered their situation hopeless. While new and aggressive challenges appeared, fully effective mobilization had to wait for another day.

Native Americans

American Indians also acted to defend their interests, but with even greater difficulties. Not only did they have to fight the forces of cultural and technological change that were eroding tribal tradition, but they also had to resist the federal government's reversal of New Deal Indian policy.

Just after the end of World War II, Native Americans achieved an important victory when Congress established the Indian Claims Commission. The commission was mandated to review tribal cases pleading that ancestral lands had been illegally taken from them through violation of federal treaties. Hundreds of tribal suits against the government in federal courts were now possible. Many of them would lead to large settlements of cash—a form of reparation for past injustices—and sometimes the return of long-lost lands.

The Eisenhower administration turned away from the New Deal policy of government support for tribal autonomy. In the Indian Reorganization Act of 1934, the government had stepped in to restore lands to tribal ownership and end their loss or sale to outsiders. In 1953, the administration adopted a new approach, known as the "termination" policy. The government proposed settling all outstanding claims and eliminating reservations as legitimate political entities. To encourage their assimilation into mainstream society, the government offered small subsidies to families who would leave the reservations and relocate in the cities.

The new policy victimized the Indians. With their lands no longer federally protected and their members deprived of treaty rights, many tribes became unwitting victims of people who wanted to seize their land. The new policy caused great disruption as the government terminated tribes like the Klamaths in Oregon, the Menominees in Wisconsin, the Alabamas and Coushattas in Texas, and bands of Paiutes in Utah. At the same time, the policy spurred Indian activism. The National Congress of American Indians mobilized opposition to the federal program. In 1958, the Eisenhower administration ended termination without a tribe's consent. The policy continued to have the force of law, but implementation ceased.

CONCLUSION

QUALMS AMID AFFLUENCE

In general, the United States during the decade and a half after World War II was stable and secure. Recessions occurred periodically, but the economy righted itself after short downturns. For the most part, business boomed. Millions of middle-class Americans moved to the suburbs to enjoy what they considered the good life.

Some Americans, however, did not share in the prosperity. Though black Americans and other minority groups were beginning to mobilize, their protests remained peaceful.

Toward the end of the 1950s, after the Soviet Union became the first nation to place a satellite in orbit, a wave of anxiety swept the nation. Some Americans began to criticize the materialism that had apparently caused the nation to fall behind.

Criticisms and anxieties notwithstanding, the standard of living remained high for many of the nation's citizens. Healthy and comfortable, upper- and middle-class Americans assumed that their society would continue to prosper. But the "other Americans" had begun to make their voices heard, and the echoes would reverberate loudly in future years.

Recommended Reading

A number of good books describe domestic developments in the years between 1945 and 1960. David Brody, *Workers in Industrial America* (1980), and James R. Green, *The World of the Worker* (1980), deal perceptively with labor issues. Kenneth T. Jackson, *Crabgrass Frontier: The Suburbanization of the United States* (1985), focuses on the growth of suburbs; William Leuchtenburg, *A Troubled Feast* (1983), is a perceptive assessment of the entire post-1945 period that focuses on the consumer culture that came into prominence after World War II.

Robert J. Donovan, *Conflict and Crisis: The Presidency of Harry S. Truman, 1945–1948* (1977), is a detailed overview of Truman's first term. *Tumultuous Years: The Presidency of Harry S. Truman* (1982), by the same author, carries the story through the second term. Harry S. Truman, *Memoirs*, 2 vols. (1955, 1956), is Truman's own account of his years at the top.

For a general introduction to the Eisenhower period, see Charles C. Alexander, *Holding the Line: The Eisenhower Era, 1952–1961* (1975). Dwight D. Eisenhower, *Mandate for Change, 1953–1956* (1963), is the first volume of Ike's memoirs of his years in office; *Waging Peace* (1965) is the concluding volume.

Stephen E. Ambrose, *Eisenhower: The President* (1984), is an excellent account of the White House years.

On women, William H. Chafe, *The American Woman: Her Changing Social, Economic, and Political Roles, 1920–1970* (1972), is an outstanding survey of women's struggle. Betty Friedan, *The Feminine Mystique* (1963), is a compelling book describing the stereotypical role of women in the 1950s as they focused on being housewives and mothers.

For further details on civil rights, see Harvard Sitkoff, *The Struggle for Black Equality, 1954–1980* (1981), a readable survey of the movement since the early 1950s. David J. Garrow, *Bearing the Cross: Martin Luther King, Jr., and the Southern Christian Leadership Conference* (1986), is a good account of King and his role. Taylor Branch, *Parting the Waters: America in the King Years, 1954–1963* (1988), vividly records the conflicts in the movement. Rodolfo Acuña, *Occupied America: A History of Chicanos*, 3d ed. (1988), gives insight into the Chicanos' struggle in the years after World War II. Alvin M. Josephy, Jr., *Now That the Buffalo's Gone* (1982), details Indian struggles over the past several decades.

Time Line

1944	GI Bill Passed	**1951**	J. D. Salinger's *Catcher in the Rye*
1945	World War II ends Wave of strikes in heavy industries	**1952**	Dwight D. Eisenhower elected president
1946	Truman vetoes bill extending Office of Price Administration Prices rise by 25 percent in 18 months Union strikes in the auto, coal, steel, and electrical industries Employment Act Dr. Spock's *Baby and Child Care*	**1953**	Submerged Lands Act
		1954	*Brown* v. *Board of Education*
		1955	Montgomery bus boycott begins First McDonald's opens in Illinois AFL and CIO merge
		1956	Eisenhower reelected Interstate Highway Act Allen Ginsberg's "Howl"
1947	Taft-Hartley Act Jackie Robinson breaks the color line in major league baseball	**1957**	Little Rock school integration crisis Civil Rights Act Baby boom peaks with 4.3 million births Soviet Union launches *Sputnik*
1948	Executive order bars discrimination in federal government Armed forces begin to desegregate "Dixiecrat" party formed Truman defeats Dewey Kinsey report on human sexuality Transistor developed at Bell Laboratories	**1959**	One-third of all Americans reside in suburbs
		1960	Three-fourths of all families own a TV Civil Rights Act GNP hits $500 billion
1949	Truman launches Fair Deal		
1950	*Asociación Nacional México-Americana* formed		

chapter 28

The Rise and Fall of the Liberal State

Ron Kovic was an all-American boy. Born in 1946, he grew up on Long Island. Life was secure in the comfortable post–World War II years, as Kovic shared the dreams of millions of others his age. "I loved baseball more than anything else in the world," he later recalled, "playing catch-a-fly-you're-up for hours with a beat-up old baseball." When baseball did not occupy him, television did.

Anxious moments occasionally intervened. Kovic, like others, wondered how the Russians had managed to put a satellite into space before the United States. He grew up fearing "the Communist threat." But, like most Americans, Kovic had an unquestioning confidence in the "American way." Caught up in the spirit of the New Frontier, Kovic was stunned when President John F. Kennedy was shot. "I truly felt I had lost a dear friend," he wrote.

After graduating from high school, Kovic enlisted in the marines. The desire to be a hero carried him through basic training and a first tour of duty in the war in Vietnam. Proud of what he was doing, he signed up for a second tour. Only then did the conflict begin to tear him apart.

Kovic was increasingly haunted by his conduct in the war. He accidently shot and killed an American corporal and, as if to atone for his deed, plunged on even more aggressively to serve his country. Yet that effort, too, ended in disaster when men in his unit shot at shadowy figures moving in a village hut, only to learn that they had killed and wounded innocent children.

Later Kovic was hit in the foot and then took a 30-caliber sniper bullet in the spine. The pain in his foot vanished, but so did all sensation below his chest. Suddenly, all he could feel was "the worthlessness of dying right here in this place at this moment for nothing."

Ron Kovic returned from the war paralyzed from the chest down. As he went from hospital to hospital, seeing the muscle tone of his legs disappear, he grew to believe that he had been trapped in a meaningless crusade and then left to dangle on his own. He became one of the many protesters who finally helped bring the war to an end.

Ron Kovic's passage through the 1960s and 1970s reflected that of American society as a whole. Millions of Americans shared his positive views as the period began. And like Ron Kovic, they were then consumed by doubts about the government's role as the United States became more and more involved in Vietnam.

This chapter describes both the climax of twentieth-century liberalism and its subsequent decline. We will examine first the Democratic initiatives, then the Republican responses, as American politics shifted course in the 1960s and 1970s. In pondering the possibilities of reform, we will outline the various efforts to devise an effective political response to structural changes in the post–World War II economy and follow the fate of those efforts as they became intertwined with the nation's ill-conceived anticommunist crusade in Vietnam.

THE HIGH-WATER MARK OF LIBERALISM

American priorities changed as Dwight Eisenhower came to the end of his second term. The Republican administration's acceptance of New Deal and Fair Deal commitments helped to create a consensus on the major role of the federal government in American life. The Democrats who won office in the 1960s wanted to broaden that role. Dismayed at the problems of poverty, unemployment, and racism, they sought to manage the economy more effectively, eradicate poverty, and protect the civil rights of all Americans. Midway through the decade they came close to achieving their goals.

In this section we will examine the personalities and leadership qualities of liberal presidents Kennedy and Johnson and the changing role of government before taking up the domestic programs of the Kennedy and Johnson administrations and supportive role played by the Supreme Court.

Liberal Leadership

The liberal Democratic leaders of the 1960s took an activist view of the presidency. They believed that the president should set national priorities and then work closely with Congress to ensure the passage of legislation. Whereas Eisenhower had been more comfortable working behind the scenes with legislators, first John Kennedy, then Lyndon Johnson, hoped to use the White House as a "bully pulpit" as Theodore Roosevelt had done. Kennedy encountered fierce resistance from the legislative branch; Johnson was far more successful in implementing his program.

John F. Kennedy, who won the presidency in 1960, seemed to symbolize the commitment to energetic leadership. At 43, he was the youngest man ever elected president. Son of a former ambassador to England and grandson of an Irish-American mayor of Boston, he appeared vigorous and articulate, able to make good on his campaign promise to get the country moving again.

Keenly aware of shifting political patterns, he recognized the need to use the techniques of advertising in his bid for the presidency. Above all he realized the power of television in taking his case to the American people.

In the 1960 campaign, Kennedy squared off against Richard Nixon, the Republican nominee, in the first televised presidential debates. Seventy million Americans turned on their sets to watch the two men in the first debate. Kennedy projected a more dynamic image; Nixon looked worn out and ill at ease.

In the election of 1960, John Kennedy squared off against Richard Nixon in the first televised presidential debates. Nearly 80 million people watched Kennedy establish his credibility with a smooth performance in the four debates.

Kennedy also had the capacity to voice his aims in understandable and eloquent language. During the campaign, he pointed to "uncharted areas of science and space, unsolved problems of peace and war, unconquered pockets of ignorance and prejudice, unanswered questions of poverty and surplus" that Americans must confront, for "the New Frontier is here whether we seek it or not." He made the same point even more movingly in his inaugural address: "The torch has been passed to a new generation of Americans—born in this century, tempered by war, disciplined by a hard and bitter peace, proud of our ancient heritage." Many were inspired by his concluding call to action: "And so, my fellow Americans: Ask not what your country can do for you—ask what you can do for your country."

For Kennedy, strong leadership was all-important. He surrounded himself with talented assistants. On his staff were 15 Rhodes scholars and several famous authors. The secretary of state was Dean Rusk, a former member of the State Department who had then served as president of the Rockefeller Foundation. The secretary of defense was Robert S. McNamara, the highly successful president of the Ford Motor Company, who had proved creative in mobilizing talented assistants—"whiz kids"—and in using computer analysis to turn the company around.

Further contributing to the attractive Kennedy image were his glamorous wife, Jacqueline, and the glittering social occasions the Kennedys hosted. Energy, exuberance, and excitement filled the air. The administration seemed like the Camelot of King Arthur's day, popularized in a Broadway musical in 1960.

Despite his charismatic appeal, Kennedy faced real problems as president. He had won office despite seemingly insuperable odds and had become the first Catholic in the White House, but his victory over Nixon was razor-thin. The electoral margin of 303 to 219 concealed the close popular tally, in which he triumphed by less than 120,000 of 68 million votes. Without an overwhelming popular mandate and without sufficient liberal support in Congress, he found it difficult to make good on his promises.

Facing reelection in 1964, Kennedy wanted not only to win the presidency for a second term but also to increase Democratic strength in Congress. In November 1963, he traveled to Texas, where he hoped to unite the state's Democratic Party for the upcoming election. Dallas, one of the stops on the trip, had a reputation as being less than cordial to the administration. On November 22, as the presidential party entered the city in an open car, the group encountered friendly crowds. Suddenly shots rang out, and Kennedy slumped forward. Desperately wounded, he died a short time later at a Dallas hospital. Lee Harvey Oswald, the assassin, was himself shot and killed a few days later in the jail where he was being held.

Vice President Lyndon B. Johnson succeeded Kennedy as president of the United States.

Though less polished, Johnson was a more effective political leader than Kennedy and brought his own special skills and vision to the presidency. Johnson was a man of energy and force. Always manipulative and often vulgar, he was, Dean Acheson once told him, "not a very likable man." But he was successful in the passion of his life—politics.

Schooled in Congress and influenced by FDR, Johnson was the most able legislative leader of the postwar years. As Senate majority leader, he became famous for his ability to get things done. Like Kennedy, Johnson was determined to wield presidential power aggressively and to use the media to shape public opinion.

Johnson ran the Senate with tight control and established a credible record for himself and his party during the Eisenhower years. He was the Democrat most responsible for keeping liberal goals alive in a conservative time, as he tried to broaden his own appeal in his quest for the presidency. Unsuccessful in 1960, he agreed to take the second spot under JFK. As vice president, he felt uncomfortable with the Kennedy crowd, useless and stifled in his new role.

Despite his ambivalence about Kennedy, Johnson sensed the profound shock that gripped the United States after the assassination and was determined to utilize Kennedy's memory to achieve his own vision of a society in which the comforts of life would be more widely shared and poverty eliminated.

The Changing Role of Government

The liberal agenda reflected the changing role of government. By 1960, government had become a major factor in ordinary people's lives. The New Deal and World War II had brought the unprecedented expansion of government's role. In the 1930s, the White House became an initiator of legislation and worked closely with Congress, while new agencies administered relief and recovery programs (see Chapter 24). The process

continued during World War II, when the number of civilians working for the federal government more than tripled between 1940 and 1945. Though the number declined somewhat at the war's end, the government still employed close to 2.5 million people throughout the 1950s. Federal expenditures, which had stood at $3.1 billion in 1929, rose to $75 billion in 1953 and passed $150 billion in the 1960s. Defense spending rose dramatically during the Cold War years, but at the same time, the government extended old-age pensions and unemployment benefits to its citizens and took increasing responsibility for other social needs.

By 1960, most Americans accepted, even embraced, government's expanded role. The major political debate revolved around the question of how far that expansion should continue and which groups should benefit from it. Demands heard in the late 1940s and the 1950s—for educational assistance, for federal health care, for more extensive welfare benefits—now became part of the political agenda in the 1960s.

The New Frontier

As president from 1961 to 1963, John Kennedy sought to maintain an expanding economic system and to extend social welfare programs. Regarding civil rights, he espoused liberal goals and social justice, although his policies were limited (see Chapter 29 for a full discussion of civil rights). On the economic front, he tried to end the lingering recession by working with the business community, while controlling price inflation at the same time.

Those two goals conflicted when, in the spring of 1962, the large steel companies sought what the administration regarded as excessive price increases. Determined to force the steel companies to back down, Kennedy pressed for a congressional investigation. When the Defense Department threatened to deny contracts to the offending companies, they gave in and reinstituted the earlier price levels. Although Kennedy

The American landing on the moon resulted from Kennedy's commitment to the space program.

won, he paid a price for his victory. Business leaders concluded that this Democratic administration, like all the others, was hostile to business. In late May, six weeks after the steel crisis, the stock market plunged in the greatest drop since the Great Crash of 1929. Kennedy received the blame.

It now seemed doubly pressing to end the recession. Adopting a Keynesian approach to economic growth, in June 1962, Kennedy announced that deficits, properly used, might help the economy. In early 1963, he called for a $13.5 billion cut in corporate taxes over the next three years. While that cut would cause a large deficit, it would also provide capital to stimulate the economy and ultimately increase tax revenues.

Opposition mounted. Conservatives refused to accept the basic premise that deficits would stimulate economic growth. Liberals, economist John Kenneth Galbraith among them, claimed that it would be better to stimulate the economy by spending for social programs rather than by cutting taxes. Why, he wondered, have "a few

more dollars to spend if the air is too dirty to breathe, the water is too polluted to drink, the commuters are losing out in the struggle to get in and out of cities, the streets are filthy, and the schools are so bad that the young, perhaps wisely, stay away?" In Congress, opponents pigeonholed the proposal in committee, and there it remained. Nor did Congress pass legislation that Kennedy proposed for federal aid for education, medical care for the elderly, housing subsidies, and urban renewal. His new minimum-wage measure passed Congress only in pared-down form.

Kennedy was more successful in securing funding for the exploration of space. As first Alan Shepard, then John Glenn, flew in space, Kennedy proposed that the United States commit itself to landing a man on the moon and returning him to earth before the end of the decade. Congress assented and increased funding of the National Aeronautics and Space Administration (NASA).

Kennedy also succeeded in establishing the Peace Corps, which sent men and women overseas to assist developing countries.

If Kennedy's successes were moderate in comparison with his failures, he had begun to set a new liberal agenda that provided a model for the administrations that followed. He had reaffirmed the importance of executive leadership in the effort to extend the boundaries of the welfare state. And he had committed himself to using modern economics to maintain fiscal stability.

The Great Society in Action

Like Kennedy, Lyndon Johnson had an expansive vision of the possibilities of reform. Using his considerable political skills, he succeeded in pushing through Congress the most extensive reform program in American history. "Is a new world coming?" the president asked. "We welcome it, and we will bend it to the hopes of man."

Johnson began to develop the support he

needed the day he took office. In his first public address, delivered to Congress and televised nationwide, he embraced Kennedy's liberal program. He began, in a measured tone, with the words, "All I have, I would have given gladly not to be standing here today." He asked members of Congress to work with him, and he underscored the theme "Let us continue" throughout his speech.

As a first step, Johnson determined to secure the measures Kennedy had been unable to extract from Congress. By the spring of 1964, the outlines of his own expansive vision were taking shape, and he had begun to use the phrase "Great Society" to describe his reform program. Successful even before the election of 1964, his landslide victory over conservative Republican challenger Barry Goldwater of Arizona validated his approach. LBJ received 61 percent of the popular vote and an electoral tally of 486 to 52 and gained Democratic congressional majorities of 68–32 in the Senate and 295–140 in the House.

Johnson provided strong executive leadership in support of his proposals. He appointed task forces that included legislators to study problems and suggest solutions, worked with them to draft bills, and maintained close contact with congressional leaders through a sophisticated liaison staff. Not since the FDR years had there been such a coordinated effort, and it resulted in the strongest legislative program since the New Deal.

Civil rights reform was an integral part of the Great Society program (see Chapter 29), along with welfare state measures. Following Kennedy's lead, Johnson pressed for a tax cut to stimulate the economy. To gain conservative support, he agreed to hold down spending; the tax bill passed. With the tax cut in hand, the president pressed for the poverty program that Kennedy had begun to plan. For the first time in American history, the government developed a program specifically directed at ending poverty. The Economic Opportunity Act of 1964 created

an Office of Economic Opportunity to provide education and training for unskilled young people trapped in the poverty cycle, VISTA (Volunteers in Service to America) to assist the poor at home, and assorted community action programs to give the poor themselves a voice in improving housing, health, and education in their own neighborhoods.

Johnson also won passage of important legislation in health, education, and aid for the poor. Medicare, a medical assistance plan, was tied to the established social security system and limited to the elderly. Medicaid met the needs of the poor below the age of 65 who could not afford private insurance. The Medicare-Medicaid program was the most important extension of federally directed social benefits since the Social Security Act of 1935. Johnson was similarly successful in his effort to provide aid for elementary and secondary schools and rent supplements for the poor.

Congress, meanwhile, reformed the restrictive immigration policy, which for decades had rested on racial and national quotas. The Immigration Act of 1965 replaced the 1924 quota system with a new yearly limit of 170,000 people from the Eastern Hemisphere and 120,000 from the Western Hemisphere. Family members of United States citizens were exempted from the quotas, as were political refugees. In the 1960s, some 350,000 immigrants entered the United States annually; in the 1970s, the number exceeded 400,000 a year. This new immigration brought different groups to America and helped revive a sense of ethnic consciousness.

Meanwhile, the federal government provided new forms of aid, such as legal assistance for the poor, financial grants to colleges and universities, and support for artists and scholars through the new National Endowments for the Arts and Humanities.

At the same time, the Great Society reflected the stirring of the environmental movement. In 1962, naturalist Rachel Carson alerted the public to the dangers of pesticide poisoning and environmental pollution in her book *Silent Spring*. Johnson recognized the need to do something about caustic fumes in the air, lethal sludge in rivers and streams, and the steady disappearance of wildlife. The National Wilderness Preservation System Act of 1964 set aside 9.1 million acres of wilderness, while Lady Bird Johnson, the president's wife, led a beautification campaign to eliminate unsightly billboards and junkyards along the nation's highways, and Congress passed other measures to limit air and water pollution.

A Sympathetic Supreme Court

The Supreme Court also supported and promoted social change in the 1960s. Under the leadership of Chief Justice Earl Warren, the Court followed the lead it had taken in 1954 in *Brown* v. *Board of Education*. Having dealt with the issue of school segregation, the Court moved against Jim Crow practices in other public establishments.

The Court also supported civil liberties. It began to protect the rights of individuals who held radical political views. Similarly, in *Gideon* v. *Wainwright* (1963), the justices decided that poor defendants in serious cases had the right to free legal counsel. In *Escobedo* v. *Illinois* (1964), they ruled that a suspect had to be given access to an attorney during questioning. In *Miranda* v. *Arizona* (1966), they argued that offenders had to be warned that statements extracted by the police could be used against them and that they could remain silent.

Other decisions similarly broke new ground. *Baker* v. *Carr* (1962) opened the way to reapportionment of state legislative bodies, according to the standard, defined a year later by Justice William O. Douglas's words, of "one person, one vote." This crucial ruling helped break the political control of lightly populated rural districts in many state assemblies and similarly made the United States House of Representatives much more responsive to urban and sub-

urban issues. Meanwhile, the Court outraged conservatives by ruling that prayer could not be required in the public schools and that obscenity laws could no longer restrict allegedly pornographic material that might have some "redeeming social value."

The Great Society Under Attack

For a few years, the Great Society worked as Johnson had hoped. The tax cut proved effective. The budget deficit dropped, unemployment fell, and inflation remained under control. Medical programs provided a measure of security for the old and the poor. Education flourished as schools were built, and salaries increased in response to the influx of federal aid.

Yet the gains proved short-lived. No real effort had been made to redistribute income. Nor was enough money allocated to the new social programs. As Michael Harrington concluded, "What was supposed to be a social war turned out to be a skirmish and, in any case, poverty won."

Although the Great Society was criticized by both the left and the right, it accomplished much in widening the web of federal activity. It might have accomplished even more had not a series of internal contradictions and external challenges intruded.

The Great Society suffered from the start from factionalism. Civil rights activists disagreed with white southern Democrats over how strongly the government should push for equal rights; the urban poor who pressed for increased political power fought with political bosses who had been the backbone of the Democratic Party and who wanted to preserve their strength.

At the same time, the Great Society suffered from the consequences of the Vietnam War (see Chapter 26 for the origins of the war and the last section of this chapter for its escalation). LBJ's decision to try to maintain the war and commitments at home without raising taxes fueled an inflation that soon jumped out of control. Congress finally got into the act and responded by slashing Great Society programs. As hard economic choices became increasingly necessary, many decided the country could no longer afford social reform on the scale Johnson had proposed.

The Decline of Liberalism

After eight years of Democratic rule, many Americans questioned the liberal agenda and the ability of the government to solve social problems. The war had polarized the country, and the Democratic Party was under attack. Republicans, capitalizing on the alienation sparked by the Vietnam War, determined to scale down the commitment to social change and pay more attention to white, middle-class Americans. While, like Dwight Eisenhower a decade and a half before, they accepted some social programs as necessary for the well-being of modern America, they were resolved to reduce spending and cut back the federal bureaucracy.

Republican Leadership

Nixon had long dreamed of holding the nation's highest office. In 1968, his chances seemed good as the Vietnam War split the Democratic Party. Americans were tired of the drawn-out, expensive war, and Johnson had announced that he would not seek another term. As Senator Eugene McCarthy promoted his candidacy, Robert F. Kennedy, the charismatic brother of the slain president, launched his own bid for the nomination. It ended in his assassination, which shook the country. Inheriting the role of leading contender was Vice President Hubert H. Humphrey.

The Democratic national convention was a disaster. Militant protesters found themselves pitted against Mayor Richard Daley, longtime boss of Chicago, who vowed to use his police force to keep order. On the climactic evening when the convention nominated Humphrey, the police ran amok, clubbing not only demonstrators but also reporters, bystanders, and anyone else in the way.

Complicating the general election was the third-party campaign of Governor George C. Wallace of Alabama, who exploited racial tensions for his own ends.

Nixon's nomination by the Republicans was a triumph in a turbulent career. Running for vice president in 1952, Nixon had almost been dropped from the ticket when charges of a slush fund surfaced. Only his maudlin televised appeal to the American public saved him then. After his loss to Kennedy in 1960 and his defeat in a race for governor of California in 1962, his political career appeared over. But after the Goldwater disaster in 1964, Nixon began to campaign for Republican candidates and reestablished a base of support.

In the election, Nixon received 43.4 percent of the popular vote, not quite one percent more than Humphrey, with Wallace capturing the rest, but it was enough to give Nixon a majority in the electoral college. The Democrats won both houses of Congress.

In and out of office, Nixon was a remote man, lacking humor and grace. As one of his speech-writers said, there was "a mean side to his nature" that he strove to conceal. Earlier in his career he was labeled "Tricky Dick." He was most comfortable alone or with a few wealthy friends. Even at work he insulated himself, preferred written contacts to personal ones, and often retreated to a small room in the executive office building to be alone.

Philosophically, Nixon disagreed with the liberal faith in federal planning and wanted to decentralize social policy. But he agreed with his liberal predecessors that the presidency ought to be the engine of the political system. Faced with a Congress dominated by Democrats and their allocations of money for programs which he opposed, he impounded, or refused to spend, funds Congress had authorized. Later commentators would see the Nixon years as the height of the "imperial presidency."

In Nixon's cabinet sat only white, male Republicans. Yet for the most part, Nixon worked around his cabinet, relying on other White House staff appointees. In domestic affairs, Arthur Burns, a former chairman of the Council of Economic Advisers, and Daniel Patrick Moynihan, a Harvard professor of government (and a Democrat), were the most important. In foreign affairs, the major figure was Henry A. Kissinger, another Harvard government professor, even more talented and ambitious, who directed the National Security Council staff and later became secretary of state.

Still another tier of White House officials insulated the president from the outside world and carried out his commands. Advertising executive H. R. Haldeman, a tireless Nixon campaigner, became chief of staff. Lawyer John Ehrlichman started as a legal counselor and rose to become chief domestic adviser. Haldeman and Ehrlichman came to be known as the "Berlin Wall" for the way they guarded the president's privacy. Another lawyer, John Mitchell, known as "El Supremo" by the staff, and as "the Big Enchilada" by Ehrlichman, assumed the post of attorney general and gave the president daily advice.

The Republican Agenda

Although Nixon had come to political maturity in Republican circles, he accepted the basic contours of the welfare state and sought to systematize its programs. Despite reservations at first, he proved willing to use economic tools to maintain stability.

The economy was faltering when Nixon assumed office. Nixon responded to inflation by tightening monetary and fiscal policy. Later he imposed wage and price controls to stop inflation and used monetary and fiscal policies to stimulate the economy. After his reelection in 1972, however, he lifted wage and price controls, and inflation began to rise again.

A number of factors besides the Vietnam War contributed to the spiral of rising prices. Large grain sales to Russia in 1972, coupled with crop disasters, caused inflation in grain prices. In 1973, events in the Middle East caused oil prices to rise dramatically. Although OPEC (the Organization of Petroleum Exporting Countries) had slowly raised oil prices in the early 1970s, the 1973 war between Israel, Egypt, and Syria led Saudi Arabia to impose an embargo on oil shipped to Israel's ally, the United States. Other OPEC nations quadrupled their prices. Dependent on imports for one-third of their energy needs, Americans faced shortages and skyrocketing prices. When the embargo ended in 1974, prices remained high.

The oil crisis affected all aspects of American economic life. Manufacturers, farmers, homeowners—all were touched by high energy prices. A loaf of bread that had cost 28 cents in the early 1970s jumped to 89 cents, and automobiles cost 72 percent more in 1978 than they had in 1973. Accustomed to filling up their cars' tanks for only a few dollars, Americans were shocked at paying 65 cents a gallon. In 1974, inflation reached 11 percent. But as higher energy prices encouraged consumers to cut back on their purchases, the nation also entered a recession. Unemployment climbed to 9 percent, the highest level since the 1930s. Inflation and high unemployment were worrisome bedfellows.

As economic growth and stability eluded him, Nixon also tried to reorganize rapidly expanding welfare programs. At the urging of domestic adviser Daniel Moynihan, Nixon endorsed an expensive but feasible work-incentive program, which would have guaranteed a minimum yearly stipend of $1,600 to a family of four, with food stamps providing about $800 more. Though promising, the program died in the Senate, but it indicated what the administration hoped to do.

As he tried to manage the economy, Nixon also worked to restore "law and order" in the United States. Political protest—and rising crime rates, increased drug use, and more permissive attitudes toward sex—brought a growing backlash on the part of working-class and many middle-class Americans. Nixon decided to use government power to silence disruption in an effort to strengthen his own political constituency. He lashed out at demonstrators—he called the students "bums" at one point. His vice president and hatchet man, Spiro Agnew, called opposition elements, and students in particular, "ideological eunuchs" who made up an "effete corps of impudent snobs."

Another part of Nixon's effort to promote stability involved attacking the media, which he regarded as biased and hostile toward him personally. Agnew spearheaded the attack on the television networks.

Most important, however, was Attorney General John Mitchell's effort to curb domestic protest by seeking enhanced powers for a campaign on crime, sometimes at the expense of individuals' constitutional rights. One part of Mitchell's plan involved reshaping the Supreme Court, which had rendered increasingly liberal decisions on the rights of defendants in the past decade and a half. In his first term, Nixon had the extraordinary opportunity to name four judges to the Court, and he nominated men who shared his views. His first choice was Warren E. Burger as chief justice to replace the liberal Earl Warren, who was retiring. Burger, a moderate, was confirmed quickly. The next two men he nominated showed such racial biases or limitations that the Senate refused to confirm them. Nixon then appointed Harry Blackmun, Lewis F. Powell, Jr., and William Rehnquist, all able and qualified, and all inclined to tilt the Court in a more conservative direction.

Over the next few years, the Court shifted to the right. It narrowed defendants' rights and upheld pornography laws if they reflected community standards. In the controversial 1973 *Roe* v. *Wade* decision, however, the Court legalized abortion, stating that women's rights included the right to control their own bodies. This deci-sion was one that feminists, a group hardly supported by the president, had ardently sought.

Watergate and Its Aftermath

Faced with a solidly Democratic Congress, the Nixon administration found its legislative initiatives blocked. In this situation, Nixon was determined to end the stalemate by winning a second term and sweeping Republican majorities into both houses of Congress in 1972. His efforts to gain a decisive Republican victory at the polls led to excesses that brought his demise.

In his reelection campaign, Nixon relied on aides who were fiercely loyal and prepared to do anything to win. He also drew on the assistance of White House counsel John Dean, former CIA agent E. Howard Hunt, and former FBI agent G. Gordon Liddy.

The Committee to Re-elect the President (CREEP), headed by John Mitchell, who resigned as attorney general, launched a massive fund-raising drive, aimed at collecting as much money as it could before the reporting of contributions became necessary under a new campaign-finance law. That money could be used for any purpose, including payments for the performance of dirty tricks aimed at disrupting the opposition's campaign. Other funds financed an intelligence branch within CREEP that had Liddy at its head and included Hunt.

Early in 1972, Liddy and his lieutenants proposed an elaborate scheme to wiretap the phones of various Democrats and to disrupt their nominating convention. Twice Mitchell refused to go along, arguing that the plan was too risky and expensive. Finally he approved a modified version of the plan to tap the phones of the Democratic National Committee at its headquarters in the Watergate apartment complex in Washington, D.C. Mitchell, formerly the top justice official in the land, had authorized breaking the law.

The wiretapping attempt took place on the evening of June 16 and ended with the arrest of those involved. They carried with them money and documents that could be traced to CREEP and incriminate the reelection campaign. Reelection remained the most pressing priority, so Nixon's aides played the matter down and used federal resources to head off the investigation. When the FBI traced the money carried by the burglars to CREEP, the president authorized the CIA to call off the FBI on the grounds that national security was at stake. Though not involved in the planning of the break-in, the president was now party to the cover-up. In the succeeding months, he authorized payment of hush money to silence Hunt and others. Top members of the administration, including Mitchell, perjured themselves in court to shield the higher officials who were involved.

Nixon won the election of 1972 in a landslide, trouncing his opponent, George McGovern, a liberal senator from South Dakota. He failed, however, to gain the congressional majorities necessary to support his programs.

When the Watergate burglars were brought to trial, they pleaded guilty and were sentenced to jail, but the case refused to die. Two zealous reporters, Bob Woodward and Carl Bernstein of the Washington *Post,* eventually linked Mitchell to Watergate. A Senate investigation then revealed that the White House had been involved in the episode.

In May 1973, the Senate committee began televised public hearings, reminiscent of the earlier McCarthy hearings of the 1950s. As millions of Americans watched, the drama built. John Dean, seeking to save himself, testified that Nixon knew about the cover-up, and other staffers revealed a host of illegal activities undertaken at the White House: Money had been paid to the burglars to silence them; State Department documents had been forged to smear a previous administration; wiretaps had been used to prevent top-level leaks. The most electrifying moment was the disclosure that the the president had in his office a secret taping system that recorded all conversations. Tapes could verify or disprove the growing rumors that Nixon had in

fact been party to the cover-up all along. But Nixon would not release the tapes.

More and more Americans now believed that the president had played a role in the cover-up. *Time* magazine ran an editorial headlined "The President Should Resign," and Congress considered impeachment. In late July 1974, the House Judiciary Committee, made up of 21 Democrats and 17 Republicans, voted to impeach the president on the grounds of obstruction of justice, abuse of power, and refusal to obey a congressional subpoena to turn over his tapes. A full House of Representatives vote still had to occur, and the Senate would have to preside over a trial before removal could take place. But for Nixon the handwriting was on the wall.

After a brief delay, on August 5 Nixon obeyed a Supreme Court ruling and released the tapes. Despite a troubling 18½-minute silence, they contained clear evidence of his complicity in the cover-up. Four days later, on August 9, 1974, Nixon became the first American president ever to resign.

Although the power of government and of the presidency had expanded greatly in the 1960s and 1970s, the Watergate episode seemed disturbing and scandalous evidence that the appropriate balance of power had disappeared. As the scandal wound down, many began to question the centralization of power in the American political system and to cite the "imperial presidency" as the cause of recent abuses. Others simply lost faith in the presidency altogether. Disillusionment over the American involvement in Vietnam and revelations concerning the Watergate affair contributed to the cumulative distrust of politics in Washington and to the steady decrease in political participation.

Gerald Ford: Caretaker President

Gerald Ford succeeded to the presidency in the aftermath of the Watergate affair. He had become vice president in 1973 when Nixon's first vice president, Spiro Agnew, resigned in disgrace for accepting bribes. An unpretentious middle-American Republican who believed in the traditional virtues, Ford faced the difficult task of trying to use his authority to restore national confidence at a time when the misuse of presidential power had caused the crisis.

Ford worked quickly to restore trust in the government. He promised to cooperate both with Congress and with American citizens. The new president then pardoned Richard Nixon barely a month after his resignation. Haldeman, Ehrlichman, Mitchell, Dean, and other Nixon administration officials faced indictment, trial, and imprisonment for their part in the Watergate affair, but their former leader, even before a hearing, was to go free of prosecution for any crimes committed while president. Ford's action raised doubts about his judgment and caused angry demonstrations.

In domestic policy, Ford followed the direction established during the Nixon years. Economic problems proved most pressing in 1974 as inflation, fueled by oil-price increases, rose to 11 percent a year, unemployment stood at 5.3 percent, and gross national product declined. Not since Franklin Roosevelt took office in the depths of the Great Depression had a new president faced economic difficulties so severe.

Ford tried to restore confidence through his WIN campaign, calling on Americans to "Whip Inflation Now" by saving more and by planting their own vegetable gardens to challenge rising prices in the stores. The plan failed and soon disappeared.

At last convinced of the need for strong governmental action, the administration introduced a tight-money policy as a means of curbing inflation. It led to the most severe recession since the Depression, with unemployment peaking at 12 percent in 1975. Congress pushed for an antirecession spending program. Recognizing political reality, Ford endorsed a multibillion-dollar tax cut coupled with higher unemployment benefits. The economy made a modest recovery, although inflation and unemployment remained high, and federal budget deficits soared.

Ford's dilemma was that his belief in limited presidential involvement set him against liberals who still argued that strong executive leadership was necessary to make the welfare state work. When he failed to take the initiative, Congress intervened, and the two branches of government became embroiled in conflict. Ford vetoed numerous bills, including those creating a consumer protection agency and expanding programs in education, housing, and health. In response, Congress overrode a higher percentage of vetoes than at any time since the presidency of Franklin Pierce more than a century before.

The Carter Interlude

In the election of 1976, the nation's bicentennial year, Ford faced Jimmy Carter, former governor of Georgia. Carter, appealing to voters distrustful of political leadership, portrayed himself as an outsider. He stressed that he was not from Washington and that, unlike many of those mired in past scandals, he was not a lawyer.

Carter won a 50 to 48 percent majority of the popular vote and a 297 to 240 tally in the electoral college. He did well with the working class, blacks, and Catholics, and he won most of the South.

Carter was a graduate of the Naval Academy, trained as a manager and an engineer. A modest man by nature, he hoped to take a restrained approach to the presidency and thereby defuse its imperial stamp.

Initially, voters saw him as a reform Democrat committed to his party's liberal goals, but he was hardly the old-line liberal some Democrats had hoped for. Though he called himself a populist, his political philosophy and priorities were never clear, and he seemed to respond to problems in a haphazard way. His status as an outsider, touted during the campaign, led him to ignore traditional political channels when he assumed power. Like Herbert Hoover, he was a technocrat in the White House at a time when liberals wanted a visionary to help them overcome hard times.

In economic affairs, Carter gave liberals some hope at first as he permitted a policy of deficit spending. When inflation rose to about 10 percent a year in 1979, he slowed down the economy and cut the deficit slightly. Contraction of the money supply led to greater unemployment and many small business failures. Budget cuts fell largely on social programs and distanced Carter from reform-minded Democrats who had supported him three years before. Yet even that effort to arrest growing deficits was not enough. When the budget released in early 1980 still showed high spending levels, the financial community reacted strongly. Bond prices fell, and interest rates rose dramatically.

Similarly, Carter disappointed liberals by his failure to construct an effective energy policy in the face of OPEC's rising oil prices. His program, bogged down in Congress for 26 months, eventually committed the nation to move from oil dependence to reliance on coal, possibly even on sun and wind, and established a new synthetic-fuel corporation. Nuclear power seemed less attractive as costs rose and accidents, such as the near disaster at Three Mile Island (see Chapter 29), occurred.

Carter further upset liberals by beginning deregulation—the removal of governmental controls in economic life. Arguing that certain restrictions established over the past century ended competition and increased consumer costs, he supported decontrol of oil and natural gas prices to spur production. He also deregulated the railroad, trucking, and airline industries.

THE CONTINUING COLD WAR AND ITS CONSEQUENCES

As executive and legislative leaders struggled to define the government's role in domestic affairs, the Cold War continued to dominate America's role abroad. Involvement in the quagmire of Vietnam was the unfortunate result. Extrication from the war demanded the same kind of redefinition of role that was occurring on the domestic front.

Kennedy's Confrontations

John Kennedy entered office determined to stand firm in the face of Russian power. During the campaign, he declared: "The enemy is the communist system itself—implacable, insatiable, unceasing in its drive for world domination."

Kennedy's most imaginative approach to the Cold War involved the promotion of "peaceful revolution" in unaligned Third World countries. By providing nonmilitary assistance programs that increased agricultural productivity and built modern transportation and communications systems, Kennedy hoped to promote stable, pro-Western governments throughout Latin America, Africa, and Asia.

While these efforts in developing nations proceeded, Kennedy saw direct challenges from the Soviet Union almost from the beginning of his presidency. The first came at the Bay of Pigs in the spring of 1961. Cuban-American relations had been strained since Fidel Castro's revolutionary army had overthrown the dictatorial Fulgencio Batista, a longtime American ally, in 1959. As Castro expropriated private property of major American corporations, which for decades had dominated the Cuban economy, the U.S. government became increasingly concerned. A radical regime in Cuba, leaning toward the Soviet Union, could provide a model for upheaval elsewhere in Latin America and threaten the venerable Monroe Doctrine.

Just before Kennedy assumed office, the United States broke diplomatic relations with Cuba. The CIA, meanwhile, was covertly training anti-Castro exiles to storm the Cuban coast at the Bay of Pigs. The American planners assumed the invasion would lead to an uprising of the Cuban people against Castro. When Kennedy learned of the plan, he approved it.

The invasion, on April 17, 1961, was an un-mitigated disaster. Cuban forces kept troops from coming ashore, and there was no popular uprising to greet the invaders. The United States stood exposed to the world, attempting to over-throw a sovereign government. It had broken agreements not to interfere in the internal affairs of hemispheric neighbors and had intervened clumsily and unsuccessfully.

Although chastened by the debacle at the Bay of Pigs, Kennedy remained determined to deal sternly with the perceived Communist threat. In June 1961, the Russians were pressing for a settlement regarding Berlin that would re-flect the reality of the city's division into eastern and western zones since World War II and pre-vent the flight of East Germans to the West. Fearful that the Soviet effort signaled designs on the Continent as a whole, Kennedy responded aggressively, seeking $3 billion more in defense appropriations, more men for the armed forces, and funds for a civil defense fallout shelter pro-gram, as if to warn of the possibility of nuclear war. After the Russians erected a wall in Berlin to seal off their section, the crisis eased.

The next year, a new crisis arose. Fidel Cas-tro, understandably fearful of the American threat to Cuban independence after the Bay of Pigs invasion, secured Russian assistance. Ac-cording to American aerial photographs in Oc-tober 1962, the Soviet Union had begun to place offensive missiles on Cuban soil. Cuba insisted that the missiles were defensive and in any event they did not change the strategic balance signifi-cantly, for the Soviets could still wreak untold damage on American targets from bases farther away, and American missiles stood on the bor-ders of the Soviet Union in Turkey. But with Russian weapons installed just 90 miles from American shores, appearance was more impor-tant than strategic balance. Kennedy was deter-mined to confront the Russians (not the Cubans) and win.

The president went on nationwide TV to tell the American people about the missiles and to demand their removal. He declared that the United States would not shrink from the risk of nuclear war and announced a naval blockade around Cuba to prevent Soviet ships from bring-ing in additional missiles. He called the move a quarantine, for a blockade was an act of war.

As the Soviet ships steamed toward the blockade and the nations stood "eyeball to eye-ball" at the brink, the American and Russian people held their breath. After several days, the tension broke, but only because Khrushchev called the Russian ships back and then sent a long letter to Kennedy pledging to remove the missiles if the United States ended the blockade and promised to stay out of Cuba altogether. The United States agreed, having already an-nounced its intention to remove its own missiles from Turkey. With that the crisis ended.

The Cuban missile crisis was the most terri-fying confrontation of the Cold War. But Kennedy emerged from the crisis as a hero who had stood firm. His reputation was enhanced, as was the image of his party in the coming con-gressional elections. One consequence of the cri-sis was the establishment of a Soviet-American hot line to avoid similar episodes in the future. Another was Russia's determination to increase its nuclear arsenal so that it would never again be exposed as inferior to the United States.

Escalation in Vietnam

Believing that the power and prestige of the United States had been damaged by the Bay of Pigs and the confrontation over the Berlin Wall, Kennedy was determined to achieve Cold War victories in other parts of the world. Thus he willingly increased American involvement in Southeast Asia. Unsympathetic to Ho Chi Minh's regime in North Vietnam, the United States had steadily increased its support to South Vietnam. By the time Eisenhower left the presi-dency in 1961, some 675 American military ad-visers were assisting the South Vietnamese. By the end of 1963, the number had risen to more than 16,000.

Despite American backing, South Vietnamese leader Ngo Dinh Diem was rapidly losing support within his own country. American officials began to realize that Diem would never reform. After receiving assurances that the United States would not object to an internal coup, South Vietnamese military leaders assassinated Diem and seized the government.

Kennedy understood the importance of popular support for the South Vietnamese government if that country were to maintain its independence. But he was reluctant to withdraw and let the Vietnamese solve their own problems. When Kennedy met with a violent death shortly after Diem's assassination, Lyndon Johnson faced a situation in flux in Vietnam.

Johnson shared many of Kennedy's assumptions about the threat of communism. Like Kennedy, Johnson believed in the domino theory, which held that if one country in a region fell, others were bound to follow. In 1965, he sent 20,000 troops to the Dominican Republic to help buttress a military junta. His flimsy claims about the threat of communism and the importance of protecting American tourists created a wedge between his administration and liberals.

That wedge would widen over the question of Vietnam. Kennedy had expanded American forces there; Johnson took the Vietnam War and made it his own. Soon after assuming office, he reached a fundamental decision that guided policy for the next four years. South Vietnam was more unstable than ever after the assassination of Diem. Guerrillas, known as Viet Cong, challenged the regime, aided by Ho Chi Minh and the North Vietnamese. "I am not going to lose Vietnam," Johnson said. "I am not going to be the President who saw Southeast Asia go the way China went."

In the election campaign of 1964, Johnson posed as a man of peace. All the while, however, he was planning to increase American involvement in the war.

In August 1964, Johnson cleverly obtained congressional authorization for the war. North Vietnamese torpedo boats, he announced, had, without provocation, attacked American destroyers in the international waters of the Gulf of Tonkin, 30 miles from North Vietnam. Only later did it become clear that the American ships had violated the territorial waters of North Vietnam by assisting South Vietnamese commando raids in offshore combat zones. With the details of the attack still unclear, Johnson used the episode to obtain from Congress the "Gulf of Tonkin Resolution," giving him authority to "take all necessary measures to repel any armed attack against the forces of the United States and to prevent further aggression."

Military escalation began in earnest in February 1965, and a few months later, the president sent American ground troops into action, marking a crucial turning point in the Americanization of the Vietnam War. Only 25,000 American soldiers were in Vietnam at the start of 1965. By the end of the year, there were 184,000, and the number swelled to 385,000 in 1966, 485,000 in 1967, 543,000 in 1968.

American forces became direct participants in the fight to prop up a dictatorial regime in faraway South Vietnam. Although a more effective government headed by Nguyen Van Thieu and Nguyen Cao Ky was finally established, the level of violence increased. Saturation bombing of North Vietnam continued. Fragmentation bombs, killing and maiming countless civilians, and napalm, which seared off human flesh, were used extensively. Similar destruction wracked South Vietnam. Yet the North Vietnamese and their revolutionary allies in South Vietnam pressed on. Like LBJ, they sought not compromise but victory.

Americans began to protest their involvement in the war. The first antiwar teach-in took place in March 1965 at the University of Michigan. Others soon followed. "Make love, not war," slogans proclaimed as more and more students became involved in political demonstrations at dozens of colleges. "Hey, hey, LBJ. How many kids did you kill today?" opponents of the war chanted. In 1967, some 300,000 people marched in New York City. In Washington, D.C., 100,000 tried to close down the Pentagon.

The Vietnam War

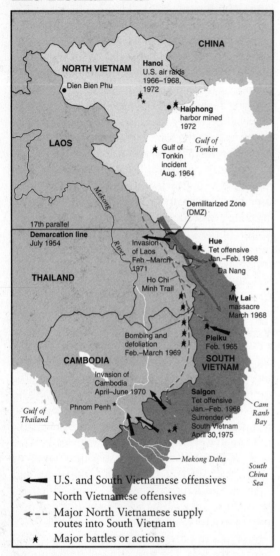

CHINA

NORTH VIETNAM

Hanoi
U.S. air raids
1966–1968,
1972

Dien Bien Phu

Haiphong
harbor mined
1972

LAOS

*Gulf of
Tonkin*

Gulf of
Tonkin
incident
Aug. 1964

Mekong River

Demilitarized Zone
(DMZ)

17th parallel
Demarcation line
July 1954

Invasion
of Laos
Feb.–March
1971

Hue
Tet offensive
Jan.–Feb. 1968

Da Nang

THAILAND

Ho Chi
Minh Trail

My Lai
massacre
March 1968

Bombing and
defoliation
Feb.–March 1969

Pleiku
Feb. 1965

CAMBODIA

SOUTH
VIETNAM

Invasion of
Cambodia
April–June 1970

Phnom Penh

*Gulf of
Thailand*

Saigon
Tet offensive
Jan.–Feb. 1968
Surrender of
South Vietnam
April 30,1975

*Cam
Ranh
Bay*

Mekong Delta

*South
China
Sea*

◀—— U.S. and South Vietnamese offensives

◀—— North Vietnamese offensives

◀- - - Major North Vietnamese supply
routes into South Vietnam

★ Major battles or actions

*This map shows the major campaigns of the Vietnam War.
The North Vietnamese Tet offensive of early 1968 turned the
tide against U.S. participation in the war and led to peace
talks. The American invasion of Cambodia in 1970 provoked
serious opposition.*

Working-class and middle-class Americans
began to sour on the war as well. Watching
nightly television reports that featured graphic
representations of the death and destruction,
they wondered about their nation's purposes and
actions.

In early 1968, the North Vietnamese
mounted the massive Tet offensive, attacking
provincial capitals and district towns in South
Vietnam. In Saigon, they struck the American
embassy, Tan Son Nhut air base, and the presidential palace. Though beaten back, they won a
psychological victory. American audiences came
to realize that the war perhaps could not be won.

When Richard Nixon assumed office in
1969, he gave top priority to extricating the
deeply divided United States from Vietnam while
still finding a way to win the war. He embarked
on the policy of Vietnamization, which entailed
removing American forces and replacing them
with Vietnamese ones. At the same time, Americans launched ferocious air attacks on North
Vietnam. "Let's blow the hell out of them,"
Nixon ordered. Between 1968 and 1972, American troop strength dropped from 543,000 to
39,000. Yet as the transition occurred, the South
Vietnamese steadily lost ground to the Viet Cong.

War protests multiplied in 1969 and 1970. In
November 1969, as a massive protest demonstration took place in Washington, D.C., stories surfaced about a massacre of civilians in Vietnam the
year before. Journalist Seymour M. Hersh had
heard rumors about an episode at My Lai and
had begun to piece together an account of what
had occurred. His efforts provided the American
people with horrifying evidence of the war's brutality.

At My Lai, a small village in South Vietnam,
American soldiers rounded up the villagers—
women, children, and old men—and gunned
them down in cold blood. Private Paul Meadlo
recalled:

> We huddled them up. We made them squat
> down. . . . I poured about four clips into the
> group. . . . The mothers was hugging their chil-

dren. . . . Well, we kept right on firing. They was waving their arms and begging. . . . I still dream about it. About the women and children in my sleep. Some days . . . some nights, I can't even sleep.

While the My Lai incident led many to wonder about American conduct of the war, incidents on several college campuses made them question the use of troops at home. Nixon's policy prompted the episodes. Still looking for victory in Vietnam, Nixon announced that American and Vietnamese troops were invading Cambodia to clear out the Communist enclaves there. The United States, he said, would not stand by as "a pitiful helpless giant" when there were actions it could take to stem the Communist advance.

Nixon's invasion of Cambodia brought renewed demonstrations on college campuses, some with tragic results. At Kent State, in Ohio, disgruntled students gathered downtown but were dispersed by local authorities. The next evening, groups of students collected around the ROTC building, began throwing firecrackers and rocks at the structure, and then set it on fire and watched it burn to the ground.

The governor of Ohio ordered the National Guard to the university. In the ensuing confrontation, the soldiers fired at the students. When the firing ceased, four students lay dead, nine wounded. Two of the dead had been demonstrators, who were more than 250 feet away when shot. The other two were innocent bystanders, almost 400 feet from the troops.

Students around the country, as well as other Americans, were outraged by the attack. Many were equally disturbed about a similar attack at Jackson State University in Mississippi. Policemen and highway patrolmen poured automatic weapon fire into a women's dormitory without warning. When the shooting stopped, two people were dead, more wounded. The dead there, however, were black students at a black institution, and white America paid less attention to that attack.

In 1971, the Vietnam War made major

headlines once more when the New York *Times* began publishing a secret Department of Defense account of American involvement in the war. The so-called Pentagon Papers, leaked by Daniel Ellsberg, a defense analyst, gave Americans a firsthand look at the fabrications and faulty assumptions that had guided the steady expansion of the struggle. Even though the study stopped with the Johnson years, the Nixon administration was furious and tried, without success, to halt publication of the series.

Vietnam remained a political football as Nixon ran for reelection in 1972. Negotiations aimed at a settlement were under way, and just days before the election, Henry Kissinger announced, "Peace is at hand." A cease-fire was finally signed in 1973, and American troops were brought home.

After Nixon left office, Gerald Ford called for more aid for the South Vietnamese, but Congress refused, leaving the crumbling government of South Vietnam to fend for itself. As the North Vietnamese consolidated their hold over the entire country, Republicans hailed Kissinger for having freed the United States from the Southeast Asian quagmire. *The New Republic* wryly observed that Kissinger brought peace to Vietnam in the same way Napoleon brought peace to Europe: by losing.

The conflict was finally over, but the costs were immense. In the longest war in its history, the United States lost almost 58,000 men, with far more wounded or maimed. Blacks and Chicanos suffered more than whites since they were disproportionately represented in combat units. The nation spent over $150 billion on the unsuccessful war. Domestic reform had slowed, then stopped. American society had been deeply divided. Only time would heal the wounds.

Détente

If the Republicans' Vietnam policy was a questionable success, accomplishments were impressive in other areas. Nixon, the Red-baiter of the past, was able to deal successfully with the Com-

When Ohio National Guardsmen fired on a crowd of antiwar demonstrators and killed four students, even prowar Americans were shocked. This photograph shows the grief and outrage of others who survived the savage shooting of innocent bystanders.

munist powers, reversing the direction of American policy since World War II. He relied heavily on Kissinger, who understood the tensions within the Communist realm, and exploited them to restore better American relations with both the Soviet Union and China.

Nixon's most dramatic step was opening formal relations with the People's Republic of China. In the two decades since Mao Zedong's victory on the Chinese mainland in 1949, the United States had never recognized the PRC, regarding Jiang Jieshi's rump government on Taiwan as the rightful government of the Chinese people. In 1971, with an eye on the forthcoming political campaign, the administration began softening its rigid stand. Nixon believed that he could open a dialogue with the Chinese Communists without political harm, for he had long been a vocal critic of communism and could hardly be accused of being "soft" on it. He knew

also that the coverage of a dramatic trip could give him a boost in the press.

Nixon went to China in February 1972. He met with Chinese leaders Mao Zedong and Zhou Enlai (Chou En-lai), talked about international problems, exchanged toasts, and saw some of the major sights. Though formal relations were not yet restored, détente between the two countries had begun.

Seeking to play one Communist state against the other, Nixon also visited Russia, where he was likewise warmly welcomed. After several cordial meetings, the president and Soviet premier Leonid Brezhnev agreed to limit missile stockpiles, work together in space, and ease long-standing restrictions on trade. Businessmen applauded the new approach, and most Americans approved of détente.

When Gerald Ford assumed office, he followed the policies begun under Nixon. Kissinger

Nixon shifted the course of Chinese-American relations by his dramatic visit to the People's Republic. He met Chinese officials for the first time, visited the Great Wall and other sites, and then reported back enthusiastically to the American people.

remained secretary of state and continued to play an influential role in foreign affairs. Ford continued the Strategic Arms Limitation Talks (SALT) that provided hope for eventual nuclear disarmament. He also accepted the Helsinki Accords, which defined European security arrangements and underscored basic human rights. He pursued friendly relations with China and elsewhere maintained the spirit of détente, even while rejecting the term.

Human Rights Diplomacy

Jimmy Carter enjoyed a number of notable successes in conducting a more modest foreign policy, though he had had little diplomatic experience when he took office. Deeply religious, he sought to make American policy adhere to the Christian standards that were part of his personal life.

Carter's major achievement involved the Middle East, where Israel and the Arab nations had fought a series of bitter wars. His personal diplomacy helped bring about a peace treaty, signed in March 1979, between Israel and Egypt. After 30 years of hostilities, the two nations were at peace.

At home, Carter fought for Senate acceptance of two treaties turning the Panama Canal over to Panama by the year 2000. Resentment had grown in Panama over the presence of a foreign power. In the agreements, accepted by the margin of a single vote, the United States retained certain rights in the event of crisis but otherwise yielded to Panamanian demands.

In Asia, Carter successfully followed Nixon's initiatives by extending diplomatic recognition to the People's Republic of China. American wheat farmers and businessmen eyed the Chinese market of nearly a billion people with enthusiasm, and American diplomats were eager to keep China and Russia at odds.

With the Soviet Union, Carter was less successful. His commitment to human rights caused him to lend verbal support to Russian dissidents, which antagonized the Soviets. One prickly issue was arms control. Negotiations for a more comprehensive strategic arms limitation treaty than the agreement of 1972 were protracted, but the SALT II agreement was reached in June 1979. The Soviet invasion of Afghanistan in December 1979, however, complicated ratification. The Russians considered internal agitation there a threat to their security and invaded the country. After a year and a half of watching the bloody involvement, Carter responded by calling the Soviet move the most serious blow to world peace since World War II. He postponed presenting SALT II to the Senate and imposed an American boycott of the 1980 Olympic Games in Moscow. Détente was effectively dead.

Carter also stumbled in his effort to defuse a major crisis with Iran. Americans had long supported the shah of Iran. Overlooking the corruption and abuse in his regime, they viewed him as a reliable supplier of oil and defender of stability in the Persian Gulf region. In January 1979, revolutionary groups drove the shah from power. In his place sat the Ayatollah Ruholla Khomeini, an Islamic priest who returned from exile in Paris to lead a new fundamentalist Islamic regime.

When Carter admitted the shah to the United States for medical treatment in October 1979, angry Iranian students seized the American embassy in Tehran and held 53 Americans hostage. The prisoners were blindfolded, bound, and beaten. Some suffered solitary confinement and endured mock executions. In the United States, their ordeal became a national cause. Unwilling to return the shah or to apologize for past American support for his now discredited regime, Carter broke diplomatic relations and froze Iranian assets, but his actions brought no results and his popularity plummeted. The Iranians finally agreed to free the hostages in early 1981, but not until the very day Carter left office did the prisoners end their 444-day ordeal. Congressional hearings in 1987 would subsequently reveal that Reagan administration officials had obtained the release of the hostages by secretly and illegally selling arms to Iran (see the discussion of the Iran-Contra affair in Chapter 30).

CONCLUSION

POLITICAL READJUSTMENT

America's political role, at home and abroad, changed significantly in the decade and a half after Dwight Eisenhower left the presidency. First Democrats, then Republicans accepted the need for large-scale government intervention to meet the social and economic problems that accompanied the modern industrial age. They endorsed a process under way since the New Deal and strengthened the nation's commitment to a capitalist welfare state. They committed the nation to a similar role in maintaining an anticommunist stability in the continuing Cold War.

Most Americans, like Ron Kovic, welcomed the nation's approach. They embraced the message of John Kennedy and the New Frontier and endorsed the programs that resulted. But over time, like Kovic, they began to question the tenets of liberalism as the economy faltered and the country became mired in Vietnam. Slowly, the optimism that had characterized the 1960s evaporated. A more conservative approach to domestic and foreign problems emerged.

Recommended Reading

For a good introduction to the basic foreign and domestic policies of the 1960s, see Jim F. Health, *Decade of Disillusionment: The Kennedy-Johnson Years* (1975). Herbert S. Parmet, *JFK: The Presidency of John F. Kennedy* (1983), is a comprehensive account of Kennedy's White House years.

Doris Kearns, *Lyndon Johnson and the American Dream* (1976), is a readable analysis of the Johnson presidency by a political scientist and former White House fellow. Robert A. Caro, *The Years of Lyndon Johnson: The Path to Power* (1983), describes LBJ's ascent. In *The Promise of Greatness* (1976), Sar A. Levitan and Robert Taggart argue that Great Society goals were realistic and that the programs enacted made a difference. Lyndon Johnson, *The Vantage Point: Perspectives of the Presidency* (1971), is LBJ's own autobiographical overview of his presidential years. An excellent appraisal of the Johnson years is Robert Dallek's *Lone Star Rising: Lyndon Johnson and His Times* (1990). For an excellent analysis of the 1960s, see Allen J. Matusow, *The Unraveling of America: A History of Liberalism in the 1960s* (1984).

On the Nixon presidency, Rowland Evans, Jr., and Robert D. Novak, *Nixon in the White House* (1972), offers the best assessment of public policy and politics in the first term. Richard Nixon, *RN: The Memoirs of Richard Nixon* (1978), is his own account of his life and achievements. Stephen Ambrose, *Nixon: The Education of a Politician, 1913–1962* (1987), is a good survey of Nixon's prepresidential period.

For the Watergate affair, J. Anthony Lukas, *Nightmare: The Underside of the Nixon Years* (1976), provides the background necessary to understand the scandal and places that crisis in the proper perspective.

On Gerald Ford, Richard Reeves, *A Ford, Not a Lincoln* (1975), is a penetrating account of how Ford functioned as president.

A great deal has been written about the Vietnam War. George C. Herring, *America's Longest War: The United States and Vietnam, 1950–1975* (1979), is the best brief account of American policy in that conflict, particularly in the 1960s and thereafter. Al Santoli, *Everything We Had: An Oral History of the Vietnam War by Thirty-three American Soldiers Who Fought It* (1981), is a collection of first-person narratives about the struggle.

Time Line

1960	John F. Kennedy elected president
1961	Bay of Pigs invasion fails Khrushchev and Kennedy meet in Vienna Berlin Wall constructed
1962	JFK confronts steel companies Cuban missile crisis
1963	Kennedy assassinated; Lyndon B. Johnson becomes president Buddhist demonstrations in Vietnam President Diem assassinated in Vietnam
1964	Gulf of Tonkin Resolution Economic Opportunity Act initiates War on Poverty Johnson reelected
1965	Vietnam conflict escalates Marines sent to Dominican Republic Teach-ins begin Department of Housing and Urban Development established Elementary and Secondary Education Act
1966	National Traffic and Motor Vehicle Safety Act Department of Transportation established
1967	Antiwar demonstrations
1968	Robert F. Kennedy assassinated Antiwar demonstrations increase Tet offensive in Vietnam Police and protesters clash at Democratic national convention Richard Nixon elected president My Lai massacre
1969	Moratorium against the Vietnam War
1969	SALT talks begin
1970	U.S. invasion of Cambodia Kent State and Jackson State shootings
1971	New York *Times* publishes Pentagon Papers
1972	Nixon visits China and the Soviet Union Watergate break-in Nixon reelected SALT I treaty on nuclear arms
1973	Vietnam cease-fire agreement Arab oil embargo Watergate hearings in Congress Spiro Agnew resigns as vice president
1974	OPEC price increases Inflation hits 11 percent Unemployment reaches 7.1 percent Nixon resigns; Gerald R. Ford becomes president Ford pardons Nixon
1975	South Vietnam falls to the Communists Unemployment reaches 12 percent
1976	Jimmy Carter elected president
1977	Carter energy program, human rights policy Panama Canal treaties
1978	Israeli-Egyptian peace accords at Camp David
1979	Russians invade Afghanistan Iranian revolution overthrows shah SALT II agreement on nuclear arms
1979–1981	Iranian hostage crisis

chapter 29
....

The Struggle for Social Reform

Ann Clarke—as she chooses to call herself now—always wanted to go to college. But girls from Italian families rarely did when she was growing up. Her mother, a Sicilian immigrant and widow, asked her brother for advice: "Should Antonina go to college?" "What's the point?" he replied. "She's just going to get married." Responsive to family needs, Ann finished the high school commercial course in three years and became a legal secretary on Wall Street. She was proud of her ability to bring money home to her family.

When World War II began, Ann wanted to join the WACS. "Better you should be a prostitute," her mother said. Ann went off to California instead, where she worked at resorts. When she left California, she vowed to return to that land of freedom and opportunity.

After the war, Ann married Gerard Clarke, a college man with an English background. Her children would grow up accepted with Anglo-Saxon names. Over the next 15 years, Ann devoted herself to her family. By the early 1960s, her three children were all in school, and she enrolled at Pasadena City College. It was not easy. Family still came first. A simple problem was finding time to study. When doing dishes or cleaning house, she memorized lists of dates, historical events, and other material for school.

Her conflict over her studies was intensified by her position as one of the first older women to go back to college. "Sometimes I felt like I wanted to hide in the woodwork," she admitted. Often her teachers were younger than she was. It took four years to complete the two-year program. But she was not yet done. She wanted a bachelor's degree. Back she went, this time to California State College at Los Angeles.

As the years passed and the credits piled up, Ann became an honors student and graduated at the top of her class. Then she returned to school for a teaching credential. Receiving her certificate at age 50, she faced the irony of social change. Once denied opportunities, Italians had been assimilated into American society. Now she was just another Anglo in Los Angeles, caught in a changing immigration wave; the city now sought Hispanics and other minorities to teach in the schools. Jobs in education were scarce, and she was close to "retirement age," so she became a substitute in Mexican-American areas for the next ten years, specializing in bilingual education.

Meanwhile, Ann was troubled by the Vietnam War and by the social adjustments that resulted. Her son grew long hair and a beard and attended protest rallies. Her daughter came home from college in boots and a leather miniskirt designed to shock. Ann accepted her children's changes as relatively superficial, confident in their fundamental values; "they were good kids." She trusted them, even as she worried.

◆──═══──◆

Ann Clarke's experience paralleled that of millions of women in the 1960s and 1970s. Caught up for years in traditional patterns of family life, these women began to recognize their need for something more. Like blacks, Hispanics, Native Americans, and other groups, American women struggled to transform the conditions of their lives and the rights they enjoyed within American society.

This chapter describes the reform impulse that accompanied the effort to define the government's responsibility for economic and social stability described in Chapter 28. Like earlier reform efforts, this modern struggle attempted to fulfill the promise of the American past and to provide liberty and equality in racial, gender, and social relations. Its voices, however, came more from those on the mudsills of society than from middle-class activists.

THE BLACK STRUGGLE FOR EQUALITY

The quest for equality by black Americans sparked all other struggles for civil rights. Stemming from an effort dating back to the Civil War and Reconstruction, the movement had gained momentum in the mid-twentieth century (see Chapter 27 for the gains of the 1950s), but change was slow.

Confrontation

A spectrum of organizations, some old, some new, spearheaded the challenge to segregation in the courts and organized nonviolent direct action that relied on grass-roots support. The National Association for the Advancement of Col-

ored People (NAACP), founded in 1910, remained committed to overturning the legal bases for segregation. Other activist organizations included the Congress of Racial Equality (CORE), established in 1942; the Southern Christian Leadership Conference (SCLC), an organization of southern black clergy, founded in 1957 by Martin Luther King, Jr., and others after their victory at Montgomery; and the Student Non-Violent Coordinating Committee (SNCC, pronounced "snick"), formed in 1960. Recruiting young Americans who had not been involved in the civil rights struggle, SNCC would become far more militant and confrontational than the older, gradualist organizations.

The importance of grass-roots efforts for reform was evident as early as 1960 when black college students sat down at a segregated Woolworth's lunch counter and deliberately violated

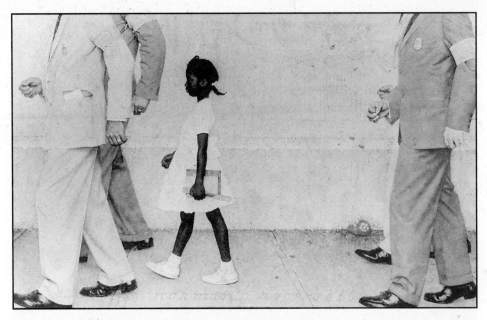

A painting by Norman Rockwell that illustrates the perception by many Americans in the North of the inequity and frustration of the initial efforts at school integration in the South. In many cases, black students were forced to run a gauntlet of white protesters under the protection of federal officials. The strict segregation that had existed in the South for so long was often highly resistant to change.

southern segregation laws by refusing to leave. The sit-ins captured media attention, and soon thousands of blacks were involved in the campaign. The following year, the sit-ins gave rise to freedom rides, aimed at testing southern transportation facilities, recently desegregated by a Supreme Court decision. Organized initially by CORE and aided by SNCC, the program sent groups of blacks and whites together on buses heading south and stopping at terminals along the way. The riders, peaceful themselves, anticipated confrontations that would publicize their cause and generate political support.

In North and South alike, consciousness of the need to combat racial discrimination grew. The civil rights movement became the most powerful moral campaign since the abolitionist crusade before the Civil War. Black and white

participants in the movement came from every direction.

Anne Moody, who grew up in a small town in Mississippi, personified the awakening of black consciousness. Through her own efforts, Moody became the first of her family to go to college. Once there, she found her own place in the civil rights movement. At Tougaloo College, near Jackson, Mississippi, she joined the NAACP and also became involved in the activities of SNCC and CORE. Slowly, she noted, "I could feel myself beginning to change. For the first time I began to think something would be done about whites killing, beating, and misusing Negroes. I knew I was going to be a part of whatever happened." She participated in sit-ins where she was thrashed and jailed for her role, but she remained deeply involved.

In violation of southern law, black college students refused to leave a lunch counter, launching a new campaign in the struggle. Here the students wait patiently for service, or forcible eviction, as a way of dramatizing their determination to end segregation.

Many whites also joined the struggle in the South. Mimi Feingold, a white student at Swarthmore College in Pennsylvania, helped picket Woolworth's in Chester, Pennsylvania, and sought to unionize Swarthmore's black dining hall workers. In 1961, after her sophomore year, she headed south to join the freedom rides sponsored by CORE.

In 1962, the civil rights movement accelerated. James Meredith, a black air force veteran and student at Jackson State College, sought to enter the all-white University of Mississippi, only to be rejected on racial grounds. Suing to gain admission, he carried his case to the Supreme Court, where Justice Hugo Black affirmed his claim. But then Governor Ross Barnett, an adamant racist, asserted that Meredith would not be admitted, whatever the Court deci-

sion. With such positions staked out, a major riot began. Tear gas covered the university grounds, and by the end of the riot, two men lay dead and hundreds hurt.

An even more violent confrontation began in April 1963, in Birmingham, Alabama, where local black leaders encouraged Martin Luther King, Jr., to launch another attack on southern segregation. Forty percent black, the city was rigidly segregated along racial and class lines. King later explained, "We believed that while a campaign in Birmingham would surely be the toughest fight of our civil rights careers, it could, if successful, break the back of segregation all over the nation."

Though the demonstrations were nonviolent, the responses were not. City officials declared that protest marches violated city regulations against parading without a license and, over a five-week period, they arrested 2,200 blacks, some of them schoolchildren. Police Commissioner Eugene "Bull" Connor used high-pressure fire hoses, electric cattle prods, and trained police dogs to force the protesters back. As the media recorded the events, Americans watching television and reading newspapers were horrified. The images of violence in Birmingham created mass sympathy for black Americans' civil rights struggle.

Kennedy's Response

John Kennedy claimed to be sickened by the pictures from Birmingham but insisted that he could do nothing, even though he had sought and won black support in 1960. The narrowness of his election victory made him reluctant to press white southerners on civil rights when he needed their votes on other issues. Kennedy failed to sponsor any civil rights legislation. Nor did he fulfill his campaign promise to end housing discrimination by presidential order, despite gifts of numerous bottles of ink. Not until November 1962, after the midterm elections, did he take a modest action—an executive order ending segregation in federally financed housing.

Events finally forced Kennedy to take bolder actions. In the James Meredith confrontation, the president, like his predecessor in the Little Rock crisis, had to send federal troops to restore control and to guarantee Meredith's right to attend. The administration also forced the desegregation of the University of Alabama and helped arrange a compromise providing for desegregation of Birmingham's municipal facilities, implementation of more equitable hiring practices, and formation of a biracial committee. And when white bombings aimed at eliminating black leaders in Birmingham caused thousands of blacks to abandon nonviolence and rampage through the streets, Kennedy readied federal troops to intervene.

The events in Birmingham helped to push Kennedy to honor the commitments he had made during the campaign. In a nationally televised address, he called the quest for equal rights "a moral issue" and asked, ". . . are we to say to the world, and much more importantly, to each other that this is a land of the free except for the Negroes. . . ?" Hours after he spoke, assassins killed Medgar Evers, a black NAACP official, in his own driveway in Jackson, Mississippi.

Kennedy sent Congress a new civil rights bill, which prohibited segregation in public places, banned discrimination wherever federal money was involved, and advanced the process of school integration. Polls showed that 63 percent of the nation supported his stand.

To lobby for passage of that measure, civil rights leaders, pressed from below by black activists, arranged a massive march on Washington in August 1963. More than 200,000 people gathered from across the country and demonstrated enthusiastically. Celebrities were present: Ralph Bunche, James Baldwin, Sammy Davis, Jr., Harry Belafonte, Jackie Robinson, Lena Horne. The folk music artists of the early 1960s were there as well. Joan Baez, Bob Dylan, and Peter, Paul, and Mary sang songs associated with the movement such as "Blowin' in the Wind" and "We Shall Overcome."

But the high point of the day was the address by Martin Luther King, Jr., the nation's preeminent spokesman for civil rights and proponent of nonviolent protest. King proclaimed his faith in the decency of his fellow citizens and in their ability to extend the promises of the Constitution and the Declaration of Independence to every American. With all the power of a southern preacher, he implored his audience to share his faith.

"I have a dream," King declared, "that one day this nation will rise up and live out the true meaning of its creed: 'We hold these truths to be self-evident, that all men are created equal.' I have a dream that one day on the red hills of Georgia, the sons of former slaves and the sons of former slave-owners will be able to sit to-gether at the table of brotherhood." It was a fervent appeal, and one to which the crowd responded. Each time King used the refrain "I have a dream," thousands of blacks and whites roared together.

Despite the power of the rhetoric, and despite large Democratic majorities, strong white southern resistance to the cause of civil rights remained, and as of November 1963, Kennedy's bill was still bottled up in committee.

Civil Rights Under Johnson

Lyndon Johnson was more successful than Kennedy in advancing civil rights. His first legislative priority on assuming office was civil rights reform, although his earlier record on the issue was mixed. A southerner from Texas, he broke with the South when he guided the Civil Rights Act of 1957 through Congress.

In 1963, Johnson revived Kennedy's civil rights proposal, which had been sidetracked in Congress. Seizing the opportunity provided by Kennedy's assassination, Johnson told Congress, "No memorial oration or eulogy could more eloquently honor President Kennedy's memory than the earliest possible passage of the civil rights bill." He pushed the bill through Congress, heading off a Senate filibuster by persuading his old colleague, minority leader Everett Dirksen, to work for cloture—a two-thirds vote to cut off debate. In June 1964, the Senate for the first time imposed cloture to advance a civil rights measure, and passage soon followed. "No army can withstand the strength of an idea whose time has come," Dirksen commented.

The Civil Rights Act of 1964 outlawed racial discrimination in all public accommodations and authorized the Justice Department to act with greater authority in school and voting matters. In addition, an equal-opportunity provision prohibited discriminatory hiring on grounds of race, gender, religion, or national origin in firms with more than 25 employees. The

legislation was one of the great achievements of the 1960s.

Johnson realized that the Civil Rights Act of 1964 was only a starting point, since widespread discrimination still existed in American society. Despite the voting rights measures of 1957 and 1960, blacks still found it difficult to vote in large areas of the South. Freedom Summer, sponsored by SNCC and other civil rights groups in Mississippi in 1964, focused attention on the problem by sending black and white students south to work for black rights. Early in the summer, two whites, Michael Schwerner and Andrew Goodman, and one black, James Chaney, were murdered. By the end of the summer, 80 workers had been beaten, 1,000 arrests had been made, and 37 churches had been bombed.

Early in 1965, Alabama police clubbed and tear-gassed demonstrators in an aborted march from Selma to the state capital at Montgomery. Events in Selma forced President Johnson first to send the National Guard to protect another march to Montgomery, led by Martin Luther King, Jr., and second to ask Congress for a voting bill that would close the loopholes of the previous two acts.

The Voting Rights Act of 1965, perhaps the most important law of the decade, singled out the South for its restrictive practices and authorized the U.S. attorney general to appoint federal examiners to register voters where local officials were obstructing the registration of blacks. In the year after passage of the act, 400,000 blacks registered to vote in the Deep South; by 1968, the number reached a million.

BLACK POWER CHALLENGES LIBERAL REFORM

Despite passage of the Civil Rights Act of 1964 and the Voting Rights Act of 1965, racial discrimination remained in both North and South. De facto segregated schools, wretched housing, and inadequate job opportunities were continuing problems. As civil rights moved north, dramatic divisions within the movement emerged.

One episode that contributed to a black sense of betrayal by white liberals occurred at the Democratic national convention of 1964 in Atlantic City. SNCC, active in the Freedom Summer project in Mississippi, had founded the Freedom Democratic Party as an alternative to the all-white delegation that was to represent the state. Before the credentials committee, black activist Fannie Lou Hamer testified that she had been beaten, jailed, and denied the right to vote. Yet the committee's final compromise, pressed by President Johnson, who worried about losing southern support in the coming election, was that the white delegation would still be seated, with two members of the protest organization offered seats at large. That response hardly satisfied those who had risked their lives and families to try to vote in Mississippi. As civil rights leader James Forman observed, "Atlantic City was a powerful lesson, not only for the black people from Mississippi, but for all of SNCC. . . . No longer was there any hope . . . that the federal government would change the situation in the Deep South." SNCC, once a religious, integrated organization, began to change into an all-black cadre that could mobilize poor blacks for militant action. "Liberation" was replacing civil rights as a goal.

Increasingly, angry blacks argued that the nation must no longer withhold the rights pledged in its founding credo. James Baldwin, a prominent black author, wrote that unless change came soon, the worst could be expected: "If we do not now dare everything, the fulfillment of that prophecy, recreated from the Bible in song by a slave, is upon us: God gave Noah the rainbow sign, No more water, the fire next time!"

Even more responsible for focusing aggressive black sentiment was Malcolm X. Born Malcolm Little and raised in ghettos from Detroit to New York, he hustled numbers and prostitutes in the big cities. Later, in prison, he became a convert to the Nation of Islam and a disciple of black leader Elijah Muhammad. He began to preach that the white man was responsible for the black man's condition and that blacks had to help themselves.

Malcolm was impatient with the moderate civil rights movement and its nonviolent sit-ins. Espousing black separatism and black nationalism for most of his public career, he argued for black control of black communities, preached an international perspective embracing African peoples in diaspora, and appealed to blacks to fight racism "by any means necessary."

Malcolm X became the most dynamic spokesman for poor blacks since Marcus Garvey in the 1920s. Though he was assassinated by a black antagonist in 1965, his perspective helped shape the ongoing struggle against racism.

One man influenced by Malcolm's message was Stokely Carmichael. Born in Trinidad, he came to the United States at the age of 11 and grew up with an interest in political affairs and black protest. He participated in pickets and demonstrations and was beaten and jailed. Frustrated with the strategy of civil disobedience, he urged field-workers to carry weapons for self-defense. It was time for blacks to cease depending on whites, he argued, and to make SNCC into a black organization. His election as head of SNCC in 1966 reflected the organization's growing radicalism.

The split in the black movement became clear in June 1966 when Carmichael's followers challenged those of Martin Luther King, Jr., during a march in Mississippi. King still adhered to nonviolence and interracial cooperation. Carmichael, just out of jail, jumped onto a flatbed truck to address the group. "This is the twenty-seventh time I have been arrested—and I ain't going to jail no more!" he shouted. "The only way we gonna stop them white men from whippin' us is to take over. We been saying freedom for six years and we ain't got nothing. What we gonna start saying now is Black

Power!" Carmichael had the audience in his hand as he repeated, "We . . . want . . . Black . . . Power!"

Meanwhile, other blacks proposed more drastic action. The Black Panthers formed a militant organization that vowed to eradicate not only racial discrimination but capitalism as well. H. Rap Brown, who followed Carmichael as head of SNCC, became known for his statement that "violence is as American as cherry pie."

Violence often accompanied the more militant calls for reform. Riots erupted in Rochester, New York City, and several New Jersey cities in 1964. In 1965, in the Watts neighborhood of Los Angeles, a massive uprising lasting five days left 34 dead, more than 1,000 injured, and hundreds of structures burned to the ground. Violence broke out again in other cities in 1966 and 1967. When Martin Luther King, Jr., fell before a white assassin's bullet in April 1968, angry blacks reacted by demonstrating once more in cities around the country.

"SOUTHERN STRATEGY" AND SHOWDOWN ON CIVIL RIGHTS

Richard Nixon, elected president in 1968, was less sympathetic to the cause of civil rights than his predecessors. In 1968, the Republicans had won only 12 percent of the black vote, leading Nixon to conclude that any effort to woo the black electorate would endanger his attempt to obtain white southern support.

From the start, the Nixon administration sought to scale back the federal commitment to civil rights. It moved, at the start of Nixon's first term, to reduce appropriations for fair-housing enforcement. Then the Department of Justice tried to block an extension of the Voting Rights Act of 1965. Although Congress approved the extension, the administration's position on racial issues was clear. When South Carolina senator Strom Thurmond and others tried to suspend federal school desegregation guidelines, the Jus-

tice Department lent support by urging a delay in meeting desegregation deadlines in 33 of Mississippi's school districts. When a unanimous Supreme Court rebuffed the effort, Nixon disagreed publicly with the decision.

Nixon also faced the growing controversy over busing as a means of desegregation, a highly charged issue in the 1970s. Transporting students from one area to another to attend school was nothing new. By 1970, over 18 million students, almost 40 percent of those in the United States, rode buses to school. Yet when busing became tangled with the question of integration, it inflamed passions.

In the South, before the Supreme Court endorsed integration, busing had long been used to maintain segregated schools. Some black students in Selma, Alabama, for example, traveled 50 miles by bus to an entirely black trade school in Montgomery, even though a similar school for whites stood nearby. Now, however, busing had become a means of breaking down racial barriers.

The issue came to a head in North Carolina, in the Charlotte-Mecklenburg school system. A desegregation plan involving voluntary transfer was in effect, but many blacks still attended largely segregated schools. A federal judge ruled that the district was not in compliance with the latest Supreme Court decisions, and in 1971, the Supreme Court ruled that district courts had broad authority to order the desegregation of school systems—by busing, if necessary.

Earlier, Nixon had opposed such busing. Now he proposed a moratorium or even a restriction on busing and went on television to denounce it. Although Congress did not accede to his request, southerners knew where the president stood.

As the busing mandate spread to the North, resistance spilled out of the South. In many of the nation's largest northern cities, schools were as rigidly segregated as in the South, largely because of residential patterns. This segregation was called *de facto* to differentiate it from the *de jure* or legal segregation that had existed in the South. Mississippi senator John C. Stennis, a bitter foe of busing, hoped to stir up the North by making it subject to the same standards as the South. His proposal, adopted in the Senate, required that the government enforce federal desegregation guidelines uniformly throughout the nation or not use them at all. Court decisions subsequently ordered many northern cities to desegregate their schools.

In Boston, the effort to integrate proved rockier than anywhere else in the North. In 1973, 85 percent of the blacks in Boston attended schools that had a black majority. More than half the black students were in schools that were 90 percent black. In June 1974, a federal judge ordered that busing begin. The first phase, involving 17,000 pupils, was to start in the fall of that year.

For many younger students, being bused to different elementary schools went smoothly. Reassigned high school students were less fortunate. A white boycott at South Boston High cut attendance from the anticipated 1,500 to less than 100 on the first day. Buses bringing in black students were stoned, and some children were injured. White working-class South Bostonians felt that they were being asked to carry the burden of middle-class liberals' racial views. Similar resentments and anger triggered racial episodes elsewhere. In many cases, white families either enrolled their children in private schools or fled the city altogether.

Nixon hoped to slow down the civil rights movement, and to a degree he did. His successor, Gerald Ford, never came out squarely against civil rights, but his lukewarm approach demonstrated a weakening of the federal commitment.

The situation was less inflamed at the college level, but the same pattern held. Blacks made significant progress until the Republican administrations in the late 1960s and 1970s slowed the movement for civil rights. Integration at the post-secondary level came easier as federal affirmative-action guidelines brought more blacks into colleges and universities. In 1950, only 83,000 black students were enrolled in institutions of higher education. A decade later, more than one million were working for college degrees. Black enrollment in colleges reached 9.3 percent of the college population in 1976, dropped back to 9.1 percent in 1980, just what it had been in 1973, then rose to 10.2 percent in 1990.

As blacks struggled on the educational and occupational fronts, some whites protested that gains came at their expense and amounted to "reverse discrimination." In 1973 and 1974, for example, Allan Bakke, a white, applied to the medical school at the University of California at Davis. Twice rejected, he sued on the grounds that a racial quota reserving 16 of 100 places for minority-group applicants was a form of reverse discrimination that violated the Civil Rights Act of 1964. In 1978, the Supreme Court ordered Bakke's admission to the medical school but also upheld the consideration of race in admissions policies, even while arguing that quotas could no longer be imposed.

Jimmy Carter, president when the *Bakke* decision was handed down, tried to adopt a more active approach than his Republican predecessors. He brought a number of qualified blacks into his administration. Some, like Andrew Young, his ambassador to the United Nations, were highly visible. But his lack of support for increased social programs for the poor hurt the majority of black citizens and strained their loyalty to the Democratic Party.

By the early 1980s, for the first time since Reconstruction, black voting rights had brought to political office a host of new leaders. Black political candidates won mayoral elections in the 1980s in major cities, including Detroit, Los Angeles, Cleveland, Chicago, and New York. In 1989, Douglas Wilder of Virginia became the first African-American ever to be elected governor of any state. Equally impressive were the presidential campaigns of the Reverend Jesse Jackson in 1984 and 1988. Though he did not win the nomination, his campaign indicated the important African-American presence in politics.

Yet cutting against the grain of those strides forward in electoral politics were backward steps in the struggle for social and economic equality.

After steady progress toward integration in the 1970s and 1980s, residential and school resegregation began to occur. Racial separation in urban neighborhoods was part of the problem. More important was the erosion of the commitment to civil rights and the economic policies (discussed in Chapter 30) pursued during the Republican administrations of the 1980s and early 1990s. Ronald Reagan opposed busing to achieve racial balance, and his attorney general worked to dismantle affirmative-action programs. Initially reluctant to support extension of the enormously successful Voting Rights Act of 1965, Reagan relented only under severe criticism from Republicans as well as Democrats. He directed the Internal Revenue Service to cease banning tax exemptions for private schools that discriminated against blacks, only to see that move overturned by the Supreme Court in 1983. He also weakened the Civil Rights Commission by appointing members who did not support its main goals.

The courts similarly weakened the commitment to equal rights. As a result of Reagan's judicial appointments, and those of his successor, George Bush, federal courts stopped pushing for school integration. The *Freeman* v. *Pitts* decision in 1992 granted a suburban Atlanta school board relief from a desegregation order on the grounds that it was not possible to counteract massive demographic shifts. This was the second time in two years that the Court granted a local board such relief.

The civil rights movement underscored the democratic values on which the nation was based, but the gap between rhetoric and reality remained. Given a wavering presidential commitment to reform in the 1970s and 1980s, only

pressures from reform groups kept the faltering civil rights movement alive.

The Women's Movement

The black struggle for equality in the 1960s and 1970s was accompanied by a women's movement that grew out of the agitation for civil rights but soon developed a life of its own. That struggle, like the struggles by Hispanics and Native Americans, employed the confrontational approach and the vocabulary of the civil rights movement to create sufficient pressure for change. Using proven strategies, it sometimes proceeded even faster than the black effort.

Attacking the Feminine Mystique

Many white women joined the civil rights movement only to find that they were second-class citizens. Men, black and white, held the policy positions and relegated women to menial chores when not actually involved in demonstrations or voter drives. Many women also felt sexually exploited by male leaders. Stokely Carmichael's comment only underscored their point. "The only position for women in SNCC," he said, "is prone."

Although the civil rights movement helped spark the women's movement, broad social changes provided the preconditions. During the 1950s and 1960s, increasing numbers of married women entered the labor force, and half of all women worked. Yet, in 1963, the average working woman earned only 63 percent of what a man could expect; in 1973, only 57 percent. Just as important, many more young women were attending college. By 1970, women earned 41 percent of all B. A.'s awarded, in comparison to only 25 percent in 1950. These educated young women held high hopes for themselves.

When women tried to rely on Title 7 of the 1964 Civil Rights bill, which prohibited discrim-

Women in the Work Force, 1920–1990

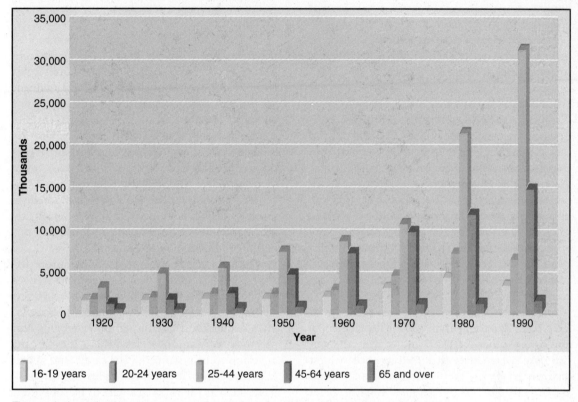

This graph shows the dramatic increase in the number of women in the work force in the 1970s, 1980s, and 1990s. Note particularly the rise in the number of working women 25–44 years old.
Source: U.S. Bureau of the Census.

ination on the basis of gender as well as race, they discovered that the Equal Employment Opportunities Commission regarded women's complaints of discrimination as far less important than those of blacks.

In 1966, a group of 28 professional women, including Betty Friedan, established the National Organization for Women (NOW) "to take action to bring American women into full participation in the mainstream of American society *now.*" By full participation the founders not only meant fair pay and equal opportunity but a new, more egalitarian form of marriage. NOW also attacked "the false image of women . . . in the media." By 1967, some 1,000 women had

joined the organization, and four years later, its membership reached 15,000.

NOW was a political pressure group. To radical feminists, who had come up through the civil rights movement, NOW's agenda failed to confront adequately the problem of gender discrimination. They tried, through the technique of consciousness raising, to help women understand the extent of their oppression and to analyze their experience as a political phenomenon.

Feminism at High Tide

A 1970 survey of first-year college students showed that men interested in such fields as business, medicine, engineering, and law out-numbered women eight to one; by 1975, the ratio had dropped to three to one. The proportion of women beginning law school quadrupled between 1969 and 1973. Women gained access to the military academies and entered senior officer ranks, but were still restricted from combat command ranks. Similarly, many employers systematically excluded women from certain positions, and women usually held "female" jobs in the clerical, sales, and service sectors. But changes were under way. For example, Title 9 of the Education Amendments of 1972 barred gender bias in federally assisted education activities and programs, made the admission of women easier, and changed the nature of intercollegiate athletics. By 1980, fully 30 percent of the participants in intercollegiate athletics were women, compared with 15 percent before Title 9 had become law.

A flurry of publications spread the ideas of the women's movement. In 1972, Gloria Steinem and several other women founded a new magazine, *Ms.*, which succeeded beyond their wildest dreams. By 1973, there were almost 200,000 subscribers. *The New Woman's Survival Catalogue* provided useful advice to women readers. *Our Bodies, Ourselves,* a handbook published by a woman's health collective, encouraged women to understand and control their bodies; it sold 850,000 copies between 1971 and 1976.

These new books and magazines differed radically from older women's magazines like *Good Housekeeping* and *Ladies' Home Journal,* which focused on women's domestic interests. *Ms.*, in dramatic contrast, dealt with abortion, employment, discrimination, and other feminist issues, such as the Equal Rights Amendment.

Women both in and out of NOW worked for congressional passage, then ratification, of the Equal Rights Amendment (ERA) to the Constitution. Passed by Congress in 1972, it stated simply, "Equality of rights under the law shall not be denied or abridged by the United States or by any State on account of sex." Thirty of the re-quired 38 states quickly ratified it, a few others followed, and for a time final approval seemed imminent.

Other feminist groups adopted more radical positions. Some insisted that legal changes were not enough. Traditional gender and family roles would have to be discarded, they maintained. Socialist feminists claimed that it was not enough to strike out at male domination, for capitalist society itself was responsible for women's plight. Only through the process of revolution could women be free.

Moderates and radicals alike attracted opposition. Nixon sided with the traditionalists when in 1971 he vetoed an appropriation for day-care centers with the argument that they undermined the sanctity of the family.

Women themselves resisted feminism for many reasons. Many felt the women's movement was contemptuous of women who stayed at home to perform traditional tasks. In politics, Phyllis Schlafly headed a nationwide campaign to block ratification of the ERA. "It won't do anything to help women," she said, "and it will take away from women the rights they already have, such as the right of a wife to be supported by her husband, the right of a woman to be exempted from military combat, and the right, if you wanted it, to go to a single-sex college." The ERA, she predicted, would lead to the establishment of coed bathrooms, the elimination of alimony, and the legalization of homosexual marriage.

Schlafly and her allies had their way. Within a few years of passage of the ERA, 35 states had agreed to the measure, but then the momentum disappeared. By mid-1982, the ERA was dead.

Even so, the 1980s brought significant gains. In politics, women won mayoral races in the nation's major cities. Far more women were elected to state legislatures and to Congress. In 1981, President Ronald Reagan appointed Sandra Day O'Connor as the first woman Supreme Court justice, and in 1984, Geraldine Ferraro, a Democratic member of Congress, became the

Women marched to mobilize support for ratification of the Equal Rights Amendment, but the campaign failed as opponents aroused public fears and blocked support in a number of key states. A decade after passage, the ERA was dead.

first woman vice-presidential candidate of a major party.

Despite substantial gains, women still faced serious problems. Access to new positions did not change their concentration in lower-paying jobs. In 1985, most women still served as secretaries, cashiers, bookkeepers, registered nurses, and waitresses. In 1985, full-time working women still earned only 63.6 cents for every dollar earned by men. Their concentration in the so-called pink-collar positions—traditional women's jobs—made further improvement difficult. Arguments that women should receive equal pay for equal work now led to demands for equal pay for different jobs of similar value. Comparable-worth cases began to work their way through the courts.

Women were likewise worried about the erosion of their right to abortion. Despite the

1973 Supreme Court decision legalizing abortion, the issue remained very much alive. The number of abortions increased dramatically in the decade after the decision. By some estimates, 10 million lawful abortions were performed in that decade, or one for every three births. In response, "pro-life" forces mobilized. They lobbied to cut off federal funds that allowed the poor to obtain the abortions that the better-off could pay for themselves; they insisted that abortions should be performed in hospitals and not in less expensive clinics; and they worked to reverse the original decision itself.

Though the Supreme Court, which included the first woman in its history, reaffirmed its judgment in 1983, the pro-life movement was not deterred. In 1989, a solidifying conservative majority on the Court ruled in *Webster* v. *Reproductive Health Services* that while women's right to abortion remained intact, state legislatures could impose limitations if they chose. With that judgment, a major legislative debate over the issue began, and numerous states began to mandate restrictions. In response, the courts heard still further cases to determine what should remain legal. In 1992, in *Planned Parenthood* v. *Casey*, the Supreme Court reaffirmed what it termed the "essence" of the right to abortion, while permitting further state restrictions.

Outside of the legal arena, pro-life groups engaged in civil disobedience campaigns and harassment tactics to discourage or prevent women from seeking abortions. They picketed and tried to block access to clinics, and many screamed epithets at women approaching the clinics. A few extremists resorted to violence, including the murder of clinic personnel and arson.

Despite counterattacks against women's right of reproductive choice, the women's movement flourished in the 1970s and 1980s. In the tenth-anniversary issue of *Ms.* magazine, in 1982, founding editor Gloria Steinem noted the differences a decade had made. "Now, we have words like 'sexual harassment' and 'battered women,'" she wrote. "Ten years ago, it was just called 'life.'"

Hispanic Rights

Hispanics, like women, profited from the example of blacks in the struggle for equality. Long denied equal access to the American dream, they became more vocal and confrontational as their numbers increased in the postwar years. Puerto Ricans in the Northeast, Cubans in Florida, and Chicanos in California and Tejanos in Texas developed a heightened sense of solidarity and group pride as they began to assert their own rights. In 1970, some 9 million people declared they were of Spanish origin; in 1980, the figure was 14.6 million; and in 1990 it was 20.8 million, as increases far outstripped the aggregate

César Chávez organized the United Farm Workers to give migrant Mexican workers representation in their struggle for better wages and working conditions.

American increase. But median household income remained less than three-fourths of that of Anglos, and inferior education and political weakness reinforced social and cultural separation.

César Chávez and the Politics of Confrontation

In the 1960s and 1970s, Mexican-Americans began to use confrontational tactics and pressure politics. In the election of 1960, Mexican-Americans supported Kennedy, helping him win Texas. In 1961, Henry B. González was elected to Congress from San Antonio. Three years later, Elizo ("Kika") de la Garza of Texas won election to the House and Joseph Montoya of New Mexico went to the Senate. Chicanos were gaining a political voice and began to anticipate the day when it could help them improve their lives.

More important than political representation, which came only slowly, was direct action. César Chávez, founder of the United Farm Workers, proved what could be done by organizing one of the most exploited and ignored groups of laboring people in the country, the migrant farm workers of the West. Chávez concentrated on migrant Mexican fieldhands, who worked long hours in the fields for meager pay. By 1965, his organization had recruited 1,700 members.

Chávez first took on the grape growers of California. Calling the grape workers out on strike, the union demanded better pay and working conditions as well as the recognition of the union. When the growers did not concede, Chávez launched a nationwide consumer boycott of their products. Although the Schenley Corporation and several wine companies came to terms, others held out. In 1966, the DiGiorgio Corporation agreed to permit a union election but then rigged the results. When California governor Edmund G. Brown, Sr., launched an investigation that resulted in another election, he became the first major political figure to support the long-powerless Chicano fieldhands. This time, the United Farm Workers won. Similar boycotts of lettuce and other products harvested by exploited labor also ended in success. In 1975, César Chávez's long struggle for farmworkers ended in the successful passage in California of a measure that required growers to bargain collectively with the elected representatives of the workers. Farmworkers had never been covered by the National Labor Relations Board. Now they had achieved the legal basis for representation that could help bring higher wages and improved working conditions. And Chávez had become a national figure.

Meanwhile, Mexican-Americans pressed for reform in other areas as well. In the West and Southwest, Mexican-American studies programs flourished. By 1969, at least 50 were available in California alone. They offered degrees, built library collections, and gave Chicanos access to their own past. The campuses also provided a network linking students together and mobilizing them for political action.

Beginning in 1968, Mexican-American students began to protest conditions in their overcrowded and run-down secondary schools. In March 1968, some 10,000 Chicano students walked out of five high schools in Los Angeles. Their actions inspired other walkouts in Colorado, Texas, and other parts of California and led to demands for Hispanic teachers, counselors, and courses and better facilities.

At the same time, new organizations emerged. A few years before, teenager David Sánchez and four Chicanos in East Los Angeles had formed a group called Young Citizens for Community Action. Gradually the organization evolved from a service club to a defensive patrol. Now known as Young Chicanos for Community Action, the group adopted a paramilitary stance. Its members became identified as the Brown Berets and formed chapters throughout the Midwest and Southwest.

Other Hispanics began to organize politically. In Texas José Angel Gutiérrez formed a cit-

izens' organization, which evolved into the La Raza Unida political party and successfully promoted Mexican-American candidates for political offices. Throughout the 1970s, it gained strength in the West and Southwest.

Hispanics made a particular point of protesting against the Vietnam War. Because the draft drew most heavily from the poorer segments of society, the Hispanic casualty rate was far higher than that of the population at large. In 1969, the Brown Berets organized the National Chicano Moratorium Committee and staged antiwar demonstrations. They argued that this was a racial war, with black and brown Americans being used against their Third World compatriots. Some of the rallies ended in confrontations with the police. News reporter Rubén Salazar, active in exposing questionable police activity, was killed in one such episode in 1970, and his death brought renewed charges of police brutality.

Aware of the growing numbers and growing demands of Hispanics, the Nixon administration sought to defuse their anger and win their support. Cuban-American refugees, strongly opposed to communism, shifted toward the Republican Party, which they assumed was more likely eventually to intervene against Fidel Castro. Meanwhile, Nixon courted Chicanos by dangling political positions, government jobs, and promises of better programs for Mexican-Americans. The effort paid off; Nixon received 31 percent of the Hispanic vote in 1972. Rather than reward his Hispanic followers, however, the president moved to cut back the poverty program, begun under Johnson, that assisted many of them.

Despite occasional gains in the 1970s and 1980s, Hispanics faced continuing problems. Spanish-speaking students often found it difficult to move through the educational system. In 1987, fully 40 percent of all Hispanic high school students did not graduate. Only 31 percent of the Hispanic seniors were enrolled in college-preparatory courses. Hispanic students frequently received little help from guidance counselors. Anel Albarran, a Mexican immigrant who arrived in East Los Angeles when she was 11, applied to UCLA when a special high school teacher encouraged her and made sure that she received help in choosing the necessary courses. By contrast, her regular counselor asked her two months before graduation whether she had considered college: "All he had wanted to do during high school was give me my classes and get me out of the room."

A growing network of Hispanic educators and programs worked to ease the way for future students. "Ten years ago, there was no national Chicano academic community," declared Arturo Madrid, president of the National Chicano Council on Higher Education, in 1982. "Now we have a professional presence in higher education." A colleague estimated that there were 5,000 Chicano faculty members in 1980, compared with 2,000 a decade before, and the numbers continued to grow.

Hispanics slowly extended their political gains as well. In San Antonio, Rudy Ortiz was appointed mayor pro tem in 1978, and Henry Cisneros was elected mayor in 1982. At the same time, Colorado state legislator Federico Peña was elected mayor of Denver. In New Mexico, Governor Toney Anaya called himself the nation's highest elected Hispanic and worked to create a national "Hispanic force." Among Hispanic administrators appointed at the national level of government, Lauro Cavazos, named U.S. secretary of education in 1988, Henry G. Cisneros, appointed secretary of housing and urban development in 1993, and Federico Peña, secretary of transportation, also appointed in 1993, are the most prominent.

NATIVE AMERICAN PROTEST

Like Hispanics, Native Americans continued to suffer second-class status as the 1960s began. But, partly inspired by the confrontational tactics of other groups, they became more aggressive in their efforts to claim their rights and to improve living and working conditions. The years saw not only a renewed aggressiveness but also phenomenal population growth—from 550,000 in 1960 to 1,959,000 in 1990.

Tribal Voices

During the Eisenhower years, the federal government's policy of termination was in effect. That effort to force Indians to assimilate into mainstream American life by relocating them in cities had worked poorly. Thousands of Native Americans traded reservation poverty for urban poverty.

In the 1960s, Indians began to assert themselves. At a conference in Chicago in 1961, several hundred Indians asked the Kennedy administration for the right to help make decisions about programs and budgets for the tribes. A group of college-educated Indians at the conference formed a National Indian Youth Council aimed at reestablishing Indian national pride. Over the next several decades, the council helped change the attitudes of tribal leaders, who were frequently called Uncle Tomahawks and "apples" (red outside, white inside) for their willingness to sacrifice their people's needs to white demands.

Indians successfully promoted their own values and designs. Native American fashions became more common, museums and galleries displayed Indian art, and Indian jewelry found a new market. The larger culture came to appreciate important work by Native Americans. In 1968, N. Scott Momaday won the Pulitzer Prize for his book *House Made of Dawn*. Vine Deloria's *Custer Died for Your Sins* (1969) had even wider readership. Meanwhile popular films like *Little Big Man* (1970) and, several decades later, the Academy Award–winning *Dances with Wolves* (1990) provided sympathetic portrayals of Indian history. Indian studies programs developed in colleges and universities. Organizations like the American Indian Historical Society in San Francisco protested traditional textbook treatment of Indians and demanded more honest portrayals.

Indian Activism

At the same time, Native Americans became more confrontational. Like other groups, they worked through the courts when they could but also challenged authority in more aggressive ways when necessary.

Led by a new generation of leaders, Native Americans tried to protect what was left of their tribal lands. "Everything is tied to our homeland," D'Arcy McNickle, a Flathead anthropologist, told other Indians in 1961.

The new activism was apparent on the Seneca Nation's Allegany reservation in New York State. Although the Senecas' right to the land was established by a treaty made in 1794, the federal government had planned since 1928 to build the Kinzua Dam there as part of a flood control project. In 1956, after hearings to which the Indians were not invited and about which they were not informed, Congress appropriated funds for the project. The dam was eventually built, and although the government belatedly passed a $15 million reparations bill, money did not compensate for the loss of 10,000 acres of land that contained sacred sites, hunting and fishing grounds, and homes.

The Seneca did somewhat better in the 1970s. When New York State tried to condemn a section of Seneca land for a superhighway running through part of the Allegany reservation, the Indians again went to court. In 1981, the state finally agreed to an exchange: state land elsewhere in addition to a cash settlement in return for an easement through the reservation. That decision encouraged tribal efforts in Montana, Wyoming, Utah, New Mexico, and Arizona to resist similar incursions on reservation lands.

Native American leaders then brought a wave of lawsuits charging violations of treaty rights. In 1967, in the first of many decisions upholding the Indian side, the U.S. Court of Claims ruled that the government had forced the Seminole in Florida to cede their land in 1823 for an unreasonably low price. The court directed the government to pay additional funds 144 years later. In other litigation, Indian tribes fought to protect their water rights and fishing rights.

The activist American Indian Movement (AIM) was founded in 1968 by George Mitchell and Dennis Banks, Chippewa living in Minneapolis. AIM sought to help neglected Indians in the city. It managed to get Office of Economic Opportunity funds channeled to Indian-controlled organizations. It also established patrols to protect drunken Indians from harassment by the police. As its successes became known, chapters formed in other cities.

The new militancy was dramatized in November 1969, when a landing party of 78 Indians seized Alcatraz Island in San Francisco Bay to protest symbolically the inability of the Bureau of Indian Affairs to "deal practically" with questions of Indian welfare. They converted the island, with its defunct federal prison, into a cultural and educational center, but in 1971 federal officials removed them.

Other, similar protests followed. In 1972, militants launched the Broken Treaties Caravan to Washington. For six days, insurgents occupied the Bureau of Indian Affairs. In 1973, AIM took over the South Dakota village of Wounded Knee, where in 1890 the U.S. 7th Calvary had massacred the Sioux. The reservation surrounding the town was mired in poverty. Half the families were on welfare, alcoholism was widespread, and 81 percent of the student population had dropped out of school. The occupation was meant to dramatize these conditions and to draw attention to the 371 treaties AIM leaders claimed the government had broken. Federal officials responded by encircling the area and, when AIM tried to bring in supplies, killed one Indian and wounded another. The confrontation

The American Indian Movement's armed occupation of Wounded Knee, South Dakota, site of a late-nineteenth-century massacre of the Sioux, resulted in bloodshed that dramatized the government's unfair treatment of Native Americans.

ended with a government agreement to reexamine the treaty rights of the Indians, although little of substance was subsequently done.

At the same time, Native Americans devoted increasing attention to providing education and developing business and legal skills. Because roughly half of the Indian population continued to live on reservations, many tribal communities founded their own colleges. In 1971, the Oglala Sioux established Oglala Lakota College on the Pine Ridge Reservation in South Dakota. Nearby Sinte Gleska College on the Rosebud Reservation was the first to offer accredited four-year and graduate programs. The number of Indians in college rose from a few hundred in the early 1960s to tens of thousands by 1980. Between 1980 and 1990, Native American enrollment in higher education institutions increased by over 23 percent.

Some tribal communities developed business skills, although traditional Indian attitudes hardly fostered the capitalist perspective. "Now we're beginning to realize that, if we want to be self-sufficient, we're going to have to become entrepreneurs ourselves," observed Iola Hayden, the Comanche executive director of Oklahomans for Indian Opportunity. The Choctaw in Mississippi were perhaps the most successful, cutting their 1979 unemployment rate of 50 percent in half by the mid-1980s.

Indians themselves studied law and acted as legal advocates for their own people in the court cases they were filing. They have worked for tribes directly and have successfully argued for tribal jurisdiction in conflicts between whites and Indians on the reservations.

Government Response

Indian protest brought results. The outcry against termination in the 1960s led the Kennedy and Johnson administrations to steer a middle course, neither endorsing nor disavowing the policy. Instead they tried to bolster reservation economies and raise standards of living by persuading private industries to locate on reservations and by promoting the leasing of reservation lands to energy and development corporations. In the 1970s, however, the Navajo, Northern Cheyenne, Crow, and other tribes sought to cancel or renegotiate such leases, fearing "termination by corporation."

The Native American cry for self-determination brought Indian involvement in the poverty program of the Great Society in the mid-1960s. Two agencies, the Area Redevelopment Administration (later the Economic Development Administration) and the Office of Economic Opportunity, responded to Indian pressure by making their resources available. Indians could devise programs and budgets and administer programs themselves. They were similarly involved with Great Society housing, health, and education initiatives. Finally, in 1975, Congress passed the Indian Self-Determination and Education Assistance acts. Though both laws were limited, they nonetheless reflected the government's decision to respond to Indian pressure.

SOCIAL AND CULTURAL PROTEST

As blacks, Hispanics, and Native Americans agitated, middle-class American society experienced an upheaval unlike any it had known before. Young people in particular rejected the stable patterns of affluent life their parents had forged in the decade before. Some embraced radical political activity; many more adopted new standards of sexual behavior, music, and dress. In time their actions spawned still other protests as Americans tried to make the political and social world more responsive than before.

The Student Movement

Among young Americans who came of age in the 1960s, many, especially from the large mid-

dle class, moved on to some form of higher education. By the end of the 1960s, college enrollment was more than four times what it had been in the 1940s.

In college, some students joined the struggle for civil rights. Hopeful at first, they gradually became discouraged by the limitations of the government's commitment, despite the rhetoric of Kennedy and the New Frontier.

Out of that disillusionment arose the radical spirit of the New Left. Civil rights activists were among those who in 1960 organized Students for a Democratic Society (SDS). In 1962, SDS issued a manifesto, the Port Huron Statement, written largely by Tom Hayden of the University of Michigan, and calling for the creation of a "New Left." "We are people of this generation, bred in at least modest comfort, housed now in universities, looking uncomfortably at the world we inherit," it began. It went on to deplore the vast social and economic distances separating people from each other and to condemn the isolation and estrangement of modern life. The document called for a better system, "a democracy of individual participation."

The first blow of the growing student rebellion came at the University of California in Berkeley. There civil rights activists became involved in a confrontation that quickly became known as the free speech movement. It began in September 1964 when the university refused to allow students to distribute protest material outside the main campus gate. The students, many of whom had worked in the movement in the South, argued that their tables were off campus and therefore not subject to university restrictions on political activity. When police arrested one of the leaders, students surrounded the police car and kept it from moving all night.

The university regents brought charges against the student leaders, including Mario Savio. When the regents refused to drop the charges, the students occupied the administration building. Then, as in the South, police stormed in and arrested the students in the building. A student strike, with faculty aid, mobilized wider support for the right to free speech.

The free speech movement at Berkeley was basically a plea for traditional liberal reform. Students sought only the reaffirmation of a long-standing right, the right to express themselves as they chose, and they aimed their attacks at the university, not at society as a whole. The attack broadened as the ferment at Berkeley spread to other campuses in the spring of 1965. Students sought a greater voice in university affairs, argued for curricular reform, and demanded admission of more minority students. Their success in gaining their demands changed the shape of American higher education.

The mounting protest against the escalation of the Vietnam War fueled and refocused the youth movement. Confrontation became the new tactic of radical students, and protest became a way of life. Between January 1 and June 15, 1968, hundreds of thousands of students staged 221 major demonstrations at more than 100 educational institutions.

The next year, in October 1969, the Weathermen, a militant fringe group of SDS, sought to show that the revolution had arrived with a frontal attack on Chicago, scene of the violent Democratic convention of 1968. The Weathermen, taking their name from a line in a Bob Dylan song—"You don't need a weatherman to know which way the wind blows"—came from all over the country. Dressed in hard hats, jackboots, work gloves, and other padding, they rampaged through the streets with clubs and pipes, chains and rocks. They ran into the police, as they had expected and hoped, and continued the attack. Some were arrested, others were shot, and the rest withdrew to regroup. For the next two days, they plotted strategy, engaged in minor skirmishes, and prepared for the final thrust. It came on the fourth day, once again pitting aggressive Weathermen against hostile police.

Why had the Weathermen launched their at-tack? "The status quo meant to us war, poverty, inequality, ignorance, famine and disease in most of the world," Bo Burlingham, a participant from Ohio, reflected. "To accept it was to condone and help perpetuate it. We felt like miners trapped in a terrible poisonous shaft with no light to guide us out. We resolved to destroy the tunnel even if we risked destroying ourselves in the process." The rationale of the Chicago "national action" may have been clear to the participants, but it convinced few other Americans. There and elsewhere, citizens were infuriated at what they saw.

The New Left was, briefly, a powerful force. Although activists never composed a majority, radicals attracted students and other sympathizers to their cause until the movement fragmented. But while it was healthy, the movement focused opposition to the Vietnam War and challenged inequities in American society.

The Counterculture

In the 1960s, many Americans, particularly young people, lost faith in the sanctity of the American system. "There was," observed Joseph Heller, the irreverent author of *Catch-22* (1961), "a general feeling that the platitudes of Americanism were horseshit." The protests exposed the emptiness of some of the old patterns, and many Americans, some politically active, some not, found new ways to assert their individuality and independence, often drawing on the example of the beats of the 1950s.

Surface appearances were most visible and, to older Americans, most troubling. The "hippies" of the 1960s carried themselves in different ways. Men let their hair grow and sprouted beards; men and women both donned jeans, muslin shirts, and other simple garments. Stressing spontaneity above all else, some rejected traditional marital customs and gravitated to communal living groups. Their example, shocking to some, soon found its way into the culture at large.

Sexual norms underwent a revolution as more people separated sex from its traditional ties to family life. A generation of young women came of age with access to "the pill"—an oral contraceptive that was easy to use and freed sexual experimentation from the threat of pregnancy. Americans of all social classes became more open to exploring, and enjoying, their sexuality. Scholarly findings supported natural inclinations. In 1966, William H. Masters and Virginia E. Johnson published *Human Sexual Response,* based on intensive laboratory observation of couples engaged in sexual activities. Describing the kinds of response that women, as well as men, could experience, they destroyed the myth of the sexually passive woman.

Nora Ephron, author and editor, summed up the sexual changes in the 1960s as she reflected on her own experiences. Initially she had "a hangover from the whole Fifties virgin thing," she recalled. "The first man I went to bed with, I was in love with and wanted to marry. The second one I was in love with, but I didn't have to marry him. With the third one, I thought I *might* fall in love."

The arts reflected both the sexual revolution and the mood of dissent. Federal courts ruled that books like D.H. Lawrence's *Lady Chatterley's Lover,* earlier considered obscene, could not be banned. Many suppressed works, long available in Europe, now began to appear. Nudity became more common on stage and screen. "Op" artists painted sharply defined geometric figures in clear, vibrant colors, starkly different from the flowing, chaotic work of the abstract expressionists. "Pop" artists like Andy Warhol, Roy Lichtenstein, and Jasper Johns made ironic comments on American materialism and taste with the representations of everyday objects like soup cans, comic strips, or pictures of Marilyn Monroe. Their paintings broke with formal artistic conventions. Some used spray guns and fluorescent paints to gain effect. Others even tried to make their pictures look like giant newspaper photographs.

Hallucinogenic drugs also became a part of the counterculture. One prophet of the "drug scene" was Timothy Leary, who aggressively asserted that drugs were necessary to free the mind. Drug use was no longer confined to an urban subculture of musicians, artists, and the streetwise. Soldiers brought experience with drugs back from Vietnam. Young professionals began experimenting with cocaine as a stimulant. Taking a "tab" of LSD became part of the coming-of-age ritual for many middle-class college students. Marijuana became phenomenally popular in the 1960s.

Music became intimately connected with these cultural changes. The rock and roll of the 1950s and the gentle strains of folk music gave way to a new kind of rock that swept the country—and the world. The Beatles were the major influence, as they took first England, then the United States, by storm. Other groups enjoyed enormous commercial success while attacking materialism and other bourgeois values. Mick Jagger of the Rolling Stones was an aggressive, sometimes violent showman on stage whose androgynous style showed his contempt for conventional sexual norms. Janis Joplin, a hard-driving, hard-drinking woman with roots in the blues, reflected the intensity of the new rock world until her early death by drugs.

The music was most important on a mid-August weekend in 1969 when some 400,000 people gathered in a large pasture in upstate New York for the Woodstock rock festival. There, despite intense heat and torrential rain, despite inadequate supplies of water and food, the festival unfolded in a spirit of affection. Some people shed their clothes and paraded in the nude, some had sex in public, and most shared whatever they had, particularly the marijuana that seemed endlessly available, while major rock groups provided ear-splitting, around-the-clock entertainment for the assembled throng. The weekend was not without problems, but supporters hailed the festival as an example of the new and better world to come.

Other Americans, however, viewed the antics of the young with distaste. Their fears seemed vindicated at another festival four months later in Altamont, California. Some 300,000 people gathered at a stock car raceway to attend a rock concert climaxing an American tour by the immensely popular Rolling Stones. Woodstock had been well planned; the Altamont affair was not. In the absence of adequate security, the Stones hired a band of Hell's Angels to maintain control. Those tough motorcyclists, fond of terrorizing the open road, prepared to keep order in their own way.

The spirit at Altamont was different from the start. "It was a gray day, and the California hills were bare, cold and dead," wrote Greil Marcus, a music critic. An undercurrent of violence simmered, Marcus observed, as "all day long people . . . speculated on who would be killed, on when the killing would take place. There were few doubts that the Angels would do the job."

With the Stones on stage, the fears were realized. As star Mick Jagger looked on, the Hell's Angels beat a young black man to death. A musician who tried to intervene was knocked senseless. Other beatings occurred, accidents claimed several more lives, and drug-overdosed revelers found no adequate medical support.

Altamont revealed the underside of the counterculture. That underside could also be seen in the Haight-Ashbury section of San Francisco, where runaway "flower children" mingled with "burned-out" drug users and radical activists. Joan Didion, a perceptive essayist, wrote of American society in 1967: "Adolescents drifted from city to torn city, sloughing off both the past and the future as snakes shed their skins, children who were never taught and would never now learn the games that had held the society together." For all the spontaneity and exuberance, the counterculture's underside could not be ignored.

Gay and Lesbian Rights

Closely tied to the revolution in sexual norms that affected sexual relations, marriage, and family life was a fast-growing and increasingly militant gay liberation movement. There had always been people who accepted the "gay" life style, but American society as a whole was unsympathetic, and many homosexuals kept their preferences to themselves. The climate of the 1970s encouraged gays to "come out of the closet." A nightlong riot in 1969, in response to a police raid on a homosexual bar in Greenwich Village in New York, helped spark a new consciousness and a movement for gay rights. Throughout the 1970s and 1980s, homosexuals made important gains in ending the most blatant forms of discrimination against them. In 1973, the American Psychiatric Association ruled that homosexuality should no longer be classified as a mental illness, and that decision was overwhelmingly supported in a vote by the membership the next year. In 1975, the U.S. Civil Service Commission lifted its ban on employment of homosexuals.

In this new climate of acceptance, many gays who had hidden or suppressed their sexuality revealed their darkest secret. Women also became more open about their sexual preferences and demanded that they not be penalized for choosing other females as partners. A lesbian movement developed, sometimes involving women active in the more radical wing of the women's movement. But many Americans remained unsympathetic to anyone who challenged traditional sexual norms. Churches and some religious groups often lashed out against gays.

The discovery of AIDS (acquired immune deficiency syndrome) in 1981 changed the situation for homosexuals dramatically. The deadly new disease struck intravenous drug users and homosexuals with numerous partners more than any other groups. The growing number of deaths—200,000 by 1992—suggested that the disease would reach epidemic proportions. Advertisements in the national media advised the use of condoms, and the U.S. surgeon general mailed a brochure, "Understanding AIDS," to every household in the United States. As knowledge—and misunderstanding—of the disease increased, many Americans felt that hostility toward homosexuality was justified. Still, homosexuals fought on for a greater governmental effort to find a cure for AIDS. The disease itself began to be better understood when heterosexual sports heroes Earvin "Magic" Johnson and Arthur Ashe were diagnosed as having the virus that causes the disease, and that understanding promised to help the gay cause.

THE ENVIRONMENTAL AND CONSUMER MOVEMENTS

Although many of the social movements that arose in the 1960s were defined by race, gender, and sexual preference, one further movement united many of these reformers across such boundaries. Emerging in the early 1960s, a powerful movement of Americans concerned with the environment began to revive issues raised in the Progressive era and to go far beyond them.

The modern environmental movement gathered momentum after the publication in 1962 of Rachel Carson's *Silent Spring*. She took aim at chemical pesticides, particularly DDT, which had increased crop yields but had disastrous side effects. As Americans learned of the pollutants surrounding them, they became increasingly worried about pesticides, motor vehicle exhaust, and industrial wastes that filled the air. Lyndon Johnson pressed for and won basic legislation to halt the destruction of the country's natural resources.

Public concern mounted further in 1969 when it was discovered that thermal pollution from nuclear power plants was killing fish in both eastern and western rivers. DDT was threatening the very existence of the bald eagle, the nation's emblem. A massive oil spill off the coast of southern California in 1969 turned white beaches black and wiped out much of the marine life in the immediate area. An even worse

oil spill occurred in Alaska in 1989 when the *Exxon Valdez* ran aground.

Concern about the deterioration of the environment increased as people learned more about substances they had once taken for granted. In 1978, the public became alarmed about the lethal effects of toxic chemicals dumped in the Love Canal neighborhood of Niagara Falls, New York. A few years later, attention focused on dioxin, one of the poisons permeating from the Love Canal, which now surfaced in other areas in more concentrated form. Dioxin, a by-product of the manufacture of herbicides, plastics, and wood preservatives, remained active after being released in the environment. Thousands of times more potent than cyanide, it was one of the most deadly substances ever made.

Equally frightening was the potential environmental damage from a nuclear accident. That possibility became more real as a result of a mishap at one of the reactors at Three Mile Island in 1979. There a faulty pressure relief valve led to a loss of coolant. Initially, plant operators refused to believe indicators showing a serious malfunction. Part of the nuclear core became uncovered, part began to disintegrate, and the surrounding steam and water became highly radioactive. An explosion releasing radioactivity into the atmosphere appeared possible, and thousands of residents of the area were evacuated. The worst never occurred and the danger period passed, but the plant remained shut down, filled with radioactive debris, a monument to a form of energy that was once hailed as the wave of the future but now appeared more destructive than any ever known.

The threat to the environment seemed even more horrifying with another nuclear accident seven years later, in 1986. This time the disaster played itself out at a plant in Chernobyl in the Soviet Union. The first reports indicated as many as a thousand people had died following a huge explosion. Though the number of deaths was later scaled down, the airborne contamination affected people thousands of miles away. Europeans plowed up freshly planted crops, warned against drinking milk, and banned imports of livestock and vegetables from the east. Some scientists predicted that one million people would develop cancer, and five years after the accident, estimates of the cancer death toll ranged from 17,000 to 475,000.

As a result of the Three Mile Island and Chernobyl accidents, public opposition to nuclear power has grown worldwide and has made it difficult to build new plants or find geologically safe and politically acceptable places in which to permanently store radioactive waste products produced by nuclear energy plants. In the United States, environmental activists mobilized opinion sufficiently that no new plants were authorized after 1978.

Environmentalists also worried about America's excessive use of water, which had risen from 40 billion gallons a day in 1900 to 393 billion gallons by 1975, though the population had only tripled. American homes, farms, and industries used three times as much water per capita as the world's average, and far more than other industrialized societies. Pointing to the destruction of the nation's rivers and streams and the severe drawing down of the water table in many areas, environmentalists launched an angry wave of protest.

Environmental agitation produced legislative results in the 1960s and 1970s. Lyndon Johnson, whose vision of the Great Society included an "environment that is pleasing to the senses and healthy to live in," won basic legislation to halt the depletion of the country's natural resources (see Chapter 28). During Nixon's presidency, Congress passed the Clean Air Act, the Water Quality Improvement Act, and the Resource Recovery Act and mandated a new Environmental Protection Agency (EPA) to spearhead the effort to control abuses.

Despite growing national sympathy for environmental goals, the movement faced fierce political resistance in the 1980s. Ronald Reagan systematically restrained the EPA in his avowed

effort to promote economic growth. James Watt, his secretary of the interior, opened forest lands, wilderness areas, and coastal waters to economic development and frankly conceded that he saw little reason to save the natural environment for future generations. George Bush initially seemed more sympathetic to environmental causes, but as the economy faltered, he proved less willing to support environmental action that he claimed might slow economic growth. In 1992, he accommodated business by easing clean air restrictions. That same year, he attended a United Nations–sponsored Earth Summit at Rio de Janeiro in Brazil with 100 other heads of state. There he stood alone in his refusal to sign a biological diversity treaty framed to conserve millions of plant and animal species.

Environmentalists were encouraged by the 1992 election of Bill Clinton as president and environmental advocate Albert Gore, Jr., as vice president. The economic recession, however, which had contributed to the defeat of Republican candidate George Bush, also hindered efforts to protect forests, waterways, and wildlife from commercial and industrial exploitation.

Related to the environmental movement was a consumer movement. Americans throughout the twentieth century, particularly in the 1950s, their appetites whetted by advertising, had bought fashionable clothes, house furnishings, and electrical and electronic gadgets. Congress had established a variety of regulatory efforts to protect citizens from unscrupulous sellers. In the 1970s, a strong consumer movement grew, led by Ralph Nader. He had become interested in the issue of automobile safety while studying law at Harvard and had pursued that interest as a consultant to the Department of Labor. His book *Unsafe at Any Speed: The Designed-in Dangers of the American Automobile* (1965) argued that many cars were coffins on wheels. Head-on collisions, even at low speeds, could easily kill, for cosmetic bumpers could not withstand modest shocks. He termed the Corvair "one of the nastiest-handling cars ever built" because of its tendency to roll over in certain situations. His efforts paved the way for the National Traffic and Motor Vehicle Safety Act of 1966.

Nader's efforts attracted scores of volunteers, called "Nader's Raiders." They turned out critiques and reports and, more important, inspired consumer activists at all levels of government—city, state, and national. Consumer protection offices began to monitor a flood of complaints as ordinary citizens became more vocal in defending their rights.

CONCLUSION

EXTENDING THE AMERICAN DREAM

The 1960s, 1970s, and 1980s were turbulent decades. Yet this third major reform era of the twentieth century accomplished a good deal for the groups fighting to expand the meaning of equality. Blacks now enjoyed greater access to the rights and privileges enjoyed by mainstream American society, despite the backlash the movement brought. Women like Ann Clarke, introduced at the start of the chapter, returned to school in ever-increasing numbers and found jobs and sometimes independence after years of being told that their place was at home. Native Americans and Hispanics mobilized too and could see the stirrings of change. Environmentalists created a new awareness of the global dangers the nation and the world faced.

But the course of change was ragged. The reform effort reached its high-water mark during Lyndon Johnson's Great Society and in the years immediately following, then faltered with the rise of conservatism and disillusionment with liberalism (see Chapter 28). Some movements were circumscribed by the changing political climate; others simply ran out of steam. Still, the various efforts left a legacy of ferment on which others could draw.

Recommended Reading

A number of books provide good introductions to the civil rights movement. Harvard Sitkoff, *The Struggle for Black Equality, 1954–1980* (1981), is a short but stimulating overview of the civil rights struggle. Taylor Branch, *Parting the Waters: America in the King Years, 1954–1963* (1988), is a much fuller account of the reform effort. David J. Garrow, *Bearing the Cross: Martin Luther King, Jr., and the Southern Christian Leadership Conference* (1986), tells King's story. William H. Chafe, *Civilities and Civil Rights: Greensboro, North Carolina, and the Black Struggle for Freedom* (1980), is an outstanding study of black southern protest. Anne Moody, *Coming of Age in Mississippi* (1968), is the eloquent autobiography of a young southern black woman who became involved in the civil rights movement.

On women's issues, Sara Evans, *Personal Politics: The Roots of Women's Liberation in the Civil Rights Movement and the New Left* (1979), contains some thoughtful observations about the women's movement in the 1960s and 1970s. Alice Kessler-Harris, *Out to Work: A History of Wage-Earning Women in the United States* (1982), is a good exploration of shifting patterns of employment.

Rodolfo Acuña, *Occupied America: A History of Chicanos,* 3d ed. (1988), is the best account of Chicanos in America, particularly in the modern period. For a thoughtful essay on César Chávez, see Cletus Daniel, "César Chávez and the Unionization of California Farm Workers," in Melvyn Dubofsky and Warren Van Tine, eds., *Labor Leaders in America* (1987).

Alvin M. Josephy, Jr., *Now That the Buffalo's Gone* (1982), is a useful starting point for further examination of recent Indian struggles. Frederick E. Hoxie, ed., *Indians in American History* (1988), contains good material on the modern period.

For the turbulence of the 1960s, see Todd Gitlin, *The Sixties: Years of Hope, Days of Rage* (1987). On the counterculture, William L. O'Neill, *Coming Apart: An Informal History of America in the 1960s* (1971), provides an engaging narrative.

Time Line

1960	Birth control pill becomes available Sit-ins begin Students for a Democratic Society (SDS) founded
1961	Freedom rides Michael Harrington publishes *The Other America;* Joseph Heller, *Catch-22*
1962	James Meredith crisis at the University of Mississippi SDS's Port Huron Statement Publication of Rachel Carson's *Silent Spring*
1963	Birmingham demonstration Civil rights March on Washington Publication of Betty Friedan's *The Feminine Mystique*
1964	Freedom Democratic Party attempts to gain recognition at the Democratic national convention Civil Rights Act Race riots in New York City Free speech movement, Berkeley
1965	Martin Luther King, Jr., leads march from Selma to Montgomery Voting Rights Act United Farm Workers' grape strike Assassination of Malcolm X Watts riot in Los Angeles Ralph Nader, *Unsafe at Any Speed*
1966	Stokely Carmichael becomes head of SNCC and calls for "black power" Black Panthers founded NOW founded Masters and Johnson, *Human Sexual Response*
1967	Urban riots in 22 cities
1968	Kerner Commission report on urban disorders Martin Luther King, Jr., assassinated Student demonstrations at Columbia and elsewhere Chicano student walkouts American Indian Movement (AIM) founded

Time Line (continued)

1969	Woodstock and Altamont rock festivals Weathermen's "Days of Rage" in Chicago Native Americans seize Alcatraz La Raza Unida founded	**1979**	Three Mile Island nuclear power plant accident
		1981	Sandra Day O'Connor appointed to the Supreme Court
1971–1975	School busing controversies in North and South	**1982**	Ratification of ERA fails
		1984	Geraldine Ferraro runs for vice president
1972	*Ms.* magazine founded Congress passes Equal Rights Amendment Broken Treaties caravan to Washington	**1986**	Chernobyl nuclear accident in Soviet Union
		1988	Lauro Cavazos appointed secretary of education
1973	*Roe* v. *Wade* AIM occupies Wounded Knee	**1989**	*Webster* v. *Reproductive Health Services*
1975	Farmworkers' grape boycott Indian Self-Determination and Education Assistance acts	**1991**	Clarence Thomas appointed to the Supreme Court
		1992	Bill Clinton elected president *Planned Parenthood* v. *Casey*
1978	*Bakke* v. *Regents of the University of California*		

chapter 30

....

The Triumph of Conservatism

David Patterson flourished in the early 1980s. An executive in the computer industry, he had risen through the ranks and now directed an entire division of his company. He enjoyed a good salary, a handsome home in the New York suburbs, and two luxury cars. Then, in the middle of the decade, his affluent world collapsed. One Friday afternoon, his boss told him he no longer had a job; his entire division and its fifty employees were all being eliminated. Fortified with but four weeks of severance pay, Patterson was on his own. At first he was optimistic about landing another position, but after nine months of futile efforts, he realized that his family was in serious financial trouble. Although his wife, Julia, had gone back to work, their combined income from her salary and his unemployment check was but a fraction of what it had been. Unable to make mortgage payments, they were forced to sell their house and move into a modest apartment in a nearby town. The emotional costs were even greater. Embarrassed at his plight, Patterson stopped calling friends, and they ceased trying to reach him in turn. He was puzzled and hurt. Computers were hailed as the magical machines of the future, so it was hard to understand the shakedown that affected firms throughout the industry. Why was he having such trouble finding another job? Was there something wrong with him?

Thousands of other executives faced the corporate downsizing that accompanied a continuing economic recession. The cover story in the March 23, 1992, issue of *Business Week* focused on the increasingly pervasive phenomenon of "Downward Mobility" and noted the growing difficulties professionals had finding new jobs as they moved through the 1980s. At the start of the decade, 90 percent of the white-collar employees who lost their positions were quickly hired in similar jobs with the same or better pay. By the late 1980s, the figure was down to 50 percent; by 1992 it had dropped to 25 percent and was still falling. Clearly David Patterson was not alone.

Patterson and thousands of others who lost their jobs were the middle-class victims of a conservative era that was marked by greed and extravagance, especially on the part of those best off. As the nation pulled out of a recession at the start of the 1980s and the economy improved, more affluent Americans prospered most from the initiatives of the Reagan administration. The nation's economic policies widened the gaps between rich and poor; poverty became more widespread; and members of minority groups encountered continued difficulty finding jobs. An even worse recession in the early 1990s brought hardship to the middle and upper-middle classes as well. The national debt skyrocketed, and finally, in reaction to questions about the stability of the economy, the stock market tumbled. At the same time, cataclysmic events shook Communist governments in the USSR and eastern Europe, ending nearly a half century of Cold War.

This chapter describes the enormous changes of the 1980s and early 1990s. It covers the public policies of the new Republican majority, which promised prosperity but brought economic catastrophe to many. It outlines the economic and demographic transformations after 1980 and examines the new role of the United States in a vastly different world order.

THE CONSERVATIVE TRANSFORMATION

In the 1980s, the Republican Party established itself as the dominant force in national politics. The transformation that had begun in the Nixon era was now largely complete. The liberal agenda that had governed national affairs ever since the New Deal of Franklin Roosevelt had lost its broad appeal and gave way to a new Republican coalition determined to scale back the social welfare state and prevent what its proponents perceived as the erosion of the nation's moral values. Firmly in control of the presidency, occasionally in control of the Senate, the Republican Party directed the new national agenda.

The New Politics

Political conservatism became respectable in the 1980s, having gained countless new adherents after the turbulence of the 1960s and the backlash of the Vietnam War. New political techniques that capitalized on national disaffection with liberal solutions to continuing social problems made the conservative movement an almost unstoppable national force.

Conservatives seized on Thomas Jefferson's maxim "That government is best which governs least." They argued that the United States in the 1980s had moved into an era of limits, and that the liberal solution of throwing money at social problems no longer worked. They therefore sought to limit the size of government, to reduce the tax burden, and to cut back the regulations they claimed hampered business competition. In the process, they would restore the focus on individual initiative and private enterprise that many Americans felt had always been the essence of the nation's strength.

The conservative philosophy had tremendous appeal. It offered hope for the revival of the basic social and religious values that many citizens worried had been eaten away by rising divorce rates, legalized abortion, openly expressed homosexuality, and mass media preoccupation with sex and violence. It attracted middle-class Americans who were concerned that they were being forgotten in the rush to assist minorities and the poor. Some members of the new conservative coalition embraced the economic doctrines of the University of Chicago's Milton Friedman, who advocated the free play of market forces and less government regulation of the economy. Other supporters embraced the social and political dictums of North Carolina Senator Jesse Helms, a tireless foe of any forms of expression in art, dance, or literature he deemed pornographic. Many others flocked to the Republican fold because they objected to affirmative action, job quotas, and school busing to promote racially integrated schools. The conservative coalition also drew in religious fundamentalists, ranging from devout Catholics to orthodox Jews to evangelical Protestants, who were worried about sexual permissiveness, the erosion of family life, and the alarming increase in crime. Between 1970 and 1980, the murder rate rose 31 percent, the robbery rate 42 percent, the burglary rate 56 percent, the assault rate 79 percent, and the rape rate 99 percent. The use of drugs spread. Members of the religious right wanted to return religion to a central place in American life and to revive traditional values.

Many of these activists belonged to the so-called Moral Majority. The Reverend Jerry Falwell of Virginia and other television evangelists underscored the concerns of religious fundamentalism and developed large followings in the 1980s. Listeners donated millions of dollars to support the call for the redemption from sin, and Moral Majority money began to fund politicians who held conservative positions on issues like school prayer, abortion, and the Equal Rights Amendment.

Conservatives also understood the importance of television advertising. They became adept at using brief "sound bites," often no more than 15 or 30 seconds, to communicate their positions. They also refined the art of negative advertising in a political campaign. Mudslinging has always been a part of the American political tradition, of course, but now carefully crafted television ads increasingly concentrated not on issues, but on subtly or even openly attacking an opponent's character.

Public relations techniques assumed great importance. Polls, sometimes taken daily, mandated which part of a candidate's image needed polishing most or where one's opponent was most vulnerable. "Spin doctors" moved into action after a candidate made a public statement to put the best possible gloss on what had been said. Small wonder that Americans became increasingly cynical about politics and stayed away from the voting booth in record numbers as the twentieth century drew to a close.

Conservatives likewise led the way in raising enormous sums of money for their campaigns. Richard Viguerie, a young Houston activist in the New Right, organized a huge direct-mail campaign, unlike anything seen before in American politics, to raise money for right-wing causes. His fund raising played a major part in the rise of conservatism as a powerful political force.

But conservatives also understood the need to provide an intellectual grounding for their positions. Numerous conservative scholars worked in think tanks and other research organizations, such as the Hoover Institution at Stanford University or the American Enterprise Institute in Washington, D.C., churning out books, articles, and reports that helped elect Ronald Reagan and other conservative politicians.

Conservative Leadership

Ronald Reagan was more responsible than any other Republican politician for the success of the conservative cause. An actor turned politician, he was elected governor of California in 1966. He failed in his first bid for the Republican nomination in 1976 but consolidated his strength over the next four years. By 1980, he had the firm support of the growing right, which applauded his effort to reduce the size of the federal government but bolster military might. Charging the Carter administration with a "litany of broken promises," he provided a soothing contrast to the incumbent. He showed real wit as he quibbled with Carter over economic definitions. "I'm talking in human terms and he is hiding behind a dictionary," Reagan said. "If he wants a definition, I'll give him one. A recession is when your neighbor loses his job. A depression is when you lose yours. A recovery is when Jimmy Carter loses his."

Reagan scored a landslide victory in 1980, gaining a popular vote of 51 to 41 percent and a 489 to 49 electoral college advantage. He also led the Republican Party to control of the Senate for the first time since 1955.

In 1984, Reagan ran for reelection against Walter Mondale, Jimmy Carter's vice president. For his running mate, Mondale selected Geraldine Ferraro, a congresswoman from New York, the first woman ever to receive a major party's nomination on the presidential ticket. Reagan benefited from the economic upturn and received 59 percent of the popular vote. He swamped Mondale in the electoral college 525 to 13, losing only Minnesota, Mondale's home

state, and the District of Columbia. While the Republicans continued to control the Senate, Democrats netted two additional Senate seats and managed to maintain superiority in the House of Representatives.

Reagan had a pleasing manner and a special skill as a media communicator. A gifted storyteller, best at relating one-liners, he seemed like a trusted uncle who spoke in soothing terms. For much of his term, people talked about a "Teflon" presidency—criticisms failed to stick, and disagreements over his policies never diminished his personal popularity.

But Reagan had a number of liabilities that surfaced over time. He was the oldest president the nation had ever had, inaugurated two weeks before his seventieth birthday. Dwight Eisenhower, who left office at just that age, once remarked, "No one should ever sit in this office

Ronald Reagan drew on his experience in the movies to project an appealing, if old-fashioned, image. Though he was the nation's oldest president, he gave the appearance of vitality. Here he is pictured with his wife, Nancy, who was one of his most influential advisers.

over 70 years old, and that I know." But Reagan remained a full eight years beyond that. His attention often drifted, and he occasionally fell asleep during meetings. At times he appeared uninterested in governing. In press conferences, he was frequently unsure about what was being asked. He delegated a great deal of authority, even if that left him unclear about policy decisions. Critics often accused him of being dependent on his wife, Nancy, for advice.

Worst of all, he suffered from charges of "sleaze" in his administration. In a period of several months during his last year in office, one former aide was convicted of lying under oath to conceal episodes of influence peddling. Another was convicted of illegally lobbying former government colleagues. Attorney General Edwin Meese escaped indictment but nonetheless came under severe criticism for improprieties that culminated in his resignation.

In 1988, Republican George Bush sought the presidency after eight years as Reagan's vice president. A businessman who had prospered in the Texas oil industry, then served in Congress, as top envoy to China, and as head of the CIA, Bush gradually overcame his public image of a political weakling by becoming something of a pit bull during a mudslinging campaign against his Democratic opponent, Michael Dukakis. As governor of Massachusetts, Dukakis had turned his state around after years in the economic doldrums. The son of Greek immigrants, he defeated challenges from several Democrats, including the charismatic black candidate Jesse Jackson, in the primaries but proved unable to counter the charges of the Republican campaign.

One particularly devastating Republican advertisement featured black convict Willie Horton, who had benefited from a Massachusetts weekend release program only to commit another brutal crime while away from prison. The advertisement never mentioned race directly, but it encouraged racial polarization and proved a blow from which Dukakis never recovered.

On election day, many Americans, believing that neither candidate had addressed the issues, stayed home to protest the victory of style over substance. Bush claimed a 54 to 46 percent popular vote victory and carried 40 states, giving him a 426–112 electoral vote win. But he did not have the kind of mandate Reagan had enjoyed eight years earlier, and Democrats controlled both houses of Congress.

Bush quickly put his own imprint on the presidency. An unpretentious man, he liked to keep busy, tearing through golf courses and appointments from morning till night. He maintained a wide network of friends and political contacts through handwritten notes, telephone calls, and personal visits. More than a year and a half into his term, he was still on his political honeymoon, with a personal approval rating of 67 percent. Support grew even stronger as he presided over the Persian Gulf War in 1991. Then, as the economy faltered and the results of the war seemed suspect, approval levels began to drop.

Republican Policies at Home

Republicans in the 1980s aimed to reverse the stagnation of the Carter years and to provide new opportunities for business to prosper. To that end Reagan proposed and implemented an economic recovery program that rested on the theory of supply-side economics. This held that the reduction of taxes would encourage business expansion, which in turn would lead to a larger supply of goods to help stimulate the system as a whole. "Reaganomics" promised a revitalized economy.

One early initiative involved pushing through regressive tax reductions. Although all taxpayers enjoyed some savings, the rich benefited far more than middle- and lower-income Americans. As a result of tax cuts and enormous defense expenditures, the budget deficit grew larger and ultimately ran out of control. The gross federal debt—the total national indebtedness—spiraled upward from $914 billion in

1980 to $3.1 trillion in 1990. When Reagan assumed office, the per capita national debt was $4,035; nine years later, in 1990, it was about $12,400.

Faced with the need to raise more money and to rectify the increasingly skewed tax code, in 1986 Congress passed and Reagan signed the most sweeping tax reform measure since the income tax began. It lowered rates, simplified brackets, and closed loopholes to expand the tax base. Though it ended up neither increasing nor decreasing the government's tax take, the measure was an important step toward treating low-income Americans more equitably, but most of the benefits still went to the rich.

At the same time, Reagan embarked on a major program of deregulation. In a campaign more comprehensive than Jimmy Carter's, he weakened agencies of the 1970s like the Environmental Protection Agency, the Consumer Product Safety Commission, and the Occupational Safety and Health Administration. He argued that regulations impeded business growth, and he appointed people like James Watt, his first secretary of the interior, who systematically relaxed enforcement of environmental rules.

Meanwhile Reagan challenged the consensus fostered by the New Deal that the national government should monitor the economy and assist the least fortunate citizens. He had won fame and fortune on his own, and others could do the same. He declared that it was time to eliminate "waste, fraud, and abuse" by cutting programs the country did not need.

Reagan needed to make cuts in social programs, both because of the sizable tax cuts and because of the enormous military expenditures. While calling for economy in government, his administration sought an unprecedented military budget of $1.5 trillion. By 1985, with a budget of $300 billion, the United States was spending half a million dollars a minute on defense and four times as much as at the height of the Vietnam War. The trade-off was clear: reduced spending for social programs.

The huge cuts in some social programs reversed the approach followed under Franklin Roosevelt and endorsed by liberals in the past 50 years. Public service jobs, mandated under the Comprehensive Employment and Training Act, were eliminated, and other aid to the cities, where the poor congregated, was severely reduced. Unemployment compensation was cut back. Medicare patients were required to pay more for treatment. Welfare benefits were lowered, and food stamp allocations were reduced. Many grants for college students gave way to loans. The Legal Services Corporation, which offered legal advice to those too poor to afford lawyers' fees, was gutted. According to the Congressional Budget Office, spending on human resources fell by $101 billion between 1980 and 1982. The process continued even after Reagan left office. Between 1981 and 1992, American spending, after adjustment for inflation, fell 82 percent for subsidized housing, 63 percent for job training and employment services, and 40 percent for community services. Middle-class Americans, aided by the tax cuts, were not hurt by the slashes in social programs. But for millions of America's poorest citizens, the administration's approach caused real suffering.

As a political conservative distrustful of central government, Reagan also yearned to place more power in the hands of state and local governments and to reduce the ways in which the federal government touched people's lives. His "New Federalism" attempted to shift responsibilities from the federal to the state level. By eliminating federal funding and making grants to the states instead, which could spend the money as they saw fit, he hoped to restore a measure of local initiative. But the program never produced the desired results. As critics charged, with some justification, the proposal was merely a backhanded way of moving programs from one place to another, while eliminating federal funding. When a prolonged recession began in 1990, this policy contributed to the near-bankruptcy of a number of states and municipalities, which constitutionally could not run deficits as could the federal government but had been handed responsibility for programs formerly funded in Washington.

Meanwhile, Reagan took a decidedly conservative approach to social issues as well. He willingly accepted the support of the New Right, speaking out for public prayer in the schools and openly demonstrating his opposition to abortion by making sure that the first nongovernmental group to receive an audience at the White House was an antichoice March for Life contingent.

George Bush followed directly in his predecessor's footsteps. Having forsworn his objection to "voodoo economics" as soon as he received the vice-presidential nomination, he faithfully adhered to Reagan's general economic policy while serving in that office and continued it once he became president in January 1989. In the 1988 campaign, he admonished voters to "read my lips" and promised "no new taxes." Though he backed down from that pledge in a bipartisan effort to bring the budget deficit under control, he later renounced his own agreement to modest tax increases when he went back on the campaign trail in 1992.

Like Reagan, Bush systematically prevented spending for social programs. Tireless in his criticism of the Democratic majorities in the Senate and the House of Representatives, he vetoed measure after measure intended to assist those caught in the ravages of a recession that sent unemployment rates up to 8 percent and left one of every four urban children living in poverty.

As president, Bush also firmly opposed abortion, although at the start of the 1980s he had been sympathetic to a woman's right to decide for herself; and his Supreme Court appointments, like Reagan's, guaranteed that the effort to roll back or overturn *Roe* v. *Wade* would continue (see Chapter 29).

The Republican philosophy under Reagan and Bush dramatically reversed America's domestic agenda. Liberalism in the 1960s had reached a high-water mark in a time of steady growth, when hard choices about where to spend money had been less necessary. As limits began to loom, decisions about social programs became more difficult, and millions of Americans came to believe that most of the Great Society programs had failed to conquer poverty and in fact had created lifelong welfare dependency. Conservatism offered a more attractive answer, particularly to those Americans in the middle and upper classes who were already comfortable.

But the conservative transformation also led to a number of serious problems that loomed in the early 1990s. As Bush assumed the presidency, his administration uncovered a scandal at the Department of Housing and Urban Development (HUD) in which highly placed Republicans received large fees from developers in return for helping wealthy clients win HUD contracts. At the same time, the new president had to deal with a crisis in the long-mismanaged savings and loan industry. The Republican deregulation policy had allowed owners of savings and loan institutions to operate without the previous restrictions, and many of them, paying themselves lavish salaries, made unwise high-risk investments that proved profitable for a while but then produced tremendous losses. To protect depositors whose assets had been lost by these questionable lending practices, Congress approved a $166 billion rescue plan (the sum soon rose above $250 billion) that committed taxpayers to bailing out the industry.

Far worse was the role Republican policy played in widening the gaps between rich and poor. Tax breaks for the wealthy, deregulation initiatives, high interest rates for investors, permissiveness toward mergers, and an enormous growth in the salaries of business executives all contributed to the shift. So did more flexible antitrust enforcement and a general sympathy for speculative finance.

The results were clear. "The 1980s," analyst Kevin Phillips observed, "were the triumph of upper America—an ostentatious celebration of wealth, the political ascendancy of the rich and a glorification of capitalism, free markets and finance." The concentration of capital increased, and the sums involved took what Phillips termed a "megaleap" forward. Now there was an extraordinary amassing of wealth at the top levels. According to one study, the share of national wealth of the richest 1 percent of the nation rose from about 18 percent in 1976 to 36 percent in 1989. The net worth of the *Forbes* magazine 400 richest Americans nearly tripled between 1981 and 1989.

Meanwhile, less fortunate Americans, ranging from foreclosed farmers to laid-off industrial workers, were hurting more than they had since the Great Depression of the 1930s. A disproportionate number of women and members of minority groups lost ground in the 1980s, despite the gains of some of the luckiest in all of those groups. While white family income and net worth rose, they fell among African-American and Hispanic families.

The growing disparity in wealth, resurgent racism, and the neglect of the urban poor became horrifyingly visible in the terrible rioting that swept through Los Angeles in the spring of 1992. The year before, Americans had watched a videotaped savage beating of black motorist Rodney King by white police officers, only the most dramatic of a long string of incidents involving police brutality. When a California jury, which contained no blacks, acquitted the policemen, people of all colors throughout the country were astonished and convinced that equal justice under the law had been proved unobtainable by people of color. In Los Angeles thousands reacted with uncontrolled fury. More than a decade of urban neglect lay in the background of the riot and so did tension between African-Americans and Korean shopkeepers and between black and Hispanic urban dwellers, who competed for jobs and living space in the city. As widespread arson and looting swept through many neighborhoods, the police proved unable to control the mayhem. Much of it was led by gang members but involved as well hundreds of

ordinary citizens who acted irresponsibly. The riot left 51 dead, 2,000 injured, and $1 billion in damage to the city. It was the worst riot in decades, more deadly even than the Watts riot that had wracked Los Angeles 27 years before. Political candidates from both parties scurried around trying to define new policies to address neglected urban problems.

THE POSTINDUSTRIAL ECONOMY

The Los Angeles riots took place against the backdrop of an economy that frequently appeared more volatile than before. For decades, the Democrats had been trying to use Keynesian tools to stabilize the economy. Now, under Republican supply-side economics, the business cycle began to follow a pattern of moving from recession to boom and back to recession again. As Reagan assumed office, the economy was reeling under the impact of declining productivity, galloping inflation, oil shortages, and high unemployment. Reagan's policies brought improvement in the early 1980s, particularly for middle- and upper-income people, but not for those of lesser means. The recession that gripped the country from 1990 to 1992 only underscored the need for renewed productivity, full employment, and more equitable distribution of wealth.

The Shift to a Service Economy

In the 1980s, the economy underwent significant restructuring. In a trend under way for more than half a century, the United States shifted from an industrial base, where most workers actually produced things, to a service base, where most provided expertise or service to others in the work force. By the mid-1980s, three-fourths of the 113 million employees in the country worked in the service sector—as fast-food workers, clerks, computer programmers, doctors, lawyers, bankers, teachers, and public employees.

In part, that shift derived from the decline of America's industrial sector. The United States, which had been the world's industrial leader since the late nineteenth century, began to lose that position by the 1970s. After 1973, productivity slowed in virtually all American industries; in the early 1980s, during the worst recession since the 1930s, economic growth virtually ceased. Real GNP fell by 0.2 percent in 1980, rose by 1.9 percent in 1981, and fell by 2.5 percent in 1982. In the midst of the Reagan boom it rose 3.0 percent in 1987 and 3.9 percent in 1988, then stagnated from 1990 to 1992 during another recession.

The causes of this decline in productivity were complex. The most important factor was a widespread and systematic failure on the part of the United States to invest sufficiently in its basic productive capacity. During the Reagan years, investment in capital goods—plants and equipment—gave way to speculation, mergers, and spending abroad. Domestic investment declined 5.7 percent in 1990 and 9.5 percent in 1991. Other factors affecting industrial productivity were rising oil prices (see Chapter 28), government policies aimed at curbing inflation by keeping machines idle, and environmental regulations intended to make industries change their methods of operation. Finally, the war in Vietnam diverted federal funds from support for research and development at the same time that Japan, Germany, and the Soviet Union were increasing their R & D expenditures.

While American industry became less productive, other industrial nations moved forward. German and Japanese industries aggressively modernized and reached new heights of efficiency. As a result, the United States began to lose its former share of the world market for industrial goods. Formerly a leader in iron and steel production, the United States found itself importing a fifth of its iron and steel from abroad. By 1980, Japanese car manufacturers

had also captured nearly a quarter of the American automobile market, and they continued to hold that substantial share in 1990. The American auto industry, which had been a mainstay of economic growth for much of the twentieth century, suffered plant shutdowns and massive layoffs. In 1991, Ford lost a staggering $2.3 billion, in its worst year ever. Although the American auto industry subsequently improved its position, foreign competition remained a major challenge.

Workers in Transition

In the 1980s and early 1990s, American labor struggled to hold on to the gains realized by the post–World War II generation of blue-collar workers. The shift to a service economy created problems for many Americans workers. Millions of men and women who had lost positions as a result of plant closings and permanent economic contractions now found themselves in low-paying jobs with few opportunities for advancement. Entry-level posts were seldom located in the central cities, where most of the poor lived, and minority residents often lacked the skills to acquire such jobs. A basic mismatch between jobs and people in the cities became more pronounced.

Meanwhile, the trade union movement faltered as the economy moved from an industrial to a service base. As the United States emerged from World War II, unions claimed 35 percent of all nonagricultural workers as members, but this percentage began to decrease steadily in the mid-1950s and continued to decline in subsequent years. Union membership rose in the public sector, but even this increase did not reverse the general decline in membership. By 1989, only 16.4 percent of nonagricultural workers belonged to unions.

The shift from blue-collar to white-collar work contributed to the contraction. The increase in the numbers of women and young people in the work force (groups that have historically been difficult to organize) was another factor, as was the more forceful opposition to unions by managers applying the provisions of the Taft-Hartley Act of 1947, which restricted the weapons labor leaders could use.

Union vulnerability could be seen early in Ronald Reagan's first term, when the Professional Air Traffic Controllers Organization went out on strike. Charging that the strike violated the law and undermined the "protective services which are government's reason for being," the president fired the strikers, decertified the union, and ordered the training of new air controllers at a cost of $1.3 billion. The message was clear: Government employees could not challenge the public interest. But antiunion sentiments reverberated throughout the nongovernment sector as well.

Everywhere unions encountered hard times. To respond to increasing foreign competition and stagnant domestic productivity rates, unions found themselves forced to make concessions. In 1984, the United Auto Workers (UAW) ended a strike at General Motors after winning a pledge that GM would guarantee up to 70 percent of the production workers' lifetime jobs in return for a smaller wage increase than they sought and also in return for a modification of the cost-of-living allowance that had been a part of UAW contracts since 1948. In the same way, in 1988, General Electric workers in the Midwest accepted a pay cut to save their jobs. That decision was part of a calculated effort to persuade GE to revitalize domestic plants rather than turn more actively to foreign labor. In 1992 the UAW called off a strike against Caterpillar Tractor and went back to the bargaining table after realizing that its contract demands would never be met.

Agricultural workers likewise had to adjust as the larger work force was reconstituted. Continuing a trend that began in the early twentieth century, the number of farmers declined steadily. When Franklin Roosevelt took office in 1933, some 6.7 million farms covered the American landscape. Fifty years later, farm families numbered only 2.4 million. In 1980, farm residents made up 2.7 percent of the total population; by 1989, that figure had fallen to 1.9 percent. As family farms disappeared, farming income became more concentrated in the hands of the largest operators. By 1983, the largest 1 percent of the nation's farmers produced 30 percent of all farm products and had average annual incomes of $572,000.

The extraordinary productivity of American farmers derived in part from the use of chemical fertilizers, irrigation, pesticides, and scientific agricultural management. Equally important were the government's price support programs, initiated during the New Deal to shield struggling farmers from unstable prices and continued thereafter.

Yet that very productivity had environmental costs and led to unexpected setbacks in the 1980s. In the 1970s, as food shortages developed in many countries, the United States became the "breadbasket of the world." Farmers increased their output to meet multibillion-bushel grain orders from India, China, Russia, and other countries and profited handsomely from high grain prices caused by global shortages. Often farmers borrowed heavily to increase production, sometimes at interest rates up to 18 percent. Then, the fourfold increase in oil prices beginning in 1973 drove up the cost of running the modern mechanized farm. When a worldwide economic slump began in 1980, overseas demand for American farm products declined sharply and farm prices fell. Farmers who had borrowed money at high interest rates, when corn sold at $3 to $4 per bushel, now found themselves trying to meet payments on these loans with corn that brought only $2 per bushel. Thousands of farmers, caught in the cycle of overproduction, heavy indebtedness, and falling prices, watched helplessly as banks and federal agencies foreclosed on their mortgages and drove them out of business.

Conditions improved little at the end of the decade. Family farms continued to disappear amid predictions that the trend would continue to the turn of the century. A drought in the Southeast in 1986 led to burned and stunted fields. An even worse drought in 1988 stretched across most of the Midwest. Devastating crops and forcing up prices, it demonstrated how vulnerable farmers remained.

The Roller Coaster Economy

During the 1980s and 1990s, the economy suffered a series of shifts. The Reagan-Bush era began with a recession, moved into an economic boom between 1983 and 1990, and then became mired in another recession as the new decade began. It appeared that the United States had embarked on another cycle of boom and bust, like that of the early years of the twentieth century.

The recession of 1980–1982 began during Jimmy Carter's administration when the Federal Reserve Board tried to deal with mounting deficits by increasing the money supply. To counter the resulting inflation and cool down the economy, Carter cut programs but succeeded only in bringing on a recession. Under Carter, the unemployment rate had hovered between 5.6 and 7.8 percent. During Reagan's first year, the job situation deteriorated further, and by the end of 1982, the unemployment rate had climbed to 10.8 percent, with joblessness among African-Americans over 20 percent. Nearly a third of the nation's industrial capacity lay idle, and 12 million Americans were out of work. Inflation also continued to be a problem, eroding the purchasing power of people already in difficulty.

The recession of 1980–1982 afflicted every region of the country. Business failures, bankruptcies, and plant closings increased. General Electric released almost 10,000 of its 23,000 workers, and International Harvester closed a plant employing 6,500 people. Detroit was one of the hardest-hit areas in the United States. An industrial city revolving around automobile manufacturing, it suffered both from Japanese competition and from the high interest rates that made car sales plummet. The Detroit unemployment rate rose to more than 19 percent, as the entire city suffered from the decline. The Sun Belt—the vast southern region stretching from coast to coast—initially seemed "recession-proof," but soon it was also stricken. The unemployment rate in California in mid-1982 reached the national average of 9.5 percent, while in Texas it was 7 percent, higher than it had been for ten years. There was more joblessness in Greenlee County, Arizona, than anywhere in the country.

As the rising price of oil led to frantic drilling in many parts of the world, supplies suddenly outstripped demand. The resulting collapse in oil prices disrupted the economy in states like Texas, Oklahoma, and Louisiana. At the same time, worldwide gluts of minerals like copper added to unemployment elsewhere in the Southwest. The threat to the overextended southwestern banking system endangered the entire nation's financial structure. Because many parts of the rural South had never prospered, a gloomy economic picture spread from the Gulf states almost to California. In Jefferson County, Mississippi, 67 percent of the population lived below the poverty line.

Economic conditions improved in late 1983 and early 1984, particularly for Americans in the middle and upper income ranges, but the economic upswing masked a growing undercurrent of poverty. A 1984 survey noted a "staggering" increase in poverty in the South. The Census Bureau reported that the net worth of a typical white household was 12 times greater than the net worth of a typical black household and 8 times greater than the net worth of a typical Latino household. In 1988, the Census Bureau reported a national poverty figure of 13.5 percent. The figure for whites was 10.5 percent, for blacks 33.1 percent. While many families continued to earn a middle-class income, they often did so only by having two full-time income earners. Blue-collar workers often had to accept lower standards of living. Single mothers were hit hardest of all.

The huge and growing budget deficits were another reflection of fundamental economic instability. The doubts those deficits caused culminated in the stock market crash of 1987. After six weeks of falling prices, it suffered a 22.6 percent drop on Monday, October 19, almost double the 12.8 percent plunge on October 28, 1929. The deficits, negative trade balances, and exposures of Wall Street fraud all combined to puncture the bubble. The stock market revived, but the crash foreshadowed further problems.

Those problems surfaced in the early 1990s, as the country experienced another recession. The combination of extravagant military spending, the uncontrolled growth of entitlements—programs like Medicare and Medicaid that provided benefits for millions of Americans on the basis of need—and the tax cut sent budget deficits skyward. As bond traders in the 1980s speculated recklessly, bought and sold companies with an eye solely toward quick gain, and pocketed huge profits, the basic productive structure of the country continued to decline. The huge increase in the size of the national debt eroded business confidence, and this time the effects were felt not simply in the stock market but in the economy as a whole, which drifted into a downturn in 1990.

American firms suffered a serious decline. In an effort to cope with declining profits and decreased consumer demand, companies scaled back dramatically. In late 1991, General Motors announced that it would close 21 plants, lay off 9,000 white-collar employees the next year, and eliminate more than 70,000 jobs in the next several years. Hundreds of other companies did the same, trimming corporate fat but also cutting thousands of jobs. In the New York City metropolitan area, more than 400,000 jobs were lost since 1989. In Manhattan alone, job losses eliminated virtually all of the private sector growth

of the 1980s. In a chilling indication of the city's economic woes, over a million New Yorkers, one out of every seven, were on the welfare rolls in July 1992. Most of the newcomers were unskilled workers who were unable to find jobs during the recession. Meanwhile, for those working, real incomes, after adjustment for inflation, began to fall. The upshot, the New York *Times* reported, was that "most Americans are entering the 1990s worse off than they were in the early 1970s." Around the nation, state governments found it impossible to balance their budgets without resorting to massive spending cuts. Reagan's efforts to move programs from the federal to the state level worked as long as funding lasted, but as national support dropped and state tax revenues declined, states found themselves in a budgetary gridlock. Most had constitutional prohibitions against running deficits, and so they had to slash spending for social services and education, even after yearly budgets had been approved.

After a number of false starts, the economy looked as though it was starting to shake off the recession in mid-1992. But deficits still haunted the nation, and grass-roots opposition to tax increases made it all the more difficult to bring the national debt under control or to balance state and local budgets. Despite some improvement, it was clear that recovery might take a long time.

The Demographic Transformation

As the American people dealt with the swings of the economy, demographic patterns changed in significant ways. The 1990 census revealed that in the previous decade the population of the United States had increased from 228 million to approximately 250 million. The rise of 9.6 percent in the 1980s, down from 11.5 percent in the 1970s, was one of the lowest rates of growth in American history. At the same time, the complexion of the country changed. As a result of increased immigration and minority birthrates significantly higher than the rate for whites, an all-time high of 25 percent of the population in 1992 was black, Hispanic, Asian, or Native American.

Urban and Suburban Shifts

Urban populations changed significantly. White families continued to leave for the steadily growing suburbs, which by 1990 contained almost half the population. As that transformation unfolded, American cities increasingly filled with members of the nation's minorities. In 15 of the nation's 28 largest cities, minorities made up at least half the population. Between 1980 and 1990, the minority population in New York rose from 48 to 57 percent, in Chicago from 57 to 62 percent, in Houston from 48 to 59 percent, in

San Diego from 31 to 41 percent. Minority representation varied by urban region. In Detroit, Washington, New Orleans, and Chicago, blacks were the largest minority, while in Phoenix, El Paso, San Antonio, and Los Angeles, Hispanics held that position, and in San Francisco, Asians outnumbered other groups.

The New Pilgrims

Another shift occurred as the United States admitted new immigrants from a variety of foreign nations. A fifth of the decade's population growth stemmed from this immigration, which was spurred by the Immigration Act of 1965. Part of Lyndon Johnson's Great Society program, this act authorized the acceptance of immigrants impartially from all parts of the world. Because the national-origins system of the 1920s

Population Shifts, 1980–1990

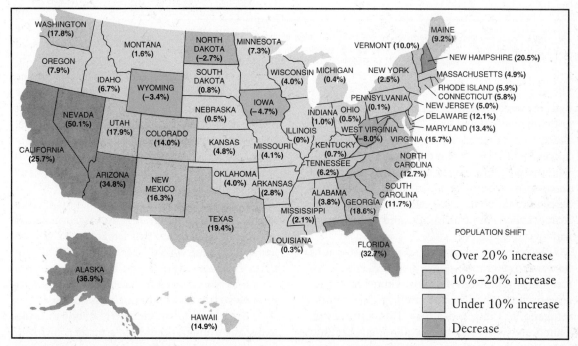

This map shows the population shifts between 1980 and 1990. Note the substantial increases in western regions of the country and the much smaller increases along the Atlantic seaboard.

Immigration: Volume and Sources, 1945–1989

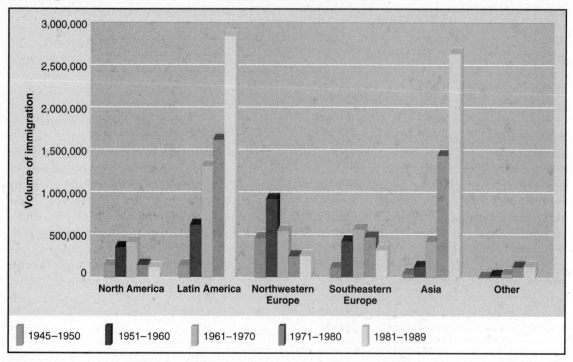

This chart shows the shifting patterns of American immigration in the postwar years. In particular, note the large increase in Asian and Latin American immigration in the past several decades.

had favored western Europeans, most immigrants between 1930 and 1960 had come from Europe or Canada. Between 1977 and 1979, however, only 16 percent came from these areas, while 40 percent came from Asia and another 40 percent from Latin America. In the 1980s, 37 percent came from Asia, and 47 percent came from Mexico, the Caribbean, and Latin America.

As had long been true, the desire for jobs fostered immigration. But foreign crises also fueled the influx. After 1975, the United States accepted more than a half million Vietnamese refugees. In 1980, more than 160,000 arrived. That same year, the nation admitted 125,000 Cubans and Haitians to southern Florida. The

official total of all immigrants in 1978 was higher than it had been in 60 years.

Millions more arrived illegally. As the populations of Latin American nations soared and as economic conditions deteriorated, more and more people looked to the United States for relief. In the mid-1970s, Leonard Chapman, commissioner of the Immigration and Naturalization Service, estimated that there might be 12 million foreigners in the United States illegally. While official estimates were lower, Attorney General William French Smith declared in 1983, "Simply put, we've lost control of our own borders."

Several legislative measures sought to rationalize the immigration process further. In 1986, Congress passed the Immigration Reform and

Control Act, aimed at curbing illegal immigration while offering amnesty to aliens who had lived in the United States since 1982. Turnout for the program was less than expected until the mid-1988 deadline approached. Then 50,000 per week applied, compared with 10,000 earlier in the year, and all-night lines became common at legalization centers.

The Immigration Act of 1990 was even more important. It raised immigration quotas by 40 percent per year, cut back on restrictions based on ideology or sexual orientation that had been used to deny entry in the past, reserved a substantial number of visas for large investors, and provided for swift deportation of aliens who committed crimes.

The United States had once again become a refuge for people from very different parts of the world. The Sun Belt in particular, from Florida to California, felt the impact of the new Asians and Hispanics. In Los Angeles, Samoans, Taiwanese, Koreans, Vietnamese, Filipinos, and Cambodians competed for jobs and apartments with Mexicans, African-Americans, and whites, just as newcomers from different countries had contended with one another in New York City a century before. Throughout the country, in Miami, in Houston, in Brooklyn, the languages heard in the schools and on the streets changed.

These groups left a new imprint on the United States. As blacks and Hispanics became major figures in the urban equation, the number of Asians in the country doubled in the 1980s. In California, they became the largest group of entering students at a number of college campuses.

Growing Up

Other demographic changes also affected Americans' lives. In the mid-1970s, the birthrate began to rise slowly after a decade and a half of decline. The baby boom, which peaked in 1960 with a rate of 24 births per 1,000 people, had created a population explosion in the years after World War II before leveling off. In 1981, the rate stood at 16, then rose to nearly 17 in 1990, as demographers viewed the new increase in births as part of a long-term trend.

But children less frequently lived in traditional homes. Despite the stereotype of the breadwinner father, the homemaker mother, and two children, the Labor Department estimated that only 7 percent of the nation's families actually matched that pattern in the late 1970s. Divorce shattered the mold, reaching a peak of nearly 1.2 million by 1980, and declining to 1.175 million divorces in 1990. For each 1,000 marriages there were 480 divorces in 1990, compared with 258 per 1,000 in 1960. The social stigma once attached to divorce disappeared, and the nation elected its first divorced president, Reagan. "Nonfamily households" became increasingly common. Between 1980 and 1990, such households increased, and single-parent families, particularly those headed by women, were now common. In 1960, 11 percent of all children lived in such homes; by 1990, the figure had reached 25 percent. For blacks, the proportion of families headed by women was three times as great as for whites. A 1986 study observed that children in such families were more likely to leave school, have children out of wedlock, and end up on welfare.

The rising rate of runaway children became another product of changed family life. According to some estimates, more than a million children between the ages of 10 and 17 were on the run. They left home for various reasons. Some were driven out. Others were victims of physical abuse. Still others fled a violent or stressed family life. In 1974, Congress passed the Runaway and Homeless Youth Act, which established telephone hot lines and temporary shelters. But the shelters served only 45,000 youths a year, leaving countless others without help.

Even more ominous was the rising death rate among the young. The Public Health Service reported in 1982 that the death rate for most

Americans had dropped significantly over a 30-year period, and it continued to drop throughout the decade, but the rate for those between 15 and 24 rose steadily after 1976. Automobile accidents, murders, and suicides caused three out of four deaths for that group.

Growing Old

As concern with the problems of the young increased, awareness of the plight of the old, the fastest-growing age group in modern America, also grew. In the 1980s, the number of Americans over 75 grew by more than 27 percent. Underlying the rapid increase was the steady advance in medical care, which in the twentieth century had increased life expectancy from 47 to 74 years. The "aging revolution" promised to become the most lasting of all twentieth-century social changes. Legislation in 1978 raised the mandatory retirement age from 65 to 70, helping older workers who wanted to keep their jobs, but decreasing employment opportunities for younger job seekers.

Generational resentment over jobs was compounded by the knotty problems faced by the social security system established a half century before. As more and more Americans retired, the system could not generate sufficient revenue to make the payments due without assistance from the general governmental fund. In the early 1980s, it appeared that the entire system might collapse. A government solution involving higher taxes for those still employed and a later age for qualifying for benefits rescued the fund.

At an intensely personal level, American families faced difficult decisions about how to care for older parents who could no longer care for themselves. In the past, the elderly might naturally have moved into their children's homes, but attitudes and family patterns had changed. Children were fewer than in earlier generations, and as women gravitated to jobs outside the home, they were less able to take care of an elderly parent. Retirement villages and nursing homes provided two alternatives, but the decision to place a parent under institutional care was often excruciating.

Margaret Stump, an occupational therapist from Tenafly, New Jersey, agonized over such a decision. For six years she flew to Lima, Ohio, every three months to see her mother, who was over 90 years old. Finally, she decided to bring her to a New Jersey nursing home. "I felt that she'd be better once she got to a home," Margaret recalled. "But I knew she wanted to be in her own house. It was a very difficult decision. I had to wait until I thought she wouldn't know where she was."

The New Students

Another group of Americans were also affected by demographic change. College students were more numerous than ever before. After World War II, partly as a result of GI education benefits, higher education became broadly accessible for the first time in American history. College enrollment, which had never exceeded 1.5 million before 1945, rose to nearly 3 million in the early 1960s and reached 13.7 million in 1990. Women entered college in unprecedented numbers, and students were often older. Students in the 1980s and early 1990s were also significantly more conservative and more willing to work within the system.

Some students, not sure of themselves or their goals, gravitated toward cults, such as the Unification Church of the Reverend Sun Myung Moon, the Way International, and the International Society for Krishna Consciousness. But most students in the 1980s coped with uncertain times by preparing for careers. Large numbers of them chose business or economics courses, while enrollment in the liberal arts dropped sharply. Once in the working world, these young urban professionals, or "yuppies," devoted themselves to upward mobility and material gain. In the

1990s, however, many of these opportunities dried up and left students contemplating further schooling until the economy improved.

THE UNITED STATES IN A CHANGED WORLD

The domestic changes experienced by the American people were in many ways less dramatic than those taking place in the international arena. In the 1980s and 1990s, the United States emerged triumphant in the Cold War that had dominated world politics since the end of World War II. In the most momentous development in modern world history, communism collapsed in Eastern Europe and in the Soviet Union, and the various republics of the Soviet system embraced both capitalism and democracy. Yet the transition to a market economy was tortuous, and several of the Soviet satellite nations fragmented into separate states based on long-standing ethnic divisions. The Soviet Union itself disintegrated into its diverse republics once Marxist-Leninist doctrine and centralized authority no longer provided the cement to keep the once-unified nation together. Similar turbulence gripped the Middle East, accompanied by the rise of religious fanaticism and fundamentalism. South Africa likewise experienced breathtaking change, as black leader Nelson Mandela was freed after more than two decades of imprisonment and led the movement to end apartheid and establish a multiracial state. In the midst of this international tumult, the United States had to shift its assumptions and its traditional approach to the rest of the world and learn to operate with a new multicultural perspective.

The United States and the Cold War

The Cold War was very much alive as Reagan assumed power in 1981. In foreign affairs, the new president asserted American interests far more aggressively than Jimmy Carter. Like most of his contemporaries, Reagan believed in large defense budgets and a militant approach toward the Soviet Union. He wanted to cripple the Russians militarily and economically by forcing them to spend more than they could afford. The massive buildup in both nuclear and conventional weapons helped undermine the Communist state but unfortunately at the cost of tremendously destabilizing budget deficits at home.

Reagan promoted an increased atomic arsenal by arguing that a nuclear war could be fought and won. Discounting scientists' studies that showed that nuclear war would cause cataclysmic destruction, he claimed that the United States could survive. T. K. Jones, deputy undersecretary of defense for strategic and theater nuclear forces, even revived the dormant notion of nuclear civil defense. "Dig a hole, cover it with a couple of doors, and then throw three feet of dirt on top," he advised. "It's the dirt that does it. . . . If there are enough shovels to go around, everybody's going to make it." That position appeared particularly cavalier as scientists began to speculate about the "nuclear winter" that could end planetary life after a nuclear war.

While promoting defense spending and nuclear superiority during his first term, Reagan persisted in viewing the Soviet Union as an "evil empire." The administration abandoned Senate ratification of SALT II, the arms reduction plan negotiated under Carter, although it observed its restrictions. Instead the administration proposed that Russia destroy certain missiles in return for an American pledge not to deploy new weapons in Europe. The Soviet Union balked at that idea, which was so different from the careful negotiation accompanying previous arms talks. As the arms race escalated, new U.S. missiles were deployed in western Europe, and in both countries, military budgets soared.

Meanwhile, Reagan proposed the Strategic Defense Initiative, popularly known as "Star Wars" after a 1977 movie, to intercept Soviet missiles by means of a shield in outer space. Scientists questioned whether the proposal was technologically feasible. Economists pointed to the extraordinary sums it would cost just to find out. But the administration pressed ahead with the project.

In his second term, Reagan softened his rigid position toward the Soviet Union and agreed to meet with the new Russian leader, Mikhail Gorbachev. Summits in both the Soviet Union and the United States led to an Intermediate-Range Nuclear Forces Treaty that provided for withdrawal and destruction of a whole category of nuclear weapons in both countries. The two nations had not yet resumed détente, but communications were better than they had been in some time.

George Bush maintained Reagan's comfortable relationship with Mikhail Gorbachev. The two leaders met in Malta in late 1989 and in the United States in mid-1990. Together they signed agreements reducing the number of long-range nuclear weapons to a maximum of 1,600 rockets and 6,000 warheads, ending their manufacture of chemical weapons, and easing trade restrictions between the two nations. The Strategic Arms Reduction Treaty (START) they signed in 1991 dramatically decreased the number of long-range weapons stockpiled during years of international hostility. "The Cold War is now behind us," Gorbachev declared at Stanford University. "Let us not wrangle over who won it." But the outcome was clear: In the final years of the twentieth century, the United States would be the dominant force.

Hailed around the world for his part in ending the Cold War, Gorbachev encountered trouble from opposition groups within the Soviet Union. In 1991, he survived a right-wing challenge, but he could not resist those who wanted to go even further to establish democracy and capitalism. The forces he had unleashed within the Soviet Union finally tore the USSR apart. In the turbulence that followed the coup, Boris Yeltsin, head of Russia, the strongest, largest,

and most populous of the Soviet republics, emerged as the dominant leader. Already independence movements in the tiny Baltic republics of Estonia, Latvia, and Lithuania had begun the disintegration of the Soviet Union, and now other republics declared their autonomy and then coalesced loosely in a Commonwealth of Independent States.

Early in 1992, Bush and Yeltsin proclaimed a new era of "friendship and partnership" and formally declared an end to the Cold War. The United States and its allies sought a new role for NATO, the North Atlantic Treaty Organization, and contemplated the extension of aid to former Soviet republics that needed help in reorganizing their economies as free enterprise systems.

While celebrating the collapse of the Soviet Union, the United States found itself facing a vastly different situation in Europe. The liberalization initiated by Gorbachev in his own country quickly spread beyond Soviet borders and soon toppled governments in most countries within the Soviet orbit. Bush spoke of a "New World Order," anticipating international stability, but the fall of communism brought growing disorder as the disintegration of central authority opened the way for intense political wrangling and the rekindling of ancient racial, cultural, and religious antagonisms.

The most dramatic chapter in the collapse of communism began in November 1989, when East Germany's Communist Party boss announced unexpectedly that citizens of his country would be free to leave East Germany. Within hours, thousands of people gathered on both sides of the 28-mile Berlin Wall, the symbol of the Cold War that divided Berlin into east and west sectors. As the border guards stepped aside, East Germans flooded into West Berlin amidst dancing, shouting, and fireworks. All through the night noisy celebrators reveled in what one observer called the "greatest street party in the history of the world." Within days, an outpouring of sledgehammer-wielding Germans pulverized the Berlin Wall, and soon the Communist

The destruction of the Berlin Wall in November 1989 was a symbolic blow to the entire Cold War structure that had grown up in Europe in the postwar years. The dismantling of the Wall touched off joyous celebrations.

government led by Erich Honnecker came tumbling down with it. In October 1990, East and West Germany were formally reunited.

The fall of the Berlin Wall marked a watershed in history. Everywhere it brought in its wake the pell-mell overthrow of Communist regimes. In Poland, the 10-year-old Solidarity movement led by Lech Walesa finally triumphed in its long struggle against Soviet domination and found itself in power, with Walesa as president. In Czechoslovakia, after over four decades of Communist rule, Czech playwright Vaclav Havel became president. But Czechoslovakia soon divided into its two main ethnic components, peacefully forming the Czech Republic and Slovakia. New regimes also swept into power in Bulgaria, Hungary, Romania, and Albania.

Yugoslavia proved to be the extreme case of resurgent ethnic hostility in the face of collapsing central authority. The Balkan region had long been a powder keg, and only dictatorship had held the diverse republics together. When Slovenia and Croatia declared their independence in 1991, the fragile nation descended into chaos.

The decision of the Muslim and Croatian majority in Bosnia to secede from Serbian-dominated Yugoslavia led Bosnian Serbs, backed by the Serbian republic, to embark upon a brutal siege of the city of Sarajevo and an even more ruthless "ethnic cleansing" campaign to eliminate opposition elements of newly independent Bosnia and Herzegovina.

The United States and the Middle East

The Middle East remained equally unstable, as the ancient Arab-Israeli conflict dragged on. In June 1982, the Israelis invaded Lebanon in an attempt to destroy the Palestine Liberation Organization (PLO). Lebanese factions sought Syrian help against the Israelis. In August, U.S. marines joined France and Italy in a peacekeeping mission to restore order and soon found themselves allied with one Lebanese faction against Syria. A year later, terrorist bombs in the American barracks killed 241 servicemen. Humiliated, the United States pulled out its forces, only to station American vessels later in the troubled Persian Gulf, as the Middle East remained as turbulent as before.

In the early 1990s Secretary of State James Baker finally secured agreement from the major parties in the region to speak to one another face to face. Though intense squabbling continued, negotiations struggled forward. A victory in the Israeli parliamentary elections in mid-1992 for Yitzhak Rabin, a less hawkish prime minister, offered further hope for peace.

Another problem in the region drew the United States into a shooting war during the Bush administration. When Saddam Hussein, ruler of Iraq, invaded and annexed the neighboring state of Kuwait in August 1990, the United States took a strong stand. Earlier, between 1985 and 1990, the United States had provided massive military support for Iraq in the war it was waging with Iran. Now, however, the Iran-Iraq war had ended, and Iraq's invasion of Kuwait threatened the flow of Saudi Arabian oil to the West. Equally troubling, Saddam seemed intent on unifying Arab nations, thereby threatening Israel and dominating the region's production of oil, upon which the United States was highly dependent.

Saddam's invasion aroused an immediate reaction. The United Nations Security Council voted 14–0 to condemn the invasion and a few days later endorsed by a 13–0 vote an embargo on trade with Iraq. The American secretary of state and the Soviet foreign minister issued a joint statement condemning the attack. Working through the UN, as Truman had done in Korea, the United States implemented a blockade and began planning for war.

Denouncing Iraq's "naked aggression," Bush mobilized American reserves, including a sizable number of women, organized a multinational army of nearly half a million troops, and secured from the Senate and House a resolution authorizing the use of force. In mid-January 1991, the 28-nation alliance struck at Iraq in Operation Desert Storm with both air and ground forces.

Unlike the costly, drawn-out, and ultimately unpopular war in Vietnam, the Persian Gulf War was swift and engrossing. Television footage showed "smart bombs" being guided to their targets by laser beams. Briefings by General H. Norman Schwarzkopf and other members of his staff carefully released information about the military operations and orchestrated a sympathetic response. Victory came quickly, as the alliance forces completely overwhelmed the Iraqis with sophisticated missiles, airplanes, and tanks. Bush's approval rating soared to 91 percent.

The mood of euphoria in the United States soon soured, however, as Saddam retained power and used his remaining military might to put down revolts of Kurds and Shiites in Iraq. Bush's unwillingness to become bogged down in an Iraqi civil war and his eagerness to bring American troops home left the conflict unfinished. A year after victory, Saddam was as strong as he had been before.

The United States and Latin America

Closer to home, the Reagan and Bush administrations intervened frequently in Latin America. Viewing Central America as a Cold War battlefield, Reagan openly opposed the left-wing guerrillas of El Salvador who fought to overthrow a repressive right-wing regime that was receiving support from the United States. Fearful that another nation might follow the Marxist examples of Cuba and Nicaragua, Reagan increased assistance to the antirevolutionary Salvadoran government, heedless of a similar course followed earlier in Vietnam. Efforts to destroy the radical Farabundo Martí National Liberation Front (FMLN) failed. Reagan rejected an FMLN offer to negotiate and for the next six years poured about $1 million a day into El Salvador. As Americans took over the economy, the CIA sought to prevent either the left wing or the far-right wing, which employed "death squads" to kill thousands of people, from gaining power. That policy failed, and in 1989, the far-right faction, Alianza Republicana Nacionalista

(ARENA), won Salvadoran elections. Peace appeared possible, however, as the government signed an agreement with the rebel FMLN in January 1992.

Nicaragua became an even bloodier battleground and one where Reagan persistently flouted international law and the U.S. Constitution when Congress refused to yield to his efforts to defeat revolutionary reformers. In 1979, revolutionaries calling themselves Sandinistas (after César Sandino, who fought in the 1920s against occupying American troops) overthrew the repressive Somoza family, which had ruled for three decades. Jimmy Carter initially extended aid to the Sandinistas and recognized the new regime, then cut off support to show his disapproval of their curbs on civil liberties and of their alleged efforts to assist rebels in El Salvador. The Reagan administration charged that the Sandinistas were driving out moderate elements, welcoming Cuban and Soviet assistance, and supplying leftist guerrillas in El Salvador. In November 1981, Reagan authorized the CIA to arm and train counterrevolutionaries known as Contras. Although this policy violated United States neutrality laws, the training continued, and the Contras began to attack from bases in Honduras and Costa Rica. As the Sandinistas built up their forces and secured aid from western Europe and the Soviet bloc, Nicaragua became enmeshed in a bitter civil war.

The war went badly for the Contras. Their failures by the end of 1983 led the CIA to assume the initiative in military operations and to mine Nicaraguan harbors in violation of international law. When Congress discovered these secret missions, it cut off military aid to the Contras. In Reagan's second term, Congress insisted on ending military aid, though humanitarian assistance to the Contras continued. American economic sanctions meanwhile disrupted the Nicaraguan economy further and led to a crippling inflation rate, but still the Sandinistas clung to power until peaceful elections in early 1990 drove them out. President Daniel Ortega gave way to Violeta Barrios de Chamorro and her National Opposition Union. Though the economy remained in desperate straits and the Sandinistas still maintained control of the armed forces and continued to be represented in the bureaucracy, the Nicaraguans were ready for democratic change, and the new regime seemed to offer some hope of healing the wounds of the bloody civil war.

The Middle Eastern and Central American crises became entangled in the Iran-Contra affair. In 1987, the nation discovered that the National Security Council had launched an effort to free American hostages in the Middle East by selling arms to Iran and then using the funds to aid the Contras, in direct violation of both the law and congressional will. Commissions and congressional hearings demonstrated the chaos and duplicity in the administration and cast doubt on the president's ability to govern. The subsequent trial of Oliver North, the National Security Council official responsible for the policy, focused on his distortions and falsifications before congressional committees and on his destruction of official documents. Convicted in 1989, North received a light sentence requiring no time in prison from a judge who recognized that North was not acting entirely on his own. His conviction was overturned the following year by the U.S. Appeals Court.

Only on the tiny Caribbean island of Grenada did Reagan win a modest victory. The president ordered 2,000 marines there in October 1983, after a military coup installed a government sympathetic to Fidel Castro's Cuba. U.S. marines invaded the island, rescued a number of American medical students, and the administration claimed triumph.

Bush took the credit for a similar incursion in Panama, ostensibly to protect American lives. The United States invaded Panama, the Bush administration said, to protect the Panama Canal, defend American citizens following a number of attacks, and stop the drug traffic. The incursion resulted in the capture of military leader Manuel Noriega, notorious for his involvement in the drug trade. Noriega was brought to the United

States, charged, and in a lengthy trial convicted of drug trafficking.

The United States and South Africa

Americans, like people around the world, applauded the black struggle against apartheid in South Africa, which grew more militant in the 1980s. Under the rigid policy of apartheid, the white minority, constituting about 15 percent of the population, segregated and suppressed the black majority and denied it voting rights. Under Reagan, the United States followed a policy of "constructive engagement," in which it relied on talk but not economic sanctions to force an end to apartheid. By 1986, the bankruptcy of that approach was evident, and Congress imposed sanctions, including a rule prohibiting new American investments, despite Reagan's objections. The economic pressure damaged the South African economy and persuaded more than half of the 300 American firms in business there to leave.

In 1989, a new president, Frederik W. De Klerk, recognized that South Africa could no longer withstand the pressure from the United States and the rest of the world. The next year he freed the 71-year-old Nelson Mandela, the symbol of militant opposition to apartheid, after 27 years in prison, and announced plans gradually to overturn apartheid. South Africa appeared to be embarking on a new path as the world looked on hopefully.

The Election of 1992

As the world changed, so the United States changed, and the election of 1992 reflected the national and international transformations taking place. After four years in office, George Bush sought a second term and found himself involved in an unusual three-way race against Democratic candidate Bill Clinton, governor of Arkansas, and Texas billionaire Ross Perot, an independent candidate. Overcoming allegations of adultery, marijuana use, and draft evasion, the 46-year-old Clinton argued that it was time for a new generation to take command. Perot pulled out of the race in July but reentered it in the fall.

The three candidates faced a disillusioned nation. A Gallup Poll reported in September that 79 percent of all Americans felt the country was in economic decline, 65 percent believed it was in moral decline, and 19 percent thought it was in military decline. To many, the deficit appeared to be choking both present and future public policy. Despite brilliant technological advances, health care was becoming prohibitively expensive and patently unfair. Crime was becoming a national epidemic.

This campaign, more than any in the past, was fought on television. There were three presidential debates, involving all three candidates, but they told only part of the story. Far more important were the candidates' appearances on talk shows and interview programs. This reliance on the electronic marketplace was visible evidence of the shift occurring in American politics. At times the campaign turned nasty, as when Bush claimed that "my dog Millie knows more about foreign affairs" than Bill Clinton. Despite such rhetoric, the contest was less ugly than Bush's victorious campaign four years before.

In the end, it became a clash of competing visions. In accepting the Republican nomination, Bush underscored his faith in the individual rather than the bureaucracy and insisted, "Government is too big and spends too much." Clinton, in contrast, claimed that the government had a necessary role to play "to make America work again."

On election day, Clinton won 43 percent of the popular vote to 38 percent for Bush and 19 percent for Perot. The electoral vote margin was even larger: 370 for Clinton, 168 for Bush, 0 for Perot. The Democrats retained control of both houses of Congress, with more women and minority members than ever before.

Since the 1960 presidential campaign, televised debates have been a popular way for the candidates to reach large numbers of the American people. In the 1992 campaign, the three major candidates—Republican George Bush, Independent H. Ross Perot, and Democrat Bill Clinton—met in a series of televised debates.

The president-elect moved quickly to demonstrate his intention of shifting America's course after 12 years of Republican rule. His Cabinet nominations included four women, four African-Americans, and two Latinos. He held a televised "economic summit" to explore national options and demonstrated a keen grasp of the details of policy. In his inaugural address in early 1993, Clinton told an eager nation that "a new season of American renewal has begun." Major problems loomed ahead, but a new generation stood ready to try whatever was necessary to resolve them.

The Clinton Presidency

Bill Clinton faced a very different world as he took office in early 1993. The end of the Cold War stimulated complex and rapid changes in countries around the world. Without the familiar framework of Soviet-American competition to guide its foreign policy, U.S. policymakers and the American public were frequently uncertain about what role the country should play in the international arena. What actions were in the national interest? Where did U.S. humanitarian responsibilities lie? These and other questions prompted debate, but no consensus emerged.

Ethnic conflicts posed particularly difficult problems for the United States. In the former Yugoslavia, ethnic and religious violence in Bosnia and Herzegovina worsened. But when Clinton pledged to send American troops to help keep peace, the American public was unwilling to honor his commitment.

Meanwhile, Africa presented other challenges to American policymakers. Somalia, in

East Africa, suffered from a devastating famine and breakdown of political order. American troops, sent by George Bush, assisted a United Nations relief effort there. Six months after Clinton became president, a firefight with a Somali faction led by Mohammed Farrah Aidid resulted in several dozen American casualties. The crisis prompted some Americans, still haunted by the memory of Vietnam, to demand withdrawal. Reluctant to back down, Clinton increased the number of American troops. The soldiers returned home the following spring without having achieved their goals.

Another crisis erupted in Rwanda, in Central Africa, when a fragile balance of power between two ethnic groups—the Tutsis and the Hutus—broke down and led to the slaughter of several hundred thousand innocent people. As the world followed the situation on television, the United States, like many European nations, debated the possibility of intervention on humanitarian grounds but decided to do nothing.

In South Africa, the news was more heartening. Nelson Mandela and Frederik W. de Klerk worked together to ensure peaceful elections in which blacks, who made up the vast majority of the population, voted for the first time. After years of struggle, the African National Congress assumed power and began to dismantle the apartheid system. Mandela himself became president of this nation that was building itself anew.

In the Middle East, Clinton played the part of peacemaker, just as Jimmy Carter had done 15 years before. On September 13, 1993, in a dramatic ceremony on the White House lawn, Palestine Liberation Organization leader Yasir Arafat and Israeli president Yitzhak Rabin took the first public step toward ending years of conflict as they shook hands and signed a peace agreement that led to Palestinian self-rule in the Gaza strip. While extremists tried to destroy the peace process by continued violence, the effort to overcome old animosities continued.

Clinton was similarly successful in Haiti, but just barely. After seeking for several years to restore deposed president Jean Bertrand Aristide to power, Clinton threatened and then authorized an American invasion of the island. At the last minute a delegation including Carter and former Joint Chiefs of Staff chairman Colin Powell secured a commitment from the military dictatorship to relinquish power, and the transition took place. While the United States wanted to nourish democracy and protect its economic interests, Americans remained wary of foreign intervention. American reluctance to become deeply involved abroad posed difficult problems for the president.

Clinton also had his hands full at home. Although the economy finally began to improve, the public gave the president little credit for the upturn. Republicans and some conservative Democrats resisted his initiatives, and he had to fight fiercely for every program he endorsed. He gained Senate ratification of the North American Free Trade Agreement (NAFTA)—aimed at promoting free trade between Canada, Mexico, and the United States—in November 1993, but only after a bitter battle. He secured passage of a crime bill after a similar struggle. But he failed to win approval of his major legislative initiative: health care reform. "This health-care system of ours is badly broken," he said in September 1993, "and it's time to fix it." Particularly troublesome were escalating costs and the lack of universal medical care. Clinton's proposal for a system of health alliances in each state to pay health claims, provide far greater coverage, and trim costs was too complex for many Americans and provoked intense opposition from the health care industry and from politicians with plans of their own. In the end he was unable to persuade Congress either to accept his approach or adopt a workable alternative.

Voters demonstrated their dissatisfaction in the mid-term elections of 1994. They demanded change and supported candidates who promised a smaller government, less regulation, and lower taxes. In a rebuff to Clinton and the Democrats, Republicans gained control of both the Senate and the House of Representatives for the first time in 40 years. Clinton acknowledged that Americans "don't like what they see when they watch us working here." Now the major parties had to see if they could work together for the next two years.

CONCLUSION

THE RECENT PAST IN PERSPECTIVE

In the 1980s and early 1990s, the United States witnessed the triumph of conservatism. The assault on the welfare state, dubbed the "Reagan Revolution," involved creating a less regulated economy, whatever the implications for less fortunate Americans. Policies inaugurated by Reagan and followed by Bush continued the trend begun by Richard Nixon in the 1970s. They reshaped the political agenda and reversed the liberal approach that had held sway since the New Deal of Franklin Roosevelt in the 1930s. There were limits to the transformation, to be sure. Such fundamental programs as Social Security and Medicare remained securely in place.

In foreign affairs, Republican administrations likewise shifted course. Reagan first assumed a steel-ribbed posture toward the Soviet Union, then moved toward détente, and watched as his successor declared victory in the Cold War.

Despite the end of the Cold War, the nation's defense budget remained far higher than many Americans wished, and the nuclear arsenal continued to pose a threat to the human race. Meanwhile, periods of deep recession wrought havoc on the lives of blue-collar and white-collar workers alike. Middle-class Americans like David Patterson, introduced at the start of the chapter, were caught in a spiral of downward mobility. Liberals and conservatives both worried about the mounting national debt and the ability of the American economy to compete with Japan, Korea, Germany, and other countries. Countless Americans were uneasy about the growing gaps between rich and poor. Children wondered for the first time in American history whether they could hope to do better than or as well as their parents had done.

In the 1980s and early 1990s, the United States struggled to adhere to its historic values in a complex and changing world. When the Democrats took command, those basic values still governed, as the American people continued their centuries-old effort to live up to the promise of the American dream.

Recommended Reading

Historians have not yet had a chance to deal in detail with the developments of the immediate past, so fuller descriptions must be found in other sources. Much of the best writing about the years in this chapter appears in the newspapers and magazines of the popular press. But a number of useful treatments about selected topics provide good starting points in various areas.

General and statistical works about this period include Barry Bluestone and Bennett Harrison, *The Deindustrialization of America: Plant Closings, Community Abandonment, and the Dismantling of Basic Industry* (1982); Peter Duignan and Alvin Rabushka, eds., *The United States in the 1980s* (1980); Andrew Hacker, ed., *U/S: A Statistical Portrait of the American People* (1983); Katherine S. Newman, *Falling from Grace: The Experience of Downward Mobility in the American Middle Class* (1988); Kevin P.

Phillips, *The Politics of Rich and Poor: Wealth and the American Electorate in the Reagan Aftermath* (1990); Neil Postman, *Amusing Ourselves to Death: Public Discourse in the Age of Show Business* (1985); U.S. Bureau of the Census, *Statistical Abstract of the United States: 1991;* and U.S. Bureau of the Census, *U.S. Census of Population, 1990.*

On the Reagan presidency, see Lawrence I. Barrett, *Gambling with History: Reagan in the White House* (1983); Paul Boyer, ed., *Reagan as President: Contemporary Views of the Man, His Politics, and His Policies* (1990); Lou Cannon, *President Reagan: A Role of a Lifetime* (1991) and *Reagan* (1982); Ronnie Dugger, *On Reagan: The Man and His Presidency* (1983); Rowland Evans and Robert Novak, *The Reagan Revolution* (1981); Fred I. Greenstein, ed., *The Reagan Presidency: An Early Assessment* (1983); Haynes Johnson, *Sleepwalking Through History: America Through the Reagan Years* (1991); Richard A. Viguerie, *The New Right: We're Ready to Lead* (1981); and Garry Wills, *Reagan's America: Innocents at Home* (1985)

The Bush years are treated in Colin Campbell, S.J., and Bert A. Rockman, eds., *The Bush Presidency: First Appraisals* (1991).

For a closer look at immigration issues, see Roger Daniels, *A History of Immigration and Ethnicity in American Life* (1990); David M. Reimers, *Still the Golden Door: The Third World Comes to America* (1985); Paul James Rutledge, *The Vietnamese Experience in America* (1992); and Virginia Yans-McLaughlin, ed., *Immigration Reconsidered: History, Sociology, and Politics* (1990).

On foreign affairs see Paul Kennedy, *The Rise and Fall of the Great Powers: Economic Change and Military Conflict from 1500 to 2000* (1987); Walter LaFeber, *America, Russia, and the Cold War, 1945–1990* (6th ed., 1991), *Inevitable Revolutions: The United States in Central America* (1983), and *The American Age: United States Foreign Policy at Home and Abroad Since 1750* (1989); Sandra Mackey, *Lebanon* (1989); Robert Scheer, *With Enough Shovels: Reagan, Bush and Nuclear War* (1982); Strobe Talbott, *The Russians and Reagan* (1984); Seth P. Tillman, *The U.S. and the Middle East* (1982); Sanford J. Ungar, ed., *Estrangement: America and the World* (1985); Mary B. Vanderlaan, *Revolution and Foreign Policy in Nicaragua* (1986); and Thomas W. Walker, ed., *Revolution and Counterrevolution in Nicaragua* (1991).

Insight into the period may also be gained from fictional accounts such as the following: Tim O'Brien, *The Nuclear Age* (1985); Anne Tyler *Dinner at the Homesick Restaurant* (1982); and Tom Wolfe, *The Bonfire of the Vanities* (1987).

Time Line

1980	Ronald Reagan elected president	1990	National debt reaches $3.1 trillion Immigration Act of 1990 passed Sandinistas driven from power in Nicaragua Nelson Mandela freed in South Africa
1980–1982	Recession		
1981	Reagan breaks air controllers' strike		
1981–1983	Tax cuts; deficit spending increases	1990–1992	Recession
1982	American invasion of Lebanon	1991	Persian Gulf War Failed coup in the Soviet Union Disintegration of the Soviet Union Department of Housing and Urban Development scandal uncovered Strategic Arms Reduction Treaty (START) signed
1983	Reagan proposes Strategic Defense Initiative		
1984	Reagan reelected		
1986	Tax reform measure passed Immigration Reform and Control Act passed		
1987	Iran-Contra affair becomes public Stock market crashes Intermediate-Range Nuclear Forces Treaty signed	1991–1992	Ethnic turbulence in a fragmented Yugoslavia
		1992	Bill Clinton elected president Czechoslovakia splits into separate republics
1988	George Bush elected president		
1989	Federal bailout of savings and loan industry Fall of the Berlin Wall		

Declaration of Independence in Congress, July 4, 1776

THE UNANIMOUS DECLARATION OF THE THIRTEEN UNITED STATES OF AMERICA

When, in the course of human events, it becomes necessary for one people to dissolve the political bonds which have connected them with another, and to assume, among the powers of the earth, the separate and equal station to which the laws of nature and of nature's God entitle them, a decent respect to the opinions of mankind requires that they should declare the causes which impel them to the separation.

We hold these truths to be self-evident: That all men are created equal, that they are endowed by their Creator with certain unalienable rights; that among these are life, liberty, and the pursuit of happiness; that, to secure these rights, governments are instituted among men, deriving their just powers from the consent of the governed; that whenever any form of government becomes destructive of these ends, it is the right of the people to alter or to abolish it, and to institute new government, laying its foundation on such principles, and organizing its powers in such form, as to them shall seem most likely to effect their safety and happiness. Prudence, indeed, will dictate that governments long established should not be changed for light and transient causes; and accordingly all experience hath shown that mankind are more disposed to suffer, which evils are sufferable, than to right themselves by abolishing the forms to which they are accustomed. But when a long train of abuses and usurpations, pursuing invariably the same object, evinces a design to reduce them under absolute despotism, it is their right, it is their duty, to throw off such government, and to provide new guards for their future security. Such has been the patient sufferance of these colonies; and such is now the necessity which constrains them to alter their former systems of government. The history of the present King of Great Britain is a history of repeated injuries and usurpations, all having in direct object the establishment of an absolute tyranny over these states. To prove this, let facts be submitted to a candid world.

He has refused his assent to laws the most wholesome and necessary for the public good.

He has forbidden his governors to pass laws of immediate and pressing importance, unless suspended in their operation till his assent should be obtained; and, when so suspended, he has utterly neglected to attend to them.

He has refused to pass other laws for the accommodation of large districts of people, unless those people would relinquish the right of representation in the legislature, a right inestimable to them, and formidable to tyrants only.

He has called together legislative bodies at places unusual, uncomfortable, and distant from the depository of their public records, for the sole purpose of fatiguing them into compliance with his measures.

He has dissolved representative houses repeatedly, for opposing, with manly firmness, his invasions on the rights of the people.

He has refused for a long time, after such dissolutions, to cause others to be elected; whereby the legislative powers, incapable of annihilation, have returned to the people at large for their exercise; the state remaining, in the mean time, exposed to all the dangers of invasions from without and convulsions within.

He has endeavored to prevent the population of these states; for that purpose obstructing the laws for naturalization of foreigners; refusing to pass others to encourage their migration hither, and raising the conditions of new appropriations of lands.

He has obstructed the administration of justice, by refusing his assent to laws for establishing judiciary powers.

He has made judges dependent on his will alone, for the tenure of their offices, and the amount and payment of their salaries.

He has erected a multitude of new offices, and sent hither swarms of officers to harass our people and eat out their substance.

He has kept among us, in times of peace, standing armies, without the consent of our legislatures.

He has affected to render the military independent of, and superior to, the civil power.

He has combined with others to subject us to a jurisdiction foreign to our constitution, and unacknowledged by our laws, giving his assent to their acts of pretended legislation:

For quartering large bodies of armed troops among us;

For protecting them, by a mock trial, from punishment for any murders which they should commit on the inhabitants of these states;

For cutting off our trade with all parts of the world;

For imposing taxes on us without our consent;

For depriving us, in many cases, of the benefits of trial by jury;

For transporting us beyond seas, to be tried for pretended offenses;

For abolishing the free system of English laws in a neighboring province, establishing therein an arbitrary government, and enlarging its boundaries, so as to render it at once an example

and fit instrument for introducing the same absolute rule into these colonies;

For taking away our charters, abolishing our most valuable laws, and altering fundamentally the forms of our governments;

For suspending our own legislatures, and declaring themselves invested with power to legislate for us in all cases whatsoever.

He has abdicated government here, by declaring us out of his protection and waging war against us.

He has plundered our seas, ravaged our coasts, burned our towns, and destroyed the lives of our people.

He is at this time transporting large armies of foreign mercenaries to complete the works of death, desolation, and tyranny already begun with circumstances of cruelty and perfidy scarcely paralleled in the most barbarous ages, and totally unworthy the head of a civilized nation.

He has constrained our fellow-citizens, taken captive on the high seas, to bear arms against their country, to become the executioners of their friends and brethren, or to fall themselves by their hands.

He has excited domestic insurrection among us, and has endeavored to bring on the inhabitants of our frontiers the merciless Indian savages, whose known rule of warfare is an undistinguished destruction of all ages, sexes, and conditions.

In every stage of these oppressions we have petitioned for redress in the most humble terms; our repeated petitions have been answered only by repeated injury. A prince, whose character is thus marked by every act which may define a tyrant, is unfit to be the ruler of a free people.

Nor have we been wanting in our attentions to our British brethren. We have warned them, from time to time, of attempts by their legislature to extend an unwarrantable jurisdiction over us. We have reminded them of the circumstances of our emigration and settlement here. We have appealed to their native justice and magnanimity; and we have conjured them, by the ties of our common kindred, to disavow these usurpations, which would inevitably interrupt our connections and correspondence. They, too, have been deaf to the voice of justice and of consanguinity. We must, therefore, acquiesce in the necessity which denounces our separation, and hold them, as we hold the rest of mankind, enemies in war, in peace friends.

We, therefore, the representatives of the United States of America, in General Congress assembled, appealing to the Supreme Judge of the world for the rectitude of our intentions, do, in the name and by the authority of the good people of these colonies, solemnly publish and declare, that these United Colonies are, and of right ought to be, FREE AND INDEPENDENT STATES; that they are absolved from all allegiance to the British crown, and that all political connection between them and the state of Great Britain is, and ought to be, totally dissolved; and that, as free and independent states, they have full power to levy war, conclude peace, contract alliances, establish commerce, and do all other acts and things which independent states may of right do. And for the support of this declaration, with a firm reliance on the protection of Divine Providence, we mutually pledge to each other our lives, our fortunes, and our sacred honor.

Constitution of the United States of America*

PREAMBLE

We the people of the United States, in order to form a more perfect union, establish justice, insure domestic tranquillity, provide for the common defense, promote the general welfare, and secure the blessings of liberty to ourselves and our posterity, do ordain and establish this Constitution for the United States of America.

ARTICLE 1

Section 1   All legislative powers herein granted shall be vested in a Congress of the United States, which shall consist of a Senate and a House of Representatives.

Section 2   The House of Representatives shall be composed of members chosen every second year by the people of the several States, and the electors in each State shall have the qualifications requisite for electors of the most numerous branch of the State Legislature.

No person shall be a Representative who shall not have attained to the age of twenty-five years, and been seven years a citizen of the United States, and who shall not, when elected, be an inhabitant of that State in which he shall be chosen.

Representatives and direct taxes shall be apportioned among the several States which may be included within this Union, according to their respective numbers, *which shall be determined by adding to the whole number of free persons, including those bonded in service for a term of years and excluding Indians not taxed, three-fifths of all other persons.* The actual enumeration shall be made within three years after the first meeting of the Congress of the United States, and within every subsequent term of ten years, in such manner as they shall by law direct. The number of Representatives shall not exceed one for every thirty thousand, but each State shall have at least one Representative; *and until such enumeration shall be made, the State of New Hampshire shall be entitled to choose three, Massachusetts eight, Rhode Island and Providence Plantations one, Connecticut five, New York six, New Jersey four, Pennsylvania eight, Delaware one, Maryland six, Virginia ten,*

---

*The Constitution became effective March 4, 1789.

NOTE: Any portion of the text that has been amended appears in italics.

North Carolina five, South Carolina five, and Georgia three.

When vacancies happen in the representation from any State, the Executive authority thereof shall issue writs of election to fill such vacancies.

The House of Representatives shall choose their Speaker and other officers; and shall have the sole power of impeachment.

Section 3   The Senate of the United States shall be composed of two Senators from each State, *chosen by the legislature thereof,* for six years; and each Senator shall have one vote.

Immediately after they shall be assembled in consequence of the first election, they shall be divided as equally as may be into three classes. The seats of the Senators of the first class shall be vacated at the expiration of the second year, of the second class at the expiration of the fourth year, and of the third class at the expiration of the sixth year, so that one-third may be chosen every second year; *and if vacancies happen by resignation or otherwise, during the recess of the legislature of any State, the Executive thereof may make temporary appointments until the next meeting of the legislature, which shall then fill such vacancies.*

No person shall be a Senator who shall not have attained to the age of thirty years, and been nine years a citizen of the United States, and who shall not, when elected, be an inhabitant of that State for which he shall be chosen.

The Vice-President of the United States shall be President of the Senate, but shall have no vote, unless they be equally divided.

The Senate shall choose their other officers, and also a President *pro tempore,* in the absence of the Vice-President, or when he shall exercise the office of President of the United States.

The Senate shall have the sole power to try all impeachments. When sitting for that purpose, they shall be on oath or affirmation. When the President of the United States is tried, the Chief Justice shall preside; and no person shall be convicted without the concurrence of two-thirds of the members present.

Judgment in cases of impeachment shall not extend further than to removal from the office, and disqualification to hold and enjoy any office of honor, thrust or profit under the United States: but the party convicted shall nevertheless be liable and subject to indictment, trial, judgment and punishment, according to law.

Section 4   The times, places and manner of holding elections for Senators and Representatives shall be prescribed in each State by the legislature thereof; but the Congress may at any time by law make or alter such regulations, except as to the places of choosing Senators.

The Congress shall assemble at least once in every year, and such meeting *shall be on the first Monday in December, unless they shall by law appoint a different day.*

Section 5   Each house shall be the judge of the elections, returns and qualifications of its own members, and a majority of each shall constitute a quorum to do business; but a smaller number may adjourn from day to day, and may be authorized to compel the attendance of absent members, in such manner, and under such penalties, as each house may provide.

Each house may determine the rules of its proceedings, punish its members for disorderly behavior, and with the concurrence of two-thirds, expel a member.

Each house shall keep a journal of its proceedings, and from time to time publish the same, excepting such parts as may in their judgment require secrecy; and the yeas and nays of the members of either house on any question shall, at the desire of one-fifth of those present, be entered on the journal.

Neither house, during the session of Congress, shall, without the consent of the other, adjourn for more than three days, nor to any other place than that in which the two houses shall be sitting.

Section 6   The Senators and Representatives shall receive a compensation for their services, to be ascertained by law and paid out of the treasury of the United States. They shall in all cases except treason, felony and breach of the peace be privileged from arrest during their attendance at the session of their respective houses, and in going to and returning from the same; and for any speech or debate in either house, they shall not be questioned in any other place.

No Senator or Representative shall, during the time for which he was elected, be appointed to any civil office under the authority of the United States, which shall have been created, or the emoluments whereof shall have been increased, during such time; and no person holding any office under the United States shall be a member of either house during his continuance in office.

Section 7 All bills for raising revenue shall originate in the House of Representatives; but the Senate may propose or concur with amendments as on other bills.

Every bill which shall have passed the House of Representatives and the Senate, shall, before it becomes a law, be presented to the President of the United States; if he approve he shall sign it, but if not he shall return it with objections to that house in which it originated, who shall enter the objections at large on their journal, and proceed to reconsider it. If after such reconsideration two-thirds of that house shall agree to pass the bill, it shall be sent, together with the objections, to the other house, by which it shall likewise be reconsidered, and, if approved by two-thirds of that house, it shall become a law. But in all such cases the votes of both houses shall be determined by yeas and nays, and the names of the persons voting for and against the bill shall be entered on the journal of each house respectively. If any bill shall not be returned by the President within ten days (Sundays excepted) after it shall have been presented to him, the same shall be a law, in like manner as if he had signed it, unless the Congress by their adjournment prevent its return, in which case it shall not be a law.

Every order, resolution, or vote to which the concurrence of the Senate and House of Representatives may be necessary (except on a question of adjournment) shall be presented to the President of the United States; and before the same shall take effect, shall be approved by him, or being disapproved by him, shall be repassed by two-thirds of the Senate and House of Representatives, according to the rules and limitations prescribed in the case of a bill.

Section 8 The Congress shall have power:

To lay and collect taxes, duties, imposts, and excises, to pay the debts and provide for the common defense and general welfare of the United States; but all duties, imposts and excises shall be uniform throughout the United States;

To borrow money on the credit of the United States;

To regulate commerce with foreign nations, and among the several States, and with the Indian tribes;

To establish an uniform rule of naturalization, and uniform laws on the subject of bankruptcies throughout the United States;

To coin money, regulate the value thereof, and of foreign coin, and fix the standard of weights and measures;

To provide for the punishment of counterfeiting the securities and current coin of the United States;

To establish post offices and post roads;

To promote the progress of science and useful arts by securing for limited times to authors and inventors the exclusive right to their respective writings and discoveries;

To constitute tribunals inferior to the Supreme Court;

To define and punish piracies and felonies committed on the high seas and offenses against the law of nations;

To declare war, grant letters of marque and reprisal, and make rules concerning captures on land and water;

To raise and support armies, but no appropriation of money to that use shall be for a longer term than two years;

To provide and maintain a navy;

To make rules for the government and regulation of the land and naval forces;

To provide for calling forth the militia to execute the laws of the Union, suppress insurrections, and repel invasions;

To provide for organizing, arming, and disciplining the militia, and for governing such part of them as may be employed in the service of the United States, reserving to the States respectively the appointment of the officers, and the authority of training the militia according to the discipline prescribed by Congress;

To exercise exclusive legislation in all cases whatsoever, over such district (not exceeding ten miles square) as may, by cession of particular States, and the acceptance of Congress, become the seat of government of the United States, and to exercise like authority over all places purchased by the consent of the legislature of the State, in which the same shall be, for erection of forts, magazines, arsenals, dockyards, and other needful buildings;—and

To make all laws which shall be necessary and proper for carrying into execution the foregoing powers, and all other powers vested by this Constitution in the government of the United States, or in any department or officer thereof.

Section 9 *The migration or importation of such persons as any of the States now existing shall think proper to admit shall not be prohibited by the Congress prior to the year 1808; but a tax or duty may be imposed on such importation, not exceeding $10 for each person.*

The privilege of the writ of habeas corpus shall not be suspended, unless when in cases of rebellion or invasion the public safety may require it.

No bill of attainder or ex post facto law shall be passed.

No capitation or other direct tax shall be laid, unless in proportion to the census or enumeration herein before directed to be taken.

No tax or duty shall be laid on articles exported from any State.

No preference shall be given by any regulation of commerce or revenue to the ports of one State over those of another; nor shall vessels bound to, or from, one State be obliged to enter, clear, or pay duties in another.

No money shall be drawn from the treasury, but in consequence of appropriations made by law; and a regular statement and account of the receipts and expenditures of all public money shall be published from time to time.

No title of nobility shall be granted by the United States: and no person holding any office of profit or trust under them, shall, without the consent of the Congress, accept of any present, emolument, office, or title, of any kind whatever, from any king, prince, or foreign state.

Section 10 No State shall enter into any treaty, alliance, or confederation; grant letters of marque and reprisal; coin money; emit bills of credit; make anything but gold and silver coin a tender in payment of debts; pass any bill of attainder, ex post facto law, or law impairing the obligation of contracts, or grant any title of nobility.

No State shall, without the consent of Congress, lay any imposts or duties on imports or exports, except what may be absolutely necessary for executing its inspection laws: and the net produce of all duties and imposts, laid by any State on imports or exports, shall be for the use of the treasury of the United States; and all such laws shall be subject to the revision and control of the Congress.

No State shall, without the consent of Congress, lay any duty of tonnage, keep troops or ships of war in time of peace, enter into any agreement or compact with another State, or with a foreign power, or engage in war, unless actually invaded, or in such imminent danger as will not admit of delay.

ARTICLE II

Section 1 The executive power shall be vested in a President of the United States of America. He shall hold his office during the term of four years, and, together with the Vice-President, chosen for the same term, be elected as follows:

Each State shall appoint, in such manner as the legislature thereof may direct, a number of electors, equal to the whole number of Senators and Representatives to which the State may be entitled in the Congress; but no Senator or Representative, or person holding an office of trust or profit under the United States, shall be appointed an elector.

The electors shall meet in their respective States, and vote by ballot for two persons, of whom one at least shall not be an inhabitant of the same State with themselves. And they shall make a list of all the persons voted for, and of the number of votes for each, which list they shall sign and certify, and transmit sealed to the seat of government of the United States, directed to the President of the Senate. The President of the Senate shall, in the presence of the Senate and House of Representatives, open all the certificates, and the votes shall then be counted. The person having the greatest number of votes shall be the President, if such number be a majority of the whole number of electors appointed; and if there be more than one who have such majority, and have an equal number of votes, then the House of Representatives shall immediately choose by ballot one of them for President; and if no person have a majority, then from the five highest on the list said house shall in like manner choose the President. But in choosing the President the votes shall be taken by States, the representation from each State having one vote; a quorum for this purpose shall consist of a member or members from two-thirds of the States, and a majority of all the States shall be necessary to a choice. In every case, after the choice of the President, the person having the greatest number of votes of the electors shall be the Vice-President. But if there should remain two or more who have equal votes, the Senate shall choose from them by ballot the Vice-President.

The Congress may determine the time of choosing the electors and the day on which they shall give their votes; which day shall be the same throughout the United States.

No person except a natural-born citizen, *or a citizen of the United States at the time of the adoption of this Constitution,* shall be eligible to the office of President; neither shall any person be eligible to that office who shall not have attained to the age of thirty-five years, and been fourteen years a resident within the United States.

In case of the removal of the President from office or of his death, resignation, or inability to discharge the powers and duties of the said office, the same shall devolve on the Vice-President, and the Congress may by law provide for the case of removal, death, resignation, or inability, both of the President and Vice-President, declaring what officer shall then act as President, and such officer shall act accordingly, until the disability be removed, or a President shall be elected.

The President shall, at stated times, receive for his services a compensation, which shall neither be increased nor diminished during the period for which he shall have been elected, and he shall not receive within that period any other emolument from the United States, or any of them.

Before he enter on the execution of his office, he shall take the following oath or affirmation:—"I do solemnly swear (or affirm) that I will faithfully execute the office of the President of the United States, and will to the best of my ability preserve, protect and defend the Constitution of the United States."

Section 2 The President shall be commander in chief of the army and navy of the United States, and of the militia of the several States, when called into the actual service of the United States; he may require the opinion, in writing, of the principal officer in each of the executive departments, upon any subject relating to the duties of their respective offices, and he shall have power to grant reprieves and pardons for offenses against the United States, except in cases of impeachment.

He shall have power, by and with the advice and consent of the Senate, to make treaties, provided two-thirds of the Senators present concur;

and he shall nominate, and by and with the advice and consent of the Senate, shall appoint ambassadors, other public ministers and consuls, judges of the Supreme Court, and all other officers of the United States, whose appointments are not herein otherwise provided for, and which shall be established by law: but Congress may by law vest the appointment of such inferior officers, as they think proper, in the President alone, in the courts of law, or in the heads of departments.

The President shall have power to fill up all vacancies that may happen during the recess of the Senate, by granting commissions which shall expire at the end of their next session.

Section 3   He shall from time to time give to the Congress information of the state of the Union, and recommend to their consideration such measures as he shall judge necessary and expedient; he may, on extraordinary occasions, convene both houses, or either of them, and in case of disagreement between them, with respect to the time of adjournment, he may adjourn them to such time as he shall think proper; he shall receive ambassadors and other public ministers; he shall take care that the laws be faithfully executed, and shall commission all the officers of the United States.

Section 4   The President, Vice-President and all civil officers of the United States shall be removed from office on impeachment for, and on conviction of, treason, bribery, or other high crimes and misdemeanors.

ARTICLE III

Section 1   The judicial power of the United States shall be vested in one Supreme Court, and in such inferior courts as the Congress may from time to time ordain and establish. The judges, both of the Supreme and inferior courts, shall hold their offices during good behavior, and shall, at stated times, receive for their services a compensation which shall not be diminished during their continuance in office.

Section 2   The judicial power shall extend to all cases, in law and equity, arising under this Constitution, the laws of the United States, and treaties made, or which shall be made, under their authority—to all cases affecting ambassadors, other public ministers and consuls;—to all cases of admiralty and maritime jurisdiction;—to controversies to which the United States shall be a party;—to controversies between two or more States;—*between a State and citizens of another State;*—between citizens of different States;—between citizens of the same State claiming lands under grants of different States, and between a State, or the citizens thereof, and foreign states, citizens or subjects.

In all cases affecting ambassadors, other public ministers and consuls, and those in which a State shall be party, the Supreme Court shall have original jurisdiction. In all the other cases before mentioned, the Supreme Court shall have appellate jurisdiction, both as to law and fact, with such exceptions, and under such regulations, as the Congress shall make.

The trial of all crimes, except in cases of impeachment, shall be by jury; and such trial shall be held in the State where said crimes shall have been committed: but when not committed within any State, the trial shall be at such places or places as the Congress may by law have directed.

Section 3   Treason against the United States shall consist only in levying war against them, or in adhering to their enemies, giving them aid and comfort. No person shall be convicted of treason unless on the testimony of two witnesses to the same overt act, or on confession in open court.

The Congress shall have power to declare the punishment of treason, but no attainder of treason shall work corruption of blood, or forfeiture except during the life of the person attainted.

ARTICLE IV

Section 1   Full faith and credit shall be given in each State to the public acts, records, and judicial proceedings of every other State. And the

Congress may by general laws prescribe the manner in which such acts, records, and proceedings shall be proved, and the effect thereof.

Section 2   The citizens of each State shall be entitled to all privileges and immunities of citizens in the several States.

A person charged in any State with treason, felony, or other crime, who shall flee from justice, and be found in another State, shall on demand of the executive authority of the State from which he fled, be delivered up, to be removed to the State having jurisdiction of the crime.

No person held to service or labor in one State, under the laws thereof, escaping into another, shall, in consequence of any law or regulation therein, be discharged from such service or labor, but shall be delivered up on claim of the party to whom such service or labor may be due.

Section 3   New States may be admitted by the Congress into this Union; but no new State shall be formed or erected within the jurisdiction of any other State; nor any State be formed by the junction of two or more States, or parts of States, without the consent of the legislatures of the States concerned as well as of the Congress.

The Congress shall have power to dispose of and make all needful rules and regulations respecting the territory or other property belonging to the United States; and nothing in this Constitution shall be so construed as to prejudice any claims of the United States, or of any particular State.

Section 4   The United States shall guarantee to every State in this Union a republican form of government, and shall protect each of them against invasion; and on application of the legislature, or of the executive (when the legislature cannot be convened), against domestic violence.

ARTICLE V

The Congress, whenever two-thirds of both houses shall deem it necessary, shall propose amendments to this Constitution, or, on the application of the legislatures of two-thirds of the several States, shall call a convention for proposing amendments, which, in either case, shall be valid to all intents and purposes, as part of this Constitution, when ratified by the legislatures of three-fourths of the several States, or by conventions in three-fourths thereof, as the one or the other mode of ratification may be proposed by the Congress; provided *that no amendments which may be made prior to the year one thousand eight hundred and eight shall in any manner affect the first and fourth classes in the ninth section of the first article; and* that no State, without its consent, shall be deprived of its equal suffrage in the Senate.

ARTICLE VI

All debts contracted and engagements entered into, before the adoption of this Constitution, shall be as valid against the United States under this Constitution, as under the Confederation.

This Constitution, and the laws of the United States which shall be made in pursuance thereof; and all treaties made, or which shall be made, under the authority of the United States, shall be the supreme law of the land; and the judges in every State shall be bound thereby, anything in the Constitution or laws of any State to the contrary notwithstanding.

The Senators and Representatives before mentioned, and the members of the several State legislatures, and all executive and judicial officers, both of the United States and of the several States, shall be bound by oath or affirmation to support this Constitution; but no religious test shall ever be required as a qualification to any office or public trust under the United States.

ARTICLE VII

The ratification of the conventions of nine States shall be sufficient for the establishment of this Constitution between the States so ratifying the same.

Done in Convention by the unanimous consent of the States present, the seventeenth day of September in the year of our Lord one thousand seven hundred and eighty-seven and of the Independence of the United States of America the twelfth. In witness whereof we have hereunto subscribed our names.

AMENDMENTS TO THE CONSTITUTION*

Amendment I [1791]

Congress shall make no law respecting an establishment of religion, or prohibiting the free exercise thereof; or abridging the freedom of speech, or of the press; or the right of the people peaceably to assemble, and to petition the government for a redress of grievances.

Amendment II [1791]

A well-regulated militia being necessary to the security of a free State, the right of the people to keep and bear arms shall not be infringed.

Amendment III [1791]

No soldier shall, in time of peace, be quartered in any house without the consent of the owner, nor in time of war, but in a manner to be prescribed by law.

Amendment IV [1791]

The right of the people to be secure in their persons, houses, papers, and effects, against unreasonable searches and seizures, shall not be violated, and no warrants shall issue but upon probable cause, supported by oath or affirmation, and particularly describing the place to be searched, and the persons or things to be seized.

Amendment V [1791]

No person shall be held to answer for a capital or otherwise infamous crime, unless on a presentment or indictment of a grand jury, except in cases arising in the land or naval forces, or in the militia, when in actual service in time of war or public danger; nor shall any person be subject for the same offense to be twice put in jeopardy of life or limb; nor shall be compelled in any criminal case to be a witness against himself, nor be deprived of life, liberty or property, without due process of law; nor shall private property be taken for public use without just compensation.

Amendment VI [1791]

In all criminal prosecutions, the accused shall enjoy the right to a speedy and public trial, by an impartial jury of the State and district wherein the crime shall have been committed, which district shall have been previously ascertained by law, and to be informed of the nature and cause of the accusation; to be confronted with the witnesses against him; to have compulsory process for obtaining witnesses in his favor, and to have the assistance of counsel for his defense.

Amendment VII [1791]

In suits at common law, where the value in controversy shall exceed twenty dollars, the right of trial by jury shall be preserved, and no fact tried by a jury shall be otherwise reexamined in any court of the United States, than according to the rules of the common law.

Amendment VIII [1791]

Excessive bail shall not be required, nor excessive fines imposed, nor cruel and unusual punishments inflicted.

Amendment IX [1791]

The enumeration in the Constitution, of certain rights, shall not be construed to deny or disparage others retained by the people.

*The first ten amendments are known as the Bill of Rights.

Amendment X [1791]

The powers not delegated to the United States by the Constitution, nor prohibited by it to the States, are reserved to the States respectively, or to the people.

Amendment XI [1791]

The judicial power of the United States shall not be construed to extend to any suit in law or equity, commenced or prosecuted against one of the United States by citizens of another State, or by citizens or subjects of any foreign state.

Amendment XII [1804]

The electors shall meet in their respective States, and vote by ballot for President and Vice-President, one of whom, at least, shall not be an inhabitant of the same State with themselves; they shall name in their ballots the person voted for as President, and in distinct ballots the person voted for as Vice-President, and they shall make distinct lists of all persons voted for as President, and of all persons voted for as Vice-President, and of the number of votes for each, which lists they shall sign and certify, and transmit sealed to the seat of government of the United States, directed to the President of the Senate;—the President of the Senate shall, in the presence of the Senate and House of Representatives, open all the certificates and the votes shall then be counted;—the person having the greatest number of votes for President shall be the President, if such number be a majority of the whole number of electors appointed; and if no person have such majority, then from the persons having the highest numbers not exceeding three on the list of those voted for as President, the House of Representatives shall choose immediately, by ballot, the President. But in choosing the President, the votes shall be taken by States, the representation from each State having one vote; a quorum for this purpose shall consist of a member or members from two-thirds of the States, and a majority of all the States shall be necessary to a choice. And if the House of Representatives shall not choose a President whenever the right of choice shall devolve upon them, before *the fourth day of March* next following, then the Vice-President shall act as President, as in the case of the death or other constitutional disability of the President.

The person having the greatest number of votes as Vice-President shall be the Vice-President, if such number be a majority of the whole number of electors appointed; and if no person have a majority, then from the two highest numbers on the list the Senate shall choose the Vice-President; a quorum for the purpose shall consist of two-thirds of the whole number of Senators, and a majority of the whole number shall be necessary to a choice. But no person constitutionally ineligible to the office of President shall be eligible to that of Vice-President of the United States.

Amendment XIII [1865]

Section 1 Neither slavery nor involuntary servitude, except as a punishment for crime whereof the party shall have been duly convicted, shall exist within the United States, or any place subject to their jurisdiction.

Section 2 Congress shall have power to enforce this article by appropriate legislation.

Amendment XIV [1868]

Section 1 All persons born or naturalized in the United States, and subject to the jurisdiction thereof, are citizens of the United States and of the State wherein they reside. No State shall make or enforce any law which shall abridge the privileges or immunities of citizens of the United States; nor shall any State deprive any person of life, liberty, or property, without due process of law; nor deny to any person within its jurisdiction the equal protection of the laws.

Section 2 Representatives shall be apportioned among the several States according to their respective numbers, counting the whole number of persons in each State, excluding Indians not taxed. But when the right to vote at any election for the choice of Electors for President and Vice-President of the United States, Representatives in Congress, the executive and judicial officers of a State, or the members of the legislature thereof, is denied to any of the male inhabitants of such State, being twenty-one years of age and citizens of the United States, or in any way abridged, except for participation in rebellion, or other crime, the basis of representation therein shall be reduced in the proportion which the number of such male citizens shall bear to the whole number of male citizens twenty-one years of age in such State.

Section 3   No person shall be a Senator or Representative in Congress, or Elector of President and Vice-President, or hold any office, civil or military, under the United States, or under any State, who, having previously taken an oath, as a member of Congress, or as an officer of the United States, or as a member of any State legislature, or as an executive or judicial officer of any State, to support the Constitution of the United States, shall have engaged in insurrection or rebellion against the same, or given aid or comfort to the enemies thereof. Congress may, by a vote of two-thirds of each house, remove such disability.

Section 4   The validity of the public debt of the United States, authorized by law, including debts incurred for payment of pensions and bounties for services in suppressing insurrection or rebellion, shall not be questioned. But neither the United States nor any State shall assume or pay any debt or obligation incurred in aid of insurrection or rebellion against the United States, or any claim for the loss of emancipation of any slave; but all such debts, obligations, and claims shall be held illegal and void.

Section 5   The Congress shall have power to enforce, by appropriate legislation, the provisions of this article.

Amendment XV [1870]

Section 1   The right of citizens of the United States to vote shall not be denied or abridged by the United States or by any State on account of race, color, or previous condition of servitude.

Section 2   The Congress shall have power to enforce this article by appropriate legislation.

Amendment XVI [1913]

The Congress shall have power to lay and collect taxes on incomes, from whatever source derived, without apportionment among the several States, and without regard to any census or enumeration.

Amendment XVII [1913]

Section 1   The Senate of the United States shall be composed of two Senators from each State, elected by the people thereof, for six years; and each Senator shall have one vote. The electors in each State shall have the qualifications requisite for electors of [voters for] the most numerous branch of the State legislatures.

Section 2   When vacancies happen in the representation of any State in the Senate, the executive authority of such State shall issue writs of election to fill such vacancies: Provided that the legislature of any State may empower the executive thereof to make temporary appointments until the people fill the vacancies by election as the legislature may direct.

Section 3   The amendment shall not be so construed as to affect the election or term of any Senator chosen before it becomes valid as part of the Constitution.

Amendment XVIII [1919]

Section 1   After one year from the ratification of this article the manufacture, sale, or transportation of intoxicating liquors within, the importation thereof into, or the exportation thereof from the United States and all territory subject to the jurisdiction thereof, for beverage purposes, is hereby prohibited.

Section 2 The Congress and the several States shall have concurrent power to enforce this article by appropriate legislation.

Section 3 This article shall be inoperative unless it shall have been ratified as an amendment to the Constitution by the legislatures of the several States, as provided by the Constitution, within seven years from the date of the submission thereof to the States by the Congress.

Amendment XIX [1920]

Section 1 The right of citizens of the United States to vote shall not be denied or abridged by the United States or by any State on account of sex.

Section 2 The Congress shall have power to enforce this article by appropriate legislation.

Amendment XX [1933]

Section 1 The terms of the President and Vice President shall end at noon on the 20th day of January, and the terms of Senators and Representatives at noon on the 3d day of January, of the years in which such terms would have ended if this article had not been ratified; and the terms of their successors shall then begin.

Section 2 The Congress shall assemble at least once in every year, and such meeting shall begin at noon on the 3d day of January, unless they shall by law appoint a different day.

Section 3 If, at the time fixed for the beginning of the term of the President, the President-elect shall have died, the Vice-President-elect shall become President. If a President shall not have been chosen before the time fixed for the beginning of his term, or if the President-elect shall have failed to qualify, then the President-elect shall act as President until a President shall have qualified, and the Congress may by law provide for the case wherein neither a President-elect nor a Vice-President-elect shall have quali-

fied, declaring who shall then act as President, or the manner in which one who is to act shall be selected, and such persons shall act accordingly until a President or Vice-President shall have qualified.

Section 4 The Congress may by law provide for the case of the death of any of the persons from whom the House of Representatives may choose a President whenever the right of choice shall have devolved upon them, and for the case of the death of any of the persons from whom the Senate may choose a Vice-President whenever the right of choice shall have developed upon them.

Section 5 Sections 1 and 2 shall take effect on the 15th day of October following the ratification of this article.

Section 6 This article shall be inoperative unless it shall have been ratified as an amendment to the Constitution by the legislatures of three-fourths of the several States within seven years from the date of its submission.

Amendment XXI [1933]

Section 1 The eighteenth article of amendment to the Constitution of the United States is hereby repealed.

Section 2 The transportation or importation into any State, Territory, or Possession of the United States for delivery or use therein of intoxicating liquors, in violation of the laws thereof, is hereby prohibited.

Section 3 This article shall be inoperative unless it shall have been ratified as an amendment to the Constitution by conventions in the several States, as provided in the Constitution, within seven years from the date of submission thereof to the States by the Congress.

Amendment XXII [1951]

Section 1 No person shall be elected to the office of President more than twice, and no person who has held the office of President, or acted as

President, for more than two years of a term to which some other person was elected President shall be elected to the office of President more than once. But this article shall not apply to any person holding the office of President when this article was proposed by the Congress, and shall not prevent any person who may be holding the office of President, or acting as President, during the term within which this article becomes operative from holding the office of President or acting as President during the remainder of such term.

Section 2   This article shall be inoperative unless it shall have been ratified as an amendment to the Constitution by the legislatures of three-fourths of the several States within seven years from the date of its submission to the States by the Congress.

Amendment XXIII [1961]

Section 1   The District constituting the seat of Government of the United States shall appoint in such manner as the Congress may direct:

A number of electors of President and Vice-President equal to the whole number of Senators and Representatives in Congress to which the District would be entitled if it were a State, but in no event more than the least populous State; they shall be in addition to those appointed by the States, but they shall be considered for the purposes of the election of President and Vice-President, to be electors appointed by a State; and they shall meet in the District and perform such duties as provided by the twelfth article of amendment.

Section 2   The Congress shall have the power to enforce this article by appropriate legislation.

Amendment XXIV [1964]

Section 1   The right of citizens of the United States to vote in any primary or other election for President or Vice-President, for electors for President or Vice-President, or for Senator or Representative in Congress, shall not be denied or abridged by the United States or any State by reason of failure to pay any poll tax or other tax.

Section 2   The Congress shall have the power to enforce this article by appropriate legislation.

Amendment XXV [1967]

Section 1   In case of the removal of the President from office or of his death or resignation, the Vice-President shall become President.

Section 2   Whenever there is a vacancy in the office of the Vice-President, the President shall nominate a Vice-President who shall take office upon confirmation by a majority vote of both houses of Congress.

Section 3   Whenever the President transmits to the President pro tempore of the Senate and the Speaker of the House of Representatives his written declaration that he is unable to discharge the powers and duties of his office, and until he transmits to them a written declaration to the contrary, such powers and duties shall be discharged by the Vice-President as Acting President.

Section 4   Whenever the Vice-President and a majority of either the principal officers of the executive departments or of such other body as Congress may by law provide, transmit to the President pro tempore of the Senate and the Speaker of the House of Representatives their written declaration that the President is unable to discharge the powers and duties of his office, the Vice-President shall immediately assume the powers and duties of the office as Acting President.

Thereafter, when the President transmits to the President pro tempore of the Senate and the Speaker of the House of Representatives his written declaration that no inability exists, he shall resume the powers and duties of his office unless the Vice-President and a majority of either the principal officers of the executive department[s] or of such other body as Congress may by law provide, transmit within four days to the President pro tempore of the Senate and the Speaker of the House of Representatives their written declaration that the President is unable to discharge the powers and duties of his office. Thereupon Congress shall decide the issue, assembling within forty-eight hours for that purpose if not in session. If the Congress, within twenty-one days after receipt of the latter written declaration, or, if Congress is not in session, within twenty-one days after Congress is required to assemble, determines by two-thirds vote of both Houses that the President is unable to discharge the powers and duties of his office, the Vice-President shall continue to discharge the same as Acting President; otherwise, the President shall resume the powers and duties of his office.

Amendment XXVI [1971]

Section 1 The right of citizens of the United States, who are eighteen years of age or older, to vote shall not be denied or abridged by the United States or by any State on account of age.

Section 2 The Congress shall have power to enforce this article by appropriate legislation.

Year	Candidates	Parties	Percent of Popular Vote*†	Electoral Vote‡	Percent of Voter Participation†
1789	GEORGE WASHINGTON	No party designations		69	
	John Adams			34	
	Other candidates			35	
1792	GEORGE WASHINGTON	No party designations		132	
	John Adams			77	
	George Clinton			50	
	Other candidates			5	
1796	JOHN ADAMS	Federalist		71	
	Thomas Jefferson	Democratic-Republican		68	
	Thomas Pinckney	Federalist		59	
	Aaron Burr	Democratic-Republican		30	
	Other candidates			48	
1800	THOMAS JEFFERSON	Democratic-Republican		73	
	Aaron Burr	Democratic-Republican		73	
	John Adams	Federalist		65	
	Charles C. Pinckney	Federalist		64	
	John Jay	Federalist		1	
1804	THOMAS JEFFERSON	Democratic-Republican		162	
	Charles C. Pinckney	Federalist		14	
1808	JAMES MADISON	Democratic-Republican		122	
	Charles C. Pinckney	Federalist		47	
	George Clinton	Democratic-Republican		6	
1812	JAMES MADISON	Democratic-Republican		128	
	DeWitt Clinton	Federalist		89	
1816	JAMES MONROE	Democratic-Republican		183	
	Rufus King	Federalist		34	

Year	Candidates	Parties	Percent of Popular Vote*†	Electoral Vote‡	Percent of Voter Participation†
1820	JAMES MONROE	Democratic-Republican		231	
	John Quincy Adams	Independent Republican		1	
1824	JOHN QUINCY ADAMS	Democratic-Republican	30.5	84	26.9
	Andrew Jackson	Democratic-Republican	43.1	99	
	Henry Clay	Democratic-Republican	13.2	37	
	William H. Crawford	Democratic-Republican	13.1	41	
1828	ANDREW JACKSON	Democratic	56.0	178	57.6
	John Quincy Adams	National Republican	44.0	83	
1832	ANDREW JACKSON	Democratic	54.5	219	55.4
	Henry Clay	National Republican	37.5	49	
	William Wirt	Anti-Masonic	8.0	7	
	John Floyd	Democratic		11	
1836	MARTIN VAN BUREN	Democratic	50.9	170	57.8
	William H. Harrison	Whig		73	
	Hugh L. White	Whig		26	
	Daniel Webster	Whig	49.1	14	
	W. P. Mangum	Whig		11	
1840	WILLIAM H. HARRISON	Whig	53.1	234	80.2
	Martin Van Buren	Democratic	46.9	60	
1844	JAMES K. POLK	Democratic	49.6	170	78.9
	Henry Clay	Whig	48.1	105	
	James G. Birney	Liberty	2.3	0	
1848	ZACHARY TAYLOR	Whig	47.4	163	72.7
	Lewis Cass	Democratic	42.5	127	
	Martin Van Buren	Free-Soil	10.1	0	
1852	FRANKLIN PIERCE	Democratic	50.9	254	69.6
	Winfield Scott	Whig	44.1	42	
	John P. Hale	Free-Soil	5.0	0	
1856	JAMES BUCHANAN	Democratic	45.3	174	78.9
	John C. Frémont	Republican	33.1	114	
	Millard Fillmore	American	21.6	8	
1860	ABRAHAM LINCOLN	Republican	39.8	180	81.2
	Stephen A. Douglas	Democratic	29.5	12	
	John C. Breckinridge	Democratic	18.1	72	
	John Bell	Constitutional Union	12.6	39	
1864	ABRAHAM LINCOLN	Republican	55.0	212	73.8
	George B. McClellan	Democratic	45.0	21	
1868	ULYSSES S. GRANT	Republican	52.7	214	78.1
	Horatio Seymour	Democratic	47.3	80	
1872	ULYSSES S. GRANT	Republican	55.6	286	71.3
	Horace Greeley	Democratic	44.0	0§	

Year	Candidates	Parties	Percent of Popular Vote*†	Electoral Vote‡	Percent of Voter Participation†
1876	RUTHERFORD B. HAYES	Republican	48.0	185	81.8
	Samuel J. Tilden	Democratic	51.0	184	
1880	JAMES A. GARFIELD	Republican	48.5	214	79.4
	Winfield S. Hancock	Democratic	48.1	155	
	James B. Weaver	Greenback-Labor	3.4	0	
1884	GROVER CLEVELAND	Democratic	48.5	219	77.5
	James G. Blaine	Republican	48.2	182	
1888	BENJAMIN HARRISON	Republican	47.9	233	79.3
	Grover Cleveland	Democratic	48.6	168	
1892	GROVER CLEVELAND	Democratic	46.0	277	74.7
	Benjamin Harrison	Republican	43.0	145	
	James B. Weaver	Populist	8.5	22	
1896	WILLIAM McKINLEY	Republican	51.1	271	79.3
	William J. Bryan	Democratic	46.7	176	
1900	WILLIAM McKINLEY	Republican	51.7	292	73.2
	William J. Bryan	Democratic; Populist	45.5	155	
1904	THEODORE ROOSEVELT	Republican	56.4	336	65.2
	Alton B. Parker	Democratic	37.6	140	
	Eugene V. Debs	Socialist	3.0	0	
1908	WILLIAM H. TAFT	Republican	51.6	321	65.4
	William J. Bryan	Democratic	43.1	162	
	Eugene V. Debs	Socialist	2.8	0	
1912	WOODROW WILSON	Democratic	41.9	435	58.8
	Theodore Roosevelt	Progressive	27.4	88	
	William H. Taft	Republican	23.2	8	
	Eugene V. Debs	Socialist	6.0	0	
1916	WOODROW WILSON	Democratic	49.4	277	61.6
	Charles E. Hughes	Republican	46.2	254	
	Allan L. Benson	Socialist	3.2	0	
1920	WARREN G. HARDING	Republican	60.4	404	49.2
	James M. Cox	Democratic	34.2	127	
	Eugene V. Debs	Socialist	3.4	0	
1924	CALVIN COOLIDGE	Republican	54.0	382	48.9
	John W. Davis	Democratic	28.8	136	
	Robert M. La Follette	Progressive	16.6	13	
1928	HERBERT C. HOOVER	Republican	58.2	444	56.9
	Alfred E. Smith	Democratic	40.9	87	
1932	FRANKLIN D. ROOSEVELT	Democratic	57.4	472	56.9
	Herbert C. Hoover	Republican	39.7	59	

Year	Candidates	Parties	Percent of Popular Vote*†	Electoral Vote‡	Percent of Voter Participation†
1936	FRANKLIN D. ROOSEVELT	Democratic	60.8	523	61.0
	Alfred M. Landon	Republican	36.5	8	
1940	FRANKLIN D. ROOSEVELT	Democratic	54.8	449	62.5
	Wendell L. Willkie	Republican	44.8	82	
1944	FRANKLIN D. ROOSEVELT	Democratic	53.5	432	55.9
	Thomas E. Dewey	Republican	46.0	99	
1948	HARRY S TRUMAN	Democratic	49.5	303	53.0
	Thomas E. Dewey	Republican	45.1	189	
	J. Strom Thurmond	States' Rights	2.4	39	
	Henry A. Wallace	Progressive	2.4	0	
1952	DWIGHT D. EISENHOWER	Republican	55.1	442	63.3
	Adlai E. Stevenson	Democratic	44.4	89	
1956	DWIGHT D. EISENHOWER	Republican	57.4	457	60.6
	Adlai E. Stevenson	Democratic	42.0	73	
1960	JOHN F. KENNEDY	Democratic	49.7	303	64.0
	Richard M. Nixon	Republican	49.6	219	
	Harry F. Byrd	Independent	0.7	15	
1964	LYNDON B. JOHNSON	Democratic	61.1	486	61.7
	Barry M. Goldwater	Republican	38.5	52	
1968	RICHARD M. NIXON	Republican	43.4	301	60.6
	Hubert H. Humphrey	Democratic	42.7	191	
	George C. Wallace	American Independent	13.5	46	
1972	RICHARD M. NIXON	Republican	60.7	520	55.5
	George S. McGovern	Democratic	37.5	17	
1976	JIMMY CARTER	Democratic	50.0	297	54.3
	Gerald R. Ford	Republican	48.0	240	
1980	RONALD REAGAN	Republican	50.8	489	53.0
	Jimmy Carter	Democratic	41.0	49	
	John B. Anderson	Independent	6.6	0	
1984	RONALD REAGAN	Republican	58.7	525	52.9
	Walter F. Mondale	Democratic	40.6	13	
1988	GEORGE BUSH	Republican	54.0	426	50.1
	Michael Dukakis	Democratic	46.0	111	
1992	WILLIAM J. CLINTON	Democratic	43.0	370	61.3
	George Bush	Republican	38.0	168	
	H. Ross Perot	Independent	19.0	0	

*Candidates receiving less than 2.5 percent of the popular vote have been omitted. Hence the percentage of popular vote may not total 100 percent.
†Prior to 1824, most presidential electors were chosen by state legislators rather than by popular vote.
‡Before the Twelfth Amendment was passed in 1804, the electoral college voted for two presidential candidates; the runner-up became the vice president.
§Greeley died before the electoral college met. His votes were divided among four other candidates.

Credits

Page abbreviations are as follows: **L** left, **R** right.

6 Library of Congress **10L** Musée de l'Homme, Paris **10R** Musée de l'Homme, Paris **16** American Museum of Natural History **17** Biblioteca Medices Laurenziana, Florence, Italy **27** Copyright the British Museum **32** Courtesy American Antiquarian Society **37** Julie Roy Jeffrey **41** Gibbes Museum of Art, Carolina Art Association, Charleston **44** National Gallery of Art, Washington, D.C. **54** From the Collection of The Detroit Institute of Art, Founders Society, Gibbs-Williams Fund **64** Peabody Museum, Harvard University **71L** Moravian Historical Society, Nazareth, Penn. **71R** Moravian Historical Society, Nazareth, Penn. **77** National Gallery of Art, Washington, D.C. **86** Copyright Yale University Art Gallery, Gift of Eugene Phelps Edwards **102** Courtesy, Virginia Historical Society, Richmond **106** Massachusetts Historical Society **110L** Library of Congress **110R** The New-York Historical Society, New York City **120** Library of Congress **126** Prints Division/New York Public Library, Astor, Lenox and Tilden Foundations **129** Library of Congress **131** Library of Congress **139** New York State Historical Association, Cooperstown **155** Mead Art Museum, Amherst College, Amherst, Mass. **165** Library of Congress **166** Copyright Yale University Art Gallery **172** The Metropolitan Museum of Art, Bequest of Cornelia Cruger, 1923 (24.19.1) **185** The Maryland Historical Society, Baltimore **192** Historical Society of Pennsylvania **201** National Museum of Natural History, Smithsonian Institution **219** Library of Congress **222** Museum of American Textile History, North Andover, Mass. **224** Public Library of Cincinnati and Hamilton County, Ohio **231** Copyright Yale University Art Gallery, Mabel Brady Garvan Collection **246** South Carolina Library, Columbia, S.C. **250** Library of Congress **255** New York Public Library/Schomburg Center for Research in Black Culture **261** Library of Congress **273** Harry T. Peters Collection/The Museum of the City of New York **279ALL** Sophia Smith Collection, Smith College, Northampton, Mass. **293** Western History Collection, Denver Public Library **295** California Society Library **299** Copyright Yale University Art Gallery, Beinecke Rare Book and Manuscript Collection **309** Library of Congress **313** New York Public Library, Astor, Lenox and Tilden Foundations **316** Courtesy of The Newberry Library, Chicago **319** Bettmann Archive **333** The National Archives, Office of the Chief Signal Officer **336** January 24, 1863/*Frank Leslie's Illustrated Newspaper* **340** Library of Congress **351** February 23, 1867/*Frank Leslie's Illustrated Newspaper* **353** May 26, 1866/*Harper's Weekly* **357** Brown Brothers **359** Valentine Museum, Richmond, Virginia **371** The Metropolitan Museum of Art, Bequest of Adele S. Colgate **374** Solomon D. Butcher Collection/Nebraska State Historical Society **377** Smithsonian Institution **396** The Museum of the City of New York **399** Library of Congress **409** July 16, 1892/*Harper's Weekly* **417** Chicago Historical Society **422** University of Illinois, Chicago/Jane Addams Memorial Collection at Hull House **428** Library of Congress **429** Library of Congress **436** Hawaii State Archives **441** The Granger Collection, New York **444** Culver Pictures **458** Records of the Children's Bureau, The National Archives, Office of the Chief Signal Officer **459** International Museum of Photography/George Eastman House **467** Chicago Historical Society **473** Library of Congress **487** U.S. Signal Corps, The National Archives, Office of the Chief Signal Officer **490** The National Archives, Office of the Chief Signal Officer **493** The National Archives, Office of the Chief Signal Officer **503** Library of Congress **508** From the collection of Whitney Museum of American Art **510** Brown Brothers **514** UPI/Bettmann **525** From the collection of Whitney Museum of American Art **530** Bettmann Archive **533** Library of Congress **551** General Records of the Navy Department/The National Archives, Office of the Chief Signal Officer **554** Library of Congress **555** Library of Congress **562** AP/Wide World **563** The Franklin D. Roosevelt Library **578** Bettmann Archive **589** UPI/Bettmann **598** Margaret Bourke-White/*Life* Magazine/Time Warner Inc. **605** UPI/Bettmann **610** Bob Henriques/Magnum Photos **617** CBS-TV **619** NASA **632** John Filo **633** Sygma **639** Printed by permission of the Estate of Norman Rockwell, Photo Courtesy of The Norman Rockwell Museum at Stockbridge **640** Bruce Roberts/Photo Researchers **649** J. L.Atlan/Sygma **650** Bob Fitch/Black Star **654** Michael Abramson/Gamma-Liaison **668** Michael Evans/The White House **683** AP/Wide World **687** Jeffrey Markowitz/Sygma

Index

Abolitionists, 71, 141, 275–277
  Emancipation Proclamation and, 335
  Kansas-Nebraska Act and, 311
  underground railroad and, 253–254
Abortion, 228, 459, 624, 649, 671
Acheson, Dean, 580, 588
Adams, Abigail, 111, 134, 138
Adams, Brooks, 421
Adams, Dudley, 385
Adams, Henry, 363, 364, 416–417, 419, 431
Adams, John, 103, 106, 108, 134, 164, 172, 180, 417
Adams, John Quincy, 174, 199, 207, 261, 262, 417
Adams, Samuel, 95, 100, 103, 106
Adamson Act, 485
Adams-Onís Treaty (1819), 285
Addams, Jane, 422, 423, 425, 431, 442, 457, 459, 461, 472, 481, 496
Adultery, 192
Advertising, 505, 600
Affirmative action, 645
Afghanistan, 634
Africa, 9, 11
African-Americans, 179–180. See also Civil rights; Suffrage
  in Civil War, 336, 339
  Colored Farmers' Alliance and, 387
  election of 1936 and, 539
  free blacks and, 254–255
  freedmen, 349–350, 353
  frontier life and, 296
  the Grand Convention and, 157
  Great Compromise and, 156–157
  Harlem Renaissance and, 510
  immigration policy's effect on, 679
  in labor movement, 465
  living conditions in cities, 398–399
  migration to cities, 395–396, 509, 607
  mob lynchings and, 383–384
  New Deal and, 536–537
  occupational mobility of, 411
  in politics, 360, 645
  in post–Civil War period, 382–384
  post–World War II, 601
  progressivism and, 472
  protests and ideologies, 384–385, 609, 611
  Reconstruction era and, 358–359
  in Revolutionary War, 132–133
  segregation and, 383, 508, 640–641
  in Spanish American War, 441
  suffrage, 354, 382, 427
  underclass and, 229–230
  unemployment and, 675
  urban racial tensions and, 228–229
  in World War I, 489–491
  in World War II, 553–554
African Methodist Episcopal Church, 358, 399
Afro-American League, 384
Agnew, Spiro, 624, 626
Agricultural Adjustment Act, 528–529
Agricultural Marketing Act (1929), 523
Agriculture and farming
  antebellum farming in East, 230–232
  in Carolinas, 40–41
  cash crops, 317
  closed field, 35
  colonial period and, 27, 29–31, 35, 40, 74–76, 79–81
  cotton. See Cotton production
  ecological transformation and, 78–79
  environment and, 233
  family farms, 371, 674
  farmers' alliances, 386–387
  on Great Plains, 372–374, 533–534
  Grangers and, 385
  Great Depression and, 528–529, 532–533
  industrialization and urbanization, 370–371
  Jefferson's land policies and, 183–188
  Native Americans and, 4, 6
  New Deal and, 528–529, 532–533
  in 1980s, 674–675
  northeast regions and, 184–185
  Northern family farms, 75–79
  open field, 35
  in post–Civil War South, 317
  post–World War II, 596
  production and prices, 372, 529, 605, 674
  productivity and, 75, 674
  railroads and, 215, 376, 385
  rice production, 80
  Southern regions and, 185–186
  sugar. See Sugar production
  technological innovation and, 239, 339
  tenant farmers, 607
  tobacco. See Tobacco production
  Trans-Appalachia, 186–187
  westward expansion and, 293–294
  wheat farming, 317–372

Du Bois, W. E. B., 348, 356, 472, 489, 509, 536, 590
Dukakis, Michael, 669
Dulles, John Foster, 579, 584, 586
Duncan, John, 374, 375
Dunkirk, 549
Du Pont, 503
Dutch, 20, 38–39, 51, 127
Dutch East Indies, 559
Dutch West India Company, 38
Dylan, Bob, 656

Eagleton, Ethie, 325
Eagleton, George, 325, 326, 331, 343
Economic Opportunity Act (1964), 620
Economy Act, 527
Economy and economics. *See also* Commerce and Trade; Debt; Depressions and recessions; Industry and manufacturing; Work force
    Bush administration and, 671
    business cycles and, 394
    Carter administration and, 627
    Civil War and, 327
    concentration of wealth, 403, 534, 595
    consumption culture, 600
    education and, 217–218
    Eisenhower administration and, 606
    factors driving growth, 215–216
    Ford administration and, 626
    foreign competition in 1980s, 673
    Great Depression and, 523–525
    growth from 1820–1860, 215
    Hamilton's policies and, 165–167
    Jackson administration and, 264–265
    Johnson administration and, 619–621
    Kennedy administration and, 618–619
    Keynesian economics, 539, 603, 619
    Lincoln administration and, 340–341
    Madison administration and, 205
    market economy, 232
    Nixon administration and, 623
    post–Civil War South, 381
    post–Revolutionary War, 141–143
    post–Seven Years' War depression, 99
    post–World War I, 503
    post–World War II, 594–595
    Reagan administration and, 669–670
    in Reconstruction era, 356–358
    Removal Act (1830) and, 263
    Roosevelt (Franklin) adnministration. *See* New Deal
    shift to service economy, 672–673
    Truman administration and, 603–604
    Washington administration and, 165–167
    World War II production, 552
Ecuador, 15
Eddis, William, 132
Education
    African-Americans and, 230, 359
    Asian-Americans and, 679
    economic growth and, 217–218
    on the frontier, 294
    GI Bill (1944), 595
    land grant colleges, 344
    Massachusetts model for, 217–218
    middle class and, 401
    Native Americans and, 201–202
    new students, 680
    in post–Civil War South, 381
    postwar conformity and, 600
    post–World War I, 503
    Puritans and, 33
    religious pluralism and, 88
    school prayer debate, 671
Education Amendments (1972), 648
Education of Henry Adams, The (Adams), 417
Edwards, Jonathan, 85
Einstein, Albert, 548
Eisenhower, Dwight D., 562, 563, 603, 616, 622, 634, 652, 668
    Cold War and, 578–579, 583
    economic expansion under, 595
    election of, 605–606
    Korean War and, 581
    World War II and, 562, 564
Electoral process, 157
Electrification, 504, 511, 512, 533
Eliot, John, 35
Eliot, T. S., 511
Elizabeth I, Queen of England, 3, 19, 20
Elkins Act (1903), 470
Ellsberg, Daniel, 631
El Salvador, 684–685
Elskwatawa (the Prophet), 203
Ely, Richard T., 422
Emancipation Proclamation (1863), 335–336
Embargo Act (1807), 195
Emergency Banking Relief Act, 527
Emerson, Ralph Waldo, 268, 309
Emigrant's Guide to Oregon and California (Hastings), 285
Emlen, Anne, 138
Employment Act (1946), 603
Entitlement programs, 676
Environment, 233
    Bush administration and, 660
    Clinton administration and, 660

Wealth, concentration of, 403, 534, 595, 672
Weathermen, 656
Weaver, James B., 387, 388, 428
Webster, Daniel, 264
Webster v. *Reproductive Health Service,* 649
Welch, Joseph, 589
Weld, Theodore Dwight, 259, 271, 275, 277, 278
Welfare state, 423
Welles, Orson, 541
Wells, Ida B., 384
Wells, Maine, 63
Western Federation of Miners (WFM), 408
Western Union, 393
West Indies, 21
Westinghouse Corporation, 503
West Jersey, 43
Westos, 39
Westward expansion, 283, 331
 annexation of New Mexico, 289
 annexation of Texas, 285–287
 California and, 289
 cotton production and, 239–240
 emigrants' motivation, 291–292
 foreign claims to, 284
 frontier life and, 293–298
 fur trade and, 97
 Louisiana Purchase and, 187
 Manifest Destiny and, 285, 287
 Native Americans and, 149–151
 Northwest Ordinance and, 149
 Oregon Territory and, 290
 overland trials, 292–293
 Plains Indians and, 298–300
 slavery and, 206
 Treaty of Guadalupe Hidalgo and, 290
Weyler, Nicolau, 439–440
Wheeling, West Virginia, 362
Whig ideology, 91–92
Whiskey Rebellion, 167–168
Whiskey Ring affair, 363
Whiskey Tax (1791), 167
White, John, 20
Whitefield, George, 67, 86, 87
Whitman, Walt, 323
Whitney, Eli, 185, 239
Wichita, 298
Wide, Wide World, The (Warner), 214
Wilder, Douglas, 645
Wilderness, battle of the, 342
Wilhelm II, Kaiser of Germany, 449, 482
Willard, Francis, 420–421
William and Mary, 88
William of Orange, 59, 60

Williams, Abigail, 61
Williams, George Washington, 399
Williams, Roger, 34
Willkie, Wendell, 549
Wilmot, David, 306
Wilmot Proviso, 306–307
Wilson, Ellen Axson, 480
Wilson, James, 155
Wilson, Wash, 251
Wilson, Woodrow, 417, 446, 456, 469, 473–475, 477, 480, 514
 Central American interventions, 484–485
 election to office, 473–475, 485–486
 immigration and, 507
 League of Nations and, 496
 Mexican interventions and, 484–485
 neutrality and, 482–484
 tariff and banking reform and, 475–476
 World War I and, 486
Winesburg, Ohio (Anderson), 511
Winthrop, John, 21, 32, 434
Wirt, William, 265
Witchcraft trials, Salem, 61–62
Wolfe, James, 98
Woman's Land Army, 493
Woman's Peace party, 481
Women in Economics (Gilman), 460
Women Rebel, The, 459
Women's Army Corps (WACS), 559
Women's Christian Temperance Union (WCTU), 273, 420
Women's International League for Peace and Freedom, 496
Women's issues. *See also* Suffrage
 abortion, 228, 459, 624, 649, 671
 birth control and, 228, 459, 511, 657
 during Civil War, 340, 341–342
 education and, 648
 Equal Rights Amendment, 648
 Anne Hutchinson and, 34
 indentured servants, 28
 labor union support for, 407
 middle class and, 227–228, 400–401
 Native Americans and, 7
 New Deal and, 537–538
 during 1960s and 1970s, 646–647
 1920s and, 511–512
 Northern colonial society and, 76–78
 polygamy and, 296–297
 postwar widowhood and, 99
 post–World War II and, 601–602
 progressive reform and, 458–459, 464, 477
 Puritan families and, 36
 Reconstruction Amendments and, 355